The Oxford Handbook of
Psychology and Law

OXFORD LIBRARY OF PSYCHOLOGY

AREA EDITORS:

Clinical Psychology
David H. Barlow

Cognitive Neuroscience
Kevin N. Ochsner and Stephen M. Kosslyn

Cognitive Psychology
Daniel Reisberg

Counseling Psychology
Elizabeth M. Altmaier and Jo-Ida C. Hansen

Developmental Psychology
Philip David Zelazo

Health Psychology
Howard S. Friedman

History of Psychology
David B. Baker

Methods and Measurement
Todd D. Little

Neuropsychology
Kenneth M. Adams

Organizational Psychology
Steve W.J. Kozlowski

Personality and Social Psychology
Kay Deaux and Mark Snyder

OXFORD LIBRARY OF PSYCHOLOGY

The Oxford Handbook of Psychology and Law

Edited by

David DeMatteo and Kyle C. Scherr

OXFORD
UNIVERSITY PRESS

OXFORD
UNIVERSITY PRESS

Oxford University Press is a department of the University of Oxford. It furthers
the University's objective of excellence in research, scholarship, and education
by publishing worldwide. Oxford is a registered trade mark of Oxford University
Press in the UK and certain other countries. .

Published in the United States of America by Oxford University Press
198 Madison Avenue, New York, NY 10016, United States of America.

Library of Congress Cataloging-in-Publication Data
Names: DeMatteo, David, 1972– editor. | Scherr, Kyle C., editor.
Title: The Oxford handbook of psychology and law / David DeMatteo, Kyle C. Scherr.
Description: New York, NY : Oxford University Press, [2023] |
Series: Oxford library of psychology series |
Includes bibliographical references and index.
Identifiers: LCCN 2022030915 (print) | LCCN 2022030916 (ebook) |
ISBN 9780197649138 (hardback) | ISBN 9780197649152 (epub) | ISBN 9780197649169
Subjects: LCSH: Law—Psychological aspects. | Law—Psychological aspects—United States. |
Forensic psychology—United States. | Mental health laws—United States.
Classification: LCC K346 .O94 2022 (print) | LCC K346 (ebook) |
DDC 340/.19—dc23/eng/20220924
LC record available at https://lccn.loc.gov/2022030915
LC ebook record available at https://lccn.loc.gov/2022030916

DOI: 10.1093/oxfordhb/9780197649138.001.0001

9 8 7 6 5 4 3 2 1

Printed by Marquis, Canada

CONTENTS

Experimental Psychology–Law

Part I · Witnesses and Victims

Part II · Evidence Gathering and Pursuit in Criminal Cases

Part III · Criminal Outcomes

PREFACE

The field of psychology–law is comprised of two distinct yet complementary disciplines. Psychologists and lawyers come from different cultures, with different interests, different approaches to solving problems, different research methodologies, different attitudes toward confrontation and argument, and different ways of arriving at the "truth." Psychologists and lawyers also have different types of education and training. Legal education facilitates an understanding of case analysis, statutory interpretation, the evolution of legal traditions, ways to structure arguments, and methods for resolving disputes, while education in psychology focuses on an understanding of human cognition and behavior, the development of research skills and statistical competence, and (sometimes) the development of assessment and intervention skills. Law, which has special rules regarding evidence and proof, relies heavily on precedent and the application of legal principles to specific facts toward the goal of settling conflicts that need resolution. By contrast, psychology looks at problems through an empirical lens, using psychometrically based tools and rigorous methodologies to systematically evaluate questions while rarely reaching a "final verdict."

Despite the differences between psychology and law, the two disciplines have a rich history of working symbiotically in a variety of clinical, research, and legal contexts. This book focuses on that intersection of psychology and law, which we refer to as the field of psychology–law. The field of psychology–law has grown considerably over the past few decades and the range of topics that falls under the psychology–law umbrella is strikingly large, so editing this *Handbook* came with several challenges and required several decisions regarding the book's structure and content.

We structured the book to reflect the two broad domains of applied psychology and experimental psychology. Whereas applied specialties in psychology, such as clinical, counseling, neuropsychology, and school, are typically grounded in the scientist-practitioner model that emphasizes both research and the provision of clinical services (e.g., assessment and therapy), experimental psychology focuses primarily on conducting empirical research grounded in theories from domains such as cognitive, developmental, and social psychology. Importantly, both applied and experimental psychologists have made meaningful contributions to the psychology–law field, and each of those domains of the psychology–law field includes a range of well-developed topic areas with robust empirical support. Although we recognize that the distinction between applied psychology and experimental psychology is somewhat arbitrary and has inherently blurry boundaries, we felt that this organizational structure would be an effective approach for grouping topics and enhancing the readability of the book.

Rather than duplicating the tables of contents from other books that have sought to provide broad coverage of topic areas in the broader field of psychology–law or the narrower field of forensic psychology, we included a mix of *traditional topics* that would be expected to be included in a comprehensive book of this type and *novel topics* in emerging content areas. There are several content areas that must be included in a book of this type because they have strong empirical support, are widely accepted by both psychologists and lawyers, and address considerations with clear relevance to the legal system. However, the field of psychology–law is dynamic, with new content areas emerging as researchers, practitioners, and legal professionals recognize the many valuable contributions that psychology can make to the legal field, with new advances in technology used in the legal system, and with current events, such as a pandemic or BIPOC movement, that meaningfully change human behavior. We believe it is important to provide coverage of those emerging areas.

This *Handbook* is broadly divided into three sections. The first section, "Foundational Psychology–Law," includes five chapters that have clear foundational relevance to both applied psychology and experimental psychology. This section has two goals. First, we wanted to highlight topics that meaningfully tie together the applied and experimental aspects of psychology–law. Second, this section introduces a primary goal of this *Handbook*—presenting emerging, cutting-edge topics in psychology–law that will continue to grow and meaningfully shape future research programs and policy reform.

The second section of this *Handbook*, "Applied Psychology–Law," includes twenty chapters that provide coverage of topics related to the provision of forensic services (broadly defined) in criminal and civil legal contexts. We further divided this section into three parts. Part I ("General Considerations") focuses on topics with general relevance to applied psychology–law practice. These three chapters, which address a framework for forensic mental health assessments, the ethical practice of forensic psychology, and forensic report writing, provide foundational content for the other chapters in this section of the *Handbook*. Part II ("Criminal and Civil Forensic Psychology") includes chapters on forensic mental health assessments in various criminal and civil contexts. In addition to including chapters on the more commonly conducted forensic mental health assessments, we included chapters on emerging practice areas that have received less coverage in books and other publications. Part III ("Consultation and Intervention") includes chapters that address the significant contribution made by applied psychologists in the areas of consultation and intervention.

The third section of this *Handbook*, "Experimental Psychology–Law," includes nineteen chapters that provide coverage of perceptions, judgments, decision-making, and behaviors that are relevant to criminal (and some civil) contexts. Although there is undoubtedly overlap of content across the sequence of events in criminal contexts, we organized this section loosely using a chronological format from occurrence to investigation through resolution and beyond. To this end, we divided the experimental section into three parts. Part I ("Witnesses and Victims") focuses on who are often directly involved with, and issues directly related to, the occurrence of legal wrongdoing. Part I comprises several emerging issues stemming from traditional and well-established areas, such as nascent issues related to eyewitness identifications, forensic interviewing, and legal decision-making among young victims and witnesses. Part II ("Evidence Gathering and Pursuit in Criminal Cases") includes chapters that address the investigative aspects of solving criminal cases. Like Part I, Part II offers several emerging issues related to traditional topics such as custody during interrogation, barriers to detecting child sexual abuse, and how innocents may be targeted for criminal wrongdoing. Part III ("Criminal Outcomes") includes chapters that address the processes associated with the resolution of criminal cases and postconviction issues. Part III also focuses heavily on emerging issues, such as novel developments in wrongful convictions, plea bargains, prosecutorial misconduct, and sentencing of minorities.

Across all forty-four chapters in this *Handbook*, there are more than 115 authors and coauthors from a variety of academic, research, clinical, legal, and other professional settings. A glance at the Table of Contents reveals that we are fortunate to include chapters from well-known contributors with established reputations who have already made significant contributions to the psychology–law field, and also from early-career professionals and other researchers and scholars who are emerging as future leaders in their respective content areas.

This *Handbook* took a proverbial village to complete, and we owe a debt of gratitude to many people. We thank the many contributors for their timely, high-quality contributions to this book. Your expertise in your respective areas yielded chapters that will "set the bar" for the psychology–law field. We also appreciate the outstanding support we received from Oxford University Press, particularly Sarah Harrington, Hayley Singer, and Emily Benitez. Finally, we thank the many researchers, clinicians, legal professionals, and students who continue to shape the psychology–law field.

Dave DeMatteo
Kyle C. Scherr

LIST OF CONTRIBUTORS

Fabiana Alceste
Department of Psychology, Butler
University

C. J. Appleton
Center for Advancing Correctional
Excellence and Department of
Criminology, Law and Society,
George Mason University

Shelby Arnold
Beck Institute

Beth C. Arredondo
Ochsner Neuroscience Institute,
Ochsner Health

Tzachi Ashkenazi
Israeli Prime Minister's Office,
Tel Aviv, Israel

Virginia Barber-Rioja
Department of Psychology, New York
University

Samantha Bean
New York University

Amanda Beltrani
Fairleigh Dickinson University

Scott D. Bender
Department of Psychiatry and
Neurobehavioral Sciences, University
of Virginia Health System

Marcus T. Boccaccini
Psychology Department, Sam
Houston State University

Brian H. Bornstein
Arizona State University &
University of Nebraska-Lincoln

Ben Bradford
Institute for Global City Policing,
Jill Dando Institute of Security
and Crime Science, University
College London

Julie M. Brovko
Gold Standard Forensic, LLC,
and Department of Psychiatry and
Behavioral Sciences at the University
of New Mexico

Mary Catlin
George Mason University

Allison E. Cipriano
Department of Psychology,
University of Nebraska, Lincoln

William Crozier
Wilson Center for Science and Justice,
Duke University School of Law

Brian L. Cutler
School of Psychology, Fielding
Graduate University

David DeMatteo
Department of Psychological and
Brain Sciences and the Thomas
R. Kline School of Law, Drexel
University

Richart L. DeMier
Independent Practice

Amy Dezember
George Mason University

Jason J. Dickinson
Department of Psychology, Montclair
State University

Park Dietz
University of California, Los Angeles

Kevin S. Douglas
Simon Fraser University

Eric Y. Drogin
Harvard Medical School

Itiel E. Dror
University College London

Karen L. Dugosh
Public Health Management
Corporation

Jaymes Fairfax-Columbo
University of New Mexico
Department of Psychiatry and
Behavioral Sciences and University of
New Mexico School of Law

Melanie B. Fessinger
Graduate Center and John Jay
College of Criminal Justice

David S. Festinger
Public Health Management
Corporation and Philadelphia
College of Osteopathic Medicine

Ronald P. Fisher
Department of Psychology, Florida
International University

Daniel J. Flack
Department of Psychological and
Brain Sciences and the Thomas
R. Kline School of Law, Drexel
University

William E. Foote
Department of Psychiatry and
Behavioral Sciences, University of
New Mexico

Alexandra Garcia-Mansilla
New York City Health + Hospitals,
Correctional Health Services

Brandon L. Garrett
L. Wilson Center for Science
and Justice, Duke University
School of Law

Phillip Atiba Goff
Yale University and Center for
Policing Equity

Deborah Goldfarb
Florida International University

Kenny Gonzalez
Department of Psychology, Montclair
State University

Jonathan W. Gould
Charlotte Psychotherapy &
Consultation Group, Charlotte,
North Carolina

Pär Anders Granhag
Department of Psychology,
University of Gothenburg, Sweden

Lauren Grove
Department of Psychology, Montclair
State University

Nicole Guevara
Department of Psychology, Montclair
State University

Max Guyll
Arizona State University

Leigh D. Hagan
Independent Practice of Forensic &
Clinical Psychology

Stephen D. Hart
Simon Fraser University

Kirk Heilbrun
Department of Psychological and
Brain Sciences, Drexel University

Sarah Hitchcock
Department of Psychology, Montclair
State University

Kathryn J. Holland
Department of Psychology and
Women's & Gender Studies
Program, University of Nebraska,
Lincoln

Jennifer S. Hunt
University of Kentucky

Saul M. Kassin
Department of Psychology, John Jay College of Criminal Justice

Christopher M. King
Department of Psychology, Montclair State University

Steven M. Kleinman
Operational Sciences Institute

Lauren E. Kois
University of Alabama

Margaret Bull Kovera
John Jay College of Criminal Justice and the Graduate Center, City University of New York

Daniel A. Krauss
Claremont McKenna College

Alexandra Kudatzky
Thomas R. Kline School of Law, Drexel University

Jeff Kukucka
Towson University

Arabella Kyprianides
Institute for Global City Policing, University College London

Casey LaDuke
John Jay College of Criminal Justice, Queens College, & The Graduate Center, City University of New York, and Department of Rehabilitation and Human Performance, Icahn School of Medicine at Mount Sinai

Sharon Leal
University of Portsmouth

JoAnn Lee
Department of Social Work, George Mason University

McCown Leggett
Texas Tech University

Lora M. Levett
University of Florida

Jessica L. Lipkin
Public Health Management Corporation

Nicole E. Lytle
Department of Social Work and Child Advocacy, Montclair State University

Benjamin J. Mackey
Center for Advancing Correctional Excellence and Department of Criminology, Law and Society, George Mason University

Stephanie Madon
Arizona State University

Lindsay C. Malloy
Ontario Tech University

Bernice A. Marcopulos
Department of Graduate Psychology, James Madison University, and Department of Psychiatry and Neurobehavioral Sciences, University of Virginia Health System

Jessica Mattera
Texas Tech University

Bradley D. McAuliff
California State University, Northridge

Christian A. Meissner
Iowa State University

Amelia Mindthoff
Iowa State University

Robert D. Morgan
Southern Illinois University

Shreya Mukhopadhyay
University of California, Irvine

Christopher Mulchay
Independent Practice

Jessica Munoz
Department of Psychology, Iowa State University

Daniel C. Murrie
Institute of Law, Psychiatry, and Public Policy, University of Virginia

Bronwyn Neeser
University of New Mexico
Department of Psychiatry and
Behavioral Sciences

Randy K. Otto
College of Psychology, Nova
Southeastern University

Ira K. Packer
University of Massachusetts
Medical School

Amanda Palardy
Department of Psychology, Montclair
State University

Minqi Pan
University of North Texas

Anthony D. Perillo
Indiana University of Pennsylvania

Jennifer T. Perillo
Indiana University of Pennsylvania

Liana C. Peter-Hagene
North Central College

Erik P. Phillips
Iowa State University

Lisa Drago Piechowski
Independent Practice

Debra Ann Poole
Department of Psychology, Central
Michigan University

Gwen Prowse
Tulane University

Jodi A. Quas
University of California, Irvine

Allison D. Redlich
George Mason University

Madelena Rizzo
Department of Psychological and
Brain Sciences and the Thomas R.
Kline School of Law, Drexel University

Richard Rogers
University of North Texas

Jesse N. Rothweiler
Iowa State University

Jessica M. Salerno
Arizona State University

Faith Scanlon
Texas Tech University

Kyle C. Scherr
Department of Psychology, Central
Michigan University

Ryan Schneider
Montclair State University

Nicholas Scurich
University of California, Irvine

Suraiya Shammi
George Mason University

Sarah Skidmore
Center for Advancing Correctional
Excellence and Department of Social
Work, George Mason University

Christopher Slobogin
Vanderbilt Law School

Andrew M. Smith
Iowa State University

Faye S. Taxman
Center for Advancing Correctional
Excellence and Schar School of
Policy and Government, George
Mason University

Alice Thornewill
Independent Practice

Chriscelyn M. Tussey
Private Practice and Department
of Psychiatry, New York University
Grossman School of Medicine

Aldert Vrij
Department of Psychology,
University of Portsmouth

Gary L. Wells
Iowa State University

Kellie Wiltsie
Department of Psychological and
Brain Sciences and the Thomas
R. Kline School of Law, Drexel
University
Joshua Wyman
Ontario Tech University
Julia A. Yesberg
Institute for Global City Policing,
University College London

Patricia A. Zapf
Palo Alto University
Heidi Zapotocky
Department of Psychological and
Brain Sciences, Drexel University
Tina M. Zottoli
Montclair State University

Foundational Psychology–Law

Training for Careers in Psychology–Law

David DeMatteo *and* Kyle C. Scherr

Abstract

There are numerous indications that the field of psychology–law has grown tremendously over the past few decades. Some of the more prominent indicators include the use of psychology–law research in influential court cases, the law's recognition that psychologists can serve as expert witnesses on mental health issues, the development of national and international professional organizations devoted to law and psychology/psychiatry, and numerous professional journals devoted to psychology–law topics. This chapter focuses on another indicator of the growth of psychology–law—training for a career in the psychology–law field. After describing the long relationship between the fields of psychology and law, this chapter discusses the varied roles for psychologists in the psychology–law field. Then, the chapter discusses the educational and training opportunities for those interested in psychology–law, including opportunities at the undergraduate, graduate, and postdoctoral levels.

Key Words: psychology–law, training, education, forensic assessment, forensic therapy, forensic research, consultation

Although there are differences between psychology and law in terms of professional interests, approaches to problem-solving, the way each profession establishes the "truth," and training models, the two disciplines have a rich history of working symbiotically in a variety of clinical and research-based contexts. There is evidence that ancient Greek, Roman, and Hebrew civilizations dating back more than two thousand years considered an individual's mental health when determining legal responsibility (DeMatteo et al., 2020), but the formal relationship between psychology and law was established much more recently due to several key events in the late 1800s and early 1900s. A seminal event was the establishment of Wilhelm Wundt's psychology–law research laboratory in the late 1870s at the University of Leipzig, which formalized the study of the relationship between psychology and law. Other key events around that time include the publication of Harvard psychologist Hugo Münsterberg's (1908) influential book, *On the Witness Stand*, which highlighted areas in which psychology and law intersect (e.g., eyewitness testimony and false confessions), and the founding of William Healy's Chicago Juvenile Psychopathic

Institute, which provided rehabilitative treatment for adolescents who committed crimes. These and other events led to the integration of mental health professionals into the legal system in the early and mid-1900s.

The psychology–law field continued to grow and evolve throughout the latter half of the twentieth century as psychological science and psychologists became more integrated in the legal system. Shortly after World War II, *amicus curiae* briefs that summarized social science research, sometimes called "Brandeis Briefs," were used in several important legal cases. In the landmark school desegregation case *Brown v. Board of Education*,[1] the US Supreme Court relied in part on psychological research summarized in a social science brief in concluding that racial segregation in schools was unconstitutional. Several years later, in *Jenkins v. United States*,[2] the US Court of Appeals for the District of Columbia Circuit held that properly trained and qualified psychologists could offer expert testimony on mental health disorders. The *Jenkins* decision, which was authored by the forward-thinking Judge David Bazelon, was a paradigm shift regarding the role of psychologists in legal proceedings. Prior to *Jenkins* and throughout most of our legal system's history, courts typically preferred the testimony of medically trained professionals when an individual's mental health was at issue. After *Jenkins*, the field of forensic psychology experienced dramatic growth, and forensic psychologists currently conduct thousands of forensic mental health assessments each year on a variety of legal issues in criminal and civil courts (Melton et al., 2018; Otto & Heilbrun, 2002).

Another indicator of the growth of the psychology–law field is the development of national and international professional organizations devoted to law and psychology/psychiatry, including the American Academy of Psychiatry and the Law; American Psychology-Law Society; Australian and New Zealand Association of Psychiatry, Psychology, and Law; European Association of Psychology and Law; International Academy of Law and Mental Health; International Association of Applied Psychology; International Association for Correctional and Forensic Psychology; International Association of Forensic Mental Health Services; and International Investigative Interviewing Research Group. Professional conferences that focus on psychology–law have experienced remarkable growth in recent years. The American Psychology-Law Society (AP-LS), which is Division 41 of the American Psychological Association, was founded in 1968 as forensic psychology's first professional association (Grisso & Brodsky, 2018). Having once had fewer than fifty members, AP-LS currently has more than three thousand members (including a large portion of students), and the AP-LS annual conference regularly attracts more than one thousand attendees.

There are also numerous professional journals devoted to publishing empirical, theoretical, and practice articles relevant to psychology–law, including *Behavioral Sciences and the Law; Criminal Justice and Behavior; International Journal of Forensic Mental Health;*

---

[1] Brown v. Bd. of Educ., 347 U.S. 483 (1954).
[2] Jenkins v. United States, 307 F.2d 637 (D.C. Cir. 1962).

Journal of the American Academy of Psychiatry and the Law; Law and Human Behavior; Psychology, Crime and Law; and *Psychology, Public Policy, and Law.* In addition to peer-reviewed journals, there are also hundreds of books devoted to various aspects of forensic psychology. Some are more academic in nature and targeted to researchers and practitioners, including the Best Practices for Forensic Mental Health Assessment series published by Oxford University Press and a book series published by the AP-LS, while other books on psychology–law are mass-marketed to the public.

This chapter focuses on another indicator of the growth of psychology–law—training for a career in the psychology–law field. The psychology–law field encompasses many different substantive areas, and psychologists working in these areas can assume a variety of roles. Given the growth and expansion of the psychology–law field, it is imperative that training opportunities keep pace. This chapter begins by describing the varied roles for psychologists in the psychology–law field and then discussing the educational and training opportunities for those interested in psychology–law.

Roles in the Psychology–Law Field

The psychology–law field is quite broad, and the varied roles assumed by psychologists working in the field reflect the field's diversity and breadth. At a broad level, which is reflected in the structure of the table of contents for this book, psychologists in the psychology–law field can be categorized as clinical (applied) or experimental (nonapplied). But this should not be viewed as a rigid dichotomy, and this book ideally demonstrates the substantial overlap between clinical and experimental specialties. This section describes some of the more common roles in the psychology–law field, which highlight differences between clinical and experimental psychologists while also demonstrating the many ways in which these specialty areas overlap.

Forensic Clinicians

FORENSIC MENTAL HEALTH ASSESSMENTS

Psychologists who are clinically trained and properly credentialed (i.e., licensed) can conduct forensic mental health assessments of criminal offenders and civil litigants in a variety of legal and administrative contexts (see Heilbrun et al., 2014; Melton et al., 2018). Unlike traditional clinical assessments, which are primarily conducted to develop a psychological treatment plan for individuals with mental health symptoms, forensic mental health assessments assist legal decision makers—typically attorneys, judges, and juries, but also administrative bodies—to make better-informed decisions in contexts in which psychological expertise can be useful to the legal process. In this role, forensic psychologists are using their expertise regarding human behavior, interviewing and testing, and legal standards to offer an expert opinion about an individual's mental health functioning or ways in which the individual's mental health is relevant to a particular legal question.

Forensic psychologists can address a variety of legal questions in a criminal context (see Heilbrun et al., 2014). Some of the legal questions addressed in criminal contexts include competence to stand trial (Zapf & Roesch, 2008),[3] competence to plead guilty,[4] competence to waive *Miranda* rights (Goldstein & Goldstein, 2010),[5] competence to be executed,[6] mental state at the time of the offense (i.e., insanity, diminished capacity; Packer 2009), juvenile waiver (Heilbrun et al., 2017), conditional release (Vitacco et al., 2014), state and federal sentencing (Atkins & Watson, 2011), violence risk assessment (Heilbrun, 2009), and capital mitigation (Cunningham, 2010; DeMatteo et al., 2011). The legal decisions in these cases are made by the court (either the judge or jury, depending on the type of case and jurisdiction), but forensic psychologists can help courts to better understand how the offender's mental health relates to the specific legal question being addressed.

Forensic psychologists in civil law contexts can evaluate individuals who are involved or may become involved in litigation or some other civil proceeding (Heilbrun et al., 2014). As with forensic mental health assessments in criminal contests, these evaluations can be requested by attorneys and courts, but they can also be requested employers and insurance companies. Some of the forensic mental health assessments conducted in civil contexts include civil competencies (e.g., competence to execute a contract and competence to consent to or refuse treatment) (Kim, 2010), workplace discrimination and harassment and disability (Goodman-Delahunty & Foote, 2011), workplace disability (Piechowski, 2011), civil commitment (Pinals & Mossman, 2011), child custody (Cooke & Norris, 2011), parenting capacity (Budd et al., 2011), child abuse and neglect (Blair & Steinberg, 2011), guardianship (Drogin & Barrett, 2010), psychological damages (Kane & Dvoskin, 2011), sexually violent predator commitment (Witt & Conroy, 2008), fitness for duty (Corey & Zelig, 2020), and malpractice (Drogin & Meyer, 2011).

FORENSIC THERAPY

Some clinically trained psychologists provide mental health treatment to justice-involved individuals. Not all therapeutic efforts with justice-involved individuals are appropriately conceptualized as being forensic in nature, but such services are properly considered forensic if they are tailored to the issues and context of a legal proceeding (American Psychological Association, 2013). Forensic therapy may involve providing "restorative therapy" in a secure forensic psychiatric hospital to criminal offenders who have been found incompetent to stand trial (Samuel & Michals, 2011). Other forensic therapy may be designed to reduce the risk of violence of an offender who has been

---

[3] See Dusky v. United States, 62 U.S. 402 (1960).
[4] Godinez v. Moran, 509 U.S. 389 (1993).
[5] See Miranda v. Arizona, 384 U.S. 486 (1966).
[6] Ford v. Wainwright, 477 U.S. 399 (1986); Panetti v. Quarterman, 551 U.S. 930 (2007).

found not guilty by reason of insanity, reduce the risk of recidivism among sexually violent predators, or address the treatment needs of adolescents in juvenile residential treatment facilities.

Forensic Researchers

We endorse a broad definition of forensic psychology that is consistent with the definitions adopted by leading psychology and forensic psychology organizations. For example, the American Board of Forensic Psychology (2020), which is the premier board certification organization for forensic psychologists in the United States, defines forensic psychology as the application of scientific, technical, or other specialized knowledge of psychology to inform matters within the judicial system, legislative bodies, and administrative agencies. The American Psychological Association adopted the *Specialty Guidelines for Forensic Psychology* as official policy in 2011, and the *Specialty Guidelines* defines forensic psychology as "professional practice by any psychologist working within any subdiscipline of psychology (e.g., clinical, developmental, social, cognitive) when applying the scientific, technical, or specialized knowledge of psychology to the law to assist in addressing legal, contractual, and administrative matters" (American Psychological Association, 2013, p. 7). These broad definitions of forensic psychology encompass clinical, research, and consultation activities, and they recognize the widely varying roles that can be assumed by forensic psychologists in a variety of settings.

In this section, we highlight the activities of psychologists who conduct research that can be useful to legal decision makers or to some other aspect of the judicial system (see DeMatteo et al., 2020, for a detailed discussion). Forensically relevant research can be conducted by clinically trained psychologists (assuming a sufficient foundation of training in research design/methodology and statistics) and experimental psychologists. Some clinically trained psychologists integrate research into their professional activities. Some psychologists do not have clinical training and instead have a doctoral degree in a research-based area of psychology, so they do not have the qualifications to conduct forensic mental health assessments or provide forensic therapy. The research conducted by these psychologists can be used in a specific criminal or civil case, applied more broadly to some aspect of the justice system, or used to effectuate changes in policy and practice.

Psychologists from a variety of subdisciplines of psychology conduct forensic-relevant research. For example, clinical psychologists might help develop valid and reliable screening measures to assess mental health functioning or violence risk among justice-involved individuals, or they may conduct outcome research to assess the efficacy of prison-based treatment programs. Experimental psychologists often apply basic cognitive, developmental, and social theories to study jury decision-making, racial discrimination, eyewitness memory and identifications, forensic evidence evaluation, false confessions, investigative interviewing, deception detection, plea bargaining, the reliability of courtroom testimony provided by children, decision-making among children and adolescents, risk and protective factors for juvenile delinquency, and the effects of divorce on children. These are just a small selection of the forensically relevant topics on which researchers focus.

Forensic Consultants

Clinical and experimental psychologists can also serve as consultants who address some aspect of the judicial system, broadly conceptualized. Psychologists from a variety of sub-disciplines (e.g., clinical, neuropsychology, developmental, social, and cognitive) can be of tremendous assistance to the legal system in a variety of contexts. On a case-specific level, psychologists might consult with attorneys regarding jury selection, or they may be retained by an attorney to evaluate a psychological report submitted by the opposing party's expert and develop cross-examination questions to highlight weaknesses in the opposing expert's report.

There are a variety of consultation opportunities for psychologists at a broader systems level. For example, in a correctional context, forensic psychologists may be asked to recommend an efficient, valid, and reliable screening tool to classify inmates based on their mental health needs, suicide risk, or potential for violence, or to assist the facility in providing evidence-based psychological treatment to improve the mental health functioning of inmates. Psychologists with expertise in industrial/organizational psychology may consult on ways to improve the staffing and administrative structure of a correctional facility, while other psychologists may be asked to consult on the negative psychological effects of solitary confinement or to train staff on deescalation strategies correctional officers can use when confronted with a potentially violent inmate. Consultation with police departments has increased in recent years. In that context, psychologists may be asked to develop valid and reliable screening procedures for hiring police officers, assist in developing mental health assessment and treatment protocols for officers involved in shootings, or train police officers and other first responders to interact more effectively with individuals who are mentally ill and/or drug involved.

Psychologists often consult with schools, courts, government agencies, and legislative bodies. For example, in educational contexts, psychologists are being asked to collaborate with schools and law enforcement agencies to develop effective "active-shooter" safety protocols. Consultation with courts might focus on developing, implementing, and evaluating judicial programs (e.g., problem-solving courts). Some psychologists consult with government agencies that focus on the well-being of children to review organizational policy and practice related to the handling of child abuse and neglect cases. Finally, psychologists may be asked to offer their expertise to legislative or administrative bodies regarding how certain laws or policies can be developed or modified based on psychological research.

Other Careers

Although many psychologists work as consultants with law enforcement agencies, both clinical and experimental psychologists can also work as in-house staff for law enforcement agencies. For example, some clinical psychologists employed by large agencies or who are solely involved in doing officer assessments perform fitness-for-duty evaluations when there is a reasonable belief that some psychological condition may be an underlying cause leading to impaired work performance or a direct threat to the officer or the publics' safety.[7] Experimental psychologists can also work in-house at various law enforcement agencies. These careers may involve conducting research solely with and for the agency or collaborations involving other agencies or academic researchers. Experimental psychologists may also work as analysts examining patterns from field data, in-house research, or collaborative endeavors with academics and other agencies.

Another career option for clinical and experimental psychologists is working for non-profit organizations whose main focus is to inform and advance public policy. These career options primarily involve conducting research and attaining grant funding to support the organizations' research endeavors. Some notable examples of these organizations include the RAND Corporation, the Innocence Project, and the Pew Research Center.

Educational and Training Opportunities in Psychology–Law

The development of educational programs that provide psychology–law training began relatively recently. Before these formal training programs were developed, psychologists typically received forensic training "on the job" (see DeMatteo et al., 2016, p. 5). The development of formal psychology–law training programs in the 1970s ushered in a new era of opportunities for psychologists interested in working at the intersection of psychology and law (e.g., Bersoff, 1999; DeMatteo et al., 2009; Krauss & Sales, 2014).

The development of formal psychology–law programs was facilitated by several key events. The 1995 National Invitational Conference on Education and Training in Law and Psychology at Villanova University identified the state of forensic education at that time and set a direction for the future development of training in psychology and law (Bersoff et al., 1997). In 2009, DeMatteo et al. described core elements, both existing and aspirational, of educational and training programs in forensic psychology. One year later, Heilbrun and Brooks (2010) utilized recommendations set by the National Research Council (2009) to propose meaningful planning in forensic psychology training. Not to be overlooked is the increased student demand for psychology–law training (Brigham, 1999; DeMatteo et al., 2016).

Currently, there are a variety of educational and training opportunities for those interested in the psychology–law field. These opportunities range from undergraduate survey courses that examine the broad intersection of psychology and law to doctoral

---

[7] Americans with Disabilities Act of 1990, Pub. L. No. 101-336, 104 Stat. 328.

programs that provide in-depth psychology–law training to postgraduate opportunities for fellowships and continuing education. Of note, the growth in educational and training opportunities in the psychology–law field has not been accompanied by a clear consensus regarding the appropriate training models, curricula, and goals of these specialized training programs. A discussion of this issue is beyond the scope of this chapter, but interested readers can refer to several resources that discuss this debate (e.g., Bersoff et al., 1997; DeMatteo et al., 2009; Krauss & Sales, 2014).

The following sections discuss the educational and training opportunities currently available to students and practitioners in psychology–law. Over the past fifty years, the educational and training opportunities for those interested in psychology–law have increased considerably, with a variety of opportunities at the undergraduate, graduate, and postdoctoral levels. We also briefly discuss opportunities for advanced credentialing, including board certification, for forensic psychologists who wish to distinguish themselves as having advanced expertise.

Undergraduate Training

Many colleges and universities offer courses that fall under the psychology–law umbrella, including courses in forensic psychology, criminal psychology, legal psychology, and child witnesses (Burl et al., 2012; Hall et al., 2010). There are no recent comprehensive surveys on how many undergraduate programs offer psychology–law courses, but several surveys conducted in the 1990s indicated that the number of such courses was rising (Ogloff et al., 1996) and that many psychology departments offered at least one psychology–law course (Bersoff et al., 1997). Also, the growing number of forensic psychology textbooks for undergraduates suggests that psychology–law courses are offered with increased regularity (e.g., Costanzo & Krauss, 2018; Greene & Heilbrun, 2019; Huss, 2014). Psychology–law courses offered at the undergraduate level are becoming more specific and nuanced. In addition to broad survey courses on the intersection of psychology and law, some colleges and universities are offering courses with a more specific focus, including eyewitness testimony, wrongful convictions, memory and the law, and the treatment and management of offenders. Some schools are also offering undergraduate degrees in forensic psychology (e.g., John Jay College of Criminal Justice).

Master's Programs

Despite increased offerings of undergraduate psychology–law courses, there are more educational and training opportunities in psychology–law at the graduate level. Graduate programs in forensic psychology can be categorized by program focus (e.g., clinical forensic psychology, legal psychology, and experimental psychology), training goals (e.g., clinical scientist-practitioner and nonclinical scientist-scholar), and degrees awarded (e.g., master's, doctorate, and joint degree) (see DeMatteo et al., 2016; DeMatteo et al., 2020; Krauss & Sales, 2014). The AP-LS periodically produces a guide to graduate programs that offer psychology–law training (see American Psychology-Law Society, 2020).

There has been considerable growth in the educational and training opportunities in psychology–law available at the master's level. For example, a 1990 survey on forensic psychology training programs by Tomkins and Ogloff revealed only one program that provided psychology–law training at the master's level, and another review article published the same year did not even address training at the master's level (Otto et al., 1990). Two decades later, Burl et al. (2012) identified seventeen master's-level training programs in the United States, and the most recent guide to graduate programs from the AP-LS identifies twenty-eight master's programs that provide psychology–law training (American Psychology-Law Society, 2020).

Master's programs, which provide students with a foundation in a particular subfield of psychology (e.g., clinical, experimental, and forensic), can typically be completed in two or three years. In contrast to most doctoral programs, master's programs are often heavily focused on coursework and may not have an applied component. Master's degrees come in two forms: Master of Arts (MA) and Master of Science (MS). Although both types of programs may provide students with research experience, MS programs typically require completion of an independent research project; by contrast, MA programs do not typically require empirical research, although students may be required to complete some other type of research project as a prerequisite for graduation. Some master's programs are designed to prepare graduates for employment in a research or clinical context, while other master's programs are primarily designed to prepare students for a doctoral program. Finally, a master's degree may be terminal (i.e., the graduate program is completed upon receipt of the degree) or earned as an intermediate step toward a doctoral degree. Although the entry-level degree in forensic psychology is typically a doctoral degree, there is growing demand for master's-level clinicians in employment settings where psychology interfaces with the law (see Krauss & Sales, 2014; Zaitchik et al., 2007).

Doctoral Programs

For researchers and clinicians, the "norm for independent professional practice" is the doctoral degree (Krauss & Sales, 2014, p. 123). There are currently more than thirty doctoral programs that provide some type of psychology–law training (American Psychology-Law Society, 2020). This represents growth in available opportunities for psychology–law training, but that is a relatively small number of programs. To put this in context, as of November 2020, there were 248 APA-accredited clinical psychology doctoral programs (American Psychological Association, 2020), and the training directory for the Society for Clinical Neuropsychology (2020) currently lists thirty-eight doctoral programs in clinical neuropsychology.

There are two primary types of doctoral programs in clinical psychology: Doctor of Philosophy (PhD) and Doctor of Psychology (PsyD). PsyD programs primarily train students to provide clinical services (e.g., assessment and treatment) and there is less focus (if any) on conducting research. By contrast, PhD programs typically adhere to the scientist-practitioner model and provide more balanced training in research and clinical work. These types of degree programs also differ in terms of costs of attendance and selectivity in admissions. Many PhD programs offer partial or full tuition remission in addition to a stipend, whereas most PsyD programs are tuition-based and offer less financial support. The differences in the financial structure of PsyD and PhD programs are associated with differences in selectivity in admissions. PhD programs often select small cohorts of students from large numbers of applicants, while PsyD programs typically accept larger cohorts. Although there is variability in admissions data based on program focus, geographic location, and other factors, PhD programs accept 7–16 percent of their applicants, while PsyD programs accept 26–50 percent of their applicants (Norcross et al., 2010). Finally, graduate program completion time also varies, with PsyD programs typically taking four to six years to complete and PhD programs taking five to seven years to complete.

Clinical psychology doctoral programs produce psychologists skilled at integrating research and clinical work. The American Psychological Association's accreditation standards require clinically oriented doctoral programs to provide instruction in history and systems of psychology; basic content areas in scientific psychology (affective, biological, cognitive, developmental, and social); advanced integrative knowledge of scientific psychology; and research methods, statistical analysis, and psychometrics (American Psychological Association Commission on Accreditation, 2020). There is also an emphasis on research, ethical and legal standards, diversity, professional values and attitudes, communication and interpersonal skills, assessment, intervention, supervision, and consultation and interprofessional/interdisciplinary skills (American Psychological Association Commission on Accreditation, 2020).

Doctoral programs in applied specialty areas (e.g., clinical, counseling, school, and neuropsychology) also provide students with real-world clinical experience via placements (or practica). Through placements, doctoral students gain experience under the supervision of experienced mental health professionals. Depending on resources relationships and location, these placements may be in college counseling centers, outpatient mental health treatment centers, state hospitals, private practices, and correctional facilities. These clinical experiences prepare students for the final stage of their doctoral training, which involves completion of an internship. Students pursuing a PhD or PsyD in clinical, counseling, and school psychology are required to complete a one-year predoctoral internship prior to receiving their degree. Over the past forty years, the percentage of predoctoral internships with either minor or major rotations in forensic psychology has increased considerably (DeMatteo et al., 2016).

Experimentally focused doctoral programs offer a single degree: PhD. Initially, experimental students interested in psychology–law were trained in basic cognitive, developmental, or social psychology and then applied those basic theories to issues in the legal system. Perhaps due to the growth of the psychology–law field, more recent programs offer training in legal psychology specifically rather than a focus on more basic background in cognitive, developmental, or social psychology. Historically, experimental programs trained and prepared students for research careers in academia. However, career options for experimentally trained PhDs in psychology–law have also evolved. Some programs now offer training that prepares students for more applied careers such as working with consulting firms or as analysts for law enforcement agencies (e.g., FBI). Regardless of the epistemological basis of the training for either academic or applied careers, all experimental students' training is primarily concentrated on conducting research.

Joint-Degree Programs

There are a handful of joint-degree options for those interested in obtaining formal training in both psychology and law. Some of these programs provide clinical training, while others are experimental. There are several different degree combinations, including (a) a Juris Doctor (JD) with either a master's degree or doctoral psychology degree, and (b) a Master of Legal Studies (MLS) degree in combination with a master's or doctoral psychology degree. Whereas a JD degree is required (along with passage of the jurisdictional Bar Exam) to practice law, the MLS is a nonpractitioner degree that provides foundational legal knowledge to help students function in fields that require an understanding of the law. Joint-degree programs range in length from four to seven years, depending on the degree combination and program structure. There are also several schools that permit students to pursue a JD and PhD concurrently, but without offering a formal integrated curriculum in law and psychology.

Other Types of Programs

There are several less traditional paths for those interested in studying psychology–law. For example, some professionals in the psychology–law field obtained doctoral degrees in fields related to psychology, such as a PhD in counseling psychology or Doctor of Education (EdD). These degree programs are similar to PhD programs in clinical psychology in that they typically adhere to the scientist-practitioner model, but there are key differences. The training in PhD programs in counseling psychology focuses on how individuals function both individually and in relationships, and the focus is somewhat different than the focus of PhD programs in clinical psychology. Whereas clinical psychology focuses on mental health disorders and behavioral health, counseling psychology focuses on multicultural training and holistic approaches to assessment and treatment (Price, 2009). Also, clinical psychologists tend to work with individuals with serious mental illness to reduce symptoms of mental health disorders, whereas counseling psychologists tend to work with healthier populations to improve overall life satisfaction. A Doctor of Education degree focuses on conducting research on the educational system as a whole.

Completion of a doctoral program in either education or counseling psychology typically makes graduates eligible to become licensed clinicians.

Postdoctoral Training, Education, and Credentialing in Psychology–Law

Psychologists interested in psychology–law can avail themselves of several training opportunities at the postdoctoral level, including formal postdoctoral fellowships in forensic psychology and continuing education programs. Postdoctoral fellowships, which offer supervised research and/or clinical experience, are appropriate for those with forensic training and experience who want to specialize in a particular area of forensic psychology as well as for those trained in nonclinical programs or nonforensic programs who want respecialization training in clinical psychology with a forensic emphasis. For those seeking licensure as a psychologist, these training opportunities are also useful because states typically require that licensure candidates obtain supervised experience after receiving their doctorate.

Practitioners can also enhance their psychology–law knowledge through continuing education (CE) training seminars. Several organizations, including the American Academy of Forensic Psychology (AAFP) and CONCEPT, offer CE and other seminars for those interested in psychology–law. CE programs, which provide CE credits (a required part of licensure as a psychologist in most jurisdictions), are available on range of topics within the psychology–law field, and they range from one-hour sessions that provide a broad overview of a topic area to intensive three-day workshops that offer highly specific training.

Psychologists in applied specialty areas are eligible to pursue board certification as a way to distinguish themselves as having advanced expertise. Although several organizations offer board certification, the most highly respected is the American Board of Professional Psychology (ABPP) (Heilbrun & Brooks, 2010). ABPP offers certification in fifteen specialty areas of psychology, including forensic psychology. The Diplomate in Forensic Psychology is the credential for identifying the highest level of competence in forensic psychology, although ABPP titling terminology is shifting from Diplomate to Board Certified Specialist. There are strict eligibility criteria for becoming eligible for board certification in forensic psychology through the American Board of Forensic Psychology, which is the ABPP specialty board that oversees forensic psychology board certification. The eligibility criteria relate to education, training, and experience, and the ABFP certification process involves a credential review, written exam, submission of two practice samples, and a three-hour oral examination. There are currently fewer than 450 ABFP-certified forensic psychologists in the United States.

Postdoctoral training is becoming more common for experimental psychologists as well. Often these opportunities are designed to advance new PhDs a program of research and provide an opportunity for them to obtain external funding. In other instances, experimental PhDs can take postdoctoral opportunities within a court system, some other organization related to the legal system (e.g., FBI), or organizations not directly a part of the legal system but very closely aligned with the legal system (e.g., Innocence Project). Although not required, engaging postdoctoral opportunities are becoming more commonplace and critical to securing a job regardless of whether the experimental PhD desires a job in or outside academia.

Conclusion

The growth of psychology–law over the past fifty years has been accompanied by an expansion of the roles and educational/training opportunities available to students and practitioners. The continuing growth of the field is attributable to its rising popularity among students, the increasing diversity of roles assumed by psychologists in the field, and the legal system's enhanced appreciation of the contribution of psychologists. These are positive indicia of a field that is primed for continued growth. With that said, it is important for the field to develop a consensus regarding what psychology training should encompass, which would provide some consistency, continuity, and quality assurance among training programs.

References

American Board of Forensic Psychology. (2020). *About*. https://abfp.com/about/.

American Psychological Association. (2013). Specialty guidelines for forensic psychology. *American Psychologist, 68*(1), 7–19.

American Psychological Association. (2020). *Search for accredited programs*. https://apps.apa.org/accredsearch/?_ga=2.74942162.1966602285.1610034446-2108069146.1604771025.

American Psychological Association Commission on Accreditation. (2020). *Implementing regulations—Section C: IRS Related to the Standards of Accreditation*. https://www.apa.org/ed/accreditation/section-c-soa.pdf.

American Psychology-Law Society. (2020). *Guide to graduate programs in forensic and legal psychology—2019-20: A resource for prospective students*. https://www.apls-students.org/uploads/4/6/5/6/46564967/guide_to_graduate_programs_in_forensic_and_legal_psychology_2020___1_.pdf.

Atkins, E. L., & Watson, C. (2011). Sentencing. In E. Y. Drogin, F. M. Dattilio, R. L. Sadoff, & T. G. Gutheil (Eds.), *Handbook of forensic assessment: Psychological and psychiatric perspectives* (pp. 49–78). John Wiley & Sons.

Bersoff, D. N. (1999). Preparing for two cultures: Education and training in law and psychology. In R. Roesch, S. D. Hart, & J. R. P. Ogloff (Eds.), *Psychology and law: The state of the discipline* (pp. 375–401). Kluwer Academic/Plenum.

Bersoff, D. N., Goodman-Delahunty, J., Grisso, T., Hans, V. P., Poythress, N. G., & Roesch, R. G. (1997). Training in law and psychology: Models from the Villanova Conference. *American Psychologist, 52*(12), 1301–1310.

Blair, G., & Steinberg, A. G. (2011). Child abuse and neglect. In E. Y. Drogin, F. M. Dattilio, R. L. Sadoff, & T. G. Gutheil (Eds.), *Handbook of forensic assessment: psychological and psychiatric perspectives* (pp. 361–389). John Wiley & Sons.

Brigham, J. C. (1999). What is forensic psychology, anyway? *Law and Human Behavior, 23*(3), 273–298.

Budd, K. S., Connell, M., & Clark, J. R. (2011). *Evaluation of parenting capacity in child protection*. Oxford University Press.

Burl, J., Shah, S., Filone, S., Foster, E., & DeMatteo, D. (2012). A survey of graduate training programs and coursework in forensic psychology. *Teaching of Psychology, 39*(1), 48–53.

Cooke, G., & Norris, D. M. (2011). Child custody and parental fitness. In E. Y. Drogin, F. M. Dattilio, R. L. Sadoff, & T. G. Gutheil (Eds.), *Handbook of forensic assessment: Psychological and psychiatric perspectives* (pp. 433–458). John Wiley & Sons.

Corey, D. M., & Zelig, M. (2020). *Evaluations of police suitability and fitness for duty*. Oxford University Press.

Costanzo, M., & Krauss, D. A. (2018). *Forensic and legal psychology: Psychological science applied to law* (3rd ed.). Worth.

Cunningham, M. D. (2010). *Evaluation for capital sentencing*. Oxford University Press.

DeMatteo, D., Burl, J., Filone, S., & Heilbrun, K. (2016). Training in forensic assessment and intervention: Implications for principles-based models. In R. Jackson & R. Roesch (Eds.), *Learning forensic assessment: Research and practice* (2nd ed., pp. 3–31). Routledge/Taylor & Francis Group.

DeMatteo, D., Fairfax-Columbo, J., & Desai, A. (2020). *Becoming a forensic psychologist*. Routledge/Taylor & Francis Group.

DeMatteo, D., Marczyk, G., Krauss, D. A., & Burl, J. (2009). Educational and training models in forensic psychology. *Training and Education in Professional Psychology, 3*(3), 184–191.

DeMatteo, D., Murrie, D. C., Anumba, N. M., & Keesler, M. E. (2011). *Forensic mental health assessments in death penalty cases*. Oxford University Press.

Drogin, E. Y., & Barrett, C. L. (2010). *Evaluation for guardianship*. Oxford University Press.

Drogin, E. Y., & Meyer, D. J. (2011). Psychiatric and psychological malpractice. In E. Y. Drogin, F. M. Dattilio, R. L. Sadoff, & T. G. Gutheil (Eds.), *Handbook of forensic assessment: psychological and psychiatric perspectives* (pp. 543–570). John Wiley & Sons.

Goldstein, A., & Goldstein, N. E. S. (2010). *Evaluating capacity to waive* Miranda *rights*. Oxford University Press.

Goodman-Delahunty, J., & Foote, W. E. (2011). *Evaluation for workplace discrimination and harassment*. Oxford University Press.

Greene, E., & Heilbrun, K. (2019). *Wrightsman's psychology and the legal system* (9th ed.). Wadsworth.

Grisso, T., & Brodsky, S. L., eds. (2018). *The roots of modern psychology and law: A Narrative history*. Oxford University Press.

Hall, T. A., Cook, N. E., & Berman, G. (2010). Navigating the expanding field of law and psychology: A comprehensive guide to graduate education. *Journal of Forensic Psychology Practice, 10*(2), 69–90.

Heilbrun, K. (2009). *Evaluation for risk of violence in adults*. Oxford University Press.

Heilbrun, K., & Brooks, S. (2010). Forensic psychology and forensic science: A proposed agenda for the next decade. *Psychology, Public Policy, and Law, 16*(3), 219–253.

Heilbrun, K., DeMatteo, D. D., Brooks Holliday, S., & LaDuke, C., eds. (2014). *Forensic mental health assessment: A casebook* (2nd ed.). Oxford University Press.

Heilbrun, K., DeMatteo, D. D., King, C., & Filone, S. (2017). *Evaluating juvenile transfer and disposition: Law, science, and practice*. Routledge/Taylor & Francis Group.

Huss, M. T. (2014). *Forensic psychology: Research, clinical practice, and applications* (2nd ed.). John Wiley & Sons.

Kane, A. W., & Dvoskin, J. A. (2011). *Evaluation for personal injury claims*. Oxford University Press.

Kim, S. Y. H. (2010). *Evaluation of capacity to consent to treatment and research*. Oxford University Press.

Krauss, D. A., & Sales, B. D. (2014). Training in forensic psychology. In I. B. Weiner & R. K. Otto (Eds.), *The handbook of forensic psychology* (4th ed., pp. 111–134). John Wiley & Sons.

Melton, G. B., Petrila, J., Poythress, N. G., Slobogin, C., Otto, R. K., Mossman, D., & Condie, L. O. (2018). *Psychological evaluations for the courts* (4th ed.). Guilford Press.

Münsterberg, Hugo. (1908). *On the witness stand: Essays on psychology and crime*. Doubleday.

National Research Council. (2009). *Strengthening forensic science in the United States: A path forward*. https://www.ncjrs.gov/pdffiles1/nij/grants/228091.pdf.

Norcross, J. C., J. L. Ellis, & Sayette, M. (2010). Getting in and getting money: A comparative analysis of admission standards, acceptance rates, and financial assistance across the research-practice continuum in clinical psychology programs. *Training and Education in Professional Psychology, 4*(2), 99–104.

Ogloff, J. R. P., Tomkins, A. J., & Bersoff, D. N. (1996). Education and training in law/criminal justice: Historical foundations, present structures, and future developments. *Criminal Justice and Behavior, 23*(1), 200–235.

Otto, R. K., & Heilbrun, K. (2002). The practice of forensic psychology. *American Psychologist, 57*(1), 5–18.

Otto, R. K., Heilbrun, K., & Grisso, T. (1990). Training and credentialing in forensic psychology. *Behavioral Sciences & the Law, 8*(3), 217–231.

Packer, I. K. (2009). *Evaluation of criminal responsibility*. Oxford University Press.

Piechowski, L. D. (2011). *Evaluation of workplace disability*. Oxford University Press.

Pinals, D. A., & Mossman, D. (2011). *Evaluation for civil commitment*. Oxford University Press.

Price, M. (2009, March). Counseling vs. clinical programs: Similarities abound. *GradPSYCH, 7*(2), 6.

Samuel, S. E., & Michals, T. J. (2011). Competency restoration. In E. Y. Drogin, F. M. Dattilio, R. L. Sadoff, & T. G. Gutheil (Eds.), *Handbook of forensic assessment: psychological and psychiatric perspectives* (pp. 79–96). John Wiley & Sons.

Society for Clinical Neuropsychology. (2020). *Training directory.* https://scn40.org/training-directory/?filter_74=Doctoral&filter_219=United+States&mode=all.

Tomkins, A. J., & Ogloff, J. R. P. (1990). Training and career options in psychology and law. *Behavioral Sciences and the Law, 8*(3), 205–216.

Vitacco, M. J., Green, D., Felthous, A. (2014). Introduction to this special issue: Conditional release. *Behavioral Sciences and the Law, 32*(5), 553–556.

Witt, P. H., & Conroy, M. A. (2008). *Evaluation of sexually violent predators.* Oxford University Press.

Zaitchik, M. C., Berman, G. L., Whitworth, D., & Platania, J. (2007). The time is now: The emerging need for master's-level training in forensic psychology. *Journal of Forensic Psychology Practice, 7*(2), 65–71.

Zapf, P. A., & Roesch, R. (2008). *Evaluation of competence to stand trial.* Oxford University Press.

Influencing Policy and Procedure with Law–Psychology Research: Why, When, Where, How, and What

Brian H. Bornstein *and* Christian A. Meissner

Abstract

Psycholegal research is, by design, a field devoted to evaluating and addressing issues that directly affect the justice system. At the same time, many scholars in the field have experienced firsthand the frustrations of bridging the divide between research and policy or practice. In this chapter we discuss key issues and challenges involved in bridging this divide by focusing on a number of cardinal questions: Why influence policy? When, where, and how might we do so? How much evidence must there be before adopting a particular policy? And what policies can (or should) we address? We argue that psycholegal research should operate within a translational research framework, and we encourage scholars to communicate their findings to a broader audience, spend time with the professionals for whom their research is intended, introduce students to best practices for conducting policy-relevant research, and reconsider how we evaluate one another's contributions in the academy.

Key Words: psycholegal research, policy, translational research, policy reform, best practices

Like all areas of science, every field of psychology has its own special allure. Some scholars are motivated by underlying scientific questions (e.g., what causes some substance users to become addicted, but not others? Are emotional experiences encoded differently in the brain compared to neutral experiences?), whereas others are motivated by the practical implications of their research efforts (e.g., How best to treat addiction and inform debates over the legalization of illicit substances? How reliable are victims' and other eyewitnesses' memories of traumatic events?). The distance between the scientific methods used and the work's generalizability to real-world situations varies both across and within psychological subdisciplines as a function of the specific research question, disciplinary conventions, and investigator choices (Banaji & Crowder, 1989). Yet for law-psychology researchers, that distance, on average, is relatively short. Put another way, the practical implications of much psycholegal research are readily apparent. Seeing how their work might influence policy and procedure in the legal system is quite appealing to many law-psychology researchers.

Unfortunately, it is not always easy to influence the workings of the legal system. The path from A (doing and even publishing the research) to B (influencing policy and practice) can be—and in our experience, usually is—long, hard, circuitous, and fraught with obstacles. Many of those obstacles pertain to the translation and utilization of research findings after the studies themselves have been conducted. Other obstacles relate to earlier decisions: conceptualization of the research question, choice of methodological and measurement approaches, and so forth. How researchers deal with both kinds of obstacles reflects the tension between basic and applied research that has been present in psychology and law since the field's origins more than a century ago (Bornstein & Meissner, 2008; Bornstein & Neuschatz, 2020).

Although achieving an optimal balance between basic and applied psycholegal research is challenging, both are important. Research that prizes ecological validity at the expense of theory testing and methodological innovation disserves the science and, in the long run, provides a weak foundation on which to base the very policy and procedural changes it seeks to advance (Lane & Meissner, 2008). Instead, we argue that psycholegal research should operate within a translational research framework, seeking to inform legal policies, practices, and procedures by systematically grounding our scholarship in theory and demonstrated efficacy before moving it toward interventions and practices that are evaluated in real-world effectiveness studies.

The legal system changes slowly (some would add "if at all"), and this has been a source of frustration for many psycholegal scholars. For every topic in which evidence-based practice has made significant inroads, like eyewitness lineup identification procedures, the interviewing of child witnesses/victims, or risk assessment, there are several others, such as death qualification, where researchers might rightly feel their recommendations are not being heard. Most others are somewhere in between—some change has occurred, as in the gradual adoption of evidence-based practices in interviewing and interrogation, yet much remains to be done. Many factors account for this variability. First and foremost, the quantity and quality of the supporting research evidence are greater for some topics than for others. Beyond that, researchers vary with respect to their approaches to influencing policy change. In this chapter, we discuss this process by focusing on a number of cardinal questions: Why influence policy? When, where, and how might we do so? And what policies can we address? Our focus is on the criminal justice system, but we believe these principles also apply to the civil justice system and to other areas of psychological science that might seek to influence policy and procedure.

There are important differences between *policy* and *procedure* within the criminal justice system, or any institution or organization, that scholars should consider when seeking to apply their research findings. Policies typically include a set of guidelines that describe an institution's principles, values, or culture. They often communicate expectations regarding the institution's purpose and goals, and serve to facilitate or regulate the actions of individuals within the institution. Whereas laws passed by legislatures and executive orders signed at the federal, state, and local levels establish the basis for policy development, specific policy is typically developed and refined by the leadership of an organization. From the psycholegal context, relevant policies could include addressing racial bias in the criminal justice system by expressly prohibiting racial profiling in police stops, requiring training on racial bias of all actors within the system, or reforming bail or sentencing guidelines to reduce disparate treatment.

As might be surmised, policies set the parameters from which specific procedures are developed within an organization. Although policies most certainly have an impact on key outcomes of concern to an organization, it is the specific procedures and manner of policy implementation that mediate this effect. Procedures provide a step-by-step guide for action across various contexts, at times restricting or broadening individual discretion. They typically address the responsible party for each action and provide specific guidance on the actions to be undertaken. Within the psycholegal context, practices influenced by research have included things like specific procedures for collecting eyewitness identification evidence, questioning techniques used to interview child witnesses and victims, or assessing offenders' risk for future violence.

Why Influence Policy and Procedure?

Most psycholegal scholars have a ready answer to this question: to make the criminal justice system *fairer*. The most obvious injustices cited by scholars include wrongful conviction of the innocent and systemic biases that lead to disparate treatment due to extralegal factors, such as an individual's race, ethnicity, or socioeconomic status. However, the costs of imperfect justice do not stop there. In signal detection terms, wrongful convictions are a "false positive" error. Just as important, there are also "misses" in the form of lawbreakers who are not held accountable for their criminal or tortious behavior. Poor policies and procedures can also be costly and inefficient, if they lead to longer processes (e.g., police investigations, pretrial detention, discovery, trials) or repeated processes (e.g., retrials following successful appeals).

These different kinds of error and hidden costs highlight the importance of not singling out only one kind of error, such as wrongful convictions, or limiting the focus simply to error reduction. Optimal procedures improve discriminant outcomes. For example, one of the more contentious eyewitness lineup reforms is the administration of a sequential versus simultaneous photo array (i.e., presenting one lineup member at a time vs. showing the entire lineup at once). Since the mid-1980s (e.g., Lindsay & Wells, 1985), experiments have shown that when compared to simultaneous lineups, sequential lineups reduce the number of false-positive identifications of innocent suspects (i.e., false alarms)—thereby reducing the risk of wrongful convictions—accompanied by a typically smaller reduction in the number of true positive identifications of guilty suspects (i.e., hits). For example, one meta-analysis found that sequential lineups produced 22 percent fewer false alarms in target-absent lineups, compared to 8 percent fewer hits in target-present lineups (Steblay et al., 2011). Although this same body of research shows that the sequential procedure yields greater diagnosticity—that is, a higher ratio of identifications of the culprit from target-present lineups to identifications of the innocent suspect from target-absent lineups (Steblay et al., 2011)—the research also highlights that witnesses tend to become more conservative overall when undergoing a sequential lineup procedure (Meissner et al., 2005; Palmer & Brewer, 2012). The trade-off seen in this research necessitates a cost-benefit analysis that accounts for different kinds of error (Clark, 2012). Our purpose in raising this example of sequential versus simultaneous lineups is not to advocate for one procedure or the other but to illustrate that the goals of policy change can be, and very often are, complicated. Owing, in large part, to the trade-off between hits and false alarms, leading eyewitness lineup reform recommendations have declined to advocate for a specific lineup presentation method (e.g., National Research Council, 2014; Wells et al., 2020).

Another, perhaps less obvious, answer to the "why" question is that poor policies and practices diminish public trust in the justice system. Trust in essentially all government institutions, including the courts, has been declining for decades (Twenge et al., 2014)—and that was before the Black Lives Matter movement, the election and tumultuous administration of President Trump, and the coronavirus pandemic with its significant public health and economic consequences. If anything, the public's trust in the justice system has diminished even more rapidly in recent years, especially in the African American community (Kochel, 2019), as a polarized American populace, widespread protests against racial disparities, and calls to defund the police make abundantly clear. Trust in various aspects of the justice system, such as law enforcement, the judiciary, and the jury system, has a great many consequences, ranging from citizens' willingness to report crime or obey the law (Jackson, 2015; Tyler, 2006) to their compliance with court decisions (Gibson, 2015) and whether they respond to a jury summons (Bornstein et al., 2020). Thus, designing evidence-based policies and procedures for the administration of justice yields a number of direct (e.g., better outcomes for justice-involved persons) and indirect benefits (e.g., greater citizen trust in the justice system).

When to Influence Policy and Procedure?

It goes without saying that evidence-based policies are preferable to those based merely on intuition or political considerations. There are numerous examples of laws enacted to combat crime that look and sound good, and may even be well-intentioned, but that turn out to be ineffective (e.g., AMBER Alerts and sex offender registration laws; Griffin & Miller, 2008, refer to such efforts as "crime control theater"). Not only do policies having an empirical foundation seem more legitimate, but policies created in the absence of relevant data can have unintended negative consequences (DeVault et al., 2016; Saks, 1992).

Nonetheless, a critical question for psycholegal researchers, as well as for policymakers and practitioners, remains: how much evidence and what kind of evidence must there be before adopting a particular policy?

Not only is there no easy answer to this question; there is no consensus on what criteria are even relevant. Malpass et al. (2008) proposed several criteria that could be used in deciding whether a given research literature provides an adequate basis for policy development: what counts as research, consistency of findings, diversity of methods, agreement among scientific peers, amount of available research, the relationship between science and implementation, and coverage of important variables. Although these criteria require subjective judgments about matters on which reasonable people can disagree (e.g., How much diversity, agreement, or research? Which variables are important?), they nonetheless provide a useful framework for approaching the question of when scientists can credibly and responsibly advocate for change.

Evaluating the sufficiency of a literature could also be approached by considering the degree to which research has addressed both theoretical and applied issues relevant to a policy or procedure. For example, Hoffman and Deffenbacher (1993) established four dimensions (validity, relevance, salience, and representativeness) along which research could be evaluated for its epistemological and ecological contributions. Further, the authors suggested that an assessment of the utility (findings help you do things), novelty (findings help you do new things), and generality (findings apply to diverse contexts) of a literature's contributions could support an assessment of application and real-world relevance. As echoed by Lane and Meissner (2008), research has the greatest potential for successful application when it has been situated and validated based upon psychological theory, has been tested using a diverse array of methodological approaches, and has been examined in both in vitro (laboratory) and in vivo (naturalistic) contexts that ensure effective translation of the available science (Dunbar & Blanchette, 2001; see Diamond, 1997, for a similar distinction).

Translational research has become the primary approach to research within the biomedical community and is the predominant framework used by the National Institutes of Health to coordinate its funding efforts. But is such a framework relevant for other areas of science, such as psycholegal research? We believe that it is and that scholars should consider such a model for moving research to policy and practice. Translational research has been defined as "the advancement of basic science research findings into application and everyday practice" (Bardo & Pentz, 2016, p. 553). A distinction is typically made between Type I and Type II research in this context, with the former related to basic research and theory testing in efficacy studies and the latter related to more applied research involving effectiveness trials and policy research in the real world (e.g., Diamond, 1997). Translational research is typically approached in an interdisciplinary manner given the research skills needed to move from basic to applied scholarship. Further, it is often noted that research can progress through the translational process both forward and backward, with basic scholars addressing issues that could only be learned via real-world effectiveness studies.

With respect to when the transition from basic research to application should occur, a number of approaches have been used to assess or establish the sufficiency of a literature, including systematic reviews and meta-analyses, consensus panels, scientific review papers by professional societies, and surveys of qualified experts (Malpass et al., 2008). By virtue of aggregating large amounts of data, such products are both compelling and potentially easier for policymakers and practitioners to digest when compared with reviewing the primary research literature. Expert surveys, such as those conducted on eyewitness identification (Kassin et al., 2001) and police interrogations (Kassin et al., 2018), offer policymakers and practitioners a consensus scientific opinion on the reliability of certain phenomena, which can diverge from the assumptions demonstrated by lay or practitioner perspectives (cf. Alceste et al., 2021). Scientific review papers on such topics (e.g., Kassin et al., 2010; Wells et al., 2020) offer a qualitative synthesis of the available research aimed more pointedly toward influencing policy and practice. Such papers tend to be widely cited within the academic literature and receive considerable attention by news and social media outlets, placing them in the top 5 percent of all research outputs on tracking sites such as Altmetric (http://www.altmetric.com). Finally, consensus panels often have a significant impact on furthering scientific research, such as the National Research Council's (2014) consensus study report on eyewitness identification. Consensus panels can also lead to measurable impacts on policy and procedure, as in the National Research Council's (2009) study on forensic science that was followed by a policy commission at the US Department of Justice (National Commission on Forensic Science) and ultimately the US National Institute for Standards and Technology's creation of the Organization of Scientific Area Committees, which now establishes evidence-based standards and guidelines for forensic practice (Butler, 2014).

From a purely empirical perspective, quantitative synthesis of a research literature allows scholars to evaluate the reliability and magnitude of a given effect and to assess whether the variance surrounding an effect size might be related to important study moderators that are of theoretical or practical relevance (Cooper et al., 2019). The conduct of meta-analyses within a literature is surely a sign of the development and maturity of the available research. For example, one of us recently reviewed the proliferation of systematic reviews and meta-analyses in research on investigative interviewing, much of which has begun to influence policy and practice on the interviewing of witnesses, victims, and suspects (Meissner, 2021). Organizations within the criminal justice (Campbell Collaborative), health care (Cochrane, PRISMA), and education (What Works Clearinghouse) sectors have also begun to develop and support the conduct of systematic reviews as a mechanism for directly informing policy and practice.

Finally, it should be rather obvious that theoretically and empirically derived recommendations for policy and procedure should be based upon findings that have been widely replicated across situations, contexts, and populations. Attempts at replication within psychological science have posed considerable challenges to the perceived reproducibility of findings (Open Science Collaboration, 2015). Current efforts aimed at improving both the generalizability and replicability of psycholegal findings, commensurate with the open science movement (Shrout & Rogers, 2018), will ensure the effective translation of research to policy and practice.

Where to Influence Policy and Procedure?

If you are a psycholegal researcher with important findings that you believe would make the justice system fairer in some respect and you want to do more than just publish them, where do you take them? The question of "where" necessarily entails a consideration of "who," as it raises the related question: Who makes policy or is responsible for enacting procedural reforms? As briefly described above, a great many individuals and bodies are responsible for the development of policies and procedures that apply in legal settings. First and foremost, perhaps, are legislative bodies at the federal, state, county, and municipal levels. Colleges and universities typically coordinate legislative communication efforts via internal state and federal relations offices; staff in these offices often provide training to faculty and can arrange meetings with legislators. For psycholegal scholars, law enforcement agencies similarly span federal, state, county, and municipal levels, with an estimated eighteen thousand police departments in the United States, across all levels of government (Banks et al., 2016). Policymakers in the executive branches and those who review or enact policies and procedures in the judicial branches (judges and prosecutors, respectively) are also important decision makers with whom to communicate.

A key consideration here is finding the right settings, venues, and influencers. Where to begin? A popular adage holds that "all politics is local." Although it might be less true in our media-(over)saturated information age than it was in the past, there are still good reasons to start locally and start small. Local officials, especially elected ones, tend to be more responsive to, and more willing to meet face to face with, their constituents—who not only vote, but also live and work in their community—than those holding statewide or federal office. They also typically have more authority to implement policy changes and enact evidence-based procedures on their own initiative; that is, local police chiefs, trial court judges, and even mayors and state legislators can make things happen faster than officials at higher levels. An added benefit of starting local is that local experiments often function as test labs—if an innovative procedure works there, it can be scaled up and implemented more broadly (in the following section, we address *how* you might strategically engage with policymakers and practitioners in these contexts).

In addition to working with policymakers directly, scholars can reach these audiences by disseminating their research products at policy or practice meetings or via professional periodicals. Of course, disseminating our findings is part and parcel of what researchers, especially those in academia, do routinely; however, our traditional academic journals and conference proceedings are rarely accessible to policymakers and justice system professionals. Success, then, depends on shifting one's perspective and meeting policymakers on their own turf. Preparing a research brief that translates the policy implications of your scholarship for legislators at the state and federal levels and coordinating a brief meeting with their appropriate legislative staff to share these ideas is an excellent approach to initiating a conversation about policy change. Professional organizations, such as the American Psychological Association's (APA) Science Government Relations Office (see Kaslow, 2015), host policy forums on Capitol Hill and provide training and support to scholars who would like to meet with their legislators to advance the translation of psychological science into policy. In recent years, psycholegal research on eyewitness identification and interviewing/interrogation were highlighted at these forums, and policy recommendations for criminal justice issues are regularly developed by the APA (e.g., https://www.apa.org/advocacy/criminal-justice). The APA has also developed a number of advocacy training tools that include information and tips for things like communicating with elected officials (see https://apa.org/apags/resources/advocacy/toolkit).

With respect to influencing procedural changes, trainings and conferences for practitioners within the criminal justice system offer important opportunities to share evidence-based recommendations. For example, attorneys and judges have continuing legal education requirements, and the organizations (local, state, and national) that coordinate these trainings are quite receptive to presentations by scientists. The American Bar Association engages in the development and advocacy of policy recommendations for criminal justice and legal practice, and organizations such as the Innocence Project play an important role in both national- and state-level policy change. There is also movement within the law enforcement, military, and intelligence communities to incorporate evidence-based practices. Organizations such as the International Association for Chiefs of Police (IACP), particularly its Center for Police Research and Policy; the National Police Foundation; and the Police Executive Research Forum support research and policy development through a variety of venues that include scholarly input. Conferences such as those held by the IACP often serve as a platform for sharing the latest evidence-based practices, and administrative and training personnel who attend are receptive to policy and procedural recommendations. There are also a surprising number of regional and national policing organizations around the country that host annual meetings—such gatherings allow for continuing education opportunities and presentations by scholars on the latest evidence-based practices. Finally, scholars can reach the law enforcement training community at such conferences as the International Law Enforcement Educators and Trainers Association or the IACP's section on International Managers of Police Academy and College Training.

Although justice system professionals might not regularly read peer-reviewed, academic journals, they do read newsletters and more practice-oriented journals. For example, the mission of *Judicature*, whose six thousand subscribers include federal judges and state appellate and supreme court judges, is "to create a forum for judges, practitioners, and academics to share ideas, best practices, perspectives, and opinions" (*Judicature*, n.d.). *Court Review*, published by the American Judges Association, is read by judges at all levels and functions similarly. Both journals regularly feature social science research. For example, *Court Review* published a scientific review paper on procedural justice—authored by two judges—that relied extensively on psychological research and offered practical recommendations for how judges could promote procedural justice in their courtrooms (Burke & Leben, 2007). The *ABA Journal* similarly reaches a wide audience of attorneys, and outlets such as the *FBI Law Enforcement Bulletin* and the IACP's *Police Chief Magazine* incorporate articles by scholars that are read nationally by law enforcement professionals.

Although speaking directly to a professional audience is important, it is also critical to author articles, books, or commentaries that might reach the general public. Policy and procedural change are difficult to initiate in many organizations, and such change is often driven by public sentiment and politics. Scholars must share their findings beyond the academy and beyond the professionals and organizations they intend to influence. This can be accomplished by authoring opinions, commentaries, or brief articles for local, state, and national publications. Prominent examples are available in the psycholegal realm, such as the opinion piece on police interrogation by Saul Kassin (2021) in *The New York Times*. Academics might also consider writing an article for *The Conversation*, an international news outlet that collaborates with scholars to translate their work and findings for the general public. You will likely be surprised at the "reach" of such an article and the impact it can have.

A challenge for researchers seeking to publish in outlets read by practitioners and policymakers is that, despite having a wide circulation, such outlets are frequently not peer-reviewed or heavily cited—criteria by which the vast majority of academic researchers, as well as hiring and promotion and tenure committees, have been conditioned to evaluate a work's merit. The situation is unfortunate, as it creates a disincentive for psycholegal scholars to invest the time and effort on activities that could bring their work to the very people they seek to influence. Although everyone recognizes the importance of such activities—for example, the Association for Psychological Science (APS) has advocated for the "giving away" of psychology essentially since its founding (see, e.g., Bjork, 1991)—such contributions are difficult to quantify and factor into faculty evaluation criteria.

One solution is to publish articles describing the same research in both peer-reviewed and practitioner-oriented outlets. The APA's *Ethical Principles of Psychologists and Code of Conduct* prohibit duplicate publication of data; however, data may be republished when accompanied by proper acknowledgment (American Psychological Association, 2017, §8.13), especially when repackaged for a substantially different audience. One of us engaged in this practice several years ago in reporting the results of a field study that examined whether written reminders would reduce courts' failure-to-appear rate: the theoretical rationale and detailed analyses were reported in peer-reviewed journals (Bornstein et al., 2013; Rosenbaum et al., 2012), and abridged summaries, with practical advice, were reported in *Court Review* and a state bar association newsletter (Herian & Bornstein, 2010; Tomkins et al., 2012). Tailoring dissemination efforts for different audiences is not cost-free, but the time required to do so is relatively modest compared to the benefits of reaching a broader audience, especially those who are best situated to put your findings into practice.

Finally, we offer a rather obvious caveat that speaking to and writing for a professional or lay audience is much different from writing for the academy (see Steblay, 2019). Contributions to outlets described above are generally brief summaries of the available research, situated in the jargon and context of the professional audience rather than the academy, that outline the practical benefits and recommendations arrived at by the scholarship. Theoretical and methodological aspects of a project are to be avoided (with appropriate reference to relevant academic publications that offer such details), and considerations of the audience's interests and perspectives are tantamount for successful engagement. The budding field of science communication offers important recommendations for scholars (Kappel & Holmen, 2019; National Research Council, 2017), and many universities have developed training opportunities to facilitate the translation and communication of science to professional and lay audiences.

How to Influence Policy and Procedure?

Having identified the relevant audiences and opportunities to share your scholarship and recommendations, it is necessary to consider an appropriate strategy for effecting change. This is very different from influencing fact-finders (i.e., juries and judges), as through expert testimony (see chapter by Cutler and Krauss, this volume). Many psycholegal researchers seem to believe that if they conduct rigorous studies using reliable and valid methods, policymakers will sit up and take notice. We refer to this as the "Field of Dreams" philosophy: If you build it, they will come. Unfortunately, as well as the Field of Dreams philosophy ultimately worked out for Ray Kinsella (the film's Kevin Costner character), it is naïve. As noted in the previous section, policymakers rarely read psychology journals (or, arguably, any scientific reports). Even if they did read about such research in a professional or practitioner-oriented journal, it is unlikely they would immediately adopt its recommendations. This is not to suggest that policymakers do not believe in science—rather, they are typically not trained in the scientific method, their jobs require them to spend time on other things, and they might have other considerations (e.g., practical or political) that make them reluctant to espouse certain positions.

Moreover, when policymakers do consider psycholegal research, they can be quite critical of it. The example of scholarship on capital punishment is illustrative. Research has identified numerous problems with death penalty jurisprudence, such as that murder suspects are more likely to be sentenced to death when the victim is White than non-White (Blume et al., 2004); death-qualified jurors are more likely to convict than non-death-qualified jurors (Yelderman et al., 2016); and comprehension of capital jury instructions is notoriously poor (Alvarez et al., 2016). While critiques of this work can legitimately include concerns regarding the methods and sampling used to produce the findings, the magnitude or importance of the findings, or even the (political or ideological) motivations of scholars who produced the research, policymaking decisions are ultimately influenced by the values, politics, and public sentiment that surround key issues. So then, how might we work to "close the deal" and facilitate change in policy or procedure?

An important consideration is whether the available scholarship simply points to problems associated with an existing policy and practice or whether it offers viable, evidence-based solutions as well. Psychological science is replete with scholarship that highlights the frailties and errors of human perception, memory, judgment, and decision-making. This certainly extends to psycholegal research, where scholars have demonstrated the failures and suggestive nature of memory, and the heuristics and extralegal biases associated with various criminal justice decisions. For decades, our focus has been to assess factors that lead to errors within the legal system, most notably including wrongful conviction of the innocent. As one of us has argued elsewhere (see Meissner et al., 2010), a focus on the problems of current practice alone is simply insufficient to influence policymakers and practitioners—what is required is a positive psychological science that offers solutions.

A common critique of scientists is that they pontificate from their ivory towers, assuming knowledge of the real world but never leaving the confines of the laboratory to understand the circumstances in situ. This stereotype may not be completely accurate, but the development of evidence-based recommendations for policy and procedure require that we engage with professionals in their context. The burden is on us to demonstrate that we understand the conditions and practices for which we offer critiques, and to generate possible solutions in this context.

Whatever the subject of your research, find opportunities to learn about actual practices on the ground—they may differ from what you have read about or seen in documentaries or popular television. If your research considers legal decision-making, ensure that you spend time in courtrooms observing trial practice and procedure to understand how jurors and judges are presented with evidence or arguments and the various constraints inherent to legal procedure. If you are interested in eyewitness identification or police interviewing, take advantage of programs that offer citizens and scholars a firsthand perspective of police practice, including ride-alongs and citizen police academies supported by many state and local agencies. If you conduct research examining the effectiveness of correctional interventions designed to reduce criminal recidivism, consider volunteering at your local prison, talking with treatment providers in correctional facilities, or interviewing parole officers or staff at halfway houses to obtain firsthand information about the benefits and challenges of certain treatment programs.

Importantly, changing policy and procedure occurs as a product of *influence*. This could involve persuading legislators and executives within local, state, or federal government that change is necessary and solutions are available, or influencing law enforcement or prosecutors to engage in evidence-based practices that improve the aims of justice—particularly with respect to key outcome metrics of interest to them. Volumes within social psychology have been written about the science of social influence, all of which are relevant to this issue. While writing for professional or lay outlets and giving talks to audiences outside academia will offer avenues to engage in rational or narrative persuasion, there is no substitute for interpersonal influence that can yield important opportunities for change. Of course, this requires developing a relationship with someone inside the policymaking body or professional organization who might be willing to champion your cause.

The process of developing professional relationships of trust and mutual respect requires time, patience, and strategic engagement. Much like any relationship, we tend to connect with those who hold similar values and interests, those who are nonjudgmental and empathetic, and those who are willing to listen to our perspective and learn from our experiences. In this process, academics must be able to suspend their critique of policy or practice. They should demonstrate a willingness to hear the expert advice of those who have years, even decades, of experience and to gain an appreciation for the multitude of factors that influence the decisions and behaviors of professionals. Indeed, many of the issues faced on the ground have not been systematically evaluated or controlled for in our research, and the recommendations we offer may fall short of accounting for the complete range of scenarios for which they were developed. Scholars should also be open to inquiring about the questions professionals would like answered and to finding ways of addressing those questions as a trust-building exercise.

As might be evident from this discussion, such professional relationships offer an opportunity both to improve our scholarship and its potential impact, and to win the support of professionals for whom our research is conducted. One of the most exciting aspects of engaging with practitioners in this manner is the potential for collaboration. Practices and procedures that have been developed in the laboratory could be examined in situ and compared with existing policies and procedures. Recent examples from the interviewing and interrogation literature include a study conducted by Rivard et al. (2014) at the Federal Law Enforcement Training Center that demonstrated the effectiveness of the cognitive interview protocol when compared with a five-step interview protocol that has been taught in federal law enforcement training for decades. Recent training studies that introduce evidence-based interviewing protocols have also involved important collaborations (and authorship) with practitioners (Brandon et al., 2019; Brimbal et al., 2021; Luke et al., 2016). On the clinical side, collaborations between universities and public behavioral health organizations have resulted in the development of clinics that provide evaluation and mental health services to justice-involved individuals (Heilbrun et al., 2021). Not only have such collaborations led to the effective translation of evidence-based practices, but engagement between scientists and practitioners has also facilitated changes in policy and procedure in these areas.

What Policies and Procedures to Focus On?

The American justice system is sufficiently imperfect and slow to change that there is no shortage of candidates for where psycholegal scholars might direct their efforts (in focusing on the American system, we acknowledge that *any* justice system is necessarily imperfect; our recommendations should apply to a large extent in other countries, though the most pressing problems and relevant policies and procedures will of course vary). Even in relatively mature research areas, like eyewitness identification and interviewing procedures, false confessions and interrogation practices, and jury procedures, putting research findings into practice has been a fitful (and at times fit-inducing) process. To some extent, this is simply a consequence of having so many jurisdictions with considerable autonomy to devise their own policies and procedures. Moreover, as newer findings accumulate, recommended best practices can change yet again. Indeed, this is one of the trickier aspects of the "when to influence policy" question, and it helps to explain, in part, the justice system's reluctance to change. But declining to adopt a better policy now because an even better one might come along in two, five, or ten years is spurious reasoning. The breadth of topics, multijurisdictional nature of the US justice system, and fluidity of the scientific process mean that there are plenty of policies on which to focus. And we are loath to say that some topics are more deserving of researchers' attention than others.

Nonetheless, we suggest four criteria that researchers seeking to effect meaningful policy change might want to consider when thinking about possible research topics: severity of consequences, vulnerable populations, disparate impact, and efficiency. First, some justice system errors are more costly than others. A false conviction for any crime can have enormous consequences for both the falsely convicted person and society. That risk raises the importance of research into factors that contribute to false convictions, such as eyewitness misidentification, false confession, flawed forensic science, and jailhouse informants, as well as policy reforms that can ameliorate those factors. Moreover, a false conviction for a crime that carries the most extreme possible penalty, such as life imprisonment or execution, is catastrophic. We suspect that a consideration of the unjust consequences that can ensue when things go awry motivates much of the research on aspects of the justice system like capital punishment and punitive damages—things that are, numerically speaking, very low in frequency yet have the most severe consequences in their respective domains.

Second, the justice system often deals with vulnerable populations: children and adolescents, the elderly, persons with mental illness, crime victims, and prisoners. These individuals deserve additional protections and policies that recognize their unique status; unfortunately, they often do not receive them, as evidenced by widespread juvenile transfer (Griffin et al., 2011) and the dearth of resources for crime victims (Lee, 2019) or offenders with mental illness (e.g., Prins, 2014). Nor does it help matters that many of the assessment tools used by forensic psychologists lack a strong empirical foundation but nevertheless are rarely challenged in court (Neal et al., 2019). There is a pressing need for better policies regulating the ways that vulnerable persons interact with the justice system.

Third, there is also demand for policies that eliminate disparate impact as a function of individuals' demographic characteristics. Public awareness that racial and ethnic minorities are disadvantaged in the criminal justice system is increasing, and reform efforts (e.g., the Black Lives Matter movement) have accompanied that awareness. Social science evidence documenting those racial and ethnic disparities (e.g., research on racial profiling) have lent credence to the reform efforts and will continue to do so. The same is true of policies having a disparate impact on members of other marginalized groups, such as sexual and gender minorities (Plumm & Leighton, 2019).

Finally, the efficiency criterion raises the question: Where can I get the biggest bang for my buck? Improving "front-end" practices, like police and prosecutorial decision-making, bail setting, forensic science, alternative dispute resolution, and plea bargaining, has the potential to affect far more individuals than "downstream" practices like trials and postconviction proceedings. Efficiency is only one criterion among many, so we are not suggesting that downstream practices are somehow less important. Nonetheless, we take it as a good sign that researchers are paying increased attention to those front-end practices (see, e.g., Mnookin, 2018; Redlich et al., 2017; Simon, 2012).

Conclusion

Psycholegal research is, by design, a field devoted to evaluating and addressing issues that directly affect the criminal justice system. At the same time, many scholars in the field have experienced firsthand the frustrations of bridging the divide between research and policy or practice. For every success story of a psycholegal policy implementation, there are likely several times as many scholars who have experienced frustrations, roadblocks, or disinterest. Successful implementation of research findings likely requires skill sets and considerations that are uncommon to the training we receive as psychological scientists. Yet, with proper motivation and guidance, we believe that all scholars can influence change by strategically disseminating the implications of their research and engaging with practitioners in effectiveness studies. We hope that this chapter offers an effective "how to" for those interested in following the translational research path.

We conclude our contribution to this *Handbook* by highlighting several issues we believe are most important to facilitate policy and procedural change. First, the foundation of any good recommendation derived from scholarship is the evidence base upon which it sits. Scholars in our area must be trained in a translational approach to research that moves from basic, theoretically informed research to implementation and evaluation in the field.

Scholars must also be encouraged to collaborate across (sub)disciplines within psychology, across the social and behavioral sciences, and even across the academy. Translational scholarship requires a variety of research skills, and team science is more likely to accomplish the necessary transitions; ensure that appropriate methods, measures, and analytics are utilized; and have a high impact (Wuchty et al., 2007).

Second, effective implementation requires that we understand the multitude of factors that drive everyday decision-making and practice. Get out of the laboratory and learn more about the context to which your scholarship relates. Start local and develop relationships with policymakers and practitioners, learn from their experiences, and spend time in their world. Doing so can enrich your scholarship, help you to develop collaborations with professionals and organizations, and allow you to recruit a champion who will support your recommendations for change.

Third, changing policy or procedure requires influence and persuasion. Sharing your research with policymakers and practitioners is critical to raising an awareness of key issues and the potential for improvement. Don't focus solely on the problem; rather, offer viable solutions and alternatives to current practice. Learn to communicate your findings and their implications in a manner that is accessible and absent academic jargon. Collaborate with professionals to ensure that any recommendations are both feasible and effective given the context in which they are used. And share your recommendations with the public to build consensus on the need for change.

Finally, we need to reconsider our process for evaluating one another's contributions in the academy so that we can reward policy work. As anyone who has submitted or reviewed annual faculty evaluations knows, performance assessments have become a bureaucratic bean-counting exercise that favors academic publications in high-impact journals, high-dollar grant awards from competitive science agencies, and near-perfect course ratings from undergraduate and graduate students. Contributions to policy and practice are rarely, if ever, considered by the evaluation committee, and when they are, such activities tend to be seen in a negative light, as they distract from those activities identified above. We believe this situation needs to change, particularly as administrators are being encouraged to highlight their university's contributions to the public good. Effective translational research requires a significant time investment on the part of the scholar. Presentations, trainings, and publications in professional outlets should be valued by the academy, and the impact of the scholar's work on policy and procedure should be highlighted. More awards for scholarly contributions to policy and practice, similar to the APA's Award for Distinguished Contributions to Research in Public Policy or the APS's James McKeen Cattell Fellow Award, should be available to recognize the contributions of scholars throughout their careers. In placing value on translational research efforts and the bridging of research and policy or procedure, we incentivize the important and significant work that is required to facilitate change in the criminal justice system.

References

Alceste, F., Luke, T., Redlich, A., Hellgren, J., Amrom, A., & Kassin, S. (2021). The psychology of confessions: A comparison of expert and lay opinions. *Applied Cognitive Psychology, 35*(1), 39–51.

Alvarez, M. J., Miller, M. K., & Bornstein, B. H. (2016). "It will be your duty . . .": The psychology of criminal jury instructions. In M. K. Miller & B. H. Bornstein (Eds.), *Advances in psychology and law* (Vol. 1, pp. 119–158). Springer.

American Psychological Association. (2017). *Ethical principles of psychologists and code of conduct.* American Psychological Association.

Banaji, M. R., & Crowder, R. G. (1989). The bankruptcy of everyday memory. *American Psychologist, 44*(9), 1185–1193.

Banks, D., Hendrix, J., Hickman, M., & Kyckelhahn, T. (2016). *National sources of law enforcement employment data.* U.S. Department of Justice/Bureau of Justice Statistics.

Bardo, M. T., & Pentz, M. A. (2016). Translational research. In A. E. Kazdin (Ed.), *Methodological issues and strategies in clinical research* (4th ed., pp. 69–84). American Psychological Association.

Bjork, R. A. (1991). On giving psychology away. *APS Observer*, November 1. https://www.psychologicalscience.org/observer/on-giving-psychology-away-2

Blume, J. H., Eisenberg, T., & Wells, M. T. (2004). Explaining death row's population and racial composition. *Journal of Empirical Legal Studies, 1*(1), 165–207.

Bornstein, B. H., Hamm, J. A., Dellapaolera, K. S., Kleynhans, A., & Miller, M. K. (2020). JUST: A measure of jury system trustworthiness. *Psychology, Crime & Law, 26*(8), 797–822.

Bornstein, B. H., & Meissner, C. A. (2008). Introduction: Basic and applied issues in eyewitness research: A Münsterberg centennial retrospective. *Applied Cognitive Psychology, 22*(6), 733–736.

Bornstein, B. H., & Neuschatz, J. S. (2020). *Hugo Münsterberg's psychology and law: A historical and contemporary assessment.* Oxford University Press.

Bornstein, B. H., Tomkins, A. J., Neeley, E. M., Herian, M. N., & Hamm, J. A. (2013). Reducing courts' failure-to-appear rate by written reminders. *Psychology, Public Policy, & Law, 19*(1), 70–80.

Brandon, S. E., Arthur, J. C., Ray, D. G., Meissner, C. A., Kleinman, S. M., Russano, M. B., & Wells, S. (2019). The High-Value Detainee Interrogation Group (HIG): Inception, evolution, and impact. In M. Staal & S. Harvey (Eds.), *Operational psychology: A new field to support national security and public safety* (pp. 263–285). ABC-CLIO.

Brimbal, L., Meissner, C. A., Kleinman, S. M., Phillips, E. P., Atkinson, D. J., Dianiska, R. E., Rothweiler, J., Oleszkiewicz, S., & Jones, M. S. (2021). Evaluating the benefits of developing rapport and trust in investigative interviews: A training study with law enforcement investigators. *Law & Human Behavior, 45*(1), 55–67.

Burke, K., & Leben, S. (2007). Procedural fairness: A key ingredient in public satisfaction. *Court Review, 44*(1-2), 4–25.

Butler, J. M. (2014). The National Commission on Forensic Science and the Organization of Scientific Area Committees. *Proceedings of the 25th International Symposium on Human Identification.*

Clark, S. E. (2012). Costs and benefits of eyewitness identification reform: Psychological science and public policy. *Perspectives on Psychological Science, 7*(3), 238–259.

Cooper, H., Hedges, L. V., & Valentine, J. C. (2019). *The handbook of research synthesis and meta-analysis* (3rd ed.). Russell Sage Foundation.

DeVault, A., Miller, M. K., & Griffin, T. (2016). Crime control theater: Past, present, and future. *Psychology, Public Policy & Law, 22*(4), 341–348.

Diamond, S. S. (1997). Illuminations and shadows from jury simulations. *Law and Human Behavior, 21*(5), 561–571.

Dunbar, K., & Blanchette, I. (2001). The in vivo/in vitro approach to cognition: The case of analogy. *Trends in Cognitive Sciences, 5*(8), 334–339.

Gibson, J. L. (2015). Legitimacy is for losers: The interconnections of institutional legitimacy, performance evaluations, and the symbols of judicial authority. In B. H. Bornstein & A. J. Tomkins (Eds.), *Motivating cooperation and compliance with authority* (pp. 81–116). Springer.

Griffin, P., Addie, S., Adams, B., & Firestin, K. (2011). *Trying juveniles as adults: An analysis of state transfer laws and reporting.* U.S. Department of Justice, Office of Justice Programs, Office of Juvenile Justice and Delinquency Prevention.

Griffin, T., & Miller, M. K. (2008). Child abduction, AMBER Alert, and crime control theater. *Criminal Justice Review, 33*(2), 159–176.

Heilbrun, K., Wright II, H. J., Giallella, C., & DeMatteo, D. (Eds.). (2021). *University and public behavioral health organization collaboration: Models for success in justice contexts.* Oxford University Press.

Herian, M. N., & Bornstein, B. H. (2010, Sept.). Reducing failure-to-appear in Nebraska: A field study. *The Nebraska Lawyer, 13*(8), 11–14.

Hoffman, R. R., & Deffenbacher, K. A. (1993). An analysis of the relations between basic and applied psychology. *Ecological Psychology, 5*(4), 315–352.

Jackson, J. (2015). On the dual motivational force of legitimate authority. In B. H. Bornstein & A. J. Tomkins (Eds.), *Motivating cooperation and compliance with authority* (pp. 145–166). Springer.

Judicature. (n.d.). *Overview: Welcome to* Judicature, *the scholarly journal about the judiciary.* https://judicature.duke.edu/about/overview/

Kappel, K., & Holmen, S. J. (2019). Why science communication, and does it work? A taxonomy of science communication aims and a survey of the empirical evidence. *Frontiers in Communication, 4*, 55.

Kaslow, N. J. (2015). Translating psychological science to the public. *American Psychologist, 70*(5), 361–371.

Kassin, S. M. (2021). It's time for the police to stop lying to suspects. *New York Times,* January 29. https://www.nytimes.com/2021/01/29/opinion/false-confessions-police-interrogation.html

Kassin, S. M., Drizin, S. A., Grisso, T., Gudjonsson, G. H., Leo, R. A., & Redlich, A. D. (2010). Police-induced confessions: Risk factors and recommendations. *Law and Human Behavior, 34*(1), 3–38.

Kassin, S. M., Redlich, A. D., Alceste, F., & Luke, T. J. (2018). On the general acceptance of confessions research: Opinions of the scientific community. *American Psychologist, 73*(1), 63–80.

Kassin, S. M., Tubb, V. A., Hosch, H. M., & Memon, A. (2001). On the "general acceptance" of eyewitness testimony research: A new survey of the experts. *American Psychologist, 56*(5), 405–416.

Kochel, T. R. (2019). Explaining racial differences in Ferguson's impact on local residents' trust and perceived legitimacy: Policy implications for police. *Criminal Justice Policy Review, 30*(3), 374–405.

Lane, S. M., & Meissner, C. A. (2008). A "middle road" approach to bridging the basic-applied divide in eyewitness research. *Applied Cognitive Psychology, 22*(6), 779–787.

Lee, S. (2019, November). Crime victim awareness and assistance through the decades. *National Institute of Justice Journal, 2019*(281), 1–10. https://www.ncjrs.gov/pdffiles1/nij/252733.pdf

Lindsay, R. C. L., & Wells, G. L. (1985). Improving eyewitness identifications from lineups: Simultaneous versus sequential lineup presentation. *Journal of Applied Psychology, 70*(3), 556–564.

Luke, T. J., Hartwig, M., Joseph, E., Brimbal, L., Chan, G., Dawson, E., Jordan, S., Donovan, P., & Granhag, P. (2016). Training in the strategic use of evidence technique: Improving deception detection accuracy of American law enforcement officers. *Journal of Police and Criminal Psychology, 31*(4), 270–278.

Malpass, R. S., Tredoux, C. G., Schreiber Compo, N., McQuiston-Surrett, D., MacLin, O. H., Zimmerman, L. A., & Topp, L. D. (2008). Study space analysis for policy development. *Applied Cognitive Psychology, 22*(6), 789–801.

Meissner, C. A. (2021). "What works?" Systematic reviews and meta-analyses of the investigative interviewing research literature [Special issue]. *Applied Cognitive Psychology, 35*(2), 322–328. https://doi.org/10.1002/acp.3808

Meissner, C. A., Hartwig, M., & Russano, M. B. (2010). The need for a positive psychological approach and collaborative effort for improving practice in the interrogation room. *Law and Human Behavior, 34*(1), 43–45.

Meissner, C. A., Tredoux, C. G., Parker, J. F., & MacLin, O. H. (2005). Eyewitness decisions in simultaneous and sequential lineups: A dual-process signal detection theory analysis. *Memory & Cognition, 33*(5), 783–792.

Mnookin, J. L. (2018). The uncertain future of forensic science. *Daedalus, 147*(4), 99–118.

National Research Council. (2009). *Strengthening forensic science in the United States: A path forward.* National Academies Press.

National Research Council. (2014). *Identifying the culprit: Assessing eyewitness identification.* National Academies Press.

National Research Council. (2017). *Communicating science effectively: A research agenda.* National Academies Press.

Neal, T. M. S., Slobogin, C., Saks, M. J., Faigman, D. L., & Geisinger, K. F. (2019). Psychological assessments in legal contexts: Are courts keeping "junk science" out of the courtroom? *Psychological Science in the Public Interest, 20*(3), 135–164.

Open Science Collaboration. (2015). Estimating the reproducibility of psychological science. *Science*, *349*(6251), Article aac4716.

Palmer, M. A., & Brewer, N. (2012). Sequential lineup presentation promotes less-biased criterion setting but does not improve discriminability. *Law and Human Behavior*, *36*(3), 247–255.

Plumm, K. M., & Leighton, K. N. (2019). Sexual orientation and gender bias motivated violent crime. In B. H. Bornstein & M. K. Miller (Eds.), *Advances in psychology and law* (Vol. 4, pp. 175–196). Springer.

Prins, S. J. (2014). Prevalence of mental illnesses in U.S. state prisons: A systematic review. *Psychiatric Services*, *65*(7), 862–872.

Redlich, A. D., Wilford, M. M., & Bushway, S. (2017). Understanding guilty pleas through the lens of social science. *Psychology, Public Policy, and Law*, *23*(4), 458–471.

Rivard, J. R., Fisher, R. P., Robertson, B., & Mueller, D. H. (2014). Testing the cognitive interview with professional interviewers: Enhancing recall of specific details of recurring events. *Applied Cognitive Psychology*, *28*(6), 917–925.

Rosenbaum, D. I., Hutsell, N., Tomkins, A. J., Bornstein, B. H., Herian, M. N., & Neeley, E. M. (2012). Using court date reminder postcards to reduce courts' failure to appear rates: A benefit-cost analysis. *Judicature*, *95*(4), 177–187.

Saks, M. J. (1992). Do we really know anything about the behavior of the tort litigation system—and why not? *University of Pennsylvania Law Review*, *140*(4), 1147–1292.

Shrout, P. E., & Rodgers, J. L. (2018). Psychology, science, and knowledge construction: Broadening perspectives from the replication crisis. *Annual Review of Psychology*, *69*, 487–510.

Simon, D. (2012). *In doubt: The psychology of the criminal justice process*. Harvard University Press.

Steblay, N. K. (2019). Translating psychological science into policy and practice. In N. Brewer & A. B. Douglass (Eds.), *Psychological science and the law* (pp. 417–443). Guilford Press.

Steblay, N. K., Dysart, J. E., & Wells, G. L. (2011). Seventy-two tests of the sequential lineup superiority effect: A meta-analysis and policy discussion. *Psychology, Public Policy, and Law*, *17*(1), 99–139.

Tomkins, A. J., Bornstein, B. H., Herian, M. N., Rosenbaum, D. I., & Neeley, E. M. (2012). An experiment in the law: Studying a technique to reduce failure to appear in court. *Court Review*, *48*(3), 96–106.

Twenge, J. M., Campbell, W. K., & Carter, N. T. (2014). Declines in trust in others and confidence in institutions among American adults and late adolescents, 1972-2012. *Psychological Science*, *25*(10), 1914–1923.

Tyler, T. R. (2006). *Why people obey the law*. Princeton University Press.

Wells, G. L., Kovera, M. B., Douglass, A. B., Brewer, N., Meissner, C. A., & Wixted, J. T. (2020). Policy and procedure recommendations for the collection and preservation of eyewitness identification evidence. *Law and Human Behavior*, *44*(1), 3–36.

Wuchty, S., Jones, B. F., & Uzzi, B. (2007). The increasing dominance of teams in production of knowledge. *Science*, *316*(5827), 1036–1039.

Yelderman, L. A., Miller, M. K., & Peoples, C. D. (2016). Capital-izing jurors: How death qualification relates to jury composition, jurors' perceptions, and trial outcomes. In B. H. Bornstein & M. K. Miller (Eds.), *Advances in psychology and law* (Vol. 2, pp. 27–54). Springer.

Preventive Justice

Christopher Slobogin

Abstract

Abstract: Preventive justice is an approach to criminal conduct aimed primarily at individual prevention rather than deterrence of the general population or ensuring that offenders receive their just desert. Preventive justice fits more comfortably than either deterrence- or retribution-driven regimes with a psychological approach to criminal justice that assumes that behavior is heavily influenced by biology and the environment and that antisocial tendencies can be reduced through appropriate interventions. It relies heavily on empirical assessments of recidivism risk and intervention needs and deemphasizes the goal of calibrating sanctions to the culpability of offenders. After describing preventive justice in skeletal form, this chapter explains why the present moment might be a propitious time to reconsider this approach as an alternative to our current system of criminal justice. It then explores a number of preventive justice-related topics that psychological researchers could investigate.

Key Words: preventive justice, prevention, deterrence, retribution, risk, interventions

Introduction

"Preventive justice," as the term is used here,[1] describes an approach to criminal conduct that is aimed primarily at individual prevention rather than deterrence of the general population or ensuring that offenders receive their just desert. Expressed in terms of the traditional purposes of punishment, its central focus is rehabilitation, specific deterrence, and, if necessary, incapacitation, as opposed to general deterrence or retribution. Preventive justice, so defined, fits more comfortably than either deterrence- or retribution-driven regimes with a psychological approach to criminal justice that assumes that behavior is heavily influenced by biology and the environment, and that antisocial tendencies can be

---

[1] I coined this phrase in 2011 to refer to the type of sentencing described in the text. *See* CHRISTOPHER SLOBOGIN & MARK R. FONDACARO, JUVENILES AT RISK: A PLEA FOR PREVENTIVE JUSTICE (Oxford University Press, 2011). Other authors have used it in a pejorative sense, primarily as a synonym for preventive detention. *See* ANDREW ASHWORTH & LUCIA ZEDNER, PREVENTIVE JUSTICE (2014); chapters by Markus Dubber, David Dyzenhaus, Matt Matravers, Bernard Harcourt and Pat O'Malley, *in* PREVENTION AND THE LIMITS OF THE CRIMINAL LAW (Andrew Ashworth, Lucia Zedner, & Patrick Tomlin, eds., 2013).

reduced through appropriate interventions. It relies heavily on empirical assessments of recidivism risk and of intervention needs and deemphasizes the goals of estimating the societal response to particular sanctions or the culpability of particular offenders.

Preventive justice is both a new idea and an old idea. It is new because for the past several decades the primary goal of the American criminal justice system has been retributive punishment, not prevention through correctional policies.[2] It is old because as recently as fifty years ago, prevention—in particular, through rehabilitation—was the predominant goal of the system.[3]

That old system deserved to wither away because it was founded on weak underpinnings and was poorly implemented. But today, a system of preventive justice could take advantage of new developments and research, including research by psychologists, to move the criminal system away from a punitive regime based on sanctioning past harm and toward a preventive one that looks to minimize future harm.

After describing preventive justice in skeletal form, this chapter explains why the present moment might be a propitious time to reconsider this approach as an alternative to our current system of criminal justice. It then explores a number of preventive justice-related topics that psychological researchers could investigate. Some of this research is already occurring, but this chapter also suggests new areas of study.

Preventive Justice Defined

Preventive justice is best understood when contrasted with justice based on desert. The latter system, the one that is dominant today, bases sentences primarily on an offender's culpability. In such a regime, the most significant criteria in determining a person's sentence have to do with the past—the current crime of conviction and past crime. The idea is to ensure that a person's sentence imposes the punishment that the offender deserves and that is proportionate to the offender's guilt or blameworthiness.[4] In commonly used, somewhat misleading, language, a desert-based system punishes the crime, not the criminal.

---

[2] Sara Steen & Rachel Bandy, *When the Policy Becomes the Problem: Criminal Justice in the New Millennium*, 9 PUNISHMENT & SOC'Y 5, 5 (2007) ("Over the past three decades, legislators have created a conversation [about punishment] in which the inclusion of principles other than retribution and revenge is virtually impossible.").

[3] Kevin Reitz, *The "Traditional" Indeterminate Sentencing Model, in* THE OXFORD HANDBOOK OF SENTENCING AND CORRECTIONS, 270, 270 (2012) ("As recently as the early 1970s, every jurisdiction in the United States operated with a traditional indeterminate sentencing structure, in which judges had broad and unregulated discretion to select criminal sentences constrained only by maximum statutory penalties [and] parole boards held broad and unregulated authority to determine actual time served . . .").

[4] The modern progenitor of this point of view is Andrew von Hirsch. *See* ANDREW VON HIRSCH, DOING JUSTICE: THE CHOICE OF PUNISHMENTS (1976). In his most recent effort, von Hirsch states that the "desert model contains two main elements . . .: the principle of proportionality, according to which a sentence's severity should be made fairly proportionate to the seriousness of the defendant's criminal conduct," and censure, or "punishment's role of conveying censure or disapprobation of a convicted person for his or her criminal misconduct." ANDREW VON HIRSCH, DESERVED CRIMINAL SENTENCES 1 (2017).

The preventive model, in contrast, is forward looking. Sentences are not proportionate to past behavior but reflect the likelihood that the offender will recidivate if some type of intervention does not occur. The goal is not retribution for past acts but prevention of future ones, through risk assessment and risk management. Reliance is placed on treatment, vocational, and other rehabilitative programs and, as a last resort, incarceration. In sound bite jargon, here we are punishing the criminal, not the crime.

Again, preventive justice is not a new idea. A famous proponent of the general concept was psychiatrist Karl Menninger, who wrote a book with a title—*The Crime of Punishment*[5]—which summed up the thinking of many social scientists of the day. Menninger argued that prevention through treatment, not punishment based on desert, should be the goal of criminal justice.[6] Before him, Barbara Wootton, who eventually became a baroness for her work, also made a strong case for jettisoning culpability as a basis for criminal liability, even at the trial stage; she argued that anyone who committed a nonjustified criminal act should be sentenced, but that sentencing should take place through a preventive prism, not a punitive one.[7] And well before both Menninger and Wootton there was Enrico Ferri, a sociologist, who argued that crime was largely the result of circumstance and that blaming offenders made little sense.[8]

In *Minding Justice*, published in 2006, I proposed a rejuvenation of the preventive justice concept.[9] However, my version is not the preventive justice of Menninger, Wootton, and Ferri. Rather it is a hybrid, based on the idea that desert is still an important concept. This hybrid has three principal features.

First, conviction for crime would still be based on desert. Before punishment could take place, the state would have to prove, beyond a reasonable doubt, that a criminal act occurred with the requisite mens rea. This feature recognizes that labeling someone a criminal should occur only when a person has engaged in a blameworthy act, with a culpable mental state such as intent, recklessness or gross negligence.

Second, desert would still also be relevant at sentencing, but only in determining sentence ranges. As is true under most other sentencing schemes, each crime would be associated with a minimum and maximum sentence based on the relative culpability of the crime in question. However, in contrast to many modern sentencing regimes, these sentence ranges would be quite broad. A model is provided by the original Model Penal Code (MPC) of the American Law Institute (ALI), promulgated in the 1950s when criminal law theorists were more rehabilitation-oriented.[10] Outside of the death penalty context

---

[5] KARL MENNINGER, THE CRIME OF PUNISHMENT (1966).

[6] *Id.* at 190–218.

[7] BARBARA WOOTTON, CRIME AND THE CRIMINAL LAW 32–84 (1963).

[8] ENRICO FERRI, CRIMINAL SOCIOLOGY (1917).

[9] CHRISTOPHER SLOBOGIN, MINDING JUSTICE: LAWS THAT DEPRIVE PEOPLE WITH MENTAL DISABILITY OF LIFE AND LIBERTY 152–77 (2006).

[10] AMERICAN LAW INSTITUTE, MODEL PENAL CODE AND COMMENTARIES (1962).

and a few other special situations, the MPC's sentence ranges were fixed at one to twenty years for first-degree felonies,[11] one to ten years for second-degree felonies, and one to five years for third-degree felonies, with courts permitted to depart below the minimum and to consider alternatives to prison within all categories.[12]

The third feature of preventive justice departs entirely from the desert model and is more closely aligned with the ideas of Menninger and Wootton. Sentences within these retributively-defined ranges would depend solely on a risk-needs assessment, carried out periodically by an assessment team using modern actuarial and structured professional judgment tools that rely on empirically-derived risk and protective factors having to do with criminal history, psychological and psychosocial characteristics, and perhaps some demographic characteristics, such as age or education.[13] Criminal justice jurisdiction for a particular crime would last no longer than the maximum term. But the sentence could be much shorter, depending on an offender's risk. Further, much, if not all, of the sentence period might be served outside of prison, in community-based programs, especially if the person is considered low risk.[14] In essence, preventive justice is a return to the indeterminate sentencing regimes that were quite popular in this country up through the 1960s and are still popular in some European countries.[15]

Why Rejuvenation of Preventive Justice May Be a Good Idea

The indeterminate sentencing regimes of yesteryear, featuring broad sentence ranges and release decision-making by parole boards, were much maligned, justifiably so in many respects. Critics voiced concerns about the inefficacy of correctional treatment, the inaccuracy of predictions, and the incompetence of parole boards, among other objections. Why argue for its return? There are two broad reasons for doing so. Both involve developments since the 1970s.

First, there are new scientific advances, in several different domains. We are rapidly learning more about the interaction of the brain and behavior, genes and behavior, and the environment and behavior.[16] To some, these developments call into question whether

---

[11] *Id.*, § 6.06 (Alternative).

[12] *Id.*, § 6.12 (1962) (allowing sentence reductions if a sentence is "unduly harsh" in light of "the nature and circumstances of the crime and . . . the history and character of the defendant.").

[13] For a general commentary on risk assessment instruments, see HANDBOOK OF VIOLENCE RISK ASSESSMENT (Kevin Douglas & Randy Otto, eds., 2nd ed. 2021).

[14] Even commentators who are more wedded to retributivism favor this approach toward low-risk offenders. *See* RICHARD FRASE, JUST SENTENCING: PRINCIPLES AND PROCEDURES FOR A WORKABLE SYSTEM 25–26 (2013); Kevin Reitz, *The Compelling Case for Low Violence-risk Preclusion in American Prison Policy*, 38 BEHAV. SCI. & L. 207 (2020).

[15] On European sentencing, see generally RELEASE FROM PRISON: EUROPEAN POLICY AND PRACTICE (Nicola Padfield, Dirk van Zyl Smit, & Firder Dunkel, eds. 2010).

[16] A special issue of *Behavioral Sciences and Law* that I edited provides several examples of these developments. *See* David Freedman & George W. Woods, *The Developing Significance of Context and Function: Neuroscience Law*, 36 BEHAV. SCI. & L. 411 (2018) (describing neuroscientific and social psychology findings); Natalie Gordon & Mark R. Fondacaro, *Rethinking the Voluntary Act Doctrine: The Implications*

we should *ever* punish based on backward-looking assessments of culpability; if behavior is truly determined, one might ask, how can we presume to assign blame for it?[17] But the free will-determinism debate is ongoing, and science will not resolve it in the foreseeable future.

In the meantime, the reason current research about human motivation has implications for criminal justice today is that, because we know more about what causes crime, we know more about how to predict and prevent it. Thus, compared to fifty years ago, we are better at both assessing risk and managing risk.[18] Although, as discussed later in this chapter,[19] we still have much to learn, today we know considerably more about how to implement preventive justice than we did when the reign of indeterminate sentencing came to an end.

A second reason for bringing preventive justice back is more practical. The United States is in the throes of hyperincarceration, a massive increase in the size of our prison population that has only recently begun to abate—and then only in the sense that it is no longer increasing. A conservative estimate is that the United States has gone from imprisoning 96 people per 100,000 to close to 600 people per 100,000; some scholars put today's rate at more than 700 out of 100,000,[20] a rate six times that of Europe's.[21]

We also are imposing much longer sentences. The number of prisoners serving life terms has quadrupled since 1986, meaning that one of nine offenders in our prison system today is serving a life sentence, either with or without parole; further, more than 10 percent of these individuals are serving sentences for something other than homicide.[22] Likewise, penalties for drug offenses have increased, on average, by more than three years between 1986 and 2012.[23] Compared to Europe, three times as many

---

from Neuroscience and Behavioral Science, 36 BEHAV. SCI. & L. 426 (2018) (same); Robert Walker et al., *Developmental Impairments in Moral Competence as Mitigation in Capital Cases*, 36 BEHAV. SCI. & L. 437 (2018) (describing social and developmental psychology findings).

[17] For an argument in this vein, see DAVID M. EAGLEMAN, INCOGNITO 151 (2011) (relying on neuroscience findings in concluding that "blameworthiness is the wrong question").

[18] See Sarah J. Desmarais, Kiersten L. Johnson, & Jay P. Singh, *Performance of Recidivism Risk Assessment Instruments in U.S. Correctional Settings*, 13 PSYCHOL. SERVS. 206, 206 (2016) available at https://doi.org/10.1002/9781119184256.ch1 ("There is overwhelming evidence that risk assessments completed using structured approaches produce estimates that are more reliable and more accurate than unstructured risk assessments."); R. Karl Hanson & Kelly E. Morton-Bourgon, *The Accuracy of Recidivism Risk Assessments for Sexual Offenders: A Meta-analysis of 118 Prediction Studies*, 21 PSYCHOL. ASSESSMENT 1, 6 (2009)("For the prediction of sexual or violent recidivism, the actuarial measures designed for violent recidivism were superior to any of the other methods.").

[19] *See infra* text accompanying notes 91–97.

[20] *See* Christopher Slobogin, *How Changes in American Culture Triggered Hyper-Incarceration: Variations on the Tazian View*, 58 HOWARD L.J. 305, 307 (summarizing research).

[21] MICHELLE ALEXANDER, THE NEW JIM CROW 7–8 (2010).

[22] The Sentencing Project, Life Goes On: The Historic Rise in Life Sentences in America 7 (2013), sentencing project.org/doc/publications/inc_Life%20Goes%20On%202013.pdf.

[23] The Sentencing Project, Trends in U.S. Corrections 3 (2012), at senteincgproject.org./doc/publications/inc_Trends_in_Corrections_Fact_sheet.pdf.

convicted offenders end up in prison, and our sentences are, on average, three times as long.[24]

There are dozens of reasons for this increase in punitiveness. But a key one is the move toward desert-based sentencing, which began in this country in the 1970s, at precisely the same time hyperincarceration began.

Desert-based sentencing is implemented in several ways. First, sentences are determinate, and usually based on "sentencing guidelines," meaning that the ultimate sentence is set not by a parole board at the back end but by a judge at the front end. The judge is given a very narrow range to work with for each crime, and punishment within that range is generally supposed to be based on proven past criminal behavior.[25] Of course, determinate sentences do not have to be long; for instance, one of the leading advocates for determinate sentencing once proposed that even serious offenders should receive a maximum sentence of only a few years.[26] But over the past few decades, politicians jockeying to demonstrate their toughness on crime have routinely increased the guidelines maxima. The result is that our sentences today are longer than they have ever been.

A second consequence of desert-based sentencing is the truth-in-sentencing movement. Even in states that retain indeterminate sentencing, offenders often serve at least 85 percent of their maximum sentence, because in the 1990s Congress decided to encourage states to make offenders serve most of their "just" sentence. While Congress directly controls only federal sentencing, it conditioned disbursement of correctional funding to the states on meeting the truth-in-sentencing mandate. Given the hunger for federal money, well over half the states have gone along with it.[27]

Third, if punishment is based on desert, mandatory minimum sentences are much more likely; when the crime, rather than the criminal, is the focus, it is easier to assign a definitive minimum in the abstract. Mandatory minima have proliferated in the desert era. As noted above, mandatory life without parole is now common for adults and, until the Supreme Court declared it unconstitutional, was also common for juveniles;[28] mandatory sentences are also routine for less serious offenses.[29]

---

[24] See Slobogin, *supra* note 20, at 309–10 (providing more specific information on the comparison).

[25] Kelly Lyn Mitchell, *State Sentencing Guidelines: A Garden Full of Variety*, 81 FED. PROB. 28, 29 (2017) (noting that, despite variations, all sentencing guidelines "express the sentence as either a fixed term or a range of time from which a term must be selected" and that the "two primary determinants of the sentence . . . are offense severity and criminal history.").

[26] Andrew von Hirsch, Equality, *"Anisonomy," and Justice: A Review of Madness and the Criminal Law*, 82 MICH. L. REV. 1093, 1105–6 (1984) (suggesting a range of two to three years for a first offense of armed robbery).

[27] PAULA M. DITTON & DORIS J. WILSON, TRUTH IN SENTENCING IN STATE PRISONS 3 (1999).

[28] Miller v. Alabama, 567 U.S. 466 (2012) (holding that imposing a mandatory life-without-parole sentence on an individual who commits the crime before age eighteen is a violation of the Eighth Amendment and noting that 2,500 individuals were currently serving such sentences).

[29] JONATHAN SIMON, GOVERNING THROUGH CRIME: HOW THE WAR ON CRIME TRANSFORMED AMERICAN DEMOCRACY AND CREATED A CULTURE OF FEAR 101 (2007) (describing the proliferation of mandatory

Fourth, several states have enacted three-strikes-and-you are-out (or even two-strikes) laws. These statutes prolong sentences upon conviction of a third felony, in some jurisdictions up to a maximum of twenty-five years, in others up to life.[30] Some have suggested that these laws are the result of an obsession with risk, not with exacting retribution.[31] But if these statutes were actually based on assessments of risk, they would not impose the same twenty-five-year-to-life sentence on *every* third-time felon, as current three-strikes laws do. That fact means that, whatever their official explanation, these statutes are based not on a prevention rationale but on a desert rationale: a person who commits a crime after being given two chances to go straight has, according to this view, thumbed their nose at the law and thus deserves more punishment, regardless of individual risk.[32]

A final development associated with determinate, desert-based sentencing—one that naturally follows from the first four—is that, because sentences are set at the front-end, parole boards become virtually irrelevant. In fact, the federal government and many states have done away with parole boards, either explicitly or in practice.[33] This is unfortunate for our bulging prisons because, by differentiating between who can be released safely and who should not be, parole was one of the primary ways states reduced pressure on prison populations.[34] When parole boards determine the length of sentences, punitive legislative enactments and tough-on-crime prosecutors cannot control the punishment outcome.

It has been suggested that recent prison growth has been just as significant in states that have retained parole as in states that moved to determinate sentencing.[35] But, in fact, the same pressures that led to truth-in-sentencing, mandatory minima, and three-strikes laws also made "indeterminate" sentencing regimes much more determinate; legislative initiatives in these jurisdictions significantly increased the proportion of prisoners who are ineligible for parole, to anywhere from 55 percent to 95 percent.[36] And although parole

---

penalties and noting that it was part of a broader shift toward a "zero tolerance" approach that applied to both severe and low-level crimes).

[30] U.S. Dep't of Justice, National Institute of Justice, "Three Strikes and You're Out": A Review of State Legislation 1 (Sept. 1996), ncjrs.gov./pdffiles/165369ppdf (stating that between 1993 and 1995, twenty-four states and the federal government enacted three-strikes laws).

[31] Paul Robinson, Joshua Baron, & Matthew Lister, *Empirical Desert, Individual Prevention and Limiting Retributivism: A Reply*, 17 NEW CRIM. L. REV. 312, 357 (2014).

[32] JULIAN V. ROBERTS, PUNISHING PERSISTENT OFFENDERS: EXPLORING COMMUNITY AND OFFENDER PERSPECTIVES 68, 163, 171–74 (2008) (stating that the "legal discourse surrounding the punishment of repeat offenders is suffused with references to culpability").

[33] Edward E. Rhine, *The Present Status and Future Prospects of Parole Boards and Parole Supervision*, *in* THE OXFORD HANDBOOK OF SENTENCING AND CORRECTIONS, 627, 631–32 (2012) (describing the abolition or "contraction" of parole in most states since the 1970s).

[34] W. David Ball, *Normative Elements of Parole Risk*, 22 STAN. L. & POL'Y REV. 395, 395 (2011) ("[S]tates can use parole as a population safety valve without indiscriminately endangering public safety, since parole boards can release only those prisoners least likely to reoffend.").

[35] Kevin Reitz, *Don't Blame Determinacy: Incarceration Growth Has Been Driven by Other Forces*, 84 TEX. L. REV. 1787, 1794 (2006).

[36] For instance, Reitz says that the top four "carceral powerhouses" were "Texas, Louisiana, Oklahoma and Georgia, all indeterminate jurisdictions." *Id.* at 1795. But all these states significantly limit the proportion

boards are certainly easily vulnerable to political pressures from governors and legislatures, that malleability works both ways; before the tough-on-crime movement in the 1980s, parole boards were more willing to release prisoners early,[37] and today the states that are leading the charge in the fledgling decarceration movement are those with parole-driven sentencing.[38] Unfortunately, however, most states still circumscribe parole authority.

In theory, a preventive justice regime should curb every one of these instruments of hyperincarceration. There would be no requirement that offenders serve 85 percent of their sentences, and there would be no mandatory minima or three-strikes laws. Parole boards would return to preeminence, so that sentences could be titrated according to risk and correctional capacity, and the public could be protected through "selective incapacitation" of high-risk individuals rather than general incapacitation based on the nature of the crime. Putting a dent in mass incarceration is thus a second reason, besides the assertion that we now know more about criminal behavior, for adopting a preventive justice regime.

The Constitution and Preventive Justice

Moving back toward preventive justice may make good sense. But some have argued that whatever the practical benefits of preventive justice, it is unconstitutional. Lengthy rebuttals of these contentions are not possible here.[39] But a summary of why the constitutional arguments against preventive justice do not fly, as well as a brief account of the constraints the Constitution *does* impose on preventive justice, are necessary to set up the remainder of this chapter.

Probably the most common complaint about any system of sentencing that relies in whole or part on risk assessment is that it permits punishment for status (the status of dangerousness), in violation of the Eighth Amendment's prohibition on cruel and unusual punishment or substantive due process.[40] For instance, in *Kansas v. Hendricks*[41]

---

of the prison population that is eligible for parole: Texas (55 percent), Louisiana (7 percent), Oklahoma (17 percent) and Georgia (39 percent), and none of them recognize presumptive parole (requiring automatic release if certain criteria are met). *See* Jorge Renaud, *Grading the Parole Release Systems of All 50 States*, Prison Pol'y Initiative (2019), https://www.prisonpolicy.org/reports/parole_grades_table.html.

[37] Kevin Reitz, *Prison-Release Reform and American Decarceration*, 104 MINN. L. REV. 2741, 2744 (2020) ("During the thirty-five year buildup period, . . . parole boards . . . became progressively more risk-averse in their decision-making and ever more fearful of external scrutiny and condemnation. Instead focusing their release discretion as often as they had done in the earlier twentieth century, parole boards transformed themselves into agencies of "release-denial discretion.").

[38] *Id.* at 131 ("it is intriguing that indeterminate states have had more than twice as much prison-rate decline as determinate states in the post-growth period. This raises the possibility that the low-friction quality of indeterminate prison-release systems could make it easier to reverse course than in stickier determinate regimes.").

[39] *See* CHRISTOPHER SLOBOGIN, JUST ALGORITHMS: USING SCIENCE TO REDUCE INCARCERATION AND INFORM A JURISPRUDENCE OF RISK 86-99 (2021).

[40] *Cf.* Robinson v. California, 370 U.S. 660, 666 (1970) (holding that punishment of a person for the status of addiction violates the Eighth Amendment).

[41] 521 U.S. 346 (1997).

the Supreme Court stated that, under the due process clause, "A finding of dangerousness, standing alone, is ordinarily not a sufficient ground upon which to justify indefinite involuntary commitment."[42] And in *Buck v. Davis*, the Supreme Court stated that "Our law punishes people for what they do, not who they are."[43] However, numerous decisions by the Court, including those involving the death penalty, have made clear that, as long as a sentence is preceded by conviction for an offense and stays within a retributively defined range—which are both requirements in a preventive justice regime—it is not cruel and unusual or unconstitutionally disproportionate to the crime.[44]

A related argument is that basing sentences on gender or age or on factors, like socioeconomic status, that are statistically correlated with race—which explicitly occurs with many risk assessment instruments and implicitly occurs with any form of prediction—violates equal protection under the law, guaranteed by the Fourteenth Amendment. Consistent with that view, in *Buck*, the Supreme Court stated: "It would be patently unconstitutional for a state to argue that a defendant is liable to be a future danger because of his race."[45] But that holding, concerning race, may be sui generis. For instance, the courts are likely to hold that the explicit use of factors such as gender and age is permissible if it adds appreciably to the ability of the instrument to identify high-risk offenders, given the compelling interest in protecting the public and in avoiding inaccurate risk designations (which is likely to occur if factors such as sex and age are not taken into account).[46] Likewise, any disparate racial impact that might result from reliance on nonracial risk factors, such as education, is probably permissible as long as it is the product of a good faith attempt to produce accurate predictions and not the result of racial animus.[47]

Finally, it could be argued that indeterminate sentencing based on judicial or parole board assessment of risk factors violates the Sixth Amendment right to jury trial which, after the Supreme Court's decision in *United States v. Booker*,[48] requires that all facts that

---

[42] *Id.* at 359.

[43] Buck v. Davis, 137 S. Ct. 759, 778 (2017).

[44] Jurek v. Texas, 428 U.S. 262 (1976) (upholding the dangerousness aggravator in Texas's death penalty statute).

[45] Buck v. Davis, 137 S. Ct. at 778.

[46] See Wisconsin v. Loomis, 881 N.W.2d 749, 765–67, 769 (2016) (holding that use of gender as a risk factor is not unconstitutional; also noting that sentencing courts using such instruments should attend to the fact that "[s]ome studies of . . . risk assessment scores have raised questions about whether they disproportionately classify minority offenders as having a higher risk of recidivism."). *See generally* Christopher Slobogin, *Risk Assessment, in* THE OXFORD HANDBOOK OF SENTENCING AND CORRECTIONS 190, 204–5 (discussing the equal protection argument).

[47] Washington v. Davis, 426 U.S. 229, 239 (1976) ("[O]ur cases have not embraced the proposition that a law or other official act, without regard to whether it reflects a racially discriminatory purpose, is unconstitutional solely because it has a racially disproportionate impact."). *Davis* might be violated, however, if disparate racial impact results from using a risk factor or outcome measure, such as drug or misdemeanor arrests, known to exaggerate black offending compared to white offending. See SLOBOGIN, *supra* note 39, at 93–95.

[48] 543 U.S. 220 (2005).

lead to aggravation of a sentence beyond the statutory or guidelines maximum be determined by a jury beyond a reasonable doubt. But *Booker* also made clear that as long as the sentence stays within the legislatively designated range, the Sixth Amendment is not implicated.[49] Lower courts have held that this rule permits within-guidelines sentence enhancements based on judicial findings of risk.[50]

In short, arguments that a preventive justice regime is unconstitutional would fail. However, that does not mean the Constitution would impose no limits on such a regime. Most importantly, under the Supreme Court's holding in *Jackson v. Indiana*,[51] the due process clause requires that the nature and duration of any deprivation of liberty by the government bear a "reasonable relationship to the purpose of the deprivation."[52] That important principle has at least three implications for preventive justice.

First, it requires that the government show that a deprivation of liberty in the name of prevention is the last drastic means of achieving its preventive aim. That would mean, for instance, that community-based programs should be the presumptive disposition unless they are demonstrably less able than prison to protect the public, and that the state should experiment with different dispositional approaches to determine the best risk-reducing programs.[53] In capital punishment states, it would also mean a death sentence based on a risk assessment is impermissible, because no offender presents such a significant threat that execution, as opposed to confinement, is necessary to prevent it.[54]

Second, *Jackson* means that the government *must* provide treatment if treatment will reduce the length of the intervention. Otherwise, the disposition is not the least restrictive means of accomplishing the state's aim. In other words, *Jackson* provides a strong basis for a right to ameliorative treatment when the sentence is preventive in focus.[55]

Finally, *Jackson's* reasonable relationship requirement means that any preventive confinement that occurs should be proportionate to the risk, and that the longer the intervention extends, the stronger the proof of risk must be.[56] Thus, individuals considered low risk, or at risk of committing only minor crimes, should never be detained for preventive purposes. Even individuals considered to be high risk could not be confined for prolonged periods of time without increasingly higher showings of risk (and, of course, no one could be detained beyond the retributively determined maximum sentence).

---

[49] *Id.* at 244.

[50] *See, e.g.*, Luttrell v. Commonwealth, Record No. 2092-02-4 (Va. Ct. App., Feb. 17, 2004).

[51] 406 U.S. 715 (1972). *See also* Seling v. Young, 531 U.S. 250, 265 (2001) (citing *Jackson*, indicating that residents of commitment facility may have a claim for release if they are not receiving treatment).

[52] 405 U.S. at 738.

[53] *See* Eric S. Janus & Wayne A. Logan, *Substantive Due Process and the Involuntary Confinement of Sexually Violent Predators*, 35 CONN. L. REV. 319, 358–59 (2003).

[54] *See* Christopher Slobogin, *Capital Punishment and Dangerousness*, *in* MENTAL DISORDER AND CRIMINAL LAW: RESPONSIBILITY, PUNISHMENT AND COMPETENCE 119, 125–26 (Robert F. Schopp et al., eds., 2009).

[55] Janus & Logan, *supra* note 53, at 358 ("the *Jackson* line of cases suggests a strong right to treatment, one in which *effective* treatment facilitates real progress toward community re-entry").

[56] See SLOBOGIN, *supra* note 9, at 143–45 (arguing for such a proportionality principle based on *Jackson*).

The Constitution would also require certain procedural protections. As construed by the Court in *Hendricks*, the due process clause requires periodic review of risk and needs assessments.[57] Further, building on the Supreme Court's parole revocation cases,[58] these review hearings would have to be open and adversarial. In a properly run preventive regime, parole boards would have to be staffed by experts on risk assessment, not the political appointees that often populated such boards in the past.[59] And although the state should have to rely on validated risk assessment instruments (about which more below), offenders should have the right to present "softer" clinical evidence that rebuts an actuarial assessment showing they are high risk, analogous to the character evidence rule that allows the defense to control when the door is opened to less probative evidence.[60]

The rest of this chapter briefly explores the type of psychological research that might be relevant to the rationale and scope of preventive justice, viewed from the perspective of the three major purposes of punishment: exacting retribution; promoting general deterrence; and ensuring individual prevention.

Preventive Justice and Desert

Although a preventive justice regime would not be unconstitutional, a subconstitutional debate still rages over whether a sentence based on risk can ever be "just." Many scholars believe that punishing a person more or less than is "deserved" is immoral, a stance that precludes use of risk as a determinant of punishment.[61] Others have suggested that a desert-based system is crucial to ensuring that offenders and victims are treated with dignity and respect.[62] Furthermore, Paul Robinson has argued that sentences that fail to adhere to commonly accepted beliefs about blameworthiness could undermine the

---

[57] *Hendricks*, 521 U.S., at 363–64.

[58] Morrissey v. Brewer, 408 U.S. 471 (1972) (requiring adversarial rights at parole revocation proceedings); Gagnon v. Scarpelli, 411 U.S. 778, 788 (1973) (requiring counsel at such hearings when "a disputed issue can fairly be represented only by a trained advocate.").

[59] Flores v. Stanford, 2019 WL 4572703 *11 (S.D.N.H., 2019) (holding that a due process claim is stated when "[p]arole Board commissioners commonly do not even read such offenders' files before conducting parole interviews or making parole determinations; make parole determinations based at least in part on a risk assessment algorithm the workings of which no defendant knows or understands; predetermine parole outcomes before conducting parole interviews; and pay no attention to other commissioners' questions and offenders' answers during interviews.").

[60] *See* CHRISTOPHER SLOBOGIN, PROVING THE UNPROVABLE: THE ROLE OF LAW, SCIENCE AND SPECULATION IN ADJUDICATING CULPABILITY AND DANGEROUSNESS 125–29 (2007) (elaborating on this "subject-first" procedure).

[61] *See, e.g.*, MICHAEL MOORE, LAW AND PSYCHIATRY: RETHINKING THE RELATIONSHIP 238–39 (1984).

[62] HERBERT MORRIS, ON GUILT AND INNOCENCE 46 (1976) (desert-based punishment is necessary to affirm the dignity of the offender); Jean Hampton, *The Retributive Idea, in* FORGIVENESS AND MERCY 111, 125 (1988) (arguing that retribution is not only a way of paying back the offender for the wrong they have done but also as an expression of society's refusal to accept the wrongdoer's implicit claim to be more important or valuable—of greater worth—than their victims).

legitimacy of the criminal justice system, and even lead to less compliance with it.[63] Each of these arguments casting doubt on the rationale of a punishment system based on risk raises interesting empirical questions.

Consider first the argument that minimizing desert as a punishment goal is immoral. This contention assumes that the culpability of an offender can be calibrated precisely, or at least pared down to a narrow range. But that conceit is belied by the centuries of debate over the grading of crimes, the role of reasonableness in defining mens rea and the defenses, the relevance of social disadvantage to sentencing, and a host of other matters that are still unresolved. It may be that, as Norval Morris observed years ago, the best we can do is ensure that a given sentence is "not undeserved."[64] At the same time, empirical study of the public's view of sentencing might help determine the *outer boundaries* of what is not undeserved. Following research on what has been called "empirical desert,"[65] and building on some of my work,[66] research aimed at identifying dispositions that the bulk of the populace find offensive might provide information that could be highly useful in establishing the minimum and maximum sentencing levels in a preventive justice regime.

The implicit hypothesis of the closely related dignity argument is that only through a desert-based sentence can the offender and the victim be recognized and treated as valuable human beings. Yet, in theory at least, preventive justice can also promote the dignity of both offenders and victims. Risk management programs, done correctly, stress the person's responsibility for their actions and the ability to change one's situation.[67] And such programs might accord victims *greater* respect than a purely desert-based system, because they often involve all parties in fashioning a disposition. For instance, restorative justice, a primary goal of which is to reduce recidivism, is premised on the idea that offenders and victims should meet each other, and that during these conferences the offender will come to understand that the victim is not just a "mark" or an object to be exploited, but a person with feelings who has been caused pain by the offender.[68]

---

[63] Paul Robinson, *The Utility of Desert*, 91 NW. U. L. REV. 451, 457 (1997).

[64] NORVAL MORRIS, THE FUTURE OF IMPRISONMENT 151 (1974).

[65] Paul H. Robinson & Robert Kurzban, *Concordance and Conflict in Intuitions of Justice*, 91 MINN. L. REV. 1829 (2007); Paul Robinson, Geoffrey Goodwin & Michael Reisig, *The Disutility of Injustice*, 85 N.Y.U. L. REV. 1940 (2010).

[66] Christopher Slobogin & Lauren Brinkley-Rubinstein, *Putting Desert in Its Place*, 65 STAN. L. REV. 77, 94–97 (2013) (presenting empirical evidence that laypeople endorse wide, but not unlimited, sentences in several crime scenarios).

[67] *See, e.g.*, Judith Becker & William D. Murphy, *What We Know and Do Not Know about Assessing and Treating Sex Offenders*, 4 PSYCHOL. PUB. POL'Y & L. 116, 128 (1998) (noting that sex offender treatments "focus on reducing denial and cognitive distortions or minimizations, which are the rationalizations that offenders use to justify and maintain their behavior").

[68] Gabrielle Maxwell & Allison Morris, *The Role of Shame, Built, and Remorse in Restorative Justice Processes for Young People, in* RESTORATIVE JUSTICE: THEORETICAL FOUNDATIONS 280 (Elmar G. M. Weitkamp & Hans-Jurgen Kerner, eds., 2002).

The possibility that, contrary to hypothesis, desert-based punishment tends to *denigrate* rather than reinforce offender and victim dignity should also be considered. For instance, a system focused on seeking revenge toward the perpetrator and justice for the victim could coarsen our discourse and behavior rather than heighten it. Neil Vidmar has suggested that a retributive message from the criminal justice system could accelerate society-wide cycles of recrimination and violence.[69] In short, research comparing a desert-based system with preventive justice in terms of a dignity or human-affirming metric would be highly worthwhile.

As to Robinson's legitimacy point, it is probably true that if the criminal justice system abandoned all pretense at assessing culpability, significant negative consequences would result. Although I have argued that Robinson exaggerates the noncompliance effects of failing to adhere to lay perceptions of desert,[70] I think his basic assertion is correct: a system that routinely failed to impose significant punishment for the most egregious crimes or that, conversely, convicts people in the absence of a criminal act or culpable mental state and routinely imposed long sentences on minor offenders, would trigger a significant loss of moral authority. As Tom Tyler's work suggests,[71] such a system could well eat away at the natural tendency to obey the law, cooperate with authorities, and comply with government mandates in other aspects of life.

At the same time, the destabilizing impact of ignoring desert is likely to occur only if departures from widely held views about culpability are radical and routine, and even then any moral offense might quickly dissipate.[72] Some research even suggests that, if informed of the many ways in which human behavior is shaped by biological and environmental forces, people's views about the importance of individual desert can change drastically.[73] All of these hypotheses are worth pursuing further.

---

[69] Neil Vidmar, *Retribution and Revenge, in* HANDBOOK OF JUSTICE RESEARCH IN LAW 54 (Joseph Sanders & V. Lee Hamilton, eds., 2002).

[70] Slobogin & Brinkley-Rubinstein, *supra* note 66, at 79.

[71] TOM R. TYLER, WHY PEOPLE OBEY THE LAW (1990).

[72] Slobogin & Brinkley-Rubinstein, *supra* note 66, at 108–10 (study finding that dissatisfaction with rules that are not consistent with desert may have no prolonged effect).

[73] Rachel R. Katz & Mark R. Fondacaro, *Fight, Flight, and Free Will: The Effect of Informed Psychoeducation on Perceived Culpability and Punishment for Juvenile and Adult Offenders*, 39 BEHAV. SCI. & L. 708, 719 (2021) (study finding that "perceived culpability of offenders was influenced by free will beliefs, and that free will beliefs were altered through a brief psychoeducational video which did not mention free will, but rather explained the biopsychosocial model and trauma's effects on behavior"); Azim F. Shariff et al., *Free Will and Punishment: A Mechanistic View of Human Nature Reduces Retribution*, 25 PSYCHOL. SCI. 1563 (2014) (studies finding that "learning about the neural bases of human behavior, through either lab-based manipulations or attendance at an undergraduate neuroscience course, reduced people's support for retributive punishment").

Preventive Justice and General Deterrence

Closely related to the legitimacy-compliance debate, but nonetheless conceptually distinct from it, is the concern that a risk-based system, especially one that often opts for community-based alternatives, will not pack sufficient deterrent wallop. Henry Hart asserted that while punishment based on desert sends the message ".If you violate the law, your conduct will receive the formal and solemn condemnation of the community as morally blameworthy," a preventive regime communicates something very different: "If you violate the law, you will merely be considered to be sick and subjected to officially-imposed rehabilitative treatment in an effort to cure you."[74] To Hart, the latter message was very unlikely to deter would-be bad actors.

Hart's description of the message a preventive justice regime communicates is inapt, however. That directive is better framed as this: "If you violate the law, you will be subject to intervention designed to prevent you from violating it again," a warning that could be quite an effective deterrent. Imagine that you have never committed a crime but are thinking about committing a theft. In a desert-based regime, you would know what your penalty would be if you are caught. In a preventive justice jurisdiction, you would not; it might be the minimum sentence, the maximum sentence (which could be quite a bit longer), or something in-between. Assume instead that you have already committed two crimes and are contemplating another one. Again, although you probably know that a third crime is likely to lengthen your punishment, you will be less sure of its precise effect than in a determinate regime. Which regime provides more deterrence?

Much work has already been done on the deterrent effect of criminal penalties, and most of it shows that manipulation of sentence lengths has little impact on crime;[75] indeed, most criminals do not think they will be caught and are relatively oblivious to penalty.[76] But to the extent punishment does deter, the minimal research carried out to date suggests that uncertainty about sanction is a better deterrent than certainty.[77] The extent to which precise knowledge of punishment schemes disincentivizes crime deserves closer study.

---

[74] Henry M. Hart Jr., *The Aims of the Criminal Law*, 23 LAW & CONTEMP. PROBS. 401, 407–8 (1958).

[75] Michael Tonry, *Purposes and Functions of Sentencing*, 34 CRIME & JUST. 1, 28 (2006) (summarizing the research of three National Academy of Sciences panels as finding that "[i]maginable increases in severity of punishments do not yield significant (if any) marginal deterrent effects.").

[76] David A. Anderson, *The Deterrence Hypothesis and Picking Pockets at the Pickpocket's Hanging*, 4 AM. L. & ECONOMICS REV. 1, 20–21 (2002)(interview study of 278 criminals finding that that most committed their crimes under the influence of alcohol, in a fit of rage, or because they needed money and rarely considered the consequences of getting caught).

[77] *See* Dan M. Kahan, *Ignorance of Law Is an Excuse—But Only for the Virtuous*, 96 MICH. L. REV. 127, 137–41 (1997) (discussing "prudent obfuscation" and vague terminology as a means of fostering law-abiding behavior).

The third major purpose of punishment is individual prevention, which is precisely what preventive justice tries to achieve. Here too controversies swirl, beyond those already canvassed in the discussion of constitutional issues. It is with respect to these controversies—involving the accuracy of risk assessment and the efficacy of risk management—that research carried out by psychologists is most likely to have an impact.

The Accuracy of Risk Assessment. The first worry is whether the factual basis for preventive justice—the assessment of risk—can be achieved with a satisfactory degree of accuracy. Four decades ago Justice Blackmun's dissenting opinion in *Barefoot v. Estelle* declared that "predictions of dangerousness are less accurate than the flip of a coin."[78] That statement was probably never true, even in the days of unstructured clinical assessment,[79] and the Area Under the Curve (AUC) values associated with today's risk assessment instruments demonstrate that these tools can provide predictive information that is much better than chance.[80] Nonetheless, it is highly likely that if forensic psychologists were forced to make the binary determination of whether an offender will or will not reoffend, they would frequently be wrong. Whereas a considerable amount of research relevant to risk and needs assessment exists, much more empirical work needs to be done if a preventive justice regime—or any sentencing scheme that relies on risk—is to function effectively. Specifically, more research is needed to ensure both that risk assessments "fit" the legal context and that they rest on sufficiently valid methodologies.[81]

Fit. In the past twenty years, research on risk assessment instruments has exploded. But much of it misses the mark because it does not address the questions the law is asking (or at least should be asking). Assessing the legal fit of a risk assessment tool requires data about (1) the proportion of people in the subject's risk category, (2) who will commit legally relevant antisocial conduct (3) within the legally relevant time frame (4) if specified interventions do not occur.

---

[78] 463 U.S. 880, 931 (1981) (Blackmun, J., dissenting) (citing Bruce Ennis & Thomas R. Litwack, *Psychiatry and the Presumption of Expertise: Flipping Coins in the Courtroom*, 62 CALIF. L. REV. 693, 737 (1974).

[79] Christopher Slobogin, *Dangerousness and Expertise*, 133 U. PA. L. REV. 97, 111–13 (1984) (explaining why "knowledgeable clinicians are much better at predicting dangerousness than the random selection process suggested by the coin-flipping").

[80] Darryl G. Kroner, Jeremy F. Mills, & John R. Redden, *A Coffee Can, Factor Analysis, and Prediction of Antisocial Behavior: The Structure of Criminal Risk*, 28 INT'L J. L. & PSYCHIATRY 360 (2005) (finding that four major risk assessment instruments, as well as combinations thereof, have AUCs over 0.65). AUC refers to the area under the curve produced by plotting the true positive rate over the false-positive rate for as many cut points as possible.

[81] For elaboration on the following points about fit and validity, see SLOBOGIN, *supra* note 39, at 37–85.

Given the near impossibility of predicting individual behavior, when a judge or parole board is attempting to estimate the probability of reoffending (issue (1)), the most useful and accurate information is not a binary declaration that the person will or will not reoffend but rather a statement about group probabilities, as in: "This person belongs to a group, roughly 30% of whom recidivated in the relevant validation study." The legal decision-maker also needs to know the outcome that is being predicted (issue (2)): for instance, is it *arrest* for *any* offense, or *conviction* for a *violent* offense? And, if the latter, how is "violent offense" defined?[82] Significant legal consequences could depend on the answers to these questions. Arguably, for instance, in felony sentencing cases the outcome measure should be conviction for a violent offense.

Further, because the legal decision-maker is often attempting to forecast reoffending within a limited period, a time frame for the prediction is important (issue (3)). For instance, if a parole board is considering the risk posed by an individual between the time of its decision and the next parole review period a year or two hence, a risk assessment based on a several-year follow-up period is not very helpful. Finally, an individual's risk of reoffending can vary enormously depending on the law's response to the risk (issue (4)). While imprisonment might reduce risk, it may not be any more effective at doing so than placement in an effective substance abuse treatment program in the community, a vocational training program in a halfway house, or a job-release program coupled with an ankle monitor. *Jackson's* parsimony principle requires consideration of such options.

Research on risk assessments needs to address all these issues. Otherwise, it will not fit legal needs, particularly those that arise in a preventive justice regime.

Validity. Of course, even if a risk assessment can address the probability, outcome, duration, and intervention issues, it will be useless unless it does so with a fair degree of accuracy. Here again, research is needed on four issues, this time focused on whether a given risk assessment instrument does what it purports to do in the following senses: (1) calibration; (2) discrimination; (3) local validation; and (4) interrater reliability.

Given the law's need for probability estimates described above, the most important measure of calibration is the positive predictive value (PPV), which indicates how often a tool's prediction that someone will recidivate is correct, within specified confidence intervals.[83] However, in a preventive justice regime, more than a single PPV is needed. A more

---

[82] *Cf.* Johnson v. United States, 576 U.S. 591, 593–94 (noting the large number of crimes that could be called violent, while finding unconstitutional language in the Armed Career Criminal Act that authorized an additional fifteen-year sentence for "conduct that presents a serious potential risk of physical injury to another").

[83] Jay P. Singh, *Predictive Validity Performance Indicators in Violent Risk Assessment*, 31 BEHAV. SCI. & L. 8, 18 (2013).

legally relevant measure of calibration is what could be called the category positive predictive value (CPPV) or category base rate, which answers the following three-part question: (1) does the risk assessment instrument (RAI) associate a person with a category (a score, decile, or risk group); (2) if so, what percentage of people in the category does it predict will recidivate in the way defined by the relevant law; and (3) to what extent can we be confident of that percentage? That is, there needs to be a PPV for every risk category. Risk assessment should try to identify as many discrete risk categories, with associated PPVs, as possible.

While calibration is a crucial metric for legal purposes, it should not be the only measure of predictive validity. Data regarding a tool's ability to differentiate high- and low-risk offenders—most commonly measured with the AUC—are also necessary, to provide some sense of its sensitivity and specificity.[84] If a risk assessment instrument does not have an AUC somewhere above 0.6, it may well be irrelevant for legal purposes.[85]

Third, both calibration and discriminant validity should be demonstrated on a legally relevant population. That means predictive validity data should be derived not only from a sample within the jurisdiction in which it will be used but also from important demographic groups within that jurisdiction, to ensure validity is maintained for those groups. For instance, although research for many of the most widely used instruments shows that predictive validity does not vary significantly among racial groups,[86] such outcomes cannot simply be assumed.[87] To be valid, an RAI should have similar positive predictive values for each risk classification across as many major demographic groups as feasible, and have a similar AUC for each demographic group as well.[88] This may require separate instruments (with different risk factors) for people of color, women, and so on.

Even an RAI that has good calibration, discriminant validity, and external validity may still not produce valid results if it cannot be administered reliably. A survey of

---

[84] *Id.* at 15.

[85] L. Maaike Helmus & Kelly M. Babchishin, *Primer on Risk Assessment and the Statistics Used to Evaluate Its Accuracy*, 44 CRIM. JUST. & BEHAV. 8, 12 (2017) (discussing acceptable AUC values).

[86] Jennifer L. Skeem & Christopher Lowenkamp, *Risk, Race, and Recidivism: Predictive Bias and Disparate Impact*, 54 CRIMINOLOGY 680, 700 (2016) ("these results indicate that risk assessment is not 'race assessment'"); Desmarais et al., *supra* note 18, at 216 (in metareview of nineteen RAIs, of the three that permitted comparison of Black and White AUCs, the measures were "identical" or "highly similar"); Jay Singh & Seena Fazel, *Forensic Risk Assessment: A Metareview*, 37 CRIM. JUST. & BEHAV. 965, 978 (2010) (finding that, of six meta-reviews, five found "no evidence that predictive validity varied by the ethnicity of participants").

[87] *See, e.g.*, Melissa Hamilton, *Judicial Gatekeeping on Scientific Validity with Risk Assessment Tools*, 38 BEHAV. SCI. & L. 226, 232–36 (2020) (providing several examples of how PPVs and AUCs can differ by race, sex, and other variables).

[88] Min Yang et al., *The Efficacy of Violence Prediction: A Meta-Analytic Comparison of Nine Risk Assessment Tools*, 136 PSYCHOL. BULL. 740, 741 (2010).

fifty-three studies in 2013 found that only two reported interrater reliability.[89] Given that many risk and needs factors are loosely defined, more empirical work is required here as well.

Finally, it must be recognized that all four measures of accuracy just described can vacillate for a particular instrument if, for instance, the population on which the RAI was normed changes significantly; the jurisdiction's crime, arrest, or conviction rates go up or down significantly; or the jurisdiction begins implementing innovative alternatives to prison that can reduce risk. Because the potential for offending is affected by these types of factors, a person rated high risk on an outdated instrument may belong to a group that is low risk, or vice versa. Tools should be audited periodically to ensure they are performing adequately.[90] Ideally, this audit should be carried out by researchers who did not develop the instrument.

CPPVs, AUCs, and reliability data that have been replicated by others, in the same setting in which the risk tool is being used, are the best means of instilling confidence that risk assessments are reliable in both the legal and scientific sense. Providing good data on all these various indicia of validity is a tall order. Nonetheless, from an empirical perspective, serious effort should be made in this regard. Otherwise, even a tool that provides answers the law wants can be irrelevant.

The Efficacy of Risk Management. The second major empirical concern associated with the individual prevention rationale of preventive justice is whether the interventions that evaluators recommend to reduce risk are effective at doing so. For many years, the accepted wisdom was that "nothing works" with respect to rehabilitation. Francis Allen, in his famous book, *The Decline of the Rehabilitative Ideal,* summarized the relevant point bluntly: "We do not know how to prevent criminal recidivism through rehabilitative effort."[91]

But Allen was writing in early 1980. More recent results from meta-analytic studies show that rehabilitation can be successful, especially if implemented through treatment programs that focus on skills rather than discipline, that concentrate on high risk offenders rather than low risk offenders, and that take place in the community rather than in prison.[92] According to Mark Lipsey: "The global question of whether rehabilitation treatment works to reduce recidivism has been answered in the affirmative by every

---

[89] Desmarais et al., *supra* note 18, at 213.

[90] Brandon Garrett & John Monahan, *Judging Risk*, 108 CALIF. L. REV. 439, 486 (2020).

[91] FRANCIS ALLEN, THE DECLINE OF THE REHABILITATIVE IDEAL: PENAL POLICY AND SOCIAL PURPOSE 57 (1981) (also noting that the programs that do exist can be very expensive).

[92] Christopher T. Lowenkamp, Edward J. Latessa, & Alexander M. Holsinger, *The Risk Principle in Action: What Have We Learned from 13,676 Offenders and 97 Correctional Programs?* 52 CRIME & DELINQ. 77, 89–90 (2006) (metareview finding that targeting offenders identified as high risk is more effective at reducing risk); Francis T. Cullen & Cheryl Lero Jonson, *Rehabilitation and Treatment Programs, in* CRIME AND PUBLIC POLICY 293, 303 (James Q. Wilson & Joan Petersilia, eds., 2011).

meta-analyst who has conducted a systematic synthesis of a broad sample of the available experimental and quasi-experimental research."[93]

At the same time, much more research is needed to identify specific methods of reducing both risk and the use of incarceration.[94] As Jennifer Skeem and John Monahan point out, risk assessment is usually divorced from "needs" assessment; "in practice, . . . the former is often subject to empirical scrutiny while 'anything goes' for the latter,"[95] because validation is easier with respect to risk assessment than risk management. Thus, some "needs" variables "do not even qualify as risk factors for recidivism, much less as 'causal' risk factors."[96] Skeem and Monahan recommend that if the goal is to inform risk reduction efforts, "needs assessments must prominently feature empirically supported, causal risk factors for recidivism."[97]

Without attention to the types of concerns identified by Skeem and Monahan, preventive justice cannot work. Instruments that can validly assess risk are very important for making determinations about whether someone should stay in prison or go to prison in the first instance. But without valid information about risk-reducing factors and the programs that can effectively deal with those needs, at most only half the empirical battle has been won.

Back to the Future?

A preventive justice regime harks back to an era when indeterminate sentencing reigned. But it contemplates significant differences from that regime as well. It would adopt sentence ranges consistent with the offender's desert and then rely on expert parole boards, assisted by validated risk assessment tools, to determine the nature and duration of sentence within this range, based on consideration of the individual prevention goals of specific deterrence, rehabilitation, and incapacitation. I have argued elsewhere that

> a system of relatively wide sentence ranges derived from retributive principles, in combination with short minimum sentences that are enhanced under limited circumstances by statistically-driven risk assessment and management, can alleviate many of the inherent tensions between desert and prevention, between deontology and political reality, and between the desire for

---

[93] Mark W. Lipsey & Francis T. Cullen, *The Effectiveness of Correctional Rehabilitation: A Review of Systematic Reviews*, 3 ANN. REV. L. & SOC. SCI. 297, 306 (2008).

[94] Jodi Viljoen et al., *Impact of Risk Assessment Instruments on Rates of Pretrial Detention, Postconviction Placements, and Release: A Systematic Review and Meta-Analysis*, 43 LAW & HUM. BEHAV. 397 (2019) (meta-analysis of studies showing only a small reduction in recidivism and restrictive conditions).

[95] Jennifer Skeem & John Monahan, *Lost in Translation: "Risks," "Needs," and "Evidence" in Implementing the First Step Act*, 38 LAW & HUM. BEHAV. 287, 288 (2020).

[96] *Id.*

[97] *Id.*

community input and the allure of expertise. If done properly, it should also significantly reduce prison populations.[98]

Achieving any of this, however, will require empirical efforts of the type identified in this chapter, aimed at bolstering both the conceptual basis of preventive justice and its ability to have real-world crime prevention impacts.

Acknowledgments

Some of this chapter is taken from Christopher Slobogin, *Preventive Justice: A Paradigm in Need of Testing*, 36 BEHAV. SCI. & L. 394 (2018).

---

[98] Christopher Slobogin, *Limiting Retributivism and Individual Prevention*, *in* THE ROUTLEDGE HANDBOOK ON THE PHILOSOPHY AND SCIENCE OF PUNISHMENT 49 (Farah Focquaert, ed., 2021).

Expert Psychological Testimony

Brian L. Cutler *and* Daniel A. Krauss

Abstract

Psychologists offer expert testimony on a variety of psychological topics in civil, criminal, and family law cases, and this testimony is often challenged by the opposing party. The laws and procedures governing the admissibility of expert psychological testimony are the same ones that determine the admissibility of other forms of expert testimony. The content of expert psychological testimony may include expert opinions about mental states relevant to legal proceedings (e.g., a criminal defendant's mental state at the time of offense), or it may be used to educate the fact-finders about scientific research findings (e.g., research on mistaken eyewitness identification). Considerable psychological research has investigated matters such as the need for expert psychological testimony and bias among experts in the adversarial system. Psychologists serving as expert witnesses must be aware of and sensitive to ethical issues governing their practices with a number of professional associations providing ethical guidelines for expert witnesses.

Key Words: experts, expert testimony, evidence, admissibility, ethics, bias

Overview of Expert Psychological Testimony Topics

Psychologists, on a regular basis, are called upon to convey their knowledge and opinions in court hearings and trials with the objectives of assisting the judge or jury with rendering a fair and just decision in the case. In this capacity, psychologists are referred to as "expert witnesses." Expert witnesses are in some ways treated differently than nonexpert, or lay witnesses, and the legal rules governing the testimony of experts are somewhat different. For example, experts are allowed to offer testimony about facts and events that they have not directly perceived, provide opinions about individuals, and base those opinions on evidence that would not be inadmissible during a trial (DeMatteo et al., 2019). However, expert witnesses are in some ways treated similarly to lay witnesses. Juries are instructed to weigh the credibility of expert witnesses and evaluate their testimony as they would that of lay witnesses.

The topics on which psychologists are called to offer expert testimony are vast and differ as a function of the psychologist's education and training. For example, clinical psychologists may testify about present mental states in cases involving the competence of a defendant or litigant (e.g., competence to stand trial, competence to consent to treatment, and competence to manage one's own financial affairs). Clinical psychologists may also testify about past mental states in a criminal responsibility evaluation, in cases in which the insanity defense is raised, or about an individual's level of risk in a sentencing hearing regarding future behavior. Neuropsychologists may testify about their assessments of traumatic brain injury in cases involving personal injuries (e.g., in civil cases arising from automobile accidents). Social and cognitive psychologists may testify about the reliability of eyewitness memory, the potential for false confessions, and the potential impact of prejudicial pretrial publicity in criminal cases. Developmental psychologists may testify about the reliability of children's memory and the suggestibility of interviews in criminal cases involving alleged child sexual abuse. Industrial-organizational psychologists may testify about the adverse impacts in employment discrimination cases and about the impact of hostile work environments in sexual harassment cases.

The types of cases and hearings in which psychologists testify likewise vary. Psychologists most commonly testify in both criminal and civil cases, but they also may testify in family court, juvenile court, problem-solving courts (e.g., drug courts, veterans' courts, and mental health courts), and military court martial cases. Psychologists testify in depositions, pretrial hearings of many kinds, arbitrations, jury trials, and bench trials in which the judge renders the verdict.

Admissibility of Expert Psychological Testimony

Before an expert of any type is permitted to testify in a hearing or trial, the judge must deem the expert an expert. State and federal courts have developed various criteria for experts and expert testimony. The purposes of these criteria are to ensure that experts have proper credentials and expertise so that they do not mislead the court and to ensure that the nature of the testimony is legitimate scientific or professional knowledge and not some form of "junk science." In practice, one party in the case proffers the expert witness, and the other party may challenge the admissibility of the expert witness. There are various grounds on which the opposing party can challenge admissibility. The opposing party may challenge the expert's credentials, for example; or, the opposing party may challenge methods used by the expert and the scientific reliability and/or validity of the testimony. Additionally, an attorney might argue that the expert testimony being offered by one side is irrelevant, prejudicial, misleading, or overly confusing. The judge then applies the appropriate admissibility criteria and determines whether the expert witness will be permitted to testify. This determination by the judge usually occurs at a pretrial hearing or without a jury present during a trial (Sales & Shuman, 2005).

In US courts for about seventy years, the "*Frye* test" often guided judges' admissibility decisions.[1] In *Frye*, the defendant proffered an expert witness to testify about the results of

---

[1] Frye v. United States, 293 F. 1013 (D.C. Cir. 1923).

a lie detection test, a precursor to the modern polygraph. The judge rendered the expert's testimony inadmissible. The defendant appealed his conviction, and the US Court of Appeals for the District of Columbia developed the *Frye* test, which stated that, for novel scientific evidence to be admitted, it must be "sufficiently established to have gained general acceptance in the field in which it belongs."[2] About fifty years later, the US Congress adopted the Federal Rules of Evidence (FRE).[3] These rules were originally developed by an advisory committee created by Chief Justice Earl Warren in 1965, were later submitted and approved by the Judicial Conference of the United States before being promulgated by the US Supreme Court, and finally passed by Congress. The FRE included new admissibility criteria for expert testimony. FRE Rule 702 states that expert testimony will be ruled admissible if the specialized knowledge conveyed by the expert will "assist the trier of fact" and the expert has been qualified on the basis of "knowledge, skill, experience, training, or education." For the next twenty years or so, both the *Frye* test and the FRE governed the admissibility of expert testimony, and there was sometimes confusion about which criteria should be used. In a series of US Supreme Court cases in the 1990s, most notably *Daubert v. Merrell Dow Pharmaceuticals*,[4] the US Supreme Court explicitly decided this controversy and held that FRE 702 supplanted the *Frye* test in federal courts.

In *Daubert*, the US Supreme Court also elaborated upon the admissibility criteria for expert testimony under FRE 702. Initially, the trial judge must determine whether the expert testimony proffered is relevant. If the expert testimony is deemed irrelevant, it is not admitted. If the testimony is deemed relevant, it must also assist the trier of fact. To do so, the judge in a gatekeeping role must ascertain whether the testimony proffered by the expert is evidentiary reliable or scientifically valid (Krauss et al., 2009). The Supreme Court provided a list of factors that the trial judge may consider but is not limited to in evaluating the scientific validity of the proffered testimony. These factors, now known as the "*Daubert* criteria," include: the falsifiability of the underlying theory, known error rates, peer review, and general acceptance within the scientific community (the sole criterion of the *Frye* test). The trial judge may consider other relevant factors as well in determining scientific reliability. The newer *Daubert* criteria potentially facilitate the admission of novel research that is scientifically valid but has not yet gained acceptance by the relevant scientific community (because it takes time for novel research to gain acceptance). The newer *Daubert* criteria also pose challenges to expert testimony that has been accepted by the relevant professional community but may not be established as scientifically valid (e.g., latent fingerprint identification, bite marks, and blood splatter) (Saks & Koehler, 2005).

---

[2] *Id.* at 1014.

[3] Federal Rules of Evidence (1975). Retrieved from https://www.uscourts.gov/sites/default/files/Rules%20of%20Evidence

[4] Daubert v. Merrell Dow Pharm., Inc., 509 U.S. 579 (1993).

The *Daubert* criteria are only directly binding on the US federal court system. Although almost all jurisdictions have adopted the FRE and FRE 702, *Daubert* involved an explicit interpretation of FRE 702 and does not control the interpretation of state courts that have adopted the same rule (Sales & Shuman, 2005). As a result, each state court in the United States has its own rules and criteria for admissibility of expert testimony. Some states have adopted the *Frye* test, or a version of it, and expressly rejected the *Daubert* criteria (e.g., California, Illinois, Maryland, New York, New Jersey, Pennsylvania, and Washington; Melton et al., 2018). Other states, in contrast, have modeled their expert testimony admissibility criteria directly after the *Daubert* decision and factors. It should be recognized that the *Frye* and *Daubert* decisions are required for admittance of expert testimony during the trial phase of criminal and civil proceedings and are rarely used to determine the admissibility of expert testimony in other aspects of the legal process (e.g., sentencing hearings) where different legal rules are employed.

Content of Expert Psychological Testimony

Admissibility decisions are based upon the content of expert psychological information provided by the expert, and these also can vary widely from one expert to another. For example, as previously noted, a social or cognitive psychologist might offer to provide expert testimony in a criminal trial concerning factors that might increase the likelihood of a false confession during a police interrogation. This testimony could be provided as general educational expert testimony to assist the trier of fact by summarizing relevant research in this content area. In such cases, the judge would not only have to determine if the evidence is reliable and would assist the trier of fact but also whether it is beyond the understanding of the average juror. In other words, why would you need an expert if most jurors already possessed such knowledge? Many forms of educational psychological expert testimony were at least initially thought to be *not* outside the knowledge base of the average juror and were as a result deemed inadmissible. However, this trend has been changing, with much more of this educational psychological expert testimony now being admitted by courts (Costanzo & Krauss, 2018).

In contrast, clinical psychologists are more likely to offer expert testimony directly relevant to an individual's mental state or abilities that are central to the legal dispute. For example, they might interview and assess whether individuals are competent to manage their finances. This individualized evaluation is specific to a particular defendant. While this clinical evaluation might borrow on psychological research and administered psychological tests' normative sample derived from groups of individuals, the expert opinion proffered will concern that individual. The clinical psychologist would then often offer an opinion to the court about whether the defendant is competent to handle their finances (i.e., the issue at the heart of the legal proceeding). Interestingly, these clinical expert opinions have received far less scrutiny and risk of being rejected by judges in their admissibility decisions, even in jurisdictions following the *Daubert* criteria, than the more general educational expert testimony by psychologists (Sales & Shuman, 2005).

Importantly, it should be noted that educational psychological expert testimony exists on a continuum in which the expert may or may not more specifically address whether particular defendants or litigants by virtue of their dispositions are particularly vulnerable or whether the conditions to which the litigants were exposed were particularly impactful. For example, returning to our example of a social or cognitive psychologist testifying about interrogation factors that may increase the likelihood of a false confession, an expert might detail how specific factors are particularly relevant to this defendant in this case. The expert might highlight that: the defendant was interviewed for more than forty hours without a break by police; the interrogator used suggestive questioning techniques; and the defendant's limited cognitive abilities all made it more likely that the defendant might falsely confess. As more of the psychological research is directly applied to the individual involved in a case, this bridging begins to approach (but ultimately falls short of) the expert testimony that is commonly offered by clinical psychologists. For example, the expert witness may testify that the interrogation procedures were highly coercive and likely to cause an innocent suspect to falsely confess, but the expert would *not* go as far as to say that the coercive interrogation procedures caused *this* suspect to falsely confess.

Whereas research suggests that this linking of expert testimony to the individual case and defendant increases jury understanding and the use of the expert testimony (this research will be discussed later in this chapter), it also raises a number of ethical and admissibility questions. One such question is whether the psychological expert testimony is usurping or taking over the role of the jury to decide important legal questions. These same concerns have been leveled against clinical psychological expert testimony addressing the central issue of legal disputes, sometimes referred to as ultimate legal opinion expert testimony. While such expert testimony is generally admitted by courts,[5] in one particular instance in the federal courts, Congress has decided that expert testimony directly answering whether a criminal defendant is insane or not is inadmissible.[6]

The Work of Psychologist Expert Witnesses

It is somewhat of a misnomer to classify the use of the title "expert witness" when describing the work of psychologists who offer expert testimony. This is because only a small percentage of the psychologist's time is actually spent giving expert testimony. Most cases, whether criminal or civil, do not go to trial. Most cases are settled before trial through the processes of plea bargaining (in criminal cases) and negotiation and pretrial settlements (in civil cases). Thus, the expert typically spends many hours working on cases that do not go to trial. That is not to say that the expert's work is unimportant or not influential,

---

[5] See FRE 704a.
[6] See FRE 704b.

however. The expert's opinions often factor into the decisions reached in plea-bargaining or pretrial settlements, and the experts therefore play important roles in the cases even though they did not testify as expert witnesses.

Let us examine how expert psychologists actually spend their time. Initially, a lawyer makes contact with the expert and engages the expert in routine conversations about availability, fees, timetables, and other logistics. The lawyer then provides the expert with case materials, or "discovery," to review. In a criminal case, the materials may include police reports of the crime, the indictment, grand jury testimony, and statements by witnesses. The purpose of sharing this information is to provide the expert with background about the case. If the expert is a clinical psychologist who expects to conduct an assessment of the defendant, the expert would be provided with (or seek out) the defendant's education, medical, and mental health records and other relevant information that informs the expert about the defendant's background. In a civil case, the discovery is usually much more voluminous. In civil cases, both parties are entitled to a lengthy period in which they may depose all witnesses in the case. These depositions amount to lengthy interviews, sometimes up to seven hours each. The depositions are recorded and transcribed by a court reporter. Sometime after the period for deposing witnesses ends, the period for deposing expert witnesses begins. The expert witness is therefore furnished with all the transcripts of relevant witness depositions.

As the expert witness is reviewing case information (and, if present, deposition transcripts), the expert witness conducts their evaluation of the case. Many expert witnesses' opinions are based solely on the evaluations of case materials. For example, an eyewitness expert reviews information about the conditions under which a crime occurred and the nature of the eyewitness identification test and identifies psychological risk factors for mistaken eyewitness identification. Clinically trained psychologists conduct forensic mental health assessments with defendants or litigants. For example, a clinical psychologist serving in the role of expert might evaluate a criminal defendant's competence to stand trial. In this role, the clinical psychologist would evaluate the defendant's educational, medical, and other personal records and would conduct a formal interview and assessment of the defendant. During the evaluation, the psychologist might administer a set of general psychological and/or specific forensic psychological tests centered around the competence question. These tests and the interview itself provide the clinical psychologist with insights about the defendant's level of competence to stand trial.

Once the expert witness completes the phase of reviewing and analyzing the relevant discovery and, if appropriate, conducting a formal assessment of the defendant or litigant, the expert integrates the information and forms expert opinions. The expert then shares the opinions with the lawyer who retained the expert, either orally (in a phone call) or in writing in the form of a report, depending on the lawyer's needs. At that point, the lawyer, who is in the position of advocating for their client, must make a decision as to whether to continue the expert's involvement in the case (i.e., if the expert's opinion is helpful to their client's case) or discontinue the expert's involvement in the case (i.e., if the expert's opinion is harmful to their client's case). In many cases, the expert's work is therefore done at this early stage in the case. However, different jurisdictions and legal contexts apply divergent rules about whether these solicited but unused expert opinions and reports may be discoverable by the other side (Melton et al., 2018).

If the lawyer decides to continue the expert's work in the case, the expert will be informed of the next stages. This next stage likely involves expert testimony in some form. The expert may be required to testify in a deposition in which the expert is questioned, on the record, by the opposing counsel. The purpose of this deposition is so that the opposing counsel can be informed about the expert's opinions and related information in advance of the trial. The expert might testify in a pretrial hearing. For example, the eyewitness expert, described above, might testify in a hearing in which the defense moves to exclude an eyewitness identification test from trial on the basis of the test's suggestiveness. In this role, the expert offers opinions about the suggestiveness of the identification test. The clinical psychologist described above might testify in a hearing designed to ascertain the defendant's competence to stand trial. In this role, the clinical psychologist explains the method they used to test the defendant's competence (i.e., the nature of the interview and the tests administered) and would convey to the judge the results of their psychological evaluation of the defendant. In some cases, the psychologist is asked directly for their opinion about the defendant's competence to stand trial.

At any point in the process, including before or after the series of pretrial hearings that takes place, the case may resolve in one of several ways. The case may be dismissed. The defendant in a criminal case may enter into a plea bargain instead of facing a trial. The parties in a civil case may enter into a pretrial settlement that resolves the matter before the court. When any of this happens, the psychologist's work is done. In some small percentage of cases, however, the case proceeds through the discovery and pretrial hearing phases and proceeds to trial. In those cases, the expert prepares and offers testimony as an expert witness in trial. Like any witness, the expert is subjected to direct examination by the lawyer who retained them, cross-examination by the opposing lawyer, and possible questioning by the judge. In some cases, the jury is invited to submit questions to the judge as well. When the trial reaches a verdict, the expert's work is typically over. Some trials result in "hung juries," that is, the juries were unable to reach unanimous verdicts, and the trial may be held again. In such cases, the expert witness may testify again at the retrial. In cases in which verdicts are reached but the defeated party chooses to appeal the verdict, the expert might be involved in posttrial appellate work, which can consist of additional testimony at hearings or the submission of written affidavits.

Research on Expert Psychologist Testimony

Expert psychological testimony itself has been the subject of considerable research. Researchers, usually psychologists in academic settings, have endeavored to provide empirical answers to such questions as: Is expert psychological testimony needed? Is there consensus among psychologists about the research findings about which experts testify? How effective are judges at keeping junk science out of the courtroom? To what extent are experts biased toward the parties that retain them? And what effect does expert testimony have on jury decision-making? We provide a summary of the research and research findings in this section.

Is expert psychological testimony needed? This question asks whether the expert witness has something to offer to the judge or jury that the judge or jury does not already know. Several studies have examined what prospective jurors know about human memory and whether their knowledge comports with scientific knowledge about human memory. These studies found that although some matters of memory are common knowledge, others are counterintuitive and not matters of common sense (e.g., Desmarais & Read, 2011; Simons & Chabris, 2011). Some research has likewise found that prospective jurors harbor misconceptions about interrogations and false confessions (e.g., Leo & Liu, 2009) and that prospective jurors and social science experts differ in their believes about the coerciveness of some critical interrogation tactics (Kaplan et al., 2020). This research demonstrates that juries, when left to their own devices, are not well informed to evaluate eyewitness evidence and confessions, and that such information is outside their common knowledge.

Likewise, jurors in criminal trials involving domestic or interpersonal violence in which a battering partner is assaulted or murdered harbor numerous misconceptions about the victim's and/or potential defendant's actions. For example, the populace (and juries) misperceives how common intimate partner violence is, the level of fear the defendant may experience in these relationships, the difficulty most defendants experience leaving such relationships, and the danger the defendant faces if they are successful in removing themselves from those relationships (e.g., Costanzo & Krauss, 2018). Expert testimony on battering and its effects has the ability to correct some of these misconceptions and orient jurors to what they may see as counterintuitive behaviors, such as returning to a relationship where battering has occurred or attacking the batterer at a moment when there is no immediate threat of imminent violence.

Is there consensus among psychologists about the research findings that form the subjects of expert testimony? As explained above, consensus among experts is one criterion for consideration under *Daubert* and served as the sole criterion for admissibility of expert testimony under the *Frye* test. Psychologists have conducted empirical research on the consensus question in two expert witness domains: eyewitness memory (Kassin et al., 2001) and false confessions (Kassin et al., 2018). In both studies, experts in the respective areas were surveyed for their opinions about the reliability of typical psychological phenomena and research findings about which experts would normally testify. Both studies demonstrated high levels of consensus among the experts for many if not most of the expert testimony content. This research suggests that consensus exists among the relevant scientific communities in at least two expert testimony domains and that lack of consensus would not be a valid reason for excluding expert testimony on the topics of eyewitness memory and false confessions.

How effective are judges at keeping junk science out of the courtroom? The *Daubert* decision shifted the burden of evaluating the science underlying expert testimony from the relevant scientific communities to the trial court judges of the cases in which the expert testimony is proposed. Many, if not most, judges are former lawyers and are not trained in the social sciences. In one national survey of judges (Gatowski et al., 2001), the judges felt qualified to perform their roles of gatekeepers but lacked the ability to define important scientific terms. Five percent or fewer of the judges understood important scientific terms, such as error rate and falsifiability.

One experiment (Kovera & McAuliff, 2000) examined judges' abilities to detect flaws in scientific research. Judges were unable to recognize three experimental defects: lack of a control group, a confound, and experimenter bias due to non-blind testing. Subsequent research by the same authors (McAuliff & Duckworth, 2010; McAuliff et al., 2009) found that prospective jurors were also likely insensitive to threats of internal validity in expert testimony.

Most recently, an analysis of the scientific validity of psychological tests used by psychologists as expert witnesses, as well as an analysis over a three-year period of the prevalence and success of admissibility challenges, indicated that psychology and the legal system are continuing to struggle with these decisions. Based upon survey data from psychological practitioners involved in legal cases, as many as one-third of assessment instruments employed by these experts were not generally accepted in the field (*Frye* criteria and the fourth *Daubert* criterion), and roughly 60 percent lacked adequate scientific validity. Further troubling was the fact that admissibility challenges to a select number of these psychological instruments happened extremely infrequently (roughly 5 percent of the time) and were rarely successful (less than one-third of the time) (Neal et al., 2019). Taken together, these findings suggest that judges continue to show difficulty in determining scientific validity, and thus the admissibility of a number of commonly used psychological tests employed by experts.

To what extent are experts biased toward the parties that retain them? The expert witness should be objective and nonpartisan. The pressures of an adversarial system, however, can push an expert toward nonobjectivity. Researchers have used the phrase "adversarial allegiance" to describe the situation in which the expert witness aligns their views with that of the lawyer who retained them. Some researchers have examined the extent of adversarial allegiance. In one study, Murrie et al. (2008) examined pairs of forensic psychological evaluations of the same individuals and using the same instrument in sex offender civil commitment trials. Murrie et al. (2008) found that the evaluation scores deviated and in the direction of adversarial allegiance. McAuliff and Arter (2016) also found evidence of adversarial allegiance among expert reviews in a simulated child sexual abuse case.

And what effect does expert testimony have on jury decision-making? Researchers have examined the influence of expert testimony of a variety of types on the decision-making of juries. Typically, this research involves the use of trial simulation experiments conducted in the laboratory or in online research forums. The expert testimony topics that have been studied include eyewitness memory, false confessions, death penalty sentencing, child sexual abuse, intimate partner violence, and sexual assault. Across these various domains, it is clear that juries attend to and make use of the content of expert psychological testimony. The research goes further and demonstrates the conditions under which expert testimony is more influential. For example, one study found that expert testimony based on clinical judgment is more influential than testimony based on actuarial prediction (Krauss & Sales, 2001). Another study found that expert testimony has more impact when it is concretely linked to trial evidence than when the link between expert testimony and the trial evidence is more implicit (Kovera et al., 1997).

Ethical Issues for Expert Witnesses

As should be apparent from some of the previous discussion, psychologists face a multitude of ethical issues in serving as expert witnesses for the legal system. For example, as previously noted, the legal system may allow and even advocate that they offer ultimate legal opinions that may be beyond their true expertise. To clarify this point further, an expert might be asked to opine whether a defendant is competent to stand trial, waive *Miranda* rights, discharge their attorney, and so on. Several commentators, however, have argued the exact point at which an individual is competent or meets any legal standard regardless of their level of mental illness and how it affects their functioning is a moral, normative, or legal judgment, not a psychological one (Melton et al., 2018). It follows that it is beyond the expertise of the psychologist performing the examination to answer these questions. Unfortunately, existing research suggests that offering such opinions is far too common for most experts, and the courts almost always follow the ultimate opinions of experts when they are proffered (Costanzo & Krauss, 2018).

Likewise, other critics caution that adversarial allegiance effects might also encourage psychologist to overstate, or perhaps even unknowingly bias, their evaluation results or testimony in favor of the side that hired them (Murrie et al., 2013). Although recent commentaries have suggested that there are several methods that might help diminish these biases in clinical evaluations (Neal & Brodsky, 2016), this area remains largely understudied. This is especially true for experimental psychologists who may find themselves engaged by an attorney for one side in civil or criminal legal proceedings and who may possess limited knowledge of how the adversarial system may affect their expert opinions.

In fact, psychologists as expert witnesses may raise more ethical issues than almost any other area of psychological practice. Given this, it should not be surprising that many aspects of *Ethical Principles of Psychologists and Code of Conduct* (EPPCC) (American Psychological Association, 2017a) have significant bearing on the practice of psychological expert witnesses, including provisions related to, but not limited to, Misuse of Psychologists' Work (1.01), Boundaries of Competence (2.01), Bases for Scientific and Professional Judgment (2.04), Multiple Relationship with Clients (3.05); Third Party Requests for Services (3.07); Informed Consent (3.10); Discussing the Limits of Confidentiality (4.02); Record Keeping and Fees (6–6.07); and Assessment (9–9.11).

A full discussion of all ethical standards enumerated in the EPPCC that are directly relevant to psychological expert witnesses is well beyond the scope of this chapter (see Pirelli et al., 2017a, for a more comprehensive discussion of many of these issues). However, it should be noted that the EPPCC standards are largely only applicable to members of the American Psychological Association (APA), and psychologists do not have to be a member of APA to serve as expert witnesses. Yet, for clinical psychologists who are licensed and serve as expert witnesses, many state licensing boards have adopted provisions from the EPPCC and may restrict or prohibit practice if practitioners are found to have violated them regardless of their membership in APA.

In addition to the ECCPP, other ethical guidelines have been promulgated to help psychologists navigate serving and acting as expert witnesses. The *Specialty Guidelines for Forensic Psychology* (SGFP) (American Psychological Association, 2010) are designed to be aspirational in nature (unlike the EPPCC's ethical standards, which are intended as enforceable rules) and were intended to improve the quality of services offered to the public as well as protect the public from unethical practices. The SGFP define forensic psychology as the

> professional practice by any psychologist working within any subdiscipline of psychology (e.g., clinical, developmental, social, cognitive) when applying scientific, technical, or specialized knowledge of psychology to the law to assist in addressing legal contractual, and administrative matters. Application of the Guidelines does not depend on the practitioner's typical area of practice or expertise, but rather on the services provided in the case at hand. (American Psychological Association, 2010, p. 7)

Clearly, the SGFP also apply to psychologists engaged as expert witnesses, and these individuals need to be aware of their provisions. Beyond the ECCPP and SGFP, there are also numerous other ethical guidelines that are specific to narrow areas of forensic clinical practice, such as child custody—Guidelines for Child Custody Proceedings in Family Law Proceedings (American Psychological Association, 2010) or ethical guidelines that may be relevant to the populations a psychologist encounters when serving as an expert witness or evaluator—Multicultural Guidelines: An Ecological Approach to Context, Identity, and Intersectionality (American Psychological Association, 2017b). At a minimum, ethical psychological expert witnesses need to be aware of the specific codes and guidelines that govern their behavior as well as jurisdictional rules that dictate their actions. Competent psychologists should also be aware of and have knowledge of some of the common ethical dilemmas that they will face when they agree to serve as expert witnesses.

Emerging Issues in Expert Psychological Testimony

The preeminent emerging areas in expert psychological testimony involve increasing the objectivity of psychologists serving as expert witnesses in an adversarial system and increasing the trier of fact's understanding of the expertise that these witnesses convey. Given that the adversary system itself rewards attorneys who select and induce experts to offer testimony most favorable to their side, some attempts have been made by the legal system and the psychological profession to lessen possible expert adversarial allegiance. Rather than having attorneys employing experts most favorable to their side, judges have the ability to appoint their own experts.[7] These court-appointed experts are not likely subject to the same financial and psychological allegiances as attorney-selected experts. Unfortunately, most surveys of judges demonstrate that they rarely use this power (Krafka et al., 2002), and in some legal contexts (e.g., criminal defense) attorneys may still be legally entitled to select their own experts even if judges appoint experts.

Professional bodies and jurisdictions have also tried to decrease the possible bias of attorney-selected psychological expert witnesses by establishing approved panels of experts, maintaining educational or training requirements for these expert panels, and requiring attorneys to select these empaneled experts. Likewise, professional organizations such as American Board of Forensic Psychology have created certification credentialing that requires certain educational, testing, and professional practice requirements before clinical psychologists can suggest that they are exceptionally qualified to perform forensic evaluations for the courts. It remains to be seen, however, if any of these procedures have decreased the biases associated with expert selection and eventual expert testimony.

A more radical approach to decreasing bias in expert witnesses was developed in Australia—concurrent expert testimony, dubbed "hot-tubbing." This procedure has been implemented in a number of different international jurisdictions, including use in Canada, New Zealand, Singapore, the United Kingdom, and in several cases in the United States (Krauss et al., 2018). In hot-tubbing, experts are selected normally by attorneys, but their expert witnesses and testimony are presented to the trier of fact concurrently rather than sequentially. The expert witnesses, before testifying, must specify what facts and opinions they agree on and where dispute still exists between them. When the experts testify together (i.e., they are in the hot tub or witness chair at the same time), attorneys, the other hot-tubbed expert, and the triers of fact are allowed to question the experts. These procedures are intended to create a more collegial atmosphere and decrease the pull of experts to overstate their opinions. To date, there has been limited review of

---

[7] See FRE 706.

the effectiveness of hot-tubbing, but qualitative surveys of the legal actors and attorneys suggest high praise for this novel procedure, with one Australian survey suggesting 95 percent overall satisfaction (Greene & Gordon, 2016). However, the incorporation of hot-tubbing into the US adversarial system is somewhat questionable on a number of legal and practical grounds. Australian courts require an oath of impartiality from its experts, a practice not followed in other countries. Implementing concurrent expert testimony would cede some control of experts from attorneys to the court (resembling more of an inquisitorial rather than adversarial legal process). Hot-tubbing would also upset the well-established procedure of prosecution/plaintiff first and defense second sequencing of most trials. Hot-tubbing has not yet been used with juries. Australian courts—where hot-tubbing was invented—do not allow for juries in most civil trials where hot-tubbing has been most extensively used. Juries are much more prevalent in US courts. There is almost no information on the effectiveness of hot-tubbing in jury trials.

Perhaps the more significant research and legal question for the innovations discussed in this section is whether any of them increase the trier of facts' understanding of the complex evidence commonly presented by expert witnesses. Although it is important to decrease the bias of experts, it is far more important for the goals of justice for the trier of fact to accurately understand the expert evidence presented to them and make legal judgments based on an accurate understanding of that information. Classically, cross-examination and opposing experts were designed to increase jurors understanding of complex expert witness testimony. Unfortunately, the vast majority of research suggests that these procedures are largely ineffective in doing so (e.g., Krauss & Sales, 2001). So, do court-appointed expert witnesses or hot-tubbed experts accomplish these goals? With regard to court-appointed experts "the jury is still out." Some research suggests that jurors place greater weight on expert testimony presented by court-appointed experts, but it is not always clear that such expert testimony leads to better understanding of complex scientific areas by jurors (e.g., Scurich et al., 2015). In one experiment, court-appointed expert testimony on the psychology of eyewitness memory made mock-jurors more skeptical about eyewitnesses rather than better enabling them to evaluate eyewitness identifications (Cutler et al., 1990).

Similarly, there has been simply too little research performed on hot-tubbing to determine if it increases juror knowledge and understanding of complex scientific issues. Yet, there is ample reason to believe it might. The presentation of conflicting expert witness testimony in a compressed time period with the allowance of questions by multiple parties to clarify areas of dispute may lead to better memory, processing, and comprehension of complex scientific evidence. We share the optimism expressed by Greene and Gordon (2016, p. 359): "On balance, we believe that hot-tubbing will enhance jurors' understanding of expert testimony and lead to more rational and predictable verdicts, particularly in cases involving complex and probabilistic evidence." Clearly more research is needed in these areas.

Conclusion

Psychologists have a great deal of knowledge, expertise, and assessment skills to assist defendants, litigants, advocates, judges, and juries with resolving matters in criminal, civil, family, and military courts and other such judicial settings. Psychologists offer their knowledge on a wide variety of matters and from diverse psychological perspectives, and some (i.e., clinically trained psychologists) conduct forensic mental health assessments with individuals in the court system and form opinions about such matters as competence and risk. The degree of acceptance of psychologists as expert witnesses varies from widely accepted (e.g., in the case of clinical psychologists) to growing acceptance (e.g., in the case of experts who testify about eyewitness memory and false confessions).

Like experts in other scientific domains, expert psychological testimony must meet established admissibility criteria. Similar to other expert witnesses, psychologists placed in an adversarial system must strive to maintain impartiality, may face challenges in their roles, and must abide by ethical codes of conduct. Unlike expert testimony in most other scientific domains, psychologists conduct empirical research on expert psychological testimony, seeking to inform the scientific and professional communities about the validity of assumptions underlying the admission of expert testimony and its effect. And finally, like other domains of expert testimony, innovations designed to improve the effect of expert testimony may apply to psychological expert testimony as well.

References

American Psychological Association. (2017a). *Ethical principles of psychologists and code of conduct.* Retrieved from https://www.apa.org/ethics/code/ethics-code-2017.pdf

American Psychological Association. (2017b). *Multicultural guidelines: An ecological approach to context, identity, and intersectionality.* Retrieved from http://www.apa.org/about/policy/multicultural-guidelines.pdf

American Psychological Association. (2010). Guidelines for child custody evaluations in family law proceedings. *American Psychologist, 65,* 863–867. https://doi.org/ 10.1037/a0021250

American Psychological Association. (2010). *Specialty guidelines for forensic psychology. American Psychologist, 68,* 7–19.

Costanzo, M., & Krauss, D. (2018). *Forensic and legal psychology: Psychological science applied to the law* (3rd ed.). Worth.

Cutler, B. L., Dexter, H. R., & Penrod, S. D. (1990). Nonadversarial methods for improving juror sensitivity to eyewitness evidence. *Journal of Applied Social Psychology, 20,* 1197–1207.

DeMatteo, D., Fishel, S., & Tansey, A. (2019). Expert evidence: The (unfulfilled) promise of *Daubert. Psychological Science in the Public Interest, 20,* 129–134.

Desmarais, S. L., & Read, J. D. (2011). After 30 years, what do we know about what jurors know? A meta-analytic review of lay knowledge regarding eyewitness factors. *Law and Human Behavior, 35*(3), 200–210.

Gatowski, S. I., Dobbin, S. A., Richardson, J. T., Ginsburg, G. P., Merlino, M. L., & Dahir, V. (2001). Asking the gatekeepers: A national survey of judges on judging expert evidence in a post-*Daubert* world. *Law and Human Behavior, 25,* 433–458.

Greene, G., & Gordon, N. (2016). Can the "hot tub" enhance jurors' understanding and use of expert testimony? *Wyoming Law Review, 16,* 359–385.

Kaplan, J., Cutler, B. L., Leach, A. M., Marion, S., & Eastwood, J. (2020). Perceptions of coercion in interrogations: A comparison of perspectives. *Psychology, Crime and Law, 26,* 384–401.

Kassin, S. M., Redlich, A. D., Alceste, F., & Luke, T. J. (2018). On the general acceptance of confession research: Opinions of the scientific community. *American Psychologist, 73,* 63–80.

Kassin, S. M., Tubb, V. A., Hosch, H. M., & Memon, A. (2001). On the "general acceptance" of eyewitness testimony research: A new survey of experts. *American Psychologist, 56,* 405–416.

Kovera, M. B., Gresham, A. W., Borgida, E., Gray, E., & Regan, P. C. (1997). Does expert testimony inform or influence juror decision-making? A social cognitive analysis. *Journal of Applied Psychology, 82*, 178–191.

Kovera, M. B., & McAuliff, B. (2000). The effects of peer review AND evidence quality on evaluations of psychological science: Are judges effective gatekeepers? *Journal of Applied Psychology, 85*, 574–586.

Krafka, C., Dunn, M. A., Johnson, M. T., Cecil, J. S., & Miletich, D. (2002). Judge and attorney experiences, practices, and concerns regarding expert testimony in federal civil trials. *Psychology, Public Policy, and Law, 8*, 251–308.

Krauss, D., Cassar, D., & Strother, A. (2009). The admissibility of expert testimony in the United States, the Commonwealth, and elsewhere. In D. Krauss & J. D. Lieberman (Eds.), *Psychological expertise in court* (Vol. II, pp. 1–24). Ashgate.

Krauss, D., Gongola, J., Scurich, N., & Busch, B. (2018). Mental state at time of offense in the hot tub: An empirical investigation of concurrent evidence in an insanity case. *Behavioral Sciences and the Law, 36*, 358–372.

Krauss, D., & Sales, B. D. (2001). The effects of clinical and scientific expert testimony on juror decision-making in capital sentencing. *Psychology, Public Policy, & Law, 7*, 267–310.

Leo, R. A., & Liu, B. (2009). What do potential jurors know about police interrogation techniques and false confessions? *Behavioral Sciences & the Law, 27*(3), 381–399.

McAuliff, B. D., & Arter, J. L. (2016). Adversarial allegiance: The devil is in the evidence details, not just on the witness stand. *Law and Human Behavior, 40*, 524–535.

McAuliff, B. D., & Duckworth, T. D. (2010). I spy with my little eye: Jurors' detection of internal validity threats in expert evidence. *Law and Human Behavior, 34*, 489–500.

McAuliff, B. D., Kovera, M. B., & Nunez, G. (2009). Can jurors recognize missing control groups, confounds, and experimenter bias in psychological science? *Law and Human Behavior, 33*, 247–257.

Melton, G. B., Petrila, J., Poythress, N. G., Slobogin, C., Otto, R., Mossman, D., & Condie, L. (2018). *Psychological evaluations for the courts: A handbook for mental health professionals and lawyers* (4th ed.). Guilford Press.

Murrie, D. C., Boccaccini, M. T., Guarnera, L. A., & Rufino, K. A. (2013). Are forensic experts biased by the side that retained them? *Psychological Science, 24*, 1889–1897.

Murrie, D. C., Boccaccini, M. T., Johnson, J. T., & Janke, C. (2008). Does interrater (dis)agreement on Psychopathy Checklist scores in sexually violent predator trials suggest partisan allegiance in forensic evaluations? *Law and Human Behavior, 32*, 352–362.

Neal, T. M. S., Slobogin, C., Saks, M. J., Faigman, D. L., & Geisinger, K. F. (2019). Psychological assessments in legal contexts: Are courts keeping "junk science" out of the courtroom? *Psychological Science in the Public Interest, 20*, 134–163.

Saks, M., & Koehler, J. (2005). The coming paradigm shift in forensic identification science. *Science, 309*, 892–894.

Sales, D. B., & Shuman, D. W. (2005). *Experts in court: Reconciling law, science, and professional knowledge.* American Psychological Association.

Scurich, N., Krauss, D., Reiser, L., Garcia, N., & Deer, L. (2015). Venire jurors' perception of adversarial allegiance. *Psychology, Public Policy, and Law, 21*, 161–168.

Simons, D. J., & Chabris, C. F. (2011). What People believe about how memory works: A representative survey of the US Population. *PloS One, 6*(8), Article e22757.

Psychology and Law, Meet Open Science

Bradley D. McAuliff, Melanie B. Fessinger, Anthony D. Perillo, *and* Jennifer T. Perillo

Abstract

As the field of psychology and law begins to embrace more transparent and accessible science, many questions arise about what *open science* actually is and how to do it. In this chapter, we contextualize this reform by examining fundamental concerns about psychological research—irreproducibility and replication failures, false-positive errors, and questionable research practices—that threaten its validity and credibility. Next, we turn to psychology's response by reviewing the concept of open science and explaining how to implement specific practices—preregistration, registered reports, open materials/ data/ code, and open access publishing—designed to make research more transparent and accessible. We conclude by weighing the implications of open science for the field of psychology and law, specifically with respect to how we conduct and evaluate research, as well as how we train the next generation of psychological scientists and share scientific findings in applied settings.

Key Words: open science, psychology, validity, replication, false-positives, QRPs

Psychological science is experiencing a fundamental paradigm shift. Whether characterized as a "crisis of confidence" (Pashler & Wagenmakers, 2012, p. 528), a "credibility revolution" (Vazire, 2018, p. 411), or "psychology's renaissance" (Nelson et al., 2018, p. 512), how researchers design, conduct, and report their work has changed dramatically in recent times. This transformation is perhaps best described as an unprecedented emphasis on transparency and accessibility. We have begun to lift the shroud of scientific discovery to evaluate the underlying processes and decisions themselves, from theory and prediction to design, measurement, and execution to analysis and conclusions. Now more than ever, it is clear that the value of psychological science depends on the integrity of those underlying processes and decisions, which should be in plain view for all to see.

The subdiscipline of psychology and law has not been exempt from this trend. The Executive Committee of the American Psychology-Law Society (AP-LS; Division 41 of the American Psychological Association) voted unanimously in March 2017 for its flagship journal *Law and Human Behavior* to become a formal signatory of the Transparency and Openness Promotion (TOP) guidelines. That same year, Editor-in-Chief Margaret

Bull Kovera introduced Open Science Badges in an effort to recognize and incentivize the public sharing of data, materials, preregistration plans, and analyses. In 2018, 19 percent of the articles published in *Law and Human Behavior* qualified for at least one badge and by the end of 2020 that number rose to 28 percent. In 2019, Editor-in-Chief Bradley McAuliff implemented the journal's first phase of the TOP Guidelines focusing on the transparency of data, design, and materials (McAuliff et al., 2019), and in 2020 the journal began accepting proposals for registered reports. Extrapolating from these milestones and recent editorials in other psychology and law journals (Lamb et al., 2021; Neuschatz, 2020), there is a growing expectation for transparent and accessible science in psychology and law.

The purpose of this chapter is to explain open science and contemplate what it means for the field of psychology and law. We begin by contextualizing the recent paradigm shift by focusing on its genesis in irreproducibility and replication failures, false-positive errors, and questionable research practices. Next, we turn to psychology's response by reviewing the open science movement and common practices that include preregistration, registered reports, open materials, open data and code, and open access publishing. We conclude by weighing the implications of open science for the field of psychology and law, specifically with respect to how we conduct and evaluate research, as well as how we train the next generation of psychological scientists and share our findings in applied settings.

How Did We Get Here?

Scholars point to a series of events involving irreproducibility and replication failures, false-positive errors, and questionable research practices that have catalyzed the open science movement (Nelson et al., 2018; Tackett et al., 2019).

Irreproducibility and Replication Failures

Recent research has revealed that most, but certainly not all, published psychological science is reproducible (see Artner et al., 2021, Table 1, for a list of published reproducibility research in psychology as of August 2020). By reproducible, we mean that an independent researcher obtained identical results as the original researcher using the same data and analyses (NAS, 2019). Across three studies that examined the reproducibility of articles appearing in prominent psychology journals, the majority of primary claims (between 60 percent and 70 percent) were, in fact, reproducible (Artner et al., 2021; Hardwicke et al., 2021; Hardwicke et al., 2018). However, the ability to reproduce findings often required consulting with the authors and receiving additional data or code because the original articles tended to report unclear, incomplete, or incorrect descriptions of data analytic procedures (Hardwicke et al., 2018). Moreover, although the majority of primary claims were reproducible, a notable proportion of claims were not (between 30 percent and 40 percent).

These initial empirical investigations reveal a mixed picture of reproducibility. It is reassuring that the statistics for most primary claims in published psychological research were reproducible. And when errors occurred, they generally did not affect the authors' original conclusions. Yet we must also consider the potential role of selection bias in yielding an overly optimistic assessment of reproducibility. All three studies examined articles for which authors made original data openly available—a practice that is increasingly common but not yet the norm. Errors may be more common in data that authors are unwilling to share. The research teams also focused on relatively basic statistics (e.g., regression, t-tests, and analyses of variance), but the reproducibility of more complicated analyses (e.g., linear regression and structural equation modeling) has proven difficult in other fields (Bergh et al., 2017). Perhaps most importantly, any attempt to evaluate reproducibility using original data is only as good as the information authors provide about key decisions, such as operationalizing variables and analyzing results. In this respect, "vagueness makes assessing reproducibility a nightmare" (Artner et al., 2021, p. 538), and we all must strive to ensure those attempting to reproduce results get a good night's sleep.

Extending beyond pure reproducibility, researchers have also begun to question the replicability of published findings. By replicability, we mean that researchers obtain the same general result across different samples and studies that vary fundamental components of the research design, such as the experimental manipulations, operational definitions, and procedures (Asendorpf et al., 2013). Reproducibility is an absolute judgment (original data + same analyses = identical result?), whereas replication is a matter of degree because it entails research design variations. It is difficult to answer the question of how replicable psychological research truly is (Maxwell et al., 2015), and scientists disagree about what level of replicability we should expect (Gordon et al., 2021). Consider, for example, the effects of interviewer rapport on witness accuracy. There are myriad ways researchers can operationalize rapport and measure accuracy, so it is unrealistic to expect that different studies will yield truly identical results. However, we can establish replicability by observing that, across different studies, the same general result emerges: interviewers' provision of rapport (however operationalized) increases witness accuracy (however measured). But how do we determine whether "the same general result emerges"? We can look at the pattern of statistical significance across studies, whether studies agree about the direction of the effects and/or whether the effect sizes of subsequent studies fall within the confidence interval of the original study (Valentine et al., 2011). How we choose to operationalize "replicability" will affect whether we conclude that results are, in fact, replicable.

Scholars have sought to quantify the replicability of psychological science despite the inherent challenges. In the largest systematic examination of replication studies to date, Nosek et al. (2022) amassed evidence from both "systematic replications" that conducted as many studies in a defined sampling frame as possible and "multisite replications" that conducted the same replication protocol in a variety of samples and settings. Across an impressive total of 307 replications, 64 percent reported statistically significant results in the same direction as the original studies with effect sizes that were 68 percent as large. Thus, the existing data suggest that the replication rates in psychological science are similar to those observed in reproducibility studies. It is encouraging that most effects replicated using two common types of replications. However, sample sizes for the replication studies were much larger than those from original studies, which resulted in more precise estimates of effect size and heterogeneity but also led to a "relatively generous definition of success" due to increased statistical power to detect significant differences in the same direction as the original effects (Nosek et al., 2022, p. 726). In other words, these findings are vexing because a larger number of lower-powered original studies detected differences compared to a smaller number of higher-powered replication studies. False-positive errors and questionable research practices likely contribute to this paradox in psychology's published literature.

False-Positive Errors and Questionable Research Practices

For decades, the scientific community has largely ignored several inconvenient truths about published psychological research. First, most studies are woefully underpowered, meaning their ability to detect true differences between groups is extremely low (Cohen, 1962; Sedlmeier & Gigerenzer, 1989). Second, psychological phenomena are complex and multidetermined (Gotz et al., 2021), and the effect of any single factor is typically small to medium in size (Lovakov & Agadullina, 2021). Third, despite the prevalence of underpowered studies and elusive effects, the rate at which studies in journals report detecting differences between groups is exceedingly high, even as high as 96 percent (Scheel et al., 2021). This reality implicates the presence of false-positive errors in which researchers mistakenly conclude that an effect or difference between groups exists when it does not (i.e., Type 1 error). False-positive errors are even more likely to occur when testing hypotheses with a lower prior probability of being true (Nosek et al., 2022), and one study calculated an average prior probability of just .088 (9 percent) across forty-four articles published in three top psychology journals (Dreber et al., 2015).

Ioannidis (2005) was among the first to formally sound the alarm with his article titled "Why Most Published Research Findings Are False." He argued that the combination of various design, data analysis, and presentation factors (collectively termed "bias") tends to produce false-positive research findings. Bias can manifest in several study characteristics that increase the likelihood a result is not true, such as small sample size, small effect sizes, testing a large number of relationships that were not preselected, and using flexible designs, definitions, outcomes, and analyses. Simmons et al. (2011) amplified these concerns by demonstrating how unacceptably easy it is to obtain statistically significant evidence for a false hypothesis (in that study, testing the ability of certain songs to change listeners' ages). Like Ioannidis, they were troubled by potential bias and focused on "researcher degrees of freedom," referring to the relatively unfettered flexibility researchers have when making data collection and analysis decisions: "Should some observations be excluded? Which conditions should be combined and which ones compared? Which control variables should be considered? Should specific measures be combined or transformed or both?" (Simmons et al., 2011, p. 1359).

Using computer simulations of experimental data, Simmons and colleagues established that four common researcher degrees of freedom are particularly pernicious in producing false-positives: selectively reporting dependent variables, using interim data analyses to determine stopping points for data collection and sample size, including covariates, and reporting subsets of experimental conditions. The combination of all four practices increased the likelihood of obtaining a false-positive result from the conventional 5 percent (alpha) to 61 percent in their simulations.

How frequently do researcher degrees of freedom lead to questionable research practices (QRPs) in the published psychological literature? Nosek et al. (2022) analyzed fourteen QRP surveys of psychology researchers worldwide and observed that 78 percent of those surveyed reported engaging in at least one of these practices in their own research. See table 5.1 for specific examples of QRPs. Almost half of researchers admitted to selectively reporting studies that "worked" (48 percent), failing to report all dependent variables (46 percent), and deciding whether to collect

Table 5.1 Questionable Research Practices	
P-hacking	• Selectively reporting studies that "worked" or failing to report studies that "didn't work" • Failing to report all of a study's conditions, dependent measures, or outcomes • Dropping participants, observations, measures, or conditions that yielded inconvenient data • Excluding data after examining the impact of doing so • Filling in missing data without identifying those values as estimated • Stopping data collection earlier than planned because results were statistically significant • Collecting additional data or analyses because results were not statistically significant • Rounding down *p* values (e.g., reporting that a *p* value of 0.054 is less than 0.05) • Applying poorly motivated and *post hoc* data transformations • Adding questionable covariates or dropping covariates selectively
HARKing	• Presenting *post hoc* hypotheses as *a priori* hypotheses • Presenting hypotheses known *post hoc* to be contradicted by the data • Suppressing initially plausible hypotheses that failed the immediate empirical test • Reassessing as plausible a hypothesis originally seen as quite impossible • Advancing a new hypothesis wholly unanticipated prior to the study • Using current results to construct *post hoc* hypotheses that are reported as *a priori* hypotheses • Retrieving hypotheses from a *post hoc* literature search and reporting them as *a priori* hypotheses • Failing to report *a priori* hypotheses that are unsupported by the current results

Note. Adapted from QRPs examined by Chin et al. (2021); John et al. (2012); Kerr (1998); Lindsay (2015); and Simmons et al. (2011).

additional data after examining whether results were statistically significant (40 percent). Roughly one-third of researchers reported hypothesizing after the results were known ("HARKing," 36 percent) and excluding data after examining its effect on the results (32 percent), and nearly one-quarter failed to report all study conditions (23 percent) and rounded p values to meet a prespecified threshold (21 percent). Far fewer reported stopping data collection earlier than planned after obtaining the expected result (12 percent), claiming results were unaffected by demographic variables such as gender when uncertain (3 percent), and falsifying data (2 percent). Although these rates are likely to be influenced by self-serving bias and respondents' limited insight into their own decisions and behaviors, the high proportion of researchers admitting to engaging in QRPs is troubling.

More objective measures show that QRPs are quite prevalent. Franco et al. (2016) compared original study registrations to final published manuscripts and found that 41 percent of manuscripts failed to report all experimental conditions and 72 percent reported fewer outcome variables than what appeared on a public study registry. Moreover, reported effect sizes were twice as large and nearly three times as likely to be significant than unreported effects. In published social psychology dissertations, Cairo et al. (2020) found that nearly one-third (32 percent) of the original hypotheses were dropped from the manuscripts. Authors were more likely to drop unsupported hypotheses and maintain fully or partially supported hypotheses. Additionally, nearly half (48 percent) of manuscripts showed evidence of other questionable (or "selective") research practices, including changing sample size (20 percent) and dropping variables (18 percent).

Both self-report and publication pipeline studies reveal that QRPs are common in the field of psychology. Though rates for specific practices are generally low, most psychological researchers admit to engaging in at least one QRP in their own research. In fact, some of the most frequently reported and observed infractions represent three of the four researcher degrees of freedom shown to dramatically increase false-positive errors (failing to report dependent variables, reporting only a subset of experimental conditions, and collecting additional data after examining statistical significance), especially when combined (Simmons et al., 2011).

The question of whether recent research findings on reproducibility, replicability, false-positive errors, and QRPs is symptomatic of a science that is "rotten to the core" or "not so bad" (Motyl et al., 2017, p. 36) remains open to healthy scholarly debate and empirical investigation. For certain, this growing body of findings has revealed that published psychological studies—much like the scientists behind them—are imperfect. Be that as it may, the stark reality is that failures to replicate impede the acquisition of knowledge, distort the truth, waste valuable resources, and can result in decisions and policies that are ineffective or even harmful (Nelson et al., 2018; Tackett et al., 2019). Suffice to say, we can do better as a discipline to improve the rigor and transparency of psychological science.

What Is Open Science?

Even though many scientists perceive transparency as a normative part of the research process (Anderson et al., 2007), recent concerns about reproducibility, replicability, and false-positive errors have called into question whether science is as open as it aspires to be (Open Science Collaboration, 2015). As one scholar aptly analogized, scientific reporting is a bit like selling a used car (Vazire, 2017). The researcher, as the salesperson, knows much more about their product than does the reader, as the consumer. The researcher knows the original hypotheses, how many unsuccessful studies were left out of the manuscript, what the raw data look like, and how many analyses were attempted. Without transparent reporting of this information, "it is difficult to tell a cherry from a lemon" (Linsday, 2017, p. 701). Researchers have responded to these concerns by calling for a radical shift in the way that science is produced and reported, commonly known as the open science movement (Klein et al., 2018; Nosek et al., 2015; Vazire, 2017).

Open science reflects the idea that scientists should produce and report knowledge in a transparent and accessible manner. These concepts are admittedly abstract because "open science" itself is an umbrella term; it describes many different practices and, as some have rightly noted, has no formal definition (Arabito & Pitrelli, 2015). This ambiguity has led to the development of several schools of thought on the purpose and goals of the movement, but they tend to converge around the same basic goals: to strengthen and accelerate scientific progress, to enhance the accessibility of scientific work, to increase representativeness and access within science, and to improve trust in the institution of science (Ledgerwood et al., 2022; Masuzzo & Martens, 2017; Roberts et al., 2020).

One challenge confronting the open science movement is the lack of strong incentives for researchers to be more transparent about their work (Nosek et al., 2015; Nosek et al., 2012). The increased time needed to engage in open science practices understandably concerns some researchers. Some open science practices can increase efficiency at other stages of research (e.g., preregistration can establish data analysis rules researchers no longer have to contemplate after collecting data and preprints allow researchers to share findings with others more quickly). Admittedly, though, open science practices require researchers to invest more time and effort into their work at most stages. Issues of time particularly affect students and early career researchers, whose research output risks being judged by admissions, search, and promotion-and-tenure committees through traditional metrics (e.g., publications) without credit for additional accomplishments (e.g., preregistrations). These practices can also expose research, and researchers themselves, to a higher degree of scrutiny. In recognition of these barriers, a collection of various stakeholders worked together to draft a set of standards that can be adopted by journals and granting agencies to encourage open practices known as the TOP Guidelines (Nosek et al., 2015).

The TOP guidelines consist of eight standards regarding citation, design and analysis, materials and methods, data sharing, preregistration, and replication that journals and granting agencies should recommend or require for publication or funding. In the few years since the creation of the TOP Guidelines, hundreds of journals across various disciplines have incorporated the standards into their policies (Mayo-Wilson et al., 2021). Additionally, many journals, including *Law and Human Behavior*, also encourage and incentivize researchers to participate in open science practices by offering badges to those who do (Kidwell et al., 2016; McAuliff et al., 2019). Those who meet the requirements receive a badge at the top of their published paper signaling to readers that the researchers participated in one or more open science practices. Some data suggest that the use of badges has led to an increase in open science practices (Kidwell et al., 2016) and trust in research among nonscientists (Schneider et al., 2020).

Many different practices fall under the umbrella of open science. In the sections that follow, we discuss preregistration, registered reports, open materials, open data and code, and open access publishing.

Preregistration

Preregistration involves documenting a research plan before conducting a study. The research plan often includes a description of the *a priori* hypotheses, methodology, and analytic plan. It can also include more detail, such as possible competing hypotheses, anticipated data transformations, analysis code, and coding schemes. Researchers have flexibility in how much information they include in their preregistrations; however, more detailed preregistration plans can lead to more confidence in the later interpretation of results (Lindsay et al., 2016). Researchers who choose to preregister their study can use one of several available templates (e.g., van't Veer & Giner-Sorolla, 2016; see table 5.2 for template links) or draft one themselves.

Table 5.2 Resources for Learning about and Incorporating Open Science Practices

General	
Open Scholarship Knowledge Database	https://www.oercommons.org/hubs/OSKB
7 Easy Steps to Open Science (annotated bibliography)	https://doi.org/10.31234/osf.io/cfzyx
TOP Evidence and Practice	https://osf.io/kgnva/#Registries_90
Improving Statistical Inferences course	https://coursera.org/learn/statistical-inferences
For Research	
Open Access Policies (journals, agencies)	https://v2.sherpa.ac.uk/
Badges to Acknowledge Open Practices	https://osf.io/tvyxz/ https://doi.org/10.1371/journal.pbio.1002456
Preprints	
PsyArXiv (psychology preprint host)	https://psyarxiv.com/
SocArXiv (social science preprint host)	https://socarxiv.org/
Templates (#PrettyPreprint)	https://osf.io/hsv6a/

Table 5.2 Continued	
Preregistration	
As Predicted	https://aspredicted.org/
Open Science Framework	https://osf.io/registries
Templates	https://osf.io/qpdth/ https://osf.io/zab38/wiki/home/
Tutorials and Webinars	https://www.cos.io/initiatives/prereg https://help.osf.io/hc/en-us/articles/36001 9738834-create-a-preregistration https://psyarxiv.com/hvfmr/ https://help.osf.io/m/registrations/l/ 546603-enter-the-preregistration-challenge
Registered Reports	
Journals accepting registered reports	https://www.cos.io/initiatives/ registered-reports
Examples	https://osf.io/8f7hy/ https://osf.io/sbr4d/ https://osf.io/jtsn4/
Checklist, Templates, Webinars	https://www.cos.io/initiatives/registered- reports https://osf.io/7pekf/
Twitter	@RegReports
Replication	
Replication Curation Websites	http://psychfiledrawer.org http://curatescience.org
Collaborative Replications and Education Project (CREP; resources to learn about replication and collaborate on replication projects)	https://osf.io/wfc6u/
Many Legal Labs (replication projects for legal psychology)	manylegallabs@gmail.com
Psychological Science Accelerator (lab networking for replication projects)	https://psysciacc.org/
Shared Data	
Guidelines	https://doi.org/10.1080/ 00224545.2021.1938811
National Institutes of Health Policy for Data Management and Sharing	https://grants.nih.gov/grants/guide/notice- files/NOT-OD-21-013.html
Databrary (video data library for behavioral scientists)	https://nyu.databrary.org/
Talkbank (shared audio and video samples of language samples and speech transcripts)	http://talkbank.org
OpenNeuro (shared brain-imaging data sets)	http://openneuro.org

(continued)

Table 5.2 Continued	
Study Swap (replication, shared data)	https://osf.io/meetings/studyswap/
Psych-DS (in-progress project promoting database sharing practices)	https://psych-ds.github.io/
Agreements/templates for permission to share identifiable data and recordings	http://databrary.org/about/agreement/agreement.html https://www.icpsr.umich.edu/icpsrweb/content/datamanagement/confidentiality/conf-language.html
Protected Access Repositories (for sharing sensitive data with qualified personnel)	https://osf.io/tvyxz/wiki/8.%20Approved%20Protected%20Access%20Repositories/
Data Codebooks	
Document data with *codebook* R package and Web app	https://rubenarslan.github.io/codebook/
SPSS	https://libguides.library.kent.edu/spss/codebooks https://stats.idre.ucla.edu/spss/modules/labeling-and-documenting-data/
R	https://rubenarslan.github.io/codebook/articles/codebook_tutorial.html https://doi.org/10.1177/2515245919838783
Data Anonymization	https://www.ukdataservice.ac.uk/manage-data/legal-ethical/anonymisation/qualitative.aspx
R	http://psychbrief.com/anonymous-data-r/ https://bookdown.org/martin_monkman/DataScienceResources_book/anonymity-and-confidentiality.html
Software Tool for Removing Patient Identifying Information from Clinical Documents	https://academic.oup.com/jamia/article/15/5/601/732612
Random Data Generators	
R synthpop	https://www.synthpop.org.uk/get-started.html
SPSS using GRD	https://www.tqmp.org/RegularArticles/vol10-2/p080/p080.pdf
Registry of Data Repositories	https://www.re3data.org
For Teaching	
Student Initiative for Open Science	@StudentIOS https://osf.io/4ekac/
Syllabi	
Teaching Open Science as a course	https://osf.io/3dp52/
Shared syllabi for open science coursework	https://osf.io/vkhbt/ https://osf.io/zbwr4/
Course Materials	
Five-week course for teaching open science practices	https://www.bitss.org/mooc-parent-page/

Table 5.2 Continued	
Best Practices Lecture and Slides	https://osf.io/mh9pe/
"How to Do Open Science" Textbook	https://www.ucpress.edu/book/9780520296954/transparent-and-reproducible-social-science-research
Open Science Massive Open Online Community (MOOC; shared templates for teaching open science)	https://github.com/OpenScienceMOOC
Replications as pedagogy	https://doi.org/10.1177/2515245917740427 https://journals.sagepub.com/doi/10.1177/1745691612460686
Open Access Textbooks	
OER Commons (Open Education Resources)	https://www.oercommons.org/
Open Science Training Handbook	https://book.fosteropenscience.eu/en/
Noba	https://nobaproject.com/
Organizations	
Berkeley Initiative for Transparency in the Social Sciences (BITSS)	https://www.bitss.org/ @UCBITSS
Center for Open Science (COS)	https://www.cos.io/ @OSFramework
Framework for Open and Reproducible Research Training (FORRT)	https://forrt.org/
Institute for Globally Distributed Open Research and Education (IGDORE)	https://igdore.org/
Project TIER	https://www.projecttier.org/
Society for the Improvement of Psychological Science (SIPS)	http://improvingpsych.org
Open Psychology & Law Science	@openpsychlaw

Note: Some resources derived from Spellman et al. (2018) and Towse et al. (2021).

Researchers typically submit their preregistrations to an external repository such as the Open Science Framework (osf.io) or AsPredicted (aspredicted.org). These repositories allow researchers to make their preregistration publicly accessible for others to verify whether they followed or deviated from their plan. Importantly, researchers have the option of making their preregistration immediately available or entering it into an embargo period during which it is only visible to the researchers or anyone with whom they shared a link (e.g., peer reviewers) until they end the embargo or a predetermined amount of time has passed. The embargo period precludes others from seeing a preregistration, which can mitigate concerns about others "scooping" a project before the researchers have finished it. Once viewable to others, the previously embargoed preregistration documents all the *a priori* study information as well as a timestamp of when the pregistration was submitted.

Preregistration is becoming an increasingly popular open science practice (Nosek & Lindsay, 2018), with many journals incentivizing (Eich, 2014) or requiring registered plans (Jonas & Cesario, 2015). Proponents of preregistration argue that it will increase the credibility and replicability of findings by decreasing the influence of motivation and biases on data analysis and interpretation (Nosek et al., 2018; van't Veer & Giner-Sorolla, 2016). It also has other benefits, such as placing an emphasis on strong theory to guide hypotheses, decreasing HARKing, and reducing reporting biases. In fact, some preliminary data show that having specific *a priori* hypotheses is related to increased replicability (Swaen et al., 2001) and that preregistration is related to a decrease in positive results (Kaplan & Irvine, 2015). Thus, preregistration is one tool that can help mitigate the prevalence of QRPs. Researchers seem to be increasingly willing to preregister their studies, and some anticipate that it may soon become the norm (Nosek & Lindsay, 2018).

Other researchers express concerns about preregistration (Goldin-Meadow, 2016). Some are concerned that preregistration takes additional time and effort not worth spending. Indeed, preregistration does require more time and effort of researchers at the beginning of a project. Yet, much of the information that goes into a research plan may be already written for a grant proposal or will eventually have to be written for a manuscript. Moreover, decisions made when preparing a preregistration can save considerable time that would be spent later in the research process, such as how to analyze the data. Therefore, it does not necessarily require much more time than what would have to be spent at some other point in the research process; it merely shifts the time commitment earlier.

Some researchers contend that preregistration is inflexible, not allowing them to make necessary adjustments to their plan or conduct exploratory analyses. This is not the case. Researchers can still make necessary adjustments to their preregistered plans or do exploratory data analyses as long as they are transparent about doing so, which allows others to assess the impact of those changes and analyses on the results (Nosek et al., 2018). In that way, the preregistration serves to make a clear distinction between decisions and inferences that were independent from or dependent on the data (Nosek et al., 2018). Finally, some express concerns that preregistration does not work for all types of research. Importantly, preregistration is certainly not a one-size-fits-all approach. Researchers can include as few or as many details in their preregistrations as they wish; they have various templates to choose from or can create one themselves if existing templates do not fit their study design. In fact, researchers analyzing archival data or conducting secondary data analysis can still preregister their studies; many templates allow researchers to document the state of their data at the time of preregistration (already collected but not analyzed, analyzed for other purposes, etc.). In these ways, preregistration is flexible enough to be a viable option for most types of research (van't Veer & Giner-Sorolla, 2016).

Registered Reports

Registered reports are an open science practice similar to preregistration but different in that they involve submitting the research plan to the peer review process before data collection has begun. Instead of a full manuscript, reviewers read and assess the research question, hypotheses, sample size, planned methodology, and analysis plan. Pilot testing may be necessary to establish that the manipulations are perceived as intended, and authors must confirm that an institutional review board has approved the proposed research. If the reviewers decide that the research question has the potential to advance the field regardless of the results and that the method is sufficiently strong to address such a question, the journal may grant the authors an "in-principle acceptance" on the final manuscript (Nosek et al., 2018). This acceptance means that if the researchers execute the study according to their articulated plan and submit a final manuscript to the journal, it will be published regardless of the specific outcomes observed. Journal editors and reviewers evaluate registered reports based on the quality of the method and execution rather than on the size and direction of their findings.

Like preregistration, registered reports are becoming increasingly more common (Chambers, 2019). Many journals, including *Law and Human Behavior* and *Legal and Criminological Psychology*, have adopted this new publishing format. Proponents argue that registered reports will decrease publication bias and increase objectivity by masking outcomes during review (Chambers & Tzavella, 2020; Nosek & Lakens, 2014). This process encourages reviewers to judge a project purely through its means, not the end results. Registered reports can also decrease the motivation to *p*-hack or to selectively report results because the authors are free to present the results the way that they are rather than having to carve out one clear but perhaps incomplete or inaccurate narrative (Chambers, 2019). Indeed, preliminary evidence shows that registered reports more often contain null results than traditional articles (Allen & Mehler, 2019). Although this may cause concerns about an eventual "null literature" with decreased journal impact factors and citation counts, some evidence suggests that registered reports receive similar or sometimes even more citations than their traditional counterparts (Hummer et al., 2017) and they may be more reproducible than traditional articles (Chambers & Tzavella, 2020). Registered reports can also benefit researchers who receive reviewer feedback before devoting their valuable resources to conducting a study. They can incorporate feedback to make revisions to the protocol that may otherwise have led reviewers to reject the final manuscript had it not been vetted up front.

As with all new innovations, there are still concerns about registered reports that must be resolved as the format evolves. Some of these concerns center on how to prepare a registered report itself. For example, what are researchers to do if, lacking a theoretical basis to anticipate potential effect sizes, they cannot reasonably anticipate the number of participants they will need for proper analysis? Other concerns involve how strictly binding an accepted registered report should be and what to do if the completed research deviates from what was registered. Zero leniency could prove detrimental to those whose institutional review boards require protocol changes to a registered study, and questions remain as to how reviewers should evaluate the merit of deviating from a registered plan. A lack of consensus on whether in-principle acceptances should include an "expiration date" (i.e., deadlines for submitting the completed study) must also be resolved. Chambers et al. (2014) offer a thorough overview and response to these concerns and several others. Even with many issues still to be resolved, registered reports serve as another tool researchers can use to work toward a more credible and reproducible literature.

Open Materials

Another open science practice is publicly sharing materials from a research project. Due to space constraints, both formal (e.g., journal page limits) and informal (e.g., reviewer expectations that a paper flow clearly and concisely), authors often omit details and contextual information from their manuscripts that are often important for understanding why a certain study produced certain results (Bowman & Spence, 2020). It is fairly common to see only a few sample dependent measures, a summary of manipulations, or an overview of the instructions given to participants. Yet many of these details are important to understanding and even replicating the results of study. As decades of research have shown, the exact wording of a question can have a profound impact on the way participants respond (Schwarz, 1999; Tversky & Kahneman, 1986). We also know that the exact order in which materials are presented to participants can affect their responses (Strack, 1992). These small but impactful details may be left out for the sake of space when authors describe their materials but are essential to evaluating the results of a study. Open materials allow readers to better evaluate whether the results may be a function of the specific question wording, the instructions given to participants, or the way the data were coded. They can also facilitate replications in a manner that would be otherwise difficult if only relying on a summary.

Researchers who share their materials have many options available to them in terms of how and where to do it. They can choose to make their materials publicly available (the purest form of "open"), available to other researchers, or available only by request (Gilmore et al., 2018). They can do so on individual lab websites, through supplemental materials to their manuscript with the publisher, or using external repositories (e.g., Open Science Framework). Different projects have different implications for sharing; therefore, researchers who share their materials need to assess the appropriate level of and venue for doing so. If materials include components that could be used to identify participants (e.g., video recordings of experimental sessions), researchers need to ensure that they have approval to share through their institutional review boards and consent to do so from participants. Researchers must curate shared materials so they are easily accessible and understood by others (Wilkinson et al., 2016).

Open Data and Code

A similar open science practice is publicly sharing the data and code from a research project. Authors often must choose which statistical results are important to include in their manuscript and omit others. Manuscripts typically only contain basic descriptive statistics, tests with significant results, or examples of open-ended data (Bowman & Spence, 2020). Readers may have questions about the data and analyses that go unanswered without access to the complete data and code, such as what may have happened if the authors chose a different statistical technique or coded their data differently (West, 2016). Access to the data and code enables others outside the research team to check for errors, attempt to reproduce the results, examine how the analytical decisions may have affected the results, assess the inferences the authors drew from their results, and in some cases conduct secondary analyses on the data to answer new questions (Gilmore et al., 2018; Lindsay, 2017; West, 2016). They can also use the data in meta-analytic work, which can ultimately lead to more confidence in an observed effect (Lindsay, 2017).

Open data have long been the practice in certain fields (MacWhinney & Snow, 1985), but is certainly not the norm in others. However, sharing data is becoming more common due to replication concerns. Many journals (e.g., *Law and Human Behavior*; *Psychology, Public Policy, and Law*; and *Legal and Criminological Psychology*) and funding agencies (e.g., National Science Foundation and National Institutes of Health) in the United States and abroad (see Borgerud & Borglund, 2020) strongly recommend or even require that researchers share their data.

Researchers must ensure their shared data and code are findable, accessible, interoperable, and reusable (FAIR; Wilkinson et al., 2016). As with sharing materials, there are many options for how and where to share data and code. Researchers can do so publicly, with other researchers, or upon request (Gilmore et al., 2018). However, sharing data and code is inherently more difficult than sharing materials because it requires extra effort to transform these materials into a shareable format. Researchers will need to ensure that all variables are clearly labeled and described in such a way that reviewers or readers who are less familiar with their project can still work with the data and code. Doing so requires additional time and effort, but that work often has the added benefit of fewer statistical errors (Wicherts et al., 2011) and increased citation counts (Piwowar et al., 2007).

Like open materials, different projects have different implications for sharing; therefore, researchers who engage in this open practice need to assess the appropriate level of and venue for sharing for their work. Sharing data and code may not be feasible or even recommended for every project. Researchers need to account for ethical, legal, and practical considerations when deciding the extent to which they make their research products publicly available. They should ensure that they have approval to do so through their institutional review boards and consent from participants if applicable. In fact, for those working with sensitive information (e.g., institutional data from correctional or forensic facilities), researchers may wish to collaborate with ethics review boards on a detailed data-sharing plan to ensure privacy (El Emam et al., 2015). There are also special considerations for those who have access to the open data and code. If researchers intend to conduct secondary analyses on open data, they should do so carefully in recognition of issues such as data ownership, alpha inflation, and confirmation biases (West, 2016).

Open Access Publishing

Another open science practice is open access publishing, which involves researchers providing some form of unrestricted access to their scholarly work. Open access publishing is an alternative to the traditional subscription-based model of academic publishing, which generally puts journal articles behind paywalls. It can take on many forms, including the sharing of manuscripts before they go through the formal peer review process (otherwise known as posting "preprints") or publishing manuscripts in an open access format or open access journal. Some journals designate certain articles as open access, allow researchers to pay an additional fee to make their article open access, or make every article in their publication open access by default. Open access publishing practices vary considerably between journals.

Similar to other open science practices, open access publishing is becoming increasingly common (Laakso et al., 2011), with many journals making all (e.g., *PLOS One*) or some of their articles (e.g., *Law and Human Behavior, Legal and Criminological Psychology*) publicly available and many researchers archiving their articles in preprint servers (e.g., PsyArXiv) or social networks (e.g., ResearchGate). There are many arguments advancing the open access publishing movement. Some focus on the idea that science is itself a collaborative venture and that open sharing among scientists would lead to faster, more efficient, and better scientific progress (Nosek & Bar-Anan, 2012). Indeed, open access articles tend to have a higher impact, as reflected in higher citation counts, than their traditional counterparts (Tennant et al., 2016). We see the same benefit with preprints, with articles preceded by a preprint receiving more views and higher citation counts than articles with no preprint (Fu & Hughey, 2019). Other arguments focus on the fact that much of scientific research is funded by taxpayers and therefore should be accessible to taxpayers without them having to pay a fee for the article or for a subscription to a journal that did not itself fund the work (Björk, 2017; Parker, 2013). Some take a broad moral position that scientific knowledge should be accessible to all who can benefit from it (Masuzzo & Martens, 2017). Regardless of which argument is leading the movement, many express optimism that open access will soon become the norm for scientific publishing (e.g., Joseph, 2013; Lewis, 2012).

Practically, open access publishing appears fairly straightforward. Authors can submit their manuscripts into a preprint server, such as PsyArXiv, prior to sending it through the peer review process. Doing so can allow the researchers to have earlier dissemination of their work as well as get earlier feedback that they may choose to incorporate before sending it to a journal for submission. These preprints can be timestamped and accompanied with digital object identifiers (DOIs) so that the work can be built upon and/or cited without authors fearing that their work will be "scooped" by those who see the prepublication manuscript. Researchers who wish to publish their manuscript as open access can either seek out a fully open access journal or find a journal that allows for open access articles.

Open access publishing comes with some challenges and complications still to be addressed. Many journals will not consider papers that have been publicly disseminated elsewhere. For some journals, preprints are considered public dissemination, so authors planning to submit their work should be mindful of journal policies on preprints (see table 5.2 for an online resource for preprint policies of different journals). Preprints also risk compromising masked review if scholars come across the preprint of a paper they have been asked to review (this happened with a preprint for two authors of this chapter, in fact). Delays in review, retraction of the preprint from servers, and rejection from the journal are all possible avenues depending on how reviewers and journals respond in those situations. There is also concern about how well people in and out of the scientific community appreciate the "in progress" status of many papers on preprint servers (Cook et al., 2019), an issue particularly apparent in the wildly variable media coverage of preprints for COVID-19 research (Fleerackers et al., 2022). Dissemination of papers before they have been vetted through peer review might risk publicizing findings that peer review later uncovers to be misleading, incomplete, or downright wrong. One question that arises from these concerns is not *whether* preprints should be publicly shared but rather *when* they should be shared. Finally, there are considerable inequities in terms of which scientists have means to publish open access in journals. Journals that offer open access publishing may charge a substantial fee to do so; therefore, those who wish to publish their article in an open access format may need to plan in advance to ensure they have the necessary funding to do so.

Where Do We Go from Here?

Irreproducibility, replication failures, false-positive errors, and QRPs have catalyzed the open science movement in psychology and other disciplines. The field of psychology and law is adapting to these changes as well. A quick glance through recent articles in the field's top peer-reviewed journals and a stroll through an American Psychology-Law Society poster session will reveal a number of open science badges or links to open materials and data.

Yet we do not know the degree to which the issues that brought about the open science movement specifically affect our field because psychology and law research on this topic is extremely sparse (cf. special issue of direct replications to be published in *Legal and Criminological Psychology*, Spring 2023). Irvine et al. (2018) took a critical first step by attempting replications of three experiments on issues relevant to civil litigation (apologies, framing effects of litigant roles, and valuations of physical and financial harms). They characterized the results of the replications as "partially successful" (p. 340) and pointed to contextual sensitivity of the original studies (e.g., one involved a bicyclist/pedestrian accident on path in a park; another used saving the dolphins as a salient exemplar of environmental advocacy) as one potential explanation for the observed differences. With respect to QRPs, a survey by John et al. (2012) included a small subsample ($n = 16$) of forensic psychologists, 28 percent of whom had engaged in at least one of these practices in their own research. A considerably higher percentage (87 percent) of respondents from the related field of criminology admitted to using QRPs as well (Chin et al., 2021).

These preliminary data suggest that the current state of psychology and law is similar to other disciplines: replicability is imperfect and QRPs are common. Whatever the case may prove to be based on future studies, there is no time to waste with so much work needed to improve psychology and law research.

Implementing Change When Conducting and Evaluating Research

Research assessing the replicability of psychology and law research is necessary and ongoing. However, adopting open science practices should improve the validity of the field's scientific findings. Our advice is to think big but to start small by creating a free account on Open Science Framework (osf.io) or AsPredicted (aspredicted.org). These websites provide resources to facilitate the process, including preregistration templates. In fact, AsPredicted even has a "Just trying it out; make this pre-registration self-destroy in 24 hours" option complete with a cartoon-style bomb emoji (see, isn't open science fun?). After familiarizing yourself with the websites, you can then use them to begin engaging in open science. When designing your next study, choose one of the templates and use it to preregister your hypotheses, method, and data-analytic plan. After collecting data, keep careful records of the analyses, including confirmatory and exploratory analyses, as well as any deviations from the original plan. Have a colleague or lab member use your data and follow your analysis plan to determine the reproducibility of your results. Better yet, have a colleague or lab member analyze simulated data to determine if you should modify your analysis plan *before* preregistration. Be thorough and transparent when drafting your manuscript by implementing the "21 word solution" to describe your methodology: "We report how we determined our sample size, all data exclusions (if any), all manipulations, and all measures in the study" (Simmons et al., 2012). Archive your deidentified data file, code, and results on a public repository and be willing to extend your work by replicating and collaborating with others. Be open about intentions to reform and admit errors—doing so can even increase public perceptions of researcher trustworthiness and credibility (Altenmüller et al., 2021).

Implementing open science practices should not be limited to one's own research program. When reviewing manuscripts or grant proposals, researchers should demand the same high level of rigor and transparency that they aspire to in their own work. For example, if a manuscript is light or unclear on methodological details, consider including this standard request from the Center for Open Science:

> I request that the authors add a statement to the paper confirming whether, for all experiments, they have reported all measures, conditions, data exclusions, and how they determined their sample sizes. The authors should, of course, add any additional text to ensure the statement is accurate. This is the standard reviewer disclosure request endorsed by the Center for Open Science. (See also http://osf.io/hadz3)

Reviewers must also recalibrate their expectations for "pretty" data that tell a "neat" story. Restricting researcher degrees of freedom, QRPs, and HARKing almost certainly will result in uglier and messier, but more valid, findings. This transition will require tolerance and patience for everyone involved. Reviewers should not be afraid to ask authors to demonstrate that results do not hinge on arbitrary analytic decisions and to request replications if authors' data collection or analysis justifications are not compelling (Simmons et al., 2011).

Training the Next Generation

Students can also benefit from incorporating open science into university courses. Beginning in introductory courses, professors can share basic information about the reproducibility crisis and open science practices, which can then be expanded upon in more advanced courses. Several modules, syllabi, and teaching resources exist for use with undergraduates (see table 5.2). Even a brief hour-long lecture teaching students about these issues can increase their comprehension without damaging their overall perceptions of the field (Chopik et al., 2018). Research methods, thesis, or capstone courses offer a unique opportunity to train students firsthand in open science practices by conducting replication studies (Frank & Saxe, 2012; Hawkins et al., 2018). With proper supervision, students could contribute to large replication databases that could provide immense benefit to the field (Grahe et al., 2012), while also increasing students' interest and enjoyment in the research process. Graduate methods courses could also take advantage of similar processes to collect replication data (Hawkins et al., 2018) and to teach open science practices (Tackett et al., 2020).

Psychology and law researchers must also be mindful that their laboratories house the next generation of psychological scientists. What we say and do undoubtedly will affect junior lab members (Krishna & Peter, 2018). Senior researchers tend to support QRPs more and open science less than their students (Chin et al., 2021). Knowledge of mentor engagement in QRPs significantly predicts students' self-reported QRPs (Swift et al., 2022) and beliefs that QRPs are normative or necessary for career success are associated with increased acceptability of QRPs (Sacco et al., 2018). The message from these data is clear: old dogs must be willing to learn new tricks. Otherwise, we risk passing on outdated and subpar research skills to the next generation of psychological scientists. Researchers can make open science practices like preregistration and preprints standard operating laboratory procedures to increase students' familiarity and normalize usage (Kathawalla et al., 2021). Creating shared lab documents and codebooks to standardize note taking and reporting data collection issues can further promote research transparency and facilitate data sharing (see table 5.2 for a list of resources). Providing students a variety of opportunities to practice open research will facilitate their development as junior scientists, ensuring the field becomes even more transparent and accessible as they progress in their own careers.

Open Science in Applied Settings

Psychology and law researchers must also consider the downstream effects of open science on their work in applied settings. One of the primary conduits for psychological science into the legal system is expert testimony. Psychology experts testify on an array of issues relevant to civil and criminal cases, including dangerousness, competency, intellectual and social functioning, eyewitness identification, confessions, and witness suggestibility. Adopting open science practices may enable psychological research to better meet the *Daubert* admissibility standards of relevant and valid (or "reliable" using the Court's terminology) expert evidence (Chin et al., 2019). A review of 364 psychological assessment tools forensic psychologists commonly use in legal cases found that only 25 percent had generally favorable evaluations of quality (Neal et al., 2019). Transparent and accessible research would offer a clearer understanding of the work needed to bring the remaining 75 percent of tools to acceptable levels of reliability and validity for courts. Moreover, peer-reviewed research that is published with inflated rates of false-positive errors associated with researcher degrees of freedom and QRPs could lead judges to erroneously admit flawed research (Hu et al., 2018). False-positive errors also skew and distort estimations of a methodology's error rate. Open science practices that decrease false-positives and increase nonsignificant results in the published literature will more accurately reflect the true state of psychological science and should result in more effective admissibility decisions by judges (Chin et al., 2020). In essence, increased transparency and accessibility in the field of psychology and law can show how robust its tools and research actually are and simultaneously set up opportunities to improve them.

Open science practices can also benefit other actors within the criminal justice and legal systems. More accurately evaluating the strength of scientific evidence in a case can enhance the ability of investigators to determine whether to follow other avenues in an investigation or attorneys to recommend their clients take a plea versus challenge the evidence in court (Chin et al., 2020). Similarly, a recent Pew Research Center (2019) survey found 54 percent of the respondents indicated they would have greater trust in scientific findings if open data practices were used. Although research has not yet explored the impact of open science practices in a field or by a particular expert witness on jurors' perceptions of scientific evidence, this finding suggests that adoption of open science practices may engender greater trust in experts and make them more effective on the witness stand.

All of this is not to say that adopting open science practices will be an easy feat for psychology and law. Our field has unique limitations that must be taken into account. For example, we often work with sensitive populations, such as individuals in prison settings, children, and survivors of crime. These populations present valuable research opportunities but also present a potential obstacle for publicly sharing data. Although there are preventive steps researchers can take to protect this sensitive data, there remains a risk of reidentification by those who share intimate knowledge of the events being studied (Campbell et al., 2019; Finkel et al., 2015; Ross et al., 2018). However, these issues are not insurmountable, and scholars have described best practices for the ethical sharing of sensitive data (e.g., Campbell et al., 2019; Gilmore et al., 2018; Meyer, 2018). Repositories can also provide protective access for data that can facilitate sharing with qualified personnel (Chin & Zeiler, 2021; Schumann et al., 2019). Some of these practices may be acceptable to organizations that typically restrict data sharing. Even when data are not shareable, this does not necessarily stop researchers from preregistering hypotheses or sharing materials. Open science is not an "all-or-nothing" endeavor—researchers can engage in one open science practice even if another is not available to them. Certainly something is better than nothing.

Conclusion

Valid science in psychology and law matters because our contributions as researchers and practitioners have great potential to meaningfully influence—in positive and negative ways—the lives of people involved in the legal and criminal justice systems. Judges, attorneys, police, jurors, victims, plaintiffs, defendants, corrections officers, and prisoners rely on us and the work we do. We owe it to these individuals and ourselves to improve psychology and law research by adopting more transparent and accessible practices. Doing so will help ensure that our conclusions are sound and lead to recommendations that promote justice for all.

References

Allen, C., & Mehler, D. M. A. (2019). Open science challenges, benefits and tips in early career and beyond. *PLOS Biology, 17*(12), Article e3000246. https://doi.org/10.1371/journal.pbio.3000246

Altenmüller, M. S., Nuding, S., & Gollwitzer, M. (2021). No harm in being self-corrective: Self-criticism and reform intentions increase researchers' epistemic trustworthiness and credibility in the eyes of the public. *Public Understanding of Science, 30*(8), 962–976. https://doi.org/10.1177/09636625211022181

Anderson, M. S., Martinson, B. C., & De Vries, R. (2007). Normative dissonance in science: Results from a national survey of U.S. scientists. *Journal of Empirical Research on Human Research Ethics, 2*(4), 3–14. https://doi.org/10.1525/jer.2007.2.4.3

Arabito, S., & Pitrelli, N. (2015). Open science training and education: Challenges and difficulties on the researchers' side and in public engagement. *Journal of Science Communication, 14*(4), Article C01_en. https://doi.org/10.22323/2.14040301

Artner, R., Verliefde, T., Steegen, S., Gomes, S., Traets, F., Tuerlinckx, F., & Vanpaemel, W. (2021). The reproducibility of statistical results in psychological research: An investigation using unpublished raw data. *Psychological Methods, 26*(5), 527–546. https://doi.org/10.1037/met0000365

Asendorpf, J. B., Conner, M., De Fruyt, F., De Houwer, J., Denissen, J. J. A., Fiedler, K., Fiedler, S., Funder, D. C., Kliegl, R., Nosek, B. A., Perugini, M., Roberts, B. W., Schmitt, M., van Aken, M. A. G., Weber, H., & Wicherts, J. M. (2013). Recommendations for increasing replicability in psychology. *European Journal of Personality, 27*(2), 108–119. https://doi.org/10.1002/per.1919

Bergh, D. D., Sharp, B. M., Aguinis, H., & Li, M. (2017). Is there a credibility crisis in strategic management research? Evidence on the reproducibility of study findings. *Strategic Organization, 15*(3), 423–436. https://doi.org/10.1177/1476127017701076

Björk, B-C. (2017). Gold, green, and black open access. *Learned Publishing, 30*(2), 173–175. https://doi.org/10.1002/leap.1096

Borgerud, C., & Borglund, E. (2020). Open research data, an archival challenge? *Archival Science, 20*(3), 279–302. https://doi.org/10.1007/s10502-020-09330-3

Bowman, N. D., & Spence, P. R. (2020). Challenges and best practices associated with sharing research materials and research data for communication scholars. *Communication Studies, 71*(4), 708–716. https://doi.org/10.1080/10510974.2020.1799488

Cairo, A. H., Green, J. D., Forsyth, D. R., Behler, A. M. C., & Raldiris, T. L. (2020). Gray (literature) matters: Evidence of selective hypothesis reporting in social psychological research. *Personality and Social Psychology Bulletin, 46*(9), 1344–1362. https://doi.org/10.1177/0146167220903896

Campbell, R., Goodman-Williams, R., & Javorka, M. (2019). A trauma-informed approach to sexual violence research ethics and open science. *Journal of Interpersonal Violence, 34*(23–24), 4765–4793. https://doi.org/10.1177/0886260519871530

Chambers, C. (2019). The registered reports revolution: Lessons in cultural reform. *Significance, 16*(4), 23–27. https://doi.org/10.1111/j.1740-9713.2019.01299.x

Chambers, C. D., Feredoes, E., Muthukumaraswamy, S. D., & Etchells, P. J. (2014). Instead of "playing the game" it is time to change the rules: Registered reports at *AIMS Neuroscience* and beyond. *AIMS Neuroscience, 1*(1), 4–17. https://doi.org/10.3934/Neuroscience.2014.1.4

Chambers, C. D., & Tzavella, L. (2020). The past, present, and future of registered reports. *MetaArXiv.* https://doi.org/10.31222/osf.io/43298

Chin, J. M., Pickett, J. T., Vazire, S., & Holcombe, A. O. (2021). Questionable research practices and open science in quantitative criminology. *Journal of Quantitative Criminology.* Advance online publication. https://doi.org/10.1007/s10940-021-09525-6

Chin, J. M., McFadden, R., & Edmond, G. (2020). Forensic science needs registered reports. *Forensic Science International: Synergy, 2*, 41–45. https://doi.org/10.1016/j.fsisyn.2019.10.005

Chin, J. M., Ribeiro, G., & Rairden, A. (2019). Open forensic science. *Journal of Law and the Biosciences, 6*(1), 255–288. https://doi.org/10.1093/jlb/lsz009

Chin, J. M., & Zeiler, K. (2021). Replicability in empirical legal research. *Annual Review of Law and Social Science, 17*(1), 239–260.

Chopik, W. J., Bremner, R. H., Defever, A. M., & Keller, V. N. (2018). How (and whether) to teach undergraduates about the replication crisis in psychological science. *Teaching of Psychology, 45*(2), 158–163. https://doi.org/10.1177/0098628318762900

Cohen, J. (1962). The statistical power of abnormal-social psychological research: A review. *The Journal of Abnormal and Social Psychology, 65*(3), 145–153. https://doi.org/10.1037/h0045186

Cook, B. G., Lloyd, J. W., & Therrien, W. J. (2019). Open science in the field of emotional and behavioral disorders. *Education and Treatment of Children, 42*(4), 579–600. https://doi.org/10.1353/etc.2019.0027

Dreber, A., Pfeiffer, T., Almenberg, J., Isaksson, S., Wilson, B., Chen, Y., Nosek, B. A., & Johannesson, M. (2015). Using prediction markets to estimate the reproducibility of scientific research. *Proceedings of the National Academy of Sciences, 112*(50), 15343–15347. https://doi.org/10.1073/pnas.1516179112

Eich, E. (2014). Business not as usual. *Psychological Science, 25*(1), 3–6. https://doi.org/10.1177/0956797613512465

El Emam, K., Rodgers, S., & Malin, B. (2015). Anonymising and sharing individual patient data. *BMJ, 350*, Article h1139. https://doi.org/10.1136%2Fbmj.h1139

Finkel, E. J., Eastwick, P. W., & Reis, H. T. (2015). Best research practices in psychology: Illustrating epistemological and pragmatic considerations with the case of relationship science. *Journal of Personality and Social Psychology*, *108*(2), 275–297. https://doi.org/10.1037/pspi0000007

Fleerackers, A., Riedlinger, M., Moorhead, L., Ahmed, R., & Alperin, J. P. (2022). Communicating scientific uncertainty in an age of COVID-19: An investigation into the use of preprints by digital media outlets. *Health Communication*, *37*(6), 726–738. https://doi.org/10.1080/10410236.2020.1864892

Franco, A., Malhotra, N., & Simonovits, G. (2016). Underreporting in psychology experiments evidence from a study registry. *Social Psychological and Personality Science*, *7*(1), 8–12. https://doi.org/10.1177/19485 50615598377

Frank, M. F., & Saxe, R. (2012). Teaching replication. *Perspectives on Psychological Science*, *7*(6), 600–604. https://doi.org/10.1177/1745691612460686

Fu, D. Y., & Hughey, J. J. (2019). Meta-research: Releasing a preprint is associated with more attention and citations for the peer-reviewed article. *eLife*, *8*, Article e52646. https://doi.org/10.7554/eLife.52646

Gilmore, R. O., Kennedy, J. L., & Adolph, K. E. (2018). Practical solutions for sharing data and materials from psychological research. *Advances in Methods and Practices in Psychological Science*, *1*(1), 121–130. https://doi.org/10.1177/2515245917746500

Goldin-Meadow, S. (2016, September). Why preregistration makes me nervous. *APS Observer*. https://www.psychologicalscience.org/observer/why-preregistration-makes-me-nervous

Gordon, M., Viganola, D., Dreber, A., Johannesson, M., & Pfeiffer, T. (2021) Predicting replicability—Analysis of survey and prediction market data from large-scale forecasting projects. *PLOS One*, *16*(4), Article e0248780. https://doi.org/10.1371/journal.pone.0248780

Götz, F. M., Gosling, S. D., & Rentfrow, P. J. (2021). Small effects: The indispensable foundation for a cumulapsychological science. *Perspectives on Psychological Science*, *17*(1), 205–215. https://doi.org/10.1177/1745691620984483

Grahe, J. E., Reifman, A., Hermann, A. D., Walker, M., Oleson, K. C., Nario-Redmond, M., & Wiebe, R. P. (2012). Harnessing the undiscovered resource of student research projects. *Perspectives on Psychological Science*, *7*(6), 605–607. https://doi.org/10.1177/1745691612459057

Hardwicke, T. E., Bohn, M., MacDonald, K., Hembacher, E., Nuijten, M. B., Peloquin, B. N., deMayo, B. E., Long, B., Yoon, E. J., & Frank, M. C. (2021). Analytic reproducibility in articles receiving open data badges at the journal *Psychological Science*: An observational study. *Royal Society Open Science*, *8*(1), Article 201494. https://doi.org/10.1098/rsos.201494

Hardwicke, T. E., Mathur, M. B., MacDonald, K., Nilsonne, G., Banks, G. C., Kidwell, M. C., Mohr, A. H., Clayton, E., Yoon, E. J., Tessler, M. H., Lenne, R. L., Altman, S., Long, B., & Frank, M. C. (2018). Data availability, reusability, and analytic reproducibility: Evaluating the impact of a mandatory open data policy at the journal *Cognition*. *Royal Society Open Science*, *5*(8), Article 180448. https://doi.org/10.1098/rsos.180448

Hawkins, R. X. D., Smith, E. N., Au, C., Arias, J. M., Catapano, R., Hermann, E., Keil, M., Lampinen, A., Raposo, S., Reynolds, J., Salehi, S., Salloum, J., Tan, J., & Frank, M. C. (2018). Improving the replicability of psychological science through pedagogy. *Advances in Methods and Practices in Psychological Science*, *1*(1), 7–18. https://doi.org/10.1177/2515245917740427

Hu, C-P., Jiang, X., Jeffrey, R., & Zuo, X-N. (2018). Open science as a better gatekeeper for science and society: A perspective from neurolaw. *Science Bulletin*, *63*(23), 1529–1531. https://doi.org/10.1016/j.scib.2018.11.015

Hummer, L. T., Singleton Thorn, F., Nosek, B. A., & Errington, T. M. (2017). Evaluating registered reports: A naturalistic comparative study of article impact. *OSF Preprints*. https://doi.org/10.31219/osf.io/5y8w7

Ioannidis, J. P. A. (2005). Why most published research findings are false. *PLOS Medicine*, *2*(8), Article e124. https://doi.org/10.1371/journal.pmed.0020124

Irvine, K., Hoffman, D. A., & Wilkinson-Ryan, T. (2018). Law and psychology grow up, goes online, and replicates. *Journal of Empirical Legal Studies*, *15*(2), 320–355. https://doi.org/10.1111/jels.12180

John, L. K., Loewenstein, G., Prelec, D. (2012). Measuring the prevalence of questionable research practices with incentives for truth telling. *Psychological Science*, *23*(5), 524–532. https://doi.org/10.1177/09567 97611430953

Jonas, K. J., & Cesario, J. (2015). How can preregistration contribute to research in our field. *Comprehensive Results in Social Psychology*, *1*(1-3), 1–7. https://doi.org/10.1080/23743603.2015.1070611

Joseph, H. (2013). The open access movement grows up: Taking stock of a revolution. *PLoS Biology*, *11*(10), Article e1001686. https://doi.org/10.1371/journal.pbio.1001686

Kaplan, R. M., & Irvine, V. L. (2015). Likelihood of null effects of large NHLBI clinical trials has increased over time. *PLoS One, 10*(8), Article e0132382. https://doi.org/10.1371/journal.pone.0132382

Kathawalla, U-K., Silverstein, P., & Syed, M. (2021). Easing into open science: A guide for graduate students and their advisors. *Collabra: Psychology, 7*(1), Article 18684. https://doi.org/10.1525/collabra.18684

Kerr, N. L. (1998). HARKing: hypothesizing after the results are known. *Personality and Social Psychology Review, 2*(3), 196–217. https://doi.org/10.1207/s15327957pspr0203_4

Kidwell, M. C., Lazarević, L. B., Baranski, E., Hardwicke, T. E., Piechowski, S., Falkenberg, L-S., Kennett, C., Slowik, A., Sonnleitner, C., Hess-Holden, C., Errington, T. M., Fiedler, S., & Nosek, B. A. (2016). Badges to acknowledge open practices: A simple low-cost effective method for increasing transparency. *PLOS Biology, 14*(5), Article e1002456. https://doi.org/10.1371/journal.pbio.1002456

Klein, O., Hardwicke, T. E., Aust, F., Breuer, J., Danielsson, H., Mohr, A. H., IJzerman, H., Nilsonne, G., Vanpaemel, W., & Frank, M. C. (2018). A practical guide for transparency in psychological science. *Collabra: Psychology, 4*(1), Article 20. https://doi.org/10.1525/collabra.158

Krishna, A., & Peter, S. M. (2018). Questionable research practices in student final theses – Prevalence, attitudes, and the role of the supervisors' perceived attitudes. *PLoS One, 13*(8), Article e0203470. https://doi.org/10.1371/journal.Pone.0203470

Laakso, M., Welling, P., Bukvova, H., Nyman, L., Björk, B-C., Hedlund, T. (2011). The development of open access journal publishing from 1993 to 2009. *PLoS One, 6*(6), Article e20961. https://doi.org/10.1371/journal.pone.0020961

Lamb, M. E., Steblay, N. K., & Neal, T. M. S. (2021). *Psychology, Public Policy, and Law* adopts further open science practices and refreshes its commitment to generalizable empirical research. *Psychology, Public Policy, and Law, 27*(3), 293–294. http://dx.doi.org/10.1037/law0000318

Ledgerwood, A., Hudson, S. T. J., Lewis, N. A., Maddox, K. B., Pickett, C. L., Remedios, J. D., Cheryan, S., Diekman, A. B., Dutra, N. B., Goh, J. X., Goodwin, S. A., Munakata, Y., Navarro, D. J., Onyeador, I. N., Srivastava, S., & Wilkins, C. L. (2022). The pandemic as a portal: Reimagining psychological science as truly open and inclusive. *Perspectives on Psychological Science, 17*(4), 937–959. https://doi.org/10.1177/17456916211036654

Lewis, D. W. (2012). The inevitability of open access. *College and Research Libraries, 73*(5), 493–505. https://doi.org/10.5860/crl-299

Lindsay, D. S. (2015). Replication in *Psychological Science. Psychological Science, 26*(12), 1827–1832. https://doi.org/10.1177/0956797615616374

Lindsay, D. S. (2017). Sharing data and materials in *Psychological Science. Psychological Science, 28*(6), 699–702. https://doi.org/10.1177/0956797617704015

Lindsay, D. S., Simons, D. J., & Lilienfeld, S. O. (2016, November 30). Research preregistration 101. *APS Observer.* https://www.psychologicalscience.org/observer/research-preregistration-101

Lovakov, A., & Agadullina, E. R. (2021). Empirically derived guidelines for effect size interpretation in social psychology. *European Journal of Social Psychology, 51*(3), 485–504. https://doi.org/10.1002/ejsp.2752

MacWhinney, B., & Snow, C. (1985). The child language data exchange system. *Journal of Child Language, 12*(2), 271–295. https://doi.org/10.1017/S0305000900006449

Masuzzo, P., & Martens, L. (2017). Do you speak open science? Resources and tips to learn the language. *PeerJ Preprints, 5*, Article e2689v1. https://doi.org/10.7287/peerj.preprints.2689v1

Maxwell, S. E., Lau, M. Y., & Howard, G. S. (2015). Is psychology suffering from a replication crisis? What does "failure to replicate" really mean? *American Psychologist, 70*(6), 487–498. https://doi.org/10.1037/a0039400

Mayo-Wilson, E., Grant, S., Supplee, L., Kianersi, S, Amin, A., DeHaven, A., & Mellor, D. (2021). Evaluating implementation of the Transparency and Openness Promotion (TOP) guidelines: The TRUST process for rating journal policies, procedures, and practices. *Research Integrity and Peer Review, 6*(9), 1–11. https://doi.org/10.1186/s41073-021-00112-8

McAuliff, B. D., Hunt, J. S., Levett, L. M., Zelechoski, A. D., Scherr, K. C., & DeMatteo, D. (2019). Taking the next steps: Promoting open science and expanding diversity in *Law and Human Behavior. Law and Human Behavior, 43*(1), 1–8. https://doi.org/10.1037/lhb0000322

Meyer, M. N. (2018). Practical tips for ethical data sharing. *Advances in Methods and Practices in Psychological Science, 1*(1), 131–144. https://doi.org/10.1177/2515245917747656

Motyl, M., Demos, A. P., Carsel, T. S., Hanson, B. E., Melton, Z. J., Mueller, A. B., Prims, J. P., Sun, J., Washburn, A. N., Wong, K. M., Yantis, C., & Skitka, L. J. (2017). The state of social and personality science: Rotten to the core, not so bad, getting better, or getting worse? *Journal of Personality and Social Psychology, 113*(1), 34–58. https://doi.org/10.1037/pspa0000084

National Academies of Sciences, Engineering, and Medicine (NAS). (2019). *Reproducibility and replicability in science*. The National Academies Press. https://doi.org/10.17226/25303

Neal, T. M. S., Slobogin, C., Saks, M. J., Faigman, D. L., & Geisinger, K. F. (2019). Psychological assessments in legal contexts: Are courts keeping "junk science" out of the courtroom? *Psychological Science in the Public Interest*, *20*(3), 135–164. https://doi.org/10.1177/1529100619888860

Nelson, L. D., Simmons, J., & Simonsohn, U. (2018). Psychology's renaissance. *Annual Review of Psychology*, *69*, 511–534. https://doi.org/10.1146/annurev-psych-122216-011836

Neuschatz, J. S. (2020). Editorial. *Psychology, Crime, and Law*, *26*(3), 207. https://doi.org/10.1080/10683 16X.2020.1729968

Nosek, B. A., Alter, G., Banks, G. C., Borsboom, D., Bowman, S. D., Breckler, S. J., Buck, S., Chambers, C. D., Chin, G., Christensen, G., Contestabile, M., Dafoe, A., Eich, E., Freese, J., Glennerster, R., Goroff, D., Green, D. P., Hesse, B., Humphreys, M., . . . Yarkoni, T. (2015). Promoting an open research culture. *Science*, *348*(6242), 1422–1425. https://doi.org/10.1126/science.aab2374

Nosek, B. A., & Bar-Anan, Y. (2012). Scientific utopia: I. Opening scientific communication. *Psychological Inquiry*, *23*(3), 217–243. https://doi.org/10.1080/1047840X.2012.692215

Nosek, B. A., Ebersole, C. R., DeHaven, A. C., & Mellor, D. T. (2018). The preregistration revolution. *Proceedings of the National Academy of Sciences*, *115*(11), 2600–2606. https://doi.org/10.1073/pnas.1708274114

Nosek, B. A., Hardwicke, T. E., Moshontz, H., Allard, A., Corker, K. S., Dreber, A., Fidler, F., Hilgard, J., Kline Struhl, M., Nuijten, M., Rohrer, J., Romero, F., Scheel, A., Scherer, L., Schönbrodt, F., & Vazire, S. (2022). Replicability, robustness, and reproducibility in psychological science. *Annual Review of Psychology*, *73*(1), 719–748.

Nosek, B. A., & Lakens, D. (2014). Registered reports: A method to increase the credibility of published results. *Social Psychology*, *45*(3), 137–141. https://doi.org/10.1027/1864-9335/a000192

Nosek, B. A., & Lindsay, D. S. (2018, February 28). Preregistration becoming the norm in psychological science. *APS Observer*. https://www.psychologicalscience.org/observer/preregistration-becoming-the-norm-in-psychological-science

Nosek, B. A., Spies, J. R., & Motyl, M. (2012). Scientific utopia II. Restructuring incentives and practices to promote truth over publishability. *Perspectives on Psychological Science*, *7*(6), 615–631. https://doi.org/10.1177/1745691612459058

Open Science Collaboration. (2015). Estimating the reproducibility of psychological science. *Science*, *349*(6251), 1–8. https://doi.org/10.1126/science.aac4716

Parker, M. (2013). The ethics of open access publishing. *BMC Medical Ethics*, *14*, Article 16. https://doi.org/10.1186/1472-6939-14-16

Pashler, H., & Wagenmakers, E-J. (2012). Editors' introduction to the special section on replicability in psychological science: A crisis of confidence? *Perspectives on Psychological Science*, *7*(6), 528–530. https://doi.org/10.1177/1745691612465253

Pew Research Center (2019). *Trust and mistrust in Americans' views of scientific experts*. https://www.pewresearch.org/science/2019/08/02/trust-and-mistrust-in-americans-views-of-scientific-experts/

Piwowar, H. A., Day, R. S., & Fridsma, D. B. (2007). Sharing detailed research data is associated with increased citation rate. *PLoS One*, *2*(3), Article e308. https://doi.org/10.1371/journal.pone.0000308

Roberts, S. O., Bareket-Shavit, C., Dollins, F. A., Goldie, P. D., & Mortenson, E. (2020). Racial inequality in psychological research: Trends of the past and recommendations for the future. *Perspectives on Psychological Science*, *15*(6), 1295–1309. https://doi.org/10.1177/1745691620927709

Ross, M. W., Iguchi, M. Y., & Panicker, S. (2018). Ethical aspects of data sharing and research participant protections. *American Psychologist*, *73*(2), 138–145. https://doi.org/10.1037/amp0000240

Sacco, D. F., Bruton, S. V., & Brown, M. (2018). In defense of the questionable: Defining the basis of research scientists' engagement in questionable research practices. *Journal of Empirical Research on Human Research Ethics*, *13*(1), 101–110. https://doi.org/10.1177/1556264617743834

Scheel, A. M., Schijen, M. R. M. J., & Lakens, D. (2021). An excess of positive results: Comparing the standard psychology literature with registered reports. *Advances in Methods and Practices in Psychological Science*, *4*(2), 1–12. https://doi.org/10.1177/25152459211007467

Schneider, J., Rosman, T., Kelava, A., & Merk, S. (2020). (Re)building trust? Journals' open science badges influence trust in scientists. *PsychArchives*. https://doi.org/10.23668/PSYCHARCHIVES.3364

Schumann, S., van der Vegt, I., Gill, P., & Schuurman, B. (2019). Towards open and reproducible terrorism studies: Current trends and next steps. *Perspectives on Terrorism*, *13*(5), 61–73.

Schwarz, N. (1999). Self-reports: How the questions shape the answers. *American Psychologist, 54*(2), 93–105. https://doi.org/10.1037/0003-066X.54.2.93

Sedlmeier, P., & Gigerenzer, G. (1989). Do studies of statistical power have an effect on the power of studies? *Psychological Bulletin, 105*(2), 309–316. https://doi.org/10.1037/0033-2909.105.2.309

Simmons, J. P., Nelson L. D., & Simonsohn, U. (2011). False-positive psychology: Undisclosed flexibility in data collection and analysis allows presenting anything as significant. *Psychological Science, 22*(11), 1359–1366. https://doi.org/10.1177/0956797611417632

Simmons, J. P., Nelson, L. D., & Simonsohn, U. (2012). A 21 word solution. *The Official Newsletter of the Society for Personality and Social Psychology, 26*(2), 4–7. https://doi.org/10.2139/ssrn.2160588

Spellman, B. A., Gilbert, E. A., & Corker, K. S. (2018). Open science. In J. T. Wixted & E.-J. Wagenmakers (Eds.), *Stevens' handbook of experimental psychology and cognitive neuroscience, methodology* (4th ed., Vol. 5, pp. 729–775). John Wiley & Sons. https://doi.org/10.1002/9781119170174.epcn519

Strack, F. (1992). "Order effects" in survey research: Activation and information functions of preceding questions. In N. Schwarz & S. Sudman (Eds.), *Context effects in social and psychological research* (pp. 23–34). Springer-Verlag. https://doi.org/10.1007/978-1-4612-2848-6_3

Swaen, G. G., Teggeler, O., & van Amelsvoort, L. G. (2001). False positive outcomes and design characteristics in occupational cancer epidemiology studies. *International Journal of Epidemiology, 30*(5), 948–954. https://doi.org/10.1093/ije/30.5.948

Swift, J. K., Christopherson, C. D., Bird, M. O., Zöld, A., & Goode, J. (2022). Questionable research practices among faculty and students in APA-accredited clinical and counseling psychology doctoral programs. *Training and Education in Professional Psychology, 16*(3), 299–305. https://doi.org/10.1037/tep0000322

Tackett, J. L., Brandes, C. M., Dworak, E. M., & Shields, A. N. (2020). Bringing the (pre)registration revolution to graduate training. *Canadian Psychology/Psychologie canadienne, 61*(4), 299–309. https://doi.org/10.1037/cap0000221

Tackett, J. L., Brandes, C. M., King, K. M., & Markon, K. E. (2019). Psychology's replication crisis and clinical psychological science. *Annual Review of Clinical Psychology, 15*(1), 579–604. https://doi.org/10.1146/annurev-clinpsy-050718-095710

Tennant, J. P., Waldner, F., Jacques, D. C., Masuzzo, P., Collister, L. B., & Hartgerink, C. H. J. (2016). The academic, economic and societal impacts of open access: An evidence-based review. *F1000Research, 5*, Article 632. https://doi.org/10.12688/f1000research.8460.3

Towse, A. S., Ellis, D. A., & Towse, J. N. (2021). Making data meaningful: Guidelines for good quality open data, *The Journal of Social Psychology, 161*(4), 395–402. https://doi.org/10.1080/00224545.2021.1938811

Tversky, A., & Kahneman, D. (1986). Rational choice and the framing of decisions. *The Journal of Business, 59*(4), S251–S278. http://www.jstor.org/stable/2352759

Valentine, J. C., Biglan, A., Boruch, R. F., Castro, F. G., Collins, L. M., Flay, B. R., Kellam, S., Mościcki, E. K., & Schinke, S. P. (2011). Replication in prevention science. *Prevention Science: The Official Journal of the Society for Prevention Research, 12*(2), 103–117. https://doi.org/10.1007/s11121-011-0217-6

van't Veer, A. E., & Giner-Sorolla, R. (2016). Pre-registration in social psychology—A discussion and suggested template. *Journal of Experimental Social Psychology, 67*, 2–12. https://doi.org/10.1016/j.jesp.2016.03.004

Vazire, S. (2017). Quality uncertainty erodes trust in science. *Collabra: Psychology, 3*(1), Article 1. https://doi.org/10.1525/collabra.74

Vazire, S. (2018). Implications of the credibility revolution for productivity, creativity, and progress. *Perspectives on Psychological Science, 13*(4), 411–417. https://doi.org/10.1177/1745691617751884

West, R. (2016). Data and statistical commands should be routinely disclosed in order to promote greater transparency and accountability in clinical and behavioral research. *Journal of Clinical Epidemiology, 70*, P254–P255. https://doi.org/10.1016/j.jclinepi.2015.06.015

Wicherts, J. M., Bakker, M., & Molenaar, D. (2011). Willingness to share research data is related to the strength of evidence and the quality of reporting statistical results. *PLoS One, 6*(11), Article e26828. https://doi.org/10.1371/journal.pone.0026828

Wilkinson, M. D., Dumontier, M., Aalbersberg, I. J., Appleton, G., Axton, M., Baak, A., Blomberg, N., Boiten, J-W., da Silva Santos, L. B., Bourne, P. E., Bouwman, J., Brookes, A. J., Clark, T., Crosas, M., Dillo, I., Dumon, O., Edmunds, S., Evelo, C. T., Finkers, R., . . . Mons, B. (2016). The FAIR guiding principles for scientific data management and stewardship. *Scientific Data, 3*, Article 160018. https://doi.org/10.1038/sdata.2016.18

Applied
Psychology–Law

General Considerations

A Framework for Forensic Mental Health Assessments: Principles, Standards of Care, and Standards of Practice

Kirk Heilbrun, Madelena Rizzo, Kellie Wiltsie, *and* Heidi Zapotocky

Abstract

This chapter describes foundational principles of forensic mental health assessment (FMHA) that have been developed and revised to describe aspects of FMHA that apply to a various kinds of FMHA. Principles are further described as they apply in two contexts: in general, and in a sequence associated with a specific case (preparation, data collection, data interpretation, communication, and testimony). The chapter also distinguishes between standard of care and standard of practice as each applies to legal decision-making and addresses how these FMHA principles might apply to each standard. In highlighting the broader questions of science, ethics, and practice that apply in legal contexts, we hope that both the maturation of FMHA as well as the remaining gaps will become clearer. It is important to pursue continuous improvement in the legal relevance, scientific foundations, ethics specificity, and practice guidance in FMHA.

Key Words: forensic mental health assessment, standards of practice, standards of care, principles, legal decision-making

Forensic mental health assessment[1] (FMHA) has matured considerably over the last three decades. It is one form of professional service provided by psychologists in a legal context. There are other professional services provided by those who engage in forensic psychology, of course. Under the definition of "forensic psychology" used by the American Psychological Association (APA), this area comprises "professional practice by any psychologist working within any subdiscipline of psychology (e.g., clinical, developmental, social, and cognitive) when applying the scientific, technical, or specialized knowledge of

---

[1] For the purposes of this chapter, forensic mental health assessment is "evaluation that is performed by mental health professionals as part of the legal decision-making process, for the purpose of assisting the decision-maker or helping one of the litigants in using relevant clinical and scientific data" (Heilbrun, 2001, p. 3).

psychology to the law to assist in addressing legal, contractual, and administrative matters" (American Psychological Association, 2013, p. 7).

This chapter is part of a book on psychology and law. Within this broad framework, there are professional services provided by those in applied psychology (e.g., trained in areas such as clinical, counseling, or school psychology) and others by those in experimental psychology (e.g., trained in social, developmental, or cognitive psychology). There is also relevant law guiding definitions and process, applicable science providing empirical support for these activities, relevant ethical standards and guidelines, and a literature helping to guide practice.

This chapter provides a broad framework that can be used to guide one professional activity—FMHA—as part of the larger practice of forensic psychology. This practice, in turn, is part of the more expansive area of psychology and law. We also underscore the distinction between *standards of practice* and *standards of care* as part of the broader consideration of what is prescribed and proscribed in the practice of FMHA. The evolution of forensic psychology has been considered in four separate accounts over the last four decades (see Poythress, 1979; followed by Grisso, 1987; then by Otto & Heilbrun, 2002; and finally by Heilbrun & Brooks, 2010), allowing those interested to track the field's development.

No single chapter can provide a detailed review of FMHA. The next twelve chapters in this book offer a more extensive review of the content and process of FMHA, including ethical considerations and supporting science. Our overriding goal in the present chapter, by describing a larger framework and considering the question of standards of practice and care, is to provide a lens through which the remaining chapters in the area of applied pschology–law can be viewed. But chapters in the experimental pschology–law areas also contain a great deal of information important in FMHA. Topics such as cognitive biases, effective interviewing strategies for both defendants and witnesses, detecting deception, developmental maturity, human memory, sexual violence, and race and police are variously applicable to different kinds of FMHA. Although it is helpful to understand certain differences between "applied" and "experimental" areas, therefore, we remain cognizant of their important areas of overlap as well.

Principles of FMHA

The thirty-eight principles described in table 6.1 were originally derived by considering the sources of authority relevant to FMHA: *law* (statutes, case law, and administrative code), *ethics* (professional standards and guidelines), *science* (theory and scientific evidence), and *practice* (literature relevant to guidelines for good practice) (Heilbrun, 2001). This work described the shared, foundational aspects of FMHA. This question involving the common aspects of FMHA has also been addressed elsewhere (Heilbrun et al., 2009; Melton et al., 2007; Melton et al., 2018), with Melton and colleagues devoting a chapter to describing principles that apply to particular FMHA legal questions addressed in other chapters of their handbook. They distinguished forensic from thera-peutic assessment by noting differences in (1) *scope* (therapeutic assessment is broader), (2) *importance of the client's perspective* (greater in therapeutic assessment), (3) *volun-tariness* (greater in therapeutic assessment), (4) *autonomy* (greater in therapeutic assess-ment), (5) *threats to validity* (less risk of conscious, intentional distortion of self-report in therapeutic assessment), and (6) *pace and setting* (therapeutic assessment does not consistently have externally imposed time limitations). They also recommended certain procedures distinctive to FMHA when contrasted with psychological testing more gen-erally: (1) tests should be selected and applied because they are relevant to functional–legal capacities (behavior or abilities that are part of a particular legal question); (2) test results should be considered in conjunction with other sources of information, allowing a "hypothesis testing" approach; (3) when reconstructing mental state at an earlier time, deemphasize psychological testing results providing present-state information and pri-oritize other sources of information that are more directly applicable to the individual's thinking, feeling, and behavior at that earlier time; (4) use tests that have face validity as well as other forms of validity; (5) use specialized measures developed specifically for addressing the functional–legal capacities that are part of the legal question at hand; and (6) consider response style, particularly that involving the exaggeration/fabrication or the defensive minimization of self-reported symptoms.

These points are comparable to much of what is described in works focusing entirely on broad, foundational principles (Heilbrun, 2001; Heilbrun et al., 2009). In discuss-ing these principles in the present chapter, we consider them particularly in the domains of impartiality, information-gathering and data interpretation, and written communica-tion and testimony (see table 6.1). These principles were originally described in 2001 as derived and supported through multiple sources of authority—law, science, ethics, and practice—but for present purposes we focus primarily on literature that is more recent and in the areas of impartiality, information-gathering and data interpretation, and writ-ten communication and testimony.

Relevant Research

The original FMHA principles described by Heilbrun (2001) were subsequently expanded (see Heilbrun et al., 2009) to include additional principles that apply generally as well as those that are specific to individual cases. It can be useful to consider how to identify and distinguish the aspects of FMHA that are generally applicable (see table 6.1, principles 1–7; see also Simon & Gold, 2004) from those that are case-specific (table 6.1, prin-ciples 8–38). The former have implications for training and the development of special-ized knowledge and skills. The latter also may be used to appraise the quality of FMHA reports (Lander & Heilbrun, 2009), avoid errors in FMHA practice (Gardner & Murrie, 2018; Grisso, 2010), and modify practice while still preserving quality during a pandemic (Heilbrun et al., 2020).

FMHA has been disaggregated into different broader domains by others. For example, Young and Brodsky (2016) have offered four principles for effective and ethical practice in FMHA: *dignity* (in all phases of forensic work), *distance* (avoiding pitfalls of adversarial divide), *data* (information gathered should be comprehensive and scientifically informed), and *determination* (considering all reliable data and addressing possible interpretations and conclusions). Specialty competencies have been discussed in the broad domains of knowledge, skills, and attitudes (see Varela & Conroy, 2012), with each domain having several components:

- *knowledge*—statutes, case law, governmental rules, and other legal authority relevant to assessment; distinctive assessment techniques used to appraise psycholegal issues; particular rights of those being evaluated; distinctive ethical issues associated with FMHA; and awareness of different racial, ethnic, and cultural characteristics of justice-involved individuals;.
- *skills*—use of collateral information, particularly that most relevant to FMHA; considering functional–legal capacities and other aspects of law when selecting assessment methods; administering and interpreting specialized forensic assessment instruments; explaining FMHA methods and their limitations to nonpsychologists in the legal system; and communicating opinions to such individuals; and
- *attitudes*—awareness of attitudes that may influence assessment and formulation of expert opinions; acceptance of challenges to FMHA in the context of an adversarial system; acceptance of limits of psychology's role in the broader context of the legal system; resistance to considering probabilistic conclusions as facts; awareness of the limits of FMHA; and understanding the limits and potential biases of records and third-party interviews.

For present purposes, we describe aspects of the research and practice literatures in the areas of impartiality, data gathering and interpretation, and communication (report writing and testimony). More extensive research and practice support for these principles is described in the primary sources (Heilbrun, 2001; Heilbrun et al., 2009; Melton et al., 2007; Melton et al., 2018) and in the chapters that follow.

IMPARTIALITY

One of the most important aspects of FMHA is the reliance on data obtained using relevant, reliable, and valid means. For this to be achieved, there must be a reasonable degree of impartiality. Sometimes termed "objectivity," this refers to the focus on data rather than a host of other influences that can affect the selection, administration, scoring, interpretation, and communication of the findings from various sources of information.

The heightened interest in bias in FMHA has undoubtedly been influenced by the work of Daniel Kahneman (2011). In describing various cognitive biases that influence decision-making under conditions of uncertainty, he provided a useful framework for considering bias in FMHA. Three forms of bias have been considered in particular by commentators during the last decade: hindsight bias, the bias blind spot (described originally by Pronin et al., 2002), and adversarial allegiance (Murrie et al., 2009).

Hindsight bias refers to the different appraisal of evidence depending on whether the outcome is known, in effect suggesting that an event could have been predicted more accurately than it actually could. For example, consider the decision to release an individual into the community who has been hospitalized following an acquittal by reason of insanity. That decision can be informed by a risk assessment conducted prior to the release decision. But it could also be considered at a different time—say, after it is known that a released individual has killed another person shortly after release. Hindsight bias would suggest that the same information—interview transcripts, testing results, review of records, collateral interviews—would be interpreted differently when the adverse outcome is known. To test this possibility, investigators (Beltrani et al., 2018) used a 2 X 2 between-groups design to consider whether an international sample of ninety-five mental health professionals would have predicted harm to self or another person. Results demonstrated that the participants provided with information that such harm occurred were significantly more likely to indicate that they would have predicted this outcome, consistent with the operation of hindsight bias. This is particularly important in FMHA cases, in which an evaluator is asked to consider whether a decision was made in a way consistent with the standard of practice even when the outcome was tragic.

The "bias blind spot" refers to the perception that one is less susceptible to various forms of bias than others are. In a two-stage survey involving qualitative interviews with experts and structured questions of other forensic evaluators, investigators (Neal & Brodsky, 2016) found evidence for the presence of the bias blind spot in FMHA. "Debiasing" strategies proposed by the first group of participants in this study and endorsed by the second group of participants ranged from empirically supported (e.g., formal and informal education, relying on data, using procedural and structural supports) to empirically unsupported (e.g., introspection). Another of these strategies (disengaging emotionally from cases) is discussed later in this section.

The recognition of cognitive biases, including the bias blind spot, appeared to be inconsistent within a cohort of 120 randomly selected psychologists with forensic interests (MacLean et al., 2019). Although most respondents were familiar with well-known biases and reported using research-identified strategies to manage them, there were other participants with limited familiarity with actual biases who endorsed "sham" biases and coping strategies. Nearly all participants, moreover, endorsed "introspection" as a bias management strategy—although there is little evidence that it is effective for this purpose (Zappala et al., 2017).

A third form of cognitive bias in FMHA was termed "allegiance bias" (Murrie et al., 2009). Referring to the tendency to favor the side that retains an expert, the study by

Table 6.1 Principles of Forensic Mental Health Assessment

Current Principles of FMHA ($N = 38$)

GENERAL

1. Be aware of the important differences between clinical and forensic domains.

2. Obtain appropriate education, training, and experience in one's area of forensic specialization.

3. Be familiar with the relevant legal, ethics, scientific, and practice literatures pertaining to FMHA.

4. Be guided by honesty and striving for impartiality, actively disclosing the limitations on as well as the support for one's opinions.

5. Control potential evaluator bias in general through monitoring case selection, continuing education, and consultation with knowledgeable colleagues.

6. Be familiar with specific aspects of the legal system, particularly communication, discovery, deposition, and testimony.

7. Do not become adversarial, but present and defend your opinions effectively.

IN SPECIFIC CASES

Preparation

8. Identify relevant forensic issues.

9. Accept referrals only within area of expertise.

10. Decline the referral when evaluator impartiality is unlikely.

11. Clarify the evaluator's role with the attorney.

12. Clarify financial arrangements.

13. Obtain appropriate authorization.

14. Avoid playing the dual roles of therapist and forensic evaluator.

15. Determine the particular role to be played within forensic assessment if the referral is accepted.

16. Select the most appropriate model to guide data gathering, interpretation, and communication.

Data Collection

17. Use multiple sources of information for each area being assessed. Review the available background information and actively seek important missing elements.

18. Use relevance and reliability (validity) as guides for seeking information and selecting data sources.

19. Obtain relevant historical information.

20. Assess clinical characteristics in relevant, reliable, and valid ways.

21. Assess legally relevant behavior.

22. Ensure that conditions for evaluation are quiet, private, and distraction-free.

23. Provide appropriate notification of purpose and obtain appropriate authorization before beginning.

24. Determine whether the individual understands the purpose of the evaluation and the associated limits on confidentiality.

Table 6.1 *Continued*
Data Interpretation
25. Use third-party information (TPI) in assessing response style.
26. Use testing when indicated in assessing response style.
27. Use case-specific (idiographic) evidence in assessing clinical condition, functional abilities, and causal connection.
28. Use nomothetic evidence in assessing clinical condition, functional abilities, and causal connection.
29. Use scientific reasoning in assessing causal connection between clinical condition and functional abilities.
30. Carefully consider whether to answer the ultimate legal question. If it is answered, it should be in the context of a thorough evaluation clearly describing data and reasoning, and with the clear recognition that this question is in the domain of the legal decision maker.
31. Describe findings and limits so that they need change little under cross-examination.
Written Communication
32. Attribute information to sources.
33. Use plain language; avoid technical jargon.
34. Write report in sections, according to model and procedures.
Testimony
35. Base testimony on the results of the properly performed FMHA.
36. Prepare.
37. Communicate effectively.
38. Control the message. Strive to obtain, retain, and regain control over the meaning and impact of what is presented in expert testimony.

Source: From Heilbrun et al. (2009), and used with permission.

Murrie et al. (2009) suggested that allegiance bias may influence even structured tasks such as the scoring of specialized measures like the MsSOST-R and the PCL-R. A measure requiring virtually no evaluator judgment (the STATIC-99) was less affected. The influence of allegiance bias was addressed in more detail in a subsequent review (Murrie & Boccaccini, 2015), yielding two conclusions. First, the commentators suggested that working when retained by one side causes some to "drift" in the direction of the interests of the retaining party. Second, they noted that this drift was likely influenced by underlying mechanisms that are similar to the cognitive biases and unconscious heuristics that affect decision-making in other contexts. The limited independence of FMHA evaluators from referring sources has been described as one of two major sources of unreliability in FMHA (Guarnera et al., 2017)—the second being the unknown or insufficient field reliability of forensic procedures.

One strategy for controlling the influence of cognitive bias in FMHA appears to be greater structure. In an encouraging finding on this point, the use of structured assessment tools to aid evaluator judgment was found to be widespread in one international survey of

434 experts and their two most recent evaluations (Neal & Grisso, 2014). Most evaluations (74 percent) employed such tools, suggesting that their usage is common—although the large number of such structured tools (286) may also reflect the need for research attention to promote the empirical testing of the relevance and reliability of these measures. Enhancing understanding through a structured approach to FMHA also underlies the approach taken by Dror and Murrie (2018), who proposed the application of Dror's (2016) Hierarchy of Expert Performance (HEP) to questions of bias susceptibility. This yielded some domains that have meaningful data, particularly on interrater reliability, but others (e.g., reliability at the level of observations and reliability and bias susceptibility within experts) that have relatively little empirical information. Such structured analysis holds considerable promise for better understanding bias in FMHA, particularly when it is expanded (see, e.g., Zapf & Dror, 2017).

Another approach involves research on indicators of potential bias. When a study of possible bias in FMHA appraised language according to valence (positive and negative) and dominance (low and high), it appeared that reports with dominant language and stronger negative valence ratings may have reflected greater bias (Neal, 2018). Interestingly, such reports were also shorter, included fewer alternative hypotheses, and used fewer sources. This raises the possibility that greater influence by cognitive biases is inversely related to certain principles of FMHA more generally—and that reports consistent with the principles described in table 6.1 are less likely to be strongly influenced by such cognitive biases. This certainly bears further investigation.

There appears to be an unfortunate perception among many conducting FMHA that cognitive bias can be controlled through introspection or willpower (Zapf et al., 2018). There is evidence that introspection is not effective in this regard (Pronin & Kugler, 2007), although many believe that it is (Neal & Brodsky, 2016; Zapf et al., 2018), and providing an intervention to decrease reliance on introspection is also ineffective (Zappala et al., 2017). Given this, it may be useful to take a closer look at what is involved in "introspection." If it involves merely thinking about whether one is influenced by bias, then it is not surprising that even those who acknowledge the impact of cognitive bias in FMHA for others do not see it as applying to themselves. But what if introspection were expanded to include a review of one's own data conducting evaluations over a substantial period to include number of referrals, number of referrals accepted, role of referring party (e.g., defense vs. prosecution or defense vs. plaintiff, court), and, most important, the percentage of cases in which findings were favorable to the referring party? Further, what if such introspection included a consultation with a colleague who was asked to identify any possible bias from these data, and in reports? Introspection alone appears ineffective. Introspection plus data might work better. It is also noteworthy that evaluators who receive training about bias were more likely to acknowledge cognitive bias as a cause for concern, but evaluators with *more* experience were *less* likely to acknowledge cognitive bias as a cause for concern in forensic evaluation as well as in their own judgments (Zapf et al., 2018).

It has been suggested that greater empathy with evaluees can improve the quality of FMHA (Shuman & Zervopoulos, 2010). Even though these commentators distinguished between empathy arising from evaluation issues ("therapeutic empathy") and empathy arising from evaluators' personal views of these issues ("empathy bias"), their position would move evaluators away from the "emotional disengagement" that has been suggested as helping to control bias and in the direction of incorporating evaluators' personal responding to evaluees. Moreover, others advocate even more strongly for the contribution of empathy to improving the quality of FMHA (e.g., Mulay et al., 2018). There are two important considerations here. First, it is quite possible that evaluators who use empathy are actually *increasing* the influence of a certain kind of bias. For instance, one study indicated that in the context of a psychopathy assessment interview, evaluees ($N = 94$, 100% male, 57.4% Caucasian) interviewed by an evaluator using expressive empathy techniques were no more likely than those interviewed by an evaluator avoiding expressive empathy techniques to admit to past instances of misbehavior. But using expressive empathy techniques seemed to affect how the evaluators saw those they evaluated—rating them as less psychopathic, more conscientious, and engaging less in impression management. In short, it was the evaluators, not the evaluees, who were affected by the evaluators' use of expressed empathy. The second consideration, however, is that behaving in a respectful and courteous manner remains an important aspect of FMHA notwithstanding the precaution about using expressed empathy. Moreover, if there are racial, ethnic, or other cultural considerations that provide important context (see McCallum et al., 2015), it is important to understand them.

DATA GATHERING AND INTERPRETATION

The second important area to consider is the approach to gathering information and interpreting findings, translating them through explicit reasoning into relevant psycholegal opinions. One of the two major sources of inaccuracy in FMHA has been described as insufficient field reliability of forensic procedures (Guarnera et al., 2017), and one principle in table 6.1 concerns the value in using relevance and reliability (validity) as guides for seeking information and selecting data sources. This has implications for the selection of empirically supported and relevant psychological tests (Archer et al., 2016; McLaughlin & Kan, 2014), structured assessment tools (Neal & Grisso, 2014), and specialized measures (e.g., Douglas et al., 2017; Melton et al., 2018; Singh & Fazel, 2010) toward the conducting of FMHA that is more structured and more reliable (Acklin et al., 2015; Gowensmith et al., 2012; Gowensmith et al., 2017). The "field utility" of specialized forensic assessment instruments, in particular, is important because such measures are often relatively new but also highly relevant to accurately appraising functional–legal capacities (Edens & Boccaccini, 2017). As collateral information is a significant part of the FMHA process, it is also important that evaluators and consumers of FMHA be familiar with the evidence on this topic as well (see Heilbrun et al., 2015).

This information should be provided in response to questions about the sources of information used in FMHA. Such questions may be asked formally—in depositions or testimony—or less formally, by a retaining attorney inquiring about the basis for using and interpreting different sources of information in FMHA. Using a particular kind of measure, such as a psychological test or a specialized measure of response style, should be undertaken only by those who are sufficiently trained, experienced, and competent in the use of this measure to both use it correctly and explain how it works. Those without the necessary expertise in a particular measure should simply not use it in FMHA. Knowledge regarding psychological tests and measures appears to vary widely across mental health professionals (see Paulson et al., 2019), suggesting that their use in FMHA should be limited accordingly. Forensic evaluators have a responsibility to educate judges and attorneys on the importance of a scientific foundation for FMHA (Redding & Murrie, 2010). Even in *Frye*[2] jurisdictions, in which the standard for admission of expert evidence depends on the general acceptance of the techniques used to provide the evidence, there is a strong argument that expert evidence should be supported by science. In *Daubert*[3] jurisdictions, that expectation is more explicit (Shapiro et al., 2015).

COMMUNICATION: REPORT WRITING AND TESTIMONY

The third major domain of FMHA principles involves communicating the findings of evaluations, both in writing reports and providing testimony. Much of the content and process of such communication flows from earlier principles. To the extent that both reports and testimony document the general competencies and specific steps described earlier in principles 1–31, these forms of communication are more consistent with an approach described by this principled-based FMHA framework. Indeed, there are only three principles associated specifically with report writing: attribute information to sources; use plain language and avoid technical jargon; and write report in sections, according to model and procedures. The remainder of the guidance for writing FMHA reports simply involves the expectation that the FMHA will use the preceding principles as well.

One of the valuable discussions held recently involves the question of whether an evaluee's race or ethnicity should be included in a written report (Romaine & Kavanaugh, 2019). This is particularly timely in light of the broader social justice focus in the United States in 2022. The authors considered the available information and discussed both advantages and disadvantages of including this information, in light of larger principles of good FMHA practice. Although there are certain advantages to including such information—with the recognition of implicit bias, the management of stereotype threat, and the limitations of colorblind approaches among them—the authors concluded that a

---

[2] Frye v. United States, 293 F. 1013 (D.C. Cir. 1923).
[3] Daubert v. Merrell Dow Pharm., Inc., 509 U.S. 579 (1993).

decision about citing race or ethnicity should ultimately be based on a culturally competent consideration of evidence.

There is great value in the expert testimony maxims provided by Brodsky (1991, 1999, 2004, 2013; Brodsky & Gutheil, 2016). They offer both empirically supported and highly relevant guidance in communicating the results of FMHA in expert testimony. Like report writing, expert testimony is conceptualized within FMHA principles as strongly linked to previous principles. To the extent that such testimony conveys the findings of FMHA conducted by individuals who are knowledgeable and competent about the evaluation at hand, and followed the principles 1–34 in particular, then effectiveness in testimony already has a strong foundation. It can be increased by stylistic maxims—guiding not so much what is said as how it is said—with the combination of substantive and stylistic maxims capturing well the approach to effective expert testimony consistent with FMHA principles.

The call to make expert testimony evidence-based, with "evidence" referring to both relevant scientific findings and data from this particular case, has been made strongly and convincingly (see, e.g., Boccaccini et al., 2016; Conroy, 2006). This has been captured well by those who suggest that since expert testimony is about evidence, it is "not about you" (Dvoskin & Guy, 2008).

Relevant Law: Standards of Practice and Care

The description of principles of FMHA in this chapter might raise the larger question of how such principles relate to the concepts of standard of care and standard of practice in forensic psychology. There is an important distinction between these two (see Heilbrun et al., 2008, for a larger discussion). This distinction applies particularly in the context of tort litigation, in which the court must ultimately decide whether the minimally acceptable standards of professional conduct have been observed in the context of a specific dispute. A standard of practice, by contrast, reflects customary or good practice within a particular field. As such, standard of care reflects a legally mandatory and enforceable set of actions that, when not observed, can contribute to a finding of civil liability. It is defined by the legal decision maker. This definition can be informed by evidence regarding the standard of practice, which is not legally enforceable but is established by the relevant profession rather than by the law.

The framework provided by a principles-based approach to FMHA is more applicable to FMHA standards of practice than to standards of care. Principles alone would not define such a standard of practice, of course. A professional standard of practice is based on standards promulgated by the representative national organizations for the profession (e.g., *Specialty Guidelines for Forensic Psychology* [American Psychological Association, 2013]; *Ethics Guidelines for the Practice of Forensic Psychiatry* [American Academy of Psychiatry and Law, 2005; American Academy of Psychiatry and Law, 2015]; *Revised Criminal Justice Mental Health Standards* [American Bar Association, 2016]), aggregated literatures on science and practice, and other published materials provided by smaller groups down to single commentators. It should incline users toward aspirational practice rather than minimally acceptable standards. But the principles described in this chapter can contribute meaningfully to helping to describe standards of practice in FMHA. These principles were derived using sources of authority that are broadly applicable within FMHA—law, science, ethics, and practice—and have been validated and modified as forensic psychology has evolved as a specialty. They do not represent the work of a single investigator, or even a single discipline. Their breadth allows these principles to provide an overarching framework within which more specific kinds of forensic evaluations, and particular questions within law, science, ethics, or practice, may be considered.

Implications and Future Directions

Foundational principles of FMHA such as those described in this chapter can provide a useful counterbalance to the tendency to focus on increasingly specific questions. An overview of a discipline such as psychology and law must document how the field has considered the myriad questions that comprise it, certainly. But providing a broader context by using a single encompassing framework can sharpen our thinking in a different way. Ideally, that is accomplished in this chapter, which can be considered as providing a framework for specific areas described in the following chapters.

Different kinds of FMHA are distinctive in important respects. But they also have common elements, and a principles-based framework requires that we consider their common features as well as their differences. How is evaluator impartiality pursued? How do we decide what approaches, tests, and specialized measures offer the optimal combination of relevance, accuracy, and parsimony? How do we most clearly communicate FMHA findings within the context of an adversarial system? We have focused on these domains as important aggregates of the thirty-eight principles in table 6.1. There are other ways to apply a set of principles, however; by considering how the principles in table 6.1 apply to the following chapters in this section, there may be different analytic strategies that can also be applied to identifying and addressing the common issues within FMHA.

By highlighting the broader questions of science, ethics, and practice as they are applied in legal contexts, we hope that both the maturation of FMHA as well as the remaining gaps will become clearer. It is important to pursue continuous improvement in the legal relevance, scientific foundations, ethics specificity, and practice guidance in a professional activity such as FMHA. This has rarely been more evident than in 2020, when the United States experienced the twin crises of a medical pandemic and a social justice upheaval.

It raises the question of whether a principles-based framework can help with the adaptations in professional activities such as FMHA when there is sudden and substantial change in the broader society. For several reasons, we think it can. It allows the consideration of an activity that has been pursued similarly for decades (the in-person evaluation of individuals confined in detention center, jails, and prisons) that can, for public health reasons, no longer be conducted in the same way. In light of the COVID-19 pandemic, it is unclear for the long term whether in-person FMHA with confined individuals will resume following the introduction of a vaccine or effective treatment in the near future—or whether such evaluations will necessarily be conducted differently for the foreseeable future. Without even the capacity to make a reasonable prediction, it falls to the field to consider how to change the process while preserving the integrity of FMHA. This can be attempted in a reasonable way by applying a broad principles-based framework (see Heilbrun et al., 2020).

There has also been a reconsideration of social justice questions involving race, ethnicity, citizens and police, and enforcement of laws on a scale not seen in the United States for fifty years. It seems very likely that some forms of FMHA will undergo substantial revision to better accommodate cultural competence, reduce the impact of racial and ethnic discrimination, and revise the expectations of law enforcement. This may be reflected in a greater emphasis on rehabilitation for individuals who are justice-involved. There may be an acceleration in the declining trend of confining justice-involved individuals. There may be a greater emphasis on using certain kinds of FMHA activities (e.g., risk assessment) to create "action groups" for rehabilitation rather than unchanging predictions of offending risk. There may be, more generally, a movement away from using FMHA to disguise larger societal disparities in services access, toward other forms that acknowledge such disparities but are designed to lessen their impact. There will certainly be an expanding recognition of the ways in which various forms of bias can limit the accuracy of FMHA. Toward these ends, we encourage the consideration of the chapters in this book as reflecting not only what psychology and law is, but what it may become.

References

Acklin, M. W., Fuger, K., & Gowensmith, W. (2015). Examiner agreement and judicial consensus in forensic mental health evaluations. *Journal of Forensic Psychology Practice, 15*(4), 318–343.

American Academy of Psychiatry and the Law. (2005). *Ethical guidelines for the practice of forensic psychiatry.* Retrieved July 13, 1920 from https://aapl.org/ethics.htm.

American Academy of Psychiatry and the Law. (2015). AAPL practice guideline for the forensic assessment. *Journal of the American Academy of Psychiatry and the Law, 43*(2), S3–S53.

American Bar Association. (2016). *Criminal justice mental health standards* (revised). American Bar Association.

American Psychological Association. (2013). Specialty guidelines for forensic psychology. *American Psychologist, 68*(1), 7–19.

Archer, R. P., Wheeler, E. M. A., & Vauter, R. A. (2016). Empirically supported forensic assessment. *Clinical Psychology: Science and Practice, 23*(4), 348–364.

Beltrani, A., Reed, A. L., Zapf, P. A., & Otto, R. K. (2018). Is hindsight really 20/20? The impact of outcome information on the decision-making process. *International Journal of Forensic Mental Health, 17*(3), 285–296.

Boccaccini, M. T., Kwartner, P. P., & Harris, P. B. (2016). Testifying in court: Evidence-based recommendations for expert-witness testimony. In R. Jackson & R. Roesch (Eds.), *International perspectives of forensic mental health. Learning forensic assessment: Research and practice* (pp. 506–520). Routledge/Taylor & Francis Group.

Brodsky, S. L. (1991). *Testifying in court: Guidelines and maxims for the expert witness.* American Psychological Association.

Brodsky, S. L. (1999). *The expert witness.* American Psychological Association.

Brodsky, S. L. (2004). *Coping with cross-examination and other pathways to effective testimony*. American Psychological Association.

Brodsky, S. L. (2013). *Testifying in court: Guidelines and maxims for the expert witness* (2nd ed.). American Psychological Association.

Brodsky, S. L., & Gutheil, T. (2016). *The expert witness: More maxims and guidelines for testifying in court.* American Psychological Association.

Conroy, M. A. (2006). Report writing and testimony. *Applied Psychology in Criminal Justice, 2*(3), 237–260.

Douglas, T., Pugh, J., Singh, J., Savulescu, J., & Fazel, S. (2017). Risk assessment tools in criminal justice and forensic psychiatry. *European Psychiatry, 42*, 134–137.

Dror, I. E. (2016). A hierarchy of expert performance (HEP). *Journal of Applied Research in Memory and Cognition, 5*(2), 121–127.

Dror, I. E., & Murrie, D. C. (2018). A hierarchy of expert performance applied to forensic psychological assessments. *Psychology, Public Policy, and Law, 24*(1), 11–23.

Dvoskin, J. A., & Guy, L. S. (2008). On being an expert witness: It's not about you. *Psychiatry, Psychology and Law, 15*(2), 202–212.

Edens, J. F., & Boccaccini, M. T. (2017). Taking forensic mental health assessment "out of the lab" and into "the real world": Introduction to the special issue on the field utility of forensic assessment instruments and procedures. *Psychological Assessment, 29*(6), 599–610.

Gardner, B. O., & Murrie, D. C. (2018). Insanity findings and evaluation practices: A state-wide review of court-ordered reports. *Behavioral Sciences & the Law, 36*(3), 303–316.

Gowensmith, W. N., Murrie, D. C., & Boccaccini, M. T. (2012). Field reliability of competence to stand trial opinions: How often do evaluators agree, and what do judges decide when evaluators disagree? *Law and Human Behavior, 36*(2), 130–139.

Gowensmith, W. N., Sessarego, S. N., McKee, M. K., Horkott, S., MacLean, N., & McCallum, K. E. (2017). Diagnostic field reliability in forensic mental health evaluations. *Psychological Assessment, 29*(6), 692–700.

Grisso, T. (1987). The economic and scientific future of forensic psychological assessment. *American Psychologist, 42*(9), 831–839.

Grisso, T. (2010). Guidance for improving forensic reports: A review of common errors. *Psychiatry Publications and Presentations, 2*, 102–115.

Guarnera, L. A., Murrie, D. C., & Boccaccini, M. T. (2017). Why do forensic experts disagree? Sources of unreliability and bias in forensic psychology evaluations. *Translational Issues in Psychological Science, 3*(2), 143–152.

Heilbrun, K. (2001). *Principles of forensic mental health assessment*. Kluwer Academic/Plenum.

Heilbrun, K., & Brooks, S. (2010). Forensic psychology and forensic science: A proposed agenda for the next decade. *Psychology, Public Policy, and Law, 16*(3), 219–253.

Heilbrun, K., Burke, S., NeMoyer, A., Durham, K., & Desai, A. (2020). A principles-based analysis of change in forensic mental health assessment in an era of global pandemic. *Journal of the American Academy of Psychiatry and Law, 48*, 1–10.

Heilbrun, K., DeMatteo, D., Marczyk, G., & Goldstein, A. M. (2008). Standards of practice and care in forensic mental health assessment: Legal, professional, and principles-based consideration. *Psychology, Public Policy, and Law, 14*(1), 1–26.

Heilbrun, K., Grisso, T., & Goldstein, A. (2009). *Foundations of forensic mental health assessment*. Oxford University Press.

Heilbrun, K., NeMoyer, A., King, C. M., & Galloway, M. (2015). Using third party information in forensic mental health assessment: A critical review. *Court Review, 51*, 16–35.

Kahneman, D. (2011). *Thinking, fast and slow*. Farrar, Straus, and Giroux.

Lander, T. D., & Heilbrun, K. (2009). The content and quality of forensic mental health assessment: Validation of a principles-based approach. *The International Journal of Forensic Mental Health, 8*(2), 115–121.

MacLean, N., Neal, T. M. S., Morgan, R. D., & Murrie, D. C. (2019). Forensic clinicians' understanding of bias. *Psychology, Public Policy, and Law, 25*(4), 323–330.

McCallum, K. E., MacLean, N., & Gowensmith, N. (2015). The impact of defendant ethnicity on the psycho-legal opinions of forensic mental health evaluations. *International Journal of Law and Psychiatry, 39*, 6–12.

McLaughlin, J. L., & Kan, L. Y. (2014). Test usage in four common types of forensic mental health assessment. *Professional Psychology: Research and Practice, 45*(2), 128–135.

Melton, G., Petrila, J., Poythress, N. G., & Slobogin, C. (2007). *Psychological evaluations for the courts: A handbook for mental health professionals and lawyers* (3rd ed.). Guilford Press.

Melton, G., Petrila, J., Poythress, N. G., Slobogin, C., Otto, R., Mossman, D., & Condie, L. (2018). *Psychological evaluations for the courts: A handbook for mental health professionals and lawyers* (4th ed.). Guilford Press.

Mulay, A. L., Mivshek, M., Kaufman, H., & Waugh, M. H. (2018). The ethics of empathy: Walking a fine line in forensic evaluations. *Journal of Forensic Psychology Research and Practice, 18*(4), 320–336.

Murrie, D. C., & Boccaccini, M. T. (2015). Adversarial allegiance among expert witnesses. *Annual Review of Law and Social Science, 11*, 37–55.

Murrie, D. C., Boccaccini, M. T., Turner, D. B., Meeks, M., Woods, C., & Tussey, C. (2009). Rater (dis)agreement on risk assessment measures in sexually violent predator proceedings: Evidence of adversarial allegiance in forensic evaluation? *Psychology, Public Policy, and Law, 15*(1), 19–53.

Neal, T. M. S. (2018). Discerning bias in forensic psychological reports in insanity cases. *Behavioral Sciences & the Law, 36*(3), 325–338.

Neal, T. M. S., & Brodsky, S. L. (2016). Forensic psychologists' perceptions of bias and potential correction strategies in forensic mental health evaluations. *Psychology, Public Policy, and Law, 22*(1), 58–76.

Neal, T. M. S., & Grisso, T. (2014). Assessment practices and expert judgment methods in forensic psychology and psychiatry: An international snapshot. *Criminal Justice and Behavior, 41*(12), 1406–1421.

Otto, R. K., & Heilbrun, K. (2002). The practice of forensic psychology: A look toward the future in light of the past. *American Psychologist, 57*(1), 5–18.

Paulson, K. L., Straus, E., Bull, D. M., MacArthur, S. K., DeLorme, J., & Dalenberg, C. J. (2019). Knowledge and views of psychological tests among psychiatrists and psychologists. *Journal of Forensic Psychology Research and Practice, 19*(2), 112–127.

Poythress, N. G. (1979). A proposal for training in forensic psychology. *American Psychologist, 34*(7), 612–621.

Pronin, E., & Kugler, M. B. (2007). Valuing thoughts, ignoring behavior: The introspection illusion as a source of bias blind spot. *Journal of Experimental Social Psychology, 43*(4), 565–578.

Pronin, E., Lin, D. Y., & Ross, L. (2002). The bias blind spot: Perceptions of bias in self versus others. *Personality and Social Psychology Bulletin, 28*(3), 369–381.

Redding, R. E., & Murrie, D. C. (2010). Judicial decision making about forensic mental health evidence. In A. M. Goldstein (Ed.), *Forensic psychology: Emerging topics and expanding roles* (pp. 683–707). Wiley.

Romaine, C. L. R., & Kavanaugh, A. (2019). Risks, benefits, and complexities: Reporting race and ethnicity in forensic mental health reports. *International Journal of Forensic Mental Health, 18*(2), 138–152.

Shapiro, D. L., Mixon, L., Jackson, M., & Shook, J. (2015). Psychological expert witness testimony and judicial decision making trends. *International Journal of Law and Psychiatry, 42–43*, 149–153.

Shuman, D. W., & Zervopoulos, J. A. (2010). Empathy or objectivity: The forensic examiner's dilemma? *Behavioral Sciences & the Law, 28*(5), 585–602.

Simon, R. I., & Gold, L. H. (2004). *The American psychiatric publishing textbook of forensic psychiatry*. American Psychiatric Association.

Singh, J. P., & Fazel, S. (2010). Forensic risk assessment: A metareview. *Criminal Justice and Behavior, 37*(9), 965–988.

Varela, J. G., & Conroy, M. A. (2012). Professional competencies in forensic psychology. *Professional Psychology: Research and Practice, 43*(5), 410–421.

Young, G., & Brodsky, S. L. (2016). The 4 Ds of forensic mental health assessments of personal injury. *Psychological Injury and Law, 9*, 278–281.

Zapf, P. A., & Dror, I. E. (2017). Understanding and mitigating bias in forensic evaluation: Lessons from forensic science. *International Journal of Forensic Mental Health, 16*(3), 227–238.

Zapf, P. A., Kukucka, J., Kassin, S. M., & Dror, I. E. (2018). Cognitive bias in forensic mental health assessment: Evaluator beliefs about its nature and scope. *Psychology, Public Policy, and Law, 24*(1), 1–10.

Zappala, M., Reed, A. L., Beltrani, A., Zapf, P. A., & Otto, R. K. (2017). Anything you can do, I can do better: Bias awareness in forensic evaluations. *Journal of Forensic Psychology Research and Practice, 18*(1), 45–56.

CHAPTER 7

Ethics in Forensic Psychology Practice

Randy K. Otto

Abstract

Psychologists' obligations and responsibilities when providing forensic services manifest differently than when they are providing therapeutic services. The sources of authority that impose obligations upon psychologists, who psychologists' clients are, to whom psychologists owe a duty, whose interests psychologists must be consider when acting, and how obligations of privacy apply are just a few examples of this. Discussed in this chapter are key sources of authority that impose obligations upon psychologists when providing forensic services, some key distinctions in how general ethical obligations manifest in forensic settings, and recommendations for how the Ethical Principles of Psychologists and Code of Conduct of the American Psychological Association can be revised to better account for these many differences.

Key Words: forensic psychology, ethics, ethical principles, forensic roles, ethical conflicts, specialty guidelines for forensic psychology

Introduction and Background

Published in 1980, *Who Is the Client? The Ethics of Psychological Intervention in the Criminal Justice System* (Monahan) is one of the first books devoted to considering the special challenges psychologists encounter when providing clinical services in forensic and correctional settings.[1] That volume presented the report of the American Psychological Association's (APA) Task Force on the Role of Psychology in the Criminal Justice System, summarized the results of a survey of psychologists who were queried about ethical dilemmas they encountered when working in the criminal and juvenile justice systems, and

---

[1] Many commentators and practitioners distinguish between *forensic* practice/services and *clinical* practice/services (e.g., Mart, 2006). I consider this to be in error insofar as most forensic practice and service involves clinical matters and expertise, including an understanding of human development, psychopathology, and psychological assessment and interventions. A more accurate distinction is between *forensic* practice/services and *therapeutic* practice/services (also see below), and it is the ethical challenges that are encountered when providing clinical services in forensic settings and contexts that are the focus of this chapter. Ethical challenges encountered when engaged in nonclinical forensic activities (e.g., jury selection, change-of venue-polling, and teaching or researching forensic issues) are not addressed here.

included background papers examining the ethical issues confronting psychologists when working with law enforcement agencies, the courts, and adult and juvenile corrections.

As significant as this publication was, important to note is that its focus was only a subset of forensic psychology practice—criminal forensic psychology. For example, ethical challenges encountered in civil forensic psychology practice (e.g., assessing civil capacities, custody, dependency, personal injury, and worker's compensation) went unaddressed. Also important to consider was when this volume was published. The American Psychology-Law Society (Division 41 of APA) was just eleven years old (Grisso, 1991), and the American Board of Forensic Psychology, which credentials psychologists as competent to provide forensic psychological services, had been established just two years prior (1978; Kaslow, 2018); it would be eleven more years before the *Specialty Guidelines for Forensic Psychologists* was published (Committee on Ethical Guidelines for Forensic Psychologists, 1991), and there was just a handful of journals and books devoted to the science and practice of forensic psychology and psychiatry (*Bulletin of the American Academy of Psychiatry and the Law* [1969]; *Journal of Psychiatry & Law*, 1972; *Criminal Justice & Behavior*, 1973; *Law & Human Behavior*, 1977; Cooke, 1980).

In the forty years since Monahan's monograph was published, and coinciding with an increase in specialty practice in forensic psychology, considerably more attention has been paid to the unique ethical challenges associated with forensic psychology practice. Most forensic psychology texts include chapters devoted to ethics (see, e.g., Drogin et al., 2011; Jackson & Roesch, 2016; Melton et al., 2018; Otto, 2012; Weiner & Otto, 2013), and a number of books devoted to the ethics of forensic psychology and psychiatry practice are now available as well (e.g., Bush et al., 2020; Griffith, 2018; Igoumenou, 2020; Otto et al., 2017; Pirelli et al., 2017). Addressed in this chapter are (1) sources of authority in forensic psychology practice, (2) key ethical obligations and how they manifest in forensic psychology practice, and (3) areas in need of additional consideration and discussion.

Source of Authority in Forensic Psychology Practice

Regardless of their specialty, psychologists' clinical work is shaped by three sources of authority: the law, professional ethics, and "professional authority." Psychologists must be familiar with and knowledgeable about all three sources to practice any area of psychological specialty competently, including forensic psychology.

Law

The law that shapes the practice of and imposes obligations upon psychologists is varied. A nonexhaustive list of the types of law that can shape forensic psychology practice specifically includes psychology practice/licensure acts, laws regarding the specific forensic activity in which the psychologist is engaged (e.g., evaluation of child custody, testamentary capacity, competence to proceed, or criminal responsibility and treatment of a defendant adjudicated incompetent to stand trial or not guilty by reason of insanity), rules of evidence and procedure, and laws regarding privilege and other privacy matters. Critical for all psychologists to appreciate, including those providing forensic services, is that the law varies across jurisdictions. So, for example, the rules of evidence or limitations on confidential and privileged communications in one state may differ from those in another, and the definition of insanity in federal courts can differ from its definition in state courts.

Ethics

The *Ethical Principles of Psychologists and Code of Conduct* (EPPCC; American Psychological Association, 2017) shapes the practice of and imposes obligations upon psychologists, regardless of the services they are providing or the activities in which they are engaged.[2] The current version of the EPPCC tries to be all things to all psychologists: "This Ethics Code applies only to psychologists' activities that are part of their scientific, educational, or professional roles as psychologists. Areas covered include but are not limited to the clinical, counseling, and school practice of psychology; research; teaching; supervision of trainees; public service; policy development; social intervention; development of assessment instruments; conducting assessments; educational counseling; organizational consulting; *forensic activities*; program design and evaluation; and administration" (American Psychological Association, 2017, p. 2 [emphasis added]). As a condition of their membership, psychologists affiliated with the APA are bound by the EPPCC. In addition, even psychologists who are not members of the APA will likely be held to standards embodied in the EPPCC by adjudicative bodies (e.g., licensing boards and courts) and other authorities (e.g., employers) that may be asked to consider the appropriateness of their actions. For example, Fisher (2017) estimated that the psychology practice acts of approximately half of the jurisdictions in the United States make specific reference to the EPPCC and require licensed psychologists to practice in a way that is consistent with the code. Interestingly, as an example of how the law can vary across jurisdictions, the Pennsylvania Psychology Practice Act directs that psychologists must follow not only the EPPCC, but the ethics code developed and adopted by that state's Board of Psychology.[3]

The EPPCC has as its goals the welfare and protection of those served by psychologists and the education of psychologists and others about the ethical standards of the discipline (American Psychological Association, 2017). The EPPCC includes general principles, aspirations, and standards—only the latter of which the APA considers to be enforceable obligations. Although the EPPCC is sometimes specific with respect to mandating some actions (e.g., competent practice) and prohibiting others (e.g., sexual contact with clients), it most typically requires application and interpretation.

---

[2] The APA is the only US-based broad membership organization of psychologists that has published an ethics code. The other US-based broad membership organization of psychologists, the Association for Psychological Science, has not published an ethics code.

[3] 49 Pa. Code §41.61 (2020).

The EPPCC's broad focus and lack of specificity are among its greatest weaknesses. In its attempt to apply to all professional activities, the EPPCC is sometimes vague, sometimes confusing, sometimes lacking, and sometimes inconsistent. Furthermore, despite the EPPCC's statement that it applies to all professional activities, a quick reading reflects a disproportionate emphasis on the obligations of psychologists when providing therapeutic services, and a lack of consideration of how the work of psychologists who provide clinical services that are not therapeutic (e.g., forensic services) may differ. To be discussed more below, this can prove problematic insofar as some may interpret this silence as indicating we should always expect the same of psychologists who are providing forensic services as we do of psychologists providing therapeutic services.

Professional Authority

Professional or clinical authority refers to what the profession considers to be appropriate practice in the matter at hand. Historically, what the profession considered to be "appropriate practice" or "competent practice" has been established by a loosely identified consensus that was reached by review of the professional literature (e.g., journal articles, books, and presentations) and consideration of the opinions of, and the direction provided by, acknowledged experts. Although these sources are still relied upon when questions of "appropriate" or "competent" psychology practice arise, within the past quarter century organized psychology has placed an increasing emphasis on practice guidelines and similar documents (e.g., "statements" and "policies"). These documents typically represent "best practice" in a particular area and are authored by a group of content-area experts empaneled by a sponsoring organization. Some psychology practice guidelines and related documents focus on populations (e.g., older adults; men and boys; women and girls; and lesbian, gay, and bisexual persons), some focus on activities (e.g., assessing dementia and age-related cognitive decline, providing services remotely using technology, recordkeeping, evaluating children in dependency proceedings, ensuring test security, using psychometrists when conducting evaluations, and using social media), some focus on conditions (e.g., treating persons with posttraumatic stress disorder and treating persons with depression), and some focus on specialty area practice (e.g., forensic psychology). A comprehensive listing of APA's practice guidelines can be accessed at https://www.apa.org/about/policy/approved-guidelines.

Exactly how much "authority" or deference practice guidelines should be accorded is debated. For example, the APA (2015) directs that its many guidelines are, by definition, aspirational and should not be used to establish a standard of care:

> Guidelines differ from standards. Standards are mandatory and, thus, may be accompanied by an enforcement mechanism; guidelines are not mandatory, definitive, or exhaustive. Guidelines are aspirational in intent. They aim to facilitate the continued systematic development of the profession and to promote a high level of professional practice by

psychologists. A particular set of guidelines may not apply to every professional and clinical situation within the scope of that set of guidelines. As a result, guidelines are not intended to take precedence over the professional judgments of psychologists that are based on the scientific and professional knowledge of the field. (p. 824)

Of course, despite this qualification, a court, licensing board, or employer is free to use practice documents published by the APA or any other organization to establish a standard of care or inform its judgments about what appropriate psychology practice is.[4] Despite the potential of practice guidelines to identify competent work or good work, psychologists and others should not consider practice guidelines and related documents as beyond reproach and follow them reflexively. Indeed, psychologists and others should adopt a perspective of "caveat emptor" when considering how much weight to give to the many practice guidelines, policies, and statements that have been published by various organizations. This is, in part, because the adequacy of the review process that different organizations employ when it comes to developing, adopting, and publishing these documents varies considerably.

Furthermore, some organizations do not make clear the process they employ to develop and adopt these documents. The APA (2015) provides a highly detailed, seven-page description of its multitiered review process that guides development of its practice guidelines, which takes place over a number of years. In the APA process, there is preliminary consideration of the need for the proposed guidelines, review of and commentary on guideline drafts by various APA constituencies and members of the public with responses by the guidelines' authors, followed by approval by the APA's Board of Directors and Council of Representatives—all of which is documented by way of a formal recordkeeping process. The National Academy of Neuropsychology (NAN; 2021) explains its position papers and how they are developed and reviewed in the following way:

> [position papers] capture the consensus opinion for various important issues that affect our profession. The topics for these papers were initially suggested by the NAN Board of Directors, members of the NAN Policy and Planning Committee, or individual Academy members. The Policy and Planning Committee facilitated the process of writing, editing, and facilitating outside peer reviews. The NAN Board of Directors approved the final paper.

The American Academy of Clinical Neuropsychology (AACN) has published a large number of "position papers" and "policy statements" devoted to neuropsychology practice, which also have implications for forensic psychology practice. Although AACN has not published a description of its review process, the organization's president, Richard Naugle, relayed that development of these documents is coordinated by the AACN's Publications

---

[4] See, e.g., 49 Pa. Code §41.61(3)(e).

Committee, AACN members have sometimes had the opportunity to provide input on document drafts via workshops held at the organization's annual meeting, and their adoption and publication requires a majority vote by the AACN Board (R. Naugle, personal communication, February 3, 2021). Table 7.1 lists an array of practice guidelines that have been published by the APA and other psychology organizations that are of particular relevance to forensic psychology practice.

Table 7.1 A Sample of Psychology Practice Guidelines and Statements

Guidelines	Date of Publication	Organization
AACN Consensus Conference Statement on the Neuropsychological Assessment of Effort, Response Bias, and Malingering	2009	AACN
APA Guidelines for Psychological Assessment and Evaluation	2020	APA
Guidelines for Child Custody Evaluations in Family Law Proceedings	2010	APA
Guidelines for the Practice of Parenting Coordination	2012	APA
Guidelines for Psychological Evaluations in Child Protection Matters	2013	APA
Independent and Court-Ordered Forensic Neuropsychological Examinations	2003	NAN
Official Position of the American Academy of Clinical Neuropsychology on Ethical Complaints Made against Clinical Neuropsychologists During Adversarial Proceedings	2010	AACN
Policy Statement on the Presence of Third Party Observers in Neuropsychological Assessments	2001	AACN
Presence of Third-Party Observers During Neuropsychological Testing	2000	NAN
Professional Practice Guidelines for Occupationally Mandated Psychological Evaluations	2017	APA
Protecting Raw Data and Psychological Tests from Wrongful Disclosure	2009	AACN
Record Keeping Guidelines	2007	APA
Secretive Recording of Neuropsychological Testing and Interviewing	2009	NAN
Specialty Guidelines for Forensic Psychology	2013	APA
Statement on Third Party Observers in Psychological Testing and Assessment: A Framework for Decision Making	20xx	APA
Symptom Validity Assessment: Practice Issues and Medical Necessity	2005	NAN
Test Security	2000	NAN

Notes. AACN, American Academy of Clinical Neuropsychology statements and policies may be found at Position Papers and Policies—AACN (theaacn.org); APA, American Psychological Association guidelines may be found at www.apa.org; NAN, National Academy of Neuropsychology position papers may be found at www.nanonline.org.

Key Ethical Obligations of Psychologists Providing Forensic Services

Because the EPPCC applies to psychologists when engaged in any professional activity, regardless of the service they are providing, all the standards, aspirations, obligations, and prohibitions in the EPPCC apply to psychologists when providing forensic services. In many circumstances this is not a problem as there are few, if any, meaningful differences between forensic psychology practice and other specialty practice areas. There are, however, some matters for which forensic psychology practice differs greatly, or for which the application of the general ethical requirement deserves special consideration. These matters are discussed next.

Competence

Standard 2 of the EPPCC requires that, with the exception of emergencies and other limited circumstances, psychologists only provide services for which they have the requisite competence. There are, of course, knowledge and skills that are generic to all clinical practice. For example, regardless of their particular specialty, all psychologists who provide clinical services must be knowledgeable about and skilled in (1) working with population(s) to whom they provide services, (2) the clinical conditions they assess or treat, and (3) the techniques or tools they employ. But, as is the case with all psychological specialties, there are knowledge and skills that are either unique or more relevant to forensic psychology practice.

Given the environment in which forensic psychologists operate, perhaps most obvious in terms of specialized knowledge is an understanding of the law and legal process (Cox & Brodsky, 2018; Massey, 2017; Melton et al., 2018). Whereas Standard 2.01(f) of the EPPCC references the need for psychologists to be familiar with the law that governs their role when providing forensic services, Guideline 2.04 of the Specialty Guidelines for Forensic Psychology (SGFP) offers more specific direction that psychologists should be knowledgeable about "legal and professional standards, laws, rules, and precedents that govern their participation in legal proceedings and that guide the impact of their services on service recipients" (American Psychological Association, 2013, p. 9). This presumably includes the law of the jurisdiction in which the psychologist is practicing that is relevant to the legal matter at hand (e.g., child custody, testamentary capacity, civil commitment, competence to stand trial, and criminal responsibility), relevant rules of evidence and civil and criminal procedure (e.g., rules pertaining to expert testimony and its admissibility), and the law regulating the practice of psychology more generally (e.g., licensing acts).

Given the disproportionate amount of forensic practice that is devoted to psychological assessment (Borum & Otto, 2000) and the unique assessment questions that psychologists are presented with in forensic settings, specialized knowledge of assessment matters is likely critical, as is knowledge of the conditions experienced by special forensic populations they may treat (e.g., victims of crime and various offender populations).

Forensic Roles and Relationships

In most cases, psychologists providing forensic services owe duties to many people and organizations including, but not limited to, their employer, persons they are evaluating or treating, and the professionals or organizations that hire them. Critical to appreciate and communicate to all to whom the psychologist provides forensic services is that the specific duties owed vary as a function of role and relationship.

UNDERSTANDING AND COMMUNICATING ONE'S ROLE AND ATTENDANT RESPONSIBILITIES

There is perhaps no issue that is more important than "role" when it comes to providing forensic services. This is because the psychologist's role directly impacts what clients and others expect of the psychologist. Most clinical services many psychologists provide are therapeutic in nature. As a result, many people picture a psychologist and client establishing a strong therapeutic alliance and voluntarily working together in order facilitate some mutually identified treatment goals that likely include improvement in some aspects of the client's functioning and adjustment. The nature of this relationship stands in marked contrast to relationships that often result when psychologists provide forensic services (Lamade, 2017; Neal, 2017).

In the case of forensic evaluation, for example, the assessment is typically initiated by a third party (e.g., attorney, court, insurer, and employer), the examinee may not be participating voluntarily, confidentiality and privilege are limited or nonexistent, and the goal of the evaluation is not improving the examinee's functioning and adjustment but, rather, informing a third party (e.g., court, attorney, and disability insurer) about some aspects of the examinee's emotional, behavioral, or cognitive functioning as it relates to some issue in dispute. As a result, it is best that the person undergoing evaluation not be considered the client but, rather, the examinee. The client is the third party who initiated the psychologist's involvement in the matter. Although psychologists still owe forensic examinees many duties (e.g., respect, competence, diligence, and privacy), the duties they have are considerably different from the duties owed to persons voluntarily seeking treatment.

Even when psychologists provide treatment in forensic contexts, their relationships with the people they treat (rightfully considered clients/patients) are much different than the relationships they establish with clients/patients they treat in nonforensic contexts (Glancy & Simpson, 2018; Wechsler, 2017). In forensic contexts, treatment may be involuntary, confidentiality and privilege may be more limited, and treatment goals may not be the client's/patient's insofar as some may be dictated by concerns in addition to any that that the client may have (e.g., in the case of a defendant who has been adjudicated incompetent and is treated with the goal of returning them to court, or in the case of a parent who has abused or neglected a child and is being treated with the goal of remedying deficits so that the child can be returned).

Some appreciation of these differences, including that not all persons with whom psychologists interact are clients, is reflected in EPPCC Standard 3.07:

> When psychologists agree to provide services to a person or entity at the request of a third party, psychologists attempt to clarify at the outset of the service the nature of the relationship with all individuals or organizations involved. This clarification includes the role of the psychologist (e.g., therapist, consultant, diagnostician, or expert witness), an identification of who is the client, the probable uses of the services provided or the information obtained, and the fact that there may be limits to confidentiality. (American Psychological Association, 2017, p. 6)

Given the many ways forensic services differ from therapeutic services and the resulting confusion that recipients of forensic services (e.g., examinees, attorneys, courts, and employers) may experience, Guideline 6 of the SGFP directs psychologists to clarify their role and the nature and extent of services "because the methods and procedures of forensic practitioners are complex and may not be accurately anticipated by the recipients of forensic services, forensic practitioners strive to inform service recipients about recipients about the nature and parameters of the services to be provided" (American Psychological Association, 2013, p. 12).

AVOIDING PROBLEMATIC OR INAPPROPRIATE ROLES

EPPCC Standard 3.06 directs that "Psychologists refrain from taking on a professional role when personal, scientific, professional, legal, financial, or other interests or relationships could reasonably be expected to (1) impair their objectivity, competence, or effectiveness in performing their functions as psychologists or (2) expose the person or organization with whom the professional relationship exists to harm or exploitation" (American Psychological Association, 2017, p. 6). Similar direction is provided in the SGFP: "Forensic practitioners refrain from taking on a professional role when personal, scientific, professional, legal, financial, or other interests or relationships could reasonably be expected to impair their impartiality, competence, or effectiveness, or expose others with whom a professional relationship exists to harm" (American Psychological Association, 2013, p. 9). Personal beliefs or experiences and prior relationships with retaining parties or potential examinees or patients are among the many factors that might present conflicts for psychologists when providing forensic services. For example, it may not be possible for some psychologists who are opposed to the death penalty to function objectively in capital proceedings. Or, some psychologists may have had personal experiences that render them unable to provide services in certain forensic contexts objectively, competently, and without risking harm to those to whom they owe a duty. It is the psychologist's obligation to ensure that their work in a forensic matter will not be negatively impacted by such beliefs, experiences, or preexisting relationships.

MANAGING MULTIPLE ROLES AND RELATIONSHIPS

According to the EPPCC, multiple relationships occur when "a psychologist is in a professional role with a person and (1) at the same time is in another role with the same person, (2) at the same time is in a relationship with a person closely associated with or related to the person with whom the psychologist has the professional relationship, or (3) promises to enter into another relationship in the future with the person or a person closely associated with or related to the person" (American Psychological Association, 2017, p. 6). The SGFP caution of the potential conflicts and threats to objectivity that can result from multiple relationships, and EPPCC Standard 4.02 prohibits multiple relationships that "could reasonably be expected to impair the psychologist's objectivity, competence, or effectiveness in performing his or her functions as a psychologist, or otherwise risks exploitation or harm to the person with whom the professional relationship exists" (American Psychological Association, 2017, p. 6).

MIXING THERAPEUTIC AND FORENSIC EXAMINATION ROLES

A practice that has long been recognized as having the potential for complications is mixing the roles of treatment provider and forensic examiner (Greenberg & Shuman, 1997, 2007; Strasburger et al., 1997). Because of the different expectations associated with these disparate roles, there appears to be a consensus that such should be avoided whenever possible. Guideline 4.02.01 of the SGFP (American Psychological Association, 2013) directs that:

> Providing forensic and therapeutic psychological services to the same individual or closely related individuals involves multiple relationships that may impair objectivity and/or cause exploitation or other harm. Therefore, when requested or ordered to provide either concurrent or sequential forensic and therapeutic services, forensic practitioners are encouraged to disclose the potential risk and make reasonable efforts to refer the request to another qualified provider. If referral is not possible, the forensic practitioner is encouraged to consider the risks and benefits to all parties and to the legal system or entity likely to be impacted, the possibility of separating each service widely in time, seeking judicial review and direction, and consulting with knowledgeable colleagues. When providing both forensic and therapeutic services, forensic practitioners seek to minimize the potential negative effects of this circumstance. (p. 11)

That some state Boards of Psychology proscribe a mixing of therapeutic and forensic roles in some circumstances provides some evidence of the consensus that has developed around this issue. For example, Florida Administrative Code §64B19-18.007(3) directs:

> It is a conflict of interest for a psychologist who has treated a minor or any of the adults involved in a custody or visitation action to perform a forensic evaluation for the purpose of recommending with which adult the minor should reside, which adult should have custody, or what visitation should be allowed. Consequently, a psychologist who treats a minor or any of the adults involved in a custody or visitation action may not also perform a forensic evaluation for custody, residence or visitation of the minor.

This perspective has not gone without criticism, however. Heltzel (2007) argued that calls for such prohibitions are without foundation and contrary to the public interest. Acknowledging that treating psychologists will likely be supportive of and empathic toward their patients, Heltzel (2007) maintained that it is unreasonable to assume that the therapeutic relationship equates to bias and impaired objectivity, "A diagnostician-therapist, whether or not providing testimony, is ethically required to maintain reasonable professional objectivity, which should not be incompatible with a supportive, accepting and empathic attitude" (p. 126). In addition, argued Heltzel, the EPPCC standards related to impaired objectivity and the legal system's safeguard of cross-examination combine to prevent and facilitate the exposure of tainted testimony of a treating professional, "If either the plaintiff's evaluator-therapist or the defendant's consultant-evaluator selectively presents only favorable or distorted facts, or makes a weak argument, this will usually become evident to the trier-of-fact. The legal system does not assume unbiased or neutral testimony" (p. 126).

MIXING FORENSIC ROLES

Another matter regarding multiple roles, which has received less attention, and about which there remains some disagreement, is that of mixing the roles of forensic examiner and litigation consultant. Some commentators argue that it is inappropriate for psychologists to offer expert testimony in a legal proceeding in which they are also serving as a litigation consultant by way of assisting the retaining attorney in matters including but not limited to case development, witness selection, jury selection, and preparation of direct- and cross-examination questions for lay and expert witnesses (see, e.g., Brodsky, 1999; Martindale, 2006a, 2006b, 2007). The reasoning underlying this perspective is that because the responsibilities that accompany each role are so divergent, taking on both roles presents too great a risk of harming others by impairing the psychologist's efficacy and/or objectivity. Martindale identified as at least one potential harm that the expert's credibility with the fact-finder can be compromised when engaged in both sets of activities in the same matter, and he expressed skepticism about experts' abilities to accurately assess whether their objectivity is impaired (personal communication, February 5, 2021).

DeMeir (personal communication, February 1, 2021) offered an alternative perspective and argued that a mixing of testifying expert and litigation consultant roles may be appropriate in some systems, including the military courts martial cases in which he participates. He asserted that it is wrong to automatically assume that the litigation consultant's role is to assist retaining counsel in "winning" the case, and that the consultant's role and perspective may actually be not too different from that of the testifying expert:

> There is the idea that if I am an evaluator, I am independent, but if I am a consultant, I am there to help one side win. This is overly simplistic. We know that many evaluators lean toward one side or the other (as a result of adversarial allegiance, or even their personal reactions to the discovery material). Moreover, I think it is an oversimplification to say that a consultant is there to help one side "win." I see my role as helping the attorneys understand the evidence, and sometimes, the best way to present (or otherwise cope with) the evidence. But, that does not necessarily mean I want to see that side win. (R. DeMier, personal communication, February 1, 2021)

Similarly, in describing her experience in military courts martial, Connell (personal communication, February 4, 2021) noted that it is general practice in these proceedings that the retained expert will assume the roles of both litigation consultant and potential testifying expert, all involved in the proceedings understand this to be the case, and both the prosecution and defense typically have available to them "evenly qualified experts." With respect to the heightened potential for bias or impaired objectivity that results from adopting these two roles, Connell (2019) identified experts' concerns about developing reputations as being biased in the relatively small community of military proceedings as serving some preventive function, and noted that just as testifying experts are expected to take steps to control other sources of bias that may operate, they can take steps to counteract any bias that may result from providing litigation consultation.

Dale and Gould (2014) argued that the appeal of the bright-line delineation of the roles of testifying expert and litigation consultant made by commentators like Brodsky and Martindale lies, in part, in its simplicity. They offered several arguments in support of their perspective that providing both testimony and litigation consultation is not necessarily problematic, including that "role concepts are not sufficiently precise for the kinds of differentiated, ethical decision-making needed in the forensic context" (p. 20), not all multiple roles and relationships are prohibited, the risk of bias and impaired efficacy does not necessarily translate into bias and impaired efficacy, such practices may be more accurately conceptualized as multiple activities rather than multiple roles, and there may not always be such a bright line between the services that a testifying expert and litigation consultant offer.

Appreciating definitions and subtleties is important insofar as one psychologist's opinion of what is appropriate to do as a testifying expert may be another's unethical mix of the testifying and litigation consultant roles. For example, many psychologists consider integral to one's responsibility as an examining and testifying expert to discuss with retaining counsel how and why the opinions they formed are different from opinions offered by the expert retained by opposing counsel. In doing this, the testifying expert may identify for the attorney problems with the other expert's approaches and opinions. To the degree that this might involve criticizing the other expert's work (e.g., "she used a test inappropriately" and "he did not offer a factual basis for the diagnosis offered") might some psychologists consider this to constitute inappropriate litigation consultation?

The distinction between litigation consultation and assisting retaining counsel to understand differences between one's opinions and the opinions offered by other experts may come down to a matter of degree, or exactly where one is comfortable drawing a line. For example, what if the above-referenced expert develops a list of questions retaining counsel can ask her at trial that will make clear to the fact-finder the adequacy of her work and the shortcomings of the other expert's work—is that inappropriate litigation consultation by a testifying expert? No, how about this? What if the expert develops a list of questions the retaining attorney can ask the *other* expert at trial that will demonstrate the shortcomings of his evaluation—is that inappropriate litigation consultation by a testifying expert? No, how about this? What if the expert identifies for the retaining attorney the type of juror who will be most receptive to her opinions—is that inappropriate litigation consultation by a testifying expert? No, how about this? What if the expert sits at the retaining attorney's table during jury selection and presents counsel with questions to ask prospective jurors—is that inappropriate litigation consultation by a testifying expert? No, how about this? What if the expert, immediately before the trial starts, coaches or works with the litigant she examined on how to act and respond when testifying—is that inappropriate litigation consultation by a testifying expert? At *some* point, all readers probably answered at least one of these questions in the affirmative.

There is no obvious way to rectify these different perspectives among those who hold them. This, in part, is because the EPPCC prohibits only a subset of multiple relationships (i.e., those that impair the psychologist's efficacy or objectivity and risk harm to others), and the discussion above makes clear that psychologists apply and interpret this prohibition differently. Of course, although there may be some circumstances in which it may not be feasible, by refusing to adopt multiple roles psychologists will never risk harm, impaired objectivity, or impaired efficacy that can result from them. At a minimum, however, if psychologists take on the dual roles of therapist and forensic examiner, or litigation consultant and testifying expert, they should communicate this to the judge or jury and the risk of harm resulting from impaired efficacy and objectivity.

Striving for Independence, Objectivity, and Accuracy

Principle C of the EPPCC directs, "Psychologists seek to promote accuracy, honesty, and truthfulness in the science, teaching, and practice of psychology. In these activities psychologists do not steal, cheat or engage in fraud, subterfuge, or intentional misrepresentation of fact" (American Psychological Association, 2017, pp. 3–4). These obligations are particularly significant when providing forensic services given some of the special challenges associated with the adversarial process.

When evaluating persons involved in litigation, psychologists are often retained by one of two parties. The "pull" resulting from working with an attorney who is advocating vigorously for her client can be significant. Yet, despite this affiliation, psychologists, when describing the examinee's functioning, are obligated to work independently and offer opinions that are objective and unbiased. Guideline 11.01 of the SGFP (American Psychological Association, 2017), in part, directs:

> When providing reports and other sworn statements or testimony in any form, forensic practitioners strive to present their conclusions, evidence, opinions, or other professional products in a fair manner. Forensic practitioners do not, by either commission or omission, participate in misrepresentation of their evidence, nor do they participate in partisan attempts to avoid, deny or subvert the presentation of evidence contrary to their own position or opinion (EPPCC Standard 5.01). This does not preclude forensic practitioners from forcefully presenting the data and reasoning upon which a conclusion or professional product is based. (p. 16)

Remaining nonpartisan and presenting one's work and opinions fairly can be especially challenging in forensic contexts given the sometimes highly adversarial nature, subtle and not-so-subtle affiliation/allegiance effects (e.g., Murrie & Boccaccini, 2015; Otto, 1989) and the tendency of some who retain psychologists to see them as "on their side." When providing forensic services, psychologists must do their best to practice in a way that minimizes threats to objectivity, impartiality, and fairness.

Ensuring Transparency and Facilitating Review of One's Work

Because of the very nature of adversarial forums, much of what is asserted or has occurred is disputed. Psychologists providing forensic services should expect that their work will always be reviewed, and sometimes challenged by those who are not happy with their findings and opinions. Because of the obligations of objectivity and impartiality, psychologists should conduct themselves, and document what they do, in a way that facilitates review and critique of their work. Too frequently, psychologists who are providing forensic services, perhaps either as a result of getting swept up in the adversarial process or out of concern that the adequacy of their work will be criticized, fail to meet these obligations.

The EPPCC imposes specific obligations upon psychologists when it comes to documenting their work, and APA's Record Keeping Guidelines provide additional guidance to psychologists that is of some relevance to forensic practice. Standard 6.01 of the EPPCC directs that

> psychologists create, and to the extent the records are under their control, maintain, disseminate, store, retain, and dispose of records and data relating to their professional and scientific work in order to (1) facilitate provision of services later by them or by other professionals . . . (4) ensure accuracy of billing and payments, and (5) ensure compliance with law. (American Psychological Association, 2017, p. 9)

APA's Record Keeping Guidelines (American Psychological Association, 2007) advise that (1) one purpose of records is to document the psychologist's decision making, (2) what is contained in the record can vary as a function of the psychologist's activity or service, and (3) psychologists maintain records to ensure their accuracy and facilitate their use by others who have a right to access them.

The SGFP provide recordkeeping guidance specific to forensic psychology practice. Guideline 10.06 directs psychologists to document all data they have considered when providing forensic services in such a way as to facilitate review and scrutiny by others. Guideline 10.08 directs that psychologists, when presented with a lawful request for records of their work, provide any and all records that "might reasonably be related" to any the opinions they have or will express (American Psychological Association, 2013, p. 16).

Further reflecting the importance of transparency and affirmative disclosure when proving forensic services are a number of SGFP guidelines (American Psychological Association, 2013) that provide guidance about what psychologists should communicate to others when memorializing their work in writing (e.g., reports) or orally (e.g., testifying). Included in Guidelines 11.02, 11.03, and 11.04 of the SGFP are directions to:

- "distinguish observations, inferences, and conclusions,"
- "explain the relationship between their expert opinions and the legal issues and facts of the case at hand,"
- "disclose all sources of information obtained,"
- "identify the source of each piece of information that was considered and relied upon in formulating a particular conclusion, opinion or other professional product," and
- "offer a complete statement of all relevant opinions that they formed within the scope of their work on the case, the basis and reasoning underlying the opinions, the salient data or other information that was considered in forming the opinions, and an indication of any additional evidence that may be used in support of the opinions to be offered." (pp. 16–17).

Psychologists who follow the guidance provided by the SGFP make it easy for interested persons (e.g., attorneys, judges, jurors, and examinees) to identify the data they did and did not consider, gather, or develop and understand the opinions they formed and the underlying logic. This, in turn, facilitates both acceptance of sound opinions and critiques or rejection of unfounded ones.

Ethical Concerns in Need of Additional Discussion and Consideration

For the benefit of forensic psychology and those who forensic psychologists serve, there remain some key ethical issues that are in need of further discussion and consideration. Some of the most pressing matters, which would ideally be addressed as the EPPCC is undergoing revision, are discussed below.

Reconsidering Whether the EPPCC Should Attempt to Be All Things to All Psychologists

The current version of the EPPCC tries to be all things to the public and all psychologists including but not limited to teachers/instructors, human subjects researchers, animal researchers, social psychology researchers, organizational consultants, treatment providers, and forensic service providers. This results in too much of the existing code (1) being irrelevant to part of its intended audience, (2) lacking clarity and specificity, (3) requiring too much interpretation, and, at times, (4) being inconsistent. The APA should consider the feasibility of developing more than one ethics code, perhaps shaped by general activity (e.g., teaching/instruction, research, clinical service provision, and organization consultation).[5] At a minimum, this would facilitate a more focused and detailed consideration of many of the matters that prove perplexing for forensic psychologists (and might benefit other psychology specialties and pursuits in similar ways as well).

Getting Clearer on What It Means to Avoid Harm

Standard 3.04 of the EPPCC directs that "Psychologists take reasonable steps to avoid harming their clients/patients . . . organizational clients, and others with whom they work, and to minimize harm where it is foreseeable and avoidable" (American Psychological Association, 2017, p. 6). Yet, in many cases, the work of forensic psychologists harms people. As a result of forensic psychological evaluations, parents in dependency proceedings can lose the right to parent their children (the children, of course, may be helped), respondents in sexually violent predator proceedings may lose their liberty for extended periods of time (society, of course, will be protected from (potential) future acts of violence), and criminal defendants may be sentenced to death and executed (the criminal justice system, of course, will have been assisted in carrying out its mission). Writing that death penalty proceedings are part of "an inequitable legal process whose inconsistencies

---

[5] Although I have no belief the APA would consider this recommendation at this point in time, I nonetheless offer it in order to begin a conversation about the possibility.

lethally violate the human rights of defendants" (p. 61) Fisher (2013) has queried whether the EPPCC should be interpreted as barring psychologists' participation in certain aspects of death penalty proceedings.

In discussing the ethics of a psychologist who assisted law enforcement agents to develop a plan that would play on the emotional vulnerability of a suspected spy and facilitate her capture, Grisso (2001) described the belief that psychologists must never do harm as "overly simplistic" (p. 458). Grisso made a number of important points, including that psychologists have obligations to both individuals and society, psychologists do not always function as healers, and psychologists' clients are sometimes organizations. Appelbaum (1990), a forensic psychiatrist, was even bolder. He wrote that forensic evaluations, in which the examinee is not rightfully considered the client, are only useful (to the legal process) if they have the potential to harm the examinee. The same rings true for forensic psychological evaluations and other forensic activities in which psychologists may engage. That psychologists sometimes cause harm and should be expected to cause harm when acting ethically should be acknowledged explicitly in the ethics code, and the circumstances in which causing harm is acceptable and unacceptable should be better delineated. Accomplishing this may be facilitated by suggestions I include immediately below.

Distinguishing Between Different Types of Service Recipients and Associated Duties and Obligations

In addition to "client" and "patient," the EPPCC uses many terms to refer to persons or entities that may receive clinical services from psychologists, including forensic services:

- "those with whom they work,"
- "those with whom they interact professionally,"
- "organizations,"
- "populations,"
- "individuals,"
- "organizational clients,"
- "others,"
- "persons who are legally incapable of providing informed consent or for whom testing is mandated by law or governmental regulations,"
- "couples,"
- "families,"
- "legally authorized persons,"
- "groups," and
- "persons with questionable capacity to consent."

Unfortunately, nowhere in the EPPCC are these various terms defined, despite what appear to be obvious distinctions and differences. More detailed discussion of these terms is important insofar as it makes explicit that the client is not always a person, and the person who receives a service from and interacts with the psychologist is not always the client. This, in turn, will facilitate a discussion of how the obligations and duties owed by the psychologists to various persons or entities vary as a function of the nature of the relationship and associated role.

Summary

What is required of psychologists when providing forensic services is informed by the law, professional authority, and professional ethics. Psychologists are obligated to be familiar with these many and varied sources of authority that can impact their work. In many circumstances, the clinical activities of psychologists, regardless of their specialty practice, are similar enough so that the general guidance and discussion offered in the EPPCC is adequate, can be applied in the forensic context, and does not prove problematic. Many key ethical obligations referenced in the EPPCC have clear application in forensic practice. In some cases, however, psychologists providing forensic services encounter special challenges and circumstances so that the EPPCC falls short. For some issues, the EPPCC fails to provide adequate guidance and, for others, the EPPCC offers conflicting guidance or can be interpreted as prohibiting what should be considered appropriate practice. As the current version of the EPPCC undergoes revision, these various shortcomings should be identified and addressed. In the meantime, psychologists providing forensic services should appreciate the many ways the forensic practice differs from other clinical specialty practice in order to ensure that they consistently meet obligations imposed upon them by the law, professional authority, and professional ethics.

References

American Psychological Association. (2007). Record keeping guidelines. *American Psychologist, 62*(9), 993–1004.

American Psychological Association. (2013). Specialty guidelines for forensic psychology. *American Psychologist, 68*(1), 7–19.

American Psychological Association. (2015). Professional practice guidelines: Guidance for developers and users. *American Psychologist, 70*(9), 823–831.

American Psychological Association. (2017). *Ethical principles of psychologists and code of conduct.* https://www.apa.org/ethics/code/ethics-code-2017.pdf

Appelbaum, P. S. (1990). The parable of the forensic psychiatrist: Ethics and the problem of doing harm. *International Journal of Law and Psychiatry, 13*(4), 249–259.

Borum, R., & Otto, R. (2000). Advances in forensic assessment and treatment: An overview and introduction to the special issue. *Law and Human Behavior, 24*(1), 1–7.

Brodsky, S. L. (1999). *The "expert" expert witness: More maxims and guidelines for testifying in court.* American Psychological Association.

Bush, S. S., Connell, M. A., & Denney, R. L. (2020). *Ethical practice in forensic psychology: A guide for mental health professionals* (2nd ed.). American Psychological Association.

Committee on Ethical Guidelines for Forensic Psychologists. (1991). Specialty guidelines for forensic psychologists. *Law and Human Behavior, 15*(6), 655–665.

Connell, M. (2019). The varied roles of the psychologist in military proceedings. In C. Stein & J. N. Younggren (Eds.), *Forensic psychology in military courts* (pp. 103–124). American Psychological Association.

Cooke, G. (1980). *The role of the forensic psychologist.* C. C. Thomas.

Cox, J., & Brodsky, S. L. (2018). Objectivity and boundaries of competence as ethical issues in forensic assessment. In E. E. H. Griffith (Ed.), *Ethics challenges in forensic psychiatry and psychology practice* (pp. 67–83). Columbia University Press.

Dale, M. D., & Gould, J. W. (2014). Science, mental health consultants, and attorney-expert relationships in child custody. *Family Law Quarterly, 48*(1), 1–34.

Drogin, E. Y., Datillio, F. M., Sadoff, R. L., & Gutheil, T. G. (2011). *Handbook of forensic assessment: Psychological and psychiatric perspectives.* John Wiley & Sons.

Fisher, C. B. (2013). Human rights and psychologists' involvement in assessments related to death penalty cases. *Ethics & Behavior, 23*(1), 58–61.

Fisher, C. B. (2017). *Decoding the ethics code: A practical guide for psychologists* (4th ed.). SAGE.

Glancy, G. D., & Simpson, A. (2018). Ethical dilemmas in correctional institutions. In E. E. H. Griffith (Ed.), *Ethics challenges in forensic psychiatry and psychology practice* (pp. 101–115). Columbia University Press.

Greenberg, S. A., & Shuman, D. (1997). Irreconcilable conflict between therapeutic and forensic roles. *Professional Psychology: Research and Practice, 28*(1), 50–57.

Greenberg, S. A., & Shuman, D. W. (2007). When worlds collide: Therapeutic and forensic roles. *Professional Psychology: Research and Practice, 38*(2), 129–132.

Griffith E. E. H. (Ed.). (2018). *Ethics challenges in forensic psychiatry and psychology practice.* Columbia University Press.

Grisso, T. (1991). A developmental history of the American Psychology-Law Society. *Law and Human Behavior, 15*(3), 213–231.

Grisso, T. (2001). Reply to Shafer: Doing harm ethically. *Journal of the American Academy of Psychiatry and the Law, 29*(4), 457–460.

Heltzel, T. (2007). Compatibility of therapeutic and forensic roles. *Professional Psychology: Research and Practice, 38*(2), 122–128.

Igoumenou, A. (Ed.). (2020). *Ethical issues in clinical forensic psychiatry.* Springer.

Jackson, R., & Roesch, R. (Eds.). (2016). *Learning forensic assessment: Research and practice* (2nd ed.). Routledge.

Kaslow, F. W. (2018). The founding and early years of the American Board of Forensic Psychology. In T. Grisso & S. Brodsky (Eds.), *The roots of psychology and law: A narrative history* (pp. 195–206). Oxford University Press.

Lamade, R. (2017). Identifying the client and professional services. In G. Pirelli, R. A. Beatty, & P. A. Zapf (Eds.), *The ethical practice of forensic psychology: A casebook* (pp. 64–88). Oxford University Press.

Mart, E. G. (2006). *Getting started in forensic psychology practice.* John Wiley & Sons.

Martindale, D. A. (2006a). Consultants and role delineation. *The Matrimonial Strategist, 24*(4), 3–4, 8.

Martindale, D. A. (2006b). Consultants and further role delineation. *The Matrimonial Strategist, 24*(7), 6.

Martindale, D. A. (2007). Forensic consultation in litigated custody disputes. *Journal of Psychiatry and Law, 35*(3), 281–298.

Massey, C. (2017). Competence. In G. Pirelli, R. A. Beatty, & P. A. Zapf (Eds.), *The ethical practice of forensic psychology: A casebook* (pp. 32–53). Oxford University Press.

Melton, G. B., Petrila, J., Poythress, N. G., Slobogin, C., Otto, R. K., Mossman, D., & Condie, L. O. (2018). *Psychological evaluations for the courts: A handbook for mental health professionals and lawyers* (4th ed.). Guilford Press.

Monahan, J. (Ed.). (1980). *Who is the client? The ethics of psychological intervention in the criminal justice system.* American Psychological Association. https://psycnet.apa.org/doiLanding?doi=10.1037%2F10051-000

Murrie, D. C., & Boccaccini, M. T. (2015). Adversarial allegiance among expert witnesses. *Annual Review of Law and Social Science, 11*(1), 37–55

National Academy of Neuropsychology. (2021). *Position papers.* https://www.nanonline.org/nan/Professional_Resources/Position_Papers/NAN/_ProfessionalResources/Position_Papers.aspx?hkey=71602191-716a-4375-8eb8-4b4e6a071e3a

Neal, T. (2017). Identifying the forensic psychologist role. In G. Pirelli, R. A. Beatty, & P. A. Zapf (Eds.), *The ethical practice of forensic psychology: A casebook* (pp. 1–15). Oxford University Press.

Otto, R. K. (1989). Bias and expert testimony of mental health professionals in adversarial proceedings: A preliminary investigation. *Behavioral Sciences & the Law, 7*(2), 267–273.

Otto, R. K. (Ed.). (2012). *Forensic psychology* (2nd ed.). John Wiley & Sons.

Otto, R., Goldstein, A. M., & Heilbrun, K. (2017). *Ethics in forensic psychology practice.* John Wiley & Sons.

Pirelli, G., Beatty, R. A., & Zapf, P. A. (Eds.). (2017). *The ethical practice of forensic psychology: A casebook.* Oxford University Press.

Strasburger, L., Gutheil, T., & Brodsky, A. (1997). On wearing two hats: Role conflict in serving as both psychotherapist and exert witness. *American Journal of Psychiatry, 154*(4), 448–456.

Wechsler, H. (2017). Treatment. In G. Pirelli, R. A. Beatty, & P. A. Zapf (Eds.), *The ethical practice of forensic psychology: A casebook* (pp. 300–320). Oxford University Press.

Weiner, I., & Otto, R. K. (Eds.). (2013). *Handbook of forensic psychology* (4th ed.). John Wiley & Sons.

Forensic Report Writing: Proposing a Research Agenda

Richart L. DeMier *and* Daniel A. Krauss

Abstract

Most guidance for forensic report writing lacks empirical support. Current recommendations have largely been derived from ethical principles, the professional literature, and, in some cases, personal experiences. This chapter briefly reviews these existing recommendations, their rationales, and, when it exists, their scientific foundations. Practical and stylistic considerations are discussed, from language choice to issues such as relevance of data and how to frame diagnoses. The chapter proposes a research agenda to investigate whether existing guidance can be empirically supported. Broad research questions are proposed to stimulate thought about additional empirical work, and some initial ideas about how to approach specific hypotheses are considered. In particular, researchers need to further investigate ways to fashion reports that legal actors and other consumers of the information will read, understand, and use appropriately.

Key Words: forensic reports, written reports, ethics, bias, psychological testing

Psychologists pride themselves on being empiricists. Whether or not their graduate schools explicitly adopted the scientist–practitioner model, they learned the scientific method, and they were socialized to value research. They were trained that assessment methods must be valid and reliable (American Educational Research Association, American Psychological Association, & National Council on Measurement in Education, 2014) and that treatments should be empirically supported (Chambless & Hollon, 1998). Despite the value placed on empiricism, however, there are contexts in forensic psychology where it is lacking, and the clearest example may be forensic report writing.

This is unfortunate, given that preparation of reports is ubiquitous among forensic psychologists, and those reports may be the most important work products they generate. Attorneys, judges, insurance companies, police commissions, regulatory boards, and others benefit from thorough and well-reasoned forensic reports that address specific psychological questions related to contested issues. More forensic cases are completed on the basis of a written report than on the basis of expert testimony at a deposition, hearing, or trial (Melton et al., 2018). It is somewhat surprising, then, that so little empirical research has focused on written forensic reports as compared to other topics, such as expert testimony. This may be an artifact of the ease with which expert testimony (or mock expert testimony) can be empirically evaluated, and the difficulties associated with studying psychological reports.

Much has been written about the task of creating forensic reports, and those who seek to improve their report-writing skills can easily find multiple sources of guidance. Abundant advice about practical matters has emerged, and that advice is largely consistent across sources (Buchanan & Norko, 2011; DeMier & Otto, 2017; Karson & Nadkarni, 2013; Melton et al., 2018; Miller & Gagliardi, 2016; Otto et al., 2014). Most of this advice, unfortunately, is not based on empirical studies. That does not mean it is wrong; each piece of advice has a rational basis which, at its core, generally has an ethical foundation. It is therefore likely that much of the guidance is useful. But, the practice of report writing would likely benefit from a greater empirical examination of some of the truths that forensic psychologists appear to hold as self-evident.

Given the wealth of good sources related to forensic report writing, this chapter will focus on unanswered empirical questions. Practical guidance with a rational and/or ethical basis that has attained broad consensus will be briefly reviewed, and the remainder of the chapter will focus on ideas for research that would address empirical questions for which there are few current answers. Note that the two categories are not mutually exclusive; some assuredly rational advice could still be bolstered by empirical study.

Rational Guidance, Informed by Ethics

A forensic report should clearly articulate the psycholegal referral question(s) being addressed. Although this is seemingly obvious, numerous reports fail to clearly identify the referral question, or they may address abilities that are not relevant to the referral question (Heilbrun & Collins, 1995; Robbins et al., 1997). Identifying the referral question provides the reader with a clear statement about what the report is and what it is not. It establishes the boundaries and contours of the report. In those cases where the referral question is unclear (and efforts to clarify it were unsuccessful), it describes what the forensic psychologist understood the question to be.

A surprising number of forensic reports lack a description of the notification process, during which an evaluee is informed of the nature and purpose of an examination and the limits of confidentiality (Budd et al., 2001; Heilbrun & Collins, 1995; Skeem et al., 1998). Some evaluations require informed consent, and that process should be described in the report; evaluations where consent is not required (e.g., a court-ordered evaluation) should nevertheless detail what was explained to the evaluee. A central component should be a statement regarding the extent to which the evaluee understood that explanation.

Sources of information should be included in the forensic report. Indeed, the *Specialty Guidelines for Forensic Psychology* (hereafter, SGFP; American Psychological Association, 2013b) indicate that examiners should "disclose all sources of information obtained in the course of the professional services, and to identify the source of each piece of information" (p. 15). Nevertheless, clinicians differ in the degree of information included. Resnick and Soliman (2011) argued that overspecificity is preferable to underspecificity. The guiding principles about what to include should be clarity and transparency. The reader of the report should have sufficient information to make a fair appraisal of the sources used, as that will inform the weight a reader should give the report.

Relevance should also dictate what is included in—and excluded from—forensic reports. Report authors will always face choices about whether a piece of information is appropriate for a report, and some psychologists struggle to find the right balance between insufficient detail and too much information. Opinions should be built upon a foundation of relevant information, carefully explained. Just as evidence in court should be probative, meaning it tends to prove something central to the issues in dispute, information included in a forensic report should lead the reader closer to the opinion offered.

The way in which information is presented in a forensic report matters. There is consensus that data should be presented that support the inferences, conclusions, and opinions reached by the psychologist. Commonly, this is accomplished by presenting the data first, then discussing how the data led to the psychologist's conclusions. Conversely, some psychologists state the conclusion first, then provide the data that support it. Regardless of the order, conclusions and opinions should be explicitly linked to the data that underlie them.

Specific words used in the report matter as well. Jargon should be avoided when possible. When avoiding jargon is simply too cumbersome, unfamiliar or technical words should be carefully explained. This begins with the recognition that lay readers will likely not understand much of the language psychologists use on a daily basis, or worse, they may have an erroneous understanding of a term and conclude that it means something other than what the report writer intends. When the psychologist defines the meaning of a term that will be used repeatedly, it is helpful to explain it carefully and bolster the explanation with examples.

Finally, most forensic reports will be strengthened by a discussion of any plausible alternative conclusions. Some novice report writers might worry that such a discussion could weaken or undermine their opinion, but the opposite is likely true. An explanation of alternative conclusions shows the reader that the psychologist considered such possibilities and rejected them in favor of the opinion presented in the report. When psychologists explain the reasons for reaching their conclusions instead of other possible alternatives, they are creating the transparency that leads to a better and more persuasive report.

Empirical Questions

Some of this practical guidance does not appear to be worth exploring empirically, as few would dispute its value. A satirical publication reported a fictitious study which concluded that intoxication increases risky behavior among teens, according to the "Center for Figuring Out Really Obvious Things" (The Onion, 2002). Although some of the practical guidance may appear to be sound on its face and rooted in common sense, there are still empirical questions worth exploring. Focused research could challenge certain assumptions about how reports are read, interpreted, and used by legal consumers.

The remainder of this chapter introduces questions that are worthy of empirical study. A recommended practice is identified, along with its rationale. In most cases, there are both practical and ethical reasons to adhere to the recommendation, and these are discussed briefly. In discussing ethics, both the American Psychological Association's *Ethical Principles of Psychologists and Code of Conduct* (EPPCC) (American Psychological Association, 2017) and SGFP (American Psychological Association, 2013b) will be explicitly referenced. While recognizing that the EPPCC only applies to APA members and the SGFP are intended as aspirational in nature, many state licensing boards have adopted aspects of the EPPCC as binding, and a few have even done so for the SGFP (e.g., Pennsylvania) (Melton et al., 2018). As a result, depending on jurisdictional rules, the ethical considerations raised by these sources may have far-reaching implications for forensic practitioners beyond their guidance as useful tools for determining appropriate standards of ethical practice.

Additionally, explicit research questions in need of further study will be offered, but the specifics of any proposed research design go well beyond the scope of the chapter; the questions are intended to spark empirical thoughts about the topics. These empirical questions are summarized in table 8.1. Finally, practical recommendations will be briefly discussed (if different from what is noted above). For ease of organization, issues will be explored in the order in which they might be expected to appear in a report. First, however, some general writing considerations will be addressed.

First-Person Voice

Although this issue has received scant attention, DeMier and Otto (2017) recommended that forensic reports adopt first-person language, using words like "I" and "me," instead of an awkward phrase like "the undersigned evaluator." Although first-person voice is encouraged by some, it should not be colloquial or casual; it should not suggest a personal relationship with the examinee that does not exist. The relationship between the forensic evaluator and the person being examined is a professional one, and that remains the case regardless of whether first-person or third-person language is used. An awkward phrase is not necessary to show that the relationship is not personal. It has been argued that using first-person voice is easier to write, easier to read and understand, and more authentic. Are these arguments valid, or are they merely a stylistic preference with no measurable advantage or disadvantage? The consumers of forensic reports, who are mostly legal actors (i.e., litigants, attorneys, judges, and jury members), are likely to possess the most useful advice about this recommendation. Surveying these individuals about first-person voice

Table 8.1 Practice Recommendations and Research Questions

Practice	Current Recommendation	Research Questions
First-person voice	Avoid awkward phrases like "the undersigned evaluator." Use "I" and "me" instead.	Will first-person voice ease reading or improve understanding of forensic reports?
Exclusion of irrelevant racial or ethnic identifiers	Only identify race or ethnicity when it is relevant to the referral question.	Can psychologists reliably determine when such information is relevant? What is the impact of including such information in forensic reports?
Avoid biased language	Avoid value-laden language. Be attuned to subtle instances of bias when choosing words.	What is the impact of biased words on the legal consumer? What words most commonly contribute to unintended perceptions?
Focus on the forensic question	Limit the report to the psycholegal referral question(s).	Do legal consumers recognize differences in quality when reports are appropriately limited in scope?
Document all sources	List all sources collected, reviewed, and relied upon.	Are reports that provide complete information viewed as more objective or more credible?
Focus on Relevant Information	Link opinions to relevant information. Exclude irrelevant information from the forensic report.	How is relevance determined? Are judgments about relevance reliable?
Separate facts, inferences, and opinions	Link opinions to underlying facts and inferences.	What are the most effective ways to frame opinions so that their logic is clear?
Minimize and explain jargon	Avoid jargon when possible. Explain jargon that is necessary.	What do legal consumers prefer regarding explanations of psychological concepts?
Psychological testing	Determine how to present test results based on the individual demands of a case.	When and how should test scores be included? Should test results be presented individually or integrated?
Include explanations of reasoning and report limitations	Carefully explain reasoning to achieve a transparent report. Candidly disclose the report's limitations.	Can legal consumers be persuaded to read complete forensic reports instead of scanning for the "bottom line"?
Presenting a diagnosis	Do not draw unnecessary attention to diagnosis, as it is often peripheral to the psycholegal referral question.	Does the way information about diagnosis is presented inadvertently give the diagnosis too much weight?
Ultimate opinion issues	Literature is mixed on whether to include ultimate issue opinions.	What are the expectations of legal consumers? Do those expectations vary based on a mediating variable?

in a report might prove useful in determining whether it makes any real difference in how reports are perceived and understood.

Exclusion of Irrelevant Racial or Ethnic Identifiers

Most forensic reports include identification of an examinee's race and/or ethnicity. Many reports begin with phrases such as, "The defendant is a 36-year-old, White woman," or "The plaintiff is a 51-year-old, African American man." The wisdom of including racial or ethnic identifiers as a matter of course, however, has been challenged. Riggs Romaine and Kavanaugh (2019) have argued that such identifiers should only be included when relevant, and they offered guidance for making such decisions.

Racial or ethnic identifiers can precipitate implicit bias. Psychologists may form hypotheses based on such an identifier (e.g., that a person is likely poor, or likely has fewer educational or vocational opportunities, or is at increased risk for unfair criminal justice practices). However, psychologists' hypotheses will not necessarily be the same as those formed by legal consumers of forensic reports. An attorney or judge, for example, might be at increased risk for erroneous conclusions based solely on implicit biases. There is no basis for assuming that the reader of the forensic report will have the same reactions to the inclusion of a racial or ethnic identifier as the psychologist who prepared the report. As psychologists prepare forensic reports, they should carefully consider whether to include or exclude ethnic or racial identifiers; decisions should be made based on the context of the case, recognizing that in some cases, such information will be crucial (e.g., a claim of workplace discrimination based on race) and that in others, they are likely irrelevant (e.g., competence to proceed in a criminal case).

Proposed research could include inquiries into how practitioners currently decide when to include or exclude such information. Can practitioners make reliable decisions regarding relevance of this information? While some research explores the impact of such information on the reader in clinical settings (Shin et al., 2016), more focused research should examine the impact on the consumer of forensic reports.

Avoid Biased Language

In recent years, forensic psychologists have paid increased attention to bias and various ways to minimize it (Neal, 2018; Neal & Grisso, 2014). Of course, doing so is consistent with the general principles of the EPPCC (American Psychological Association, 2013b). It is hoped that few forensic reports contain egregious examples of biased language; it would be unusual, for example, to read a custody report that referred to a "deadbeat dad." In reality, indications of bias tend to be much more subtle, and thus, more difficult for the writer to combat and more difficult for the reader to identify.

However, the reader of a forensic report does not need to be aware of biasing words for them to have an effect (see generally Kahneman, 2013). Consider, for example, the words "admit" and "deny." Although seemingly neutral words, admissions and denials are usually associated with something negative. People admit criminal histories and drug use; they do not tend to "admit" graduating from college or being exonerated.

Careful word choice is essential to avoid biasing effects. Taking care to choose exactly the right word likely helps a writer control for bias as well. Neal and Brodsky (2016) included the removal of value-laden language from reports as one way to address bias.

Do such subtleties make a difference in the minds of legal consumers who read forensic reports? Careful research in this area, where clinicians, laypeople, and legal professionals read excerpts with and without biased language could reveal whether such effects are present, and the impact of any effects found. Such research could also provide insight into the best word choices to avoid unintended consequences.

Focus on the Forensic Question

Some of the earliest criticisms of forensic report writing focused on the fact that mental health professionals tended to focus on clinical issues rather than psycholegal referral questions (Bazelon, 1974; Elwork, 1984; Vann, 1965). Rather than addressing the narrow issue of interest to the court, mental health practitioners would often complete a standard clinical evaluation with a focus on diagnosis, which was often inappropriately equated with the relevant psycholegal issue. Some reports even went well beyond the limits of the psychologists' expertise (Morse, 1978).

The SGFP (American Psychological Association, 2013b) direct, "In reports and testimony, forensic practitioners typically provide information about examinees' functional abilities, capacities, knowledge, and beliefs, and address their opinions and recommendations to the identified psycholegal issues" (p. 15). Allan and Grisso (2014) argued that the ethical principles of fidelity and responsibility dictate that "clinician's reports should clearly define the legal and forensic questions they were asked, which establishes the boundaries and purpose of the evaluation" (p. 470).

Do the consumers of forensic reports appreciate the meaningful difference between a report that addresses the psycholegal question and limits itself to only those questions that were posed? This has been an area of significant focus for report authors, and some legal commentators have remarked about it in scholarly works (Morse, 1978). What is not known, however, is the degree to which the everyday legal or lay consumer favors this distinction. How much attention do legal consumers pay to this aspect of report fidelity, and does it affect their decisions to rely on experts whom they perceive to clearly state the referral questions and limit their reports to the relevant issues?

Research could examine judges' and attorneys' reactions and ratings of reports that offer mere psychological diagnosis as compared to reports that adhere to the psycholegal question posed, to determine if legal decision makers are aware of this important differentiation. Regardless of the outcome, it is important that forensic reports continue to make such distinctions. However, if no differences in ratings of report quality are found, it may be incumbent on the profession to explain to the legal world why such differences in focus are important.

Document All Sources

The SGFP (American Psychological Association, 2013b) note that forensic practitioners should use multiple sources to corroborate their data points. A complete and detailed list of all the sources that were collected, reviewed, and relied upon will lead to a more credible report. Listing sources which were sought but not obtained makes clear the information the clinician thought might be useful, but which was unavailable. This demonstrates the good faith and due diligence of the examiner, and it also reveals potential weaknesses in the report.

It is doubtful that any research finding would change the recommendation to provide a clear and comprehensive list of the materials reviewed. What is unknown is whether there is a difference in how such reports are perceived. Are reports that include this information perceived as more transparent? Would they be rated as better, more objective, or more credible? A comparison of reports that lack such detail could be compared with those that provide it. Raters could be legal consumers, forensic psychologists, and psychologists who have no particular forensic expertise. In addition to developing evidence that the practice is indeed a good one, such research could illuminate differences in the way forensic reports are perceived as a function of one's expertise or role.

Focus on Relevant Information

A clear ethical basis exists for relying on relevant information. The EPPCC assert, "Psychologists include in written and oral reports and consultations only information germane to the purpose for which the communication is made" (American Psychological Association, 2017, Standard 4.04). The SGFP (American Psychological Association, 2013b) further define that purpose: "Forensic examiners seek to assist the trier of fact to understand evidence or determine a fact in issue, and they provide information that is most relevant to the psycholegal issue" (p. 15). Failure to abide by these principles can have consequences in real life. As Griffith et al. (2010) noted, "Including in the report pejorative or embarrassing information that is irrelevant to the legal issue may demonstrate a completeness of the interview, but it does so at the cost of the client's dignity" (p. 39). (For an excellent discussion of this guidance as an ethical duty, see Allan & Grisso, 2014).

Relying on relevant information will lead to opinions that are better understood. Opinions that make intuitive sense will also be more defensible. Despite such sound ethical and practical rationales for linking one's opinions to relevant information, multiple sources have noted deficits in this area (Heilbrun, 2001; Heilbrun & Collins, 1995; Otto et al., 2014; Resnick & Soliman, 2011; Robbins et al., 1997).

What is unknown is the degree to which people can discern relevant from irrelevant information. A host of potential research questions emerge. How is relevance determined? Can this be operationalized in any meaningful way? Would clinicians agree about the relevance of certain facts in a given report? Would legal consumers of reports rate relevance in the same manner as clinicians? What is the reliability of judgments of relevance? To what extent would individuals from different professions value this principle?

Separate Facts, Inferences, and Opinions

A fact is something that is known to be true in reality. An inference is a reasonable conclusion drawn from the facts through reasoning. A forensic opinion involves the application of facts and inferences to reach a position on a psycholegal question. Without facts and their accompanying inferences, there is no basis for a psychologist to form an opinion on a disputed psycholegal matter.

Care should be taken to link opinions to their underlying facts and inferences (Allan & Grisso, 2014; Otto et al., 2014). Not only is such practice consistent with the SGFP (American Psychological Association, 2013b), it mirrors the thought process of many attorneys and judges. Unlike other types of testimony allowed in the courtroom, experts are allowed to go beyond mere facts and offer opinions based on those facts and their professional inferences. Federal Rule of Evidence 703, Bases of an Expert, explicitly acknowledges the importance of the relationship between facts and expert opinions, highlighting that the facts or inferences that underlie the expert's opinion must be the type that experts in the field would reasonably rely upon in forming their opinions (Federal Rules of Evidence, 2020). In other words, the courts are very much interested in how the expert connects facts and inferences to their expert opinions in determining the admissibility of expert testimony at trial.

It is not a far reach to assume these same considerations are important for conclusions and opinions offered in forensic reports. What are the facts, and do those facts and inferences support a particular position in a legal dispute? Differentiating facts, inferences, and opinions makes for a transparent report, with conclusions dictated by logic in a way that should appeal to the legal consumer.

Whether it does appeal to the legal consumer, however, is an unanswered empirical question. Psychologists who take pains to adhere to this guidance presumably do so to write better and more persuasive reports. Whether such reports are more persuasive is an open question, and one that would lend itself easily to experimental study where reports containing the same facts could be manipulated. A comparison of reports with and without an explicit link between the facts, inference, and opinions could be conducted with both clinicians and legal consumers. Further studies could explore whether the order of presentation leads to differences in understanding or persuasiveness, or in some cases, the admissibility of expert testimony. Common sense dictates that opinions should be framed in such a manner that the logic is clear and understandable, but experiments could shed light on the most effective ways of doing so.

Minimize and Explain Jargon

When speaking, a person sending a message can gauge whether the message is accurately received via both verbal and nonverbal feedback; if the message is not understood as intended, there is often an opportunity for clarification. No such immediate feedback loop exists for the psychologist preparing a forensic report. Forensic report writers need to use words and terms that are known to their intended readers. They should be careful not to assume that their readers will know technical terms that are used routinely within the mental health community. Nevertheless, jargon is rampant in psychological reports in general (Groth-Marnot & Horvath, 2006; Harvey, 1997, 2006) and in forensic reports in particular (Allnut & Chaplow, 2000; Conroy, 2006).

Research could inform the profession regarding the best ways to communicate complicated or unfamiliar ideas to legal consumers and laypeople. Would legal consumers prefer explanations of psychological concepts without any jargon, with jargon that is explained, or with jargon without explanation? Beyond what they prefer, what would lead to the highest degree of understanding? Similar to work performed on *Miranda* warnings (Rogers, Hazelwood, Sewell, Harrison, & Shuman, 2008a; Rogers, Hazelwood, Sewell, Shuman, & Blackwood, 2008b; Rogers et al., 2010), the comprehensibility of the language used in forensic reports could be examined, and the necessary education to comprehend these reports could be studied. Could jargon be explained more efficiently, such that lengthy or cumbersome explanations do not deter the reader?

Psychological Testing

There is no discernible consensus about how psychological testing should be presented in a forensic report; indeed, there is no consensus on whether specific test scores should be included in forensic reports, or what level (if any) of both normative comparisons (e.g., standard deviations from mean, percentiles) and error intervals (e.g., standard errors, confidence intervals) should be included with those scores. This area is ripe for empirical investigation. What should be presented, and how? Should specific scores be included? If so, should they be presented in the narrative of the report or appended as a technical supplement? Should test scores be integrated into a coherent synopsis, or should they be addressed individually? What are the advantages of disadvantages of each approach?

Some data would suggest that psychologists are not particularly adept at the complex cognitive task of integrating test results (Garb, 1998, 2005). It is therefore reasonable to assume that a lay reader or legal consumer would be even less suited to this task than a psychologist.

There are types of evaluations where specific test scores are likely crucial (e.g., whether an individual education plan is mandated for a child, or whether an individual is ineligible for execution due to intellectual disability). However, specific scores are less important in other types of psychological testing (e.g., personality assessment). Psychologists need to determine the best approach based on the individual demands of a case and the anticipated knowledge base of the intended recipient. Empirical findings to guide such decisions would be a boon to the profession.

Include Explanations of Reasoning and Report Limitations

Experts in legal settings sometimes use *ipse dixit* reasoning, although "reasoning" is a misnomer. This Latin phrase is loosely translated as "because I said so." Experts who do not explain their reasoning, and instead aim to rely on their credentials as a source of authority, are not helpful to the court. To have value to an adversarial legal system, an opinion must be susceptible to challenge on its merits. When the explanation is not explicit, those merits are hidden, and the expert's conclusions cannot be properly challenged.

Such a shortcoming is explicitly addressed by the SGFP (American Psychological Association, 2013b), which direct that forensic psychologists "strive to offer . . . the basis and reasoning underlying the opinions" (p. 17) and that they "avoid partisan presentation of unrepresentative, incomplete, or inaccurate evidence that might mislead finders of fact" (p. 9). Moreover, to be of the greatest value to the legal consumer, the report's limitations should be explicit. The SGFP advise, "[F]orensic practitioners strive to have readily available for inspection all data which they considered, regardless of whether the data supports their opinion" (p. 16).

Forensic clinicians appear to accept that such guidance is sound (Neal & Grisso, 2014; Otto et al., 2014; Robinson & Acklin, 2010; Skeem et al., 1998). But, whether legal consumers of forensic reports agree is unclear. Some forensic practitioners speculate that some attorneys and judges fail to carefully read forensic reports; instead, they skip to the last page looking for the bottom line. Practitioners can likely support such suspicions with anecdotal evidence. Are reports that explicitly address inconsistent data and/or alternate hypotheses viewed more positively by other forensic clinicians? Do legal consumers perceive the advantages noted by psychologists?

For both ethical and practical reasons, psychologists should continue to include explicit and transparent explanations of their reasoning. Similarly, they should continue to include, where appropriate, data that are inconsistent with or contrary to the report's conclusion. A discussion of the reasons that alternative hypotheses were rejected will strengthen the report's conclusions by showing that the psychologist was alert to other conclusions and that those conclusions were considered prior to reaching a more appropriate one.

The "last page problem" merits attention. If some judges, attorneys, and other consumers of forensic reports are indeed skimming the reports in search of the bottom line, are there ways to frame reports that will alter this behavior? Researchers could evaluate various strategies to encourage more people to read the complete report.

Presenting a Diagnosis

Prior to the publication of the fifth edition of *Diagnostic and Statistical Manual of Mental Disorders* (DSM-5; American Psychiatric Association, 2013a), mental health disorders were generally offered within the multiaxial system. As a result, many reports had diagnoses set apart, often indented, like so:

Axis I:	Adjustment disorder with depressed mood
Axis II:	Dependent personality disorder
Axis III:	No significant findings
Axis IV:	Death of parent; housing insecurity
Axis V:	GAF = 75

Now that the DSM has abandoned the multiaxial system of diagnosis, perhaps it is through force of habit that many psychologists still separate or otherwise highlight diagnoses, such that the eye is drawn to them in the report. Sometimes, the diagnosis is simply discussed in the narrative of the report, but even in such instances, the diagnosis may be highlighted via boldface, or perhaps the words in the diagnosis are capitalized. (If cancer is not capitalized, why should schizophrenia be?)

Does the manner in which a diagnosis is presented have an impact on how much attention or importance is ascribed to it by the lay reader or legal consumer? Although this may be a subtle point, it is worth considering whether readers react in a different manner depending on whether or not the diagnosis is highlighted or set aside in a way that is easy to see.

Ultimate Opinion Issues

This well-worn "controversy" is familiar to most forensic psychologists. Some authorities (e.g., Melton et al., 2018) argue that forensic reports should not offer opinions on the ultimate legal issue, as doing so infringes on the province of the fact-finder. Others (e.g., Rogers & Ewing, 1989) argue that sidestepping the psycholegal referral question results in imprecise or confusing opinions. Otto et al. (2014) termed the issue a "red herring" and a distraction from the critical issue of explanation of an opinion. They wrote, "When forensic reports contain adequate explanations of the examiner's reasoning, the legal factfinder is free to draw conclusions independent of any that might be proposed by the expert" (Otto et al., p. 84).

What forensic psychologists recommend is inconsistent; what legal consumers want and need appears to be variable at best. When a forensic psychologist was asked his ultimate opinion about insanity during a federal trial, he explained that the Federal Rules of Evidence prevented him from expressing that opinion on the stand. The judge responded, "Why do you think we brought you here?" (R. L. Denney, personal communication, December 1, 2020).

A survey of attorneys and judges could result in a better understanding of their positions. Do attorneys vary in their expectations about whether forensic reports should address ultimate issues? Do their expectations vary by type of case, or by jurisdiction, or by some other mediating variable? When do legal consumers find ultimate opinions helpful and when do they find them harmful? Are their expectations consistent with the law?

Conclusion

The existing literature in forensic psychology provides abundant guidance on writing forensic reports, but much of that guidance relies on experience rather than empirical data. Psychologists have developed what appears to be sound advice that will lead to reports that are clear and transparent, and psychologists have assumed that such reports will be most helpful to the courts and other entities that resolve disputes. However, that guidance appears to come solely from the perspective of report writers. Psychologists offer advice about what they *believe* will be most helpful to courts, but that advice is rarely verified by the legal consumers of reports.

A useful research agenda should focus on legal consumers as much as it does on the perspectives of psychologists. The way legal consumers use forensic reports, their perceptions of and reactions to such reports, and the differential effects of word choices within reports should be investigated to determine how best to serve the legal community.

References

Allan, A., & Grisso, T. (2014). Ethical principles and the communication of forensic mental health assessments. *Ethics and Behavior, 24*(6), 467–477.

Allnutt, S. H., & Chaplow, D. (2000). General principles of forensic report writing. *Australian and New Zealand Journal of Psychiatry, 34*(6), 980–987.

American Educational Research Association, American Psychological Association, & National Council on Measurement in Education. (2014). *Standards for educational and psychological testing* (5th ed.). American Educational Research Association, American Psychological Association, & National Council on Measurement in Education.

American Psychiatric Association. (2013a). *Diagnostic and statistical manual of mental disorders* (5th ed.). American Psychiatric Press.

American Psychological Association. (2013b). Specialty guidelines for forensic psychology. *American Psychologist, 68*(1), 7–19.

American Psychological Association. (2017). *Ethical principles of psychologists and code of conduct* (2002, amended effective June 1, 2010, and January 1, 2017). https://www.apa.org/ethics/code

Bazelon, D. L. (1974). Psychiatrists and the adversary process. *Scientific American, 230*(6), 18–23.

Buchanan, A., & Norko, M. A. (2011). *The psychiatric report: Principles and practice of forensic writing.* Cambridge University Press.

Budd, K. S., Poindexter, L. M., Felix, E. D., & Naik-Polan, A. T. (2001). Clinical assessment of parents in child protection cases: An empirical analysis. *Law and Human Behavior, 25*(1), 93–108.

Chambless, D. L., & Hollon, S. D. (1998). Defining empirically supported therapies. *Journal of Consulting and Clinical Psychology, 66*(1), 7–18.

Conroy, M. A. (2006). Report writing and testimony. *Applied Psychology in Criminal Justice, 2*(3), 237–260.

DeMier, R. L., & Otto, R. K. (2017). Forensic report writing: Principles and challenges. In R. Roesch & A. N. Cook (Eds.) *Handbook of forensic mental health services* (pp. 216–234). Routledge.

Elwork, A. (1984). Psycholegal assessment, diagnosis, and testimony: A new beginning. *Law and Human Behavior, 8*(3-4), 197–203.

Federal Rule of Evidence. (2020). https://www.law.cornell.edu/rules/fre/rule_703

Garb, H. N. (1998). *Studying the clinician: Judgment research and psychological assessment.* American Psychological Association.

Garb, H. N. (2005). Clinical judgment and decision making. *Annual Review of Clinical Psychology, 1*(1), 67–89.

Griffith, E. E. H., Stankovic, A., & Barnoski, M. (2010). Conceptualizing the forensic psychiatry report as performative narrative. *Journal of the American Academy of Psychiatry and the Law, 38*(1), 32–42.

Groth-Marnat, G., & Horvath, L. S. (2006). The psychological report: A review of current controversies. *Journal of Clinical Psychology, 62*(1), 73–81.

Harvey, V. S. (1997). Improving readability of psychological reports. *Professional Psychology: Research and Practice, 28*(3), 271–274.

Harvey, V. S. (2006). Variables affecting the clarity of psychological reports. *Journal of Clinical Psychology, 62*(1), 5–18.

Heilbrun, K. (2001). *Principles of forensic mental health assessment.* Kluwer Academic/Plenum.

Heilbrun, K., & Collins, S. (1995). Evaluations of trial competency and mental state at the time of offense: Report characteristics. *Professional Psychology: Research and Practice, 26*(1), 61–67.

Kahneman, D. (2013). *Thinking, fast and slow.* Farrar, Straus, and Giroux.

Karson, M., & Nadkarni, L. (2013). *Principles of forensic report writing.* American Psychological Association.

Melton, G. B., Petrila, J., Poythress, N. G., Slobogin, C., Otto, R. K., Mossmon, D., & Condie. L. O. (2018). *Psychological evaluations for the courts: A handbook for mental health professionals and lawyers* (4th ed.). Guilford Press.

Miller, A. K., & Gagliardi, G. J. (2016). Writing forensic psychological reports. In R. Jackson & R. Roesch (Eds.), *Learning forensic assessment: Research and practice* (2nd ed., pp. 487–505). Routledge.

Morse, S. J. (1978). Law and mental health professionals: The limits of expertise. *Professional Psychology, 9*(3), 389–399.

Neal, T. M. S. (2018). Discerning bias in forensic psychological reports in insanity cases. *Behavioral Sciences and the Law, 36*(3), 325–338.

Neal, T. M. S., & Brodsky, S. L. (2016). Forensic psychologists' perceptions of bias and potential correction strategies in forensic mental health evaluations. *Psychology, Public Policy, and Law, 22*(1), 58–76.

Neal, T. M. S., & Grisso, T. (2014). The cognitive underpinnings of bias in forensic mental health evaluations. *Psychology, Public Policy, and Law, 20*(2), 200–211.

Otto, R. K., DeMier, R. L., & Boccaccini, M. T. (2014). *Forensic reports and testimony: A guide to effective communication for psychologists and psychiatrists.* Wiley.

Resnick, P. J., & Soliman, S. (2011). Draftmanship. In A. Buchanan & M. A. Norko (Eds.), *The psychiatric report: Principles and practices of effective report writing* (pp. 81–92). Cambridge University Press.

Riggs Romaine, C. L., & Kavanaugh, A. (2019). Risks, benefits, and complexities: Reporting race and ethnicity in forensic mental health reports. *International Journal of Forensic Mental Health, 18*(2), 138–152.

Robbins, E., Waters, J., & Herbert, P. (1997). Competency to stand trial evaluations: A study of actual practice in two states. *Journal of the American Academy of Psychiatry and the Law, 25*(4), 469–483.

Robinson, R., & Acklin, M. W. (2010). Fitness in paradise: Quality of forensic reports submitted to the Hawaii judiciary. *International Journal of Law and Psychiatry, 33*(3), 131–137.

Rogers, R., & Ewing, C. P. (1989). Ultimate opinion proscriptions: A cosmetic fix and a plea for empiricism. *Law and Human Behavior, 13*(4), 357–374.

Rogers, R., Hazelwood, L., Sewell, K., Harrison, K., & Shuman, D. (2008a). The language of Miranda warnings in American jurisdictions: A replication and vocabulary analysis. *Law and Human Behavior, 32*(2), 124–136.

Rogers, R., Hazelwood, L., Sewell, K., Shuman, D., & Blackwood, H. (2008b). The comprehensibility and content of juvenile Miranda warnings. *Psychology, Public Policy, and Law, 14*(1), 63–86.

Rogers, R., Rogstad, J., Gillard, N., Drogin, E., Blackwood, H., & Shuman, D. (2010). "Everyone knows their *Miranda* rights": Implicit assumptions and countervailing evidence. *Psychology, Public Policy, and Law, 16*(3), 300–318.

Shin, R. Q., Smith, L. C., Welch, J. C., & Ezeofor, I. (2016). Is Allison more likely than Lakisha to receive a callback from counseling professionals? A racism audit study. *The Counseling Psychologist, 44*(8), 1187–1211.

Skeem, J. L., Golding, S. L., Cohn, N. B., & Berge, G. (1998). Logic and reliability of evaluations of competence to stand trial. *Law and Human Behavior, 22*(5), 519–547.

Teen sex linked to drugs and alcohol, reports Center for Figuring Out Really Obvious Things. *The Onion*, May 1, 2002. https://www.theonion.com/teen-sex-linked-to-drugs-and-alcohol-reports-center-fo-1819566423.

Vann, C. (1965). Pre-trial determination and judicial decision-making: An analysis of the use of psychiatric information in the administration of criminal justice. *University of Detroit Law Journal, 43*(1), 13–33.

PART I I

Criminal and Civil Forensic Psychology

Emerging Issues in Competence to Stand Trial Evaluation

Patricia A. Zapf *and* Amanda Beltrani

Abstract

Recent data indicate that *at least* 90,000 evaluations of competency to stand trial are conducted each year in the United States, making this the most prevalent type of forensic evaluation ordered by the courts. A robust literature exists regarding the evaluation of competency to stand trial, but less work has been done on issues related to the restoration of competency, with researchers calling for more evidence regarding effective techniques for improving competence-related functioning. This chapter discusses the topic of emerging issues in competency evaluation, specifically addressing the use of videoconferencing technology and the issue of bias and unreliability in competency evaluation. The available research and commentary on these two emerging issues is reviewed and suggestions for a path forward are provided, with a focus toward a more nuanced understanding of the interplay between evaluator characteristics, evaluation methods, and training.

Key Words: competence to stand trial, forensic mental health assessments, videoconferencing, bias, reliability, evaluations

For the last two decades, it has been estimated that approximately 60,000 evaluations of competence to stand trial are conducted annually in the United States, making competency assessment the most prevalent forensic evaluation ordered by the courts (see Bonnie & Grisso, 2000). More recent estimates, compiled by submitting Freedom of Information Act requests for competence to proceed data for the 2019 fiscal or calendar year from fifty-two US judiciaries (all state systems, as well as Washington, DC and federal systems), suggest that the number of competency evaluations ordered annually in the United States is considerably higher than 60,000 and likely double that number (Kois, Potts, et al., 2020). Preliminary data from twenty states reporting complete data (i.e., data from all counties) indicate that 56,198 competency evaluations were conducted during the 2019 fiscal or calendar year. To calculate a more accurate national estimate, evaluation by arrest base rates were calculated, suggesting that an average 0.011 percent of adult arrestees were evaluated for competency evaluations in 2019. Extrapolating from these data, the best conservative estimate is that *at least* 91,927 adult competence evaluations were conducted in the United States in 2019 and this number is likely to be closer to ~150,000 (Kois, Potts, et al., 2020).

A relatively robust literature on competency to stand trial exists, with more than twelve hundred journal articles and book chapters published on this topic. Historically, this literature has primarily been focused on the evaluation of competence, the development of tools to assist in the evaluation of competence, and the differences between competent and incompetent defendants. Numerous articles, chapters, and texts have been written on the evaluation of competence to stand trial (also called adjudicative competence; see Grisso, 2003, 2014; Melton et al., 2018; Zapf & Roesch, 2009) and multiple tools and instruments have been developed to structure competency evaluations and provide relevant normative data regarding the performance of a particular defendant on competence-related abilities (see Acklin, 2012; Blake et al., 2019; Melton et al., 2018; Zapf & Roesch, 2009, for summaries of these tools and instruments).

With respect to the characteristics of competent and incompetent defendants, two meta-analyses of the competency literature have been published, decades apart, with consistent results. Nicholson and Kugler (1991) examined thirty studies that compared 8,170 competent and incompetent criminal defendants and found the characteristics most strongly related to incompetence were "(a) poor performance on psychological tests or interviews specifically designed to assess defendants' legally relevant functional abilities, (b) a psychotic diagnosis, and (c) psychiatric symptoms reflective of severe psychopathology" (p. 355). Pirelli et al. (2011) examined sixty-eight studies comparing 26,139 competent and incompetent defendants and found: (a) "defendants diagnosed with a psychotic disorder were approximately eight times more likely to be found incompetent than defendants without a psychotic disorder diagnosis," (b) "the likelihood of being found incompetent was approximately double for unemployed defendants as compared to employed defendants," and (c) "the likelihood of being found incompetent was also double for defendants with a previous psychiatric hospitalization compared to those without a hospitalization history" (p. 1). In addition, the base rate of incompetence was 27.5 percent.

Less robust than the competency evaluation literature, however, is the literature on competency restoration. Approximately one-quarter of defendants who are evaluated for competency are found incompetent; considering Kois, Potts, et al.'s (2020) extrapolations from preliminary data of between 90,000 and 150,000 defendants evaluated for competency each year, this means that in excess of 25,000 defendants are being court ordered to restoration services annually in the United States. Zapf and Roesch (2011) summarized the research on competency restoration, noting the piecemeal nature of published research on this topic, highlighting the deficiencies in our knowledge in this area and the promise of a cognitive remediation approach to restoration, and calling for future research on restoration and related issues. Pirelli and Zapf (2020) attempted to meta-analyze the competency restoration literature—examining data from fifty-one independent competency restoration samples, spanning a forty-year period, with 12,781 defendants—finding a base rate for competency restoration of 81 percent and a median length of stay of 147 days. Beyond these (important) data, however, these authors ultimately concluded that "the restoration literature does not currently lend itself to meta-analysis" (p. 134), calling for more specific reporting of competency restoration procedures, the use of pre- versus posttreatment designs to assess treatment effectiveness, and more clinical research on restoration techniques.

More recently, systemic issues related to competency evaluation and restoration have begun to receive increased attention as legal actions against several states have ensued as a result of lengthy wait lists and overburdened forensic systems. Across the United States, a backlog of defendants on waiting lists for competency evaluation or restoration has resulted in deprivation of individual liberty and a call for reform of the forensic system to become more aligned with the needs of those it serves. These systemic issues are driving new ways of thinking about the forensic system and the implications for practice (Beltrani & Zapf, 2020). Litigation in various states and the resulting consent decrees have created interesting changes in the way we think about and practice competency evaluation and restoration (Gowensmith, 2019), including: implementing triage protocols for evaluating only those who pose a risk to themselves or others on an inpatient basis with outpatient evaluation as the default, leaving inpatient beds for more critically ill defendants and those in need of restoration (Fader-Towe & Kelly, 2020); applying different models, such as jail-based or community-based, for competency restoration services (Gowensmith et al., 2016); diverting mentally ill defendants from the criminal justice system at various intercepts (Pinals & Callahan, 2020); changing statutory timelines to be more aligned with empirical evidence indicating that forty-five days might be a sweet spot for evaluations (Schwermer, 2020); and limiting competency to felony defendants (Murrie et al., 2020a; Schwermer, 2020).

Systemic research is difficult, especially at a statewide or national level, and it takes time and coordination, requiring the reorganization of systems in some instances or the implementation of different policies, procedures, or protocols in others. While we await a more robust literature and a national coordination of efforts to learn more about ways in which forensic systems across the country can be improved, we watch the efforts of groups such as the National Association of State Mental Health Program Directors (NASMHPD) and the collaborative learning communities established by Policy Research Associates and the Substance Abuse and Mental Health Services Administration's (SAMHSA's) GAINS Center working toward a more wholistic understanding of the needs of mentally ill individuals within the criminal justice system and decriminalizing mental illness. Although competency evaluation is a clinical/applied issue, the research that informs this issue is both applied and experimental. These are complex, systematic issues with extensive implications and the interplay of applied and experimental work is key.

To address the topic of emerging issues in the evaluation of competence to stand trial, we focus on two issues that have been stimulating research and commentary: (1) the use of videoconferencing technology for competency evaluation; and (2) the issue of bias and unreliability in competency evaluation. The remainder of this chapter addresses these two emerging issues, with a review of the research and relevant case law, followed by a discussion of implications, next steps, and future directions.

Use of Videoconferencing Technology for Competency Evaluation

Telepsychology is defined as "the provision of psychological services using telecommunication technologies" (Joint Task Force for the Development of Telepsychology Guidelines for Psychologists, 2013, p. 791) and includes videoconferencing as well as telephone and e-mail communications. It is not a specialized area of practice but rather a method for delivering mental health services and information. The release of the *Guidelines for the Practice of Telepsychology* (2013) has facilitated practitioners' incorporation of telepsychology into their practice and has stimulated research and discussion regarding when, with whom, and under what circumstances telepsychology should be used along with considerations for delivering various mental health services using this method. Recently, a primer for the practice of telepsychology was published, describing the clinical, technical, and logistical steps necessary to prepare, initiate, and participate in telepsychology and providing risk management and other practical tips for practitioners (Martin et al., 2020). Similarly, a primer on forensic e-mental health describing research priorities and reporting how to plan for and overcome logistical obstacles in implementing forensic e-mental health policies and practices (Kois, Cox, et al., 2020). The current coronavirus pandemic has further increased interest in and necessity for telepsychology services in many areas of practice but specifically with respect to competency evaluation and other forensic services. Here, we review the available research on the use of videoconferencing (VC) technology for evaluations of adjudicative competence along with relevant legal precedent.

Antonacci et al. (2008) reviewed the early research on telepsychiatry—including a dozen articles from forensic settings—and concluded, "there are no data that demonstrate that telepsychiatric services are harmful, either to general psychiatric patients, children, or to prisoners" (p. 266) noting that "telepsychiatric assessments are acceptable to individuals in forensic and correctional facilities, and that telepsychiatric services can be used effectively with prisoners with certain psychiatric disorders" (p. 266). These authors called for more comparisons regarding specific psychiatric subgroups and treatment interventions to "optimally match the technological medium of intervention with particular prisoner or patient problems" (p. 266).

Several studies comparing the use of standardized psychological tests and measures administered in person and by VC indicate that clinical assessments conducted using VC are generally as reliable as those conducted in person for the majority of adult psychiatric patients (Brearly et al., 2017; Luxton et al., 2014; Sharp et al., 2011). With respect to establishing rapport between the evaluator and interviewee, comparable levels of rapport have been established during video-based and in-person interviews (Antonacci et al.,

2008; Luxton et al., 2014). Factors that influence the reliability and validity of remote psychological assessments—remote physical presence and setting; technology issues; user acceptance; cultural considerations; ethical, privacy, and safety considerations; psychometric considerations for selecting assessment measures—were reviewed by Luxton et al. (2014) and best practice recommendations offered for conducting remote assessments. These authors highlight the importance of practitioners' familiarity with the available research and guidelines regarding remote assessment and describe the need to consider the applicability and appropriateness of assessment measures or techniques on a case-by-case basis when conducting remote evaluations.

Batastini et al. (2016) conducted a series of meta-analytic investigations on five studies examining telepsychology and related services using in-person comparison groups with justice-involved and substance abuse clients published between 2000 and 2014 (*n* = 342 participants). These researchers sought to examine outcomes in five domains: mental health symptoms, therapeutic process, program performance, program engagement, and service satisfaction. While carefully delineating the limitations in generalizing from these data, these authors concluded that the results "provide cautious optimism for implementing technology-based interventions" (p. 27), elaborating that assessment and treatment outcomes for in-person and video-conferencing services are grossly equivalent. Physical presence in the room "does not appear to be a necessary therapeutic component for gathering adequate clinical information or producing desired treatment effects" (p. 27) and "does not seem to inhibit clients' willingness to participate and engage in services" (p. 27).

Regarding evaluations of adjudicative competence specifically, Lexcen et al. (2006) investigated whether the quality of results from video interviews was comparable to that obtained from in-person interviews. The results of in-person and video-based interviews using the Brief Psychiatric Rating Scale (BPRS) and the MacArthur Competence Assessment Tool—Criminal Adjudication (MacCAT-CA) were compared in a sample of seventy-two pre- and posttrial defendants diagnosed with severe mental illness. Results indicated high levels of interrater reliability between conditions, with these authors concluding that "this study provides the first available data to demonstrate that structured forensic interviews conducted with video conferencing equipment are generally comparable with interviews conducted in person" (Lexcen et al., 2006, p. 715).

Manguno-Mire et al. (2007) investigated whether forensic evaluations could be reliably performed using telemedicine by conducting competency evaluations using the Georgia Court Competency Test (GCCT) with twenty-one inpatient defendants where half were evaluated using an in-person interview and half with a VC interview. Results showed high levels of agreement in total GCCT scores between the two interview conditions. Regarding satisfaction, they found that "although patients did not express a preference for a particular interview modality, providers reported greater satisfaction with live [in-person] interviews" (Manguno-Mire et al., 2007, p. 481).

After reviewing and summarizing the available information on using VC technology to conduct evaluations of adjudicative competence—including legal considerations, validity and reliability of video assessments, evaluator competence, defendant characteristics and appropriateness for videoconferencing, limits of confidentiality, and safety/duty-to-warn considerations—Luxton and Lexcen (2018) concluded that VC appears to be a viable approach to meeting the demand for timely competency evaluations. Consideration of legal, ethical, and practice standards in determining the appropriateness of VC for a particular client is necessary and VC evaluations should meet the standards and expectations of professional practice, as well as applicable policy and law. "VC-based evaluations make the most sense when they improve the efficiency of services while maintaining the same standards of quality of traditional evaluations" (p. 129).

Adjorlolo and Chan (2015) provided practice considerations for enhancing forensic assessments conducted remotely through videoconferencing, addressing issues such as testing and assessment, competence with technology, informed consent, privacy and confidentiality, standard of practice and professional liability, and reporting assessment results. In addition to all the information that would typically go into a competency evaluation report (see Zapf & Roesch, 2009), Adjorlolo and Chan (2015) advocated that evaluators also include a section that details why the assessment medium was chosen, the features of the technology, and the possible impact on the assessment, as well as means taken to ensure privacy and confidentiality. "This section of the report should explicitly state whether, in the opinion of the evaluator, the use of the VC medium negatively influenced the result obtained" (p. 198).

The use of telepsychology, in general, as well as its specific use for the provision of forensic services will continue to stimulate research and commentary as telepsychology practice develops (see, e.g., recent commentary on conducting child custody evaluations using VC by Dale & Smith, 2020). Indeed, before the current pandemic, Batastini et al. (2020) reported that approximately 28 percent of 156 forensic mental health evaluators surveyed indicated they had conducted a competency-to-proceed evaluation via videoconference; the coronavirus pandemic has only spurred on the use of VC for competency evaluation in states across the nation. As researchers begin to present the results of their data on this practice, we will learn more about the various issues that arise and how to best address these in practice. Currently, the largest limitation is a small—but growing—research base. As this literature continues to develop, we will be able to further generalize about the practice of telepsychology and the use of VC for forensic evaluation.

The courts have used videoconferencing in a variety of proceedings—both criminal and civil—for more than two decades (McMillan, 2010; National Center for State Courts, 2017). Despite this, there does not appear to be any current case law regarding the use of VC technology for the evaluation of adjudicative competence, nor are there any federal guidelines regarding the use of VC during pretrial evaluations.

A review of legal considerations and court acceptance of videoconferencing by Luxton and Lexcen (2018) concluded that although there are currently no rules or case law regarding the use of VC as an evaluation method for competency evaluations, it is clearly becoming an accepted method for conducting clinical, civil, and criminal matters. Consideration of the pros and cons of using VC in a particular case along with review of whether it impairs due process rights of the defendant is required.

As we navigate the current coronavirus pandemic, we are sure to see legal cases raising issues of fairness, access, and due process that will impact the ways in which VC is used in forensic assessment.

Bias and Unreliability in Competency Evaluation

Three decades ago, in describing the results of the first meta-analysis of competency-to-stand trial research, Nicholson and Kugler (1991) noted the then-current body of research's focus on the correlates of competency status and defendant demographic variables and called attention to the need for future research to move the field forward by examining clinical decision-making processes in formulating opinions about a defendant's competency status. Since that time, several studies have examined different facets of opinion formulation, with a focus on the reliability of evaluator opinions regarding adjudicative competence (Gowensmith et al., 2012; Morris et al., 2004; Skeem et al., 1998).

In studies where evaluator opinions of competency are compared to court determinations, there is strong agreement (well over 0.90) between these two outcomes (Cruise & Rogers, 1998; Gowensmith et al., 2012; Zapf et al., 2004). In experimental research designs where evaluators are given a circumscribed case vignette or other case information and asked to arrive at an opinion regarding competence, there is generally good agreement between evaluator opinions overall regarding competence (Rosenfeld & Ritchie, 1998). Skeem et al. (1998) reported good levels of agreement (0.81–0.83) between evaluators regarding overall competency status but decreasing levels of agreement between evaluators as the level of specificity of the inquiry increases. That is, rates of agreement were highest when evaluators were opining about a defendant's overall competency status (competent/incompetent) but decreased (to 0.25 or lower) when evaluators were opining about specific abilities or domains of competence that served as the basis for the competency opinion.

Murrie, Boccaccini, Zapf, et al. (2008) examined the rates of incompetency opinions across sixty clinicians who had completed more than seven thousand forensic evaluation reports. Although aggregate rates of incompetency across the United States are around 27.5 percent (Pirelli et al., 2011), Murrie et al. reported wide variability in clinician rates of incompetency opinions, ranging from 0 percent to 62 percent. More than a decade later, Murrie et al. (2020b) reviewed 3,644 competency evaluation reports completed by 126 evaluators and found an average incompetence rate of 38.8 percent in Virginia. Rates of incompetency opinions were calculated for twenty-six evaluators who had each submitted at least thirty reports, ranging from 9 percent to 77 percent across evaluators. Further, rates of reports opining a defendant incompetent but restorable ranged from 0 percent to 77 percent and rates of reports opining a defendant incompetent and unrestorable ranged from 0 percent to 40 percent. This variability in evaluators' rates of opining incompetence can be attributed to multiple possible causes—including referral stream, case difficulty, ambiguity, and other case-relevant variables in addition to a host of evaluator-specific variables—thus field research examining agreement between evaluators regarding the same case provides an externally valid means of examining reliability and isolating the potential causes of variability in evaluator opinions.

Gowensmith et al. (2012) examined 216 cases in Hawaii, where three independent competency evaluations were completed for each defendant. In 29 percent of these cases, the three evaluators did not agree on the defendant's overall competency status. Further, Gowensmith et al. (2017) examined diagnostic reliability between evaluators for 240 cases where three independent evaluators provided diagnoses for the same defendant. Perfect agreement across six different diagnostic categories was found in only 18 percent of cases. Evaluators agreed on the presence of a psychotic, mood, or substance use disorders in approximately 65 percent of cases and on the presence of developmental or cognitive disorders in approximately 90 percent of cases, but agreement dropped to about 47 percent for the combination of psychotic and substance use disorders. These authors concluded that "evaluators are more likely to disagree than agree on a defendant's total diagnostic picture in pretrial forensic mental health evaluations" (Gowensmith et al., 2017, p. 692). To date, it does not appear that research investigating the combined considerations of diagnostic formulation and competency opinion on evaluator reliability has been published; even research addressing the reliability of competency opinions in actual practice appears lacking (Guarnera & Murrie, 2017).

Discrepancies in evaluator agreement for the same defendant raise the question of what accounts for this variability. In a review of the sources of disagreement in forensic evaluations, Guarnera et al. (2017) highlighted that, in addition to individual evaluator differences, inherent task difficulty, and allegiance to the retaining party (discussed below), disagreement often results from limited training and certification and the use of unstandardized methods. Using computer stimulation, Mossman (2013) explored whether bias accounts for differences in evaluator opinions regarding competency. Results indicated that between-examiner disagreements might be attributable to random error rather than examiner biases that imply different thresholds for conceptualizing a defendant's competency status and that fair to moderate agreement in the field could be reasonably expected given the complexity of the task. Dror and Murrie (2018) postulated that this overall variability is a function of both reliability and biasability. Moving beyond simply thinking about reliability to also consider issues of biasability has opened up a broader line of inquiry regarding the extent to which and under what conditions evaluators can become biased in their decision-making and the degree to which this impacts the outcome in a particular case (see Zapf et al., 2017).

There is a growing body of literature examining issues of bias in many forensic sciences, including forensic psychology. Indeed, the reports of the National Research Council's Committee on Identifying the Needs of the Forensic Science Community (2009) and the President's Council of Advisors on Science and Technology (2016) concluded that forensic scientists are prone to a variety of contextual biases and that the error rates of many of their techniques are unknown. Within forensic psychology, there has been increased attention to issues of bias and unreliability, including delineation of the sources of bias and how these might apply in the context of forensic evaluation (see Dror & Murrie, 2018; Zapf & Dror, 2017). Neal and Grisso (2014) described the various heuristics and possible sources of bias as they might apply to forensic evaluation, several of which—such as hindsight bias (Beltrani et al., 2018), bias awareness (Zappala et al., 2018), and the anchoring effect (Murrie, Boccaccini, Johnson, et al., 2008; Murrie et al., 2009; Murrie et al., 2013)—have been the subject of research with forensic evaluators.

With respect to the issue of bias in forensic evaluation, Neal and Brodsky (2016) interviewed twenty board-certified forensic psychologists regarding their experiences with, awareness of, and efforts to correct bias in forensic evaluation. They found that bias awareness falls on a continuum, ranging from complete dismissal of the idea of bias in one's own work to a belief that bias is inevitable, and that participants reported more concern about bias in their colleagues' work than in their own. To better understand beliefs about the scope and nature of cognitive bias, Zapf et al. (2017) surveyed 1,099 forensic mental health evaluators and found that many acknowledged the impact of cognitive bias on the forensic sciences in general (86 percent) and on forensic evaluation specifically (79 percent), but fewer were willing to acknowledge bias in their own forensic evaluations (52 percent). This bias blind spot—the tendency to perceive oneself as less vulnerable to bias than others (see Pronin et al., 2002)—has been demonstrated in a variety of contexts, with experts and laypersons alike. Similar to Neal and Brodsky, who found that most evaluators indicated using introspection to combat bias (a technique that has been demonstrated to be ineffective; see Nisbett & Wilson, 1977; Pronin & Kugler, 2007), Zapf et al. (2017) also found that most evaluators expressed concern over cognitive bias but held an incorrect view that mere willpower can reduce bias. Evaluators who had received training about bias were more likely to acknowledge cognitive bias as a cause for concern, whereas evaluators with more experience were less likely to acknowledge cognitive bias as a cause for concern in forensic evaluation as well as in their own judgments.

There is mounting evidence to suggest that there is at least some risk for bias to impact forensic evaluations, either with respect to the outcome (i.e., ultimate opinion) or with respect to the interpretation of specific instruments or measures used in the evaluation. A series of studies by Murrie, Boccaccini, and colleagues has demonstrated the presence of an adversarial allegiance through results showing that variability in test scores, norm selection and reporting, and ultimate opinions between evaluators was not solely attributable to a lack of reliability but was also a function of a bias in favor of the side for which the experts worked (Chevalier et al., 2015; Murrie, Boccaccini, Johnson, et al., 2008; Murrie et al., 2009; Murrie et al., 2013). This adversarial allegiance effect was demonstrated using an experimental research design wherein the manipulated variable was whether the evaluator believed they were retained by the prosecution or the defense, with all other procedures and materials consistent between the two conditions (Murrie et al., 2013). Although the context in this experiment was with respect to risk assessment, the wide range of reliability estimates found in the available field research on forensic evaluation underscores the importance of understanding the extent to which different evaluation contexts produce different reliability rates (see Guarnera & Murrie, 2017).

As evidence for various types of bias in forensic evaluation continues to emerge, there will be a continual need to devise ways in which we can limit the impact of these biases on decision outcomes. Structured evaluations with systematic methods (see Neal & Grisso, 2014), context management (see Zapf & Dror, 2017; Zapf et al., 2017), tracking one's own evaluation data and understanding one's own base rates (see Gowensmith & McCallum, 2019), and a host of other strategies have been proposed; additional research is needed to understand implications, determine best practices, and calculate known error rates for evaluations conducted in various contexts.

Current limitations of research on sources of unreliability and bias in forensic evaluation include a disjointed understanding of the extent to which unreliability in competency evaluation is a result of individual evaluator variables—including their training and experience—evaluation methods, or other contextual considerations. Future research will need to focus on practical applications for mitigating bias and increasing reliability in a variety of contexts.

Perhaps the most concerning implications of unreliability and bias in evaluations of competency to stand trial surround the issue of admissibility of expert opinion testimony. Rule 702 of the Federal Rules of Evidence indicates that "a witness qualified as an expert by knowledge, skill, experience, training, or education, may testify thereto in the form of an opinion or otherwise, if (1) the testimony is based on sufficient facts or data, (2) the testimony is the product of *reliable principles and methods*, and (3) the witness has *applied the principles and methods reliably to the facts of the case*."[1] Prior to 1993, admissibility of expert testimony was guided by the standard set out in *Frye v. United States*,[2] in which the court held that the criterion for admissibility was whether the foundation on which the expert evidence was based had been sufficiently established to gain general acceptance in the field. In 1993, however, the US Supreme Court decided *Daubert v. Merrell Dow Pharmaceuticals*,[3]

---

[1] 28 U.S.C. FRE 702 (emphases added).
[2] Frye v. United States, 293 F. 1013 (D.C. Cir. 1923).
[3] Daubert v. Merrell Dow Pharm., Inc., 509 U.S. 579 (1993).

which provided a more expansive standard going beyond mere determination of whether the methods used by an expert are generally accepted in the field to also gauge the scientific foundation supporting an expert's methods. This requires the trial court judge to "assess the factual, methodological, and theoretical basis of the testimony, as well as the 'fit' of that testimony with the case at hand, all through the prism of 'reliability'" (Melton et al., 2018, p. 21). *Daubert* is now the admissibility standard in the federal jurisdiction and in more than half of the states. As such, it underscores the need for accurate estimates of known reliability and error rates for the methods and techniques used in forensic evaluation.

Implications, Next Steps, and Future Directions

Despite extensive and varied research on the topic of adjudicative competency spanning multiple decades, there are still numerous aspects of the competency evaluation process that are understudied or unknown. Fogel et al. (2013) noted that there is still scant research addressing issues relating to ethnic and cultural diversity in competency (e.g., use of interpreters in evaluations). And, despite Nicholson and Kugler's (1991) call for more research on the decision-making process in competency evaluation three decades ago, there is still much to be done in this area. Indeed, one of the conclusions from this early meta-analysis was that "although these results are generally consistent with the legal standard for competency to stand trial, some of the correlates of competency may reflect potential biases in the decision-making process" (Nicholson & Kugler, 1991, p. 355). Research since this meta-analysis has shown that Black and Hispanic defendants are more likely to be referred for inpatient evaluation in a secure facility than their White counterparts (Pinals et al., 2004); that Black defendants are more likely than White defendants to be opined incompetent (Cooper & Zapf, 2003); and that Spanish-speaking defendants are rated as less mentally ill by attorneys than English-speaking defendants, who are more likely to be referred for evaluation (Varela et al., 2011). With respect to sex differences, results have been mixed with studies finding women more likely to be found incompetent than men (Crocker et al., 2002), less likely to be incompetent than men (Pirelli et al., 2011), and others finding no differences (Warren et al., 2006). As Kois et al. (2013) observed, variables that have historically been associated with competency status (i.e., minority status and age) in predominately male samples may not transfer across demographic groups. The extent to which demographic characteristics are reflective of biases on the part of forensic evaluators or others involved in the criminal justice system remains an area in need of further investigation.

Regarding emerging issues such as conducting evaluations using videoconferencing technology or attempting to better understand the sources of bias or unreliability in competency evaluation, we provide three areas of consideration for a path forward.

Evaluator Characteristics

The available competency research has focused primarily on examining defendant characteristics and how these might be related to competency status with little regard to the characteristics of evaluators and how these might contribute to case conceptualization and opinion formation. Nicholson and Kugler (1991) called for future research to examine the decision-making process more closely; three decades later, we still have gaps in our knowledge regarding how forensic evaluators conceptualize cases and formulate opinions. The research that has been conducted has shown wide variability in rates of evaluation outcomes by evaluator (see Murrie, Boccaccini, Johnson et al., 2008b; Murrie et al., 2009; Murrie et al., 2013) and wide variability in reliability estimates depending on the evaluation context (Guarnera et al., 2017). The need for reliability among evaluators (as well as by the same evaluator at different times) is a cornerstone for establishing forensic evaluation as a defensible science that meets legally required admissibility criteria for evidence and expert testimony. Better understanding of evaluator characteristics—including training, culture, and experience—that contribute to opinion formulation will result in better strategies for limiting the impact of these characteristics on objective observation and inferences in forensic evaluation. "Understanding and characterizing the abilities required for the specialized task of forensic evaluation will ultimately allow further development of profiles for selecting evaluators or for developing necessary evaluation skills" (Zapf & Dror, 2017, p. 236).

Evaluation Methods

Systematic research on the methods and procedures used in forensic evaluation and the impact of these on evaluation outcomes will ultimately allow for development and refinement of those most effective for forensic evaluation. As telepsychology evolves and the use of alternative or nontraditional methods increase, we must continue to explore the impact of various evaluation methods and techniques on a variety of relevant outcomes. These outcomes should include both the actual outcome of the evaluation (i.e., the evaluator's opinion regarding competence) and also relevant outcomes such as satisfaction (evaluator and defendant), cost, convenience, time, and other ways in which to gauge consumer and system impact. In addition, exploring the interrelations between evaluator characteristics and evaluation methods will further increase our understanding of the interplay between personal and situational variables in forensic evaluation.

Standardized evaluation methods and structured tools result in higher field reliability (Miller et al., 2012); however, surveys of forensic clinicians indicate that many are not using any tools or standardized methods and are instead relying on clinical judgment alone (Neal & Grisso, 2014). Further work needs to be done to elevate the level of practice among forensic clinicians and to implement best practices gleaned from the available research base.

Systemically, reevaluation of common policies, procedures, and practices in light of emerging evidence will likely become necessary in some jurisdictions. For example, although it is common in many jurisdictions to order and conduct competency and insanity evaluations concurrently for a defendant, research suggests that rates of evaluator opinions on the issue of competency vary according to whether the evaluation conducted was competency alone or competency in conjunction with an insanity evaluation. Better understanding of evaluation methods and contexts will allow for better forensic evaluations.

Training

The issue of evaluator training is important enough to stand on its own as an area in need of further investigation, but it is also related to evaluator characteristics and evaluation methods. Extrinsic sources of expert disagreement include limited training and certification for forensic evaluators (Guarnera et al., 2017). Although specialized training programs and board certifications have been established, the typical training and certification for conducting forensic evaluations remains variable and often poor (DeMatteo et al., 2009). Wettstein (2005) demonstrated that certification programs for forensic evaluators improve the reliability and quality of forensic evaluation reports; however, only about one-third to one-half of states have any state-level certification in forensic mental health assessment and, even among those that do, many have weak standards (Gowensmith et al., 2014). In addition to initial training and certification, Gowensmith et al. (2015) also highlight the importance of ongoing training and recertification. Research suggesting that evaluators with more training produce more reliable forensic opinions (Guarnera et al., 2017) underscores the importance of initial and ongoing training in this specialty area of practice. Indeed, when interrater reliability rates for forensic opinions regarding competence (insanity and risk) were compared before and after a more stringent certification standard was implemented in Hawaii, results showed improved reliability rates postcertification (Gowensmith et al., 2014). This natural experiment provides "the first direct evidence that more stringent state-level certification standards can improve the field reliability of forensic opinions" (Guarnera et al., 2017, p. 146).

Regarding the issue of bias in forensic evaluation, a survey of more than one thousand forensic evaluators indicated that most evaluators are not provided any formal, direct training on the ways in which bias can impact their work (Zapf at al., 2017). Further, although most evaluators recognized bias as a cause for concern in forensic evaluation, far fewer saw themselves as vulnerable to bias and many showed a limited understanding of how to effectively mitigate bias (Neal & Brodsky, 2016; Zapf et al., 2017). Understanding the most effective ways of training evaluators to perform forensic evaluations in a consistent and reliable way while limiting the impact of bias will allow for the implementation of best practices, both with respect to the evaluations themselves as well as with respect to training procedures and outcomes.

References

Acklin, M. W. (2012). The forensic clinician's toolbox I: A review of competency to stand trial (CST) instruments. *Journal of Personality Assessment, 94*(2), 220–222.

Adjorlolo, S., & Chan, H. C. (2015). Forensic assessment via videoconferencing: Issues and practice considerations. *Journal of Forensic Psychology Practice, 15*(3), 185–204.

Antonacci, D. J., Bloch, R. M., Saeed, S. A., Yildirim, Y., & Talley, J. (2008). Empirical evidence on the use and effectiveness of telepsychiatry via videoconferencing: Implications for forensic and correctional psychiatry. *Behavioral Sciences and the Law, 26*(3), 253–269.

Batastini, A. B., King, C. M., Morgan, R. D., McDaniel, B. (2016). Telepsychological services with criminal justice and substance abuse clients: A systematic review and meta-analysis. *Psychological Services, 13*(1), 20–30.

Batastini, A. B., Pike, M., Thoen, M. A., Jones, A. C. T., Davis, R. M., & Escalera, E. (2020). Perceptions and use of videoconferencing in forensic mental health assessments: A survey of evaluators and legal personnel. *Psychology, Crime & Law, 26*(6), 593–613.

Beltrani, A., Reed, A. L., Zapf, P. A., & Otto, R. K. O. (2018). Is hindsight really 20/20? The impact of outcome information on decision making. *International Journal of Forensic Mental Health, 17*(3), 285–296.

Beltrani, A., & Zapf, P. A. (2020). Competence to stand trial and criminalization: an overview of the research. *CNS Spectrums, 25*(2), 161–172.

Blake, G. A., Ogloff, J. R. P., & Chen, W. S. (2019). Meta-analysis of second generation competency to stand trial assessment measures: Preliminary findings. *International Journal of Law and Psychiatry, 64*, 238–249.

Bonnie, R. J., & Grisso, T. (2000). Adjudicative competence and youthful offenders. In T. Grisso & R. G. Schwartz (Eds.), *Youth on trial: A developmental perspective on juvenile justice* (pp. 73–103). University of Chicago Press.

Brearly, T. W., Shura, R. D., Martindale, S. L., Lazowski, R. A., Luxton, D. D., Shenal, B. V., & Rowland, J. A. (2017). Neuropsychological test administration by videoconference: A systematic review and meta-analysis. *Neuropsychology Review, 27*(2), 174–186.

Chevalier, C. S., Boccaccini, M. T., Murrie, D. C., & Varela, J. G. (2015). Static-99R reporting practices in sexually violent predator cases: Does norm selection reflect adversarial allegiance? *Law and Human Behavior, 39*(3), 209–218.

Cooper, V. G., & Zapf, P. A. (2003). Predictor variables in competency to stand trial decisions. *Law and Human Behavior, 27*(4), 423–436.

Crocker, A. G., Favreau, O. E., & Caulet, M. (2002). Gender and fitness to stand trial: A 5-year review of remands in Quebec. *International Journal of Law and Psychiatry, 25*(1), 67–84.

Cruise, K. R., & Rogers, R. (1998). An analysis of competency to stand trial: An integration of case law and clinical knowledge. *Behavioral Sciences and the Law, 16*(1), 35–50.

Dale, M. D., & Smith, D. (2020). Making the case for videoconferencing and remote child custody evaluations (RCCES): The empirical, ethical, and evidentiary arguments for accepting new technology. *Psychology, Public Policy, and Law.* Advance online publication. https://.doi.org/10.1037/law0000280

DeMatteo, D., Marczyk, G., Krauss, D. A., & Burl, J. (2009). Educational and training models in forensic psychology. *Training and Education in Professional Psychology, 3*(3), 184–191.

Dror, I. E., & Murrie, D. C. (2018). A hierarchy of expert performance applied to forensic psychological assessments. *Psychology, Public Policy, and Law, 24*(1), 11–23.

Fader-Towe, H., & Kelly, E. (2020). *Just and well: Rethinking how states approach competency to stand trial.* The Council of State Governments Justice Center.

Fogel, M. H., Schiffman, W., Mumley, D., Tillbrook, C., & Grisso, T. (2013). Ten year research update (2001–2010): Evaluations for competence to stand trial (adjudicative competence). *Behavioral Sciences and the Law, 31*(2), 165–191.

Gowensmith, W. N. (2019). Resolution or resignation: The role of forensic mental health professionals amidst the competency services crisis. *Psychology, Public Policy, and Law, 25*(1), 1–14.

Gowensmith, W. N., Frost, L. E., Speelman, D. W., & Therson, D. E. (2016). Lookin' for beds in all the wrong places: Outpatient competency restoration as a promising approach to modern challenges. *Psychology, Public Policy, and Law, 22*(3), 293–305.

Gowensmith, W. N., & McCallum, K. E. (2019). Mirror, mirror on the wall, who's the least biased of them all? Dangers and potential solutions regarding bias in forensic psychological evaluations. *South African Journal of Psychology, 49*(2), 165–176.

Gowensmith, W. N., Murrie, D. C., & Boccaccini, M. T. (2012). Field reliability of competence to stand trial opinions: How often do evaluators agree, and what do judges decide when evaluators disagree? *Law and Human Behavior, 36*(2), 130–139.

Gowensmith, W. N., Pinals, D. A., & Karas, A. C. (2015). States' standards for training and certifying evaluators of competency to stand trial. *Journal of Forensic Psychology Practice, 15*(4), 295–317.

Gowensmith, W. N., Sessarego, S. N., McKee, M. K., Horkott, S., MacLean, N., & McCallum, K. E. (2017). Diagnostic field reliability in forensic mental health evaluation. *Psychological Assessment, 29*(6), 692–700.

Gowensmith, W., Sledd, M., & Sessarego, S. (2014, August). *Impact of stringent certification standards on forensic evaluator reliability*. Paper presented at the annual meeting of the American Psychology Association, Washington, DC.

Grisso, T. (2003). *Evaluating competencies: Forensic assessments and instruments* (2nd ed.). Kluwer Academic/Plenum.

Grisso, T. (2014). *Competence to stand trial evaluations: Just the basics*. Professional Resource Press.

Guarnera, L. A., & Murrie, D. C. (2017). Field reliability of competency and sanity opinions: A systematic review and meta-analysis. *Psychological Assessment, 29*(6), 795–818.

Guarnera, L. A., Murrie, D. C., & Boccaccini, M. T. (2017). Why do forensic experts disagree? Sources of unreliability and bias in forensic psychology evaluations. *Translational Issues in Psychological Science, 3*(2), 143–152.

Joint Task Force for the Development of Telepsychology Guidelines for Psychologists. (2013). Guidelines for the practice of telepsychology. *American Psychologist, 68*(9), 791–800.

Kois, L. E., Cox, J., & Peck, A. T. (2020, December 3). Forensic E-mental health: Review, research priorities, and policy directions. *Psychology, Public Policy, and Law*. Advance online publication. http://dx.doi.org/10.1037/law0000293

Kois, L., Pearson, J., Chauhan, P., Goni, M., & Saraydarian, L. (2013). Competence to stand trial among female inpatients. *Law and Human Behavior, 37*(4), 231–240.

Kois, L. E., Potts, H., Cappello, V., Cox, J., & Zapf, P. (2020, March). *Updating the "magic number:" Contemporary competence to proceed metrics reported by U.S. judiciaries*. [Paper presentation]. Annual meeting of the American Psychology-Law Society, New Orleans, LA.

Lexcen, F. J., Hawk, G. L., Herrik, S., & Blank, M. B. (2006). Use of videoconferencing for psychiatric and forensic evaluations. *Psychiatric Services, 57*(5), 713–715.

Luxton, D. D., & Lexcen, F. J. (2018). Forensic competency evaluations via videoconferencing: A feasibility review and best practice recommendations. *Professional Psychology, Research and Practice, 49*(2), 124–131.

Luxton, D. D., Pruitt, L. D., & Osenbach, J. E. (2014). Best practices for remote psychological assessment via telehealth technologies. *Professional Psychology: Research and Practice, 45*(1), 27–35.

Manguno-Mire, G. M., Thompson, J. W., Jr., Shore, J. H., Croy, C. D., Artecona, J. F., & Pickering, J. W. (2007). The use of telemedicine to evaluate competency to stand trial: A preliminary randomized controlled study. *Journal of the American Academy of Psychiatry and the Law, 35*(4), 481–489.

Martin, J. N., Millan, F., & Campbell, L. F. (2020). Telepsychology practice: Primer and first steps. *Practice Innovations, 5*(2), 114–127.

Melton, G. B., Petrila, J., Poythress, N. G., Slobogin, C., Otto, R. K., Mossman, D., & Condie, L. O. (2018). *Psychological evaluations for the courts: A handbook for mental health professionals and lawyers* (4th ed.). Guilford Press.

McMillan, J. (2010). Videoconferencing survey of 2010 results. National Center for State Courts. Retrieved from http://www.ncsc.org/services-and-experts/areas-of-expertise/technology/ncsc-video-conferencing-survey.aspx

Miller, C. S., Kimonis, E. R., Otto, R. K., Kline, S. M., & Wasserman, A. L. (2012). Reliability of risk assessment measures used in sexually violent predator proceedings. *Psychological Assessment, 24*(4), 944–953.

Morris, G. H., Haroun, A. M., & Naimark, D. (2004). Assessing competency competently: Toward a rational standard for competency-to-stand-trial assessments. *Journal of the American Academy of Psychiatry and the Law, 32*(3), 231–245.

Mossman, D. (2013). When forensic examiners disagree: Bias, or just inaccuracy? *Psychology, Public Policy, and Law, 19*(1), 40–55.

Murrie, D. C., Boccaccini M. T., Guarnera, L. A., & Rufino, K. A. (2013). Are forensic experts biased by the side that retained them? *Psychological Science, 24*(10), 1889–1897.

Murrie, D. C., Boccaccini, M. T., Johnson, J. T., & Janke, C. (2008). Does interrater (dis)agreement on Psychopathy Checklist scores in sexually violent predator trials suggest partisan allegiance in forensic evaluations? *Law and Human Behavior, 32*(4), 352–362.

Murrie, D. C., Boccaccini, M. T., Turner, D., Meeks, M., Woods, C., & Tussey, C. (2009). Rater (dis)agreement on risk assessment measures in sexually violent predator proceedings: Evidence of adversarial allegiance in forensic evaluation? *Psychology, Public Policy, and Law, 15*(1), 19–53.

Murrie, D. C., Boccaccini, M. T., Zapf, P. A., Warren, J. I., & Henderson, C. E. (2008). Clinician variation in findings of competence to stand trial. *Psychology, Public Policy, and Law, 14*(3), 177–193.

Murrie, D. C., Gardner, B. O., & Torres, A. N. (2020a). The impact of misdemeanor arrests on forensic mental health services: A state-wide review of Virginia competence to stand trial evaluations. *Psychology, Public Policy, and Law*. Advance online publication. https://doi.org/10.1037/law0000296

Murrie, D. C., Gardner, B. O., & Torres, A. N. (2020b). Competency to stand trial evaluations: A state-wide review of court-ordered reports. *Behavioral Sciences & the Law, 38*(1), 32–50.

National Center for State Courts. (2017). NCSC Video Conferencing Survey. Retrieved from http://www.ncsc.org/services-and-experts/areas-of-expertise/technology/ncsc-video-conferencing-survey.aspx

National Research Council, Committee on Identifying the Needs of the Forensic Science Community. (2009). *Strengthening forensic science in the United States: A path forward*. National Academies Press. Retrieved from https:// www.ncjrs.gov/pdffiles1/nij/grants/228091.pdf

Neal, T., & Brodsky, S. L. (2016). Forensic psychologists' perceptions of bias and potential correction strategies in forensic mental health evaluations. *Psychology, Public Policy, and Law, 22*(1), 58–76.

Neal, T., & Grisso, T. (2014). Assessment practices and expert judgment methods in forensic psychology and psychiatry: An international snapshot. *Criminal Justice and Behavior, 41*(12), 1406–1421.

Nicholson, R. A., & Kugler, K. (1991). Competent and incompetent criminal defendants: A quantitative review of comparative research. *Psychological Bulletin, 109*(3), 355–370.

Nisbett, R. E., & Wilson, T. D. (1977). Telling more than we can know: Verbal reports on mental processes. *Psychological Review, 84*(3), 231–259.

Pinals, D. A., & Callahan, L. (2020). Evaluation and restoration of competence to stand trial: Intercepting the forensic system using the Sequential Intercept Model. *Psychiatric Services, 71*(7), 698–705.

Pinals, D. A., Packer, I. K., Fisher, W., & Roy-Bujnowski, K. (2004). Relationship between race and ethnicity and forensic clinical triage dispositions. *Psychiatric Services, 55*(8), 873–878.

Pirelli, G., Gottdiener, W. H., & Zapf, P. A. (2011). A meta-analytic review of competency to stand trial research. *Psychology, Public Policy, And Law, 17*(1), 1–53.

Pirelli, G., & Zapf, P. A. (2020). An attempted meta-analysis of the competency restoration research: Important findings for future directions. *Journal of Forensic Psychology Research and Practice, 20*(2), 134–162.

President's Council of Advisors on Science and Technology (PCAST). (2016). *Report to the President: Forensic science in the criminal courts: Ensuring scientific validity of feature-comparison methods*. Executive Office of the President of the United States. Retrieved from https://www.whitehouse.gov/sites/default/files/microsites/ostp/PCAST/pcast_forensic_science_report_final.pdf

Pronin, E., & Kugler, M. B. (2007). Valuing thoughts, ignoring behavior: The introspection illusion as a source of the bias blind spot. *Journal of Experimental Social Psychology, 43*(4), 565–578.

Pronin, E., Lin, D. Y., & Ross, L. (2002). The bias blind spot: Perceptions of bias in self versus others. *Personality and Social Psychology Bulletin, 28*(3), 369–381.

Rosenfeld, B., & Ritchie, K. (1998). Competence to stand trial: Clinician reliability and the role of offense severity. *Journal of Forensic Sciences, 43*(1), 151–157.

Schwermer, R. (May, 2020). *State Justice Institute-Improving the justice system response to mental illness: Competence to stand trial, interim report*. State Justice Institute. Retrieved from https://www.ncsc.org/__data/assets/pdf_file/0025/38680/Competence_to_Stand_Trial_Interim_Final.pdf

Sharp, I. R., Kobak, K. A., & Osman, D. A. (2011). The use of videoconferencing with patients with psychosis: A review of the literature. *Annals of General Psychiatry, 10*, 14.

Skeem, J. L., Golding, S. L., Cohn, N., & Berge, G. (1998). Logic and reliability of evaluations of competence to stand trial. *Law and Human Behavior, 22*(5), 519–547.

Varela, J. G., Boccaccini, M. T., Gonzalez, E., Jr., Gharagozloo, L., & Johnson, S. M. (2011). Do defense attorney referrals for competence to stand trial evaluations depend on whether the client speaks English or Spanish? *Law and Human Behavior, 35*(6), 501–511.

Warren, J. I., Murrie, D. C., Stejskal, W., Colwell, L. H., Morris, J., Chauhan, P., & Dietz, P. (2006). Opinion formation in evaluating the adjudicative competence and restorability of criminal defendants: A review of 8,000 evaluations. *Behavioral Sciences & the Law, 24*(2), 113–132.

Wettstein, R. M. (2005). Quality and quality improvement in forensic mental health evaluations. *Journal of the American Academy of Psychiatry and the Law, 33*, 158–175.

Zapf, P. A., & Dror, I. E. (2017). Understanding and mitigating bias in forensic evaluation: Lessons from forensic science. *International Journal of Forensic Mental Health, 16*(3), 227–238.

Zapf, P. A., Hubbard, K. L., Cooper, V. G., Wheeles, M. C., & Ronan, K. A. (2004). Have the courts abdicated their responsibility for determination of competency to stand trial to clinicians? *Journal of Forensic Psychology Practice, 4*(1), 27–44.

Zapf, P. A., Kukucka, J., Kassin, S. M., & Dror, I. E. (2017). Cognitive bias in forensic mental health assessment: Evaluator beliefs about its nature and scope. *Psychology, Public Policy, and Law, 24*(1), 1–10.

Zapf, P. A., & Roesch, R. (2009). *Best practices in forensic mental health assessment. Evaluation of competence to stand trial.* Oxford University Press.

Zapf, P. A., & Roesch, R. (2011). Future directions in the restoration of competency to stand trial. *Current Directions in Psychological Science, 20*(1), 43–47.

Zappala, M., Reed, A. L., Beltrani A., Zapf, P. A., & Otto, R. K. (2018). Anything you can do, I can do better: Bias awareness in forensic evaluators. *Journal of Forensic Psychology Research and Practice, 18*(1), 45–56.

Criminal Responsibility Evaluations

Ira K. Packer *and* Lauren E. Kois

Abstract

Criminal responsibility (sanity) is a complex concept at the intersection of mental health and the law, which is then contextualized by societal standards. Although sanity is not a clinical concept per se, the legal system frequently calls on mental health professionals' expertise to inform triers of fact in their decision-making: on account of severe mental illness, should a particular defendant be found not culpable for criminal behavior? This review is broad in scope and covers a range of issues that are pertinent for mental health and legal practitioners and scholars. We begin with commentary on the historical antecedents that have led to the contemporary conceptualization of the insanity defense in the United States. We discuss issues of quality of criminal responsibility evaluation and report writing, and call for standardized evaluator training and certification standards. Following an appraisal of the empirical literature, we cite its systematic limitations and conclude with specific recommendations for future research in this area.

Key Words: criminal responsibility, insanity, insanity defense, training, certification, criminal behavior

Presentation of Topic/Legal Overview

The term "insanity" is a legal not a psychological or psychiatric term. It is not synonymous with mental illness but, rather, reflects a societal decision that certain individuals, due to severe mental impairments, are not considered legally responsible for their behavior. In order to be criminally liable, the individual must be found not only to have committed an illegal act (*actus reus,* which is Latin for "bad act"), but also to have done so with the requisite mental state (*mens rea,* which means "guilty mind"). This general proposition is not particularly controversial, as it has been recognized for centuries and across cultures. However, the more complex issue is deciding on the level of impairment that would qualify an individual to be found not guilty of a crime by reason of insanity, and developing a standard that can be applied reliably in all cases. Psychologists and psychiatrists can provide relevant knowledge about psychopathology, brain functioning, and human behavior that can inform the legal system's approach to development of standards to be adopted for an insanity defense. However, it is up to legislatures and courts to make the final decision about the wording to be used.

Furthermore, once a decision has been made about the standard, the role of the mental health professional is to evaluate the defendant and educate the trier of fact about the individual's mental functioning and how it may or may not have impacted the capacities relevant to the legal standard. Courts have clarified that it is then up to jury or judge to decide how much weight to give the expert testimony, and how to apply it to make their determination. For instance: "[T]he issue of insanity is not strictly medical; it also invokes both legal and ethical [referring actually to "moral"] considerations. Otherwise the issue of sanity would be decided in the hospitals and not the courtrooms."[1] In addition, as the conscience of the community, juries are given great leeway: "[U]ltimately the issue of insanity at the time of the offense excusing criminal responsibility lies in the province of the jury, not only as to the credibility of the witnesses and the weight of the evidence, but also as to the limits of the defense itself."[2]

Complicating matters even further, each state (as well as the federal courts and military courts) can set its own standard (Packer, 2009). Therefore, two individuals who commit the exact same offense, with the exact same mental state, may have different outcomes depending on where the crime was committed. Indeed, four states (Idaho, Kansas, Montana, and Utah) have effectively abolished the insanity defense. The US Supreme Court has recently addressed the issue of the constitutionality of the legal standard in Kansas.[3] In that case, Mr. Kahler claimed that the Kansas statute which eliminated the insanity defense should be considered unconstitutional. This was the first time that the Supreme Court had agreed to address this issue, having denied *certiorari* (i.e., did not accept the case for review) in previous cases from Montana and Idaho.[4]

Formulations of the Insanity Defense

The *Kahler* Court recognized a long history, embedded in both American and English Law (from which the insanity defense was derived), of the concept that mental illness may deprive individuals of those abilities necessary to be considered criminally responsible for their actions. However, the specific formulations of the defense change and evolve over time, in conjunction with changes in understanding of mental illness. For instance, in the English case of *Rex v. Arnold*,[5] the following standard was adopted: "a man must be *totally deprived* of his understanding and memory, and doth not know what he is doing, no more than an *infant, brute, or a wild beast*" (emphasis added). This admittedly vague standard was modified in England in 1843, following the acquittal of Daniel M'Naghten

---

[1] *Bigby v. State*, 892 S.W.2d 864, 877 (Tex. Crim. App. 1994).

[2] *Graham v. State*, 566 S.W.2d 941, 949 (1978).

[3] *Kahler v. Kansas*, 140 S. Ct. 1021, 1038 (2020) (Breyer, J., dissenting).

[4] *State v. Cowan*, 861 P.2d 884 (Mont. 1993), cert. denied, 511 U. S. 1005 (1994); *State v. Delling*, 267 P. 3d 709 (Ida. 2011), cert. denied, 568 U.S. 1038 (2012).

[5] *Rex v. Arnold*, 16 How. St. Tr. 695 (1724).

who, attempting to kill the prime minister, instead shot and killed his secretary, Edward Drummond. In response to public pressure, the House of Lords then developed what has come to be known as the "M'Naghten standard":

> "[T]o establish a defense on the ground of insanity, it must be proved that, at the time of the committing of the act, the party accused was laboring under such a defect of reason, from disease of the mind, as not to know the nature and quality of the act he was doing or if he did know it, that he did not know he was doing what was wrong."[6]

This case became the basis for the insanity defense in the United States as well. However, in the twentieth century, in response to concerns that this narrow focus on the cognitive ability to know right from wrong no longer reflected scientific and clinical advances, attempts were made to broaden the definition. One approach was to add a volitional component; that is, recognizing that mental illness could impair an individual's capacity to control behavior, even if he or she knew that such behavior was illegal. Initial formulations used the term "irresistible impulse," but the American Law Institute (ALI) updated the terminology when it developed the Model Penal Code in 1962.[7] This language modified both the volitional as well as the cognitive prongs, indicating that a defendant could be found legally insane if "as a result of mental illness or mental defect he lacked the capacity either to appreciate the wrongfulness of his conduct or to conform his conduct to the requirements of the law."

The Supreme Court noted that changes in the standards reflected ongoing developments in the fields of psychology and psychiatry, and thus the majority chose to address the issue in a narrow sense. Rather than directly address whether abolition of the insanity defense is unconstitutional, the *Kahler* Court ruled that the Kansas statute did not constitute abolition. Specifically, the Kansas statute included language that "it shall be a defense to a prosecution under any statute that the defendant, as a result of mental disease or defect, lacked the culpable mental state required as an element of the offense charged."[8] The majority equated this provision with what they called the cognitive incapacity prong of the *M'Naghten* standard (i.e., not knowing the nature and quality of the act), and concluded that since Kansas did provide for mental illness to be considered both a factor negating criminal responsibility as well as a mitigating factor at sentencing, there was no constitutional violation. It should be noted that the minority opinion strongly disagreed with this formulation.

The dissenting opinion, authored by Justice Stephen Breyer, noted that the Kansas statute effectively limited the analysis to whether a defendant formed the requisite intent,

---

[6] M'Naghten, (1843) 8 E.R. 718.
[7] American Law Institute, Model Penal Code (1962).
[8] Kan. Stat. Ann. §21-5209 (2018).

which does not accurately reflect the impact of mental illness. Almost all mentally ill defendants (even those who are psychotic and delusional) can form intent to commit the act, but they may do so based on misperceptions that impact their motivation. Thus, the dissent argued, the effect of this ruling is to allow states to abolish the insanity defense as we typically understand it and replace it with a defense of lack of intent. In practice, according to the dissent, this amounts to abolition.

Justice Breyer illustrated his point by offering two hypothetical scenarios. In the first scenario, the defendant shot and killed another person, believing (due to severe mental illness) that he was shooting a dog, not a human being. In the second scenario, the defendant believed (due to a severe mental illness) that that a dog had ordered him to kill the victim. Under most standards for insanity, both individuals would be acquitted. Justice Breyer noted that the hypothetical defendants are comparably severely mentally ill, and should be considered equally not blameworthy. However, under the Kansas statute, only the first defendant would be acquitted (since he had no intention of killing a human being), while the second defendant would be convicted (as he clearly intended to kill the victim but was psychotically motivated). These scenarios thus encapsulate the distinction between an insanity defense focused on impairment of capacity to appreciate wrongfulness, and a standard that absolves only individuals who could not form the requisite intent. An important focus of the dissent is that the majority's formulation is not consistent with the current state of scientific knowledge. As Justice Breyer wrote: "Mental illness typically does not deprive individuals of the ability to form intent. Rather, it affects their *motivations* for forming such intent."[9] Nevertheless, the impact of the Supreme Court decision does not impact the vast majority of jurisdictions that maintain such an option.

The Volitional Prong

Another controversial element of the insanity defense relates to the volitional prong (impairment in capacity to conform conduct). There is more limited scientific and clinical knowledge bearing on the assessment of ability to control behavior (as opposed to simply choosing not to refrain from the action). Although individuals experiencing a manic episode are most likely to demonstrate impairments in volitional capacity, there is considerable controversy regarding whether psychologists and psychiatrists can reliably determine the requisite level of impairment. Following John Hinckley's acquittal by reason of insanity in 1983 for shooting President Ronald Reagan and his press secretary, James Brady, the American Psychiatric Association endorsed the elimination of the volitional prong, writing that "the line between an irresistible impulse and an impulse not resisted is probably no sharper than that between twilight and dusk" (American Psychiatric Association, 1983,

---

[9] Kahler, 140 S. Ct. at 1048.

p. 685). The American Bar Association also supported this change, which was incorporated into federal standards for insanity[10] as well as adopted by a number of individual states.

Opposition to the inclusion of the volitional prong has included not only these pragmatic concerns but also conceptual and philosophical objections. For instance, Morse (1994) argued against the volitional prong on the grounds that that although an individual's subjective experience may include a feeling of compulsion, this does not equate to a determination that the individual's capacity to resist the urge to act was beyond their control. Alternatively, the situation could be conceptualized as a choice faced by the actor between conflicting alternatives, either acting on the impulse or avoiding doing so in order to avoid negative consequences. Rather than frame this conflict in terms of capacity to control one's urges, Morse suggested that the relevant issue should be the irrationality of the individual's thinking about the alternatives. Nonetheless, at present sixteen states still include the volitional prong, but there is little evidence that this significantly impacts adjudications. For instance, in a review of more than five thousand insanity defense evaluations in Virginia over a ten-year period, Warren et al. (2004) found that in only 9 percent of cases where evaluators opined that a defendant met the insanity defense criteria, did they rely solely on the volitional prong (as compared to 44 percent sole reliance on the cognitive prong, and the remainder were deemed to be impaired on both).

Substance Use and the Insanity Defense

Another aspect of the insanity defense that revolves around volitional behavior relates to the effects of substance use on mental status. From a legal perspective, if an individual's cognitive or volitional capacities were impaired due to the acute effects of voluntary intoxication, the defendant is typically not eligible for the insanity defense. Again, the basis for this caveat is a legal/moral one, not necessarily a clinical one. The legal position is articulated clearly in the case of *Kane v. United States*,[11] in which the court stated that mental illnesses that qualify for the insanity defense are "brought about by circumstances beyond the control of the actor,"[12] but intoxication is the result of purposeful behavior. Addictions specialists might disagree with this characterization, instead considering substance use disorders to be a brain disease, thus impacting the individual's capacity to choose not to drink or take the drug. The competing arguments were articulated in competing *amicus curia* briefs in the Massachusetts case of *Commonwealth v. Eldred*.[13]

The *Eldred* case involved a probationer who was ordered to abstain from substance use as a condition of probation, and who was detained due to violation of that condition.

---

[10] Insanity Defense Reform Act of 1984, 18 U.S.C. §17.
[11] *Kane v. United States*, 399 F.2d 730 (9th Cir. 1968).
[12] *Id.* at 735.
[13] *Commonwealth v. Eldred*, 101 N.E.3d 911 (Mass. 2018).

The *amicus* for Ms. Eldred argued that abstinence should not be imposed as a condition of probation, as the individual is unable to abstain due to addiction being a disease of the brain. The *amicus* for the defendant (in this case, the Commonwealth of Massachusetts) argued that those addicted to substances could nonetheless respond to consequences, demonstrating volitional capacity. They further noted that if the court agreed with the plaintiff, this could open the door to defendants addicted to substances being deemed to lack criminal responsibility for possession of illegal substances. The Massachusetts court decided the case on narrow grounds and did not resolve the competing scientific and medical arguments about how addiction should be treated by the criminal justice system. However, this case likely presages further disputes, particularly as more refined scientific knowledge of addiction is developed.

Neuroscience and the Insanity Defense

These differing approaches to understanding the impact of brain mechanisms on behavior have emerged in other areas as well. There is a tension between biomechanistic explanations of behavior and their application to the criminal justice system. The implications have been highlighted by several studies and articles. For instance, Aspinwall et al. (2012) conducted a study with trial judges, presenting them with vignettes and asking what sentences they would give. They found that the judges gave lesser sentences to defendants identified as psychopaths when they were told that psychopathy was caused by a "biomechanism" (i.e., a biological explanation tied to brain functioning) compared to no such explanation. Although this did not involve the insanity defense, this type of thinking (that evidence of biological mechanisms reduces culpability) could be used in such cases.[14] However, this approach has been critiqued on both conceptual and scientific grounds. For instance, Miller (2012) noted that attributing a lower level of culpability simply because there is a correlation with a biological mechanism, as opposed to behavior brought about by environmental factors (e.g., a history of abuse), is not warranted. Furthermore, he pointed out that the state of the science is that it is premature to apply research findings to particular cases. In the *Montgomery* case, the appeals court agreed with the trial judge that the proposed expert testimony based on a PET scan was neither scientifically proven nor probative to the insanity defense.

Prevalence of Insanity Pleas and Acquittals

No national database tracks insanity pleas, let alone outcomes of defendants who plead insanity at trial. Thus far, very little empirical work has examined the prevalence of insanity pleas and acquittals. Perhaps the most well-known and frequently cited study on the volume of insanity pleas and acquittals examined county court dockets between 1976 and

---

[14] E.g., *United States v. Montgomery*, 635 F.3d 1074 (8th Cir. 2011).

1987. After reviewing nearly 1 million indictments in forty-nine counties that spanned eight states, Callahan et al. (1991) found that felony defendants raised insanity pleas in 0.93 percent (Range = 0.30–5.74 percent) of cases, with an acquittal rate of 26 percent (Range = 7.3–87 percent). This project, funded by the National Institute of Mental Health, was an enormous research endeavor that made a significant contribution to the burgeoning insanity literature. Yet its findings are now several decades old, did not parse out pleas and acquittals by time or insanity statute, and excluded defendants solely charged with misdemeanors, who can account for a significant portion of criminal responsibility evaluation referrals (22.3 percent in one study; Gardner et al., 2020). It will not be an easy feat, but tracking these data will be critical to our further understanding of when the insanity defense is raised, and by whom.

The best statistical proxies we have for trends in insanity acquittals are from a study commissioned by the National Association of State Mental Health Program Directors (NASMHPD). Wik et al. (2020) requested forensic inpatient data for defendants undergoing pretrial evaluations, defendants opined incompetent to proceed, defendants found not guilty by reason of insanity,[15] civilly committed sex offenders, and state prison transfers from state-level directors of mental health for all fifty states and Washington, DC. Response rates varied depending on the location and forensic population of interest, but overall 76 percent of directors returned some portion of the data requested. Although there were significant variations across jurisdictions, Wik and colleagues identified a 6 percent overall increase in the census of NGRI (not guilty by reason of insanity) inpatients from 1999 to 2014. A closer examination revealed differing admission trends across states and over time. For example, after controlling for population size, eleven states had an increase in NGRI patients, ten states had a decrease, and the census for three states was stable across the fifteen-year time span. Findings such as these offer more questions than answers, and it is important to acknowledge that an inpatient census equates to the yearly average number of NGRI patients hospitalized on a given day, not the number of yearly acquittals, nor does it include acquittees on conditional release.

What about the base rate of evaluators' insanity opinions among defendants referred for evaluation, or for those who plead insanity at trial? In the first meta-analysis of the criminal responsibility literature, Kois and Chauhan (2018) found that evaluators opined that 13.55 percent of defendants evaluated for criminal responsibility were opined to meet criteria for NGRI (SD = 5.84). The base rate was higher for defendants acquitted at trial: approximately one-quarter of these defendants were found NGRI by a judge or jury (M = 25.58%, SD = 6.96). The authors posited that evaluators serve a "filtering" role in this process. That is, defendants opined sane by evaluators are less likely to be acquitted and

---

[15] The authors combined guilty but mentally ill (GBMI) and NGRI pleas into a "NGRI" category, given that some states did not differentiate between the two, some states did not allow for the GBMI plea, and the base rate of GBMI pleas in the sample were likely negligible.

so are less likely to pursue the insanity defense, while those opined insane are more likely to succeed, and proceed with mounting a defense. As a result, the pool of defendants who plead insanity are more often opined insane by the courts.

Conducting Criminal Responsibility Research

First steps in criminal responsibility research design include the selection of (1) comparison samples, (2) outcome/criterion variables, and (3) correlates (predictor variables; Zapf et al., 2011). Decisions at this step in the research process have profound significance for the interpretation and generalizability of the study.

By matching a study's comparison samples to their populations of interests, researchers maximize the extent to which their findings can generalize to applied settings. Researchers wishing to address the question of which defendants are referred for evaluation and opined insane should sample a pool of defendants evaluated for sanity, and compare defendants according to whether they were found sane or insane. Likewise, researchers aiming to elucidate which defendants who plead insanity at trial are acquitted should sample these defendants and compare whether they are acquitted or found guilty. However, researchers often select comparison groups that do not address these research questions directly. In their meta-analysis of correlates of criminal responsibility outcomes, Kois and Chauhan (2018) found that when researchers selected their "insane" comparison groups, most utilized acquittee samples (twelve/fifteen studies in the meta-analysis), with the remaining studies utilizing pretrial defendants opined insane by evaluators (three/fifteen studies). There was more variability among "sane" comparison groups, and slightly more than half (eight/fifteen) of the studies utilized groups that did not lend generalizability to evaluation or trial contexts. For instance, researchers incorporated clinical (civil psychiatric patients), forensic (defendants opined incompetent to proceed or inmates with mental illness), and correctional (individuals convicted of a crime who never raised the insanity defense) samples as "sane" comparison groups. Only seven studies that met inclusion criteria could inform insanity base rates (three studies in the context of evaluator opinions and four in the context of trial). Unfortunately, when research is conducted without population-valid samples, extrapolating findings to real-world questions of criminal responsibility is questionable. It is imperative to consider how sampling lends or threatens external validity when conducting and interpreting this area of research.

The second methodological issue, selection of outcome/criterion variables, is also key. Policymakers have modified what it means to be "criminally responsible" at the jurisdictional level, and these criteria can evolve even within the same jurisdiction. In theory, the United States could have more than 50 insanity defense statutes, considering all states, territories, military courts, and the federal system. Although this is not quite the case, there are significant statutory nuances across jurisdictions that should not be overlooked (Packer, 2009). Although some experimental research has demonstrated that varying insanity prongs may be "much ado about nothing" (Finkel, 1989), clinical research suggests that evaluators do indeed differentiate between cognitive and volitional prongs when drawing opinions (Warren et al., 2004). This indicates that a defendant opined insane in an ALI variant jurisdiction may not be opined insane when evaluated under *M'Naghten* criteria. Researchers should intentionally select and clearly define the study outcome (insanity statute variant x sane/insane) in criminal responsibility research.

The final fundamental tasks in study design are deciding which correlates to examine and how to analyze them. Correlates of interest typically fall into demographic, clinical, or legal domains and are defined rather broadly. For example, in much of the insanity research, race is dichotomized into "White/non-White," diagnoses are dichotomized into "psychotic disorder/nonpsychotic disorder," and offense type is dichotomized into "violent/nonviolent." In practice, there is both gradation and overlap in race, diagnoses, and offense type, as well as countless other defendant/case characteristics. Most criminal responsibility research is conducted using bivariate analyses (Zapf et al., 2011), but with this simplistic approach, important features and interactions of a defendant's demographic, clinical, and legal makeup are lost. Researchers should examine variables that have psycholegal relevance (theoretically tied to criminal responsibility decision-making) in sufficient detail. This approach will require more meticulous data collection along with more sophisticated analyses but will allow for a finer understanding of criminal responsibility correlates.

Correlates of Insanity Acquittals

Kois and Chauhan (2018) conducted their meta-analyses with all eligible studies (regardless of comparison group) and again with only "psycholegal cases" (studies in which defendants were referred for evaluation or who went to trial). Notably, effect sizes changed substantially across these two approaches, which further supports the call for appropriate sampling in criminal responsibility research. The authors found that older defendants were significantly more likely to be found insane ($d = 0.24$), as were females relative to males (Odds Ratio [OR] = 1.66), high school graduates relative to those with lower educational level (OR = 1.56), and individuals who were unemployed relative to those who were employed at the time of the offense (OR = 1.87). Considering that mental health impairment is requisite for a successful acquittal, it is not surprising that psychosis is one of the most robust predictors of insanity outcomes. In the Kois and Chauhan study, defendants with psychiatric treatment histories were significantly more likely to be found insane (OR = 2.70); however, diagnosis of a psychotic disorder was a particularly robust correlate of insanity outcomes (OR = 12.53). Defendants without criminal histories were more likely associated with insanity (OR = 1.51), as were individuals who had been opined incompetent to proceed in the past (OR = 14.45). Although defendants' race was not a significant correlate overall, high heterogeneity suggested that the variable's measurement (White/non-White) may have obscured findings.

Evaluation and Report Practices

Criminal responsibility evaluations can involve extensive review of collateral sources, clinical interviewing, and administration of psychological tests (Packer, 2009), with the defendant's clinical presentation at the time of the alleged crime(s) of utmost importance. Depending on the jurisdictional standard, evaluators should target cognitive and volitional prongs of insanity in addition to assessing for the presence of a psychiatric diagnosis. It appears that clinical interviews, psychological testing, and review of mental health and criminal records are quite common, while contact with collateral sources and academic records review is less common in actual practice (Neal & Grisso, 2014a; Warren et al., 2004).

Practitioner surveys have indicated that evaluators use multiscale personality inventories in approximately 40 percent of their criminal responsibility evaluations, forensic-relevant and forensic-assessment instruments in 20–50 percent, and cognitive/ neuropsychological testing in another 15–20 percent (McLaughlin & Kan, 2014; Neal & Grisso, 2014a). However, evaluators report less test usage when assessing Hispanic defendants low in English proficiency relative to those fluent in English (Canales et al., 2017). The Rogers Criminal Responsibility Assessment Scales (R-CRAS; Rogers, 1984) standardizes the evaluation of criminal responsibility by measuring specific defendant and case characteristics. It has been validated for use with ALI, *M'Naghten,* and GBMI criteria (Rogers et al., 1986). According to Lally's (2003) survey of forensic evaluators, 94 percent found the R-CRAS "acceptable" for use in insanity evaluations. Archer et al. (2006) found that among their sample of forensic evaluators, 44 percent reported ever using the R-CRAS, while only three evaluators (0.03 percent) reported using it in all insanity evaluations. In Neal and Grisso's (2014a) international practitioner survey, the R-CRAS was not among the top 10 tools evaluators reported administering during insanity evaluations. Despite its low reported use, the R-CRAS does shed light on which domains deserve consideration in criminal responsibility evaluations.

In terms of reporting findings, the length of report varies significantly across evaluators (Neal, 2018; Neal & Grisso, 2014a). Heilbrun and Collins (1995), in their survey of criminal responsibility evaluations in Florida, found that 73 percent of evaluators neglected to address defendants' understanding of the alleged offenses' consequences, 71 percent did not address the defendants' understanding of wrongfulness of the alleged offense, and 59 percent did not address defendants' understanding of the offense itself. This lack of comprehensiveness is concerning, as evaluators should elucidate the reasoning behind their opinions when submitting reports to the court. Interested readers can consult practitioner guides for details on criminal responsibility report writing best practice (Grisso, 2010; Heilbrun et al., 2014; Packer, 2009).

Field Reliability of Insanity Opinions

The interrater reliability (agreement between independent raters) for sanity-related questions is generally low. Guarnera and Murrie (2017) meta-analyzed nine criminal responsibility field reliability studies and found that evaluator pairs disagreed in 25–35 percent of sanity cases. What could account for the difference in opinions? Guarnera et al. (2017) proposed the following for disagreement in forensic evaluations more generally: answering a forensic referral question is an inherently difficult task to begin with; training among forensic evaluators is inconsistent; evaluators use unstandardized methods when approaching forensic referrals; individual differences (e.g., personality and values) among evaluators; and adversarial allegiance. Evaluator experience and setting may also influence decision-making (Homant & Kennedy, 1987; Murrie & Warren, 2005; Neal, 2018).

Mock Juror Research

A systematic review indicated that in mock juror studies, defendants diagnosed with psychotic disorders are significantly more likely to be acquitted compared to defendants diagnosed with nonpsychotic disorders, however, no research considered a "control" condition in which the mock defendant had no diagnostic label (van Es et al., 2020). The influence of defendant sex may play a nuanced role in mock juror verdicts. Although this characteristic does not appear to directly impact verdicts, it may interact with offense behavior and defendants' race and mental health diagnoses (Breheney et al., 2007; Dunn et al., 2006; Mossière & Maeder, 2016). Data on defendant race have been mixed, but more recent work suggests that the interaction of defendant race and diagnosis may impact verdicts. In one study, there were no significant differences in acquittal versus conviction for Black versus White defendants, nor was there an overall main effect for diagnosis (schizophrenia vs. depression; Maeder et al., 2020). However, for Black defendants, those diagnosed with schizophrenia were significantly more likely to be convicted by the mock jurors than Black defendants with depression. For White defendants, those with depression were more likely to be convicted than those with schizophrenia, but this difference was not statistically significant.

Research examining the relationship between specific juror traits and trial verdicts has indicated that religious fundamentalism and death penalty qualification are robust predictors of guilty verdicts in mock insanity trials (Bloechl et al., 2007; Kivisto & Swan, 2011). Overall, however, jurors' attitudes toward the insanity defense are the most robust predictor of verdict type. Research consistently demonstrates that the Insanity Defense Attitude–Revised (IDA-R; Skeem et al., 2004) scale is more predictive of mock juror verdicts than defendant race and mock jurors' perceptions of the criminal justice system, conviction proneness, and position on the death penalty (Maeder et al., 2020; Peters & Lecci, 2012; Vitacco et al., 2009). These findings indicate that many prospective jurors hold preexisting biases against the defense, and they raise the question of whether defendants pleading insanity can have a fair jury trial. Concern over juror bias is further complicated in capital cases, which requires death qualification, a factor that is also correlated with guilty verdicts in insanity cases (Kivisto & Swan, 2011; Peters & Lecci, 2012).

Crocker and Kovera (2010) attempted to "rehabilitate" mock jurors who had expressed bias against the insanity defense using a "rehabilitative questioning" intervention. They found that explicitly biased jurors and those with higher IDA-R scores were more likely to choose guilty verdicts in a mock insanity trial. Jurors who received rehabilitative instructions demonstrated a decrease in IDA-R scores compared to those who received standard juror instructions, regardless of whether or not they expressed any initial bias. Although instructions had an impact on participants' ratings of defendants' appreciation and understanding of wrongfulness, they did not influence dichotomous verdicts, that is, insane or guilty (i.e., the ecologically valid outcomes). These findings were replicated using a Canadian insanity statute (Maeder et al., 2015). The resounding takeaway message from this body of research is worrisome, as there is strong evidence that pretrial juror bias threatens defendants' opportunity for a fair trial, and attempts to rehabilitate these biases may be futile.

Civil Commitment and Conditional Release

Perlin (1994) reviewed several "myths of the insanity defense" harbored by the public: (1) the defense is frequently raised, (2) it is usually successful, (3) acquittees are released from commitment after only a brief period of time, and (4) acquittees are particularly dangerous. However, empirical data have indicated that the defense is hardly "used and abused" (Callahan et al., 1991; Jeffrey & Pasewark, 1983). In fact, acquittees are often civilly committed longer than if they had been convicted and incarcerated, regardless of whether charges were violent (Braff et al., 1983; Dirks-Linhorst & Kondrat, 2012; Harris et al., 1991).

Conditional release programs aim to balance acquittees' freedom along with state oversight in order to protect the public's safety, and are also cost-saving tactics for treating offenders with mental illness (Weinstein, 2014). These programs are distinct from outpatient civil commitment, given their dual emphasis on maintaining psychiatric stability while also reducing the likelihood of recidivism. In general, acquittees undergoing conditional release violently recidivate at extremely low rates (Vitacco et al., 2018), although revocation of conditional release is not uncommon (33.6 percent over a nine-year period in one study; Vitacco et al., 2018). Research indicates that the mandated nature of conditional release stipulations (e.g., living arrangements, substance use monitoring, regular psychotherapy, and medication management) can have a significant role in reducing the likelihood of recidivism among community-dwelling acquittees. McDermott et al. (2020) found that acquittees who reentered the community without mandated treatment were nine times more likely to reoffend than acquittees mandated to treatment. In terms of specific conditions, research indicates that acquittees who are released to step-down settings (secure residential treatment settings) fare better than those released directly into the community (Novosad et al., 2016).

Future Directions

In the Kois and Chauhan (2018) criminal responsibility meta-analysis, the average year of data collection was 1985 and the average publication year was 1993. Although data in this area are somewhat dated, it is inadequate to simply call for "new research." Key topics for the specific research agenda should include defendant diversity and interevaluator agreement.

The United States has grown increasingly diverse in terms of race and ethnicity, and the general (as well as offender) population has aged considerably (Vespa et al., 2018). Further, the female offender population has grown over 700 percent since 1980 (The Sentencing Project, 2020). The present criminal responsibility research base does not reflect these demographic changes (Kois & Chauhan, 2018). Future research should attend to nuances in demographic characteristics, for example, by recognizing that age, race, ethnicity, sex, and gender may play important intersecting roles in forensic mental health research, including criminal responsibility. For example, one study found that when considering defendants referred for criminal responsibility or competency evaluations, Black but not Hispanic defendants were significantly more likely than White defendants to be referred for inpatient evaluations following an outpatient screening (Pinals et al., 2004). However, when considering only *male* defendants, both Black and Hispanic defendants were more likely than Whites to be referred for inpatient evaluations in a higher-security hospital, rather than a medium-security hospital. Attending to defendants' intersecting identities such as these will be an important research development that is long overdue (Carter & Forsyth, 2007; McAuliff et al., 2019).

In recent years, research on practitioners' interevaluator agreement and potential sources of bias have flourished (Gowensmith et al., 2013; Gowensmith et al., 2017; Neal & Grisso, 2014b), and work should continue to explore factors that contribute to disagreement. For example, in the Gowensmith studies that revealed low field reliability, evaluators tended to agree on insanity outcomes more often when they agreed on diagnosis, specifically psychotic disorder, and less often agreed when the defendant was under the influence of substances at the time of the offense. At present, it is unknown whether such disagreements are any more or less common in forensic settings as compared to general (civil) psychiatric contexts. Further, although some research points to adversarial allegiance as a source of evaluator bias in sex offender evaluations (Murrie et al., 2009), the Gowensmith et al. studies examined interevaluator agreement in the context of criminal responsibility evaluations. These evaluators were all court-appointed, so the impact of adversarial allegiance on diagnostic and forensic opinions could not be discerned.

Potentially, training and certification may enhance field reliability. Yet relatively few training programs are available to meet the demand for forensic training, and forensic mental health examiners are not trained, certified, or regulated in any consistent way across (and sometimes within) jurisdictions (DeMatteo et al., 2019; Gowensmith et al.,

2015; Packer, 2008). Training should instruct evaluators to adopt a consistent, systematic approach to forensic evaluations, which would likely increase interevaluator agreement and improve quality of work. Training could also integrate structured self-monitoring approaches with the goal of decreasing evaluator bias (Gowensmith & McCallum, 2019), although bias in forensic evaluation may be inevitable (Neal & Grisso, 2014b).

The criminal justice and mental health systems strive to use the least restrictive means possible to maintain an individual's safety and security. With this in mind, as research on conditional release programming builds, policymakers should consider cultivating more community-based programming for insanity acquittees that utilize appropriate monitoring (i.e., supervision tailored to an individual's risk and needs, rather than a one-size-fits-all approach). Bloom and Novosad (2017) proposed a national database for tracking individuals acquitted by reason of insanity, committed for dangerousness (sexual or otherwise), or incompetent to stand trial. Merging administrative datasets from mental health, social service, and criminal justice agencies to map patterns of offender entry and exist across the sequential intercepts could inform diversion and intervention practices as well as public policy more broadly.

References

American Law Institute. (1962). *Model penal code and annotations*. American Law Institute.

American Psychiatric Association. (1983). APA statement on the insanity defense. *American Journal of Psychiatry, 140*, 681–688.

Archer, R. P., Buffington-Vollum, J. K., Stredny, R. V., & Handel, R. W. (2006). A survey of psychological test use patterns among forensic psychologists. *Journal of Personality Assessment, 87*(1), 84–94.

Aspinwall, L. G., Brown, T. R., & Tabery, J. (2012). The double-edged sword: Does biomechanism increase or decrease judges' sentencing of psychopaths? *Science, 337*, 846–849.

Bloechl, A. L., Vitacco, M. J., Neumann, C. S., & Erickson, S. E. (2007). An empirical investigation of insanity defense attitudes: Exploring factors related to bias. *International Journal of Law and Psychiatry, 30*(2), 153–161.

Bloom, J. D., & Novosad, D. (2017). The forensic mental health services census of forensic populations in state facilities. *Journal of the American Academy of Psychiatry and the Law, 45*(4), 447–451.

Braff, J., Arvanites, T., & Steadman, H. J. (1983). Detention patterns of successful and unsuccessful insanity defendants. *Criminology, 21*(3), 439–448.

Breheney, C., Groscup, J., & Galietta, M. (2007). Gender matters in the insanity defense. *Law & Psychology Review, 31*, 93.

Callahan, L. A., Steadman, H. J., McGreevy, M. A., & Robbins, P. C. (1991). The volume and characteristics of insanity defense pleas: An eight-state study. *Journal of the American Academy of Psychiatry and the Law Online, 19*(4), 331–338.

Canales, E. J., Kan, L. Y., & Varela, J. G. (2017). Forensic assessment with hispanic and limited english-proficient hispanic evaluees: A survey of practice. *Professional Psychology: Research and Practice, 48*(2), 122–130.

Carter, R. T., & Forsyth, J. M. (2007). Examining race and culture in psychology journals: The case of forensic psychology. *Professional Psychology: Research and Practice, 38*(2), 133–142.

Crocker, C. B., & Kovera, M. B. (2010). The effects of rehabilitative voir dire on juror bias and decision making. *Law and Human Behavior, 34*(3), 212–226.

DeMatteo, D., Fairfax-Columbo, J., & Desai, A. (2019). *Becoming a forensic psychologist*. Routledge.

Dirks-Linhorst, P. A., & Kondrat, D. (2012). Tough on crime or beating the system: An evaluation of missouri department of mental health's not guilty by reason of insanity murder acquittees. *Homicide Studies, 16*(2), 129–150.

Dunn, K. F., Cowan, G., & Downs, D. (2006). Effects of sex and race of perpetrator and method of killing on outcome judgments in a mock filicide case. *Journal of Applied Social Psychology, 36*(10), 2395–2416.

Finkel, N. J. (1989). The insanity defense reform act of 1984: Much ado about nothing. *Behavioral Sciences & the Law, 7*(3), 403–419.

Gardner, B. O., Murrie, D. C., & Torres, A. N. (2020). The impact of misdemeanor arrests on forensic mental health services: A state-wide review of virginia sanity evaluations. *Law and Human Behavior, 44*(4), 286–299.

Gowensmith, W. N., & McCallum, K. E. (2019). Mirror, mirror on the wall, who's the least biased of them all? Dangers and potential solutions regarding bias in forensic psychological evaluations. *South African Journal of Psychology, 49*(2), 165–176.

Gowensmith, W. N., Murrie, D. C., & Boccaccini, M. T. (2013). How reliable are forensic evaluations of legal sanity? *Law and Human Behavior, 37*(2), 98–106.

Gowensmith, W. N., Pinals, D. A., & Karas, A. C. (2015). States' standards for training and certifying evaluators of competency to stand trial. *Journal of Forensic Psychology Practice, 15*(4), 295–317.

Gowensmith, W. N., Sessarego, S. N., McKee, M. K., Horkott, S., MacLean, N., & McCallum, K. E. (2017). Diagnostic field reliability in forensic mental health evaluations. *Psychological Assessment, 29*(6), 692–700.

Grisso, T. (2010). Guidance for improving forensic reports: A review of common errors. *Open Access Journal of Forensic Psychology, 2*, 102–115.

Guarnera, L. A., & Murrie, D. C. (2017). Field reliability of competency and sanity opinions: A systematic review and meta-analysis. *Psychological Assessment, 29*(6), 795–818.

Guarnera, L. A., Murrie, D. C., & Boccaccini, M. T. (2017). Why do forensic experts disagree? Sources of unreliability and bias in forensic psychology evaluations. *Translational Issues in Psychological Science, 3*(2), 143–152. https://doi.org/10.1037/tps0000114

Harris, G. T., Rice, M. E., & Cormier, C. A. (1991). Length of detention in matched groups of insanity acquittees and convicted offenders. *International Journal of Law and Psychiatry, 14*(3), 223–236.

Heilbrun, K., & Collins, S. (1995). Evaluations of trial competency and mental state at time of offense: Report characteristics. *Professional Psychology: Research and Practice, 26*(1), 61–67.

Heilbrun, K., DeMatteo, D., Holliday, S. B., & LaDuke, C. (Eds.). (2014). *Forensic mental health assessment: A casebook* (2nd ed.). Oxford University Press.

Homant, R. J., & Kennedy, D. B. (1987). Subjective factors in the judgment of insanity. *Criminal Justice and Behavior, 14*(1), 38–61.

Jeffrey, R. W., & Pasewark, R. A. (1983). Altering opinions about the insanity plea. *The Journal of Psychiatry & Law, 11*(1), 29–40.

Kivisto, A. J., & Swan, S. A. (2011). Attitudes toward the insanity defense in capital cases: (Im)partiality from *Witherspoon* to *Witt. Journal of Forensic Psychology Practice, 11*(4), 311–329.

Kois, L. E., & Chauhan, P. (2018). Criminal responsibility: Meta-analysis and study space. *Behavioral Sciences & the Law, 36*(3), 276–302.

Lally, S. J. (2003). What tests are acceptable for use in forensic evaluations? A survey of experts. *Professional Psychology: Research and Practice, 34*(5), 491–498.

Maeder, E. M., Yamamoto, S., & Fenwick, K. L. (2015). Educating canadian jurors about the not criminally responsible on account of mental disorder defence. *Canadian Journal of Behavioural Science [Revue canadienne des sciences du comportement], 47*(3), 226–235.

Maeder, E. M., Yamamoto, S., & McLaughlin, K. J. (2020). The influence of defendant race and mental disorder type on mock juror decision-making in insanity trials. *International Journal of Law and Psychiatry, 68*, Article 101536.

McAuliff, B. D., Hunt, J. S., Levett, L. M., Zelechoski, A. D., Scherr, K. C., & DeMatteo, D. (2019). Taking the next steps: Promoting open science and expanding diversity in *Law and Human Behavior. Law and Human Behavior, 43*(1), 1–8.

McDermott, B. E., Ventura, M. I., Juranek, I. D., & Scott, C. L. (2020). Role of mandated community treatment for justice-involved individuals with serious mental illness. *Psychiatric Services, 71*(7), 656–662.

McLaughlin, J. L., & Kan, L. Y. (2014). Test usage in four common types of forensic mental health assessment. *Professional Psychology: Research and Practice, 45*(2), 128–135.

Miller, G. (2012). Science and the courts: In mock case, biological evidence reduces sentences. *Science, 337*, 788.

Morse, S. J. (1994). Causation, compulsion, and involuntariness. *Bulletin of the American Academy of Psychiatry and Law, 22*(2), 159–180.

Mossière, A., & Maeder, E. M. (2016). Juror decision making in not criminally responsible on account of mental disorder trials: Effects of defendant gender and mental illness type. *International Journal of Law and Psychiatry, 49*, 47–54.

Murrie, D. C., Boccaccini, M. T., Turner, D. B., Meeks, M., Woods, C., & Tussey, C. (2009). Rater (dis) agreement on risk assessment measures in sexually violent predator proceedings: Evidence of adversarial allegiance in forensic evaluation? *Psychology, Public Policy, and Law, 15*(1), 19–53.

Murrie, D. C., & Warren, J. I. (2005). Clinician variation in rates of legal sanity opinions: Implications for self-monitoring. *Professional Psychology: Research and Practice, 36*(5), 519–524.

Neal, T. M. S. (2018). Discerning bias in forensic psychological reports in insanity cases. *Behavioral Sciences & the Law, 36*(3), 325–338.

Neal, T. M. S., & Grisso, T. (2014a). Assessment practices and expert judgment methods in forensic psychology and psychiatry: An international snapshot. *Criminal Justice and Behavior, 41*(12), 1406–1421.

Neal, T. M. S., & Grisso, T. (2014b). The cognitive underpinnings of bias in forensic mental health evaluations. *Psychology, Public Policy, and Law, 20*(2), 200–211.

Novosad, D., Banfe, S., Britton, J., & Bloom, J. D. (2016). Conditional release placements of insanity acquittees in Oregon: 2012–2014. *Behavioral Sciences & the Law, 34*(2-3), 366–377.

Packer, I. K. (2008). Specialized practice in forensic psychology: Opportunities and obstacles. *Professional Psychology: Research and Practice, 39*(2), 245–249.

Packer, I. K. (2009). *Evaluation of criminal responsibility.* Oxford University Press.

Perlin, M. L. (1994). *The jurisprudence of the insanity defense.* Carolina Academic Press.Peters, M., & Lecci, L. (2012). Predicting verdicts, adherence to judge's instructions, and assumptions about the disposition of the defendant in a case involving the insanity defense. *Psychology, Crime & Law, 18*(9), 817–831.

Pinals, D. A., Packer, I. K., Fisher, W., & Roy-Bujnowski, K. (2004). Relationship between race and ethnicity and forensic clinical triage dispositions. *Psychiatric Services, 55*(8), 873–878.

Rogers, R. (1984). *Rogers Criminal Responsibility Assessment Scales (R-CRAS) and test manual.* Psychological Assessment Resources.

Rogers, R., Seman, W., & Clark, C. R. (1986). Assessment of criminal responsibility: Initial validation of the R-CRAS with the M'Naghten and GBMI standards. *International Journal of Law and Psychiatry, 9*(1), 67–75.

Skeem, J. L., Louden, J. E., & Evans, J. (2004). Venirepersons's attitudes toward the insanity defense: Developing, refining, and validating a scale. *Law and Human Behavior, 28*(6), 623–648.

The Sentencing Project. (2020, November 24). Incarcerated women and girls. The Sentencing Project. https://www.sentencingproject.org/publications/incarcerated-women-and-girls/

van Es, R. M. S., Kunst, M. J. J., & de Keijser, J. W. (2020). Forensic mental health expert testimony and judicial decision-making: A systematic literature review. *Aggression and Violent Behavior, 51*, Article 101387. https://doi.org/10.1016/j.avb.2020.101387

Vespa, J., Armstrong, D. M., & Medina, L. (2018). *Demographic turning points for the united states: Population projections for 2020 to 2060.* U.S. Department of Commerce, Economics and Statistics Administration.

Vitacco, M. J., Balduzzi, E., Rideout, K., Banfe, S., & Britton, J. (2018). Reconsidering risk assessment with insanity acquittees. *Law and Human Behavior, 42*(5), 403–412.

Vitacco, M. J., Malesky Jr, L. A., Erickson, S., Leslie, W., Croysdale, A., & Bloechl, A. (2009). Measuring attitudes toward the insanity defense in venirepersons: Refining the IDA-R in the evaluation of juror bias. *International Journal of Forensic Mental Health, 8*(1), 62–70.

Warren, J. I., Murrie, D. C., Chauhan, P., Dietz, P. E., & Morris, J. (2004). Opinion formation in evaluating sanity at the time of the offense: An examination of 5175 pre-trial evaluations. *Behavioral Sciences & the Law, 22*(2), 171–186.

Weinstein, N. M. (2014). The legal aspects of conditional release in the criminal and civil court system. *Behavioral Sciences & the Law, 32*(5), 666–680.

Wik, A., Hollen, V., & Fisher, W. H. (2020, Apr). Forensic patients in state psychiatric hospitals: 1999-2016. *CNS Spectrums, 25*(2), 196–206.

Zapf, P., Green, D., & Rosenfeld, B. (2011). Competency to stand trial and criminal responsibility research. In B. Rosenfeld & S. D. Penrod (Eds.), *Research methods in forensic psychology* (pp. 156–173). John Wiley & Sons.

Of Capital Importance: Considerations in Capital Sentencing Contexts

Jaymes Fairfax-Columbo, Bronwyn Neeser, Alexandra Kudatzky, *and* David DeMatteo

Abstract

Capital sentencing is the legal process by which homicide offenders are determined to be deserving either of a sentence of life imprisonment or a sentence of death. Due to the severe and irrevocable liberty deprivation that a death sentence represents, the US Supreme Court has gone to great lengths to ensure that death sentences are not levied in arbitrary and capricious fashion. In addition, they have restricted the classes of individuals the death penalty can apply to. This chapter reviews key Supreme Court case law pertaining to capital sentencing as well as highlights several vital factors for forensic mental health professionals to consider in conducting evaluations in accordance with the trial phase of capital sentencing proceedings. Said factors include assessment of mitigating factors for sentencing, assessment of intellectual disability in *Atkins* evaluations, and assessment of future dangerousness.

Key Words: death penalty, capital sentencing, sentencing, risk assessment, intellectual disability, future dangerousness, mitigation, homicide, murder

Providing Psycholegal Context: An Overview of Capital Sentencing

To analyze capital sentencing in a psycholegal context, it is essential to understand the purpose of criminal sentencing. Sentencing is the imposition of sanctions by a judicial authority, and may include economic sanctions (e.g., fines), community supervision (e.g., probation), incarceration, or, in the most extreme of cases, death. The severity of the sentence typically depends on the crime committed, aggravating/mitigating circumstances, and theories and legal limitations of punishment, among other factors. Sentencing goals are derived from philosophical and psychological theories about human behavior, and include retribution (idea that offenders are morally deserving of punishment), deterrence (idea that punishment dissuades future crime), incapacitation (limiting ability to reoffend), rehabilitation (reforming offenders into law-abiding citizens), and restitution (repaying society/victims for wrongdoings) (Seiter, 2017).

Historically, judges gave indeterminate sentences in which the length of a sentence was outlined by a minimum and maximum length. In contrast, the "tough on crime" attitude of the 1980s saw demand for determinate sentences to ensure offenders faced certain consequences (Seiter, 2017). However, recent research and calls for sentencing reform have prompted reexamination of sentencing policies and growing concern for how offenders are evaluated throughout sentencing. The change from the past to the present has focused on degree of culpability rather than the past's more black-and-white sentencing system. To that end, today's sentencing model relies on *aggravating* (increase culpability/increase sentence) and *mitigating* (decrease culpability/lessen sentence) circumstances to determine an individual's degree of culpability. Aggravating factors must be statutorily enumerated and their existence either admitted by the defendant or proven to a fact-finder beyond a reasonable doubt.[1] Common examples include prior criminal history, use of a weapon, or a victim suffering severe injuries. In contrast, mitigating factors do not need to be proven to a fact-finder beyond a reasonable doubt. Examples include lack of a criminal record, acceptance of responsibility for one's actions, or a defendant suffering from behavioral health problems.

Notably, sentencing patterns/schemes evolve to reflect changes in political climate, public opinion, and advances in psycholegal research—perhaps nowhere is this more evident than in the realm of capital sentencing jurisprudence. Beginning with 1972's *Furman v. Georgia*, the Supreme Court of the United States (SCOTUS) has rendered numerous decisions governing the procedures by which the death penalty can be imposed, as well as restricting its imposition.[2] In *Furman*, the Court opined that the death penalty must not be implemented in a cruel and unusual fashion; multiple Justices expressed feeling the decision as to which capital offenders were sentenced to death appeared to be being made in arbitrary and capricious fashion. A four-year moratorium on the death penalty ensued, eventually concluding with the Court's decision in *Gregg v. Georgia*.[3] In *Gregg*, SCOTUS approved a capital sentencing scheme utilized by the State of Georgia in which (1) trial proceedings were bifurcated, such that guilt and sentencing were considered separately; (2) aggravating and mitigating circumstances were considered in order to aid the fact-finder in rendering a punishment decision; and (3) an automatic appeals process existed to review whether the death penalty was assigned arbitrarily. In *Gregg*'s wake, states worked to reformulate their capital sentencing procedures and the death penalty re-emerged as a viable criminal sanction.

Since *Gregg*, SCOTUS has issued several decisions impacting the procedural imposition of the death penalty and restricting the class of individuals to whom the death penalty can apply. Procedurally, SCOTUS applied its decisions from *Apprendi* and its progenies to capital sentencing in *Ring v. Arizona* (2002) and *Hurst v. Florida* (2016), in which

---

[1] See Alleyne v. United States, 570 U.S. 99 (2013); Apprendi v. New Jersey, 530 U.S. 466 (2000); Blakely v. Washington, 542 U.S. 296 (2004); United States v. Booker, 543 U.S. 220 (2005).

[2] Furman v. Georgia, 408 U.S. 238 (1972).

[3] Gregg v. Georgia, 428 U.S. 153 (1976).

SCOTUS declared Arizona's and Florida's death penalty statutes unconstitutional because they used elements of larger offenses as aggravating factors at sentencing for a judge to consider or find beyond a reasonable doubt.[4] SCOTUS said because these states' aggravating factors for imposing the death penalty operated as a "functional equivalent of an element of a greater offense than the one covered by the jury's guilty verdict," under the *Apprendi* rule, the Sixth Amendment requires these factors to be found by a fact-finder (jury) beyond a reasonable doubt, and not only by a judge.[5] Additionally, SCOTUS's decisions in *Lockett v. Ohio*, *Eddings v. Oklahoma*, and *Tennard v. Dretke* dictated that though aggravating factors must be enumerated, a sentencing authority must consider *any relevant* aspect of a defendant's character, history, or record as a mitigating factor.[6] In other words, mitigating factors for the death penalty cannot be restricted.

Concerning restriction of the populations upon which the death penalty can be imposed, several groups are *categorically excluded* from being sentenced to death: juveniles, nonhomicide offenders, offenders who committed nonintentional murder, and individuals who have an intellectual disability. *Enmund v. Florida* banned a death sentence for someone who did not commit murder, attempt to commit murder, or intend to commit murder.[7] The 2002 case of *Atkins v. Virginia* barred individuals with an intellectual disability from being sentenced to death, reasoning that the limitations of these individuals prevented the death penalty from serving any true principle of punishment (such as deterrence or retribution);[8] this bar was further affirmed in *Hall v. Florida* and *Moore v. Texas*.[9] In 2005's *Roper v. Simmons*, SCOTUS ruled that it is unconstitutional to execute individuals who committed their offense prior to the age of 18, reasoning minors to be ineligible for the death penalty because of their transitory personality traits, susceptibility to negative influences, and developmental immaturity as compared to adults.[10] In 2008's *Kennedy v. Louisiana*, SCOTUS indicated that the death penalty was an inappropriate sentence for nonhomicide offenders—including child rapists—because societal standards of decency do not measure nonhomicide crimes with the severity and irrevocability of murder.[11]

Finally, one SCOTUS decision—*Ford v. Wainwright*—held it unconstitutional to execute someone who had psychologically decompensated to the point of not being competent to be executed because being unable to appreciate one's sentence rendered the death penalty ineffectual in serving a principle of punishment.[12] This was affirmed in

---

[4] *Apprendi*, 530 U.S. 466; Ring v. Arizona, 536 U.S. 584 (2002); Hurst v. Florida, 537 U.S. 977 (2016).

[5] *Apprendi*, 530 U.S. at 494.

[6] Lockett v. Ohio, 438 U.S. 586 (1978); Eddings v. Oklahoma, 455 U.S. 104 (1982); Tennard v. Dretke, 542 U.S. 274 (2004).

[7] Enmund v. Florida, 458 U.S. 782 (1982).

[8] Atkins v. Virginia, 536 U.S. 304 (2002).

[9] Hall v. Florida, 572 U.S. 701 (2014); Moore v. Texas, 127 S. Ct. 1039 (2017).

[10] Roper v. Simmons, 543 U.S. 551 (2005).

[11] Kennedy v. Louisiana, 554 U.S. 407 (2008).

[12] Ford v. Wainwright, 477 U.S. 399 (1986).

Panetti v. Quarterman, in which SCOTUS clarified that determination of competence to be executed compelled consideration of factual understanding and rational understanding of impending execution and the reasoning underlying it.[13] SCOTUS also noted that inability to recall committing a crime was not a de facto bar to rational understanding, though it recognized that dementia may undermine rational understanding—as in *Madison v. Alabama*.[14] In the aforementioned cases, SCOTUS defined the non-negotiable circumstances under which the death sentence is cruel and unusual. Table 11.1 presents a brief summary of the case law just discussed.

Table 11.1 Summary of Key Supreme Court Death Penalty Cases

Case	Year	Holding
Furman v. Georgia	1972	The death penalty cannot be imposed in arbitrary and capricious manner. Resulted in a moratorium on the death penalty.
Gregg v. Georgia	1976	The death penalty is not unconstitutional in all cases. A bifurcated trial process in which guilt and sentencing are separate proceedings, consideration of aggravating and mitigating factors to help distinguish offenders deserving of death from those not deserving of death, and an automatic review process to make sure a death sentence was not imposed in arbitrary and capricious fashion was sufficient to address concerns in Furman v. Georgia. Moratorium on the death penalty lifted.
Lockett v. Ohio	1978	Mitigating factors cannot be restricted for consideration; rather, sentencing authorities must be allowed to consider all mitigating circumstances pertinent to the defendant.
Eddings v. Oklahoma	1982	Reaffirmed *Lockett*, noting that any and all mitigating circumstances pertaining to a defendant must be able to be considered. In this specific case, the Court held that the trial court erred in failing to consider evidence of Eddings's difficult childhood and emotional issues.
Enmund v. Florida	1982	Cannot sentence an individual to death if she is not directly involved in the committing of a murder (no intent to kill, does not attempt to kill, does not actually kill). In essence, restricted the use of the felony murder rule/transferred intent in rendering a defendant eligible for the death penalty.
Ford v. Wainwright	1986	Cannot carry out the death penalty on someone who is incompetent to be executed.
Atkins v. Virginia	2002	Individuals with an intellectual disability are not eligible for the death penalty.
Ring v. Arizona	2002	Aggravating factors rendering a defendant eligible for the death penalty must be proven to a fact-finder beyond a reasonable doubt.

(continued)

---

[13] Panetti v. Quarterman, 551 U.S. 930 (2007).
[14] Madison v. Alabama, 138 S. Ct. 718 (2019).

	Table 11.1 *Continued*	
Case	Year	Holding
Roper v. Simmons	2005	Juveniles are not eligible for the death penalty.
Panetti v. Quarterman	2007	The standard for competence to be executed includes more than just factual understanding of an impending execution; rational understanding is also key to a determination of competency to be executed.
Kennedy v. Louisiana	2008	Nonhomicide offenders are not eligible for the death penalty (though did not consider federal high crimes, such as treason).
Hall v. Florida	2014	Jurisdictions must consider measurement error in the assessment of intellectual impairments for purposes of *Atkins* determinations.
Hurst v. Florida	2016	A fact-finder—not a sentencing authority—need find the existence of all elements necessary to support a sentence of death. Reaffirmed *Ring*.
Moore v. Texas	2017	Jurisdictions cannot rely on outdated clinical definitions of intellectual disability for purposes of *Atkins* determinations.
Madison v. Alabama	2019	Rational understanding is key to a determination of competency to be executed. An individual being unable to remember committing her crime may still exhibit rational understanding of her impending execution and the reasons underlying it; however, dementia may also undermine rational understanding.

To further illustrate the evolving nature of sentencing—particularly capital sentencing—it is important to realize that not every state uses the death penalty as its most severe punishment. Public opinion about the death penalty has fluctuated over time. In the 1960s, polls reported that more than 40 percent of the U.S. population opposed the death penalty (Death Penalty Information Center, 2019). However, tailing the "tough on crime" mentality of the 1980s, the country demanded harsher crime control and saw the public approval of the Violent Crime Control and Law Enforcement Act of 1994 and the onset of mass incarceration (Death Penalty Information Center, 2019). In 1994, 80 percent of the population approved of the use of the death penalty in the justice system. Since then, approval has been steadily declining, and, according to a 2020 Gallup Poll, only 55 percent of Americans supported the death penalty for someone convicted of murder, with 43 percent outright opposing it (Death Penalty Information Center, 2020). Policy-wise, since 2007, eleven states have abolished the death penalty, generating a total of twenty-three states and the District of Columbia that have outlawed capital punishment. Although public opinion has seemingly shifted to disapprove of the death penalty, twenty-seven states, the federal government, and the US military still allow the death penalty as a maximum sentence (Death Penalty Information Center, 2021).

Forensic Mental Health Assessment in Sentencing Contexts—Mitigation

Before addressing the two key components of an Forensic Mental Health Assessment (FMHA) in capital sentencing contexts—assessing intellectual disabilities for *Atkins* evaluations and assessing future dangerousness—we must address the primary mitigating factors relevant to moral culpability and sentencing in general. We define moral culpability as the fundamental psycholegal conceptualization underlying mitigation (i.e., persons who were developmentally disadvantaged and/or whose psychological resources are limited are judged less harshly than persons who are not disadvantaged and have greater psychological resources), and mitigation as any factor or reason for a less severe sentence (Cunningham, 2010). Therefore, it is important to consider possible social issues (e.g., employment and education), trauma, psychological issues, and cognitive issues as key factors in FMHA conceptualization related to sentencing evaluations. Please note that this discussion is but a *snapshot* of factors to consider—an exhaustive exploration of potential mitigating factors in sentencing evaluations is beyond the scope of this chapter.

Research suggests *social insecurities* (e.g., food, housing, employment, and healthcare) in conjunction with low socioeconomic status correlate with greater risk of legal involvement and limited moral autonomy (Blacksher, 2002). Individuals suffering from social insecurities tend to have greater involvement with law enforcement and the legal system in general. Unfortunately, social insecurity has been positively correlated with greater instances of traumatic life events and adverse childhood experiences (ACEs). It should be noted that this is a much larger topic and there is increasing research pertaining to early childhood neglect and brain development, specifically within the limbic system (survival responses) and the frontal lobe (executive functioning: planning, organizing, decision making, etc.). Research suggests that children who experience abuse and neglect tend to experience over- or underarousal of these brain regions, often making it difficult to make logical and stepwise decisions (De Bellis et al., 2009; Moreno-Manso et al., 2020). Exposure to traumatic events, abuse, and neglect often forces individuals to engage in their environment in a survivalist manner, looking to meet immediate needs rather than having the stability to plan for the future (De Bellis et al., 2009; Moreno-Manso et al., 2020).

Additionally, much research has been done regarding early attachment and the impact of attachment style on later social engagement. Those who experience disorganized or avoidant attachment styles in early childhood are more outwardly aggressive and impulsive and demonstrate increased risk-taking behaviors (Fonagy et al., 2003); all these behaviors have been positively correlated with greater legal involvement. Although social insecurities are risk factors to consider, they are dynamic—meaning they can be changed. The literature supports findings that when individuals' basic needs are met, they demonstrate more self-confidence, have higher self-esteem, and generally exhibit greater autonomy and less involvement with the legal system (Blacksher, 2002). Although slightly more complex, evidence-based practices for the treatment of trauma have been proven effective and efficacious. The experience of significant early childhood trauma as well as lifetime traumatic events can also impact psychological functioning.

Psychopathology requires attention when considering moral culpability, as it impacts the psychological resources that individuals possess. Individuals with severe and persistent mental illnesses—such as psychotic disorders, bipolar disorder, or other serious mood/anxiety disorders—may experience symptoms that, although not excusing criminal behavior, may help to explain it and suggest that an individual be held less culpable for a criminal action than those not experiencing such symptoms. Such symptoms may be a detachment from reality, disorganization, increased impulsivity and impetuous decision-making, or irrational decision-making. These symptoms can reduce an offender's moral culpability by impairing their ability to think as clearly about the offense compared to those with greater psychological resources. An example may include a defendant with a delusion about being sick who stole some medication she could not afford. If the individual recognized that stealing was wrong and was in sufficient control of their actions, she likely cannot be said to be insane at the time of the offense. However, because the crime was in part motivated by a delusion, the delusion can play a mitigating role, providing context that may help a sentencing authority to better conceptualize and understand the individual's behavior. In other words, if criminal involvement may be partially attributable to some unmet behavioral health need, a sentencing authority may be more likely to be lenient in sentencing.

Cognitive impairments can have a profound impact on an individual's knowledge or comprehension of the law, decision-making abilities, rational judgment, and comprehension of punishment. Therefore, these individuals may not have the same level of moral culpability as those with greater cognitive power. In sentencing evaluations, it is important consider an individual's educational experiences and cognitive abilities, including learning disability diagnoses, participation in special education classes, use of an Individualized Education Program (IEP), behavioral difficulties, academic performance, and prior testing that assessed for learning and intelligence deficits. Cognitive abilities are discussed in greater detail later in this chapter as they pertain to *Atkins* evaluations. Again, this is a snapshot of these domains, all of which are more complex than presented and deserve additional attention during sentencing evaluations.

Atkins Evaluations

The inclusion of forensic psychologists in capital sentencing has increased exponentially over the last two decades. This is due in large part to seminal case law surrounding the assessment of intellectual disability (still referred to as "mental retardation" in some jurisdictions). Perhaps the most notable of these cases is *Atkins v. Virginia*.[15] *Atkins* involved the case of Daryl Renard Atkins, sentenced to death following convictions for murder, abduction, and armed robbery. Atkins had a full-scale IQ score of 59; defense counsel argued that sentencing an individual with such low intellectual functioning to death constituted cruel and unusual punishment under the Eighth Amendment. SCOTUS agreed, noting that in light of evolving standards of decency, many jurisdictions at the time either

---

[15] *Atkins*, 536 U.S. 304.

prohibited individuals with an intellectual disability from being sentenced to death, or, in states where individuals with an intellectual disability could be executed, the practice of sentencing intellectually disabled defendants to death was uncommon. Additionally, the Court held that sentencing an individual with an intellectual disability to death did not serve any penological purpose, noting that the severity of the cognitive deficits experienced by individuals with an intellectual disability limited the retributive value and deterrent effect of the death penalty. However, though the Court prohibited individuals with an intellectual disability from being sentenced to death, it left it up to individual states to decide appropriate ways to define an intellectual disability.

From a clinical perspective (i.e., per the *Diagnostic and Statistical Manual of Mental Disorders, 5th Edition, Test Revision* [DSM-5-TR; American Psychiatric Association, 2022]), the definition of intellectual disability includes three components: (1) significant limitations in intellectual functioning, (2) significant limitations in adaptive behavior, and (3) onset of these deficits in the developmental period. These categories are discussed in more detail later. With SCOTUS allowing jurisdictions to decide how to approach defining intellectual disability, it perhaps comes as no surprise that states took a variety of approaches post-*Atkins*, with many states adopting definitions that did not fully comport with accepted clinical standards (DeMatteo et al., 2007). This generated several *Atkins* progeny cases, as the Court attempted to course-correct and create some uniformity in the assessment of intellectual disability in capital contexts.

In *Hall v. Florida*,[16] defendant Freddie Lee Hall was denied the ability to present evidence of intellectual disability because he scored 1 point above the state IQ score cutoff of 70 points. SCOTUS determined that a strict cutoff of 70 violated the Eighth Amendment because it failed to account for measurement error inherent in IQ tests, noting specifically that the evolving trend among states was to consider measurement error when determining if someone was intellectually disabled. In effect, this decision widened the range of individuals who might be found to have an intellectual disability for capital sentencing purposes, in recognition that IQ scores are better interpreted as falling within a range as opposed to being affixed at a set number.

SCOTUS further clarified how intellectual disability should be defined in 2017's *Moore v. Texas*.[17] In *Moore*, Bobby James Moore challenged his death sentence in Texas on the grounds that he had an intellectual disability and thus was not eligible to be sentenced to death. A state habeas court agreed with Moore, finding him intellectually disabled based on a substandard IQ score (74) and substandard adaptive functioning per the eleventh edition of the American Association on Intellectual and Developmental Disabilities (AAIDD) clinical manual. However, the Texas Criminal Court of Appeals disagreed with the habeas court, holding that under Texas law—which incorporated an outdated clinical

---

[16] *Hall*, 572 U.S. 701
[17] *Moore*, 127 S. Ct. 1039.

standard for intellectual disability—Moore did not qualify as having an intellectual disability. SCOTUS held that though states had discretion in defining intellectual disability, they could not define it according to outdated clinical standards.

Atkins's progenies highlight the complexity of assessing individuals for intellectual disability when they fall in the *mild* range of functional impairment. Clinically, roughly 2 percent of the population qualifies for a diagnosis of intellectual disability and, of that 2 percent, roughly 75–85 percent fall in the mild intellectual disability range (Fabian et al., 2011). However, research has shown that individuals with mild intellectual disability tend to have an intense motivation to mask their limitations due to the significant stigma surrounding the diagnosis (Ellis et al., 2018). With case law in mind, the role of the forensic mental health evaluator in an *Atkins* case is to provide information to the fact-finder regarding the explanation and contextualization of intellectual disability, and more specifically, the impairments of the defendant. Again, the information reviewed is a broad brushstroke of what to consider when approaching these assessments, and the references cited herein are great resources to gain deeper knowledge. That being said, the three diagnostic criteria for the diagnosis of intellectual disability—significant intellectual impairment, significant adaptive functioning impairment, and onset of limitations within the developmental period—provide scaffolding for the assessment (American Psychiatric Association, 2022; AAIDD, n.d.).

Intellectual impairment is generally assessed via standardized intelligence testing (IQ tests), along with corroborating behavioral observations and consultation of collateral sources. Two of the most used IQ tests are the Wechsler Adult Intelligence Scale—Fourth Edition (WAIS-IV) (Wechsler, 2008) and the Stanford Binet—Fifth Edition (SB-5) (Roid, 2003). Both tests are based on a standard distribution with an average IQ of 100 and a standard deviation of 15. Approximately 68 percent of the population will fall within one standard deviation of the mean (85–115). An individual is considered to exhibit gross intellectual impairment if they score two standard deviations below the average, generally corresponding with scores ≤ 70. Additionally, as stated in *Hall*, the standard error of measurement (SEM, or the range of scores that the true score likely falls within) must be considered. The SEM corresponds to a range of the IQ score ± 5, meaning that scores as high as 75 might be within the range of gross intellectual impairment.

Adaptive behavior is the collection of conceptual, social, and practical skills learned by people to enable them to function in their everyday lives. For a diagnosis of intellectual disability, the individual must evidence a significant impairment in at least one of these domains. Per DSM-5-TR, these adaptive domains encompass several abilities (see table 11.2). Multiple tests purport to measure at least some aspects of adaptive functioning; three comprehensive and standardized measures are reviewed here. The Scales of Independent Behavior—Revised (SIB-R; Bruininks et al., 1996) is appropriate for use with individuals up to eighty years in age. The SIB-R is a self-report measure that contains both a Short

Table 11.2 Adaptive Abilities	
Domain	Abilities Encompassed (Not Exhaustive)
Conceptual	"competence in memory, language, reading, writing, math reasoning, acquisition of practical knowledge, problem solving, and judgement in novel situations"
Social	"awareness of others' thoughts, feelings, and experiences; empathy; interpersonal communication skills; friendship abilities; and social judgement"
Practical	"learning and self-management across life settings, including personal care, job responsibilities, money management, recreation, self-management of behavior, and school and work task organization"

Source: American Psychiatric Association (2022, p. 42).

Form (administered in roughly twenty minutes) and a more comprehensive Full Scale form (completed in roughly forty-five to sixty minutes). The SIB-R measures skills across fourteen subscales (Social Interaction, Language Comprehension, Language Expression, Eating and Meal Preparation, Toileting, Dressing, Personal Self-Care, Domestic Skills, Time and Punctuality, Money and Value, Work Skills, Home/Community Orientation, Gross Motor Skills, and Fine Motor Skills) spanning four adaptive functioning domains: Social Interaction and Communication Skills, Personal Living Skills, Community Living Skills, and Motor Skills. The SIBS-R also measures maladaptive behaviors pertaining to Asocial, Externalizing, and Internalizing domains. Norm-referenced scores are generated for each adaptive domain, as well as for a Broad Independence Score composite.

The Adaptive Behavior Assessment System—Third Edition (ABAS-3; Harrison & Oakland, 2015) is appropriate for use in individuals up to eighty-nine years of age and assesses several functional capacities across eleven skill areas: communication, community use, functional academics, health and safety, home or school living, leisure, self-care, self-direction, social, work, and motor. It has a self-report form, and parent/caregiver- and teacher-report forms; all forms are also available in Spanish and are relatively quick to complete (approximately fifteen to twenty minutes). Norm-referenced standard scores are generated for the three adaptive behavior domains—Conceptual, Social, and Practical—as well as for a General Adaptive Composite.

Finally, the Vineland Adaptive Behavior Scales—3rd Edition (Vineland-3) (Sparrow et al., 2016) is appropriate for use with individuals aged ninety and below. It can be administered in self-report and other-report formats (parent/caregiver and teacher). Administration time typically ranges between ten and forty minutes; answer forms can also be obtained in Spanish. The answer forms assess abilities across four domains: Communication (Receptive, Expressive, and Written language skills), Daily Living Skills (Personal, Domestic, Community), Socialization (Interpersonal Relationships, Play and Leisure, Coping Skills), and Motor Skills (Gross Motor and Fine Motor skills). As with the SIB-R and the ABAS-3, the Vineland-3 produces norm-referenced scores in each domain, as well an Adaptive Behavior Composite score.

In the assessment of adaptive functioning—and in FMHA more generally—it is important to note that evaluators should not rely on a single source but rather focus on the convergence of information. This increases confidence that any adaptive behavior deficits that are reported—or not reported—are accurate. This convergence may refer to convergence within an adaptive functioning measure—for example, having at least two sources provide information for the ABAS-3 and the Vineland-3, given that each allows for information to be obtained from multiple sources—but also via such methods as interviewing the defendant's family, friends, employers, and teachers. Additionally, archival data can be useful to gain a better understanding of a defendant's adaptive behavior such as prior school testing, school records, and other medical records. Finally, the evaluator can typically gather enough information from the adaptive behavior inventory and additional archival data to elucidate—or at least hypothesize—if the onset of difficulty in fact occurred in the developmental period (the third diagnostic criterion for an intellectual disability), or if present cognitive difficulties instead reflect decline secondary to some precipitating factor (such as substance use, a dementing process, a traumatic brain injury, etc.).

As with all FMHAs, *Atkins* evaluations have particular nuances to be aware of and consider. Fabian et al. (2011) provided a list of concerns related to best practices in *Atkins* cases. For the purposes of this chapter, we discuss practice effects, the Flynn Effect, cultural and ethnic considerations, and malingering versus cognitive suboptimal performance; for deeper understanding, practitioners are encouraged to consult the source articles. *Practice effects* refer to the possible increase in IQ scores due to a short test-retest interval. IQ scores have the potential to increase by 10 points when the same instrument is administered within a three-month window, but this effect diminishes within six to twelve months after the initial administration (Bartles et al., 2010). Evaluators should consider practice effects in *Atkins* cases, particularly as each side typically will want its expert to assess the defendant separately. Utilizing a different IQ test—for example, administering the WAIS-IV if you are aware a different expert administered the SB-5—may limit these effects. It is also important to remain in strong communication with the referral source, encouraging them to find out if previous IQ tests have been administered, which test was administered, and when that test was administered. It may also be advisable to gauge the defendant's own experience with IQ testing during the actual evaluation.

The *Flynn Effect* describes the phenomenon of increasing fluid and crystalized intelligence over the twentieth century. IQ tests are therefore re-normed every fifteen to twenty years to account for this increase and to maintain test averages at 100. Important for capital sentencing evaluations, the calibration of these tests may have direct impact on defendants qualifying for intellectual disability. Research suggests that at the end of a norming cycle, the IQ test may underqualify individuals as intellectually disabled due to the perceived ease of the test in comparison to collective gains in intelligence over time. The reverse is true for newly normed instruments, indicating that these tests may overqualify individuals as intellectually disabled due to the perceived difficulty of the test in comparison to population knowledge (Kanaya et al., 2003). Therefore, evaluators should be aware of what part of the test cycle they are in during administration and scoring; a 2014 meta-analysis by Trahan and colleagues suggested that the Flynn Effect can account for IQ score fluctuations of roughly 3 points.

Cultural and ethnic considerations during IQ testing have long been discussed and researched with findings suggesting the need for possible various norms for different ethnic and cultural groups. Studies have long found significant differences in IQ scores between White, Hispanic, and Black individuals (see Reynolds et al., 2021, for a review). Navajo children have obtained performance scale scores that exceed verbal scale scores by approximately 30 points. Furthermore, children who learn English as a second language or learn two languages simultaneously frequently obtain performance scores that are significantly higher than verbal scores (McLellan & Nellis, 2003). Resultantly, failing to account for cultural differences in testing—regarding either test selection or appropriately caveating/interpreting results—risks distorting the cognitive picture for nonmajority individuals.

Finally, a large component of the accuracy of IQ testing is the *effort* that the defendant puts forward. For capital sentencing—where there may be clear incentive to either put forth poor effort or attempt to feign cognitive impairment—it is vital to consider performance validity. Performance validity can be gauged via stand-alone measures such as the Test of Memory Malingering (TOMM; Tombaugh, 1996) or the Dot Counting Test (DCT; Boone et al., 2002), or via embedded measures, such as the WAIS-IV Reliable Digit Span. Of note, Ellis et al. (2018) suggest that there is limited or insufficient support for the reliable use of many performance validity tests to detect potential malingering in individuals who are truly intellectually disabled; this is certainly true if appropriate adaptations—such as consulting research to determine if cutoff scores need to be adjusted to more accurately classify noneffortful performance in cognitively impaired populations, or if certain measures are more predictive in cognitively impaired populations than others—are not undertaken. Regardless, the most significant and substantial measurement of effort for this population is generally the comparison of multiple IQ tests across time, particularly given that IQ is typically conceptualized as a relatively stable construct (barring intervening factors such as aging, substance use, organic brain damage, psychopathology, etc.). As above, convergence of information is key to assessing performance validity specifically and response style generally. Review of medical records, comparing and contrasting previous testing, collateral interviews, and behavioral observations can all provide useful information in determining if someone is accurately representing their cognitive abilities during an *Atkins* evaluation.

In total, assessment of intellectual disability in a capital sentencing case is complex and requires the evaluator to have fundamental and specific knowledge related to case law, the legal standard of intellectual disability in the jurisdiction in which the evaluation is being conducted, the clinical standard for diagnosis of intellectual disability, knowledge of developmental psychology, and knowledge related to forensic psychology (Olley, 2009). The role of the forensic examiner in *Atkins* cases is to provide clinical information and to describe intellectual disability-associated level of impairment to a legal audience. One of the difficulties of this may be the misalignment of the legal standard being utilized by a jurisdiction and the current clinical standard for the diagnosis of intellectual disability. Therefore, it is imperative that forensic examiners consider this tension and provide education to courts and legal professionals regarding these differences. Further, research regarding limitations and concerns of IQ testing is vast and consistently has implications for capital sentencing. Adaptive behavior research—though less prevalent than research on IQ testing—also continues to expand and should be followed closely.

Assessment of Future Dangerousness in Capital Contexts

In death penalty contexts, assessment of future dangerousness refers to the likelihood that an individual, absent a penalty of death, will engage in future serious violent behavior in prison. Currently, only four states *expressly* consider future dangerousness to be an aggravating factor for the death penalty (see table 11.3; of note, Texas requires a finding of future dangerousness and another aggravating circumstance to sentence an offender to death), prosecutors may still present evidence of future dangerousness as a non-statutorily enumerated aggravating factor that jurors might consider as well as rebuttal evidence to an assertion that the defendant does not present as a future danger (Dorland & Krauss, 2005). Additionally, research suggests that even if evidence of future dangerousness is not

Table 11.3 Jurisdictions that Provide Future Dangerousness as an Explicit Aggravating Factor

Jurisdiction	Code	Aggravating Factor Language
Idaho	Idaho Code §19-2515(9)(i) (2021)	"(i) The defendant, by his conduct, whether such conduct was before, during or after the commission of the murder at hand, has exhibited a propensity to commit murder which will probably constitute a continuing threat to society."
Oklahoma	Oklahoma Statutes Annotated, Title 21, §701.12(7) (2020)	"7. The existence of a probability that the defendant would commit criminal acts of violence that would constitute a continuing threat to society."
Texas	Texas Code of Criminal Procedure, Article 37.071. Procedure in Capital Case, Sec. 2. (2021)	"(b) On conclusion of the presentation of the evidence, the court shall submit the following issues to the jury: (1) whether there is a probability that the defendant would commit criminal acts of violence that would constitute a continuing threat to society."
Wyoming	Wyoming Statutes Title 6. Crimes and Offenses §6-2-102 (2020)	"(xi) The defendant poses a substantial and continuing threat of future dangerousness or is likely to commit continued acts of criminal violence."

presented during capital proceedings, future dangerousness is nearly always considered by a jury in its decision-making (Blume et al., 2001).

Assessing future dangerousness in capital sentencing contexts poses unique challenges. First, though the field of violence risk assessment has progressed substantially in recent decades—allowing forensic examiners to much more accurately predict risk than when unstructured clinical judgment was the predominant approach to risk assessment (see Heilbrun et al., 2017, for a review)—this does not hold for the prediction of institutional violence specifically. This is inherently problematic, as institutional violence is generally the type of violence at issue when deciding if an offender is worthy of a sentence of life imprisonment or death (see Edens et al., 2005).[18]

The most notable challenge in accurately assessing likelihood of serious institutional violence is the low-base-rate problem. Any assessment of violence risk is incomplete without first anchoring it to a base rate of violence in a population or context. Given a lack of other pertinent information about an individual, the base rate of violence in a context/population will serve as the most accurate predictor of violence for that person; varying from the base rate is only indicated if that individual exhibits empirically derived risk factors (Cunningham, 2010). However, if the base rate of a behavior in a population/context is low to begin with, departing from the base rate may not provide much pertinent information regarding future dangerousness. For example, converging studies suggest that, at most, fewer than one in five prison inmates convicted of murder will carry out an act of serious institutional violence, and at the least, fewer than 2 percent of this group will commit an act of serious violence (see Cunningham, 2010, for a more comprehensive review). The lower end of that spectrum, suggesting that a particular offender may be two times more likely to commit an act of serious institutional violence than other homicide offenders, only corresponds to a 4 percent likelihood of a serious violent act. In other words, the low-base-rate problem suggests that even if the chance of an individual committing an act of serious institutional violence is much greater than that of other offenders comparatively speaking, it is still quite unlikely absolutely speaking.

Further, research does not suggest that individuals eligible for capital punishment are disproportionately likely to commit an act of serious violence than are other offenders. Studies of capital offenders who had their sentences commuted, studies of life-sentenced capital offenders, studies of capital offenders housed in general population, and studies of capital offenders housed in segregation all revealed roughly equivalent and low rates of serious institutional violence (see Cunningham, 2010, for a review). Additionally, studies exploring the accuracy of predictions of future dangerousness in capital sentencing contexts have consistently revealed high error rates (again, see Cunningham, 2010, for a comprehensive review)—suggesting, as indicated above, that though the field of FMHA

---

[18] See Shafer v. South Carolina, 532 U.S. 36 (2001); Simmons v. South Carolina, 512 U.S. 154 (1994).

has progressed in its ability to predict violence more generally, its ability to predict institutional violence among capital offenders specifically is still suspect.

A second unique challenge of assessing risk of institutional violence in capital offenders is an overreliance on factors that are not empirically related to institutional violence. Per Cunningham (2010), the following factors empirically demonstrate a negative relationship with institutional violence: age, educational attainment, and sentence length. In contrast, having had previous prison bids and a history of institutional violence is positively associated with institutional violence. Further, both having been convicted of a property crime and being male are associated with institutional violence. Notably, neither psychopathology nor personality disorders appear to reliably predict institutional violence. Regardless, expert testimony is often offered to demonstrate that a defendant is a future danger (Krauss & Sales, 2001), particularly testimony that a capital offender is psychopathic as demonstrated by scores of 30 + on the Psychopathy Checklist-Revised (PCL-R; Hare, 2003). In fact, case law reviews suggest that the use of the PCL-R for such purposes has increased in recent years (e.g., DeMatteo et al., 2014).

A full critique of issues with the use of the PCL-R in risk assessment is beyond the scope of this chapter. Undoubtedly, the PCL-R has value in predicting violence and recidivism in many contexts, and its use in FMHA can provide great value to the criminal justice system (see Hare, 2016, for a review). However, one area in which the PCL-R notably lacks predictive validity regards institutional violence, the primary outcome of interest in the assessment of future dangerousness in capital contexts. Converging meta-analyses indicate that the relationship between PCL-R total and factor scores and institutional violence/institutional aggression is nonexistent at worst and weak at best (Guy et al., 2005; Leistico et al., 2008; Walters, 2003).

Compounding the issue of the PCL-R's poor predictive validity for institutional violence is accumulated evidence suggesting that (1) PCL-R scores, while showing strong interrater reliability in experimental settings, do not show strong interrater reliability in field settings (where capital sentencing evaluations are conducted) (see DeMatteo et al., 2020, for a review); (2) PCL-R scores may be subject to adversarial allegiance effects, meaning PCL-R scores in the field may be biased toward the side requesting the evaluation (see Murrie & Boccaccini, 2015, for a review); and (3) attributing a "psychopath" label or traits to capital defendants makes them more likely to receive the death penalty (Berryessa & Wohlstetter, 2019; Kelley et al., 2019).

Concerning this last point, converging meta-analyses demonstrate this psychopath labeling effect (Berryessa & Wohlstetter, 2019; Kelley et al., 2019). Further, though some independent studies have failed to produce data supporting the psychopath labeling effect in capital contexts, it appears that these results may have been triggered by weak experimental manipulations that did not produce perceptions of the mock defendant as psychopathic. Indeed, when mock jurors do perceive defendants to exhibit psychopathic traits, they are significantly more likely to be supportive of a death sentence (Truong et al., 2021).

Taken together, these concerns have prompted some experts to express a high level of skepticism regarding use of PCL-R to predict future dangerousness in capital cases, with some going so far as to issue a Statement of Concerned Experts and recommend that use of the PCL-R in death penalty cases no longer be considered appropriate and no longer be "generally accepted in the field of forensic mental health as a reliable and valid means of predicting serious institutional violence, that is, of estimating or determining the likelihood that a person will commit such violence in the future" (DeMatteo et al., 2020, p. 140). Though this Statement of Concerned Experts has prompted debate regarding the utility of the PCL-R in capital cases (see Olver et al., 2020), the elucidated concerns suggest that critical consideration of the role the PCL-R may play in such evaluations appears warranted.

Summary/Conclusions

This chapter reviewed key case law pertaining to FMHAs in capital sentencing and illustrated key concerns that forensic examiners may encounter when conducting evaluations corresponding to the sentencing phase of capital sentencing proceedings. Common referrals at this stage include evaluation for mitigation, evaluation of intellectual disability (per *Atkins* and its progenies), and assessment of future dangerousness as an aggravating factor. Each evaluation context presents unique challenges and nuances to be keenly aware of. Summarized concisely, key takeaways are as follows:

- Pertaining to mitigation, broad exploration of factors relevant to moral culpability is necessary. Key factors may include social issues, trauma, psychological issues, and cognitive issues. The goal of such evaluations is not to excuse criminal behavior but to provide context for sentencing authorities regarding who the defendant is and what may have contributed to their wrongdoing.
- Regarding *Atkins* evaluations, assessment of intellectual disability is complex. In assessing IQ score, forensic examiners must consider the standard error of measurement, and be aware of and account for practice effects, the Flynn Effect, cultural and ethnic differences in testing, and effort/performance validity. Assessing adaptive functioning is a key component of assessing for intellectual disability, as is exploration of whether observable deficits occurred in the developmental period. Given the field's consistently evolving understanding of intellectual disability, practitioners must be avid consumers of research.
- Considering assessment of future dangerousness in capital contexts, forensic examiners need be aware of the myriad difficulties in accurately predicting risk of serious institutional violence. Of particular concern are the low-base-rate problem and the limitations of the PCL-R in predicting institutional violence, especially when balanced with concerns of poor interrater reliability in the field, adversarial allegiance, and the psychopath labeling effect.

References

American Association on Intellectual and Developmental Disabilities. (n.d.). *Definition of intellectual disability*. American Association on Intellectual and Developmental Disabilities. https://www.aaidd.org/intellectual-disability/definition

American Psychiatric Association. (2022). *Diagnostic and statistical manual of mental disorders* (5th ed.). American Psychiatric Association.

Bartles, C., Wegrzyn, M., Wiedl, A., Ackermann, V., & Ehrenreich, H. (2010). Practice effects in healthy adults: A longitudinal study on frequent repetitive cognitive testing. *BMC Neuroscience 11*, Article 118.

Berryessa, C. M., & Wohlstetter, B. (2019). The psychopathic "label" and effects on punishment outcomes: A meta-analysis. *Law and Human Behavior, 43*(1), 9–25.

Blacksher, E. (2002). On being poor and feeling poor: Low socioeconomic status and the moral self. *Theoretical Medicine, 23*(6), 455–470.

Blume, J. H., Garvey, S. P., & Johnson, S. L. (2001). Future dangerousness in capital cases: Always "at issue." *Cornell Law Review, 86*(2), 397–410.

Boone, K. B., Lu, P., & Herzberg, D. (2002). *The Dot Counting Test.* Western Psychological Services.

Bruininks, R. H., Woodcock, R. W., Weatherman, R. F., & Hill, B. K. (1996). *Scales of Independent Behavior-Revised (SIB-R).* Riverside.

Cunningham, M. D. (2010). *Evaluation for capital sentencing.* Oxford University Press.

De Bellis, M. D., Hooper, S. R., Spratt, E. G., & Woolley, D. P. (2009). Neuropsychological findings in childhood neglect and their relationships to pediatric PTSD. *Journal of the International Neuropsychological Society, 15*(6), 868–878.

DeMatteo, D., Edens, J. F., Galloway, M., Cox, J., Smith, S. T., Koller, J. P., & Bersoff, B. (2014). Investigating the role of the Psychopathy Checklist-Revised in United States case law. *Psychology, Public Policy, and Law, 20*(1), 96–107.

DeMatteo, D., Hart, S. D., Heilbrun, K., Boccaccini, M. T., Cunningham, M. D., Douglas, K. S., Dvoskin, J. A., Edens, J. F., Guy, L. S., Murrie, D. C., Otto, R. K., Packer, I. K., & Reidy, T. J. (2020). Statement of concerned experts on the use of the Hare Psychopathy Checklist-Revised in capital sentencing to assess risk for institutional violence. *Psychology, Public Policy, and Law, 26*(2), 133–144.

DeMatteo, D., Marczyk, G., & Pich, M. (2007). A national survey of state legislation defining mental retardation: Implications for policy and practice after *Atkins. Behavioral Sciences and the Law, 25*(6), 781–802.

Dorland, M., & Krauss, D. (2005). The danger of dangerousness in capital sentencing: Exacerbating the problem of arbitrary and capricious decision-making. *Law and Psychology Review, 29*, 63–104.

Edens, J. F., Buffington-Vollum, J. K., Keilen, A., Roskamp, P., & Anthony, C. (2005). Predictions of future dangerousness in capital murder trials: Is it time to "disinvent the wheel?" *Law and Human Behavior, 29*(1), 55–86.

Ellis, J. W., Everington, C., & Delpha, A.M. (2018). Evaluating intellectual disability: Clinical assessments in *Atkins* cases. *Hofstra Law Review, 46*(4), 1305–1419.

Executions Overview. (2021, February 22). Death Penalty Information Center. https://deathpenaltyinfo.org/executions/executions-overview.

Fabian, J., Thompson, W., & Lazarus, J. B. (2011). Life, death, and IQ: It's much more than just score: Understanding and utilizing forensic psychological and neuropsychological evaluations in *Atkins* intellectual disability/mental retardation cases. *Cleveland State Law Review, 59*(3), 399–430.

Fonagy, P., Target, M., Gergely, G., Allen, J. G., & Bateman, A. W. (2003). The developmental roots of borderline personality disorder in early attachment relationships: A theory and some evidence. *Psychoanalytic Inquiry, 23*(3), 412–459.

Gallup Poll. (2019, November 25). *For first time, majority of Americans prefer life sentence to capital punishment.* Death Penalty Information Center. https://deathpenaltyinfo.org/news/gallup-poll-for-first-time-majority-of-americans-prefer-life-sentence-to-capital-punishment

Gallup Poll. (2020, November 24). *Public support for the death penalty lowest in a half-century.* Death Penalty Information Center. https://deathpenaltyinfo.org/news/gallup-poll-public-support-for-the-death-penalty-lowest-in-a-half-century

Guy, L. S., Edens, J. F., Anthony, C., & Douglas, K. S. (2005). Does psychopathy predict institutional misconduct among adults? A meta-analytic investigation. *Journal of Consulting and Clinical Psychology, 73*(6), 1154–1163.

Hare, R. D. (2003). *The Hare Psychopathy Checklist-Revised technical manual* (2nd ed.). Multi-Health Systems.

Hare, R. D. (2016). Psychopathy, the PCL-R, and criminal justice: Some new findings and current issues. *Canadian Psychology, 57*(1), 21–34.

Harrison, P., & Oakland, T. (2015) *Adaptive Behavior Assessment System (ABAS-3).* Psychological Corporation.

Heilbrun, K., Fairfax-Columbo, J., Wagage, S., & Brogan, L. (2017). Risk assessment for future offending: The value and limits of expert evidence at sentencing. *Court Review, 53*(3), 116–125.

Kanaya, T., Ceci, S. J., & Scullin, M. H. (2003). The rise and fall of IQ in special ed: Historical trends and their implications. *Journal of School Psychology, 41,* 453–465.

Kelley, S. E., Edens, J. F., Mowle, E. N., Penson, B. N., & Rulseh, A. (2019). Dangerous, depraved, and death-worthy: A meta-analysis of the correlates of perceived psychopathy in jury simulation studies. *Journal of Clinical Psychology, 75*(4), 627–643.

Krauss, D., & Sales, B. (2001). The effects of clinical and scientific expert testimony on juror decision making in capital sentencing. *Psychology, Public Policy, and Law, 7*(2), 267–310.

Leistico, A. M. R., Salekin, R. T., DeCoster, J., & Rogers, R. (2008). A large-scale meta-analysis relating the Hare measures of psychopathy to antisocial conduct. *Law and Human Behavior, 32*(1), 28–45.

McLellan, M. J., & Nellis, L. (2003). Using the WISC-III with Navajo children: A need for local norms. *Journal of American Indian Education, 42*(2), 50–60.

Moreno-Manso, J. M., Garcia-Baamonde, M. E., Murillo, M. R., Blazquez-Alonso, M., Guerrero-Barona, E., & Garcia-Gomez, A. (2020). Differences in executive functions in minorsuffering physical abuse and neglect. *Journal of Interpersonal Violence,* 1–17. Advanced online publication.

Murrie, D. C., & Boccaccini, M. T. (2015). Adversarial allegiance among expert witnesses. *Annual Review of Law and Social Science, 11,* 37–55.

Olley, J. G. (2009). Knowledge and experience required for experts in *Atkins* cases. *Applied Neuropsychology, 16*(2), 135–140.

Olver, M. E., Stockdale, K. C., Neumann, C. S., Hare, R. D., Mokros, A., Baskin-Sommers, A., Brand, E., Folino, J., Gacono, C., Gray, N. S., Kiehl, K., Knight, R., Leon-Mayer, E., Logan, M., Meloy, J. R., Roy, S., Salekin, R. T., Snowden, R., Thomson, N., Tillem, S., Vitacco, M., & Yoon, D. (2020). Reliability and validity of the Psychopathy Checklist-Revised in the assessment of risk for institutional violence: A cautionary note on DeMatteo et al. *Psychology, Public Policy, and Law, 26*(4), 490–510.

Reynolds, C. R., Altmann, R. A., & Allen, D. N. (2021). *Mastering modern psychological testing: Theory and methods* (2nd ed.). Springer.

Roid, G. H. (2003). *Stanford-Binet Intelligence Scales, fifth edition, examiner manual.* Riverside.

Seiter, R. (2017). *Corrections: An introduction.* Pearson.

Sparrow, S. S., Cicchetti, D. V., & Saulnier, C. A. (2016). *Vineland Adaptive Behavior Scales, Third Edition (Vineland-3).* Pearson.

Tombaugh, T. N. (1996). *Test of memory malingering.* Multi-Health Systems.

Trahan, L., Stuebing, K. K., Hiscock, M. K., & Fletcher, J. M. (2014). The Flynn Effect: A meta-analysis. *Psychological Bulletin, 140*(5), 1332–1360.

Truong, T. N., Kelley, S. E., & Edens, J. F. (2021). Does psychopathy influence juror decision-making in capital murder trials? "The devil is in the (methodological) details." *Criminal Justice and Behavior, 48*(5), 690–707.

Walters, G. D. (2003). Predicting institutional adjustment and recidivism with the Psychopathy Checklist factor scores: A meta-analysis. *Law and Human Behavior, 27*(5), 541–558.

Wechsler, D. (2008). *WAIS-IV administration and scoring manual.* Psychological Corporation.

Forensic Evaluation in Civil Litigation: A Case Example

Julie M. Brovko *and* William E. Foote

Abstract

The Five-Stage Model is an assessment tool that is used for guiding the evaluator in their review of records, their clinical interviews, their psychological testing and testing interpretation, their report writing, and their testimony in evaluations that are conducted in the context of tort and civil rights cases. Although the Five-Stage Model has been detailed at great length in previous work, the purpose of this chapter is to apply this model to personal injury case example. In this chapter, we demonstrate how it can assist the evaluator in producing a comprehensive and coherent opinion that is forensically useful.

Key Words: civil litigation, forensic evaluation, five-stage model, personal injury, forensic reports

Over the past forty years, the US legal system has called on the skills of mental health professionals to assist in decision-making in a range of criminal cases. Significant print has been devoted to the ethical, professional, and evidence-based conduct of these forensic evaluations (e.g., Heilbrun et al., 2014; Melton et al., 2018; Otto et al., 2014). As some have recently noted (Foote et al., 2020), forensic attention has only recently turned to evaluations conducted in civil cases, such as those arising in tort cases, civil rights litigation, and regulatory settings (Foote, 2017, 2020; Foote & Goodman-Delahunty, 2021; Foote et al., 2020; Foote & Lareau, 2013; Kane & Dvoskin, 2011; Kane et al., 2013; Young & Brodsky, 2016). Although some attempts have been made to provide processes for conducting assessments in civil contexts (Greenberg et al., 2003; Wilson & Moran, 2004), a model focusing on the sequential evaluation process has been developed for use in both tort and civil rights cases (Foote, 2017, 2020; Foote & Goodman-Delahunty, 2021; Foote & Lareau, 2013; Goodman-Delahunty et al., 2012).

The Five-Stage Model has developed into an assessment tool for guiding the evaluator in record review, clinical and collateral interviews, psychological test interpretation, report writing, and testimony. This chapter applies this model to a personal injury case example, demonstrating how such a model can assist the evaluator in producing a comprehensive, coherent, and forensically useful opinion. It is important to note that while a summary of the model's sequence is described, a full description and explanation of the model is outside the scope of this chapter. For more information and explanation of the model stages, please see Foote (2020) and Foote and Goodman-Delahunty (2021).

The five-Stage Model (see fig. 12.1) is a systematic and comprehensive process that is used to reach evidence-based conclusions about causation and the extent of damages. Its purpose is to guide the evaluation and to help the evaluator maximize the probability of including information that is relevant to the case. This model is especially helpful because it allows the evaluator to use an individualized approach to the evaluation while still applying consistent principles and language so that it is easily digested by the finder of fact.

The model has three aspects that render it helpful to the mental health professional conducting civil evaluations (Foote, 2020; Foote & Goodman-Delahunty, 2021; Foote et al., 2020). First, each stage focuses on the causation of symptoms or problems that the plaintiff claims arose from the litigation-related event(s) (LRE). To prevail in a tort case, the plaintiff must prove a causal connection between the putative cause of the plaintiff's injuries and the plaintiff's claimed emotional responses. Second, each stage provides data concerning the nature and extent of the plaintiff's damages. Third, the model provides a system for exploring alternative explanations for the plaintiff's symptoms and problems. The model is designed to serve as a guide to the evaluation process, as a method for sorting data, as a system for arriving at defensible opinions, and as an organized procedure for presenting data to the finder of fact in reports and testimony.

According to this model, stage 1 deals with the period before the LRE, or the "day before" analysis. Stage 2 examines the evaluee's experiences during the LRE, a period varying from seconds to years, depending on the case. Stage 3 spans the interval between the end of the LRE and the date of the evaluation. Stage 4 is the evaluation interval, and stage 5 extrapolates from the evaluation to determine future damages.

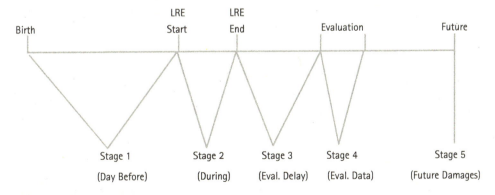

Figure 12.1 The Five-Stage Model Timeline.

The Case of JM

At the time of the evaluation, John Martin was a 32-year-old White male. The purpose of the evaluation was to assist the court in dealing with issues related to Mr. Martin's mental health and damages related to a recent police assault.[1] This plaintiff's case will serve as an example of the five-stage process, and the chapter will proceed in examining his case using the model and illustrating with facts from this anonymized case from the files of Dr. Brovko.

Stage 1

This first phase of the evaluation process focuses on what happened in the period before the alleged LRE began. This analysis is important for subsequent stages of the model, as it provides a baseline of the individual's functioning before the LRE. Assessment of preexisting psychopathology is part of this stage because such problems and symptoms can affect the complainant's reaction to alleged LRE in later stages. In addition to clinical interviews with the complainant and collateral witnesses, a review of records is an essential source of information. At the completion of this stage, the evaluator should have a clear picture of the individual's previous functioning and especially their functioning immediately before the alleged LRE (i.e., "day before" status). This knowledge sets the stage for an appraisal of the claimant's experiences during the alleged LRE.

DEVELOPMENTAL, FAMILY, AND SOCIAL HISTORY

Mr. Martin reported he was born and raised in New Mexico. He stated he spent his time moving between his parents' houses. There was no history of interpersonal violence in his home, nor did he report any physical abuse or neglect. However, his father drank "a lot" of alcohol and used drugs, but he was never incarcerated.

Mr. Martin's pre-LRE history featured his father's death from a stroke in 2016, which the plaintiff experienced as quite traumatic. He reported he came into the room and found his father "on the floor and I picked him up. He was still talking. He said, 'I can't breathe.'" In spite of his provision of CPR, by the time the ambulance arrived, his father had died. Mr. Martin stated his father's death "messed me up." He reported "for a long time, I didn't believe he was gone. I was lying to myself, and I kinda gave up taking care of myself. I was waiting to die. I didn't know what was going to happen next in life. I was doing drugs, and I wasn't taking care of myself. I was at a standstill. I'd go from place to place. I wasn't living. I was being sicker. I was constantly depressed." Mr. Martin reported, "It's been downhill since."

---

[1] This case material has been deidentified in accordance with American Psychological Association ethical and publication guidance (American Psychological Association, 2017, 2019) and HIPAA guidelines (Health Information Portability and Accountability Act, Pub. L. No. 104-191, §264, 110 Stat.1936 [1996]).

RELATIONSHIP HISTORY

As an adult, Mr. Martin has had difficulty developing or maintaining relationships and has never been married. He does have one son, whom he has not seen since his son was six months old.

EDUCATION AND WORK HISTORY

Mr. Martin said he completed the tenth grade and stopped attending school in the eleventh grade. He denied ever obtaining a GED. Records confirm Mr. Martin's report that he received special education services. He said he has not worked since "way before" his father passed away because he has trouble with motivation.

SUBSTANCE ABUSE HISTORY

Mr. Martin reported a history of alcohol and marijuana use but stated he has not used them since his adolescent years. He said he has also used "a lot" of methamphetamine.

LEGAL HISTORY

Mr. Martin reported, and records confirm, he does not have a juvenile legal history, but he has been to jail for various adult misdemeanor charges, including possession of a controlled substance, petty theft, trespassing, and public intoxication Prior to the LRE, Mr. Martin had a warrant out for his arrest due to a probation violation (failure to report). He was on probation after being found guilty of possession of methamphetamine.

MENTAL AND MEDICAL HEALTH HISTORY

Mr. Martin indicated that before the dog-bite incident, he had no history of medical problems, including head injuries. However, records indicate that he did have a history of mental health diagnoses, including major depression, posttraumatic stress disorder (PTSD), attention deficit hyperactivity disorder (ADHD), and cannabis use disorder. He had also been prescribed a number of psychotropic drugs, including Prozac (antidepressant), Wellbutrin (antidepressant), Trazodone (antidepressant and sedative), Tegretol (mood stabilizer), Ritalin (for ADHD), clonidine (for ADHD), Risperdal (antipsychotic), and Seroquel (antipsychotic). Mr. Martin denied a history of suicide attempts but noted a history of suicidal ideation and incidents of self-harm, including punching walls and hitting his head against the wall.

EVENTS LEADING UP TO THE POLICE ASSAULT

When asked to describe his circumstances before the police assault took place, Mr. Martin reported he had been homeless since his father's death four years before the current evaluation, and his mother was concerned for his welfare. His father's death had left him disorganized and distraught. He stated, "I lost him (father) and everything in one day." He reported, "I was about to break down." When asked to describe his emotional condition,

Mr. Martin reported he was "sad" and "tired of dealing with everything and nothing getting better, so I was literally giving up. I was breaking down. Something was about to happen, in my mind." He noted he spent most of his time "sitting there."

Mr. Martin was queried for mental health symptoms that he experienced prior to the police assault using criteria from the *DSM-5* (American Psychiatric Association, 2013). He endorsed symptoms including negative cognitions and depressed mood. He felt emotionally distant or cut off from other people ("it was like I didn't have a connection with them"). He had lost interest in activities he used to enjoy and had trouble experiencing positive feelings. In addition, he reported impairments in arousal and reactivity including reckless behavior (methamphetamine use and criminal behavior), sleep problems ("I've always had trouble falling asleep"), and childhood problems in anger management.

When asked about his early experiences related to police, Mr. Martin reported "they used to take me away when I was little, so I never liked any kind of law enforcement around me." Although Mr. Martin had been arrested several times for misdemeanor offenses, he had experienced his contacts with the police as relatively neutral, and, on some occasions when he was unhoused, the police were helpful in getting him into safer circumstances at local shelters.

Stage 2

Stage 2 focuses on the interval in which the evidence indicates the psychological injury took place. In this stage, the evaluator should have a clear picture of what occurred during the LRE.

When asked to describe the circumstances leading up to the police assault on February 22, 2019, Mr. Martin reported he had been homeless since his father's death. He stated, "I lost him (father) and everything in one day. I was staying at friends and family. I didn't have clothes. I didn't have personal things. I didn't know what I was doing." He reported, "I went to my mom's place and I was about to break down." Records indicate Mr. Martin's mother (Ms. Calvin) was concerned for his welfare prior to the police attack in part because she believed he was suicidal. He was generally distraught, and he recalls he was "sad" and "tired of dealing with everything and nothing getting better, so I was literally giving up. I was breaking down. Something was about to happen, in my mind." He recalls feeling suicidal at that time. Mr. Martin said he fell asleep and his mother, concerned about his condition, left to talk to her neighbor and friend at her apartment complex. Ms. Calvin stated that she was at her neighbor's apartment at the time of the police attack. She said she went there because she was concerned. She reported, "I could see he was really down, and I know it was because of his dad and he didn't have anywhere to go." Upon hearing her concerns, the neighbor called the police.

Mr. Martin stated the police came to the door to "check" on him. He said he told them he was all right, but they refused to leave. He said, "They busted in" and "attacked me and tazed me and punched me. One of them beat me with a baton, and I was just screaming my head off. I don't know. I couldn't believe it. It was a shock." When asked what the experience was like for him, Mr. Martin stated, "I never been hurt like that or attacked like that in my life. I never bled like that in my whole life. I never been afraid or scared or I never been put in a position like that my whole life." Mr. Martin said the experience "changed me."

Police videos and reports were generally consistent with the plaintiff's account. Upon breaking in the door of the house, the officers physically assaulted Mr. Martin with a taser gun, with their fists, and with their feet. After he was on the floor, they hit his legs multiple times with a baton. Mr. Martin was handcuffed while screaming and placed on a stretcher, put in an ambulance, and then taken to the hospital. Records state Mr. Martin had an "injury of lower limb," and his symptoms were noted to be "localized swelling, mass and lump, unspecified lower limb." Upon contact with Mr. Martin, EMS staff observed Mr. Martin's bones in his leg to be broken and noted Mr. Martin to be "screaming in pain." Records note Mr. Martin was taken to Central Medical Center, and his injuries were of sufficient severity and complexity as to merit his transfer via helicopter to Copper Medical Center in Springfield for a higher level of care. He was discharged to Green Health Care and Rehabilitation on February 27, 2019, five days after the incident.

Stage 3

In Stage 3, the evaluator forms a clear picture of what transpired in the interval between the date the LRE ended and the date of the complainant's evaluation. Because people in litigation are still living their daily lives, automobile accidents, problems with children or parents, marital distress, bankruptcies, and other negative events may very well have occurred during this sometimes two- to three-year interval. These require discussion and an attempt by the evaluator to determine their impact.

When asked about his emotional condition after the event, Mr. Martin reported, "I was scared. It messed me up." He noted he lost interest in pleasurable activities because all he was doing was "living, walking, talking, and being awake." He used to "see the benefit in doing certain things. It would be worth it, and I'd go do it. It would be normal for me to do them, and I wouldn't have no problems." He noted trouble with concentration and stated he had thoughts about suicide. Mental health treatment records from that period included symptoms of depression and staff were concerned that Mr. Martin was at risk for "distressed/fluctuating" mood symptoms related to "sadness/depression." Additionally, he was noted to exhibit anger toward medical staff and his medical center roommate. Mr. Martin was prescribed Trazodone (antidepressant and sedative) to address depression and sleep impairment.

Mr. Martin reported that after he was released from the hospital and the rehabilitation center, he moved into his grandparent's home and was cared for by his aunt. He said it took him "a long time" to heal, and it was a month before he was able to walk with assistance.

He said he was "almost healed" and "barely starting to walk" by himself again at the time of his arrest for an outstanding warrant for a probation violation (failure to report).

Detention center records summarized two admissions. The first detainment took place between July 18, 2019 and August 10, 2019. Upon admission, Mr. Martin reported to staff he was being treated for a police attack. Staff observed Mr. Martin's mood to be depressed. On July 23, 2019, Mr. Martin made "suicidal comments" to staff, resulting in his being placed on suicide watch. During this detainment, Mr. Martin was prescribed hydroxyzine (antihistamine, for anxiety). This medication was started on August 2, 2019 and discontinued on August 13, 2019. Mr. Martin was also prescribed Augmentin (anti-biotic). Documentation suggests he refused his medication. Mr. Martin was released on bond. When asked what jail was like for him, Mr. Martin said, "It wasn't good. I was having my issues still." Mr. Martin returned to the detention center on August 20, 2019 for a probation violation. His mood was noted to be depressed. Mr. Martin was released on August 30, 2019, and his probation was documented as complete. When asked about his detainment, Mr. Martin reported he felt depressed while in jail and like "nothing mattered" except his release.

Not long after his release from the detention center, Mr. Martin was able to walk without assistance, albeit slowly and with a limp, for short periods of time. He could complete basic activities of daily living on his own. He reported that during that time, he believed he would never be able to walk "normally" again and was looking for ways to accept this loss of function. He reported, "It made me sad and have no hope." He said that during periods of depression or frustration, he would engage in self-harm, such as stabbing himself with a screwdriver. Although he contends that he had been abstinent from methamphetamine use in the interval before the LRE, he said he started using again in the weeks after the incident.

In the interval between September 22, 2019 and May 22, 2020, Mr. Martin was twice hospitalized for symptoms related to trauma, depression, and amphetamine use for a total of eleven days. In the course of these admissions, he reported incidents of suicidal ideation and self-harm in the form of stabbing himself with a screwdriver. He was noted to experience mood swings, insomnia, racing thoughts, trouble with concentration, irritability, outbursts, difficulty trusting others, and hypervigilance that interfere with his functioning. Mr. Martin stated he felt angry and depressed when he was not taking his medication. He was prescribed a broad range of antidepressant and anxiolytic medications. His PTSD symptoms included nightmares, sleep impairment, panic attacks, and avoidance of crowds and loud noises.

The current interview included questions about DSM-5 PTSD symptoms in the LRE-interview interval. Taken together, these symptoms indicate he met the criteria for PTSD over a period of ten months. These symptoms were stable, did not increase after his detainment, and then began to decrease over time. He endorsed the following:

- **Intrusion:** (1) repeated, disturbing and unwanted memories ("different racing thoughts. What if? How come? All kinds of things. They are all different and one after another. I get mad and try to force them out. I stress myself out and try to wait for it to go away and it won't leave me alone. There is nothing I can do to help it. It comes and goes." "I get tired of thinking"); (2) repeated, disturbing dreams ("getting attacked by the police, running, and like, fear."); (3) physiological stress at exposure to cues (racing heart); and (4) psychological distress at exposure to cues ("I'm bothered and agitated." "I got different problems that I don't understand yet." "I start feeling like I need to fight." "I get undecisive").

- **Avoidance:** (1) avoidance of memories, thoughts, and feelings ("I try to stop myself from thinking altogether and sometimes, I can't at all. Sometimes, I try to concentrate on nothing"; and (2) avoidance of external reminders ("going outside, walking, everything." "If I see cops, I don't want to be seen or be around. That's why I'm home. Unfamiliar places, I start thinking outside of my comfort zone").

- **Negative cognitions and mood:** (1) negative beliefs about self, other, world ("I'm scared. I'm looking for something I never looked for. It changed me all the way. I don't even look the same."); (2) persistent negative emotional state (depression); (3) loss of interest in activities; (4) feeling emotionally distant or cut off from other people ("I can't connect like I used too. Even with eye contact. Little things, like gestures. I could tell my mom, 'I love you, Mom.' Now, it's not normal."); (5) loss of interest in previously enjoyed activities ("always"); and (6) trouble experiencing positive feelings ("when things are ok, they are ok. When I'm troubled or going through something, anxiety or whatever, then I can't feel positive feelings").

- **Arousal and reactivity:** (1) irritability or angry outbursts ("I get real angry and I'll walk around just cussing." "I never punched or socked myself up out of anger. It's a mix of anger and things that are overwhelming me."); (2) reckless or self-destructive behavior (methamphetamine relapse); (3) hypervigilance ("I'm paying attention to things." "I'm alert to, to how other people are watching me."); (4) problems with concentration ("I can't focus. I'm too busy being bothered or I'm uncomfortable and I have to settle down."); and (5) sleep difficulties.

Stage 4

By the time the evaluator reaches stage 4, a picture of many significant aspects of the evaluee's case should be emerging. All of the previously gathered information sets the stage for the assessment of the complainant's current status and it is time to produce a final product, which is usually a written evaluation report. Keep in mind how the stages flow, and how they may be used in the report.

When asked about his current emotional condition, Mr. Martin reported he is doing "a lot better." He stated his "life is pretty much in order. I can maintain without getting out of control." He reported he is being treated by a medical professional and a mental health professional. Mr. Martin said he is taking his psychiatric medication as prescribed and noted it is helpful. He admitted that he currently uses methamphetamine when he needs "to feel better," and he asserted he is not "hooked." When asked if his dislike of being around others has changed since immediately after the police attack, Mr. Martin reported it has improved. He stated his trust in others and depression has also improved.

In responding to interview questions focusing on the long-lasting effects of the police attack, Mr. Martin reported he lost trust in the police but stated this lack of trust has not impacted his life or kept him from going places because "I don't really do nothing wrong. It's not nothing bad I'm doing for them to be there. They are just regular people too." When asked about his current feelings toward police officers, Mr. Martin reported they are "alright" and noted he can be near them if they are not looking for him, specifically. When asked about his current medical condition, Mr. Martin reported he is currently taking medication to address stomach problems. Mr. Martin said he still experiences pain in his leg. He reported he cannot walk for long periods of time and stated his leg becomes "tight and numb."

In response to queries about his current social functioning and relationships, Mr. Martin said he is currently living with one of his aunts and his relationship with his family is positive. When asked about friendships, Mr. Martin stated he has friends that are "cool" with him and "that care"; however, he said they are "never around each other. I need to open up a bit. I don't know when that will be." He said, "I don't do stuff everyone else does." Mr. Martin indicated that he is currently unemployed and described his current finances as "the same situation I always been in." When asked how he supports himself, Mr. Martin reported he receives food stamps. When asked how he spends his current leisure time, Mr. Martin said, "I wake up and I eat breakfast, clean, do laundry, eat lunch, just eat and try to take care of myself. The basics. The little things." Mr. Martin stated he is "on my feet" much less than he used to be and said he has difficulty exercising.

PSYCHOLOGICAL ASSESSMENT

As part of the evaluation, Mr. Martin was administered the Test of Memory Malingering (TOMM), the Wechsler Adult Intelligence Scale, Fourth Edition (WAIS-IV), the Wide Range Achievement Test, Fifth Edition (WRAT5), the Personality Assessment Inventory (PAI), and the Detailed Assessment of Posttraumatic Stress (DAPS).

The TOMM distinguishes between true and feigned memory impairment. Mr. Martin's scores on this measure indicate he exerted adequate effort during testing, suggesting the cognitive data most likely reflect his current level of functioning.

The WAIS-IV is a test that is often used to establish an estimate of an individual's cognitive functioning. Scores indicate that Mr. Martin functions at borderline to high average cognitive abilities with an estimated Full Scale Intelligence Quotient (FSIQ) of 77. His summary scores are within a few points of this score, except for his scores on tasks requiring motor speed, which were above average.

The WRAT5 is an achievement test. The Sentence Comprehension subtest was administered to Mr. Martin. His score on this subtest placed him at the 11.8 grade level. This score indicates the self-report measures were likely within his reading ability.

The PAI is an objective, self-report measure of personality and psychological functioning. Validity scores indicate the profile was valid. Mr. Martin's responses on the measure indicated clinical elevations on scales indicative of anxiety and anxiety-related disorders. Responses suggest broad impairment due to anxiety and psychological turmoil and suggest his symptoms may be related to trauma.

The DAPS is a self-report measure that assesses trauma exposure and posttraumatic response. Mr. Martin's response pattern on this measure did not appear to exhibit positive or negative bias. His responses on the DAPS suggest that he has been exposed to traumatic events in his life. Mr. Martin indicated that the trauma most upsetting or clinically important was the police assault. Overall, Mr. Martin reported clinically significant symptoms of traumatic stress, including intense negative emotions (e.g., helplessness, horror, shame, and humiliation), dissociation, intrusive reexperiencing, avoidance/numbing, hyperarousal, and deficits in psychosocial functioning. Results indicate Mr. Martin is experiencing some suicidal ideation. The overall severity of his posttraumatic stress symptoms is in the severe range.

COLLATERAL INTERVIEWS

Ms. Calvin, Mr. Martin's mother, reported Mr. Martin lived with both biological parents until approximately 1991 when she divorced his father. Ms. Calvin said after Mr. Martin's father passed away, Mr. Martin had "issues." She reported "that (father) was his best friend. He had a hard time."

When asked how the police assault impacted Mr. Martin, Ms. Calvin reported Mr. Martin's depression had worsened after the police attack. She stated, "He feels like he wasn't doing anything, and the police are supposed to protect us, and it's hard cause he's at my house and that's where it happened." When asked about Mr. Martin's motivation before and after the police attack, Ms. Calvin said "it's worse now. He goes through his stages where he is okay for a little while. It's okay and he smiles and eats good, and sometimes he doesn't want to get up, but he's trying and trying to get his meds right." She said she believes he will always have "trust issues because of the police attack. He was already kind of like that, but it's more now. He doesn't really trust anyone." She reported Mr. Martin's mental health symptoms did not appear to exacerbate after his detainment.

Ms. Garcia, Mr. Martin's therapist, reported she saw him for his initial assessment in November 2019. When asked about mental health diagnoses, Ms. Garcia reported Mr. Martin met the criteria for major depressive disorder (MDD) and PTSD. She stated Mr. Martin has "trouble stabilizing his moods" due to symptoms of depression. She said after the police attack, Mr. Martin experienced more "issues" with sleep, nightmares, and flashbacks. She reported he also became more hypervigilant. Ms. Garcia stated Mr. Martin has trouble "going out" and being around people without his family. She said this has always been the case with Mr. Martin, but it was exacerbated after the police attack.

His therapist stated that Mr. Martin isolates himself "often," and she noted "the hypervigilance is a part of that. If he is afraid something will happen to him or he doesn't feel safe outside of home, he isolates which means he is more prone to depression." She said Mr. Martin has trouble with anger and irritability. When asked about the etiology of these symptoms, Ms. Garcia reported "this (police attack) is not his first trauma. With PTSD, the more trauma you have, the worse it gets. He has trauma from his dad that we've talked about and this situation (police attack) triggered something." She stated "it's (police attack) not the source of everything but it exacerbated everything." Ms. Garcia reported that their treatment includes increasing Mr. Martin's coping skills, his ability to communicate with others, and his ability to "take care of himself."

When asked if Mr. Martin has shown improvement, Ms. Garcia said, "It goes back and forth." She reported he has times when he is doing better and then there are other times that his mental health symptoms are exacerbated. She stated Mr. Martin is currently taking medication and is generally medication compliant. His therapist reported Mr. Martin is "good about managing" his symptoms of PTSD and depression, but "the paranoia and social anxiety has increased due to the incident (police attack)." Ms. Garcia stated Mr. Martin has problems building trust with others. She said he also avoided talking about what happened. When asked if Mr. Martin is exhibiting symptoms of depression, Ms. Garcia said he was "spiraling" before he moved into his aunt's home. She reported now that he is living with his aunt and his medication has been stabilized, he is doing "a lot better."

DIAGNOSTIC IMPRESSION

Substance use disorder (SUD) is defined not only by heavy substance consumption but also by difficulties controlling substance use, negative consequences of substance use (and continued use despite these consequences), and physiological changes. Data from the current evaluation suggest that Mr. Martin meets diagnostic criteria for stimulant use disorder, amphetamine-type substance, severe.

PTSD is defined by the DSM-5 as the development of psychological distress, such as intrusive thoughts, avoidance, diminished mood or cognition, and reactive behavior, following exposure to traumatic or stressful events. Mr. Martin reported some symptoms that are consistent with PTSD prior to the police attack. It is important to note that the police attack constituted a DSM-5 criterion A stressor that would be a necessary predicate for the development of posttraumatic symptoms. During the incident, Mr. Martin directly experienced serious injury. This experience caused him extreme fear, horror, and pain. Mr. Martin endorsed symptoms immediately after the police attack that are consistent with intrusive thoughts, avoidance, diminished mood or cognition, and reactive behavior. Additionally, psychological testing suggests Mr. Martin was experiencing high levels of anxiety and other symptoms of PTSD. Symptoms noted in psychological testing appear to be consistent with Mr. Martin's self-report and with symptoms noted by collaterals. At the time immediately after the police attack, he met the criteria for PTSD.

The typical course of PTSD is characterized by the most severe symptoms in the period immediately following trauma exposure. Although many people completely recover within six months, it is also common for symptoms to improve but continue to persist at a lower frequency or severity. Mr. Martin's course generally followed this path in that he reported that his posttraumatic symptoms have generally improved over time, save some persistent symptoms. For example, Ms. Garcia reported he continues to experience symptoms such as paranoia, hypervigilance, anger, and irritability. Although Mr. Martin may not be experiencing all categories of symptoms that are needed to merit a current PTSD diagnosis, the symptoms that he is currently experiencing are debilitating and negatively impact his functioning. This condition constitutes what is referred to as "partial PTSD" (Breslau et al., 2004; McLaughlin et al., 2015) or the DSM-5 designation of "Other Specified Trauma-and-Stressor-Related Disorder" in which an individual does not meet the full PTSD criteria but the trauma symptoms they do experience, nevertheless, generate considerable distress and impairment.

Major depressive disorder (MDD) is characterized by a disruptive mood for a two-week period or longer. Common symptoms of the disorder include sadness, feelings of emptiness, or irritability together with cognitive and somatic changes. The cluster of symptoms contributes to notable functional impairment in an individual. It is possible for MDD to be preceded by a traumatic event, and although some symptoms of MDD overlap with PTSD (e.g., diminished interest in activities and sleep disturbance), other symptoms are more unique to a diagnosis of MDD (e.g., appetite disturbance, and diminished energy). Mr. Martin reported and collateral sources indicated Mr. Martin has a long history of depression that antedated the police attack on February 22, 2019.

Additionally, depressive symptoms were noted at the time of the interview. Specifically, Mr. Martin reported a depressed mood, feeling "slow," hopelessness, trouble with sleep, trouble with concentration, anxiety, and some suicidal ideation. Records suggest Mr. Martin has experienced symptoms of depression and has a history of medication use to address depressed mood and sleep trouble. Collateral sources support the depression diagnosis indicating that Mr. Martin is experiencing symptoms of depression that include feeling down and lacking motivation. Importantly, he noted he was doing "alright" and "better" at the time of the second interview. Taken together, Mr. Martin meets the criteria for major depressive disorder, severe, with anxious distress.

SUMMARY

Mr. Martin is an individual with a complicated history. He was noted to have suffered from mental health problems that included depression and PTSD for a large portion of his life before the police attack incident that is the focus of the current lawsuit. Mr. Martin reported some mood symptoms related to his father's death prior to the police attack, but he did not appear to meet the criteria for PTSD. The symptoms he experienced prior to the police attack included negative cognition and mood as well as symptoms of arousal and reactivity. Specifically, he reported a persistent negative emotional state and feeling distant from others, loss of interest in pleasurable activities, and trouble experiencing positive experiences. Mr. Martin also noted sleep difficulties. Both by his report and from information from his family, he did not show intrusion and avoidance symptoms prior to the police assault.

PTSD is an especially complex disorder because it combines both anxious, depressive, and a mix of other symptoms. These symptoms of trauma fall into various clusters or categories. Some of the categories are specific to the source of the trauma (e.g., intrusive recollections, nightmares, and avoidance), although other categories are more general and not directly linked to any one specific traumatic event (e.g., numbing symptoms, irritability, and sleep difficulties). In some cases, these symptoms may not be linked to a specific instance, except in cases where they emerge after a specific event. During the evaluation, Mr. Martin reported that after the police assault, he experienced PTSD symptoms that were specific to the police attack. These symptoms included intrusion, avoidance, and arousal and reactivity. Specifically, Mr. Martin reported intrusion symptoms such as "racing thoughts" about why the police attack happened and stated he sometimes feels "tired of thinking." He said he experienced nightmares related to the police attack that include him feeling frightened. He reported that he feels stress and experiences psychological distress when reminded of the police attack or when he is exposed to cues related to the police attack. He also reported avoidance symptoms such as avoiding memories. In his daily life, in spite of his experience of several arrests and incarcerations, he did his best to avoid external reminders of the police attack by avoiding situations in which he had contact with police officers. Avoidance directly related to the police attack was also noted by Ms. Garcia. New symptoms related to trauma included being hypervigilant or feeling "more alert to how other people are watching me" and having trouble with concentration and being able to focus.

Although Mr. Martin experienced some more diffuse symptoms of PTSD prior to the police assault, many of the symptoms persisted and were exacerbated immediately after the police attack. For example, his preexisting negative emotional state worsened following the attack. Although he previously felt distant from others, both his therapist and Mr.

Martin stated he had trouble connecting with others in the same way to the extent that he had trouble making eye contact with others. He also noted he had trouble expressing himself to others and even has trouble telling his mother that he loves her. Mr. Martin noted that even before the attack he "always" experienced a loss of interest in or pleasure from activities. His inability to experience positive feelings changed from not caring about the feelings to, at times, not being able to experience them. Regarding arousal and reactivity symptoms, they also were exacerbated immediately after the police attack. Additionally, he continued to experience sleep difficulties.

It is important to note that in most cases, individuals experience the most severe symptoms of trauma immediately after or in close proximity to the traumatic event. For most people who are presenting an accurate picture of their symptoms, most symptoms will resolve or decrease in frequency or severity over time. This pattern is exemplified by Mr. Martin. As noted above, he reported worse symptoms immediately after the police attack. However, his symptoms had improved somewhat at the time of the in-person interview with the undersigned evaluator. Based upon his report during the follow-up with him and the report of Mr. Martin's therapist, Ms. Garcia, the symptoms have continued to improve over time. However, it should be noted that there are some trauma-related symptoms that have continued to persist, including isolation, hypervigilance, methamphetamine use, anger, and irritability.

Just prior to the police attack, Mr. Martin was experiencing acute depression. He noted feeling depressed, sleeping most of the day, and experiencing some thoughts of suicide. He stated that he spent his time between the homes of various family members, where he would sit until it was time to leave to go to the next home. Collateral sources indicate that Mr. Martin continued to grieve for his father. Importantly, collateral sources suggest the reason the police were called to Mr. Martin's mother's apartment the night of the police attack was because his mother was concerned for Mr. Martin's welfare.

After the police attack, some of Mr. Martin's depressive symptoms persisted at about the same level as before the incident. For example, he continued to feel "slow," hopeless, and anxious. He continued to have trouble with sleep and concentration and to experience some suicidal ideation. However, after the police attack, some symptoms of depression were exacerbated and became so severe that Mr. Martin was hospitalized twice. At the time of the interview, Mr. Martin's symptoms of depression appeared manageable. Taken together, Mr. Martin appeared to be severely depressed prior to the police assault, but data suggest his depression worsened immediately after the police assault leading to hospitalization. Since that time, in response to effective interventions through medication and psychotherapy, his symptoms of depression have somewhat improved. This improvement shows evidence of the plaintiff's active attempts to mitigate his damages.

Mr. Martin indicates that he had a substantial history of methamphetamine use before the February 22, 2019 police assault, and most likely would have met the criteria for stimulant use disorder, amphetamine-type substance, severe. However, he had been abstinent for approximately four weeks before the attack. In the interval following the attack (stage 3), Mr. Martin returned to methamphetamine use at a severe level. With the interventions of his psychotherapist, in addition to several hospitalizations and periods of incarceration, he was able to reduce his use somewhat, although he was still sporadically using methamphetamine at the time of the interview.

One way that preexisting conditions that are evident in stage 1 affect the stage 4 analysis is that they may make the person more vulnerable to developing a new disorder or they weaken a person's functioning that can break down following a traumatic incident. Considerations of comorbidity become important in this context. PTSD and SUDs are highly correlated such that the most common comorbid disorder for men with trauma symptoms is substance use. Given Mr. Martin's history of methamphetamine use, it is not surprising that he relapsed after the police attack and began using methamphetamine again. PTSD and depression are also highly related such that the exacerbation of trauma symptoms and depressive symptoms are related to one another. The evidence is clear that the stress of the police attack exacerbated Mr. Martin's symptoms of depression. Taken together, although Mr. Martin was already vulnerable to depression, his methamphetamine use, the exacerbation of his depressive symptoms, and the stress caused by the police attack and subsequent events triggered suicidal episodes that prompted two hospitalizations for Mr. Martin. These episodes further exacerbated Mr. Martin's symptoms of depression, trauma, and substance use, as if it were all a vicious cycle.

Data obtained during the current evaluation suggest that Mr. Martin's social functioning declined, and relationships were negatively impacted immediately after the police attack. Collateral information suggested that family members were not sure how to interact with Mr. Martin or how to help him cope with his mental health symptoms. He felt isolated and alone and because of his mental health needs, he was asked not to return to his aunt's home. Currently, Mr. Martin reported his relationship with his family is positive and stated he feels supported by them.

Outside the family sphere, since the police attack, Mr. Martin continues to minimize his interactions with others who are not his family, which has kept him from fostering friendships. Additionally, Mr. Martin no longer engages in relationship-building activities with individuals other than his mother or very close family. His aunt noted Mr. Martin no longer spends time with his cousins. Since the police attack, Mr. Martin said his financial and employment situations have not changed.

Prior to the police attack, his leisure appeared minimal, such that he spent his time at the homes of family and friends, where he would "rest." After the police attack, Mr. Martin stated he was "stuck" laying down and spent his time "dwelling" on his circumstances. He also reported he stopped spending time outside because he was too fearful. He noted he began using substances again, including methamphetamine. Mr. Martin reported he currently spends his time attempting to care for himself.

In sum, on the day of the police attack incident central to this lawsuit, Mr. Martin experienced several mental health symptoms, including depression, symptoms of trauma, and methamphetamine use. The evidence indicates that all these conditions became worse following the February 22, 2019 police attack incident. He developed symptoms consistent with PTSD that were related to the police attack and the events that followed. His depression exacerbated, leading to two psychiatric hospitalizations. His methamphetamine use resumed and complicated his treatment for PTSD and depression. His housing circumstances continued to be unstable and attempts for him to live with relatives were complicated by more severe PTSD and depression symptoms. His mental health symptoms caused him to become alienated from his extended family, which had been an important source of social contact before the police attack incident. Taken together, it is clear that the police attack exacerbated symptoms of substance abuse and depression and also caused Mr. Martin to experience additional symptoms consistent with depression and PTSD.

Stage 5

In stage 5, the examiner utilizes the data collated in stage 4 to determine the prognosis and future treatment and care needs for the plaintiff.

PTSD, MDD, and SUD often co-occur and are associated with greater functional impairment as compared to any disorder alone. Several empirically supported treatments have been shown to be effective in treating PTSD and depression. These methods focus on cognitive-behavioral strategies and devote attention to identifying, challenging, and modifying negative cognitive appraisals (e.g., "I am not safe in the world"). Although less is known about the treatment of comorbid PTSD and depression relative to the treatment of either disorder alone, there is growing empirical support for the use of integrated and concurrent treatments among individuals with symptom comorbidity. In fact, initial research suggests that cognitive-behavioral therapies may be effective in treating comorbid PTSD and depression.

Dialectical behavior therapy (DBT) is a cognitive-behavioral treatment designed to target deficits in emotion regulation and distress tolerance. The treatment encompasses skill building in the areas of mindfulness, distress tolerance, emotion regulation, and interpersonal effectiveness. It is also likely to aid in the reduction of his trauma and depressive symptoms, such that DBT emotion regulation skills emphasize increasing emotional processing and behavioral activation. Given Mr. Martin's history of depression and other mental health difficulties, he will likely need ongoing, prolonged treatment to address his symptoms.

Research has shown that the recommended treatments discussed here are effective in reducing symptoms of PTSD and depression. It should be noted that individuals undergoing PTSD treatment often experience an initial increase in symptoms as they begin to fully process their trauma. Because of this, dropout rates tend to be relatively high for trauma-focused treatment; however, if individuals continue to engage in the treatment, symptoms are likely to then decline. Moreover, engagement in DBT will likely aid in improving Mr. Martin's abilities in emotion regulation and distress tolerance, which will also prove helpful when he is encouraged to process his trauma. Additionally, in light of his current substance use, it is important that Mr. Martin talk to his treatment providers about the use of methamphetamine. It is likely that integrated treatment for PTSD, MDD, and substance use is warranted.

In conclusion, at this time, it appears Mr. Martin would benefit from a highly structured, outpatient, empirically supported dual-diagnosis treatment program for PTSD and depression, as well as DBT. This program should include individual and group mental health counseling, as well as coordinated medication management at the discretion of his mental health provider(s). It should be noted that he appears to have a positive and trusting relationship with his current mental health provider. This is also imperative to treatment and should be taken into consideration when choosing future treatment for Mr. Martin.

Conclusion

This modified evaluation report provides an example of how the Five-Stage Model can be used to explicate a complex personal injury case. In this example, the plaintiff had an extensive mental health history, and, in fact, the incident that generated the lawsuit occurred in the midst of a mental health crisis. The Five-Stage Model is designed to take into account preexisting disorders, and to account for their continued occurrence or exacerbation after the LRE, or to account for them leading to a subsequent stressor to have a greater impact—the "eggshell skull" (Renka, 2007). In addition, preexisting impairments in social functioning may leave the evaluee with few social support resources following a litigation-related stressor. In Mr. Martin's case, all these patterns were evident. However, the trauma he experienced at the time of the police incident was extensive and resulted in serious medical consequences. Accordingly, the PTSD literature would suggest that anyone's reactions to these events would likely include some posttraumatic reactions, in addition to symptoms of depression. The extensive comorbidity literature (see Debell et al., 2014; Horesh et al., 2017; Kessler et al., 2009) indicates that a person diagnosed with PTSD is more likely than not to have a substance use disorder, depression, or anxiety diagnosis as well. That was the case with Mr. Martin, not only after the police incident but, indeed, before.

One feature of the Five-Stage Model is a focus on function, particularly changes in function following an LRE. Mr. Martin's history indicates that he had seriously impaired functioning before the police incident. He had no effective work history, had never been married, and experienced periods of homelessness. He occasionally used methamphetamine and had been arrested and adjudicated for a number of misdemeanors, including possession of methamphetamine. In this case, the model indicates that some of these things improved following the LRE. He entered into psychotherapy and was more closely followed for his ongoing mental health problem. This increased mental health involvement most likely mitigated the negative impact of the police assault-related PTSD and depression.

In all, the five-stage model provided a framework for structuring the large amount of information coming from Mr. Martin's prior medical, legal, and life history. The model guided the examiner through the plaintiff's account of the police assault, paying close attention to aspects of that account that may have increased the severity of subsequent emotional reactions. Focus on the interval between the relatively brief, but severe, traumatic episode allowed for a nuanced appreciation of factors that both exacerbated and mitigated his emotional reactions to this severely stressful event. A complete and thorough evaluation, including interviews with the plaintiff and collateral sources, along with psychological testing, provided a clear picture of his current status, and a basis for determining functional changes as compared to his "day before" status.

All this information allowed the evaluator to provide the court with a picture of viable future treatment courses and their effectiveness. A clear report of this analysis can assist in retaining counsel in decision-making regarding the case, opposing counsel in the determination of their response, and mediators in their attempts to resolve the case in a manner acceptable to the parties. Although as many as 98 percent of personal injury cases are resolved out of court (Foote & Goodman-Delahunty, 2021; Hadfield, 2004), in complex cases such as Mr. Martin's, the case may be bound for trial. In the pretrial deposition, the preparation of a clear report that clearly indicates that the examiner took into account alternative sources of causation for the plaintiff's complaint provides a basis for withstanding close scrutiny. In the trial, the Five-Stage Model can serve as a systematic approach for presenting the data to the judge and jury that helps the examiner withstand cross-examination because of the attention to data that both support and detract from the expert's stated opinions.

References

American Psychological Association. (2013). *Diagnostic and statistical manual of mental disorders* (5th ed.). American Psychological Association.

American Psychological Association. (2017). *Ethical principles of psychologists and code of conduct (2002, Amended June 1, 2010 and January 1, 2017)*. Retrieved from http://www.apa.org.libproxy.unm.edu/ethics/code/index.aspx.

American Psychological Association. (2019). *Publication manual of the American Psychological Association* (7th ed.). American Psychological Association.

Breslau, N., Lucia, V. C., & Davis, G. C. (2004). Partial PTSD versus full PTSD: An empirical examination of associated impairment. *Psychological Medicine, 34*(7), 1205–1214.

Debell, F., Fear, N. T., Head, M., Batt-Rawden, S., Greenberg, N., Wessely, S., & Goodwin, L. (2014). A systematic review of the comorbidity between PTSD and alcohol misuse. *Social Psychiatry and Psychiatric Epidemiology, 49*(9), 1401–1425.

Foote, W. E. (2017). Personal injury evaluations. In S. Walfish, J. E. Barnett, & J. Zimmerman (Eds.), *Handbook of private practice: Keys to success for mental health practitioners* (pp. 641–646). Oxford University Press.

Foote, W. E. (2020). Assessing trauma in personal injury evaluations. In R. A. Javier, E. A. Maddux, & J. A. Maddux (Eds.), *Assessing trauma in forensic contexts* (pp. 297–324). Springer.

Foote, W. E., & Goodman-Delahunty, J. (2021). *Understanding sexual harassment: Evidence-based forensic practice*. American Psychological Association.

Foote, W. E., Goodman-Delahunty, J., & Young, G. (2020). Civil forensic evaluation: Professional and ethical considerations in litigation related assessment. *Psychological Injury and Law, 13*, 327–353.

Foote, W. E., & Lareau, C. R. (2013). Psychological evaluation of emotional damages in tort cases. In R. K. Otto & I. B. Weiner (Eds.), *Handbook of psychology: Forensic psychology* (pp. 172–200). John Wiley & Sons.

Goodman-Delahunty, J., Saunders, P., & Foote, W. (2012). *Evaluating claims for workplace discrimination: A five-stage model* [Paper presentation]. Proceedings of the 2011 APS Forensic Psychology Conference, Australian Psychological Society Ltd, Sydney.

Greenberg, S. A., Otto, R. K., & Long, A. C. (2003). The utility of psychological testing in assessing emotional damages in personal injury litigation. *Assessment, 10*(4), 411–419.

Hadfield, G. K. (2004). Where have all the trials gone? Settlements, nontrial adjudications, and statistical artifacts in the changing disposition of federal civil cases. *Journal of Empirical Legal Studies, 3*(1), 705–734.

Heilbrun, K., DeMatteo, D., Brooks Holliday, S., & LaDuke, C. (Eds.). (2014). *Forensic mental health assessment: A casebook* (2nd ed.). Oxford University Press.

Horesh, D., Lowe, S. R., Galea, S., Aiello, A. E., Uddin, M., & Koenen, K. C. (2017). An in-depth look into PTSD-depression comorbidity: A longitudinal study of chronically-exposed Detroit residents. *Journal of Affective Disorders, 208*, 653–661.

Kane, A. W., & Dvoskin, J. A. (2011). *Evaluation for personal injury claims*. Oxford University Press.

Kane, A. W., Nelson, E. M., Dvoskin, J. A., & Pitt, S. E. (2013). Evaluation for personal injury claims. In R. Roesch & P. A. Zapf (Eds.), *Forensic assessments in criminal and civil law: A handbook for lawyers* (pp. 148–160). Oxford University Press.

Kessler, R. C., Ruscio, A. M., Shear, K., & Wittchen, H.-U. (2009). Epidemiology of anxiety disorders. In M. M. Antony & M. B. Stein (Eds.), *Oxford handbook of anxiety and related disorders* (pp. 19–33). Oxford University Press.

McLaughlin, K. A., Koenen, K. C., Friedman, M. J., Ruscio, A. M., Karam, E. G., Shahly, V., Stein, D. J., Hill, E. D., Petukhova, M., Alonso, J., Andrade, L. H., Angermeyer, M. C., Borges, G., de Girolamo, G., de Graaf, R., Demyttenaere, K., Florescu, S. E., Mladenova, M., PosadaVilla, J., . . . Kessler, R. C. (2015). Subthreshold posttraumatic stress disorder in the World Health Organization World Mental Health Surveys. *Biological Psychiatry, 77*(4), 375–384.

Melton, G. B., Petrila, J., Poythress, N. G., Slobogin, C., Otto, R. K., Mossman, D., & Condie, L. O. (2018). *Psychological evaluations for the courts: A handbook for mental health professionals and lawyers* (4th ed.). Guilford Press.

Otto, R. K., DeMier, R. L., & Boccaccini, M. T. (2014). *Forensic reports and testimony: A guide to effective communication for psychologists and psychiatrists*. John Wiley & Sons.

Renka, C. (2007). The presumed eggshell plaintiff rule: Determining liability when mental harm accompanies physical injury. *Thomas Jefferson Law Review, 29*, 289–311.

Wilson, J. P., & Moran, T. A. (2004). Forensic/clinical assessment of psychological trauma and PTSD in legal settings. In J. P. Wilson & T. M. Keane (Eds.), *Assessing psychological trauma and PTSD* (pp. 603–636). Guilford Press.

Young, G., & Brodsky, S. L. (2016). The 4 Ds of forensic mental health assessments of personal injury. *Psychological Injury and Law, 9*(3), 278–281.

Evaluating Workplace Disability

Lisa Drago Piechowski

Abstract

Forensic disability evaluations occur in different contexts, each with its own legal standards. The common basis is establishing the presence of a valid psychological condition, assessing the functional impairments that derive from that condition, and comparing those impairments with the examinee's work demands. This requires drawing a connection between the manifestations of the individual's mental health condition and specific impairments in their functioning, then extrapolating these functional impairments to the requirements of their job. Research has begun to identify factors relevant to understanding these connections. However, the methodology for applying these factors to predict outcomes in individual cases has not yet been developed. Additional research is needed to identify specific methods and practices associated with more accurate outcomes in disability evaluations. The development of an actuarial model of prediction for return to work could improve the accuracy of disability assessments beyond reliance on clinical judgment.

Key Words: disability evaluations, fitness for duty, forensic evaluations, malingering, best practices

Work disability is not uncommon, affecting approximately 10 percent of working-age adults in the United States. Mental health issues are the second leading cause of disability after neck and back problems, and they account for about one in five cases of disability (Theis et al., 2018). Being legally designated "disabled" can have significant consequences for the individual involved and for the institutions with which that individual interacts in terms of entitlement to benefits, conferring legally protected rights, and securing employment opportunities. Incorrect determinations of disability can prevent individuals from receiving financial benefits or legal protections to which they are entitled. Incorrect determinations are also costly to society, such as when limited resources are misdirected to the wrong parties.

The forensic assessment of workplace disability occurs in several different contexts. These include claims for disability benefits (e.g., disability insurance and workers' compensation), fitness-for-duty evaluations, and determining eligibility for legal protection (e.g., Americans with Disabilities Act). Each context has its own standards, requirements, procedures, and laws. However, the common basis among all of these is establishing the presence of a valid psychological condition, assessing the functional impairments that derive from that condition, and comparing those impairments with the demands of the examinee's job or their overall work capacity. In essence, a disability evaluation is an attempt to answer the question, given this individual's mental health condition, to what extent can they work?

Legal Definitions of Disability

The term "disability," used in the context of a forensic evaluation, always has a specific legal definition. The relevant legal definition is determined by the specific policy, contract, statute, or program relevant to the circumstances of the evaluation. To be considered "disabled," the examinee must meet this specific legal definition of disability. Regardless of the context, all forensic disability evaluations require comparing the examinee's presentation and circumstances with this legal standard.

Claims for Benefits

When an individual's capacity to work is compromised due to an illness or injury, they may seek disability benefits to compensate them for their lost income. Sources of benefits vary depending on the circumstances of the claimant. These sources include private disability insurance, employer-paid disability, worker's compensation, and Social Security Disability Insurance (SSDI). Each source of benefits is controlled by a different set of laws, regulations, statutes, and rules.

"Private" or "individual" disability insurance refers to an insurance policy purchased by an individual (often self-employed) to provide monetary benefits if an illness or injury prevents the policyholder from being able to work or to work at full capacity. This policy is a contract between the policyholder and the insurance company. In exchange for premiums paid by the policyholder, the insurance company agrees to provide a monetary benefit if the insured party becomes disabled as defined under the terms of the policy. State laws govern the relationship between policyholders and insurance companies. Disputes can be litigated in state courts or in federal courts applying state laws.

Employer-paid or "group" disability policies are sometimes provided by an employer as part of the employee's benefits. As such, they are governed by the federal Employee Retirement Income Security Act[1] (ERISA). ERISA, which preempts state laws that otherwise apply to private disability insurance policies, establishes a set of administrative procedures that must be followed in the event of a dispute between the claimant and the company. Like individual policies, the definition of disability for employer-paid disability is determined by the policy language. The claimant is required to provide proof of loss,

---

[1] Employee Retirement Income Security Act of 1974 (ERISA), Pub. L. No. 93-406, 88 Stat. 829.

and the insurance company must then evaluate the claim. Claim denials can be appealed but must follow the guidelines and timeframes set by ERISA.

Workers' compensation is intended to provide benefits for workers who become ill or are injured on the job. Thus, workers' compensation differs from other kinds of disability benefits in that the causation of the illness or injury is a critical factor. The injured worker must demonstrate that the illness or injury was the direct outcome of their employment. Workers' compensation benefits are handled differently in each state and are governed by statutes, case law, and administrative practices. Disputed claims are decided by special administrative agencies utilizing administrative law judges. Although worker's compensation was developed with the intention of compensating for physical injuries, most states recognize compensation for some types of mental injuries as well. Claims involving emotional stress are categorized as: (1) *physical-mental*, referring to psychological problems arising from a physical illness or injury; (2) *mental-physical*, which describes a physical condition caused by psychological stress arising in the course of employment; or (3) *mental-mental*, referring to mental injuries arising from employment in the absence of a physical injury.

SSDI is governed by a vast body of federal law consisting of statutory law, regulatory law, rulings, and court decisions. To be disabled under SSDI, the claimant must have a severe disability (or combination of disabilities) that has lasted, or is expected to last, at least twelve months or result in death, and which prevents the claimant from working at a "substantial gainful activity" level (Social Security Act).[2] Mental health conditions are listed in eleven categories. To be considered disabled, the claimant's impairment must have been "medically determined" by a physician or psychologist based on an examination or treatment of the claimant. In addition, the claimant's condition must cause marked impairment in one or more mental capacities: the ability to learn and remember task instructions, sustain mental effort; interact appropriately with others, and/or accommodate and adapt to unexpected changes.

Fitness for Duty

Fitness-for-duty evaluations are typically initiated by an employer to assess an employee's capacity to perform their job duties in a safe and competent manner in the context of a possible mental impairment. These evaluations are often prompted by changes in an employee's behavior that is seen as being disruptive, bizarre, or threatening; or when other issues presumed to involve the employee's mental health interfere with their work performance. These evaluations focus on questions about the employee's mental or emotional condition and its impact on the employee's ability to perform the essential functions of the position safely and effectively, with or without reasonable accommodation (American Psychological Association, 2018). Like other types of disability evaluations,

---

[2] Social Security Act, 42 U.S.C. §423.

fitness-for-duty evaluations involve comparing the employee's functional capacity to the requirements of their job.

However, there are some important distinctions that set fitness for duty evaluations apart from other disability evaluations. Federal law requires employers to provide employees with a workplace free from recognized hazards likely to cause death or serious physical harm.[3] This obligates employers to address potential threats in the workplace related to the behavior of their employees. Because fitness-for-duty evaluations are almost always mandated by the employer, this can pose potentially significant legal, financial, and safety consequences for all parties involved, including the forensic evaluator (American Psychological Association, 2018). In essence, the context of a fitness-for-duty evaluation creates a tension between the needs of the employer to maintain a safe and productive workplace and the privacy rights of the employee (Piechowski & Drukteinis, 2011).

Eligibility for Legal Protection

The third context in which workplace disability evaluations take place, is when an individual seeks legal protection as a disabled person under the Americans with Disabilities Act (ADA).[4] The ADA is a federal law designed to protect the rights of individuals with disabilities who wish to have access to or participate in certain aspects of American society, including the competitive labor market. Persons who meet the definition of disability under ADA are entitled to protection from discrimination by employers, either for having a disability, having a history of a disability, or being perceived as disabled. The ADA defines disability as a physical or mental impairment that substantially limits one or more of the major life activities, a record of such impairment, or being regarded as having such an impairment.[5]

Several different circumstances can trigger an ADA evaluation. For example, an evaluation may be requested by an employee who self-identifies as having a disability and requests accommodations from their employer. Alternatively, an employer may want to accommodate an employee's disability but is unsure as to what accommodations would be most appropriate and practical. Sometimes, an employer requests an evaluation when the employer wants to understand the cause of an employee's behavior, especially when this behavior is atypical of the employee, becomes distracting or concerning to other employees, or raises questions of workplace safety. The employer seeks to understand if the employee's behavior is due to a disability rather than being a reflection of a lack of motivation, negative personality traits, poor interpersonal skills, or antisocial behavior. This latter circumstance generally falls under the category of a fitness-for-duty evaluation.

---

[3] Occupational Safety and Health Act (OSHA) of 1970, 29 U.S.C. §654, Pub. L. 91–596, 84 Stat. 1590, 91st Cong., S. 2193 (1970).

[4] Americans with Disabilities Act of 1990 (ADA), 42 U.S.C. §§12101 et seq. (1990).

[5] ADA, 42 U.S.C. §12102(2).

Similarly, an evaluation may be triggered by an employee seeking to return to work after a long absence due to mental health issues. The employer may want to know if the employee is now able to return to work and what, if any, specific accommodations may be required in light of the employee's disability (Piechowski & Rehman, 2011).

Conceptualizing Disability

Disability is not an enduring characteristic of an individual. It is best understood as a complex interaction of person and situational variables. These variables include the individual's clinical condition and their functional capacity in a given situation in light of this condition.

Functional capacity, as defined by Grisso (2003), refers to what an individual can do or accomplish. Although the presence of a mental health condition is required for a determination of disability, diagnosis alone is insufficient. The fact that an individual meets the diagnostic criteria for a mental health disorder does not necessarily mean that they meet the legal definition of disability, as functioning cannot be directly inferred from diagnosis. There are several reasons for this. First, there are very few mental health disorders that preclude all types of functioning. Second, because there is considerable variability with respect to symptom presentation, premorbid capacity, and situational demands, two individuals with the same diagnosis might function quite differently (Piechowski, 2011). Third, many mental health disorders are chronic or episodic. Symptoms can wax and wane over time. During periods of relative stability, when an individual manifests few or no symptoms, their functioning may be unimpaired; during periods of exacerbation, functioning may be seriously compromised (Anfang et al., 2018).

Functioning needs to be understood within a specific context in order to have meaning. The specific aspects of functioning relevant in a disability evaluation are determined by the nature and purpose of the disability evaluation and the specific requirements of the examinee's work situation. Some evaluations require a comparison of the examinee's functioning to the demands of their specific position or occupation, while others focus on the ability to work in any gainful employment. Although many functional abilities are "generic" and are necessary for the performance of almost any job (e.g., following directions), many jobs, especially highly skilled jobs, also require specific functional abilities in addition to these generic requirements (e.g., managing the work of others). Moreover, the specific setting of the job may demand certain functional abilities not required to perform the same job in another setting.

Several schemas have been proposed for categorizing aspects of work functioning. SSDI, as mentioned previously, focuses on generic functional capacities that would be required for any job: the ability to learn and remember task instructions, sustain mental effort, interact appropriately with others, and/or accommodate and adapt to unexpected changes. The World Health Organization Disability Assessment Schedule (WHODAS 2.0) (Üstün, 2010), which is not limited to work functioning, consists of six domains:

understanding and communicating, getting around, self-care, getting along with people, life activities, and participation. The American Medical Association in the AMA *Guides to the Evaluation of Permanent Impairment* (Rondinelli et al., 2008) lists seven categories of functioning: self-care, role functioning, travel, interpersonal relationships, concentration, persistence and pace, and resilience. Long et al. (2019) proposed ten domains of functional assessment related to mental health disability: social competence and/or teamwork, adaptability/flexibility, conscientiousness/dependability, impulse and behavioral control, integrity, emotional regulation, decision-making and judgment, substance use proclivity, risk-taking behavior, and cognition. A simpler schema, focusing specifically on work functioning related to mental health conditions, consists of three domains: cognitive functioning (e.g., memory, concentration, and problem solving), interpersonal functioning (e.g., role boundaries, communication, and reliability), and emotional functioning (e.g., stress tolerance, emotional control, and mood stability) (Piechowski, 2013).

Mental Health and Work Functioning

Forensic disability evaluations are essentially about explaining how an individual's mental health condition interacts with the demands of their work environment and the extent to which their work capacity is affected as a result of this interaction. This requires drawing a connection between the manifestations of the individual's mental health condition and specific impairments in their functioning, then extrapolating these functional impairments to the requirements of their job. Research has begun to identify factors relevant to understanding these connections. However, the methodology for applying these factors to predict outcomes in individual cases has not yet been developed. What is apparent is that the relationship between mental health and work functioning is extremely complex and involves variables related to the severity and symptoms of the illness, the work environment, personal characteristics, and situational factors.

A 2017 meta-analysis looked at the association between various predictive factors and return to work among employees with depression (Ervasti et al., 2017). Eleven published studies from five different countries were included in the analysis. Older age, somatic comorbidity, psychiatric comorbidity, and more severe depression were associated with a lower rate of return to work. The authors noted the dearth of observational studies on predictors of return to work after depression and the significant heterogeneity between the studies that were included.

Gaines et al. (2017) investigated the relationship between sociocultural factors and length of work disability. Utilizing data from 216,162 private disability insurance claims and census-tract sociocultural data, a number of geographically based factors were identified that were related to the length of disability. Specifically, communities with higher unemployment rates, greater median household income, increased poverty status, increased length of work commute, lower educational attainment, lower percentage of residents living alone, a higher percentage of residents age fifty-five and older, a higher percentage of disabled adults, and a lower percentage of White and a higher percentage of Hispanic residents were all associated with longer periods of disability.

Using data from the Netherlands Study of Depression and Anxiety ($N = 2731$), Bokma et al. (2017) examined the comorbidity between psychological disorders (anxiety and depression) and chronic somatic diseases. They found that psychological disorders and chronic somatic diseases each significantly impacted disability, but the impact was substantially larger for psychological disorders. The prognosis was most unfavorable for individuals with comorbid psychological and somatic conditions.

Using a database of disability claims in the United States, Gaspar et al. (2018) investigated rates and predictors of recurrent work disability for individuals with common mental disorders. They found that individuals with bipolar disorder and depressive disorders were most likely to experience a recurrence of disability leave. The rate of disability recurrence for these groups was significantly larger than the rate for chronic (e.g., diabetes) or acute (e.g., injury) somatic disorders.

Hiilamo et al. (2019) conducted a ten-year follow up study of midlife public-sector employees with and without common mental health disorders at baseline, with respect to the incidence of sick leave and disability retirement. Three trajectories of work disability were identified (none, stable/low, and high/increasing). Results indicated that female gender, childhood adversity, low occupational class, lifestyle-related risk factors, and chronic ill-health were associated with the poorer work disability trajectories regardless of mental health status. Having a mental health disorder was strongly associated with a trajectory leading to early exit from employment.

Corbière et al. (2016) conducted a qualitative study of twenty-two individuals who experienced depression while employed and subsequently took sick leave. When interviewed, all participants reported that their depression was partially or completely related to their work. Three themes emerged regarding their decision to take sick leave: work-related psychosocial risk factors, such as supervisors' attitudes; their experiences during employment, such as reactions to their symptoms; and their experience preceding the sick leave, such as communication with supervisors.

Milanovic et al. (2018) investigated the differences between those with major depressive disorder and healthy comparisons on measures of competence, functional disability, and self-perceived competence. It was found that individuals with depression were less likely to accurately evaluate their own abilities. For this group, lower self-perception of competence was significantly related to greater interpersonal dysfunction.

A longitudinal study compared long-term work disability and absenteeism between individuals with anxiety disorders and individuals with depressive disorders over a four-year period (Hendriks et al., 2015). It was found that a history of or current anxiety and/or depressive disorders were associated with increasing work disability and absenteeism in comparison to healthy controls. The highest rates of disability and absenteeism were found in individuals with comorbid anxiety and depression, followed by individuals with depressive disorders. Rates were lowest among individuals with anxiety disorders without comorbidity.

Adler et al. (2006) investigated the relationship between depression severity and job performance among employed primary care patients over eighteen months. Patients with depression ($N = 286$) were compared with 93 individuals with rheumatoid arthritis and 193 healthy control subjects. Results indicated that the depression group had significantly greater deficits in managing mental-interpersonal time and output tasks. Additionally, the job performance of those in the depression group did not improve even when their symptoms of depression were clinically improved.

Evans et al. (2016) conducted a meta-analysis of forty-two randomized controlled trials of antidepressant medication regarding the effects on occupational functioning for individuals with depression. They found that antidepressants had a small, positive impact on occupational impairment in the short term, but they indicated the clinical significance of this finding was questionable.

O'Donnell et al. (2017) investigated predictors of poor occupational functioning of individuals with bipolar disorder in a longitudinal study of 273 adults with bipolar disorder. Over a five-year period, the participants underwent an annual assessment including a clinical assessment, neuropsychological testing, and work functioning measures. Results indicated that individuals with higher levels of depression and more severe deficits in cognitive flexibility were more likely to experience poorer work attendance, lower quality of work, and reduced satisfaction from work.

Functional outcomes over the course of bipolar disorder were investigated by Martino et al. (2017). Fifty-five individuals with bipolar disorder were clinically and functionally assessed over at least forty-eight months. Those with euthymic bipolar disorder showed significant improvement in their level of psychosocial functioning and employment status. Having more affective episodes was associated with worse functioning. Over a mean follow-up period of seventy-seven months, measures of functioning tended to remain stable or slightly improve. It was noted that functional outcome was highly variable, with some individuals having difficulty achieving full functional recovery, while others kept a high level of social and occupational functioning despite their illness.

Burton et al. (2019) investigated the relationship between prospective memory and disability among individuals with severe mental illness. The results indicated that prospective memory performance was negatively affected by severe mental illness and was associated with greater illness burden and functional disability. Individuals with worse prospective memory performances had higher amounts of disability entitlements, more months of hospitalization, worse functional capacity, and worse employment outcomes.

Although research has been accumulating about the effects of various mental health conditions on work capacity, to date, there has been no method identified for reliably combining these data to make accurate predictions about present and future work capacity. Schultz et al. (2016) proposed developing an actuarial model to predict future work functioning and disability related to musculoskeletal injury and pain, depression, post-traumatic stress disorder, and traumatic brain injury. They identified research-based worker factors (modifiable and nonmodifiable) and workplace factors (modifiable and nonmodifiable) for each of these conditions. Nonmodifiable worker factors included demographic variables, clinical/medical factors, and psychosocial factors. Modifiable worker factors consisted of psychiatric predictors and personality and coping variables. The authors cautioned, however, that the evidence of predictors of disability for workers with depression, anxiety, and PTSD is emerging, but not strong. They suggested studies be replicated with larger sample sizes and better designs.

Assessment Considerations

The purpose of a disability evaluation is to generate objective data about the validity of the examinee's condition, the functional impairments resulting from this condition, and the extent to which these impairments compromise the examinee's ability to function in a work setting (Piechowski, 2015). Consistent with the standard of practice in forensic assessment, a disability evaluation should incorporate data from multiple sources (Heilbrun, 2001). Typical elements include a clinical interview, behavioral observations, psychological testing, and reviewing records and documents. This allows the evaluator to cross-validate information among sources to obtain a more complete and objective understanding of the examinee.

Unfortunately, no research has been done in terms of identifying accurate and appropriate methodology for disability assessment or comparing the relative efficacy of different approaches. The National Institute of Medicine (2015) was asked by the Social Security Administration (SSA) to evaluate the value of and provide guidance on the use of psychological testing in SSA disability determinations. The authors concluded that the results of standardized cognitive and noncognitive psychological tests, appropriately administered, interpreted, and validated, could provide objective evidence to help identify and document the presence and severity of mental health impairments and help identify and assess the severity of work-related cognitive functional impairment and mental residual functional capacity. However, they noted that no data existed on the rates of false positives and false negatives in SSA disability determinations, making it difficult to verify if the use of testing would improve the accuracy of these determinations. In considering disability evaluations in other contexts (military, Veterans Administration, private disability insurance), the authors noted that these systems left the question of test selection to the discretion of the professional performing the evaluation. With the exception of SSA, all these symptoms permitted, or in the case of private disability insurance required, the use of symptom validity testing in disability evaluations.

Estimates of the base rates of malingering in disability evaluations vary widely. Mittenberg et al. (2002) examined the rate of probable malingering and symptom exaggeration through a survey of neuropsychologists certified by the American Board of Clinical Neuropsychology. Based on a review of 3,688 disability cases, the survey participants estimated that malingering or symptom exaggeration was present in 30 percent of these cases. In a review of the literature, Samuel and Mittenberg (2005) reported that estimates of the base rate for malingering ranged from 7.5 to 33 percent of disability claimants. Sumanti et al. (2006) investigated the presence of noncredible psychiatric and cognitive symptoms in 233 "stress claim" worker's compensation litigants and reported that between 9 and 29 percent of the sample endorsed noncredible psychiatric symptoms, and between 8 and 15 percent of the sample displayed noncredible cognitive symptomatology. Larrabee et al. (2009) estimated the base rate of malingering to be 40 +/- 10 percent based on a review of the literature and his own research that identified malingering based on atypical performance patterns on neuropsychological tests. Cottingham et al. (2014) found differences in patterns of feigning between personal injury litigants and disability claimants. Disability claimants tended to perform in a less sophisticated manner in comparison to personal injury litigants. They attributed some of these differences to the type of diagnosis feigned. Specifically, they found that those seeking compensation for mental health diagnoses were more likely to feign or exaggerate a wide variety of cognitive deficits, whereas those with claimed medical diagnoses (i.e., traumatic brain injury) were more targeted in their attempts to feign and/or exaggerate neurocognitive compromise. Young (2015) conducted a review of the literature on malingering in psychological injury cases. He concluded that the percentage of malingering found in the empirical research was about 23 percent, far less than the 40+/-10 percent suggested by Larrabee et al.

Disability assessments are high-stakes evaluations with monetary benefits, access to legal protections, and participation in employment at risk. Several studies have identified that financial incentives and the context of litigation can influence the accuracy of self-report data (Lees-Haley et al., 1997; Williams et al., 1999). In situations in which financial compensation is at stake, examinees are more likely to report superior premorbid functioning and poorer current functioning and are more likely to exaggerate the number and severity of their symptoms (Greiffenstein et al., 2002; Williams et al., 1999).

Inaccuracies in self-reported data are not limited to intentional attempts at distortion. The examinee may incorrectly report material due to misunderstanding or inaccurately recalling information. Personality factors or the nature of the condition itself may lead the examinee to take an unnecessarily pessimistic view of their abilities or prognosis. For example, as discussed previously, Milanovic et al. (2018) found that individuals with depression tended to be inaccurate in the self-assessment and had a lower perception of their competence.

Misinformation can come from other sources as well. A study of SSDI applicants and their treating providers by Marfeo et al. (2015) found poor concordance and systematic inconsistency between the claimants' and their providers' perceptions of their behavioral health functioning. Specifically, in terms of behavioral control and self-efficacy, providers tended to rate their patients as lower functioning than did the patients themselves. Stevens et al. (2018) evaluated the validity of clinicians' diagnoses of major depression. In this study, 127 claimants whose treating clinicians had established the diagnosis of major depression underwent an assessment consisting of a psychiatric interview, physical examination, self-report symptom questionnaires, and performance and symptom validity testing. It was found that only 31 percent of the claimants' self-reported symptoms fulfilled the diagnostic criteria for major depression. None of the claimants' depression diagnoses were confirmed by psychiatric evaluation. Additionally, 40 percent of the claimants were identified as having significant overreporting of symptoms on a symptom validity test (Self-Report Symptom Inventory).

Recommendations for Best Practices and Future Directions

In the absence of research to support assessment methodologies and test selection in disability evaluations, the best source of guidance is from the principles and practices of forensic assessment in general. These recommendations include clarifying the forensic question and the legal context for the evaluation, approaching the evaluation objectively and without bias, seeking data from multiple sources, selecting valid and reliable psychological tests based on the appropriateness to the questions of the evaluation and the characteristics and situation of the examinee, assessing response style, interpreting data systematically, and testing alternative hypotheses (Heilbrun, 2001). More research is needed to determine which specific methods and practices are associated with more accurate outcomes in disability evaluations.

Dissimulation in disability evaluations has received more attention in the literature, but the results have been highly variable. Base rates of malingering ranging from 7 percent to greater than 40 percent have been reported. One of the reasons for this disparity has been the differing methods that have been used in various studies to classify subjects as malingering. Some studies have used failure on one Symptom Validity Test (SVT)/Performance Validity Test (PVT), others have relied on multiple failures, while others appear to have been based on clinical judgment or a variety of methods. It is reasonable to conclude, however, that dissimulation occurs frequently enough in disability evaluations to warrant an assessment of response style in every evaluation. It is recommended that multiple embedded and/or stand-alone measures be used along with cross-validation of data across sources.

An area that has received little attention is the development of valid, reliable methods for assessing functional capacity in a forensic context. Current methods rely primarily on the examinee's self-report of their functioning. Given the potential for misperception or misrepresentation, the accuracy of this approach is highly questionable. The development of standardized, systematic methods for assessing work-related functioning would be extremely useful.

Although research has made some headway in identifying person and situational variables associated with the work functioning of individuals with mental health issues, additional studies are needed to replicate and expand these findings. The existing literature suggests that having more severe symptoms, comorbidity (both psychological and somatic), and cognitive impairments are associated with poorer outcomes. However, a number of noncondition-specific factors appear to influence the likelihood that an individual with mental health issues will return to work, including communications with one's supervisor, demographic factors, and characteristics of the community in which the one lives. The goal of eventually developing an actuarial model of prediction for return to work could improve the accuracy of disability assessments beyond reliance on clinical judgment.

Author Note

Lisa Drago Piechowski https://orcid.org/0000-0002-1497-0089

The author has no conflicts of interest to disclose.

References

Adler, D. A., McLaughlin, T. J., Rogers, W. H., Chang, H., Lapitsky, L., & Lerner, D. (2006). Job performance deficits due to depression. *American Journal of Psychiatry, 163*(9):1569–1576. http://ajp.psychiatryonline.org/doi/abs/10.1176/ajp.2006.163.9.1569

American Psychological Association. (2018). Professional practice guidelines for occupationally mandated psychological evaluations. *American Psychologist, 73*(2), 186–197.

Anfang, S. A., Gold, L. H., & Meyer, D. J. (2018). AAPL practice resource for the forensic evaluation of psychiatric disability. *Journal of the American Academy of Psychiatry and the Law Online, 46*(1 Suppl.), S2–S47.

Bokma, W. A., Batelaan, N. M., van Balkom, A. J. L. M., & Penninx, B. W. J. H. (2017). Impact of anxiety and/or depressive disorders and chronic somatic diseases on disability and work impairment. *Journal of Psychosomatic Research, 94*, 10–16.

Burton, C. Z., Vella, L., & Twamley, E. W. (2019). Prospective memory, level of disability, and return to work in severe mental illness. *The Clinical Neuropsychologist, 33*(3), 594–605.

Corbière, M., Samson, E., Negrini, A., St-Arnaud, L., Durand, M.-J., Coutu, M.-F., Sauvé, G., & Lecomte, T. (2016). Factors perceived by employees regarding their sick leave due to depression. *Disability and Rehabilitation, 38*(6), 511–519.

Cottingham, M. E., Victor, T. L., Boone, K. B., Ziegler, E. A., & Zeller, M. (2014). Apparent effect of type of compensation seeking (disability versus litigation) on performance validity test scores may be due to other factors. *The Clinical Neuropsychologist, 28*(6), 1030–1047.

Ervasti, J., Joensuu, M., Pentti, J., Oksanen, T., Ahola, K., Vahtera, J., Kivimäki, M., & Virtanen, M. (2017). Prognostic factors for return to work after depression-related work disability: A systematic review and meta-analysis. *Journal of Psychiatric Research, 95*, 28–36.

Evans, V. C., Alamian, G., McLeod, J., Woo, C., Yatham, L. N., & Lam, R. W. (2016). The effects of newer antidepressants on occupational impairment in major depressive disorder: A systematic review and meta-analysis of randomized controlled trials. *CNS Drugs, 30*(5), 405–417.

Gaines, B., Besen, E., & Pransky, G. (2017). The influence of geographic variation in socio-cultural factors on length of work disability. *Disability and Health Journal, 10*(2), 308–319.

Gaspar, F. W., Zaidel, C. S., & Dewa, C. S. (2018). Rates and predictors of recurrent work disability due to common mental health disorders in the United States. *PLoS ONE, 13*(10), 1–14.

Greiffenstein, M. F., Baker, W. J., & Johnson-Greene, D. (2002). Actual versus self-reported scholastic achievement of litigating postconcussion and severe closed head injury claimants. *Psychological Assessment, 14*(2), 202–208.

Grisso, T. (2003). *Evaluating competencies: Forensic assessments and instruments* (2nd ed.). Kluwer Academic/Plenum Press.

Hendriks, S. M., Spijker, J., Licht, C. M. M., Hardeveld, F., de Graaf, R., Batelaan, N. M., Penninx, B. W. J. H., & Beekman, A. T. F. (2015). Long-term work disability and absenteeism in anxiety and depressive disorders. *Journal of Affective Disorders, 178*, 121–130.

Heilbrun, K. (2001). *Principles of forensic mental health assessment.* Kluwer Academic/Plenum Publishers.

Hiilamo, A., Shiri, R., Kouvonen, A., Mänty, M., Butterworth, P., Pietiläinen, O., Lahelma, E., Rahkonen, O., & Lallukka, T. (2019). Common mental disorders and trajectories of work disability among midlife public sector employees—A 10-year follow-up study. *Journal of Affective Disorders, 247*, 66–72.

Institute of Medicine. (2015). *Psychological testing in the service of disability determination.* National Academies Press.

Larrabee, G. J., Millis, S. R., & Meyers, J. E. (2009). 40 plus or minus 10, a new magical number: Reply to Russell. *The Clinical Neuropsychologist, 23*(5), 841–849.

Lees-Haley, P. R., Williams, C. W., Zasler, N. D., Marguilies, S., English, L. T., & Stevens, K. B. (1997). Response bias in plaintiffs' histories. *Brain Injury, 11*(11), 791–800.

Long, B., Brown, A. O., Sassano-Higgins, S., & Morrison, D. E. (2019). Functional assessment for disability applications: Tools for the psychiatrist. *Psychiatric Times, 36*(6), 19–20.

Marfeo, E. E., Eisen, S., Ni, P., Rasch, E. K., Rogers, E. S., & Jette, A. (2015). Do claimants over-report behavioral health dysfunction when filing for work disability benefits? *Work, 51*(2), 187–194.

Martino, D. J., Igoa, A., Scápola, M., Marengo, E., Samamé, C., & Strejilevich, S. A. (2017). Functional outcome in the middle course of bipolar disorder: A longitudinal study. *The Journal of Nervous and Mental Disease, 205*(3), 203–206.

Milanovic, M., Holshausen, K., Milev, R., & Bowie, C. R. (2018). Functional competence in major depressive disorder: Objective performance and subjective perceptions. *Journal of Affective Disorders, 234*, 1–7.

Mittenberg, W., Patton, C., Canyock, E.M., Condit, D.C. (2002). Base rates of malingering and symptom exaggeration. *Journal of Clinical & Experimental Neuropsychology, 24*(8), 1094.

O'Donnell, L. A., Deldin, P. J., Grogan-Kaylor, A., McInnis, M. G., Weintraub, J., Ryan, K. A., & Himle, J. A. (2017). Depression and executive functioning deficits predict poor occupational functioning in a large longitudinal sample with bipolar disorder. *Journal of Affective Disorders, 215*, 135–142.

Piechowski, L. D. (2011). *Evaluation of workplace disability.* Oxford University Press.

Piechowski, L. D. (2013). Disability and worker's compensation. In I. B. Weiner (Series Ed.) & R. Otto (Vol. Ed.), *Handbook of psychology: Vol. 11. Forensic psychology* (2nd ed., pp. 201–224). John Wiley & Sons.

Piechowski, L. D. (2015). Identifying examiner-related threats to validity in the forensic assessment of disability. *International Journal of Law and Psychiatry, 42–43*, 75–80.

Piechowski, L. D., & Drukteinis, A. M. (2011). Fitness for duty. In E. Y. Drogin, F. M. Dattilio, R. L. Sadoff, & T. G. Gutheil (Eds.), *Handbook of forensic assessment: Psychological and psychiatric perspectives* (pp. 571–591). John Wiley & Sons.

Piechowski, L. D., & Rehman, U. (2011). Americans with disabilities act evaluations. In E. Y. Drogin, F. M. Dattilio, R. L. Sadoff, & T. G. Gutheil (Eds.), *Handbook of forensic assessment: Psychological and psychiatric perspectives* (pp. 459–478). John Wiley & Sons.

Rondinelli, R. D., Genovese, E., & Brigham, C. R. (2008). *Guides to the evaluation of permanent impairment* (6th ed.). AMA Press.

Samuel, R. Z., & Mittenberg, W. (2005). Determination of malingering in disability evaluations. *Primary Psychiatry, 12*(12), 60–68.

Schultz, I. Z., Law, A. K., & Cruikshank, L. C. (2016). Prediction of occupational disability from psychological and neuropsychological evidence in forensic context. *International Journal of Law and Psychiatry, 49*(Pt. B), 183–196.

Stevens, A., Schmidt, D., & Hautzinger, M. (2018). Major depression—A study on the validity of clinicians' diagnoses in medicolegal assessment. *The Journal of Forensic Psychiatry & Psychology, 29*(5), 794–809.

Sumanti, M., Boone, K., Savodnik, I., & Gorsuch, R. (2006). Noncredible psychiatric and cognitive symptoms in a workers' compensation—Stress||claim sample. *The Clinical Neuropsychologist, 20*(4), 754–765.

Theis, K. A., Roblin, D. W., Helmick, C. G., & Luo, R. (2018). Prevalence and causes of work disability among working-age U.S. adults, 2011–2013, NHIS. *Disability and Health Journal, 11*(1), 108–115.

Üstün, T. B. (Ed.). (2010). *Measuring health and disability: Manual for WHO Disability Assessment Schedule WHODAS 2.0.* World Health Organization.

Williams, C. W., Lees-Haley, P. R., & Djanogly, S. E. (1999). Clinical scrutiny of litigants' self- reports. *Professional Psychology: Research and Practice, 30*(4), 361–367.

Young, G. (2015). Malingering in forensic disability-related assessments: Prevalence 15 ± 15%. *Psychological Injury and Law, 8*(3), 188–199.

Child Custody Evaluations

Jonathan W. Gould *and* Christopher Mulchay

Abstract

This chapter describes current research and practice for conducting a child custody assessment. Although not intended as an in-depth discussion of all relevant issues in the arena, this chapter will direct readers to published, peer-reviewed literature, empirical research, professional practice guidelines, and current models that will provide a greater understanding of relevant topics. The chapter includes discussions of bias, best interests standards, procedures for conducting an evaluation, psychological testing, questionnaires, behavioral observations, collateral record review, and interviews. The chapter concludes with current trends in child custody research, which include gatekeeping, relocation, child maltreatment, resist/refusal dynamics, domestic violence, attachment, and parenting plans.

Key Words: child custody evaluation, child custody, forensic psychological assessment, best interests, parenting plans, domestic violence, child sexual abuse, child alienation

Introduction

When child custody is contested, parents are often referred to *alternative dispute resolution* (ADR) specialists, such as mediators, parent coordinators, special masters, arbitrators, and family therapists. When ADR attempts fail to resolve conflict about child custody, often a court will appoint a mental health professional to conduct a child custody evaluation (CCE).

What Is a Child Custody Evaluation?

The purpose of a CCE is to assist the court in determining the best interests of the child. The role of the evaluator is to conduct a psychological investigation (Austin & Kirkpatrick, 2004) examining specific individual and family factors associated with parenting attributes, co-parenting, the child's psychological needs, the ability of the parent to meet the child's needs, and other related factors. From these data, the evaluator develops expert opinions about the psychological best interests of the child that are communicated to the court to assist in its efforts to resolve the parents' custodial dispute. The American Psychological Association (2010) and the Association of Family and Conciliation Courts (2007) have promulgated professional practice guidelines concerning the purpose of a CCE, the role of the evaluator, and recommended procedures. Simply put, a CCE includes information about the psychological needs of the child, the parenting attributes of the parents, and the fit between them. More recent literature has stressed the need to assess other factors that might affect parenting of the child that includes cultural, ethnic, religious, extended family, and other family system variables (Garber, 2020).

Relevant Psychological Theory and Principles

CCEs are often conducted in an atmosphere of distrust and animosity (Martindale, 2004). Therefore, everything that an evaluator does should reflect a fundamental commitment toward being *transparent,* and their entire file should be available to both attorneys and the court for review.

Increasing Consensus

An emerging consensus about how CCEs should be conducted emphasizes the critical role of the scientific process (Drozd et al., 2013). Continuing research focuses on factors associated with children's postdivorce adjustment (Deutsch et al., 2020; Garber, 2020; Morrison et al., 2020; Saini et al., 2020) and the application of these factors to developing parenting access plans (Drozd et al., 2016)—the schedules identifying when children reside with each parent. Although judges and attorneys report that information from a CCE can be helpful (Ackerman et al., 2019) and often leads to settlement rather than trial, there is also increasing frustration among attorneys and the courts about the variability in quality of CCEs (Feinberg & Gould, 2012). Moreover, some scholars question the usefulness of mental health professionals conducting CCEs (Emery et al., 2005; Melton et al., 2018), and others question the scientific integrity of expert opinions about custodial placement based on CCEs (Tippins & Wittman, 2005a, 2005b). Scholars caution mental health professionals conducting CCEs to be particularly aware of bias (Gould & Dale, 2022; Martindale, 2005).

Bias and Child Custody Evaluations

There is a high rate of concordance between expert opinions and judicial decisions, suggesting that courts rely heavily on opinions proffered by forensic evaluators. An assumption implicit in courts' reliance on expert opinions is that such opinions have been formulated based on objectivity and accuracy (Zappala et al., 2018). The past decade has shown increasing awareness of factors that affect objectivity and accuracy both in how evaluations are conducted and how evaluators may be affected by factors that undermine their objectivity. One significant factor is the threat posed by bias in its various forms.

Bias factors might operate in selecting questions to investigate, selecting assessment tools used to gather data, choosing what data to gather and what data to ignore, choosing procedures to analyze data, choosing among the analyzed data that will be included in a report and that will be excluded from a report, choosing which data to rely upon as a foundation for expert opinions, and choosing how the expert opinion is presented both in writing and in oral testimony. Bias factors affect how we conduct an evaluation. Bias factors affect not only how we approach the investigative task but also how we think about ways in which we approach the investigative task.

Human beings hold biases. We develop ways to think about self, others, and the world. We are affected by our education, our family system, our current context, our perception of self and others, our understanding of our task, and many other factors. Bias allows for us to use algorithms or heuristics to more quickly process data. This process makes experts especially prone to bias. The most common reason evaluators experience bias occurs due to our cognitive architecture and the way information is formatted in the brain. "Being an expert entails using schemas, selective attention, chunking information, automaticity and more reliance on top-down information, all of which allows experts to perform quickly and efficiently; however, these very mechanisms restrict flexibility and control, may cause the experts to miss and ignore important information, introduce tunnel vision and bias and can cause other effects that degrade performance" (Dror et al., 2011, p. 177). In short, evaluators are affected by both explicit and implicit bias factors (Zappala et al., 2018).

Research findings have been sobering as we learn more and more about ways in which forensic psychological specialists are affected by bias. Murrie et al. (2013) have brought to our attention the powerful effects of retention or adversary bias, suggesting that retained experts are influenced by the side that retains them, despite efforts to remain neutral and objective. Zappala et al. (2018) identify other possible bias factors to include evaluator discipline and training, personal attitudes and values, and variations in personality traits. Other forms of bias affecting how we think about our evaluation task include overreliance on memory, underutilization of base rate data, anchoring effects, overconfidence, overreliance on unique data that might affect the accuracy of evaluations, hindsight bias, fundamental attribution error, confirmation bias, and illusory correlation (Borum et al., 1993). "An overreliance on memory in forensic evaluations can result not only in a decrease in information with which to make a judgment, but also in an increase in judgment bias" (Borum et al., 1993, p. 38).

Overconfidence refers to individuals expressing their opinions with more confidence than is actually warranted by the data. Gross and Mnookin (2003) raised concerns about the ways in which overconfident expert testimony might mislead the court, giving the false impression that the underlying data provide a more solid basis for the opinion than is warranted.

Evaluators review significant amounts of data during CCEs, so it can be difficult to determine which data are relevant. Unique or interesting data may stand out. **Overreliance on unique data** refers to the tendency to give excessive attention to specific behaviors that are unique, interesting, or highly unusual. This is the shiny object phenomenon. Evaluators often are drawn to that which is unusual or different and might assume that such unusual behaviors have greater predictive validity than more familiar ones (Borum et al., 1993). Infrequently occurring events are difficult to predict precisely because they are infrequent. Child custody evaluators are often asked to make judgments about behaviors that infrequently occur in our society. These low-frequency events occur at a low base rate, making prediction very difficult, which can results in a failure to consider base rates.

Hindsight bias refers to the tendency for outcome data to affect one's perception and judgment about the predictability of the outcome. **Fundamental attribution error** refers to the tendency for a person to emphasize person-centered factors over contextual factors when explaining and judging the behavior of others. In a forensic evaluation, the fundamental attribution error might influence an evaluator when moving from a role of observer to participant. Custody evaluators often engage in interviewing a parent or child while engaged in observing the parent–child relationship. The fundamental attribution error would predict that the evaluator's attributions change from attributions about person-centered factors when engaged in observation to attributions about contextual/environmental factors when engaged in the interactions among parent and child.

Confirmatory bias refers to the tendency to seek out data that supports or confirms one's hypotheses or preliminary impressions and to overlook (neglect, exclude) information that might challenge to disconfirm these impressions. A related concept is the **anchoring effect.** Anchoring occurs when information obtained earlier in the data-gathering process is weighed more heavily despite having information gathered later in the process that does not support the weight assigned to these initial pieces of information.

A critically important bias factor is **blind spot bias** (Zappala et al., 2018). Blind spot bias refers to the tendency for individuals to see bias in others as a greater cause for concern than in oneself. Zapf and her colleagues found that 79 percent of forensic evaluators acknowledged bias as a cause of concern in the forensic evaluations of their colleagues while only 52 percent were concerned about bias as a concern in their evaluations (Zapf et al., 2017). Noting the robust nature of blind spot bias, Pronin and Kurgler (2007) examined strategies people use to counter the effect of bias. They found the most frequent strategy used to combat bias was self-reflection (introspection). Research has demonstrated, however, that introspection is an ineffective bias reduction strategy (Boccaccini et al., 2017; Neal & Brodsky, 2016; Zaft et al., 2017; Zappala et al., 2018). One remedy to counter blind spot bias is to consult colleagues, develop and investigate rival alternative hypotheses, and gather collateral information intended to challenge the initial hypotheses. Simply put, one remedy to blind spot bias is reliance on the scientific method of hypothesis generation. Remember: science is a form of arrogance control.

Bias can affect all phases of the evaluation process. Biased data gathering can affect where we seek additional information. Biased data gathering can also affect our interpretation of those data. Biased interpretation of data can affect development of hypotheses that, in turn, can affect subsequent data gathering and interpretation of data. The effect of bias on one phase of the evaluation process can effect subsequent bias other phases of the evaluation process, undermining the legal presumption of evidentiary independence (Hasel & Kassin, 2009). At the earliest stages of an evaluator's data gathering, a belief in the credibility of one parent over the credibility of the other parent might lead an evaluator to erroneously interpret subsequent information, limit data gathering by ignoring reasonable alternative hypotheses that are inconsistent with the initial beliefs, or evaluate neutral data in a manner that is consistent with the original belief. In the custody literature, the above description is discussed as an example of confirmatory bias. In a recent case in which one of us (JG) was involved, the custody evaluator determined at the early stages of the data-gathering process that one parent's twenty-year-old traumatic brain injury (TBI) was the primary factor that affected the dysfunction in the family. The evaluator informed the psychologist who was retained to conduct the psychological tests about his beliefs about the effects of TBI on the family system and the parent's parenting. The testing psychologist chose psychological tests seeking confirmatory data to support the evaluator's belief rather than gathering a more comprehensive, parenting-focused set of data. All collateral interviews with professionals involved with the family were structured to obtain information only about the effects of the parent's TBI. The evaluator's questions of the professional collaterals were closed-ended, yes/no questions with no opportunities for the collaterals to elaborate upon their initial answers.

At the initial stages of a child custody evaluation, much of the data gathered are ambiguous. Data from parents, children, collaterals, and record reviews are often subject to significant interpretation of their meaning. Unlike fingerprint analysis in which one can objectively examine the degree to which one set of fingerprints match the fingerprints found at a crime scene, data from those involved in custody dispute are often more subjective and ambiguous. Ambiguous and subjective data are more likely to be vulnerable to bias, especially vulnerable to the evaluator's expectations, beliefs, and initial responses to each party. Those initial impressions can affect every phase of the evaluation process from the initial meeting through courtroom testimony.

Much of the bias literature in child custody has focused on the effects of evaluator beliefs, expectations, and emotional responses to the parties in development of confirmatory bias and associated bias factors such as anchoring effects, primary effects, and recency effects (Gould & Dale, 2022; Martindale, 2005). It is not just beliefs, expectations, and emotional responses that affect bias in evidence data gathering. Information that appears to imply a logical conclusion can also shape data gathering, data interpretation, and opinion formation.

Another consideration is how the need for coherent narrative might create bias. "The nature of the adversarial process encourages hostile, polarized, black-and-white thinking with little challenge, presents perceived truths as facts and fuels and channels rage in a scripted manner" (Kelly & Johnston, 2001, p. 258). Although individual pieces of evidence might not be tainted by bias, the ways in which we integrate information into a coherent narrative can be subject to bias. "The torn loyalties, grief, rage, humiliation, and anxiety commonly generated by these matters, compounded by zealous advocates and exacerbated by the adversarial court system can compromise rational thinking for all involved. The response is often a regression to more primitive, emotion-driven, and biased positions" (Garber, 2020, p. 389). The natural need for coherence in narrative may affect how pieces of evidence are strung together. A narrative that allows for a coherent assimilation of information may lead an evaluator to place greater weight on interpretation of that information relative to the value of the information, *even if the original value placed on the information was fair and balanced and free from bias.*

Bias in evidence integration refers to how the final assessment can be biased putting together the individual puzzle pieces to form a coherent narrative. Most linear models of evidence compilation suggest that the order in which the information is encountered should not make a difference. The *coherence model* (Charman et al., 2019) suggests that our interpretation of evidence is influenced by the information preceding it and by the hypotheses we develop as we encounter and evaluate those data. The coherence model is an interactive systems model, recognizing that interpretation of evidence occurs at every stage of data collection and interpretations of the meaning of those data are also influenced by the continuous changes in data collection and interpretation. Charman et al. (2019) suggest that our decision-making is most significantly influenced by the last information we encounter, the recency effect. This interpretation runs contrary to previously held beliefs that primacy and recency had relatively similar effects on memory. The theoretical basis of the coherence model is various data points must be integrated over time. The connection between and among data point is represented as a network of nodes that are interconnected via a network of excitatory and inhibitory links that represent positive or negative links between the nodes. There is a natural tendency to seek coherence among the nodes, leading to excitation in some nodes and inhibition in other nodes, creating a sense of a coherent narrative. "The very fact that the various pieces of evidence are presented within the context of a single case . . . lead the evaluations of that evidence to become correlated with one another, not because of the features of evidence itself, but because of the psychological coherence imposed upon the evaluation of those pieces of evidence" (Charman et al., 2019, p. 43).

The Best Interests of the Child Standard

A primary task of the custody evaluator is to offer an expert opinion about the psychological best interests of the child. Each state legislature controls its own child custody laws, and these vary considerably from state to state, with some states relying on specific statutory or case law, and other states having no statutory guidance. A frequently cited and as yet unsolved problem in this area is the lack of uniform consensus about the meaning of the term "best interests of the child" (Elrod & Dale, 2008).

Procedures for Conducting a CCE

A competently conducted CCE must be based on data gathered by reliable methods obtained from multiple independent sources (American Psychological Association, 2010).

The data must be gathered according to sound scientific methods and evaluated using valid techniques. Additionally, information about parenting behavior, child behavior, or parent–child interactions should have a reasonable expectation of assisting the court (Gould & Martindale, 2013). Performing an evaluation for the purpose of assisting the trier of fact with allocating parental rights and responsibilities (e.g. comparative custodial fitness) and the allocation of parental time poses several challenges, including the fact that "there is no clear consensus among attorneys, judges, and mental health professionals as to the dimensions to be examined in formulating opinions concerning the child's best psychological interests within the context of custodial suitability evaluation" (Gould & Martindale, 2007, p. 42).

"The relevance of the information gathered in the evaluation is directly tied to the clarity and scope of the questions that guide the investigation" (Gould & Martindale, 2009, p. 1). "Clearly defined questions lead the evaluator to choose methods of assessment that measure behaviors directly relevant to questions of concern to the court" (Gould & Martindale, 2007, p. 101). By including specific questions in court orders or stipulations, judges and attorneys increase the likelihood that evaluators will stay on course, investigate the issues of concern, and, in preparing their reports, provide information that bears directly upon the issues before the court (Gould & Martindale, 2009).

A CCE should follow the scientific process of observation, inference, and hypothesis generation (American Psychological Association, 2013). A CCE advisory report should help readers to differentiate the observational data from the evaluator's inferences and show how the data and inferences logically lead to the opinions. The methodology used to conduct a CCE includes (a) formulating specific questions to guide the scope of the evaluation; (b) interviewing each parent and each child; (c) observing each child with each parent and each parent with all the children; (d) reviewing relevant historical and current records; (e) interviewing collateral informants; and (f) when necessary, administering, scoring, and interpreting psychological tests.

Courts are best served when evaluators focus on issues relevant to the particular case. For example, if there are concerns about domestic violence, the interviewer should use a peer- reviewed domestic violence interview protocol in conducting interviews and should interview each family member about each alleged event. If there are concerns about how a parent disciplines a child, the evaluator might investigate factors such as parenting style, discipline style, parenting philosophy, religious affiliation and philosophy, corporal punishment, anger expression, impulsivity, and alternative disciplinary strategies. Children should be asked about these issues and to provide specific examples. In light of the research on reliability of children's self-report, it is advisable to interview each child more than once. The evaluator should carefully note similarities and differences between children's statements after having been transported by one parent versus the other. Interviewing children and parents together provides an opportunity to talk about allegations of concern.

There is a myth about children's reluctance to participate in legal proceedings regarding their custodial placement (Parkinson & Cashmore, 2008). Recent studies have shown that children want their opinions to be taken seriously; however, they do not want to be the decision makers. Children are more accepting of custody decisions when they perceive the process as fair, even if the outcome is not desirable. In other words, when children see that decision makers have listened, they are more satisfied with the outcome (Parkinson & Cashmore, 2008). As children's accounts of family life are often overshadowed by those of their parents, it is important for evaluators to give children's stories equal legitimacy to those of their parents (Gould & Martindale, 2009; Smart, 2002).

PSYCHOLOGICAL TESTS

Psychological tests can provide a set of data that can compare each parent's scores against those from a normative population and against each other. "Used within a multi-method approach to data gathering, psychological testing often helps evaluators develop hypotheses about the parties' behavioral tendencies, mental health issues, and psychological functioning as they may affect parenting, parent-to-parent communication, and other custody-related areas of concern" (Rappaport et al., 2018, p. 405). In this way, psychological testing can provide information to support or disconfirm an evaluator's speculations. Evaluators need to be sure that the measurement tool is reliable and valid with regard to the specific issue in dispute (see Otto et al., 2000, for a discussion of forensic criteria). Psychological tests offer the custodial evaluator distinct sources of information that do not share method variance with self-report or other collateral informants (Youngstrom & de los Reyes, 2015), which allows the tests to provide a powerful convergent measure of latent constructs (Campbell & Fiske, 1959). Tests often can address concerns posed by problems of social desirability, malingering, lack of insight, or other variables that might affect self-presentation and other sources of information (Youngstrom & de los Reyes, 2015).

There is an increasing awareness of limitations of some psychological tests used in CCEs (Garber & Simon, 2017; Hynan, 2004; Rappaport et al., 2018), particularly in measures of parent–child attachment (Ludolph, 2012) and the still too-often-administered projective techniques (Gould et al., 2009, 2013). Interpretation of any psychological test requires an understanding of variables that may affect performance well as the psychometric integrity of the test (American Psychological Association, 2017). For example, the stress on family members of custody litigation can be enormous. Litigants often believe that the most important element of their lives—their relationship to their children—is at stake (Galatzer-Levy et al., 2009). Many parents react negatively to having their parenting abilities investigated or become angry that someone outside the family may influence who makes decisions about access to their children. Such anxious, negative, and/or defensive reactions may affect parents' scores on psychological tests. Studies have demonstrated that positive bias leads to distorted and invalid profiles on measures of personality, parenting attitudes, and ratings of children (Carr et al., 2005).

Martindale and Flens (2011) "hypothesize that if attorneys, judges, and psychologists were asked to rate the usefulness of data from psychological tests administered in the context of family law matters, attorneys and judges would assign higher ratings than would psychologists" (p. 3). Neal et al. (2019) recently found that many psychological tests admitted into legal contexts as scientific evidence had poor or unknown scientific foundations, were rarely challenged and were not subject to legal scrutiny. Survey research revealed many custody evaluators continue to use assessment tools with weak or nonexistent psychometric integrity. "The forensic use of psychological tests needs, not only research support on the specific application but also clarity in demonstrating the best interest of the child or children. In other words, forensic custody testing needs to have the type of research support of risk assessment now commonly part of police investigations and court proceedings" (Posthuma, 2016, p. 67). The most recent survey data suggest child custody evaluators are more mindful of administering psychological tests perceived to be capable of surviving a *Daubert* challenge[1] (Ackerman et al., 2021).

When examining how psychological tests were used in courtrooms across the country, Neal et al. (2019) reported that nearly all the assessment tools used by psychologists and offered as expert evidence in legal settings have been subjected to empirical testing (90 percent). However, only about 67 percent were identified as generally accepted in the field and only about 40 percent have generally favorable reviews of their psychometric and technical properties in authorities such as the *Mental Measurements Yearbook*. Another important finding in the Neal et al. (2019) study was the lack of context-validation studies of the psychological tests being used by psychologists in forensic cases, which refers to the practice of using psychological tests for purposes other than what how they were intended to be used. Data need to be available demonstrating the test's reliability and validity when used with the population under scrutiny. That is, are there data to support an evidence-informed understanding of the meaning of test results with a particular population? The Minnesota Multiphasic Personality Measure, 2nd Edition (MMPI-2), Minnesota Multiphasic Personality Inventory 2nd Edition-Restructured Form (MMPI-2-RF), Personality Assessment Inventory (PAI), Personality Assessment Inventory Plus (PAI Plus), Millon Clinical Multiaxial Inventory, 3rd Edition (MCMI-III), and Parenting Stress Index, 4th Edition (PSI-4) have normative data describing male and female custody litigants' performance. Similar data should be available for each of the measures used by the evaluator.

It is critical to look at the nature and quality of the psychological test data. It is dangerous to assume that use of reliable data-gathering techniques will yield relevant

---

[1] Daubert v. Merrell Dow Pharm., Inc., 509 U.S. 579 (1993).

information. Reliable data-gathering techniques such as psychological tests may yield inaccurate or incomplete information. The US Supreme Court decision in *Griggs v. Duke Power Company*, a matter only remotely related to custody evaluations, holds important implications for evaluators and their choice of tests.[2] The *Griggs* case focused on industrial tests used for the purpose of guiding decisions regarding employment, placement, or promotion. The *Griggs* court declared that our assessment "devices and mechanisms" must be demonstrably reasonable measures of job performance.[3] Individuals who employ psychological tests must "measure" and describe only those aspects of the person that relate directly to the job for which the person is being evaluated (Gould & Martindale, 2013). The lesson that custody evaluators can take from the *Griggs* decision is that our attempts to assess the characteristics that bear directly upon parenting are more likely to meet with success if we conceptualize parenting as a job and focus our attention on those attributes, behaviors, attitudes, and skills that are reliably related to the demands of the job. Examining an attribute in the absence of evidence of its connection to parenting effectiveness leaves an evaluator open to criticism on several fronts (Gould & Martindale, 2013). The application of *Griggs* to review of an evaluator's selection of tests pertains to relevance.

QUESTIONNAIRES AND SELF-REPORT INVENTORIES

Custody evaluators often administer questionnaires or self-report inventories (Dies, 2008; Gould & Martindale, 2013; Garber et al., 2022). Some self-report measures have well-established reliability and validity and have been supported for use in CCEs. Others have no proper scientific foundation yet have been used for years in CCEs. How the evaluator uses information obtained from self-report measures is critical in understanding the relative weight assigned to such information. Results from self-report measures are best treated like information obtained from face-to-face interviews, subject to verification from independent data sources.

BEHAVIORAL OBSERVATIONS OF PARENTS AND CHILDREN

The evaluator's behavioral observations of each parent with each minor child and, if appropriate, with all minor children (Lampl, 2009), are critical. When no restraining orders or other legal impediments to face-to- face contact would make such observations unwise or potentially dangerous, direct observation of parent–child communication may be an important source of information.

Currently, there is no standard in the CCE field that addresses how to conduct the observation. The Association of Family and Conciliation Courts' (AFCC) *Model Standards* (2007) direct evaluators not to become participants in the observation. If the simple fact of their presence has a distorting effect, becoming an active participant increases the

---

[2] Griggs v. Duke Power Co., 401 U.S. 424 (1971).
[3] *Id.* at 436.

distortion exponentially. The evaluator should attempt to create a context that as closely as possible represents how the parent and child interact in the real world. The more that the evaluator interacts during the parent–child observation, the less the observation is a measure of what the parent and child do when alone. It is a valid criticism that the act of observing creates enough change for the parent–child interactions to be deemed unrepresentative.

After the parent–child observation, evaluators are encouraged to speak with each parent and child about how the observed interaction was or was not similar to their typical means of interacting. It is important that the evaluator describe in the report how the observation was conducted and their degree of involvement with different family members during the observation. Evaluators are wise to set ground rules for the observation, such as that the evaluator will not engage in conversations with, or accept any documents or other materials from, the parent or child during the observation, and that only parents and/or caretakers who are parties to the litigation can attend and participate. Other important areas targeted for assessment include identification of specific aspects of parent–child interaction and how they are assessed. The evaluator should take contemporaneous notes or make an audio or video recording of parent–child observations. These data should be descriptive rather than interpretative.

COLLATERAL RECORD REVIEW AND INTERVIEWS

Acquisition of reliable and relevant collateral information is one of the most important components of any forensic psychological evaluation (Greenberg & Shuman, 1997), including CCEs (Ackerman et al., 2019; Gould & Martindale, 2013; Hynan, 2016). The idea is to obtain information representative of day-to-day parent–child experiences from people with personal knowledge who are outside the immediate family (Austin, 2002; Kirkland et al., 2005). Similarly, historical records may shed light on parental cooperation and conflict, challenges, difficulties, or triumphs, as well as historical components to the parent–child relationship.

Several authors have described limitations and cautions associated with the use of collateral informants (Heilbrun et al., 2003). Austin and Kirkpatrick (2004) pointed out that those most emotionally distant from the custodial dispute are likely to be the most objective. Information obtained from them is therefore likely to be more accurate than that from relatives or close friends. Martindale (Gould & Martindale, 2013) reminds us of the term "collateral source information" and to value it as stimulus material: Some of the most useful information obtained from parents emerges when they respond to statements offered by collaterals. Evaluators may be asked to review volumes of e-mails, texts, or social media posts. Data from social networking sites are considered records, and best practices for record collection should be applied to data from social networking sites (Knuth, 2020). Compared to other psycholegal referrals, forensic psychologists are most likely to review social media evidence when conducting a CCE (Coffey et al., 2018).

There is a direct relationship between the number of independent data sources that converge on a conclusion and, therefore, support a hypothesis and the confidence the evaluator holds in the certainty that the data support the hypothesis. The nature and source of information also needs to be considered, with some types of data being assigned greater weight (meaning) than others (Gould & Martindale, 2013).

Integrating Peer-Reviewed Research with Evaluation Findings

The skilled evaluator must decide what research is applicable to the current case, apply the research, and explain how the cited research sheds light on the particular issues in dispute (Martindale & Gould, 2007). Standard 2.04 of APA's Ethics Code (American Psychological Association, 2002, p. 1064) directs psychologists to base their work "upon established scientific and professional knowledge of the discipline . . . [and] established scientific and professional knowledge" found in peer-reviewed literature. When writing a custody report or offering oral testimony, evaluators are encouraged to cite relevant research when their opinion is based, in part, upon the findings of those studies (Martindale & Gould, 2007).

Current Trends in Child Custody Research

The trend in peer-reviewed literature and conference presentations is on addressing the empirical foundation for many of the most relevant areas of concern to child custody evaluators. Drozd et al. (2016) summarize state-of-the-art scholarship and research on parenting plans. Kuehnle and Connell (2009) address allegations of child sexual abuse within the context of a child custody dispute. Lamb (2010) summarizes the literature on the role of fathers, within both intact and divorced families. Drozd et al. (2013) write about how to determine good research upon which to base expert opinions. Kelly and Ramsey (2007) address the need for judges and attorneys to learn how to differentiate good research from bad.

Gatekeeping

Children are best served when they have strong and healthy relationships with both parents (Kelly & Emery, 2003). In child custody disputes, among the most frequently occurring assessment issue is how to develop and maintain a child's unfettered access to each parent. Many child custody disputes concern the extent of paternal involvement in parenting children and/or the degree to which parental gatekeeping either permits or restricts the child's access to the father (Austin et al., 2013). Gatekeeping is defined as "attitudes and actions by a parent that are expected to affect the involvement and quality of the other parent–child relationship, either positively or negatively" (Austin et al., 2013, p. 486). Gatekeeping is a nondirectional concept, as gate closing can describe actions that restrict a parent's engagement with children, and gate opening can describe behaviors that enhance the co-parent's involvement (Austin et al., 2013). Restrictive gatekeeping occurs when a parent's actions interfere with or impede the other parent's access to and involvement with the child. There is justified and unjustified restrictive gatekeeping, the distinguishing factor in determining whether there is justified restrictive gatekeeping is whether there is a fact-based reason to protect a child from contact with a parent, i.e., abuse (Ganong et al., 2016).

Relocation Assessment

Among the most difficult challenges facing divorcing families is relocation. Nearly half of children of divorce relocate after the divorce is finalized. Evaluators should become familiar with jurisdiction-specific statutory requirements and case law pertaining to relocation (Austin, 2000c; Stahl, 2010). A move occurring within the context of divorce is one factor among many that may significantly impact a child. A request to move away must not be examined in isolation but as part of the larger story of a child's emerging life (Shear, 1996). How the child has coped with previous stressors informs us of the tolerance/resilience the child may have to another significant change. Austin (2000b, 2000c, 2000d; Austin & Drozd, 2013) developed a relocation risk assessment model identifying empirically determined risk factors to the child associated with relocation. One such factor is social capital, defined as the psychological, emotional, and social contributions that are provided to the child by the parents, extended family, peers, organizations, and groups (Coleman, 1988). The application of a social capital analysis to a child custody disputes allows for a comparative analysis of the expected types and degrees of social capital or human resources that will be available to the child in the two alternative residential living arrangements and with competing parenting time arrangements (Parkinson et al., 2016).

Child Maltreatment

Many of the complex issues that are examined in a CCE are related to allegations of child maltreatment and the potential risks such behavior poses to the child and the parent–child relationship. When there are allegations of child maltreatment, the evaluator must simultaneously consider whether the parent alleging the maltreatment is attempting to interfere with or thwart the child's relationship with the alleged perpetrator. Allegations of sexual abuse are particularly challenging for child custody evaluators who are often asked to offer opinions to the court about whether a child is at risk of sexual abuse.[4] The behavioral science literature provides little, if any, foundation upon which to make clear,

---

[4] See North Carolina v. Ronnie Lane Stancil, 559 S.E.2d 788 (2002), in which the Supreme Court of North Carolina declared that "an expert witness may testify, upon a proper foundation, as to the profiles of sexually abused children and whether a particular complainant has symptoms or characteristics consistent therewith" (p. 267).

consistent statements about our ability to identify the victims, perpetrators, or timeline of abuse (Kuehnle & Connell, 2009).

The use of sexually anatomically correct (AC) dolls was widespread in the late 1980s. Today, the general trend is to be cautious when using AC dolls. AC dolls should be used only after the entire interview process is completed, for clarification purposes alone. Any other use is not supported by research. Many different models describe how to conduct an evaluation of alleged child sexual abuse (CSA) within the context of a custody determination (see American Professional Society on the Abuse of Children, 1995; Kuehnle, 1996; Kuehnle & Connell, 2009).

Kuehnle (1996) challenged the field to think in a complex manner about CSA allegations and proposed a multi-hypothetical model to guide decision makers. She reports that the most frequent child sexual abuse allegation comes from a parent who truly believes the abuse occurred as a function of misreading the data.

Resist/Refusal Dynamics

Over the past twenty-five years, considerable discussion has centered on child alienation. Several different models describe child alienation (Garber, 2020; Johnston & Sullivan, 2020; Garber et al., 2021). Wallerstein and Kelly (1980) were the first to identify, in a population of divorced families, a child's irrational rejection of a parent and her resistance to visiting the parent. The initial formulation of an alienated child posited a pathological alignment between an angry parent and an older child or adolescent that sprang from the dynamics of the separation, including the child's reaction to the divorce (Wallerstein & Kelly, 1980). Gardner (1985) developed a more elaborate description of this alienation process, offering a series of criteria for assessing this alienation process and describing a continuum of alienating behaviors ranging from mild to severe. Parental Alienation Syndrome (PAS) was defined as a conscious or unconscious attempt by one parent to alienate the child from the other parent to force the other parent out of the child's life (Gardner, 1985). PAS includes, but is not limited to, conscious, intentional programming techniques. Gardner described a process over time in which the longer the alienating parent has control over the child, the more the child adopts the rejecting attitudes of the alienating parent toward the target parent (Gardner, 1992). Several authors have argued for the usefulness of the PAS concept, most notably Bernet (2020), Lorandos and Bernet (2020), and Warshak (2001, 2010). However, Gardner's formulation of PAS has come under fire (Bruch, 2001; Milchman et al., 2020) and, today, PAS is considered a controversial concept.

There is a lack of consensus on the definitions of alienation. The use of nonstandardized measures and procedures has limited the ability of researchers to study it. In 1997, Sullivan wrote: "Parental alienation has become the 'complaint du jour' in high-conflict family court disputes . . . [It is . . .] an emotionally charged, high stakes and frequently misunderstood process. It often leads to over-identification and a backlash of skepticism about it and when it should be a significant consideration in custody determinations" (p. 3). In 2001, Kelly and Johnston's reformulation of alienation dynamics proposed a multifactorial model that has been widely discussed and elaborated. They described a continuum of child–parent relationships after separation and divorce that distinguished the alienated child (who persistently refuses visitation because of unreasonable negative feelings) from other children who also resist contact with a parent after separation based upon normal, realistic and/or developmentally predictable reasons. Kelly and Johnston (2001) also described how everybody in the family system contributes to the resist/refuse process. Often, the rejected parent has been less involved in the child's life or possesses somewhat less robust parenting competencies. The child's complaints about the rejected parent may reflect a gross distortion or exaggeration of some true incident, resulting in highly negative feelings. The distortion makes this a *pathological* response.

Many scholars have begun to use the terms "resist/refuse" or "parent–child conduct problems" to define these dynamics. There is a complex spectrum of reasons for children to resist contact with one parent and favor the other parent, "ranging from, at one end, a child's adaptive response to abuse by a rejected parent to, at the other end, the malicious influence of a parent seeking to undermine a child's relationships with the other parent because of anger over the failure of the parents' romantic relationship" (Drozd & Bala, 2017, p. 6). Continuing to build off Kelly and Johnston's work, multifactor models make more useful, valid, and differentiated clinical predictions of children's rejection of a parent because they are informed by basic and applied research on children and families, yet these models are complex and difficult to argue in court (Johnston & Sullivan, 2020). Even though they are complex, multifactorial theoretical models increasingly draw upon a wide range of basic and applied social science research (Garber, 2020; Johnston & Sullivan, 2020; Judge & Deutsch, 2017; Fidler & Bala, 2010; Fidler et al., 2013). Garber (2020) has proposed a set of rationally developed factors to consider when evaluating allegations of resist/refusal in a family. The dynamics to investigate include the characteristics of the child, the parents' relationship with the child before litigation, the child's response to the pressures of litigation, whether the child's responses are event dependent or time dependent, whether the child experiences separation anxiety from a favored parent, anxiety related to transitions between homes, culture shock, and the sensitivity and responsiveness of the unfavored parents.

Children who resist or refuse contact often have rigid, dependent, and enmeshed perspectives and their family may avoid challenging these perspectives. As we know from behavioral psychological, avoidant behavior such as this reinforces the child's beliefs. "Without new experiences to challenge old thoughts, feelings, and behaviors, the children remain stuck with cognitive distortions and antiquated problem-solving strategies" (Drozd & Bala, 2017, p. 6) which maintains the resist/refuse dynamics.

Domestic Violence

The forensic assessment of allegations of domestic violence (DV) remains among the hottest topics for researchers (Austin, 2000a; Morrison et al., 2020) and is critical in CCEs for several reasons. First, children living in homes in which parental violence occurs are more likely to be targets of violence themselves (Jaffe et al., 2003). Second, they are psychologically affected by their exposure to parental violence (Davies & Cummings, 2006). Third, parents involved in DV tend to be poorer supervisors of their children's behavior. Fourth, the victim of the parental violence may be depressed and focused on his or her safety more than on the needs of the child (Gould & Martindale, 2007). Fifth, children raised in homes in which DV occurs often identify with the aggressor, resulting in children attributing less parenting legitimacy to the victimized parent (Bancroft & Silverman, 2002).

Research findings suggested that those who allege DV while undergoing custody evaluations are drawn from a different population than those who allege DV while living in domestic violence shelters (Dutton, 2005). Understanding differences between these populations on factors such as lethality risk and the type, frequency, and intensity of DV may be important for the evaluator to explore and the court to understand (Dutton et al., 2010). Several peer-reviewed DV interview protocols (Drozd et al., 2004) and evaluation protocols (Austin, 2000a; Drozd & Olesen, 2004; Drozd et al., 2004) may be useful in guiding a forensic evaluation of allegations of DV within the context of a child custody dispute.

Attachment and Parenting Plans

Initial formulations of attachment theory stressed the importance of the caretaker's relationship to the child during the infancy and toddler years as critical to developing secure attachment. It was believed that a securely attached infant or toddler would be well prepared for life. Over the past several decades, research findings have revealed that children's attachments are not necessarily stable over time (Thompson, 2000). Attachments may change over time, and there are predictable, fact-based reasons for this, especially if the child's environment changes, as often happens, in separating and divorcing families. The first thirty-six months of life are critically important, and a child is best served by safe, secure, and consistent caretaking from parents. The less disruption there is to the child's attachment to either caretaker, the better for the child. Disrupted attachments can most often be rehabilitated. Children need to spend time with each parent to develop the view that each parent and each parent's home is safe. Children need to engage in a variety of activities with each parent, across different contexts.

Recent researchers describe insightfulness as among the most important components of sensitive caregiving and developing a secure child–parent attachment. Insightfulness involves a parent's ability to see things from the child's point of view and to empathically think about and consider the motives underlying their child's behavior (Oppenheim &

Koren-Kare, 2016). Attachment research has often been used as the basis for developing parenting plans. There is little, if any, empirical research demonstrating which parenting plan is best for which children (Tippins & Wittmann, 2005). For many years, child development specialists and child custody evaluators have tried to develop commonsense parenting plans based on research (Drozd et al., 2016; Kelly & Lamb, 2000).

Summary

A child custody evaluator asks specific questions to define the scope of the evaluation; observes parent–child interactions; talks with collateral contacts; reviews records; administers, scores, and interprets psychological tests; and interviews parents, children, and significant others. Integration of the obtained data with behavioral science research provides a scientifically informed foundation for expert opinions. Child custody evaluators often examine complex issues including relocation requests, allegations of child maltreatment, child alienation, DV, and sexual abuse. Research findings are often used as the basis for expert opinions about parenting access schedules despite the lack of specific research addressing which particular parenting plan is best for which particular child or particular family system.

References

Ackerman, M. J., Bow, J. N., & Mathy, N. (2021). Child custody evaluation practices: Where we were, where we are and where we are going. *Professional Psychology: Research and Practice, 52*(4), 406–417.

Ackerman, M. J., Kane, A. W., & Gould, J. W. (2019). *Psychological experts in divorce actions* (7th ed.). Aspen.

American Professional Society on the Abuse of Children. (1995). *Psychosocial evaluation of suspected psychological maltreatment in children and adolescents*. APSAC.

American Psychological Association. (2010). Guidelines for child custody evaluations in family law proceedings. *American Psychologist, 65*(9), 863–867.

American Psychological Association. (2013). Specialty guidelines for forensic psychology. *American Psychologist, 68*(1), 7–19.

American Psychological Association. (2017). Ethical principles of psychologists and code of conduct (2002, amended effective June 1, 2010, and January 1, 2017). https://www.apa.org/ethics/code/

Association of Family and Conciliation Courts, Task Force for Model Standards of Practice for Child Custody Evaluations. (2007). Model standards of practice for child custody evaluations. *Family Court Review, 45*(1), 70–91.

Austin, W. G. (2000a). Assessing credibility in allegations of marital violence in the high-conflict child custody case. *Family & Conciliation Courts Review, 38*(4), 462–477.

Austin, W. G. (2000bc). A forensic psychology model of risk assessment for child custody relocation law. *Family & Conciliation Courts Review, 38*(2), 192–207.

Austin, W. G. (2000c). Relocation law and the threshold of harm: Integrating legal and behavioral perspectives. *Family Law Quarterly, 34*(1), 63–82.

Austin, W. G. (2000d). Risk reduction interventions in the child custody relocation case. *Journal of Divorce & Remarriage, 33*(1-2), 65–73.

Austin, W. G. (2002). Guidelines for utilizing collateral sources of information in child custody evaluations. *Family Court Review, 40*(2), 177–184.

Austin, W. G., & Drozd, L. M. (2013). Judge's bench book for application of the integrated framework for the assessment of intimate partner violence in child custody disputes. *Journal of Child Custody, 10*(2), 99–119.

Austin, W. G., & Kirkpatrick, H. D. (2004). The investigation component in forensic mental health evaluations: Considerations for parenting time. *Journal of Child Custody, 1*(2), 23–46.

Austin, W. G., Pruett, M., Kirkpatrick, H. D., Flens, J. R., & Gould, J. W. (2013). Parental gatekeeping and child custody: Child access evaluation: Part I. *Family Court Review, 51*(3), 485–501.

Bancroft, L., & Silverman, J. G. (2002). The batterer as parent: Assessing the impact of domestic violence on family dynamics. *Psychiatry, Psychology & Law, 9*(2), 284–285.

Bernet, W. (2020). Response to the "Ideology and rhetoric replace science and reason in some parental alienation literature and advocacy: A critique" by Milchman, Geffner, and Meier. *Family Court Review*, *58*(2), 362–367.

Boccaccini, M., Chevalier, C., Murrie, D., & Varela, J. G. (2017). Psychopathy Checklist–Revised use and reporting practices in sexually violent predator evaluations. *Sexual Abuse: A Journal of Research and Treatment*, *29*, 592–614.

Borum, R., Otto, R., & Golding, S. (1993). Improving clinical judgment and decision making in forensic evaluation. *The Journal of Psychiatry and Law*, *21*(1), 35–76.

Bruch, C. S. (2001). Parental alienation syndrome and parental alienation: Getting it wrong in child custody cases. *Family Law Quarterly*, *35*(3), 527–552.

Campbell, D., & Fiske, D. (1959). Convergent and discriminant validation by the multitrait-multimethod matrix. *Psychological Bulletin*, *56*(2), 81–105.

Carr, G. D., Moretti, M. M., & Cue, B. J. H. (2005). Evaluating parenting capacity: Validity problems with the MMPI-2, PAI, CAPI, and Ratings of Child Adjustment. *Professional Psychology: Research and Practice*, *36*(2), 188–196.

Charman, S., Douglass, A. B., & Mook, A. (2019). Cognitive bias in legal decision making. In N. Brewer & A. B. Douglass (Eds.). *Psychological science and the law* (pp. 30–53). Guilford Press.

Coffey, C. A., Batastini, A. B., & Vitacco, M. J. (2018). Clues from the digital world: A survey of clinicians' reliance on social media as collateral data in forensic evaluations. *Professional Psychology: Research and Practice*, *49*(5–6), 345–354.

Coleman, J. S. (1988). Social capital in the creation of human capital. *American Journal of Sociology*, *94*(Suppl.), S95–S120.

Davies, P. T., & Cummings, E. M. (2006). Interparental discord, family process, and developmental psychopathology. In D. Cicchetti & D. J. Cohen (Eds.), *Developmental psychopathology: Vol. 3. Risk, disorder, and adaptation* (2nd ed., pp. 86–128). John Wiley & Sons.

Deutsch, R., Drozd, L., & Ajoku, C. (2020). Trauma-informed interventions in parent-child contact cases. *Family Court Review*, *58*(2), 470–487.

Dies, R. R. (2008). The use of questionnaires in child custody evaluations. *Journal of Child Custody: Research, Issues, and Practices*, *4*(1-2), 103–122.

Dror, I. E., Pascual-Leone, A., & Ramachandran, V. (2011). The paradox of human expertise: why experts get it wrong. *The Paradoxical Brain* (p. 177).

Drozd, L. M., & Bala, N. (2017). Introduction. In A. Judge & R. Deutsch (Eds.), *Overcoming parent-child contact problems* (pp. 1–8). Oxford University Press.

Drozd, L. M., Kuehnle, K., & Walker, L. E. (2004). Safety first: A model for understanding domestic violence in child custody and access disputes. *Journal of Child Custody*, *1*(2), 75–103.

Drozd, L. M., & Olesen, N. W. (2004). Is it abuse, alienation, and/or estrangement? A decision tree. *Journal of Child Custody*, *1*(3), 65–105.

Drozd, L. M., Olesen, N. W., & Saini, M. (2013). *Parenting plan & child custody evaluations: Increasing evaluator competence & avoiding preventable errors*. Professional Resource Press.

Drozd, L., Saini, M., & Olesen, N. (Eds.). (2016). *Parenting plan evaluations: Applied research for the family court* (2nd ed.). Oxford University Press.

Dutton, D. G. (2005). Domestic abuse assessment in child custody disputes: Beware the domestic violence research paradigm. *Journal of Child Custody*, *2*(4), 23–42.

Dutton, D. G., Hamel, J., & Aaronson, J. (2010) The gender paradigm in family court processes: Re-balancing the scales of justice from biased social science. *Journal of Child Custody*, *7*, 1–31.

Elrod, L. D., & Dale, M. D. (2008). Paradigm shifts and pendulum swings in child custody: The interests of children in the balance. *Family Law Quarterly*, *42*(3), 381–418.

Emery, R. E., Otto, R. K., & O'Donahue, W. T. (2005). A critical assessment of child custody evaluations: Limited science and a flawed system. *Psychological Science in the Public Interest*, *6*(1), 1–29.

Feinberg, J. M., & Gould, J. W. (2012, June 7). *The credible and helpful child custody report*. Workshop presented at the 49th Annual Conference of the Association of Family & Conciliation Courts, Chicago, IL.

Fidler, B. J., & Bala, N. (2010). Children resisting post separation contact with a parent: Concepts, controversies, and conundrums. *Family Court Review*, *48*(1), 10–47.

Fidler, B. J., Bala, N., & Saini, M. A. (2013). *Children who resist postseparation parental contact: A differential approach for legal and mental health professionals*. Oxford University Press.

Galatzer-Levy, R. M., Kraus, L., & Galatzter-Levy (Eds.). (2009). *The scientific basis of child custody decisions* (2nd ed.). John Wiley & Sons.

Ganong, L., Coleman, M., & Chapman, A. (2016). Gatekeeping after separation and divorce. In L. Drozd, M. Saini, & N. Olesen (Eds.), *Parenting plan evaluations: Applied research for the family court* (pp. 308–345). Oxford University Press.

Garber, B. D. (2007). Conceptualizing visitation resistance and refusal in the context of parental conflict, separation and divorce. *Family Court Review, 45*(4), 588–599.

Garber, B. (2020). Sherlock Holmes and the case of resist/refuse dynamics: Confirmatory bias and abductive inference in child custody evaluations. *Family Court Review, 58*(2), 386–402.

Garber, B. D., Mulchay, C., & Knuth, S. (2022). Questionnaires in child custody evaluations: The forgotten ubiquitous medium. *Journal of Family Trauma, Child Custody & Child Development,* 1–17.

Garber, B. D., Prescott, D. E., & Mulchay, C. (2021). *A family law professional's field guide to high conflict litigation: Dynamics, not diagnoses.* American Bar Association.

Garber, B. D., & Simon, R. A. (2017). Individual adult psychometric testing and child custody evaluations: If the shoe doesn't fit, don't wear it. *Journal of the American Academy of Matrimonial Lawyers, 30,* 325–341.

Gardner, R. A. (1985). Recent trends in divorce and custody litigation. *Academy Forum, 29*(2), 3–7.

Gardner, R. A. (1992). *The parental alienation syndrome: A guide for mental health and legal professionals.* Creative Therapeutics.

Gould, J. W., & Dale, M. (2022). Reviewing child custody evaluations: Using science to maximize reliability & minimize bias. In H. Hall & J.G. Poirier (Eds.), *Forensic psychology and neuropsychology for criminal and civil cases* (2nd ed., pp. 575–604). Taylor & Francis.

Gould, J. W., & Martindale, D. A. (2007). *The art and science of child custody evaluations.* Guilford Press.

Gould, J. W., & Martindale, D. A. (2009, May). Specific questions guide child custody investigations. *The Matrimonial Strategist, 2*(5), 1ff.

Gould, J. W., & Martindale, D. A. (2013). Child custody evaluations: Current literature and practical applications. In R. K. Otto (Ed.). *Handbook of psychology: Volume 11: Forensic psychology* (pp. 101–138). John Wiley & Sons.

Gould, J. W., Martindale, D. A., & Flens, J. R. (2009). Responsible use of psychological tests in child custody assessment. In R. Galatzer-Levy, L. Kraus, & B. Galatzer-Levy (Eds.), *Scientific basis of child custody decisions* (2nd ed., pp. 85–124). Wiley.

Gould, J. W., Martindale, D. A., & Flens, J. R. (2013). Responsible use of psychological tests: Ethical and professional practice concerns. In D. Saklofske, C. Cecil Reynolds, & V. Schwean (Eds.), *The Oxford handbook of child psychological assessment.* Oxford University Press.

Greenberg, S. A., & Shuman, D. W. (1997). Irreconcilable conflict between therapeutic and forensic roles. *Professional Psychology: Research and Practice, 28*(1), 50.

Gross, R., & Mnookin, J.L. (2003). Expert information and expert evidence: A preliminary taxonomy. *Seton Hall Law Review, 34*(1), 141–189.

Hasel, L. E., & Kassin, S. M. (2009). On the presumption of evidentiary independence: Can confessions corrupt eyewitness identifications? *Psychological Science, 20,* 122–126.

Heilbrun, K., Warren, J., & Picarello, K. (2003). Third party information in forensic assessment. In A. M. Goldstein (Vol. Ed.), & I. B. Weiner (Chief Ed.), *Handbook of psychology: Vol. 11. Forensic psychology* (pp. 69–86). John Wiley & Sons.

Hynan, D. J. (2004). Unsupported gender differences on some personality disorder scales of the Millon Clinical Multiaxial Inventory-III. *Professional Psychology: Research and Practice, 35,* 105–110.

Hynan, D. J. (2016). Observing parents interact with children: All too infrequently asked questions (and answers). In Mark L. Goldstein (Ed.), *Handbook of child custody* (pp. 49–56). Springer, Cham.

Jaffe, P. G., Lemon, N. K. D., & Poisson, S. E. (2003). *Child custody & domestic violence: A call for safety and accountability.* SAGE.

Johnston, J. R., & Sullivan, M. S. (2020). Parental alienation: In search of common ground for a more differentiated theory. *Family Court Review, 58*(2), 270–292.

Judge, A., & Deutsch, R. (2017). *Overcoming parent-child contact problems.* Oxford University Press.

Kelly, J. B., & Emery, R. E. (2003). Children's adjustment following divorce: Risk and resilience perspectives. *Family Relations, 52*(4), 352–362.

Kelly, J. B., & Johnston, J. R. (2001). The alienated child: A reformulation of parental alienation syndrome. *Family Court Review, 39*(3), 249–266.

Kelly, J. B., & Lamb, M. E. (2000). Using child development research to make appropriate custody and access decisions for young children. *Family and Conciliation Courts Review, 38*(3), 297–311.

Kelly, R. F., & Ramsey, S. H. (2007). Assessing and communicating social science information in family and child judicial settings: Standards for judges and allied professionals. *Family Court Review, 45*(1), 22–41.

Kirkland, K., McMillan, E. L., & Kirkland, K. L. (2005). Use of collateral contacts in child custody evaluations. *Journal of Child Custody, 2*(4), 95–109.

Knuth, S. B. (2020). Child Custody Litigation and Psychological Evaluations. In A. B. Batastini & M. J. Vitacco (Eds.), *Forensic mental health evaluations in the digital age: A practitioner's guide to using internet-based data* (pp. 143–167). Springer.

Kuehnle, K. (1996). *Assessing allegations of child sexual abuse.* Professional Resource Press.

Kuehnle, K., & Connell, M. (2009). *The evaluation of child sexual abuse allegations: A comprehensive guide to assessment and testimony.* Wiley.

Lamb, M. E. (2010). *The role of the father in child development* (5th ed.). John Wiley & Sons.

Lampl, A. (2009). Observations of parents, care takers, and children for child custody assessment. In R. M. Galatzer-Levy, L. Kraus, & J. Galatzer-Levy (Eds.), *The scientific basis of child custody decisions* (2nd ed., pp. 71–84). Wiley.

Lorandos, D., & Bernet, W. (Eds.). (2020). *Parental alienation: Science and Law.* C. C. Thomas.

Ludolph, P. (2012). Special issue on attachment: Overreaching and theory. *Family Court Review, 50*(3), 486–495.

Martindale, D. A. (2004). Integrity and transparency: A commentary on record keeping in child custody evaluations. *Journal of Child Custody, 1*(1), 33–42.

Martindale, D. A. (2005). Confirmatory bias and confirmatory distortion. In J. R. Flens & L. Drozd (Eds.) *Psychological testing in child custody evaluations* (pp. 31–48). Routledge.

Martindale, D. A., & Flens, J. R. (2011). Test item transparency: the undisclosed threat to test validity. *The Matrimonial Strategist, 29*(7), 3–4.

Martindale, D. A., & Gould, J. W. (2007) Custody evaluation reports: The case for empirically- derived information. *Journal of Forensic Psychology Practice, 7*(3), 87–99.

Melton, G. B., Petrila, J., Poythress, N. G., Slobogin, C., Otto, R. K., Mossman, D., & Condie, L. O. (2018). *Psychological evaluations for the courts: A handbook for mental health professionals and lawyers* (4th ed.). Guilford Press.

Milchman, M. S., Geffner, R., & Meier, J. S. (2020). Ideology and rhetoric replace science and reason in some parental alienation literature and advocacy: A critique. *Family Court Review, 58*(2), 340–361.

Morrison, F., Tisdall, E. K. M., & Callaghan, J. E. M. (2020). Manipulation and domestic abuse in contested contact: Threats to children's participation rights. *Family Court Review, 58*(2), 403–416.

Murrie, D. C., Boccaccini, M. T., Guarnera, L. A., & Rufino, K. A. (2013). Are forensic experts biased by the side that retained them? *Psychological Science, 24*(10), 1889–1897.

Neal, T. M., & Brodsky, S. L. (2016). Forensic psychologists' perceptions of bias and potential correction strategies in forensic mental health evaluations. *Psychology, Public Policy, and Law, 22*(1), 58–76.

Neal, T. M., Slobogin, C., Saks, M. J., Faigman, D. L., & Geisinger, K. F. (2019). Psychological assessments in legal contexts: Are courts keeping "junk science" out of the courtroom? *Psychological Science in the Public Interest, 20*(3), 135–164.

Oppenheim, D., & Koren-Karie, N. (2016). Parents' insightfulness: The importance of keeping the inner world of the child in mind for parenting plan evaluations. In L. Drozd, M. Saini, & N. Olesen (Eds.), *Parenting plan evaluations: Applied research for the family court* (pp. 47–59). Oxford University Press.

Otto, R. K., Edens, J. F., & Barcus, E. H. (2000). The use of psychological testing in child custody evaluations. *Family & Conciliation Courts Review, 38*(3), 312–340.

Parkinson, P., & Cashmore, J. (2008). *The voice of a child in family law disputes.* Oxford University Press.

Parkinson, P., Taylor, N., Cashmore, J., & Austin, W. G. (2016). Relocation, research, and child custody disputes. In L. Drozd, M. Saini, & N. Olesen (Eds.), *Parenting plan evaluations: Applied research for the family court* (pp. 431–459). Oxford University Press.

Posthuma, A. (2016). Current and new developments in psychological testing for child custody disputes. In M. I. Goldstein (Ed.). *Handbook of child custody* (pp. 67–84). Springer.

Pronin, E., & Kugler, M. (2007). Valuing thoughts, ignoring behavior: The introspection illusion as a source of the bias blind spot. *Journal of Experimental Social Psychology, 43,* 565–578.

Rappaport, S., Gould, J., & Dale, M. (2018). Psychological testing can be of significant value in child custody evaluations: Don't buy the "anti-testing, anti-individual, pro-family systems" woozle. *Journal of the American Academy of Matrimonial Lawyers, 30*(2), 405–436.

Saini, M., Laajasalo, T., & Platt, S. (2020). Gatekeeping by allegations: An examination of verified, unfounded, and fabricated allegations of child maltreatment within the context of resist and refusal dynamics. *Family Court Review, 58*(2), 417–431.

Shear, L. E. (1996). Life stories, doctrines and decision making: Three high courts confront the move-sway dilemma. *Family & Conciliation Court Review, 34*(4), 439–458.

Smart, C. (2002). From children's shoes to children's voices. *Family Court Review, 40*(3), 307–319.

Stahl, P. M. (2010). *Conducting child custody evaluations: From basic to complex issues.* SAGE.

Sullivan, M. J. (1997). Parental alienation process in post-divorce cases. *Association of Family and Conciliation Courts Newsletter, 16*(2/3), 3–4.

Thompson, R. (2000). The legacy of early attachments. *Child Development, 71*(1), 145–152.

Tippins, T. M., & Wittmann, J. P. (2005a). Empirical and ethical problems with custody recommendations: A call for clinical humility and judicial vigilance. *Family Court Review, 43*(2), 193–222.

Tippins, T. M., & Wittmann, J. P. (2005b). A third call: Restoring the noble empirical principles of two professionals. *Family Court Review, 43*(2), 270–282.

Wallerstein, J. S., & Kelly, J. B. (1980). *Surviving the breakup: How children and parents cope with divorce.* Basic Books.

Warshak, R. A. (2001).Current controversies regarding parental alienation syndrome. *American Journal of Forensic Psychology, 19*(3), 29–59.

Warshak, R. A. (2010). *Divorce poison: How to protect your family from bad-mouthing and brainwashing* (2nd ed.). Harper-Collins.

Youngstrom, E. A. & De Los Reyes, A. (2015) Commentary: Moving toward cost-effectiveness in using psychophysiological measures in clinical assessment: Validity, decision making, and adding value. *Journal of Clinical Child & Adolescent Psychology, 44*(2), 352–361.

Zapf, P. A., Kukucka, J., Kassin, S. M., & Dror, I. E. (2017). Cognitive bias in forensic mental health assessment: Evaluator beliefs about its nature and scope. *Psychology, Public Policy, and Law, 24*(1), 1–10.

Zappala, M., Reed, A. L., Beltrani, A., Zaft, P. A., & Otto, R. K. (2018). Anything you can do, I can do better: Bias awareness in forensic evaluators. *Journal of Forensic Psychology Research and Practice, 18*(1), 45–56.

Forensic Mental Health Assessment in Immigration Court

Virginia Barber-Rioja *and* Alexandra Garcia-Mansilla

Abstract

Under US immigration law, individuals without valid immigration legal status and legal permanent residents convicted of certain crimes can face removal proceedings (i.e., deportation) and be detained. Immigration Court (IC) is civil in nature and therefore respondents (i.e., immigrants in deportation proceedings) have limited constitutional protections (e.g., right to counsel) despite the severe penalties imposed (e.g., detention and deportation). Many of the legal issues involved in IC decisions include mental health concepts (e.g., fear of persecution, mental abuse, credibility, competency for self-representation, and dangerousness). Forensic mental health assessment (FMHA) in IC proceedings requires specialized knowledge of immigration law, forensic and cross-cultural assessment, and psychological impact of trauma. Despite the crucial role of psychological evaluations in this context, FMHA in IC proceedings has received little attention. This chapter provides an overview of the legal context of immigration law, the psycholegal issues involved in immigration-related FMHA, and recommendations for best practices and future research.

Key Words: Immigration Court, immigration evaluations, cross-cultural assessment, trauma, asylum Violence Against Women Act

It is estimated that approximately eleven million individuals who live in the United States lack US documentation (Pew Research Center, 2019). This includes both foreign-born nationals who unlawfully entered the country and those who remained in the country beyond the expiration of their visas. Many of these immigrants have left their countries escaping armed conflicts, violence, torture, persecution, or poverty. Under US immigration law, anyone who lacks valid immigration status, as well as legal permanent residents (LPR) convicted of certain crimes, can be placed under removal proceedings (i.e., deportation proceedings). Before being removed, noncitizens have the right to an immigration hearing.[1] Deportation and detention release decisions are made by an Immigration Judge (IJ) in Immigration Court (IC), or in some circumstances by immigration officers from the US Citizenship and Immigration Service (USCIS). For the purposes of this chapter,

---

[1] Yamataya v. Fisher, 189 U.S. 86 (1903).

all cases in front of an immigration adjudicator will be referred to as IC. In 2018, 434,159 removal proceedings were initiated in ICs across the country, which represents a 41 percent increase from 2014 (Executive Office for Immigration Review, 2018). Immigration proceedings are a matter of civil law, but ICs constitute a separate court system that is significantly different from criminal and other civil courts in the United States (Filone & King, 2015).

Mental health professionals can play an essential role in helping immigration adjudicators resolve legal matters (e.g., removal, adjustment of status, and bond). Psychological evidence is crucial in many applications for removal-relief (e.g., asylum and hardship). Psychological evaluations in IC were first described as a type of forensic mental health assessment (FMHA) almost three decades ago (Frumkin & Friedland, 1995). At that time, Frumkin and Friedland (1995) noted that "the legal and psychological communities have given little attention to forensic evaluations in immigration cases" (p. 477). Unfortunately, not much has changed since then. The referral questions and psycholegal issues involved in immigration-related FMHA continue to lack specificity, there is poor understanding of the practices used by mental health professionals conducting evaluations in IC, and limited progress has been made in extending the empirical evidence required to develop specialized tools or establish the cross-cultural validity of clinical assessment instruments. Only recently, some books and chapters have begun to cover this topic (e.g., Butcher et al., 2015; Evans & Hans, 2018; Shapiro & Walker, 2019), and to date, none of the most important compendiums on psychology and law have described these evaluations as a type of FMHA (Heilbrun et al., 2009; Melton et al., 2018; Roesch & Zapf, 2013). This chapter provides an overview of the legal context of immigration law, the psycholegal issues involved in immigration-related FMHA, and recommendations for best practices and future research.

The Legal Context of Immigration Proceedings

Immigration courts are under the management of the Executive Office for Immigration Review (EOIR) within the Department of Justice (DOJ). After the Department of Homeland Security (DHS) charges a noncitizen with a violation of immigration laws, the EOIR decides whether the individual is removable, and if so, whether they qualify for any protection or removal relief. Once DHS has initiated removal proceedings, noncitizens will be served with a Notice to Appear (NTA) before an IJ (in 2018, DHS served more than 300,000 NTA [Department of Justice, 2018]). Noncitizens facing removal proceedings, or respondents, have the right to be provided with a reasonable opportunity to examine the evidence against them, to present evidence on their own behalf, and to cross-examine witnesses presented by the government.[2]

---

[2] See 8 U.S.C. §1229(a).

Removal proceedings are adversarial in nature and noncitizens are expected to present their cases in front of the IJ. The government is represented by a DHS attorney from US Immigration and Customs Enforcement (ICE), an entity created in 2003 as the enforcement arm of DHS, which is charged with detaining and removing noncitizens who have violated immigration law (De Jesús-Rentas et al., 2010). Even though removal proceedings are civil and considered nonpunitive,[3] they have been referred to as "quasi-criminal" given the severe penalties involved (Marouf, 2014, p. 931). This is particularly the case for individuals with mental illness or other medical conditions, who may not be able to get appropriate treatment in their countries of origin, or for those facing torture or persecution in their home countries. In fact, the US Supreme Court in *Padilla v. Kentucky,* acknowledged that deportation is a serious consequence of criminal pleas, both for undocumented and documented (LPR) immigrants.[4] Despite the high stakes, respondents are not guaranteed the same constitutional rights provided to those in criminal court, including the Sixth Amendment right to the assistance of counsel.[5]

In addition to being vulnerable to removal, noncitizens can be placed in detention upon apprehension by ICE and while undergoing removal proceedings. Immigration detention, unlike detention within the criminal justice system, does not have a punitive or rehabilitative purpose, but instead it is used to prevent the immigrants from absconding and to protect the public. In addition, it is the respondent, and not the state, who bears the burden of proof; the immigrant must affirmatively demonstrate that they are not a flight risk or a danger to the community. They also must face this legal burden without right to counsel. Immigration detention has increased exponentially in recent decades (85,000 in 1995 to more than 450,000 in 2012) due in part to the Illegal Immigration Reform and Immigrant Responsibility Act of 1996, which increased the penalties for immigration violations (Ochoa et al., 2010). Noncitizens in immigration detention are held in DHS facilities, privately run detention centers, or state and local jails that lease bed space to DHS. There are approximately 34,000 immigration detention beds in almost 200 facilities across the country (American Civil Liberties Union, n.d.).

Forensic Mental Health Concepts

There are different types of FMHAs that can inform IC decisions. The psycholegal issues involved are typically based on the type of removal relief for which the noncitizen is applying. Most forms of relief require the establishment of special facts or circumstances by statutory requirement (e.g., hardship and persecution), whereas others are solely based on a balancing of positive and negative equities by the legal decision maker (e.g., consideration of mitigating factors) (Kamhi et al., 2017). Most forms of immigration relief

---

[3] See INS v. Lopez-Mendoza, 468 U.S. 1032 (1984).
[4] Padilla v. Kentucky 559 U.S. 356 (2010).
[5] See Lopez-Mendoza, 468 U.S. 1032.

are discretionary, which means that after noncitizens have demonstrated that they meet eligibility for relief, the adjudicator still has the discretion to decide whether they deserve such relief (EOIR, 2004). As a result, FMHAs sometimes serve to contextualize behavior (e.g., to provide evidence that symptoms of mental illness contributed to a crime). Finally, FMHA in the form of risk assessment can aid adjudicators in making decisions about detention since they are asked to consider dangerousness.[6] The next sections cover the most common forensic mental health concepts in IC.

Persecution-Based Relief: Asylum, Withholding of Removal, and Convention Against Torture

Under US immigration law, immigrants who fear persecution in their native countries can request political asylum and two other related forms of protection: Withholding of Removal (WOR) and Convention Against Torture (CAT). To be eligible for asylum, immigrants must demonstrate that they meet the definition of a refugee, which involves being unable or unwilling to return because of "*persecution* or *well-founded fear* of persecution on account of race, religion, nationality, political opinion, or membership in a particular social group."[7] Applicants can meet the criteria by either demonstrating that persecution has already taken place or that they have a well-founded fear it will occur in the future. Court cases agree that persecution requires severe harm (e.g., more than trivial) but disagree on what type of harm is severe enough to constitute persecution (Meffert et al., 2010). For example, some courts have held that psychological harm meets the definition of persecution whereas others have rejected severe forms of physical harm (Meffert et al., 2010). Finally, noncitizens who have experienced torture can apply for removal relief through the United Nations CAT, which prohibits the return of an individual to a place where they are likely to be tortured (i.e., severe pain or suffering intentionally inflicted on a person).[8] Both WOR, which is similar to asylum, and CAT require a preponderance of the evidence (as opposed to 10 percent in asylum) and are not discretionary.

Given the high volume of refugee claims, psychological evaluations in the context of persecution-relief are the most common type of FMHAs conducted in IC. The primary purpose is to provide psychological evidence of the impact of persecution or torture. Although the documented presence of trauma related symptoms, such as those found in posttraumatic stress disorder (PTSD), can bolster the claim, whether the trauma is considered to be persecution or torture is a legal question decided by the adjudicator. The evaluator can certainly comment on whether the examinee fears return to their native country based on a subjective fear of reexperiencing the harm; however, the veracity of the reason for the fear is the purview of the fact-finder (De Jesús-Rentas et al., 2010).

---

[6] See In re Fatahi, 26 I & N. Dec. 791 (B.I.A. 2016).
[7] 8 U.S.C. §1101(a).
[8] 8 CFR §208.16.

Forensic evaluators can also document psychological symptoms (e.g., avoidance and cognitive impairment) that may have prevented the immigrant from applying for asylum within the required one-year period from the time of arrival. Finally, FMHA can play an important role in providing information that aids the adjudicator in making credibility decisions (see under "Credibility and Malingering").

The Istanbul Protocol (Office of the United Nations High Commissioner for Human Rights, 2004) provides international guidelines for the evaluation of survivors of human rights abuses; however, little is known about common practices in persecution-relief evaluations. A recent study found that most evaluations include a history of torture, current psychiatric complaints, diagnoses, and a consideration of malingering (Bayne et al., 2019). Although there is limited information about the extent to which adjudicators rely on these evaluations, preliminary research suggests that FMHAs may contribute to better outcomes in asylum claims. One study found that 89 percent of asylum or WOR claims that included a forensic evaluation from Physicians for Human Rights were granted, compared to the national average of 37.5 percent (Lustig et al., 2008).

Victimization-Based Relief: U/T Visas and Violence Against Women Act

There are certain nonimmigrant forms of admission that provide temporary status to noncitizens who have been victims of specific crimes (U-Visa) or human trafficking (T-Visa). Both visas can be granted as long as the noncitizen is willing to collaborate with the government during the criminal investigation. The U-Visa requires that the immigrant "has suffered *substantial mental or physical abuse* as a result of having been a victim of criminal activity, and T-Visas are available for individuals who have been "a victim of severe form of trafficking" defined as sex or labor trafficking,[9] including *psychological coercion*.[10] Finally, under the Violence Against Women Act (VAWA),[11] immigrant victims of domestic violence, child abuse, or elder abuse may self-petition for LPR status without the cooperation of the abusive spouse, parent, or child if they can prove that they have been battered or been subjected to *extreme cruelty*,[12] among other requirements.

Similar to personal injury evaluations, the forensic issue common to victimization-based relief is the assessment of psychological harm resulting from a traumatic event (i.e., victimization of crime, human trafficking, or family violence). The literature has broken down the forensic concepts in personal injury evaluations into three different issues: what are the mental health disorders or symptoms that are present, what are the functional abilities affected by the trauma, and what is the nature and strength of the connection between the traumatic experience and psychological harm (Heilbrun, 2001).

---

[9] 8 U.S.C. §1101(a).

[10] 22 U.S.C. §7102(2).

[11] Violence Against Women Act of 2000, Pub. L. No. 106-386, § 7101, 114 Stat. 464 (2000).

[12] 8 C.F.R. §204.2(c).

Best practices for personal injury evaluations (see Schultz, 2013) can be applied to victimization-based evaluations in IC, but there are additional challenges in this context. First, given high levels of trauma found in immigrant groups, it can be difficult to establish a post hoc connection between the traumatic event that is part of the victimization-based claim and the mental health symptoms (e.g., whether mental health symptoms are the result of victimization suffered in the United States, versus migration trauma, versus a history of persecution). This can be addressed by providing information about clinical functioning prior to any potential persecution suffered in the country of origin, prior to migration, and prior to the victimization-qualifying event, as well as currently. With respect to the strength of the connection, it is important to document the potential contribution and relative importance of different traumatic experiences, including the event at the base of the claim, to current symptoms and functioning (Koch et al., 2009). The questions of whether the level of psychological harm is considered *substantial* and directly connected to the event in question, or the form of trafficking or abuse resulting in symptoms *severe* or *extreme*, are the purview of the adjudicator. Second, the law does not require a diagnosis in the definition of harm (this is also the case for persecution). Often, individuals exposed to trauma do not meet diagnostic criteria for any disorder but still experience substantial functional impairment (Marshall et al., 2001), so information about changes in functioning observed since the victimization event may be more relevant than a specific diagnostic label.

Hardship-Based Relief

Legal adjudicators in IC may cancel removal of a respondent who violates immigration law if it is established that removal would cause adversity or *exceptional* and *extremely unusual hardship* to the spouse, child, or parent who is a citizen or a LPR.[13] Hardship is also a requirement in other forms of relief, such as T-Visas. The different degrees of hardship depend on the form of removal relief; hardship can take several forms, including economic, social, or psychological. The concept of hardship is not well defined by law, particularly with respect to psychological parameters, and thus decision makers have wide discretion (Frumkin & Friedland, 1995). Although there is limited empirical research on the psychological impact of family separation on immigrants and their families, this topic has received increased attention in recent years (see Rojas-Flores et al., 2017; Wylonis & Billick, 2021). It is estimated that about five million children living in the United States have one or more immigrant parents, and almost 80 percent of these children are US citizens. These children are already more vulnerable to poverty, lower education attainment, and limited English proficiency (Capps et al., 2016), and deportation of one or both parents can have a potentially significant psychological impact, particularly if the citizen or LPR has other vulnerabilities (e.g., mental illness

---

[13] 8 U.S.C §1229(b).

and neurodevelopmental disability). Hardship evaluations are complex and require not only the evaluation of the respondent but, more importantly, of the US citizen or LPR who would suffer the hardship.

Credibility and Malingering

The concept of credibility is at the core of many types of immigration evaluations, particularly in the context of relief-based claims. It is common for asylum-seekers to lack any physical or other type of evidence of the persecution they suffered and therefore the entire claim relies on their own testimony and whether that testimony is perceived as credible by the decision maker (Meffert et al., 2010). Studies have found that 40–77 percent of denied asylum claims include credibility as a reason (Anker, 1992; Kagan, 2003; McKinnon, 2009). The concept of credibility is not well defined by law, and decision makers consider different factors when making credibility decisions, especially whether there are inconsistencies in the applicant's statement. Even inconsistencies that are not central to the basis for the asylum application can be used as evidence for noncredible findings (Eyster, 2012). FMHAs can educate the court on the extensive research that points to the imperfections in human memory and on evidence showing that individuals tend to recall details that are central to an event with a high level of emotional content, often at the expense of peripheral details (Christianson & Safer, 1996). There are also individual factors specific to the experiences of asylum-seekers that can affect memory retrieval, including trauma-related symptoms, depression, sleep difficulties, or malnutrition (Cohen, 2001). Inconsistent recollections in refugees have been empirically examined in two studies. Herlihy et al. (2002) found that discrepancies in repeated descriptions of traumatic events were common in a sample of Kosovan and Bosnian refugees. In addition, they found that discrepancies in recounting of peripheral details were more common than for central details, and that symptoms of posttraumatic stress contributed to an increase in discrepancies. In a group of twenty-eight individuals who had been granted asylum in the United States, Filone and DeMatteo (2017b) also found high levels of discrepancies with no significant differences between genuine and exaggerated reports.

Related to credibility is the concept of malingering. Avoiding deportation is a potential external incentive for exaggeration or feigning. Malingering of trauma-related symptoms or PTSD is a particularly relevant psychological construct in IC, and ruling out malingering is a strategy used by immigration attorneys to support their clients' credibility (Prabhu & Baranoski, 2012). However, limited research in this area presents tremendous challenges for forensic evaluators. There is a paucity of research on assessing malingering of trauma-related symptoms or PTSD cross-culturally and in the context of IC (Weiss & Rosenfeld, 2017). In addition, some studies have found that individuals who experienced childhood abuse or veterans with PTSD can report trauma-related symptoms that can be misinterpreted as malingering in psychological testing (Elhai et al., 2002; Klotz et al., 2003), raising concerns about whether cultural manifestations of trauma could be misinterpreted as malingering. In fact, Weiss and Rosenfeld (2017) examined the ability of the Trauma Symptom Inventory-2's (TSI-2; Briere, 2011) overreporting (ATR) scale to detect PTSD feigning among West African asylum-seekers and found a 10 percent rate of false positives among those with high levels of PTSD, and only a 40 percent rate of sensitivity among those instructed to feign. On the other hand, Filone and DeMatteo (2017a) examined the TSI-2's utility among immigrants with histories of trauma and found that the ATR (Atypical Response) scale likely functions similarly in the standardization sample compared with the immigrant sample. Further research will clarify the utility of this scale and other instruments in IC.

Cross-Cultural Assessment of Trauma

There are more than 276 different languages spoken in immigration proceedings (Department of Justice, 2012). Immigrants are widely diverse with respect to race, ethnicity, language, gender and sexual orientation, disability, religious beliefs, socioeconomic status, education level, migration experiences, and acculturation, among others. This emphasizes the need for FMHAs to be culturally valid, which requires consideration of the respondents' cultural background and the intersectionality of their multiple identities (Lee et al., 2020). This requires training and self-reflection; an understanding that culture (including that of the evaluator) affects the manifestation of symptoms in the respondent and how information is interpreted by the evaluator; and the use of assessment methods that are sensitive to multiculturalism.

The cross-cultural assessment of trauma is a central component of most forms of FMHA in IC. Although studies have used different methodologies, it is estimated that refugees are ten times more likely to experience PTSD than the general population (Vallières et al., 2018). For example, in a sample of 420 refugees and immigrants, Steel et al. (2017) found that 47 percent reported clinically significant PTSD and 20 percent clinically significant depressive symptoms. Although the cross-cultural applicability of PTSD to non-Western cultures has been questioned, extensive research has demonstrated the cross-cultural validity of the PTSD diagnostic criteria. However, there is substantial variability in symptom expression, specifically with respect to avoidance symptoms, which may present less consistently across cultures (Hilton & Lewis-Fernandez, 2011). In addition, research has found that somatic symptoms are more common in individuals who are exposed to repeated traumatic events, torture, or genocide (Hilton & Lewis-Fernandez, 2011). This distinct trauma-related presentation was recently included in the *International Classification of Diseases* (ICD) under the label "Complex PTSD" (World Health Organization, 2018), and it involves exposure to a severe traumatic event of an extreme or prolonged nature and for which escape is difficult or impossible (e.g., captivity and torture). Although this disorder has not yet been included in the *Diagnostic and Statistical Manual of Mental Disorders* (DSM-5) (American Psychiatric Association, 2013) and there is substantial debate within the field as to whether it constitutes a distinct clinical entity, preliminary research suggests that it may be a relevant diagnosis for immigrants who have experienced persecution. For example, Vallières et al. (2018) found that Complex PTSD was more common (36.1 percent) than PTSD (25.2 percent) in a sample of 112 Syrian refugees.

Conducting FMHA in IC requires a thorough understanding of how cultural factors affect trauma-related clinical presentations and the different threats to cultural validity, including cross-cultural variability in symptom expression, language differences, evaluators' bias in clinical judgment, and inappropriate use of psychological tests that have only been validated with Western, educated, industrialized, rich, and democratic (WEIRD) samples (Leong & Kalibatseva, 2016). In addition, given the diversity of languages and dialects spoken by respondents, FMHA in IC often requires the use of interpreters. This limits the possibility of using psychological testing and requires a number of additional considerations. For example, if the interpreter is not certified and has no prior experience with mental health evaluations, a pre-meeting with the evaluator may be needed (Barber Rioja & Rosenfeld, 2018). Lack of formal education, which is not unusual in respondents, can also limit the use of clinical assessment instruments. The challenges to the use of psychometric instruments in IC can be such that evaluators are often forced to rely on a clinical interview and collateral sources (Weiss & Rosenfeld, 2012). When this is the case, the Cultural Formulation Interview (CFI; American Psychiatric Association, 2013) represents a more structured way of conducting culturally informed interviews. Comparative efficacy research is needed to determine the specific contribution of the CFI over other assessment methods, and its specific utility in forensic contexts. However, growing research has suggested that it is useful for rapport building, eliciting information, and improving the clinicians' understanding of cross-cultural symptom presentation (DeSilva et al., 2018).

Competency

Although there are no official statistics on this topic, it is estimated that about 15 percent of all immigrants involved in IC have a mental illness (Human Rights Watch, 2010). As in criminal proceedings, it is expected that a number of detained immigrants with mental illness or cognitive deficits may not be able to effectively participate in court proceedings or understand the consequences of deportation. This matter is likely exacerbated by the limited access to mental health treatment in immigration detention facilities. The issue of competency to participate in removal proceedings has only recently begun to receive attention from ICs (see Filone & King, 2015, for a review). Since respondents do not have the constitutional right to assistance of counsel, competency evaluations in this context mostly involve the question of whether the respondent is competent to appear pro se. Similar to the standards set forth by *Dusky v. United States*,[14] the Board of Immigration Appeals's decision In *M-A-M* set forth the following competency standard for IC:

---

[14] Dusky v. United States, 362 U.S. 402 (1960).

The test for determining whether an alien is competent to participate in immigration proceedings is whether he or she has a rational and factual understanding of the nature and object of the proceedings, can consult with an attorney or representative if there is one, and has a reasonable opportunity to examine and present evidence and cross-examine witnesses.[15]

Later, in *Franco-Gonzalez v. Holder*, [16]a federal district court included the appointment of a *qualified representative* as a reasonable safeguard for incompetent respondents (e.g., attorney, law student, accredited individual, or other "reputable" person[17]). In addition, in 2013 the DOJ and DHS announced a nationwide policy to enhance procedural protections for unrepresented respondents, which included implementation of mental health screening to identify individuals with serious mental illness in detention facilities, competency hearings, and independently conducted competency evaluations. The EOIR published guidelines ("Phase I," 2013) that define of mental disorder and further elaborate on the legal standard and psycholegal issues involved in competency for removal evaluations. It also provides guidelines to ICs on how to determine if respondents are competent to represent themselves, a system of referral for a mental health examination, a list of qualifications for the examining professional, and procedural protections and safeguards that IJs can consider for noncompetent respondents (see "Phase I," 2013). Unlike within the criminal court process, in IC, cases are not automatically suspended after the respondent is found incompetent (Filone & King, 2015) and there is no formal process for competency restoration (Marouf, 2014).

The EOIR's guidelines provide an important and necessary tool for ICs and forensic evaluators, but many questions remain. It has been argued that respondents in IC must be "more" competent for self-representation than those in criminal court because, unlike criminal proceedings, in IC the burden of proof in seeking relief resides with respondents. This may require more active participation because they have to affirmatively prove the case (Wilson et al., 2015). In addition, the functional abilities required may vary depending on the qualifications of the qualified representative or guardian that may be advocating for the respondent. Furthermore, the EOIR guidelines or the mental health trainings have not been applied to all jurisdictions. In jurisdictions like New York, where all detained immigrants can receive free legal representation (The Bronx Defenders, n.d.), it is unclear how to apply the existing standard.

Given that the issue of competency in IC has only recently begun to receive attention, there is no empirical research with respect to clinicians' practices, or knowledge of the clinical or demographic variables that make respondents more likely to be found incompetent. There are also no forensic assessment tools that have been validated for use in IC.

---

[15] In re M-A-M-, 25 I. & N. Dec. 474, at 479 (B. I. A. 2011).
[16] Franco-Gonzalez v. Holder, No. CV 10–02211 DMG (DTBx), 2013 WL 3674492 (C.D. Cal. 2013).
[17] 8 C.F.R. §1292.1 (2014).

However, Shapiro (2014) developed a competency-for-removal instrument that included questions relevant to the psycholegal abilities required in IC while leaving room for clinical judgment. This instrument has been used in some deportation proceedings after being approved by IJs and attorneys (see Shapiro & Walker, 2019).

As previously mentioned, cultural considerations are crucial in IC. This is true not only for mental health evaluators but also for lawyers and adjudicators during the competency process. Research on competency in criminal proceedings has found that attorneys are more likely to rate Spanish-speaking defendants as less mentally ill and therefore, less likely to refer them for competency evaluations (Valera et al., 2011). This raises concerns about the potential for underidentification of respondents with competency issues, particularly considering that Spanish is the most frequent language spoken in IC (Department of Justice, 2012).

Summary and Future Considerations

There has been a dramatic increase in the number of removal proceedings and associated detentions for non-citizens in the United States over the past few years. Although considered to fall under civil law, immigration procedures follow their own guidelines, with limited constitutional protection for respondents (e.g., right to counsel). While civil in nature, these cases are extremely high stakes for the individuals involved and their families. The role of mental health experts in these cases is multifaceted and extremely important as many of the legal issues involved in adjudicators' decisions include mental health concepts. Mental health professionals are equipped to help the IC understand the effects of torture and persecution on an individual, or the potential consequences of removal on a family. Psychologists are important in assessing competency to proceed and risk for future violence. They can offer context to explain behaviors, provide relevant mental health diagnoses, and offer information related to credibility of self-reported symptoms.

As the number of immigrants in removal proceedings and detention has increased, so has the need for mental health professionals needed in IC (Evans & Hass, 2018). Unlike other areas of law, it is very common for clinicians to engage in this work pro bono. For example, in a survey of fifteen clinicians who work in this context, almost all reported waiving their fees (Baranowski et al., 2018) and many others accept reduced fees; many psychologists see this work as fulfilling a humanitarian role (Sidhu & Boodoo, 2017). The terrible stories of trauma, torture, and persecution that are often elicited during these evaluations can induce significant emotional reactions in the evaluator (Evans & Hass, 2018). The reasons clinicians choose to do this work in combination with the emotions it can induce run the risk of diminishing objectivity and thus credibility (Morgan, 2017). This reinforces the need for mental health professionals to develop additional expertise. While answering psychological questions related to diagnosis or functioning is part of psychologists' general area of competence, conducting evaluations in IC requires specialized knowledge in the areas of immigration law, forensic assessment, cross-cultural assessment, and assessment of the psychological effects of trauma and torture. Although there is limited literature regarding the application of the principles of FMHA to IC, psychologists need to be thoroughly familiar with these principles (Heilbrun, 2001), and the *Specialty Guidelines for Forensic Psychology* (American Psychological Association, 2013), *Ethical Principles of Psychologists and Code of Conduct* (American Psychological Association, 2017a), the *Guidelines on Multicultural Education, Training, Research, Practice and Organizational Change for Psychologists* (American Psychological Association, 2003) and *Multicultural Guidelines: An Ecological Approach to Context, Identity, and Intersectionality* (American Psychological Association, 2017b).

Despite the increased use of psychological expertise in IC, there is a significant deficit in theoretical and empirical literature about this forensic subspecialty. The field of FMHA has mostly neglected the context of immigration law, and the field of cross-cultural assessment has rarely paid attention to forensic issues (Weiss & Rosenfeld, 2012). Although a limited number of studies have shown some promising results with respect to the cross-cultural utility of psychometric instruments in IC (e.g., Filone & DeMatteo, 2017a; Weiss & Rosenfeld, 2017), there is a substantial need for further research on the cross-cultural validity of existing clinical assessment and forensically relevant instruments, particularly those that assess trauma-related clinical presentations and malingering of trauma symptoms and response style. In addition, forensic assessment instruments need to be developed to assess specific immigration legal constructs (e.g., competency for removal). Furthermore, given IC's overreliance on complete consistency and accuracy as a reflection of credibility, more research into memory of accounts of persecution in the context of ongoing trauma is needed. Survey research can help understand the current practices employed by mental health experts in IC as well as factors contributing to decision-making in immigration adjudicators, including any potential for cultural biases. Until more research is developed in these areas, evaluators in IC need to acknowledge the limitations of their data and opinions. The limited body of research paired with the lack of specificity with respect to psycholegal constructs in immigration law (Frumkin & Friedland, 1995), suggest that evaluators should avoid answering the ultimate legal question. This also appears to be the recommendation of the EOIR with respect to competency. The guidelines state that the role of the mental health professional is "to provide information to the court about the mental health of the respondent so the court can make an informed decision about the respondent's competency" (Phase I, 2013, p. 10).

The EOIR has provided important guidelines for IJs and mental health professionals in the area of competency that will hopefully be extended nationwide. Furthermore, we suggest that EOIR develops similar guidelines and related trainings for other areas of FMHA in IC. To improve quality and facilitate consistency, principles and guidelines for the practice of FMHA in IC need to be developed (Filone & King, 2015). Finally, there is significant opportunity for psychologists to provide consultation to the immigration law system with respect to formal pathways to competency restoration and improvement of mental health treatment offered in immigration detention centers.

References

American Civil Liberties Union. n.d. ACLU fact sheet on alternatives to immigration detention. https://www.aclu.org/other/aclu-fact-sheet-alternatives-immigration-detention-atd.

American Psychiatric Association. (2013). *Diagnostic and statistical manual of mental disorders* (5th ed.). American Psychiatric Association.

American Psychological Association. (2003). Guidelines on multicultural education, training, research, practice, and organizational change for Psychologists. *American Psychologist, 58*(5), 377–402.

American Psychological Association. (2013). *Specialty guidelines for forensic psychology. American Psychologist, 68*(1), 7–19.

American Psychological Association. (2017a). *Ethical principles of psychologists and code of conduct.* https://www.apa.org/ethics/code.

American Psychological Association. (2017b). *Multicultural guidelines: An ecological approach to context, identity, and intersectionality.* http://www.apa.org/about/policy/multicultural-guidelines.pdf

Anker, D. (1992). Determining asylum claims in the United States: A case study on the implementation of legal norms in an unstructured adjudicatory environment. *N.Y.U. Review of Law and Social Change, 19*(3), 433–528.

Barber Rioja, V., & Rosenfeld, B. (2018). Addressing linguistic and cultural differences in the forensic interview. *International Journal of Forensic Mental Health, 17*(4), 377–386.

Baranowski, K. A., Moses, M. H., & Sundri, J. (2018). Supporting asylum seekers: Clinician experiences of documenting human rights violations through forensic psychological evaluation. *Journal of Traumatic Stress, 31*(3), 391–400.

Bayne, M., Sokoloff, L., Rinehart, R., Epie, A., Hirt, L., & Katz, C. (2019). Assessing the efficacy and experience of in-person versus telephonic psychiatric evaluations for asylum seekers in the U.S. *Psychiatry Research, 282*, Article 112612. https://doi.org/10.1016/j.psychres.2019.112612

Briere, J. (2011). *Trauma Symptom Inventory-2 professional manual.* Psychological Assessment Resources.

The Bronx Defenders. n.d. New York Immigrant Family Unity Project. https://www.bronxdefenders.org/programs/new-york-immigrant-family-unity-project/

Butcher, J. N., Hass, G. A., Greene, R. L., & Nelson, L. D. (2015). *The MMPI-2 in immigration evaluations.* In J. N. Butcher, G. A. Hass, R. L. Greene, & L. D. Nelson, *Using the MMPI-2 in forensic assessment* (pp. 145–168). American Psychological Association.

Capps, R., Fix, M., & Zong, J. (2016). A profile of U.S. children with unauthorized immigrant parents. *Migration Policy Institute. Fact Sheets.* https://www.migrationpolicy.org/research/profile-us-children-unauthorized-immigrant-parents

Cohen, J. (2001). Errors of recall and credibility: Can omissions and discrepancies in successive statements reasonably be said to undermine credibility of testimony? *Medico-Legal Journal, 69*(Pt. 1), 25–34.

Christianson, S. A., & Safer, M. A. (1996). Emotional events and emotions in autobiographical memories. In D. C. Rubin (Ed.), *Remembering our past: Studies in autobiographical memory* (pp. 218–241). Cambridge University Press.

De Jesús-Rentas, G., Boehnlein, J., & Sparr, L. (2010). Central American victims of gang violence as asylum seekers: The role of the forensic expert. *Journal of the American Academy of Psychiatry and the Law, 38*(4), 490–498.

DeSilva, R., Aggarwal, N. K., & Lewis-Fernández, R. (2018). The DSM-5 cultural formulation interview: Bridging barriers toward a clinically integrated cultural assessment in psychiatry. *Psychiatric Annals, 48*(3), 154–159.

Elhai, J. D., Ruggiero, K. J., Frueh, B. C., Beckham, J. C., Gold, P. B., & Feldman, M. E. (2002). The Infrequency-Posttraumatic Stress Disorder scale (Fptsd) for the MMPI-2: Development and initial validation with veterans presenting with combat-related PTSD. *Journal of Personality Assessment, 79*, 531–549.

Evans, F. B. III., & Hass, A. G. (2018). *Forensic psychological assessment in immigration court: A guidebook for evidence-based and ethical practice.* Routledge.

Executive Office for Immigration Review (EOIR). (2004). *Fact sheet.* U.S. Department of Justice. https://www.justice.gov/sites/default/files/eoir/legacy/2004/08/05/ReliefFromRemoval.pdf

Executive Office for Immigration Review (EOIR). (2018). *FY 2018: Statistics yearbook.* U.S. Department of Justice. https://www.justice.gov/eoir/file/1198896/download

Eyster, J. P. (2012). Searching for the key in the wrong place: Why common sense credibility rules consistently harm refugees. *Boston University International Law Journal, 30,* 1–54.

Filone, S., & DeMatteo, D. (2017a). Assessing "credible fear": A psychometric examination of the Trauma Symptom Inventory-2 in the context of immigration court evaluations. *Psychological Assessment, 29*(6), 701–709.

Filone, S., & DeMatteo, D. (2017b). Testimonial inconsistencies, adverse credibility determinations, and asylum adjudication in the United States. *Translational Issues in Psychological Science, 3*(2), 202–213.

Filone, S., & King, C. M. (2015). The emerging standard of competence in immigration removal proceedings: A review for forensic mental health professionals. *Psychology, Public Policy, and Law, 21*(1), 60–71.

Frumkin, I. B., & Friedland, J. (1995). Forensic evaluations in immigration cases: Evolving issues. *Behavioral Sciences & the Law, 13*(4), 477–489.

Heilbrun, K. (2001). *Principles of forensic mental health assessment.* Kluwer/Plenum.

Heilbrun, K., Grisso, T., & Goldstein, A. M. (2009). *Best practices in forensic mental health assessment.* Oxford University Press.

Herlihy, J., Scragg, P., & Turner, S. (2002). Discrepancies in autobiographical memories—Implications for the assessment of asylum seekers: Repeated interviews study. *British Medical Journal, 324*(7333), 324–327.

Hinton, D. E., & Lewis-Fernández, R. (2011). The cross-cultural validity of posttraumatic stress disorder: Implications for DSM-5. *Depression and Anxiety, 28*(9), 783–801.

Human Rights Watch. (2010). Deportation by default. https://www.hrw.org/sites/default/files/reports/usdeportation0710webwcover_1_0.pdf

Klotz Flitter, J. M., Elhai, J. D., & Gold, S. N. (2003). MMPI-2 F scale elevations in adult victims of child sexual abuse. *Journal of Traumatic Stress, 16,* 269–274.

Kagan, M. (2003). Is truth in the eye of the beholder? Objective credibility assessment in refugee status determination. *Georgetown Immigration Law Journal, 17,* 367–415

Kamhi, A., Davenport, A., Maruez, N., & Quinn, E. (2017). Introductions to hardship and the manual. In *Hardship in immigration law.* Immigration Legal Resource Center. https://www.ilrc.org/sites/default/files/sample-pdf/hardship-14th-2017-ch_01.pdf

Koch, W. K., Nader, R., & Harring (2009). The science and pseudoscience of assessing psychological injuries. In J. Skeem, K. Douglas, & S. Lilienfeld (Eds.), *Psychological science in the courtroom: Controversies and consensus* (pp. 263–283). Guilford Press.

Lee, D. J., Kleiman, S. E., & Weathers, F. W. (2020). Assessment of trauma-and stressor-related disorders. In M. Sellbom & J. A. Suhr (Eds.), *The Cambridge handbook of clinical assessment and diagnosis* (pp. 347–359). Cambridge University Press.

Leong, F. T. L., & Kalibatseva, Z. (2016). Threats to cultural validity in clinical diagnosis and assessment: Illustrated with the case of Asian Americans. In N. Zane, G. Bernal, & F. T. L. Leong (Eds.), *Cultural, racial, and ethnic psychology book series. Evidence-based psychological practice with ethnic minorities: Culturally informed research and clinical strategies* (pp. 57–74). American Psychological Association.

Lustig, S. L., Kureshi, S., Delucchi, K. L., Iacopino, V., & Morse, S. C. (2008). Asylum grant rates following medical evaluations of maltreatment among political asylum applicants in the United States. *Journal of Immigrant and Minority Health, 10*(1), 7–15.

Marshall, R. D., Olfson, M., Hellman, F., Blanco, C., Guardino, M., & Struening, E. L. (2001). Comorbidity, impairment, and suicidality in subthreshold PTSD. *The American Journal of Psychiatry, 158*(9), 1467–1473.

Marouf, F. E. (2014). Incompetent but deportable: The case for a right to mental competence in removal proceedings. *Hastings Law Journal, 65,* 929–998.

McKinnon, S. L. (2009). Citizenship and the performance of credibility: Audiencing gender-based asylum seekers in U.S. immigration courts. *Text and Performance Quarterly, 29,* 205–221.

Meffert, S. M., Musalo, K., McNiel, D. E., & Binder, R. L. (2010). The role of mental health professionals in political asylum processing. *Journal of the American Academy of Psychiatry and the Law, 38*(4), 479–489.

Melton, G. B., Petrila, J., Poythress, N. G., Slobogin, C., Otto, R. K., Mossman, D., & Condie, L. O. (2018). *Psychological evaluations for the courts: A handbook for mental health professionals and lawyers.* Guilford Press.

Morgan, C. A. (2007). Psychiatric evaluations of asylum seekers: Is it ethical practice or advocacy? *Psychiatry 4*(4), 26–33.

Ochoa, K. C., Pleasants, G. L., Penn, J. V., & Stone, D. C. (2010). Disparities in justice and care: Persons with severe mental illnesses in the U.S. immigration detention system. *Journal of the American Academy of Psychiatry and the Law, 38*(3), 392–399.

Office of Planning, Analysis & Technology. 2013. FY 2012: Statistical year book. U.S. Department of Justice. http://www.justice.gov/eoir/statspub/fy12syb.pdf.

Office of the United Nations High Commissioner for Human Rights. (2004). *Manual on the effective investigation and documentation of torture and other cruel, inhuman or degrading treatment or punishment.* https://www.ohchr.org/Documents/Publications/training8Rev1en.pdf

Pew Research Center. (2019, July 2). *Facts on U.S. Immigrants, 2017.* https://www.pewhispanic.org/2019/06/03/facts-on-u-s-immigrants/

Phase I. (2013, December 31). Plan to provide enhanced procedural protections to unrepresented detained respondents with mental disorders. http://immigrationreports.files.wordpress.com/2014/01/eoir-phase-i-guidance.pdf

Prabhu, M., & Baranoski, M. (2012). Forensic mental health professionals in the immigration process. *Psychiatric Clinics of North America, 35*(4), 929–946.

Roesch, R., & Zapf, P. A. (Eds.). (2013). *Forensic assessments in criminal and civil law: A handbook for lawyers.* Oxford University Press.

Rojas-Flores, L., Clements, M. L., Hwang Koo, J., & London, J. (2017). Trauma and psychological distress in Latino citizen children following parental detention and deportation. *Psychological Trauma: Theory, Research, Practice, and Policy, 9*(3), 352–361.

Schultz, I. Z. (2003). Psychological causality determination in personal injury and worker's compensation contexts. In I. Z. Schultz & D. O. Brady (Eds.), *Psychological injuries at trial* (pp. 102–125). American Bar Association.

Shapiro, D. L. (2014). *Development of a competency assessment instrument for deportation proceedings* [Conference session abstract]. 122nd American Psychological Association Annual Convention, Washington, DC. https://doi.org/10.1037/e542302014-001

Shapiro, D. L., & Walker, L. E. (2019). *Forensic practice for the mental health clinician.* TPI Press.

Sidhu, S. S., & Boodoo, R. (2017). U.S. case law and legal precedent affirming the due process rights of immigrants fleeing persecution. *Journal of the American Academy of Psychiatry and the Law, 45*(3), 365–373.

Steel, J. L., Dunlavy, A. C., Harding, C. E., & Theorell, T. (2017). The psychological consequences of pre-emigration trauma and post-migration stress in refugees and immigrants from Africa. *Journal of Immigrant and Minority Health, 19*(3), 523–532.

Vallières, F., Ceannt, R., Daccache, F., Abou Daher, R., Sleiman, J., Gilmore, B., Byrne, S., Shevlin, M., Murphy, J., & Hyland, P. (2018). ICD-11 PTSD and omplex PTSD amongst Syrian refugees in Lebanon: The factor structure and the clinical utility of the International Trauma Questionnaire. *Acta Psychiatrica Scandinavica, 138*(6), 547–557.

Varela J. G., Boccaccini, M. T., Gonzalez, J. E.,Gharagozioo, L., & Johnson, S. M. (2011). Do defense attorney referrals for competence to stand trial evaluations depend on whether the client speaks English or Spanish? *Law and Human Behavior, 35*(6), 501–511.

Weiss, R. A., & Rosenfeld, B. (2012). Navigating cross-cultural issues in forensic assessment: Recommendations for practice. *Professional Psychology: Research and Practice, 43*(3), 234–240.

Weiss, R. A., & Rosenfeld, B. (2017). Identifying feigning in trauma-exposed African immigrants. *Psychological Assessment, 29*(7), 881–889.

Wilson, A., Prokop, N. H., & Robins, S. (2015). Addressing all heads of the hydra: Reframing safeguards for mentally impaired detainees in immigration removal proceedings. *New York Review of Law & Social Change, 39*, 313–368.

World Health Organization. (2018). *International classification of diseases for mortality and morbidity statistics* (11th rev.). World Health Organization. https://icd.who.int/browse11/l-m/en

Wylonis, N. T., & Billick, S. B. (2021). Child and adolescent forensic psychiatry examination and analysis of U.S. citizen children with illegal immigrant parents facing deportation. *Psychiatric Quarterly, 92*(1), 397–406. https://doi.org/10.1007/s11126-020-09801-x

Forensic Mental Health Assessments in Juvenile Justice Contexts

Christopher M. King, Lauren Grove, Sarah Hitchcock, Kenny Gonzalez, Amanda Palardy, *and* Nicole Guevara

Abstract

Psychologists, criminologists, lawyers, and other professionals have made and continue to make important contributions to the structure and functioning of the juvenile justice system in the United States. Within the modern-day juvenile justice system—which generally seeks to be developmentally sensitive and balanced as to accountability and rehabilitation—several issues arise in the processing and management of youth's cases in juvenile and criminal courts that prompt referrals for forensic mental health assessments. These referred evaluations inform preadjudication (transfer to or from adult court and competence to proceed), adjudication (waiver of *Miranda* rights and reliability of confession evidence), and postadjudication decision-making (juvenile disposition or adult sentencing). This chapter reviews seminal and contemporary research and legal precedent as relevant to these juvenile forensic mental health assessments. In addition, future directions for research, policy, and best practice are discussed.

Key Words: juveniles, juvenile justice, family court, forensic mental health assessment, juvenile transfer, juvenile dispositions

In the United States, justice and social service systems have long been tasked with differentially responding to and managing cases of youth involved in crime—including prior to the existence of a formal, distinct juvenile justice system (e.g., Heilbrun et al., 2017). Since the advent of juvenile courts circa the early twentieth century, practicing psychologists and other mental health professionals have played an important role with justice-involved youth (e.g., Melton et al., 2018). So too have the circumstances of such youth long been of interest to criminologists, experimental psychologists, and other professionals, who have made important contributions to evidence-based public policies (e.g., recent US Supreme Court cases concerning juvenile interrogations and sentencing) and to individual cases as nonevaluating expert witnesses.

Today, juvenile defendants may be referred for one or more of several primary types of forensic mental health assessments (FMHAs) relevant to preadjudication case management (transfer to or from adult court and competence to proceed), adjudication (admissibility of self-incriminating evidence), and postadjudication management (juvenile disposition or adult sentencing; e.g., Grisso, 2013). This chapter summarizes seminal and contemporary research and legal precedent bearing on each of these juvenile FMHAs in the United States, while also highlighting limitations in the evidence base in need of further research, areas of legal vagueness in need of shifts in policy, and best practice resources. The matters of juvenile diversion and detention prior to adjudication, status offense cases, and mental state defenses are beyond the scope of this chapter, since these issues are less often referred to psychologists for FMHAs.

Research Review

Fortunately, reasonably sized bodies of research have developed relevant to the different types of juvenile FMHAs discussed in this chapter. Nonetheless, some pressing future directions are also highlighted.

Transfer

Notwithstanding the advent of juvenile courts around the turn of the twentieth century, the cases of some justice-involved youth were and continue to be processed in adult court (e.g., Griffin et al., 2011). There are several mechanisms by which a juvenile's case may be transferred to criminal court. The annual estimate of youth transferred to adult court via any mechanism, circa the start of the twenty-first century, approached 200,000 (American Bar Association Criminal Justice Section, 2001). Though this number has likely fallen somewhat since then (see Office of Juvenile Justice and Delinquency Prevention [OJJDP], 2020, for such a trend for one mechanism, judicial waiver). The prevalence of transfer FMHAs is unclear. Although an international survey of forensic mental health practitioners (45 percent from the United States) found that transfer was rarely endorsed (less than 1 percent) as one of the two most recently evaluated referral questions (Neal & Grisso, 2014), a survey of forensic psychologists found that, among those who had conducted juvenile risk assessments, 53 percent had done so for transfer evaluations (Viljoen et al., 2010a).

An analysis of multijurisdictional data revealed a complex picture of the relationship between different transfer mechanisms and sentencing outcomes for juveniles in adult court (Zane, 2017). And a meta-analysis of transfer studies found that transfer overall was not significantly related to recidivism (Zane, Welsh, & Mears, 2016). However, subgroup analyses suggested that transfer was associated with increased odds of violent recidivism, and that the judicial waiver mechanism was associated with increased odds of any recidivism. Though the potential for uncontrolled selection effects (such as transferred youth potentially being higher risk than retained youth) clouded the interpretation of these latter effects. Another meta-analysis found that race was not significantly related to transfer, though this finding was interpreted with caution, in part due to sizable heterogeneity among the contributing studies (Zane, Welsh, & Drakulich, 2016).

A recent study of juveniles from one state found that gender predicted judicial waiver (males being more likely to be waived than females); interactive effects between gender and race were also observed (Bryson & Peck, 2020). Another study found similar demographic effects for sentence severity among transferred youth in a different state (Lehmann et al., 2017). A longitudinal study of youth in detention in one large city found high rates of mental health disorders among both transferred and nontransferred youth; demographic variables that yielded increased odds of transfer (males, minority youth, older age); and a relationship between externalizing disorders and comorbid internalizing disorders, on the one hand, and receipt of a harsher sentence, on the other (Washburn et al., 2008). Another longitudinal study of justice-involved boys from two large cities in two states found that transfer predicted worse employment outcomes at seven-year follow-up, owing to reduced time in the community, but slightly better educational outcomes (Sharlein, 2018).

Randall Salekin was responsible for a line of seminal transfer research with particular relevance to FMHA. These studies, which analyzed surveys conducted with child psychologists, forensic psychologists, and juvenile court judges, collectively helped to refine a three-factor model of functional legal capacities for transfer FMHAs, consisting of risk, developmental maturity and criminal sophistication, and amenability to treatment (Salekin et al., 2001; Salekin et al., 2002). The model lent itself to validation in the form of a specialized forensic assessment tool for transfer evaluations, the Risk–Sophistication–Treatment Inventory (RSTI; Salekin, 2004; see also Ang et al., 2018; Gillen et al., 2015). As risk is considered one of the key psycholegal factors in transfer evaluations, the performance of juvenile risk assessment tools is of note. Several meta-analyses have examined the predictive validity of such tools in general (e.g., Olver et al., 2009). All available meta-analyses found that juvenile risk assessment tools generally demonstrated statistically significant and clinically meaningful predictive utility. Though in a survey of forensic psychologists who had conducted juvenile risk assessments, only 61 percent always or almost always used risk assessment tools (Viljoen et al., 2010a).

Competence

Juveniles must be competent to proceed to trial in adult court (Wall et al., 2018), and typically also to proceed to adjudication in juvenile court (Juvenile Justice Geography, Policy, Practice & Statistics [JJGPS], n.d.-b). Surveys of legal professionals have found that the competence issue is raised in juvenile cases with some regularity, though there may be strategic reasons or legal barriers that cut against it (Bryant et al., 2015; NeMoyer et al., 2018; Viljoen et al., 2010b). Data from one state indicated that although the total number of delinquency cases declined by about 25 percent from 2006 to 2011, the number of juveniles found incompetent per every 1,000 delinquency cases remained fairly stable (e.g., from 5 of 1,000 to 7 of 1,000; Florida Legislature, 2013). Results of an international survey of forensic mental health practitioners suggest that referrals for juvenile competence FMHAs are common (Neal & Grisso, 2014).

A seminal study concerning the competence abilities of youth of differing ages found that those age fifteen or younger scored significantly worse, and showed elevated rates of impairments, on an adult competence assessment tool relative to older adolescents and young adults (Grisso et al., 2003). This pattern of effects was especially true among detained youth (vs. youth in the community) and youth with lower levels of intellectual functioning. Moreover, younger adolescents also tended to evidence more indicators of legally relevant developmental immaturity. Significant effects were not, however, observed for prior experience with the legal system or mental health problems. A subsequent study did not find sizable differences as to the competence abilities of adolescents ages 16–17 whose cases were processed in adult court versus juvenile court, or in comparison to justice-involved young adults (Poythress et al., 2006). Other studies have yielded similar results as to age and cognitive functioning, though some studies have also found effects for certain mental health symptoms and time spent with attorneys, among other variables (Cunningham, 2020; Viljoen & Roesch, 2005).

In one state, a high rate of agreement between evaluators and judges as to juvenile competence was observed (Kruh et al., 2006). Surveys of juvenile forensic psychologists and juvenile and criminal court judges found some variability as to which components of FMHAs for juvenile competence are deemed most important (Viljoen et al., 2008). However, all three groups roughly agreed as to the essentialness of reporting information about current mental status, understanding of charges and penalties, opinions about mental illness and competence abilities, and ultimate opinions about competence. A review of juvenile competence reports by forensic mental health professionals in one state found that most evaluators' reports addressed the factors in the local competency standard, but many did not offer clear or thorough descriptions of the employed assessments techniques or examinees' clinical and legally relevant functioning, or provide mandated opinions about the ultimate question of incompetence and its cause (Christy et al., 2004). Promisingly, a study of mental health professionals participating in a certification program required to conduct juvenile FMHAs in that jurisdiction found that the practitioners' final reports showed improvements relative to their mid-training reports, on which they had received feedback about deficiencies (DiCataldo et al., 2020).

Researchers have examined which traditional clinical measures forensic mental health professionals use in their juvenile competence evaluations (e.g., Ryba et al., 2003). In addition, use of a structured interview for juvenile competence, the Juvenile Adjudicative Competence Interview (JACI; Grisso, 2005), has seemingly become common in practice (Neal & Grisso, 2014). A study found that age, intellectual functioning, and certain mental health disorders related to the competence abilities opinions of evaluators who used the JACI (Lexcen & Heavin, 2010).

Four states have been identified with well-established juvenile remediation programs (Heilbrun et al., 2016). A study conducted in one of these states found that 65 percent of surveyed judges had previously ordered a juvenile to competence remediation services (Jackson et al., 2014). The results also indicated that youth were generally satisfied with the remediation services received, though the satisfaction of legal professionals appeared more mixed. A subsequent report indicated that a majority of youth received community-based remediation services, and that a large majority of cases were disposed of (i.e., a determination of remediation, unrestorability, or dismissal) within six months (Warren et al., 2019). Data from another state indicated that costs decreased for community-based remediation programs and increased for residential remediation programs between 2002 and 2011 (Florida Legislature, 2013). Over the same time period, the average residential length of stay decreased by twenty days, the number of hours of services received in community-based programs decreased, and the time spent in community-based programs increased (from an average of seven to fifteen months).

Studies have found that most youth in remediation programs achieve competence, though lower levels of intellectual functioning lessen rates of successful remediation (e.g., Chien et al., 2016). Results have been mixed with respect to age (McGaha et al., 2001; Warren et al., 2019). Regarding reoffending, data from one state indicated that 7 percent of youth originally referred for remediation services were subsequently rereferred (Warren et al., 2019). Overrepresentation of minority youth in remediation programs has been reported for two jurisdictions (Jackson, 2018; Warren et al., 2019).

Miranda *Waiver and False Confessions*

Cases involving self-incriminating evidence may prompt referrals for FMHAs concerning youth's capacities to have waived their *Miranda* rights, and factors bearing on the reliability of youth's admissions or confession. It has long been evident that juveniles waive their *Miranda* rights at very high rates (e.g., Ferguson & Douglas, 1970), and research using different methodologies continues to replicate this finding (e.g., Cleary & Vidal, 2016). This is true even though studies of recorded police interrogations have found that police officers often deliver *Miranda* warnings in a neutral manner, rather than deemphasizing or emphasizing the importance of those warnings (e.g., Feld, 2013). The frequency of referrals for evaluations of juveniles' *Miranda* waivers is less clear. An international survey of forensic mental health professionals with a significant minority of respondents from the United States found that *Miranda* rights evaluations were the least likely of all examined referral questions to have been endorsed as one of the two most recently evaluated (Neal & Grisso, 2014). However, in another survey of forensic psychologists about juvenile competence evaluations, 11 percent reported using a specialized forensic assessment instrument for *Miranda* rights (Ryba et al., 2003), and yet another survey of forensic psychologists found that about 25 percent reported conducting *Miranda* evaluations (Ryba et al., 2007).

A sizable body of literature has developed concerning juveniles and *Miranda* rights. Early seminal research concerning juveniles' capacities as to *Miranda* rights was conducted by Grisso (1981), who found that youth age fourteen and below, and older youth with lower levels of intellectual functioning, had elevated rates of *Miranda*-related functional impairments. Subsequent studies have replicated these findings with respect to age and intellectual functioning (Grisso et al., 2003; Zelle et al., 2015). Some research has identified other factors that relate to *Miranda* capacities, such as psychosocial maturity, prior experience with the justice system, and race (Grisso, 1981; Rogers et al., 2014; Sharf et al., 2017a; Viljoen & Roesch, 2005).

Researchers have also examined the language demands presented by variable juvenile *Miranda* warnings, finding sizable jurisdictional variability as to the content, length, and reading level required of different warnings used by law enforcement (e.g., Rogers et al., 2012). Since police might deliver *Miranda* warnings in verbal, written, or hybrid formats (Cleary & Vidal, 2016), recent research examined these three modalities and easy and moderate warning complexity (Rogers et al., 2016). It was found that easy, written warnings slightly outperformed the other two formats for both immediate and delayed recall, though recall of *Miranda* warnings was poor (about 40 percent of key information or less) across the formats and warning difficulties.

Research on the susceptibility of juveniles to false admissions or confessions overlaps somewhat with juvenile *Miranda* research, though it is a distinct issue, both legally and scientifically (Frumkin, 2014). Seminal research examined cases of proven false confessions and found that a significant minority of cases involved juveniles (Drizen & Leo, 2004). Later studies of exonerees found that younger juveniles were especially likely to have falsely confessed (Gross & Schaffer, 2012; Tepfer et al., 2010). In an amicus brief filed in the case of *Dassey v. Dittman*, which was appealed to the US Supreme Court in 2018[1] (though the Court did not take up the case), the American Psychological Association (APA) and other professional organizations stressed that available research indicated that certain interrogation techniques (fabricating or exaggerating the strength of inculpatory evidence or downplaying the seriousness of the situation the accused is in) increase the risk of false confessions for both juveniles and adults; lower intelligence is a risk factor for false confessions; and juveniles are more likely than adults to falsely confess due to immaturity and vulnerability to pressure (see Kassin et al., 2010).

A validated specialized forensic assessment tool for *Miranda* waivers, with adult and youth norms, is available in the form of the *Miranda* Rights Comprehension Instruments (MRCI; Goldstein et al., 2014), though some have pointed out some limitations of the tool (Frumkin & Sellbom, 2013). A new Juvenile Miranda Quiz (JMQ; Sharf et al., 2017b) has also demonstrated promise. Recent research has also found that justice-involved juveniles were readily able to feign impairment on the MRCI and JMQ, with additional analyses suggesting promising feigning detection strategies embedded within these tools (Rogers et al., 2018). In addition, the Gudjonsson Suggestibility Scales (GSS;

---

[1] Brief for American Psychological Association et al., as Amicus Curiae Supporting Petitioner, Dassey v. Dittman, 138 S. Ct. 2677 (2018) (No. 17–1172).

Gudjonsson, 1997) and Gudjonsson Compliance Scale (GCS; Gudjonsson, 1989) are also available for the assessment of suggestibility and acquiescence as relevant totality-of-the-circumstances factors bearing on youth's capacities for waiving their *Miranda* rights, and vulnerability to a disingenuous admission or confession.

Disposition and Sentencing

The US Supreme Court specifically appealed to social science research[2] (Steinberg & Scott, 2003) in deciding that those who committed crimes as juveniles could not be sentenced to death. The effect this research has had on the Court, at least for severe sanctioning, has resulted in the characterization of contemporary juvenile justice jurisprudence as reflecting a developmental or rehabilitative era (National Research Council, 2013; Salekin, 2015). The Court has been persuaded that juveniles are generally more impulsive and less skilled in regulating emotions, more risk-prone and biased toward short-term versus long-term consequences, less self-reliant and more susceptible to the influence of others, less empathically skilled, and more transient in their personalities (Melton et al., 2018). Other current mission descriptors or recommendations for juvenile justice include balanced and restorative justice, evidence-based justice, and preventive justice (Howell et al., 2019; National Campaign to Reform State Juvenile Justice Systems, 2013; Slobogin & Fondacaro, 2011). All reflect insights gleaned from the risk–need–responsivity (RNR) model (Bonta & Andrews, 2017).

Meta-analytic evidence concerning whether jurisdictions' adoption of risk assessment tools reduce secure placements following adjudication is mixed (Viljoen et al., 2019). Data also suggest that demographic disparities are evident in juvenile dispositions and sentences (e.g., National Research Council, 2013), but meta-analytic evidence is currently mixed about the influence of risk assessment tools on such disparities (Viljoen et al., 2019). Meta-analyses have found that well-conceived treatment programs for justice-involved youth tend to reduce recidivism, including more sizable effects for programs that target higher-risk youth and criminogenic needs (Dowden & Andrews, 1999; Lipsey, 2009). Longitudinal research has cast doubt on the effects of custodial sanctions on recidivism at four-year follow-up over community-based alternatives (Loughran et al., 2009), though meta-analytic evidence suggests that the effects of custodial versus community-based treatment programs may be nuanced (Lipsey, 2009). Treatment programs for juveniles who commit sex offenses have yielded promising meta-analytic results (Kettrey & Lipsey, 2018). Regarding the risk of youth facing potential commitment as sexually dangerous persons, youth who received such a petition did not differ in rates of sexual recidivism at approximately five-year follow-up relative to youth who were screened out of commitment proceedings (Caldwell, 2013).

---

[2] Brief for American Psychological Association & Missouri Psychological Association, as Amicus Curiae Supporting Respondent, Roper v. Simmons, 543 U.S. 551 (2005) (No. 03–633).

Research Limitations

Examples of limitations in the available research that inform juvenile FMHAs include the following. For transfer, more studies with strong matching designs are needed about the long-term effects of differential case management decisions, and choices for specialized measures of sophistication–maturity and treatment amenability are limited. For competence, a juvenile-specific competence tool and juvenile remediation programs have been understudied, and research on the competence abilities of juveniles in the context of guilty pleas has only recently been emerging. For *Miranda* waiver and false confessions, the frequency and quality of FMHAs in juvenile cases involving self-incriminating evidence is unclear, and independent validations of the JMQ and the MRCI would be helpful. For disposition and sentencing, the extent to which access to community-based rehabilitation is equitable across demographic groups is unclear (which may partially account for mixed findings about differential performance of some juvenile risk assessment tools across demographic groups), and meta-analytic evidence is needed concerning the effects of tailoring treatment to justice-involved youth's various personal and environmental circumstances.

Relevant Legal Precedent

Each of the juvenile FMHAs discussed in this chapter have some seminal legal precedent available for broad guidance. However, some legal issues in need of research are also highlighted.

Transfer

The seminal US Supreme Court case concerning juvenile transfer is *Kent v. United States*,[3] which held that juvenile defendants have certain procedural due process rights in judicial waiver hearings. The Court also included as an appendix a policy memorandum from the District of Columbia that set forth a listing of eight legal and psycholegal factors to be considered by a juvenile court judge contemplating waiver in Washington, DC. While the waiver criteria were not mandatory for other jurisdictions to adopt, the listing proved influential for most jurisdictions (King, 2018; Salekin et al., 2016). The Court also held in *Breed v. Jones*[4] that a juvenile cannot be waived to adult court after an adjudication on the merits in juvenile court, as such runs afoul of the prohibition against double jeopardy.

One or more transfer mechanisms are available in all US jurisdictions (Juvenile Justice Geography, Policy, Practice & Statistics, n.d.-a; Office of Juvenile Justice and Delinquency Prevention, 2020). Legislatively, jurisdictions may exclude by statute certain cases from juvenile court jurisdiction based on age and offense criteria, and some have "once an adult, always an adult" laws, which require youth who were convicted or sanctioned as adults to be processed in adult court for later cases. Executive-branch decision-making may be employed in the form of laws that grant prosecutors the discretion (structured or

---

[3] Kent v. United States, 383 U.S. 541 (1966).
[4] Breed v. Jones, 421 U.S. 519 (1975).

unstructured) to directly file cases in either juvenile or adult court, with both systems having concurrent jurisdiction over certain cases based on combinations of age and offense criteria. Prosecutors may also charge youth or direct grand juries in certain ways in light of offense-related statutory exclusion criteria. Judicial transfer mechanisms include juvenile waiver, whereby a juvenile court judge may or must waive jurisdiction discretionarily, presumptively, or mandatorily based on certain criteria. A significant minority of jurisdictions also utilize reverse waiver, whereby an adult court judge may or must return a case to juvenile court based on certain criteria. Finally, blended sentencing provisions, such as extended jurisdiction, suspended sentencing, and youthful offender laws, may empower juvenile or adult court judges to impose different permutations of juvenile and adult sanctions.

Competence

Juveniles whose cases are transferred to adult court must be competent to proceed to the determination of guilt pursuant to adult standards and rules, and some states require that competence be determined at the same time as a transfer decision (Larson & Grisso, 2011). The US Supreme Court has decided several cases that set the standard for competence to proceed in adult court. In *Dusky v. United States*,[5] the Court promulgated the understand and assist standard for competence to stand trial, the satisfaction of which also empowers a defendant to knowingly, intelligently, and voluntarily waive the right to counsel,[6] and to plead guilty.[7] However, when a defendant's competency at trial is contingent upon being represented by counsel, a court can require that a defendant have the assistance of an attorney.[8] A defendant remanded for competence restoration can only be held for a reasonable period of time to determine whether there is a substantial probability of restoration within the foreseeable future.[9]

Competence to proceed in juvenile court was originally rationalized to be irrelevant given the juvenile court's alignment with a *parens patriae* philosophy (Larson & Grisso, 2011). However, evolving recognition of the often-harsh consequences facing juveniles in that system gave rise to the requirement that youth be afforded some procedural protections in juvenile court.[10] Most jurisdictions have a competence standard for juveniles—either a particularized one for juveniles (that may be somewhat relaxed as to requisite abilities) or one parallel to the adult standard (Juvenile Justice Geography, Policy, Practice & Statistics, n.d.-b; Panza et al., 2020). However, fewer jurisdictions have explicitly expanded the scope of a qualifying condition for incompetence from a mental health disorder to developmental immaturity (Juvenile Justice Geography, Policy, Practice & Statistics, n.d.-b; Panza et al., 2020).

---

[5] Dusky v. United States, 362 U.S. 402 (1960).
[6] Faretta v. California, 422 U.S. 806 (1975).
[7] Godinez v. Moran, 509 U.S. 389 (1993).
[8] Indiana v. Edwards, 554 U.S. 164 (2008).
[9] Jackson v. Indiana, 406 U.S. 715 (1972).
[10] See *In re* Gault, 387 U.S. 1 (1967).

Miranda *Waiver and False Confessions*

Individuals subjected to interrogation may waive their rights to the assistance of an attorney and to remain silent when in the custody of law enforcement or their proxy. But only after first being apprised of those and related rights. If the accused is not so warned, or the waiver of rights is not otherwise knowing, intelligent, and voluntary, the remedy may be suppression of evidence stemming from the interrogation, as held by the US Supreme Court in the 1966 case of *Miranda v. Arizona* and its progeny[11] (e.g., the juvenile case of *Fare v. Michael C*[12]).

The *Miranda* protections were explicitly extended to youth in juvenile court in the US Supreme Court case of In re *Gault*;[13] the Court therein also referenced its prior special concerns about the reliability and voluntary nature of juvenile confessions.[14] The triggering event for the need for *Miranda* protections is custodial interrogation, and the Supreme Court has held that a youth's age is an appropriate consideration in determining, under the totality of the circumstances, whether a reasonable youth would not have felt free to leave.[15] In *J. D. B.*, the Court continued to note its concerns about the risk of false confessions, especially among juveniles, and included references to false confession research beyond just the Court's prior anecdotal observations (e.g., Drizin & Leo, 2004). Some jurisdictions have implemented special custodial interrogation procedures for juveniles, such as adding juvenile-specific *Miranda* warnings (e.g., about the possibility of transfer to adult court), requiring the presence of an interested adult during interrogation (e.g., a parent or legal guardian), and videotaping interrogations (International Association of Chiefs of Police, 2012; Rogers et al., 2008).

One defense strategy for coping with self-incriminating evidence is to challenge the admissibility of evidence stemming from a *Miranda* waiver that was not made knowingly, intelligently, or voluntarily. But even if a waiver is determined to have been valid, the US Supreme Court held in *Crane v. Kentucky*[16] that a defendant must still be permitted to challenge the credibility of that evidence at trial. However, a review of lower court opinions identified a split among courts as to the admissibility of expert testimony concerning false confessions (Frumkin, 2014).

Disposition and Sentencing

Seminal US Supreme Court decisions have held that those convicted of crimes committed while minors can neither be sentenced to death[17] nor mandatory life without parole.[18] Furthermore, adults who were earlier sentenced to mandatory life without parole for

---

[11] Miranda v. Arizona, 384 U.S. 436 (1966).
[12] Fare v. Michael C., 442 U.S. 707 (1979).
[13] *In re* Gault, 387 U.S. 1 (1967).
[14] Gallegos v. Colorado, 370 U.S. 49 (1962); Haley v. Ohio, 332 U.S. 596 (1948).
[15] J. D. B. v. North Carolina, 564 U.S. 261 (2011).
[16] Crane v. Kentucky, 476 U.S. 683 (1986).
[17] Roper v. Simmons, 543 U.S. 551 (2005).
[18] Miller v. Alabama, 567 U.S. 460 (2012).

crimes committed while minors must be resentenced.[19] But it was recently decided that a court making a discretionary decision about whether to sentence someone to life without parole, for a crime committed while they were a juvenile, only need generally take youthfulness into account, rather than making an explicit or implicit finding on the record that the individual is permanently incorrigible.[20] Beyond these two types of especially severe sentences, youth can receive a sentence in adult court or a disposition in juvenile court (or a conditional suspended sentence or disposition) involving a wide range of community-based (e.g., referral for treatment services, community service, restitution and fines, probation) or custodial (out-of-home) sanctions or monitoring options (e.g., Salekin, 2015).

Moreover, in sex offense cases, juveniles in a few jurisdictions may be included within the scope of commitment laws for sexually dangerous persons and indeterminately civilly committed (DeMatteo et al., 2015). Evidentiary rules are typically relaxed at sentencing and disposition hearings, relative to adjudication, and the amount of discretion afforded the sentencer, while frequently broad, may carry some limits in different jurisdictions (Heilbrun et al., 2017). There are also jurisdictional age limits (often extending a few years beyond age 18) for dispositions meted out in juvenile court, with some flexibility afforded by blended sentencing laws (Juvenile Justice Geography, Policy, Practice & Statistics, n.d.-a). Many jurisdictions indicate that rehabilitation is one of the purposes of their juvenile justice system—as part of an overall *parens patriae* or balanced and restorative justice mission—which translates to various dispositional policies and practices in juvenile court meant to further that aim (Juvenile Justice Geography, Policy, Practice & Statistics, n.d.-b). Rehabilitation is also often regarded as one of the purposes of adult sentencing (Branham, 2017).

Existing and Emerging Legal Questions

For transfer, more research is needed about how judges and prosecutors weigh different transfer factors that statutes or other policies direct them to consider. Moreover, the extent to which competence is addressed in juvenile court and the standards for such a requirement—including whether developmental immaturity is regarded as a qualifying condition (including in adult court)—remains unclear. For *Miranda* waivers and confessions, how jurisdictions have adapted to the US Supreme Court's decision in *J. D. B.* (i.e., that the age of a juvenile suspect must be considered in the *Miranda* custodial analysis) is not yet clear. More research is also needed about the extent to which other protective mechanisms that jurisdictions have implemented for juvenile interrogations impact rights waivers and admissions and confessions. Similarly, the practical consequences of the split among lower courts as to the admissibility of expert testimony about risks for unreliable confession evidence are in need of study. For disposition and sentencing, the extent to which the US Supreme Court's reasoning in *Roper* and its progeny has been extended or

---

[19] Montgomery v. Louisiana, 136 S. Ct. 718 (2016).
[20] Jones v. Mississippi, 141 S. Ct. 1307 (2021).

limited by lower courts for less severe sanctions is in need of clarification. Relatedly, more research is needed about the extent to which judges in adult court versus juvenile court are sensitive to developmental issues.

Implications, Next Steps, and Future Directions

There are many intersections between psychology and juvenile justice, and several matters tend to prompt referrals for juvenile FMHAs. Forensic mental health professionals currently have comprehensive best practices resources available for transfer and disposition and sentencing (e.g., Heilbrun et al., 2017), competence (e.g., Kruh & Grisso, 2009), and *Miranda* waiver (e.g., Goldstein & Goldstein, 2010). Best practice resources are also available for diversion (e.g., Models for Change Juvenile Diversion Workgroup, 2011) and preadjudication detention (e.g., Steinhart, 2006)—though these resources are not directed at mental health professionals per se. Forensic mental health professionals are in need of comprehensive best practice resources for evaluations of false confessions (but see Frumkin, 2014) and mental state defenses (but for adults, see, e.g., Packer, 2009).

These and other best practice resources include numerous policy recommendations for the intersections of psychology and juvenile justice. At a broad level, many of these recommendations relate to the limitations in the current evidence base (e.g., calls for better data tracking and reporting to facilitate further research). Others entail suggestions for policy reforms to target laws or practices in jurisdictions that may be vague or inconsistent with evidence-based solutions. Collectively, they call for a juvenile justice system that continues to evolve in ways that are sensitive to the developmental circumstances presented by youth and in line with evidence-based strategies for responding to such youth.

References

American Bar Association Criminal Justice Section. (2001). *Youth in the criminal justice system: Guidelines for policymakers and practitioners*. American Bar Association.

Ang, X., Salekin, R. T., Sellbom, M., & Coffey, C. A. (2018). Risk-Sophistication-Treatment Inventory-Self Report (RSTI-SR): A confirmatory factor analysis and exploration of factor relations. *Psychological Assessment, 30*(1), 130–142.

Bonta, J., & Andrews, D. A. (2017). *The psychology of criminal conduct* (6th ed.). Routledge.

Branham, L. S. (2017). *The law and policy of sentencing and corrections in a nutshell* (10th ed.). West Academic.

Bryant, A., Matthews, G., & Wilhelmsen, B. (2015). Assessing the legitimacy of competence to stand trial in juvenile court: The practice of CST with and without statutory law. *Criminal Justice Policy Review, 26*(4), 371–399.

Bryson, S. L., & Peck, J. H. (2020). Understanding the subgroup complexities of transfer: The impact of juvenile race and gender on waiver decisions. *Youth Violence and Juvenile Justice, 18*(2), 135–155.

Caldwell, M. F. (2013). Accuracy of sexually violent person assessments of juveniles adjudicated for sexual offenses. *Sexual Abuse: A Journal of Research and Treatment, 25*(5), 516–526.

Chien, J., Coker, K. L., Parke, S., Tejani, N., Sirken, R. A., Sanchez-Jaquez, C., Rausch, F., & Azeem, M. W. (2016). Predictors of competency to stand trial in Connecticut's inpatient juvenile competency restoration program. *Journal of the American Academy of Psychiatry and the Law, 44*(4), 451–456.

Christy, A., Douglas, K. S., Otto, R. K., & Petrila, J. (2004). Juveniles evaluated incompetent to proceed: Characteristics and quality of mental health professionals' evaluations. *Professional Psychology: Research and Practice, 35*(4), 380–388.

Cleary, H. M. D., & Vidal, S. (2016). *Miranda* in actual juvenile interrogations: Delivery, waiver, and readability. *Criminal Justice Review, 41*(1), 98–115.

Cunningham, K. A. (2020). Advances in juvenile adjudicative competence: A 10-year update. *Behavioral Sciences & the Law, 38*(4), 406–420.

DeMatteo, D., Murphy, M., Galloway, M., & Krauss, D. A. (2015). A national survey of United States sexually violent person legislation: Policy, procedures, and practice. *International Journal of Forensic Mental Health, 14*(4), 245–266.

DiCataldo, F., Serafinski, R. L., Beam, D. C., & Grisso, T. (2020). Feedback on forensic mental health assessments in a juvenile court clinic certification program. *Juvenile & Family Court Journal, 71*(4), 35–51.

Dowden, C., & Andrews, D. A. (1999). What works in young offender treatment: A meta-analysis. *Forum on Corrections Research, 11*(2), 21–24.

Drizin, S. A., & Leo, R. A. (2004). The problem of false confessions in the post-DNA world. *North Carolina Law Review, 82*(3), 891–1007.

Feld, B. C. (2013). *Kids, cops, and confessions: Inside the interrogation room.* New York University Press.

Ferguson, A. B., & Douglas, A. C. (1970). A study of juvenile waiver. *San Diego Law Review, 7,* 39–54.

Florida Legislature. (2013). *Juvenile and adult incompetent to proceed cases and costs* (Report No. 13–04). Office of Program Policy Analysis and Government Accountability http://www.oppaga.state.fl.us/MonitorDocs/Reports/pdf/1304rpt.pdf

Frumkin, I. B. (2014). Expert testimony in juvenile and adult alleged false confession cases. *Court Review, 50*(1), 12–19.

Frumkin, I. B., & Sellbom, M. (2013). *Miranda* rights comprehension instruments: A critical review. *Assessment, 20*(5), 545–554.

Gillen, C. T. A., MacDougall, E. A. M., Salekin, R. T., & Forth, A. E. (2015). The validity of the Risk-Sophistication-Treatment Inventory–Abbreviated (RSTI-A): Initial evidence in support of a measure designed for juvenile evaluations. *Psychology, Public Policy, and Law, 21*(2), 205–212.

Goldstein, A., & Goldstein, N. E. S. (2010). *Evaluating capacity to waive* Miranda *rights.* Oxford University Press.

Goldstein, N. E. S., Zelle, H., & Grisso, T. (2014). Miranda *Rights Comprehension Instruments (MRCI): Manual for juvenile and adult evaluations.* Professional Resource Press.

Griffin, P., Addie, S., Adams, B., & Firestine, K. (2011). Trying juveniles as adults: An analysis of state transfer laws and reporting. *Juvenile offenders and victims: National report series.* https://www.ncjrs.gov/pdffiles1/ojjdp/232434.pdf

Grisso, T. (1981). *Juveniles' waiver of rights: Legal and psychological competence.* Springer.

Grisso, T. (2005). *Evaluating juveniles' adjudicative competence: A guide for clinical practice.* Professional Resource Press.

Grisso, T. (2013). *Forensic evaluation of juveniles* (2nd ed.). Professional Resource Press.

Grisso, T., Steinberg, L., Woolard, J., Cauffman, E., Scott, E., Graham, S., Lexcen, F., Reppucci, N. D., & Schwartz, R. (2003). Juveniles' competence to stand trial: A comparison of adolescents' and adults' capacities as trial defendants. *Law and Human Behavior, 27*(4), 333–363.

Gross, S. R., & Shaffer, M. (2012). *Exonerations in the United States, 1989–2012* (University of Michigan Public Law Working Paper No. 277). Retrieved January 15, 2021, from https://papers.ssrn.com/sol3/papers.cfm?abstract_id=2092195

Gudjonsson, G. H. (1989). Compliance in an interrogative situation: A new scale. *Personality and Individual Differences, 10*(5), 535–540.

Gudjonsson, G. H. (1997). *The Gudjonsson Suggestibility Scales manual.* Psychology Press.

Heilbrun, K., DeMatteo, D., & Goldstein, N. E. S. (Eds.). (2016). *APA handbook of psychology and juvenile justice.* American Psychological Association.

Heilbrun, K., DeMatteo, D., King, C., & Filone, S. (2017). *Evaluating juvenile transfer and disposition: Law, science, and practice.* Routledge.

Howell, J. C., Lipsey, M. W., & Wilson, J. J., Howell, M. Q., & Hodges, N. J. (2019). *A handbook for evidence-based juvenile justice systems* (rev. ed.). Lexington Books.

International Association of Chiefs of Police. (2012). *Reducing risks: An executive's guide to effective juvenile interview and interrogation.* International Association of Chiefs of Police. https://www.theiacp.org/sites/default/files/all/p-r/ReducingRisksAnExecutiveGuidetoEffectiveJuvenileInterviewandInterrogation.pdf

Jackson, S. L. (2018). Juvenile competency law and remediation programming: Santa Clara County's experience replicating the Virginia model. *Journal of Applied Juvenile Justice Services, 2018,* 54–74.

Jackson, S. L., Warren, J. I., & Coburn, J. J. (2014). A community-based model for remediating juveniles adjudicated incompetent to stand trial: Feedback from youth, attorneys, and judges. *Juvenile & Family Court Journal, 65*(2), 23–38.

Juvenile Justice Geography, Policy, Practice & Statistics. (n.d.-a). *Jurisdictional boundaries.* Juvenile Justice, Geography, Policy, Practice & Statistics. Retrieved October 26, 2020, from http://www.jjgps.org/jurisdictional-boundaries

Juvenile Justice Geography, Policy, Practice & Statistics. (n.d.-b). *Juvenile court.* Juvenile Justice, Geography, Policy, Practice & Statistics. Retrieved January 15, 2021, from http://www.jjgps.org/juvenile-court

Kassin, S. M., Drizin, S. A., Grisso, T., Gudjonsson, G. H., Leo, R. A., & Redlich, A. D. (2010). Police-induced confessions: Risk factors and recommendations. *Law and Human Behavior, 34*(1), 3–38.

Kettrey, H. H., & Lipsey, M. W. (2018). The effects of specialized treatment on the recidivism of juvenile sex offenders: a systematic review and meta-analysis. *Journal of Experimental Criminology, 14*(3), 361–387.

King, C. M. (2018). The psycholegal factors for juvenile transfer and reverse transfer evaluations. *Behavioral Sciences & the Law, 36*(1), 46–64. https://doi.org/10.1002/bsl.2298

Kruh, I., & Grisso, T. (2009). *Evaluation of juveniles' competence to stand trial.* Oxford University Press.

Kruh, I. P., Sullivan, L., Ellis, M., Lexcen, F., & McClellan, J. (2006). Juvenile competence to stand trial: A historical and empirical analysis of a juvenile forensic evaluation service. *International Journal of Forensic Mental Health, 5*(2), 109–123.

Larson, K., & Grisso, T. (2011). *Developing statutes for competence to stand trial in juvenile delinquency proceedings: A guide for lawmakers.* Models for Change. http://modelsforchange.net/publications/330/Developing_Statutes_for_Competence_to_Stand_Trial_in_Juvenile_Delinquency_Proceedings_A_Guide_for_Lawmakers.pdf

Lehmann, P. S., Chiricos, T., & Bales, W. D. (2017). Sentencing transferred juveniles in the adult criminal court: The direct and interactive effects of race and ethnicity. *Youth Violence and Juvenile Justice, 15*(2), 172–190.

Lexcen, F., & Heavin, S. (2010). Evaluating for competence to proceed in juvenile court: Findings with a semi-structured interview. *Open Access Journal of Forensic Psychology, 2*, 359–376.

Lipsey, M. W. (2009). The primary factors that characterize effective interventions with juvenile offenders: A meta-analytic overview. *Victims & Offenders, 4*(2), 124–147.

Loughran, T. A., Mulvey, E. P., Schubert, C. A., Fagan, J., Piquero, A. R., & Losoya, S. H. (2009). Estimating a dose-response relationship between length of stay and future recidivism in serious juvenile offenders. *Criminology, 47*(3), 699–740.

McGaha, A., Otto, R. K., McClaren, M. D., & Petrila, J. (2001). Juveniles adjudicated incompetent to proceed: a descriptive study of Florida's Competence Restoration program. *Journal of the American Academy of Psychiatry and the Law, 29*(4), 427–437.

Melton, G. B., Petrila, J., Poythress, N. G., Slobogin, C., Otto, R. K., Mossman, D., & Condie, L. O. (2018). *Psychological evaluations for the courts: A handbook for mental health professionals and lawyers* (4th ed.). Guilford Press.

Models for Change Juvenile Diversion Workgroup. (2011). *Juvenile diversion guidebook.* National Center for Youth Opportunity and Justice. https://ncyoj.policyresearchinc.org/img/resources/Juvenile_Diversion_Guidebook-012652.pdf

National Campaign to Reform State Juvenile Justice Systems. (2013). *The fourth wave: Juvenile justice reforms for the twenty-first century.* Models for Change. http://www.modelsforchange.net/publications/530/The_Fourth_Wave_Juvenile_Justice_Reforms_for_the_TwentyFirst_Century.pdf

National Research Council. (2013). *Reforming juvenile justice: A developmental approach.* National Research Council. Retrieved January 15, 2021, from https://www.nap.edu/catalog/14685/reforming-juvenile-justice-a-developmental-approach

Neal, T. M. S., & Grisso, T. (2014). Assessment practices and expert judgment methods in forensic psychology and psychiatry: An international snapshot. *Criminal Justice and Behavior, 41*(12), 1406–1421.

NeMoyer, A., Kelley, S., Zelle, H., & Goldstein, N. E. S. (2018). Attorney perspectives on juvenile and adult clients' competence to plead guilty. *Psychology, Public Policy, and Law, 24*(2), 171–179.

Office of Juvenile Justice and Delinquency Prevention. (2020). *Statistical briefing book.* U.S. Department of Justice. https://www.ojjdp.gov/ojstatbb/

Olver, M. E., Stockdale, K. C., & Wormith, J. S. (2009). Risk assessment with young offenders: A meta-analysis of three assessment measures. *Criminal Justice and Behavior, 36*(4), 329–353.

Packer, I. B. (2009). *Evaluation of criminal responsibility.* Oxford University Press.

Panza, N. R., Deutsch, E., & Hamann, K. (2020). Statutes governing juvenile competency to stand trial proceedings: An analysis of consistency with best practice recommendations. *Psychology, Public Policy, and Law, 26*(3), 274–285.

Poythress, N., Lexcen, F. J., Grisso, T., & Steinberg, L. (2006). The competence-related abilities of adolescent defendants in criminal court. *Law and Human Behavior, 30*(1), 75–92.

Rogers, R., Blackwood, H. L., Fiduccia, C. E., Steadham, J. A., Drogin, E. Y., & Rogstad, J. E. (2012). Juvenile *Miranda* warnings: Perfunctory rituals or procedural safeguards? *Criminal Justice and Behavior, 39*(3), 229–249.

Rogers, R., Hazelwood, L. L., Sewell, K. W., Shuman, D. W., & Blackwood, H. L. (2008). The comprehensibility and content of juvenile Miranda warnings. *Psychology, Public Policy, and Law, 14*(1), 63–87. https://doi.org/10.1037/a0013102

Rogers, R., Sharf, A. J., Henry, S. A., & Drogin, E. Y. (2018). Feigned *Miranda* impairment by legally involved juveniles: The vulnerability of forensic measures and the development of effective screens. *Criminal Justice and Behavior, 45*(8), 1269–1287.

Rogers, R., Steadham, J. A., Carter, R. M., Henry, S. A., Drogin, E. Y., & Robinson, E. V. (2016). An examination of juveniles' *Miranda* abilities: Investigating differences in *Miranda* recall and reasoning. *Behavioral Sciences & the Law, 34*(4), 515–538.

Rogers, R., Steadham, J. A., Fiduccia, C. E., Drogin, E. Y., & Robinson, E. V. (2014). Mired in *Miranda* misconceptions: A study of legally involved juveniles at different levels of psychosocial maturity. *Behavioral Sciences & the Law, 32*(1), 104–120.

Ryba, N. L., Brodsky, S. L., & Shlosberg, A. (2007). Evaluations of capacity to waive *Miranda* rights: A survey of practitioners' use of the Grisso instruments. *Assessment, 14*(3), 300–309.

Ryba, N. L., Cooper, V. G., & Zapf, P. A. (2003). Juvenile competence to stand trial evaluations: A survey of current practices and test usage among psychologists. *Professional Psychology: Research and Practice, 34*(5), 499–507.

Salekin, R. T. (2004). *Risk–Sophistication–Treatment Inventory (RST-I)*. Psychological Assessment Resources.

Salekin, R. T. (2015). *Forensic evaluation and treatment of juveniles: Innovation and best practice*. American Psychological Association.

Salekin, R. T., Grimes, R. D., & Adams, E. W. (2016). Clinical forensic evaluations for juvenile transfer to adult criminal court. In R. Jackson & R. Roesch (Eds.), *Learning forensic assessment: Research and practice* (pp. 294–323). Routledge.

Salekin, R. T., Rogers, R., & Ustad, K. L. (2001). Juvenile waiver to adult criminal courts: Prototypes for dangerousness, sophistication–maturity, and amenability to treatment. *Psychology, Public Policy, and Law, 7*(2), 381–408.

Salekin, R. T., Yff, R. M. A., Neumann, C. S., Leistico, A.-M. R., & Zalot, A. A. (2002). Juvenile transfer to adult courts: A look at the prototypes for dangerousness sophistication-maturity and amenability to treatment through a legal lens. *Psychology, Public Policy, and Law, 8*(4), 373–410.

Sharf, A. J., Rogers, R., & Williams, M. M. (2017a). Reasoning your way out of *Miranda* rights: How juvenile detainees relinquish their Fifth Amendment protections. *Translational Issues in Psychological Science, 3*(2), 121–130.

Sharf, A. J., Rogers, R., Williams, M. M., & Drogin, E. Y. (2017b). Evaluating juvenile detainees' *Miranda* misconceptions: The discriminant validity of the Juvenile Miranda Quiz. *Psychological Assessment, 29*(5), 556–567.

Sharlein, J. (2018). Beyond recidivism: Investigating comparative educational and employment outcomes for adolescents in the juvenile and criminal justice systems. *Crime & Delinquency, 64*(1), 26–52.

Slobogin, C., & Fondacaro, M. (2011). *Juveniles at risk: A plea for preventive justice*. Oxford University Press.

Steinberg, L., & Scott, E. S. (2003). Less guilty by reason of adolescence: Developmental immaturity, diminished responsibility, and the juvenile death penalty. *American Psychologist, 58*(12), 1009–1018.

Steinhart, D. (2006). *Juvenile detention risk assessment: A practice guide for juvenile detention reform*. Annie E. Casey Foundation. https://www.aecf.org/m/resourcedoc/aecf-juveniledetentionfacilityassessment-2014.pdf

Tepfer, J. A., Nirider, L. H., & Tricarico, L. M. (2010). Arresting development: Convictions of innocent youth. *Rutgers Law Review, 62*, 887–941.

Viljoen, J. L., Jonnson, M. R., Cochrane, D. M., Vargen, L. M., & Vincent, G. M. (2019). Impact of risk assessment instruments on rates of pretrial detention, postconviction placements, and release: A systematic review and meta-analysis. *Law and Human Behavior, 43*(5), 397–420.

Viljoen, J. L., McLachlan, K., & Vincent, G. M. (2010a). Assessing violence risk and psychopathy in juvenile and adult offenders: a survey of clinical practices. *Assessment, 17*(3), 377–395.

Viljoen, J. L., McLachlan, K., Wingrove, T., & Penner, E. (2010b). Defense attorneys' concerns about the competence of adolescent defendants. *Behavioral Sciences & the Law, 28*(5), 630–646.

Viljoen, J. L., & Roesch, R. (2005). Competence to waive interrogation rights and adjudicative competence in adolescent defendants: Cognitive development, attorney contact, and psychological symptoms. *Law and Human Behavior, 29*(6), 723–742.

Viljoen, J. L.., Wingrove, T., & Ryba, N. L. (2008). Adjudicative competence evaluations of juvenile and adult defendants: Judges' views regarding essential components of competence reports. *International Journal of Forensic Mental Health, 7*(2), 107–119.

Wall, B. W., Ash, P., Keram, E., Pinals, D. A., & Thompson, C. H. (2018). AAPL Practice resource for the forensic psychiatric evaluation of competence to stand trial. *Journal of the American Academy of Psychiatry and the Law, 46*(3), 373.

Warren, J. I., Jackson, S. L., Skowysz, B. E., Kiefner, S. E., Reed, J., Leviton, A. C. R., Nacu, M. F., Jiggetts, C. G., & Walls, G. G. (2019). The competency attainment outcomes of 1,913 juveniles found incompetent to stand trial. *Journal of Applied Juvenile Justice Services, 2019*, 54–74.

Washburn, J. J., Teplin, L. A., Voss, L. S., Simon, C. D., Abram, K. M., & McClelland, G. M. (2008). Psychiatric disorders among detained youths: A comparison of youths processed in juvenile court and adult criminal court. *Psychiatric Services, 59*(9), 965–973.

Zane, S. N. (2017). Do criminal court outcomes vary by juvenile transfer mechanism? A multi-jurisdictional, multilevel analysis. *Justice Quarterly, 34*(3), 542–569.

Zane, S. N., Welsh, B. C., & Drakulich, K. M. (2016a). Assessing the impact of race on the juvenile waiver decision: A systematic review and meta-analysis. *Journal of Criminal Justice, 46*, 106–117.

Zane, S. N., Welsh, B. C., & Mears, D. P. (2016b). Juvenile transfer and the specific deterrence hypothesis. *Criminology & Public Policy, 15*(3), 901–925.

Zelle, H., Romaine, C. L. R., & Goldstein, N. E. S. (2015). Juveniles' *Miranda* comprehension: Understanding, appreciation, and totality of circumstances factors. *Law and Human Behavior, 39*(3), 281–293.

Neuropsychological Considerations in Forensic Mental Health Assessment

Casey LaDuke, Chriscelyn M. Tussey, Bernice A. Marcopulos, Scott D. Bender, and Beth C. Arredondo

Abstract

Neuropsychological considerations can arise in any forensic mental health assessment (FMHA), and all practitioners engaging in FMHA will therefore benefit from being able to recognize and respond to neuropsychological issues in their practice. The first section of this chapter focuses on *relevance,* including a discussion of how to recognize neuropsychological consideration in forensic referrals; a summary of the most relevant neuropsychological considerations of a clinical, practical, and legal nature within FMHA; and review of some of the most common brain-based disorders encountered in contemporary forensic practice. The second section focuses on *competence,* including an introduction to general and specialty competencies in neuropsychology, and a further discussion of selected practical concerns in the field. The chapter concludes with guidance on responding to neuropsychological considerations in forensic cases, and introduces a decision-making model to help forensic practitioners consider whether independent evaluation, consultation, or referral is the most effective response in these cases.

Key Words: neuropsychology, forensic mental health assessments, forensic neuropsychology, competence, relevance

Neuropsychological considerations are increasingly common in forensic mental health assessment (FMHA). This is perhaps due to growing recognition that brain injuries and illnesses can help explain behaviors associated with certain criminal offenses, and can be caused by a compensable injury in civil law. *Neuropsychology* refers to the scientific understanding of brain–behavior relationships through the assessment of cognition and behavior, diagnosis of brain-based disorders, and determination of effective interventions and other recommendations (American Psychological Association, 2020). Neuropsychological considerations are not distinct psycholegal questions but rather represent topics that can arise in any forensic evaluation. Psychologists and other mental health practitioners engaging in FMHA will therefore benefit from being able to recognize and respond to neuropsychological issues in their practice.

This chapter is written for practitioners who encounter neuropsychological elements while conducting FMHA.[1] The first section focuses on *relevance* and is informed by a discussion of how to recognize neuropsychological consideration in forensic referrals, a summary of the most relevant neuropsychological considerations within FMHA, and review of some of the most common brain-based disorders encountered in contemporary forensic practice. The second section focuses on *competence*, including an introduction to general and specialty competencies in neuropsychology, and a further discussion of selected practical concerns in the field. The chapter concludes with guidance on responding to neuropsychological considerations in forensic cases, and introduces a decision-making model to help forensic practitioners consider whether independent evaluation, consultation, or referral is the most effective response in these cases.

Relevance

Recognizing Neuropsychological Considerations in Forensic Mental Health Assessment

Neuropsychological considerations are common in civil and criminal forensic contexts. For example, individuals with cognitive disorder make up a significant subset of those being evaluated in cases of competence to stand trial (Arredondo et al., 2017) and mental state at the time of the offense (Gardner et al., 2018). Comprehensive assessment of the validity, scope, and pattern of cognitive deficits may be crucial to inform decisions in civil litigation where a plaintiff is claiming brain injury. In addition to informing specific referral questions, incorporating neuropsychological assessment practices to address performance validity questions can aid in reducing bias by providing a standardized method of assessing performance (Marcopulos et al., 2008), with documented error rates and patterns of performance in different known clinical groups (Boone, 2012; Larrabee, 2012). These are just some of the many examples where neuropsychological practice can inform FMHA.

However, a traditional neuropsychological evaluation is not always necessary to answer psycholegal questions, may not be feasible, or may provide extraneous information not relevant to the specific issue. If a diagnosis and symptom presentation is well established and well documented, for example, assessment of cognitive abilities may not provide an additional explanation of the nexus between the symptoms and the psycholegal question. Further, in situations where the available tests do not include adequate normative comparison groups (e.g., LaDuke et al., 2017), or the examiner does not have adequate cultural and language familiarity with the background of the examinee, neuropsychological evaluation may not be appropriate (Board of Directors, 2007). Overall, deciding whether to include neuropsychological evaluation in FMHA requires consideration of multiple factors.

---

[1] Readers interested in specializing in clinical neuropsychology or forensic neuropsychology are directed to readings in these allied fields (esp. Bush et al., 2017; LaDuke, 2022; Larrabee, 2012; Morgan & Ricker, 2018).

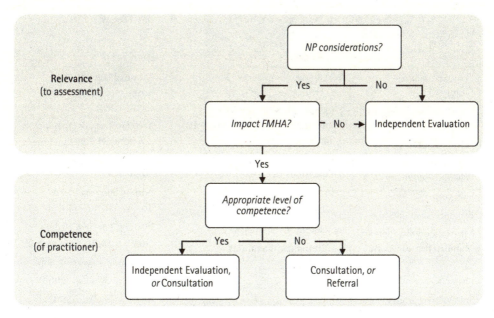

Figure 17.1 Model for Responding to Forensic Referrals with Neuropsychological Considerations.
Note: NP = Neuropsychological. FMHA = Forensic Mental Health Assessment.

Neuropsychological Considerations

There are a number of considerations relating to neuropsychological assessment that may have a significant impact on the practice of psychologists and other mental health practitioners engaging in FMHA. Figure 17.1 summarizes clinical, practical, and legal considerations that appear regularly in the neuropsychological literature related to forensic practice. Although a comprehensive review of all these issues is beyond the scope of this chapter, a number of common clinical considerations are discussed further, and several practical considerations are addressed in the next section. All forensic practitioners are expected to be knowledgeable about the legal standards, laws, rules, and precedents governing their practice, including those summarized in table 17.1 related to neuropsychological considerations in FMHA.

COMMON CLINICAL DISORDERS

Serious Mental Illness

Forensic psychologists are well trained to evaluate and diagnose serious mental illness in a majority of FMHAs, and this chapter does not argue that every individual with a serious mental illness should be evaluated by a neuropsychologist. However, many psychiatric disorders include a cognitive component (Tussey et al., 2018), which may persist even when other symptoms are adequately treated (Marcopulos & Kurtz, 2012). Cognitive abilities that may be impaired in common psychotic and mood disorders include attention,

Table 17.1 Summary of Major Neuropsychological Considerations for Forensic Mental Health Assessment

Clinical	Practical	Legal
Traumatic brain injury (TBI)	Training, competence, & board certification	Criminal law (esp. competence, sanity, & sentencing)
Dementia/Neurodegenerative disorders	Identifying & responding to referral questions involving NP considerations	Civil law (esp. competence & personal injury)
Seizure disorders		
Neurotoxic injury & multiple chemical sensitivity	Formulating referral questions to NPs	Administrative law (esp. disability)
Substance use	Evaluating data from NPs	Admissibility standards (*Frye, Daubert,* & FRE)
Psychotic disorders	Selection of tests & normative data	
Major mood disorders (esp. bipolar, depressive, & posttraumatic stress)	Relevant psychometrics	Relevant case law, including:
	Cultural considerations	*Jenkins v. United States* (1962)[a]
	Ethical considerations	*Simmons v. Mullen* (1974)[b]
Dissociative disorders	Cognitive bias/heuristics	*Grenitz v. Tomlian* (2003)[c]
Somatic symptom disorders	Flexible vs. fixed battery approach	*Atkins v. Virginia* (2002)
Chronic pain	Performance validity	*Dusky v. United States* (1960)[d]
Intellectual disability (ID)	Computerized assessment	*Jackson v. Indiana* (1972)[e]
Specific learning disorders	Remote assessment	*Wiggins v. Smith* (2003)[f]
Attention Deficit Hyperactivity Disorder (ADHD)	Independent medical evaluations (IMEs)	*Baxter v. Temple* (2008)[g]
		Madison v. Alabama (2019)
Fetal alcohol syndrome disorder (FASD)	Third party observers	
	Release of raw data	
Autism spectrum disorders (ASD)	Report writing & testimony	
Personality disorders		
Other neurological conditions		

[a] Jenkins v. United States, 307 F. 2d 637 (1962).

[b] Simmons v. Mullens, 231 Pa. Superior Ct. 199, 331 A.2d 892 (Pa. Super. Ct. 1974).

[c] Grenitz v. Tomlian, 858 So. 2d 999 (Fl. Supreme Court 2003).

[d] Dusky v. United States, 362, U.S. 402 (1960).

[e] Jackson v. Indiana, 406 U.S. 715 (1972).

[f] Wiggins v. Smith, 539 U.S. 510 (2003).

[g] Baxter v. Temple, 949 A. 2d 167 (NH Supreme Court 2008).

Note. FP = Forensic psychology. FPs = Forensic psychologists. NP = Neuropsychology/Neuropsychological. NPs = Neuropsychologists.

processing speed, executive functions, and memory. Further, individuals with serious mental illness also often have comorbid medical and social factors that further impair cognition.

In criminal forensic settings, schizophrenia spectrum disorders are most often associated with incompetence to stand trial (Pirelli et al., 2011) and impaired mental state at the time of the offense (Gardner et al., 2018). Cognitive deficits may also be significant elements in risk assessment, as they may be a distal risk factor that impacts attempts to modify direct risk factors for engaging in violent behaviors (O'Reilly et al., 2015) and can impact treatment decision-making due to the impact of cognitive dysfunction on functional outcomes in schizophrenia treatment (Green et al., 2015). Performance validity must be carefully assessed in individuals with chronic schizophrenia spectrum disorders and prominent cognitive dysfunction (Tussey et al., 2018), as they may be a population at risk for false positives on common performance validity tests. Referring for a neuropsychological consultation or evaluation may be warranted if cognitive deficits are prominent, there are concerns for validity, or in-depth assessment of strengths and weaknesses is necessary to guide treatment planning.

Traumatic Brain Injury

Traumatic brain injury (TBI) encompasses a wide range of injury causes, severity, cognitive deficits, and functional outcomes. Particularly relevant injury characteristics used in the determination of TBI severity and expected outcome include the resulting length of altered mental status (AMS) including both loss of consciousness (LOC) and posttraumatic amnesia (PTA), behavioral functioning (e.g., as measured by the Glasgow Coma Scale [GCS]), and neuroradiological evidence of structural damage to the skull, blood vessels, or brain tissue.

Moderate-to-severe TBI is associated with several significant cognitive, emotional, and physical changes that are worst immediately following the injury and relatively improve over the course of several months or years but are generally associated with long-term difficulties requiring specialized rehabilitation and accommodation strategies (Roebuck-Spencer & Sherer, 2018). The specific symptoms and course are strongly related to the site and severity of the injury and associated medical complications such as edema, hemorrhage, and seizures.

The expectation with *mild TBI* is that symptoms generally resolve in weeks or months, after which other noninjury factors likely contribute to persistent symptoms (e.g., premorbid cognitive functioning, premorbid and subsequent mood disorder, litigation; Belanger et al., 2018). However, certain injury characteristics complicate mild TBI diagnosis and recovery. Specifically, mild TBI with neuroradiological evidence of cranial fractures and intracranial hemorrhage (colloquially termed "breaks or bleeds") are better captured as *complicated mild TBI*, whose symptoms, course, and prognosis are more similar to TBIs of a moderate severity. Additionally, the short- and long-term effects of multiple subconcussive injuries are another area of much empirical, clinical, legal, and popular media interest (Belanger et al., 2018).

TBI is a common referral question for neuropsychologists in both forensic and general clinical practice (96.6 percent and 82.7 percent, respectively; Sweet et al., 2020), and has been the focus of frequent debate and discussion in the field. This is not surprising given the compensability of TBI-related disability in civil law, and the prevalence of TBI among individuals involved in the criminal justice system. Regarding the latter, TBI is much more common among incarcerated individuals (i.e., 40–60 percent; Farrer & Hedges, 2011; Shiroma et al., 2010) compared to the general population (e.g., 12–43 percent; Farrer & Hedges, 2011; Frost et al., 2013; Whiteneck et al., 2016). However, many of these reports may not include undocumented and untreated blows to the head in the distant past. A thorough history, record review, and collateral interviews are essential to validate self-report of TBI, particularly in the context of FMHA.

Additionally, a history of TBI appears to be a risk factor for involvement with the criminal justice system, and more negative outcomes during and after such involvements. Studies show that those with a history of TBI experience higher rates of arrests (Elbogen et al., 2015), certain convictions (Fazel et al., 2011), and incarcerations (McIsaac et al., 2016); more frequent problems in correctional facilities (Piccolino & Solberg, 2014) and under community supervision (i.e., probation and parole) (Brown et al., 2018); and more frequent and quicker reoffending (Piccolino & Solberg, 2014; Ray & Richardson, 2017). Importantly, some of these findings are shown after controlling for related variables such as age, gender, and social factors (Elbogen et al., 2015), and genetic influence (Fazel et al., 2011). However, many pre-TBI factors such as criminal history and prior/comorbid substance use also play an important role, complicating the connection between TBI and criminal justice involvement (Elbogen et al., 2015).

Epilepsy

One of the earliest case law examples related to competence to stand trial involved an individual who claimed memory impairment due to "a severe attack of epilepsy" in which the appeals court reversed his conviction.[2] *Epilepsy* is characterized by abnormal brain activity causing a seizure. Seizures are classified as generalized, focal, or unknown, with additional variations depending on the level of consciousness during the event (Scheffer et al., 2017). Cognitive impacts of epilepsy vary, with greater impairment expected with more frequent seizures or events of longer duration.

Forensic evaluators may face individuals with epilepsy in mental state at the time of the offense cases, particularly those in which the individual claims automatisms (involuntary movements) or seizure-related aggressive behaviors (see Melton et al., 2018, p. 277, for a discussion of epilepsy and mental state at the time of the offense evaluations). Epilepsy is also related to psychosis in a small subgroup of individuals (6 percent; Clancy et al., 2014). Regarding violence risk assessment, although prior literature reported a correlation between epilepsy and violent behaviors, more recent and rigorous investigations have not identified a clear relationship (e.g., Fazel et al., 2011; Fazel et al., 2009). Management of seizures and seizure-related mood and behavior changes may pose a challenge to discharge/risk planning. In civil forensic settings, epilepsy may be an important factor in disability determinations.

Dementia

Dementia is a particularly large and increasing concern in the United States and around the world. *Dementia* is a syndrome characterized by the pathological deterioration of

---

[2] Youtsey v. United States, 97 F. 937 (6th Cir. 1899).

cognitive abilities and functioning over time, with the specific symptoms, course, interventions, and prognosis determined primarily by the underlying neurodegenerative disease process.

Alzheimer's disease (AD) is the most common cause of dementia, accounting for approximately 60–70 percent of all dementia cases (Alzheimer's Association, 2018). Symptoms associated with AD vary, but commonly include memory loss, confusion, decreased judgment, social withdrawal, and challenges with problem-solving. Frontotemporal dementia (FTD) is a leading cause of dementia developing in midlife or earlier, and one particularly worthy of attention in forensic work given that changes in behavior, personality, and mood are typically among the first symptoms. FTD may mimic psychiatric disorders such as schizophrenia, bipolar disorder, and major depression (Velakoulis et al., 2009), as well as other disorders in later life (Baborie et al., 2012). One study (Liljegren et al., 2015) found significantly higher rates of both criminal behavior (14 percent) and violence (6.4 percent) among patients with the behavioral variant of FTD (bvFTD) compared to those with AD (both 2 percent). Common manifestations of criminal behavior in the bvFTD group included theft, traffic violations, sexual advances, trespassing, and public urination; in contrast, those in the AD group commonly committed traffic violations.

Understanding dementia in criminal forensic practice is particularly important as aging individuals are the fastest-growing segment of the incarcerated population (Carson & Sabol, 2016; Maschi et al., 2012). This trend is likely to continue over the next several decades, with estimates that the number of individuals with dementia in correctional institutions will double between 2010 and 2030, and triple by 2050 (Wilson & Barboza, 2010, as cited in Maschi et al., 2012). These statistics and recent case law (e.g., confirming that dementia meets the standard for mental disease or defect in competency for execution[3]) highlight the importance of recognizing and addressing dementia in the US criminal justice system.

Intellectual Disability

Deficits in intellectual ability can impact multiple areas of FMHA, such as *Miranda* comprehension, competence, mental state at the time of an offense, risk assessment, mitigation, and capital sentencing, to name a few. A diagnosis of intellectual disability (ID) bars a defendant from the death penalty in the United States[4] but otherwise does not automatically equate to incompetence, insanity, or other ultimate issues. Nevertheless, an accurate understanding of ID offers other information worthy of legal consideration, can lead to appropriate disposition planning and aftercare, and have implications for mitigating recidivism. For example, it may help the court to appreciate why a defendant may

---

[3] Madison v. Alabama, 586 U.S. ___, 203 L. Ed. 2d 103 (2019).
[4] Atkins v. Virginia, 536 U.S. 304 (2002).

be failing to participate in relevant procedures, assist an attorney with securing proper treatment, and inform collaborations across legal and other systems based on the expected nature and course of the observed difficulties.

Competency

General and Specialty Competencies in Clinical Neuropsychology

Clinical neuropsychological training begins at the doctoral level and consists of extensive training in brain–behavior relationships based on the widely accepted training model known as the "Houston Conference guidelines" (Bieliauskas & Mark, 2018; Hannay et al., 1998). To be competent in the practice of neuropsychology requires advanced knowledge of functional neuroanatomy, neurological disorders, and medical conditions that affect brain functioning; neurodiagnostic techniques (e.g., neuroimaging and EEG); and the neurochemical basis of behavior (Lamberty & Nelson, 2012). Neuropsychological practice requires one to learn to administer and interpret specialized tests of brain functioning (Lezak et al., 2012; Strauss et al., 2006). Specifically, one must be able to evaluate the psychometric properties and discern the neurocognitive constructs measured by the tests, select the best tests to evaluate the suspected brain dysfunction, and interpret these tests from both idiographic and nomothetic standpoints using appropriate normative comparisons and cultural considerations. These competencies are acquired at the predoctoral level through courses and clinical training experiences (i.e., practica, externships, and internship), at the postdoctoral level through a formal two-year fellowship, and later through continuing education (Lamberty & Nelson, 2012; Sperling et al., 2017). Of note, these competencies cannot be acquired through continuing education alone.

More recently, the field of clinical neuropsychology has embraced a competency-based approach to both training and evaluation (Hessen et al., 2018; Rey-Casserly et al., 2012). Sets of competencies within neuropsychology have been established at the postdoctoral level (Heffelfinger et al., 2020), and efforts have been made to standardize training across developmental levels (Smith, 2019). These include *foundational competencies* in scientific knowledge and methods; evidence-based practice; individual and cultural diversity; ethical legal standards and policy; professional identity; reflective practice, self-assessment, and self-care; relationships; and interdisciplinary systems. Additional *functional competencies* include assessment, intervention, consultation, research and evaluation, teaching and supervision, management and administration, and advocacy. Additionally, these efforts have resulted in taxonomy for education and training in clinical neuropsychology, as well as a set of entry-level and core competencies in the field (Smith, 2019; Sperling et al., 2017). These entry-level competencies again highlight the education and training outcomes from the aforementioned Houston Conference guidelines (Bieliauskas & Mark, 2018; Hannay et al., 1998). None of the current training models and competencies explicitly include forensic practice, even though many licensed practitioners in neuropsychology are involved in forensic work (Greiffenstein & Kaufmann, 2018; Sweet et al., 2020). Additionally, there are no formal training programs specializing in forensic neuropsychology at any level of training.

Nevertheless, forensic practice is a well-established specialty area within clinical neuropsychology, as illustrated by the growth of neuropsychological testimony in US courts (Farahany, 2016; Kaufmann, 2009, 2013; Kaufmann & Larrabee, 2012) and the robust practice literature devoted to this specialty. Recent publications provide specific guidance for conducting competent forensic neuropsychological evaluations in both civil and criminal settings (Bush et al., 2017; Greiffenstein & Kaufmann, 2018; Sweet et al., 2018), as do several prior publications centering both scientific (Boone, 2012; Larrabee, 2012) and principle-based approaches (Heilbrun et al., 2003). As with forensic practitioners engaging in neuropsychological work, neuropsychological practitioners engaging in forensic work must have the requisite competence in the clinical, practical, and legal considerations involved in this practice. This is consistent with ethical guidelines (American Psychological Association, 2017) and standards of practice in forensic psychology (American Psychological Association, 2011) and neuropsychology (e.g., Heilbrun et al., 2003; Kaufmann, 2013; Sweet et al., 2018).

Board certification remains the best indication that an individual has the requisite training and experience to perform a competent neuropsychological evaluation. There are currently more than 1,400 psychologists certified by the American Board of Clinical Neuropsychology (ABCN), which is a specialty board of the American Board of Professional Psychology (ABPP) (American Board of Clinical Neuropsychology, 2020). Additional specialty boards recognized within the field include the American Board of Professional Neuropsychology (ABN) and the American Board of Pediatric Neuropsychology (ABPdN). There is currently no subspecialty board certification in forensic neuropsychology within the fields of neuropsychology or forensic psychology, though this is being considered. Currently, board certification in both clinical neuropsychology and forensic psychology is certainly a viable option to demonstrating advanced competence in the subspecialty of forensic neuropsychology.

Relevant Practical Considerations

Several functional competencies within neuropsychological practice are particularly relevant to the practice of FMHA. Not surprisingly, discussion of these considerations is also prevalent in the neuropsychological practice literature (see "Practical Considerations" in table 17.1), further highlighting the importance of maintaining competence in these areas for any psychologists and other mental health practitioners engaging in FMHA with relevant neuropsychological components. Fortunately, given their relevance to forensic practice, those engaging in FMHA will already be well versed in some or all these areas. One practical consideration of particular historical and contemporary importance is *performance validity*, the development and refinement of which have been and continue to be largely driven by the fields of neuropsychology and forensic psychology.

Performance Validity

For neuropsychological testing to be useful it must be based on valid data. As a result of this fundamental reliance on validity, the past twenty years has witnessed the development and validation of a large number of instruments designed to detect invalid neuropsychological test performance, commonly referred to as performance validity tests (PVTs). Nearly 25 percent of all the research published in two major neuropsychology journals between 1995 and 2014 involved studies of PVTs (Martin et al., 2015). The majority of studies indicate that PVTs are useful as measures of neurocognitive performance validity, and associated with increased probabilities of malingering. Additionally, the neuropsychology practice literature is clear that the use of PVTs is considered standard practice in both clinical and forensic assessments (Sweet et al., 2021; Sweet et al., 2020).

In general, PVTs are effective because they detect noncredible performance without detecting genuine deficits. Their effectiveness relies on a number of issues, not the least of which is the fact that examinees do not know which tests are designed to detect performance validity. This makes test security a priority within clinical neuropsychology, as dissemination of information about PVTs could undermine their utility.

Rogers and Bender (2018) reviewed the current state of the clinical assessment of malingering and deception and cautioned against common misconceptions. First, contrary to what some believe, malingering is not rare; it is estimated to occur in 15–30 percent of forensic and nonforensic cases, with higher estimates in forensic settings. Second, some practitioners believe malingering is a static response style, but most attempts to malinger are actually situational and related to specific objectives. These objectives rarely persist across all contexts and times. A third misconception is that malingering is a tip-of-the-iceberg phenomenon, in which any evidence of noncredible performance is sufficient to conclude the examinee is malingering. Rather, a more evidence-based approach here incorporates current statistical and conceptual bases (see Sherman et al., 2020) when classifying behavior as malingered. Fourth, feigning of a specific symptom or syndrome is not always evident on a specific validity scale. Validity scales may not measure malingering of a specific syndrome as well as they measure general invalidity or generic feigning (Sharf et al., 2017). A finding of invalidity is still useful, but it is not the same as a determination of malingering. Finally, forensic practitioners are cautioned to be vigilant for reports concluding that evidence of malingering precludes the presence of genuine symptoms. These two presentations are not mutually exclusive, and years of research and clinical experience indicate that very often at least some symptoms are either genuine or involve both genuine and feigned symptoms.

Responding to Forensic Referrals with Neuropsychological Considerations

Practitioners engaging in FMHA will respond to referrals with neuropsychological considerations based on their *relevance* to the assessment at hand, and the practitioners' level of *competence* with each identified clinical, practical, and legal consideration. What constitutes a relevant neuropsychological consideration within FMHA is a sizable and ever-evolving list, requiring practitioners to remain informed about the contemporary state of the field and emerging etiologies of cognitive impairment (e.g., COVID-19; Wilson & Jack, 2020), advancements in field practices (e.g., computerized assessment and remote assessment; Bauer et al., 2012; Bilder et al., 2020, respectively), and new and refined legal foundations.[5] Relatedly, the areas and requisite levels of foundational and functional competencies within neuropsychology also continue to be defined and refined by the field (e.g., Smith, 2019). Given the large, complex, and rapidly developing nature of neuropsychological considerations impacting FMHA, forensic practitioners would benefit from a flexible decision-making model to help them determine how to best respond to such referrals (see fig. 17.1).

Forensic practitioners are first encouraged to consider whether any of the clinical, practical, or legal considerations described in this chapter are present, and, if so, whether this will have a significant impact on the FMHA process. If neuropsychological considerations are absent or do not appear to have a significant role in the FMHA, then the practitioner would appear supported in their decision to conduct an *independent evaluation*.[6] In these cases, the practitioner would retain sole responsibility to conduct each element of the FMHA, without consultation with or referral to other experts.

For example, conducting one's own assessment may be appropriate if a case appears relatively straightforward with low stakes, the neuropsychological deficits in question are not the sole reason for the FMHA, the relevant brain-based disorder is well documented in the existing record, or evidence to help answer the psycholegal question can be reasonably derived from standard psychological assessment practices. In these cases, it would be especially helpful if there was prior testing or other documentation to compare one's findings. Of course, forensic practitioners are encouraged to be mindful of the relevant clinical, practical, and legal considerations during their initial record reviews, interviews with clients and collaterals, any testing, and any communication of their findings and related opinions.

If neuropsychological considerations appear likely to play a significant role in the FMHA, forensic practitioners are encouraged to consider whether they possess the requisite level of foundational and functional competence in the relevant clinical, practical, and legal areas. If so, a decision to conduct an *independent evaluation* may still be supported, though the forensic practitioner might also consider seeking *consultation* from a neuropsychologist with case-relevant expertise. Together, the retained forensic practitioner and their consulting colleague would determine the extent and nature of each

---

[5] E.g., Madison, 586 U.S. ___, L. Ed. 2d 103.

[6] Not to be confused with the defined area of forensic practice known as independent medical examinations (IMEs) or more specifically independent neuropsychological examinations (INEs) (Oakes et al., 2017).

of their contributions to each stage of the FMHA at the outset of the consultation, to include their involvement in developing, conducting, and communicating the results of the evaluation (e.g., whether the consulting expert will serve as a consultant only, write a report, or write a section of a report). Consultation may also be supported if the forensic practitioner determines that they do not possess a sufficient level of foundational or functional competence in the neuropsychological considerations present, but that these can be reasonably addressed working with a neuropsychologist. Again, the level of the neuropsychologist's involvement would likely be inversely related to the competence of the forensic practitioner with respect to the neuropsychological factors of the case, with relatively more competence resulting in a more circumscribed role by the consultant (and vice versa).

Conversely, *referral* to another expert may be more supported given the specific nature of the neuropsychological considerations and the forensic practitioner's competence in each area. Psychologists and other mental health practitioners engaging in FMHA should never accept referrals outside their area of competence, including those with neuropsychological considerations. Forensic practitioners would likely decide to refer a case to a neuropsychologist when the psycholegal question is related to a neuropsychological disease or disorder in which in-depth knowledge about brain–behavior relationships and comprehensive neuropsychological evaluation is indicated. This may be the case when deficits are not clear, the evaluator lacks familiarity with the presenting or possible underlying cognitive conditions, or there are nuanced and consequential questions regarding prognosis. Further, when deciding to refer, forensic practitioners are strongly encouraged to carefully formulate the referral questions with the retaining party, and clarify these referral questions as needed with the external expert. Forensic practitioners should also be careful to refer to appropriately trained neuropsychologists who have knowledge and experience in forensic matters.

This decision-making is again best viewed as flexible, and able to be revisited as the forensic practitioner becomes more knowledgeable about the referral itself, the individual being evaluated, or the psycholegal needs of the case. As such, forensic practitioners are encouraged to consider seeking consultation if the case becomes more complex than initially expected, if a second opinion is needed, if the retained expert desires a review of their data interpretation, or if they need assistance reviewing previous evaluation reports and data.

Illustrative Examples

Neuropsychological considerations of a clinical nature (rather than practical or legal) are likely to be the most apparent within forensic referrals. For example, an independent evaluation may be supported if a client has a known and well-documented history of epilepsy, their symptoms are well controlled on medications that are tolerated with minimal side effects, and neither the epilepsy nor the medications appear to be significantly related to the psycholegal question. Consultation may be more supported if the epilepsy history, related symptoms, or medication tolerance is less well documented or more equivocal, and if these considerations may be somewhat relevant but not central to the forensic capacities involved in the referral.

What if a criminal defendant is pursuing a sanity evaluation claiming they were in the middle of an extended seizure during their alleged crime? The decision to consult or refer in this case depends on the forensic practitioner's foundational and functional competencies in epilepsy, and ability to consider relevant evidence from the medical record, clinical interview, collateral information, and psychological testing data (if deemed necessary) to render an opinion about the defendant's mental state at the time of the alleged offense. As the forensic practitioner's levels of relevant competencies decrease, the role played in the case by a consulting neuropsychologist would increase. If the forensic practitioner determines that they do not have the requisite level of competence in these areas (whether independently or in consultation with a neuropsychologist), they will refer the case to a neuropsychologist with expertise in epilepsy and FMHA, being sure to clearly indicate the need for characterization of cognitive strengths and weaknesses, differential diagnosis, and an opinion relating to the forensic capacities in the original referral.

Responding to forensic referral questions involving other brain injuries or illnesses would follow a similar process, although the details and related competencies to be considered would change based on the specific clinical disorder and psycho-legal question. For example, specific TBI characteristics (e.g., LOC, PTA, GCS, and structural abnormality) may be vital if the injury was the focus of a personal injury lawsuit or criminal competency evaluation, but it would be less relevant if the injury was remote in occurrence, mild in severity, and unrelated to relevant legal capacities. Determining the etiology of a client's dementia may be less important in determining criminal or civil competencies, but an understanding of the specific nature of their symptoms and course would be crucial to referrals related to future considerations (e.g., competence restoration, medical decision-making, and violence risk) or past behaviors (e.g., postmortem evaluations of testamentary capacity or the effect of preclinical sequalae on mental status at the time of an offense). In all cases, the forensic practitioner is responsible for determining the relevance of these clinical considerations and their level of competence when deciding how to respond to the referral. This preliminary determination may be aided by the consultation of a neuropsychologist.

Practical considerations also influence how forensic practitioners will respond to forensic referrals. For example, forensic practitioners must analyze their level of competence and ability to testify about relevant psychological measures, taking care to understand differences between screening tests and comprehensive neuropsychological evaluations. Screening measures can at times be useful but include the risk of overestimating or underestimating impairment (Roebuck-Spencer et al., 2017), which can have substantial implications for one's legal circumstances. Cultural factors must also always be considered. Testing may not be possible or useful for individuals with significant language and educational differences, and norm selection warrants careful attention (e.g., Guàrdia-Olmos et al., 2015; Manly, 2005). When feasible, an individual should be referred to a competent expert who also speaks their native or primary language and can conduct the assessment in that language. All caveats regarding test interpretation must be thoroughly noted. Finally, evaluators are cautioned when offering diagnoses or etiological statements related to unfamiliar symptom presentations or disorders. Since variability in neuropsychological testing is common (Binder et al., 2009) and deficits in testing do not necessarily equate to deficits in areas relevant to FMHA, forensic practitioners must always analyze this nexus. The necessity, nature, and amount of neuropsychological testing are pivotal decisions that will benefit from the assistance of a knowledgeable expert. As always, when in doubt forensic practitioners are encouraged to consult a neuropsychologist.

Conclusion

Psychologists and other mental health practitioners engaging in FMHA are very likely to receive referrals with neuropsychological considerations, and deciding how to best respond to such referrals is not always straightforward. Deliberate attention to the relevance of these clinical, practical, and legal considerations to the FMHA is foundational, and should lead to further reflection around one's level of competence in these areas whenever applicable. With relevance and competence as their guides, forensic practitioners can make informed decisions about whether it is best to respond to such referrals by conducting evaluations themselves, consulting with other experts, or referring to other providers. Practitioners in forensic mental health assessment and neuropsychological assessment have much to learn from one another, and these allied fields will continue to benefit from formal and informal interaction in their pursuit of bringing the best in psychological science to bear on legal decision-making.

Authors' Note

Correspondence should be addressed to Casey LaDuke, PhD, Department of Psychology, 524 West 59th Street, 10th Floor, New York, NY 10019. Email: claduke@jjay.cuny.edu. All additional authors contributed equally to this chapter and the printed order was randomly determined.

References

Alzheimer's Association. (2018). 2018 Alzheimer's disease facts and figures. *Alzheimer's & Dementia, 14*(3), 367–429. 10.1016/j.jalz.2018.02.001

American Board of Clinical Neuropsychology. (2020). *Directory.* https://theaacn.org/directory/

American Psychological Association. (2011). *Specialty guidelines for forensic psychology.* American Psychological Association. https://www.apa.org/practice/guidelines/forensic-psychology

American Psychological Association. (2017). *Ethical principles of psychologists and code of conduct.* American Psychological Association. https://www.apa.org/ethics/code

American Psychological Association. (2020). *Clinical neuropsychology.* Specialties and Subspecialties. https://www.apa.org/ed/graduate/specialize/neuropsychology

Arredondo, B. C., Marcopulos, B. A., Brand, J. G., Campbell, K. T., & Kent, J.-A. (2017). Cognitive functioning and adjudicative competence: Defendants referred for neuropsychological evaluation in a psychiatric inpatient setting. *The Clinical Neuropsychologist, 31*(8), 1432–1448. https://doi.org/10.1080/13854046.2017.1317032

Baborie, A., Griffiths, T. D., Jaros, E., Momeni, P., McKeith, I. G., Burn, D. J., Keir, G., Larner, A. J., Mann, D. M., & Perry, R. (2012). Frontotemporal dementia in elderly individuals. *Archives of Neurology, 69*(8), 1052–1060. https://doi.org/10.1001/archneurol.2011.3323

Bauer, R. M., Iverson, G. L., Cernich, A. N., Binder, L. M., Ruff, R. M., & Naugle, R. I. (2012). Computerized neuropsychological assessment devices: Joint position paper of the American Academy of Clinical Neuropsychology and the National Academy of Neuropsychology. *The Clinical Neuropsychologist, 26*(2), 177–196. https://doi.org/10.1080/13854046.2012.663001

Belanger, H. G., Tate, D. F., & Vanderploeg, R. D. (2018). Concussion and mild traumatic brain injury. In J. E. Morgan & J. H. Ricker (Eds.), *Textbook of Clinical Neuropsychology* (2nd ed., pp. 411–448). Routledge.

Bieliauskas, L. A., & Mark, E. (2018). Specialty training in clinical neuropsychology: History and update on current issues. In J. E. Morgan & J. H. Ricker (Eds.), *Textbook of Clinical Neuropsychology* (2nd ed., pp. 14–21). Routledge.

Bilder, R. M., Postal, K. S., Barisa, M., Aase, D. M., Cullum, C. M., Gillaspy, S. R., Harder, L., Kanter, G., Lanca, M., Lechuga, D. M., Morgan, J. M., Most, R., Puente, A. E., Salinas, C. M., & Woodhouse, J. (2020). InterOrganizational Practice Committee recommendations/guidance for teleneuropsychology in response to the COVID-19 pandemic. *Archives of Clinical Neuropsychology, 35*(6), 647–659. https://doi.org/10.1093/arclin/acaa046

Binder, L. M., Iverson, G. L., & Brooks, B. L. (2009). To err is human: "Abnormal" neuropsychological scores and variability are common in healthy adults. *Archives of Clinical Neuropsychology, 24*(1), 31–46. https://doi.org/10.1093/arclin/acn001

Board of Directors. (2007). American Academy of Clinical Neuropsychology (AACN) practice guidelines for neuropsychological assessment and consultation. *The Clinical Neuropsychologist, 21*(2), 209–231. https://doi.org/10.1080/13825580601025932

Boone, K. B. (2012). *Clinical practice of forensic neuropsychology: An evidence-based approach.* Guilford Press.

Brown, J., Luckhardt, B., Harr, D., Poser, T., & Fenrich, A. (2018). Traumatic brain injury (TBI): A guide for probation officers. *Journal of Trauma & Treatment, 7*(1), 1–9. https://doi.org/10.4172/2167-1222.1000417

Bush, S. S., Demakis, G. J., & Rohling, M. L. (Eds.). (2017). *APA handbook of forensic neuropsychology.* American Psychological Association.

Carson, E. A., & Sabol, W. J. (2016, May). Aging of the state prison population (NCJ 248766). US Department of Justice, Bureau of Justice Statistics. https://www.bjs.gov/content/pub/pdf/aspp9313.pdf

Clancy, M. J., Clarke, M. C., Connor, D. J., Cannon, M., & Cotter, D. R. (2014). The prevalence of psychosis in epilepsy: A systematic review and meta-analysis. *BMC Psychiatry, 14*(1), 75. https://doi.org/10.1186/1471-244X-14-75

Elbogen, E. B., Wolfe, J. R., Cueva, M., Sullivan, C., & Johnson, J. (2015). Longitudinal predictors of criminal arrest after traumatic brain injury: Results from the Traumatic Brain Injury Model System National Database. *The Journal of Head Trauma Rehabilitation, 30*(5), Article E3. https://doi.org/10.1097/HTR.0000000000000083

Farahany, N. A. (2016). Neuroscience and behavioral genetics in US criminal law: An empirical analysis. *Journal of Law and the Biosciences, 2*(3), 485–509. https://doi.org/10.1093/jlb/lsv059

Farrer, T. J., & Hedges, D. W. (2011). Prevalence of traumatic brain injury in incarcerated groups compared to the general population: A meta-analysis. *Progress in Neuro-Psychopharmacology and Biological Psychiatry, 35*(2), 390–394. https://doi.org/10.1016/j.pnpbp.2011.01.007

Fazel, S., Lichtenstein, P., Grann, M., & Långström, N. (2011). Risk of violent crime in individuals with epilepsy and traumatic brain injury: A 35-year Swedish population study. *PLOS Medicine, 8*(12), e1001150. https://doi.org/10.1371/journal.pmed.1001150

Fazel, S., Philipson, J., Gardiner, L., Merritt, R., & Grann, M. (2009). Neurological disorders and violence: A systematic review and meta-analysis with a focus on epilepsy and traumatic brain injury. *Journal of Neurology, 256*(10), 1591–1602. https://doi.org/10.1007/s00415-009-5134-2

Frost, R. B., Farrer, T. J., Primosch, M., & Hedges, D. W. (2013). Prevalence of traumatic brain injury in the general adult population: A meta-analysis. *Neuroepidemiology, 40*(3), 154–159. https://doi.org/10.1159/000343275

Gardner, B. O., Murrie, D. C., & Torres, A. N. (2018). Insanity findings and evaluation practices: A state-wide review of court-ordered reports. *Behavioral Sciences & the Law*, *36*(3), 303–316. https://doi.org/10.1002/bsl.2344

Green, M. F., Llerena, K., & Kern, R. S. (2015). The "right stuff" revisited: What have we learned about the determinants of daily functioning in schizophrenia? *Schizophrenia Bulletin*, *41*(4), 781–785. https://doi.org/10.1093/schbul/sbv018

Greiffenstein, M. F., & Kaufmann, P. M. (2018). Basics of forensic neuropsychology. In J. E. Morgan & J. H. Ricker (Eds.), *Textbook of clinical neuropsychology* (2nd ed., pp. 887–926). Routledge.

Guàrdia-Olmos, J., Peró-Cebollero, M., Rivera, D., & Arango-Lasprilla, J. C. (2015). Methodology for the development of normative data for ten Spanish-language neuropsychological tests in eleven Latin American countries. *NeuroRehabilitation*, *37*(4), 493–499. https://doi.org/10.3233/NRE-151277

Hannay, H. J., Bieliauskas, L. A., Crosson, B., Hammeke, T., Hamsher, K. D., & Koffler, S. P. (1998). The Houston conference on specialty education and training in clinical neuropsychology – Policy statement. *Archives of Clinical Neuropsychology*, *13*(2), 160–166.

Heffelfinger, A. K., Janecek, J. K., Johnson, A., Miller, L. E., Nelson, A., & Pulsipher, D. T. (2020). Competency-based assessment in clinical neuropsychology at the post-doctoral level: Stages, milestones, and benchmarks as proposed by an APPCN work group. *The Clinical Neuropsychologist*. Advance online publication. https://doi.org/10.1080/13854046.2020.1829070

Heilbrun, K., Marczyk, G. R., DeMatteo, D., Zillmer, E. A., Harris, J., & Jennings, T. (2003). Principles of forensic mental health assessment: Implications for neuropsychological assessment in forensic contexts. *Assessment*, *10*(4), 329–343. https://doi.org/10.1177/1073191103258591

Hessen, E., Hokkanen, L., Ponsford, J., Zandvoort, M. van, Watts, A., Evans, J., & Haaland, K. Y. (2018). Core competencies in clinical neuropsychology training across the world. *The Clinical Neuropsychologist*, *32*(4), 642–656. https://doi.org/10.1080/13854046.2017.1413210

Kaufmann, P. M. (2009). Protecting raw data and psychological tests from wrongful disclosure: A primer on the law and other persuasive strategies. *The Clinical Neuropsychologist*, *23*(7), 1130–1159. https://doi.org/10.1080/13854040903107809

Kaufmann, P. M. (2013). Neuropsychologist experts and neurolaw: Cases, controversies, and admissibility challenges. *Behavioral Sciences & the Law*, *31*(6), 739–755. https://doi.org/10.1002/bsl.2085

Kaufmann, P. M., & Larrabee, G. A. (2012). Admissibility of expert opinions based on neuropsychological evidence. In S. S. Bush, M. L. Rohling, & G. J. Demakis (Eds.), *Forensic neuropsychology: A scientific approach* (2nd ed., pp. 70–100). Oxford University Press.

LaDuke, C. (2022). Forensic neuropsychology. In R. Roesch (Ed.), *Routledge Encyclopedia of Psychology in the Real World: Psychology and Law*. Routledge. https://doi.org/10.4324/9780367198459-REPRW176-1

LaDuke, C., DeMatteo, D., Heilbrun, K., Gallo, J., & Swirsky-Sacchetti, T. (2017). The neuropsychological assessment of justice-involved men: Descriptive analysis, preliminary data, and a case for group-specific norms. *Archives of Clinical Neuropsychology*, *32*(8), 929–942. https://doi.org/10.1093/arclin/acx042

Lamberty, G. J., & Nelson, N. W. (2012). *Specialty competencies in clinical neuropsychology*. Oxford University Press.

Larrabee, G. J. (2012). *Forensic neuropsychology: A scientific approach*. Oxford University Press.

Lezak, M. D., Howieson, D. B., Bigler, E. D., & Tranel, D. (2012). *Neuropsychological assessment* (5th ed.). Oxford University Press.

Liljegren, M., Naasan, G., Temlett, J., Perry, D. C., Rankin, K. P., Merrilees, J., Grinberg, L. T., Seeley, W. W., Englund, E., & Miller, B. L. (2015). Criminal behavior in frontotemporal dementia and Alzheimer disease. *JAMA Neurology*, *72*(3), 295–300. https://doi.org/10.1001/jamaneurol.2014.3781

Manly, J. J. (2005). Advantages and disadvantages of separate norms for African Americans. *The Clinical Neuropsychologist*, *19*(2), 270–275. https://doi.org/10.1080/13854040590945346

Marcopulos, B. A., & Kurtz, M. M. (Eds.). (2012). *Clinical neuropsychological foundations of schizophrenia*. Psychology Press.

Marcopulos, B. A., Morgan, J. E., & Denney, R. L. (2008). Neuropsychological evaluation of competency to proceed. In R. L. Denney & J. P. Sullivan (Eds.), *Clinical neuropsychology in the criminal forensic setting* (pp. 176–203). Guilford Press.

Martin, P. K., Schroeder, R. W., & Odland, A. P. (2015). Neuropsychologists' validity testing beliefs and practices: A survey of North American professionals. *The Clinical Neuropsychologist*, *29*(6), 741–776. https://doi.org/10.1080/13854046.2015.1087597

Maschi, T., Kwak, J., Ko, E., & Morrissey, M. B. (2012). Forget me not: Dementia in prison. *The Gerontologist*, *52*(4), 441–451. https://doi.org/10.1093/geront/gnr131

McIsaac, K. E., Moser, A., Moineddin, R., Keown, L. A., Wilton, G., Stewart, L. A., Colantonio, A., Nathens, A. B., & Matheson, F. I. (2016). Association between traumatic brain injury and incarceration: A population-based cohort study. *CMAJ Open*, *4*(4), E746–E753. https://doi.org/10.9778/cmajo.20160072

Melton, G. B., Petrila, J., Poythress, N. G., Slobogin, C., Otto, R. K., Mossman, D., & Condie, L. O. (2018). *Psychological evaluations for the courts: A handbook for mental health professionals and lawyers*. Guilford Press.

Morgan, J. E., & Ricker, J. H. (Eds.). (2018). *Textbook of clinical neuropsychology* (2nd ed.). Routledge.

Oakes, H. J., Lovejoy, D. W., & Bush, S. S. (2017). *The independent neuropsychological evaluation*. Oxford University Press.

O'Reilly, K., Donohoe, G., Coyle, C., O'Sullivan, D., Rowe, A., Losty, M., McDonagh, T., McGuinness, L., Ennis, Y., Watts, E., Brennan, L., Owens, E., Davoren, M., Mullaney, R., Abidin, Z., & Kennedy, H. G. (2015). Prospective cohort study of the relationship between neuro-cognition, social cognition and violence in forensic patients with schizophrenia and schizoaffective disorder. *BMC Psychiatry*, *15*(1), 155. https://doi.org/10.1186/s12888-015-0548-0

Piccolino, A. L., & Solberg, K. B. (2014). The impact of traumatic brain injury on prison health services and offender management. *Journal of Correctional Health Care*, *20*(3), 203–212. https://doi.org/10.1177/1078345814530871

Pirelli, G., Gottdiener, W. H., & Zapf, P. A. (2011). A meta-analytic review of competency to stand trial research. *Psychology, Public Policy, and Law*, *17*(1), 1–53. https://doi.org/10.1037/a0021713

Ray, B., & Richardson, N. J. (2017). Traumatic brain injury and recidivism among returning inmates. *Criminal Justice and Behavior*, *44*(3), 472–486. https://doi.org/10.1177/0093854816686631

Rey-Casserly, C., Roper, B. L., & Bauer, R. M. (2012). Application of a competency model to clinical neuropsychology. *Professional Psychology: Research and Practice*, *43*(5), 422–431. https://doi.org/10.1037/a0028721

Roebuck-Spencer, T. M., Glen, T., Puente, A. E., Denney, R. L., Ruff, R. M., Hostetter, G., & Bianchini, K. J. (2017). Cognitive screening tests versus comprehensive neuropsychological test batteries: A National Academy of Neuropsychology education paper. *Archives of Clinical Neuropsychology*, 32(4), 491–498. https://doi.org/10.1093/arclin/acx021

Roebuck-Spencer, T. M., & Sherer, M. (2018). Moderate and severe traumatic brain injury. In J. E. Morgan & J. H. Ricker (Eds.), *Textbook of clinical neuropsychology* (2nd ed., pp. 387–410). Routledge.

Rogers, R., & Bender, S. D. (Eds.). (2018). *Clinical assessment of malingering and deception* (4th ed.). Guilford Press.

Scheffer, I. E., Berkovic, S., Capovilla, G., Connolly, M. B., French, J., Guilhoto, L., Hirsch, E., Jain, S., Mathern, G. W., Moshé, S. L., Nordli, D. R., Perucca, E., Tomson, T., Wiebe, S., Zhang, Y.-H., & Zuberi, S. M. (2017). ILAE classification of the epilepsies: Position paper of the ILAE Commission for Classification and Terminology. *Epilepsia*, *58*(4), 512–521. https://doi.org/10.1111/epi.13709

Sharf, A. J., Rogers, R., Williams, M. M., & Henry, S. A. (2017). The effectiveness of the MMPI-2-RF in detecting feigned mental disorders and cognitive deficits: A meta-analysis. *Journal of Psychopathology and Behavioral Assessment*, *39*(3), 441–455. https://doi.org/10.1007/s10862-017-9590-1

Sherman, E. M. S., Slick, D. J., & Iverson, G. L. (2020). Multidimensional malingering criteria for neuropsychological assessment: A 20-year update of the malingered neuropsychological dysfunction criteria. *Archives of Clinical Neuropsychology*, *35*(6), 735–764. https://doi.org/10.1093/arclin/acaa019

Shiroma, E. J., Ferguson, P. L., & Pickelsimer, E. E. (2010). Prevalence of traumatic brain injury in an offender population: A meta-analysis. *Journal of Correctional Health Care*, *16*(2), 147–159. https://doi.org/10.1177/1078345809356538

Smith, G. (2019). Education and training in clinical neuropsychology: Recent developments and documents from the Clinical Neuropsychology Synarchy. *Archives of Clinical Neuropsychology*, *34*(3), 418–431. https://doi.org/10.1093/arclin/acy075

Sperling, S. A., Cimino, C. R., Stricker, N. H., Heffelfinger, A. K., Gess, J. L., Osborn, K. E., & Roper, B. L. (2017). Taxonomy for education and training in clinical neuropsychology: Past, present, and future. *The Clinical Neuropsychologist*, *31*(5), 817–828. https://doi.org/10.1080/13854046.2017.1314017

Strauss, E., Sherman, E. M., & Spreen, O. (2006). *A compendium of neuropsychological tests: Administration, norms, and commentary* (3rd ed.). Oxford University Press.

Sweet, J. J., Heilbronner, R. L., Morgan, J. E., Larrabee, G. J., Rohling, M. L., Boone, K. B., Kirkwood, M. W., Schroeder, R. W., Suhr, J. A., & Conference Participants (2021). American Academy of Clinical Neuropsychology (AACN) 2021 consensus statement on validity assessment: Update of the 2009 AACN consensus conference statement on neuropsychological assessment of effort, response bias, and malingering. *The Clinical Neuropsychologist, 35*(6), 1053–1106. https://doi.org/10.1080/13854046.2021.1896036

Sweet, J. J., Kaufmann, P. M., Ecklund-Johnson, E., & Malina, A. C. (2018). Forensic neuropsychology: An overview of issues, admissibility, and directions. In J. E. Morgan & J. H. Ricker (Eds.), *Textbook of clinical neuropsychology* (2nd ed., pp. 857–886). Routledge.

Sweet, J. J., Klipfel, K. M., Nelson, N. W., & Moberg, P. J. (2020). Professional practices, beliefs, and incomes of U.S. neuropsychologists: The AACN, NAN, SCN 2020 practice and "salary survey." *The Clinical Neuropsychologist, 35*(1), 7–80. https://doi.org/10.1080/13854046.2020.1849803

Tussey, C. B., Caillouet, B. A., & Richards, P. (2018). Assessment of psychiatric disorders in forensic neuropsychological evaluations. In S. S. Bush, G. J. Demakis, & M. L. Rohling (Eds.), *APA handbook of forensic neuropsychology* (pp. 223–250). American Psychological Association.

Velakoulis, D., Walterfang, M., Mocellin, R., Pantelis, C., & McLean, C. (2009). Frontotemporal dementia presenting as schizophrenia-like psychosis in young people: Clinicopathological series and review of cases. *The British Journal of Psychiatry, 194*(4), 298–305. https://doi.org/10.1192/bjp.bp.108.057034

Whiteneck, G. G., Cuthbert, J. P., Corrigan, J. D., & Bogner, J. A. (2016). Prevalence of self-reported lifetime history of traumatic brain injury and associated disability: A statewide population-based survey. *Journal of Head Trauma Rehabilitation, 31*(1), E55.

Wilson, M. P., & Jack, A. S. (2020). Coronavirus disease 2019 (COVID-19) in neurology and neurosurgery: A scoping review of the early literature. *Clinical Neurology and Neurosurgery, 193*, 105866. https://doi.org/10.1016/j.clineuro.2020.105866

Violence Risk Assessment and Management

Stephen D. Hart *and* Kevin S. Douglas

Abstract

In this chapter, we provide an overview of the "state of the field" with respect to the topic of violence risk. The chapter is divided into four sections. In the first section, we define and discuss the concept of violence risk and discuss the importance of violence risk assessment and management in psychology and law. In the second section, we summarize research on violence risk, including both applied and experimental research. In the third section, we consider legal views and treatment of violence risk, focusing primarily (but not exclusively) on statutory and case law from the United States. Finally, in the fourth section, we make recommendations for research, practice, and public policy concerning violence risk.

Key Words: violence risk assessment, management of violence, legal decision-making, actuarial, structured professional judgment

Conceptual Issues

The possibility that people will engage in violence is of relevance in many instances of legal decision-making before courts, review boards, tribunals, and administrative bodies. For example, in criminal law, violence risk plays an important role in decisions about search and surveillance, arrest, juvenile transfer and decertification, bail, diversion, peace bonds, sentencing, parole, and community supervision, and in civil law, in decisions about involuntary treatment and hospitalization, protection of health and safety in employment and educational settings, immigration and deportation, child protection, parental custody and access, privacy law, and issues under tort law or law of obligations. In these decision-making contexts, diverse groups—including but not limited to mental health, law enforcement, corrections, national security, social service, human resources, and corporate security professionals—consult regarding violence risk assessment and management. The practice of *violence risk assessment and management* is sometimes referred to as *threat assessment and management*. Although some people draw distinctions between these terms (see discussion by Meloy et al., 2021), for the purpose of this chapter we consider them to be synonymous.

The fact that violence risk is a ubiquitous concern in legal decision-making would be sufficient to justify its inclusion in any handbook of psychology and law. But two additional facts provide further justification. First, legal decisions regarding violence risk have high stakes. Indeed, quite literally, decisions about violence risk can be matters of life and death. As violence is among the leading causes of injury and death worldwide (Krug et al., 2002), decisions about violence risk, depending on their quality, may protect or threaten public safety. Furthermore, the consequences of decisions about violence risk may include long-term or indefinite deprivation of rights and freedoms, and even capital sentencing (DeMatteo et al., 2020a, 2020b). Second, applied and experimental psychologists have made important contributions to the understanding of violence risk, both by studying violence itself or by developing, implementing, and evaluating assessment and management practices.

The Nature of Violence Risk

What do we mean by *violence risk*? To clarify the definition, we analyze its constituent elements, *violence* and *risk*.

VIOLENCE

Risk always involves reference to some hazard ("Risk for what?"), and violence is the relevant hazard here. Here, we define violence as *acts that cause or have the potential to cause bodily harm and are intentional and unauthorized*. *Acts* means actions or deeds committed by people on their own or in collaboration with others. The acts may be inchoate, incomplete, or complete. *Bodily harm* means physical or psychological (mental, emotional, or social) harm that is more than incidental or fleeting. *Intentional* means the acts are nonaccidental; the people who committed them either deliberately caused bodily harm or were reckless as to the possibility of causing bodily harm. *Unauthorized* means the acts are without legal consent, justification, or excuse. This definition is obviously complex, and that complexity places fundamental limits on our ability to understand, explain, assess, and manage violence risk.

RISK

Uncertainty is the essence of risk. For example, in the *Stanford Encyclopedia of Philosophy* risk is defined as "a state of affairs in which an undesirable event may or may not occur" (Hansson, 2018, p. 1, ¶ 8) and by the International Standards Organization (2018, p. 1) as the "effect of uncertainty on objectives." Risk is a multifaceted, contextual, and dynamic concept. It reflects uncertainty regarding the nature of the hazard, the seriousness of the hazard's consequences, the likelihood that the hazard will occur, the imminence of the hazard, and the frequency or duration of the hazard; it also recognizes that the hazard will arise in circumstances that are undetermined, unique, and evolving (Bernstein, 1996). Risk is not a characteristic of the physical world that can be evaluated objectively but rather a subjective perception—something that exists not in fact but in the eye of the beholder.

SYNTHESIS

Violence risk, then, is *uncertainty* regarding people's potential for violence—not just the likelihood they will commit some act of violence, but what kinds of violence they might commit, for what reasons, against whom, with what consequences, when, how many times, and so forth. The risk will also depend on such things as the person's motivation and capacity to establish a prosocial adjustment in the future, where and under what conditions the person will reside in the future, and whether the person may experience important adverse life events.

Approaches to Violence Risk Assessment and Management

The ultimate goal of assessing and managing violence risk is to synthesize and analyze relevant information to understand people's potential to commit violence and determine what steps could be taken to prevent them from committing such violence. Thus, the process of violence risk assessment and management comprises two phases (Hart et al., 2016; see Hart, 2001; Heilbrun, 1997). The first, often referred to as forecasting or prediction, involves thinking about possible futures. In this phase, evaluators identify, synthesize, and analyze relevant information to characterize the potential for violence. As part of this phase, the law may also require consideration of the extent to which any risk is attributable to specified putative causal factors, such as mental disorder (as in some decisions regarding involuntary hospitalization, for example). The second phase, often referred to as management, involves developing plans to mitigate the potential for violence. As part of this phase, the law may also require consideration of the extent to which any risk may be managed with conditions short of incapacitation (once again, as in some decisions regarding involuntary hospitalization). In this phase, evaluators consider various interventions and select a set that is likely to be successful in mitigating risk and, importantly, feasible to implement considering relevant legal, situational, and practical constraints.

There are three general approaches to the task of violence risk assessment and management. First, the *unstructured clinical judgment* (UCJ) approach is defined as the absence of formal (i.e., explicit) procedures or rules for making decisions regarding violence risk. The UCJ approach is actually a nonapproach—that is, practice in the absence of an explicit, structured, and evidence-based decision tool, although some practitioners may actually name their practice (e.g., anamnestic violence risk assessment or behavioral threat assessment). The rationale underlying UCJ is that the complexity of violence risk assessment is best dealt with by relying solely on an expert evaluator. The lack of a priori guidance concerning what information to gather, which risk factors to consider, how to define or operationalize risk factors, and how to combine risk factors to yield decisions regarding risk means that the practice of an evaluator is guided solely by professional discretion, itself a reflection of the evaluator's education, training, experience, and intuition. Although the UCJ approach has several strengths (e.g., Hart, 2001; Otto, 2000), including individualization (strong idiographic focus) and flexibility (adaptability to new problems and contexts), its limitations are serious and include a lack of transparency, low reliability (consistency, reproducibility), and low predictive validity (accuracy).

Second, the *nondiscretionary approach* is defined as the use of fixed and explicit rules established a priori in the form of decision support tools based on algorithms, such as mathematical formulas or decisions trees, that specify exactly which information elements shall be considered and how they shall be combined. Some of these decision support tools, referred to as *actuarial risk assessment instruments* (ARAIs), are developed to estimate the probability or absolute likelihood of violence by comparing the person being evaluated to some known reference group. The rationale underlying the nondiscretionary approach is that the complexity and uncertainty inherent in violence risk assessment and management is a tractable problem, one that stems from the limited cognitive abilities and resources of human evaluators and can be solved through simplification and automatization of the assessment process. Thus, the nondiscretionary approach relies on what might be called *scientific* or *statistical authority*. The strengths and limitations of the nondiscretionary approach are directly opposite to those of UCJ. The nondiscretionary approach yields violence risk assessments that have high transparency, moderate to high reliability, and moderate predictive validity. But at the same time, its reliance on fixed and restricted sets of risk factors means that it may be judged incomplete or inadequate for clinical and legal decision making. As well, its combinatoric algorithms are optimized for use in specific outcomes and in specific settings. This results in two major problems. First, the combinatoric algorithm is designed to work "on average" (i.e., across subjects). This means it suffers in terms of individualization and flexibility. The algorithm cannot be changed or adapted to recognize the diversity or uniqueness of populations and settings, or people within populations or settings. Second, because they are optimized in their validation or construction samples, combinatoric algorithms are by definition nonoptimal when used in new samples. This is sometimes referred to as "shrinkage" upon cross-validation or calibration.

Third, the *structured professional judgment* (SPJ) approach is defined as the use of guidelines to systematize the exercise of discretion by evaluators. SPJ guidelines for violence risk may be considered evidence-based because they are founded on a careful review of the relevant clinical, scientific, and legal literature. The rationale underlying SPJ is that the complexity of violence risk assessment is best dealt with by supporting the exercise of discretion by an expert evaluator. SPJ guidelines provide some structure and systematization, at the same time helping to tailor the assessment to the characteristics and context of the case at hand. The SPJ approach may be characterized as relying on *rational-legal authority*. SPJ guidelines provide an organizational scheme that increases the transparency, reliability, and predictive validity of violence risk assessments without sacrificing their individualization and flexibility. But the SPJ approach still has limitations, of course.

First, like the UCJ approach, the SPJ approach assumes evaluators have some basic level of competence. Merely giving evaluators a set of SPJ guidelines cannot overcome limitations in their knowledge, skill, or experience. Second, like the nondiscretionary approach, the SPJ approach assumes the content of evaluative devices (i.e., the procedural details, and most importantly the risk factors included) is optimal. Changes in knowledge about risk, as well as changes in society itself, may require revisions to SPJ guidelines.

Research Issues

Most research on violence risk addresses the predictive validity of decision support tools. Although fundamental, this focus captures only part of the overall domain of what ought to be addressed in risk assessment research. As such, we first will provide a brief overview of major research trends and findings in the risk assessment field, relying heavily on comprehensive reviews and meta-analyses, and then devote space to areas that are lacking adequate research focus. We do not devote space to consideration of reliability (it is acceptable for most commonly used measures—see chapters within Douglas & Otto, 2021), or topics of secondary importance when it comes to measure validation in the risk assessment field (i.e., concurrent validity).

Predictive Validity: Major Trends

The first point to make is that structured approaches to risk assessment, on average, have stronger predictive validity (and better reliability) than unstructured approaches (Guy et al., 2015, but cf. Viljoen et al., 2021). We do not go into detail, as we simply do not recommend unstructured approaches. What follows is a summary of major meta-analytic findings on structured risk assessment instruments. For a comprehensive discussion, see Guy et al. (2015); for in-depth research summaries of the most commonly used individual risk assessment instruments, see Douglas and Otto (2021).

Meta-analyses can be organized according to whether they focus on certain types of perpetrators or offenses or whether they are broad and inclusive. For instance, some focus on mentally disordered offenders (Bonta et al., 1998), offenders generally (Campbell et al., 2009), sexual offenders (Hanson & Morton-Bourgon, 2009), or adolescent sexual offenders (Viljoen et al., 2012). Others focus on specific instruments, such as the Short-Term Assessment of Risk and Treatability (START; O'Shea & Dickens, 2014), the Hare Psychopathy Checklist-Revised (PCL-R) and its derivate instruments (Leistico et al., 2008), or the Level of Service instruments (Olver et al., 2014). Others are intended to cover the field more broadly to compare instruments or approaches (Fazel et al., 2012; Singh et al., 2011; Yang et al., 2010).

We draw the following conclusions about the state of the research on risk assessment based on our review of the above-cited meta-analyses and systematic reviews, as well as the primary research literature:

- Most contemporary instruments have, on average, moderate to moderate-large associations with subsequent outcomes such as violence or crime, with

correlation coefficients of around 0.25 to 0.30 and AUC coefficients of
around 0.65 to 0.75.

- Instruments that focus on specific forms of outcomes (violence, as opposed
  to crime broadly) tend to have slightly larger effect sizes.
- Instruments that include a substantial proportion of dynamic (i.e., changeable)
  risk factors tend to have larger effect sizes than those including primarily historical
  risk factors measured in a static way.
- Few instruments have been shown to consistently outperform PCL-R
  instruments (for exceptions, see Guy et al., 2010; Yang et al., 2010).
- Instrument-specific meta-analyses have tended to be consistent with omni-
  bus meta-analyses in terms of average effect sizes.
- There is not strong evidence for consistent moderator effects within meta-
  analyses (for instance, that instruments work better for institutional compared to community violence; or better for males compared to females).
  One possible exception to this is that instruments may have lower predictive
  validity in the United States compared to other countries.
- SPJ and actuarial instruments tend to perform comparably in terms of predictive validity, although SPJ instruments have not been tested as intended
  for use in practice in most studies or meta-analyses.

To expand on this last point, in many studies, and hence meta-analyses, the total
number of risk factors is used as the predictive index for SPJ instruments. Although this
approach tests the basic SPJ assumption that, in general, the presence of a greater rather
than smaller number of risk factors leads to greater risk, it fails to test the more uniquely
SPJ assumption that, in general, humans can actually make better decisions than algorithms or total scores. That is, every SPJ instrument encourages evaluators to come to
decisions of low, moderate, or high risk, and such decisions, as reviewed earlier in this
chapter, are for many reasons not tied to scores or derived through algorithms.

In a recent overview of the violence risk field, Heilbrun et al. (2021) reported that
thirty-nine of forty-five published investigations of these summary risk ratings (SRRs)
showed support for their predictive validity. Importantly, sixteen of eighteen published
studies that evaluated whether SRRs added incremental predictive validity to the numeric
total of risk factors on a given SPJ instrument indeed found incremental validity. What
this means is that the human (structured) decisions outperformed the actuarial use of a
list of risk factors.

DYNAMIC RISK

A number of instruments contain dynamic—or potentially changeable—risk factors. The
rationale for inclusion of such risk factors is to guide intervention, with the logic being

that if such factors can be ameliorated, there will be a concomitant reduction in violence. Although there are far fewer studies on this topic than on predictive validity generally, the majority of such studies support the concept of dynamic risk (see, e.g., de Vries Robbé et al., 2015; Hogan & Olver, 2016, 2019). That is, in most such studies, when change in risk factors occurs, such change is statistically predictive of changes in violence that follows. Typically, the pattern of change is reductions in risk factors being associated with lower rates of violence in the follow-up periods.

FAIRNESS AND BIAS

In terms of fairness issues, the body of research is unfortunately thinner than the issue warrants. But it is growing. From some perspectives, there is good evidence that risk factors and instruments perform comparably across diverse cultures, countries, and continents. Meta-analyses have shown that the predictive validity of instruments is comparable across countries and continents. Further, predictive validity studies of non-English translations of commonly used instruments tend to report comparable levels of validity to the original measures.

Similarly, meta-analytic reviews would suggest that, in terms of basic predictive validity, contemporary instruments perform comparable for males and females (except the VRAG-[R]). There is some meta-analytic evidence that the greater the proportion of ethnic minority people within risk assessment samples, the lower the average effect size, although this is a small effect (Singh et al., 2011).

However, there are many fewer studies that dig deeper to evaluate claims and arguments made in the literature that contemporary instruments systematically overestimate risk for certain minority groups, and that they contain risk factors that are "proxies for race," and hence are unfair on legal or moral grounds (see Starr, 2014, and discussion that ensues in the section "Recent Legal Precedent"). We do note that these arguments have been directed primarily against pretrial actuarial instruments developed by state prison agencies, and not widely evaluated or used outside those systems. Nonetheless, ensuring fairness and lack of bias is relevant to all instruments (although testing for bias must differ, logically, based on how an instrument is constructed and intended to be used).

Vincent and Viljoen (2020) provided a review and critical analysis of the question of whether risk assessment instruments are, in general, racially biased. They made the important observation that most of the instruments under scrutiny and specifically namechecked as problematic are pretrial actuarial instruments that focus largely on criminal history variables. Further, very few of these instruments, and indeed very few of any type of instrument, have been subjected to comprehensive, detailed analysis of racial bias. At the time of their review, they were able to identify only nine such studies with nonoverlapping samples, and only two of these were pretrial instruments. The authors concluded that "there is currently no valid evidence that instruments in general are biased against individuals of color" (p. 1580). They also discussed that unbiased instruments (that is, instruments that show comparable predictive accuracy between groups) might, and likely will, detect disparities in the quantum of certain risk factors (such as more extensive criminal histories for individuals of color) that reflect larger systemic biases.

More recently, Desmarais et al. (2021) reviewed eighteen studies of pretrial risk assessment instruments used in the United States (the type most often highlighted by critics). They reported roughly comparable predictive validity across both gender and race. However, in three studies, predictive validity was lower—although still strong—for defendants of color.

In Canada, a number of recent reviews of this issue have been published, particularly focusing on predictive validity and potential bias of actuarial risk assessment instruments for Indigenous offenders within the Correctional Service of Canada. As we review elsewhere in this chapter, this issue was under its brightest spotlight ever as a result of the *Ewert* case.[1] There were a number of take-home conclusions by risk assessment scholars on point, often conflicting with one another: Lack of racial bias has not yet been adequately demonstrated for certain actuarial risk assessment tools (VRAG; Static-99R) and the PCL-R (Hart, 2016); although more research is needed, there is enough research to demonstrate that such tools have reasonable predictive validity for Indigenous offenders, despite having somewhat lower effect sizes for this group (Gutierrez et al., 2016; Haag et al., 2016); factor analysis of the PCL-R has shown invariance (at least by some metrics) across Indigenous and non-Indigenous offenders, and some assessment instruments show nonmeaningful differences in predictive validity across groups (Olver, 2016).

Gaps in the Research and an Agenda for Future Risk Assessment Research

Despite the extensive evaluation of risk assessment instruments in some regards, the field is sorely lacking in others. Indeed, in our view, the basic predictive validity of instruments is well established, and we encourage researchers to shift gears, *en masse*, to more pressing topics.

First, as discussed in the opening section of this chapter, one of the understudied yet vital topics concerns race and other bases of diversity. Most research on this topic has focused on actuarial instruments. Nonetheless, it will be important to evaluate how SPJ instruments fare in terms of fairness and bias. Although they perform comparably across countries, little research has investigated how they perform across different groups of people within countries. Clearly, how SPJ instruments are evaluated will differ from how actuarial instruments are evaluated, given that they do not use algorithms. Research should focus on potential differences in predictive validity of risk factors; decisions of levels of risk (low, moderate, high); quality of formulation, generally and in terms of diversity; and appropriateness of risk reduction efforts. Finally, we urge researchers to conceptualize diversity broadly, focusing not only on issues of race, ethnicity, and gender

---

[1] Ewert v. Canada, 2 S.C.R. 165 (Can. 2018).

but on all bases of individual difference that might impact a person's functioning in a risk-relevant manner (i.e., age, sexual orientation, immigration/acculturation, and socio-economic status).

Second, we recommend increased focus on how well risk assessment instruments, routines, and policies work in the field, embedded within systems, completed by agency staff as part of overall professional services. And these services and routines themselves vary greatly, from large, complicated state hospital or prison systems to small boutique private practices. This is a matter of applying the rich field of implementation science to our field. As yet, we are in a nascent stage in this regard. The key question here is: when adopted in practice—regardless of what that practice looks like—do our models and instruments work as intended? Do they reliably identify higher risk evaluees? Do they guide intervention adequately? Do they lead to reduced risk through specification and application of appropriate management?

Third, and following, the field needs more research that ties assessment to intervention, and whether we reliably reduce actual violence as a result of using contemporary risk assessment approaches. The research on dynamic risk certainly provides strong evidence for this goal, by showing that reductions in risk factors tend to forecast reduced rates of future violence. But it is typically at least one step removed from actual intervention research (for instance, lack of control groups, vulnerability to methodological confounds such as maturation). We would also recommend that research focuses on whether assessment improves the quality of intervention plans (for instance, does the use of a comprehensive risk assessment approach lead to interventions that target the most important, or relevant risk factors for a person?).

Finally, we recommend that research addresses the *process* of risk assessment much more so than has been done to date. This includes decision-making processes; formulation; scenario planning; as well as further attention to the complexities and various elements of risk other than likelihood (such as imminence); and various aspects of violence other than mere occurrence (such as severity). A small amount of research has started to address such factors. For instance, Hopton et al. (2018) demonstrated that the use of the Version 3 of the Historical-Clinical-Risk Management-20 (Douglas et al., 2013) led to better-quality risk formulations than its predecessor, V2 (Webster et al., 1997).

Legal Review

There have been many comprehensive reviews of legal principles surrounding violence risk assessment, and the legal settings in which risk assessment transpires (for reviews, see Douglas et al., 2014; Guy et al., 2015; Slobogin, 2021).

Legal Contexts

Risk assessment is firmly embedded in numerous legal contexts, by statute. Although such statutes do not typically require that certain instruments are used, they call for decisions to be made about future risk of crime, violence, or violation of supervisory rules. Common contexts include, inter alia, pretrial decisions pertaining to bail and placement; presentence evaluations to determine type and level of correctional supervision; release decisions (parole from prison; conditional or absolute discharge from forensic hospitalization); determinations of sexually violent predator status; civil psychiatric hospitalization and discharge; death sentence eligibility; juvenile raise decisions; and workplace violence/safety decisions.

One of the core legal areas that spurred attention to violence risk assessment is civil commitment. Until the early 1970s, civil commitment typically only required a medical opinion that people had a mental disorder and needed treatment—that was sufficient to hold them against their will in a psychiatric facility (Melton et al., 2018).

In the landmark federal district case of *Lessard v. Schmidt*,[2] the US District Court for the Eastern District of Wisconsin held that there must be, in addition to a mental disorder and need for treatment, a dangerousness element (to self or others) to hospitalize a person involuntarily. This case also afforded persons many of the same due process protections available in criminal cases (i.e., the right to counsel and to a jury), and deemed that the standard of evidence should be "beyond a reasonable doubt" rather than "preponderance of evidence." Some years later, the US Supreme Court lowered the standard of proof to "clear and convincing evidence."[3] In 1975, the US Supreme Court held that the state cannot indefinitely hold a person who is not dangerous and is capable of living safely in the community.[4]

These legal cases cemented the role of violence risk assessment within civil commitment law. Most states followed suit in the 1970s to require a dangerousness element (Melton et al., 2018). Currently, this varies across jurisdictions, but typically requires a serious risk of imminent physical harm to self or others, and a recent overt act of physical harm to self or others. In a similar way, the US Supreme Court has held that the state cannot hold a person who has been found not guilty by reason of insanity if that person no longer has a mental disorder.[5] As such, under either criminal or civil hospitalization, a person must both have a mental disorder and pose a danger to self or others.

Moreover, *Baxstrom v. Harold* determined some years earlier that a person sentenced to prison cannot be held indeterminately after the expiration of their sentence merely because they had a mental disorder.[6] Such persons must be afforded the same rights and protections as others who are subject to civil commitment proceedings (i.e., both mental

---

[2] Lessard v. Schmidt, 349 F. Supp. 1078 (E.D. Wis. 1972), *vacated on other grounds*, 414 U.S. 473 (1974).

[3] Addington v. Texas, 441 U.S. 418 (1979);

[4] O'Connor v. Donaldson, 422 U.S. 563 (1975).

[5] Foucha v. Louisiana, 504 U.S. 71 (1992).

[6] Baxstrom v. Herold, 383 U.S. 107 (1966).

STEPHEN D. HART AND KEVIN S. DOUGLAS

disorder and dangerousness must be present). That same principle applies to the contemporary instantiation of postsentence civil commitment for so-called sexual predators (Guy et al., 2015). In that context, as well, there must be a causal nexus between the mental disorder (or abnormality) and risk for future sexual violence.[7]

Common Law Duty to Protect

In many jurisdictions, there are additional common law duties for mental health professionals with respect to the duty to protect third parties from reasonably foreseeable violence posed by patients or clients. In the landmark case of *Tarasoff v. Regents of the University of California*, the California Supreme Court held that mental health professionals who know or ought to know that a patient or client has a likelihood of injuring an identifiable third party must take reasonable steps to protect that person.[8] Such steps could involve warning the potential victim, civilly committing the patient, contacting the police, or doing whatever is reasonable in the circumstances. Some states have extended this duty to nonidentifiable victims (Guy et al., 2015). This duty exists in different forms—more or less strict—across jurisdictions (Melton et al., 2018). The importance for practitioners is to know that they must be able to determine whether their patients or clients pose a risk of violence to others, and hence whether they must take reasonable steps to protect potential victims. Again, the role of violence risk assessment has been cemented, by law, into clinical practice.

Admissibility of Risk Assessment Testimony

Of course, for risk assessment to address the various statutory and common law requirements and duties, it must be considered acceptable by courts and other legal decision makers. Although the reliability and hence potential admissibility of risk assessment has been challenged many times in court, such challenges typically have failed. Indeed, most risk assessment testimony is admissible in court, under the various rules of admissibility. This is true of clinical testimony that is not based on particular tools, as well as testimony based on both actuarial instruments and SPJ guidelines.

This topic has a lengthy legal history, but courts have generally declined to hold that mental health professionals—regardless of their method of risk assessment—are as poor at the task as to render their opinions inadmissible. Indeed, even before the existence of contemporary risk assessment approaches, all reasonably well validated, courts upheld the constitutionality and admissibility of expert testimony on risk assessment. Perhaps the most notable case was *Barefoot v. Estelle*, where the US Supreme Court upheld the constitutionality of a death sentence based on expert opinion about future risk, despite the fact that the "expert" psychiatrist had not even interviewed the defendant.[9] Subsequent

---

[7] Kansas v. Crane, 534 U.S. 407 (2002).
[8] Tarasoff v. Regents of the Univ. of Cal., 551 P.2d 334 (Cal. 1976).
[9] Barefoot v. Estelle, 463 U.S. 880 (1983).

cases have followed suit,[10] essentially showing considerable deference to mental health professionals, and that cross-examination and judicial scrutiny can help to identify faulty testimony, as originally held in *Barefoot* (Douglas et al., 2014; Guy et al., 2015).

As Slobogin (2021) has described, courts have been reluctant to deviate from *Barefoot's* acceptance of expert testimony on risk assessment. Further, given that they were deemed constitutional for purposes of execution, it is difficult to see how they could not be constitutional for other purposes (Slobogin, 2021). Indeed, Slobogin (2021) has argued that there is a "judicial nonchalance" (p. 70) with respect to the admissibility of risk assessment testimony of any type. Although courts have acknowledged the difficulty of such decisions, they have also typically concluded that such decisions are possible. Indeed, they are required in many legal settings—hence, they *must* be possible (Slobogin, 2021). As concluded by Douglas et al. (2014), "Whether in *Frye* or in *Daubert* jurisdictions, courts have been receptive to violence risk assessments, whether clinical or actuarial, by mental health professionals" (p. 423). For a thorough discussion of admissibility issues based on constitutional concerns and rules of evidence, see Slobogin (2021).

Legal Treatment of Bias in Risk Assessment

Currently, there is no legal precedent in the United States that risk assessment tools, or, more broadly, risk assessment practice, is inherently biased against any particular groups of people (see Slobogin, 2021, for a review). Although there has been considerable legal academic commentary on point, as reviewed earlier, and despite a recent ruling of the US Supreme Court that decisions of risk based on race would be unconstitutional,[11] challenges in the United States to the use of risk assessment instruments on the basis of discrimination (equal protection) have failed, at least to date (Slobogin, 2021). Starr's (2014) argument that many risk factors are proxies for race, and hence ought not to be used in risk assessment on grounds of equal protection, has been rebutted by other legal scholars on the basis that unless there was a clear race-related motivation on the part of the government to use such factors, their inclusion is not unconstitutional (Slobogin, 2021). We would argue, despite any legal opinions or findings on the fairness of risk assessment instruments, that the field does have a positive duty to ensure that their use is fair across different groups of people.

In Canada, the picture is somewhat different. In Canada, the primary legal argument has been that certain risk assessment tools have not been adequately validated on offenders of Indigenous heritage. And, indeed, the Supreme Court of Canada has concurred with this argument.[12] Professional opinions diverge in terms of whether there is enough

---

[10] Kansas v. Crane, 534 U.S. 407 (2002); Kansas v. Hendricks, 521 U.S. 346 (1997); Schall v. Martin, 467 U.S. 253 (1984); United States v. Salerno, 481 U.S. 739 (1987).

[11] Buck v. Davis, 580 U.S. ___, 137 S. Ct. 759 (2017).

[12] Ewert v. Canada, 2 S.C.R. 165 (Can. 2018).

evidence of acceptable validation (contrast Hart, 2016, and Olver, 2016). There is some agreement that the risk assessment instruments in question (certain actuarial instruments, as well as the PCL-R) perform less well in terms of predictive validity for Indigenous offenders compared to other offenders, but that the level of performance is still adequate (Haag et al., 2016; Olver, 2016; cf. Hart, 2016). However, all parties would appear to agree that more research is needed, both on the impugned instruments as well as SPJ instruments.

Recommendations for Practice

In light of the issues discussed in this chapter and more general discussions of principles of forensic mental health assessment (in particular, Grisso, 2003; Heilbrun, 2001), following we provide recommendations for best practices with respect to violence risk assessment and management. For the sake of brevity, we refer to those who deliver services related to violence risk assessment and management (synonymously, threat assessment and management) as "professionals" and those whose risks are assessed and managed by professionals as "people."

1. **Professionals strive to gather and integrate all the information that is reasonably necessary to do their work.** They identify the information that is reasonably necessary and then attempt to gather it. They gather information from diverse sources, including interviews, observations, official records, and other documents. They use or rely on specialized information-gathering techniques where relevant and appropriate. They attempt to corroborate critical information. They acknowledge in their communications when critical information they relied on was unavailable, incomplete, or outdated. They do not:
   1.1. Rely on a single source of information in their work, and in particular do not rely on uncorroborated statements made by people.
   1.2. Rely solely on indirect information unless gathering information about people directly via interview or observation would be inappropriate, unfeasible, or unsafe.
   1.3. Rely on information that is or is likely to be outdated, unless gathering updated information would be inappropriate, unfeasible, or unsafe.
2. **Professionals strive to identify and use decision support tools relevant to violence risk assessment.** They acknowledge the limitations of unaided or unstructured professional judgment, seek education and training about decision support tools germane to their work, and use decision support tools, where relevant and appropriate. They use decision support tools only as recommended by authorities in the field, such as the developers. They

acknowledge in their communications the strengths and limitations of any decision support tools they used. They do not:

2.1. Rely solely on unaided or unstructured professional judgment when decision support tools germane to their work exist and could be appropriately used.

2.2. Rely on decision support tools without integrating into their final judgments relevant information not considered by those tools.

2.3. Use decision support tools unless adequately trained and experienced in their application, administration, and interpretation.

2.4. Use decision support tools unless familiar with the literature regarding their reliability (precision) and validity (accuracy).

2.5. Report the findings of decision support tools without a full interpretation or explanation of the findings.

3. **Professionals strive to develop comprehensive violence risk management plans.** They develop plans that identify potentially effective management strategies, tactics, and logistics. They ensure that plans target important risk factors. They recognize the need for and facilitate coordination with other professionals responsible for risk management, where relevant and appropriate. They acknowledge in their communications the need to evaluate and revise management plans. They do not:

3.1. Deliver risk management services without adequate training and experience in those specific services.

3.2. Deliver risk management services without involving and collaborating with other professionals, as relevant and appropriate.

4. **Professionals strive to communicate with others about their violence risk assessment and management services in a manner that is complete, accurate, and clear.** They include in their oral or written communications all the information necessary, but only the information necessary, to describe their actions, findings, or opinions. They use nontechnical language when communicating with people who are not threat assessment professionals, as relevant and appropriate. They acknowledge the limitations of their work. They do not:

4.1. Misrepresent or distort information included in their communications.

4.2. Ignore or omit potentially relevant information from their communications.

4.3. Use jargon in their communications unless necessary and unless they provide adequate definition or explanation.

4.4. Present findings or opinions without qualification in light of limitations in the information on which they were based and the contextual and dynamic nature of risk.

5. **Professionals strive to recognize and mitigate the potential of bias based on human diversity in the delivery of their violence risk assessment, management, and communication services.** They seek to identify and understand the possible influence of diversity—including but not limited to such things as people's age, gender, culture (or related concepts such as race, ethnicity, and language), physical or mental health problems, and ideology (such as religious or political affiliation)—in their work. They recognize that all human judgment is susceptible to bias and, furthermore, decision support tools that are quantitative in nature may also have bias inherent in their underlying algorithms or statistics. They take steps to reduce susceptibility to bias when delivering assessment and management services. They explicitly acknowledge in their violence risk communications the susceptibility to bias of human judgment generally and any decision support tools they used, as well as any steps they took to mitigate potential bias when delivering violence risk assessment and management services. They do not:

   5.1. Discriminate on the basis of diversity by assuming themselves or encouraging others to assume that the mere presence of a diversity they believe may be relevant to violence risk indicates that diversity is equally relevant for every person or, indeed, relevant at all for any given person.

   5.2. Ignore special responsibilities when delivering violence risk assessment, management, or communication services to or about people whose diversities are considered protected statuses under relevant international, constitutional, civil (human) rights, or statutory law.

Recommendations for Research

Below we present some recommendations for future research on violence risk, based in part on the issues discussed in this chapter and on some of our previous writings (e.g., Guy et al., 2015; Hart et al., 2016). There is no need for us to highlight topics such as the prevalence of and risk factors for various forms of violence or the validity generalizations of specific decisions support tools, as these are areas where research is active. We therefore focus on topics that remain unexplored or underexplored. Once again, we refer to those who deliver services related to violence risk assessment and management (synonymously, threat assessment and management) as "professionals" and those whose risks are assessed and managed by professionals as "people."

1. **Consumer satisfaction research**. There is a need for research on the extent to which various stakeholders such as professionals, people, and other interested parties view various violence risk assessment and management practices (e.g., decision support tools; management strategies, tactics, and logistics; methods of communication) as acceptable, useful, in need

of improvement, and so forth. This could take the form of surveys, legal reviews, focus groups, comparative outcome studies, and so forth. Examples of specific topics include:

1.1. *Training of professionals.* What background knowledge, skills, or experience best prepare professionals to engage in various risk assessment and management practices? What do professionals with different levels of experience perceive to be critical needs that would prepare them for practice? Which training curricula, delivered by which methods, do professionals find most helpful to acquire the knowledge and skills required for practice?

1.2. *Usefulness of practices.* How often are various violence risk assessment and management practices considered by experienced professionals to be clearly appropriate, clearly inappropriate, or questionably appropriate for use in various settings? For what decision-making purposes or with which types of people are those practices considered to be especially helpful or unhelpful? What kinds of revisions or modifications would make the practices more useful?

1.3. *Acceptability of practices.* How are various violence risk assessment and management practices perceived by people, allied professionals, and the public with respect to such issues as face validity, fairness, and relevance to decision-making? What could be done to improve the perceived acceptability of practices?

2. **Research on integrative judgments by professionals**. Research is needed to explore how professionals make sense of information about violence risk. This could take the form of "talk-aloud" and focus groups studies where professionals, working alone or in teams, are asked to describe their thought processes in real time as they work on cases. Examples of specific topics include:

2.1. *Process of making judgments.* How do professionals construct mental models of the violence risk posed by people or develop plans for managing that risk? For example, how do they decide which risk factors are most relevant and how they act synergistically to cause violence? How do they develop management plans? How do they communicate their judgments?

2.2. *Approaches for structuring judgments.* Which implicit theories or framework guide the judgments of untrained or novice versus trained or experienced professionals? Can professionals be trained to use different theories or frameworks? Are there other ways to improve the quality of judgments by increasing their interrater reliability, reducing their susceptibility to bias, and improving their justification or logical foundation?

3. **Field studies of violence risk.** More research is needed concerning the effectiveness of various violence risk assessment and management practices in real-world settings. This could take the form of qualitative and quantitative research. Examples of specific topics include:

   3.1. *Implementation of practices.* What policies, initial and continuing education, and quality assurance procedures support successful adoption of new risk assessment and management practices in field settings? What is the fidelity with which those practices are implemented? What barriers to successful implementation are most common, and how can they be overcome?

   3.2. *Interrater reliability of risk assessments.* What level of agreement or consistency is observed across professionals with respect to the various ratings and judgments they make using various decision support tools? To what degree is it affected by factors such as the training or experience of professionals, the adequacy or completeness of the information base available to them, and so forth?

   3.3. *Impact of risk assessments on case management decisions.* In what ways, to what degree, and how do violence risk assessments influence the risk management plans recommended or implemented in cases?

   3.4. *Dynamic aspects of risk assessment and management.* In what ways, to what degree, and how do professionals respond to potential changes in violence risk over time? How do changes in risk assessment guide changes in risk management, and vice versa? How do professionals communicate to stakeholders about changes in violence risk?

Conclusion

Violence risk is an important area of psycholegal research and practice, and there is no indication its importance will diminish in the coming years. Despite the advances the field has seen in the last thirty years, there remains a strong need for both basic and applied research to guide the development, implementation, and evaluation of decision support tools for practice.

Authors' Notes

The authors declare the following conflicts of interest: They profit from providing public presentations, training, consultation, assessment and management, and expert witness service related to in violence risk assessment, as well as from royalties for the sales of books and manuals on violence risk assessment.

References

Bernstein, P. L. (1996). *Against the gods: The remarkable story of risk.* Wiley.

Bonta, J., Law, M., & Hanson, R. K. (1998). The prediction of criminal and violent recidivism among mentally disordered offenders: A meta-analysis. *Psychological Bulletin, 123*(2), 123–142.

Campbell, M. A., French, S., & Gendreau, P. (2009). The prediction of violence in adult offenders: A meta-analytic comparison of instruments and methods of assessment. *Criminal Justice and Behavior, 36*(6), 567–590.

de Vries Robbé, M., de Vogel, V., Douglas, K. S., & Nijman, H. L. I. (2015). Changes in dynamic risk and protective factors for violence during inpatient forensic psychiatric treatment: Predicting reductions in postdischarge community recidivism. *Law and Human Behavior, 39*(1), 53–61.

DeMatteo, D., Hart, S. D., Heilbrun, K. S., Boccaccini, M. S., Cunningham, M. D., Douglas, K. S., Dvoskin, J. A., Edens, J. F., Guy, L. S., Murrie, D. C., Otto, R. K., Packer, I. K., & Reidy, T. J. (2020a). Consensus statement on the use of the Hare Psychopathy Checklist-Revised (PCL-R) in capital sentencing to assess risk for institutional violence. *Psychology, Public Policy, and Law, 26*(2), 133–144.

DeMatteo, D., Hart, S. D., Heilbrun, K. S., Boccaccini, M. S., Cunningham, M. D., Douglas, K. S., Dvoskin, J. A., Edens, J. F., Guy, L. S., Murrie, D. C., Otto, R. K., Packer, I. K., & Reidy, T. J. (2020b). Death is different: Reply to Olver et al. (2020b). *Psychology, Public Policy, and Law, 26*(4), 511–518.

Desmarais, S. L., Zottola, S. A., Clarke, S. E. D., & Lowder, E. M. (2021). Predictive validity of pretrial risk assessments: A systematic review of the literature. *Criminal Justice and Behavior, 48*(4), 398–420.

Douglas, K. S., Hart, S. D., Groscup, J. L., & Litwack, T. R. (2014). Assessing violence risk. In I. Weiner & R. K. Otto (Eds.), *The handbook of forensic psychology* (4th ed., pp. 385–441). John Wiley & Sons.

Douglas, K. S., Hart, S. D., Webster, C. D., & Belfrage, H. (2013). *HCR-20^{V3}: Assessing risk for violence.* Mental Health, Law, and Policy Institute, Simon Fraser University.

Douglas, K. S., & Otto, R. K. (Eds.). (2021). *Handbook of violence risk assessment* (2nd ed.). Routledge/Taylor & Francis.

Fazel, S., Singh J. P., Doll, H., & Grann, M. (2012). Use of risk assessment instruments to predict violence and antisocial behaviour in 73 samples involving 24,827 people: Systematic review and meta-analysis. *British Medical Journal, 345*, Article e4692

Grisso, T. (2003). *Evaluating competencies: Forensic assessments and instruments* (2nd ed.). Kluwer Academic/Plenum Press.

Gutierrez, L., Helmus, M., & Hanson, R. K. (2016). What we know and don't know about risk assessment with offenders of Indigenous heritage. *Journal of Threat Assessment and Management, 3*(2), 97–106.

Guy, L. S., Douglas, K. S., & Hart, S. D. (2015). Risk assessment and communication. In B. Cutler & P. Zapf (Eds.), *APA handbook of forensic psychology* (Vol. 1, pp. 35–86). American Psychological Association.

Guy, L. S., Douglas, K. S., & Hendry, M. (2010). The role of psychopathic personality disorder in violence risk assessments using the HCR-20. *Journal of Personality Disorders, 24*(5), 551–580.

Haag, A. M., Boyes, A., Cheng, J., MacNeil, A., & Wirove, R. (2016). An introduction to the issues of cross-cultural assessment inspired by *Ewert v. Canada. Journal of Threat Assessment and Management, 3*(2), 65–75.

Hanson, R. K., & Morton-Bourgon, K. E. (2009). The accuracy of recidivism risk assessments for sexual offenders: A meta-analysis of 118 prediction studies. *Psychological Assessment, 21*(1), 1–21.

Hansson, S. O. (2018). Risk. In E. N. Zalta (Ed.), *The Stanford encyclopedia of philosophy* (Fall 2018 ed., pp. 1–33). https://plato.stanford.edu/archives/fall2018/entries/risk/

Hart, S. D. (2001). Assessing and managing violence risk. In K. S. Douglas, C. D. Webster, S. D. Hart, D. Eaves, & J. R. P. Ogloff (Eds.), *HCR-20 violence risk management companion guide* (pp. 13–25). Mental Health, Law, & Policy Institute, Simon Fraser University.

Hart, S. D. (2016). Culture and violence risk assessment: The case of *Ewert v. Canada. Journal of Threat Assessment and Management, 3*(2), 76–96.

Hart, S. D., Douglas, K. S., & Guy, L. S. (2016). The structured professional judgment approach to violence risk assessment: Origins, nature, and advances. In L. Craig & M. Rettenberger (Volume Eds.) & D. Boer (Series Ed.), *The Wiley handbook on the theories, assessment, treatment of sexual offending: Volume II. Assessment* (pp. 643–666). John Wile & Sons.

Heilbrun, K. S. (1997). Prediction versus management models relevant to risk assessment: The importance of legal decision-making context. *Law and Human Behavior, 21*(4), 347–359.

Heilbrun, K. S. (2001). *Principles of forensic mental health assessment.* Kluwer Academic/Plenum Press.

Heilbrun, K., Yasuhara, K., Shah, S., & Locklair, B. (2021). Approaches to violence risk assessment: Overview, critical analysis, and future directions. In K. S. Douglas & R. K. Otto (Eds.), *Handbook of violence risk assessment* (2nd ed., pp. 3–27). Routledge/Taylor & Francis.

Hogan, N. R., & Olver, M. E. (2016). Assessing risk for aggression in forensic psychiatric inpatients: An examination of five measures. *Law and Human Behavior, 40*(3), 233–243.

Hogan, N. R., & Olver, M. E. (2019). Static and dynamic assessment of violence risk among discharged forensic patients. *Criminal Justice and Behavior, 46*(7), 923–938.

Hopton, J., Cree, A., Thompson, S., Jones, R., & Jones, R. (2018). An evaluation of the quality of HCR-20 risk formulations: A comparison between HCR-20 Version 2 and HCR-20 Version 3. *International Journal of Forensic Mental Health, 17*(2), 195–201.

International Standards Organization. (2018). *Risk management: Principles and guidelines* (2nd ed.). International Standards Organization .

Krug, E. G., Dahlberg, L. L., Mercy, J. A., Zwi, A. B., & Lozano, R. (Eds.). (2002). *World report on violence and health*. World Health Organization.

Leistico, A. M., Salekin, R. T., DeCosta, J., & Rogers, R. (2008). A large-scale meta-analysis relating the Hare measures of psychopathy to antisocial conduct. *Law and Human Behavior, 32*(1), 28–45.

Meloy, J. R., Hoffmann, J., Deisinger, E. R. D., & Hart, S. D. (2021). Threat assessment and threat management. In J. R. Meloy & J. Hoffmann (Eds.), *International handbook of threat assessment* (2nd ed., pp. 3–21). Oxford University Press.

Melton, G. B., Petrila, J., Poythress, N. G., & Slobogin, C., Otto, R. K., Mossman, D., & Condie, L. O. (2018). *Psychological evaluations for the courts: A handbook for mental health professionals and lawyers* (4th ed.). Guilford Press.

Olver, M. E. (2016). Some considerations on the use of actuarial and related forensic measures with diverse correctional populations. *Journal of Threat Assessment and Management, 3*(2), 107–121.

Olver, M. E., Stockdale, K. C., & Wormith, J. S. (2014). Thirty years of research on the level of service scales: A meta-analytic examination of predictive accuracy and sources of variability. *Psychological Assessment, 26*(1), 156–176.

O'Shea, L. E., & Dickens, G. L. (2014). Short-Term Assessment of Risk and Treatability (START): Systematic review and meta-analysis. *Psychological Assessment, 26*(3), 990–1002.

Otto, R. K. (2000). Assessing and managing violence risk in outpatient settings. *Journal of Clinical Psychology, 56*(10), 1239–1262.

Singh, J. P., Grann, M., & Fazel, S. (2011). A comparative study of violence risk assessment tools: A systematic review and meta-regression analysis of 68 studies involving 25,980 participants. *Clinical Psychology Review, 31*(3), 499–513.

Slobogin, C. (2021). Constitutional and evidentiary issues concerning violence risk assessment. In K. S. Douglas & R. K. Otto (Eds.), *Handbook of violence risk assessment* (2nd ed., pp. 70–90). Routledge/Taylor & Francis.

Starr, S. B. (2014). Evidence-based sentencing and the scientific rationalization of discrimination. *Stanford Law Review, 66*(4), 803–872.

Viljoen, J. L., Mordell, S., & Beneteau, J. L. (2012). Prediction of adolescent sexual reoffending: A meta-analysis of the J-SOAP-II, ERASOR, J-SORRAT-II, and Static-99. *Law and Human Behavior, 36*(5), 423–438.

Viljoen, J. L., Vargen, L. M., Cochrane, D. M., Jonnson, M. R., Goossens, I., & Monjazeb, S. (2021). Do structured risk assessments predict violent, any, and sexual offending better than unstructured judgment? An umbrella review. *Psychology, Public Policy, and Law, 27*(1), 79–97.

Vincent, G. M., & Viljoen, J. L. (2020). Racist algorithms or systemic problems? Risk assessments and racial disparities. *Criminal Justice and Behavior, 47*(12), 1576–1584.

Webster, C. D., Douglas, K. S., Eaves, D., & Hart, S. D. (1997). *The HCR-20 scheme: The assessment of dangerousness and risk* (Version 2). Mental Health, Law, and Policy Institute, Simon Fraser University.

Yang, M., Wong, S. C. P., & Coid, J. (2010). The efficacy of violence prediction: A meta-analytic comparison of nine risk assessment tools. *Psychological Bulletin, 136*(5), 740–767.

Response Styles within the Forensic Context: Conceptual Issues and Assessment Methods

Richard Rogers, Minqi Pan, *and* Eric Y. Drogin

Abstract

This chapter emphasizes the critical importance of clarity and specificity when identifying and defining response styles in forensic contexts. When differentiating "malingering" from "feigning," and "defensiveness" from "impression management," forensic practitioners must convey their findings with scientific rigor and unambiguous concision. Empirically validated detection strategies constitute the foundation of response-style research. They are systematically applied genuine responding as well as feigned and other intentionally distorted presentations. The clinical usefulness of strategy-based scales is illustrated with multiscale inventories and such specialized measures as the SIRS-2. In forensic practice, it is particularly important to minimize shortcuts, such as initial screens, that may jeopardize the validity and accuracy of response-style conclusions. Instead, forensic practitioners are asked to adopt more comprehensive multimethod and multistrategy approaches. This chapter concludes with specific recommendations for improved investigation of response styles in forensic contexts.

Key Words: response styles, malingering, feigning, defensiveness, impression management, SIRS-2, forensic mental health assessments

Forensic practitioners sometimes fall victim to the *full-disclosure fallacy* with the strong yet implicit assumption that examinees will be entirely forthcoming despite the high-stakes nature of most forensic evaluations. This same fallacy also appears to be in place when forensic assessment instruments are carefully developed over years but with virtually no attention paid to malingering and other response styles (e.g., MacArthur Competence Assessment Tool for Criminal Adjudication; Poythress et al., 1999). To put intentional distortions in a broader clinical context, Rogers (2018b) observed that deceptions are common in mental health services even including therapeutic relationships, supposedly a bastion of trust and self-disclosure. For instance, patients commonly lie about the effectiveness of therapy, reasons for missed appointments, and completion of homework (Blanchard & Farber, 2016). Moreover, to provide a balanced perspective, forensic psychologists and psychiatrists are also not likely to be entirely forthcoming about the true import of some clinical inquiries (e.g., possible malingering) or their preliminary conclusions (e.g., heightened concerns in a risk assessment). Rather than full disclosures, some forms of impression management and other response styles should be expected from forensic examinees as entirely understandable under stressful and often nonvoluntary circumstances.

Overview of Response Styles

Most intentional response styles (Rogers, 2018b) can be principally categorized along a single continuum in two opposite directions (i.e., overstated pathology and simulated adjustment). This continuum covers three main domains: (1) mental disorders or psychopathology, (2) cognitive issues, and (3) medical symptoms and complaints. This chapter focuses primarily on overstated pathology, especially in the form of feigned or malingered mental disorders.

Overstated Presentations

There are three common terms for overstated (exaggerated or fabricated) presentations, outlined here with brief comments:

1. *Malingering* is defined by the American Psychiatric Association (2013, p. 726) as "the intentional production of false or grossly exaggerated physical or psychological symptoms, motivated by external incentives."
   a. Two comments: First, the severity of the overstated presentation must be marked or even extreme (i.e., clearly fabricated or grossly exaggerated). Second, the motivation must be investigated and established, and never facilely inferred (e.g., all examinees for criminal responsibility want to be found legally "insane").
2. *Feigning* parallels the overstated presentation of malingering (i.e., fabrication or gross exaggeration) but does not address motivation.
   a. Comment: Through empirically validated detection strategies, specialized feigning measures and several psychological tests may be used to determine false and grossly exaggerated presentations. However, no measure has been developed to systematically evaluate complex motivations involved in feigning presentations.
3. *Poor effort* (or suboptimal effort) is typically inferred from unexpectedly low performance, especially on cognitive measures.
   a. Two comments: First, when stated explicitly, psychologists and psychiatrists can easily discern the inherent problem of equating effort with outcome. Second, given the often interactive nature of performance-based psychological testing, solely blaming the examinee for poor results appears one-sided and professionally misguided.

For *malingering*, the second comment regarding motivation merits a brief explanation. What considerations might be contemplated by examinees in deciding whether or not to malinger insanity? Reflect on this partial list: (1) their perceptions of the evaluator (e.g., gullible vs. skeptical), (2) comparative conditions and programming (i.e., state hospitals versus penitentiaries), (3) legal defenses being relinquished by fully admitting to the offenses; (4) if "successful" (i.e., undetected malingering), likelihood of receiving an insanity acquittal; (5) if "unsuccessful" (detected malingering), likelihood of punitive actions, such as longer sentences. Although most would-be malingerers are not so deliberative, just these five considerations underscore the potential complexity of malingering motivations in deciding when and what should be feigned.

For *poor effort*, the second comment echoes similar views to those expressed in the previous paragraph. Like malingering, effort needs to be fully investigated by itself and not facilely inferred from performance. In some cognitive and neuropsychological assessments, tests of verbal and nonverbal abilities are occasionally piled on examinees with little effort by evaluators to motivate their best performances. The unintended irony of this double standard for poor effort does not lessen the gravity of any subsequent misclassifications.

Simulated Adjustment

Forensic researchers and practitioners have paid comparatively little attention to examinees who may be presenting in an overly positive manner. This disregard of response styles is especially concerning with specialized forensic populations, such as psychopaths and offenders with substance use or paraphilias. Following a general description, we briefly address these three populations.

Specific types of forensic assessments should take into account whether some examinees may be motivated to engage in simulated adjustment to avoid negative consequences. Examples included risk assessments and sentencing evaluations, such as sex offenders targeting children. Regarding the latter, the use of highly transparent measures with no indicators of simulated adjustment (Tierney & McCabe, 2001) jeopardizes the accuracy of forensic conclusions and implicitly suggests that the full-disclosure fallacy may be operating.

Three types of simulated adjustment have been identified. Each is defined here and followed by brief comments.

1. *Defensiveness* is conceptualized as the polar opposite of malingering (Rogers, 2018b) in the denial or gross minimization of psychological and physical symptoms with the motivation obtaining an unwarranted, yet desired, external incentive.
   a. Comment: Unlike many studies of malingering, research on defensiveness is often less explicit in its attention to *unwarranted*

incentives. This distinction is important, because persons are generally expected to "put their best foot forward" in an effort to secure a desired objective, such as being hired for a competitive position.

2. *Social desirability* tends to be viewed as an ongoing effort to align oneself with positive public or societal expectations with the explicit goal of being positively valued by many persons.

    a. Two comments: First, social desirability may be more situationally focused than broadly experienced, such as attempting to appear as the "better" parent in a contested custody evaluation. Second, social desirability may need to be rethought in culturally diverse environments involving complex interplays of social expectations.

3. *Impression management* is often construed as matching or exceeding the expectations of a particular situation or setting. In many cases, impression management may almost completely correspond to social desirability. In other circumstances (e.g., sales on a commission), the two constructs may have little in common.

    a. Comment: As an innovative approach (Blasberg et al., 2014), impression management has been conceptualized in two dimensions: (1) overly positive presentations plus (2) purportedly strong denials of values and conduct not conforming to targeted group/setting.

In particular, impression management may be an overlooked response style in forensic contexts because much of the sophisticated research has been focused on personnel selection. As a valuable resource, Levashina (2018) has systematically identified eleven models of deceptive impression management in work-related settings addressing common beliefs, motivations, and justifications for impression management. Detection methods for positive impression management may include (1) extreme responses patterns (e.g., an unlikely number of highest scores on virtuous items), (2) overclaiming of abilities or experiences, and (3) inclusion of bogus items (e.g., plausible sounding but nonexistent terms). For the latter two methods, adolescents have sometimes been asked to disclose their own substance use with a fictitious drug being embedded in a list of actual substances to assess for impression management (Farrell et al., 1991).

MINIMIZED PSYCHOPATHY

Individuals with psychopathic characteristics undergoing forensic evaluations may be understandably motivated to engage in impression management and appear comparatively more prosocial and a smaller risk to others. Positive impression management is easily achievable on self-report measures of psychopathy (Kelsey et al., 2015). What is known about simulated adjustment on versions of the Psychopathy Checklist (PCL; Hare, 1980), widely considered the standard in forensic practice? Rogers et al. (2002) conducted the only available study directly addressing response styles; it utilized the PCL Youth Version (PCL-YV; Forth et al., 2003). With virtually no preparation, they found that juvenile detainees in their mid-teens could substantially suppress their PCL scores. In more than three decades of studies (Hare, 1991, 2003), rigorous research regarding the effects of simulated adjustment on PCL-R results appears to have been entirely neglected. As argued by Hare (2003), record reviews might help in uncovering some denied psychopathic features.

Three points are worthy of consideration. First, beyond official reports on arrests and convictions, records are often incomplete and may be inaccurate sources of information, based on nonsystematic impressions by nonprofessionals of a particular offender (Gillard, 2018). Second, the effectiveness of records at detecting simulated adjustments should not be simply assumed. Instead, experimental investigations should be conducted on psychopaths engaging in positive impression management to see if the presence or absence of collateral records assist in their detection. As the third and most basic point, PCL-R research on simulated adjustment should be a very high priority. With 1,798 peer-reviewed articles citing the PCL-R (PsychINFO search on September 15, 2020), it could be argued that it is now time to adopt rigorous simulation designs (Rogers, 2018b). As a parallel, Gillard and Rogers (2015) tested simulated adjustment by detainees on a semistructured interview for risk assessment, Historical-Clinical-Risk Management-20 (HCR-20; Webster et al., 1997). Those detainees with moderate to high psychopathy on the PCL-R more effectively engaged in simulated adjustment ($M\ d$ = 1.51) than those with low psychopathy ($M\ d$ = 1.01).

The two take-home messages should be considered. First, all assessments involving psychopathy should seek to integrate multiple sources of data from sources beyond the examinees. Some consideration might be given to the selective use of the Personality Assessment Inventory (PAI; Morey, 2007), which assesses several constructs related to psychopathy as well as positive impression management (see Gardner & Boccaccini, 2017). Without other sources of data, forensic practitioners may be naively expecting persons skilled at manipulations to put aside these undeniably self-serving skills and imperil their own futures via self-disclosures. Second, even the PCL-R, arguably the best-validated measures of psychopathy, is vulnerable to manipulation. As a valuable resource, Gillard (2018) provided a comprehensive review of psychopathy and deception.

MINIMIZED SUBSTANCE USE.

The underreporting of substance use should be acknowledged as a frequent issue in forensic evaluations, which may span these three types of simulated adjustment. Most psychological measures of substance abuse ask face-valid, easily foiled, test items (Stein et al., 2018), such as the method and frequency of cocaine use. Thus, they appear to have inadvertently adopted the *full-disclosure fallacy*. As a singular exception, the Substance Abuse Subtle Screening Inventory-4 (SASSI-4; Lazowski & Geary, 2019) included subtle items (i.e., not face-valid) and validity scales for denied substance abuse. However, research has raised questions about the SASSI's effectiveness in detecting undisclosed substance use (Stein et al., 2018).

Recent research (Hartigan et al., 2021) found that many offenders in treatment with substance abuse could successfully suppress their SASSI-4 scores and, thus, avoid detection.

As a very positive finding, Hartigan and her colleagues established the response-style ratio (RSR) based on the relationship between two SASSI-4 scales under two conditions of positive impression management (i.e., social desirability and denials of substance-abuse impairment). For simulators, one scale was dramatically decreased while the second scale evidenced a modest opposite trend. For the initial validation, the RSR produced excellent sensitivity (0.87) and specificity (0.94). Given its sophistication (i.e., divergent changes in two scales), the RSR may prove resistant to simulation. These same researchers also found promising results for the Inventory of Drug Use Consequences (InDUC; Tonigan & Miller, 2002). The InDUC's Control scale involves the denial of most positive experiences stemming from the use of drugs or drinking (e.g., being more relaxed). Extensive denials are likely indicative of defensiveness in relationship to substance. Forensic practitioners are encouraged to examine and likely implement specialized indicators of simulated adjustment particularly focused on denied or minimized substance use.

MINIMIZED PARAPHILIAS

Defensiveness and social desirability are commonly observed in forensic evaluations of sex offenders. These pretrial assessments typically are used to generate sentencing recommendations. Examinees are often highly motivated to minimize the number and nature of illegal sexual behaviors. Focusing on psychological measures, Witt and Neller (2018) found that the Minnesota Multiphasic Personality Inventory-2 (MMPI-2; Butcher et al., 1989) and specialized measures could often find significant differences between admitters and deniers for sex offenders using measures of general defensiveness. According to these authors, however, a critical determination in many forensic assessments occurs "between *guilty* non-admitters (men falsely denying their offenses) and *innocent* non-admitters (men falsely accused)" (Lanyon & Thomas, 2008, p. 287). Besides rapport-building, Witt and Neller (2018) recommended that evaluations involving denied sex offenses (1) applying cognitive-interview methods to increase the amount of relevant details, and (2) cautiously using evidence after the examinee's open-ended account, such as probing without disclosing evidence from police investigative reports. Regarding the latter point, denying sex offenders may see comparatively little harm in sharing what already appears to be known, based on the strength of the perceived evidence.

In summary, this major section provided a broad conceptual framework for understanding both overstated presentations and simulated adjustment. It also addressed three important assessment issues (i.e., the minimization of psychopathy, substance use, and paraphilias). The next major section is focused almost exclusively on the domain of feigned mental disorders and the application of detection strategies.

Assessment of Feigned Mental Disorders: Empirically Validated Strategies

Evaluations and empirical bases for feigned presentations have progressed from early case studies to more systematic approaches (Rogers & Correa, 2008). Fluidity in scale development was common in early studies. As an example, the Lie scale of the original Minnesota Multiphasic Personality Inventory (MMPI; Hathaway & McKinley, 1940) was originally developed to detect intentionally dishonest responses. However, subsequent research generally established its usefulness in identifying social desirability (e.g., Graham, 2012). As a further example, the Infrequency (F) scale for the original MMPI was first developed to measure careless or inconsistent responding (Buechley & Ball, 1952). Only years later, the F scale was repurposed for feigned mental disorders (see quasi-rare detection strategy). To provide a more conceptually and grounded approach to feigning, Rogers (1984) identified detection strategies focused primarily on feigned mental disorders. This section outlines the components of detection strategies and then selectively describes six strategies with salient examples.

Building on Rogers (1984), Rogers (1997, 2008, 2018a) refined the description of detection strategies with their essential components. They are defined as "a conceptually based, empirically validated standardized method for systematically differentiating a specific response style from other response styles" (Rogers, 2018a, p. 20). These components are briefly reviewed in the next paragraphs, with key words titled for easy reference.

Conceptual basis is utilized as a methodological safeguard against accidental findings, such as highly unexpected scores being used as an indicator of feigning. The nonconceptual approach is often used in cognitive assessments of feigning, such as a lower-than-expected performance on (1) a specialized feigning measure Word Memory Test (WMT; Green, 2003), or (2) a specific scale of standardized test. Regarding the latter, for example, Young et al. (2012) found that likely feigners scored lower than others on the Symbol Span of the Wechsler Memory Scale-IV (WMS-IV; Wechsler, 2008). As a nonconceptual approach, it is not surprising that the highest sensitivities on the Symbol Span only approximated chance levels (i.e., .50 and .52).

Conceptually based strategies are especially important in differentiating between closely related response styles. For instance, Velsor et al. (2021) sought to discriminate between two types of feigned mental disorders. They were comprised to factitious psychological presentations (FPP) from malingered mental disorders. For the FPP condition, inpatients sought to portray strongly dependency and overinvolvement in healthcare providers, whereas those malingering were not invested in these issues. Thus, a thorough understanding of the clinical literature led to the initial development of conceptually relevant methods.

Empirically validated standardized methods should include clear operationalization of a specific detection strategy, which subsequently informs item development. For the original Structured Interview of Reported Symptoms (SIRS; Rogers et al., 1992), eight malingering experts in addition to Rogers independently categorized individual SIRS items by detection strategy. For construct validity, the minimum concordance was set at 67 percent with a much higher level of independent agreement being achieved (i.e., 88.2 percent).

Beyond initial item development, empirical validation clearly applies to subsequent scale validation. At the most basic level, scale homogeneity must be empirically demonstrated (e.g., alphas and inter-item correlations). Also, of critical importance, validation of feigning measures should integrate both convergent and discriminant validity. On this point, many studies have focused only on convergent validity and appear to be satisfied by moderate correlations. However, as described subsequently, discriminant validity becomes unquestionably essential in correctly identifying feigned mental disorders from other response styles.

The use of *standardized methods* and the demand for *empirical validation* together highlight the scientific basis of detection strategies. Rogers (2018b) outlined in detail the specific methods used in applying simulation designs to feigned mental disorders. Put simply, flawed research design will likely yield uninterpretable but often very misleading results. Consider for the moment a simulation study without the inclusion of a clinical comparison group. Elevated test scores could reflect either feigned or genuine psychopathology (Rogers, 2018b). As documented by Nijdam-Jones et al. (2020), clinical comparison samples produce much smaller effect sizes for the MMPI-2 and feigned PTSD. Possibly because of their vested interest, researchers sometimes naively assume elevated scores must be evidence of feigning. This fundamental flaw in empirical validation has been known for decades (Rogers, 1997). Despite its very real risk of life-changing harm in forensic cases (i.e., wrongly classifying a genuine patient as malingering), this substandard practice is still observed. For a recent and striking example, see the meta-analysis of the Structured Inventory of Malingered Symptomatology (SIMS; van Impelen et al., 2014) with some simulation studies expediently and inappropriately comprised solely of presumably healthy undergraduates (see van Impelen et al., 2014, table 2).

The final component involves *systematically differentiating a specific response style from other response styles*. Statistical significance sets only the minimal threshold but provides no estimation about the magnitude of the observed difference. In research on response styles, Cohen's d is generally accepted as the effect size for measuring the magnitude of differences. Cohen's original work was content with relaxed standards (e.g., 0.50 for a medium effect). More recently, Rogers et al. (2003) proposed more rigorous standards for feigning and other specific response styles: ≥ 0.75 for moderate, large ≥ 1.25, and very large ≥ 1.50. Small effect sizes were viewed as too lax for clinical classifications. Originally focused on response styles, these standards have now been applied more broadly to psychological assessments, such as the validation of empirical correlates (Rogers et al., 2018).

The importance of such rigor is clearly underscored in light of the continuing replication crisis in the social sciences.

At its core, the accurate differentiation of specific response styles relies firmly on the establishment of utility estimates. Although a discussion of specific terms (e.g., sensitivity and specificity) are beyond the scope of this chapter, forensic practitioners must bear in mind the investigators' objectives. The simplest objective focuses on overall correct classification (OCC) or achieving the best "hit rate," irrespective of the potential consequences of inaccuracies. However, Rogers et al. (2010) has argued that false positives should be minimized to avoid the far-reaching consequences of misclassifying a genuine examinee as a feigner. When base-rates are considered, false-positive rates reaching 20 percent or more are likely to increase drastically the number of misclassified examinees with genuine disorders. Imagine for the moment conceding on the witness stand that an expert's accuracy is no better than a coin toss.[1] As a general notion, the most severely impaired examinees may be at higher risk of misclassification than others because of increased likelihood of misunderstanding bogus items and responding to them affirmatively.

Two broad categories have been empirically established via confirmatory factor analysis to classify detection strategies within the domain of feigned mental disorder (Rogers et al., 2005). The *unlikely strategies* address the presence of very unusual symptoms or clinical features that are generally uncharacteristic of patients with genuine disorders. In comparison, *amplified strategies* are identified by the magnitude of their faked presentations. In particular, feigners have "too much" in the frequency and breadth of what otherwise might be genuine symptoms and clinical characteristics.

Rogers (2018a) provided a comprehensive review of both unlikely and amplified detection strategies covering three domains of feigning (i.e., mental disorders, cognitive impairments, and medical presentations). The following two sections provide a sampling of three detection strategies each for feigned mental disorders. They are organized by unlikely and amplified detection strategies, respectively. Table 19.1 defines each strategy, with salient examples from leading feigning measures and inventories being included.

Unlikely Detection Strategies

These three unlikely strategies were selected for their central importance to the assessment of feigned mental disorders. As explained in subsequent paragraphs, it is essential that forensic practitioners clearly understand the crucial differences between *rare* and *quasi-rare* detection strategies (see also table 19.1). In addition, *symptom combinations* represent an innovative and sophisticated approach to accurately classifying feigned mental disorders (Rogers, 2018a).

---

[1] For the sake of simplicity, assume 100 examinees and a 20 percent base rate of feigning. Optimistically, assume an 80 percent accuracy (i.e., sensitivity and specificity). Sixteen feigners (0.80 X 20 feigners) are correctly classified; sixteen genuine examinees (0.20 X 80 genuine examinees) are misclassified.

Table 19.1 Unlikely and Amplified Detection Strategies for the Assessment of Feigned Mental Disorders: A Selected Review with Definitions, Examples, and Commentaries

Unlikely strategies	Definition	Examples	Commentary
Rare Symptoms	Symptoms that are potentially genuine yet infrequently (e.g., < 10%) reported by patients with genuine disorders	SIRS-2 RS scale, MMPI-2 Fp scale, and PAI NIM scale	This widely used detection strategy often yields large to very large effect size. However, care must be taken to have a diverse clinical sample so that rare symptoms have been adequately tested across a spectrum of disorders.
Quasi-Rare Symptoms	Symptoms that are rarely reported by normative and nonclinical samples, but can vary substantially in relevant setting and populations (e.g., clinical and forensic samples)	MMPI-2 F and Fb scales	Sometimes confused with rare symptoms, quasi-rare are best construed as "nonnormative" items infrequently observed in a cross-section of the community. As noted in the text, they may have variable success in patient samples.
Symptom Combinations	Individual symptoms are common in patients with genuine disorders but are rarely observed co-occurring in the same genuine responder. Thus, symptom pairs constitute the unlikely detection strategy.	SIRS-2 SC scale, M-FAST RC scale, and SIMS SC scale	Symptom combinations represents a sophisticated approach that is likely resistant to preparation and coaching. It tends to produce large effect sizes. While probably feasible, it has not been adapted to multiscale inventories.
Amplified strategies	**Definition**	**Examples**	**Commentary**
Indiscriminant Symptom Endorsement	This strategy, also called "symptom selectivity," refers to reporting a large proportion of symptoms across broad array of clinical presentations	SIRS SEL scale, SADS SEL scale, PAI MFI	The breadth of coverage is essential. Otherwise, a narrow focus (only mood disorders) is conceptually misguided and may lead to false positives.
Symptom Severity	This strategy is based on exaggerated presentations with a high proportion of clinical characteristics being reported at high if not intolerable intensity.	SIRS-2 SEV scale	This strategy can be easily adapted to various measures and scales (such as the PAI). It can produce large effect sizes.

(continued)

		Table 19.1 *Continued*	
Unlikely strategies	Definition	Examples	Commentary
Erroneous Stereotypes	Common misconceptions about a diagnosis or group of diagnoses (e.g., psychotic disorders) can be used to differentiate between genuine and feigned presentations	MMPI-2-RF Ds-ADHD	This sophisticated strategy works best with multiscale inventories, when items are not directly aligned to diagnoses. Given their non-transparent nature, lists of symptoms should not be helpful making the strategy resistant to preparation. At present, this strategy has only been tested with the MMPI and the MMPI-2.

Note. Adapted from Rogers (2018a, pp. 25–26) with recent research integrated in the text. For measures, M-FAST = Miller Forensic Assessment of Symptoms Test; MMPI = Minnesota Multiphasic Personality Inventory; SIMS = Structured Inventory of Malingered Symptomatology; SADS = Schedule of Affective Disorders and Schizophrenia; PAI = Personality Assessment Inventory; SIRS = Structured Interview of Reported Symptoms. For feigning scales, RS = Rare Symptoms; Fp = Infrequency Psychopathology; NIM = Negative Impression Management; F = Infrequency; Fb = Back Infrequency; SC = Symptom Combinations; RC = Rare Combination; SEL = Symptom Selectivity; MFI = Multiscale Feigning Index, SEV = Symptom Severity; Ds-ADHD = Dissimulation scale for ADHD.

Rare Symptoms are clearly defined by their well-established infrequencies across genuine responders in patient samples and clinical settings. For rare symptoms to effectively differentiate feigned and genuine presentations, their occurrence must be very limited in patients with genuine disorders. The general benchmark has been $\leq 10\%$. For the SIRS-2, clinical-forensic samples averaged 1.88 of a possible score of 16 or 11.8%, slightly over the 10 percent benchmark (Rogers et al., 2010). In stark contrast, the Infrequent Somatic Responses (Fs) scale of the Minnesota Multiphasic Personality Inventory-2-Restructured Form (MMPI-2-RF; Tellegen & Ben-Porath 2008) adopted a much laxer criterion (i.e., < 25%). To be well informed, forensic practitioners are encouraged to perform such simple calculations for each scale utilizing rare symptoms as an empirically based detection strategy. This simple preparation can protect against potentially troubling cross-examination.

Sharf et al. (2017) conducted a MMPI-2-RF meta-analysis of feigning. Several findings were especially noteworthy for the Infrequent Psychopathology Responses (Fp-r) scale, the stronger of the two rare-symptom scales. First, because of its rigorous development, patients with genuine disorders do not tend to have problematically elevated Fp-r scores. Second, Fp-r produces the highest effect sizes when compared to other MMPI-2-RF validity scales, achieving a high moderate range ($M\ d = 1.11$) for mixed diagnoses, outstripping the other feigning indicators (ds ranging from 0.53 to 0.85). As a result, its specificity for feigned mental disorders was outstanding (0.92 to 0.98; see Sharf et al.,

2017, table 6). Contrastingly, Fs tended mild–moderate elevations across samples with genuine disorders (M = 66.01) but still performed well for simulators of feigned medical complaints.

Quasi-rare symptoms adopted a less rigorous approach by using items rarely endorsed by nonclinical or normative samples, who are much less likely to report unusual characteristics than their clinical counterparts. The meta-analysis by Sharf et al. (2017) allowed direct comparisons between the Fp-r (rare) and F-r (quasi-rare). Unlike Fp-r, problematic F-r elevations among patient samples with genuine disorders varied from concerning to alarming. As an example of the latter, major depression (M = 84.16 for genuine) slightly edged out mixed diagnoses (M = 81.31). As an additional issue, the F-r is not specific to feigned mental disorders; instead, F-r $\geq$ 100T classifies at least half of those feigning cognitive impairment and medical issues.

Symptom combinations move beyond individual test items to examine infrequent symptom pairs. For example, hyperactivity and increased sleep are both common in clinical populations; however, their co-occurrence in the same examinee is not ordinarily expected. This detection strategy was pioneered by Rogers et al. (1992) with the development of the SIRS Symptom Combinations (SC) scale. For infrequent symptom pairs, SC items meet the 10 percent benchmark when tested across more than 1,100 clinical-forensic cases (Rogers et al., 2010). It has subsequently been applied as Rare Combinations for the Miller Forensic Assessment of Symptoms Test (M-FAST; Miller, 2001) and the SC scale of the SIMS (Widows & Smith, 2005). With the latter measure, Rogers et al. (2014) applied a statistically based approach for identifying SC pairs. They selected thirteen item-pairs (1) uncorrelated or negatively correlated in patients with genuine disorders and (2) positively correlated ($\geq$ 0.35) in feigners. This methodology could be implemented with multiscale inventories and tested extensively. When further tested with three archival samples, the SIMS SC still misclassified very few patients with genuine disorders (Edens et al., 2020) and raised the possibility of a lower SC cut score.

Amplified Strategies

As noted, amplified strategies focus on the magnitude rather than the presence of symptoms and clinical characteristics. Therefore, care must be taken to test amplified strategies with severely impaired genuine clinical samples in order to minimize misclassifications. The subsequent paragraphs feature three detection strategies (i.e., indiscriminant symptom endorsement, symptom severity and erroneous stereotypes).

The strategy of *indiscriminant symptom endorsement* is self-explanatory in simply examining the proportion of reported symptoms. As an important caveat, examinees must be presented with a very broad array of symptoms and associated features. Otherwise, examinees with genuine disorders, such as major depressive disorder, may be responding genuinely on scale focused on this disorder. On the SIRS-2 (Rogers et al., 2010), this strategy is described as Symptom Selectivity (SEL). With a range from 0 to 32, clinical forensic samples tend to average 30.0 percent as compared to 57.3 percent for simulators.

The strategy of *symptom severity* focuses on intensity of the reported symptoms and clinical features. Extreme ratings and qualitative statements, such as describing unbearable effects, often characterize this strategy. The SIRS-2 the Symptom Severity (SEV) scale is composed of thirty-two items that are reported at a comparatively lower rate than the SEL: 14.9 percent in clinical forensic samples and 41.9 percent for simulators (Rogers et al., 2010). Because of their complementary nature, SEV and SEL can be considered together. With the PAI, Gaines et al. (2012) created the Multiscale Feigning Index (MFI), which calculates the average elevation across seven clinical scales that could be viewed as less stigmatizing than the other four (e.g., Antisocial Features and Drug Problems). While showing promise (Boccaccini & Hart, 2018), the MFI requires much more extensive validation.

Gough (1954) first adopted the strategy of *erroneous stereotypes* for examining "neurotic" stereotypes as a detection strategy. It was later operationalized on the MMPI as the Dissimulation (Ds) scale, which was subsequently applied more specifically to feigned mental disorders. Logically, erroneous stereotypes are difficult to successfully feign because feigners are generally unaware of which of their general perceptions/stereotypes are accurate and which are erroneous. For the MMPI-2, a meta-analysis (Rogers et al., 2003) produced large effect sizes for the Ds scale. The Ds is recommended in conjunction with the Fp-r so that forensic practitioners may apply two proven but very different detection strategies (erroneous stereotypes and rare symptoms) in assessing feigned mental disorders. Although generally disregarded by the MMPI-2-RF, Robinson and Rogers (2018) applied the erroneous-stereotypes strategy specifically to feigned ADHD. Their work resulted in the Ds-ADHD scale. Interestingly, ADHD feigners produced a very large effect size when compared to more general feigners of mental disorders, and an extremely large difference ($d = 2.65$) between feigned and genuine ADHD conditions.

Recommendations for Better Practices

Assessment methods for response styles continue to evolve, although rarely as a simple linear progression. Thus, these recommendations are clearly described as *better* and not *best* practices. Moreover, the term "best practices" appears as a definite overstatement— perhaps an example of positive impression management—that would be deeply ironic, given the focus of this chapter. In the following paragraphs, four recommendations for improved forensic practices are summarized. Each paragraph includes a brief heading to facilitate their future use as reference points.

Multimethod and Multistrategy Approach. A disturbing trend has been observed in forensic practice, especially in high-volume settings. It involves cutting corners, rather than a careful integration of multiple measures with well-validated detection strategies. When clinically feasible (e.g., sufficient language and reading skills), both interview-based and examinee-administered (e.g., paper-and-pencil and online formats) measures should be evaluated together. Moreover, feigning indicators preferably should include scales with both unlikely and amplified detection strategies.

Confusion of Screens with Comprehensive Measures. Simply put, feigning screens and comprehensive measures are intended to serve very different purposes, each valuable for their expressed purpose (Rogers et al., 2020). Feigning screens (e.g., the M-FAST) are designed to minimize false negatives because possible feigners were overlooked. As a clear-cut comparison, comprehensive feigning measures (e.g., the SIRS-2) have a diametrically opposite purpose. They are designed to minimalize false positives (i.e., genuine responders misclassified as feigners), given the far-reaching consequences of such grave errors. This contrasting of the M-FAST and the SIRS-2 is intentional. A recent study (Tarescavage & Glassmire, 2016) attempted to assess the accuracy of the SIRS and SIRS-2 with the M-FAST as their primary external measure, apparently unaware of their cross-purposes (see Rogers et al., in press).

Professional Integrity About Feigning Errors. All feigning measures have measurement and classification errors. Using multiscale inventories as an example, the standard error of measurement (SEM) for the MMPI-2-RF F-r and Fp-r is 10T points. Moreover, when the measurement and classification errors are combined, the overall error rate can easily exceed 50 percent for scores close to the feigning cut score; this pattern has clearly been demonstrated with the PAI and feigned mental disorders (Rogers et al., 2012). Forensic practitioners should be aware of two related concepts integrally tied to cut scores and classifications: *indeterminate group* and *well-defined cut scores*. The indeterminate group is composed of too-close-to-call cases (e.g., ± 5 T points of the cut score). To avoid 50 percent or more misclassifications, well-defined cut scores are not applied to too-close-to-call cases. It is our impression that many forensic practitioners routinely ignore measurement and classification errors, putting at considerable risk the accuracy of their results. Any intentional nondisclosure of inaccuracies is ethically concerning.

Evidence of Genuine Responding. Although often overlooked, nonelevated feigning indicators are often more accurate at classifying genuine responding than are nonextreme elevations at feigning. For example, the PAI Negative Impression Management (NIM) scores ≤ 65 T—although not common among genuine responders—almost always signifies a nonfeigned response style[2] (Rogers et al., 2012). Simply put, forensic practitioners should be bound both by ethics and sworn testimony to tell the whole truth.

Concluding Thoughts

The foundation for the assessment of response styles centers on empirically tested detection strategies. This chapter mostly features feigned mental disorders. The same diligence

---

[2] Choice of the term, "nonfeigned" is intentional, because NIM scores in this range are expected with defensiveness.

is deserved across different response styles, (e.g., simulated adjustment) and different domains (e.g., cognitive abilities).

References

American Psychiatric Association. (2013). *Diagnostic and statistical manual of mental disorders* (5th ed.). American Psychiatric Press.

Blanchard, M., & Farber, B. A. (2016). Lying in psychotherapy: Why and what clients don't tell their therapist about therapy and their relationship. *Counselling Psychology Quarterly, 29*(1), 90–112. https://doi.org/10.1080/09515070.2015.1085365

Blasberg, S. A., Rogers, K. H., & Paulhus, D. L. (2014). The Bidimensional Impression Management Index (BIMI): Measuring agentic and communal forms of impression management. *Journal of Personality Assessment, 96*(5), 523–531. https://doi.org/10.1080/00223891.2013.862252

Boccaccini, M. T., & Hart, J. R. (2018). Response style on the personality assessment inventory and other multiscale inventories. In R. Rogers & S. D. Bender (Eds.), *Clinical assessment of malingering and deception.*, *4th ed.* (pp. 280–300). Guilford Press.

Buechley, R., & Ball, H. (1952). A new test of "validity" for the group MMPI. *Journal of Consulting Psychology, 16*(4), 299–301. https://doi.org/10.1037/h0053897

Butcher, J. N., Dahlstrom, W. G., Graham, J. R., Tellegen, A. M., & Kaemmer, B. (1989). *Minnesota Multiphasic Personality Inventory-2 (MMPI-2):* Manual for administration and scoring. University of Minnesota Press.

Edens, J. F., Truong, T. N., & Otto, R. K. (2020). Classification accuracy of the rare symptoms and symptom combinations scales of the Structured Inventory of Malingered Symptomatology in three archival samples. *Law and Human Behavior, 44*(2), 167–177. https://doi.org/10.1037/lhb0000361

Farrell, A. D., Danish, S. J., & Howard, C. W. (1991). Evaluation of data screening methods in surveys of adolescents' drug use. *Psychological Assessment: A Journal of Consulting and Clinical Psychology, 3*(2), 295–298.

Forth, A., Kosson, D., & Hare, R. (2003). *The Hare Psychopathy Checklist: Youth Version, technical manual.* Multi-Health Systems

Gaines, M. V., Giles, C. L., & Morgan, R. D. (2012). The detection of feigning using multiple PAI scale elevations: A new index. *Assessment, 20*, 437–447.

Gardner, B. O., & Boccaccini, M. T. (2017). Does the convergent validity of the PAI Antisocial Features Scale depend on offender response style? *Journal of Personality Assessment, 99*(5), 481–493. https://doi.org/10.1080/00223891.2017.1296846

Gillard, N. D. (2018). Psychopathy and deception. In R. Rogers & S. D. Bender (Eds.), *Clinical assessment of malingering and deception* (4th ed., pp. 174–187). Guilford Press.

Gillard, N. D., & Rogers, R. (2015). Denial of risk: The effects of positive impression management on risk assessments for psychopathic and non-psychopathic offenders. *International Journal of Law and Psychiatry, 42–43*, 106–113. https://doi.org/10.1016/j.ijlp.2015.08.014

Gough, H. G. (1954). Some common misconceptions about neuroticism. *Journal of Consulting Psychology, 18*, 287–292.

Graham, J. R. (2012). *MMPI–2: Assessing personality and psychopathology* (5th ed.). Oxford University Press.

Green, P. (2003). *Word memory test for windows: User's manual and program.* Green's Publishing.

Hathaway, S. R., & McKinley, J. C. (1940). A multiphasic personality schedule (Minnesota): I. Construction of the schedule. *Journal of Psychology: Interdisciplinary and Applied, 10*(2), 249–254. https://doi.org/10.1080/00223980.1940.9917000

Hare, R. D. (1980). A research scale for the assessment of psychopathy in criminal populations. *Personality and Individual Differences, 1*, 111–119. https://doi.org/10.1016/0191-8869(80)90028-8

Hare, R. D. (1991). *The Hare Psychopathy Checklist—Revised.* Multi-Health Systems.

Hare, R. D. (2003). *The Hare Psychopathy Checklist—Revised* (2nd ed.). Multi-Health Systems.

Hartigan, S. E., Rogers, R., Williams, M. M., and Donson, J. E. (2021). Challenges for the SASSI-4 and InDUC-2R: Positive Impression Management in Offenders with Substance Use Histories. *Journal of Psychopathology and Behavioral Assessment, 43*, 924–936. https://doi.org/10.1007/s10862-021-09909-9

Kelsey, K. R., Rogers, R., & Robinson, E. V. (2015). Self-report measures of psychopathy: What is their role in forensic assessments? *Journal of Psychopathology and Behavioral Assessment, 37*(3), 380–391. https://doi.org/10.1007/s10862-014-9475-5

Lanyon, R. I., & Thomas, M. L. (2008). Detecting deception in sex offender assessment. In R. Rogers & S. D. Bender (Eds.) *Clinical assessment of malingering and deception* (p. 285–296). Guilford Press.

Lazowski, L. E., & Geary, B. B. (2019). Validation of the Adult Substance Abuse Subtle Screening Inventory-4 (SASSI-4). *European Journal of Psychological Assessment, 35*(1), 86–97. https://doi.org/10.1027/1015-5759/a000359

Levashina, J. (2018). Evaluating deceptive impression management in personnel selection and job performance. In R. Rogers & S. D. Bender (Eds.), *Clinical assessment of malingering and deception* (p. 530–551). Guilford Press.

Miller, H. A. (2001). *Miller-Forensic Assessment of Symptoms Test (M-FAST): Professional manual*. Psychological Assessment Resources.

Morey, L. C. (2007). *The Personality Assessment Inventory professional manual* (2nd ed.). Psychological Assessment Resources.

Nijdam-Jones, A., Chen, Y., & Rosenfeld, B. (2020). Detection of feigned posttraumatic stress disorder: A meta-analysis of the Minnesota Multiphasic Personality Inventory-2 (MMPI-2). *Psychological Trauma: Theory, Research, Practice and Policy, 12*(7), 790–798. https://doi.org/10.1037/tra0000593

Poythress, N., Nicholson, R., Otto, R. K., Edens, J. F., Bonnie, R. J., Monahan, J., & Hoge, S. K. (1999). *The MacArthur Competence Assessment Tool—Criminal adjudication: Professional manual*. Psychological Assessment Resources.

Robinson, E. V., and Rogers, R. (2018). Detection of feigned ADHD across two domains: The MMPI-2-RF and CAARS for faked symptoms and TOVA for simulated attention deficits. *Journal of Psychopathology and Behavioral Assessment, 40*, 376–385. https://doi.org/10.1007/s10862-017-9640-8

Rogers, R. (1984). Towards an empirical model of malingering and deception. *Behavioral Sciences & the Law, 2*(1), 93–111. https://doi.org/10.1002/bsl.2370020109

Rogers, R. (1997). Researching dissimulation. In R. Rogers (Ed.), *Clinical assessment of malingering and deception* (2nd ed., pp. 398–426). Guilford Press.

Rogers, R. (Ed.). (2008). *Clinical assessment of malingering and deception* (3rd ed.). Guilford Press.

Rogers, R. (2018a). Detection strategies for malingering and defensiveness. In R. Rogers & S. D. Bender (Eds.), *Clinical assessment of malingering and deception* (4th ed., pp. 18–41). Guilford Press.

Rogers, R. (2018b). An introduction to response styles. In R. Rogers & S. D. Bender (Eds.), *Clinical assessment of malingering and deception* (4th ed., pp. 3–17). Guilford Press.

Rogers, R., Bagby, R. M., & Dickens, S. E. (1992). Structured Interview of Reported Symptoms (SIRS) and professional manual. Psychological Assessment Resources.

Rogers, R., & Correa, A. A. (2008). Determinations of malingering: Evolution from case-based methods to detection strategies. *Psychiatry, Psychology and Law, 15*(2), 213–223. https://doi.org/10.1080/1321871080 2014501

Rogers, R., Gillard, N. D., Wooley, C. N., & Ross, C. A. (2012). The detection of feigned disabilities: The effectiveness of the Personality Assessment Inventory in a traumatized inpatient sample. *Assessment, 19*(1), 77–88. https://doi.org/10.1177/1073191111422031

Rogers, R., Jackson, R. L., Sewell, K. W., & Salekin, K. L. (2005). Detection strategies for malingering: A confirmatory factor analysis of the SIRS. *Criminal Justice and Behavior, 32*(5), 511–525. https://doi.org/ 10.1177/0093854805278412

Rogers, R., Pan, M. & Drogin, E. Y. (2020) *Feigned mental disorders: The identification of biases and inaccuracies affecting forensic practice* [Manuscript in preparation]. Department of Psychology, University of North Texas.

Rogers, R., Robinson, E. V., & Gillard, N. D. (2014). The SIMS screen for feigned mental disorders: The development of detection-based scales. *Behavioral Sciences and the Law, 32*(4), 455–466.

Rogers, R., Sewell, K. W., & Gillard, N. D. (2010). *Structured Interview of Reported Symptoms–2 (SIRS-2) and professional manual*. Psychological Assessment Resources.

Rogers, R., Sewell, K. W., Martin, M. A., & Vitacco, M. J. (2003). Detection of feigned mental disorders: A meta-analysis of the MMPI-2 and malingering. *Assessment, 10*(2), 160–177. https://doi.org/10.1177/1073 191103010002007

Rogers, R., Velsor, S. F., Williams, M. M. (in press). A detailed analysis of the SIRS versus SIRS-2 critiques. *Psychological Injury and Law*.

Rogers, R., Vitacco, M. J., Jackson, R. L., Martin, M., Collins, M., & Sewell, K. W. (2002). Faking psychopathy? An examination of response styles with antisocial youth. *Journal of Personality Assessment, 78*(1), 31–46. https://doi.org/10.1207/S15327752JPA7801_03

Rogers, R., Williams, M. M., Winningham, D. B., & Sharf, A. J. (2018). An examination of PAI clinical descriptors and correlates in an outpatient sample: Tailoring of interpretive statements. *Journal of Psychopathology and Behavioral Assessment, 40*(2), 259–275. https://doi.org/10.1007/s10862-017-9627-5

Sharf, A. J., Rogers, R., Williams, M. M., & Henry, S. A. (2017). The effectiveness of the MMPI-2-RF in detecting feigned mental disorders and cognitive deficits: A meta-analysis. *Journal of Psychopathology and Behavioral Assessment, 39*, 441–455. https://doi.org/10.1007/s10862-017-9590-1

Stein, L. A. R., Rogers, R., & Henry, S. (2018). Denial and misreporting of substance abuse. In R. Rogers & S. D. Bender (Eds.), *Clinical assessment of malingering and deception* (4th ed., pp. 151–173). Guilford Press.

Tarescavage, A. M., & Glassmire, D. M. (2016). Differences between Structured Interview of Reported Symptoms (SIRS) and SIRS-2 sensitivity estimates among forensic inpatients: A criterion groups comparison. *Law and Human Behavior, 40*(5), 488–502. https://doi.org/10.1037/lhb0000191

Tellegen, A., & Ben-Porath, Y. S. (2008). *MMPI-2-RF: Technical manual.* University of Minnesota Press.

Tierney, D. W., & McCabe, M. P. (2001). The assessment of denial, cognitive distortions, and victim empathy among pedophilic sex offenders: An evaluation of the utility of self-report measures. *Trauma, Violence, & Abuse, 2*(3), 259–270. https://doi.org/10.1177/1524838001002003004

Tonigan, J. S., & Miller, W. R. (2002). The Inventory of Drug Use Consequences (InDUC): Test–retest stability and sensitivity to detect change. *Psychology of Addictive Behaviors, 16*(2), 165–168. https://doi.org/10.1037/0893-164X.16.2.165

van Impelen, A., Merckelbach, H., Jelicic, M., & Merten, T. (2014). The Structured Inventory of Malingered Symptomatology (SIMS): A systematic review and meta-analysis. *The Clinical Neuropsychologist, 28*(8), 1336–1365. https://doi.org/10.1080/13854046.2014.984763

Velsor, S. F., Rogers, R., Donnelly, J. W. II, & Tazi, K. (2021). Assessment of factitious psychological presentations: An overlooked response style in forensic practice. *Psychological Injury and Law, 14*, 201–212.

Webster, C. D., Douglas, K. S., Eaves, D., & Hart, S. D. (1997). *HCR-20: Assessing risk for violence (version 2).* Simon Fraser University, Mental Health, Law, and Policy Institute.

Wechsler, D. (2008). *Wechsler Memory Scale, Fourth edition.* Pearson Education.

Witt, P. H., & Neller, D. J. (2018). Detection of deception in sex offenders. In R. Rogers & S. D. Bender (Eds.), *Clinical assessment of malingering and deception* (4th ed., pp. 401–421). Guilford Press.

Widows, M., & Smith, G. P. (2005). Structured Inventory of Malingered Symptomatology (SIMS) and professional manual. Psychological Assessment Resources.

Young, J. C., Caron, J. E., Baughman, B. C., & Sawyer, R. J. (2012). Detection of suboptimal effort with symbol span: Development of a new embedded index. *Archives of Clinical Neuropsychology, 27*(2), 159–164. https://doi.org/10.1093/arclin/acr109

CHAPTER

20

How Reliable and Objective are Forensic Mental Health Evaluators?

Daniel C. Murrie *and* Marcus T. Boccaccini

Abstract

Are forensic mental health evaluators reliable with one another? Can they remain objective when retained by one side in adversarial legal proceedings? Emerging research suggests reliability is strongest when answering well-defined questions such as adjudicative competence, but weaker on more inferential questions such as sanity or risk. Studies of assessment instruments as applied in the field reveal poorer reliability than typically reported in formal research studies or instrument manuals, particularly for instruments that require more subjectivity. Studies that examine evaluator *patterns* of findings across cases reveal meaningful differences in how often evaluators offer certain forensic opinions and how they score instruments. Finally, field studies and a rigorous experiment align to suggest *adversarial allegiance*—a form of bias toward the retaining party—may influence forensic evaluators. Though the field has made progress in identifying these sources of unreliability, there remains the more challenging task of minimizing their effect in forensic practice.

Key Words: forensic mental health evaluators, reliability, bias, adversarial allegiance, forensic opinions

How reliable are forensic mental health evaluators? Will two different evaluators independently evaluating the same defendant reliably come to the same conclusions? Are evaluators so reliable as to be interchangeable, such that the court can expect the same answer regardless of who performs the evaluation? Or does the outcome of an evaluation depend, at least to some degree, on which evaluator performs the evaluation? Further, does reliability depend on role or context? For example, can evaluators who are retained by one side in adversarial legal proceedings offer the court genuinely objective findings and expert opinions? Or are these evaluators inevitably biased by the adversarial arrangements in which they work?

Questions like these are fundamental to considering the value of forensic mental health evidence and the contributions of mental health professionals to legal proceedings. Of course, reliability is a fundamental condition for any science-based procedure. Reliability is often defined broadly as the degree of consistency in scientific work, with the implication that any inconsistency is error (American Educational Research Association et al., 2014). Thus reliability statistics quantify the level of consistency and provide information about the extent to which results from the procedure are free of error.

Reliability is also the touchstone for scientific evidence and expert testimony to be admitted in court.[1] For example, *Daubert* specified that the "trial judge must ensure that any and all scientific testimony or evidence admitted is not only relevant, but reliable," and suggested a list of factors to consider when establishing "evidentiary reliability," including the "known or potential rate of error" of any scientific theory or technique.[2] These factors are applicable to evidence from the social sciences as well,[3] including forensic mental health evidence.

Finally, questions about the reliability of forensic mental health evaluations are relevant to aspirational goals of equitable justice. The legal disposition for a criminal defendant or civil litigant should not—if a system is equitable—depend upon which clinician was assigned to conduct an evaluation, or which side in adversarial proceedings retained the evaluation. Similarly, state psychiatric hospitals or mental health systems should not, in an equitable system, find far fewer (or more) individuals eligible for forensic mental health services simply because they hired one forensic evaluator versus another to examine competence, sanity, or violence risk.

Despite their importance, questions about the reliability of forensic mental health evaluations have historically prompted little research. But recent, broad trends suggest the fields of forensic psychology and psychiatry may be overdue to self-examine the reliability of forensic evaluation, particularly as routinely applied in the field. First, the National Research Council (NRC; 2009), the President's Council of Advisors on Science and Technology (PCAST; 2016), and other authorities have reviewed the state of forensic science, addressing a wide range of disciplines including analyses of DNA, fingerprints, hair, and ballistics. Authorities concluded that the basic reliability and error rates of many forensic techniques are unknown, and that forensic scientists are prone to a variety of contextual biases. Second, broad reviews of the psychological sciences have revealed a "replicability crisis," in which well-accepted research findings fail to generalize during replication attempts, and many lab-based studies fail to generalize to the field (Mitchell, 2012). Initially separate from these broader trends, the field of forensic psychology began exploratory studies addressing the reliability of forensic mental health evaluations in the field (e.g., Boccaccini et al., 2008; Gowensmith et al., 2012, 2013; Murrie, Boccaccini, Johnson, et al., 2008), ultimately leading to a broader discussion of "field reliability" in forensic mental health assessment (Edens & Boccaccini, 2017). All these trends converge in suggesting that some generally accepted clinical or scientific practices may not be

---

[1] E.g., Daubert v. Merrell Dow Pharm., 509 U.S. 579 (1993).
[2] *Id.* at 580.
[3] Kumho Tire Co. v. Carmichael, 526 U.S. 137 (1999).

sufficiently reliable, particularly when translated from research contexts to routine field contexts, and that the human "instruments" (forensic analysts or evaluators) are not perfectly objective, or independent of contextual pressures.

In this chapter, we summarize the research addressing the reliability—particularly the *field reliability*—of forensic mental health assessment and instrument results. We consider reliability in terms of traditional interrater reliability, but also in terms of evaluator patterns of findings across cases. Finally, we examine whether the reliability of forensic evaluators is influenced by the adversarial legal system in which they work, a phenomenon we label *adversarial allegiance* (Murrie & Boccaccini, 2015).

Reliability and "Field Reliability" in Forensic Assessment

Ideally, forensic mental health evaluators could provide opinions, diagnoses, and instrument scores that are completely free of error. If this was the case, any evaluator-assigned score or evaluator opinion would reflect only the examinee's true standing on what the evaluator was asked to assess (e.g., competence, violence risk, or psychopathy) and nothing else. If all evaluators were able to provide these error-free assessments, different evaluators would always come to the same conclusion when asked to evaluate the same person. Of course, error-free assessments are impossible for many reasons. The phenomena that evaluators assess always require some level of subjective judgment, leaving room for reasonable people to disagree. Evaluators also bring their own differences or idiosyncrasies to each case, and of course, examinees (and their records) may be inconsistent in what they report to evaluators.

Nevertheless, the goal for researchers and evaluators is to develop and use procedures that *minimize* the extent to which these differences influence evaluation results. In forensic mental health, researchers focus on findings from rater-agreement studies to quantify the (hopefully small) impact of measurement error on assessment results. In these studies, two or more evaluators independently assess the same set of examinees and provide opinions, diagnoses, or instrument scores. There are many types of rater agreement study designs and reliability coefficients (e.g., kappa and intraclass correlation), but all are designed to provide information about the extent to which the assessment results are affected by measurement error (i.e., inconsistency). A reliability coefficient of 1.00 means that there was no evidence of measurement error in the study. A coefficient of .00 indicates that the results were completely a product of measurement error. High reliability coefficients (e.g., 0.80 to 1.00) indicate an evaluation or scoring process that has relatively little measurement error. Low reliability coefficients (e.g., < 0.50) indicate a process in which evaluator differences, adversarial allegiance, or any other type of measurement error may better explain evaluator opinion or scores differences than just the characteristics of the examinee.

To be clear, the field of psychology generally—and forensic psychology specifically—has often placed an admirable focus on reliability, but this focus has usually been limited to the reliability of assessment *instrument* results. For example, instrument manuals report reliability values, and authorities offer guidelines for qualifying those reliability values as moderate, good, excellent, and so on (Cicchetti & Sparrow, 1981; Heilbrun, 1992). This focus on reliability, even in forensic psychology, has left two significant gaps. First, the focus has been almost exclusively on instrument scores, rather than on the broader opinions or conclusions that evaluators far more often offer the justice system (Guarnera & Murrie, 2017). Second, the focus has been on how high reliability *can be*, in relatively controlled research settings, with a select set of evaluators and examinees, rather than on what reliability *normally is*, in the field, when those instruments are applied to inform real decisions about real people (Edens & Boccaccini, 2017).

There are many reasons why findings from formal research studies of instruments may not generalize to the real-world field settings in which the instruments are applied (Edens & Boccaccini, 2017; Guarnera & Murrie, 2017; Guarnera et al., 2017). For example, researchers overseeing a formal study usually ensure that the instrument raters have ample training and maintain fidelity to instrument administration and scoring guidelines. Adequate interrater reliability is usually a prerequisite to research publication, so researchers may ensure that less-reliable raters are retrained or replaced until all raters demonstrate adequate reliability. In the field, there is rarely oversight to ensure adequate training or fidelity to instrument guidelines, and there are rarely procedures for maintaining adequate reliability across clinicians.

For the clinician, pressures may differ in formal studies versus the field. In research, the primary goal or pressure is simply accuracy, or attaining reliability with other raters. In contrast, clinicians in the field may experience various subtle contextual pressures, due to the institutions they serve or their role in an adversarial legal system. Research studies differ from field studies in several important ways, particularly for assessment procedures that require examinee participation. In research, the examinees are usually assured confidentiality/anonymity and assured there are no consequences of refusing to participate or the results of the assessment. In the field, there is no assurance of anonymity, participation is rarely by choice, and examinees know that statements are not protected as confidential or anonymous. Thus, consequences of participation and responses are almost certain; indeed, the point of any forensic evaluation procedure is to inform or influence important, life-altering decisions about examinees.

Although this distinction between research development and field application is not new, only recently have studies explicitly, intentionally addressed "field reliability" (e.g., Guarnera & Murrie, 2017) or "field validity" (e.g., Gowensmith et al., 2017; Murrie et al., 2012) of forensic assessment instrument scores and evaluator opinions. Of course, both traditional research studies and field studies are crucial. The former details whether evaluators' scores and opinions *can* demonstrate reliability and validity under optimal conditions. The latter demonstrates the extent to which evaluators' scores and opinions *do* demonstrate reliability and validity as commonly applied under routine practice conditions in the field (Boccaccini & Murrie, 2014).

Field Reliability of Opinions in Common Forensic Evaluations

The field reliability of common forms of forensic mental health evaluation is probably best summarized in a recent meta-analysis that reviewed studies examining the interrater reliability of competency and sanity opinions (Guarnera & Murrie, 2017). Of the fifty-nine studies that addressed the reliability of competence or sanity opinions, only nine addressed the field reliability of competency opinions and only eight addressed the field reliability of sanity opinions.

Those few studies that addressed "real world" reliability of competence or sanity evaluations presented a wide range of reliability estimates; pairwise percentage agreements ranged from 57 percent to 100 percent and kappa reliability coefficients ranged from 0.28 to 1.0. In other words, agreement among clinicians ranged from poor to perfect. Meta-analytic combination of field reliability estimates returned estimates of kappa = 0.49 (95% CI: 0.40–0.58) for competency opinions and kappa = .41 (95% CI: 0.29–0.53) for sanity opinions (Guarnera & Murrie, 2017). This wide range of reliability estimates underscores the extent to which different evaluation contexts tended to produce different reliability rates. Not surprisingly, reliability was stronger in contexts where evaluators worked together and even discussed their conclusions, and reliability was weaker in those contexts where evaluators were truly independent.

The individual studies that shed the best light on the field reliability of forensic evaluations are probably those from Hawaii, which assigns three independent evaluators to each evaluation of competence, sanity, or conditional release.[4] Indeed, "if researchers were designing the ideal field reliability study, they could do no better than Hawaii's 'natural experiment,' in which *three* evaluators are court-appointed (rather than selected by attorneys) at the outset for *all* felony defendants, not just particularly contentious cases" (Guarnera & Murrie, 2017, p. 809).

Regarding field reliability of competence to stand trial opinions (*N* = 216), trios of independent evaluators reached perfect agreement in 71 percent of initial competence evaluations (kappa = 0.65) and in 61 percent of subsequent competence evaluations (i.e., evaluations after a defendant was found incompetent and received some period of competence restoration services; kappa = 0.57; Gowensmith et al., 2012). In short, trios of evaluators in routine practice appeared to agree about a defendant's trial competence in roughly two-thirds of cases, suggesting that the majority of competency-to-stand trial (CST) evaluations are fairly straightforward, but a substantial minority—particularly those that occur after some restoration services—are more difficult, ambiguous, or otherwise complicated (such that different evaluators may arrive at different conclusions). Agreement appeared comparable to results from the most similar available study: a review of competence evaluator agreement in fifty Utah cases (Skeem et al., 1998). Regarding the field reliability of sanity evaluations in Hawaii (*N* = 165), agreement was

---

[4] Haw. Rev. Stat. Vol. 14, 704–404 (2003).

lower (55%, kappa = 0.56), as compared to competence evaluations, perhaps because competence is a more straightforward assessment of present abilities, and sanity requires a more inferential, retrospective assessment of a past mental state (Gowensmith et al., 2013).

Reliability was even weaker (53%, kappa = 0.35) for another inferential type of evaluation in Hawaii: those in which clinicians offered an opinion about whether an individual who was formerly found not guilty by reason of insanity (NGRI) and committed to the state hospital was ready for conditional release (Gowensmith et al., 2017). These evaluations are poorly operationalized in statute, so evaluators may operationalize readiness for release in various ways, considering violence risk, recovery from illness, and other factors (Gowensmith et al., 2014). Though from a different state system, evaluator agreement on whether sexual offenders met the Florida criteria for civil commitment as a "sexually violent predator"—another psycholegal construct that some argue is poorly defined—was similarly weak (kappa = 0.54) (Levenson, 2004). Thus, studies suggest evaluator reliability is likely poorest when the psycholegal construct is operationalized more vaguely or requires more evaluator inference.

Additional findings from the Hawaii conditional release study show an important connection between reliability and validity. When the evaluators unanimously agreed that conditional release was appropriate, only 34.5 percent of released acquittees were rehospitalized within three years of release, but when the evaluators disagreed about whether release was appropriate, 71.4 percent were rehospitalized. Overall, results suggested poor reliability among independent evaluators in routine practice but also suggested that opinions may be more accurate when evaluators agree than when they disagree (Gowensmith et al., 2017).

The poorer field reliability on more complex or inferential evaluations is not surprising, but it does underscore another limitation to the available research. The slim research base on field reliability addresses only evaluators' forensic *conclusions*, which is a reasonable place to start (indeed, no further research would be necessary of all conclusions were perfectly reliable). But almost no research in forensic psychology addresses the underlying observations, inferences, or evaluation processes, which are important to understanding how and why evaluators may ultimately reach different conclusions (Dror & Murrie, 2018).

Field Reliability of Instrument Scores from Forensic Evaluations

Beginning in the 1980s, scholars began developing a variety of assessment tools aimed at structuring and reducing subjectivity in evaluator decision-making. Indeed, research consistently documents that popular instruments in forensic assessment demonstrate strong reliability in research contexts. Forensic evaluators increasingly administer these tests and describe test results when providing their opinions to the court. They cite the research describing an instrument's strong reliability, typically reported in the instrument's technical manual, to help justify presenting instrument scores as part of their expert opinions. Indeed, some jurisdictions even *mandate* particular assessment instruments for particular evaluation or screening procedures.[5]

Although the widespread use of these instruments may seem likely to *reduce* unreliability or bias among experts, this development also provides a new opportunity to *study* reliability among experts. Specifically, the well-documented rater agreement and error values for assessment instruments in research contexts can provide a point of comparison for the rater-agreement findings on these instruments when administered in real-world evaluation contexts. These well-documented rater-agreement values provide a clear expectation for the reliability we *should* observe if research findings generalize to the field.

Recent studies have used this strategy of examining instrument scores to explore the possibility of attenuated field reliability among forensic evaluators. Often, researchers examined scores on Hare's (2003) Psychopathy Checklist-Revised (PCL-R), a twenty-item instrument designed to assess psychopathic features, scored by clinicians on the basis of an interview and record review, and the Static-99/Static-99R (Hanson & Thornton, 2000), a ten-item instrument scored on the basis of record review designed to provide information about risk for sexual recidivism.

Despite some subjectivity in rating PCL-R items (Rufino et al., 2011), the PCL-R manual reports an excellent intraclass correlation (ICC) rater-agreement coefficient of 0.87 for total scores (Hare, 2003). In other words, when offenders in research studies receive different PCL-R scores, it appears that about 87 percent of this variability in scores is explained by true differences in psychopathic traits as measured by the PCL-R, as opposed to evaluator unreliability or measurement error. But findings from a recent meta-analysis of thirteen PCL-R field reliability studies reported weaker reliability in the field, with a mean ICC of only 0.69, and a 95 percent confidence interval (0.66 to 0.72) that does not include the 0.87 value from the manual (Olver et al., 2020).

For the Static-99/R, which requires less subjective judgment to score, the instrument developers have reported an ICC of 0.90 across twelve studies (Hanson & Morton-Bourgon, 2009). Field reliability findings typical fall slightly below this median value, in the 0.75 to 0.90 range (Boccaccini, Murrie, et al., 2012; Rice et al., 2014), but have been lower in some studies (e.g., ICC = 0.58 to 0.64; Murrie et al., 2009).

Summary and Discussion: What Contributes to Attenuated Field Reliability?

Finding attenuated reliability in opinions and instrument scores from the field is perhaps not surprising, given what the larger field of psychology has already learned about disseminating procedures, such as psychotherapy, from the lab to the field (i.e., efficacy vs. effectiveness; Clarke, 1995; Weisz et al., 1992). Similarly, the inherent complexity of most

---

[5] Va. Code Ann. §37.2-903; or Tex. Health & Safety Code §841.023.

forensic evaluations, along with differences in evaluator perspective, training, and methods, virtually ensure that reliability in the field will never match reliability "in the lab" (Guarnera et al., 2017). The relatively recent move to study and document field reliability findings in forensic assessment presents both a challenge and opportunity for researchers and forensic evaluators. If reliability is weaker in the field than in controlled studies, evaluators need to know that the reliability findings reported in instrument manuals may not apply to their field scoring practices, and openly acknowledge these differences to courts and other consumers of forensic evaluations. Conversely, evaluators should encourage instrument developers to provide information about field reliability, which better corresponds with real-world forensic practice.

For researchers, the challenge is to better understand why reliability is weaker in the field and how to improve it. Although the uncontrollable and varying circumstances of real-world assessment means that there will always be some attenuation as an instrument or assessment procedure moves from more-controlled to less-controlled settings, there may be ways to avoid dramatic differences between field and nonfield studies. The first step is to identify potentially controllable factors that may be leading to attenuation. These include aspects of instruments, but also potentially aspects of the evaluators, or ways the evaluators perform their work.

Evaluator Differences in Forensic Mental Health Evaluation

Researchers have begun to study factors that may help explain weaker reliability in the field. One of these factors is the idiosyncratic instrument scoring and opinion formation tendencies that any evaluator brings to each case (Boccaccini et al., 2008; Murrie, Boccaccini, Zapf, et al., 2008). For example, evaluators may differ in the threshold for impairment they require before opining a defendant is incompetent, or they may differ in the level of a behavior or trait they expect an examinee to demonstrate before assigning that examinee the highest possible score on a PCL-R item. These types of individual differences in scoring and opinion formation tendencies among evaluators are a form of measurement error and lead to disagreement among evaluators with different tendencies. A primary goal of rater training and reliability checks in controlled research studies is to eliminate, or at least minimize, these tendencies, but there is no similar process for eliminating them in routine practice in the field.

Thus researchers have studied evaluator *patterns* across cases to gauge the extent to which evaluator differences may impact scores and opinions in the field. If evaluators are working within in the same system and assigned cases, essentially at random, from the same "referral stream"—the type of scenario that is common for evaluators working in the same forensic hospital or contracting with the same state system—we would expect them to have similar rates of findings (e.g., similar rates of competence or sanity opinions or similar average instrument scores). However, if they were assigned a similar subsample, or referral stream, of cases and yet demonstrate very different patterns of findings, this might suggest that the evaluators somehow differ, perhaps in their procedures or in their threshold for opining a defendant is incompetent or insane.

Evaluator Differences in Opinions from Common Forensic Evaluations

Studies that compare patterns of findings in forensic opinions clearly suggest evaluator differences. For example, in a two-state study of sixty evaluators and more than seven thousand CST evaluations, individual evaluators had rates of finding incompetence that varied from 0 percent to 62 percent (Murrie, Boccaccini, Zapf, et al., 2008). Likewise, a recent Virginia study examined twenty-six evaluators who completed at least thirty competence evaluations each, and found that individual evaluators opined anywhere from 9 percent to 77 percent of the defendants they evaluated were incompetent (Murrie et al., 2020). Although some evaluator differences could be explained by their employment context (e.g., private practice vs. psychiatric hospital), rates of incompetence findings still varied considerably among evaluators in the same employment context.

Similar evaluator differences emerge in evaluations of legal sanity. Among fifty-nine Virginia evaluators who conducted more than twenty sanity evaluations each, most opined that 5–25 percent of the defendants they evaluated met criteria for legal insanity (Murrie & Warren, 2005). However, a few evaluators found that *no* defendant met insanity criteria, and a few found that more than 50 percent did, suggesting meaningful differences in how those evaluators opined insanity. In a more recent study of seventy-four Virginia evaluators, rates of insanity findings among those who evaluated ten or more cases once again varied from 0 percent to 50 percent, but among those who evaluated twenty or more insanity cases rates varied from only 10 percent to 31 percent, which may assuage some concerns about wide evaluator variability (Gardner et al., 2018).

These system-wide studies of evaluator rates of competence and sanity findings strongly suggest evaluator differences, but they do not rule out many of the contextual factors (beyond evaluator differences) that may contribute to different rates: jurisdictional differences within states, exact referral stream, evaluator specialty, and so on. The study of evaluator differences that best controlled for these contextual factors examined nine evaluators who contracted with the same state correctional department to conduct evaluations of inmates who were under consideration for civil commitment as sexually violent predators (Harris et al., 2016). Evaluators assigned diagnoses they considered applicable, and then opined whether the inmate manifested a "behavioral abnormality," the statutory term for a condition that ostensibly renders them eligible for civil commitment. In this study, the referring agency assigned inmates to evaluators essentially at random; there was no reason to believe any evaluator received a systematically different subsample of inmates to evaluate. Yet among evaluators with the same referral stream from the same correctional system, their patterns of findings differed markedly. Specifically, evaluator patterns of diagnosing a paraphilia ranged from 29–70 percent of cases, and their patterns of finding a "behavioral abnormality" ranged from 49–95 percent (Harris et al., 2016). One evaluator found that just under half the inmates he evaluated manifested the condition necessary for indefinite civil commitment, whereas other evaluators found, for example, 89 percent, 94 percent, or 95 percent of the inmates were eligible for civil commitment. Again, because the study context was a small system in which case assignments essentially occurred at random, results strongly suggest that evaluator differences in patterns of diagnoses and opinions reflect something about the evaluators, not just the person evaluated.

Evaluator Differences in Instrument Scores from Forensic Evaluations

The limited research available reveals evaluator differences on unstructured or conclusory opinions like competence, sanity, or paraphilia diagnosis. But might the field reduce evaluator differences by using well-designed, structured instruments? After all, a primary purpose of assessment instruments is to enhance the structure and reliability of inferences or diagnoses. To explore these questions, researchers have examined whether evaluators differ in their pattern of scoring a widely used instrument, Hare's (2003) PCL-R, in sexually violent predator evaluations.

In an initial study, researchers examined PCL-R total scores for 321 sex offenders, evaluated by one or more of twenty different state-contracted evaluators (Boccaccini et al., 2008). More than 30 percent of the variability in PCL-R scores was attributable to differences among evaluators, even though there was no reason to believe those evaluators were assigned systematically different subsamples of offenders. For example, the mean PCL-R Total score assigned by one evaluator who had scored sixty offenders was 27.10, which falls at about the seventy-first percentile for the PCL-R. The mean PCL-R Total score from another evaluator, who had scored forty offenders, was 17.50, which falls around the thirtieth percentile (Boccaccini et al., 2008). Further research in the same system found large evaluator differences in scoring each PCL-R factor and facet (i.e., not just the total score), even after controlling for offenders' self-reported antisocial traits (Boccaccini et al., 2014).

To further explore the role of training in reducing evaluator differences, Harris et al. (2015) examined potential evaluator differences in a sample of twenty-four well-trained research assistants scoring a psychopathy measure solely for research purposes in the rigorous MacArthur Violence Risk Assessment Study (Monahan et al., 2001). The proportion of variance in Psychopathy Checklist: Screening Version (PCL:SV Hart, Cox, & Hare, 1995) scores attributable to raters ($\approx 10\%$) was smaller than observed in field studies ($\approx 30\%$), but not entirely absent, suggesting that some evaluator differences may remain even under optimal conditions.

Summary and Discussion: What Contributes to Evaluator Differences?

Many factors may contribute to evaluator differences (Guarnera et al., 2017) including differences in evaluator training, experience, attitudes, personality traits, (Homant & Kennedy, 1987; Miller et al., 2011; Neal, 2016), and even expressed empathy during interviews (Vera et al., 2019). But if formal research and instrument development studies constrain these influences through training, practice, and refining rating procedures, it may be that some "field version" of these strategies could reduce evaluator differences in the field. Field research provides some indirect evidence for these practices. In the field, PCL scores from more experienced raters also appear to be stronger predictors of recidivism than those from less experienced raters, possibly suggesting more reliable scores from more experienced raters (Boccaccini, Rufino, et al., 2017; Jeon et al, 2020; Murrie et al., 2012). In the largest PCL-R evaluator-differences study, differences were smaller (20 percent vs. 32 percent in overall sample) when analyses were limited to evaluators who reported completing a formal PCL-R training workshop (Boccaccini et al., 2014). Although not a field study per se, a study of 280 raters who completed the Hare PCL-R Training Program (i.e., the type of training reported by field evaluators) found that only 6 percent of the variance in scores was attributable to consistent rater differences on the scoring of posttraining practice cases (Blais et al., 2017), suggesting that training may be useful for reducing—even if not completely eliminating—these differences.

Field research findings for the Static-99/R—an instrument that requires little subjective inference to score items—underscore the potential benefits of refining scoring procedures to minimize subjectivity. There is little evidence of systematic evaluator differences in Static-99R scoring, with the one existing study reporting that only 3 percent of the variance in Static-99 scores assigned by 160 different evaluators (N = 45,283) was attributable to evaluator differences (Rice et al., 2012). Researchers have also reported that field reliability improved (i.e., ICC increased from 0.73 to 0.88; Rice et al., 2014) for the Static-99 scores after the introduction of an improved scoring manual in 2003, which corresponded with an improvement in field validity (AUC improved from 0.61 to 0.66; Boccaccini, Rice, et al., 2017).

Adversarial Allegiance in Forensic Assessment

Of course, the most commonly recognized reason that the reliability of forensic evaluators may be weaker in the field is because the adversarial context in which they work. If evaluators retained by different parties come to view examinees differently, and in a manner that favors the retaining party—a phenomenon we label *adversarial allegiance* (Murrie & Boccaccini, 2015)—these differences will lead to disagreement and poor reliability. Legal scholars have long assumed that retained expert witnesses are inevitably biased by the party who pays their fees (e.g., Foster, 1897). Judges and attorneys who observe expert testimony seem similarly skeptical (Shuman et al., 1994). Indeed, in a large-scale survey of federal judges and attorneys, the most frequently cited concern about expert witnesses was that they "abandon objectivity and become advocates for the side that retained them" (Krafka et al., 2002, p. 328).

Adversarial Allegiance Findings in Opinions from Common Forensic Evaluations

Perhaps the easiest way to study the possibility of allegiance is a field study reviewing opposing expert opinions from actual cases. For example, in what appears to be the first (and for decades, the *only*) field study, researchers examined expert opinions relating to a lawsuit against a coal mining company following a 1972 disaster in West Virginia. The authors compared a set of psychiatric evaluations from plaintiff-retained and defense-retained experts for the same forty-two litigants (Zusman & Simon, 1983). They observed that plaintiff-retained psychiatrists arrived at findings that supported the plaintiffs and defense-retained psychiatrists arrived at findings that supported the defendants. Of course, expert opinions in civil litigation are often more qualitative (descriptive) than quantitative (measurable), and there are many limitations to such observational studies of opinions. Indeed, this may be why there were no other such observational studies for decades.

Adversarial Allegiance in Instrument Scores from Forensic Evaluators

More recently, a research strategy has been to examine real-world situations in which opposing experts administer the same assessment instruments to the same defendant. If adversarial contexts reveal poorer agreement, or more error, on instrument scores than is found in research from instrument manuals or well-designed studies, we might assume that the instrument or procedure simply has poorer reliability in field settings than in research settings. Such a finding, by itself, would be unsurprising, given "field reliability" research demonstrating the ways that high reliability values in research studies rarely generalize fully to field settings. However, if we were to find that the instrument has poorer agreement in the field *and* that the direction of disagreement appears *systematically* related to the evaluator's side of retention, then we may infer that the poorer agreement is somehow attributable to "adversarial allegiance" (Murrie & Boccaccini, 2015).

In the first instrument-focused field study, researchers collected PCL-R scores assigned by prosecution-retained and defense-retained psychologists in twenty-three sexually violent predator (SVP) cases (Murrie, Boccaccini, Johnson, et al., 2008). The difference between PCL-R scores assigned by prosecution-retained and defense-retained evaluators was large (Cohen's d = 1.03), leading to poor rater agreement (ICC = 0.39). In 61 percent of the cases, there was a difference of more than 6.0 points between the two PCL-R scores, when differences this large should have occurred in fewer than 5 percent of all cases, according to the instrument manual. In each of these cases, the prosecution-retained evaluator assigned a higher score and the defense-retained evaluator assigned a lower score.

In a series of follow-up studies, researchers found continued disagreements in PCL-R scoring when they updated the sample to include thirty-five SVP cases (Murrie et al., 2009), with these differences being large enough that it appears that scores from different evaluators may need to be interpreted differently to provide the same information about future misbehavior (Boccaccini, Murrie, et al., 2012). They also found evidence of bias in the scores assigned on two measures designed to predict future sexual offending, the

Minnesota Sex Offender Screening Tool Revised (MnSOST-R; Epperson et al., 1998) and the Static-99 (Hanson & Thornton, 2000), which evaluators score on the basis of information in offender's correctional files. The effect size for the MnSOST-R was similar to that for the PCL-R ($d \approx .80$), but somewhat smaller for the Static-99 ($d \approx .35$).

Similar patterns of score discrepancies have emerged in case law reviews of the PCL-R scores evaluators assigned in Canadian criminal cases (Edens et al., 2015; Lloyd et al., 2010). Although the size of the apparent allegiance effect varies somewhat from study to study, scores from prosecution-retained evaluators are consistently higher, and scores from defense-retained evaluators are consistently lower. Other researchers have compared scores assigned by defense and prosecution evaluators, although not necessarily to the same offenders, and found significantly higher scores from prosecution than defense evaluators ($d \approx .90$), in both sex offender and non-sex offender cases (DeMatteo, Edens, Galloway, Cox, Smith, & Formon, 2014, DeMatteo, Edens, Galloway, Cox, Smith, Koller, et al., 2014).

Limitations of Field Studies

Although the pattern of discrepant opinions in field studies *strongly suggests* adversarial allegiance, such field research cannot rule out other plausible explanations. One possibility is that experts may have had access to different information, perhaps because attorneys provided them with different records or other sources, and therefore *appropriately* reached different conclusions based on the data available to them. It is also possible that defendants or litigants respond differently to an expert retained by "their side" versus the opposing side and—consciously or unconsciously—convey different information or clinical presentation.

Another possible explanation for the discrepant opinions involves the most important limitation of field studies of expert bias: because experts are not randomly assigned to sides, the field studies demonstrating differences in expert opinions may be a product of how attorneys select experts for their cases (selection effects), rather than the experts' decision-making after they begin work on the cases (allegiance effects). A savvy defense attorney might select an expert known to more often reach opinions that support insanity, incompetence, or low violence risk; a prosecuting attorney might select for the opposite tendencies. In short, good attorneys may capitalize on preexisting evaluator differences, which may explain some of the differences between opposing experts that we observe in the field.

Even if attorneys have little prior information about evaluators' leanings, attorneys with ample funding can still take advantage of evaluator differences by retaining multiple experts. In most jurisdictions, the court is never exposed to opinions offered by "discarded experts" whom attorneys may retain for an initial evaluation but not subsequent reports or testimony.[6] Only in some jurisdictions are prosecutors allowed access to experts whom

---

[6] See United States v. Alvarez, 519 F. 2d 1036 (3d Cir. 1975).

the defense has decided not to use.[7] Therefore, another type of selection effect that could explain field study findings is that attorneys select only a subset of their retained experts (i.e., those who reached favorable conclusions) to present to the court. "Expert shopping"—plausible only in a minority of litigation with extensive resources—means that courts (and therefore the public) are likely to see an overrepresentation of disagreeing experts and an underrepresentation of agreeing experts.

Of course, attorney selection effects are not the only selection effects that might contribute to apparent disagreements among experts. Evaluators themselves may choose to work with one side of litigation but not the other, potentially skewing expert opinions to be more favorable to the retaining side. For example, evaluators who oppose the death penalty may select to work only for the defense in capital cases (Neal, 2016).

Findings from Adversarial Allegiance Experiments

The best way to control for any type of attorney or expert selection effect is to use an experimental design. To demonstrate the phenomenon of adversarial allegiance—as distinct from selection effects—would require a situation in which attorneys are randomly assigned forensic experts, experts are randomly assigned to attorneys, experts have access to exactly the same materials, and researchers have access to data from all experts who conducted an evaluation. Only in such a scenario would discrepant scores from opposing evaluators be clearly attributable to adversarial allegiance, rather than attorney selection effects, expert selection effects, or differences in the data available to opposing parties.

To explore this possibility, researchers recruited more than one hundred practicing, doctoral-level forensic psychologists and psychiatrists and deceived them to believe they were performing a formal, large-scale forensic consultation (Murrie et al., 2013). These evaluators were—unbeknownst to them—randomly assigned to either a prosecution-allegiance or defense-allegiance group, in which they believed that they were paid by either a public defender service or a special prosecution unit. Evaluators met briefly with an attorney who posed as leading either a public defender service or a specialized prosecution unit, and requested that they score particular risk instruments based on extensive offender records (a common type of consultation). In truth, each participant was scoring the same four case files, which spanned low risk to high risk. Each set of case materials was authentic (i.e., from an actual case), including extensive records (e.g. police, court, correctional, and mental health) of the sort that evaluators typically use to score risk instruments. Thus, participating forensic experts were able to score the same two commonly used risk instruments that served as the metrics for bias in earlier field studies (Murrie et al., 2008, 2009): that is, the PCL-R (Hare, 2003) and Static-99R (Hanson & Thornton, 2000; Helmus et al., 2012).

---

[7] See United States *ex rel.* Edney v. Smith, 425 F. Supp. 1038 (E.D.N.Y 1976).

Overall, the risk measure scores assigned by prosecution and defense experts showed a clear pattern of adversarial allegiance. Allegiance effects were stronger for the PCL-R, which requires more subjective clinical judgment, than for the more structured Static-99R, which requires less inference. For the PCL-R Total score, prosecution evaluators assigned significantly higher scores than defense evaluators for three of four cases, with statistical effect sizes in the medium to large range (Cohen's d of 0.55 to 0.85) and similar in magnitude to effects ($d = 0.63$ to 0.83) documented in a sample of actual proceedings (Murrie et al., 2009). Findings from this rigorous experiment provide strong and unambiguous evidence that even scores on ostensibly objective forensic instruments can be compromised by adversarial allegiance, at least among some experts (Murrie et al., 2013).

Of course, in the field, allegiance effects probably *combine* with selection effects to produce more discrepant opinions across experts. Evaluators vary in their scoring tendencies, attitudes, and opinion formation (as described earlier), and savvy attorneys may recognize these differences and select experts strategically (or experts may self-select the side where they are more aligned). But once selected, experts may seek data, interpret data, and form opinions in a manner biased toward the side that retained them (Neal & Grisso, 2014), and this adversarial allegiance may increase disagreement between experts (Murrie & Boccaccini, 2015).

Allegiance in Score Interpretation

Across studies (Murrie et al., 2008, 2009, 2013), allegiance effects were always stronger for the PCL-R, a more subjective instrument than the Static-99R, a briefer and more straightforward instrument that leaves much less room for clinician inference. This pattern of findings seems to suggest that allegiance effects may be more problematic for a subset of assessment instruments, and could be reduced by using only strict, objective instruments. But findings from a study of Static-99R use in SVP cases suggest that opposing evaluators may draw different conclusions from ostensibly objective instrument results, even when they assign exactly the same score (Chevalier et al., 2015). In other words, adversarial allegiance may influence score *interpretation*, even when it does not (or cannot) influence score *assignment*.

Even highly structured instruments like the Static-99R allow some clinician discretion in interpreting the level of risk represented by a numerical score. An earlier version of the Static-99R manual (Phenix et al., 2012) provided separate sets of normative sample recidivism rates ("norms") for what they labeled "routine" and "high risk" offenders, and the manual provided separate rates for five-year and ten-year follow-up periods. In a survey of 109 SVP evaluators, those who routinely worked for the prosecution were more likely to endorse score interpretation practices indicating the highest possible level of risk (i.e., using high risk norms, ten-year recidivism rates), while those who tended to work for the defense were much more likely to endorse interpretation practices indicating the lowest possible level of risk (i.e., using the routine risk norms, five-year recidivism rates;

Boccaccini et al., 2017). These findings suggest assessment procedures that allow discretion in interpretation—no matter how objective in administration and scoring—leave room for allegiance effects to influence the conclusions that experts provide to the court. Unfortunately, the field has no data to shed light on whether similar allegiance effects operate on other instruments (e.g., neuropsychological tests) that require subjective decisions about norm selection.

Summary and Discussion: Allegiance Effects

Findings from field studies, surveys, and an experiment converge to show that performing an evaluation for one side in an adversarial setting can influence some evaluator's decisions. Why? No empirical study examined the mechanisms driving allegiance effects, but broad and overlapping theories may help explain. The first is relational; adversarial allegiance may result from social–psychological processes that encourage evaluators to think of themselves as being on a side or team (Brodsky, 2013). A second broad theory is that allegiance results from common, unintentional decision-making errors that plague all human judgment (Neal & Grisso, 2014). Although the relational and cognitive-error explanations are conceptually distinct, they may function in complementary ways. A third viewpoint presupposes that allegiance results from more intentional processes and motives that can probably be best summarized as *greed* or overt self-serving bias (Hagen, 1997). Although adversarial pressures do not appear to influence every evaluator score or opinion, it remains unclear which evaluators are most vulnerable to allegiance effects, or how to minimize these effects.

Broad Conclusions

Despite recent efforts to study field reliability, evaluator differences, and bias in forensic mental health assessment, we are only beginning to understand how these may interact to produce differences between opposing evaluators. Figure 20.1 depicts how some of these factors may compound to contribute to clear disagreements among opposing evaluators (Murrie & Boccaccini, 2015). In any adversarial case, there is a pool of possible evaluators that an attorney might retain. These evaluators differ to some extent in their attitudes, their thresholds for reaching certain conclusions, and the typical scores they assign on forensic assessment instruments. Attorneys who are familiar with these differences can take advantage of them by selecting an expert who appears more favorable toward their side. After an attorney retains an expert, the expert's opinion—at least in some cases— begins to favor the retaining party to a greater extent than the case data warrant. In short, adversarial allegiance effects are distinct from selection effects, evaluator differences, measurement error, and other possible of causes of differences between opposing evaluators; but all of these may interact to compound differences. Though the field has made recent progress in identifying these effects, there remains the more challenging task of disentangling and minimizing each of these sources of unreliability.

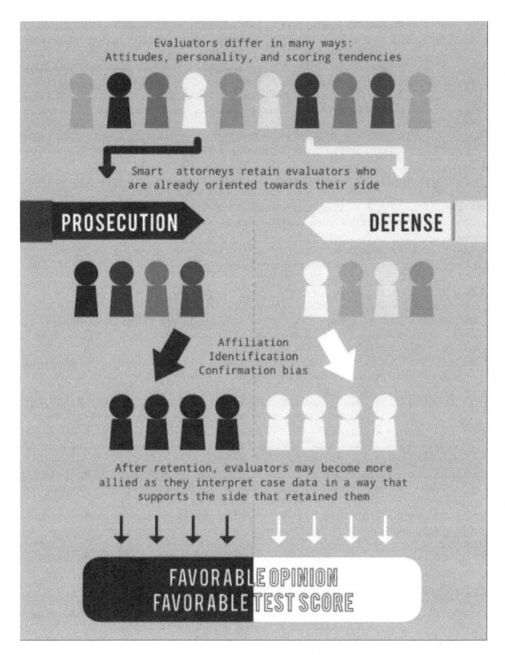

Figure 20.1 Factors Contributing to Disagreement Among Evaluators.

References

American Educational Research Association, American Psychological Association, & National Council on Measurement in Education (Eds.). (2014). *Standards for educational and psychological testing*. American Educational Research Association.

Blais, J., Forth, A. E., & Hare, R. D. (2017). Examining the interrater reliability of the Hare Psychopathy Checklist–Revised across a large sample of trained raters. *Psychological Assessment, 29*(6), 762–775.

Boccaccini, M. T., Chevalier, C. S., Murrie, D. C., & Varela, J. G. (2017). Psychopathy Checklist use and reporting practices in sexually violent predator evaluations. *Sexual Abuse: A Journal of Research and Treatment, 29*(6), 592–614.

Boccaccini, M. T., & Murrie, D. C., (2014). Keeping up with the field in "field reliability" risk assessment research. In A. Schlank (Ed.). *The sexual predator* (Vol 5) (pp. 7-1–7-15). Civic Research Institute.

Boccaccini, M. T., Murrie, D. C., Mercado, C., Quesada, S., Hawes, S., Rice, A. K., & Jeglic, E. (2012). Implications of Static-99 field reliability findings for score use and reporting. *Criminal Justice and Behavior, 39*(1), 42–58.

Boccaccini, M. T., Murrie, D. C., Rufino, K. A., & Gardner, B. O. (2014). Evaluator differences in PCL-R factor and facet level scoring. *Law and Human Behavior, 38*(4), 337–345.

Boccaccini, M. T., Rice, A. K., Helmus, L. M., Murrie, D. C., & Harris, P. B. (2017). Field validity of Static-99/R scores in a statewide sample of 34,687 convicted sexual offenders. *Psychological Assessment, 29*(6), 611–623.

Boccaccini, M. T., Rufino, K. A., Jeon, H., & Murrie, D. C. (2017). Does the predictive validity of psychopathy ratings depend on the clinical experience of the raters? *International Journal of Forensic Mental Health, 16*(2), 130–138.

Boccaccini, M. T., Turner, D. B., & Murrie, D. C. (2008). Do some evaluators report consistently higher or lower PCL-R scores than others? Findings from a statewide sample of sexually violent predator evaluations. *Psychology, Public Policy, and Law, 14*(4), 262–283.

Brodsky, S. L. (2013). *Testifying in court: Guidelines and maxims for the expert witness* (2nd ed.). American Psychological Association.

Chevalier, C., Boccaccini, M. T., Murrie, D. C., & Varela, J. G. (2015). Static-99R reporting practices in sexually violent predator cases: Does norm selection reflect adversarial allegiance? *Law and Human Behavior, 39*, 209–218. doi: 10.1037/lhb0000114

Cicchetti, D. V., & Sparrow, S. A. (1981). Developing criteria for establishing interrater reliability of specific items: Applications to assessment of adaptive behavior. *American Journal of Mental Deficiency, 86*(2), 127–137.

Clark, G. N. (1995). Improving the transition from basic efficacy research to effectiveness studies: Methodological issues and procedures. *Journal of Consulting and Clinical Psychology, 63*(5), 718–725.

DeMatteo, D., Edens, J. F., Galloway, M., Cox, J., Smith, S. T., & Formon, D. (2014a). The role and reliability of the Psychopathy Checklist-Revised in U.S. sexually violent predator evaluations: A case law survey. *Law and Human Behavior, 38*(3), 248–255.

DeMatteo, D., Edens, J. F., Galloway, M., Cox, J., Smith, S. T., Koller, J. P., & Bersoff, B. (2014b). Investigating the role of the Psychopathy Checklist-Revised in United States case law. *Psychology, Public Policy, and Law, 20*(1), 96–107.

Dror, I., & Murrie, D.C. (2018). A hierarchy of expert performance applied to forensic psychology. *Psychology, Public Policy, and Law, 24*(1), 11–23.

Edens, J. F., & Boccaccini, M. T. (2017). Taking forensic mental health assessment "out of the lab" and into "the real world": Introduction to the special issue on the field utility of forensic assessment instruments and procedures. *Psychological Assessment, 29*(6), 710–719.

Edens, J. F., Cox, J., Smith, S. T., DeMatteo, D., & Sörman, K. (2015). How reliable are Psychopathy Checklist–Revised scores in Canadian criminal trials? A case law review. *Psychological Assessment, 27*(2), 447–456.

Epperson, D. L., Kaul, J. D., Huot, S. J., Hesselton, D., Alexander, W., & Goldman, R. (1998). *Minnesota sex offender screening tool-revised (MnSOST-R)*. Minnesota Department of Corrections.

Foster, W. L. (1897). Expert testimony, prevalent complaints and proposed remedies. *Harvard Law Review, 11*(3), 169–186.

Gardner, B. O., Murrie, D. C., & Torres, A. (2018). Insanity findings and evaluation practices: A state-wide review of court-ordered reports. *Behavioral Sciences & the Law, 36*(3), 303–316.

Gowensmith, W. N., Bryant, A. E., & Vitacco, M. J. (2014). Decision-making in post-acquittal hospital release: How do forensic evaluators make their decisions? *Behavioral Sciences & the Law, 32*(5), 596–607.

Gowensmith, W. N., Murrie, D. C., & Boccaccini, M. T. (2012). Field reliability of competency to stand trial evaluations: How often do evaluators agree, and what do judges decide when evaluators disagree? *Law and Human Behavior, 36*(2), 130–139.

Gowensmith, W., Murrie, D. C., & Boccaccini, M. T. (2013). How reliable are forensic evaluations of legal sanity? *Law and Human Behavior, 37*(2), 98–106.

Gowensmith, W., Murrie, D. C., & Boccaccini, M. T. (2017). Field reliability influences field validity: Risk assessments of individuals found not guilty by reason of insanity. *Psychological Assessment, 29*(6), 786–794.

Guarnera, L., Murrie, D. C., & Boccaccini, M. T. (2017). Why do forensic experts disagree? Sources of unreliability and bias in forensic psychology evaluations. *Translational Issues in Psychological Science, 3*(2), 143–152.

Guarnera, L. & Murrie, D. C. (2017). Field reliability of competence and sanity opinions: A systematic review and meta-analysis. *Psychological Assessment, 29*(6), 795–818.

Hanson, R. K., & Morton-Bourgon, K. E., (2009). The accuracy of recidivism risk assessments for sexual offenders: A meta-analysis. *Psychological Assessment, 21*(1), 1–21.

Hagen, M. A. (1997). Whores of the court: *The fraud of psychiatric testimony and the rape of American justice*. Regan.

Hanson, R. K., & Thornton, D. (2000). Improving risk assessment for sex offenders: A comparison of three actuarial scales. *Law and Human Behavior, 24*(1), 119–136.

Hare, R. D. (2003). *The Hare Psychopathy Checklist–Revised* (2nd ed.). Multi-Health Systems.

Harris, P. B., Boccaccini, M. T., & Murrie, D. C. (2015). Rater differences in psychopathy measure scoring and predictive validity. *Law and Human Behavior, 39*(4), 321–331.

Harris, P. B., Boccaccini, M. T., & Schrantz, K. (2016, March). *Evaluator differences in behavioral abnormality conclusions and paraphilia diagnoses in sexually violent predator cases* [Paper presentation]. Annual meeting of the American Psychology-Law Society, Atlanta, GA.

Hart, S. D., Cox, D. N., & Hare, R. D. (1995). *The Hare Psychopathy Checklist: Screening Version (PCL:SV)*. Multi-Heath Systems.

Heilbrun, K. (1992). The role of psychological testing in forensic assessment. *Law and Human Behavior, 16*(3), 257–272.

Helmus, L., Thornton, D., Hanson, R. K., & Babchishin, K. M. (2012). Improving the predictive accuracy of Static-99 and Static-2002 with older sex offenders: revised age weights. *Sexual Abuse: A Journal of Research and Treatment, 24*, 64–101.

Homant, R. J., & Kennedy, D. B. (1987). Subjective factors in clinicians' judgments of insanity: Comparison of a hypothetical case and an actual case. *Professional Psychology: Research and Practice, 18*(5), 439–446.

Jeon, H., Boccaccini, M. T., Jo, E., Jang, H., & Murrie, D. C. (2020). Rater experience and the predictive validity of Psychopathy Checklist: Youth Version scores. *Psychiatry, Psychology and Law, 27*(5), 912–923. https://doi.org/10.1080/13218719.2020.1751330

Krafka, C., Dunn, M. A., Johnson, M. T., Cecil, J. S., & Miletich, D. (2002). Judge and attorney experiences, practices, and concerns regarding expert testimony in federal civil trials. *Psychology, Public Policy, and Law, 8*(3), 309–332.

Levenson, J. S. (2004). Reliability of sexually violent predator civil commitment criteria in Florida. *Law and Human Behavior, 28*(4), 357–368.

Lloyd, C., Clark, H., & Forth, A. E. (2010). Psychopathy, expert testimony, and indeterminate sentences: Exploring the relationship between Psychopathy Checklist-Revised testimony and trial outcome in Canada. *Legal and Criminological Psychology, 15*(2), 323–339

Miller, A. K., Rufino, K. A., Boccaccini, M. T., Jackson, R. L., & Murrie, D. C. (2011). On individual differences in person perception: Raters' personality traits relate to their Psychopathy Checklist-Revised scoring tendencies. *Assessment, 18*(2), 253–260.

Mitchell, G. (2012). Revisiting truth or triviality: The external validity of research in the psychological laboratory. *Perspectives in Psychological Science, 7*(2), 109–117.

Monahan, J., Steadman, H., Silver, E., Appelbaum, P., Robbins, P., Mulvey, E., Roth, L., Grisso, T., & Banks, S. (2001). *Rethinking risk assessment: The MacArthur Study of Mental Disorder and Violence*. Oxford University Press.

Murrie, D. C., & Boccaccini, M. T. (2015). Adversarial allegiance among forensic experts. *Annual Review of Law and Social Science, 11*, 37–55.

Murrie, D. C., Boccaccini, M. T., Caperton, J. D., & Rufino, K. A. (2012). Field validity of the Psychopathy Checklist-Revised in sex offender risk assessment. *Psychological Assessment, 24*(2), 524–529.

Murrie, D. C., Boccaccini, M. T., Guarnera, L. A., & Rufino, K. A. (2013). Are forensic experts biased by the side that retained them? *Psychological Science, 24*(10), 1889–1897.

Murrie, D. C., Boccaccini, M. T., Johnson, J. T., & Janke, C. (2008). Does interrater (dis) agreement on Psychopathy Checklist scores in sexually violent predator trials suggest partisan allegiance in forensic evaluations? *Law and human behavior, 32*(4), 352–362.

Murrie, D. C., Boccaccini, M. T., Turner, D. B., Meeks, M., Woods, C., Tussey, C. (2009). Rater (dis)agreement on risk assessment measures in sexually violent predator proceedings: Evidence of adversarial allegiance in forensic evaluation? *Psychology, Public Policy, and Law, 15*(1), 19–53.

Murrie, D. C., Boccaccini, M. T., Zapf, P. A., Warren, J. I., & Henderson, C. E. (2008). Clinician variation in findings of competence to stand trial. *Psychology, Public Policy, and Law, 14*(3), 177–193.

Murrie, D. C., Gardner, B. O., & Torres, A. N. (2020). Competency to stand trial evaluations: A state-wide review of court-ordered reports. *Behavioral Sciences and the Law, 38*(1), 32–50.

Murrie, D. C., & Warren, J. I. (2005). Clinician variation in rates of legal sanity opinions: Implications for self-monitoring. *Professional Psychology: Research and Practice, 36*(5), 519–524.

National Research Council, Committee on Identifying the Needs of the Forensic Science Community. (2009). *Strengthening forensic science in the United States: A path forward*. NRC.

Neal T. M. S. (2016) Are forensic experts already biased before adversarial legal parties hire them? *PLoS ONE 11*(4), Article e0154434.

Neal T., & Grisso T. (2014). The cognitive underpinnings of bias in forensic mental health evaluations. *Psychology, Public Policy, and Law, 20*(2), 200–211

Olver, M. E., Neumann, C. S., Mokros, A. Brand, E., Gacono, C., Kiehl, K., Leon-Mayer, E., Meloy, J. R., Salekin, R. T., Thomson, N., Vitacco, M., Stockdale, K. C., Hare, R. D., Baskin-Sommers, A., Folino, J., Gray, N. S., Knight, R., Logan, M., Roy, S. . . . Yoon, D. (2020). Reliability and validity of the Psychopathy Checklist-Revised in the assessment of risk for institutional violence: A cautionary note on DeMatteo et al. (2020). *Psychology, Public Policy, and Law, 26*(4), 490–510.

Phenix, A., Helmus, L., & Hanson, R. K. (2012). *Static-99R and Static-2002R evaluators' workbook*, July. http://static99.org/

President's Council of Advisors on Science and Technology (PCAST). (2016). *Report to the President: Forensic science in the criminal courts: Ensuring scientific validity of feature-comparison methods*. Executive Office of the President of the United States.

Rice, A. R., Boccaccini, M. T., & Collier, T. L. (2012, March). *Evaluator differences in assigning Static-99 scores* [Poster presentation]. Meeting at the American Psychology Law Society, San Juan, PR.

Rice, A. K., Boccaccini, M. T., Harris, P. B., & Hawes, S. W. (2014). Does field reliability for Static-99 scores decrease as scores increase? *Psychological Assessment, 26*(4), 1085–1094.

Rufino, K., Boccaccini, M. T., & Guy, L. (2011). Scoring subjectivity and item performance on measures used to assess violence risk: The PCL-R and HCR-20 as exemplars. *Assessment, 18*(4), 453–463.

Shuman D. W., Whitaker E., & Champagne A. (1994). An empirical examination of the use of expert witnesses in the courts—Part II: A three city study. *Jurimetrics, 34*(2), 193–208

Skeem, J., Golding, S., Cohn, N., & Berge, G. (1998). The logic and reliability of expert opinion on competence to stand trial. *Law and Human Behavior, 22*(5), 519–547.

Vera, L. M., Boccaccini, M. T., Laxton, K., Bryson, C., Pennington, C., Ridge, B., & Murrie, D. C. (2019). How does evaluator empathy impact a forensic interview? *Law and Human Behavior, 43*(1), 56–68.

Weisz, J. R., Weiss, B. & Donenberg, G. R. (1992). The lab versus the clinic: Effects of child and adolescent psychotherapy. *American Psychologist, 47*(12), 1578–1585.

Zusman, J., & Simon J. (1983). Differences in repeated psychiatric examinations of litigants to a lawsuit. *The American journal of psychiatry, 140*(10), 1300–1304.

Consultation and Intervention

Trial Consultation

Eric Y. Drogin *and* Leigh D. Hagan

Abstract

Trial consultation is a form of applied forensic psychology that is most easily distinguished from the work of the testifying expert when one focuses on the identities of target audiences. Whereas expert witnesses conduct, report on, and testify about the results of evaluations for the benefit of judges and juries, trial consultants educate lawyers about how to win cases. In support of—but never usurping—counsel's advocacy role, trial consultants investigate and explain the testifying expert's credentials, publications, reports, prior testimony, and more. The trial consultant's activities remain subject to mandatory ethical codes and advisory professional guidelines. Such sources help to ensure that that the trial consultant's contributions remain far more than a mere extension of counsel's adversarial approach. The trial consultant's acknowledged and assiduously promoted ambition is to investigate diligently, report accurately, and advise appropriately, with an eye toward eliminating surprises and supporting the efficacy of ethically grounded advocacy.

Key Words: trial consultation, forensic psychology, ethics, professional guidelines, testifying experts, specialty guidelines for forensic psychology

The easiest way to distinguish trial consultation from other avenues of applied psychology–law is to focus on the identities of target audiences. In criminal and civil forensic psychology, expert witnesses conduct, report on, and testify about evaluations for the benefit of judges and juries. Other psychologists conduct community-based interventions, treat justice-involved people, and provide a broad range of clinical and administrative services to jails, prisons, diversion programs, and problem-solving courts.

Trial consultants educate lawyers about how to win cases.

There are those for whom such a job description will have instant appeal. Some were drawn to forensic psychology in the first place by the combative energy of the adversarial system and feel that trial consultation would afford them a more influential and impactful role in the process. Others never cared much for courtroom jousting and welcome the opportunity to develop their theories and share their expertise without having to subject themselves and their work product to the crucible of cross-examination. Still others, confident in their witnessing skills but weary of the daily forensic grind, find themselves at a point in their storied careers where the time has come to start "getting paid for what I know, instead of getting paid for what I do" (Drogin & Barrett, 2013, p. 648).

One essential function of the trial consultant is to translate the often dense and obscure language of professional psychology into counsel's vernacular. The trial consultant's investigative skills are always welcome when these illuminate and demystify the testifying expert's credentials (e.g., education, training, licensure, professional affiliation, ethical standing, board certification, published scholarship, prior testimony, and appellate-level review of work product). These and other forms of trial consultation will inform counsel's efforts during each phase of legal proceedings, including obtaining pretrial discovery, deposing experts, preparing motions, selecting juries, arguing against admissibility, developing direct and cross-examination strategies, arguing the weight of the evidence, and styling closing arguments.

Investigating the Testifying Expert

The trial consultant and the testifying expert labor under three fundamental obligations: to tell the truth, to be fair, and to be accurate (American Psychological Association, 2013, 2017; Baker, 1983). No one becomes a testifying expert until the trial judge accords that honor, and qualification as a testifying expert is a privilege that must be earned anew in each case. The trial consultant can assist counsel by investigating the testifying expert's claimed credentials, by identifying genuine strengths as well as otherwise opaque compromises to qualification, and by pointing out issues that might reasonably and fairly undermine the weight of adverse testimony. Such scrutiny can prove valuable—even essential—when applied to counsel's testifying expert, the opposing side's testifying expert, or both.

Degrees, Titles, and Experience

Asserted credentials and qualifications can be investigated by reviewing such sources of information as websites, social media postings, transcripts of prior testimony, publication and presentation biographies, professional listservs, opposing counsel's expert disclosure documentation, and elsewhere. When researching the authenticity of the testifying expert's credentials and qualifications, the trial consultant should alert counsel to public representations that are accurate and defensible, as well as to those that appear inflated, erroneous, misleading, vague, out of date, or the apparent product of mere oversight.

Members of the legal profession, for whom "J.D." and the occasional "L.L.M." are typically sufficient, can be mystified—as well as impressed, intimidated, entertained, or moved to cynicism—by the morass of academic and board designations in the testifying expert's letterhead and signature block. Such material may represent genuine academic scholarship and professional accomplishment, whereas others, to misquote *Macbeth*, are "full of sound and fluff, signifying nothing." Counsel will usually be easy to convince that all "doctors" are not the same, despite the fact that the lay consumers may have little appreciation of the distinctions among psychiatrists, psychologists, counselors, and the like. The trial consultant can decipher the panoply of designations and help counsel grasp the boundaries of the respective areas of specialized knowledge and the limits that are not usually recognized in the context of the deference that typically accompanies the honorific of "doctor." For example, the trial consultant may point out that the opposing side's testifying M.D. is a pediatrician licensed by the state to practice medicine and surgery but is not a psychiatrist with specialized knowledge of mental disorders and mental health treatment.

The title of "doctor" is not one for counsel to accept blindly. There are important but often unrecognized and unappreciated distinctions to be made among PhD, PsyD, EdD, DSW, DMin, and other academic credentials. While the use of "A.B.D.," might be accurate and create a mystique of prestige, counsel may recognize that this means "all but dissertation," signifying that a doctoral program has not been completed. The trial consultant can assist counsel in understanding the requisite training underpinning each degree, and in differentiating between traditional brick and mortar and online educational institutions—as well as between fully accredited programs and "diploma mills" (Piña, 2010). The trial consultant's investigation might demonstrate, for example, that a testifying expert, who has been qualified on numerous occasions as an expert in sex offender risk assessment and treatment, holds a degree in divinity and has been certified as a sex offender treatment provider but is not licensed for the independent practice of any profession.

The testifying expert's assertions concerning postdegree speaking activities merit investigation as well. Some curricula vitae (CVs) copiously document the attendance of continuing education events. Those outside the mental health professions might mistakenly conclude that these are presentations made by the testifying expert when, in fact, the CV is simply identifying the passive experience of sitting in a conference hall. Some presentations that may appear to have been delivered to sophisticated audiences at prestigious gatherings of scientific societies may actually represent little more than an appearance on a location television or radio talk show.

Some testifying expert publications reflect a high standard of peer review, or may display other indicia—such as inclusion in a prestigious journal or an edited book with esteemed editors and fellow authors—that the underlying research was properly conducted and compellingly conveyed, with the finished product constituting a contribution of sufficient importance to earn a place in the established professional literature. By contrast, other testifying expert publications may lack objective merit and could find no means of dissemination other than pay-to-publish outlets that are derided in academic circles as "predatory journals" (Demir, 2018).

The substantive positions advanced in a testifying expert's publications and presentations may undermine or even contradict the testimony that expert intends to offer in the case at hand. The trial consultant can be of immeasurable assistance to counsel in ferreting out inconsistencies and shortcomings, and generally distinguishing genuine scientific merit from the insubstantial dressed in scientific clothing.

Licensure

Decoding licensure status is another opportunity for the trial consultant to identify and convey the truth to counsel with fairness and accuracy. Information obtained from a licensing board will disclose a wealth of general information that is potentially relevant to counsel's voir dire of the testifying expert, including precise designation of the license, requisite qualifications to sit for the exam, the licensee's scope of permissible practice, continuing education requirements, and regulatory practice standards. Counsel will also appreciate it when the trial consultant cross-references the testifying expert's licensure status—for example, supervised residency status versus independent practice—across such case-specific points in time as when examinations were conducted, opinions were formed, reports were written, and testimony is anticipated.

In keeping with the adage that prophets are never accepted in their hometowns, opposing counsel will often engage a testifying expert from another jurisdiction. This will prompt the trial consultant to investigate the unique statutes, regulations, case law, local court customs, and licensing board proclivities with respect to the practice of psychology by persons who are not licensed locally. Although recent developments have eased certain barriers to interstate mental health forensic practice—such as the Association of the State and Provincial Psychology Boards (ASPPB; 2021) "Mobility Program"—testifying experts are still responsible for abiding by the laws and regulations of the jurisdiction in which they render psychological services.

Each jurisdiction has the latitude to define the practice of psychology and to specify when normal licensing rules may not apply. For example, Virginia law enables the testimony of "any person duly licensed as a psychologist in another state or the District of Columbia who testifies as a treating psychologist or who is employed as an expert for the purpose of possibly testifying as an expert witness."[1] This, of course, is distinct from conducting an evaluation that may form the *basis* for such testimony—a situation that may require adherence to additional guidance. For example, Florida law allows visiting psychologists from another jurisdiction to practice in Florida for a specified number of days without a local license, if that other jurisdiction's licensing requirements meet or exceed Florida's own.[2]

Federal license requirements differ from state regulations. For example, psychologists employed by Department of Veterans Affairs may practice without a local state license if they hold a license in another state,[3] such that a psychologist licensed in one state

---

[1] Code of Va. §54.1-3601 (2000).
[2] Fla. Stat. §490.014 (2010).
[3] 38 C.F.R. p. 17 (2002).

and employed by the Veterans Administration (VA) in another state could conduct an inpatient trial competency evaluation in a second state and then testify at a federal court hearing in a third state.

The burgeoning of telepsychology—involving the provision of clinical or forensic services via telephone, video, instant messaging, electronic mail, and other media—has inspired concerns regarding health, safety, cost containment, logistical convenience, personnel resources, and other considerations (Martin et al., 2020). Although some states have modified practice regulations regarding telepsychology, it is incumbent on the practitioner to comport with the jurisdictional requirements where they practice as well as with those in the locality of the person they are serving. In instances in which the opposing side's expert relied on telecommunications technologies when treating or evaluating a party, the consulting psychologist's investigation might advise the engaging attorney whether the other expert's procedures aligned with applicable jurisdictional requirements (Drogin, 2020).

Counsel will be interested—even anxious—to learn whether a licensing board's public record shows any history of actions against the testifying expert, especially when this record is accompanied by findings of fact, orders of reprimand, or delineated practice restrictions, and all the more so if complaints were occasioned, as is increasingly the case, by expert witness practices (Marett & Mossman, 2017). Discovery of public actions could be particularly noteworthy if the violations of regulations are germane to the matter the testifying expert is anticipated to address, such as sanctions for excessive billing practices, offering services for which competency has not been demonstrated, engaging in dual-role conflicts, or exceeding professional boundaries. Information about a complaints taken under advisement, impaired provider interventions, unfavorable malpractice judgments, and retracted publications could also be uncovered by this form of investigation.

Board Certification

Whereas a valid practice license is a minimal requirement for forensic work, board certification is an optional enhancement. With a shrinking market for clinical practices that are dependent on insurance reimbursement, with recurring threats of reductions in allowable fees, with a lowering of the credentialing threshold to permit certified as well as licensed practice, and with the arrival of even more licensees into the marketplace (DeAngelis, 2014), many practitioners have turned to the forensic arena to broaden their revenue streams. Board certification has become one way for practitioners to distinguish themselves in the crowded field of newly minted testifying experts. Several new boards have arisen to support credential enhancements. This has led to a plethora of character extenders in signature blocks, which laypersons and lawyers alike are often unable to decipher, much less discern comparative value.

Not all boards hold their specialists to the same standard. Some boards have multistep screening processes and written examinations that scrutinize the candidate's grasp of subject matter and ethical obligations (Packard & Simon, 2006), whereas others require little more than a brief application process and a check that clears the bank. The latter, sometimes referred to as "vanity boards" (Dattilio et al., 2003; Ecklund-Johnson & Pearson, 2019), are of dubious value to the testifying expert beyond puffery. The proliferation of such boards might give the appearance of distinctive qualifications, but in actual practice they give the public little assurance of superior skills. Revelations about the dubious policies and practices of some credential mills have just the opposite effect and have undermined the public's trust in the board certification enterprise generally (Hansen, 2000).

Concerns about false impressions created by such credentials have led at least one judicial commission to put attorneys on notice about their responsibility to address the validity of board certification during the qualification process. "To the extent that certain credentials may be misleading, the Commission strongly urges the court and bar to carefully review the potential expert's resume, curriculum vitae and application and be informed about the nature of the accreditations included therein. . . . In the event that an evaluator gets to the point of testifying in court, it is the responsibility of the attorney to conduct a voir dire to clarify the question of validity of such credentials during the qualifying process" (Matrimonial Commission, 2006).

In support of the qualification question, "Doctor, in which professional organizations do you hold membership?" the trial consultant can assist counsel by investigating the testifying expert's current membership status as well the granting organization's membership thresholds, mission statement, ethics code, and published advocacy positions. The consultant can bring value by distinguishing between boards that require demonstrated knowledge and skill from those that simply require professional interest and dues payment. For boards that hold their members accountable to an ethics code, it could be helpful for the trial consultant to investigate any negative findings concerning a specific testifying expert—discovering, perhaps, that the board in question was so minimally invested in its ethics code that it had never seen fit to discipline a single member on that basis.

Multiple Examiners

Moving beyond credentials in the signature block, the consultant should take note of the number of signatures and the order in which they appear in any report or other work product. By custom and convention, the author featured last among the signatories is the person with ultimate responsibility for the work product. This is the person who, quite literally, has the last word. In many instances, the preceding signature is that of a student, a resident in training, or some other supervisee who conducted the evaluation and wrote the majority content of the report. In larger practices and institutional settings, a psychometrician or technical assistant might have performed the actual psychological testing but is not credited with a signature.

Whereas licensing regulations[4] and multijurisdictional practice standards such as those promulgated by the ASPPB (2018) allow for the use of technical assistants or doctoral candidates working under the supervision of a licensee, the supervisor is ethically and legally responsible for all of the supervisee's professional activities. The trial consultant's investigation may include obtaining all materials associated with the evaluation and the report in order to determine the respective contributions of those involved in the evaluation. This information will assist counsel in determining upon whom discovery demands should be served, and whom to depose or call as a witness at trial.

Conflicts of Interest

Conflicting responsibilities can emerge in clinical and forensic practice settings alike. Both the trial consultant and the testifying expert are duty-bound to remain alert to conflicts stemming from any of a variety of circumstances not limited to prior personal and professional relationships, current engagements, financial interests, and personal problems (American Psychological Association, 2013, 2017). Beyond more apparent conflicts in fact, the trial consultant should remain alert to the possibility that the testifying expert may have run afoul of an equally important but more nuanced *appearance* of a conflict. Professionals must be guided not only by the true state of their impartiality but also by the public perception of their fairness, in order to maintain the public's confidence in the integrity of the judicial process. The expert's obligation to avoid the perception of bias is analogous to legal canons applicable to judges. In Virginia, for example, "[t]he test for appearance of impropriety is whether the conduct would create in reasonable minds a perception that the judge's ability to carry out judicial responsibilities with integrity and impartiality is impaired" (Judicial Ethics Advisory Committee, 2019).

Trial consultants and testifying experts must respect and honor the public trust and strive to enhance and maintain confidence in the legal system. All involved should determine if they can remain faithful to their fundamental obligations for truth, fairness, and accuracy to all parties in the proceeding. An affirmative answer to this question does not end the inquiry. Testifying experts must also consider how their conduct will be perceived by the general public. The trial consultant may assist counsel with advice regarding the potential conflicts in fact as well the perception of conflicts that might undermine the public's trust in the field of psychology generally, and of psychologists' role in litigation specifically.

Prior Testimony

Transcripts of prior testimony and appellate reviews can reveal information relevant to voir dire and cross-examination of the testifying expert. Counsel has every reason to insist that a position, finding, or opinion proffered by a testifying expert in a prior

---

[4] See, e.g., Va. Admin. Code §125-20-150 (2012).

case should be substantially the same in a subsequent legal matter as long as the facts, circumstances, and data are similar. The same holds for the testifying expert's in-court references to published works—those authored by the testifying expert, and those authored by someone else. Based upon the trial consultant's investigation, the testifying expert's deviation from prior testimony, in the absence of a reasonable justification, should be brought to counsel's attention promptly. Trial transcripts would also show if a prior court had found the testifying expert not qualified as an expert, limited the scope of the testifying expert's qualification, or rejected the testifying expert's subject matter as not sufficiently scientific under *Frye v. United States*, *Daubert v. Merrell Dow Pharmaceuticals*, applicable portions of the Federal Rules of Evidence (2014), or other admissibility standards.[5]

Ethical Obligations and Opportunities

Having wrested consultant funding from the client or from the court—with the latter constitutionally guaranteed in some serious criminal matters by the US Supreme Court in *Ake v. Oklahoma*[6]—counsel exults in having procured, at long last, an experienced expert dedicated from the outset to seeing the case through counsel's eyes. Emboldened by a mutual understanding that what happens in counsel's office stays in counsel's office, surely the trial consultant can be untethered now from obscure, guild-driven requirements that every helpful opinion be bundled with a stated list of reasons why that opinion might actually be wrong. In counsel's mind, the assistance the trial consultant provides will remain shielded from report writing, courtroom testimony, depositions, or other avenues of disclosure (Shuman, 2007)—unless, of course, counsel elects to utilize the expert in that context as well.

The legal profession knows where the lines are supposed to be drawn. According to *Black's Law Dictionary* (Garner, 2019), a "testifying expert" is one "identified by a party as a potential witness at trial," with opinions that are subject to "initial disclosures" consisting of "all information that the witness considered" when forming such opinions (p. 274). In contrast, a "consulting expert" (also termed by this source a "nontestifying expert") is one who "though retained by a party, is not expected to be called as a witness at trial," with opinions that are "generally exempt from the scope of discovery" (Garner, 2019, p. 724).

Counsel may, however, seek to blur these and other distinctions in support of a lawyer's primary obligation to provide "zealous advocacy" (Brown, 2010), although "taking both roles (consultant and testifying expert) can easily undermine the apparent, if not actual, objectivity of the clinician as a testifying witness" (Melton et al., 2018, p. 87).

---

[5] Frye v. United States, 293 F. 1013 (D.C. Cir. 1923); Daubert v. Merrell Dow Pharm., Inc., 509 U.S. 579 (1993); Fed. Rules of Evid. (2014), https://www.uscourts.gov/sites/default/files/Rules%20of%20Evidence

[6] Ake v. Oklahoma, 470 U.S. 68 (1985).

Otto et al. (2017) have asserted that while "simultaneously serving as an examiner and consultant increases the risk of loss of impartiality," this is a problem that "vanishes if the examiner and consultant roles are combined sequentially in a single case" (pp. 73–74). Brodsky (1999) first observed more than two decades ago that for psychologists, this sequence represents "a one-way street" that "works only to change their role from evaluating expert to trial consultant," since "once committed to an advocacy role, the alliance with the attorneys includes a commitment to help win the case" (p. 134). It is worth noting that many forensic mental health professionals may be ignorant of such distinctions (Gutheil et al., 2012).

Whereas trial consultation draws upon the psychologist's knowledge of treatment, assessment, and social scientific research, such expertise will ultimately be applied in the context of another profession's rules, aspirations, and fundamental principles. Counsel needs to "win" on the behalf of the client. This is not an abstract notion from counsel's perspective. Winning is measured in such concrete terms as delineated rights preserved, sums of money obtained, and terms of incarceration avoided or imposed. Counsel understands—and can grudgingly afford to respect, within limits—the testifying expert's codified obligations to assess, report, and testify within certain guild-determined boundaries. Less patience can be expected, however, with the reservations of those trial consultants who are cast unambiguously as members of the "team," but who still seem inclined to hold back, for reasons difficult to fathom, just as victory threatens to elude counsel's grasp.

Despite such real and imagined pressures, the trial consultant will do well to note that, while counsel is the client, "psychologists have ethical obligations toward every party in a case, no matter how many or how named" (Fisher, 2009, p. 1). Further, "because psychologists' scientific and professional judgments and actions may affect the lives of others, they are alert to and guard against personal, financial, social, organizational, or political factors that might lead to misuse of their influence" (American Psychological Association, 2017, p. 3). These obligations remain in place even if the trial consultant's roles and work remain undisclosed in the course of litigation.

Following is an exploration of sources of ethical guidance that serve a dual purpose for the trial consultant: they identify pitfalls directly relevant to this mode of applied service provision, and they also serve as objective evidence—for an audience that prides itself in its expertise regarding such matters—of what lines must still be drawn, even when pursuing shared interdisciplinary goals.

Ethical Principles of Psychologists and Code of Conduct

The American Psychological Association's Ethical Principles of Psychologists and Code of Conduct (EPPCC; American Psychological Association, 2017) is that organization's sole source of mandatory ethical direction for its members (American Psychological Association, 2015). In many jurisdictions, trial consultants seeking to lend weight to their reliance on this resource can remind counsel that the EPPCC has been adopted ("incorporated by reference") into that state's licensing statutes or practice regulations, thus giving rules the force of law (Drogin, 2019, p. 36). The following paragraphs consist of a selection of EPPCC standards with particular relevance to trial consultation.

STANDARD 1.01: MISUSE OF PSYCHOLOGISTS' WORK

When psychologists "learn of misuse or misrepresentation of their work, they take reasonable steps to correct or minimize the misuse or misrepresentation" (American Psychological Association, 2017, p. 4). Proactively notifying counsel of this obligation can help to prevent future problems in this regard. For example, it may be necessary to discourage counsel from making erroneous in-court assertions based upon—and perhaps even referring—to the trial consultant's opinions. In anticipation of such problems, counsel can be informed of the consultant's own duty to correct such errors whether the assertions are directly ascribed to the consultant or not, and even though the consultant is not expected to be testifying in court or at a pretrial hearing.

STANDARD 1.04: INFORMAL RESOLUTION OF ETHICAL VIOLATIONS

If psychologists "believe that there may have been an ethical violation by another psychologist," then they "attempt to resolve the issue by bringing it to the attention of that individual," but this obligation is only translated into action when "an informal resolution appears appropriate and the intervention does not involve any confidentiality rights that may be involved" (American Psychological Association, 2017, p. 4). Counsel will be reassured to learn of this exception, and in any event would already be quick to assert that contact with the other side's expert witness—or with a psychologist who is not an expert witness but rather a party to the proceedings in question—would be anything but appropriate, and that the trial consultant's opinions (and perhaps his or her very presence on the legal team at all) should be treated as confidential.

STANDARD 1.05: REPORTING OF ETHICAL VIOLATIONS

Behavior that "has substantially harmed or is likely to substantially harm" some third party may be too serious to be resolved informally, and might normally compel the filing of a report with various "committees," "boards," or other "institutional authorities." Here, however, one finds another exception for situations involving "confidentiality rights," as well as an exception for "when psychologists have been retained to review the work of another psychologist whose professional conduct is in question" (American Psychological Association, 2017, p. 4). A reasonable difference of opinion could arise between counsel and the trial consultant concerning the import of this "retained to review" clause. Counsel would naturally construe this clause as pertaining to all situations in which the specter of misconduct has arisen in the *course* of any form of legal proceedings. The trial consultant might counter that this clause was specifically intended to avoid redundant reporting in *ongoing* disciplinary or malpractice proceedings. This potential interpretative clash makes it all the more fortunate that the "confidentiality rights" exception initially surfacing in Standard 1.04 remains in effect for Standard 1.05 as well.

STANDARD 9.01: BASES FOR ASSESSMENTS

When psychologists provide opinions in the form of "recommendations," "reports," or "diagnostic or evaluative statements," such pronouncements must be based upon "information and techniques sufficient to substantiate their findings" (American Psychological Association, 2017, pp. 12–13). Psychologists may "provide opinions of the psychological characteristics of individuals only after they have conducted an examination of the individuals adequate to support their statements or conclusions," unless such an examination is not "practical," which would be determined on the basis of "reasonable efforts" to conduct it (American Psychological Association, 2017, p. 13). A specific exception is carved out for those instances in which the psychologists "conduct a record review or provide consultation or supervision," but only when an examination "is not warranted or necessary for the opinion" in addition to which the psychologist must "explain this" and identity the "sources of information" upon which any "conclusions and recommendations" are based (American Psychological Association, 2017, p. 13). What counsel needs to gather from all of this is that the trial consultant could wind up in significant ethical and—by extension—legal jeopardy by rendering a diagnostic or other forensically oriented opinion without having examined the litigant directly.

STANDARD 9.11: MAINTAINING TEST SECURITY

Psychologists are required to "make reasonable efforts to maintain the integrity and security of test materials and other assessment techniques," in a manner that is "consistent with law and contractual obligations" and "permits adherence to this Ethics Code" (American Psychological Association, 2017, p. 14). Due to this particular standard, counsel may have moved heaven and earth in order to compel production of copies of the opposing psychologist's work product, with the compromise typically being that this material is sent directly to the trial consultant as another qualified mental health professional (Vanderpool, 2014). This does not mean, however, that once the trial consultant has obtained the test materials in question, these can be shared freely with counsel. Counsel may well ask, "Well, how am I supposed to fashion a cross-examination when I can't see what I'm asking about?" The trial consultant's challenge under such circumstances is to convey a sense of the opposing psychologist's errors—if any—and to outline what the opposing psychologist would be expected to know, without compromising the confidential contents and future viability of the tests themselves.

The American Psychological Association's Specialty Guidelines for Forensic Psychology (SGFP; American Psychological Association, 2013) were "designed to be national in scope" and were "intended to be consistent with state and federal law," but carry less objective weight than the EPPCC, as the SGFP were "not intended to serve as a basis for disciplinary action or civil or criminal liability" (American Psychological Association, 2013, p. 8). This having been noted, counsel will hardly be in a position to dismiss SGFP-based concerns as irrelevant, and indeed lawyers are typically more likely than trial consultants to recognize that guidelines promulgated and distributed by a national guild organization are going to be viewed as informing standards of practice and care (Meyer & Drogin, 2015), even when such guidelines are explicitly described as "advisory" by their authors (American Psychological Association, 2013, p. 8). The SGFP applies whether one self-identifies as a "forensic" psychologist or not (American Psychological Association, 2013, p. 7), and is far more explicit than the EPPCC when it comes to the activities of trial consultants, as reflected in the following paragraphs.

GUIDELINE 4.01: RESPONSIBILITIES TO RETAINING PARTIES

Forensic psychologists are advised, "at the initiation of any request for service," to "seek to clarify the nature of the relationship and the services to be provided" including whether the role in question will be "trial consultant" or "expert witness" (American Psychological Association, 2013, p. 11). Other issues to be settled at that time include "the probable uses of the services provided or information obtained" as well as "any limitations to privacy, confidentiality, or privilege" (American Psychological Association, 2013, p. 11). This provides as good an opportunity as any for the trial consultant to describe the various mandatory obligations imposed by the EPPCC, and to prevail upon counsel to commit to a mutual understanding regarding the contours of their collaboration from this point forward.

GUIDELINE 9.01: USE OF APPROPRIATE METHODS

Consistent with their attempts to "utilize appropriate methods and procedures in their work," forensic psychologists—when providing "consultation" as well other services—are encouraged to "maintain integrity by examining the issue or problem at hand from all reasonable perspectives," and to "seek information that will differentially test rival hypotheses" (American Psychological Association, 2013, pp. 14–15). This overt emphasis on evenhandedness is almost guaranteed to test the patience of those who win or lose by the rules of an adversary system, until counsel can be reminded that in trial consultation, the potential identification of unhelpful conclusions serves two potentially useful purposes. Not only can lawyers anticipate on this basis how their own testifying experts may go astray, but lawyers can also begin preparing right away to cross-examine—or, perhaps, to try to draw as little attention as possible to—forensic psychologists who are working for the other side.

GUIDELINE 9.03: OPINIONS REGARDING PERSONS NOT EXAMINED

Forensic psychologists are reminded of "their obligations to only provide written or oral evidence about the psychological characteristics of particular individuals" when there is "sufficient information or data" to develop "an adequate foundation for those opinions or to substantiate their findings" (American Psychological Association, 2013, p. 15). Such "obligations" are directly ascribed to Guideline 9.01 of the EPPCC (American Psychological Association, 2017, pp. 12–13), and similarly, forensic psychologists are further advised that those providing "consultation" that "does not warrant an individual examination" should "seek to identify the sources of information on which they are basing their opinions and recommendations, including any substantial limitations to their recommendations" (American Psychological Association, 2013, p. 15). It is helpful that the above-noted "obligations" are linked directly to the EPPCC in a fashion that reminds counsel that these are mandatory for forensic as well as other psychologists; however, it is rather less helpful that exceptions pertaining to "consultation" are not similarly linked, thus creating the presumably unintended perception that these are *not* intended to be mandatory for forensic psychologists.

GUIDELINE 10.06: DOCUMENTATION AND COMPILATION OF DATA CONSIDERED

Encouraged to recognize "the importance of documenting all data they consider with enough detail and quality to allow for reasonable judicial scrutiny and adequate discovery by all parties," forensic psychologists are informed that "consultations" are among a substantial list of items to be documented in this fashion, along with "assessment and test data" and "scoring reports and interpretations" (American Psychological Association, 2013, p. 16). Presumably, the last thing on counsel's mind is any desire to make the trial consultant's file prone to either "scrutiny" or "discovery." This Guideline is helpful in that it reminds counsel of the perils inherent in transforming the trial consultant into a testifying expert, in addition to which it appears to signal to the trial consultant, conversely, that it would be a mistake either to fail to develop or to jettison a file on the basis of no examinations being conducted or no testimony being anticipated.

GUIDELINE 11.05: COMMENTING UPON OTHER PROFESSIONALS AND PARTICIPANTS IN LEGAL PROCEEDINGS

Forensic psychologists seek, "when evaluating or commenting upon the work or qualifications of other professionals involved in legal proceedings," to "represent their disagreements in a professional and respectful tone," in addition to basing such disagreements on "a fair examination of the data, theories, standards, and opinions of the other expert or party" (American Psychological Association, 2013, p. 17). This Guideline provides what is perhaps the most direct advice of any in the SGFP when it comes to addressing not only the trial consultant's demeanor when interacting with counsel but also the trial consultant's need for both diligence and restraint when appraising and characterizing the adverse work product being reviewed.

Conclusion

In fairness to counsel and all others involved, it is equally important for the trial consultant to indicate when the testifying expert's license status is intact and credentials are accurate and unimpeachable. The trial consultant's ambition is to investigate diligently, report accurately, and advise appropriately, with an eye toward eliminating surprises and supporting the efficacy of ethically grounded advocacy. Prevailing with respect to the ultimate legal issue before the court is counsel's concern. Collaboration with counsel—despite counsel's own adversarial agenda—should never cloud the trial consultant's vision concerning obligations to truth and fairness.

References

American Psychological Association. (2013). Specialty guidelines for forensic psychology. *American Psychologist, 68*(1), 7–19.

American Psychological Association. (2015). Professional practice guidelines: Guidance for developers and users. *American Psychologist, 70*(9), 823–831.

American Psychological Association. (2017). *Ethical principles of psychologists and code of conduct.* American Psychological Association. https://www.apa.org/ethics/code/ethics-code-2017.pdf

Association of State and Provincial Psychology Boards. (2018). *Supervision guidelines.* Association of State and Provincial Psychology Boards. https://www.asppb.net/page/SupGuidelines

Association of State and Provincial Psychology Boards. (2021). *Mobility program overview.* Association of State and Provincial Psychology Boards. https://www.asppb.net/page/Moboverview

Baker, T. O. (1983). *Operator's manual for a witness chair.* Defense Research Institute.

Brodsky, S. L. (1999). *The expert witness: More maxims and guidelines for testifying in court.* American Psychological Association.

Brown, L. T. (2010). Drawing the ethical line: Controversial cases, zealous advocacy, and the public good. *Georgia Law Review, 44*(4), 913–920.

Dattilio, F. M., Sadoff, R. L., & Gutheil, T. G. (2003). Board certification in forensic psychiatry and psychology: Separating the chaff from the wheat. *Journal of Psychiatry & Law, 31*(1), 5–19.

DeAngelis, T. (2014). Is it time to specialize? *Monitor on Psychology, 45*(2), 50.

Demir, S. B. (2018). Predatory journals: Who publishes in them, and why? *Journal of Infometrics, 12*(4), 1296–1311.

Drogin, E. Y. (2019). *Ethical conflicts in psychology* (5th ed.). American Psychological Association.

Drogin, E. Y. (2020). Forensic mental telehealth assessment (FMTA) in the context of COVID-19. *International Journal of Law and Psychiatry, 71*, Article 101595. https://doi.org/10.1016/j.ijlp.2020.101595

Drogin, E. Y., & Barrett, C. L. (2013). Trial consultation. In I. B. Weiner (Series Ed.) & R. K. Otto (Vol. Ed.), *Handbook of psychology, Vol. 11: Forensic psychology* (2nd ed., pp. 648–663). John Wiley & Sons.

Ecklund-Johnson, E., & Pearson, C. M. (2019). Foundations of contemporary neuropsychology. In C. M. Pearson, E. Ecklund-Johnson, & Gale, S. D. (Eds.), *Neurosurgical neuropsychology* (pp. 27–37). Elsevier/Academic Press.

Fisher, M. A. (2009). Replacing "who is the client?" with a different ethical question. *Professional Psychology: Research and Practice, 40*(1), 1–7.

Garner, B. (Ed.). (2019). *Black's law dictionary* (11th ed.). Thomson Reuters.

Gutheil, T. G., Commons, M. L., Drogin, E. Y., Hauser, M. J., Miller, P. M., & Richardson, A. M. (2012). Do forensic practitioners distinguish between testifying and consulting experts? A pilot study. *International Journal of Law and Psychiatry, 35*(5–6), 452–455.

Hansen, M. (2000). Expertise to go. *ABA Journal, 86*(2), 44–52.

Judicial Ethics Advisory Committee. (2019). *Canons of judicial conduct for the Commonwealth of Virginia.* Judicial Ethics Advisory Committee.http://www.courts.state.va.us/courts/scv/canons_of_judicial_cond uct.pdf

Marett, C. P., & Mossman, D. (2017). Considering work as an expert witness? Look before you leap! *Current Psychiatry, 16*(9), 44–48.

Martin, J. N., Millán. F., & Campbell, L. F. (2020). Telepsychology practice: Primer and first steps. *Practice Innovations, 5*(2), 114–127.

Matrimonial Commission. (2006). *Report to the Chief Judge of the State of* New York. http://ww2.nycourts.gov/ sites/default/files/document/files/2018-06/matrimonialcommissionreport.pdf

Melton, G. B., Petrila, J., Poythress, N. G., Slobogin, C. S., Otto, R. K., Mossman, D. M., & Condie, L. O. (2018). *Psychological evaluations for the courts: A handbook for mental health professionals and lawyers* (4th ed.). Guilford Press.

Meyer, D. J., & Drogin, E. Y. (2015). Expert testimony and cross-examination. In R. Cautin & S. Lilienfeld (Eds.), *Encyclopedia of clinical psychology, Vol. II* (pp. 1173–1183). John Wiley & Sons.

Otto, R. K., Goldstein, A. M., & Heilbrun, K. (2017). *Ethics in forensic psychology practice.* John Wiley & Sons.

Packard, T., & Simon, N. P. (2006). Board certification by the American Board of Professional Psychology. In T. J. Thomas (Ed.), *Psychology licensure and certification: What students need to know* (pp. 117–126). American Psychological Association.

Piña, A. A. (2010). Online diploma mills: Implications for legitimate distance education. *Distance Education, 31*(1), 121–126.

Shuman, D. W. (2007). Discovery of consulting psychiatric and psychological experts. *Journal of Psychiatry and Law, 35*(3), 245–260.

Vanderpool, D. (2014). Requests for disclosure of psychological testing information. *Innovations in Clinical Neuroscience, 11*(11–12), 41–44.

Managerial Justice, Community Supervision, and Treatment Mandates: The Intersection of Clinical Practice and Social Control

Benjamin J. Mackey, JoAnn Lee, C. J. Appleton, Sarah Skidmore, *and* Faye S. Taxman

Abstract

Probation and parole comprise the largest arm of the US criminal legal system, supervising nearly 4.4 million individuals, or more than twice the number incarcerated in prisons and jails. Individuals under community supervision must comply with numerous requirements to remain in good standing with the legal system. Failure to comply with requirements such as drug, alcohol, and psychosocial treatment mandates can result in sanctions and/or incarceration, creating a revolving door whereby individuals circulate between community supervision, carceral facilities, and their respective systems of formal social control. This chapter frames the revolving door of community supervision as part of an emergent form of penality termed "managerial supervision." The chapter details how changing social and economic conditions in the latter half of the twentieth century facilitated the rise of managerial supervision, and how it manifests in modern supervision systems at macro- and microlevels through treatment mandates. Used as a means to test an individual's compliance and governability, treatment mandates imposed under managerial supervision not only frequently depart from evidence-based principles but can expose individuals to more opportunities to incur a sanction or term of incarceration. After describing these iatrogenic consequences of treatment under managerial supervision, the chapter concludes with recommendations for future research and evidence-based practice.

Key Words: managerial justice, community supervision, mandated treatment, probation, parole, social control, managerial supervision

On April 3, 2020, the coronavirus disease 2019 (COVID-19) claimed the life of Raymond Rivera in New York City's Rikers Island jail system (Ransom, 2020). Rivera was incarcerated for violating his parole, having left a residential drug treatment without notifying his parole officer (Ransom, 2020). This act constituted a "technical violation," causing his supervision to be "revoked" and returning him to incarceration. Rather than an isolated incident, Rivera's story is representative of a broader pattern whereby people on community supervision experience incarceration as a result of a technical violation. Technical violations accounted for nearly a quarter of state prison admissions in 2017 (Council of State Governments, 2019) and can occur when an individual on supervision breaches a "standard" supervision condition or a "special" condition. Supervision conditions and technical violations create a "revolving door" as individuals alternate between community supervision and incarceration not as a result of new criminal behavior but through noncompliance with the conditions of their supervision. As Rivera's case illustrates, this revolving door can have detrimental—even life-threatening—consequences for those caught in its cycle.

Rather than a true alternative to incarceration, parole and probation supervision represents a prolonged form of punishment that promotes a revolving door due to technical violations and revocations. Technical violations are often seen as a proxy for a new crime (Campbell, 2016), meaning that people on supervision can be revoked and incarcerated for engaging in activity for which the nonsupervised public cannot be sanctioned (Taxman, 2005). Probation and parole officers (POs) often respond to noncompliance issues and/or violations by subjecting individuals to increased scrutiny, thereby raising the likelihood that the officer will impose a sanction—often from revocation leading to incarceration (Lattimore et al., 2016). Revocation is a common experience for those on supervision. According to a recent report by the Pew Public Safety Performance Project,

[n]early a third of the roughly 2.3 million people who exit probation or parole annually fail to successfully complete their supervision for a wide range of reasons, such as committing new crimes, violating the rules, and absconding. Each year almost 350,000 of those individuals return to jail or prison, often because of rule violations rather than new crimes. (Horowitz et al., 2018, p. 2)

Many of the conditions violated by individuals on supervision are ostensibly therapeutic in nature. In Rivera's case, this occurred when his parole was revoked for leaving treatment without notifying his parole officer (Ransom, 2020). Rivera's experience is indicative of the ways in which treatment-based conditions may have iatrogenic effects for people on supervision. When mandated as conditions of supervision, these interventions widen the net of the penal system by empowering legal actors to incarcerate people for failures related to treatment-related conditions. Individuals experience incarceration and its pernicious consequences for their mental and physical health (Massoglia, 2008; Porter & DeMarci, 2019), employment and wages (Pager, 2007), and families (Foster & Hagan, 2014) *as a result* of their noncompliance with supervision conditions.

This chapter explores how supervision that includes treatment-based conditions can be a component of *meaningful* supervision promoting positive life change(s) (see Taxman et al., 2020) or a mode of state control using managerial justice strategies. Therapeutic conditions may operate as a form of meaningful supervision when used to benefit the individual, rather than challenge them. Meaningful supervision interventions have the potential to promote desistance from substance use, improve interpersonal skills, establish or repair healthy relationships, promote an increase in general life satisfaction and other quality-of life-outcomes beyond recidivism (Taxman et al., 2020). However, treatment conditions may extend state control when they are implemented under the rubric of managerial justice—an emergent form of penality which is concerned primarily with the efficient management of groups rather than the punishment or rehabilitation of individuals subject to carceral control (Feeley & Simon, 1992). The state has responded to changing social and economic conditions in late modernity by adopting managerial justice practices to surveil and control the burgeoning populations involved in the criminal legal system, often using the rhetoric and methods of therapeutic interventions. In the process, correctional authorities can use these interventions to focus on an individual's "accountability" by examining compliance with the intervention and its programmatic elements.

To theorize managerial justice in the context of community supervision, this chapter has five sections. The first section overviews the current state of community supervision and evidence-based treatment practices, revealing how treatment entailed in the former often diverges from the principles of the latter. Section 2 examines how this divergence came to be by charting the rise of managerial justice in the context of changing social and economic conditions in the late twentieth century. Section 3 describes managerial justice as it manifests in the community supervision system at both macro- and microlevels. Section 4 focuses on how managerial justice contributes to the revolving door of supervision. Section 5 concludes with recommendations for supervision practice and future research.

The Current State of Community Supervision and Treatment

The revolving door produced by technical violations operates in a context where community supervision has grown in recent decades. While beginning to decline, in 2018, there were 4.4 million people on community supervision in the United States—3,540,000 on probation and 878,000 on parole (Maruschak & Minton, 2020). While on supervision, the average individual is subject to seventeen to twenty conditions (Corbett, 2015); some must conform with as many as forty-one (Werth, 2012). Supervision conditions not only restrict an individual's activities but mandate them to programs to which they must devote limited time and energy. In this way, supervision conditions are "simultaneously responsibilizing and de-responsibilizing" (Turnbull & Hannah-Moffat, 2009, p. 537), not only taking away responsibilities but creating new ones. If an individual on supervision does not comply, they may experience court- or PO-imposed sanctions such as written assignments, increased drug testing or PO contacts, curfews, formal community service, home confinement with or without electronic monitoring, heavy fines, boot camp, or incarceration (Taxman et al., 1999). Sanctions often create even more responsibilities, which adds to the difficulty for an individual to comply with their many supervision conditions.

Thus, technical probation and parole violations have proliferated since the 1980s (Parent et al., 1994), as the average number of supervision conditions has increased in lockstep (Travis & Stacey, 2010). In 2017, technical violations comprised 25 percent of new state prison admissions nationally (Council of State Governments, 2019) and at least three in four prison admissions from community supervision revocation in Mississippi and North Carolina (Pew Charitable Trusts, 2019). Technical violations are especially common among certain subpopulations. In a study of 44,987 people on parole, Eno Louden and Skeem (2011) found that those with a diagnosed mental illness are more than 120 percent more likely to return to prison for a technical violation than their counterparts without such a diagnosis. Further, individuals with a diagnosis are 15.6 times more likely to return to prison for failing to attend mandated treatment conditions.

Drug, alcohol, and/or psychological treatment conditions have become increasingly popular in recent decades (Travis & Stacey, 2010). However, individuals face many barriers to accessing treatment due to financial, transportation, and other resource limitations (Horowitz, Williams, & Utada, 2020). They must often seek treatment from community service agencies, rather than from supervision agencies themselves (Taxman et al., 2007). This adds to the list of responsibilities imposed on those with treatment conditions, as they must now navigate additional service systems outside the formal probation and parole structure.

Scientific studies document that treatment offers greater potential than control-centric methods to enhance positive outcomes (Lipsey & Cullen, 2007). Meta-analytic evidence comparing the effects of each approach overwhelmingly supports the efficacy of treatment over control in reducing recidivism (see table 22.1), with expected reductions in recidivism in the range of 10–38 percent. Control-based interventions are often associated with *increases* in recidivism or, at best, small reductions ranging from 2 percent to 8 percent. These findings hold true across a variety of age groups, treatment settings, and control-based interventions. Beyond recidivism, treatment has the potential to increase an individual's quality of life by helping them manage or overcome mental illness, achieve sobriety, and connect with supportive peers (Adekson, 2018).

The potential for treatment to facilitate positive outcomes is largely contingent upon its adherence to evidence-based principles. However, the current trend in supervision may be reflective of "a resurgence of interest in 'treatment,' if not rehabilitation" (Travis & Stacey, 2010, p. 605) due to divergence from these principles. To discuss how treatment can lose its rehabilitative potential, it is essential to first review the principles of evidence-based treatment to understand how its use in community supervision may align with or depart from them.

Evidence-Based Treatment

Due to the plethora of psychosocial and/or health issues that treatment may target, specific principles detailing the ideal type(s) of treatment (e.g., cognitive-behavioral therapy,

Table 22.1 Meta-Analyses of Treatment and Control Intervention Effects on Recidivism

Meta-Analysis	Age Group	Intervention	Change in Recidivism
Treatment			
Garrett, 1985	Juveniles	Residential treatment	-10%
Whitehead & Lab, 1989	Juveniles	Community and residential treatment	-24%
Andrews et al., 1990	Juveniles & adults	Community and residential treatment	-20%
	Juveniles	Community and residential treatment	-20%
	Adults	Community and residential treatment	-22%
	Juveniles & adults	Community treatment	-22%
	Juveniles & adults	Residential treatment	-14%
Petrosino, 1997	Juveniles & adults	Community and residential treatment	-20%
	Juveniles	Community and residential treatment	-24%
	Adults	Community and residential treatment	-14%
Cleland et al., 1997	Juveniles & adults	Community and residential treatment	-16%
	Juveniles	Community and residential treatment	-16%
	Adults	Community and residential treatment	-14%
Lipsey & Wilson, 1998	Juveniles	Community treatment	-26%
	Juveniles	Residential treatment	-14%
Illescas et al., 2001	Juveniles & adults	Community and residential treatment	-34%
	Juveniles	Community and residential treatment	-38%
	Adults	Community and residential treatment	-20%
Latimer et al., 2003	Juveniles	Community and residential treatment	-18%
Supervision			
Pearson et al., 1997	Adults	Community supervision	-8%
Lipsey & Wilson, 1998	Juveniles	Community supervision	-8%
Aos et al., 2001	Juveniles	Intensive community supervision	-4%
	Adults	Intensive community supervision	-2%
Intermediate Sanctions			
Andrews et al., 1990	Juveniles & adults	Criminal sanctions	+14%
Petrosino, 1997	Juveniles & adults	Deterrence	0%
Cleland et al., 1997	Juveniles	Criminal sanctions	-8%
	Adults	Criminal sanctions	-4%
Smith et al., 2002	Juveniles & adults	Intermediate sanctions	-2%
Lipsey & Wilson, 1998	Juveniles	Prison visitation	+2%

Table 22.1 Continued			
Meta-Analysis	Age Group	Intervention	Change in Recidivism
Aos et al., 2001	Juveniles	Prison visitation	+12%
Petrosino et al., 2003	Juveniles	Prison visitation	+26%
Confinement			
Pearson et al., 1997	Adults	Incarceration	+4%
Smith et al., 2002	Juveniles & adults Juveniles & adults	Longer vs. shorter prison sentences Incarceration vs. community supervision	+6% +14%
Villettaz et al., 2006	Juveniles & adults	Custodial vs. noncustodial sentences	+4%
MacKenzie et al., 2001	Juveniles & adults	Boot camp	0%
Aos et al., 2001	Juveniles Adults	Boot camp Boot camp	+10% +0%

Note. Table adapted from Lipsey and Cullen (2007).

medication-assisted treatment, and couples therapy) and program-specific factors (e.g., duration of treatment, number of treatment sessions, and characteristics of practitioners) are often unique to the population and condition they target. Perhaps the most salient and overarching evidence-based principle of effective treatment is that it be *appropriate* for the condition in question. According to Weisz et al. (2004),

> evidence-based practice [. . .] is not a specific treatment or even a set of treatments [. . .] Thus, a critical element of evidence-based care will need to be periodic assessment, to gauge whether the treatment selected initially is in fact proving helpful. If it is not, adjustments in procedures will be necessary, perhaps several times over the course of treatment. (pp. 302–303)

A growing body of empirical literature supports this finding that treatment must be individualized (Lei et al., 2012; Liu et al., 2018) and adaptive to the individual's changing needs (Almirall & Chronis-Tuscano, 2016; Jones, 2005) to be effective. Further evidence suggests that voluntary treatment entry and relationships between POs and individuals on supervision that emphasize autonomy, collaboration, and consideration of the individual's circumstances are most effective in securing long-term engagement with treatment in correctional settings (Parhar et al., 2008; Skeem et al., 2003; Ugwudike, 2011).

In sum, the preceding suggests that effective correctional treatment is noncoercive, tailored to the individual's needs, and adaptable as those needs change. Treatment in community supervision does not closely adhere to these principles: treatment is often highly coercive, mandated by courts which may require intensive treatment or drug-testing regimens for individuals who demonstrate little need for them (Horowitz et al., 2020). When an individual on supervision does demonstrate a clear need for treatment, POs often receive little guidance on how to navigate complex behavioral health care service environments, making it difficult for them to connect individuals with high-quality treatment programming (Skeem et al., 2003; Taxman, 2008). In many cases, then, treatment in community supervision adds to the conditional responsibilities that can lead to increased opportunity for an individual to incur technical violations. This perpetuates the revolving door of community supervision and incarceration produced by these violations.

We argue that the divergence of treatment in community supervision from the principles of evidence-based practice can be viewed as part and parcel of a larger pattern of punishment. Drawing upon the work of Feeley and Simon (1992, 1994; see also Simon, 1993; Simon & Feeley, 2003), this pattern of punishment, "managerial supervision," is an emergent form of penality, which, following the principles of managerial justice (see next section), uses an individual's compliance with treatment as a test of their governability.

Rehabilitation, Retribution, and Managerialism in Community Supervision

Managerial justice is best understood in the context of the rehabilitative and punitive models of justice that preceded it.[1] The modern form of rehabilitative justice emerged in the United States during the Progressive Era of the late nineteenth and early twentieth centuries (Cullen & Gendreau, 2000). Grounded in a clinical conception of the "offender" as an unwilling subject of various social and psychological maladies, rehabilitative justice replaced the tradition of vengeful, torturous punishments long used in Europe and the colonial United States. (Cullen & Gilbert, 2012; Foucault, 1975/1995). Progressive Era policymakers held that the "supreme aim of prison discipline is the reformation of criminals, not the infliction of vindictive suffering" (as cited in Cullen & Gendreau, 2000, p. 116)—goals that were reflected in altered modalities and rhetoric of state intervention. That is, policymakers and practitioners sought to integrate punishment with treatment (Allen, 1981; Cullen & Gilbert, 2012); to rebrand carceral institutions as quasi-clinical facilities rather than sites of punishment or incapacitation (Cullen & Gendreau, 2000); and to christen the community as a potentially more effective location in which to reform the individual, thereby spurring in part the rise of treatment embedded into community supervision (Petersilia, 2009; Wodahl & Garland, 2009).

This "rehabilitative ideal" (see Allen, 1981) held sway as the dominant model of penality through the mid-twentieth century, even if the actions of practitioners did not

---

[1] Although we treat managerial, rehabilitative, and punitive models of justice as discrete forms in this discussion, they are in reality ideal types (Weber, 1904/1949) with significant overlap and local variation (Goodman et al., 2017).

always live up to such lofty rhetoric (Petersilia, 1997; Simon, 1993). However, growing empirical and ideological critique of the rehabilitative ideal rose to a crescendo in the 1970s with the publication of Robert Martinson's (1974) now-famous study, *What Works? Questions and Answers about Prison Reform*; implicit in Martinson's answer to the titular question was the proposition that "nothing works." As a result—not solely of Martinson's (1974) work but rather of the sustained critique it represented (Cullen & Gendreau, 2000)—US carceral policy took a decidedly punitive turn in the 1970s (Garland, 2001; Parent et al., 1994), with scholars advancing a model of punishment based on retribution and "just deserts" (von Hirsch, 1976). For community supervision, this moved the field to a more punitive stance designed not to rehabilitate but to supervise and punish in the community (Parent et al., 1994; Taxman, 2005).

The Antecedents of Managerial Justice
The punitive shift in correctional policy did not occur in a vacuum. Accompanying it were macrolevel social shifts that would shape the subsequent form and function of community supervision. Though not an exhaustive list, the most salient of these shifts are (a) the redefinition of penal goals, (b) the expansion of the penal state, and (c) the crystallization of urban poverty. These shifts would ultimately move supervision toward a model of managerial control.

THE REDEFINITION AND EXPANSION OF THE PENAL STATE
The first shift that would mold the subsequent form of community supervision is the redefinition of the goals of the criminal legal system—a process initiated in part by the growing salience of violent crime in the lives of the middle class (Garland, 2001). While the crime rate had been rising steadily throughout the United States following World War II, an intensive and sustained influx in criminal offending began in the 1960s and continued for over a decade (LaFree, 1999). This uptick was especially prominent with respect to violent crime, as the murder and robbery rates respectively increased 113 percent and 222 percent from the early 1960s to the mid-1970s (LaFree, 1999). Capitalizing on the panic generated by this influx, media outlets and politicians propagated the idea of supposedly ubiquitous "superpredators" threatening the lives and livelihoods of the growing suburbanite middle class (Bogert & Hancock, 2020; Simon & Feeley, 2003). This gave crime a new salience in the daily routines of the middle-class, as it was "no longer an aberration or an unexpected, abnormal event. Instead, the threat of crime [had] become a routine part of modern consciousness, a standing possibility that [was] constantly to be 'kept in mind'" (Garland, 2001, p. 106).

The salience of high crime rates in the lives of the politically empowered middle class, coupled with the state's actual or perceived inability to mitigate them, pressured legal actors to "change the criteria by which failure and success are judged" (Garland, 2001, p. 119). Rather than reassert their capacity to lower the crime rate, state agencies sought to redefine the goals of punishment as crime *control* by deemphasizing their ability to mitigate crime through rehabilitation. Successful crime control was viewed and measured as "zero-tolerance" policing; revocation and (re)incarceration of "dangerous" individuals on community supervision; and incapacitation of a criminalized underclass (Feeley & Simon, 1992; Garland, 2001).

Simultaneous with this redefinition of goals, the scope of punishment expanded exponentially in the United States. Thus, the second social shift relevant to the development of managerial supervision is the rise of mass incarceration and supervision. Between 1973 and 2009, the US prison population rose from about 200,000 to 1.5 million—a 7.5-fold increase—with an additional 700,000 held on an average day in local jails in 2009 (Travis et al., 2014). Whereas the United States incarcerated 161 per 100,000 of its residents in 1972, that figure had increased to 767 per 100,000 by 2007 (Travis et al., 2014). As the carceral population expanded, so too did the populations under community supervision. While initially framed as a rehabilitative alternative to incarceration (Petersilia, 2009), community supervision achieved significant growth in the punitive era by appearing as a "prison[] without walls" (Citizens' Inquiry on Parole and Criminal Justice, 1975), providing policymakers and legal actors eager to curb the rising incarceration rate and its attendant costs with a politically viable alternative (Phelps, 2017, p. 67). Consequently, mass incarceration and mass supervision grew in tandem: whereas about 1.1 million adults were on probation in 1980, by 2007 there were some 4.3 million, or one in every fifty-three US adult residents (Phelps, 2020).

The redefinition of the goals of the criminal legal system coupled with its rapid expansion gave rise to what Feeley and Simon (1992) term the "new penology" of managerial justice. Managerial justice emerged partially as consequence of the redefinition of goals of the criminal legal system, as the state deemphasized its ability to lower the crime rate by altering the traditional rhetoric of rehabilitation and punishment (see above; Garland, 2001). Rather than discard rehabilitation and punishment wholesale, however, the penal state instead modified and commingled them to produce a rhetoric of "personal accountability" (Bosworth, 2007; Lynch, 2000). This rhetoric offloads the responsibility to change the subject of punishment, redefining it as the duty of the individual and their community, instead of the duty of the state (Miller, 2014).

This shift in responsibility was reinforced by the growth of the penal state during the neoliberal era. Traditional programs of rehabilitation or punishment are both expensive enterprises, requiring the state to carefully study the subject to reform them through therapeutic intervention or to tailor punishments to fit their crimes (Beccaria, 1764/1992; Foucault, 1975/1995). Intensive and individualized study was irreconcilable with the fiscal austerity championed in the ascendant neoliberal era of the 1980s (Harvey, 2007); to engage in such an individualized program of penality would require unjustifiable public spending due to the massive populations under penal control. The penal state aligned itself with austerity rhetoric by defining the subject of punishment as "one who is dispositionally flawed, and who is ultimately responsible for [their] own improvement" (Lynch, 2000, p.

40). Adopting this new definition transferred responsibility for rehabilitation to the individual through the language of accountability and personal responsibility, thereby relieving the state of some measure of liability (Bosworth, 2007; Lynch, 2000; Miller, 2014).

Transferring the locus of responsibility for rehabilitation redefines the penal relationship, as correctional authorities serve not as "strict guardians or disciplinarians" (Bosworth, 2007, p. 80) but as managers of a growing criminalized underclass (Feeley & Simon, 1992). In this new managerial relationship, the correctional actor has to identify and distinguish those who they deem capable of conforming to the social order from those that are not. However, traditional indicators of such conformity increasingly lost their delineative capabilities due to the crystallization of urban poverty.

THE CRYSTALLIZATION OF URBAN POVERTY

As the penal state expanded year over year throughout the last quarter of the twentieth century, it came to represent a new form of poverty management (Wacquant, 2009). Directed primarily at society's racialized and marginalized populations, incarceration supplanted the welfare state as the preferred method to "stem the disorders generated by the diffusion of social insecurity" (Wacquant, 2009, p. 6). This is reflected in the offset of funding from the welfare state to the penal state: whereas the United States spent 50 percent more on the federal assistance program Aid to Families with Dependent Children (AFDC) than on jails and prisons in 1980, by 1995 correctional budgets had swelled 2.3 times larger than AFDC funds (Wacquant, 2009). Attacks on social welfare programs continued throughout the 1980s and 1990s, reaching their zenith with the passage of the Personal Responsibility and Work Opportunity Reconciliation Act of 1996 (PRWORA). Through unprecedented measures such as time limits for those enrolled in welfare programs, the PRWORA explicitly aligned with President Bill Clinton's promise to "end welfare as we know it" by getting welfare recipients off state assistance and into the labor force, where they often found low-wage and insecure employment paying between $5.67 and $8.42 per hour (Handler, 2006; Wacquant, 2009).

Significantly, the decline of social welfare occurred during a time when changes in the labor market led to growing employment insecurity in the inner city. The 1970s initiated a period of large-scale deindustrialization across the United States; between 1969 and 1976 alone, some 22.3 million manufacturing jobs vanished, leaving local economies grounded in the manufacturing and construction industries in a growing state of crisis (Bluestone, 1983; Wilson, 1987/2012). For communities dependent on these industries for employment—particularly those in which residents were unable to adapt to the new economy—deindustrialization and its attendant rises in insecure, under-, and unemployment (see Bluestone, 1983; Handler, 2006; Wacquant, 2009) was associated with increases in extreme poverty (Strait, 2001) and residents receiving welfare programs like AFDC (Brady & Wallace, 2001). Yet, while the need for welfare programs was arguably greater than ever, average AFDC payments dropped by nearly half, from $221 in 1970 to $119 in 1995 (when measured in constant dollars;

Wacquant, 2009). Thus, the simultaneous decline of the welfare state and expansion of deindustrialization in the United States crystalized urban poverty in the inner city, as its residents increasingly fell through widening gaps in the social welfare net (Simon, 1993; Wilson, 1987/2012).

The collective effect of the changing industrial landscape and the decline of social welfare led to a "hardening of urban poverty" (Simon, 1993, p. 138).[2] Bereft of economic security, facing widespread disinvestment, and ravaged by mass incarceration, cracks in social institutions—schools, community centers, public health facilities, and the family—grew, thereby decreasing the inner-city community's ability to promote collective well-being and solve localized problems (Sampson et al., 1997; Simon, 1993; Wacquant, 2009). These cracks persist in the present day, as the median net worth of families in low-income communities has fallen from $12,300 in 1983 to $11,300 in 2016—all while middle- and upper-income families' net worth increased from $102,000 to $115,200 and $344,100 to $848,400, respectively (Horowitz et al., 2020, p. 19).

For community supervision, the hardening of urban poverty left POs with a declining number of community-based indicators through which to determine the ability of an individual to integrate and comply with the social order. That is, whereas POs could once make such determinations by examining an individual's potential to find employment and be reabsorbed into the community through the collaborative efforts of its social institutions, these indicators of success had lessened utility due to the scarcity of employment and ineffectuality of inner-city social institutions (Simon, 1993). As a result, POs "seeking effective predictors of future behavior must rely more and more on the light that [supervision] itself is able to throw on the parolee [. . .] [i]n many cases the [individual's] compliance with supervision requirements is the only opportunity for evaluating his capacity to successfully carry out social interactions" (Simon, 1993, p. 224). Rather than using employment, community support, and the individual's success in developing prosocial connections as the primary litmus test to determine compliance with the social order, POs increasingly rely upon the individual's compliance with the formal conditions of community supervision to make such determinations. In particular, conditions like treatment mandates help delineate the compliant from the resistant "by supplying richer and more complicated fields of interactions with which to engage and evaluate the [individual]" (Simon, 1993, p. 262).

Managerial Supervision at Macro and Micro Levels

The preceding social shifts and their implications for community supervision outline both the impetus for and rough contours of a new model of managerial justice and supervision. Divorced from the ideologies of either rehabilitation or punitiveness, managerial justice is concerned primarily with the cost-effective management of the perceived risks

---

[2] Although our focus is on the effect of deindustrialization and welfare decline on supervision in an urban setting, rural communities experienced similar effects.

these individuals pose to the social order (Simon & Feeley, 2003). Underlying this specific goal is a more general and long-standing goal of the penal state: to ensure continued governance through the selective use of penality (Foucault, 1975/1995; Hay, 1975). The managerial model accomplishes this via differentiation—separating the compliant and governable from the resistant and ungovernable.

Although its methods may represent a new penology of managerial control (Feeley & Simon, 1992), the raison d'être of managerial justice reflects the function of the state to reinforce the social order *through the differentiation of classes*. Indeed, describing an earlier era and reaching generally different conclusions, Foucault (1975/1995) nonetheless anticipated and aptly captured this trend toward differentiation, writing that punishments are

> not intended to eliminate offences, but rather to distinguish them, to distribute them, to use them; that it is not so much that they render docile those who are liable to transgress the law, but that they tend to assimilate the transgression of the laws in a general tactics of subjection. Penality would then appear to be a way of handling illegalities, of laying down the limits of tolerance, of giving free rein to some, of putting pressure on others, of excluding a particular section, of making another useful, of neutralizing certain individuals and of profiting from others. In short, penality does not simply "check" illegalities; it "differentiates" them. (p. 272)

Essentially, penality serves not solely to reduce crime but to differentiate people based on their behaviors, segregating and neutralizing those who are seen to pose a threat to the social order.

The state's ability to achieve differentiation and subsequent neutralization through traditional means was attenuated by social shifts rendering obsolete the discourses of rehabilitation or punitiveness that supported these means (Feeley & Simon, 1992; Simon & Feeley, 2003). A new model of managerial justice emerged throughout the legal system (Simon, 1993; Simon & Feeley, 2003). Managerial justice entails a near-myopic focus on efficiency to supervise some 4.4 million individuals (Maruschak & Minton, 2020). This is accomplished through (1) a lessened focus on the individual and a heightened focus on groups; (2) use of actuarial strategies such as risk-need assessments; and (3) use of supervision conditions such as treatment mandates to differentiate compliant (governable) individuals from resistant (ungovernable) ones, instead of as a means to change their behavior and promote positive life change (Feeley & Simon, 1992).

Managerial supervision is therefore a practice involving multiple legal actors, ranging from the courts, which impose supervision conditions, to POs who use these conditions as a way to determine compliance and adjust their supervision styles accordingly (Corbett, 2015; Klingele, 2013; Simon, 1993). Indeed, POs tend to use an individual's ability to "program"—to follow the requirements of supervision such as attending treatment, counseling, and drug testing check-ins—to adjust the intensity of supervision (Lynch, 1998, p. 860). As such, the ways in which individual POs practice supervision are important to understand how managerial supervision manifests at the microlevel (Klingele, 2013).

This requires a narrower analysis of microlevel PO behavior to complement the preceding macrolevel overview of managerial supervision.

Managerial Supervision in Practice: Microlevel Considerations

Due to the rehabilitative origins of community supervision and the blend of psychology and correctional treatment which it came to entail (Petersilia, 2009; Simon, 1993), POs are often expected not only to supervise individuals but to play an active role in treatment. The result is a double burden for POs: they must be law enforcers and treatment providers, simultaneously balancing care and control responsibilities in their work (Clear & Latessa, 1993; Miller, 2015). This balancing act is a complex one, as it requires POs to form a "dual-role relationship" with individuals on supervision that is more intricate than traditional therapeutic alliances formed in nonsupervision settings (Skeem et al., 2007).

In bureaucratic environments wherein complex expectations like the dual-role relationship exist, front-line workers often rely upon extensive discretion or human agency to translate high-level policy into realistic practice (Lipsky, 1980). They exercise human agency to shape *how* they translate policy into practice, thereby imbuing that practice with their own personal orientations and philosophies (Cheliotis, 2006; Lipsky, 1980). As front-line workers in the supervision environment, the ways that POs translate policy into practice are imbued (to the extent possible; see below) with their own perspectives on the ideal purpose and means of supervision. Due to their differing orientations along the continuum of care and control, these perspectives are quite heterogeneous (Clear & Latessa, 1993; Miller, 2015).

That POs hold orientations to supervision which may conflict with the managerial model and its focus on aggregates, actuarial classifications, and compliance suggests that managerial supervision may be less of an "iron cage" structuring POs' every action (Cheliotis, 2006), and more of an external pressure to which they differentially respond. Indeed, POs often exercise human agency in ways that contradict managerial supervision—such as continuing to hold the rehabilitative ideal and its emphasis on individualized treatment (Allen, 1981) as central to their activities (Appleton, 2020; Lynch, 1998, 2000). As such, POs sometimes resist the actuarial practices (viz. risk assessments) of the new penology, which may conflict with their notions of individualized rehabilitation (Viglione et al., 2015). In sum, the complexity of the supervision environment facilitates and often requires POs to exercise human agency. This implies POs have autonomy to use treatment conditions as a managerial tactic to test governability, or as a component of meaningful probation intended to benefit the recipient (Taxman et al., 2020).

THE STRUCTURAL CONSTRAINTS OF THE SUPERVISION ENVIRONMENT

However, the structural constraints of the supervision environment may lead POs to use their agency to favor a managerial approach to supervision. Indeed, the massive number of individuals on supervision (discussed in Part One) means that POs are often under intense strain to manage excessively large caseloads. Average supervision caseloads are at a ratio of 100 or more individuals assigned to each PO (Skeem et al., 2017), and POs with rehabilitative orientations may find themselves in conflict with the structural constraints imposed by this environment (Sabbe et al., 2021). POs unable to overcome this conflict may experience burnout, leading some to resign their positions in favor of work providing more opportunities for individualized interactions (Ortiz & Wrigley, 2020). To balance the care and control aspects of the dual-role relationship (Skeem et al., 2007), POs who remain often rely upon techniques of technocratic management—prioritization, routinization, and optimization—to cope with their immense caseloads (Sabbe et al., 2020, 2021). These methods often entail the use measures such as treatment conditions as a way to gauge an individual's governability and to adjust the intensity of supervision accordingly (Lynch, 1998; Simon, 1993). However, when used in such managerial fashion, treatment conditions can produce iatrogenic consequences.

The Consequences of Treatment under Managerial Supervision

As an element of managerial supervision, treatment conditions may contribute to negative consequences by (1) attenuating the individuality, appropriateness, and efficacy of treatment; and (2) perpetuating the revolving door of community supervision.

Lack of Treatment Individualization and Efficacy

According to the principles of evidence-based practice, treatment must be individualized and adaptive to a person's changing needs to be effective (see section "The Current State of Community Supervision and Treatment"). This conclusion has significant implications for the use of treatment under managerial supervision. As described above, treatment conditions under managerial supervision function primarily as a test of compliance and governability, rather than interventions that individually benefit the individual. However, treatment provides this test of compliance regardless of whether it is effective or appropriately tailored to the needs of the individual. Treatment and drug-testing requirements may be imposed—sometimes repeatedly—not because the individual exhibits a need for them but because they provide another field of interaction for legal actors to determine compliance and governability (Simon, 1993). As a result, treatment and testing conditions in supervision often lack individualization as they are misaligned with and irrelevant to the needs of individuals, primarily due to a lack of resources, which results in more standardized protocols (Horowitz et al., 2020; Taxman et al., 2007). Treatment mandates under managerial supervision are thus problematic as they place a burden on individuals to attend programming which may be nonindividualized, inappropriate, and ultimately ineffective for them. When this occurs, treatment represents more so a barrier to than a facilitator of effective community integration—all while making it more likely for an individual to incur a sanction or revocation.

Treatment as a Barrier to Integration and a Facilitator of Sanctions

When used as a field of interaction by which to test compliance and governability, treatment mandates may represent another onerous requirement to be overcome, rather than an intervention promoting personal change. By responsibilizing individuals with a host of new and potentially onerous requirements to follow, supervision conditions—particularly time-intensive ones such as participation in drug, alcohol, or mental health treatment programs—may attenuate individuals' ability to achieve community integration and effect behavior change through civic and economic participation. Requirements to attend in-patient treatment programs—and sanctions imposed for failure to attend—may be a key contributor to residential instability for people on postincarceration supervision, thereby attenuating their ability to build prosocial ties and effect community adjustment (Herbert et al., 2015). Further, supervision conditions can make responsibilities such as voting, participating in community networking, finding or maintaining employment, and familial duties difficult or impossible to fulfill. Weekly or even daily check-ins with POs can occupy an individual's entire day—especially if transportation options are expensive and limited (Klingele, 2013; Ortiz & Wrigley, 2020). Even when the office is close to an individual's home, they may still be subject to long waiting times, with individuals in one study reporting that they often wait two to five hours to attend a twenty-minute parole check-in (Halushka, 2020). Even more demanding than twenty-minute check-ins, treatment mandates may conflict with survival needs, such as finding employment, securing housing, or accessing assistance programs (Halushka, 2020; Ortiz & Wrigley, 2020).

The numerous conditions of supervision may also conflict with one another, as people on supervision must choose between attending a drug treatment program or a job-readiness training program—both of which might be mandated by supervision conditions (Halushka, 2020). Excessive conditions may simultaneously present people on supervision with more opportunities to commit a technical violation while making it more likely they will commit that violation by virtue of their inability to juggle myriad and potentially conflicting requirements. Treatment conditions that carry the threat of revocation for noncompliance may thus help explain the prominent role of technical violations in perpetuating mass incarceration.

It is not treatment itself that produces these consequences but rather the manner it is used under managerial supervision. Because it is used as a test of governability, treatment compliance under managerial supervision is typically viewed dichotomously—either the individual is successfully engaging with treatment or they are not. This is problematic as treatment is a process where positive outcomes often occur over time, and they may be commingled with events such as relapse. System actors may review compliance from an actuarial lens of whether a person has performed a certain action or not, instead of recognizing that successful solutions to chronic and entrenched issues such as drug use and unemployment are frequently accompanied by events such as relapse and firings on the pathway to positive outcomes. For example, drug testing is a routine accountability tool in managerial supervision. If an individual tests positive, that can be actionable requiring notification of the judge. Yet, for individuals with an addiction disorder, relapse is common and may be part of recovery. Managerial supervision often does not employ alternative means to address the nuanced nature of events like relapse, relying instead on technical violations and, thereby, perpetuating the revolving door of managerial supervision. However, alternatives to managerial supervision exist—alternatives which may assist in deconstructing this revolving door.

Deconstructing the Revolving Door of Managerial Supervision

The preceding discussion of the iatrogenic potential of treatment under managerial supervision returns this chapter to its starting point. Raymond Rivera's death presents a graphic example of an iatrogenic consequence. His "crime" was not an offense against the public but rather against the supervision system itself through his noncompliance with its conditions. In response, the system classified him as noncompliant and, thus, ungovernable under the logic of managerial supervision. This in turn provided impetus for the legal system to manage the risk he posed to the social order by neutralizing him—not through discipline of the mind, as Foucault (1975/1995) suggests, but through simple incapacitation (Feeley & Simon, 1992; Simon, 1988). That he subsequently contracted COVID-19 and died undercuts the counterargument that the state was acting in a rehabilitative capacity by initially mandating him to treatment.

Although this conclusion may appear to be an argument against the incorporation of treatment in community supervision, this is not necessarily the case. Indeed, managerial control is not the *sine qua non* of treatment. In community supervision, emerging modes of less coercive, individualized treatment are evident in specialty models of substance use or mental health supervision. These models forefront the provision of appropriate care with less emphasis on expecting perfection or accountability from the individual. Specialty models contrast with traditional supervision models not only in their emphases but in the training provided to POs. In traditional models, POs are required to "implement treatment mandates, often in complex and overburdened mental health care systems" (Skeem et al., 2006, p. 159). Oftentimes, however, POs receive little direct guidance on how to implement these mandates (Skeem et al., 2003), potentially promoting the technocratic methods of managerial supervision to deal with this uncertain bureaucratic environment. In contrast, specialty mental health probation models are operated by POs who are trained to recognize and address the needs of the individuals they serve (Manchak et al., 2014).

Further, qualitative differences exist between the methods used by specialty POs and their generalist counterparts. Specialty mental health POs are more likely to focus on general mental health concerns rather than merely criminogenic needs, often using strategies of questioning, affirmation, and support to engage in discussions with individuals on supervision (Eno Louden et al., 2012). And, representing a stark departure from managerial supervision, specialty mental health POs are more likely to employ incentive-based approaches to secure compliance, instead of relying on technical violations (Eno Louden et al., 2012; Skeem et al., 2003, 2006). This is especially important given data on the current prevalence of technical violations among individuals with mental illness, who are greater than 120 percent more likely to return to prison for a technical violation than their counterparts without such a diagnosis (Eno Louden & Skeem, 2011).

Specialty probation models may exemplify the benefits of mitigating structural constraints, which can restrict POs from taking an individualized approach to supervision. Caseload sizes under these models are typically fifty or fewer individuals assigned to one PO, making them roughly half the size of traditional caseloads (Manchak et al., 2014; Skeem et al., 2017). This has the potential to attenuate the structural constraints of the supervision environment, providing POs greater opportunity to individualize case plans. Perhaps a reflection of the benefits of taking an individualized approach, preliminary evaluations of specialty probation models have produced positive findings on a range of recidivism and quality-of-life outcomes (Manchak et al., 2014; Skeem et al., 2017). In these ways, specialty mental health probation may take a nonmanagerial approach to treatment, using it not to assess governability, but rather as a pathway to more positive and meaningful outcomes (see Taxman et al., 2020).

Still, specialty mental health probation—particularly in its potential to lessen the structural constraints of the supervision environment—is not a panacea. Whereas evidence suggests many front-line POs still rely upon rehabilitative notions of supervision in interacting with individuals (Appleton, 2020; Lynch, 1998, 2000), studies have not systematically examined POs' attitudes in this regard to determine how their demographic and professional characteristics may be associated with their agreement with managerial supervision practices (but see Deering, 2011, for a close example from the United Kingdom). Indeed, the preponderance of literature examining PO attitudes has conceptualized them along a spectrum, with rehabilitative supervision on one end and punitive supervision on the other (e.g., Clear & Latessa, 1993; Miller, 2015). These conceptualizations are inadequate inasmuch as managerial supervision departs from both rehabilitative and punitive ideologies (Feeley & Simon, 1992). The possibility remains, therefore, that removing structural constraints of the supervision environment will do little to mitigate managerial supervision practices if POs generally agree with these practices. Further research is therefore necessary to examine the extent to which POs agree with managerial supervision practices.

Conclusion

This chapter details a new penological strategy of managerial community supervision and its use of treatment as a mode of state control. POs have come to rely upon conditions of supervision to delineate individuals deemed compliant with the social order from those deemed noncompliant. The use of supervision conditions like drug, alcohol, and psychological treatment as an indicator of governability has contributed to the proliferation of technical violations, creating iatrogenic consequences for ostensibly therapeutic interventions. Yet this does not need to be the case. Models of supervision that emphasize individualized, noncoercive approaches to treatment have the potential to alter the form of supervision, moving it toward a more meaningful approach designed to improve quality-of-life outcomes (Taxman et al., 2020). But changing the form of supervision will be insufficient if not accompanied by constraints on its scope—including decriminalization and alternatives to arrest—which may help reduce the 4.4 million individuals on supervision (Maruschak & Minton, 2020). Such reforms can make a world of difference not only at the highly aggregated level but also to individuals like Raymond Rivera, whose lives may literally depend on them.

References

Adekson, B. (2018). *Supervision and treatment experiences of probationers with mental illness: Analyses of contemporary issues in community corrections.* Routledge.

Allen, F. A. (1981). *The decline of the rehabilitative ideal: Penal policy and social purpose.* Yale University Press.

Almirall, D., & Chronis-Tuscano, A. (2016). Adaptive interventions in child and adolescent mental health. *Journal of Clinical Child and Adolescent Psychology, 45*(4), 383–395.

Andrews, D. A., Zinger, I., Hoge, R. D., & Bonta, J. (1990). Does correctional treatment work—A clinically relevant and psychologically informed meta-analysis. *Criminology, 28*(3), 369–404. https://doi.org/10.1111/j.1745-9125.1990.tb01330.x

Aos, S., Miller, M., & Drake, E. (2001). *Evidence-based adult correction programs: What works and what does not.* Washington State Institute for Public Policy. http://www.wsipp.wa.gov/ReportFile/924/Wsipp_Evidence-Based-Adult-Corrections-Programs-What-Works-and-What-Does-Not_Preliminary-Report.pdf

Appleton, C. (2020). Understanding rapport in supervision settings. In P. K. Lattimore, B. M. Huebner, & F. S. Taxman (Eds.), *Handbook on moving corrections and sentencing forward: Building on the record* (pp. 174–184). Routledge.

Beccaria, C. (1992). *An essay on crimes and punishments.* Branden Press. (Original work published 1764)

Bluestone, B. (1983). Deindustrialization and unemployment in America. *The Review of Black Political Economy, 12*(3), 27–42.

Bogert, C., & Hancock, L. (2020, November 20). Superpredator: The media myth that demonized a generation of Black youth. *The Marshall Project.* https://www.themarshallproject.org/2020/11/20/superpredator-the-media-myth-that-demonized-a-generation-of-black-youth

Bosworth, M. (2007). Creating the responsible prisoner: Federal admission and orientation packs. *Punishment & Society, 9*(1), 67–85.

Brady, D., & Wallace, M. (2001). Deindustrialization and poverty: Manufacturing decline and AFDC recipiency in Lake County, Indiana 1964-93. *Sociological Forum, 16*(2), 321–358.

Campbell, C. M. (2016). It's not technically a crime: Investigating the relationship between technical violations and new crime. *Criminal Justice Policy Review, 27*(7), 643–667.

Cheliotis, L. K. (2006). How iron is the iron cage of new penology? The role of human agency in the implementation of criminal justice policy. *Punishment & Society, 8*(3), 313–340.

Citizens' Inquiry on Parole and Criminal Justice. (1975). *Prisons without walls: Report on New York parole.* Praeger.

Clear, T. R., & Latessa, E. J. (1993). Probation officers' roles in intensive supervision: Surveillance versus treatment issues in corrections. *Justice Quarterly, 10*(3), 441–462.

Cleland, C. M., Pearson, F. S., Lipton D. S., & Yee, D. (1997). *Does age make a difference? A meta-analytic approach to reductions in criminal offending for juveniles and adults* [Conference session]. American Society of Criminology.

Corbett, R. P., Jr. (2015). The burdens of leniency: The changing face of probation. *Minnesota Law Review, 99,* 1697–1732.

Council of State Governments. (2019). *Confined and costly: How supervision violations are filling prisons and burdening budgets.* https://csgjusticecenter.org/wp-content/uploads/2020/01/confined-and-costly.pdf

Cullen, F. T., & Gendreau, P. (2000). Assessing correctional rehabilitation: Policy, practice, and prospects. In J. Horney (Ed.), *Criminal justice 2000: Vol. 3. Policies, processes, and decisions of the criminal justice system* (pp. 109–175). National Institute of Justice.

Cullen, F. T., & Gilbert, K. E. (2012). *Reaffirming rehabilitation* (2nd ed.). Routledge.

Deering, J. (2011). *Probation practice and the new penology: Practitioner reflections.* Ashgate.

Eno Louden, J., & Skeem, J. L. (2011). *Parolees with mental disorder: Toward evidence-based practice.* UC Irvine Center for Evidence-Based Corrections. https://cpb-us-e2.wpmucdn.com/sites.uci.edu/dist/0/1149/files/2013/06/Parolees-with-Mental-Disorder.pdf

Eno Louden, J., Skeem, J. L., Camp, J., Vidal, S., & Peterson, J. (2012). Supervision practices in specialty mental health probation: What happens in officer–probationer meetings? *Law and Human Behavior, 36*(2), 109–119.

Feeley, M. M., & Simon, J. (1992). The new penology: Notes on the emerging strategy of corrections and its implications. *Criminology, 30*(4), 449–474.

Feeley, M. M., & Simon, J. (1994). Actuarial justice: The emerging new criminal law. In D. Nelken (Ed.), *The futures of criminology* (pp. 173–201). SAGE.

Foster, H., & Hagan, J. (2014). Punishment regimes and the multilevel effects of parental incarceration: Intergenerational, intersectional, and interinstitutional models of social inequality and systemic exclusion. *Annual Review of Sociology, 41*, 135–158.

Foucault, M. (1995). *Discipline and punish: The birth of the prison* (A. Sheridan, Trans.). Vintage Books. (Original work published 1975)

Garland, D. (2001). *The culture of control: Crime and social order in contemporary society.* Oxford University Press.

Garrett, C. J. (1985). Effects of residential treatment on adjudicated delinquents: A meta-analysis. *Journal of Research in Crime and Delinquency, 22*(4), 287–308. https://doi.org/10.1177/0022427885022004002

Goodman, P., Page, J., & Phelps, M. (2017). *Breaking the pendulum: The long struggle over criminal justice.* Oxford University Press.

Halushka, J. M. (2020). The runaround: Punishment, welfare, and poverty survival after prison. *Social Problems, 67*(2), 233–250.

Handler, J. F. (2006). On welfare reform's hollow victory. *Daedalus, 135*(3), 114–117.

Harvey, D. (2007). *A brief history of neoliberalism.* Oxford University Press.

Hay, D. (1975). Property, authority and the criminal law. In D. Hay, P. Linebaugh, J. G. Rule, E. P. Thompson, & C. Winslow (Eds.), *Albion's fatal tree: Crime and society in 18th century England* (pp. 17–63). Pantheon Books.

Herbert, C. W., Morenoff, J. D., & Harding, D. J. (2015). Homelessness and housing insecurity among former prisoners. *The Russell Sage Foundation Journal of the Social Sciences, 1*(2), 44–79.

Horowitz, J. M., Igielnik, R., & Kochhar, R. (2020). *Most Americans say there is too much economic inequality in the U.S., but fewer than half call it a top priority.* Pew Research Center. https://www.pewresearch.org/social-trends/2020/01/09/trends-in-income-and-wealth-inequality/

Horowitz, J., Utada, C., & Fuhrmann, M. (2018). *Probation and parole systems marked by high stakes, missed opportunities: 1 in 55 U.S. adults is under community supervision.* Pew Charitable Trusts. https://www.pewtrusts.org/-/media/assets/2018/09/probation_and_parole_systems_marked_by_high_stakes_missed_opportunities_pew.pdf

Horowitz, J., Williams, M., & Utada, C. (2020). *Policy reforms can strengthen community supervision: A framework to improve probation and parole.* Pew Charitable Trusts. https://www.pewtrusts.org/-/media/assets/2020/04/policyreform_communitysupervision_report_final.pdf

Illescas, S. R., Sánchez-Meca, J., & Genovés, V. G. (2001). Treatment of offenders and recidivism: Assessment of the effectiveness of programmes applied in Europe. *Psychology in Spain, 5*(1), 47–62.

Jones, A. (2005). Perceptions on individualized approaches to mental health care. *Journal of Psychiatric and Mental Health Nursing, 12*(4), 396–404.

Klingele, C. (2013). Rethinking the use of community supervision. *The Journal of Criminal Law & Criminology, 103*(4), 1015–1069.

LaFree, G. (1999). Declining violent crime rates in the 1990s: Predicting crime booms and busts. *Annual Review of Sociology, 25*, 145–168.

Latimer, J., Dowden, C., & Morton-Bourgon, K. E. (2003). *Treating youth in conflict with the law: A new meta-analysis.* Department of Justice Canada. https://www.justice.gc.ca/eng/rp-pr/cj-jp/yj-jj/rr03_yj3-rr03_jj3/rr03_yj3.pdf

Lattimore, P. K., MacKenzie, D. L., Zajac, G., Dawes, D., Arsenault, E., & Tueller, S. (2016). Outcome findings from the HOPE demonstration field experiment: Is swift, certain, and fair an effective supervision strategy? *Criminology & Public Policy, 15*(4), 1103–1141.

Lei, H., Nahum-Shani, I., Lynch, K., Oslin, D., & Murphy, S. A. (2012). A "SMART" design for building individualized treatment sequences. *Annual Review of Clinical Psychology, 8*, 21–48.

Lipsey, M. W., & Cullen, F. T. (2007). The effectiveness of correctional rehabilitation: A review of systematic reviews. *Annual Review of Law and Social Science, 3*(1), 297–320.

Lipsey, M. W., & Wilson, D. B. (1998). Effective intervention for serious juvenile offenders: A synthesis of research. In R. Loeber & D. P. Farrington (Eds.), *Serious & violent juvenile offenders: Risk factors and successful interventions* (pp. 313–345). Sage.

Lipsky, M. (1980). *Street-level bureaucracy: Dilemmas of the individual in public services.* Russell Sage Foundation.

Liu, P., Currie, S., & Adamyk-Simpson, J. (2018). What are the most important dimensions of quality for addiction and mental health services from the perspective of its users? *Patient Experience Journal, 5*(1), 106–114.

Lynch, M. (1998). Waste managers? The new penology, crime fighting, and parole agent identity. *Law & Society Review, 32*(4), 839–870.

Lynch, M. (2000). Rehabilitation as rhetoric: The ideal of reformation in contemporary parole discourse and practices. *Punishment & Society, 2*(1), 40–65. https://doi.org/10.1177/14624740022227854

Mackenzie, D. L., Wilson, D. B., & Kider, S. B. (2001). Effects of correctional boot camps on offending. *The ANNALS of the American Academy of Political and Social Science, 578*(1), 126–143. https://doi.org/10.1177/000271620157800108

Manchak, S. M., Skeem, J. L., Kennealy, P. J., & Eno Louden, J. (2014). High-fidelity specialty mental health probation improves officer practices, treatment access, and rule compliance. *Law and Human Behavior, 38*(5), 450–461.

Martinson, R. (1974). What works? Questions and answers about prison reform. *The Public Interest, 35*, 22–54. https://www.nationalaffairs.com/public_interest/detail/what-works-questions-and-answers-about-prison-reform

Maruschak, L. M., & Minton, T. D. (2020). *Correctional populations in the United States, 2017-2018*. Bureau of Justice Statistics. https://www.bjs.gov/content/pub/pdf/cpus1718.pdf

Massoglia, M. (2008). Incarceration as exposure: The prison, infectious disease, and other stress-related illnesses. *Journal of Health and Social Behavior, 49*(1), 56–71.

Miller, J. (2015). Contemporary modes of probation officer supervision: The triumph of the "synthetic" officer? *Justice Quarterly, 32*(2), 314–336.

Miller, R. J. (2014). Devolving the carceral state: Race prisoner reentry, and the micro-politics of urban poverty management. *Punishment & Society, 16*(3), 305–335.

Ortiz, J. M., & Wrigley, K. (2020). The invisible enclosure: How community supervision inhibits successful reentry. *Corrections*. Advance online publication. https://doi.org/10.1080/23774657.2020.1768967

Pager, D. (2007). *Marked: Race, crime, and finding work in an era of mass incarceration*. University of Chicago Press.

Parent, D. G., Wentworth, D., Burke, P., & Ney, B. (1994). *Responding to probation and parole violations* (NJC No. 149473). National Institute of Justice. https://www.ojp.gov/pdffiles1/Digitization/149473NCJRS.pdf

Parhar, K. K., Wormith, J. S., Derkzen, D. M., & Beauregard, A. M. (2008). Offender coercion in treatment: A meta-analysis of effectiveness. *Criminal Justice and Behavior, 35*(9), 1109–1135.

Pearson, F. S., Lipton, D. S., & Cleland, C. M. (1997). *Rehabilitative programs in adult corrections: CDATE meta-analysis* [Conference session]. American Society of Criminology.

Petersilia, J. (1997). Probation in the United States. *Crime and Justice, 22*, 149–200.

Petersilia, J. (2009). *When prisoners come home: Parole and prisoner reentry*. Oxford University Press.

Petrosino, A. J. (1997). *'What works?' revisited again: A meta-analysis of randomized field experiments in rehabilitation, deterrence, and prevention* (Publication No. 9809031) [Doctoral dissertation, Rutgers University]. ProQuest Dissertations Publishing.

Petrosino, A., Turpin-Petrosino, C., & Buehler, J. (2003). Scared straight and other juvenile awareness programs for preventing juvenile delinquency: A systematic review of the randomized experimental evidence. *Annals of the American Academy of Political and Social Science, 589*, 41–62.

Pew Charitable Trusts. (2019). *To safely cut incarceration, states rethink responses to supervision violations: Evidence-based policies lead to higher rates of parole and probation success*. Pew Charitable Trusts. https://www.pewtrusts.org/-/media/assets/2019/07/pspp_states_target_technical_violations_v1.pdf

Phelps, M. S. (2017). Mass probation: Toward a more robust theory of state variation in punishment. *Punishment & Society, 19*(1), 53–73.

Phelps, M. S. (2020). Mass probation from micro to macro: Tracing the expansion and consequences of community supervision. *Annual Review of Criminology, 3*(1), 261–279.

Porter, L. C., & DeMarco, L. (2019). Beyond the dichotomy: Incarceration dosage and mental health. *Criminology, 57*(1), 136–156

Ransom, J. (2020, April 9). Jailed on a minor parole violation, he caught the virus and died. *The New York Times*. https://www.nytimes.com/2020/04/09/nyregion/rikers-coronavirus-deaths-parolees.html

Sabbe, M., Moyson, S., & Schiffino, N. (2021). Citizen-agency versus state-agency at the frontline in prisons and probation services: A systematic literature review. *Social Policy & Administration, 55*(1), 206–225.

Sabbe, M., Schiffino, N., & Moyson, S. (2020). Walking on thin ice: How and why frontline officers cope with managerialism, accountability, and risk in probation services. *Administration & Society*. Advance online publication. https://doi.org/10.1177/0095399720970899

Sampson, R. J., Raudenbush, S. W., & Earls, F. (1997). Neighborhoods and violent crime: A multilevel study of collective efficacy. *Science, 277*(5328), 918–924.

Simon, J. (1988). The ideological effects of actuarial practices. *Law & Society Review, 22*(4), 771–800.

Simon, J. (1993). *Poor discipline: Parole and the social control of the underclass, 1890-1990*. University of Chicago Press.

Simon, J., & Feeley, M. M. (2003). The form and limits of the new penology. In T. G. Blomberg & S. Cohen (Eds.), *Punishment and social control* (2nd ed., pp. 75–116). Aldine de Gruyter.

Skeem, J. L., Emke-Francis, P., & Eno Louden, J. (2006). Probation, mental health, and mandated treatment: A national survey. *Criminal Justice and Behavior, 33*(2), 158–184.

Skeem, J. L., Encandela, J., & Eno Louden, J. (2003). Perspectives on probation and mandated mental health treatment in specialized and traditional probation departments. *Behavioral Sciences & the Law, 21*(4), 429–458.

Skeem, J. L., Eno Louden, J., Polaschek, D., & Camp, J. (2007). Assessing relationship quality in mandated community treatment: Blending care with control. *Psychological Assessment, 19*(4), 397–410.

Skeem, J. L., Manchak, S., & Montoya, L. (2017). Comparing public safety outcomes for traditional probation vs specialty mental health probation. *JAMA Psychiatry, 74*(9), 942–948.

Smith, P., Goggin, C., & Gendreau, P. (2002). *The effects of prison sentences and intermediate sanctions on recidivism: General effects and individual differences.* Public Works and Government Services Canada. https://www.publicsafety.gc.ca/cnt/rsrcs/pblctns/ffcts-prsn-sntncs/ffcts-prsn-sntncs-eng.pdf

Strait, J. (2001). The disparate impact of metropolitan economic change: The growth of extreme poverty neighborhoods, 1970–1990. *Economic Geography, 77*(3), 272–305.

Taxman, F. S. (2002). Supervision—Exploring the dimensions of effectiveness. *Federal Probation, 66*(2), 14–27. https://www.uscourts.gov/sites/default/files/66_2_3_0.pdf

Taxman, F. S. (2005). Brick walls facing reentering offenders. *International Journal of Comparative and Applied Criminal Justice, 29*(1), 5–18.

Taxman, F. S. (2008). No illusion, offender and organizational change in Maryland's proactive community supervision model. *Criminology and Public Policy, 7*(2), 275–302. https://doi.org/10.1111/j.1745-9133.2008.00508.x

Taxman, F. S., Perdoni, M. L., & Harrison, L. D. (2007). Drug treatment services for adult offenders: The state of the state. *Journal of Substance Abuse Treatment, 32*(3), 239–254.

Taxman, F. S., Smith, L., & Rudes, D. S. (2020). From mean to meaningful probation: The legacy of intensive supervision programs. In P. K. Lattimore, B. M. Huebner, & F. S. Taxman (Eds.), *Handbook on moving corrections and sentencing forward: Building on the record* (pp. 61–78). Routledge.

Taxman, F. S., Soule, D., & Gelb, A. (1999). Graduated sanctions: Stepping into accountable systems and offenders. *The Prison Journal, 79*(2), 182–204.

Travis, J., Western, B., & Redburn, S. (2014). *The growth of incarceration in the United States: Exploring causes and consequences.* National Academies Press.

Travis, L. F., & Stacey, J. (2010). A half century of parole rules: Conditions of parole in the United States, 2008. *Journal of Criminal Justice, 38*(4), 604–608.

Turnbull, S., & Hannah-Moffat, K. (2009). Under these conditions: Gender, parole and the governance of reintegration. *The British Journal of Criminology, 49*(4), 532–551.

Ugwudike, P. (2011). Compliance with community penalties: The importance of interactional dynamics. In F. McNeill, P. Raynor, & C. Trotter (Eds.), *Offender supervision: New directions in theory, research and practice* (325–343). Routledge.

Viglione, J., Rudes, D. S., & Taxman, F. S. (2015). Misalignment in supervision: Implementing risk/needs assessment instruments in probation. *Criminal Justice and Behavior, 42*(3), 263–285.

Villettaz, P., Killias, M., & Zoder, I. (2006). The effects of custodial vs. noncustodial sentences on reoffending: A systematic review of the state of knowledge. *Campbell Systematic Reviews, 2*(1), 1–69. https://doi.org/10.4073/csr.2006.13

von Hirsch, A. (1976). *Doing justice: The choice of punishments.* Farrar, Strauss, and Giroux.

Wacquant, L. (2009). *Punishing the poor: The neoliberal government of social insecurity.* Duke University Press.

Weber, M. (1949). Objectivity in social science and social policy. In E. A. Shils & H. A. Finch (Eds. and Trans.), *Max Weber on the methodology of the social sciences* (pp. 49–112). The Free Press. (Original work published 1904)

Weisz, J. R., Chu, B. C., & Polo, A. J. (2004). Treatment dissemination and evidence-based practice: Strengthening intervention through clinician-researcher collaboration. *Clinical Psychology: Science and Practice, 11*(3), 300–307.

Werth, R. (2012). I do what I'm told, sort of: Reformed subjects, unruly citizens, and parole. *Theoretical Criminology, 16*(3), 329–346.

Whitehead, J. T., & Lab, S. P. (1989). A meta-analysis of juvenile correctional treatment. *Journal of Research in Crime and Delinquency, 26*(3), 276–295. https://doi.org/10.1177/0022427889026003005

Wilson, W. J. (2012). *The truly disadvantaged: The inner city, the underclass, and public policy.* University of Chicago Press. (Original work published 1987)

Wodahl, E. J., & Garland, B. (2009). The evolution of community corrections. *The Prison Journal, 89*(Suppl. 1), 81S–104S.

Treating Justice-Involved Populations with Severe Mental Illness

Robert D. Morgan, Faith Scanlon, Jessica Mattera, *and* McCown Leggett

Abstract

This chapter outlines several topics relevant to the treatment of justice-involved persons with serious mental illness (SMI). We begin with a historical overview, detailing previous work in conceptualizing and treating this population, followed by a review of contemporary practices and strategies. We describe the proposed co-occurring and reciprocal relation between mental illness and criminal risk, and discuss implications for correctional rehabilitation and psychiatric recovery. Building on the five-level model of risk assessment, we propose an integrated assessment model to advance service matching and delivery for justice-involved persons with SMI, an expansion necessary for holistic consideration of this population's needs. Finally, we provide recommendations for practice and future research addressing co-occurring criminal risk and mental illness to enhance services for this underserved population.

Key Words: justice-involved individuals, severe mental illness, criminal risk, mental illness, correctional psychology, correctional rehabilitation, co-occurring criminal risk and mental illness

It is commonly understood in scientific and mainstream media outlets that persons with serious mental illness (SMI) are overrepresented in the criminal justice system. This includes all sectors of corrections including jails, prisons, probation, and parole. In fact, the statistics are startling. In two acute psychiatric facilities, approximately 50 percent of patients had a history of criminal justice involvement (Scanlon et al., 2021), and 40 percent of persons with SMI have been incarcerated during their lifetime (Torrey et al., 2010). Sadly, persons with mental illness are 2.6 times more likely to be charged with a crime and 3.8 times more likely to be incarcerated compared to persons without mental illness (James & Glaze, 2006). Not surprising then, approximately 10 percent of prison inmates suffer from a serious mental illness (Prins, 2014). Clearly justice-involved persons with SMI warrant special considerations.

In this chapter, we review historical efforts at treating this vulnerable population, review proposed best practices for service delivery, examine the relation between mental illness and criminalness (i.e., behaviors that violate the rights and well-being of others;

Morgan et al., 2018), and propose an assessment model to tie services to needs consistent with effective correctional rehabilitation models. We conclude the chapter with recommendations for important lines of future research to increase success for justice-involved persons with SMI across the co-occurring domains of mental illness and criminal risk.

Persons with SMI in Corrections and Forensic Mental Health Units

Mental health services provided to justice-involved individuals vary based on their legal status and setting. Jails are short-term facilities that hold individuals with a diverse set of circumstances, including those awaiting trials, pending transfers, and serving short sentences (typically two years or less). Jails are operated by local (county) governments, leading to high variability in available services and service-related policies and procedures between jurisdictions (Scheyett et al., 2009; Torrey et al., 2014). Jail-based mental health services typically include medication management, screening (e.g., suicide and mental health), assessment, crisis management, and short-term therapy (Jacobs & Giordano, 2018; Scheyett et al., 2009). Due to high inmate turnover and limited resources, there is a dearth of empirically supported interventions for persons with SMI in jails (AbuDagga et al., 2016; Osher & Steadman, 2007). In fact, much more is known about the provision of mental health services in prisons than jails (Walker et al., 2016).

Prisons house inmates who are convicted of felonies and are serving two years of an incarceration sentence or more. Whereas jail stays are relatively acute with high turnover, prisons have a more static population. As a result, mental health services provided in prisons tend to be much more comprehensive than those provided in jail, as prison services include not only basic mental health services but also rehabilitative services (Morgan, 2003). Basic mental health services are required by law to be available to all incarcerated individuals[1]; these services are geared toward stabilization by providing inmates strategies to adapt to the facility and reduce psychological symptoms (Morgan, 2003; Morgan et al., 2014). Alternatively, rehabilitative services focus their efforts on community reentry and reducing criminal recidivism (Morgan, 2003).

Notwithstanding the numerous advancements that have been made in correctional rehabilitation, practitioners in the field still tend to emphasize issues related to justice-involved persons' mental health stability and adjustment to the prison environment (Bewley & Morgan, 2011). Unfortunately, this focus appears misguided, as evidence suggests that effective institutional adjustment does not always translate to effective community reentry (Goodstein, 1979; Skeem & Peterson, 2012). While numerous programs for general prison populations result in lowered recidivism (Landenberger & Lipsey, 2005; Lipsey & Cullen, 2007; Wilson et al., 2005), less research has focused on the effectiveness of programming for justice-involved persons with mental illness (Rice & Harris,

---

[1] E.g., Ruiz v. Estelle, 503 F. Supp. 1265 (S.D. Tex. 1980).

1997; Snyder, 2007). Accordingly, this population has few evidence-based programs. The National Institute of Justice (2020) utilizes a multistep evaluation process to rate and review various programs and practices targeted toward criminal justice populations. Of the 626 evaluated programs, three adult correctional programs target mental illness. All three programs offer continuity in services from prerelease to postrelease; however, only one was deemed effective, the Mentally Ill Offender Community Transition Program (Washington), indicating the program is strongly associated with a significant reduction in recidivism (National Institute of Justice, 2020). The other two programs, Modified Therapeutic Community for Offenders with Mental Illness and Chemical Abuse Disorders (MICA) and Offender Reentry Community Safety Program, were both deemed promising. Other programs, such as Seeking Safety, have had promising justice outcomes with specific disorders (Wolff et al., 2012; Zlotnick et al., 2009). *Changing Lives and Changing Outcomes* (*CLCO*), a theoretically transdiagnostic treatment program for justice-involved people with severe mental illness, has shown promising results in both symptom reduction and factors associated with criminal risk (Gaspar et al., 2019; Morgan et al., 2014).

Forensic psychiatric units or secure forensic hospitals house forensic mental health patients as opposed to inmates. Persons in forensic psychiatric units are typically committed to a forensic hospital for a pretrial psychiatric evaluation, or because they were adjudicated not guilty by reason of insanity or not competent to stand trial and participating in competency restoration. In some jurisdictions, forensic mental health patients are correctional inmates transferred to the hospital setting due to mental health service needs that exceed what correctional facilities can provide. Regardless of one's legal status, forensic mental health patients are similar to general psychiatric patients in that they have complex mental health needs that are compounded by their justice involvement (McInerny & Minne, 2004). Unfortunately, a paucity of evidence-based interventions remain available to the forensic mental health population (Grossi et al., 2021; MacInnes & Masino, 2019), as available treatments and interventions have typically been validated on general psychiatric patients and then modified for forensic involved persons (Barnao & Ward, 2015).

Contemporary Approaches for Criminal Justice-Involved People with SMI

Prior to the large-scale closures of US psychiatric hospitals in the 1960s, a phenomenon known as deinstitutionalization, people with SMI were largely treated in psychiatric hospitals. In 1989, Bachrach described deinstitutionalization as a three-step process: (1) reducing the number of people in psychiatric hospitals, (2) diverting people who might have previously been hospitalized into community mental health settings, and (3) expanding the duty of mental health care from one institution to multiple settings. Thirty years later, one of the three largest mental health providers in the United States are jails (Roth, 2018), and the responsibility of mental health care again is placed on one institution: the criminal justice system. There is dispute about transinstitutionalization contributing to the high rates of justice involvement for people with SMI (see Prins, 2011, for a review).

In the 1990s, there was another push to divert people with SMI away from institutionalization and toward treatment, this time through mental health courts (MHC; see Lowder et al., 2018). In MHCs, arrested people with mental illness are diverted from traditional sanctions (e.g., incarceration) to an MHC-specific court docket where they regularly attend hearings and participate in mental health treatment (see Canada et al., 2019; Lowder et al., 2018). Consistent with Bachrach's (1989) specifications, MHCs accomplish deinstitutionalization by (1) reducing the number of people involved in the criminal justice system, (2) diverting people who would otherwise be incarcerated to community mental health settings, and (3) expanding the duty of mental health care into what Canada et al. (2019, p. 73) call "collaborative efforts between criminal justice, mental health, and substance use treatment systems." MHCs were quickly adopted, with little evidence of their effectiveness (Steadman et al., 2001). In an evaluation of seven MHCs in the United States, Steadman and Redlich (2005) found the programs were unstandardized, and conclusions could not be drawn about MHC best practices or what defendants are best-suited for MHCs. In fact, the report closed with a caution to "slow the tide of new mental health courts until the specified effectiveness of current ones can be demonstrated" (Steadman & Redlich, 2005, p. 50).

Today, there are more than 470 MHCs in the United States (GAINS Center, 2015) but with more robust empirical evidence. A 2011 meta-analysis of MHCs showed promising evidence with moderate mean effect sizes (mean effect sizes = -0.54, -0.55) that the courts were effective in reducing recidivism (Sarteschi et al., 2011). A more recent meta-analysis, however, found smaller effect sizes (d = -0.2) on recidivism reduction (Lowder et al., 2018). Although even small reductions of the number of people in jails and prisons with SMI are important, as is increasing community mental health treatment utilization in this population (see Sarteschi et al., 2011), MHCs may not be maximally impactful (Campbell et al., 2015). In fact, Campbell et al. (2015) concluded that, like other correctional interventions (see Morgan et al., 2012), improvements in MHC outcomes might be achieved by integrating traditional correctional rehabilitation efforts in the mental health recovery process.

Integrating Correctional Rehabilitation and Mental Illness Recovery—A Necessary Step for Improved Outcomes

Morgan and colleagues have proposed that psychiatric and criminal justice outcomes for justice-involved persons with SMI are complicated, in part, because the nature of the mental illness and criminalness relationship is, in and of itself, complicated (e.g., Bartholomew & Morgan, 2015; Morgan et al., 2020). A series of studies across settings and populations showed that incarcerated justice-involved persons with SMI shared criminogenic risk factors with their non-SMI peers (Bolaños et al., 2020; Gross & Morgan, 2013; Morgan et al., 2010; Wilson et al., 2014; Wolff et al., 2013; Wolff et al., 2011) and these risk factors are equally predictive of antisocial behavior for justice-involved persons with SMI as they are for justice-involved persons without SMI (Bonta et al., 1998). Conversely, Bonta et al. (1998) found that clinical factors (i.e., mental illness) have limited value when predicting recidivism, as criminogenic risk is a better predictor of both general and violent recidivism than mental illness (Bonta et al., 2014). In fact, justice-involved persons with SMI have even more general risk factors for recidivism than justice-involved persons without SMI (Skeem et al., 2014).

Bartholomew and Morgan (2015) then proposed that criminalness and mental illness are reciprocal—one exacerbates the other (see fig. 23.1); this is similar to the pathoplasticity model of psychopathology, wherein psychopathology and personality mutually influence one another (Widiger & Smith, 2008). In other words, an individual's personality can shape the expression, content, and focus of their pathology; likewise, an individual's pathology can also shape their personality (Millon, 1996, 2000, 2005). For example, Morgan et al. (2020) found that antisocial cognitions were not only associated with antisocial behavioral outcomes (e.g., violent and nonviolent disciplinary infractions) but also severity of self-reported symptoms of psychopathology. Pathoplasticity then, if taken from a risk–need–responsivity (RNR) perspective (see Bonta & Andrews, 2017), could have important implications for correctional rehabilitation, in that mental illness may act as a responsivity factor for criminogenic risk and vice versa (Morgan et al., 2020).

This mental illness–criminalness relationship, though, remains misunderstood. Historically, the public has believed that mental illness directly causes violence and

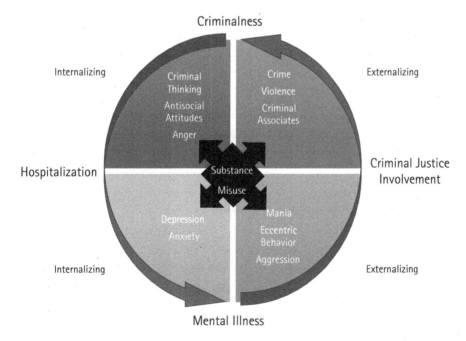

Figure 23.1 Proposed model of reciprocal criminalness and mental illness relationship.
Source: From Scanlon et al. (2021).

criminal behavior (Markowitz, 2011; Pescosolido et al., 1999). This perception is misinformed, as research continues to indicate a weak relationship between mental illness and crime (Bonta et al., 1998; Draine et al., 2002). Furthermore, of those who do engage in crime, most do so for reasons unrelated to their mental illness (Peterson et al., 2014). The finding that mental illness is not the primary casual factor for criminal behavior has also been found in criminal defendants deemed not guilty by reason of insanity, whose engagement in crime is, by definition, the direct result of their mental illness (Callahan & Silver, 1998; Monson et al., 2001). In other words, mental illness alone does not significantly increase criminal risk—rather, other factors (i.e., criminogenic risk factors) better account for people with mental illness who engage in criminal behavior.

To reduce recidivism, then, criminal justice-related treatment programs designed for persons with SMI should target symptoms associated with not only mental illness but also criminogenic needs (Epperson et al., 2011; Morgan et al., 2010; Skeem et al., 2014); however, in a comprehensive systematic review, only 17 percent of twenty-six interventions for persons with SMI included treatment efforts specifically designed to reduce criminal risk (Morgan et al., 2012). To better inform and implement integrated service delivery for this population, we must continue work in this area, beginning with mental health and criminal risk assessment.

RNR and the Five-Level Approach to Treatment and Managing Justice-Involved Persons with SMI

First published in 1990 (Andrews et al., 1990), the RNR model is built on three fundamental principles. The Risk principle: individuals should be assessed using valid and reliable actuarial assessments of risk, and resources allocated should be compatible with individual level of risk, concentrating more intensive resources on higher-risk individuals (Andrews et al., 1990). The Need principle: programs should target factors that are directly related to reduced recidivism (criminogenic needs) and are amenable to change (dynamic) (Andrews & Bonta, 2010). The Responsivity principle: programs will utilize cognitive, behavioral, and social learning methods (Andrews & Bonta, 2010; Smith et al., 2009), and service providers will adjust their approach based on an individual's characteristics (e.g., age, mental status, cognitive ability, and learning styles) to better allow for treatment effectiveness (Andrews et al., 1990).

Therefore, the assessment of criminal risk is central to managing and treating justice-involved persons with SMI. A new development in the area of criminal risk assessment is the Five-Level Risk and Needs System (Hanson et al., 2017). Consistent with an RNR framework, this system goes beyond mere identification of risk by incorporating the explicit goal of matching justice-involved people with the level and type of interventions that fit their needs. Although centered on risk, the Five-Level Risk and Needs system considers an individual's psychological, interpersonal, and lifestyle domains and is tied directly to level and type of services (see table 23.1).

Table 23.1 Five-Level Risk and Needs System

Level	Criminogenic Needs	Profile and 2-Year Recidivism Rate without Intervention	Supervision Dose	Correctional Treatment Dose	Treatment Effect	Prognosis Following Intervention
I	None or few—if any, mild and/or transitory	Non-offending profile: similar to people with no criminal record Average = 3% Range = less than 5%	Minimal or no monitoring	None—if needed, refer to community services	Risk so low that it will not be reduced further	Excellent, will stay in Level I
II	A few—some mild and transitory, or possibly acute	Vulnerable prosocial profile: higher risk than non-offending profile but lower than average Average = 19% Range = 5%–29%	Some—monitor for compliance, provide some change-focused interventions	Minimal—if any, very short term, refer to community services if needed	Risk so low that intervention can only have a minor impact	Very good, most move from Level II to I
III	Multiple—some severe	Average offending profile: the middle of the risk and needs distribution Average = 40% Range = 30%–49%	Considerable—monitor for compliance and provide change-focused interventions	Significant—100–200 hours	Intervention impact is significant and can meaningfully reduce reoffending	Good, many will move from Level III to II
IV	Multiple—some chronic and severe	Persistent offending profile: chronic and lengthy involvement in crime Average = 65% Range = 50%–84%	Intensive—monitor for safety and compliance, provide change-focused interventions	Very Significant—200–300 hours	Intervention impact can be significant but reduction will not quickly result in the lowest levels of risk	Improvement, some will move from Level IV to III, and as low as II after a significant period of time (i.e., 10+ years)
V	Multiple—chronic, severe, and entrenched, likely across psychological, interpersonal, and lifestyle domains	Entrenched criminal profile: virtually certain to reoffend Average = 90% Range = 85% or higher	Very intensive—monitor for safety and compliance, provide long-term and intensive change-focused interventions	Extensive—well over 300 hours, provided over years	Intervention can have an impact but initial risk so high that emphasis is on treatment readiness and behavioral management	Initial risk so high that reoffending will still be above average, some will move to Level IV or III, possibly as low as II in advanced age

Note. From *A Five-Level Risk and Needs System: Maximizing Assessment Results in Corrections Through the Development of a Common Language*, by R. K. Hanson, G. Bourgon, R. J. McGrath, D. Kroner, D. A. D'Amora, S. S. Thomas, and L. P. Tavarez, 2017, New York: The Council of State Governments Justice Center, p. 13. Copyright © 2017 by Council of State Governments Justice Center. Reprinted with permission.

Missing from this system and table 23.1 is the relevant psychiatric and mental health services needed for the treatment of justice-involved persons with SMI. We submit that an evidence-based service for justice-involved persons with SMI will necessitate the integration of risk assessment (specifically the inclusion of risk for psychiatric relapse risk) and psychiatric rehabilitation services. Specifically, we advocate for a conceptualization of RNR, and by extension the Five-Level Risk and Needs System, that is not limited to criminal justice considerations. Instead, these frameworks should holistically integrate issues related to justice involvement with co-occurring issues related to mental illness. Only then can we truly impact the totality of the clinical picture for this population and begin working in a manner that reflects the complexity of the mental illness–criminalness relationship. To accomplish this, table 23.1 must be expanded to include assessment of mental health needs, and necessary psychiatric treatments and services for these needs. Importantly, this suggestion would not be resolved by simply creating new columns in table 23.1. Instead, by integrating information related to psychiatric needs into existing columns, we can avoid perpetuating the siloed service model that is predominant today. This integration is especially important for the treatment of justice-involved persons with SMI, given a recent finding that services aimed at treating mental illness and criminal risk simultaneously resulted in greater improvement than services aimed at treating mental illness or criminal risk in isolation (Scanlon & Morgan, 2020).

A new model of ideal service delivery for justice-involved persons with SMI would also span criminal justice system involvement—from arrest to parole and continuing into the community. The Sequential Intercept Model is a framework that has identified intervention opportunities, or intercepts, that can be utilized to reduce the "criminalization of people with mental illness" (Munetz & Griffin, 2006, p. 544) in the United States (e.g., pretrial detention and community reentry; Griffin et al., 2015). Building from this model, Bonfine et al. (2020) proposed a reconceptualization of the existing model's first sector, Intercept 0. In the Sequential Intercept Model, Intercept 0 is labeled "Community Services," and focuses on managing people with severe mental illness crisis through responding behavioral health clinicians and police officers and diverting people in crisis from traditional hospital emergency departments and jails. Bonfine et al. (2020) offered that crisis response should be one component of a larger, integrated, behavioral health system-based Intercept 0. Other components of this reconceptualized Intercept 0, aimed at improving the health of people with SMI and reducing and/or preventing their incarceration and hospitalization, also include treatment of physical and mental health care, substance use, criminal risk, and social needs (i.e., housing and employment), in addition to provision of trauma-informed services (Bonfine et al., 2020).

Another Treatment Consideration for Justice-Involved Persons with SMI: Trauma

An important consideration that has not been integrated into specified treatments for justice-involved persons with SMI is trauma. Although not a primary risk factor, the prevalence of trauma for justice-involved persons as well as persons with SMI necessitates clinical consideration. For example, some estimates have indicated a near universal trauma rate for men (99 percent; Wolff et al., 2014) and women (98 percent; Green et al., 2005). Similarly, rates of trauma exposure among people with SMI are significantly higher than rates found in the general population (Mauritz et al., 2013). Notably, trauma-informed mental healthcare is important and feasible in clinical work with justice-involved persons with SMI (see Miller & Najavits, 2012). Specific trauma-focused treatment programs for justice-involved persons include Seeking Safety (Najavits, 2002), Trauma Affect Regulation: Guide for Education and Therapy (TARGET; Ford & Russo, 2006), Trauma, Addictions, Mental Health and Recovery (TAMAR; National Association of State Mental Health Program Directors, 2019), and Narrative Exposure Therapy for Forensic Offender Rehabilitation (FORNET; Hecker et al., 2015). Based on our current understanding of trauma and RNR, we submit that trauma is currently best classified as a responsivity issue and should be integrated into interventions for justice-involved persons with SMI.

Future Directions for Correctional Intervention Practice & Research

In this chapter, we have outlined effective treatment and management strategies for justice-involved persons with SMI, and proposed advances for enhancing the effectiveness of existing services. But much work remains, and most importantly, this work must be informed by research. A failure in the field has been using treatment programs for this population before we have sufficient evidence that it works (Skeem et al., 2015, Steadman et al., 2001; effectiveness research), how it works (process research), or if it works within our systems (implementation research). In corrections, this effectiveness research should go beyond pre–post treatment improvements, meeting the scientific bar of program evaluation through randomized controlled trials. To correct these oversights and intervene more intentionally, additional front-end effectiveness and process research prior to implementation in forensic and correctional sites is integral. Finally, the lack of a concrete conceptual model to guide treatment development and treatment research for people with SMI in forensic and correctional settings is another challenge. We need look no further than medical settings for guidance in rigorously evaluating interventions prior to implementation when treating vulnerable populations with complex disorders.

After establishing the effectiveness of an intervention, expanding program evaluations to include testing group differences is the next step. For example, because racial and sexual disparities exist in the criminal justice system (see Baćak et al., 2018; Harris, 2003; Meyer et al., 2017; Sentencing Project, 2018), it is important to consider these factors in treatment and in our evaluations of treatment. Treatment research generally is limited, and treatment research specifically examining responsivity factors like culture (racial/ethnic) and identities (gender/sexual) is even more so—in fact, Tadros et al. (2020) illustrate the lack in this area with a clarion call for psychiatric interventions for transgender people in correctional settings.

Similar to behavioral health programs in the general health sector, we must examine not only if treatments or programs work, but how to effectively utilize them in correctional settings. Ensuring that best-practice programs that are effective (e.g., reducing recidivism, improving skills, and decreasing mental illness symptoms) are the programs used in the justice system is the goal of implementation science; this goal is met by collecting information about how well a treatment program works in a setting (Proctor et al., 2009). The need for implementation research in criminal justice settings has been acknowledged (Proctor et al., 2011; Zielinksi et al., 2020), though extant implementation research in this area remains limited. As we continue to test how well our programs work for people in the criminal justice system, we must also focus our attention on how well our programs work in the settings in which they were designed to be used—courts, jails, prisons, probation, and parole.

References

AbuDagga, A., Wolfe, S., Carome, M., Phatdouang, A., & Torrey, E. F. (2016). *Individuals with serious mental illnesses in county jails: A survey of jail staff's perspectives*. Public Citizen's Health Research Group. https://www.treatmentadvocacycenter.org/storage/documents/jail-survey-report-2016.pdf

Andrews, D. A., & Bonta, J. (2010). Rehabilitating criminal justice policy and practice. *Psychology, Public Policy, and Law, 16*(1), 39–55.

Andrews, D. A., Bonta, J., & Hoge, R. D. (1990). Classification for effective rehabilitation: Rediscovering psychology. *Criminal Justice and Behavior, 17*(1), 19–52.

Baćak, V., Thurman, K., Eyer, K., Qureshi, R., Bird, J. D., Rivera, L. M., & Kim, S. A. (2018). Incarceration as a health determinant for sexual orientation and gender minority persons. *American Journal of Public Health, 108*(8), 994–999.

Bachrach, L. L. (1989). Deinstitutionalization: A semantic analysis. *Journal of Social Issues, 45*(3), 161–171.

Barnao, M., & Ward, T. (2015). Sailing uncharted seas without a compass: A review of interventions in forensic mental health. *Aggression and Violent Behavior, 22*, 77–86.

Bartholomew, N. R., & Morgan, R. D. (2015). Comorbid mental illness and criminalness implications for housing and treatment. *CNS Spectrums, 20*(3), 231–240.

Canada, K., Barrenger, S., & Ray, B. (2019). Bridging mental health and criminal justice systems: A systematic review of the impact of mental health courts on individuals and communities. *Psychology, Public Policy, and Law, 25*(2), 73–91.

Bewley, M. T., & Morgan, R. D. (2011). A national survey of mental health services available to offenders with mental illness: Who is doing what? *Law and Human Behavior, 35*(5), 351–363.

Bolaños, A. D., Mitchell, S. M., Morgan, R. D., & Grabowski, K. E. (2020). A comparison of criminogenic risk factors and psychiatric symptomatology between psychiatric inpatients with and without criminal justice involvement. *Law and Human Behavior, 44*(4), 336–346.

Bonfine, N., Wilson, A. B., & Munetz, M. R. (2020). Meeting the needs of justice-involved people with serious mental illness within community behavioral health stems. *Psychiatric Services, 71*(4), 355–363.

Bonta, J., & Andrews, D. A. (2017). *The psychology of criminal conduct*. Taylor & Francis.

Bonta, J., Blais, J., & Wilson, H. A. (2014). A theoretically informed meta-analysis of the risk for general and violent recidivism for mentally disordered offenders. *Aggression and Violent Behavior, 19*(3), 278–287.

Bonta, J., Law, M., & Hanson, K. (1998). The prediction of criminal and violent recidivism among mentally disordered offenders: A meta-analysis. *Psychological Bulletin, 123*(2), 123–142.

Callahan, L. A., & Silver, E. (1998). Factors associated with the conditional release of persons acquitted by reason of insanity: A decision tree approach. *Law and Human Behavior, 22*(2), 147–163.

Campbell, M. A., Canales, D. D., Wei, R., Totten, A. E., Macaulay, W. A. C., & Wershler, J. L. (2015). Multidimensional evaluation of a mental health court: Adherence to the risk-need-responsivity model. *Law and Human Behavior, 39*(5), 489–502.

Draine, J., Salzer, M. S., Culhane, D. P., & Hadley, T. R. (2002). Role of social disadvantage in crime, joblessness, and homelessness among persons with serious mental illness. *Psychiatric Services, 53*(5), 565–573.

Epperson, M., Wolff, N., Morgan, R., Fisher, W., Frueh, B. C., & Huening, J. (2011). *The next generation of behavioral health and criminal justice interventions: Improving outcomes by improving interventions.* Center for Behavioral Health Services and Criminal Justice Research, Rutgers, the State University of New Jersey.

Ford, J. D., & Russo, E. (2006). Trauma-focused, present-centered, emotional self-regulation approach to integrated treatment for post-traumatic stress and addiction: TARGET. *American Journal of Psychotherapy, 60*, 335–355.

GAINS Center. (2021). *Adult Mental Health Treatment Courts Locator.* Substance Abuse and Mental Health Services Administration. https://www.samhsa.gov/gains-center/mental-health-treatment-court-locator/adults

Gaspar, M., Brown, L., Ramler, T., Scanlon, F., Gigax, G., Ridley, K., & Morgan, R. D. (2019). Therapeutic outcomes of changing lives and changing outcomes for male and female justice involved persons with mental illness. *Criminal Justice and Behavior, 46*(12), 1678–1699.

Goodstein, L. (1979). Inmate adjustment to prison and the transition to community life. *Journal of Research in Crime and Delinquency, 16*(2), 246–272.

Green, B. L., Miranda, J., Daroowalla, A., & Siddique, J. (2005). Trauma exposure, mental health functioning, and program needs of women in jail. *Crime & Delinquency, 51*(1), 133–151.

Griffin, P. A., Munetz, M., Bonfine, N., & Kemp, K. (2015). Development of the Sequential Intercept Model. In P. A. Griffin, K. Heilbrun, E. P. Mulvey, D. DeMatteo, & C. A. Schubert (Eds.), *The Sequential Intercept Model and criminal justice: Promoting community alternatives for individuals with serious mental illness.* (pp. 21–36) Oxford University Press.

Gross, N. R., & Morgan, R. D. (2013). Understanding persons with mental illness who are and are not criminal justice involved: A comparison of criminal thinking and psychiatric symptoms. *Law and Human Behavior, 37*(3), 175–186.

Grossi, L., Osborn, L., Joplin, K., & O'Connor, B. (2021). Clinical interventions in state psychiatric hospitals: Safety and logistical considerations. *Journal of Forensic Psychology Research and Practice, 21*(2), 152–170. https://doi.org/10.1080/24732850.2020.1843105

Hanson, R. K., Bourgon, G., McGrath, R. J., Kroner, D., D'Amora, D. A., Thomas, S. S., & Tavarez, L. P. (2017). *A five-level risk and needs system: Maximizing assessment results in corrections through the development of a common language.* The Council of State Governments Justice Center.

Harris, D. A. (2003). The reality of racial disparity in criminal justice: The significance of data collection. *Law and Contemporary Problems, 66*(3), 71–98.

Hecker, T., Hermenau, K., Crombach, A., & Elbert, T. (2015). Treating traumatized offenders and veterans by means of narrative exposure therapy. *Frontiers in Psychiatry, 6*, 80.

Jacobs, L. A., & Giordano, S. N. (2018). "It's not like therapy": Patient-inmate perspectives on jail psychiatric services. *Administration and Policy in Mental Health and Mental Health Services Research, 45*(2), 265–275.

James, D. J., & Glaze, L. E. (2006). *Mental health problems of prison and jail inmates.* U.S Department of Justice, Bureau of Justice Statistics. https://www.bjs.gov/content/pub/pdf/mhppji.pdf

Landenberger, N. A., & Lipsey, M. W. (2005). The positive effects of cognitive–behavioral programs for offenders: A meta-analysis of factors associated with effective treatment. *Journal of Experimental Criminology, 1*(4), 451–476.

Lipsey, M. W., & Cullen, F. T. (2007). The effectiveness of correctional rehabilitation: A review of systematic reviews. *Annual Review of Law and Social Science, 3*, 297–320.

Lowder, E. M., Rade, C. B., & Desmarais, S. L. (2018). Effectiveness of mental health courts in reducing recidivism: A meta-analysis. *Psychiatric Services, 69*(1), 15–22.

MacInnes, D., & Masino, S. (2019). Psychological and psychosocial interventions offered to forensic mental health inpatients: A systematic review. *BMJ Open, 9*(3), Article e024351.

Markowitz, F. E. (2011). Mental illness, crime, and violence: Risk, context, and social control. *Aggression and Violent Behavior, 16*(1), 36–44.

Mauritz, M. W., Goossens, P. J., Draijer, N., & Van Achterberg, T. (2013). Prevalence of interpersonal trauma exposure and trauma-related disorders in severe mental illness. *European Journal of Psychotraumatology, 4*(1), Article 19985.

McInerny, T., & Minne, C. (2004). Principles of treatment for mentally disordered offenders. *Criminal Behavior and Mental Health, 14*, S43–S47.

Meyer, I. H., Flores, A. R., Stemple, L., Romero, A. P., Wilson, B. D., & Herman, J. L. (2017). Incarceration rates and traits of sexual minorities in the United States: National Inmate Survey, 2011–2012. *American Journal of Public Health, 107*(2), 267–273.

Miller, N. A., & Najavits, L. M. (2012). Creating trauma-informed correctional care: A balance of goals and environment. *European Journal of Psychotraumatology, 3*(1), 17246.

Millon, T. (1996). *Disorders of personality* (2nd ed.). John Wiley & Sons.

Millon, T. (2000). Toward a new model of integrative psychotherapy: Psychosynergy. *Journal of Psychotherapy Integration, 10*(1), 37–53.

Millon, T. (2005). Reflections on the future of personology and psychopathology. In S. Strack (Ed.), *Handbook of personology and psychopathology* (pp. 527–546). John Wiley & Sons.

Monson, C. M., Gunnin, D. D., Fogel, M. H., & Kyle, L. L. (2001). Stopping (or slowing) the revolving door: Factors related to NGRI acquittees' maintenance of a conditional release. *Law and Human Behavior, 25*(3), 257–267.

Morgan, R. D. (2003). Basic mental health services: Services and issues. In T. Fagan & R. K. Ax (Eds.), *Correctional mental health handbook* (pp. 59–71). SAGE.

Morgan, R. D., Fisher, W. H., Duan, N., Mandracchia, J. T., & Murray, D. (2010). Prevalence of criminal thinking among state prison inmates with serious mental illness. *Law and Human Behavior, 34*(4), 324–336.

Morgan, R. D., Flora, D. B., Kroner, D. G., Mills, J. F., Varghese, F., & Steffan, J. S. (2012). Treating offenders with mental illness: A research synthesis. *Law and Human Behavior, 36*(1), 37–50.

Morgan, R. D., Kroner, D., & Mills, J. F. (2018). *A treatment manual for justice involved persons with mental illness: Changing lives and changing outcomes.* Routledge.

Morgan, R. D., Kroner, D. G., Mills, J. F., & Batastini, A. B. (2014). Treating criminal offenders. In I. B. Weiner & R. K. Otto (Eds.), *The handbook of forensic psychology* (pp. 795–837). John Wiley & Sons.

Morgan, R. D., Kroner, D. G., Mills, J. F., Bauer, R. L., & Serna, C. (2014). Treating justice involved persons with mental illness: Preliminary evaluation of a comprehensive treatment program. *Criminal Justice and Behavior, 41*(7), 902–916.

Morgan, R. D., Scanlon, F., & Van Horn, S. A. (2020). Criminogenic risk and mental health: A complicated relationship. *CNS Spectrums, 25*(2), 237–244.

Munetz, M. R., & Griffin, P. A. (2006). Use of the sequential intercept model as an approach to decriminalization of people with serious mental illness. *Psychiatric Services, 57*(4), 544–549.

Najavits, L. (2002). *Seeking safety: A treatment manual for PTSD and substance abuse.* Guilford Press.

National Association of State Mental Health Program Directors. (2019). *Trauma Addictions Mental Health and Recovery (TAMAR) treatment manual and modules.* National Association of State Mental Health Program Directors. https://www.nasmhpd.org/sites/default/files/TAMAR%20NYS%20DOCCS%20Final.pdf

National Institute of Justice. (2020, July 31). *Rated practices.* Crime Solutions. https://crimesolutions.ojp.gov/rated-practices

Osher, F. C., & Steadman, H. J. (2007). Adapting evidence-based practices for persons with mental illness involved with the criminal justice system. *Psychiatric Services, 58*(11), 1472–1478.

Pescosolido, B. A., Monahan, J., Link, B. G., Stueve, A., & Kikuzawa, S. (1999). The public's view of the competence, dangerousness, and need for legal coercion of persons with mental health problems. *American Journal of Public Health, 89*(9), 1339–1345.

Peterson, J. K., Skeem, J., Kennealy, P., Bray, B., & Zvonkovic, A. (2014). How often and how consistently do symptoms directly precede criminal behavior among offenders with mental illness? *Law and Human Behavior, 38*(5), 439–449.

Prins, S. J. (2011). Does transinstitutionalization explain the overrepresentation of people with serious mental illnesses in the criminal justice system? *Community Mental Health Journal, 47*(6), 716–722.

Prins, S. J. (2014). Prevalence of mental illnesses in US state prisons: A systematic review. *Psychiatric Services, 65*(7), 862–872.

Proctor, E. K., Landsverk, J., Aarons, G., Chambers, D., Glisson, C., & Mittman, B. (2009). Implementation research in mental health services: An emerging science with conceptual, methodological, and training challenges. *Administration and Policy in Mental Health and Mental Health Services Research, 36*(1), 24–34.

Proctor, E., Silmere, H., Raghavan, R., Hovmand, P., Aarons, G., Bunger, A., Griffey, R., & Hensley, M. (2011). Outcomes for implementation research: Conceptual distinctions, measurement challenges, and research agenda. *Administration and Policy in Mental Health and Mental Health Services Research, 38*(2), 65–76.

Rice, M. E., & Harris, G. T. (1997). The treatment of mentally disordered offenders. *Psychology, Public Policy, and Law, 3*(1), 126–183.

Roth, A. (2018). *Insane: America's criminal treatment of mental illness.* Basic Books.

Sarteschi, C. M., Vaughn, M. G., & Kim, K. (2011). Assessing the effectiveness of mental health courts: A quantitative review. *Journal of Criminal Justice, 39*(1), 12–20.

Scanlon, F., & Morgan, R. D. (2020). The active ingredients in a treatment for justice-involved persons with mental illness: The importance of addressing mental illness and criminal risk. *Psychological Services.* Advance online publication. https://doi.org/10.1037/ser0000411

Scanlon, F., Morgan, R. D., Mitchell, S. M., Bolaños, A. D., & Gross, N. (2021). *The criminal justice system and community mental health: Institutions of justice-involved people with mental illness [Manuscript submitted for publication].*

Scheyett, A., Vaughn, J., & Taylor, M. F. (2009). Screening and access to services for individuals with serious mental illnesses in jails. *Community Mental Health Journal, 45*(6), 439–446.

Skeem, J. L., & Peterson, J. (2012). Identifying, treating, and reducing risk for offenders with mental illness. In J. Petersilia & K. R. Reitz (Eds.), *The Oxford handbook on sentencing and corrections* (pp. 521–543). Oxford University Press.

Skeem, J. L., Steadman, H. J., & Manchak, S. M. (2015). Applicability of the risk-need-responsivity model to persons with mental illness involved in the criminal justice system. *Psychiatric Services, 66*(9), 916–922.

Skeem, J. L., Winter, E., Kennealy, P. J., Louden, J. E., & Tatar II, J. R. (2014). Offenders with mental illness have criminogenic needs, too: Toward recidivism reduction. *Law and Human Behavior, 38*(3), 212–224.

Smith, P., Gendreau, P., & Swartz, K. (2009). Validating the principles of effective intervention: A systematic review of the contributions of meta-analysis in the field of corrections. *Victims and Offenders, 4*(2), 148–169.

Snyder, H. (2007). Nothing works, something works—But still few proven programs. *Corrections Today, 69*(6), 6–28.

Steadman, H. J., Davidson, S., & Brown, C. (2001). Law & psychiatry: Mental health courts: Their promise and unanswered questions. *Psychiatric Services, 52*(4), 457–458.

Steadman, H. J., & Redlich, A. D. (2005). *An evaluation of the Bureau of Justice Assistance mental health court initiative.* National Institute of Justice. https://www.ncjrs.gov/pdffiles1/nij/grants/213136.pdf

Tadros, E., Ribera, E., Campbell, O., Kish, H., & Ogden, T. (2020). A call for mental health treatment in incarcerated settings with transgender individuals. *The American Journal of Family Therapy, 48*(5), 495–508.

The Sentencing Project. (2018). *Report of the sentencing project to the United Nations special rapporteur on contemporary forms of racism, racial discrimination, xenophobia, and related intolerance: Regarding racial disparities in the United States criminal justice system.* https://www.sentencingproject.org/wp-content/uploads/2018/04/UN-Report-on-Racial-Disparities.pdf

Torrey, E. F., Kennard, A. D., Eslinger, D., Lamb, R., & Pavle, J. (2010). *More mentally ill persons are in jails and prisons than hospitals: A survey of the states.* Treatment Advocacy Center, National Sheriffs' Association. https://knox.oh.networkofcare.org/library/final_jails_v_hospitals_study.pdf

Torrey, E. F., Zdanowicz, M. T., Kennard, A. D., Lamb, H. R., Eslinger, D. F., Biasotti, M. C., & Fuller, D. A. (2014). *The treatment of persons with mental illness in prisons and jails: A state survey.* Treatment Advocacy Center, National Sheriffs' Association. https://www.treatmentadvocacycenter.org/storage/documents/treatment-behind-bars/treatment-behind-bars.pdf

Walker, L. E., Pann, J. M., Shapiro, D. L., & Van Hasselt, V. B. (2016). *Best practices for the mentally ill in the criminal justice system.* Springer International Publishing.

Widiger, T. A., & Smith, G. T. (2008). Personality and psychopathology. In O. P. John, R. W. Robins, & L. A. Pervin (Eds.), *Handbook of personality: Theory and research* (pp. 743–769). Guilford Press.

Wilson, D. B., Bouffard, L. A., & MacKenzie, D. L. (2005). A quantitative review of structured, group-oriented, cognitive-behavioral programs for offenders. *Criminal Justice and Behavior, 32*(2), 172–204.

Wilson, A. B., Farkas, K., Ishler, K. J., Gearhart, M., Morgan, R., & Ashe, M. (2014). Criminal thinking styles among people with serious mental illness in jail. *Law and Human Behavior, 38*(6), 592–601.

Wolff, N. B., Frueh, C., Shi, J., & Schumann, B. E. (2012). Effectiveness of cognitive–behavioral trauma treatment for incarcerated women with mental illnesses and substance abuse disorders. *Journal of Anxiety Disorders, 26*(7), 703–710.

Wolff, N., Huening, J., Shi, J., & Frueh, B. C. (2014). Trauma exposure and posttraumatic stress disorder among incarcerated men. *Journal of Urban Health, 91*(4), 707–719.

Wolff, N., Morgan, R. D., & Shi, J. (2013). Comparative analysis of attitudes and emotions among inmates: Does mental illness matter? *Criminal Justice and Behavior*, *40*(10), 1092–1108.

Wolff, N., Morgan, R. D., Shi, J., Huening, J., & Fisher, W. H. (2011). Thinking styles and emotional states of male and female prison inmates by mental disorder status. *Psychiatric Services*, *62*(12), 1485–1493.

Zielinski, M. J., Allison, M. K., Brinkley-Rubinstein, L., Curran, G., Zaller, N. D., & Kirchner, J. A. E. (2020). Making change happen in criminal justice settings: Leveraging implementation science to improve mental health care. *Health & Justice*, *8*(1), 1–10.

Zlotnick, C., Johnson, J., & Najavits, L. M. (2009). Randomized controlled pilot study of cognitive-behavioral therapy in a sample of incarcerated women with substance use disorder and PTSD. *Behavior Therapy*, *40*(4), 325–336.

Key Considerations for Pre-arrest Diversion Programs

Karen L. Dugosh, Jessica L. Lipkin, Daniel J. Flack, David DeMatteo, *and* David S. Festinger

Abstract

This chapter reviews the extant literature to identify empirically proven strategies that pre-arrest diversion (PAD) programs could employ to improve outcomes. PAD programs generally refer low-risk individuals who use drugs to community-based services and rehabilitation in lieu of formal entry into the criminal justice system. Preliminary data indicate that these programs can reduce incarceration rates, recidivism, and drug use, and that they result in cost savings relative to standard engagement in the criminal justice system. Although the early verdict is that these programs reduce public harm, existing programs often use arbitrary criteria for determining eligibility, making evaluation and replication unreliable. PAD programs may serve to improve both public health and public safety by utilizing empirically proven practices. Nevertheless, there are still many challenges to the development, implementation, and operations of PAD programs. Although preliminary data from these programs support their utility, continued research is necessary to identify what practices facilitate their short- and long-term success.

Key Words: pre-arrest diversion, community-based treatment, rehabilitation, low-risk offenders, police-assisted diversion, substance use, criminal justice

More than 30 million individuals have been arrested for drug-related offenses during the last three decades, and nearly half of all inmates in federal prisons were convicted on drug charges during this time (US Sentencing Commission, 2016). From 1980 to 2014, the number of drug arrests increased by a startling 175 percent from 581,000 per year to 1.6 million per year (Department of Justice, 2015; King, 2008), yet there is little evidence that imprisonment reduces drug use, overdose deaths, or recidivism, or that it increases public safety (Kleiman, 2004; Marlowe, 2002; Pew Charitable Trusts, 2012, 2017). Rates of relapse and recidivism for people who use drugs in the criminal justice system are high, with 60–80 percent reoffending within three years following their release from prison and overdose accounting for about one in four deaths postrelease (Binswanger et al., 2007; Chandler et al., 2009; Langan & Levin, 2002). It is estimated that 58 percent of adults who have been to state prison and 63 percent of adults who have been to jail meet the criteria for substance use disorder (Bronson et al., 2017). In addition, 63–83 percent of justice-involved individuals test positive for drugs at the time of their arrest (Office of National Drug Control Policy, 2014).

Drug policy in the United States continuously fluctuates between prioritizing public safety and public health. The goal of the public safety approach is to protect communities from drugs and crime by utilizing the criminal justice system's punitive mechanisms, such as house arrest, electronic monitoring, and incarceration, on people who use drugs who are caught offending. Alternatively, drug policies that follow a public health approach address substance use disorder as a chronic, relapsing disease and generally rely on treatment and rehabilitation as opposed to strict sanctions. Generally, neither of these one-dimensional approaches has been effective in reducing criminal activity and recidivism (Marlowe, 2002; Pugh et al., 2013).

Research suggests that effective strategies for reducing substance use and criminal recidivism tend to use components of both the public safety and public health approaches and take into consideration the person's individual needs. Without tailored disposition and treatment placements, fewer than one in four people who use drugs in the criminal justice system satisfy their treatment and supervisory obligations. Such tailoring must be based on both their functional status and static life factors including age, sex, adolescent onset of substance use or delinquency, prior felony convictions, previously unsuccessful attempts at treatment, comorbid mental health problems, and time spent with antisocial peers (Andrews & Bonta, 2010; Festinger et al., 2002; Marlowe et al., 2003; University of California, 2007).

New criminal justice approaches continue to evolve that attempt to strike a balance between public health and public safety in addressing drug-related crime. More recently, many jurisdictions in the United States have begun to implement a new strategy, pre-arrest diversion (PAD), in which police officers connect individuals who have substance use disorders with a range of services, including substance use treatment, rather than arresting them. In this chapter, we provide an overview of the theoretical basis for PAD and other types of diversion programs, descriptions of existing programs and their effectiveness, key principles and considerations for PAD programs based on the extant literature, and challenges that programs may face during both initial implementation and ongoing operations.

Sequential Intercept Model

The Sequential Intercept Model (SIM; Munetz & Griffin, 2006) provides a conceptual framework for the continuum of entry points into the criminal justice system. It identifies different points at which an intervention can be made to prevent individuals from entering or moving further into the system and facing more complicated and lasting legal consequences, including loss of liberty and lifelong stigma. Optimally, individuals would be intercepted at the earliest possible points, with decreasing numbers at each sequential, more intensive, and more restrictive point. The series of sequential intercepts include (1) arrest and emergency services; (2) initial detention and initial hearings; (3) jail, courts, forensic evaluations, and forensic commitments; (4) reentry from jails, state prisons, and forensic hospitalization; and (5) community corrections and community support.

Drug Courts

Drug courts were one of the first strategies developed to integrate the public safety and public health approaches to substance use (Huddleston & Marlowe, 2011). Drug courts represent intervention at Intercept 3 in the SIM as they offer an alternative to prosecution and incarceration. Drug courts are diversionary programs that provide a judicially supervised regimen of substance use disorder treatment, substance use monitoring, and necessary ancillary services in lieu of criminal prosecution or incarceration (National Association of Drug Court Professionals, 1997). In preadjudication drug courts, graduates have their criminal arrest charges dropped and may be eligible for record expungement after remaining arrest-free for an additional waiting period (Marlowe et al., 2011). In postadjudication drug courts, defendants enter a guilty plea, and graduates can have their sentence deferred, modified, or suspended, or have their record expunged (Open Society Foundation, 2015). This combined public health and public safety model has been successful in reducing drug use, program attrition, and criminal recidivism as demonstrated through randomized controlled trials (RCTs) and meta-analyses (e.g., DeMatteo et al., 2019; Festinger et al., 2002; Mitchell et al., 2012; Sevigny et al., 2013; Shaffer, 2011).

Drug courts are generally designed for individuals who require a high level of judicial oversight and intensive treatment for their substance use disorders (National Association of Drug Court Professionals, 2013). However, the mandated requirements of drug courts (e.g., judicial status hearings, drug screening schedules, and probation visits) may create unnecessary challenges for clients who do not require such intensive supervisory services. These program requirements may interfere with important obligations and prosocial activities (e.g., employment, family, and social). Furthermore, formally entering these individuals into the criminal justice system may waste valuable resources, expose them to antisocial peers, and have lasting negative effects on their prospects (DeMatteo et al., 2006; Dugosh et al., 2014; Festinger et al., 2002; Fletcher, 2007). Although drug courts have proven to be an effective strategy for people who use drugs who require more intensive treatment and accountability, it is likely that many individuals may benefit from PAD programs in which the intervention occurs at an earlier point in the SIM.

Pre-arrest Diversion

In traditional criminal justice encounters, lower-level justice-involved individuals are generally processed similarly to others, necessitating detainment, prosecution, and potentially jail or prison. However, some jurisdictions have shifted their attention to diverting individuals who have committed lower-level crimes, such as those who are nonviolent, to community-based services and rehabilitation instead of formal involvement with the criminal justice system. In PAD programs, eligible individuals are connected with community services (e.g., substance use disorder treatment, housing support, and employment services) *prior to* formal arrest by law enforcement (Hartford et al., 2006; Munetz & Griffin, 2006). Unlike other types of diversion programs that divert individuals from criminal justice involvement *after* the point of arrest or after charges are filed (e.g., drug courts), PAD programs may reduce or eliminate the logistical complexity and resource burden on law enforcement agencies associated with the arrest, detainment, and litigation of certain lower-level justice-involved individuals. Preventing any penetration into the criminal justice system is often referred to as Intercept 0 in the SIM (Munetz & Griffin, 2006). Furthermore, this prevents the individual from having a criminal record which often limits future opportunities including higher education and employment.

PAD programs are becoming more common throughout the United States since their inception in 2011. According to a recent report, there are now thirty-nine jurisdictions with operating PAD programs, five in the launch phase, eighteen in the development phase, and fifty-one in the exploration phase (LEAD National Support Bureau, 2020b). Furthermore, several collaboratives and organizations centered on PAD principles have been created including the Police, Treatment, and Community Collaborative (PTACC) and the Police-Assisted Addiction Recovery Initiative (PAARI; Charlier, 2019).

Seattle's Law Enforcement Assisted Diversion (LEAD) program was the first PAD program in the United States. LEAD allows individuals stopped by the police for lower-level drug or prostitution offenses to receive community-based services instead of being arrested, jailed, and prosecuted (Collins et al., 2015a, 2015b). PAD-provided services include substance use and mental health treatment, case management, housing, healthcare, and job training. The goal of LEAD is to reduce criminal recidivism by addressing the individual needs of the participant, thus improving the safety and order of the community. Notably, this aligns closely with the overarching goals of most law enforcement agencies. A non-randomized controlled evaluation of Seattle's LEAD program suggested that the program's participants had significantly fewer arrests and felony charges in the first six months; significant reductions in costs associated with legal system utilization; and significantly better outcomes related to housing, employment, and income relative to individuals who were processed as usual (Clifasefi et al., 2016; Collins et al., 2015a, 2015b, 2019). As the first PAD program in the United States., LEAD has developed core principles for various stakeholders to promote successful implementation (LEAD National Support Bureau, 2020a) and several jurisdictions have adopted the LEAD model.

Santa Fe, New Mexico was the first jurisdiction to replicate and adapt the Seattle LEAD model in 2014. Their program is very similar to that implemented in Seattle with one exception—it additionally allows individuals to enter the program via a *social contact diversion* in which officers refer individuals they perceive at risk of future arrest or in need of help for a substance use issue. In an evaluation of the first six months of the program (New Mexico Sentencing Commission, 2018), participants showed a statistically significant decrease in number of arrests, and higher engagement in the program was associated with fewer arrests for new charges. Notably, no LEAD participants were charged with a violent crime postprogram. Participants reported decreased use of heroin, increased quality of life, and better prospects in obtaining permanent housing. When counting pre- and postdiversion costs, including criminal justice and emergency medical costs, the LEAD program saved 17 percent compared to systems as usual, totaling a savings of $1,558 per participant per year.

Other jurisdictions have developed somewhat different approaches to PAD. For instance, Leon County Florida implemented the Pre-arrest Diversion/Adult Civil Citation (PAD/ACC) program in 2013. In this program (Kopak & Frost, 2017), citations are issued to individuals who have committed a qualifying misdemeanor offense and have no prior arrests. Participants must complete a ninety-day individualized intervention plan delivered by a behavioral health provider and engage in twenty-five hours of community service. Upon successful completion of program requirements, the case is closed, and the individual maintains an arrest-free criminal record. An evaluation of participant behavioral assessment and formal arrest data (Kopak, 2018) demonstrated that the PAD/ACC program had an 84 percent completion rate and an 18 percent recidivism rate overall. Among those who successfully completed the program, only 9 percent recidivated (Kopak, 2018).

Although preliminary data suggest that PAD programs can be effective, critical questions remain about their optimal structure and best practices, including how to determine program eligibility. In most programs, individuals are deemed eligible for PAD based on their current criminal involvement, criminal history, medical conditions, ability to consent, and relatively subjective judgments of how amenable to diversion they appear (LEAD Policy Coordinating Group, 2015). When officers are given this level of discretion in making determinations of who may be suitable for the program, situational and person-level factors (e.g., offense seriousness; strength of evidence; the individual's gender, race, and demeanor) coupled with officer attitudes and explicit and implicit biases they hold may unduly influence officer decision-making about who should be diverted and who should be arrested, leading to less than optimal outcomes for individuals (Worden & McLean, 2018). Using a more standardized and systematic approach to determining PAD eligibility that includes identifying risk of recidivism and treatment responsivity may help to ensure that PAD participants are matched to the optimal level of services. Moreover, further standardization of eligibility determination will reduce bias in PAD admissions and more easily facilitate program implementation in other jurisdictions. Research is needed to determine best practices, but there are many long-standing evidence-based strategies for justice-involved individuals who use drugs that PAD programs can utilize to facilitate these efforts.

Key Principles and Considerations for PAD Programs:

Stakeholders should consider a number of key principles when developing and implementing PAD programs.

Principle I: Eligibility Criteria

First, eligibility criteria regarding level and severity of offenses and threat to public safety should be clearly established. According to the risk–need–responsivity model, individuals may require different levels of treatment and criminal justice oversight depending on their level of criminogenic risk and clinical need (e.g., Andrews & Bonta, 2010; Marlowe et al., 2011; Taxman & Marlowe, 2006). Criminogenic risks typically include static, immutable factors that have been shown to reduce the likelihood of success in standard forms of rehabilitation and increase the risk of recidivism. Clinical needs are those areas of psychosocial dysfunction that, if effectively ameliorated, can substantially reduce the likelihood of continued involvement in substance use and crime. Because PAD programs offer little oversight or accountability, low-risk/high-need individuals should have the most success due to the provision of treatment for their substance use disorders without the complex legal entanglements of the criminal justice system that may compete with important role obligations and the potential iatrogenic effects of interacting with justice-involved individuals with more serious criminal histories and antisocial characteristics.

Principle II: Structured Triage to Determine Eligibility

To avoid selection bias, an individual's eligibility for the program should be determined by a standardized, structured, and brief assessment to determine their levels of criminogenic risk and clinical need. Administering a validated assessment tool prior to making a formal arrest could provide law enforcement with an evidence-based, objective way to quickly and effectively determine which individuals they stop would be most appropriate for immediate diversion to treatment. The triage should ideally be conducted as close as possible to the point of arrest. Several validated tools exist that could be used to screen individuals for PAD eligibility, including the Risk and Needs Triage (Dugosh et al., 2014; Marlowe et al., 2006, 2011), the Proxy Triage Risk Screener (Bogue et al., 2006), and the Texas Christian University Drug Screen (Knight et al., 2002).

Principle III: Comprehensive Assessment

Following determination of eligibility, individuals should complete a comprehensive psychosocial assessment to identify their level of treatment and ancillary service needs. Because of the multifaceted nature of substance use disorders, no single course of treatment is right for everyone (Institute of Medicine, 1990; Leshner, 1999). To promote optimal outcomes, this comprehensive assessment should take into consideration at least four factors that have been found to be important in treatment matching: demographics, addiction-specific characteristics, intrapersonal characteristics, and interpersonal function (Gastfriend & McClellan,

1997). Currently, the American Society of Addiction Medicine (ASAM) criteria are a widely used guideline to help clinicians determine individualized services and treatment across all levels of care (ASAM, 2017). The ASAM criteria have been studied extensively since their inception with several controlled studies supporting their predictive validity and cost-effectiveness (American Society of Addiction Medicine, 2016; Magura et al., 2003; Sharon et al., 2003; Stallvik & Gastfriend, 2014). Research shows that clients who are placed into treatment based on ASAM criteria recommendations have less morbidity, higher functioning, and more efficient service utilization than clients who were not matched (American Society of Addiction Medicine (ASAM), 2017; Gastfriend & Mee-Lee, 2004).

Principle IV: Structured Support

Although clients who enter PAD programs may not require a high level of judicial oversight, structured support is still indicated to ensure accountability. People in substance use treatment are frequently assigned support personnel, such as clinical case managers or peer recovery support specialists, as part of the continuum of services. These personnel can act as mentors, educators, and advocates for the client as they engage them in the recovery process and oversee the coordination of their care (LEAD National Support Bureau, 2020a; Substance Abuse and Mental Health Services Administration, 2015). Utilization of support personnel has been shown to increase service utilization and retention and decrease drug use and relapse rates (Bassuk et al., 2016; Chapman et al., 2018; McLellan et al., 1999; Rapp et al., 2014; Reif et al., 2014). Given that individuals with substance use disorders may often find it difficult to follow through with scheduled activities and obligations, providing a level of oversight and accountability is essential in helping clients achieve their treatment goals.

Principle V: Objective Monitoring of Substance Use

Clients should also be objectively and regularly monitored for substance use to increase their accountability and to ensure accurate oversight of client progress. Urine drug screening is a routine diagnostic monitoring tool that can be used to identify the use or misuse of specific drugs. Consistent, random drug testing has been shown to increase the detection of and act as a deterrent to drug use (Borack, 1998; Kilpatrick et al., 2000). Although client self-reports have also shown some reliability (Darke, 1998; Vakili et al., 2009; Zanis et al., 1994), people who use drugs often deny or minimize their use. As such, a combination of both methods is recommended (Zanis et al., 1994).

In drug courts, rewards for abstinence and sanctions for positive test results have been shown to lead to better outcomes (Hawken & Kleiman, 2009; Marlowe et al., 2005). A positive test result should not automatically prompt termination from the program. Although criminal sanctions cannot be used in a PAD program, other responses to noncompliance, such as more frequent counseling or treatment sessions, written assignments, community service, or educational classes, may deter future drug use. Graduated sanctions may be used for habitual use. However, given the voluntary nature of PAD programs, clients ultimately may choose not to comply with program rules and related sanctions for violations. PAD participants should also be rewarded for negative drug test results. Incentives may include less frequent treatment or counseling sessions, day trips or outings, tangible rewards to increase involvement in prosocial activities, or sobriety tokens.

Challenges:

Use first sentence of Challenge 1 as transition sentence (i.e., Stakeholders face several challenges in the development and implementation of PAD programs.)

Challenge I: Leverage

Stakeholders face several challenges in the development and implementation of PAD programs. An important consideration is how to prevent clients from dropping out of the program. Because clients have not been charged with a crime, mandating clients to comply with program requirements is a challenge. Programs should optimally include some leverage to keep clients engaged in treatment. Individuals who have substance use disorders often have difficulty following through with treatment obligations. Even drug court clients, who generally have greater judicial oversight and may face criminal sanctions for noncompliance, frequently fail to meet their program requirements (Marlowe et al., 2003). As discussed, there are several noncriminal sanctions that may be employed to deter clients from future noncompliance, assuming they have sufficient program buy-in and agree to be held responsible for program violations.

Challenge II: Funding and Sustainability

Another challenge that stakeholders may encounter is sustainability and continued funding. Many of the existing PAD programs are largely supported by federal, state, and local grants, but unfortunately, this funding in most cases is not indefinite. If stakeholders want their program to continue, they must consider new innovative ways to ensure sustainability. One benefit of PAD programs is that they are more cost-effective than more intensive criminal justice responses, saving jurisdictions money on prosecution, defense, and incarceration. For example, a cost analysis found that LEAD participants produced reduced costs in criminal justice and legal system utilization and other associated costs compared to system-as-usual controls (Collins et al., 2015a). With this cost-offset, jurisdictions could use public funds to sustain their PAD programs. It is important for stakeholders to consider alternative funding sources prior to grant support ending to help ensure that their programs can continue uninterrupted.

Challenge III: Law Enforcement Training and Buy-in

Police officers play a central role in PAD programs. People who use drugs can present police with difficult challenges, particularly if they are currently under the influence of drugs or alcohol. The PAD approach is, to a large extent, inconsistent with the traditional policing approach in which officers are charged with arresting individuals who are in violation of laws. Although officers may recognize that arresting people who use drugs often does not achieve the underlying goal of community safety, there remains a perception of diversion to treatment as outside of the role of police officers that is best left to social workers and other behavioral health staff (Barberi & Taxman, 2019; Goetz & Mitchell, 2006). Furthermore, officers often receive limited training on substance use, mental health issues, and harm reduction, which may negatively impact how they interact with people who use drugs.

LEAD Bureau's core principles for successful implementation (LEAD National Support Bureau, 2020a) underscore the importance of early investment from police officers in building program momentum. From the beginning of program development, police officers should be included as equal partners in decision-making around the design, implementation, and improvement of the program. San Francisco's initial LEAD program report (Perrone et al., 2018) recommended that stakeholders identify LEAD-specific officers who are charged with implementing the program, as this approach does not require the difficult task of securing buy-in from the entire police department. This may involve establishing a crisis intervention team (CIT), a group of police officers who are specially trained on how to interact with individuals with mental illness, including substance use. CITs increase the likelihood that individuals who are experiencing a mental health crisis receive the necessary treatment and care rather than having punitive sanctions imposed (Teller et al., 2006).

A number of PAD program reports (e.g., Albany LEAD Policy Coordinating Group, 2017; Bastomski et al., 2019; New Mexico Sentencing Commission, 2018; Perrone et al., 2018) encourage the provision of ongoing training for officers on program procedures and operations as well as harm reduction and trauma-informed approaches, which are not typically part of police training. This ongoing education may promote a shift in officer attitudes about people who use drugs and allow officers to view these individuals in a nonjudgmental, nonthreatening way.

Trainings should also focus on therapeutic jurisprudence, a concept that takes into consideration how law enforcement and criminal justice procedures impact individuals' emotional and psychological well-being (Wexler, 1999). At the police level, therapeutic jurisprudence involves offender engagement and deescalation techniques, which include minimizing force, communicating effectively, and having patience (Police Executive Research Forum, 2012). For PAD programs to be successful, it is imperative for officers to understand that addiction is a chronic relapsing disease, similar in many ways to chronic conditions such as diabetes, asthma, or hypertension rather than a moral failure.

Challenge IV: Community Buy-in

The community must also be helped to better understand addiction as a chronic health condition that requires treatment, rather than a moral failing requiring punishment. Without support from the community, individuals who have substance use disorders may have a difficult time reintegrating into society, which is an important component of their recovery. Although PAD programs typically offer support services such as housing, healthcare, and job training, the social stigma surrounding addiction may act as a barrier to utilizing these services. For example, landlords may not want people who use drugs living in their housing, and employers may be reluctant to hire individuals in substance use treatment. Additionally, stigma has the potential to adversely affect the mental and physical health of individuals with a substance use disorder, which could further impede progress in treatment (Ahern et al., 2007; Link et al., 1997).

PAD programs may serve as a mechanism to reduce stigma associated with addiction and involvement in the criminal justice system. To facilitate this, outreach and advocacy efforts should be made to garner community support for these programs. These outreach efforts should focus on stressing that addiction is a chronic, relapsing condition and that not all people who use drugs pose a threat to public safety. A systematic review of existing research has shown that having individuals share their recovery stories is an effective way to improve individual and community attitudes about people who use drugs (Livingston et al., 2012). The community should also be involved in decision-making during the development and operation of these programs. For example, LEAD utilizes a Community Advisory Board that includes representatives from business interest groups, housing and employment initiatives, churches, and recovery centers who provide feedback about the program (LEAD, n.d.). Community-backed PAD programs will not only benefit people who use drugs but the community itself.

Conclusion

The overreliance on incarceration and other restrictive criminal justice solutions for drug-related crimes in the United States calls for innovative and multidimensional solutions to better serve people who use drugs. Effective strategies such as drug courts have combined public safety and public health approaches to drug policy that are tailored to the individual. PAD programs were created for lower-risk individuals who use drugs who may not require or benefit from the structure and high level of oversight that drug courts or incarceration offer. Existing PAD programs have been shown to reduce rates of incarceration, recidivism, and drug use and be more cost-effective than standard criminal justice responses. Nevertheless, these novel programs may benefit from more standardized approaches. Utilizing empirically proven strategies will enable these programs to maximize their success and serve as a model for other jurisdictions considering adoption of these programs. As there are still many challenges that make development, implementation, and operations difficult, additional research is needed to determine the key mechanisms of action responsible for the short- and long-term success of these innovative programs.

References

Ahern, J., Stuber, J., & Galea, S. (2007). Stigma, discrimination and the health of illicit drug users. *Drug and Alcohol Dependence, 88*(2), 188–196.

Albany LEAD Policy Coordinating Group. (2017). *Report to Albany on the LEAD program: One-year anniversary.* https://d3n8a8pro7vhmx.cloudfront.net/katal/pages/1743/attachments/original/1517565036/2017_Albany_LEAD_First_Year_Report.pdf?1517565036

Andrews, D. A., & Bonta, J. (2010). *The psychology of criminal conduct* (5th ed.). Anderson.

American Society of Addiction Medicine. (2017). *The ASAM criteria.* http://asamcontinuum.org/wp-content/uploads/2017/05/The-ASAM-Criteria_2017_pg1n2_PRINT_FINAL_v9_small.pdf

American Society of Addiction Medicine. (2016). *The ASAM criteria & continuum—The ASAM criteria decision engine.* http://asamcontinuum.org/wp-content/uploads/2016/07/CONTINUUMTM-BriefDescriptionBibliography-2016_01-27.pdf

Barberi, D., & Taxman, F. S. (2019). Diversion and alternatives to arrest: A qualitative understanding of police and substance users' perspective. *Journal of Drug Issues, 49*(4), 703–717.

Bassuk, E. L., Hanson, J., Greene, R. N., Richard, M., & Laudet, A. (2016). Peer-delivered recovery support services for addictions in the United States: A systematic review. *Journal of Substance Abuse Treatment, 63,* 1–9.

Bastomski, S., Cramer, L., & Reimal, E. (2019). *Evaluation of the Contra Costa County Law Enforcement Assisted Diversion Plus Program: Interim evaluation report.* Urban Institute.

Binswanger, I. A., Stern, M. F., Deyo, R. A., Heagerty, P. J., Cheadle, A., Elmore, J. G., & Koepsell, T. D. (2007). Release from prison—A high risk of death for former inmates. *New England Journal of Medicine, 356*(2), 157–165.

Borack, J. I. (1998). An estimate of the impact of drug testing on the deterrence of drug use. *Military Psychology, 10*(1), 17–25.

Bogue, B., Woodward, W., & Joplin, L. (2006). *Using a proxy score to pre-screen offenders for risk to reoffend.* Center for the Study and Prevention of Violence.

Bronson, J., Stroop, J., Zimmer, S., & Berzofsky, M. (2017). *Drug use, dependence, and abuse among state prisoners and jail inmates, 2007–2009.* United States Department of Justice, Office of Juvenile Justice and Delinquency Prevention.

Chandler, R. K., Fletcher, B. W., & Volkow, N. D. (2009). Treating drug abuse and addiction in the criminal justice system: Improving public health and safety. *Journal of the American Medical Association, 301*(2), 183–190.

Chapman, S. A., Blash, L. K., Mayer, K., & Spetz, J. (2018). Emerging roles for peer providers in mental health and substance use disorders. *American Journal of Preventive Medicine, 54*(6), S267–S274.

Charlier, J. (2019, July). Legislative opportunities for justice: innovation, reform, and the basics. *Midwestern Legislative Conference.* Talk conducted at the meeting of the Council of State Governments, Chicago, IL.

Clifasefi, S. L., Lonczak, H. S., & Collins, S. E. (2016). *LEAD program evaluation: the impact of LEAD on housing, employment and income/benefits.* http://static1.1.sqspcdn.com/static/f/1185392/27047605/1464389327667/housing_employment_evaluation_final.PDF?token=jH%2BIkci5zJgC%2Bpldu1NI%2FATFJKY%3D

Collins, S. E., Lonczak, H. S., & Clifasefi, S. L. (2015a). *LEAD program evaluation: Criminal justice and legal system utilization and associated costs.* http://static1.1.sqspcdn.com/static/f/1185392/26401889/1437170937787/June+2015+LEAD-Program-Evaluation-Criminal-Justice-and-Legal-System-Utilization-and-Associated-Costs.pdf?token=qljoeExWHAzc5kNLv2K2CP7yD8w%3D

Collins, S. E., Lonczak, H. S., & Clifasefi, S. L. (2015b). *LEAD program evaluation: Recidivism report.* http://static1.1.sqspcdn.com/static/f/1185392/26121870/1428513375150/LEAD_EVALUATION_4-7-15.pdf?token=nF67fmYBtdKVr8gfiUwwQqbKDR0%3D

Collins, S. E., Lonczak, H. S., & Clifasefi, S. L. (2019). Seattle's law enforcement assisted diversion (LEAD): Program effects on criminal justice and legal system utilization and costs. *Journal of Experimental Criminology, 15*(2), 201–211.

Darke, S. (1998). Self-report among injecting drug users: A review. *Drug and Alcohol Dependence, 51*(3), 253–263.

DeMatteo, D., Heilbrun, K., Thornewill, A., & Arnold, S. (2019). *Problem-solving courts and the criminal justice system.* Oxford University Press.

DeMatteo, D. S., Marlowe, D. B., & Festinger, D. S. (2006). Secondary prevention services for clients who are low risk in drug court: A conceptual model. *Crime & Delinquency, 52*(1), 114–134.

Department of Justice. (2015). *Crime in the United States 2014—Arrests, FBI Uniform Crime Report.* http://www.drugwarfacts.org/cms/Crime#sthash.uWQETMYZ.dpuf

Dugosh, K. L., Festinger, D.S., Clements, N. T., & Marlowe, D. B. (2014). Alternative tracks for low-risk and low-need participants in a misdemeanor drug court: Preliminary outcomes. *Drug Court Review, 9*(1), 43–55.

Festinger, D. S., Marlowe, D. B., Lee, P. A., Kirby, K. C., Bovasso, G., & McLellan, A. T. (2002). Status hearings in drug court: when more is less and less is more. *Drug and Alcohol Dependence, 68*(2), 151–157.

Fletcher, D. R. (2007). Offenders in the post-industrial labour market: lubricating the revolving door? *People, Place & Policy Online, 1/2*, 80–89. http://doi.org/10.3351/ppp.0001.0002.0004

Gastfriend, D. R., & McLellan, A. T. (1997). Treatment matching: Theoretic basis and practical implications. *Medical Clinics of North America, 81*(4), 945–966.

Gastfriend, D. R., & Mee-Lee, D. (2004). The ASAM patient placement criteria: Context, concepts and continuing development. *Journal of Addictive Diseases, 22*(Suppl. 1), 1–8.

Goetz, B., & Mitchell, R. E. (2006). Pre-arrest/booking drug control strategies: Diversion to treatment, harm reduction and police involvement. *Contemporary Drug Problems, 33*(3), 473–520.

Hartford, K., Carey, R., & Mendonca, J. (2006). Pre-arrest diversion of people with mental illness: Literature review and international survey. *Behavioral Sciences & the Law, 24*(6), 845–856.

Hawken, A., & Kleiman, M. (2009). *Managing drug involved probationers with swift and certain sanctions: Evaluating Hawaii's HOPE: executive summary.* National Criminal Justice Reference Services.

Huddleston, W., & Marlowe, D.B. (2011). *Painting the current picture: A national report on drug courts and other problem solving court programs in the United States.* National Drug Court Institute. http://www.ndci.org/sites/default/files/nadcp/PCP%20Report%20FINAL.PDF

Institute of Medicine. (1990). *Broadening the base of treatment for alcohol problems.* National Academy Press.

Kopak, A. M. (2018). An initial assessment of Leon County Florida's Pre-Arrest Adult Civil Citation Program. *Journal of Behavioral Health Services & Research, 46*, 177–186.

Kopak, A. M., & Frost, G. A. (2017). Correlates of program success and recidivism among participants in an adult pre-arrest diversion program. *American Journal of Criminal Justice, 42*(4), 727–745.

Kilpatrick, B., Howlett, M., Sedgwick, P., & Ghodse, A. H. (2000). Drug use, self-report and urinalysis. *Drug and Alcohol Dependence, 58*(1), 111–116.

King, R. S. (2008). *Disparity by geography: The war on drugs in America's cities.* https://www.opensocietyfoundations.org/sites/default/files/disparity_geography_20080501.pdf

Kleiman, M.A.R. (2004). Toward (more nearly) optimal sentencing for drug offenders. *Criminology & Public Policy 3*(3), 435–440. https://doi.org/10.1111/j.1745-9133.2004.tb00051.x

Knight, K., Simpson, D. D., & Morey, J. T. (2002). *An evaluation of the TCU Drug Screen.* National Institute of Justice, Office of Justice Programs, U.S. Department of Justice.

Langan, P. A., & Levin, D. J. (2002). Recidivism of prisoners released in 1994. *Federal Sentencing Reporter, 15*(1), 58–65.

LEAD. (n.d.) *About LEAD.* http://leadkingcounty.org/about/#faq

LEAD National Support Bureau. (2020a). *Core principles and fact sheet.* https://www.leadbureau.org/resources

LEAD National Support Bureau. (2020b). *LEAD: Advancing criminal justice reform in 2020 [U.S. map illustrating locations of PAD programs].* http://leadbureau.org

LEAD Policy Coordinating Group (2015). *Law Enforcement Assisted Diversion (LEAD) referral and diversion protocol June 2015.* http://leadkingcounty.org/about

Leshner, A. I. (1999). Science-based views of drug addiction and its treatment. *Journal of the American Medical Association, 282*(14), 1314–1316.

Link, B. G., Struening, E. L., Rahav, M., Phelan, J. C., & Nuttbrock, L. (1997). On stigma and its consequences: evidence from a longitudinal study of men with dual diagnoses of mental illness and substance abuse. *Journal of Health and Social Behavior, 38*(2), 177–190.

Livingston, J. D., Milne, T., Fang, M. L., & Amari, E. (2012). The effectiveness of interventions for reducing stigma related to substance use disorders: A systematic review. *Addiction, 107*(1), 39–50.

Magura, S., Staines, G., Kosanke, N., Rosenblum, A., Foote, J., DeLuca, A., & Bali, P. (2003). Predictive validity of the ASAM Patient Placement Criteria for naturalistically matched vs. mismatched alcoholism patients. *American Journal on Addictions, 12*(5), 386–397.

Marlowe, D. B. (2002). Effective strategies for intervening with drug abusing offenders. *Villanova Law Review, 47*, 989–1025.

Marlowe, D. B., DeMatteo, D. S., & Festinger, D. S. (2003). A sober assessment of drug courts. *Federal Sentencing Reporter, 16*(2), 153–157.

Marlowe, D. B., Festinger, D. S., Dugosh, K. L., Caron, A., Podkopacz, M. R., & Clements, N. T. (2011). Targeting dispositions for drug-involved offenders: a field trial of the Risk and Needs Triage (RANT™). *Journal of Criminal Justice, 39*(3), 253–260.

Marlowe, D. B., Festinger, D. S., Foltz, C., Lee, P. A., & Patapis, N. S. (2005). Perceived deterrence and outcomes in drug court. *Behavioral Sciences & the Law, 23*(2), 183–198.

Marlowe, D. B., Festinger, D. S., Lee, P.A., Dugosh, K. L., & Benasutti, K. M. (2006). Matching judicial supervision to clients' risk status in drug court. *Crime & Delinquency, 52,* 52–76.

Marlowe, D. B., Patapis, N. S., & DeMatteo, D. S. (2003). Amenability to treatment of drug offenders. *Federal Probation, 67*(2), 40–46.

McLellan, A. T., Hagan, T. A., Levine, M., Meyers, K., Gould, F., Bencivengo, M., Durell, J., & Jaffe, J. (1999). Does clinical case management improve outpatient addiction treatment? *Drug and Alcohol Dependence, 55*(1), 91–103.

Mitchell, O., Wilson, D. B., Eggers, A., & MacKenzie, D. L. (2012). Assessing the effectiveness of drug courts on recidivism: A meta-analytic review of traditional and non-traditional drug courts. *Journal of Criminal Justice, 40*(1), 60–71.

Munetz, M. R., & Griffin, P. A. (2006). Use of the sequential intercept model as an approach to decriminalization of people with serious mental illness. *Psychiatric Services, 57*(4), 544–549.

National Association of Drug Court Professionals. (1997). *Defining drug courts: The key components.* Office of Justice Programs, U.S. Department of Justice.

National Association of Drug Court Professionals. (2013). *Adult drug court best practice standards, Volume 1.* Office of Justice Programs, U.S. Department of Justice.

http://www.nadcp.org/sites/default/files/nadcp/AdultDrugCourtBestPracticeStandards.pdf

New Mexico Sentencing Commission. (2018). *Evaluation of LEAD Santa Fe: A summary report of findings of a 3-year pilot period.* https://www.lead-santafe.org/wp-content/uploads/2018/10/LEAD-Report-_Final_10 818.pdf

Office of National Drug Control Policy (2014). *2013 Annual report: Arrestee Drug Abuse Monitoring Program II.* Executive Office of the President.

Open Society Foundation. (2015). *Drug courts: Equivocal evidence on a popular intervention.* Csete, J., & Tomasini-Joshi, D.

Perrone, D., Malm, A., Magana, E., Bueno, E. (2018). *Law Enforcement Assisted Diversion (LEAD) external evaluation: San Francisco LEAD fidelity assessment.* California State University Long Beach, School of Criminology, Criminal Justice and Emergency Management.

Pew Charitable Trusts. (2012). Time served: The high cost, low return on prison terms. http://www.pewtrusts. org/~/media/assets/2012/06/06/time_served_report.pdf

Pew Charitable Trusts. (2017). *The lack of a relationship between drug imprisonment and drug problems. Letter to Governor Chris Christie.* https://www.pewtrusts.org/~/media/assets/2017/06/the-lack-of-a-relationship-between-drug-imprisonment-and-drug-problems.pdf

Police Executive Research Forum. (2012). *An integrated approach to de-escalation and minimizing use of force.* http://www.policeforum.org/assets/docs/Critical_Issues_Series/an%20integrated%20approach%20to%20 de-escalation%20and%20minimizing%20use%20of%20force%202012.pdf

Pugh, T., Frederique, K., Netherland, J., Meeks, S.M., Finkelstein, R., & Sayegh, G. (2013). *Blueprint for a public health and safety approach to drug policy.* http://www.countthecosts.org/sites/default/NY-Academy-of-medicine-Blueprint.pdf

Rapp, R. C., Van Den Noortgate, W., Broekaert, E., & Vanderplasschen, W. (2014). The efficacy of case management with persons who have substance abuse problems: A three-level meta-analysis of outcomes. *Journal of Consulting and Clinical Psychology, 82*(4), 605–618.

Reif, S., Braude, L., Lyman, D. R., Dougherty, R. H., Daniels, A. S., Ghose, S. S., Salim, O., & Delphin-Rittmon, M. E. (2014). Peer recovery support for individuals with substance use disorders: Assessing the evidence. *Psychiatric Services, 65*(7), 853–861.

Sevigny, E. L., Fuleihan, B. K., & Ferdik, F. V. (2013). Do drug courts reduce the use of incarceration? A meta-analysis. *Journal of Criminal Justice, 41*(6), 416–425.

Shaffer, D. K. (2011). Looking inside the black box of drug courts: A meta-analytic review. *Justice Quarterly, 28*(3), 493–521.

Sharon, E., Krebs, C., Turner, W., Desai, N., Binus, G., Penk, W., & Gastfriend, D. R. (2003). Predictive validity of the ASAM Patient Placement Criteria for hospital utilization. *Journal of Addictive Disease, 22*(Suppl. 1), 79–93.

Stallvik, M. & Gastfriend, D.R. (2014). Predictive and convergent validity of the ASAM criteria software in Norway. *Addiction Research & Theory, 22*(6), 515–523.

Substance Abuse and Mental Health Services Administration. (2015). *Law enforcement and behavioral health partnerships for early diversion.* http://www.samhsa.gov/gains-center/grants-grantees/early-diversion

Taxman, F. S., & Marlowe, D. (2006). Risk, needs, responsivity: In action or inaction? *Crime and Delinquency, 52*(1), 3–6.

Teller, J. L., Munetz, M. R., Gil, K. M., & Ritter, C. (2006). Crisis intervention team training for police officers responding to mental disturbance calls. *Psychiatric Services, 57*(2), 232–237.

US Sentencing Commission. (2016). *Recidivism among federal offenders: A comprehensive overview.* https://www.ussc.gov/sites/default/files/pdf/research-and-publications/research-publications/2016/recidivism_overview.pdf

University of California, Los Angeles. (2007). *Evaluation of the Substance Abuse and Crime Prevention Act: Final report.* UCLA Integrated Substance Abuse Programs.

Vakili, S., Currie, S., & el-Guebaly, N. (2009). Evaluating the utility of drug testing in an outpatient addiction program. *Addictive Disorders & Their Treatment, 8*(1), 22–32.

Wexler, D. B. (1999). *Therapeutic jurisprudence: An overview.* https://law2.arizona.edu/depts/upr-intj/intj-o.html

Worden, R. E., & McLean, S. J. (2018). Discretion and diversion in Albany's LEAD program. *Criminal Justice Policy Review, 29*(6–7), 584–610.

Zanis, D. A., McLellan, A. T., & Randall, M. (1994). Can you trust patient self-reports of drug use during treatment? *Drug and Alcohol Dependence, 35*(2), 127–132.

Rehabilitative Justice: Problem-Solving Courts

Shelby Arnold, Alice Thornewill, Kirk Heilbrun, *and* David DeMatteo

Abstract

This chapter reviews the context, history, and development of problem-solving courts. We describe common components, the Risk-Needs-Responsivity model and clinical interventions, the range of courts and their unique focus, along with the strengths and limitations of the problem-solving court model. We then review the research base for key types of problem-solving courts (e.g., drug courts and mental health courts), with a focus on meta-analytic research whenever possible and a discussion of methodological challenges and limitations of the literature. The chapter also highlights the ethical and legal considerations for problem-solving courts and outlines areas for future research and development.

Key Words: rehabilitative justice, problem-solving courts, drug courts, mental health courts, veterans treatment courts, reentry courts, therapeutic jurisprudence, risk--need--responsivity

The overrepresentation of individuals with behavioral health challenges in the criminal justice system is striking. An estimated 25–40 percent of individuals with mental health disorders will become involved with the criminal justice system at some point in their lives (Hasselbrack, 2001), and a recent estimate found that approximately 1 million individuals with a major mental disorder are currently justice involved (Peterson et al., 2014). These figures increase when substance abuse is taken into account, with more than 80 percent of criminal offenders presenting with a substance-related offense or a substance abuse problem (DeMatteo et al., 2015).

Research indicates, however, that mental illness does not have a clear or direct relationship with criminal offending (Andrews et al., 2006). Rather, offenders with mental illness may be more likely to recidivate based on factors such as insecure housing, lack of employment, ongoing substance abuse problems, and victimization (Skeem et al., 2011). With regard to substance abuse, research shows that an estimated 95 percent of offenders relapse within three years of release from incarceration (DeMatteo et al., 2015). These data are concerning given the high rates of recidivism among offenders with substance abuse problems, with some studies showing a 200–400 percent increase in reoffense risk for substance-using offenders (Bennett et al., 2008). Research also shows that co-occurring mental health and substance use disorders are related to even higher levels of recidivism and criminogenic risk (e.g., Balyakina et al., 2014).

This chapter focuses on problem-solving courts, a judicial intervention developed to address the high rates of offenders with behavioral health challenges. We begin by discussing common elements, strengths, and limitations across various types of problem-solving courts. We then review the research for key types of problem-solving courts, with a focus on meta-analytic research whenever possible and a discussion of methodological challenges and limitations of the literature. Finally, we discuss the ethical and legal considerations for problem-solving courts and areas for future research and development.

Therapeutic Jurisprudence and Alternatives to Standard Prosecution

The overrepresentation of mental health and substance use disorders in the criminal justice system can be usefully considered through the model of therapeutic jurisprudence, a rehabilitative legal approach that relies on behavioral science to increase the therapeutic impact of the legal system (Winick, 2013; Wexler & Winick, 1996). Problem-solving justice represents an outgrowth of therapeutic jurisprudence and is guided by the following principles: (1) enhanced information to allow courts to make more informed decisions regarding rehabilitation; (2) increased community engagement, especially between justice-involved individuals and the public; (3) collaboration between legal partners and community stakeholders; (4) individualized approach to treatment and legal consequences; (5) increased accountability and monitoring for justice-involved individuals; and (6) ongoing research to evaluate effectiveness of problem-solving interventions and facilitate ongoing improvements (see Berman, 2009; Wolf, 2007).

Standard criminal justice processing for offenders with mental health or substance use challenges has not produced significant improvement in terms of drug abuse, mental health, or recidivism rates (Heilbrun et al., 2012). Partly as a result, a paradigm shift toward a rehabilitative justice model has been taking place over the last two decades that has included the development of a variety of alternative methods to standard prosecution. These alternative methods typically consist of individualized interventions tailored to address the unique behavioral health needs and specific risk factors of certain offenders (DeMatteo et al., 2013). This rehabilitative approach aims to identify and target the criminogenic and behavioral health needs of an offender, and as a result reduce the likelihood of future offending (Skeem & Monahan, 2011).

History and Development of Problem-Solving Courts

Problem-solving courts (PSCs) were developed for offenders with mental health and substance use disorders. PSCs are an alternative to standard prosecution that focus on treating the psychological issues underlying criminal behavior. In 1989, the first PSC was established in Dade Country, Florida. This court, a drug court, targeted the revolving door of drug-related cases facing criminal courts in that county. Since then, there has been a proliferation of drugs courts across the country. As of 2016, there were more than 3,000 operational drugs courts in the United States serving more than 125,000 offenders each year (Marlowe et al., 2016). These drug courts were unique from typical criminal courts in that they provided judicial oversight over treatment, mandatory drug testing, and rehabilitative treatment. On the heels of the rapid growth and success of drug courts came the development of several other types of PSCs, including mental health courts, veterans courts, DUI courts, family dependency courts, co-occurring disorder courts, reentry courts, gambling courts, community courts, truancy courts, and domestic violence courts.

Given the distinctive nature of PSCs, only certain offenders are eligible for participation; violent offenders or those with certain charges (e.g., sex offenses and arson) are typically precluded (DeMatteo et al., 2019). However, there is substantial variability among PSCs in terms of inclusion/exclusion criteria for participants. Some PSCs accept participants with certain types of felony charges whereas others only include those with misdemeanors (Hiday & Ray, 2010). Some PSCs require participants to plead guilty as a condition of participation whereas others do not have any plea requirements (DeMatteo et al., 2019). Mental health courts typically require that participants have a DSM-5 (*Diagnostic and Statistical Manual of Mental Disorders*, 5th edition) diagnosis, whereas participants in drugs courts typically need an established substance use history (Wolff et al., 2011). Finally, PSC participants are typically required to agree to comply with prescribed treatment and heightened court supervision.

General Strengths and Limitations of Problem-Solving Courts

To better understand the nature of the specific types of PSCs (discussed later in this chapter), it is useful to describe the strengths and limitations of these courts. In terms of strengths, empirical evidence suggests that the PSC model is effective in addressing drug use, mental health symptoms, and recidivism. Moreover, these courts increase offender access to treatment and services, lead to better-informed judges and legal actors, and enhance public confidence in the criminal justice system (Berman & Feinblatt, 2002). Moreover, the public appears to support the paradigm shift away from traditional punishment and toward a rehabilitative model. Criticisms include concerns about potential violations of the constitutional rights of participants, a lack of clarity on how to blend traditional roles of legal actors with the collaborative team approach, and potential judicial overreach (Berman & Feinblatt, 2002).

Problem-Solving Court Stakeholders

Given the distinctive nature of PSCs, stakeholders, including the judge, defense attorney, prosecutor, case managers, and community treatment providers, play unique roles. PSC judges work collaboratively with the legal actors and community providers to address the needs of participants, a major departure from the standard criminal court approach that involves imposing a punishment based almost entirely on the defendant's charge (Wolf,

2007). While the judge takes a more active role, defense attorneys in PSCs typically take a less active role to allow the participant and judge to communicate and support the treatment recommendations of the PSC team (Berman & Feinblatt, 2002). Prosecutors are also encouraged to relinquish the adversarial approach and work collaboratively with defense attorneys and the rest of the team (Faraci, 2004). PSCs often include case managers to gather detailed information about the mental health and/or substance use issues of participants and help legal stakeholders make informed treatment decisions (Wolf, 2007). Finally, active involvement of community treatment providers is essential to facilitate treatment referrals, educate legal actors, and provide services (Wolf, 2007).

The Risk–Needs–Responsivity Model and Clinical Interventions

The aim of PSCs is to reduce recidivism by targeting behavioral health needs underlying criminal behavior, so it is important to understand the risk–need–responsivity (RNR) model as a framework for evaluating criminogenic risk factors and addressing clinical needs (Andrews et al., 1990). According to the *risk* principle, those with higher risk levels should receiver higher levels of intervention or treatment (Andrews et al., 1990). The *need* principle posits that treatment should target an individual's specific criminogenic risk factors, which may include antisocial personality patterns, criminal thinking, problematic peer relationships, substance abuse, poor family relationships, limited educational/vocational achievements, and lack of prosocial leisure activities (Andrews et al., 2006). Finally, according to the *responsivity* principle, treatment should be evidence-based and individualized to meet the unique needs of each individual (Andrews et al., 2006).

Several empirically-supported interventions may be used in PSCs. Cognitive-behavioral treatment (CBT) interventions focus on identifying and reframing distorted thoughts that may cause distressing emotions and in turn lead to problematic behavior (Beck, 1976). In criminal justice settings, CBT interventions may help offenders identify and reframe criminal thinking, such as justification of offending behavior, blame displacement, entitlement, or irrational optimism (Heilbrun et al., 2016; Lipsey et al., 2007). Such interventions also focus on skill developing, such as anger management, relapse prevention, and social skills training (Lipsey et al., 2007). Examples of justice-specific CBT interventions include *Thinking for a Change* (Bush et al., 1997) and *Reasoning and Rehabilitation* (Ross et al., 1986).

Problem-solving interventions are used to address poor problem-solving skills that may lead to risky behavior patterns such as drug use or aggression (Heilbrun et al., 2016). These interventions focus on training based on cognitive problem-solving models (e.g., Spivack et al., 1976) and therapy using the social problem-solving framework (e.g., D'Zurilla & Goldfried, 1971) to help offenders recognize problematic thinking and develop skills to apply in challenging situations. Examples of specific problem-solving interventions include *Think First* (McGuire & Hatcher, 2001) and *Stop & Think* (McMurran et al., 2008). Given the relationship between substance use and risk, recommended substance use interventions include therapeutic communities, which incorporate intensive individual and group therapy focused on addiction and developing strategies to manage urges and triggers (Inciardi et al., 2004), or twelve-step programs (e.g., Alcoholics Anonymous) (DeMatteo et al., 2019).

Research Summary

The research base supporting the effectiveness of PSCs has grown considerably over the past twenty-five years, but it is not without its challenges and limitations. This section reviews the evidence for key types of PSCs, with a specific focus on large-scale, multisite, and meta-analytic research. Although there are more specific types of PSCs than those addressed below (e.g., gambling courts and gun courts), there was little to no available research on their effectiveness, so they are not included in the summary. We also discuss methodological considerations and shortcomings within the available literature.

Drug Courts

The research base on drug courts is the largest among PSCs and includes several large-scale or meta-analytic reviews. Unlike other types of PSCs, many of these studies also evaluate the impact of drug courts on target clinical outcomes (e.g., substance use and relapse). In general, research supports drug courts as an effective intervention for reducing substance use and recidivism.

Several randomized controlled trials (RCTs) conducted on drug courts show generally positive outcomes (reduced recidivism) for drug court graduates despite some limitations in the data (e.g., Deschenes et al., 1995; Gottfredson et al., 2003). A fifteen-year follow-up study was recently published for the RCT conducted in Baltimore City's Drug Treatment Court, and it found reduced rates of arrest, charges, and convictions for drug court participants, but no significant differences in length of time spent incarcerated (Kearley & Gottfredson, 2020).

Summative research on drug courts began approximately ten years after their creation, and these early reports concluded they were successful at reducing recidivism (e.g., Belenko, 2001). Numerous studies on individual drug courts have been used as the basis for several key meta-analytic studies, most of which report positive outcomes for drug court graduates. A meta-analysis by Mitchell et al. (2012) included ninety-two evaluations of drug courts and found an average drop in recidivism from 50 percent to 38 percent at a three-year follow-up. Prior meta-analyses that included both experimental and quasi-experimental evaluations showed effect sizes representing an 8–26 percent decrease in recidivism, with most in the 8–14 percent range (Drake et al., 2009; Lowenkamp et al., 2005; Shaffer, 2011; Wilson et al., 2006). Though positive outcomes are seen on a larger scale, individual studies show mixed results, with approximately 15 percent of drug courts showing no significant impact on recidivism (Logan & Link, 2019). Further, a small percentage of programs (6 percent) have been associated with increases in recidivism (Lowenkamp et al., 2005; Shaffer, 2006).

Mitchell et al. (2012) conducted the only meta-analysis that includes future substance use as an outcome. However, of the ninety-two studies included in this meta-analysis, only nine incorporated a measure of participants' substance use in follow-up research and only four looked at adult drug courts (Mitchell et al., 2012). Multisite studies show that drug court graduates experience overall reductions in substance use but not consistently to the extent of statistical significance (e.g., Green & Rempel, 2012; Rossman, Rempel, et al., 2011).

As noted above, recidivism outcomes are somewhat less promising. In a meta-analysis by Sevigny et al. (2013), participants were less likely to be reincarcerated but did not show a reduction in the length of time spent incarcerated, suggesting the possibility that those who fail drug court programs face equally long, if not longer, sentences that offset the overall reduction in reincarceration rates. In a recent multisite national study of approximately 2,300 drug court participants, older age and employment emerged as protective factors against rearrests (Wilson et al., 2018).

Some studies have also examined the impact of drug courts on additional social and economic outcomes. The Multisite Adult Drug Court Evaluation (MADCE) found that drug courts improve access to educational/vocational and treatment-related services for offenders, and that they positively affect family and other social relationships (Green & Rempel, 2012; Rossman, Rempel, et al., 2011). Drug court participation does not appear to have a significant impact on housing, financial status, and mental health (Rossman, Rempel, et al., 2011). Cost-benefit analyses show mixed results on whether drug courts save money for their respective communities (Belenko et al., 2005; Bhati et al., 2008; Government Accountability Office, 2011).

In summary, the drug court literature is the most well developed of all problem-solving courts. Drug courts appear to be an effect intervention for reducing recidivism, while also improving substance use outcomes for participants. Though the research on additional outcomes (e.g., jail time, social service access, and cost-effectiveness) is mixed, these outcomes are less frequently evaluated and thus would be a useful area for the development of the research base.

Mental Health Courts

The research on mental health courts is notably limited compared to drug courts, especially considering their widespread proliferation. Although many single court studies have been published, very little aggregate research has been conducted. Meta-analyses have a limited sample size due to significant methodological flaws of the individual studies. (For a summary of single-court program evaluations and peer-reviewed articles, see DeMatteo et al., 2019.)

The focus of meta-analyses and systematic reviews has been on mental health courts' impact on recidivism. The first meta-analysis of mental health courts included eighteen studies and showed that mental health courts are moderately effective in reducing recidivism (d = 0.54), but this study had notable limitations in inclusion criteria and statistical methods (Sarteschi et al., 2011). A 2015 systematic review found that most studies (twelve of fifteen) reported significant recidivism reduction for participants (Honegger, 2015). A 2018 meta-analysis (which included studies through 2015) analyzed seventeen studies and found a small effect of mental health court participation on recidivism reduction (d = 0.20), but the methodological limitations of the individual studies should be considered when interpreting these results (Lowder et al., 2018). An additional meta-analysis that included twenty-four studies supports the conclusion that mental health courts have a small effect on recidivism (Arnold, 2019).

Mental health–related outcomes are a less common focus of research despite being a treatment goal of mental health courts. Less than half of the studies included in meta-analyses evaluated a mental health outcome in addition to a recidivism outcome (Arnold, 2019; Honnegger, 2015). Though many single court studies included a measure of mental health, the heterogeneity of how this was operationally defined (e.g., well-established measures vs. locally developed symptom ratings, connection to treatment services, crisis service utilization, and hospitalization rates) makes it challenging to synthesize findings on a broad level (see DeMatteo et al., 2019, for a summary).

Overall, the research on mental health courts shows a small to moderate impact on recidivism and suggests promise as an intervention. However, the research base has notable methodological flaws. All the meta-analyses discussed are limited by idiosyncrasies within the individual studies, suggesting that these courts are more challenging to research. Furthermore, the evidence that mental health courts have a positive impact on mental health–related outcomes is limited and mixed, highlighting a need for future research.

Veterans Treatment Courts

There is very little research on veterans treatment courts. There are fewer such courts—and they are relatively new. A survey of fourteen veterans treatment courts conducted just a few years after their inception revealed a recidivism rate of less than 2 percent, but the limited number of graduates across the courts (N = 59) limits meaningful conclusions (Holbrook & Anderson, 2011). A few single court and large-scale studies show promising reductions in recidivism, but they did not use a comparison group in their analyses and must be interpreted with caution (Commaroto et al., 2011; Tsai et al., 2018). Veterans treatment courts show promise in reducing symptoms of substance abuse and posttraumatic stress disorder (PTSD) (Slattery et al., 2013; Tsai et al., 2018), but many studies of veterans treatment courts have significant methodological limitations (e.g., use of qualitative or anecdotal data, lack of or biased comparison groups; see Christy et al., 2012), and there is a great need for future research to better gauge their effectiveness.

Reentry Courts

Reentry court research is less developed than that of drug courts and mental health courts, with very few multisite or meta-analytic studies. The research focuses primarily on process evaluations or implementation lessons rather than outcomes (Lindquist et al., 2004, 2013). Although some studies report reductions in recidivism rates for participants (e.g., Administrative Office of the Courts, 2012; Hamilton 2010; Spelman, 2003), some research shows poorer outcomes for reentry court participants (e.g., Severson et al., 2011; Wilson & Davis, 2006). One large-scale multisite study across sixteen reentry courts did not find any significant differences in recidivism between reentry court participants and nonparticipants (Lattimore & Visher, 2009, 2014). However, researchers found improvements across other domains for reentry court participants, such as substance abuse, housing, and employment (Lattimore & Visher, 2009). For a thorough discussion of model reentry courts and a summary of process evaluations, see DeMatteo et al., 2019. Overall, researchers note that the support for reentry courts is promising, but not enough to draw robust conclusions about their effectiveness (Lindquist et al., 2013; Marlowe et al., 2016).

Methodological Challenges

Research supporting PSCs has grown considerably in recent decades, but not all courts are as well studied as others and many evaluations have notable limitations that impact the ability to draw conclusions about effectiveness. Drug courts are well researched and well supported, but the expansion of mental health courts seems to have outpaced the research, though they show promise. There is a small body of research on other types of PSCs (e.g., reentry courts and veterans treatment courts), highlighting a great area of need within the field. PSC research is challenging due to logistical, ethical, and legal concerns, and this section discusses key limitations in the PSC literature.

One key limitation of PSC research is the lack of RCTs (DeMatteo et al., 2011, 2019). True random selection and assignment in these settings is challenging and raises ethical and legal concerns about fair criminal justice processing (Government Accountability Office, 2005). As a result, most PSC evaluations are quasi-experimental, focusing on participants in the court and a similar group of nonparticipants. Although quasi-experimental studies can provide important information, these studies must be interpreted with caution and do not permit defensible causal inferences (Kazdin, 2017).

Within existing studies, sample-related issues also limit generalizability of findings. Many studies are comprised of relatively small samples. This limitation is seen among drug courts (e.g., Latimer et al., 2006), mental health courts (e.g., Arnold, 2019), reentry courts (Listswan, 2008), and DUI courts (Miller et al., 2015). Small sample size and high attrition rates also complicate the ability to conduct longitudinal research, highlighting an additional limitation of many studies. Further, samples included in PSC research often do not accurately represent the demographic characteristics in the criminal justice system. For example, researchers have observed an overrepresentation of White female participants in drug courts and mental health courts, suggesting that results from studies relying on these samples may not apply to the criminal justice population (Hiday et al., 2005; Sarteschi et al., 2011).

Another important limitation of many PSC studies relates to comparison groups. Many published studies do not use a comparison group, and many of the studies that include comparison groups struggle to accurately match samples. Moreover, due to the lack of randomization, there may be unique differences between individuals who choose versus decline to participate in PSCs (DeMatteo et al., 2019). Differences between groups may also be reflected in idiosyncratic inclusion criteria (e.g., some courts choose to accept only lower-risk offenders), which can skew or artificially inflate positive outcomes (DeMatteo et al., 2019).

Another issue frequently raised with PSC research is the process by which data are collected. Critics have suggested researchers rely on biased control groups, withhold data from participants who do not successfully complete court requirements, and overuse self-report measures (Fischer, 2003; Rowland, 2016). Further, outcome variables between studies may appear to be similar but may involve differences in how the variables are measured. Also, although recidivism is an important outcome, some studies focus exclusively on recidivism to the exclusion of other important outcomes. Further, although PSCs include many similar elements, there are multiple models for each type of PSC, and the services offered vary based on the resources available in a given community, which impacts the ability to conduct meta-analyses. Finally, research is limited by funding and permissions; many evaluations have been conducted on government-funded courts using government funding, but conducting research on courts without such funding may be challenging.

Legal and Constitutional Issues

Given that PSCs represent a major component of the paradigm shift toward a rehabilitative model within the justice system, particular emphasis must be placed on the legal considerations that accompany these courts. Considerations in this domain include how specialty courts impact constitutional rights in pleadings and competency, the role of the judge and the defense attorney, and the implications for procedural justice.

Constitutional rights are particularly relevant in PSCs because participants are typically required to waive some of their constitutional rights to enter the court (e.g., Hoffman, 1999; Nolan, 2003). According to the First Amendment's establishment clause, the state cannot coerce an individual to engage in a religious activity,[1] and several PSCs have been prohibited from requiring participants to engage in treatment programs with religious elements, such as Alcoholics Anonymous.[2] As such, a specialty court may only

---

[1] US Const. amend. I.

[2] E.g., Griffin v. Coughlin, 673 N.E.2d 98 (N.Y. 1996); Kerr v. Farrey, 95 F.3d 471 (7th Cir. 1996); Inouya v. Kemma, 504 F.3d 705 (9th Cir. 2007).

mandate treatment if participants are presented with a range of treatment programs that include secular options.[3] Specialty courts may ban participants from certain geographical locations or associating with certain people (Meyer, 2011), but restrictions that are not reasonable or not narrowly prescribed may violate the Freedom of Speech and Association Clause of the First Amendment.[4] For instance, a geographical restriction requiring the defendant to avoid any place where alcohol was sold, provided, or consumed was found to be overly broad and thus in violation of the First Amendment by an Ohio appellate court.[5] An overly broad association restriction was identified by an Alaska appellate court when it overturned a requirement that a defendant be prohibited from engaging in any unsupervised interactions with his wife, who was an active drug user.[6]

The Fourth Amendment, which prohibits the state from performing searches without probable cause, has also been considered as it relates to PSCs.[7] For instance, the Supreme Court has found it constitutional for drug courts to require participants to waive their Fourth Amendment rights and undergo searches without probable cause as a condition of participating in the court (Meyer, 2011).[8] In addition, courts have found it constitutional to search specialty court participants based on "reasonable suspicion" alone (rather than the stricter standard of probable cause)[9] and to protect public safety.[10] Some courts have found that specialty court participants who waive their Fourth Amendment rights may be searched even without any reason or suspicion of wrongdoing.[11] The Fourth Amendment also protects participants with regard to drug testing, as conditional drug testing must be reasonable and tailored to the participant.[12]

Several concerns have arisen regarding the ability PSCs to adhere to the Fourteenth Amendment's due process clause, which entitles all criminal defendants to equal treatment under the law and procedural protections.[13] These concerns include the nonadversarial

---

[3] American United v. Prison Fellowship, 509 F.3d 406 (8th Cir. 2007); Destefano v. Emergency Hous. Group, Inc., 247 F.3d 397 (2d Cir. 2001); O'Conner v. California, 855 F. Supp. 202 (C.D. Cal. 1994).

[4] E.g., Andrews v. State, 623 S.E.2d 247 (Ga. Ct. App. 2005).

[5] State v. Wright, 739 N.E.2d 1172 (Ohio Ct. App. 2000). For examples of cases where geographical restrictions were upheld, see Johnson v. State, 547 So. 2d 1048 (Fla. Dist. Ct. App. 1989); State v. Morgan, 389 So. 2d 364 (La. 1980).

[6] Dawson v. State, 894 P.2d 672 (Alaska Ct. App. 1995). For examples of cases where association restrictions were upheld, see 623 S.E.2d 247 (Ga. Ct. App. 2005); People v. Jungers, 25 Cal. Rptr. 3d 873 (Ct. App. 2005); People v. Forsythe, 43 P.3d 652 (Colo. Ct. App. 2001).

[7] U.S. Const. amend. IV)

[8] See Samson v. California, 547 U.S. 843 (2006).

[9] Griffin v. Wisconsin, 483 U.S. 888 (1987).

[10] Payne v. State, 615 S.E. 2d 564 (Ga. Ct. App. 2005); State v. Patton, 119 P.3d 250 (Ore. Ct. App. 2005).

[11] State v. Kouba, 709 N.W. 2d 299 (Minn. Ct. App. 2006); State v. McAuliffe, 125 P.3d 276 (Wyo. 2005).

[12] See Oliver v. United States, 682 A. 2d 186 (D.C. Cir. 1996); State v. Ullring, 741 A.2d 1045, 1045 (Me. 1999); Steiner v. State, 763 N.E. 2d 1024 (Ind. Ct. App. 2002).

[13] U.S. Const. amend. XIV.

method, potential paternalism of the judge, and increased oversight over participants' behaviors (Meyer, 2011).

The nonadversarial approach of PSCs emphasizes collaboration among the legal actors and stakeholders, which raises concerns regarding the defense attorney's ability to be a zealous advocate, especially as it relates to plea bargaining or interacting with the judge (Lane, 2002). A defense attorney who is collaborating with the prosecutor and the judge to determine the best court of action for the participant may risk losing vigor in exercising their duty to protect the best interests of the defendant.

Similarly, a PSC judge may struggle to adhere to their due process requirement to remain impartial,[14] as PSC judges are not only expected to have an active role in the proceedings,but to engage in informal communications with the PSC team and participant (Meyer, 2011). Although this more involved role may lead to positive outcomes for participants, including individualized treatment plans, it also creates more opportunity for judicial bias and may cloud a judge's ability to recognize when recusal is appropriate. Based on these considerations, some courts have held that a judge other than the PSC judge overseeing a participant's case should oversee termination hearings,[15] while other courts have found no need for an alternate judge.[16]

The Fourteenth Amendment's equal protection clause requires that similarly situated individuals be treated equally under the law.[17] As such, this right may be at issue when only certain individuals are permitted to engage in a PSC program. For drug courts, most challenges on this basis have been rejected; courts have found it is permissible for drugs courts to only accept certain individuals on the basis that they have a legitimate government interest in doing so.[18] Similarly, the fact that PSCs are not available in all jurisdictions has not been deemed an equal protection violation. In several cases, the rationale for these findings is that a jurisdiction's decision to not fund such a court can be rationally related to a legitimate government interest.[19]

Given the distinctive nature of PSCs, the role of procedural justice—defined as a defendant's rights to be treated with respect, have their voice heard in court, and be approached with impartiality—is particularly important. Research demonstrates that PSC participants feel they are treated fairly and respectfully (Dollar et al., 2018; Gottfredson et al., 2007; Poythress et al., 2002; Redlich & Han, 2014; Wales et al., 2010). Studies have shown that perceptions of procedural justice in mental health courts is related to improvement of mental health symptoms (Kopelovich et al., 2013), improved coping

---

[14] U.S. Cont. amend. XIV.

[15] Alexander v. State, 48 P.3d 110 (Okla. Crim. App. 2002).

[16] E.g., State v. Belyea, No. 2009-038, 2010 N.H. LEXIS 49 (N.H. May 20, 2010).

[17] U.S. Const. amend. XIV)

[18] E.g., Jim v. State, 911 So. 2d 658 (Miss. Ct. App. 2005); Evans v. State, 667 S.E.2d 183 (Ga. Ct. App. 2008).

[19] State v. Harner, 103 P.3d 738 (Wash. 4002); Lomont v. State, 852 N.E.2d 1002 (Ind. Ct. App. 2006).

skills (Ray & Dollar, 2014), and increased compliance (Redlich & Han, 2014). Research on procedural justice within drug courts has produced similar results (Rossman, Rempel, et al., 2011). Notably, however, a recent study found that Black PSC participants perceived significantly less procedural justice than their White counterparts (Atkin-Plunk et al., in press).

Future Directions

As more jurisdictions develop PSCs, it is important to clarify best practices in establishing and running these courts. Jurisdictions seeking to establish specialty courts should (1) develop the court based on the principles of therapeutic jurisprudence, (2) partner with providers who can administer evidence-based treatment, (3) design courts to meet the specific needs of a jurisdiction, and (4) clearly define the roles of stakeholders involved to effectively shift into a collaborative model.

Those working toward the establishment and expansion of PSCs should focus on incorporating components that have been supported by empirical evidence, specifically the evidence-based RNR model. The RNR model provides a valuable framework for identifying risks and needs and developing appropriate treatment to meet the individual needs of PSC participants (DeMatteo et al., 2019). Specialty courts should consider using this model to streamline certain elements of PSCs, including establishing efficient processes, defining clear inclusion/exclusion criteria, selecting evidence-based treatments to be used, and identifying clear outcome measures for program evaluation (DeMatteo et al., 2019).

As noted above, a major concern in studying PSCs relates to the significant variability among these courts. Not only do the various types of specialty courts differ from one another (i.e., drug courts primarily target substance abuse while mental health courts primarily target psychological disorders), but there is substantial variability within each type of specialty court. Although PSCs broadly adhere to a nonadversarial approach and aim to provide enhanced supervision and treatment to participants, there is wide variability in terms of composition and size of the courts, methods of referrals, inclusion criteria for participation, level/types of community partnerships, use of sanctions/rewards, and levels of oversight/monitoring (DeMatteo et al., 2019). It is important to recognize this variability and its impact on research and program evaluation.

Although there is a robust and broad evidence base supporting drugs courts, other specialty courts have not been researched to the same extent. As the number of these courts continue to grow, conducting more empirical research will be vital to their success. Specifically, mental health courts could benefit from more large-scale studies and meta-analyses of the current research base. In addition, research and program evaluation should be conducted on the many specialized PSCs that have been established in the last few decades, including reentry courts, veterans courts, domestic violence courts, and gun courts. Such research is essential to determining the effectiveness of these courts on recidivism reduction and improvement of clinical functioning, as well as facilitating future growth and dissemination of problem-solving justice (DeMatteo et al., 2019). Finally, perhaps the most important future consideration for PSCs has to do with their chronic underrepresentation of minority populations (see Marlowe et al., 2016). Given the rampant racial inequity currently permeating the criminal justice system, researching this underrepresentation and identifying means of combating it should be a top priority (DeMatteo et al., 2019).

References

Administrative Office of the Courts. (2012). *A preliminary look at California parolee reentry courts*. http://www.courts.ca.gov/documents/AOCBriefParolee0612.pdf

Andrews, D. A., Bonta, J., & Hoge, R. D. (1990). Classification for effective rehabilitation: Rediscovering psychology. *Criminal Justice and Behavior, 17*(1), 19–52.

Andrews, D. A., Bonta, J., & Wormith, J. S. (2006). The recent past and near future of risk and/or need assessment. *Crime and Delinquency, 52*(1), 7–27.

Arnold, S. (2019). *A meta-analysis of mental health courts: State of the research and recommendations*. (Publication No. 13903275) [Doctoral dissertation, Drexel University]. Proquest Dissertations.

Atkin-Plunk, C. A., Peck, J. H., & Armstrong, G. S. (in press). Do race and ethnicity matter? An examination of racial/ethnic differences in perceptions of procedural justice and recidivism among problem-solving court clients. *Race and Justice*.

Balyakina, E., Mann, C., Ellison, M., Sivernell, R., Fulda, K. G., Sarai, S. K., & Cardarelli, R. (2014). Risk of future offense among probationers with co-occurring substance use and mental health disorders. *Community Mental Health Journal, 50*(3), 288–295.

Beck, A. T. (1976). *Cognitive therapy and the emotional disorders*. International Universities Press.

Belenko, S. (2001). *Research on drug courts: A critical review: 2001 update*. National Center on Addiction and Substance Abuse at Columbia University.

Belenko, S., Patapis, N., & French, M. T. (2005). *Economic benefits of drug treatment: A critical review of the evidence for policy makers*. Treatment Research Institute.

Bennett, T., Holloway, K., & Farrington, D. (2008). The statistical association between drug misuse and crime: A meta-analysis. *Aggression and Violent Behavior, 13*(2), 107–118.

Berman, G. (2009). Problem-solving justice and the moment of truth. In P. Higgins & M. B. Mackinem (Eds.), Problem-solving courts: Justice for the twenty-first century? (pp. 1–11). Praeger.

Berman, G., & Feinblatt, J. (2002). *Judges and problem-solving courts*. http://www.courtinnovation.org/sites/default/files/JudgesProblemSolvingCourts1.pdf.

Bhati, A., Roman, J. K., & Chalfin, A. (2008). *To treat or not to treat: Evidence on the prospects of expanding treatment to drug-involved offenders*. Urban Institute.

Bush, J., Glick, B., & Taymans, J. (1997, revised 1998). *Thinking for a change: Integrated cognitive behavior change program*. https://nicic.gov/t4c

Christy, A., Clark, C., Frei, A., & Rynearson-Moody, S. (2012). Challenges of diverting veterans to trauma informed care: The heterogeneity of Intercept 2. *Criminal Justice and Behavior, 39*(4), 461–474.

Commaroto, L., Jewell, T., & Wilder, A. (2011). *Rochester Veterans Court: An expanded service of the Rochester Drug Court: Evaluation summary report*. Coordinated Care Services.

D'Zurilla, T. J., & Goldfried, M. R. (1971). Problem solving and behavior modification. *Journal of Abnormal Psychology, 78*(1), 107–126.

DeMatteo, D., Filone, S., & Davis, J. (2015). Substance use and crime. In B. L. Cutler & P. A. Zapf (Eds.), *APA handbook of forensic psychology – Vol. I: Individual and situational influences in criminal and civil contexts* (pp. 325–349). American Psychological Association.

DeMatteo, D., Filone, S., & LaDuke, C. (2011). Methodological, ethical, and legal considerations in drug court research. *Behavioral Sciences and the Law, 29*(6), 806–820.

DeMatteo, D., Heilbrun, K., Thornewill, A., & Arnold, S. (2019). *Problem-solving courts and the criminal justice system*. Oxford University Press.

DeMatteo, D., LaDuke, C., Locklair, B. R., & Heilbrun, K. (2013). Community-based alternatives for justice-involved individuals with severe mental illness: Diversion, problem-solving courts, and reentry. *Journal of Criminal Justice, 41*(2), 64–71.

Deschenes, E. P., Turner, S., & Greenwood, P. W. (1995). Drug court or probation? An experimental evaluation of Maricopa County's drug court. *Justice System Journal, 18*(1), 55–73.

Dollar, C. B., Ray, B., Hudson, M. K., & Hood, B. J. (2018). Examining changes in procedural justice and their influence on problem-solving court outcomes. *Behavioral Sciences and the Law, 36*(1), 32–45.

Drake, E. K., Aos, S., & Miller, M. G. (2009). Evidence-based public policy options to reduce crime and criminal justice costs: Implications in Washington State. *Victims & Offenders, 4*(4), 170–196.

Faraci, S. M. (2004). Slip slidin' away? Will our nation's mental health court experiment diminish the rights of the mentally ill? *Quinnipiac Law Review, 22*, 811–848.

Fischer, B. (2003). Doing good with a vengeance: A critical assessment of the practices, effects, and implications of drug treatment courts in North America. *Criminology and Criminal Justice, 3*(3), 227–248.

Gottfredson, D. C., Kearley, B. W., Najaka, S. S., & Rocha, C. M. (2007). How drug treatment courts work an analysis of mediators. *Journal of Research in Crime and Delinquency, 44*(1), 3–35.

Gottfredson, D. C., Najaka, S. S., & Kearley, B. W. (2003). A randomized study of the Baltimore City Drug Treatment Court: Results from the two-year follow-up. *Criminology and Public Policy, 2*(2), 171–196.

Government Accountability Office. (2005). *Adult drug courts: Evidence indicates recidivism reductions and mixed results for other outcomes*. GAO.

Government Accountability Office. (2011). *Adult drug courts*. GAO.

Green, M., & Rempel, M. (2012). Beyond crime and drug use: Do adult drug courts produce other psychosocial benefits? *Journal of Drug Issues, 42*(2), 156–177.

Hamilton, Z. (2010). *Do reentry courts reduce recidivism? Results from the Harlem Parole Reentry Court*. http://www.courtinnovation.org/sites/default/files/Reentry_Evaluation.pdf

Hasselbrack, A. M. (2001). Opting in to mental health courts. *Corrections Compendium, 26*(10), 4–25.

Heilbrun, K., DeMatteo, D., King, C., Thornewill, A., & Phillips, S. (2016). Risk-reducing interventions for justice-involved individuals: A critical review. In B. H. Bornstein & M. K. Miller (Eds.), *Advances in psychology and law, Volume 2* (pp. 271–304). Springer.

Heilbrun, K., DeMatteo, D., Yasuhara, K., Brooks-Holliday, S., Shah, S., King, C., DiCarlo, A.B., Hamilton, D., & Laduke, C. (2012). Community-based alternatives for justice-involved individuals with severe mental illness: Review of the relevant research. *Criminal Justice and Behavior, 39*(4), 351–419.

Hiday, V. A., Moore, M. E., Lamoureaux, M., & de Magistris, J. (2005, Spring/Summer). North Carolina's mental health court. *Popular Government, 70*(3), 24–30.

Hiday, V., & Ray, B. (2010). Arrests two years after exiting a well-established mental health court. *Psychiatric Services, 61*(5), 463–468.

Hoffman, M. B. (1999). Drug court scandal. *North Carolina Law Review, 78*, 1437–1532.

Holbrook, J. G., & Anderson, S. (2011). Veterans courts: Early outcomes and key indicators for success. *Widener Law School Legal Studies Research Paper, Series, 11*, 1–52.

Honegger, L. N. (2015). Does the evidence support the case for mental health courts? A review of the literature. *Law and Human Behavior, 39*(5), 478–488.

Inciardi, J. A., Martin, S. S., & Butzin, C. A. (2004). Five-year outcomes of therapeutic community treatment of drug-involved offenders after release from prison. *Crime and Delinquency, 50*(1), 88–107.

Kazdin, A. E. (2017). *Research design in clinical psychology* (5th ed.). Pearson Education.

Kearley, B., & Gottfredson, D. (2020). Long term effects of drug court participation: Evidence from a 15-year follow-up of a randomized controlled trial. *Journal of Experimental Criminology, 16*(1), 27–47.

Kopelovich, S., Yanos, P., Pratt, C., & Koerner, J. (2013). Procedural justice in mental health courts: Judicial practices, participant perceptions, and outcomes related to mental health recovery. *International Journal of Law and Psychiatry, 36*(2), 113–120.

Lane, E. (2002). Due process and problem-solving courts. *Fordham University Law Journal, 30*, 955–1026.

Latimer, J., Morton-Bourgon, K., & Chrétien, J. A. (2006). *A meta-analytic examination of drug treatment courts: Do they reduce recidivism?* Department of Justice Canada.

Lattimore, P. K., & Visher, C. A. (2009). The multisite evaluation of SVORI: Summary and synthesis (Report No. NJC 230421). https://www.ncjrs.gov/pdffiles1/nij/grants/230421.pdf

Lattimore, P. K., & Visher, C. A. (2014). The impact of prison reentry services on short-term outcomes: Evidence from a multisite evaluation. *Evaluation Review, 37*(3–4), 274–313.

Lindquist, C., Hardison, J., & Lattimore, P. K. (2004). The reentry court initiative: Court-based strategies for managing released prisoners. *Justice Research and Policy, 6*(1), 97–118.

Lindquist, C., Walters, J., Rempel, M., & Carey, S. (2013). *The National Institute of Justice's evaluation of second chance act adult reentry courts: Program characteristics and preliminary themes from year 1* (Report No. NJC 241400). https://www.ncjrs.gov/pdffiles1/nij/grants/241400.pdf

Lipsey, M. W., Landenberger, N. A., & Wilson, S. J. (2007). Effects of cognitive-behavioralprograms for criminal offenders. *Campbell Systematic Reviews, 3*(1), 1–27.

Listswan, S. J. (2008). Reentry for serious and violent offenders: An analysis of program attrition. *Criminal Justice Policy Review, 20*(2), 154–169.

Logan, M. W., & Link, N. W. (2019). Taking stock of drug courts: Do they work? *Victims & Offenders, 14*(3), 283–298.

Lowder, E. M., Rade, C. B., & Desmarais, S. L. (2018). Effectiveness of mental health courts in reducing recidivism: A meta-analysis. *Psychiatric Services, 69*(1), 15–22.

Lowenkamp, C. T., Holsinger, A. M., & Latessa, E. J. (2005). Are drug courts effective: A meta-analytic review. *Journal of Community Corrections, 15*(1), 5–11.

Marlowe, D. B., Hardin, C. D., & Fox, C. L. (2016). *Painting the current picture: A national report on drug courts and other problem-solving courts in the United States.* National Drug Court Institute.

McGuire, M., & Hatcher, R. (2001). Offence-focused problem solving: Preliminary evaluation of a cognitive skills program. *Criminal Justice and Behavior, 28*(5), 564–587.

McMurran, M., Huband, N., & Duggan, C. (2008). A comparison of treatment completers and non-completers of an in-patient treatment programme for male personality-disordered offenders. *Psychology and Psychotherapy: Theory, Research and Practice, 81*(2), 193–198.

Meyer, W. G. (2011). Constitutional and legal issues in drug courts. In D. B. Marlowe & W. G. Meyer (Eds.), *The drug court judicial benchbook* (pp. 160–180). National Drug Court Institute.

Miller, P. G., Curtis, A., Sonderlund, A., Day, A., & Droste, N. (2015). Effectiveness of interventions for convicted DUI offenders in reducing recidivism: A systematic review of the peer-reviewed scientific literature. *American Journal of Drug and Alcohol Abuse, 41*(1), 16–29.

Mitchell, O., Wilson, D. B., Eggers, A., & MacKenzie, D. L. (2012). Assessing the effectiveness of drug courts on recidivism: A meta-analytic review of traditional and nontraditional drug courts. *Journal of Criminal Justice, 40*(1), 60–71.

Nolan Jr, J. L. (2003). Redefining criminal courts: Problem-solving and the meaning of justice. *American Criminal Law Review, 40*(4), 1541–1565.

Peterson, J. K., Skeem, J., Kennealy, P., Bray, B., & Zvonkovic, A. (2014). How often and how consistently do symptoms directly precede criminal behavior among offenders with mental illness? *Law and Human Behavior, 38*(5), 439–449.

Poythress, N. G., Petrila, J., McGaha, A., & Boothroyd, R. A. (2002). Perceived coercion and procedural justice in the Broward mental health court. *International Journal of Law and Psychiatry, 25*(5), 517–533.

Ray, B., & Dollar, C. B. (2014). Exploring stigmatization and stigma management in mental health court: Assessing modified labeling theory in a new context. *Sociological Forum, 29*(3), 720–735.

Redlich, A. D., & Han, W. (2014). Examining the links between therapeutic jurisprudence and mental health court completion. *Law and Human Behavior, 38*(2), 109–118.

Ross, R. R., Fabiano, E. A., & Ross, R. D. (1986). *Reasoning and rehabilitation: A handbook for teaching cognitive skills.* T3 Associates.

Rossman, S. B., Rempel, M., Roman, J. K., Zweig, J. M., Lindquist, C. H., Green, M., Downey, P. M., Yahner, J., Bhati, A. S., & Farole, Jr., D. J. (2011). *The Multisite Adult Drug Court Evaluation: Volume 4. The impact of drug courts.* Urban Institute Justice Policy Center. https://www.ncjrs.gov/pdffiles1/nij/grants/237112.pdf

Rowland, M. G. (2016, December). Assessing the case for the formal recognition and expansion of federal problem-solving courts. *Federal Probation, 80*(3), 2–14.

Sarteschi, C. M., Vaughn, M. G., & Kim, K. (2011). Assessing the effectiveness of mental health courts: A quantitative review. *Journal of Criminal Justice, 39*(1), 12–20.

Severson, M. E., Bruns, K., Veeh, C., & Lee, J. (2011). Prisoner reentry programming: Who recidivates and when? *Journal of Offender Rehabilitation, 50*(6), 327–348.

Sevigny, E. L., Fuleihan, B. K., & Ferdik, F. V. (2013). Do drug courts reduce the use of incarceration? A meta-analysis. *Journal of Criminal Justice, 41*(6), 416–425.

Shaffer, D. K. (2006). *Reconsidering drug court effectiveness: A meta-analytic review*. Unpublished PhD Dissertation. University of Cincinnati.

Shaffer, D. K. (2011). Looking inside the black box of drug courts: A meta-analytic review. *Justice Quarterly, 28*(3), 493–521.

Skeem, J. L., Manchak, S., & Peterson, J. K. (2011). Correctional policy for offenders with mental illness: Creating a new paradigm for recidivism reduction. *Law and Human Behavior, 35*(2), 110–126.

Skeem, J., & Monahan, J. (2011). Current directions in violence risk assessment. *Current Directions in Psychological Science, 20*(1), 38–42.

Slattery M., Dugger M. T., Lamb T. A., & Williams L. (2013). Catch, treat, and release: Veteran treatment courts address the challenges of returning home. *Substance Use and Misuse, 48*(10), 922–932.

Spelman, J. (2003). An initial comparison of graduates and terminated clients in America's largest re-entry court. *Corrections Today, 65*, 74–77, 83.

Spivack, G., Platt, J. J., & Shure, M. B. (1976). *The problem solving approach to adjustment*. Jossey-Bass.

Tsai, J., Finlay, A., Flatley, B., Kasprow, W. J., & Clark, S. (2018). A national study of veterans treatment court participants: Who benefits and who recidivates. *Administration and Policy in Mental Health and Mental Health Services Research, 45*(2), 236–244.

Wales, H., Hiday, V., & Ray, B. (2010). Procedural justice and the mental health court judge's role in reducing recidivism. *International Journal of Law and Psychiatry, 33*(4), 265–271.

Wexler, D. B., & Winick, B. J. (1996). *Law in a therapeutic key: Developments in therapeutic jurisprudence*. Carolina Academic Press.

Wilson, D. B., Mitchell, O., & MacKenzie, D. L. (2006). A systematic review of drug court effects on recidivism. *Journal of Experimental Criminology, 2*(4), 459–487.

Wilson, J., & Davis, R. (2006). Good intentions meet hard realities: An evaluation of the Project Greenlight reentry program. *Criminology and Public Policy, 5*(2), 303–308.

Wilson, J. L., Bandyopadhyay, S., Yang, H., Cerulli, C., & Morse, D. S. (2018). Identifying predictors of substance use and recidivism outcome trajectories among drug treatment court clients. *Criminal Justice and Behavior, 45*(4), 447–467.

Winick, B. J. (2013). Problem solving courts: Therapeutic jurisprudence in practice. In Wiener, R. L., & Brank, E. M. (Eds.) *Problem solving courts: Social science and legal perspectives* (pp. 211–236). Springer.

Wolf, R. V. (2007). *Principles of problem-solving justice*. http://www.courtinnovation. org/sites/default/files/Principles.pdf.

Wolff, N., Fabrikant, N., & Belenko, S. (2011). Mental health courts and their selection processes: Modeling variation for consistency. *Law and Human Behavior, 35*(5), 402–412.

Experimental Psychology–Law

PART I

Witnesses and Victims

The Emerging Investigative Practice of Tele-Forensic Interviewing: Implications for Children's Testimony

Jason J. Dickinson, Nicole E. Lytle, *and* Debra Ann Poole

Abstract

Safety concerns during the COVID-19 pandemic prompted the release of provisional guidelines for interviewing child witnesses via videoconference applications, and some interview centers became early demonstration sites for tele-forensic interviewing (tele-FI). This chapter discusses four cornerstones that underlie emerging support for tele-FI: investigative challenges predating the pandemic, increased access to and familiarity with digital media, encouraging results from studies that compared children's performance across face-to-face and tele-FI modes, and the legal defensibility of tele-FI. The future of tele-FI will depend on results from future studies that evaluate children's and interviewers' reactions to tele-FI in the field, how tele-FI influences perceptions of child witness credibility and case trajectories, and the impact of tele-FI on the well-being of children, families, and communities served by the practice.

Key Words: tele-forensic interviewing, interviewing children, child witnesses, forensic interview, children's testimony

Law enforcement personnel, child welfare workers, and center-employed forensic interviewers elicit testimony from children that informs an array of criminal and civil matters, including allegations of domestic violence and child maltreatment, custody disputes, immigration proceedings, and claims of wrongful harm. Numerous interview protocols suggest ways to begin these conversations and ask questions about the matters under investigation (e.g., Lamb et al., 2018; Ministry of Justice, United Kingdom, 2011; National Children's Advocacy Center, 2019). Despite differences across protocols, there is consensus that child forensic interviews are (a) fact-finding conversations conducted to inform legal decision-making, that are (b) developmentally sensitive (Newlin et al., 2015). Knowledge of child development, cultural influences on conversation, and how disabilities impact children's ability to discuss personally experienced events inform best-practice standards for creating interview spaces, adopting a socially supportive demeanor, and using question forms that encourage children to share their experiences in ways that maximize the clarity, accuracy, and completeness of their testimonies (Lamb et al., 2018; Poole, 2016).

In step with a developmentally sensitive perspective, forensic interviewers have long encouraged self-disclosure and memory retrieval by speaking with children face to face (i.e., in person) and, when possible, in child-friendly spaces that minimize distractions. (For an early discussion, see Spaulding, 1987.) In the wake of the COVID-19 pandemic, however, some quarters of the child protection community questioned their ability to safely serve children, families, and the professionals who investigate cases if they continued conducting face-to-face interviews. While many jurisdictions modified in-person procedures to reduce the risk of virus transmission, a few organizations issued preliminary guidelines for interviewing via videoconference applications, and some interviewing centers adopted tele-forensic interviewing (tele-FI; National Children's Alliance, 2020; State of Michigan Governor's Task Force on Child Abuse and Neglect and Department of Health and Human Services, 2020; Vieth et al., 2020).

In this chapter, we explain why investigative needs and social changes could shift tele-FI from an emergency practice to a standard option when the benefits of interviewing from a distance outweigh limitations. Next, we review research on tele-FI to consider whether this practice meets the defining features of child forensic interviews and to identify concerns. After discussing legal considerations for tele-FI guidelines and practice, we conclude with unanswered questions and directions for research as technological change ushers in a new chapter in the history of children's eyewitness testimony.

Investigative and Social Backdrop for Tele-FI

We became interested in tele-FI when professionals in Alaska told us how challenging it can be to arrange in-person interviews in their state (Alaska Children's Alliance, 2016). Many Alaskan communities are geographically isolated, and less than a third of the population has access to interstate roadways. Even the capital, Juneau (population 32,000), lacks a roadway connecting it to the rest of the state. Because 19 percent of the US population lives in rural areas distributed over 97 percent of the nation's landmass (US Census Bureau, 2016), travel to an interview site burdens many families and can delay investigations. Around the world, accessibility issues prompted some jurisdictions to allow alternative investigative practices for children in remote areas, such as conversations between children and health workers or teachers (instead of incurring delays to provide interviewers with statutory power) and teleconferencing (Government of South Australia, 2016).

In addition to connecting forensic interviewers with children in rural areas, tele-FI can facilitate interviews of children impacted by natural disasters and those who are out of local jurisdiction. Onscreen interviews can also deliver specialized skills that are not available locally (e.g., interviewers who speak children's home languages and disability experts) and protect investigative teams when children have, or might have, a communicable disease.

When social distancing recommendations during the COVID-19 pandemic motivated some agencies to adopt tele-FI, two important cultural shifts had already lessened concerns about how adults and children would react to onscreen conversations. One was the steady rise of the tele-health industry. Well before the COVID-19 pandemic, the normalization of screen-to-screen interactions between children and helping professionals was already underway as hospitals leveraged tele-conferencing applications to deliver clinical care to geographically isolated or immunocompromised children (Hernandez et al., 2016; Olson et al., 2018). Outside medicine, helping professionals had already used tele-conferences with patients to diagnose learning disabilities (Waite et al., 2010), conduct hearing screenings (Lancaster et al., 2008), and treat childhood depression and conduct disorders (Gloff et al., 2015; Hilty et al., 2013). Though forensic interviews of children have traditionally been conducted face to face, some rurally located children's advocacy centers in the United States already used video technology to assist with medical examinations of suspected victims (Miyamoto et al., 2014) and to deliver trauma treatment (Kohrumel & Neufeld, 2019).

A related benefit for tele-FI that emerged from the health industry was the development of videoconferencing options that met the privacy requirements of the Health Insurance Portability and Accountability Act of 1996 (HIPAA).[1] Today, HIPAA compliance remains the minimal level of security required for many agencies that conduct tele-FIs, though some agencies require stronger minimum-security measures (e.g., end-to-end encryption, or E2EE).

A second cultural shift that paved the way for tele-FI was children's increased familiarity with digital media. Even before the COVID-19 pandemic forced the migration of school and social activities online, digital media had become "a constant and major presence in children's lives" (Smith, 2020, p. 1). In the United States, infants as young as four months viewed screens (Smith, 2020), two- to four-year-olds spent an average of two and a half hours per day interacting with screens, and screen time occupied five- to eight-year-olds more than three hours per day (Rideout & Robb, 2020). Children in lower-income families spent more time on screens than those in higher-income families did, and the digital divide (differential access to computers and the internet among low- and high-income families) had narrowed. The pandemic drew attention to remaining income inequities, but 74 percent of lower-income children had internet access at home by 2020 (Rideout & Robb, 2020). Moreover, only a minority of the four- to eight-year-olds in two samples—one from a small town and the other from a large metropolitan region—had never video chatted prior to the pandemic (23 percent and 7 percent, respectively; Dickinson et al., 2021).

---

[1] Health Insurance Portability and Accountability Act of 1996, Pub. L. No. 104–191, § 264, 110 Stat.1936. (1996). https://www.govinfo.gov/content/pkg/PLAW-104publ191/pdf/PLAW-104publ191.pdf

For many children, the migration of school and social functions to online delivery during the pandemic made onscreen conversations a familiar feature of everyday life. Nonetheless, professionals occasionally asked us whether tele-FI was less desirable than in-person interviewing due to inequities created by the lack of universal access to high-speed internet. Often this question reflected an assumption that it would be common-place for professionals to interview children who were using a device at home. Contrary to this scenario, provisional tele-FI guidelines cautioned against home interviews (National Children's Alliance, 2020), and tele-interviews usually occurred in interviewing centers where children and interviewers sat in separate rooms. (This configuration provided a consistent technology platform and more reliable internet access while reducing the need for face masks and acrylic shields.) Thus, one way policymakers can provide tele-FI to unconnected families is to conduct interviews at a nearby interviewing center (or partner agency; e.g., police department) that has high speed internet.

In sum, investigative needs and widespread familiarity with digital devices and media expedited conversations about tele-FI during the COVID-19 pandemic. Long-term sup-port for the practice will depend on the strength of two other cornerstones, however: the quality of testimony elicited by tele-FI and the legal defensibility of onscreen interviews.

Children's Behavior during Face-to-Face vs. Digitally Mediated Interactions

Basic research on children's interactions with digital media provides little that helps pre-dict their performance in tele-FIs. Studies of children's television viewing documented developmental improvements in attention (Anderson & Levin, 1976), the production features that capture attention (e.g., movement and purposeful behavior, Schmitt et al., 1999), and a remarkable ability to comprehend content while simultaneously playing with toys (Lorch et al., 1979). But television viewing—like watching video on computers and tablets—is not interactive. Information about children's attention to and comprehen-sion of interactive media is surprisingly thin because, as Smith (2020) concluded in a review for Common Sense Media, "research in this field has not been able to keep up with the rate at which digital media has been incorporated into childhood" (p. 2).

Nonetheless, findings from studies of toddlers provide some evidence that in-person and onscreen social interactions might be largely interchangeable. In one study, children ages twelve to twenty-five months engaged in videoconference conversations with an assis-tant who taught novel words, actions, and patterns repeated in a book. Children assigned to a second condition watched prerecorded videos of the same content. As Myers et al. (2017) explained,

> children were attentive and responsive in both conditions, but only children in the FaceTime group responded to the partner in a temporally synced manner. After one week, children in the FaceTime condition (but not the Video condition) preferred and recognized their

Partner, learned more novel patterns, and the oldest children learned more novel words. Results extend previous studies to demonstrate that children under 2 years show social and cognitive learning from video chat because it retains social contingency. (p. 1)

In a similar study, twenty-four- to thirty-month-olds learned words via video chat, live interactions, or yoked video (passive watching of video from another child's video chat session; Roseberry et al., 2014). The children learned novel words only in live and video-chat sessions, which were similarly effective. Of course, learning from video chat is not the same as recalling and sharing personal experiences, but these findings provide reassurance that even young children attend to screens and engage memory when interacting contingently with an onscreen person.

Few studies have compared children's autobiographical reports across interview modes. Analog studies of children who described an event in a courtroom versus a room equipped with closed-circuit television found better memory performance and reduced stress when children testified virtually, but courtroom conversations, unlike well-conducted forensic interviews, are highly confrontational (see Chong & Connolly, 2015, and Davies, 1999, for reviews). Therefore, conclusions about the impact of digital devices on autobiographical recall come from two other types of studies: research on novel uses of devices (i.e., animated interviewers and digital media aids in interviews) and research that compared children's performance across in-person and tele-FI modes using typical interview procedures.

Children's Reactions to Animated Interviewers and Digital Media Aids

Studies that compared in-person interviews with those containing animated interviewers or digital media aids do not directly address whether in-person interviews and tele-FIs are comparable. However, these studies did test whether screens promote event recall by better engaging children, or, conversely, whether digital content is a distractor that impairs children's ability to conduct thorough memory searches or resist leading questions.

When children (five to eight years) answered questions about a classroom event that had occurred three to four days earlier, there were few differences in reports elicited by an animated versus human interviewer (Donahue et al., 1999). During those interviews, each child answered recall and recognition questions in one of three conditions: (a) with target questions delivered by an animated figure on the computer, (b) with target questions delivered by an animated figure with the research assistant present, or (c) with target questions delivered by an in-person research assistant. (For both computer conditions, the assistant voiced the animated figure.) At the end of each interview, children could revisit questions and add to their responses with the assistant present. There were no differences between interview conditions in the number of correct details reported or children's willingness to mention a secret their teacher had asked them not to disclose. Children interviewed by the animated figure only were more likely to revise their answers, however, and these children repeated more correct information when they revisited questions compared to children interviewed face to face.

For a follow-up study, children (five to eight years) twice answered questions (four days and fourteen days later) delivered by an animated figure on the computer or a research assistant (Powell et al., 2002). The completeness and accuracy of reports was similar across conditions, but in the first interview children questioned by an animated figure rejected fewer activities that had not occurred, and children in that condition were less consistent across interviews and less frequently disclosed the secret during the follow-up interview. Finally, children in the computer condition revisited more questions than their peers in the face-to-face condition did, but the amount of new information elicited in this final interview phase was not significantly different across conditions. Thus unlike older children and adults, who are sometimes more forthcoming about sensitive issues when they are not reporting to a person (Powell et al., 2002), these younger children did not benefit from a computerized interview.

Because children with autism spectrum disorder (ASD) may feel overwhelmed by sensory information during social interactions, Hsu and Teoh (2017) asked whether an animated interviewer with simplified social gestures would promote event recall. Children with and without ASD (fifteen per group) individually participated in a staged event and, a week later, answered questions about that event during interviews modeled after the National Institute of Child Health and Human Development (NICHD) protocol (Lamb et al., 2018). Children assigned to an avatar interviewer spoke to a computer-presented cartoon-like face and torso controlled and voiced by an adult interviewer who sat in another room, whereas the other children spoke to an in-person interviewer. Both conditions ended with the interviewer asking misleading questions. Bayesian analyses, conducted due to the small sample size, suggested that the avatar benefited recall for all children (accuracy), although benefits were more pronounced for children with ASD (accuracy and number of details reported). The avatar interviewer did increase acquiescence to misleading questions, however. Collectively, studies using animated interviewers document that children readily report information to screens and maintain accuracy in response to nonmisleading questions even when the interview environment is cartoon-like. These findings could be useful for confronting defense claims that children associate screens with make-believe and, therefore, that event reports elicited via screens are inherently unreliable.

Researchers have also asked whether adding screen-based aids to in-person interviews improves children's reports. One innovation, In My Shoes (IMS), is a three-way interaction (child/computer/interviewer) in which an interviewer uses the computer to facilitate talk about emotion and emotional events. For one IMS study, an interviewer asked children (four to five years) about a wellness exam using a modified version of a standard interview structure or a structure with IMS elements (Fängström et al., 2016). For example, the children chose representational figures of people and selected emotions to superimpose on the figures, and the interviewer delivered follow-up questions about the individuals and emotions as needed. The accuracy of children's reports was not significantly different across IMS versus nonmediated interview modes, but children interviewed with IMS said more about people present during the event (perhaps because IMS interviews posed more questions than the standard interview).

As with animated interviews, these findings show that even young children stay focused on the topic of conversation and do not respond more impulsively when interviewers incorporate digital content into conversations. Moreover, even shy children are engaged when interacting with digital media (Fängström et al., 2017).

Studies of Forensic-Style Interviews

Only a few studies have compared traditional face-to-face and tele-FI modes. In one early study, children (ages six and ten years) participated in a standard, phased interview about an event either face to face or on screen, followed by leading questions (Doherty-Sneddon & McAuley, 2000). There was no difference between conditions in the amount of information children reported, although older children said more in the narrative phase when interviewed face to face. Contrary to this advantage, subsequent cued recall questions elicited more information from older children in the video-mediated condition. The children provided more incorrect information when questioned face to face, which the researchers suggested could have resulted from a greater tendency to guess when in-person interviewers ask specific questions.

Another study incorporated a survey about the frequency of interactions with electronic devices and digital applications (Hamilton et al., 2017). The children (five to twelve years) participated in scripted activities before a face-to-face or video-feed interview, one to two days later, modeled after the NICHD protocol (Lamb et al., 2018) and followed by leading and misleading questions. Children who had more digital experience were more accurate than those who had less, but there were no differences between conditions in informativeness (word counts and number of target details reported) or performance on leading or misleading questions. Interviewers in the video-feed condition delivered more clarification prompts, however, which was likely due to audiovisual complications (e.g., echoes and dropped sound) inherent to speaking and listening online.

A large tele-FI study enrolled 71 children from small towns in the Midwest along with 190 children from a large metropolitan region (four to eight years; Dickinson et al., 2021). Demographic differences across sites and different recruitment procedures produced a varied sample of lower- to higher-income children. During an initial laboratory session, the children individually participated in a hands-on educational program about germs and good hygiene. Before these activities, a female assistant described the laboratory's new germ rule, which was that Mr. Science (the man delivering the program) should not touch children while helping with the activities. Mr. Science then broke this rule when he purportedly brushed water off the child's cheek, and at the end of the session he reached for a handshake but caught his mistake before touching the child. Later at home, the child heard a story, read by a parent, that had accurate and inaccurate information about the laboratory visit, including false narrative that Mr. Science shook the child's hand. These procedures converted innocuous touches into salient transgressions, with more than a quarter of the children disclosing a germ-rule transgression to laboratory staff or a parent before a second-session interview.

About two weeks after the germ education program, the children described their experiences with the interviewer (a) sitting across a table or (b) by videoconference. (In the tele-FI condition, a female "helper" remained in the room but sat to the side of the child and farther back from the screen.) Interviewers began by delivering rapport-building questions, open-ended questions about a typical school day, and a ground rules discussion. After introducing the topic, they progressed from open-ended prompts about the germ education program to focused questions about what children liked and disliked about Mr. Science, whether someone did something wrong, and whether someone touched the child. Two challenging question sets completed the interview. First interviewers asked whether each of ten events had happened, including experienced, suggested (by the story), and novel events. These questions measured source monitoring, which is the ability to distinguish information from personal experience from information learned through some other source (e.g., the misleading story). Next, interviewers asked direct questions about event details, such as the color of an object. While children completed the interview, parents provided demographic information about themselves and their child prior to filling out questionnaires about the child's temperament and exposure to digital devices in the home (using a questionnaire modified with permission from Common Sense Media; Rideout, 2015).

Despite the young age of this sample, there were no significant differences in the accuracy of answers to difficult source-monitoring questions, the amount of accurate or inaccurate information elicited by detail questions, or the numbers of accurate and inaccurate touch reports. There were some advantages to face-to-face interviews, however. Compared to children interviewed via tele-FI, those in the face-to-face condition were more talkative about a typical school day. For younger children (four-, five-, and six-year-olds), this tendency to talk more to in-person interviewers had two repercussions: (a) They said more in response to open-ended prompts about the germ education program when conversing face to face, and (b) they disclosed the face touch and noncompleted handshake earlier in interviews. Older children disclosed earlier in the tele-FI condition, however. Thus, both interview modes elicited disclosures about inappropriate touch, but interviewers worked harder to elicit disclosures from younger children in the tele-FI condition.

An unanswered question is why young children were less forthcoming during onscreen interviews. Because children were equally accurate across modes for challenging source-monitoring and detail questions, it is unlikely that screens simply taxed cognitive resources or led children to exert less effort. Furthermore, there was no evidence that the face-to-face advantage among young children was due to the reactions of lower-income children or children who were behaviorally inhibited, had less video-chat experience, or scored lower on a battery of developmental tests (Dickinson et al., 2021). But despite some increased reticence when young children viewed interviewers on screen, reactions to tele-FI among children with different characteristics, along with the small number of performance differences across conditions, provide encouraging evidence that tele-FI can be a reasonable alternative to face-to-face interviewing.

The lack of consistent differences between face-to-face and on-screen interviews bolsters the conclusion that on-screen interviews can embody best-practice standards for questioning children. Because interviewers can deliver the same dialog in face-to-face and tele-FI modes, both formats support a neutral, fact-finding approach. There is a higher risk that low-quality audio/video could lead interviewers to misunderstand children during tele-FIs, but camera angles that capture children's gestures and good interview practices (e.g., asking children to repeat unclear answers) can reduce these risks. Diverse findings document the developmental appropriateness of tele-FI, including evidence of toddler learning from videoconference conversations and the accuracy of children's event reports—even in the face of challenging source-monitoring and detail questions.

Legal Considerations for Tele-FI Policy and Practice

Policy groups that released early guidelines reassured professionals that tele-FI was legally defensible. For one initiative, the National Children's Alliance (2020) assembled an ad hoc committee consisting of child eyewitness researchers, interviewing experts, prosecuting attorneys, and representatives from the FBI and Homeland Security Investigations. Their preliminary guidelines reflected expert consensus that tele-FI "is an effective and legally defensible alternative to face-to-face interviewing when appropriate guidelines are followed and external factors that could impact the reliability of the children's testimony are effectively addressed" (p. 1).

The State of Michigan Governor's Task Force on Child Abuse and Neglect and Department of Health and Human Services (2020) concurred that "tele-forensic interviewing (interviewing via a videoconference application) is a legally defensible alternative to face-to-face interviewing" (p. 2). Anticipating that modifications to usual practice would likely result in challenges from the defense, Vieth et al. (2020), writing for the National District Attorneys Association and the Zero Abuse Project, advised that "when considering a tele-forensic interviewing option, the overriding principle should be the best interests of the child. Ultimately, that is the best standard for also defending the decision in court" (p. 10).

An important caution is that tele-FI "does not alter the fundamental structure of interviews or waive interviewers' training requirements or agency policies" (State of Michigan Governor's Task Force on Child Abuse and Neglect and Department of Health and Human Services, 2020, p. 2). There is a risk of procedural violations if investigative teams fail to stay mindful of practice standards, which can easily occur if professionals mimic tele-FI practices designed for legal environments different from their own. For example, videoconferencing does not generally satisfy the statutory provisions of Title IV of the federal Social Security Act,[2] which requires monthly visitation by caseworkers for children in foster care. Though an in-person visitation requirement can be waived in cases of public health emergencies or other extenuating circumstances (e.g., a family member has a communicable disease), state and tribal Title IV-B organizations (child protective agencies that receive federal funding) may nevertheless require caseworkers to have face-to-face contact with children. Requirements for recording and labeling witness statements, and evidence storage requirements, can also differ across domains (e.g., criminal vs. juvenile) and jurisdictions, making it challenging to write tele-FI policy that includes these procedural elements.

A striking example of the risk of thoughtlessly substituting tele-FI for in-person interviews involves the use of physical evidence. Although presenting physical evidence to children is not a universal or even typical practice, interviewers sometimes encourage children to disclose by presenting photographs of the inside of a home (for neglect cases), medical photographs of bruises, or other evidence, such as belts (see State of Michigan Governor's Task Force on Child Abuse and Neglect and Department of Health and Human Services, 2017, for a discussion). To minimize trauma to children, some investigative teams mask explicit images or make copies of original images to mask. When images and recordings are sexually explicit, masking, copy, and display procedures must adhere to laws that prohibit possession, production, and distribution of child pornography. In face-to-face interviews in the United States, this is accomplished when law enforcement is the custodian of images. Early in the pandemic, some interviewers displayed physical evidence by having a staff member enter the child's interview room briefly to show an image (C. Barocca, personal communication January 8, 2021) and, for overseas interviews, by holding images up to the screen (for interviews recorded to a DVD; K. Connell, personal communication, December 20, 2020).

Like many services that turned to online solutions during the COVID-19 pandemic, the tele-FI guidelines that were fast-tracked to accommodate emerging cases will likely be modified to prevent investigative errs by better addressing the diversity of cases involving child witnesses. But even with clear guidelines and a regulatory green light, decisions to use tele-FI will inevitably be influenced by judicial decisions and case outcomes as the first wave of pandemic-era cases moves through the courts. Anticipating implications for children, and defense challenges, professionals who participated in early policy conversations about tele-FI often expressed concern that interviews conducted with children in their homes would make it more difficult to keep conversations private and, therefore,

---

[2] Social Security Act of 1935, 42 U.S.C. § 622 (2021). https://uscode.house.gov/view.xhtml?req=granul eid:USC-prelim-title42-section622&num=0&edition=prelim

ensure children's safety. A related concern was that children would be more susceptible to adult influence if they remained at home during interviews. These concerns motivated early advice to avoid home interviews (National Children's Alliance, 2020) and suggestions for documenting the steps investigative teams took to minimize adverse influence (Vieth et al., 2020).

Future Directions for Tele-FI Research and Policy

Before tele-FI transitions from an emergency practice to a generally accepted alternative to face-to-face interviewing, policymakers will want to know about three broad issues: (a) how children and interviewers adapt to onscreen conversations in the field, (b) how tele-FI influences case trajectories (the frequency and nature of defense challenges, judicial decisions about the practice, and case outcomes), and (c) the impact of tele-FI on the well-being of the children, families, and communities served by the practice.

Children and Interviewers On Screen

Although analog research supports the efficacy and safety of tele-FI, there are unanswered questions about feasibility and how this delivery mode functions in practice. Our early conversations with the interviewing community revealed a common concern that tele-FI might make it more challenging to establish rapport and that children would thus be less likely to disclose maltreatment or other stressful events. The finding that four- and five-year-olds more often required prompts about wrongdoing and touching before disclosing a transgression (Dickinson et al., 2021) shows the importance of capturing disclosure patterns in future field studies. Early data provided encouraging anecdotal evidence, however. The Center for Hope (a children's advocacy center that was an early adopter of tele-FI during the pandemic) conducted more than 400 tele-FIs by early 2021 with virtually no change in disclosure rates compared to pre-pandemic face-to-face interviews (Center for Hope Forensic Services, personal communication, February 12, 2021). Future research that integrates information about children's informativeness and disclosure patterns with case features (e.g., the child's relationship to the suspect) may help identify situations where the expected benefit of face-to-face interviews outweighs the convenience of tele-FI (or vice versa).

Concerns about the ability of tele-FIs to facilitate rapport with children foreshadow another avenue of research for this emerging practice. Although some professionals worried that children would be less comfortable communicating on screen, conversations during the pandemic revealed that interviewers were often anxious about migrating to tele-FI. Although analog research on tele-FI has understandably focused on children's eyewitness performance, future research should also consider differences in interviewers' verbal and nonverbal behaviors across interview modes and ask whether variability in behavior influences children's reports.

Because interviewers may be more comfortable with tele-FI if they can continue to use a familiar protocol, research on whether and how to use interview aids could influence acceptance of tele-FI. For example, anatomical dolls and diagrams are popular for clarifying reports of touching (Lytle et al., 2019), but early tele-FI guidelines were largely silent on the use of interviewing aids. The Emergency Tele-Forensic Interview Guidelines published by the National Children's Alliance (2020) noted only that prop use had not been tested and that interviewers should be prepared to respond to questions about their use. There are well-documented concerns about the developmental appropriateness of eliciting disclosures from young children using aids (see Lytle et al., 2015; Poole & Bruck, 2012), along with concerns about how interviewers question children with aids (e.g., pairing aids with leading questions; Dickinson et al., 2005). It is unknown, however, whether tele-FI compounds these problems or how best to document what interviewers presented and how children responded.

Case Trajectories

The future of tele-FI will inevitably hinge on the nature of defense challenges, judicial decisions about the practice, and case outcomes. A related question for researchers is whether tele-FI influences perceptions of child witnesses. A wide camera angle capturing the child and interviewer is the default in most interviewing centers and, typically, these images do not focus attention on children's facial details and may not reveal subtle expressions. When interviewers use videoconference applications, however, one camera typically faces the child, and proximity to the camera may allow third-party observers to better see their faces. Could this impact the credibility of children's statements?

Previous research on the effects of interrogation room camera angles on perceptions of suspect culpability suggests it can. When the camera focuses exclusively on the suspect, observers perceive a confession to be more voluntary (and the suspect more likely to be guilty) compared to when the camera angle focuses on both the suspect and interrogator (Lassiter, 2010). Lassiter argued that focusing on one actor in a two-actor dynamic creates a perceptual bias (illusory causation) whereby observers attribute the outcome of the situation to the most salient actor. Generalizing these findings to the child forensic interview context, it seems possible—perhaps even likely—that a tele-FI camera angle focused on a child could induce a similar perceptual bias in third-party observers, such that they will attribute the outcome of an interview (disclosure or nondisclosure) more often to the child while minimizing the impact of the interviewer's behavior (leading and suggestive questions) or pre-interview conversations. Although early tele-FI guidelines underscored the need to follow existing best-practice standards, we are not aware of tele-FI policy suggesting optimal camera configurations, and future challenges regarding the provision of child-focused recordings to triers-of-fact seem likely.

Broad Impacts

Finally, policy and research should look beyond case outcomes to consider the impact of tele-FI on the well-being of children, their families, and communities, including the professionals who serve them. For example, visits to interview centers often include conversations that promote cooperation and connect families with other services. Whether multidisciplinary teams achieve these goals with online contact is an important consideration for future tele-FI policy. And while tele-FI implementation has had unplanned benefits, such as making it easier for multidisciplinary team members to attend interviews, the practice could also displace jobs and erode the financial well-being of community-based interview centers. For these reasons, inviting diverse stakeholders who work with child witnesses to inform the research agenda will reduce the risk of unintentional harm from a practice that originated to keep children, and communities, safe.

References

Anderson, D. R., & Levin, S. R. (1976). Young children's attention to "Sesame Street." *Child Development*, *47*(3), 806–811.

Chong, K., & Connolly, D. A. (2015). Testifying through the ages: An examination of current psychological issues on the use of testimonial supports by child, adolescent, and adult witnesses in Canada. *Canadian Psychology*, *56*(1), 108–117.

Davies, G. (1999). The impact of television on the presentation and reception of children's testimony. *International Journal of Law and Psychiatry*, *22*(3–4), 241–256.

Dickinson, J. J., Lytle, N. E., & Poole, D. A. (2021). Tele-forensic interviewing can be a reasonable alternative to face-to-face interviewing of child witnesses. *Law and Human Behavior*, *45*(2), 97–111.

Dickinson, J. J., Poole, D. A., & Bruck, M. (2005). Back to the future: A comment on the use of anatomical dolls in forensic interviews. *Journal of Forensic Psychology Practice*, *5*(1), 63–74.

Doherty-Sneddon, G., & McAuley, S. (2000). Influence of video-mediation on adult-child interviews: Implications for the use of the live link with child witnesses. *Applied Cognitive Psychology*, *14*(4), 379–392.

Donohue, A., Powell, M. B., & Wilson, J. C. (1999). The effects of a computerised interview on children's recall of an event. *Computers in Human Behavior*, *15*(6), 747–761.

Fängström, K., Bokström, P., Dahlberg, A., Calam, R., Lucas, S., & Sarkadi, A. (2016). In My Shoes—Validation of a computer assisted approach for interviewing children. *Child Abuse & Neglect*, *58*, 160–172.

Fängström, K., Salari, R., Eriksson, M., & Sarkadi, A. (2017). The computer-assisted interview In My Shoes can benefit shy preschool children's communication. *PLoS One*, *12*(8), Article e0182978.

Gloff, N. E., LeNoue, S. R., Novins, D. K., & Myers, K. (2015). Telemental health for children and adolescents. *International Review of Psychiatry*, *27*(6), 513–524.

Government of South Australia. (2016). *Interagency code of practice: Investigation of suspected child abuse or neglect*. https://www.childprotection.sa.gov.au/__data/assets/pdf_file/0014/107051/interagency-code-of-practice.pdf

Hamilton, G., Whiting, E. A., Brubacher, S. P., & Powell, M. B. (2017). The effects of face-to-face versus live video-feed interviewing on children's event reports. *Legal and Criminological Psychology*, *22*(2), 260–273. https://doi.org/10.1111/lcrp.12098

Hernandez, M., Hojman, N., Sadorra, C., Dharmar, M., Nesbitt, T. S., Litman, R., & Marcin, J. P. (2016). Pediatric critical care telemedicine program: A single institution review. *Telemedicine and e-Health*, *22*(1), 51–55.

Hilty, D. M., Ferrer, D. C., Parish, M. B., Johnston, B., Callahan, E. J., & Yellowlees, P. M. (2013). The effectiveness of telemental health: A 2013 review. *Telemedicine and e-Health*, *19*(6), 444–454.

Hsu, C., & Teoh, Y. (2017). Investigating event memory in children with autism spectrum disorder: Effects of a computer-mediated interview. *Journal of Autism and Developmental Disorders*, *47*(2), 359–372.

Kohrumel, J., & Neufeld, J. (2019). The challenges of tele-mental health: Technology and cross-state considerations [Webinar]. National Children's Advocacy Center. https://www.youtube.com/watch?v=r2jfSaRXxb4&feature=youtu.be&t=214

Lamb, M. E., Brown, D. A., Hershkowitz, I., Orbach, Y., & Esplin, P. W. (2018). *Tell me what happened: Questioning children about abuse* (2nd ed.). John Wiley & Sons.

Lancaster, P., Krumm, M., Ribera, J., & Klich, R. (2008). Remote hearing screenings via telehealth in a rural elementary school. *American Journal of Audiology, 17*(2), 114–122.

Lassiter, G. D. (2010). Psychological science and sound public policy: Video recording of custodial interrogations. *American Psychologist, 65*(8), 768–779.

Lorch, E. P., Anderson, D. R., & Levin, S. R. (1979). The relationship of visual attention to children's comprehension of television. *Child Development, 50*(3), 722–727.

Lytle, N. E., Dickinson, J. J., & Poole, D. A. (2019). Techniques for interviewing reluctant child witnesses. In J. J. Dickinson, N. S. Compo, R. N Carol, B. L. Schwartz, & M. R. McCauley (Eds.), *Evidence-based Investigative Interviewing: Applying cognitive principles* (pp. 193–215). Routledge.

Lytle, N. E., London, K., & Bruck, M. (2015). Young children's ability to use two-dimensional and three-dimensional symbols to show placements of body touches and hidden objects. *Journal of Experimental Child Psychology, 134,* 30–42.

Ministry of Justice, United Kingdom. (2011). *Achieving best evidence in criminal proceedings: Guidance on interviewing victims and witnesses, and guidance on using special measures.* https://www.cps.gov.uk/sites/default/files/documents/legal_guidance/best_evidence_in_criminal_proceedings.pdf

Miyamoto, S., Dharmar, M., Boyle, C., Yang, N. H., MacLeod, K., Rogers, K., Nesbitt, T., & Marcin, J. P. (2014). Impact of telemedicine on the quality of forensic sexual abuse examinations in rural communities. *Child Abuse & Neglect, 38*(9), 1533–1539.

Myers, L. J., LeWitt, R. B., Gallo, R. E., & Maselli, N. M. (2017). Baby FaceTime: Can toddlers learn from online video chat? *Developmental Science, 20,* Article e12430.

National Children's Advocacy Center. (2019). *National Children's Advocacy Center's child forensic interview structure.* https://www.nationalcac.org/wp-content/uploads/2019/02/NCAC_CFIS_Feb-2019.pdf

National Children's Alliance. (2020). *Emergency tele-forensic interview guidelines: A guide for the Children's Advocacy Center response during the COVID-19 pandemic.* https://4a3c9045adefb4cfdebb-852d241ed1c54e70582a59534f297e9f.ssl.cf2.rackcdn.com/ncalliance_e171953af194996033620560a119f562.pdf

Newlin, C., Cordisco Steele, L., Chamberlin, A., Anderson, J., Kenniston, J., Russell, A., Stewart, H., & Vaughan-Eden, V. (2015, September). *Child forensic interviewing: Best practices* [Juvenile Justice Bulletin]. US Department of Justice, Office of Juvenile Justice and Delinquency Prevention. http://www.ojjdp.gov/pubs/248749.pdf

Olson, C. A., McSwain, S. D., Curfman, A. L., & Chuo, J. (2018). The current pediatric telehealth landscape. *Pediatrics, 141*(3), Article e20172334.

Poole, D. A. (2016). *Interviewing children: The science of conversation in forensic contexts.* American Psychological Association.

Poole, D. A., & Bruck, M. (2012). Divining testimony? The impact of interviewing props on children's reports of touching. *Developmental Review, 32*(3), 165–180.

Powell, M. B., Wilson, J. C., & Thomson, D. M. (2002). Eliciting children's recall of events: How do computers compare with humans? *Computers in Human Behavior, 18*(3), 297–313.

Rideout, V. (2015). *The Common Sense census: Media use by tweens and teens.* Common Sense Media. https://www.commonsensemedia.org/sites/default/files/uploads/research/census_researchreport.pdf

Rideout, V., & Robb, M. B. (2020). *The Common Sense census: Media use by kids age zero to eight.* Common Sense Media. https://www.commonsensemedia.org/research/the-common-sense-census-media-use-by-kids-age-zero-to-eight-2020

Roseberry, S., Hirsh-Pasek, K., & Golinkoff, R. M. (2014). Skype me! Socially contingent interactions help toddlers learn language. *Child Development, 85*(3), 956–970.

Schmitt, K. L., Anderson, D. R., & Collins, P. A. (1999). Form and content: Looking at visual features of television. *Developmental Psychology, 35*(4), 1156–1167.

Smith, H. (2020). *Children, executive functioning, and digital media: A review.* Common Sense Media. https://www.commonsensemedia.org/research/children-executive-functioning-and-digital-media-a-review-2020

Spaulding, W. (1987). *Interviewing child victims of sexual exploitation.* National Center for Missing and Exploited Children.

State of Michigan Governor's Task Force on Child Abuse and Neglect and Department of Health and Human Services. (2020). *Provisional tele-forensic interview guidelines.* https://www.michigan.gov/documents/mdhhs/Provisional_Tele-Forensic_Interview_Guidelines_704784_7.pdf

State of Michigan Governor's Task Force on Child Abuse and Neglect and Department of Health and Human Services. (2017). *State of Michigan Governor's Task Force on Children's Justice and Department of Health and Human Services forensic interviewing protocol* (4th ed.). https://www.michigan.gov/mdhhs/-/media/Project/Websites/mdhhs/Adult-and-Childrens-Services/Abuse-and-Neglect/Childrens-Protective-Services/DHS-PUB-0779_211637_7.pdf?rev=891e339e51134ff79f2e01bad1ccc6df&hash=611EBAE27609B546D54D1D3641FE4B04

US Census Bureau. (2016, December 8). *New census data show differences between urban and rural populations* [Press release]. https://www.census.gov/newsroom/press-releases/2016/cb16-210.html

Vieth, V., Farrell, R., Johnson, R., & Peters, R. (2020). *Conducting and defending a pandemic-era forensic interview.* National District Attorneys Association and the Zero Abuse Project. https://cdn2.zeroabuseproject.org/wp-content/uploads/2020/05/Conducting-and-Defending-Pandemic-Era-Forensic-Interview-FINAL-1.pdf

Waite, M. C., Theodoros, D. G., Russell, T. G., & Cahill, L. M. (2010). Assessment of children's literacy via an internet-based telehealth system. *Telemedicine and e-Health, 16*(5), 564–575.

Using Reflector Variables to Determine Whether the Culprit Is Present in or Absent from a Police Lineup

Andrew M. Smith *and* Gary L. Wells

Abstract

Psychological scientists have long taken two approaches to combatting mistaken identifications: the system-variable approach and the estimator-variable approach. The system-variable approach involves developing lineups that prevent mistaken identifications. The estimator-variable approach involves estimating the reliability of an identification given all factors that may have affected memory in that case. The system-variable approach has had a tremendous impact on reducing mistaken identifications, but the estimator-variable approach has not. This chapter explains why, despite their import, estimator variables have failed to distinguish reliable from unreliable identifications in real cases, and then introduces a new class of variables that fill the void—reflector variables. Reflectors reveal how strongly the suspect matches the witness's memory for the culprit. Because guilty suspects tend to provide a stronger match-to-memory than do innocent suspects, reflector variables reflect whether the suspect in a lineup is guilty. This chapter argues that the reflector-variable approach requires videorecording lineups in their entirety.

Key Words: eyewitness identifications, reflector-variable, estimator-variable, system-variable, lineups, witness memory

Mistaken eyewitness identification was the primary evidence used to convict approximately 69 percent of the people who were initially convicted and then later exonerated using forensic DNA testing (Innocence Project, n.d.). Historically, cognitive and social psychologists who study eyewitness identification have relied on two general approaches to combat the mistaken-identification problem. The first approach involves developing lineup procedures that better discriminate between guilty suspects and innocent suspects and encouraging police investigators to implement these superior procedures. This is a *prospective* approach to reducing innocent-suspect identifications and missed culprit identifications before they happen. The second approach involves examining the witnessing conditions *after the witness makes an identification decision* and estimating the probability that the witness made an accurate decision (witness reliability) given the witnessing conditions. This is a *retrospective* approach of trying to assess witness reliability. This distinction between *prospective* and *retrospective* approaches to combatting the mistaken-identification problem typifies an early distinction in the eyewitness science literature between *System* and *Estimator* variables (Wells, 1978). System variables are those variables that affect the accuracy of eyewitness identification over which the police investigator has control and estimator variables are variables that affect the accuracy of eyewitness identification over which the police investigator has no control.

Researchers have placed a premium on system variables (e.g., prelineup instructions to witnesses, proper selection of lineup fillers) because system variables can be used in actual cases to increase the capacity of the investigator to discriminate between guilty suspects and innocent suspects. System variables can be used to prevent innocent-suspect identifications before they occur. Estimator variables (e.g., lighting conditions and distance), in contrast, are not under the control of the investigator and therefore can, at best, be used only in a retrospective manner to estimate the probability that the eyewitness made an accurate identification decision. By 1998, eyewitness scientists agreed broadly on a set of recommendations about how to use system variables to improve the capacity of the investigator to discriminate between guilty suspects and innocent suspects, such as the use of double-blind administration (Wells et al., 1998). Based on this same body of research, plus the expertise of police, prosecutors, eyewitness researchers, and defense attorneys, the National Institute of Justice (1999) published a guide for law enforcement, *Eyewitness Evidence*. Since the publication of the NIJ Guide there has been a great deal of progress in reforming eyewitness identification procedures in a large number of jurisdictions across the United States. For example, as of 2019, twenty-six states have passed statutes (or administrative orders) requiring lineups to be conducted using double-blind procedures, warning witnesses in pre-lineup instructions that the culprit might not be in the lineup, and using lineup fillers who are carefully selected so that the suspect does not stand out. Even in states that have not made state-wide reforms, individual jurisdictions have made these reforms, especially in larger cities. Encouraged by this progress, the American Psychology-Law Society (which includes the world's top eyewitness scientists) recently published a new scientific review paper that expands system-variable recommendations to encompass all the latest research developments (Wells et al., 2020).

But there is a clear limit to how much of the mistaken identification problem can be cleared up using system-variable improvements alone. In a telling field study that collected photo-lineup outcome data in four jurisdictions (police departments in Austin, San Diego, Charlotte, Tucson), the study revealed that eyewitnesses picked a known-innocent filler 36 percent of the time that they made an identification. This high rate of known-innocent filler identifications occurred despite the fact that each of the four police jurisdictions used the best system-variable procedures. In fact, the photo-identification procedures were carefully implemented by using standardized computer software (Wells et al., 2015).

Analyses of actual lineups conducted by police are extremely telling in terms of the surprising frequency with which victim and bystander eyewitnesses to serious crimes make identification errors. Identification errors can be studied in actual lineups because proper lineups contain fillers. Lineup fillers are known-innocent individuals who are included in a lineup simply to "fill it out" and not let the suspect stand out. When a witness picks the suspect, it might or might not be an accurate identification, but when the witness picks a filler it is definitively known as a mistaken identification. Figure 27.1 represents witness performance in the real world aggregated across eleven peer-reviewed field studies (Wells, 2018). Especially noteworthy for current purposes are how often witnesses who identify someone from a lineup pick a known-innocent filler. Overall, 4,345 of the 7,734 total

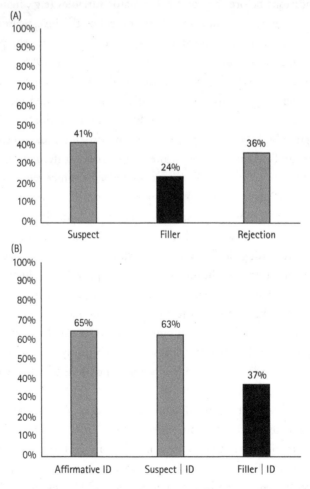

Figure 27.1 Panel A. Lineup outcomes (*N* = 6,734) from peer-reviewed published field studies on eyewitness identification. Panel B. Percent of witnesses making an ID, percent of those making an ID who picked the suspect, and percent of those making an ID who picked a filler.

eyewitnesses made an affirmative identification. Of these 4,345 affirmative identifications, 1,599 (36.8 percent) identified a known-innocent filler.

Figure 27.1 helps illustrate the point that mistaken identifications are common in police lineups, even when the procedures used to secure those identifications are following best practices (which was definitely the case in the field studies of Klobuchar et al., 2006; Wells et al., 2015; Wixted et al., 2016). Clearly, there are also some mistaken identifications landing on innocent suspects, but there is no way to separate those from accurate identifications of guilty suspects in these field data.

Importantly, these field studies have yielded some striking surprises when they attempt to look at estimator variables (e.g., exposure duration, presence of a weapon, delay between witnessing and the lineup, and viewing distance). Although there is little doubt these estimator variables affect eyewitness identification in fully randomized laboratory settings (Lampinen et al., 2014; Memon et al., 2003; Sauer et al., 2010) the capacity of these estimator variables to distinguish between suspect identifications and filler identifications in the field is inconsistent at best. Horry et al. (2014, p. 95), for instance, concluded that when it comes to using estimator variables to distinguish between suspect identifications and filler identifications in the field, the "inconsistencies outweigh the consistencies." Most of these field studies, for example, have failed to show that the presence of a weapon can predict suspect versus filler identifications. In fact, in a prominent study of a wide range of estimator variables, researchers found that lighting conditions, viewing distance, viewing obstructions, weapon presence, and ethnicity all failed to predict whether the witness had identified a suspect or a filler from their lineups (Valentine et al., 2003). This is in spite of the fact that each of these variables has been shown to do so in laboratory settings.

Why Do Estimator Variables Fail to Discriminate in Field Data?

Why have estimator variables proven less successful at discriminating between suspect identifications and filler identifications in the field compared to in laboratory settings? Most likely, this is attributable to the fact that the real world is "fraught with multicollinearities" (Wilford & Wells, 2013) that do not exist in a fully randomized lab experiment. For example, in the lab, both stress and witnessing distance have been shown to decrease the accuracy of eyewitness identification; however, in the real world, stress will tend to be negatively correlated with distance in the sense that witness stress is undoubtedly higher when distance between the witness and the culprit is closer. Hence, a closer viewing distance to the culprit might favor greater eyewitness identification accuracy, but being closer to the culprit might also produce greater stress, thereby canceling the advantage of a closer distance. Whereas viewing distance and witness stress are likely confounded in the real world, they are unconfounded in laboratory settings. For example, in the lab, an experimenter examining the impact of viewing distance manipulates viewing distance independently of all other variables in a fully randomized design (e.g., Lampinen et al., 2014). In this context, viewing distance is unconfounded (uncorrelated) with all other possible variables and so when researchers estimate the impact of viewing distance on identification performance in the lab, they get an estimate that is independent of the variables that might covary with viewing distance in the real world.

These complex multicollinearities among estimator variables in field studies create serious problems for using estimator variables to predict suspect versus filler identifications, especially because no study can account for all possible variables and their higher-order multicollinear relations (see Horry et al., 2014, for a more extensive discussion on this issue). This problem with not being able to measure and account for all possible collinear variables is particularly true of the culprit-present versus culprit-absent variable. No variable has a greater impact on the chances of identifying a suspect versus a known-innocent filler than whether the culprit is present versus absent in the lineup; suspect identifications are far more likely when the culprit is present than when the culprit is absent, and filler identifications are far more likely when the culprit is absent than when the culprit is present (Wells et al., 2015; Wells & Lindsay, 1980; Wells & Turtle, 1986). And, of course, it is not known with certainty in field studies whether the culprit is in the lineup or not. Moreover, whether or not the culprit is in the lineup can be correlated in complex ways with various estimator variables. For example, to the extent that crime investigators put more resources into finding a criminal suspect for robberies involving a weapon than they do for those not involving a weapon, we might expect the culprit to be more likely to be in the lineup for a weapon-involved crime than for a no-weapon crime. Hence, suspect identifications might be more common for cases in which a weapon is involved merely because the suspect is more likely to be the actual culprit. Or, this increased likelihood that the lineup's suspect is guilty in weapon cases might simply cancel the typical weapon-focus effect. Consider as well that witnesses have difficulty estimating many of the estimator-variable factors (such as distance and time) reliably (Lindsay et al., 2008; Loftus, Schooler, et al., 1987) and witnesses' self-reports on these estimator variables are malleable as a function of feedback that witnesses inevitably get over time (e.g., Steblay et al., 2014; Wells & Bradfield, 1998). In hindsight, perhaps we should not have been surprised that estimator variables (such as distance, lighting, and delay to identification) would not be good predictors of suspect versus filler identifications in actual cases given the complex multicollinearities involved. Of course, sorting between filler identifications and suspect identifications in field studies can be improved by taking into consideration corroborative (noneyewitness) evidence (Horry et al., 2014). But that is to be expected given that witnesses are more likely to identify the suspect if guilty and identify a filler if the suspect is not guilty.

Filler vs. Suspect as a Real-World Proxy for Innocent vs. Guilty
Why should we care that estimator variables do a weak and inconsistent job of sorting between filler identifications and suspect identifications in field studies with actual

cases? We care because the capacity to distinguish between suspect identifications and filler identifications serves as a proxy for the capacity to distinguish between guilty-suspect identifications and innocent-suspect identifications in actual cases; *if estimator variables cannot distinguish between suspect identifications and filler identifications in actual cases, then they cannot be expected to effectively distinguish between guilty-suspect identifications and innocent-suspect identifications actual cases either.* The logic is relatively simple; although the identification of a suspect will sometimes be mistaken, all identifications of fillers are mistaken identifications. Because a critical mass of suspect identifications are accurate identifications of the culprit whereas none of the filler identifications are accurate identifications, any assessment variable that cannot effectively sort between suspect identifications and filler identifications will also be unable to effectively sort between guilty-suspect identifications and innocent-suspect identifications.

The weak and inconsistent capacity of estimator variables to sort between suspect and filler identifications does not mean that these estimator variables are not affecting eyewitness identification accuracy (lab studies are the best test of that proposition). Instead, the field data indicate that there are complex multicollinearities among the estimator variables in the real world that can cancel and even reverse the predictive nature of any given estimator variable in actual cases. Even more central to the failure of estimator variables to effectively sort between filler identifications and suspect identifications in the real world is the fact that estimator variables are largely independent of whether the lineup contains the culprit, which is ultimately the question that the legal system is trying to answer. So, if police, prosecutors, and others who are trying to sort between accurate and mistaken identifications of suspects cannot rely on traditional estimator variables, what are they to do?

We suggest that there is a different type of variable, a type that is neither a traditional estimator variable not a traditional system variable. We call this third type of variable a *reflector variable*, because these variables reflect whether the culprit is present in or absent from the police lineup (Wells, 2020). In what is to follow, we further define reflector variables and explain the rationale for this third type of eyewitness variable. Finally, we argue that maximizing the efficacy of reflector variables requires video recording all identification procedures in their entirety.

Reflector Variables: The Right Variable for the Problem

Although most eyewitness researchers, police, lawyers, and courts tend to sort all eyewitness identification variables into the system versus estimator variable categories originally proposed by Wells (1978), there is a third and distinct class of eyewitness variables called *reflector* variables (Wells, 2020). Reflector variables have traditionally been referred to as *postdiction* variables because they can be used to retroactively predict whether the witness made a reliable identification decision; however, each of system, estimator, and *reflector* variables can be used to postdict the reliability of an identification decision, but only reflector variables REFLECT whether the culprit is present in or absent from the lineup. Reflector variables are qualitatively distinct from system and estimator variables. System variables and estimator variables are both defined as variables that affect the discriminability and/or reliability of eyewitness identification (Wells, 1978). Reflector variables, in contrast, do not AFFECT the reliability of eyewitness identification accuracy but instead REFLECT the reliability of eyewitness identification.

A key to understanding the special value of reflector variables is to appreciate the fact that the purpose of a lineup is not to test the memory of the eyewitness. Rather, the purpose of a lineup is to test the police investigator's hypothesis that the suspect in the lineup is the culprit (Smith et al., 2020; Wells & Luus, 1990). Hence, a lineup is not a test of the witness' memory but rather is a tool for collecting information that can inform on whether the suspect is likely guilty or likely innocent. The witness's decision, confidence, decision speed, and a host of other *reflector* variables all provide data that the investigator can use to help test their hypothesis that the suspect is the culprit.

Reflector variables include both verbal and nonverbal behaviors emitted by eyewitnesses in the course of performing the eyewitness identification task. These include such behaviors as verbal utterances about comparison processes, the witness's expressed level of confidence, the amount of time that an eyewitness takes to make an identification decision, visible evidence of effort, use of elimination strategies, and references to mere familiarity rather than recollection, among others (Sporer, 1992, 1993; Weber et al., 2004).

Historically, the eyewitness identification literature has not fully appreciated or described the reflect/affect distinction between reflector variables on the one hand and system and estimator variables on the other hand. Returning to the distinction between AFFECTING reliability and REFLECTING reliability, estimator variables *AFFECT the strength and accuracy of the witness's memory trace for the culprit during the initial encounter.* But estimator variables are largely orthogonal to the presence or absence of the culprit in the lineup. A poor view, for example, results in a weak memory regardless of whether the witness encounters a culprit-present lineup or a culprit-absent lineup, and in that sense, knowing that the witness had a poor view is not all that helpful for determining whether the culprit is present in the lineup. Reflector variables, by contrast, *REFLECT the strength of the witness's recognition experience during the lineup.* And, the primary factor influencing whether the witness has a strong or weak recognition experience during the lineup is whether the culprit is present or absent from the lineup. Indeed, a witness cannot have a strong recognition experience unless the culprit is present in the lineup. This is extremely important because a proper lineup contains only one suspect (all others are fillers); accordingly, whether the culprit is present or not is the same as whether the suspect is guilty or not (Wells & Turtle, 1986). Hence, unlike system and estimator variables, reflector variables are designed to more directly answer the question that police are asking—is the culprit present in the lineup?

A Theoretical Rationale for the Reflector-Variable Approach

The rationale for conducting a lineup is that if the suspect is the culprit, this person should provide a relatively strong match to the witness's memory for the culprit, and the witness should pick this person out of the lineup. Conversely, if the suspect is not the culprit, this person should not provide a strong match to the witness's memory for the culprit, and the witness should not pick this person out of the lineup. Hence, a lineup is a tool for measuring the perceptual overlap between the suspect's appearance and the witness's memory for the culprit, and the information extracted from this procedure sheds light on the likely guilt or innocence of the suspect. But a categorical identification decision is a very crude measure of the extent to which the suspect matches the witness's memory for the culprit. This is where reflector variables come into play. Reflector variables reflect the *degree* of match between a witness's memory for the culprit and the suspect and, hence, reflect the likelihood that the suspect is the culprit.

There are a number of verbal and nonverbal behaviors exhibited by the eyewitness that reflect whether the culprit is present in the lineup (e.g., Dunning & Stern, 1994; Lindsay et al., 1998; Sporer, 1992). But these variables that appear to have reflective value in the lab were not borne out of mere "dustbowl empiricism." Instead, these reflector variables tend to have been derived from general theoretical understandings of recognition memory and broad conceptualization of automatic versus deliberative processing. These variables are based on what we know about the behavioral manifestations of strong versus weak recognition experiences and the simple observation that strong versus weak recognition experience correlate with whether the culprit is versus is not in the lineup.

Reflector variables of eyewitness identification accuracy can be understood in terms of a general model of relatively automatic versus deliberative processes (Dunning & Stern, 1994; Sauerland & Sporer, 2007; Wells, 1984). Reliable visual recognition memory is generally considered an automatic process in the sense that it is relatively rapid, effortless, and nonverbal. This is especially true in the recognition of faces. It has long been established that faces are recognized not by analysis of individual features but instead "holistically" or configurally (Diamond & Carey, 1986; Wells & Hryciw, 1984; Wilford & Wells, 2010). Hay et al. (1986), for example, discovered that people recognized the faces of celebrities almost immediately, and without cognitive deliberation. Recognition of a celebrity's face is unaffected by the number of distractor faces and people are largely unable to explain verbally how they made the recognition decision. Deliberative processes, in contrast to automatic processes, are relatively slow, effortful, verbal, and not configural (not holistic).

This general conceptualization of face recognition processes is the guiding theoretical framework underlying our understanding of reflector variables. Reliable visual recognition memory is based on the strength of the ecphoric experience (i.e., the perceptual overlap between a stimulus face and an individual's memory trace for some target person; Tulving, 1983), which is an automatic, rapid, effortless process, especially for faces. It follows from this framework, for example, that reliable eyewitness identifications from lineups will be relatively rapid (measured in seconds, not minutes; e.g., see Dunning & Perretta, 2002; Sporer, 1992). It also follows from this type of framework that reliable identifications from lineups tend to result from "pop-out" experiences rather than deliberative back and forth comparisons of faces to determine who looks most like the culprit (Wells, 1984), or the use of elimination strategies (e.g., "couldn't be number 3, 4, or 5, so I believe it is number 2"; see Dunning & Stern, 1994). It follows from our understanding of face recognition that reliable identifications from lineups typically do not involve deliberations about facial features (e.g., "his nose looks like number three's nose), or the use of deliberate elimination processes.

What Is the Evidence That Reflector Variables Are Useful for Determining If the Culprit Is Present?

The eyewitness's expressed level of confidence has been studied more than any other reflector variable. Although it has long been known that confidence can be useful for sorting between culprit identifications and innocent-suspect identifications (Juslin et al., 1996; Lindsay et al., 1998; Sporer et al., 1995), eyewitness scientists have, historically, been hesitant to conclude that confidence reflects culprit presence (e.g., Sporer et al., 1995). This hesitation was attributable to the fact that if certain system-variable safeguards are not in place then an eyewitness might come to identify even an innocent suspect with high confidence. For example, when the police suspect stands out from the remaining lineup members, both guilty suspects and innocent suspects are relatively likely to be identified with high confidence, thereby rendering confidence to be a poor reflector of culprit presence (Wixted & Wells, 2017). In a landmark paper, Wixted and Wells (2017) demonstrated that under "pristine" lineup conditions, high-confidence suspect identifications imply culprit presence and low-confidence suspect identifications do not imply culprit presence. Among the pristine conditions needed are that the lineup includes only one suspect embedded among known-innocent fillers, the suspect does not stand out from the fillers, the witness is admonished that the culprit might not be present in the lineup, the administrator is blinded to the identity of the suspect, and the confidence statement is collected immediately after the identification decision. When these conditions are in place, high-confidence suspect identifications imply culprit presence and low-confidence suspect identifications do not imply culprit presence (Brewer & Wells, 2006; Wixted & Wells, 2017).

The second most commonly studied reflector variable is decision time. Because reliable recognition memory is generally automatic, rapid, and effortless, a fast suspect identification generally implies culprit presence and a slower suspect identification does not imply culprit presence (Brewer & Wells, 2006; Dodson & Dobolyi, 2016; Sporer, 1993). Both culprit identifications and innocent-suspect identifications can result from deliberative strategies such as rule of elimination. Deliberative strategies are time-consuming and suspect identifications that result from these strategies are relatively slow. Hence, slow suspect identifications do not provide strong evidence of culprit presence. Conversely, assuming pristine conditions and barring coincidental resemblance, only a culprit identification is likely to result from the much faster automatic, rapid, and effortless process. Hence, relatively fast suspect identifications imply culprit presence.

There is also some work examining how well confidence and decision time, together, can sort between the presence and absence of the culprit in the lineup (e.g., Dodson & Dobolyi, 2016). The key finding is that fast suspect identifications made with high confidence strongly imply culprit presence, but slower suspect identifications made with high confidence are less diagnostic of culprit presence. Hence, decision time might be an important moderator of the confidence-accuracy relationship for suspect identifications.

What about Rejections and Filler Identifications?

One notable shortfall in both the reflector-variable literature and the eyewitness identification literature more generally is the myopic focus on suspect identifications and the lack of empirical attention devoted to lineup rejections and filler identifications (Wells et al., 2015; Wells & Lindsay, 1980; Wells & Turtle, 1986). In comparing the relative worth of identification procedures, eyewitness scientists have focused almost exclusively on suspect identifications and have largely ignored filler identifications and rejections. The rationale is that only a suspect is at risk of arrest and conviction and that we ought to prevent the erroneous arrest and conviction of innocent persons. But identification procedures also have an immense capacity to demonstrate innocence. Consider the rates of suspect identifications in Table 27.1. Suspect identifications are far more likely when the culprit is present than when the culprit is absent, which means that they are diagnostic of guilt. But the reverse is true for filler identifications and rejections. Both of these behaviors are more likely when the culprit is absent than when the culprit is present. Because these behaviors are more likely when the culprit is absent than when the culprit is present, they are diagnostic of innocence. Whereas a suspect identification has the capacity to inculpate the guilty, filler identifications and rejections have the capacity to exculpate the innocent. Indeed, if the police investigator had the right guy in the lineup, then why is the witness not recognizing and identifying him? In our view, exculpating the innocent is every bit as important as inculpating the guilty, and any decision about which of two lineup procedures is superior must factor not only their

Table 27.1 Suspect Identification, Filler Identification, and Rejection Rates as a Function of Culprit Presence and Culprit Absence for the Clear Viewing Condition

	Suspect ID	Filler ID	Rejection
Culprit Present	73%	8%	20%
Culprit Absent	4%	21%	75%

Source: From Smith et al. (2019, Experiment 1).

relative capacities to incriminate but also their relative capacities to exculpate. While this argument is beyond the scope of the current work, we refer the interested reader to Smith et al. (2020) and to Wells et al. (2015).

That a rejection is diagnostic of culprit absence is quite intuitive. In theory, a witness rejects a lineup when none of its members provide a sufficiently strong match to their memory for the culprit. Because this phenomenology is more likely to occur when a witness encounters a culprit-absent lineup than when a witness encounters a culprit-present lineup, rejections are diagnostic of culprit absence. It takes a bit more thought to understand why filler identifications are diagnostic of culprit absence. When a witness identifies someone from a lineup, they are both explicitly identifying that individual and implicitly rejecting the remaining lineup members. When a witness identifies a filler, they are simultaneously rejecting the suspect. Of course, the witness should be more likely to reject the suspect—in one form or another—when that suspect is innocent compared to when that suspect is guilty. Hence, both rejections and filler identifications are diagnostic of culprit absence.

In addition to ignoring exculpating behaviors when making inferences about which of two lineup procedures is superior, the capacity of reflector variables to demonstrate culprit absence has also been understudied. As with incriminating behaviors, confidence and decision time are the two most studied reflector variables associated with exculpatory behaviors. Yet, neither confidence nor decision time has proven particularly successful at demonstrating the absence of the culprit in a lineup (Brewer & Wells, 2006; Sauerland & Sporer, 2007; Sporer, 1992). What is more, when it comes to demonstrating the absence of the culprit in a lineup, the examination of reflector variables has been limited almost entirely to rejection decisions whereas filler identifications have been almost entirely ignored. This is in spite of the fact that filler identifications are typically diagnostic of culprit absence (Wells et al., 2015).

A Call to Video Record Eyewitness Identification Procedures

Another shortfall of the reflector-variable literature is the utter failure to establish the extent to which combinations of reflector variables can better distinguish between the presence and absence of the culprit in a lineup than can isolated reflector variables. The evidence suggests that, when used together, confidence and decision time do a better job of sorting between culprit-present and culprit-absent lineups than does either variable on its own (e.g., Dodson & Dobolyi, 2016). But confidence and decision time are only two of a large corpus of reflector variables and most other reflector variables (e.g., pop-outs, elimination strategies, hedging, and spontaneous utterances) have only been examined in isolation. Given that no reflector variable can perfectly sort between culprit-present and culprit-absent lineups, it is somewhat surprising that researchers have not done more to look at the extent to which a set of reflector variables can be used to sort between the presence and absence of the culprit in a lineup.

There are logical reasons that might explain why researchers typically have not focused on measuring the incremental validity of using multiple reflector variables. Eyewitness lineup experiments typically require large numbers of participants. This is attributable to the fact that eyewitness experiments are typically conducted between participants and the dependent measure is typically binary (e.g., culprit present or culprit absent)[1] or categorical (e.g., suspect identification, filler identification, and rejection). The result is that adequately powering eyewitness experiments typically requires more than 1,000 participants. Given the sheer number of participants required to carry out the typical lineup experiment, data collection often proceeds online (with participants recruited from SONA or crowdsourcing platforms like Amazon's Mechanical Turk) and even when carried out in a laboratory setting the experimental protocol is often one of convenience in which the participant has little interaction with the experimenter and instead completes the experiment in relative isolation on a computer. Confidence and decision time are easy to measure with computer-administered lineup experiments, but other reflector variables (e.g., pop-outs, elimination strategies, hedging, spontaneous utterances) are much more difficult to measure with computer-administered experiments.

Capturing reflector variables other than eyewitness confidence and decision time means both observing and documenting the witness's verbal and nonverbal behaviors as she completes the lineup task. The only way to create a complete and accurate record of the witness's behaviors is to video record the witness during the identification task. Of course, sitting a participant in front of a computer screen and recording that individual is unlikely to elicit the sort of nonverbal and verbal behaviors that would be useful for sorting between culprit-present and culprit-absent lineups. Instead, it would probably be necessary to accompany the witness with an experimenter who acts in the role of a lineup administrator and coaxes information out of the witness or at least to have the participant complete some sort of think-aloud procedure. Once video records of participants completing lineups have been secured, raters who are blind as to whether the witness viewed a culprit-present or culprit-absent lineup would code the verbal and nonverbal behaviors of each eyewitness-participant. After building the data set, the compendium of reflector variables would then be subject to statistical analyses designed to determine which combinations of reflector variables best distinguish between the presence and absence of the culprit in the lineup and the absolute capacity of these reflector variables to sort between the presence and absence of the culprit in the lineup.

Because all of these reflector variables reflect the strength of the witness's recognition experience, they will, of course, be correlated with each other. Hence, of course there will

---

[1] Given that culprit presence and culprit absence is an experimentally manipulated variable, the attentive reader might be taken aback by reference to this variable as a dependent measure; however, when examining the usefulness of reflector variables for purposes of trying to assess ground truth (the real-world problem), culprit presence is used as the dependent measure.

be some redundant variance that is explained by confidence, decision time, and verbalized strategies, for instance. But none of these variables perfectly reflects the strength of the witness's recognition experience and each of these variables is also associated with some degree of measurement error. Hence, there will be instances in which we observe divergence, such as rapid decisions with low confidence or slow decisions with high confidence. What do these mean? When there is a discrepancy, which is more trustworthy, the self-report of confidence or the rapidity of the decision? What we do know is that because all individual measures have some measurement error, multiple measures should be a more reliable predictor than any single measure. It comes back to the idea that we are trying to measure the strength of the witness's recognition experience with the understanding that a strong recognition experience should only occur when the culprit is present in the lineup. Because we cannot measure the strength of a witness's recognition experience directly, a better approach is to measure all of the behavioral manifestations of that underlying latent construct and to integrate those behaviors into a comprehensive reflector model.

In the end, the goal is to answer the question of which combination of reflector variables best distinguishes between lineups that include the culprit and lineups that do not include the culprit and the absolute capacity of this combination of reflector variables to do so. Our proposal to video record eyewitness-participants as they complete lineup tasks in the lab is in line with recent calls for police agencies to video record all lineup procedures. Motivations for past calls to video record identification procedures primarily concerned preserving a faithful record of what happened during the identification procedure and encouraging law enforcement personnel to follow best-practice recommendations (Kassin, 1998; National Research Council, 2014; Wells et al., 2020). Preserving faithful records and encouraging use of best practices are certainly good reasons for video recording identification procedures; however, we believe that the greatest potential that might come from video recording lineup procedures is the potential to extract reflector-variable information that might be used to sort between the presence and absence of the culprit in the lineup. There is a lot of lab work that needs to be done before we can begin extracting reflector-variable information from video recordings of real-world eyewitnesses and using these variables to make inferences about culprit presence, but in this respect, video recordings have the potential to revolutionize eyewitness science in the real world.

Conclusion

For forty years, research on eyewitness identification has been guided by the distinction between system variables and estimator variables. Here, we introduce a third class of eyewitness variables—*reflector variables*. Whereas system variables and estimator variables affect witness accuracy, reflector variables reflect witness accuracy. Reflector variables reflect whether the culprit is present in or absent from the lineup identification procedure. Past research on reflector variables has focused on their isolated capacity to sort between the presence and absence of the culprit in the lineup. Because no measure perfectly reflects the presence or absence of the culprit in a police lineup, future work must put more emphasis on examining the relative capacity of multiple reflector variables to distinguish between culprit-present and culprit-absent lineups. We suggest that the only way to effectively encode and preserve all the valuable reflector-variable information that is available during a lineup procedure is to video record the lineup procedure in its entirety and to have coders score the witness on the compendium of reflector variables. Whereas past arguments in favor of video recording identification procedures have focused on transparency and promoting adherence to best-practice administration, we suggest that the greatest potential from video recording identification procedures is the potential to distinguish between lineups that include the culprit and lineups that do not include the culprit.

References

Brewer, N., & Wells, G. L. (2006). The confidence-accuracy relationship in eyewitness identification: Effects of lineup instructions, foil similarity, and target-absent base rates. *Journal of Experimental Psychology: Applied*, *12*(1), 11–30.

Diamond, R., & Carey, S. (1986). Why faces are and are not special: An effect of expertise. *Journal of Experimental Psychology: General*, *115*(2), 107–117.

Dodson, C. S., & Dobolyi, D. G. (2016). Confidence and Eyewitness Identifications: The Cross-Race Effect, Decision Time and Accuracy: Confidence and eyewitness identifications. *Applied Cognitive Psychology*, *30*(1), 113–125.

Dunning, D., & Perretta, S. (2002). Automaticity and eyewitness accuracy: A 10- to 12-second rule for distinguishing accurate from inaccurate positive identifications. *Journal of Applied Psychology*, *87*(5), 951–962.

Dunning, D., & Stern, L. B. (1994). Distinguishing accurate from inaccurate eyewitness identifications via inquiries about decision processes. *Journal of Personality and Social Psychology*, *67*(5), 818–835. https://doi.org/10.1037/0022-3514.67.5.818

Hay, D. C., Young, A. W., & Ellis, A. W. (1986). What happens when a face rings a bell? Automatic processing of famous faces. In H. D. Ellis, M. A. Jeeves, F. Newcombe, & A. W. Young (Eds.), *Aspects of face processing*. Martinus Nijhoff.

Horry, R., Halford, P., Brewer, N., Milne, R., & Bull, R. (2014). Archival analyses of eyewitness identification test outcomes: What can they tell us about eyewitness memory? *Law and Human Behavior*, *38*(1), 94–108.

Juslin, P., Olsson, N., & Winman, A. (1996). Calibration and diagnosticity of confidence in eyewitness identification: Comments on what can be inferred from the low confidence–accuracy correlation. *Journal of Experimental Psychology: Learning, Memory, and Cognition*, *22*(5), 1304–1316.

Kassin, S. M. (1998). Eyewitness identification procedures: The fifth rule. *Law and Human Behavior*, *22*(6), 649–653.

Klobuchar, A., Steblay, N. K., & Caligiuri, H. L. (2006). Improving eyewitness identifications: Hennepin County's Blind Sequential Lineup Pilot Project. *Cardozo Public Law, Policy, and Ethics Journal*, *2*, 381–414.

Lampinen, J. M., Erickson, W. B., Moore, K. N., & Hittson, A. (2014). Effects of distance on face recognition: Implications for eyewitness identification. *Psychonomic Bulletin & Review*, *21*(6), 1489–1494.

Lindsay, D. S., Read, J. D., & Sharma, K. (1998). Accuracy and confidence in person identification: The relationship is strong when witnessing conditions vary widely. *Psychological Science*, *9*(3), 215–218.

Lindsay, R. C. L., Semmler, C., Weber, N., Brewer, N., & Lindsay, M. R. (2008). How variations in distance affect eyewitness reports and identification accuracy. *Law and Human Behavior*, *32*(6), 526–535.

Loftus, E. F., Schooler, J. W., Boone, S. M., & Kline, D. (1987). Time went by so slowly: Overestimation of event duration by males and females. *Applied Cognitive Psychology*, *1*(1), 3–13.

Memon, A., Hope, L., & Bull, R. (2003). Exposure duration: Effects on eyewitness accuracy and confidence. *British Journal of Psychology*, *94*(3), 339–354.

National Institute of Justice. (1999). *Eyewitness evidence: A guide for law enforcement* (NCJ No. 178240). US Department of Justice, Office of Justice Programs.

National Research Council. (2014). *Identifying the culprit: Assessing eyewitness identification.* The National Academies Press. https://www.nap.edu/catalog/18891/identifyingtheculprit-assessing-eyewitness-identification

Sauer, J., Brewer, N., Zweck, T., & Weber, N. (2010). The effect of retention interval on the confidence–accuracy relationship for eyewitness identification. *Law and Human Behavior, 34*(4), 337–347.

Sauerland, M., & Sporer, S. L. (2007). Post-decision confidence, decision time, and self-reported decision processes as postdictors of identification accuracy. *Psychology, Crime & Law, 13*(6), 611–625.

Smith, A. M., Wilford, M. M., Quigley-McBride, A., & Wells, G. L. (2019). Mistaken eyewitness identification rates increase when either witnessing or testing conditions get worse. *Law and Human Behavior, 43*(4), 358–368.

Smith, A. M., Yang, Y., & Wells, G. L. (2020). Distinguishing between investigator discriminability and eyewitness discriminability: A method for creating full receiver operating characteristic curves of lineup identification performance. *Perspectives on Psychological Science, 15*(3), 589–607.

Sporer, S. L. (1992). Post-dicting eyewitness accuracy: Confidence, decision-times and person descriptions of choosers and non-choosers. *European Journal of Social Psychology, 22*(2), 157–180.

Sporer, S. L. (1993). Eyewitness identification accuracy, confidence, and decision times in simultaneous and sequential lineups. *Journal of Applied Psychology, 78*(1), 22–33.

Sporer, S. L., Penrod, S., Read, D., & Cutler, B. (1995). Choosing, confidence, and accuracy: A meta-analysis of the confidence-accuracy relation in eyewitness identification studies. *Psychological Bulletin, 118*(3), 315–327.

Steblay, N. K., Wells, G. L., & Douglass, A. B. (2014). The eyewitness post identification feedback effect 15 years later: Theoretical and policy implications. *Psychology, Public Policy, and Law, 20*(1), 1–18.

Tulving, E. (1983). Ecphoric processes in episodic memory. *Philosophical Transactions of the Royal Society of London. B, Biological Sciences, 302*(1110), 361–371.

Valentine, T., Pickering, A., & Darling, S. (2003). Characteristics of eyewitness identification that predict the outcome of real lineups. *Applied Cognitive Psychology, 17*(8), 969–993.

Weber, N., Brewer, N., Wells, G. L., Semmler, C., & Keast, A. (2004). eyewitness identification accuracy and response latency: The unruly 10-12-second rule. *Journal of Experimental Psychology: Applied, 10*(3), 139–147.

Wells, G. L. (1978). Applied eyewitness-testimony research: System variables and estimator variables. *Journal of Personality and Social Psychology, 36*(12), 1546–1557.

Wells, G. L. (1984). The psychology of lineup identifications. *Journal of Applied Social Psychology, 14*(2), 89–103.

Wells, G. L. (2018). Eyewitness identification. In E. Luna (Ed.), *Reforming criminal justice: Policing* (pp. 259–278). (Vol. 2, pp. 259–278). Iowa State University Press.

Wells, G. L. (2020). Psychological science on eyewitness identification and its impact on police practices and policies. *American Psychologist, 75*(9), 1316–1329.

Wells, G. L., & Bradfield, A. L. (1998). "Good, you identified the suspect": Feedback to eyewitnesses distorts their reports of the witnessing experience. *Journal of Applied Psychology, 83*(3), 360–376.

Wells, G. L., & Luus, E. C. A. (1990). Police lineups as experiments: Social methodology as a framework for properly conducted lineups. *Personality and Social Psychology Bulletin, 16*(1), 106–117.

Wells, G. L., & Hryciw, B. (1984). Memory for faces: Encoding and retrieval operations. *Memory & Cognition, 12*(4), 338–344.

Wells, G. L., Kovera, M. B., Douglass, A. B., Brewer, N., Meissner, C. A., & Wixted, J. T. (2020). Policy and procedure recommendations for the collection and preservation of eyewitness identification evidence. *Law and Human Behavior, 44*(1), 3–36.

Wells, G. L., & Lindsay, R. C. (1980). On estimating the diagnosticity of eyewitness nonidentifications. *Psychological Bulletin, 88*(3), 776–784.

Wells, G. L., Small, M., Penrod, S., Malpass, R. S., Fulero, S. M., & Brimacombe, C. A. E. (1998). Eyewitness identification procedures: Recommendations for lineups and photospreads. *Law and Human Behavior, 22*(6), 603–647.

Wells, G. L., Steblay, N. K., & Dysart, J. E. (2015). Double-blind photo lineups using actual eyewitnesses: An experimental test of a sequential versus simultaneous lineup procedure. *Law and Human Behavior, 39*(1), 1–14.

Wells, G. L., & Turtle, J. W. (1986). Eyewitness identification: The importance of lineup models. *Psychological Bulletin, 99*(3), 320–329.

Wells, G. L., Yang, Y., & Smalarz, L. (2015). Eyewitness identification: Bayesian information gain, base-rate effect equivalency curves, and reasonable suspicion. *Law and Human Behavior, 39*(2), 99–122.

Wilford, M. M., & Wells, G. L. (2010). Does Facial Processing Prioritize Change Detection? Change Blindness Illustrates Costs and Benefits of Holistic Processing. *Psychological Science, 21*(11), 1611–1615.

Wilford, M. M., & Wells, G. L. (2013). Eyewitness system variables. In B. L. Cutler (Ed.), *Reform of eyewitness identification procedures.* (pp. 23–43). American Psychological Association.

Wixted, J. T., Mickes, L., Dunn, J. C., Clark, S. E., & Wells, W. (2016). Estimating the reliability of eyewitness identifications from police lineups. *Proceedings of the National Academy of Sciences, 113*(2), 304–309.

Wixted, J. T., & Wells, G. L. (2017). The Relationship Between Eyewitness Confidence and Identification Accuracy: A New Synthesis. *Psychological Science in the Public Interest, 18*(1), 10–65.

Interviewing Cooperative Forensic Witnesses and Mediation: Areas of Overlap and Potential for Future Research

Deborah Goldfarb *and* Ronald P. Fisher

Abstract

Although recent work has expanded research on empirically informed forensic interviewing techniques outside the criminal context, no work that we are aware of has considered potential synergies for this research within the realm of alternative dispute resolution (ADR). The current chapter addresses the relation between forensic interviewing and ADR, and more specifically how techniques developed to interview forensic witnesses might be adapted for mediation. In so doing, we first review the research on mediation and forensic interviewing. Next we compare and contrast the two contexts on both psychological and legal dimensions. Finally, we examine areas of potential growth and future directions. By bringing together the work on potential synergies between the two realms, we hope to inspire others to expand further this nascent area of research.

Key Words: forensic interviews, alternate dispute resolution, interviewing, cognitive interview, mediation

Legal psychology has a long history of conducting research on the best techniques to help elicit memories of specific, episodic events or experiences. Research on forensic interviewing previously was applied primarily to criminal settings. Indeed, numerous law enforcement agencies have adopted forensically informed interviewing techniques, such as the Cognitive Interview (CI; Fisher & Geiselman, 1992, 2019) or, in the context of interviewing children, the National Institute of Child Health and Human Development (NICHD) (Lamb et al., 2007) or Ten-Step (Lyon, 2005) protocols, as part of their investigative practice. Recent work, however, has expanded research on empirically informed forensic interviewing techniques into the civil and administrative realms as well. No work that we are aware of, however, has considered applying techniques for interviewing cooperative witnesses to alternative dispute resolution (ADR).

Although academics debate the exact definition of ADR (Eisenberg, 2020), at its most colloquial and simplest sense, ADR is the process whereby parties attempt to resolve disputes outside of trial. ADR processes can include (1) negotiation, when parties meet to informally settle a case; (2) arbitration, when cases are heard and decided by a third-party neutral rather than a judge; and (3) mediation, when parties meet with a third-party neutral in an attempt to work together to reach a mutually agreed upon resolution.

Despite their separate empirical evolutions, research on forensic interviewing has several potential benefits for ADR, and vice versa. Indeed, both contexts seek to encourage parties, where possible, to establish rapport with each other and, to some extent, to exchange relevant information. Given potential areas of overlap, we consider how psychological research on interviewing witnesses to legally relevant events could apply to the ADR context, focusing here on mediation, and, correspondingly, how research on mediation might benefit either research on or the practice of interviewing cooperative forensic witnesses.

The chapter first outlines the roles of forensic interviewing and ADR in their respective domains and then provides a brief overview of the existing research. We then compare the two interview contexts, examining both their similarities and the differences, and we do so in terms of both the underlying psychological processes engaged and also their legal ramifications. We then examine possible symbiotic relations between the two contexts. Finally, we conclude with suggestions about future directions.

Overview of Forensic Interviewing and Research

Eliciting information from victims and witnesses to crime is the lifeblood of criminal investigation. Analyses of shoeprints, fabrics, and abandoned cigarette butts makes for compelling television programming, but these analyses alone rarely solve real-world criminal cases. More prosaic, but characteristic of reality, the best predictor of whether police close cases is the quantity and quality of verbal information provided by witnesses (Baskin & Sommers, 2010; Rand Corporation, 1975). Unfortunately, victims and witnesses frequently do not provide as much information as police need to solve crimes. Reasons for witnesses providing limited information abound: Crimes occur quickly, so there is minimal opportunity to encode the event; the perpetrator may be unknown to the witness, who, naturally, finds it difficult to describe strangers; a weapon may be used during the commission of the crime, drawing victims' and witnesses' attention to the weapon—and not to the perpetrator. Whereas these factors certainly limit witness descriptions, there is nothing police can do to overcome these limitations (estimator variables; Wells, 1978). One factor that police have control over, and therefore can improve upon, is their method of conducting interviews.

In general, police interviews have been less than ideal, to be kind. Earlier reviews showed that police interviewers likely elicited considerably less information than was available and that they made some avoidable errors, including not developing adequate rapport, asking too few open-ended questions and too many closed questions, and, especially, asking suggestive questions. Moreover, interviewers did little to facilitate witness memory when witnesses were unable to access information from memory (e.g., Fisher et al., 1987). This pattern held for American, Canadian, and German police (Fisher et al., 2014). This less-than-optimal performance may have been the natural byproduct of providing minimal training for police to interview cooperative witnesses (Molinaro et al., 2019; but see Kebbell et al., 2013 for a description of more thorough training in the UK).

Over the last three decades, researchers have attempted to provide empirically informed methods that can improve the quality of police interviews by incorporating scientific principles of cognitive and social psychology into interviewing techniques. The most successful of these interviewing techniques, and the protocol that has been tested most thoroughly, is the CI (Fisher & Geiselman, 1992, 2019). See Table 28.1 for a summary of the major elements of the CI.

Table 28.1 Important CI Techniques

CI Element	Description
Rapport	Develop rapport between respondent and interviewer
Active respondent participation	Respondent actively to generate information (not merely to answer Interviewer's questions)
Report everything	Include all recollections in response; do not edit out unimportant details
Reinstate context	Reinstate the context of the original experience
Describe in detail	Instruct respondents to provide a detailed account
Close eyes	Instruct respondents to close their eyes
No interruptions	Do not interrupt the respondent's narration
Don't guess	Instruct respondents not to guess (OK to say "I don't know")
Open-ended questions	Ask primarily open-ended questions (closed questions as follow-up)
Multiple retrieval	Encourage respondents to search through memory more than once
Varied retrieval	Encourage respondents to search through memory in different ways
Respondent-compatible questions	Ask questions that are compatible with respondent's currently accessible information
Avoid suggestive questions	Avoid asking questions that suggest a specific answer
Code-compatible output	Allow respondents to output their knowledge in the same form as it is stored (often non-verbal)

Note. Additional explanations of and support for each of the elements and descriptions above can be found in "Expanding the Cognitive Interview to Non-criminal Investigations" by R. P. Fisher and R. E. Geiselman, in J. J. Dickinson, N. Schreiber Compo, R. Carol, B. L. Schwartz, and M. McCauley (Eds.), *Evidenced-Based Investigative Interviewing: Applying Cognitive Principles* (p. 3), 2019, Routledge. Copyright © 2019 by Routledge.

Research Methodology

Most of the research testing the CI entails presenting a videotape of a simulated crime to undergraduate college students and then interviewing the students about their recollection of the crime details. To allow for analysis of the effect of the interview techniques, the interviews are conducted either as a CI or as a Structured Interview, which is composed of generally considered good interview techniques (e.g., rapport and nonsuggestive questions) but without the unique memory- and communication-enhancing elements of the CI. Variations on the test procedures also include live, innocuous events, sometimes to nonstudent adults (or to children). The interviewers are usually student assistants—although, on occasion, professional law enforcement conduct the interviews. The delay between seeing the event and interview varies from a few minutes (the most common procedure) to several days. In these laboratory studies, standard measures of the interview's success are the amount of information (number of statements) produced by the witnesses and the accuracy rate (proportion of statements that are correct).

A limited number of studies have been conducted in the field in the United States and Europe, with victims and witnesses of real crimes or road accidents (e.g., Dodier et al., 2021). Currently, Ashkenazi and Fisher (2022) are exploring police/security investigations of crime and terrorist activity in Israel. The obvious advantage of real-world investigations is that they extend the range of investigative events to include highly arousing and fearful experiences, which are prohibited in laboratory studies. The disadvantages of examining real-world investigations are that (a) the researcher usually cannot measure accuracy, because there is no record of the actual event (e.g., no videotape of the crime), which researchers normally have in laboratory studies; and (b) researchers cannot experimentally control any of the variables that might influence witness recollection (e.g., proximity to the event; perpetrator's physical characteristics). Interestingly, the patterns of results found in the zoo of real-world investigations are remarkably similar to those found in the tightly choreographed laboratory studies.

Research Findings

Of the roughly 130 studies on the effects of the CI, the most common finding is that the CI elicits approximately 30–70 percent more information than does the Structured Interview (SI), and at comparable accuracy rates (see Memon et al., 2010, for a meta-analysis, and Fisher & Geiselman, 2019, for a recent review). Of the 130 studies, only three did not reveal the CI superiority effect: In two studies, there were no differences in the amount of information gathered and in one study, more information was gathered with the CI, but the accuracy rate was lower (Fisher & Geiselman, 2019).

Increasing the number of facts would seem, at first blush, to be presumptively valuable to forensic investigations, as more facts are better than fewer facts. Some facts, however, may not be particularly useful (e.g., the robber was wearing shoes). Moreover, we can imagine that there is a tipping point at which additional facts may be counterproductive, as they may overwhelm the investigator. Better than measuring the number of facts gathered, it would be more valuable to measure the utility of the elicited facts to accomplish the investigator's goal.

Two recent studies, one conducted in the laboratory and one conducted as part of real-world criminal and terrorist investigations, did just that, assessing the utility of the gathered information. In Satin and Fisher (2019), student witnesses were interviewed with either a CI or SI to provide descriptions of the perpetrator of a live, simulated crime. Another set of investigators (other students in Experiment 1, and police officers in Experiment 2) then attempted to find the perpetrator (from a collection of photographs) based on the CI-elicited or SI-elicited descriptors. The investigators were approximately 35 percent more likely to find the perpetrators using the CI-elicited than the SI-elicited descriptors. In Ashkenazi and Fisher (2022), victims and witnesses of violent crimes (shootings, stabbings, and others) were interviewed by experienced Israeli interviewers who conducted either a CI or SI. Other, professional investigators rated the intelligence value of the CI-elicited information to be considerably greater (more than 3 points higher on a 10-point scale) than the SI-elicited information. We encourage other researchers to measure not only the number of facts elicited but, more important, the utility of the facts in an investigatively relevant task.

Although the CI has been effective, it has drawbacks. First, it takes longer to train investigators to learn the CI than to learn the simpler SI. Second, it generally takes more time to conduct a CI than an SI, which limits using the CI to very serious cases (e.g., murders, armed robberies, child abductions, and sexual assaults), where investigators have more time to conduct the interview. Of course, one might make the counterargument that if an investigator spends dozens of hours to complete all of the subtasks in a complex case (e.g., conducting interviews, writing reports, giving depositions, and testifying—and waiting—in court), then the additional thirty minutes or so required to conduct a CI is only a "drop in the bucket." Finally, Westera et al. (2017) have argued that the CI may not be appropriate for sexual assault cases, because the flood of additional information may tax jurors' limited abilities to process very detailed accounts. In keeping with our earlier recommendation, investigators should decide how to conduct interviews based on the utility of the information gathered, which may vary from one case to another. Alternatively, if testimony is presented via the recording rather than live, prosecutors should be judicious when deciding which of the many statements elicited in the original witness interview will be presented to jurors.

Overview of Mediation and Research on Mediation

Substantial research has also been conducted on the benefits of ADR, including whether it saves time and resources for the contending parties. For instance, the Department of Justice (DOJ) regularly analyzes the number of cases it resolves via ADR and the potential upsides from deciding cases outside the courtroom. In 2017, the DOJ estimated that it resolved 75 percent of its cases via ADR, resulting in a savings of approximately $14 million and almost two thousand months of litigation time (Department of Justice, 2020; see also Bingham et al., 2008).

As of the time of writing this chapter, the COVID-19 pandemic of 2020 and 2021 caused closures throughout the United States and the world. Courts were among those impacted and, although legal professionals worked valiantly to move portions of proceedings online, trials were put on hold for months (Chan, 2021). Indeed, during the pandemic, many courthouses had not conducted either in-person or online jury trials for approximately eight months. One proposed solution to these delays and backlog is ADR.

Decreasing costs and time spent on litigation are not the only benefits to ADR. Resolving cases outside of adversarial hearings may also be the parties' preference. Parties often enter disputes with a preference for adversarial proceedings, including trial. Scientists posit that this may be due to parties' familiarity with such procedures (see Shestowsky, 2020). Preferences, however, seem to change as cases progress. Despite their initial preference, many parties report *ex ante* (after their case has resolved) that they prefer settlement or other cooperative dispute resolution procedures (Shestowsky, 2020). Advocates also argue that ADR allows individuals to have more of a voice in both the process and the outcome of their case.

Concerns do exist, however, that resolving almost all cases outside the court system has downsides. For instance, cases decided via mediation do not create case law, which helps establish precedent upon which other courts may rely and with which lawyers may advise their clients. Indeed, many mediated agreements contain nondisclosure clauses that prevent disclosure of the facts of the case and its outcome. By moving outcomes into the parties' hands, we often sacrifice the public nature of resolving a case.

Although how ADR is conducted varies greatly depending on the procedure utilized and the facts and posture of the case (e.g., multiple parties vs. two parties and prelitigation vs. during the course of litigation), central to almost all forms of dispute resolution is a retelling or discussion of each party's beliefs about the facts in a case. For instance, elicitive mediation requires mediators to encourage parties to state their premises and perspectives (Goldfien & Robbennolt, 2006). In discussing their own premises, parties will rely on their memories for the prior interactions and the dispute itself, and, as discussed above, memory can often be incomplete.

Research on Mediation

Research on mediation has grown within the past few decades; indeed, a review of the past sixty years of research on negotiation and mediation noted that articles were discussing the contours of mediation as early as 1957 (Druckman & Wall, 2017). Researchers have empirically analyzed a vast range of topics within the mediation realm, from the effectiveness of mediator techniques to analyzing individuals' preferences for various alternative dispute resolution techniques (see ABA Dispute Resolution Task Force Report, 2017).

A systematic review of the research on mediator techniques found that, as of around 2017, approximately forty-seven studies had been conducted on this subject (Task Force Report, 2017). In the intervening years since the 2017 systematic review, other studies have analyzed either the role mediators' techniques place on case outcomes or other factors influencing the impact of mediation, including work on party preferences in mediation (Storrow & Coleman, 2020).

Research Methodology

Studies on mediators' techniques have focused primarily on the effect of such techniques on whether a dispute is resolved (Task Force, 2017). Many studies that analyzed mediator techniques look specifically at mediator behaviors in actual cases and often use pre- and post-surveys to determine whether they predict case outcomes (Charkoudian et al., 2018). Other studies analyze techniques either in the laboratory through the use of mock conflicts or in the real-world using quasi-experimental designs. Few studies have utilized randomized control trials to analyze effects of mediators' behaviors. Across all these studies, a wide variety of case facts and disputes have been analyzed, including family, general civil, and small claims court.

Perhaps the most common thread in the methodology used in mediation studies is the lack of a common thread. For example, methods for quantifying mediators' techniques mirror the variety seen in the types of cases analyzed. Many researchers have attempted to develop underlying taxonomies of mediator behaviors (Druckman & Wall, 2017). In their review of the literature, Druckman and Wall (2017) proposed that at least twenty-four categories of such behaviors have been identified, varying from communicative behaviors to facilitative movements.

Studies also vary as to how they measure outcomes in the mediation process. For instance, even quantifying whether a case is resolved is not always clear; many mediations end in a partial resolution or require additional steps to solidify the case. Other studies do not attempt to quantify resolution but, instead, consider the relationship between the parties and whether the mediators' behaviors influence how the parties interact with one another (increasing quality communications, views of the other party in a favorable light, likelihood of interacting together in the future). Finally, other studies consider how mediators' behaviors relate to litigants' views of either the mediation process itself or the legal system generally.

Scholars have noted the need for standardizing outcomes and developing validated measures of mediator techniques (Boyle, 2017; Task Force, 2017). Model Mediation Surveys have been developed to create more consistency in the measurements used across these studies (Task Force, 2017). These surveys gather standardized information from the various parties in a mediation proceeding. The goal is to allow for comparative analyses across case types and different mediation platforms.

Mediation has been shown repeatedly to have beneficial effects on case outcomes, with approximately 60 percent of cases reaching an agreement (Druckman & Wall, 2017). No clear connection between mediators' behaviors and techniques during the mediation process and case resolution has been shown: Some studies reveal a positive relation to case resolution (with a particular behavior increasing the likelihood of resolving a case); others showing a negative relation (decreasing the likelihood of case resolution), and others no benefit at all (Task Force, 2017). Indeed, the most recent review of the literature found that no one technique revealed a clear benefit for either case outcomes or the parties' relationships with one another.

The Task Force did identify a number of mediator techniques that studies showed had "greater potential for positive effects than negative effects" (Task Force, 2017, p. 4). These specific techniques were:

> (1) eliciting disputants' suggestions or solutions; (2) giving more attention to disputants' emotions, relationship, and sources of conflict; (3) working to build trust and rapport, expressing empathy or praising the disputants, and structuring the agenda; and (4) using premediation caucuses focused on establishing trust.

Thus, of the mixed results found so far, it appears that the techniques that encourage the parties to talk more about their past, current, and future experiences appear to have the most beneficial effect on case outcomes.

Elicitation of information about past experiences is also a goal of forensic interviewing, albeit from the interviewee rather than a party to a mediation. There is thus the potential for shared overlap and distinction between the two areas.

Comparing and Contrasting Mediation and Forensic Interviews of Witnesses: Psychological Similarities and Differences:

We explore in this section points of similarity and points of contrast between mediation and forensic interviewing.

Common Elements

Both mediators and forensic interviewers attempt to elicit information from people who, at the outset, are unknown to the interviewers, a condition that normally militates against effective communication. This is especially the case for events that carry emotional overtones. Both mediators and forensic interviewers are therefore encouraged to establish rapport and a good working relationship to begin their conversations.

Forensic witnesses and parties to a mediation may have incorrect beliefs about their respective tasks, which will misdirect the conversations. Forensic witnesses may believe, because of the imbalance of power between witnesses and law enforcement interviewers, that the interviewer will dominate the interview and ask many questions, and that the witness's task is merely to answer the interviewer's questions by providing concise answers. In fact, forensic respondents could perform their tasks more effectively, and be more informative, if they actively generated extensive details in the form of a rich narrative. Similarly, parties to a mediation may incorrectly believe that the mediator's function is to help them win their dispute against the other party—when, in fact, the mediator's role is to help the disputants attempt to reach an agreement that satisfies both (or all) their needs. In both cases, mediators and interviewers will need to educate their interviewees about the goals of the interview, including disabusing litigants as to incorrect beliefs about the process, and then guide the respondent's behavior to help maximize the interview's goals.

Mediators in many jurisdictions are currently required under their rules of ethics to provide an opening statement that outlines the purpose and format of the mediation. For instance, in Florida, mediators must "describe the mediation process and the role of the mediator."[1] The mediator must then go on to inform the parties that mediation is consensual and confidential, and that the mediator is impartial and cannot require resolution.

One CI technique that could help bolster the required "opening statement" that mediators provide is through a model statement, or an example of what a rich, detailed response sounds like—but not using an event that is semantically related to the police investigation. The model statement has been shown to elicit considerably more detailed descriptions from witnesses (Leal et al., 2015). Mediators might educate their respondents by modeling the kinds of statements or discussions that promote agreement among the disputants. For instance, mediators might say "When I disagree with my cousin, we both indicate one area where we are firm, but also other areas that are open to negotiation, as I realize that we may both have different goals."

Witnesses and parties to a mediation will likely think about their experiences in a limited manner—in part reflecting that human beings have only limited capacity to process information (e.g., Kahneman, 1973). For instance, the witness may think about a bank robbery only from the witness's perspective of waiting in line, whereas the ADR disputant thinks about the disputed event only from their perspective. To overcome the limitation of thinking about experiences only from one's perspective, forensic investigators might ask witnesses to think about the bank robbery also from the bank robber's perspective (the CI's principle of Varied Retrieval). Similar tools are also used in mediation, including reframing, which is to encourage the parties to think about an experience or a position in a different way. For instance, mediators might instruct parties also to consider the financial losses associated with not reaching an agreement quickly.

---

[1] Fla. R. for Certified Mediators Rule 10.420.

Contrasting Elements

The goals of forensic and ADR interviews differ considerably. Ideally, forensic interviews will yield a historically accurate account of the critical event that occurred in the past, whereas discussions during a mediation are intended to yield an agreement between two contesting parties as to a future goal. As such, forensic interviewers focus on processes associated with the witness's memory retrieval, whereas mediators focus on processes associated with the parties' social (awareness of the other party involved) and decision-making processes (whether to agree or not, or to modify a settlement).

The sequences of events leading up to forensic interviews and mediation differ considerably, and these differences have important implications for recall accuracy. Forensic interviews are often conducted shortly after a critical event—although some interviews may be delayed by months or years—and in many cases provide the first opportunity for a witness to think about and describe the event to an authority. By comparison, mediations arise potentially after a long-standing dispute and after prior unsuccessful meetings by the disputants to reach a solution. The parties thus have likely had many opportunities to retrieve the event from memory. Delaying a mediation is not likely to significantly further alter the respondent's recollection of the critical event, but delaying a forensic interview, even by a day or two, may have deleterious effects on remembering a recently experienced crime event.

Differences in timing between mediation and forensic interviewing can also result in differences between the contact that the parties have prior to the ultimate meeting (either the mediation or the forensic interview). Mediators often speak with the parties ahead of the mediation. Sometimes mediators meet with the parties before mediation, which is often referred to as a premediation caucus. When premediation caucuses focus on establishing trust between the mediator and the parties, they have been found to be effective at resolving the case (Task Force Report, 2017). Forensic interviewers are often under greater time pressures and may not have as much time to conduct pre-interview discussions. That being said, spending additional time to establish rapport and trust prior to the interview may yield similar benefits in the forensic context. Further research is needed on this issue.

The relationship between the people involved is also likely to vary considerably between forensic interviews and mediations. In forensic interviews, and especially with bystander witnesses, the respondent's role is to provide the investigator with information that will help to solve the crime. The obligation to reach a conclusion falls on the shoulders of the law enforcement investigator, with the bystander witness merely helping the investigator by providing factual information. By comparison, in mediation, the parties may feel that the mediator's role is to help each party win the argument with the competing complainant. Whether the police interviewer is seen as the primary actor, with the witness playing only a "helper" role, or the party is seen as the primary actor, with the mediator playing the helper role, is likely to influence whether respondents view themselves as passive responders (forensic interviews) or as active controllers of the dialog (mediation). We note that the aforesaid analysis, of the bystander witness assisting the law enforcement investigator, may break down depending on the nature of the crime and the parties to the investigation (e.g., whether the individual is a victim or a bystander or a witness who is related to one of the parties in the case).

Legal Similarities and Differences

Mediation and bystander witness interviews share a number of legal similarities. First, both proceedings occur prior to the trial and, as such, are procedural attempts to move the case in a new direction. Eyewitness interviews are part of the evidence-gathering mechanisms in legal proceedings.[2] These interviews allow eyewitnesses to provide relevant facts and exchange potential sources of information. Although mediation is not primarily meant as an information-gathering mechanism, as discussed more below, legal mechanisms are in place, such as provisions of confidentiality, to encourage the parties to freely exchange information.

Second, both eyewitness interviews and mediation proceedings can occur either voluntarily or under compulsion of a legal authority. Many eyewitness interviews can and do proceed without legal compulsion. If witnesses refuse to cooperate, a subpoena may be issued requiring that the witness testifies.[3] In some states, such subpoenas can be served prior to an indictment or a charge being filed, and many statutes allow witnesses to be held in contempt for failing to appear.[4] The ability to require testimony, however, is not without limits; eyewitnesses maintain their right against self-incrimination and can move to limit the scope of the inquiry and may seek to quash the subpoena in its entirety.[5]

Mediation can be conducted voluntarily and at the parties' own request.[6] Courts also can and do order parties to attend mediation in an attempt to resolve the suit.[7] Indeed, as discussed earlier in the chapter, many courts have now instituted some form of mandated early dispute resolution, including mediation. As with compelled interviews, parties also have procedural protections during the mediation process. Mediation is a voluntary process, and the mediator cannot order the parties to resolve the dispute (but see Nolan-Haley, 2009, arguing that parties are often implicitly or explicitly encouraged to settle).

In addition to their psychological or empirical differences, mediation and forensic interviewing also share several legal differences. These differences can help guide our understanding of when research from one realm may help inform the other. Here, we cover three key differences: Use of information gathered during the two procedures as evidence in the underlying trial, duty of confidentiality, and mandatory nature of the proceedings.

---

[2] See 18 U.S.C. § 3502.

[3] Fed. R. of Crim. Proc. Rule 17.

[4] Id.

[5] Fed. R. Crim. Proc. R. 17(c)(2).

[6] See Dist. Ct. Alaska Local R. 6.2; Dist. Ct. of Me. Local R. 83.11.

[7] Dist. Ct. Alaska Local R. 16.2.

In almost all jurisdictions, the information provided during mediation cannot be offered into evidence. For instance, under the California Rules of Evidence,

> No evidence of anything said or any admission made for the purpose of, in the course of, or pursuant to, a mediation or a mediation consultation is admissible or subject to discovery, and disclosure of the evidence shall not be compelled, in any arbitration, administrative adjudication, civil action, or other noncriminal proceeding in which, pursuant to law, testimony can be compelled to be given.[8]

The goal of such protections is to allow parties to communicate freely and exchange information without concerns about how it may later be portrayed in a court of law or by a fact-finder.

Forensic interviews, however, are conducted for the purpose of information gathering that can be later used during a courtroom proceeding. Ironically, of course, most cases do not end in trial and, instead, are resolved in some form of ADR. As such, one might fairly argue that the purpose of forensic interviewing is most often preparation for ADR. That being said, the specter of the courtroom remains a driving force for most litigators and parties.

A related difference between mediation and forensic interviewing is that the mediator is bound by the duty of confidentiality for any statements made during the course of the mediation.[9] Many states prohibit mediators from being called to testify about statements that were said to them or in their presence during the mediation.[10] Confidentiality's goals mimic those of prohibiting admission of evidence from the mediation proceedings in that they seek to foster an environment where participants feel that they can be fully transparent with the mediator, including about potential weaknesses in their case.

Forensic interviewers, in contrast, are frequently called to testify in criminal or civil proceedings about the information that was gathered. Most forensic interviewers are not prohibited from testifying or bound by any duty of confidentiality. To the contrary, most rules of criminal procedure require a broad disclosure of information gathered by the government during the investigation.[11] Civil proceedings also take a similar view toward the open exchange of information.[12] Almost all information provided during a forensic interview could be the subject of testimony by any of the parties' present, subject to limitations by the rules of evidence and hearsay.

Finally, mediation and forensic interviewing differ about whether the law enforces or encourages participation. Previously, mediation was a fully voluntary procedure engaged in by the parties to a case. Although mediation continues to be voluntary and parties can withdraw at any point, many courts require parties to engage in some form of ADR,

---

[8] Cal. Evid. Code § 1119(a); Fed. R. Evid. 408(a); Fla. 44.405; S.C. R. Alternative Dispute Resolution Rule 8.
[9] See Cal. Evid. Code § 1119(b).
[10] S.C. R. Alternative Dispute Resolution Rule 8(g).
[11] See Fed. R. Evid. Rule 16(a); Fla. R. Crim. Proc. 3.220(a).
[12] See Fed. R. Civ. Proc. Rule 26.

including mediation.[13] Forensic interviews are generally voluntary in statement (as cooperative witnesses often do participate with law enforcement of their own volition), but individuals can and are sometimes compelled to provide information.[14] For example, some states allow criminal depositions to be taken and for the court to compel such depositions.[15] Even where criminal depositions are limited to exceptional circumstances and court order (as is the case in the majority of the states and the federal courts), parties are permitted to discover the names of all parties who may have information and, in most cases, try to obtain statements from those individuals.[16]

Future Directions:

A number of potential directions exist as to future research on issues related to both forensic interviewing of witnesses and mediation.

Forensic Interviewing of Witnesses

Much of the research on the CI has been to validate it in different settings (e.g., across witness populations and episodic events). The findings are robust enough so that one more validation test will not advance our knowledge much. Greater advances are to be found by developing new memory- or communication-enhancing techniques that can be incorporated into an improved version of the CI. For instance, only recently has the "model statement" been incorporated into the CI. It is time to advance the protocol even further. Certainly, we have not exhausted our collective knowledge of social, cognitive, and communication processes so that we cannot find new techniques to incorporate into an ever-improving version of the technique.

Although the principles of forensic interviewing are relatively easy to understand, actually implementing the principles has proven to be more challenging. Part of the problem is that many police academies allocate precious little or no time to interviewing cooperative witnesses—as opposed to interrogating suspects (Molinaro et al., 2019). The first step to improving forensic interviewing, then, is to realize that investigators need to receive more formal training to interview cooperative witnesses and to incorporate such training into the police academy curriculum. The follow-up is to ensure that the training is effective by treating interviewing as a skill, which must be practiced, and not merely to describe the techniques as if they were to be memorized.

Mediation

Many areas of future research similarly exist within the mediation realm. For instance, mediation sessions often begin as joint sessions where all of the parties and the mediator are in the

---

[13] See N.D. Cal. ADR Local R. 3; Fla. Stat. Ch. 44.
[14] Fed. R. Civ. Proc. R. 45.
[15] Fla. R. Crim. Proc. 3.220(a).
[16] Fed. R. Evid. R. 16(a).

same room. Mediators can also choose to separate the parties into separate rooms and move back and forth between them, relaying information. This split session is often referred to as caucus or caucusing. Caucusing occurs for several reasons, including if the mediator feels that the parties are too emotionally volatile to keep in the same room. Research has revealed several potential downsides to caucus, including that it raises feelings in the parties that the mediation was not fair, that they lacked control, and that they were forced to settle (Task Force, 2017). Additional research is necessary to determine techniques that mediators and law enforcement can use during mediation or interviews to help individuals regulate emotions, such as taking breaks or changing the topic of the interview, enabling mediators to keep the parties in joint session rather than splitting them into separate rooms.

Relatedly, forensic-interviewing research has focused on ways to increase self-disclosure and participation in the legal process, including rapport techniques that establish affiliation between the parties (Dianiska et al., 2021). These techniques could be beneficial for mediators when they do need to split the parties into caucus. Mediators already work to establish ground rules and rapport during the start of mediation. Introducing these additional techniques could strengthen the parties' trust in both the mediator and the mediation process, potentially decreasing the distrust experienced during caucus. Given differences in the party structure of the mediation process (e.g., the introduction of a nongovernmental actor), additional research is necessary to determine whether their efficacy transfers into an ADR context.

Conclusion

The breadth of areas covered and the techniques used by the legal system present a unique challenge and opportunity for scholars and practitioners. Techniques developed in one arena, with a particular set of procedural, legal, and psychology assumptions, may or may not transfer to a new arena. For instance, it may not be clear at first glance that research and techniques generated under the context of the criminal system will apply when transferred to bankruptcy or family court. In this chapter, we queried whether applying research developed within the contexts of mediation and interviewing of cooperative forensic witnesses were transferrable to each other. Although there are several areas of unique distinction between the two, there are also definite potential areas for growth and synergies, including work on establishing rapport. In reviewing these two contexts, we hope to stimulate further research in the two arenas and to encourage conversation across research traditions.

References

ABA Section of Dispute Resolution Task Force on Research on Mediator Techniques. (2017). *ABA section of dispute resolution report of the task force on research on mediator techniques*. American Bar Association. https://www.americanbar.org/content/dam/aba/administrative/dispute_resolution/med_techniques_tf_report.authcheckdam.pdf

Ashkenazi, T., & Fisher, R. P. (2022). Field test of the cognitive interview to enhance eyewitness and victim memory in intelligence investigations of terrorist attacks. *Journal of Applied Research in Memory and Cognition, 11*(2), 200–208.

Baskin, D. & Sommers, I. (2010). The influence of forensic evidence on the case outcomes of homicide incidents *Journal of Criminal Justice, 38*(6), 1141–1149.

Bingham, L. B., Nabatchi, T., Senger, J. M., & Jackman, M. S. (2008). Dispute resolution and the vanishing trial: Comparing federal government litigation and ADR outcomes. *Ohio State Journal on Dispute Resolution, 24*(2), 225.

Boyle, A. (2017). Effectiveness in mediation: A new approach. *Newcastle Law Review, 12,* 148.

Chan, M. (2021, February 23). 'I want this over." For victims and the accused, justice is delayed as COVID-19 snarls courts. *Time.* https://time.com/5939482/covid-19-criminal-cases-backlog/

Charkoudian, L., Walter, J. L., & Eisenberg, D. T. (2018). What works in custody mediation? Effectiveness of various mediator behaviors. *Family Court Review, 56*(4), 544–571.

Department of Justice. (2020, July 24). Use and benefits of alternative dispute resolution by the Department of Justice. https://www.justice.gov/archives/olp/alternative-dispute-resolution-department-justice.

Dianiska, R. E., Swanner, J. K., Brimbal, L., & Meissner, C. A. (2021). Using disclosure, common ground, and verification to build rapport and elicit information. *Psychology, Public Policy, and Law, 27*(3), 341.

Dodier, O., Ginet, M., Teissedre, F., Verkampt, F., & Fisher, R. P. (2021). Using the cognitive interview to recall real-world emotionally stressful experiences: Road accidents. *Applied Cognitive Psychology, 35,* 1099–1105.

Druckman, D., & Wall, J. A. (2017). A treasure trove of insights: Sixty years of JCR research on negotiation and mediation. *Journal of Conflict Resolution, 61*(9), 1898–1924.

Eisenberg, D. T. (2020). The "genericide" of ADR: What dispute resolution is (is not) and should be, *Ohio State Journal on Dispute Resolution, 35*(5), 705–736.

Fisher, R. P., & Geiselman, R. E. (1992) *Memory-enhancing techniques in investigative interviewing: The cognitive interview.* C.C. Thomas.

Fisher, R. P., & Geiselman, R. E. (2019). Expanding the cognitive interview to non-criminal investigations. In J. Dickinson, N. Schreiber Compo, R. Carol, B. Schwartz, & M. McCauley (Eds.), *Evidence-based investigative interviewing: Applying cognitive principles* (pp. 1–28). Routledge: Taylor & Francis.

Fisher, R. P., Geiselman, R. E., & Raymond, D. S. (1987). Critical analysis of police interviewing techniques. *Journal of Police Science & Administration, 15*(3), 177–185.

Fisher, R. P., Schreiber Compo, N., Rivard, J., & Hirn, D. (2014). Interviewing witnesses. In T. Perfect & S. Lindsay (Eds.), *The SAGE handbook of applied memory* (pp. 559–578). SAGE.

Goldfien, J. H., & Robbennolt, J. K. (2006). What if the lawyers have their way—An empirical assessment of conflict strategies and attitudes toward mediation styles. *Ohio State Journal on Dispute Resolution, 22*(2), 277–320.

Kahneman, D. (1973). *Attention and effort.* Prentice-Hall.

Kebbell, M. R., Milne, R, & Wagstaff, G. (2013). The cognitive interview in forensic investigations: A review. In G. Traverso & L. Bagnoli (Eds.), *Psychology and law in a changing world: New trends in theory, practice and research* (pp. 185–197). Psychology Press.

Lamb, M. E., Orbach, Y., Hershkowitz, I., Esplin, P. W., & Horowitz, D (2007). Structured forensic interview protocols improve the quality and informativeness of investigative interviews with children: A review of research using the NICHD Investigative Interview Protocol. *Child Abuse and Neglect, 31*(11–12), 1201–1231.

Leal, S., Vrij, A., Warmelink, L., Vernham, Z., & Fisher, R. P. (2015). You cannot hide your telephone lies: Providing a model statement as an aid to detect deception in insurance telephone calls. *Legal and Criminological Psychology, 20*(1), 129–146.

Lyon, T. D. (2005). *Ten step investigative interview.* Retrieved from http://works.bepress.com/thomaslyon/5

Memon, A., Meissner, C. A., & Fraser, J. (2010). The Cognitive Interview: A meta-analytic review and study space analysis of the past 25 years. *Psychology, Public Policy, and Law, 16*(4), 340–372.

Molinaro, P. F., Fisher, R. P., Mosser, A. E., & Satin, G. E. (2019). Train-the-trainer: Methodology to learn the Cognitive Interview. *Journal of Investigative Psychology and Offender Profiling, 16*(1), 32–43.

Nolan-Haley, J. (2009). Mediation exceptionality. *Fordham Law Review, 78*(3), 1247–1264.

Rand Corporation. (1975). *The criminal investigative process*: Vols. 1-3. Technical Report R-1777-DOJ. Rand Corporation.

Satin, G. E., & Fisher, R. P. (2019). Investigative utility of the cognitive interview: Describing and finding perpetrators. *Law and Human Behavior, 43,* 491–506.

Shestowsky, D. (2020). Great expectations? Comparing litigants' attitudes before and after using legal procedures. *Law and Human Behavior, 44*(3), 179.

Storrow, R., & Coleman Jr., H. (2020). Exploring research regarding mediation party preferences and mediation within commercial arbitration. *Conflict Resolution Quarterly, 37*(4), 289–303.

Wells, G. L. (1978). Applied eyewitness testimony research: System variables and estimator variables. *Journal of Personality and Social Psychology, 36*(12), 1546–1557.

Westera, N., Powell, M., & Milne, B. (2017). Lost in the detail: Prosecutors' perceptions of the utility of video recorded police interviews as rape complaint evidence. *Australian and New Zealand Journal of Criminology, 50*(2), 252–268.

Emerging Policy Issues Related to Sexual Violence in Higher Education: Investigation and Adjudication Procedures and Mandatory Reporting Policies

Allison E. Cipriano *and* Kathryn J. Holland

Abstract

In this chapter, we review two emerging policy issues regarding sexual misconduct in institutions of higher education: investigation and adjudication procedures and mandatory reporting policies. First, we review key policymaking regarding sexual misconduct investigation and adjudication, contextualizing policymaking on sexual misconduct in higher education within its historical, sociopolitical background. We then discuss a current and controversial issue in investigation and adjudication procedures—due process and the use of live hearings with direct cross-examination. Second, we provide an overview of mandatory reporting policies for sexual misconduct, reviewing federal guidance and state legislation that have shaped these policies and discuss the important issue of survivor autonomy and control in reporting decisions. Finally, we discuss recommendations for policy reforms and future research on these two policy issues regarding sexual misconduct in higher education.

Key Words: sexual violence, higher education, mandatory reporting policies, sexual misconduct, sexual harassment, gender discrimination, Title IX

Sexual misconduct is a pervasive and harmful issue within universities across the United States (Coulter et al., 2017; Fedina et al., 2016). The term "sexual misconduct," used throughout this chapter, refers to all forms of sex- and gender-based discrimination that institutions of higher education must address according to federal and state laws, including rape, sexual assault, sexual harassment, gender-based harassment, stalking, and intimate partner violence. In this chapter, we review two emerging policy issues regarding sexual misconduct in institutions of higher education: (1) investigation and adjudication procedures and (2) mandatory reporting policies.

We first clarify terminology that will be used in this chapter when referring to those who have experienced and been accused of sexual misconduct. Next, we review key policymaking regarding sexual misconduct investigation and adjudication and discuss a current and controversial issue in these procedures—due process and the use of live hearings with direct cross-examination. We then provide an overview of mandatory reporting policies for sexual misconduct, reviewing federal guidance and state legislation that have shaped these policies and discuss the important issue of survivor autonomy and control in reporting decisions. Finally, we discuss recommendations for policy reforms and future research on these two issues.

Terminology

When describing those who have experienced sexual misconduct, there is continued debate regarding using the terms "victim" versus "survivor." Both terms, "victim" and "survivor," are used by those who have experienced misconduct (Hockett & Saucier, 2015), and we use them interchangeably to describe those who have experienced sexual misconduct. The term "complainant" is used when referring to victims who have reported sexual misconduct, and the term "respondent" is used when referring to those who have been accused of sexual misconduct. The terms "college" and "university" are used interchangeably for institutions of higher education.

Investigation and Adjudication Procedures

In this section, we begin by outlining federal laws regarding responses to university sexual misconduct in US institutions of higher education before introducing current issues in university reporting, investigation, and adjudication of sexual misconduct under Title IX.

Background

Two main federal laws have shaped how universities investigate and adjudicate sexual misconduct after it has been reported, Title IX and the Clery Act. Title IX of the Educational Amendments of 1972 is a civil rights statute prohibiting discrimination on the basis of sex within educational institutions receiving federal funding. The application of Title IX to cases of sexual misconduct has been established through case law and federal guidance. In 1980, Yale students successfully argued that sexual harassment was a form of sex discrimination prohibited under Title IX.[1] Following *Alexander v. Yale University*, the Supreme Court ruled multiple times that students who report instances of sexual misconduct perpetrated by an employee or fellow student are able to sue their school for monetary damages under Title IX if the educational institution does not demonstrate an adequate response to their report.[2] In addition, the Department of Education Office for Civil Rights (OCR)—the federal office responsible for enforcing Title IX—has issued guidance on investigation and adjudication procedures for sexual misconduct. In 1997, the OCR first provided guidance regarding how educational institutions must respond to student reports of sexual misconduct under Title IX; for instance, schools must adopt and publish grievance procedures providing for

---

[1] Alexander v. Yale University, 631 F.2d 178 (1980).
[2] Including in Franklin v. Gwinnett County Pub. Schs., 503 U.S. 60 (1992); Gebser v. Lago Vista Independent Sch. Dist., 524 U.S. 274 (1998); and Davis v. Monroe County Bd. of Educ., No. 97–843 (11th Cir. 1999).

prompt and equitable resolution of sex discrimination complaints, including complaints of sexual harassment (US Department of Education, 1997). The OCR released revised guidance in 2001, clarifying that the requirements for institutional response to sexual misconduct must be enforced even in circumstances where the complainant is not eligible for a monetary damage claim under Title IX (US Department of Education, 2001). Ten years later, President Obama's administration took significant steps to ensure that educational institutions were adequately responding to sexual misconduct. In 2011, the OCR issued a *Dear Colleague Letter* (DCL) reminding schools of their responsibility to take immediate and effective action in response to sexual misconduct reports and issued new recommendations for investigation and adjudication processes (e.g., training all persons involved in implementing grievance procedures in handling complaints of sexual misconduct, using the preponderance of evidence standard, aiming to resolve complaints within sixty days, providing equal opportunity to complainants and respondents to present witnesses and evidence, providing complainants and respondents written and concurrent notice of outcomes and the opportunity to appeal a decision; US Department of Education, 2011). The 2011 DCL also reiterated that informal processes (e.g., mediation) would not be appropriate for resolving sexual misconduct reports involving sexual assault, which was originally established in the OCR 2001 revised guidance on sexual harassment. In 2014, the OCR released a *Questions and Answers* (Q&A) document further clarifying universities' obligations under Title IX (US Department of Education, 2014). These guidance documents provided specific recommendations for creating investigation and adjudication procedures that are equitable for complainants and respondents (US Department of Education, 2011, 2014).

The second federal law that has substantially shaped sexual misconduct reporting procedures is the Clery Act. In 1990, Congress passed the Student Right-to-Know and Campus Security Act (later termed the Clery Act),[3] which requires colleges and universities receiving federal funding to collect and distribute information about the prevalence of sex-related crimes on and near campus (US Department of Education, 2016). Institutions are required to publish an Annual Security Report (ASR) that summarizes statistics on the types and locations of crimes committed and describes information about the institution's procedures for reporting sexual misconduct. In 2014, the Campus SaVE Act was signed into law as part of the 2013 reauthorization of the Violence Against Women Act (VAWA).[4] The Campus SaVE Act amended the Clery Act, expanding its legislative scope with regard to university response to sexual misconduct. For instance, the Campus SaVE Act required that institutional policy include a statement of the standard of evidence used to determine responsibility (although, it does not prescribe an evidentiary standard) and the sanctions that may be imposed after a determination of responsibility. Additionally,

---

[3] Clery Act, 20 U.S.C.A. § 1092.

[4] Violence Against Women Act of 1994 (Title IV of the Violent Crime Control and Law Enforcement Act, H.R 3355, signed by President Bill Clinton on September 13, 1994).

this law required that university officials conducting the investigation and adjudication proceedings be trained to investigate and conduct hearings with methods that protect the safety of the victim and promote accountability, allow both complainants and respondents to have an advisor of choice present during a disciplinary proceeding, and simultaneously notify the complainant and respondent of the outcome in writing.

In addition, states have introduced laws relating to sexual misconduct on college campus, including investigation and adjudication procedures (Richards & Kafonek, 2016). For example, *Massachusetts HB 1041* required that university employee training around sexual misconduct be trauma-informed, *Virginia SB 1193* required that a transcript notation of disciplinary proceedings be provided for sexual violence convictions, and *Louisiana A 255* mandated a transcript hold during the sexual misconduct disciplinary process (Richards & Kafonek, 2016). Although not all of the introduced legislation will become law, there is a clear trend of increasing state intervention in university investigation and adjudication procedures for sexual misconduct.

Current Issues

The increased attention to improving the investigation and adjudication of sexual misconduct within institutions of higher education via federal and state policymaking was driven, in large part, by survivor activists. College students who experienced and reported sexual misconduct shared their personal stories of how the inadequate and inequitable university responses often exacerbated their trauma (Behre, 2020). For instance, survivors described being discouraged from initiating an investigation and being retaliated against when they reported (e.g., Huckabee, 2013; Kingkade, 2016). An article published in the *Huffington Post* detailed how rarely students found responsible for sexual misconduct were suspended or expelled (Kingkade, 2014) and the documentary *The Hunting Ground* (Ziering & Dick, 2015) drew further public attention to universities failing to appropriately investigate and adjudicate sexual misconduct. Students also helped increase the public's awareness of Title IX and the OCR's role in holding universities accountable for failing to respond appropriately to sexual misconduct reports (Pérez-Peña, 2013), resulting in hundreds of Title IX complaints being filed with the OCR.[5] These efforts were a call to establish investigation and adjudication procedures that are equitable for complainants and respondents but also avoid retraumatizing victims during the process.

For example, the 2011 DCL and 2014 Q&A documents did not require live hearings and discouraged direct cross-examination (i.e., a respondent or an advisor for the respondent is able to directly question a complainant and witnesses). The use of direct cross-examination of complainants in sexual misconduct cases takes advantage of common myths about sexual violence (Smith & Skinner, 2012, 2017) and exacerbates trauma responses in sexual misconduct survivors (Chou et al., 2018; Konradi 2007; Parsons & Bergin, 2010; Valentine & Maras, 2011). Cross-examination in sexual misconduct cases is not intended

---

[5] *California v. Green, 399* U.S. 149, 158 (1970).

to uncover an accurate and unbiased account of the reported incident; instead, defense lawyers (or in the case of university disciplinary procedures, a respondent's chosen "advisor") frequently use leading and close-ended questions to interrogate complainants in an effort to control evidence and offer a plausible alternative story (Smith & Skinner, 2012, 2017; Zajac & Cannan, 2009). Cross-examination frequently draws on deeply held myths and misunderstandings of sexual violence, depicting the complainant's behavior as inconsistent with a "real victim" (Smith & Skinner, 2012, 2017). Legal scholars have argued that "cross-examination, by definition, represents an attempt to discredit the witness" (Zajac & Cannan, 2009, p. 48). Thus, in the effort to establish equitable procedures and avoid further trauma for survivors, the OCR recommended indirect questioning in which the complainant and respondent could submit questions to a trained hearing panel who would determine the relevance of the questions and ask the questions of the respective parties (US Department of Education, 2014)—a procedure that was already in use by universities and was determined to offer respondents sufficient opportunity to probe complainant and witness statements (Migler, 2017).

However, in response to the OCR's renewed focus on university response to sexual misconduct, a "disciplined student" narrative emerged (Behre, 2019, 2020). So-called men's rights groups (e.g., Families Advocating for Campus Equality, the National Coalition for Men Carolinas, and Stop Abusive and Violence Environments) openly opposed the 2011 DCL and lobbied for increased due process rights for respondents (see Barthélemy, 2020, for review). These groups asserted that universities have overcorrected for their earlier failures by "adopting a presumption of guilt for all male students reported for sexual misconduct violations" (Behre, 2020, p. 110). For instance, they contend that the preponderance-of-the-evidence standard of proof can yield greater consequences (e.g., expulsion and suspension) than typically results from civil cases where the preponderance-of-the-evidence standard is used and that investigation and adjudication procedures are not in line with the procedural safeguards they are constitutionally guaranteed (Johnson, 2012; New, 2015). This narrative has been bolstered by some university faculty who penned open letters and books supporting these positions (Bartholet et al., 2017; Kipnis, 2017). Those accused of sexual misconduct have positioned themselves as victims of overzealous and wrongful discipline by universities (Behre, 2020). US courts have received a substantial influx of litigation from students accused of sexual misconduct, alleging their due process rights were infringed upon in the investigation and adjudication of sexual misconduct (Buzuvis, 2017). Men's rights activists also met a sympathetic ear from OCR leadership under the Trump administration (Barthélemy, 2020).

In 2017, the Department of Education released a new *Dear Colleague Letter*, which rescinded both the 2011 DCL and 2014 Q&A documents and stated its intention to develop new Title IX regulations, citing concerns about adequate due process rights for students accused of sexual misconduct (US Department of Education, 2017). The OCR released proposed regulations in 2018, which included myriad requirements for investigation and adjudication procedures, including a mandate that postsecondary institutions conduct live hearings with direct cross-examination to resolve formal sexual misconduct complaints (US Department of Education, 2018). A sixty-day Notice and Comment period followed the proposal of new regulations, during which over 124,000 public comments were received by the Department of Education (US Department of Education, 2020). In May 2020, the Department of Education released a 2,033-page document detailing the final regulations, discussing the public comments on the proposed regulations submitted during the Notice and Comment period, and providing justifications for the final regulations (US Department of Education, 2020). Several notable changes have been made in the new regulations. Institutions of higher education are no longer required to resolve sexual misconduct complaints within sixty days, use the preponderance-of-the-evidence standard in disciplinary hearings, or avoid informal mediation for sexual assault reports (US Department of Education, 2020). Although, one of the most controversial changes was the requirement that universities conduct live hearings with direct cross-examination (§ 106.45 (b)(6)(i)).[6] The Department of Education asserted that adversarial cross-examination was needed to ensure due process protections for respondents due to "credibility" issues within sexual misconduct allegations (US Department of Education, 2020).

Two Supreme Court cases in the 1970s established initial parameters on the due process protections that must be afforded to students accused of misconduct within a disciplinary hearing. *Goss v. Lopez* ruled that (public school) students who may be temporarily suspended from school are entitled to notice of the case against them and an opportunity to have their account heard prior to disciplinary action.[7] *Mathews v. Eldridge* then established a "balancing test" that lower courts can use to determine whether or not a respondent received adequate due process within a disciplinary proceeding.[8] While private colleges enjoy a greater level of discretion in investigating and adjudicating student code violations, they are not able to dismiss a student "arbitrarily or capriciously" and must provide the students accused of misconduct with procedural protections that meet a "basic fairness" standard (Behre, 2020).

Although the recent Department of Education regulations on Title IX frame cross-examination as a due process right for students accused of sexual misconduct, courts are split on this issue. A few recent cases have ruled in favor of cross-examination as a means of ensuring due process for respondents in sexual misconduct disciplinary proceedings. In *Doe v. University of Cincinnati*, the Sixth Circuit Court of Appeals ruled that due process rights require the opportunity to cross-examine one's accuser to assess their "credibility" in the "most serious cases" (i.e., sexual assault).[9] In *Doe v. Baum*, the Sixth Circuit Court of Appeals again ruled that "if a public university has to choose between competing narratives to resolve a case, the university must give the accused student or his agent an opportunity

---

[6] § 106.45(b)(6)(i).
[7] Goss v. Lopez, 419 U.S. 565 (1975).
[8] Mathews v. Eldridge, 424 U.S. 319 (1976).
[9] Doe v. Univ. of Cincinnati, 872 F.3d 393 (6th Cir. 2017).

to cross examine the accuser and adverse witnesses in the presence of a neutral factfinder."[10] Additionally, in *Doe v. Allee*, the California Court of Appeal, Second Appellate District ruled that when a student accused of sexual misconduct faces "severe" disciplinary sanctions and the "credibility" of witnesses is central to the adjudication of the allegation, "fundamental fairness requires, at a minimum, that the university provide a mechanism by which the accused may cross-examine those witnesses, directly or indirectly, at a hearing in which the witnesses appear in person or by other means (e.g., videoconferencing) before a neutral adjudicator with the power independently to find facts and make credibility assessments."[11]

However, far more courts have ruled that live and direct cross-examination is not required to provide due process for an accused student in university disciplinary procedures, including the First, Second, Fourth, Fifth, Tenth, and Eleventh Circuit, and district courts in the Seventh and Eighth Circuits (Migler, 2017). For instance, in *Plummer v. University of Houston*, the Fifth Circuit determined that the university had granted respondents adequate due process rights by allowing the respondents to cross-examine witnesses through written questions, testimony, and witness presentation.[12] Further, the First Circuit decision in *Haidak v. University of Massachusetts-Amherst* explicitly contradicts *Doe v. Baum* and *Doe v. Allee*, asserting that direct cross-examination is not required for due process in sexual misconduct proceedings.[13] Instead, the court ruled that due process of law was satisfied if the university conducted "reasonably adequate questioning," such as indirect cross-examination through a hearing panel.[14]

In sum, although some courts have ruled that live hearings with cross-examination are necessary to provide accused students their due process rights, many others have determined that live and direct cross-examination is not necessary for due process and that indirect questioning sufficiently allows respondents to probe complainants' allegations. Some state lawmakers have attempted to intervene on this issue as well, for instance, California Senate Bill 493 (passed in 2020) states that cross examination cannot be conducted directly by a party or a party's advisor, in direct contradiction to the Department of Education's 2020 regulations on Title IX. Criticism of university response to sexual violence has continued alongside these inconsistent legislative decisions, with student survivors asserting that universities are not addressing their sexual misconduct claims well enough while accused students argue that university adjudication procedures are acting against their constitutional due process rights (Goldman, 2020). Scholars have also continued to weigh in on this issue, with recent arguments stating that students accused of sexual misconduct actually have more due process rights than students accused of other types of code violations (Goldman, 2020), and that the centering of respondent rights has resulted in student survivors being "pushed off the scales of justice" (Goldman 2020, p. 319).

---

[10] Doe v. Baum, 903 F.3d 575 (6th Cir. 2018).
[11] Doe v. Allee, 30 Cal. App. 5th 1036 (2019).
[12] Plummer v. Univ. of Houston, 860 F.3d 767, 774 & n.6 (5th Cir. 2017).
[13] Haidak v. Univ. of Mass.-Amherst, 933 F.3d 56 (1st Cir. 2019).
[14] *Id.* at p. 70.

Mandatory Reporting Policies:

In this section, we turn from summarizing current issues in the investigation and adjudication of college sexual misconduct under Title IX to taking a deeper look at the component of university sexual misconduct policies that often sets these processes into motion—mandatory reporting policies.

Background

Mandatory reporting policies refer to university policies that require certain employees to report experiences of sexual misconduct that they learn about to university officials—or, in some cases, law enforcement—regardless of whether or not the victim wants their experience to be reported (Holland et al., 2018). Mandatory reporting policies have been shaped by federal law, including the Clery Act and Title IX. The Clery Act requires colleges to assign individuals to the role of Campus Security Authority, who are responsible for reporting aggregate information about crimes (e.g., crime type and location) to inform the university's ASR (US Department of Education, 2016). Because the Clery Act does not require reporting of victims' names or other identifying information, we will not be focusing on campus security authorities in this chapter. Title IX guidance has also driven mandated reporting. In the 2001 revised guidance on sexual harassment, the OCR required universities to assign some employees into the role of "responsible employee" (US Department of Education, 2001). Responsible employees were defined as employees with the *"authority to take action to redress the harassment, who has the duty to report to appropriate school officials sexual harassment or any other misconduct by students or employees, or an individual who a student could reasonably believe has this authority or responsibility"* (US Department of Education, 2001, p. 13). These employees would be required to report any sexual misconduct they learn about to university officials (e.g., the Title IX Coordinator) and reports may include identifying information about the victim, perpetrator, and witnesses, when it is known. The OCR retained this definition of responsible employees in the 2014 Q&A guidance, with the slight adjustment of using the term "sexual violence" instead of "sexual harassment," and offered best practices for training responsible employees (US Department of Education, 2014).

Neither the Clery Act nor Title IX guidance requires universities to report sexual misconduct cases to the police. In fact, the Campus SaVE Act stipulates that victims must retain the choice to report to the university, the police, both, or neither. However, state lawmakers have introduced bills that would require universities to report sexual misconduct to law enforcement. In 2015, both California and Virginia passed laws that require university administrators to report sexual misconduct to local law enforcement under certain circumstances and other states have introduced similar bills.[15] California Assembly

---

[15] E.g., Utah House Bill 326 (Campus Sexual Violence Protection Act, H.B. 326. (2017), https://le.utah.gov/~2020/bills/static/HB0326.html); and Georgia House Bill 51 (Postsecondary institutions; reporting

Bill 636 states that postsecondary institutions must report sexual assault to law enforcement when the victim has made a report "for purposes of notifying the institution or law enforcement," but that the institution should not identify the victim "unless the victim consents to being identified." However, the alleged assailant can be identified "even if the victim does not consent to being identified, if the institution determines both that the alleged assailant represents a serious or ongoing threat to the safety of students, employees, or the institution."[16] Virginia House Bill 1930, on the other hand, offers no option for victim anonymity. University Title IX Coordinators are required to refer sexual assault reports to a committee that will review the report and will then disclose the incident to law enforcement—including personally identifiable information—if they determine that it is necessary to "protect the health and safety of the victim or other individuals."[17]

Current Issues

A major issue around mandatory reporting policies that has been raised by survivor-activists and scholars is that they strip survivors of autonomy and control (Deamicis, 2013; Holland et al., 2018). After experiencing sexual violence, regaining one's sense of autonomy and control is an important component of the healing process (Frazier, 2003; Walsh & Bruce, 2011). Survivors report increased symptoms of posttraumatic stress and depression when support providers respond by taking away their control (Orchowski et al., 2013; Peter-Hagene & Ullman, 2014). Researchers find that survivors are less supportive of mandatory reporting policies compared to non-victims (Holland et al., 2019; Newins et al., 2018; Newins & White, 2018) and survivors overwhelmingly prefer policies that grant them autonomy and control over the decision to report (Holland et al., 2020b). Moreover, many student survivors lack knowledge about their university's sexual misconduct reporting policy (Amin, 2019; Holland et al., 2020b), which means they may disclose experiences of sexual misconduct to university employees without adequate knowledge about the employees' reporting requirements.

Despite these concerns, institutions of higher education across the United States have implemented expansive mandatory reporting requirements. The majority of institutions require all or nearly all of their employees to report any instance of sexual misconduct they learn about to university officials, even if the victim does not consent to the report (Holland et al., 2018). The move toward these *"universal"* or *"wide-net"* reporting

---

and investigation of certain crimes by officials and employees; provide manner, H.B. 51. Ga. Gen. Assembly (2017–2018), http://www.legis.ga.gov/Legislation/en-US/display/20172018/HB/51), although neither have been signed into law.

[16] Cal. Assembly Bill 636 (2015) (Postsecondary education: student safety, A.B. 636. (2015), https://leginfo.legislature.ca.gov/faces/billNavClient.xhtml?bill_id=201520160AB636).

[17] Va. House Bill 1930 (2015).

policies is based on assumptions that mandated reporting will benefit survivors and increase reports of sexual misconduct, thereby allowing universities to investigate and resolve more sexual misconduct cases (Holland et al., 2018). However, available empirical evidence does not support these assumptions (see Holland et al., 2018, for review). Fewer institutions have taken a more nuanced approach to crafting mandatory reporting policies. For example, some schools have implemented *selective* mandatory reporting policies, which limit those who are required to report to employees in leadership positions and employees in other roles with significant responsibility over student welfare (e.g., housing staff; Holland et al., 2018). In addition, at least one university (University of Oregon) has implemented a *student-directed* reporting policy, which designates a limited list of employees as mandatory reporters and requires all other employees to provide survivors who disclose with information, resources, and support (Holland et al., 2020a; Holland et al., 2018).

The OCR defined responsible employees but did not provide a prescriptive mandate about which campus community members should be assigned this role, leading to the variability in how colleges and universities have interpreted and implemented the mandatory reporter mandate (Holland et al., 2018). The most recent regulations on Title IX from the OCR more explicitly states that institutions do not need to designate all employees as mandatory reporters, leaving "each institution flexibility to decide whether the institution desires all (or nearly all, or some subset) of its employees to be 'mandatory reporters' who must report notice of sexual harassment to the Title IX Coordinator" (US Department of Education, 2020, pp. 1959–1960). The 2020 regulations made another notable change regarding mandated reporting of sexual misconduct, which deserves some explanation.

The 2020 regulations removed the title of "Responsible Employee" and introduced the role of "Official with Authority" (US Department of Education, 2020). The regulations stipulate that institutions are only obligated to respond to sexual misconduct when "any official of the recipient who has authority to institute corrective measures on behalf of the recipient" (referred to herein as 'officials with authority') conveys *actual knowledge* to the recipient" (Department of Education, 2020, p. 30039 [emphasis added]). Complainants are only able to sue their school for monetary damages under Title IX if the institution had *actual knowledge* of the misconduct,[18] but all previous Title IX guidance has stated that schools can be considered in violation of Title IX guidance by the OCR if they *knew or should have known* about the misconduct (e.g., due to its pervasiveness) and failed to respond. Thus, within the 2020 regulations, the explicit statement that schools can limit the number of mandatory reporters is coupled with a reduction in institutional responsibility to address sexual misconduct.

---

[18] Davis v. Monroe County Bd. of Educ., No. 97–843 (11th Cir. 1999); Gebser v. Lago Vista Independent Sch. Dist., 524 U.S. 274 (1998).

State laws have also introduced more expansive and restrictive policies. For instance, Texas Senate Bill 212 (passed in 2019)[19] requires all college employees to report any sexual misconduct involving a student to the institution's Title IX coordinator, and those who fail to report can be fired and charged with a class B misdemeanor punishable by up to 180 days in jail and a $2,000 fine. Passed in August 2020, California Senate Bill 493[20] requires federally funded institutions of higher education to designate nearly all their employees as mandatory reporters, including (but not limited to) housing staff, faculty members, lecturers, graduate student instructors, lab directors and principal investigators, and internship and study-abroad directors. In effect, nearly every university employee in the state of California is now mandated to report sexual misconduct, regardless of the wishes of the survivor disclosing to them. These state laws could serve as a model for other states, leading to increased imposition of universal mandated reporting and severe consequences for noncompliance (e.g., employment termination and incarceration), without recognition of how such policies may harm survivors (e.g., stripping their autonomy). As of the writing of this chapter, the Department of Education has released new proposed regulations on Title IX related to sexual misconduct (US Department of Education, 2022); while the regulations will be revised following a 60-day notice and comment period, the proposed regulations would mandate broad mandatory reporting policies within all institutions of higher education (e.g., requiring all instructors and advisors to report any instance of sexual misconduct they learn about in any way to Title IX). This would effectively reverse the current Department of Education regulations enacted in 2020, greatly limiting institutional discretion in mandatory reporting policy creation.

Recommendations for Policy and Future Research

When examining current issues concerning investigation and adjudication procedures and mandatory reporting policies, a common problem is that these mechanisms intended to address sexual misconduct do not consider those who experience sexual misconduct. There has been a shift toward centering the rights of those accused of misconduct in university investigation and adjudication procedures. Further, most university mandatory reporting policies offer few options for survivors to control what happens to their personal information when they disclose to university employees. In these policy decisions, the wishes and consent (or lack thereof) of survivors are not being considered, whether they want their sexual misconduct experience to be reported or whether they want to endure live cross-examination in disciplinary proceedings. As previously stated, policies that do

---

[19] Tex. S.B. 212. (2019), https://capitol.texas.gov/tlodocs/86R/billtext/html/SB00212I.htm
[20] Education: Sex equity, S.B. 493. (2020), https://leginfo.legislature.ca.gov/faces/billTextClient.xhtml?bill_id=201920200SB493

not consider survivors' needs can be harmful, as regaining control and autonomy are key components of the healing process following sexual victimization (Frazier, 2003; Walsh & Bruce, 2011). The recommendations outlined below shifts the focus back to those who have experienced sexual misconduct.

Policy Recommendations

First, we recommend investigation and adjudication procedures that allow for indirect cross-examination, which entails both parties submitting questions to a trained investigator and/or hearing panel who will determine the relevance of the submitted questions and ask the questions of the respective parties. Requiring adversarial cross-examination in this context—which is explicitly aimed at interrogating and undermining the "credibility" of those who have reported sexual misconduct—offers inadequate due process protections for complainants and can further traumatize survivors (Holland et al., 2020b; Konradi, 2007; O'Toole, 2017). Case law overwhelmingly allows indirect cross-examination to probe complainant, respondent, and witness statements (Migler, 2017).

Second, we recommend survivor-centered mandatory reporting policies that (1) limit the number of employees who are designated as mandatory reporters and clearly communicate which employees are mandatory reporters, (2) set reporting exemptions (e.g., a report is not required if an employee learns about misconduct in a class assignment), and (3) afford survivors control over whether a report will be made to university officials and/or law enforcement. While (currently) uncommon, survivor-centered policies do exist. The University of Oregon is an excellent example of a survivor-centered policy, in that most employees are required to provide a survivor who discloses sexual misconduct with information about campus resources and reporting options, ask whether the survivor wants a report to be made, and respect the survivor's decisions.[21] A different approach has been taken by Tulane University's "care connection" policy, in which employees are required to report sexual misconduct disclosures to victim support services. While the Title IX coordinator is informed of incidents (i.e., copied on the care connection message), it is trained advocacy staff who reach out to survivors instead of Title IX investigators (Tulane University, 2020). Both the University of Oregon and Tulane University policies outline reporting exceptions, including disclosures made within an academic context (e.g., discussions and assignments). These policies serve as helpful models for other universities interested in shifting to a more survivor-centered policy approach.

---

[21] US16/17–07 (2016): University of Oregon Prohibited Discrimination and Retaliation, Policy V.11.02. Retrieved from https://policies.uoregon.edu/vol-5-human-resources/ch-11-human-resources-other/prohibited-discrimination-and-retaliation. University of Oregon, 2022.

Future Research Recommendations

Additional research is needed to further our understanding of the policy issues outlined in this chapter. First, research is needed to further understand survivors' experiences with university investigation and adjudication procedures, particularly their experiences in live hearings with cross-examination. Given the new Department of Education Title IX regulations requiring live hearings allowing for cross-examination in university sexual misconduct cases, students will be increasingly subjected to this type of hearing process. While research on cross-examination of sexual violence survivors already exists, there is a lack of research on live hearings with cross-examination of survivors within the university disciplinary hearing context. Research is needed to understand the actions (or lack of actions) that institutions are taking to minimize harm to survivors in disciplinary hearings. For instance, the new Title IX Regulations did not require universities to implement trauma-informed training for those who are conducting or presiding over cross-examination in disciplinary hearings (Holland et al., 2020b). This work will be helpful in informing policymakers about the experiences of students seeking justice through university investigation and adjudication procedures and ways to improve these processes.

Future research might also investigate survivors' perceptions of different mandatory reporting policy models. There is limited research on this topic, but some recent evidence suggests that survivors prefer student-directed approaches over other models (e.g., selective, universal; Holland et al., 2020a). Further, research is needed to understand the factors that drive people's support for expansive mandatory reporting policies, including survivors (i.e., which survivors support mandatory reporting and why?) and other key groups (e.g., university administrators and state lawmakers). For example, some research suggests that survivors are less supportive of mandatory reporting because they lack trust in how the university responds to sexual assault reports (Holland, 2019). Larger, more representative samples examining the reasons why people support policies that mandate reporting without victim consent will be helpful in informing efforts to create more survivor-centered reporting policies.

References

Amin, D. M. (2019). *Students' awareness, knowledge, and perceptions of mandatory reporting of sexual victimization on college campuses* [Unpublished doctoral dissertation]. Virginia Commonwealth University.

Barthélemy, H. (2020). How men's rights groups helped rewrite regulations on campus rape. *The Nation.* Retrieved from https://www.thenation.com/article/politics/betsy-devos-title-ix-mens-rights/

Bartholet, E., Gertner, N., Halley, J. & Gersen, J. S. (2017). Fairness for all students under Title IX. *Digital Access to Scholarship at Harvard.* Retrieved from http://nrs.harvard.edu/urn-3:HUL.InstRepos:33789434

Behre, K. A. (2019). Deconstructing the disciplined student narrative and its impact on campus sexual assault policy. *Arizona Law Review, 61*(4) 885–903. https://arizonalawreview.org/pdf/61-4/61arizlrev885.pdf

Behre, K. A. (2020). Rape exceptionalism returns to California: Institutionalizing a credibility discount for college students reporting sexual misconduct. *Oklahoma Law Review, 73*(1), 101–119.

Buzuvis, E. E. (2017). Title IX and procedural fairness-why disciplined student litigation does not undermine the role of Title IX in campus sexual assault. *Montana Law Review, 78,* 71–108.

Chou, C. Y., La Marca, R., Steptoe, A., & Brewin, C. R. (2018) Cardiovascular and psychological responses to voluntary recall of trauma in posttraumatic stress disorder. *European Journal of Psychotraumatology, 9*(1), 147–298.

Chronicle of Higher Education. (n.d.). Title IX: Tracking sexual assault investigations. Retrieved from http://projects.chronicle.com/titleix/

Coulter, R. W., Mair, C., Miller, E., Blosnich, J. R., Matthews, D. D., & McCauley, H. L. (2017). Prevalence of past-year sexual assault victimization among undergraduate students: Exploring differences by and intersections of gender identity, sexual identity, and race/ethnicity. *Prevention Science, 18*(6), 726–736.

DeAmicis, C. (2013, May 20). Which matters more: Reporting assault or respecting a victim's wishes? *The Atlantic.* Retrieved from https://www.theatlantic.com/national/archive/2013/05/which-matters-more-reporting-assault-or-respecting-a-victims-wishes/276042/

Fedina, L., Holmes, J. L., & Backes, B. L. (2016). Campus sexual assault: A systematic review of prevalence research from 2000 to 2015. *Trauma, Violence, & Abuse, 19*(1), 76–93.

Frazier, P. A. (2003). Perceived control and distress following sexual assault: A longitudinal test of a new model. *Journal of Personality and Social Psychology, 84*(6), 1257–1269.

Goldman, R. A. (2020). When is due process due?: The impact of Title IX sexual assault adjudication on the rights of university students. *Pepperdine Law Review, 47*(5), 185–228.

Higher educational institutions; review committees, reporting of acts of sexual violence, report, H.B. 1930 (2015). https://lis.virginia.gov/cgi-bin/legp604.exe?151+sum+HB1930

Hockett, J. M., & Saucier, D. A. (2015). A systematic literature review of "rape victims" versus "rape survivors": Implications for theory, research, and practice. *Aggression and Violent Behavior, 25*(Pt. A), 1–14.

Holland, K. J. (2019). Examining responsible employees' perceptions of their sexual assault reporting requirements under federal and institutional policy. *Analyses of Social Issues and Public Policy, 19*(1), 133–149.

Holland, K. J., Bedera, N., & Webermann, A. (2020). The selective shield of due process: An analysis of the U.S. department of education's 2020 Title IX regulations on live cross-examination. *Analyses of Social Issues and Public Policy, 20*(1), 584–612.

Holland, K. J., Cipriano, A. E., & Huit, T. Z. (2020a). "The fear is palpable": service providers' perceptions of mandatory reporting policies for sexual assault in higher education. *Analyses of Social Issues and Public Policy, 20*(1), 66–89.

Holland, K. J., Cipriano, A. E., & Huit, T. Z. (2020b). "A victim/survivor needs agency": Sexual assault survivors' perceptions of university mandatory reporting policies. *Analyses of Social Issues and Public Policy, 21*(1), 488–508.

Holland, K. J., Cortina, L. M., & Freyd, J. J. (2018). Compelled disclosure of college sexual assault. *American Psychologist, 73,* 256–268.

Holland, K. J., Cortina, L. M. & Freyd, J. J. (2019) Advocating alternatives to mandatory reporting for college sexual assault: Reply to Newins (2018). *American Psychologist, 74*(2), 250–251.

Huckabee, C. (2013). Occidental and Swarthmore Colleges are accused of mishandling assault cases. *Chronicle of Higher Education.* Retrieved from https://www.chronicle.com/blogs/ticker/occidental-college-is-accused-of-failing-toprotect-women-from-sexual-assault/58833

Johnson, A (2012). Opinion, against the preponderance of evidence standard. *Stanford Daily.* Retrieved from https://www.stanforddaily.com/2012/05/21/op-ed-against-the-preponderance-of-evidence-standard/.

Kingkade, T. (2016). Why don't sexual assault victims report? Ask these college women. *BuzzFeed News.* Retrieved from https://www.buzzfeed.com/tylerkingkade/retaliation-reporting-sexualassault?utm_term=.leJBGq59oK#.ogBjRXmMyK

Kingkade, T. (2014, September 29). Fewer than one-third of campus sexual assault cases result in expulsion. *Huffington Post.* Retrieved from https://www.huffingtonpost.com/2014/09/29/campus-sexual-assault_n_5888742.html

Kipnis, L. (2017). Eyewitness to a Title IX witch trial. *Chronicle of Higher Education.* Retrieved from https://www.chronicle.com/article/eyewitness-to-a-title-ix-witch-trial/

Konradi, A. (2007). *Taking the stand: Rape survivors and the prosecution of rapists.* Praeger.

Migler, W. J. (2017). An accused student's right to cross-examination in university sexual assault adjudicatory proceedings. *Chapman Law Review, 20*(2), 357–392.

New, J. (2015). Suits from the accused. *Inside Higher Ed.* Retrieved from https://www.insidehighered.com/news/2015/05/01/students-accused-sexual-assault-struggle-win-gender-bias

Newins, A., Bernstein, E., Peterson, R., Waldron, J., & White, S. (2018). IX mandated reporting: The views of university employees and students. *Behavioral Sciences, 8*(11), 106–124.

Newins, A. R., & White, S. W. (2018). Title IX sexual violence reporting requirements: Knowledge and opinions of responsible employees and students. *Journal of Aggression, Conflict and Peace Research, 10*(2), 74–82.

Orchowski, L. M., Untied, A. S., & Gidycz, C. A. (2013). Social reactions to disclosure of sexual victimization and adjustment among survivors of sexual assault. *Journal of Interpersonal Violence, 28*, 2005–2023.

O'Toole, S. (2017). Campus sexual assault adjudication, student due process, and a bar on direct cross-examination. *University of Pittsburgh Law Review, 79*, 511–542.

Parsons, J., & Bergin, T. (2010). The impact of criminal justice involvement on victims' mental health. *Journal of Traumatic Stress, 23*(2), 182–188.

Pérez-Peña, R. (2013, March 19). College groups connect to fight sexual assault. *New York Times*. Retrieved from http://www.nytimes.com/2013/03/20/education/activists-at-colleges-network-to-fight-sexual-assault.html

Peter-Hagene, L. C., & Ullman, S. E. (2014). Social reactions to sexual assault disclosure and problem drinking: Mediating effects of perceived control and PTSD. *Journal of Interpersonal Violence, 29*, 1418–1437.

Richards, T. N., & Kafonek, K. (2016). Reviewing state legislative agendas regarding sexual assault in higher education proliferation of best practices and points of caution. *Feminist Criminology, 11*, 91–129.

Smith, O., & Skinner, T. (2012). Observing court responses to victims of rape and sexual assault. *Feminist Criminology, 7*(4), 298–326.

Smith, O., & Skinner, T. (2017). How rape myths are used and challenged in rape and sexual assault trials. *Social & Legal Studies, 26*(4), 441–466.

US Department of Education Office for Civil Rights. (1997). *Sexual harassment guidance: Harassment of students by school employees, other students, or third parties*. https://www.govinfo.gov/content/pkg/FR-1997-03-13/pdf/97-6373.pdf

US Department of Education Office for Civil Rights. (2001). *Revised sexual harassment Guidance: Harassment of students by school employees, other students, or third parties*. https://www2.ed.gov/about/offices/list/ocr/docs/shguide.pdf

US Department of Education Office for Civil Rights. (2011). *Dear colleague letter: Sexual violence*. https://www2.ed.gov/about/offices/list/ocr/letters/colleague-201104.pdf

US Department of Education. (2014, May 1). *US Eepartment of Education releases list of higher education institutions with open title IX sexual violence investigations*. Retrieved from https://www.ed.gov/news/pressreleases/us-department-education-releases-list-higher-educationinstitutions-open-title-ix

US Department of Education, Office for Civil Rights. (2020). *Title IX and sex discrimination*. https://www.federalregister.gov/documents/2020/05/19/2020-10512/nondiscrimination-on-the-basis-of-sex-in-education-programs-or-activities-receiving-federal

US Department of Education, Office for Civil Rights. (2022). *Federal Register Notice of Proposed Rulemaking Title IX of the Education Amendments of 1972*. https://www2.ed.gov/about/offices/list/ocr/docs/t9nprm.pdf

Valentine, T., & Maras, K. (2011). The effect of cross-examination on the accuracy of adult eyewitness testimony. *Applied Cognitive Psychology, 25*(4), 554–561.

Walsh, R. M., & Bruce, S. E. (2011). The relationships between perceived levels of control, psychological distress, and legal system variables in a sample of sexual assault survivors. *Violence Against Women, 17*, 603–618. https://doi.org/10.1177/1077801211407427

Zajac, R., & Cannan, P. (2009). Cross-examination of sexual assault complainants: A developmental comparison. *Psychiatry Psychology and Law, 16*(Suppl.), S36–S54.

Ziering, A. (Producer), & Dick, K. (Director). (2015). *The hunting ground* [Motion picture]. The Weinstein Company.

Legal Decision-Making among Youth Defendants, Victims, and Witnesses: Emerging Issues, Research, and Theory

Lindsay C. Malloy, Joshua Wyman, Shreya Mukhopadhyay, *and* Jodi A. Quas

Abstract

Adolescence is characterized by multifaceted growth, change, and vulnerability. Several developmental characteristics of adolescence, such as youths' tendencies to engage in exploratory and risk-taking behaviors, susceptibility to peer influence, and desire for autonomy, increase the likelihood that they will come into contact with the legal system not only as perpetrators but also as victims and witnesses. Those same characteristics then influence their experiences. In the present chapter, we describe these influences, focusing on how they likely influence legally relevant decisions adolescents make in interviews and in court as suspects and defendants and as victims and witnesses. We close by highlighting important new directions for research on how developmental characteristics shape legal decisions in unique subsets of adolescents (e.g., those who are both delinquent and victims) and by offering practical recommendations regarding the need for more in-depth training of legal professionals on how adolescent development affects youth involvement in the legal system.

Key Words: adolescent decision making, victims, witnesses, delinquency

Within the field of psychology and the law, there has been long-standing scientific and practical interest in youths' experiences and functioning within the legal system. This interest has led to incredible advances in knowledge regarding youth vulnerabilities in legal contexts, suggestibility, decision-making, and criminal culpability (see Owen-Kostelnik et al., 2006; Steinberg, 2009, for reviews), and to significant changes in policy and laws that fundamentally alter justice for youth. For example, California Assembly Bill 1423 allows Californian youth to have their case returned to juvenile court following their conviction in criminal court, and *Roper v. Simmons*[1] eliminated the death penalty for adolescent defendants ages sixteen to seventeen, characterizing them as categorically different from

---

[1] Roper v. Simmons, 543 U.S. 551 (2005).

adults who commit comparable crimes. Similar arguments were made in the cases that abolished mandatory juvenile life without parole sentences.[2] Psychological research on youth functioning was featured prominently in these decisions, which, in essence, fundamentally change the lives of youth immersed in the legal system.

Despite what one could argue is the enormous success of the research, important questions remain about the specifics of youths' legal involvement, particularly ways to facilitate that involvement, especially in less-well studied populations of adolescents (e.g., adolescent-age victims). It is not enough simply to document the challenges legally involved youth face; research needs to identify strategies that improve their involvement. The overarching purpose of the current chapter is to review research relevant to both adolescents' experiences in the legal system and questions in need of answers about how best to help adolescents who become involved. The goal of this chapter is not to provide an exhaustive review of the literature on adolescents' involvement in the legal system; instead, we provide a framework and discuss several examples of how developmental characteristics shape adolescent responses and decisions in legal settings. Of note, our focus on decision-making in adolescent suspects/defendants' and victims/witnesses' cases is not to imply that decision-making is the only important aspect to consider in relation to these youth's legal experiences. Instead, our intent is to provide an example of how developmental processes shape facets of adolescents' legal involvement.

Hallmarks of Adolescent Development Relevant to Their Legal Decision-Making

A useful place to start, before discussing adolescents' experiences in the legal system, is with a brief discussion of several hallmark characteristics of adolescence, a developmental window defined by rapid changes in biological processes, cognitive abilities, social relationships, and motivational and emotional functioning (see Boyer, 2006). Characteristics particularly relevant to adolescent legal decision-making as well as their likelihood of coming into contact with the legal system include their tendencies toward exploratory, risk-taking, sensation-, and reward-seeking behaviors (especially in emotional contexts), alongside their susceptibility to peer influence and desire for autonomy (Steinberg, 2009).

First, with regard to exploratory behaviors, across cultures, adolescents gradually become more independent as they develop their own identity, tendencies captured in classic (e.g., Erikson's Psychosocial Model of Personality Development; Erikson, 1968) and modern (e.g., Luyckx et al., 2006) models of psychosocial development. Exploratory behaviors are key components of this independence, and society offers ample opportunities for adolescents to test new beliefs, boundaries, and behaviors. Adolescents may change schools (e.g., from middle to high school) and begin working, as their roles and responsibilities

---

[2] I.e., Graham v. Florida, 560 U.S. 48 (2010); Miller v. Alabama, 567 U.S. 460 (2012).

shift. Their social networks expand as they form new relationships. Adolescents also transition to spending more time with friends than parents. In combination, these experiences expose adolescents to religious, political, and sexual views or behaviors that may be novel or diverge from those of parents, offering ample opportunity for exploration and testing of behaviors. For some adolescents, these behaviors include experimentation with risky or even illegal activities, such as alcohol use (Simons-Morton et al., 2010). Although common practice among many adolescents (Sebastian et al., 2008), such behaviors also carry risk and may increase youths' likelihood of legal contact.

Adolescents' exploratory behaviors are motivated not only by a drive toward independence and identity development but also by socioemotional processes associated with high reward-seeking. For example, adolescents evidence a greater likelihood of making risky decisions that have the potential for high-reward payouts (e.g., in a gambling game), especially when those rewards are immediate, rather than decisions that involve less payout or for which payouts extend over time (Braams et al., 2015; Levenson & Galvan, 2014). These risky decisions, moreover, are most likely to occur in high-emotion contexts when there is little time for deliberation, as is likely the case when adolescents are in social interactions with peers or potentially experimenting with illegal activities (Albert et al., 2013). As we discuss shortly, certain aspects of the legal system may also be high-emotion contexts in which decisions need to be made quickly with minimal deliberation.

A second characteristic common to adolescents, the salience of peers, may also affect their likelihood of exposure to activities that bring them into contact with the legal system and then their decisions once that contact occurs. As mentioned, adolescents gradually spend more time with peers than parents (Crone & Dahl, 2012), and peers become a primary reference group regarding behavioral norms and expectations (Steinberg & Silverberg, 1986). Thus, adolescents increasingly want to engage in behaviors valued by peers, and both their decisions and actions are consistent with those that they believe their peers will value (van Hoorn et al., 2016).

Not only do adolescents act in ways consistent with the type of behavior they think peers will endorse, but adolescents' actual behavior varies as a function of peers' presence. Research in both laboratory and real-life settings show that adolescents take more risks in the presence of peers than when by themselves. For instance, they are more likely to try drugs or alcohol when with friends than when alone and to make poor or risky decisions while driving when peers are versus are not present (Albert et al., 2013; Allen & Brown, 2008). When adolescents' expanding peer networks, peer affiliations, and affinity for behavior valued by peers are combined with their sensation-seeking and risk-taking tendencies, their vulnerability to making poor and possibly harmful decisions that could lead to legal involvement becomes even more pronounced.

Autonomy is a third characteristic of adolescence that plays a particularly important role in shaping youths' legally relevant behaviors and decisions. Adolescents, much more than children, express a growing desire for autonomy (Steinberg & Silverberg, 1986). This is reflected in their tendency to make more independent decisions over time, about who their friends and romantic partners are, about what to do, and about where to go (Simons-Morton et al., 2010). These decisions are accompanied by greater feelings of responsibility for those decisions. That same drive for autonomy though, could also lead adolescents to take responsibility for decisions and behaviors into which they were manipulated or pressured, either because they fail to recognize that they were manipulated or because they do not want to present themselves as vulnerable to others' manipulations (Grandpre et al., 2003). Feelings of autonomy, likewise, may reduce adolescents' willingness to tell others (e.g., adults) about risky situations or experiences, again either because the adolescents want to appear independent or they feel that whatever happened is their responsibility or fault. Expressing fear or reluctance to engage in risky behavior, or seeking help after negative events occurred might be viewed as signs of weakness or immaturity, undermining adolescents' desire for independence.

Adolescent Decision-Making in Legal Contexts

In combination, these hallmark characteristics of adolescence, along with many others, affect their decision-making when it comes to engaging in risky behaviors, which includes committing crimes and experiencing contexts where crimes or exposure to harm may occur (e.g., Connolly et al., 2017). Moreover, these same hallmark characteristics affect what happens after the crime, that is, once adolescents are questioned by the authorities and become immersed in the legal system. In particular, reward-seeking, the salience of peers, and desire for independence shape the decisions adolescents make as their involvement progresses—decisions that profoundly affect the progression of cases and their ultimate outcome.

Adolescent Suspects and Defendants

From the moment adolescents are identified as suspects of delinquent or criminal behavior, their decisions play significant and long-lasting roles in how their contact with the legal system unfolds. In particular, after adolescents are identified for suspicion of having committed a crime, they must decide what they want to disclose about the crime and their knowledge to the authorities, whether to waive *Miranda* rights while being questioned, and whether to admit guilt while being questioned. Similar decisions, that is, what to tell to whom, extend to adolescents' attorney and to the judge, and even their parents. All these decisions are affected by adolescents' perceptions of the rewards (vs. risk), affiliation with peers, and desire for independence. Here we review some of these important potential effects.

DECISIONS IN THE INTERROGATION ROOM

When apprehended on suspicion of criminal or delinquent activity, adolescents, like adults, are informed of their rights to remain silent and to access legal counsel (e.g., as specified in their "*Miranda* Rights" in the United States or the Canadian Charter of Rights and Freedoms in Canada), along with other rights designed to protect them from or during interrogations. Ample research, however, shows that adolescents often waive their rights and submit to police questioning in interrogations, often with no supportive adult present (e.g., Grisso, 1980, 1981; Viljoen et al., 2005). Adolescents, especially those who are younger, waive their rights even though they do not fully understand or appreciate their rights (Kelley et al., 2018). For example, Zelle et al. (2015) evaluated nearly 200 juvenile justice–involved youths' (ages twelve to nineteen) understanding of their *Miranda* rights. A majority failed to understand and appreciate the different components of the warning (e.g., right to remain silent), and nearly half (48 percent) reported not remembering the *Miranda* rights being explained when they were detained. Only 20 percent reported having discussed these rights with their attorneys.

Adolescents' lack of complex knowledge about the justice system, plus possible difficulties with attention or listening in a high-stress interrogation context, may limit their ability to follow law enforcement's explanation of their *Miranda* rights or reason about how those rights apply to their situation (Eastwood et al., 2015; Grisso et al., 2003). Many justice-involved youth are significantly delayed academically or have learning disabilities or cognitive deficits (Grigorenko, 2006) that can further inhibit their ability to understand legal jargon, potentially complex topics, or discussion of personal rights, whether presented verbally or in written form (Eastwood et al., 2015; Lieser et al., 2019). Thus, a sizable number of adolescents may not have the requisite cognitive capabilities to fully understand and appreciate the rights that they may be forgoing when they submit to an interrogation. Nor will many ask for clarification. They may want to appear independent, and not speak up when they do not understand and waive their right to have someone else, such as a parent or attorney, present during the interrogation (Malloy et al., 2014; Viljoen et al., 2005). For example, Cleary (2014) found that, among youth suspects charged with a felony offense in the United States, parents were present in 21 percent of interrogations, and no defense attorneys were present in any.

In the interrogation therefore, all on their own, adolescents are making crucial decisions about what to share with law enforcement; and whether to confess to what they did, deny involvement, or perhaps claim falsely to have committed the alleged offense as a way of ending pressure from law enforcement to tell. Adolescents' reward sensitivity may lead them to overemphasize the short-term benefit of ending the stressful or coercive interrogation and underemphasize the longer-term consequences of confession. They may try to explain their behavior with inferences or falsely confess, believing that these are reasonable options to help "end" the interrogation. Grisso et al. (2003), for instance, presented community and justice system–involved juveniles and young adults with police interrogation vignettes and asked them whether the suspect's "best choice" was to confess, remain silent, or deny involvement in a crime. Nearly 60 percent of the eleven- to thirteen-year-olds and more than 40 percent of the fourteen- to fifteen-year-olds chose "confess" as the best option, compared to only 20 percent of the young adults. Likewise, Pimentel et al. (2015) conducted a laboratory study of adolescents' (ages fourteen to seventeen) and adults' willingness to falsely confess to cheating to protect someone else. When deliberating about whether to sign the confession, significantly more adults (49 percent) than adolescents (32 percent) asked questions or made comments about potential consequences to themselves. The adolescents were thinking less about the potential consequences of confession or perhaps were simply less likely to ask about such consequences, potentially as a way of demonstrating their autonomy. This inclination may be similar to adolescents' tendency not to request the presence of a parent in real-life (Malloy et al., 2014) and analogue interrogations (Pimentel et al., 2015), again in an attempt to be independent.

Even though it is unlikely adolescents would be with peers during an interrogation, peer affiliation and influence may nonetheless exert an influence in this context. When asked, for instance, adolescents say that they would lie to the police to protect their friends (Warr, 1993) and that they have confessed to a crime to protect a peer (Gudjonsson et al., 2008; Viljoen et al., 2005). Such was demonstrated in an investigation by Malloy et al. (2014) in regard to false confessions. Among nearly two hundred incarcerated adolescents interviewed about their confession behavior, thirty-three said that they had falsely confessed to police to a crime in the past, over half of whom then claimed to have done so to protect someone else, such as a friend or family member. Pimentel et al. (2015) demonstrated this same phenomenon empirically in the aforementioned study of adolescents' and adults' willingness to falsely confess to cheating committed by a similar-aged confederate. Whereas 39 percent of adults signed the confession statement admitting to learning the answers to the test ahead of time, 59 percent of adolescents did so. The developmentally normative immediate reward-seeking tendencies (i.e., "just sign it to get it over with") combined with a desire to affiliate with and be valued by peers are instrumental in shaping adolescents' interactions with law enforcement, including in terms of not only what they ultimate decide to disclose but also their willingness to provide false information as a way of protecting peers.

DECISIONS IN THE COURTROOM

Another example of how characteristics of adolescence directly and profoundly shape their decisions in legal settings comes from the courtroom, notably when adolescents decide whether to accept a plea or not (which in some US state juvenile courts is termed "admitting guilt"). Pleas, in theory, can reduce punishment associated with delinquent or criminal behavior. But they also carry a number of consequences (Redlich et al., 2019). Depending on the severity of the crime and the age of the defendant, youth who plead guilty may be giving up the rights to a trial in front of a judge (or if transferred, a jury) and appeal their conviction. Their immigration status, access to services (e.g., food stamps and federal aid), and voting rights may also be affected. Finally, having a criminal record can make applying for jobs and educational opportunities more challenging later in life

(Edkins, 2019). Given the collateral consequences of pleading guilty, youth, like adults, must have a clear understanding of what their decision means now and in the future. In legal terms, they must knowingly, intelligently, and voluntarily decide to plea.[3]

On the one hand, adolescents appear able to make slow and deliberative decisions when deciding whether to take a plea. That is, they do not just accept a plea because it will end the case, a potentially high immediate reward: Viljoen et al. (2005) found that, among youth defendants ages eleven to seventeen, those ages fifteen to seventeen years reported taking the evidence against them into account when deciding to plea. According to Peterson-Badali and Abramovitch (1993), even ten-year-olds knew not to take a plea, in a hypothetical scenario, when the purported evidence against them was weak. On the other hand, adolescents' actual understanding of the plea, especially its consequences, is much more limited compared to adults, and it is unclear how well adolescents deliberate in the moment when deciding to plea. Adolescents may be at risk for pleading guilty to a crime, even when they are innocent, in part due to their relatively high impulsivity (Redlich, 2009). This impulsivity is related to, and motivated by, the high value of immediate reward for adolescents, which overrides their ability to evaluate and appreciate longer-term consequences that result from their decisions. Redlich and Shteynberg (2016), for example, asked adolescents (ages thirteen to seventeen) and young adults (ages eighteen to twenty-four) to consider the short- and long-term consequences of hypothetical plea decisions after they were asked to assume their own innocence or guilt. Adolescents were less likely than adults to consider the overall quality of the hypothetical plea deal and impact of the plea on their longer-term future. They were two and a half times more likely than the young adults to falsely plead guilty when they were actually innocent.

Finally, adolescents' desire for autonomy can shape their plea decisions. Redlich et al. (in press) observed actual plea hearings involving juvenile defendants and found that they were often only minimally engaged. They rarely asked questions. When questions were asked of them, most instead just provided the bare minimum answer. Adolescents may be too intimidated to ask questions, or may also not want to appear naïve or as though they do not understand what is happening. They may not know what is appropriate to say to, or ask of, whom. Viljoen et al. (2005) found that, of approximately 150 detained adolescents awaiting trial, only 35 percent reported that they would respond assertively if they disagreed with their attorney, and nearly a third reported that they would not or may not share important case information with their attorney.

In summary, developmentally normative processes, like immediate reward-seeking and need for autonomy, influence adolescent defendants' decision-making processes in the courtroom similar to the processes influencing other legally relevant decisions adolescents

---

[3] Godinez v. Moran, 509 U.S. 389 (1993).

make. Although not directly tested, research examining how adolescents' decisions to plea in cases where multiple adolescent-aged peers are involved could shed light on whether these decisions, again like other legal decisions, are shaped by wanting to protect peers or peer affiliation.

Adolescent Victims and Witnesses

While most work on adolescents' decision-making in the legal system has been devoted to understanding adolescents suspected of committing crimes, adolescents who have witnessed or experienced crime must also make important decisions that affect their involvement and experiences in the justice system. The same developmental processes that affect adolescent defendants shape adolescent witnesses and victims. Examples, similar to those for adolescent suspects, emerge when considering witness decisions in the interview room and the courtroom.

DECISIONS IN THE INTERVIEW ROOM

Given adolescents' gradual tendency to engage in riskier behavior, and to spend more time exploring and with peers rather than parents, it is perhaps unsurprising that they are at increased risk not only to commit crimes, but also to witness or experience them. They may witness peers or friends engaged in delinquency or be victimized themselves. In fact, with the exception of young adults (aged eighteen to twenty-four), adolescents are the second most likely age group to experience violent crime (Morgan & Truman, 2020). This means that they often encounter law enforcement and are questioned about their experiences.

A crucial decision for adolescents, therefore, is what to tell the police. Evidence indicates that adolescents are not especially forthcoming in disclosing to adults in general about their negative and risky behaviors, such as sexual activity, alcohol or drug use, automobile accidents or encounters with gun violence (Jaccard et al., 1998; Johnson 2014). This reluctance to tell extends to their own victimization. Adolescents tend to delay disclosing sexual abuse or will flatly deny it occurred much more often than children do (Goodman-Brown et al., 2003). Leander et al. (2008), for instance, found that among sixty-eight adolescent victims, ages eleven to nineteen, of internet-initiated sexual abuse, only three (4 percent) told someone before the crime was discovered. The remaining sixty-five disclosed only later, after the police questioned them often in conjunction with the presentation of corroborative evidence of the abuse. Katz (2013) reported a similar trend in forensic interviews of adolescents victimized by online adult sexual predators. Not one disclosed the abuse prior to it being discovered via online chats and images.

When considering why adolescents do not disclose or delay disclosure, multiple sources of influence, including those reflective of characteristics common to adolescent development, are likely. First, compared to children, adolescents are more advanced cognitively and socioemotionally. Thus, when not under pressure to make immediate decisions, adolescents can reason about the potential consequences to themselves and others of sharing details about their experiences (e.g., having been sexually assaulted by a "friend"). Consistent with developmental improvements in reasoning, adolescents are more likely to delay disclosing, while children are more likely to retract prior claims, possibly due to the latter's realization, after telling, about the consequences (Goodman-Brown et al., 2003; Malloy et al., 2007).

Second, adolescents' desire to be autonomous may, at least under some circumstances, inhibit their willingness to report victimization. By disclosing sexual abuse, for instance, adolescents may believe that they will be seen as weak or vulnerable, as has been reported retrospectively in former male victims of child sexual abuse regarding why they had never told anyone. Or, adolescents may be experimenting with risky behaviors. In an effort to be independent, they may take responsibility for negative consequences of their behaviors, failing to recognize that, in some circumstances, they may have been manipulated or coerced into behaving in a particular manner. Even child victims of sexual abuse, for example, sometimes feel complicit or blame themselves, which discourages their disclosures (Hershkowitz et al., 2007). Such feelings may be exacerbated in adolescents who could assume that they made the decision to be involved with a particular perpetrator. Or, they may believe that they have a bond with the perpetrator and do not want to tell or get them in trouble (Katz, 2013; Leander et al., 2008).

One group for whom the latter situations may be especially common is victims of sex trafficking. They are at a particularly high risk for nondisclosure in interviews with law enforcement (Lavoie et al., 2019). Many of these victims have histories of child abuse, as well as involvement in the child welfare and dependency system, and many have lived in foster or group homes or been homeless (see Choi, 2015, for a review). Trafficking, for them, is a way to survive. Some have been in romantic relationships with their trafficker and hence feel the need to protect them (Moore et al., 2020; Reid, 2016), whereas others bond with or feel committed to the other victims, which ultimately can serve as a source of peer affiliation. Given trafficked adolescents' life history and potential encounters with law enforcement (e.g., for prostitution, delinquency, and running away), they are unlikely to trust authorities, even those purportedly there to help them (Lacks & Gordon, 2005). Finally, trafficked adolescents likely have a strong need for autonomy, having had to survive, over time, incredibly challenging circumstances, with no or minimal support from others. All this leads to high levels of reluctance in interviews (Nogalska et al., 2021), demonstrated by the adolescents' strategic decisions either to flat out refuse to answer some questions or to employ evasive tactics such as answering questions with questions, or answering questions by rephrasing them as statements. These decisions result in protection of the trafficker and possibly others involved at the expense of the adolescent victim.

Peer alliance may also shape reporting decisions in other types of victims and witnesses as well. Adolescents see peers as confidants. They often select peers over adults when deciding who to tell about past wrongdoings or exposure to harm, including that which is extreme, like sexual assault (e.g., Schaeffer et al., 2011). Adolescents may make this selection because they trust and value their friend's support more so than that of an adult (Ungar et al., 2009). Yet, once peers know about a friend's victimization, there is no clear evidence that they will tell an adult. That is, adolescents' commitment to their friends is strong when deciding not only how to act but also whether to tell someone else information gained in confidence (Rotenberg, 2010). That same commitment, though, could extend to situations within which the friend or peer was the perpetrator of a crime, as in situations involving "date rape" or interpersonal violence. Evidence indicates that, although such experiences are common in teens (Young et al., 2009), disclosure to authorities is rare. Adolescents may feel responsible for being in compromising situations or for allowing friends to be in compromising positions, or may be afraid of causing problems or telling on friends (Hershkowitz et al., 2007). Finally, for some, peers may be preferred disclosure recipients for victimization because the disclosure is *not* expected to lead to formal intervention.

In summary, adolescent victims and witnesses are also questioned by law enforcement about their experiences. Although the questioning techniques are likely quite different from those used with youth suspects (who may be interrogated to elicit a confession), in both settings, adolescents make crucial decisions about what to tell about their experiences, truthfully or falsely. Multiple factors influence those decisions, some of which include those common to adolescence, such as a desire for autonomy and allegiance to peers. Ultimately, adolescents' decisions about disclosure affect not only the immediate consequences of the interview itself but potentially the progression and outcome of any legal action taken. Even if adolescents are only witnesses and minimally involved in the legal action, what unfolds has the potential to affect them for years to come (Quas et al., 2005).

DECISIONS IN THE COURTROOM

Perhaps the least well-studied aspect of adolescent decision-making in legal contexts concerns decisions of victims and witnesses as a legal case unfolds. There is no easily and identifiable example of a singular and especially important decision that victims and witnesses make, like the decision whether to accept a plea that is made by adolescent defendants. Instead, adolescent victims and witnesses make multiple decisions about cooperativeness and engagement throughout a case, such as whether they will take the stand and what they will say; and whether they will contact social workers, attorneys, victim advocates, and others. Because these decisions are more diffuse and their precise and immediate effects less clear, they have not been studied as often as decisions about the plea.

One area of research, however, that has received attention with regard to adolescent victim decision making concerns when they are involved in dependency cases, that is, cases that arise following exposure to maltreatment and removal from home and placement in temporary out-of-home care. Such involvement is not limited to adolescents. Large numbers of children also suffer maltreatment and may be placed in out-of-home care as a result (Child Welfare Information Gateway, 2020). Yet, for adolescents, dependency cases take on special meaning, legally and psychologically. Legally, across many states, the dependency system distinguishes adolescents from children. Justification for this distinction relies on the cognitive maturity during adolescence that, at least according to the dependency system, warrants their more direct involvement in decisions that affect their lives. One salient example is that several states and some countries require the courts to solicit placement opinions from foster youth, at least those age twelve years and older, who have been removed from their caregivers and are being placed in out-of-home care and to give some weight to these opinions when finalizing placement decisions.[4]

Not only are adolescents presumed capable of expressing a reasonable preference by approximately age twelve (Child Welfare Information Gateway, 2020), but soliciting their input can confer benefits. Youth are valuable sources of knowledge about their experiences and needs across a range of contexts, including custody cases (Kelly, 1994; Saywitz et al., 2010), and they may be able to provide information relevant to their placement that has been overlooked or was unknown to the courts. In addition, by being able to provide input about their placement, foster youths' feelings of control, empowerment, and autonomy may be enhanced (Merritt, 2008; Pitchal, 2008). Given that such feelings are especially salient to adolescents, finding ways to promote those feelings in an otherwise extremely challenging and potentially confusing process is likely to facilitate their adjustment not only to their placement but to their removal and the dependency case more broadly. Finally, multiple studies have demonstrated that both children and adolescents *want* their voice to be heard and to be given the opportunity to provide input (see Ang et al., 2006).

Other dependency court procedures similarly promote engagement in youth, which may be especially important to adolescents. For instance, although not required in most jurisdictions, some county dependency courts explicitly request youth be present at ongoing hearings and facilitate youth attendance (other jurisdictions allow youth to attend, but do very little other than notify youth of hearing times). Regardless of age, youth typically welcome such attendance and report feeling positive afterward about having participated (Quas et al., 2009; Salazar et al., 2020). Youth feel that their voice mattered, even when the ultimate decision by the courts was not one that they had wanted (Pitchal, 2008). For adolescents, being able to attend and decide what to share while in attendance may play a significant role in their legal experiences.

---

[4] E.g., Child Welfare Information Gateway (2020); UK Children Act 1989 c.41, § 25B, https://www. legislation.gov.uk/ukpga/1989/41/section/25B/2013-06-24; UN Committee on the Rights of the Child (UNCRC) art. 12 (2009) (Switzerland), https://www2.ohchr.org/english/bodies/crc/docs/AdvanceVersions/ CRC-C-GC-12.pdf.

Among the other characteristics that seem particularly important in adolescent defendant decision-making in the courtroom, namely, the salience of immediate rewards and peer allegiance, it is perhaps more difficult to see how these play out for adolescent victims and witnesses. However, peer influences can occur: Adolescents may be reluctant to testify against a peer who committed a crime. Conversely, adolescents may feel more empowered to testify if they know other youth are taking the stand. Although these possibilities have yet to be examined directly, hints of the significant role that peers might play have emerged in a recent investigation of disclosure decisions in adolescent victims of sex trafficking. Henderson et al. (2021) compared disclosure in police interviews and in court in a unique sample of eight victims, all of whom had been trafficked by the same perpetrator, the defendant in the trial. Victims who were most reluctant during police interviews were the least likely to show up in court. One, for instance, did not want to be called a snitch, and another considered herself a part of a "team" and refused to disclose information. Among the six who showed up in court, 11 percent of their answers reflected reluctance. Thus, adolescents may make decisions in the courtroom that are shaped by their feelings of loyalty to peers. In this case, that included the other victims and the trafficker.

In sum, adolescent victims and witnesses make crucial decisions in the courtroom—decisions that are likely influenced by the same hallmarks of adolescent development that affect adolescent defendants. Additional research is sorely needed, however, on the nature of these diverse decisions, how they may interact with their developmental capacities and limitations, and methods for facilitating their decision-making in this particular legal context.

Future Research, Practical Implications, and Conclusions

Adolescence is a unique period of human development characterized by multifaceted growth, change, and vulnerability. The developmental characteristics of adolescents covered in this chapter—namely, their tendencies to engage in exploratory and risk-taking behaviors, susceptibility to peer influence, and desire for autonomy—increase the likelihood that they will experiment with or engage in risky or delinquent behavior, be exposed to or engage in criminal and delinquent behaviors, and experience crime, especially violent crime and exploitation, all of which increase the likelihood that adolescents will come into contact with the legal system. Once that contact begins, the developmental characteristics continue to exert an influence, shaping how adolescents interact with others within the context of the legal system. That influence, in turn, affects the progression and ultimate outcome of the adolescents' contact, in terms of both legal action itself and adolescents' functioning and future. In the present chapter, we described how these developmental characteristics influence some of the legally relevant decisions adolescents make in interviews and in court when they are suspects/defendants or victims/witnesses. We sought to provide a few examples that highlight the need to consider development when evaluating adolescents' behaviors and decisions in legal settings. These examples also offer suggestions for future research and for policy and practice.

First, greater attention needs to be paid to adolescent decision-making in legal contexts that extend beyond those in which they are defendants. Adolescent victims and witnesses interact with attorneys, but also social workers and victim advocates. How their impulsiveness and emphasis on immediate rewards influence their interactions is unclear, but important to determine, given the significance of these interactions for the progression of a case. As an example, in dependency cases, when asked about whom they would like to live with following removal from their parent because of maltreatment, adolescents' responses vary considerably. Some want to return home whereas others want to remain with kin or with foster families (Mukhopadhyay et al., 2022), and the reasons underlying their placement preferences is not clear. Whether such preferences are shaped by immediate concerns about stability, rules, or even proximity to peers, has never been explored, but is worthwhile to consider.

A second topic in need of more direct empirical attention concerns testing methods of questioning adolescents about their experiences in ways that recognize adolescent development. For instance, when interviewers establish a positive and supportive rapport with suspected child victims via open-ended rapport, back channeling, and providing ground rules, children's eyewitness reports increase in detail and accuracy (Saywitz et al., 2019). Rapport building with adult victims has similarly been shown to increase the amount of detail provided (Meissner, 2021). A key component of rapport with adults, though, is self-disclosure by an interviewer, which leads to mutual trust and enhanced disclosures. Which approach or combination of approaches would be best for adolescent-age victims, and perhaps witnesses and suspects, is unknown but may depend on the extent to which the precise rapport approach used capitalizes on knowledge of adolescent development. Perhaps approaches that emphasize mutual disclosure are more effective with adolescents if the interviewer is seen as someone similar rather than as an authority figure, a testable hypothesis that suggests interviewer age might matter. Likewise, interview approaches that acknowledge adolescents' need for autonomy may be more effective than those that provide detailed instruction or ground rules. Such empirical tests would help guide interviewing practices toward increasing adolescent disclosures and details provided.

Third, there is a need to focus on understudied vulnerable adolescent populations who perhaps do not clearly fall into the category of suspect, victim, or witness. This is perhaps most obvious with adolescent victims of trafficking, many of whom are picked up on suspicions of delinquent or criminal activity, including prostitution (Halter, 2010). They may be interrogated, with law enforcement who only learn of their trafficking as the victim responds. Even when their victim status is known, they are at times still treated as suspects, for instance, placed in juvenile detention, while law enforcement decides how best to proceed (e.g., Nogalska et al., 2021). In addition to possessing the normative characteristics of adolescence that shape their perceptions and interactions with the authorities, they also have significant trauma histories (e.g., Moore et al., 2020), repeated negative encounters with law enforcement, and often experience in the foster care system; all these experiences shape their behaviors and decisions throughout a legal case. Other adolescents may be in similar precarious positions, having witnessed criminal activity while perhaps having been peripherally involved. Whether they are interrogated as accomplices or considered bystander witnesses may impact how they are questioned and how they respond. Scientific research on these populations, including on factors that shape their decisions and behaviors, as well as methods of ensuring that those decisions are made thoughtfully in a way that protects the adolescents, is needed.

Regarding policy, perhaps the most straightforward implication of this review is the need for the legal community, considered broadly to include law enforcement, social services, and legal professionals, to be better trained on the diverse ways that development shapes adolescents' behaviors and decisions. This training is possible, evidenced by the courts and attorneys regularly citing adolescents' immature brain circuitry and the prolonged development of neural systems across adolescence in relation to their criminal culpability. This training should be expanded to ensure that professionals are aware of how the same neural processes, as well as exploratory and reward-seeking behaviors, influence of peers, and desire for autonomy influence decisions and behaviors throughout a legal case, among adolescents who may have committed a crime, adolescents who have experienced crime, and all adolescents in between.

Despite the considerable advances in research, policy, and practice concerning adolescents' legal decision making, several new or emerging issues remain that warrant further scientific inquiry, many of which we have highlighted in this chapter. Those who study adolescent development and the intersection of psychology and the law will undoubtedly continue to grapple with the best ways to facilitate adolescents' involvement in the legal system for decades to come. We hope that future work involves increased collaboration between legal and law enforcement agencies and scientists. Such collaborations would allow researchers to conduct large-scale studies that could be used to determine the best methods for facilitating adolescents' legal decision-making while simultaneously protecting their rights and guarding against miscarriages of justice.

References

Albert, D., Chein, J., & Steinberg, L. (2013). The teenage brain: Peer influences on adolescent decision making. *Current Directions in Psychological Science, 22*(2), 114–120.

Allen, J. P., & Brown, B. B. (2008). Adolescents, peers, and motor vehicles: The perfect storm? *American Journal of Preventive Medicine, 35*(3), S289–S293.

Ang, F., Berghmans, E., Cattrijsse, L., Delens-Ravier, I., Delplace, M., Staelens, V., Vandewiele, T., Vandresse, C., & Verheyde, M. (2006). *Participation rights of children.* Intersentia.

Boyer, T. W. (2006). The development of risk-taking: A multi-perspective review. *Developmental Review, 26*(3), 291–345.

Braams, B. R., van Duijvenvoorde, A. C., Peper, J. S., & Crone, E. A. (2015). Longitudinal changes in adolescent risk-taking: A comprehensive study of neural responses to rewards, pubertal development, and risk-taking behavior. *Journal of Neuroscience, 35*(18), 7226–7238.

Child Welfare Information Gateway. (2020). *Determining the best interests of the child*. U.S. Department of Health and Human Services, Administration for Children and Families, Children's Bureau.

Choi, K. R. (2015). Risk factors for domestic minor sex trafficking in the United States: A literature review. *Journal of Forensic Nursing, 11*(2), 66–76.

Cleary, H. (2014). Police interviewing and interrogation of juvenile suspects: A descriptive examination of actual cases. *Law and Human Behavior, 38*(3), 271–282.

Connolly, E. J., Lewis, R. H., & Boisvert, D. L. (2017). The effect of socioeconomic status on delinquency across urban and rural contexts: Using a genetically informed design to identify environmental risk. *Criminal Justice Review, 42*(3), 237–253.

Crone, E. A., & Dahl, R. E. (2012). Understanding adolescence as a period of social–affective engagement and goal flexibility. *Nature Reviews Neuroscience, 13*(9), 636–650.

Eastwood, J., Snook, B., & Luther, K. (2015). Measuring the reading complexity and oral comprehension of Canadian youth waiver forms. *Crime and Delinquency, 61*(6), 798–828.

Edkins, V. A. (2019). Collateral consequences and disenfranchisement. In V. A. Edkins & A. D. Redlich (Eds.), *A system of pleas: Social sciences contributions to the real legal system* (pp. 168–183). Oxford University Press.

Erikson, E. H. (1968). *Identity: Youth and crisis*. W. W. Norton.

Goodman-Brown, T. B., Edelstein, R. S., Goodman, G. S., Jones, D. P., & Gordon, D. S. (2003). Why children tell: A model of children's disclosure of sexual abuse. *Child Abuse & Neglect, 27*(5), 525–540. https://doi.org/10.1016/S0145-2134(03)00037-1

Grandpre, J., Alvaro, E. M., Burgoon, M., Miller, C. H., & Hall, J. R. (2003). Adolescent reactance and anti-smoking campaigns: A theoretical approach. *Health Communication, 15*, 349–366.

Grigorenko, E. L. (2006). Learning disabilities in juvenile offenders. *Child and Adolescent Psychiatric Clinics, 15*(2), 353–371.

Grisso, T. (1980). Juveniles' capacities to waive *Miranda* rights: An empirical analysis. *California Law Review, 68*(6), 1134–1166.

Grisso T. (1981). Juveniles' comprehension of *Miranda* warnings. In *Juveniles' waiver of rights. Vol. 3. Perspectives in law & psychology* (pp 59–93). Springer.

Grisso, T., Steinberg, L., Woolard, J., Cauffman, E., Scott, E., Graham, S., Lexcen, F., Reppucci, N. D., & Schwartz, R. (2003). Juveniles' competence to stand trial: A comparison of adolescents' and adults' capacities as trial defendants. *Law and Human Behavior, 27*(4), 333–363. doi: 10.1023/A:1024065015717

Gudjonsson, G. H., Sigurdsson, J. F., Sigfusdottir, I. D., & Asgeirsdottir, B. B. (2008). False confessions and individual differences: The importance of victimization among youth. *Personality and Individual Differences, 45*(8), 801–805.

Halter, S. (2010). Factors that influence police conceptualizations of girls involved in prostitution in six US cities: Child sexual exploitation victims or delinquents? *Child Maltreatment, 15*(2), 152–160.

Henderson H., Cho S., Nogalska A., & Lyon T. D. (2021). Identifying novel forms of reluctance in commercially sexually exploited adolescents. *Child Abuse & Neglect, 115*, 104994.

Hershkowitz, I., Lanes, O., & Lamb, M. E. (2007). Exploring the disclosure of child sexual abuse with alleged victims and their parents. *Child Abuse & Neglect, 31*, 111–123.

Jaccard, J., Dittus, P. J., & Gordon, V. V. (1998). Parent-adolescent congruency in reports of adolescent sexual behavior and in communications about sexual behavior. *Child Development, 69*(1), 247–261.

Johnson S.D. (2014). Comparing factors associated with maternal and adolescent reports of adolescent traumatic event exposure. *Family Process, 53*, 214–224. https://doi.org/10.1111/famp.12050

Katz, C. (2013). Internet-related child sexual abuse: What children tell us in their testimonies. *Children and Youth Services Review, 35*(9), 1536–1542.

Kelley, S., Zelle, H., Brogan, L., & Goldstein, N. E. (2018). Review of research and recent case law on understanding and appreciation of *Miranda* warnings. In M. Miller & B. Bornstein (Eds.), *Advances in psychology and law* (pp. 77–117). Springer.

Kelly, J. B. (1994). The determination of child custody. *The Future of Children, 4*(1), 121–142.

Lacks, R. D., & Gordon, J. A. (2005). Adults and adolescents: The same or different? Exploring police trust in an inner-city adolescent population. *Criminal Justice Studies, 18*(3), 271–280.

Lavoie, J., Dickerson, K. L., Redlich, A. D., & Quas, J. A. (2019). Overcoming disclosure reluctance in youth victims of sex trafficking: New directions for research, policy, and practice. *Psychology, Public Policy, and Law, 25*(4), 225.

Leander, L., Christianson, S. Å., & Granhag, P. A. (2008). Internet-initiated sexual abuse: adolescent victims' reports about on-and off-line sexual activities. *Applied Cognitive Psychology*, *22*(9), 1260–1274.

Levenson, E., & Galván, A. (2014). Neural representation of expected value in the adolescent brain. *Proceedings of the National Academy of Sciences*, *111*(4), 1646–1651.

Lieser, A. M., Van der Voort, D., & Spaulding, T. J. (2019). You have the right to remain silent: The ability of adolescents with developmental language disorder to understand their legal rights. *Journal of Communication Disorders*, *82*, Article 105920.

Luyckx, K., Goossens, L., Soenens, B., & Beyers, W. (2006). Unpacking commitment and exploration: Preliminary validation of an integrative model of late adolescent identity formation. *Journal of Adolescence*, *29*(3), 361–378.

Malloy, L. C., Lyon, T. D., & Quas, J. A. (2007). Filial dependency and recantation of child sexual abuse allegations. *Journal of the American Academy of Child & Adolescent Psychiatry*, *46*(2), 162–170.

Malloy, L. C., Shulman, E. P., & Cauffman, E. (2014). Interrogations, confessions, and guilty pleas among serious adolescent offenders. *Law and Human Behavior*, *38*(2), 181–193.

Meissner, C. A. (2021). "What works?" Systematic reviews and meta-analyses of the investigative interviewing research literature. *Applied Cognitive Psychology*, *35*(2), 322–328.

Merritt, D. H. (2008). Placement preferences among children living in foster or kinship care: A cluster analysis. *Children and Youth Services Review*, *30*(11), 1336–1344.

Moore, J. L., Houck, C., Hirway, P., Barron, C. E., & Goldberg, A. P. (2020). Trafficking experiences and psychosocial features of domestic minor sex trafficking victims. *Journal of Interpersonal Violence*, *35*(15-16), 3148–3163.

Morgan, R., & Truman, J. (2020, September). *Criminal victimization, 2019*. Bureau of Justice Statistics. https://www.bjs.gov/content/pub/pdf/cv19.pdf

Mukhopadhyay, S., Dickerson, K. L., Lyon, T. D., & Quas, J. A. (2022). Foster youth's placement preferences: The roles of kin, siblings, and age. *Child Abuse & Neglect*, *131*, 105761. https://doi.org/10.1016/j.chiabu.2022.105761

Nogalska, A. M., Henderson, H. M., Cho, S. J., & Lyon, T. D. (2021). Police interviewing behaviors and commercially sexually exploited adolescents' reluctance. Psychology, *Public Policy, and Law*, *27*(3), 328–340. https://doi.org/10.1037/law0000315

Owen-Kostelnik, J., Reppucci, N. D., & Meyer, J. R. (2006). Testimony and interrogation of minors: Assumptions about maturity and morality. *American Psychologist*, *61*, 286–304.

Peterson-Badali, M., & Abramovitch, R. (1993). Grade related changes in young people's reasoning about plea decisions. *Law and Human Behavior*, *17*(5), 537–552.

Pimentel, P. S., Arndorfer, A., & Malloy, L. C. (2015). Taking the blame for someone else's wrongdoing: The effects of age and reciprocity. *Law and Human Behavior*, *39*(3), 219–231.

Pitchal, E. S. (2008). Where are all the children? Increasing youth participation in dependency proceedings. *UC Davis Journal of Juvenile Law & Policy*, *12*(1), 233–262.

Quas, J. A., Cooper, A., & Wandrey, L. (2009). Child victims in dependency court. In B. L. Bottoms, C. J. Najdowski, & G. S. Goodman (Eds.), *Children as victims, witnesses, and offenders: Psychological science and the law* (pp. 128–149). Guilford Press.

Quas, J. A., Goodman, G. S., Ghetti, S., Alexander, K. W., Edelstein, R., Redlich, A. D., Cordon, I. M., Jones, D. P. H., & Haugaard, J. J. (2005). Childhood sexual assault victims: Long-term outcomes after testifying in criminal court. *Monographs of the Society for Research in Child Development*, *70*, i–139. https://www.jstor.org/stable/3701439

Redlich, A. D. (2009). The susceptibility of juveniles to false confessions and false guilty pleas. *Rutgers Law Review*, *62*, 943–957.

Redlich, A. D., Domagalski, K., Woestehoff, S. A., Dezember, A., & Quas, J. A., (in press). Guilty plea hearings in juvenile and criminal court. *Law and Human Behavior*.

Redlich, A. D., & Shteynberg, R. V. (2016). To plead or not to plead: A comparison of juvenile and adult true and false plea decisions. *Law and Human Behavior*, *40*(6), 611.

Redlich, A. D., Zottoli, T., & Daftary-Kapur, T. (2019). Juvenile justice and plea bargaining. In V. A. Edkins & A. Redlich (Eds.), *A system of pleas: Social science contributions to the real legal system* (pp. 107–131). Oxford University Press.

Reid, J. A. (2016). Entrapment and enmeshment schemes used by sex traffickers. *Sexual Abuse*, *28*(6), 491–511.

Rotenberg, K. J. (2010). The conceptualization of interpersonal trust: A basis, domain, and target framework. In K. J. Rotenberg (Ed.), *Interpersonal trust during childhood and adolescence* (pp. 8–27). Cambridge University Press.

Salazar, A. M., Spiers, S. S., & Pfister, F. R. (2020). Authentically engaging youth with foster care experience: Definitions and recommended strategies from youth and staff. *Journal of Youth Studies, 24*, 1015–1032.

Saywitz, K. J., Camparo, L. B., & Romanoff, A. (2010). Interviewing children in custody cases: Implications of research and policy for practice. *Behavioral Sciences & the Law, 28*(4), 542–562.

Saywitz, K. J., Wells, C. R., Larson, R. P., & Hobbs, S. D. (2019). Effects of interviewer support on children's memory and suggestibility: Systematic review and meta-analyses of experimental research. *Trauma, Violence, & Abuse, 20*, 22–39.

Schaeffer, P., Leventhal, J. M., & Asnes, A. G. (2011). Children's disclosures of sexual abuse: Learning from direct inquiry. *Child Abuse & Neglect, 35*(5), 343–352.

Sebastian, C., Burnett, S., & Blakemore, S. J. (2008). Development of the self-concept during adolescence. *Trends in Cognitive Sciences, 12*(11), 441–446.

Simons-Morton, B., Pickett, W., Boyce, W., Ter Bogt, T. F., & Vollebergh, W. (2010). Cross-national comparison of adolescent drinking and cannabis use in the United States, Canada, and the Netherlands. *International Journal of Drug Policy, 21*, 64–69.

Steinberg, L. (2009). Adolescent development and juvenile justice. *Annual Review of Clinical Psychology, 5*, 459–485.

Steinberg, L., & Silverberg, S. B. (1986). The vicissitudes of autonomy in early adolescence. *Child Development, 57*(4), 841–851.

Ungar, M., Tutty, L. M., McConnell, S., Barter, K., & Fairholm, J. (2009). What Canadian youth tell us about disclosing abuse. *Child Abuse & Neglect, 33*(10), 699–708.

van Hoorn, J., Fuligni, A. J., Crone, E. A., & Galvan, A. (2016). Peer influence effects on risk-taking and prosocial decision-making in adolescence: Insights from neuroimaging studies. *Current Opinion in Behavioral Sciences, 10*, 59–64.

Viljoen, J. L., Klaver, J., & Roesch, R. (2005). Legal decisions of preadolescent and adolescent defendants: Predictors of confessions, pleas, communication with attorneys, and appeals. *Law and Human Behavior, 29*(3), 253–277.

Warr, M. (1993). Age, peers, and delinquency. *Criminology, 31*(1), 17–40.

Young, A. M., Grey, M., & Boyd, C. J. (2009). Adolescents' experiences of sexual assault by peers: Prevalence and nature of victimization occurring within and outside of school. *Journal of Youth and Adolescence, 38*, 1072–1083.

Zelle, H., Romaine, C. L. R., & Goldstein, N. E. (2015). Juveniles' Miranda comprehension: Understanding, appreciation, and totality of circumstances factors. *Law and Human Behavior, 39*(3), 281–293.

Why Seeing the Big Picture in the Study of Public Safety Is Necessary for Combatting Racism within It

Gwen Prowse *and* Phillip Atiba Goff

Abstract

Quantitative social science has primarily studied policing in general and racial disparities in policing specifically by focusing on micro- and mesolevel phenomena rather than engaging macrolevel phenomena. Policy recommendations informed by quantitative social science therefore end up focused on reforming what are framed as patterns of errors rather than on the broader systems that produce the conditions for these interactions. The current approach places quantitative social science out of step with contemporary debates about public safety, including when and whether to deploy police at all. This chapter examines why quantitative social science has thus far missed the big picture, the consequences, and what integrating macrolevel approaches in our research might look like.

Key Words: racial disparities, policing, macrolevel structures, public safety, methodology

In the summer of 2020, the world bore witness to communities calling for fundamental changes to the ways the United States produces public safety. Previously, when communities had demanded change, there had been a significant quantitative social science literature from which to draw solutions. Scholars of race and crime had research on community policing in response to the uprisings in Los Angeles of 1992 (Friedmann, 1992; Greene & Mastrofski, 1988). Similarly, there was research on implicit bias and procedural justice that was responsive to public outcry following the shooting of Amadou Diallo and the rebellions that followed Ferguson (Eberhardt et al., 2004; Sunshine & Tyler, 2003). These literatures demonstrated how policing produced worse outcomes for subjugated communities and suggested methods to reduce that burden. In other words, these literatures largely addressed the question of how to deploy police better. Yet, as the national conversation turned from asking how to make policing better to asking when and whether to deploy police, there was simply not a robust quantitative social science literature up to the task.

Political historians have begun to ask questions about the reasons the United States governs more through crime than the welfare of its citizens (Hinton, 2016; Schrader,

2019; Simon, 2007). Some social psychologists have begun framing questions of unequal outcomes in terms of both personal bias and structural features (Glaser et al., 2015; Goff & Godsil, 2016; Swencionis et al., 2021). And political scientists have begun asking questions about the role of profit motive in policing (Christiani et al., 2021; Sances & You, 2017) and the costs of policing to democratic participation (Weaver & Lerman, 2014). But as to the following questions—Why do police respond to mental health crises rather than healthcare workers? Why does an armed first responder issue traffic violations? What are the consequences of those policy choices? Can policing be democratic in a sociopolitically stratified society? When, if ever, are police necessary?—the quantitative literature is thin to nonexistent.

The purpose of this chapter is to discuss one reason why: that quantitative social science has been far more concerned with micro- and mesostructural approaches to race and public safety than macrostructural approaches. In other words, the field has literally missed the big picture. The result is that the questions occasioned by lower-level considerations— questions of behavioral interventions and policy regulations—have trumped consideration of broader questions of policing's mission. If quantitative social science hopes to be relevant to policy discussions of race and public safety going forward, integrating macro-level approaches to the issue will be critical.

This chapter is organized into four sections. We begin by putting the current landscape in historical context. We articulate what we mean by micro-, meso-, and macrolevel approaches to studying racial disparity in public safety, outline popular approaches in the quantitative study of public safety, and then contrast these approaches to dissident scholars such as W. E. B. Du Bois, who have implored their peers to focus on the big-picture relationships between anti-Blackness and public safety. Second, we describe how micro- and mesolevel approaches have become inscribed into law, namely, through courts' interpretations of the Fourth and Fourteenth Amendments. Third, we identify common ways that quantitative social scientists measure racial bias in public safety and the consequences of ignoring the big picture. We conclude by considering how quantitative scholars can take up a more macrolevel approach by studying the consequences of public safety practices, evolving our methods, and investigating how communities heal from the harms of state violence.

Background

Critical incidents of police misconduct are often discussed in popular media at the level of the individual officer and their individual actions. We define the empirical focus on individual-level actions and interactions as a *micro*level of inquiry. This focus on the microlevel organization of officer misconduct is mirrored in a preponderance of the scholarship and policy recommendations on the topic (e.g., President's Task Force on 21st Century Policing; Lum et al., 2016). If the individual encounter is the microlevel framing of policing, then we might think of neighborhoods, local healthcare, school districts, and community surveillance—what Monica Bell (2020) terms "located institutions"—as *mesolevel* factors. The mesolevel may comprise individual neighborhoods, or even single blocks. This framing is appealing because policing is exceptionally place-driven; norms surrounding police/community engagement in one neighborhood may be unrecognizable from norms in another, even if both are in the same city (Groff et al., 2010; Eck & Weisburd, 2015). Economic variance across cities, climate variance across regions, political contexts and histories, and cultural variance across countries are also likely to shape policing in substantive ways, exerting *macro*structural influence on public safety phenomena (Christiani et al., 2021; Sampson et al., 2018; Sances & You 2017). These levels are similar to what economists Alford and Friedland (1985) term "structural, institutional, and situational" levels of analysis, where structural-level analyses concern "what game should we play," institutional-level analyses concern "what are the rules," and situational-level analyses concern "what moves can I make within the game."

For decades, the focal point of quantitative social science's investigation of race and policing has been at the microlevel. This may have been a natural starting point for researchers interested in whether individual officers are biased (Eberhardt et al., 2004). As calls for police reform grew, these tools pivoted toward the study of how bias affects police officer behavior toward citizens and, in turn, how citizens perceive this behavior. In this approach, reducing racism in policing boils down to reducing patterns of error via procedural interventions that improve police behavior. But this level of inquiry leads to policy recommendations too individualized to solve structural problems. It leaves little room for consideration of how the history of racism in policing influences non-White communities' sense of civic belonging, dignity, and autonomy (Justice & Meares, 2014; Soss & Weaver, 2017). We provide examples of how these shortcomings play out in the chapter's subsequent sections.

Other scholarship in quantitative social science considers questions at the mesolevel (Goff, 2016), treating violence and crime as a concentrated place-based phenomenon (Braga et al., 2019; Meares, 1997; Papachristos & Hureau, 2013). The preponderance of the quantitative scholarship engaging meso-levels of analysis concerns reducing crime in neighborhoods (Braga & Weisburd, 2010; Braga et al., 2014). Yet, without a historical lens, a mesolevel approach risks overlooking structural forces that produce neighborhood crime, violence, and even geography (Rothstein, 2017). In contrast, a macrolevel lens might consider what historical factors (though they may persist) contribute to violence and the perception thereof, such as housing policies, unemployment, and neighborhood disinvestment. A macrostructural orientation to crime and violence can shape the questions asked at the neighborhood level. How, for example, might historical racial disparities in access to mental health resources shape neighborhood violence? What about contemproary forces, such as housing insecurity? And, is crime even the most appropriate metric for measuring, analyzing, evaluating, or even describing community safety?

Fortunately, mesolevel research is in a unique position to evolve toward macrolevel engagement. Research on policing sits easily alongside other studies of neighborhood welfare concerning matters of health, education, and sociopolitical infrastructure. As we expound on later in the chapter, recent work at the intersection of meso- and macrolevel studies of racism and policing has uncovered the deleterious health and educational consequences of living in a neighborhood with a high concentration of Terry stops (Sewell & Jefferson, 2016), as well as how the availability of "social infrastructure" (i.e., park and libraries) correlates with reduced violent crime in communities (Klinenberg, 2018); and how Black representation on city councils appears to mitigate the use of fines, fees, and traffic stops on city residents (Christiani, 2021; Sances & You, 2017). Through its engagement with the historical and structural features of policing and punishment in the United States, this work represents a promising direction for quantitative social scientists.

Macrolevel studies of racism and public safety have largely remained at the margins of quantitative social science. Yet for more than a century, Black social scientists in particular have argued that this work be at the center. In his early years as a scholar, W. E. B. Du Bois (1899) spent eighteen months living in Philadelphia's majority-Black seventh ward to conduct the most extensive social scientific study of Black urban life of its time, which included the topic of crime. He concludes in his findings that White Philadelphians' overly narrow understanding of racism was one of the greatest barriers to Black progress in the Northern city and beyond. Du Bois explains that in the mind of the Black Philadelphian, racial prejudice "is that widespread feeling of dislike for his blood, which keeps him and his children out of decent employment, from certain public conveniences and amusements, from hiring houses in many sections, and in general, from being recognized as a man" (p. 229). He contrasts this with the views of White people, who regard racism solely as an aversion to intimate (i.e., sexual) relations with people of a lower status. Here, Du Bois draws a distinction between the macrolevel understanding of racism held by Black residents and the microlevel understanding held by Whites. To Du Bois, Whites' refusal to view racism as an active form of domination instead of a passive, individual-level aversion at the turn of the twentieth century was a refusal to take responsibility for the structural conditions that create and compound Black poverty, insecurity, and overall subjugated citizenship. This abdication would destine White elites to overstate Black criminality, to treat it as a matter of individual responsibility, and to attribute it to the defect of (the politically constructed identity that is) Blackness itself (for more, see Muhammad, 2010).

Du Bois was not the last multimethod researcher to challenge what safety was afforded to Black people within a racist society. Ten years later, Ida B. Wells-Barnett would publish "On Lynching: Our National Crime" (1909), which drew from decades of her prior research, urging the federal government to systematically count the prevalence of lynching and sanction it accordingly. Arthur Raper, a White sociologist and admirer of Wells-Barnett's research, would launch the nation's first quantitative study of police killings across more than two hundred police departments, which he found resulted in four times more Black deaths in the South than lynch mobs (O'Flaherty & Sethi, 2019). Raper's findings would form the basis of Gunnar Myrdal's chapter on police in *An American Dilemma*, where he described the policeman as "personification of White authority in the Negro community" (1944, p. 535). Thirty years after Myrdal's book, the National Conference of Black Political Scientists published the first issue of their journal, *The Journal on Political Repression*. The inaugural topic: police repression (Jones, 1975). In a series of multimethod case studies, Black political scientists criticized the 1968 creation of the Law Enforcement Assistance Administration (LEAA) using the "War on Crime," as a guise for quashing Black liberation projects:

> The cry for "law and order" can be better understood as a code, which deciphered means things are changing too fast and "stop the niggers." The abstract, unbiased belief in justice and order was absent since crimes and violence were quite visible for a decade before there developed a concern for demanding that everyone obey all laws. It need not even be mentioned that under certain material conditions justice and order are contradictory. Those forces that gave rise to the new anti-crime bureaucracy were motivated more by a concern for order than justice, and even support order without justice. (Trice, 1975, p. 93)

To summarize, a minority of researchers in the first half of the twentieth century illustrated the magnitude of Black deaths caused by police. By 1970, Black social scientists sounded alarms as the definition of public safety narrowed to the use of armed first responders. At neither point did quantitative social science respond proportionally in its research agendas. Nor did policymakers in their laws, which we turn to now.

Inquiry Levels and the Law

How courts interpret safety, society's responsibility for providing it to residents, and an individual's responsibility for compliance with the law, has implications for how we study it. Much of the focus in constitutional law is at the individual level, and much of the focus on the state's provision of public safety is framed as negative rights: protection *from* unreasonable searches and seizures (see Guyll et al., this volume), protection *from* cruel and unusual punishment, protection *from* coercion (expressed as a right to legal counsel; see Alceste & Kassin, this volume), and protection *from* self-incrimination (expressed in *Miranda* as a right to remain silent). Stated another way, constitutional law, and the legal precedent that follows, generally lives at the microlevel by prioritizing an individual's protection (or lack thereof) from the overreach of state abuses. Here, we describe several examples of how this approach to constitutional interpretation manifests in public safety policy.

The legal area where the focus on the microlevel is perhaps most acute is surrounding the Fourth Amendment. In *Whren v. United States,*[1] the Court held that a violation of

---

[1] Whren v. United States, 517 U.S. 806 (1996).

traffic laws justifies the temporary detention of the driver and does not violate the Fourth Amendment protection against unreasonable seizure.[2] This Court based its decision on defendants Michael Whren and James L. Brown committing a traffic violation (failure to signal a turn), which led to a plain view search and confiscation of drugs by two plain-clothes police officers in an unmarked vehicle. At the microlevel, the case is fairly straight-forward. Even for those who dispute the grounds of the officers' search and the Court's final decision, the precedent to stop and search a traffic-violating individual need not create or exacerbate racial disparities. However, when officers are more likely to administer traffic stops, citations, and searches to non-White people, perhaps the legal question is better situated within a macrolevel framework (Quattlebaum, 2018). Regardless of whether these racial disparities stem from real or perceived criminality, the very fact that they exist demands consideration of the underlying reasons for these existing disparities, as well as their implications. A macrolevel legal focus might consider the history of police stopping and searching Black people and other non-White groups. It might pay closer attention to the political arrangements that promote or discourage the use of so-called *Terry* stops (Christiani et al., 2021). It might reflect on the disproportionate likelihood of police using excessive force against Black people during Terry stops (Carbado, 2017). All these approaches would demand viewing racial disparity within policing not as an aberration but as endemic feature of how we currently practice public safety.

There have been some, albeit few, exceptions to this individualized approach to legal interpretation. In contrast to the microlevel lens from which the Supreme Court decided *Whren* is *Illinois v. Wardlow*.[3] Here, the Court found that reasonable suspicion for an investigative stop existed based on factors specific to the suspect and the location of the encounter. The defendant in *Wardlow* was a pedestrian in a "high crime neighborhood" who fled upon seeing the police. When the police caught Mr. Wardlow, they conducted a pat-down search and found a firearm. The Court based its opinion to uphold the reason-ableness of this search, in part, on Mr. Wardlow's "unprovoked flight upon noticing the police" while living in a high crime neighborhood.[4] Quantitative scholarship focusing on the mesolevel relationship between place and crime—"hotspots"—arguably provided an empirical justification for the decision in *Wardlow* (National Academy of Sciences 2018; Braga & Weisburd, 2010). However, in a recent test of *Wardlow*'s central legal claim using a data set of two million investigative stops in New York City between 2002 and 2007, Grunwald and Fagan (2019) found that police invoking high-crime area (HCA) to justify a stop is only weakly correlated with the area's crime rate. Instead, a suspect's race, the racial composition of the area, and the racial identity of the officer are more predictive of the designation of HCA than crime rate itself. Further, the authors find that when an

---

[2] *Id.* at 809–819.
[3] Illinois v. Wardlow, 528 U.S. 119 (2000),
[4] *Id.* at 124.

officer invokes HCA to justify a stop, their "hit rate" for contraband is no higher than non-HCAs, and even negative across certain measures. These finding at the mesolevel have macrolevel implications: a city policy that allows police officers to rely on intuition alone to determine an area's criminality creates racial disparities in police stops, which in turn, increases the prospect of criminalization and violence for those stopped.

While courts have done little to curb the power of police to stop, search, and use force against residents, they have also done little to mandate that the state protect people at risk of serious harm (Bell, 2020; Prowse et al., 2020). In *DeShaney v. Winnebago County*,[5] the DeShaney family sued Winnebago County for the failure of Child Protective Services to intervene before four-year-old Joshua DeShaney was nearly beaten to death by his father. The Court ruled that the due process clause of the Fourteenth Amendment does not mandate that the state protect citizens from private violence. Monica Bell (2020) describes in an essay how cases like *DeShaney* have (thus far) foreclosed legal claims by communities who argue that safety hazards in public housing were "state-created dangers that the state had an affirmative duty to alleviate" (p. 717). This case illustrates how the administration of public safety—when capaciously defined—is a far murkier feature of the constitution, where federal courts are apprehensive to provide broad interpretations. This murkiness at the macro-level impedes the legal remediation of state-created safety hazards that disproportionately affect entire neighborhoods and poor, non-White people.

In summary, dominant approaches to constitutional interpretation have also missed the big picture when it comes to public safety, focusing on individual rights to the detriment of macrostructural sources of the problem. As we demonstrate in the next section, this parallels dominant approaches to the topic in quantitative social science.

The Perils of Ignoring the Big Picture

This section outlines dominant approaches in quantitative methods to studying racial disparities in policing. Here, we illustrate how these predominantly micro- and mesolevel approaches cannot sufficiently attend to macrolevel safety issues. Then in the subsequent section, we provide recommendations for where quantitative scholars may be able to adjust course. We focus primarily on racial bias in officer-initiated stops, often known as proactive policing (National Academies of Sciences, 2018). We do so because a majority of scholarship in the field focuses on (1) whether there is racial disparity in an officer's decision to stop and search an individual or (2) whether an officer used force following their decision to stop and search a resident.

Counterfactual Analysis

Conceptualizing "the causal effect of race" is a central constitutive task of diagnosing racism in policing (National Academies of Sciences, 2018). This is no easy task and one with

---

[5] DeShaney v. Winnebago County, 489 U.S. 189 (1989).

limited consensus. Some schools of thought suggest that because race is an "immutable" characteristic, it cannot be manipulated—that is, a person who is Black cannot become White, or vice versa (Hernan, 2016; Holland, 1986; Pearl & Mackenzie, 2018; though see Penner & Saperstein, 2008). Others suggest that measuring the causal effect of race in quantitative studies requires an understanding that race is a socially and politically constructed category irreducible to phenotypical features (Fields & Fields, 2014; Omi & Winant, 2014; Sen & Wasow, 2016). In the latter frame, race is a "bundle of sticks": an array of variables that include skin tone, name, neighborhood, power relations, wealth, class, religion, and so on. Thus, race as a treatment "affects nearly every social-economic variable typically included in standard regression analysis" (Sen & Wasow, 2016, p. 504).

Because of both the lack of conceptual consensus on what race is and the methodological difficulties of measuring the causal effect of race, racism, and other racially relevant mechanisms on racial disparities, counterfactual analysis is increasingly used for measuring racial bias in policing. Greiner and Rubin (2011) most famously proposed shifting the focus from the person who is being racialized to the person at risk of making a racially biased decision. In the case of policing, the race of the resident of potential bias is determined by the subjective criteria in which a police officer discerns their race. This approach typically employs an experimental design that takes place in a laboratory setting, where the only variable randomly assigned to condition is the race of the officer or target. This randomization makes ruling out confounds easier—though not absolute (National Academies of Sciences, 2018).

A common research design for counterfactual analysis among social psychologists can be found in the study of implicit bias: often measured in terms of automatic associations between groups and stereotypes about that group (Greenwald et al., 1998). This research has demonstrated that when shown pictures of Black faces—even beneath awareness—police, like everyone else, are prone to misperceive neutral objects as crime-related (Eberhardt et al., 2004; though training may reduce these errors, Sim et al., 2013). Social psychologists have also demonstrated that implicit dehumanization predicts endorsement of violence and even death sentences (Goff et al., 2008), in addition to establishing the robust ways in which situations (such as cognitive depletion, time pressure, and lack of practice; Swencionis & Goff, 2017) render officers more vulnerable to making stereotypical errors.

Findings from these counterfactual models may be crucial for substantiating the deadly consequences of unjust assumptions, particularly when they are held (consciously or unconsciously) by armed first responders. And these findings may be especially attractive because of the policy recommendations that they imply: address the racism of individual officers and workforce conditions that exacerbate stereotypic errors, then disparities diminish. What these microlevel solutions cannot resolve are the macrolevel conditions that encourage police officers to respond in racially disparate ways in the name of public safety. These macrolevel conditions include the ever-evolving laws that disproportionately criminalize behaviors that have come to be associated with stereotypes of racial and ethnic groups, such as Blackness (e.g., crack cocaine, sagging pants, and, most recently, public protest) (Hinton & Cook, 2021) or Latinidad (e.g., citizenship) (Macias-Rojas, 2016). In the best-case scenario, microlevel interventions that reduce officer bias may work, but they run the risk of obscuring the forest for the trees.

Outcomes-Based Testing

Outcomes-based tests are statistical tests used by quantitative social scientists seeking to understand the underlying motivation for racial disparities in police-resident interactions. The primary benefit of outcomes testing is that it prevents the need to wrangle (statistically) with selection bias in a sample. For instance, if one observes that Black motorists are six times more likely to be stopped by police than are White motorists, it is not clear how much that disparity owes to police bias or how much to the demographics of a jurisdiction (for instance). However, if one observes that Black motorists who have been stopped are searched six times more often than White motorists who have been stopped, that difference logically cannot be because of racial disparities in demographics or regional demographics. In this way, analyzing conditional probabilities produces at least the appearance of stronger causal inference (Knowles et al., 2001; National Academies of Sciences, 2018).

The primary way in which outcomes testing misses the "big picture" is that it focuses on identifying biases in aggregated officer behaviors that occur downstream within police/community contacts. Even if outcomes testing does not reveal bias conditioned on (for instance) stops, racial disparities in stops can still have devastating and unjust consequences within communities (Del Toro et al., 2019). This is especially true for youth. Young people who make contact with the criminal-legal system experience lower academic achievement on test scores and are more likely to drop out of school (Kirk & Sampson, 2013). They are also more likely to self-report experiencing psychological distress and engaging in future acts of delinquent behavior six, twelve, and eighteen months after police contact (Del Toro et al., 2019). Qualitative research helps to animate the psychic harms of criminalization on Black and Latino youth, namely, how proactive policing practices affect how youth come to understand their place and value in this world (Jones, 2014; Morris, 2016; Rios, 2011). In a three-year-long ethnography of Black and Latino youth in Oakland, sociologist Victor Rios (2011) portrays this process through the eyes of one of his youth informants, Tyrell. Here, Tyrell describes how his growth spurt in the sixth grade led to him being punished by the teachers in school and by the police outside:

> The five-o [police] stopped me all the time. They checked me for drugs and guns most of the time. At first I was scared and told them I was only twelve. They didn't believe me and kept asking me where I was hiding the drugs. That made me hella mad 'cause I wasn't slanging [selling drugs] or anything. On mama's [I promise] I wasn't slanging. I said, fuck it. So a few months later I started selling weed. (p. 73)

Here, Tyrell attributes these adversarial experiences with authorities to his turning to street involvement, not the other way around. The microlevel approach of distinguishing between statistical discrimination and racial animus in the outcomes-based test fails to account for the macrolevel consequences of racially disparate traffic stops such as the alienation and estrangement described by Tyrell (see also Bell 2017).

Interventions in Police Culture

A growing body of quantitative social science tests how to improve police-resident interactions and mitigate racial bias in policing by targeting elements of police culture. Using advanced methodologies and large sample sizes, researchers have been able to identify how interventions at the individual level affect both resident trust of police and police conduct toward different racial and ethnic groups. These interventions often prioritize processes that improve fairness and respect for human dignity—what is often described as procedural justice (see Bradford et al., this volume).

The literature on procedural justice in public safety demonstrates that interactions with police shape how residents perceive their performance in solving crime, as well as acting lawfully and fairly. These perceptions shape how individuals perceive the police and, by extension, view the law as legitimate. To increase legitimacy, procedural justice policing recommends that interactions between residents and law enforcement include neutrality, respect, trustworthiness, and giving residents the ability to voice their perspective during an encounter with an officer (Tyler, 2003; Tyler et al., 2014). A recent staggered-adoption study of a single-day procedural justice training of Chicago Police Department officers found that this intervention reduced officers' use of force, reduced the volume of citizen complaints (Wood, 2020) and increased officer support for procedural justice practices (Skogan et al., 2015).

Recently, quantitative social scientists have also been able to test the use of community-oriented policing (COP) principles to increase citizen trust in police. Rather than the punitive enforcement of the law, COP promotes police-resident cooperation through "nonenforcement interactions" such as friendly neighborhood interactions, shared community meetings, and other venues for problem-solving community safety issues (Peyton et al., 2019; Lum et al., 2016; Skogan, 2006). In a community policing field experiment conducted in New Haven, Connecticut, Peyton et al. (2019) found that a single positive interaction initiated by a police officer could improve self-reported attitudes toward police for Black and White residents, including resident perception of legitimacy and willingness to cooperate with law enforcement.

As promising as this research literature is, focusing on micro and mesolevel reforms might be read as treating trust in police and racially equitable public safety as leading indicators. In other words, the goal is to "get the community to trust the police." In reality, they may better be conceptualized as lagging indicators—communities will trust public systems such as police that have earned that trust. While the difference in framing may seem semantic in a policy journal, the difference in policy can easily be felt by residents who are told the goal of an intervention is to improve trust rather than reduce police brutality.

Another microlevel intervention is building a more representative police force—what is commonly known as descriptive representation (Pitkin, 1967). One study of seven thousand Chicago police officers found that Black and Hispanic officers make fewer stops and arrests than their White counterparts by focusing less on low-level offenses, and they also use comparatively less force. Women across racial and ethnic groups used less force than all men officers in the study. Nevertheless, police officers across groups are more likely to use force against Black residents than against any other group of residents (Ba et al., 2021). These findings lend insight into the role of racial and gender composition in reducing racial disparity in policing. However, they should be understood only as a partial achievement of contemporary and historical political demands made by communities affected by the disparate provision of public safety (Hinton, 2016). They should also be understood within the macrolevel structures at play that lead the state to lean on armed first responders as their primary mode of public safety (Goff, 2021). In other words, evidence that officer demographics matter should not preclude discussion about whether any should be sent.

Toward a Macrolevel Lens

How might quantitative social science as a field get better at seeing the forest from the trees of our research on public safety? How can we ensure that the big picture is accounted for in the questions we ask, the data we gather, and the policy recommendations we propose? Here, we reflect on three potential paths forward: (1) study the consequences of policing, (2) innovate methodologically, and (3) investigate how communities heal from the harms of policing.

Study Consequences of Contemporary Public Safety Practices

Police violence contributes to and takes place within an ecosystem of racial harm. More than one third of people in the United States killed by police have a disability (Perry & Long, 2016). This includes Eric Garner, who had asthma and a heart condition and Sandra Bland, who suffered from epilepsy and depression (Bradley & Katz, 2020). If we visit their neighborhoods, we find their stories are more common than they are unique. Freddie Gray was one of 65,000 mostly Black children living in Baltimore between 1993 and 2013 exposed to dangerously high levels of lead paint (Barry-Jester, 2015). Erica Garner died four years after her father (who was famously killed by New York City police officers) from heart failure, an illness associated with acute stress (Sewell et al., 2021). Other harms are economic. Walter Scott's decision to flee the officer who shot him in the back was no doubt informed by a fear of becoming of the approximately 50,000 noncustodial parents incarcerated for unpaid child support arrears (Hager, 2015). Public safety in Michael Brown's hometown was "shaped by the City's focus on revenue rather than by public safety needs," according to the Justice Department's Ferguson Report (2015). We know the names and faces of those subjected to the rarest and most severe manifestations of police use of force, but quantitative social science has largely overlooked the more quotidian harm public safety deprivation causes their neighbors.

Fortunately, there is a growing body of quantitative scholarship from which the field can draw inspiration for future work (see also Hunt, this volume). Some researchers are turning to the very neighborhoods designated in our data sets as "high crime" or "hot spots" and examining the association between current public safety practices and mental and physiological welfare of residents. Their findings suggest that living in neighborhoods with frequent crime, police contact, or high levels of incarceration result in physical symptoms associated with acute stress for Black women in particular (Lee et al., 2014; Sewell et al., 2021) as well as higher rates of depression and posttraumatic stress disorder (Weisburd et al., 2018) for Black men in particular (Sewell, 2017). Similarly, research on the political economy of public safety illuminates how the dramatic changes to local finance and governance over the last fifty years has been to the detriment of poor, non-White residents (Atuahene, 2020; Hinton, 2016). Among the consequences of disinvestment is the role that law enforcement plays in using fines and fees to recover revenue (Beckett & Harris, 2011; Beckett et al., 2008; Harris, 2016: Harris et al., 2010), a pattern robustly associated with a higher proportion of Black people living in a city (Sances & You, 2017).[6] And recent quantitative work has found that not only does this revenue-raising model exacerbate economic equality for non-White residents, but it also correlates with inequality in public safety, namely, a lower clearance rate of violent crimes and homicides (Goldstein et al., 2020). How criminal legal systems shape political participation and perception of citizenship is another urgent matter, made more urgent by a period of rising political polarization (Iyengar et al., 2019). Survey research from administrative records demonstrates how arrests and brief jail spells reduce the likelihood of an individual voting (Manza & Uggen, 2008; White, 2019) and promote a broader "system avoidance," in which individuals living in communities with persistent and negative contact with the criminal-legal system are more likely to withdraw from other bureaucratic institutions (Brayne, 2014) and experience "legal estrangement" from the very institutions purported to protect them (Bell, 2017).

Quantitative social scientists can continue to investigate the relationship between local revenue raising and public safety. We can consider how coercive revenue-generating models affect the financial, physical, and mental health of residents, and the effect that these practices have on the safety of all residents. To address the political consequences of policing, quantitative social science might choose to examine whether police are even the most effective street-level bureaucrat to respond to certain public safety calls. Perhaps,

---

[6] These outcomes are attenuated by Black representation on city councils (Christiani et al., 2021; Sances & You, 2017).

for example, non-White communities would experience public safety institutions as more democratic if unarmed public servants wrote traffic violations or responded to welfare visits. There are numerous municipalities rushing to provide natural experiments in the wake of the 2020 uprisings (Goff, 2021). It would be a shameful waste if quantitative social scientists did not provide assessments of those frontiers in democratic change.

Regardless of how quantitative social scientists take up these questions, there would appear to be merit in the field rediscovering the work of Du Bois and Myrdal that clearly identified policing as a key mechanism of White supremacist state power—and building on the too-long-neglected portions of that tradition. This will require that macrolevel theorizing about the structures of White supremacy is integrated with micro- and meso-level demonstrations of its mechanisms. Failure to do so segregates hypotheses about root causes from the evidence necessary to prove it.

Innovate Methodologically

A durable way that quantitative social science can incorporate macrolevel sensibilities into our work is through our methods and research designs. This may include leveraging existing relationships with bureaucratic agencies to generate new measures for public safety and gathering these data. The Center for Policing Equity (CPE) has recommended innovating COMPSTAT, the data-driven tool that police departments use to focus resources and energies toward stopping crime, to begin collecting data that help mesolevel institutions better understand the origins of racial disparities in public safety—and foreground the macrostructural consequences of police contact. This new measurement paradigm, COMPSTAT for Justice, would assist government bodies in differentiating between racial disparities caused by officer-initiated interactions versus other racially inequitable features of public safety such as forces that contribute to poverty and poor health (Goff & Buchanan, 2020).

In addition to innovating with regard to our methods of data capture, the field would do well to innovate in terms of our conceptual framework for quantitative analysis. Recent work by Knox and Mummolo (2020) outlines a framework for what can, and cannot, be used as evidence of bias in police behavior in order to resolve decades-long disagreements on the topic. A similar emphasis on updating our approaches to the historical legacy of disparate policies (at least as difficult an inferential problem) would advance the field significantly.

The field can also center the experiences that are often excluded from quantitative studies: those living in neighborhoods most adversely affected by safety deprivation. We can employ survey methods that ask residents about their most urgent public safety needs. Or, we can go a step further and ensure vulnerable communities have a seat at the table through community-based participatory action research (CBPAR): a practice more common in public health literatures on vulnerable populations (Minkler & Wallerstein, 2003).

Just as the United States must build public safety systems worthy of trust, so too must quantitative researchers build research paradigms worthy of trust. Doing so does not happen overnight or through pristine research plans. It happens instead with time, humility, and deference—to the (mostly qualitative, non-White) scholars whose work has garnered such trust and, most certainly, to the communities for whom our work has historically fallen short in serving.

Investigate How Communities Heal from the Harms of Policing

An understanding of the generations of racial harm caused by contemporary policing practices is essential for our field, as is engagement with the path toward repair. One way that our field might do so is by joining the growing cadre of scholars examining the role that community-based organizations play in creating public safety. We can systematically study the efforts by grass-roots organizers who have been personally affected by the criminal legal system to mobilize for better state responsiveness or community-driven public safety (Walker, 2020; Weaver et al., 2020). We can also use our skills in mesolevel analysis to examine how community-based organizations create and maintain safety through violence prevention, health and wellness service, and dignity-affirming jobs (Jones, 2019; Sharkey, 2018; Owens & Walker, 2018). This approach can reflect the work of Patrick Sharkey (2018) who describes how indigenous neighborhood institutions play a complementary role to state-sanctioned safety measures, or even act more effectually; or Eric Klinenberg (2018) who performed a comparable study of community resilience and its relationship to the availability of "social infrastructure" such as accessible libraries, parks, and other public space. It can speak to the ethnographic work of Nikki Jones (2018), who illustrates the path toward redemption sought by formerly incarcerated Black men and the community institutions that are responsive to and representative of those whom they serve. These mesolevel approaches consider the macroforces contributing to contemporary safety deprivation for non-White and marginalized people; one step further would be to address the legacies of state-created harms.

What does facing history look like for quantitative researchers? One framework from which to draw and study is transitional justice, a field devoted to studying and facilitating societal shifts "oppression and violence toward a more just and peaceful order" (Joshi, 2020, p. 1186). It creates systems of accountability, promotes nonrepetition of harm, builds forums for reconciliation, and creates formal opportunities for marginalized people to express and transform their political and social identities. Transitional justice has been implemented in international contexts following acts of ethnic cleansing, apartheid, and war but has yet to be formally employed in the United States. Legal scholar Yuvraj Joshi (2020) points out that the United States leveraged courts to transition from slavery and Jim Crow but "has largely eschewed transitional justice in response to racist human rights violations" (p. 1187). Community organizers and survivors have pursued these processes in instances of interpersonal violence through restorative justice practices (e.g., Balanji et al., n.d.) and have sought larger-scale reparations and transitional processes for victims of racialized state violence at the local, state, and national levels, but few have been formally implemented (e.g., Ritchie et al., 2020). Just as a macrolevel approach necessitates viewing public safety beyond policing, so too must reconciliation efforts in their path to repair by engaging state actors (and histories) outside the criminal legal system complicit in harm.

Conclusion

Activists and academics questioning the necessity of armed first responders for just, equitable, and effective public safety do so from the understanding that generations of political decisions created contemporary injustices. They join a legacy of rigorous researchers like Du Bois, Wells-Barnett, and Myrdal who called attention to policing's historic relationship to chattel slavery, patrolling borders, and White vigilante violence against non-White people (for a review, see Hinton & Cook, 2020). They draw linkages between public safety and the macrolevel forces that have produced urban inequality. Their work is vigilant to the ways public safety policies have affected the health, civic identity, and economic mobility of marginalized people (Rios, 2011; Sewell, 2016; Weaver et al., 2020). And they often provide evidence that the road to repair requires institutional accountability, collective responsibility, and centering those most harmed by centuries of state violence in all processes (Kaba, 2021). In this chapter, we reflected on how quantitative social science might leverage similar premises to answer questions in public safety most relevant to the contemporary moment.

We began by arguing that a key problem in quantitative social science is its focus on individual, neighborhood, or institution-level interactions—what we term the "micro-" and "mesolevels" of public safety. Naturally, these approaches to public safety often focus primarily on the role of police in responding to or deterring crime. We contrasted this approach with a macrolevel approach that considers the economic, political, cultural, and historical forces at play in a particular city that produce racially inequitable outcomes in public safety. The macrolevel approach invites a more capacious understanding of public safety. We also consider legal origins that promote individualized approaches to public safety and punishment that are instantiated in the Fourth Amendment and interpretations thereof.

Next, we identified competing ways that quantitative social scientists have measured race and racial bias in policing. Central to the drawbacks of contemporary methods is their inability to understand racial disparity in public safety as historically rooted or something that can be mitigated outside systems dedicated to criminal punishment. We concluded by describing a growing body of quantitative scholarship that examines the racial harms caused by contemporary public safety practices and proposed scholarly interventions that can support a path toward repair. Should the field fail to heed this moment, it risks not only policy irrelevance but a moral dereliction of responsibility to be seekers of truth and interpreters of the world. A guide who literally misses the forest for the trees is a poor guide. So too is a field of social scientists that literally misses the big picture because they have failed to engage with questions on that level.

Acknowledgments

The authors would like to thank Minali Aggarwal (Yale University) for her thoughtful feedback on this chapter.

References

Alford, R. R., & Friedland, R. (1985). *Powers of theory: Capitalism, the state, and democracy*. Cambridge University Press.

Atuahene, B. (2020). Predatory cities. *California Law Review, 108*, 107–182.

Ba, B. A., Knox, D., Mummolo, J., & Rivera, R. (2021). The role of officer race and gender in police-civilian interactions in Chicago. *Science, 371*(6530), 696–702.

Balaji, S., Bruenn, L., Cuba, J., Herzing, R., Kang, I., Kim, M., Pusey, O. (n.d.). *Creative Interventions Toolkit*. Creative Interventions.

Barry-Jester, A. M. (2015, May 7). Baltimore's Toxic Legacy of lead paint. *FiveThirtyEight*.

Beckett, K. A., & Harris, A. (2011). On cash and conviction: Monetary sanctions as misguided policy. *Criminology & Public Policy, 10*(3), 505–507.

Beckett, K. A., Harris, A. M., & Evans, H. (2008). *The assessment and consequences of legal financial obligations in Washington state*. Washington State Minority and Justice Commission Olympia.

Bell, M. C. (2017). Police reform and the dismantling of legal estrangement. *Yale Law Journal, 126*, 2054–2150.

Bell, M. C. (2020). Located Institutions: Neighborhood Frames, Residential Preferences, and the Case of Policing. *American Journal of Sociology, 125*(4), 917–973.

Bradley, D., & Katz, S. (2020, June 9). Sandra Bland, Eric Garner, Freddie Gray: The toll of police violence on disabled Americans. *The Guardian*. https://samedifference1.com/2020/06/09/sandra-bland-eric-garner-freddie-gray-the-toll

Braga, A. A, Brunson, R. K., & Drakulich, K. M. (2019). Race, place, and effective policing. *Annual Review of Sociology, 45*, 535–555.

Braga, A. A., Papachristos, A. V., & Hureau, D. M. (2014). The effects of hot spots policing on crime: An updated systematic review and meta-analysis. *Justice Quarterly, 31*(4), 633–663.

Braga, A. A., & Weisburd, D. (2010). *Policing problem places: Crime hot spots and effective prevention*. Oxford Scholarship Online.

Brayne, S. (2014). Surveillance and system avoidance: Criminal justice contact and institutional attachment. *American Sociological Review, 79*(3), 367–391.

Carbado, D. W. (2017). From stopping Black people to killing Black people: The Fourth Amendment pathways to police violence. *California Law Review, 105*, 125–166.

Christiani, L., Shoub, K., Baumgartner, F. R., Epp, D. A., & Roach, K. (2021). Better for everyone: Black descriptive representation and police traffic stops. *Politics, Groups, and Identities*. Advance Online Publication. https://doi.org/10.1080/21565503.2021.1892782

Del Toro, J., Lloyd, T., Buchanan, K. S., Robins, S. J., Bencharit, L. Z., Smiedt, M. G., Reddy, K. S., Pouget, E. R., Kerrison, E. M., & Goff, P. A. (2019). The criminogenic and psychological effects of police stops on adolescent black and Latino boys. *Proceedings of the National Academy of Sciences, 116*(17), 8261–8268.

Du Bois, W. E. B. (1899). *The Philadelphia Negro*. Cosimo.

Eberhardt, J. L., Goff, P. A., Purdie, V. J., & Davies, P. G. (2004). Seeing black: Race, crime, and visual processing. *Journal of Personality and Social Psychology, 87*(6), 876.

Eck, J., & Weisburd, D. L. (2015). Crime places in crime theory. Crime and place: *Crime Prevention Studies, 4*.

Fields, K. E., & Fields, B. J. (2014). *Racecraft: The soul of inequality in American life*. Verso Trade.

Friedmann, R. R. (1992). *Community policing: Comparative perspectives and prospects*. St. Martin's Press.

Gelman, A., Kiss, A., & Fagan, J. (2006). An analysis of the NYPD's stop-and-frisk policy in the context of claims of racial bias. *Columbia Public Law Research Paper No. 05–95*. https://scholarship.law.columbia.edu/faculty_scholarship/1390

Glaser, J., Martin, K. D., & Kahn, K. B. (2015). Possibility of death sentence has divergent effect on verdicts for Black and White defendants. *Law and human behavior, 39*(6), 539.

Goff, P. A. (2016). Identity traps: How to think about race & policing. *Behavioral Science & Policy, 2*(2), 10–22.

Goff, P. A. (2021). Asking the right questions about race and policing. *Science, 371*(6530), 677–678.

Goff, P. A., & Buchanan, K. S. (2020). A data-driven remedy for racial disparities: Compstat for justice. *NYU Annual Survey of American Law, 76*(2), 375–396.

Goff, P. A., Eberhardt, J. L., Williams, M. J., & Jackson, M. C. (2008). Not yet human: Implicit knowledge, historical dehumanization, and contemporary consequences. *Journal of Personality and Social Psychology, 94*(2), 292–306.

Goff, P. A., & Godsil, R. (2016). The moral ecology of policing. In J. Jacobs & J. Jackson (Eds.), *The Routledge handbook of criminal justice ethics* (pp. 348–369). Taylor & Francis.

Goldstein, R., Sances, M. W., & You, H. Y. (2020). Exploitative revenues, law enforcement, and the quality of government service. *Urban Affairs Review, 56*(1), 5–31.

Greene, J. R., & Mastrofski, S. D. (Eds.). (1988). *Community policing: Rhetoric or reality.* Praeger.

Greenwald, A. G., McGhee, D. E., & Schwartz, J. L. (1998). Measuring individual differences in implicit cognition: The implicit association test. *Journal of Personality and Social Psychology, 74*(6), 1464.

Greiner, D. J., & Rubin, D. B. (2011). Causal effects of perceived immutable characteristics. *Review of Economics and Statistics, 93*(3), 775–785.

Groff, E. R., Weisburd, D., & Yang, S.-M. (2010). Is it important to examine crime trends at a local "micro" level?: A longitudinal analysis of street to street variability in crime trajectories. *Journal of Quantitative Criminology, 26*(1), 7–32.

Grunwald, B., & Fagan, J. (2019). The end of intuition-based high-crime areas. *California Law Review, 107,* 345–405.

Hager, E. (2015, April 10). Why was Walter Scott running? *The Marshall Project.* https://www.themarshallproject.org/2015/04/10/

Harris, A. (2016). *A pound of flesh: Monetary sanctions as punishment for the poor.* Russell Sage Foundation.

Harris, A., Evans, H., & Beckett, K. (2010). Drawing blood from stones: Legal debt and social inequality in the contemporary United States. *American Journal of Sociology, 115*(6), 1753–1799.

Hernán, M. A. (2016). Does water kill? A call for less casual causal inferences. *Annals of Epidemiology, 26*(10), 674–680.

Hinton, E. (2016). *From the war on poverty to the war on crime: The making of mass incarceration in America.* Harvard University Press.

Hinton, E., & Cook, D. (2021). The mass criminalization of Black Americans: A historical overview. *Annual Review of Criminology, 4*(1), 261–286.

Holder, J., Calaff, I., Maricque, B., & Tran, V. C. (2022). Concentrated incarceration and the public-housing-to-prison pipeline in New York City neighborhoods. *Proceedings of the National Academy of Sciences, 119*(36), e2123201119.

Holland, P. W. (1986). Statistics and causal inference. *Journal of the American Statistical Association, 81*(396), 945–960.

Iyengar, S., Lelkes, Y., Levendusky, M., Malhotra, N., & Westwood, S. J. (2019). The origins and consequences of affective polarization in the United States. *Annual Review of Political Science, 22,* 129–146.

Jones, M. H. (Ed.). (1975). *The Journal on Political Repression* (Vol. 1).

Jones, N. (2014). "The regular routine": Proactive policing and adolescent development among young, poor black men. *New Directions for Child and Adolescent Development, 2014*(143), 33–54.

Jones, N. (2018). *The chosen ones: Black men and the politics of redemption* (Vol. 6). University of California Press.

Joshi, Y. (2020). Racial transition. *Washington University Law Review, 98,* 1181.

Justice, B., & Meares, T. L. (2014). How the criminal justice system educates citizens. *The Annals of the American Academy of Political and Social Science, 651*(1), 159–177.

Kaba, M. (2021). *We do this' til we free us: Abolitionist organizing and transforming justice.* Haymarket Books.

Kirk, D. S., & Sampson, R. J. (2013). Juvenile arrest and collateral educational damage in the transition to adulthood. *Sociology of Education, 86*(1), 36–62.

Knowles, J., Persico, N., & Todd, P. (2001). Racial bias in motor vehicle searches: Theory and evidence. *Journal of Political Economy, 109*(1), 203–229.

Klinenberg, E. (2018). *Palaces for the people: How social infrastructure can help fight inequality, polarization, and the decline of civic life.* Crown.

Knox, D., & Mummolo, J. (2020). Toward a general causal framework for the study of racial bias in policing. *Journal of Political Institutions and Political Economy, 1*(3), 341–378.

Lee, H., Wildeman, C., Wang, E. A., Matusko, N., & Jackson, J. S. (2014). A heavy burden: The cardiovascular health consequences of having a family member incarcerated. *American Journal of Public Health, 104*(3), 421–427.

Lerman, A. E., & Weaver, V. M. (2014). *Arresting citizenship.* University of Chicago Press.

Lum, C. M., Koper, C. S., Gill, C., Hibdon, J., Telep, C., & Robinson, L. (2016). *An evidence-assessment of the recommendations of the President's Task Force on 21st Century Policing: Implementation and research priorities.* International Association of Chiefs of Police.

McCarthy, M., Trinkner, R., & Goff, P. (2021). The threat of appearing racist: Stereotype threat and support for coercion among Australian police officers. *Criminal Justice and Behavior, 48*(1), Article 0093854821993513.

Macías-Rojas, P. (2016). *From deportation to prison.* New York University Press.

Manza, J., & Uggen, C. (2008). *Locked out: Felon disenfranchisement and American democracy.* Oxford University Press.

Meares, T. L. (1997). Place and crime. *Chicago-Kent Law Review, 73,* 669–710.

Minkler, M., & Wallerstein, N. (2003). Part one: introduction to community-based participatory research. In M. Minkler & N. Wallerstein (Eds.), *Community-based participatory research for health* (pp. 5–24). Jossey-Bass.

Morris, M. (2016). *Pushout: The criminalization of Black girls in schools.* New Press.

Muhammad, K. G. (2019). *The condemnation of Blackness: Race, crime, and the making of modern urban America, with a new preface.* Harvard University Press.

Myrdal, G. (1944). *An American dilemma; the Negro problem and modern democracy* (2 vols.). Routledge.

National Academies of Sciences, Engineering, and Medicine. (2018). *Proactive policing: Effects on crime and communities.* National Academies Press.

O'Flaherty, B., & Sethi, R. (2019). *Shadows of doubt: Stereotypes, crime, and the pursuit of justice.* Harvard University Press.

Omi, M., & Winant, H. (2014). *Racial formation in the United States.* Routledge.

Owens, M. L., & Walker, H. L. (2018). The civic voluntarism of "custodial citizens": involuntary criminal justice contact, associational life, and political participation. *Perspectives on Politics, 16*(4), 990–1013.

Pearl, J., & Mackenzie, D. (2018). *The book of why: The new science of cause and effect.* Basic books.

Penner, A. M., & Saperstein, A. (2008). How social status shapes race. *Proceedings of the National Academy of Sciences, 105*(50), 19628–19630.

Perry, D. M., & Carter-Long, L. (2016). *The Ruderman white paper on media coverage of law enforcement use of force and disability.* Ruderman Foundation. https://rudermanfoundation.org/wp-content/uploads/2017/08/MediaStudy-PoliceDisability_final-final.pdf

Pitkin, H. (1967). *The concept of representation.* University of California.

Prowse, G., Weaver, V. M., & Meares, T. L. (2020). The state from below: Distorted responsiveness in policed communities. *Urban Affairs Review, 56*(5), 1423–1471.

Peyton, K., Sierra-Arévalo, M., & Rand, D. G. (2019). A field experiment on community policing and police legitimacy. *Proceedings of the National Academy of Sciences, 116*(40), 19894–19898.

Quattlebaum, M. (2018). Let's get real: Behavioral realism, implicit bias, and the reasonable police officer. *Stanford Journal of Civil Rights & Civil Liberties, 14,* 1–49.

Rios, V. M. (2011). *Punished: Policing the lives of Black and Latino boys.* New York University Press.

Ritchie, A., Smith, D., Johnson, J., Ifetayo, J., Stahly-Butts, M., Kaba, M., Simmons, M., Taifa, N., Herzing, R., Wallace, R., & Obuya, T. (2020). Reparations Now Toolkit. Movement for Black Lives.

Rothstein, R. (2017). *The color of law: A forgotten history of how our government segregated America.* Liveright.

Sampson, R. J., Wilson, W. J., & Katz, H. (2018). Reassessing "Toward A Theory of Race, Crime, and Urban Inequality": Enduring and new challenges in 21st century America. *Du Bois Review: Social Science Research on Race, 15*(1), 13–34.

Sances, M. W., & You, H. Y. (2017). Who pays for government? Descriptive representation and exploitative revenue sources. *The Journal of Politics, 79*(3), 1090–1094.

Sen, M., & Wasow, O. (2016). Race as a "bundle of sticks": Designs that estimate effects of seemingly immutable characteristics. *Annual Review of Political Science, 19,* 499–522.

Sewell, A. A. (2016). The racism-race reification process: A mesolevel political economic framework for understanding racial health disparities. *Sociology of Race and Ethnicity, 2*(4), 402–432.

Sewell, A. A. (2017). The illness associations of police violence: Differential relationships by ethnoracial composition. *Sociological Forum, 32,* 975–997.

Sewell, A. A., Feldman, J. M., Ray, R., Gilbert, K. L., Jefferson, K. A., & Lee, H. (2021). Illness spillovers of lethal police violence: The significance of gendered marginalization. *Ethnic and Racial Studies, 44*(7), 1089–1114.

Sewell, A. A., & Jefferson, K. A. (2016). Collateral damage: The health effects of invasive police encounters in New York City. *Journal of Urban Health, 93*(1), 42–67.

Sewell, A. A., Jefferson, K. A., & Lee, H. (2016). Living under surveillance: Gender, psychological distress, and stop-question-and-frisk policing in New York City. *Social Science & Medicine, 159*, 1–13.

Schrader, S. (2019). *Badges without Borders*. University of California Press.

Sharkey, P. (2018). *Uneasy peace: The great crime decline, the renewal of city life, and the next war on violence.* W. W. Norton.

Shedd, C. (2015). *Unequal city: Race, schools, and perceptions of injustice.* Russell Sage Foundation.

Sim, J. J., Correll, J., & Sadler, M. S. (2013). Understanding police and expert performance: When training attenuates (vs. exacerbates) stereotypic bias in the decision to shoot. *Personality and Social Psychology Bulletin, 39*(3), 291–304.

Simon, J. (2007). *Governing through crime: How the war on crime transformed American democracy and created a culture of fear.* Oxford University Press.

Skogan, W. G. (2006). Advocate: The promise of community policing. In D. Weisburd (Ed.), *Police innovation: Contrasting perspectives* (pp. 27–43). Cambridge University Press.

Skogan, W. G., Van Craen, M., & Hennessy, C. (2015). Training police for procedural justice. *Journal of Experimental Criminology, 11*(3), 319–334.

Soss, J., & Weaver, V. (2017). Police are our government: Politics, political science, and the policing of race–class subjugated communities. *Annual Review of Political Science, 20*, 565–591.

Sunshine, J., & Tyler, T. R. (2003). The role of procedural justice and legitimacy in shaping public support for policing. *Law & Society Review, 37*(3), 513–548.

Swencionis, J. K., & Goff, P. A. (2017). The psychological science of racial bias and policing. *Psychology, Public Policy, and Law, 23*(4), 398.

Swencionis, J. K., Pouget, E. R., & Goff, P. A. (2021). Hierarchy maintenance policing: Social dominance and police use of force. Proceedings of the National Academy of Sciences, *118*(18).

Institute for Justice. *The size and scope of Philadelphia's civil forfeiture machine.* (n.d.). https://ij.org/philadelphia-facts-and-figures/

Trice, L. (1975). The black community and law enforcement in St. Louis. Journal on Political Repression, *1*(1), 79–96.

Tyler, T. R. (2003). Procedural justice, legitimacy, and the effective rule of law. *Crime and Justice, 30*, 283–357.

Tyler, T. R., Fagan, J., & Geller, A. (2014). Street stops and police legitimacy: Teachable moments in young urban men's legal socialization. *Journal of Empirical Legal Studies, 11*(4), 751–785.

Walker, H. L. (2020). Targeted: The mobilizing effect of perceptions of unfair policing practices. *The Journal of Politics, 82*(1), 119–134.

Weaver, V., Prowse, G., & Piston, S. (2020). Withdrawing and drawing in: Political discourse in policed communities. Journal of Race, *Ethnicity, and Politics, 5*(3), 604–647.

Weisburd, D., Cave, B., Nelson, M., White, C., Haviland, A., Ready, J., Lawton, B., & Sikkema, K. (2018). Mean streets and mental health: Depression and post-traumatic stress disorder at crime hot spots. *American Journal of Community Psychology, 61*(3–4), 285–295.

White, A. (2019). Misdemeanor disenfranchisement? The demobilizing effects of brief jail spells on potential voters. *American Political Science Review, 113*(2), 311–324.

Wood, G., Tyler, T. R., & Papachristos, A. V. (2020). Procedural justice training reduces police use of force and complaints against officers. *Proceedings of the National Academy of Sciences, 117*(18), 9815–9821.

Evidence Gathering and Pursuit in Criminal Cases

Procedural Justice Theory: Challenges and New Extensions

Ben Bradford, Arabella Kyprianides, *and* Julia A. Yesberg

Abstract

Understanding why and on what basis people cooperate with police and comply with the law is vital for the formulation of legal policy and, indeed, the functioning of the justice system. Procedural justice theory (PJT) has emerged as arguably the dominant account in this area. Stressing the centrality of fairness judgments in police-public relations, PJT provides a detailed account of the ways trust and legitimacy are formed, are reproduced, and feed into cooperation and compliance. In this chapter, we outline the existing evidence base for PJT, consider recent critiques of the theory, and explore some new developments and avenues for future research and practice. We conclude that although PJT has contributed enormously to our understanding of police-public relations, to demonstrate its applicability where it really counts for policing, those working within the paradigm need to develop a more expansive theoretical and methodological framework.

Key Words: procedural justice theory, fairness, police-public relations, legal policy, trust, legitimacy

What do people want from police and justice institutions? What motivates their trust or distrust? Why do they cooperate with legal authorities? What drives widespread compliance with rules and regulations? Such questions are of central concern to practitioners, policy-makers, and indeed all those engaged with issues of crime, law, and policing. Without public support, cooperation, and engagement, and without widespread voluntary compliance, the criminal justice systems of democratic states would quickly cease to function, and indeed cease to be "democratic" in any meaningful sense of that word. Procedural justice theory (PJT) provides a compelling set of answers to these questions that revolve around the importance of fair process, group values, and social norms in generating public trust, legitimacy, cooperation, and compliance in policing and legal contexts; and it provides a model for the establishment of consensual rather than coercive relationships between criminal justice actors and the publics they serve (Sunshine & Tyler, 2003; Tyler & Fagan, 2008; Tyler & Jackson, 2014).

The account offered by PJT comprises, in essence, four stages (see Tyler, 2006; Tyler & Huo, 2002, for "classic" statements of the theory). First, in interactions with legal authorities such as police officers, the *style* of social interaction and the *neutrality* of decision-making are central to peoples' experiences and judgments. Second, social bonds between individual and authority are strengthened by fair and neutral decision-making, and by treatment that is fair, respectful, legal, and not based on bias and stereotypes. Third, these social bonds encourage trust and legitimacy (that the institution has the right to power and the authority to govern, the right to dictate appropriate behavior, and is morally justified in expecting cooperation and compliance). Fourth, trust and legitimacy promote normative modes of compliance and cooperation that are both more stable and more sustainable than compliance and cooperation based on deterrence, sanction, and fear of punishment.

The idea of procedural justice (in the sense used in PJT) is now nearly fifty years old (Thibaut & Walker, 1975). However, it has recently moved to the center of policy debates and formation, particularly in the realm of policing (Her Majesty's Inspectorate of Constabulary and Fire and Rescue, 2018; President's Task Force on 21st Century Policing, 2015). In some senses the question of legitimacy lies at the heart of all police activity. But relatively widespread uptake, or at least engagement with, ideas central to PJT is both a relatively new phenomenon and something that *may* comprise an important shift in police policy and practice.

Concentrating on policing as our primary example, we set out in this chapter to do three things: outline the existing evidence base for PJT, consider some of the challenges posed to the theory, and describe some new developments and avenues for future research and practice. Broadly speaking, we conclude that PJT has contributed enormously to our understanding of police-public relations, and it provides a compelling set of answers to the questions posed above. Yet, to move forward, and to demonstrate its applicability where it really counts for policing—in relation to the groups and communities with whom police have most contact—those working within the paradigm need to develop a more expansive theoretical and methodological framework.

Procedural Justice Theory—Research Review

PJT is premised on the social psychology of group relations and an understanding of how people view, comprehend, and react to the actions of power holders within social groups. As such, it has wide relevance and has been used to explore relationships between employer and employee (Blader & Tyler, 2009; Skarlicki & Folger, 1997), teacher and pupil (Chory-Assad, 2002; Lenzi et al., 2014), and parent and child (Thomas et al., 2020; Trinkner et al., 2012). In recent years, it has also become an increasingly popular theoretical approach through which to view police-community relations. In short, PJT posits that: (1) in their interactions with police, people want to feel they have been treated fairly, been given a voice, been treated with dignity and respect, and feel they have been dealt with in an impartial manner during personal encounters; (2) that such "procedural justice" is strongly linked to trust and legitimacy; and (3) that trust and legitimacy are linked to cooperation between police and public, compliance with the law, and other "prosocial" behaviors (e.g., Tyler, 2006; Tyler et al., 2015; Tyler & Huo, 2002). The theory is explicitly bidirectional: more procedural justice is linked to more trust and legitimacy, and less procedural justice is linked to less trust and legitimacy.

PJT is premised on the idea that people attend closely to the fairness of the processes through which those with power—bosses, teachers, police officers—interact with them. There are a number of reasons why this should be the case. The experience of procedural justice indicates that the interaction or procedure was conducted appropriately, in line with widespread norms concerning how authorities should treat subordinates (Tyler & Trinkner, 2017), and that the individual was treated as being *worthy* of respect and dignity (Tyler et al., 1996). Process fairness can also serve to reassure that unobservable characteristics of the interaction were appropriate; for example, that decisions were made without bias (Tyler & Wakslak, 2004), or that the individual had a meaningful influence on the interaction and its outcome (Thibaut & Walker, 1975). Individually and collectively, these types of experiences generate satisfaction with decision makers, acceptance of their decisions, trust, and legitimacy.

It is also important to note that a perception that the police *generally* behave procedurally fairly is also linked to trust and legitimacy (Bradford et al., 2018). On many accounts, evaluations that police operate fairly are a close antecedent of trust, if not part of the concept itself (Hardin, 2006; but see PytlikZillig & Kimborough, 2015). While PJT is at its core a model of interaction, studies have regularly identified robust correlations between overall assessments of police procedural justice, trust, and legitimacy (e.g., Hough et al., 2013; Jackson, 2018; Peacock, 2021). It is a further important claim of the theory that assessments and evaluations of procedural justice are more important predictors of trust and legitimacy than instrumental concerns with effectiveness or the distribution of outcomes (Jackson, 2018).

With its central focus on the generation of consensual rather than coercive relationships, PJT resonates strongly with the ideology of policing by consent: that the trust of the public, and the legitimacy granted *to* the police *by* the policed, are fundamental to the proper and effective functioning of the police in a democratic society. PJT also foregrounds the idea that most people obey the criminal law most of the time because they think it is the "right thing" to do, and not simply because it is in their own best interests. Crucially, such judgments are grounded in the institutional frameworks people encounter and operate within as they move through their lives (Justice & Meares, 2014; Tyler & Trinkner, 2017). "Normative" compliance is premised, in part, on trust and the legitimacy of legal institutions; in turn, trust and legitimacy are shaped by encounters with individual legal actors.

Research across a wide range of contexts seems to confirm that perceptions of procedural justice are strongly linked to perceptions of police legitimacy, and that perceptions of police legitimacy drive important behaviors, such as deference to authority, compliance with the law, and cooperation in achieving community goals (Bolger & Walters, 2019; Higginson & Mazerolle 2014; Walters & Bolger, 2019). While the stronger claims of the theory—particularly relating to compliance behavior—are not uncontested (see "Limitations and Critiques"), the evidence from PJT research suggests we should focus on process fairness in encounters between police and public partly because of the benefits it generates for the police and wider society. Cooperation and normative compliance based on social bonds between individual and institution are the foundation of social order in a general sense, and in specific instances where, for example, police and communities need to work together to solve problems.

The benefits to the individual are important, too. The experience of fair process at the hands of authority figures such as police officers motivates a sense of identification with and inclusion in the group(s) those authorities symbolically and materially represent (Tyler & Blader, 2003). The police, for example, are frequently cited as "prototypical" (Sunshine & Tyler, 2003) representatives of the nation-state and its communities (e.g., Loader & Mulcahy, 2003; Reiner, 2010), making encounters with police officers "identity relevant" to many. Studies have shown that thinking police are procedurally just in a general sense, and experiencing specific encounters with officers as fair, is linked to stronger identification with superordinate social categories—such as "Britishness" or "Australianness"— and a stronger sense of belonging or inclusion (Bradford 2014; Bradford et al., 2014). Conversely, procedural *in*justice can exclude, marginalize, and/or alienate (Blackwood et al., 2015). The implication here is that procedurally just policing can promote a sense of secure belonging among the policed, or at least reinforce membership founded in a wider set of processes (e.g., childhood socialization and economic inclusion).

Finally, procedural justice is important in and of itself. Behavior in line with principles of fairness is, according to almost all accounts, simply the best and most appropriate way for police officers to behave. The idea of procedural justice integrates closely with—although by no means exhausts—categories such as democratic policing (e.g., Jones et al., 1996) and rights-based policing (e.g., Miller & Redhead, 2019), at the same time corresponding closely to lay perspectives on the right way for police to behave (Stoutland, 2001).

Limitations and Critiques of PJT

The core tenets of PJT have become widely accepted among academics and policymakers (e.g., Her Majesty's Inspectorate of Constabulary and Fire and Rescue, 2018; President's Task Force on 21st Century Policing, 2015). However, there is a growing recognition of the need to acknowledge and address the limitations of PJT and to develop some of the more nuanced aspects of the theory (Martin & Bradford, 2020; Tyler, 2017). In this section, we outline some broad areas of current debate.

First, some scholars have argued that the available evidence may not warrant the widespread adoption of PJT as a *crime-reduction* policy. In two recent reviews of the literature,

Nagin and Telep (2017, 2020) argue that research has not plausibly demonstrated a causal connection between procedurally just treatment, perceptions of legitimacy, and compliance with the law. In particular, they note a dearth of randomized control trials testing PJT in policing, and argue that perception-based research tells us little about whether experiences of "objectively" procedurally just treatment by police leads to changes in perceived legitimacy and compliance *behaviors*. Others, however, have pointed out that experimental research in other contexts (e.g., workplace organizations and courts) has found strong support for the procedural justice model (Tyler, 2017), and that there is some direct evidence from policing contexts (see below).

Two important aspects of this debate are, on the one hand, the extent to which change in the *objective* fairness of police activity causes change in *perceptions* of procedural justice (Nagin & Telep, 2020; Waddington et al., 2015; Worden & Maclean, 2017). PJT is primarily concerned with how people experience their relations with power holders, and as such is less concerned with the "reality" of the interactions concerned. But from a policy perspective, it is clearly important to understand whether making officer activity more procedurally fair will lead to enhanced perceptions of procedural justice. Although it is clear there is a robust, and in all likelihood causal, link between *subjective experiences* of police activity (at earlier time points) and *perceptions* of procedural justice (at later time points; e.g., Augustyn, 2015; Oliveira et al., 2021), studies that have systematically altered police activity and then picked up a resulting change in perceptions are rare (Worden & McLean, 2017); however, as noted, they do exist (e.g., Demir et al., 2020; MacQueen & Bradford, 2015; Mazerolle et al., 2013).

On the other hand, the extent to which change in perceptions of procedural justice leads to change in legitimacy judgments has also been called into question (Pina-Sánchez & Brunton-Smith, 2020). There are good reasons to suggest that perceptions of procedural justice and legitimacy are mutually constitutive, such that the legitimacy ascribed to police will affect how officer behavior is experienced. Both also seem likely to be anchored in a set of psychological, sociological, and political needs, attitudes, and orientations that comprise a wide range of potential "third common causes" that might explain the association between procedural justice perceptions and legitimacy (Nagin & Telep, 2020). Yet, despite this, there is a significant weight of evidence linking prior experiences of procedural justice with subsequent legitimacy judgments, including from longitudinal (Bradford et al., 2014; Oliveira et al., 2021; Tyler & Fagan, 2008) and experimental (Posch et al., 2021) studies.

Another reason why the nature of the relationship between procedural justice and legitimacy remains a thorny question is debate around the concept of legitimacy itself (see Cao & Graham, 2019; Jackson & Bradford, 2019; Sun et al., 2018; Tankebe, 2013; Trinkner, 2019), and huge variation across studies in how it is measured. PJT as posited by Tyler and colleagues argues that perceptions of procedurally fair treatment are foundational to perceptions of police legitimacy but are distinct from them. This is necessarily the case if the claim is that procedural justice is a *cause* of legitimacy. However, others have questioned the extent to which procedural justice, trust, and legitimacy are separate constructs (Jonathan-Zamir et al., 2015; Tankebe, 2013). Tankebe (2013) and Bottoms and Tankebe (2012), for example, argued that procedural justice is a component of legitimacy rather than one of its sources.

Key to this discussion is the role of obedience in the concept of legitimacy. There is widespread agreement that what legitimacy "does" for power holders is secure the right to issue commands and expect obedience. It follows that an authority can be seen as legitimate when those subordinate to it feel they have a duty to obey its instructions (Kelman & Hamilton, 1989). Bottoms, Tankebe, and others argue on broadly methodological grounds, however, that obedience cannot be part of the concept of legitimacy itself, because it may stem from sources other than legitimacy, most obviously prudence (people who do not obey police instructions know they can, and may well actually be, physically forced to comply). For this reason, obedience may flow from legitimacy but is not part of it. Recent studies have responded to this debate by recalibrating the concept of duty to obey, underlining that it is something experienced as a moral imperative by those who grant police legitimacy (Jackson, 2018; Posch et al., 2021). Doing so focuses on the part of obedience that is constitutive of the empirical legitimacy of an institution such as police, and distinguishes it from prudential and other factors.

The nature and role of social identity and intergroup relations as mediators (and/or moderators) of fairness and legitimacy, cooperation, and compliance are also contested. Despite core aspects of PJT relying on social identity as the underlying psychological mechanism (Tyler & Huo, 2002), and despite group membership clearly being central to the dynamics of police-community relations in a wide range of contexts, there has been a relative dearth of police-specific research that has properly taken into account this aspect of PJT (Radburn & Stott, 2018). Extant studies have tended to conclude that although identity may be important as a mediator (Bradford, 2014) or moderator (Murphy et al., 2015; Radburn et al., 2016; Sergeant et al., 2013) of the association between procedural justice and legitimacy, more work in this area is needed. In particular, the way in and extent to which social identity mediates the effect of procedural justice is likely to be complex and highly context dependent. Is it identification with police as a social category in their own right, with the superordinate categories they may or may not represent, or some combination of the two, that is important (Radburn et al., 2016)? Are any mediating effects invariant across groups (Wolfe et al., 2016), or do other and possibly competing categorizations have an effect (Madon et al., 2017)? These and related questions largely await definitive answers.

Finally, PJT research tends to focus on general population samples, and only infrequently on subpopulations such as minority group members, the socially excluded, or offenders. Of the eighty-eight samples in Walters and Bolger's (2019) recent meta-analysis of procedural justice, legitimacy, and cooperation, only twelve covered populations considered at least potentially marginal or socially excluded. Most of the latter were ethnic minority, immigrant, or "youth" populations (e.g., Huq et al., 2011; Murphy et al.,

2015), and only a few were offenders (e.g., White et al., 2016) or victims (Kochel et al., 2013). We therefore know little about whether (and how) PJT replicates to those parts of the population who have most at stake in their interactions with officers, have sometimes long histories of problematic relations with police, and who are increasingly the focus of strategic police priorities (e.g., safeguarding, counterradicalization, antisocial behavior, and protest groups; see also Hunt; Prowse & Goff, this volume).

Experiences of police activity might be differentially meaningful for people in the social "mainstream," with a relatively strong sense of identification with dominant social categories associated with the police, compared with others whose individual and group status is more marginal. This is a significant concern given the reliance on group membership and identification as a causal psychological mechanism within PJT. It has also been argued that there has been a lack of adequate attention given to social and cultural context in the PJT literature (Nagin & Telep, 2017; Tankebe, 2009), and on the potential importance of individual and collective histories with and in relation to police (Kyprianides et al., in press).

Implications, Next Steps, and Future Directions:

In this section, we consider potential developments in PJT research that may expand the theories purchase and help address some of the issues outlined above.

PJT and Marginalized Groups

It is on this last set of critiques that we focus the remainder of this chapter, not least because exploring it in more detail further illuminates many of the other points raised earlier. In short, we suggest that aspects of PJT may limit its policy relevance to the policing of those marginalized groups with whom police have most contact. The relationship between the police and marginalized or disenfranchised communities is more complex than has thus far been accounted for, particularly when it comes to issues of social identity and police-initiated encounters involving officers engaging in a regulatory role (as opposed to public-initiated encounters, like reporting a crime; see Guyll et al., this volume; Hunt et al., this volume).

In addition to the fact that most of the research that provides the empirical underpinning of PJT relies on general population samples, comprised primarily of individuals and groups more or less safely "on the inside" of society, in most extant studies, police and public are conceptualized as belonging to the same social group, such that encounters are conceived as *intra*group. In many cases, of course, police interact with people who *do* see police as an ingroup, not least because in many interactions (e.g., with victims of crime), the outgroup is clearly defined (e.g., offenders). However, marginalized or minority groups may not have a strong sense of identification with social categories associated with the police, not least because of a history of unjust treatment by police and other state agents (Nagin & Telep, 2017). It might be more meaningful, therefore, to describe interactions between police and such groups as *inter*group as opposed to *intra*group (Radburn et al., 2016). The extent to which police behavior is identity relevant for those who may only feel a weak bond with the social group the police represent has been underexplored, although there is of course a rich social psychological literature on the underlying issues involved (Radburn & Stott, 2018; Turner et al., 1987).

Relatedly, few PJT studies have paid sufficient attention to the fact that contact between police and public is an *embedded process*, not simply a one-off interaction (the most important exception here is research that has considered the long-term relationship between police and black communities in the United States; e.g., Blount-Hill, 2020; Brunson, 2007; Gau & Brunson, 2010). To adequately comprehend this process we need to understand all its features: the geographic, social, and political context in which it occurs and the history of the people involved, as well as how they judge the encounter itself. Salient here is the paucity of ethnographic and in-depth observational studies focused on procedural justice (for exceptions, see Gau & Brunson, 2010; Ilan, 2016; Kyprianides et al., in press). Quantitative longitudinal studies have demonstrated that, for example, perceptions of police contact are shaped but not determined by prior attitudes, and in turn shape but do not determine subsequent attitudes (e.g., Tyler & Fagan, 2008), but these have been limited in the extent to which they can consider the longer histories and specific contexts involved. There is a danger of simply assuming that procedural justice can be "applied" by police to promote perceptions of fairness across individuals and contexts (Jonathan-Zamir et al., 2015; Savigar-Shaw et al., 2021).

Extending PJT Research

In addition to the long-standing interest in US criminology in the implications of race for PJT (for recent examples, see Atkin-Plunk et al., 2019; Johnson et al., 2017; Wheelock et al., 2019), recent research has begun to populate some of the gaps identified above. Murphy and colleagues (Murphy et al., 2017, 2020; Murphy et al., 2015) have explored how PJT can be applied to Muslim minority communities in Australia. Their research is set within the context of new counterterrorism laws leading to feelings of stigmatization, an "us" versus "them" mentality and a perception among Muslims that they are being unfairly targeted by the new laws (Cherney & Murphy, 2016). Kyprianides, Bradford, Jackson, and Stott (2022) explored the identity dynamics of PJT among a sample of people living on the streets of London and examined how processes of identification and legitimation might shape homeless people's willingness to cooperate with police. Other research has considered the relevance of police procedural justice and legitimacy to people marginalized by crime victimization (Elliot et al., 2014; Murphy & Barkworth, 2014) or their status as offenders (Papachristos et al., 2012; Pina-Sánchez & Brunton-Smith, 2020).

Taken together, findings from this research generally shows support for the relevance of PJT among such marginalized communities. For example, Murphy et al. (2017) found procedural justice had a strong relationship with Muslims' cooperation, but only for those who questioned the legitimacy of police. For those who viewed the police as legitimate, procedural justice had no impact (in other words, the way in which procedural justice promotes cooperation may vary depending on arguably "deeper" legitimacy beliefs). In another study, Murphy et al. (2020) found that procedural justice moderated the relationship between feelings of stigmatization and crime-reporting intentions. Individuals who felt highly stigmatized placed more salience on procedural justice when deciding whether or not to report information to police. Similarly, Murphy et al. (2019) found that procedural justice was a more important predictor of reporting intentions for Muslims who felt socially excluded. Kyprianides, Bradford, Jackson, and Stott (2022) found that police behavior was also identity relevant to the street population participating in their research, and that even people experiencing the extreme precariousness of homelessness were attuned to the messages of inclusion/exclusion encoded in police activity.

However, there appear to be different mediating and moderating variables throughout the process envisaged by PJT, which suggests that its application to marginalized groups may not be straightforward. Murphy et al. (2015) found that for Muslims with a separatist identity (i.e., who believed it was important to retain a separate culture from the dominant Australian culture), police performance was a more important factor than procedural justice, potentially highlighting the importance of instrumentality for those who feel most disengaged from, or even antagonistic toward, mainstream society. Studies conducted in some developing countries have likewise identified a greater interest in the effectiveness of police in contexts where they have been historically and currently viewed as ineffective and corrupt (e.g., Bradford et al., 2014; Tankebe, 2009).

The importance of instrumentality was also highlighted by Kyprianides, Bradford, Jackson, Yesberg, et al. (2022), who contrasted relational and instrumental perspectives on compliance among people experiencing homelessness. They found little association between legitimacy judgments and self-reported compliance. Instead, instrumental concerns (deterrence) seemed more important; although a key message from this research was that since they needed to offend in order to survive, neither deterrence *nor* legitimacy perceptions had much relationship with behavior. By contrast, Papachristos et al. (2012), working with a sample of active offenders in Chicago, found that those who granted police *more* legitimacy offended *less* than those who granted less legitimacy (specifically, they were less likely to carry a gun).

Next Steps and Future Directions—"Doing" Procedural Justice

In addition to deepening its focus on those individuals and groups that have most contact with police, another very obvious next step for PJT research is to move into the much more applied arena of designing and implementing interventions aimed at improving the way police officers treat members of the public. Indeed, this concern would, at the present time, seem pressing. Although in most developed democracies, and indeed many other societies around the world, large numbers of people do experience policing as procedurally just, this is of course not always the case. In a disturbingly large number of cases, officer behavior has been marked by egregious *unfairness* (see inter alia Schwartz & Jahn, 2020), poisoning the relationship between police and the communities they are meant to serve. Yet despite this, training-based efforts to enhance procedural justice in practice have been limited; and there are a number of reasons why police might be reluctant to adopt (more) procedurally just policing in practice.

These include, first, concerns about the difficulty inherent in generating incremental change within police organizations (Skogan, 2008). It has yet to be definitively established that changes in policy, training, and elsewhere can be effective in shifting the way officers treat the public and translate into improved legitimacy and compliance with the law (Nagin & Telep, 2020). Procedural justice is not straightforward to "implement," and the effectiveness of interventions will depend on how they are viewed/used by individual officers. For example, a randomized field trial—the Scottish Community Engagement Trial (ScotCET)—involved an experimental condition where police officers used a series of key messages that incorporated procedural justice into road traffic stops (MacQueen & Bradford, 2015). Results offered no support for the efficacy of the procedural justice script. If anything, the intervention had backfire effects on citizen perceptions of police legitimacy. Based on interviews with officers who were tasked to deliver the script to the drivers, MacQueen and Bradford (2017) identified a series of issues, including poor communication from management about the project and lack of officer buy-in, which threatened consistent implementation. Officers resisted using the messages because of concerns they made them look inept to the public. Additionally, many felt as though the project was sprung on them from management and was not grounded in their experience.

Relatedly, police may be reluctant to adopt procedurally just policing approaches with those marginalized members of the population they believe might not be "worth it." A recent study by Savigar-Shaw et al. (2021) explored the capacity of PJT to explain the dynamic interactions between police and citizens in the context of police detention. From the perspective of officers, procedural justice can be conceptualized as a "reward" offered to those who are already acquiescent: observation and interviews in police custody suites suggested procedural justice was often a "gift to the compliant." Noncompliant individuals could expect harsher treatment. Such variation may also be visible outside the police station: Radburn et al. (2022) report that officers sometimes are unable or unwilling to engage in "procedurally fair" interpersonal encounters when, for example, working in economically deprived areas. They would instead carry with them expectations of a risk of immediate collective hostility and threat, which they felt needed a different kind of approach (see also Alceste & Kassin, this volume).

The second cause of doubt about the implementation of PJT-oriented reform may be concerns that heavily policed populations are not "receptive" to procedurally just policing.

Research has suggested that the association between procedural justice and legitimacy, for example, is relatively consistent across key demographic categories such as age, gender, and ethnicity (Wolfe et al., 2016), as well as across different group affiliations (Huo et al., 1996). More broadly, the sheer consistency of "procedural justice effects" across multiple, indeed global, contexts suggests that it is only at the extremes that procedural justice reforms might not "work." But the issue is that police often find themselves working at the extremes. Moreover, perceptions of procedurally just treatment are reflective of an accumulation of a lifetime of cultural, community, and familial influences, not just one or more interactions with the police. Particularly in the most disadvantaged communities, separating out the impact of procedurally just treatment on legitimacy perceptions and legal compliance from other influences, such as extreme poverty, racial isolation, and various forms of social dysfunction, is a daunting challenge (Nagin & Telep, 2017; Weitzer & Tuch, 2005). Indeed, a wide range of factors are likely to come together to shape legitimacy judgments, only a few of which are susceptible to police-led intervention. In addition to those listed above, these range from people's migration histories (Bradford & Jackson, 2018), deep-seated worldviews (Mehozay & Factor, 2017), and group identities (Gerber et al., 2018). This work suggests that policy interventions based on procedural justice must overcome a lot of "background noise" to have an effect.

All that said, emerging research based on robust experimental and other evidence is offering support to the idea that PJT reforms can shift public attitudes and opinions. Mazerolle et al. (2013) found that providing a script to officers, based on procedural justice concepts, was sufficient to alter perceptions of procedural justice in the highly formalized context of roadside breath-testing in Australia. Langley et al. (2020) used a checklist approach to improving the procedural justice of officers conducting counterterrorism interventions at airports, and found a significant effect on the perceptions of those targeted across dimensions of procedural justice, distributive justice, and self-reported intentions to obey the law. Finally, Owens et al. (2018) found that officers involved in a training program based on principles of procedural justice were less likely to resolve incidents with an arrest and less likely to use force during a six-week to six-month follow up period.

Conclusion

PJT has gained significant traction in police research, policy, and practice in recent years. Despite concerns about the viability of core causal pathways envisaged by the theory, systematic reviews of the evidence base tend to conclude that at least at the level of individual perception, procedural justice really does cause legitimacy. There is also growing evidence that procedural justice and legitimacy together motivate cooperation and compliance. Moreover, studies that deliberately target excluded and marginalized groups draw broadly similar conclusions. Quite aside from the ethical imperative that police should treat people with dignity and respect, it therefore seems that PJT is a viable "policy option" to those interested in maximizing consensual policing and normative compliance with the law.

There are two deeper issues here, though, on which we will close and to which more attention needs to be paid in the future. First, as Worden and Maclean (2017, p. 33) argued, "street-level procedural justice probably cannot be achieved through the formulation and promulgation of administrative rules." It is the culture of police organizations, rather than their formal structures and training regimes, which will do most to promote and/or inhibit procedurally just practice. Moreover, negative attitudes toward the police among some communities in the United States, United Kingdom, and elsewhere have been caused, in part, by long histories of unfair policing founded in precisely those same police cultures. To undo this will take time, and it is possible that what is at stake is *generational* change, as improvements in police behavior take years to filter through into the "consciousness" of particular groups. The returns achieved by checklist and even training approaches may not be enough to address such issues.

Second, police reform is plainly not a magic wand that will on its own solve deeper structural issues of racism, inequality, deprivation, exclusion, and so forth. Even a perfectly fair police department would, when operating within a society shaped by structural racism, likely serve to reproduce the hierarchies that racism defines—and so, inevitably, face challenges to its legitimacy among those it polices.

However, to say that something is hard to do, and that it does not provide an all-encompassing answer to the problems it confronts, is not to say it should not be attempted. Many of the studies noted here suggest that incremental change is possible. Indeed, just as negative relations with police in some communities are likely to be the result of an accretion of poor experiences over time, a slow accretion of positive experiences may, even if individually minor, accumulate to something more significant over a longer time period. Such a shift, if based not only on principles of procedural justice but also an appropriate ethics of policing, may even be an effective part of wider efforts to confront historical and ongoing wrongs. A key challenge for police and others will therefore be embedding reforms in such a way as to open up the possibility of long term change.

References

Atkin-Plunk, C. A., Peck, J. H., & Armstrong, G. S. (2019). Do race and ethnicity matter? An examination of racial/ethnic differences in perceptions of procedural justice and recidivism among problem-solving court clients. *Race and Justice*, *9*(2), 151–179.

Augustyn, M. B. (2015). The (ir)relevance of procedural justice in the pathways to crime. *Law and Human Behavior*, *39*(4), 388–401.

Blackwood, L., Hopkins, N., & Reicher, S. D. (2015). Flying while Muslim: Citizenship and misrecognition at the Airport. *Journal of Social and Political Psychology*, *3*(2), 148–170.

Blader, S. L., & Tyler, T. R. (2009). Testing and extending the group engagement model: Linkages between social identity, procedural justice, economic outcomes, and extra role behavior. *Journal of applied psychology*, *94*(2), 445.

Blount-Hill, K. L. (2020). Exploring a social identity theory of shared narrative: Insights from resident stories of police contact in Newark, New Jersey, and Cleveland, Ohio. *Criminal Justice and Behavior*, *48*(6), 810–827.

Bolger, P. C., & Walters, G. D. (2019). The relationship between police procedural justice, police legitimacy, and people's willingness to cooperate with law enforcement: A meta-analysis. *Journal of Criminal Justice*, *60*, 93–99.

Bottoms, A., & Tankebe, J. (2012). Beyond procedural justice: A dialogic approach to legitimacy in criminal justice. *The Journal of Criminal Law and Criminology*, *102*(1), 119–170.

Bradford, B. (2014). Policing and social identity: Procedural justice, inclusion, and cooperation between police and public. *Policing and Society*, *22*(1), 22–43.

Bradford, B, & Jackson J. (2018). Police legitimacy among immigrants in Europe: Institutional frames and group position. *European Journal of Criminology*, *15*, 567–588.

Bradford, B., Jackson, J., & Hough, M. (2018). Trust in justice. In E. Uslaner (Ed.), *The Oxford handbook of social and political trust* (pp. 633–646). Oxford University Press.

Bradford, B., Murphy, K., & Jackson, J. (2014). Officers as mirrors: Policing, procedural justice and the (re) production of social identity. *British Journal of Criminology*, *54*(4), 527–550.

Brunson, R. K. (2007). "Police don't like black people": African American young men's accumulated police experiences. *Criminology & Public Policy*, *6*(1), 71–101.

Cao, L., & Graham, A. (2019). The measurement of legitimacy: a rush to judgment? *Asian Journal of Criminology*, *14*, 291–299.

Cherney, A., & Murphy, K. (2016). Being a "suspect community" in a post 9/11 world: The impact of the War on Terror on Muslim communities in Australia. *Australian & New Zealand Journal of Criminology*, *49*, 480–496.

Chory-Assad, R.M. (2002). Classroom justice: Perceptions of fairness as a predictor or student motivation, learning, and aggression. *Communication Quarterly*, *50*(1), 58–77.

Demir, M., Braga, A. A., & Apel, R. (2020). Effects of police body-worn cameras on citizen compliance and cooperation: Findings from a quasi-randomized controlled trial. *Criminal Public Policy*, *19*, 855–882.

Elliott, I., Thomas, S., & Ogloff, J. (2014). Procedural justice in victim-police interactions and victims' recovery from victimisation experiences. *Policing and Society*, *24*(5), 588–601.

Gau, J. M., & Brunson, R. K. (2010). Procedural justice and order maintenance policing: A study of inner-city young men's perceptions of police legitimacy. *Justice Quarterly*, *27*(2), 255–279.

Gerber, M. M., González, R., Carvacho, H., Jiménez-Moya, G., Moya, C., & Jackson, J. (2018). On the justification of intergroup violence: The roles of procedural justice, police legitimacy, and group identity in attitudes toward violence among indigenous people. *Psychology of Violence*, *8*(3), 379.

Hardin, R. (2006), *Trust and trustworthiness*. Russell Sage Foundation.

Her Majesty's Inspectorate of Constabulary and Fire and Rescue. (2018) *State of policing. The annual assessment of policing in England and Wales 2017*. HMICFRS.

Higginson, A., & Mazerolle, L. (2014). Legitimacy policing of places: The impact on crime and disorder. *Journal of Experimental Criminology*, *10*(4), 429–457.

Hough, M., Jackson, J., & Bradford, B. (2013). The drivers of police legitimacy: Some European research. *Journal of Policing, Intelligence and Counter Terrorism*, *8*(2), 144–165.

Huo, Y. J., Smith, H. J., Tyler, T. R., & Lind, E. A. (1996). Superordinate identification, subgroup identification, and justice concerns: Is separatism the problem; is assimilation the answer?. *Psychological Science*, *7*(1), 40–45.

Huq, A. Z., Tyler, T. R., & Schulhofer, S. (2011). Mechanisms for eliciting cooperation in counterterrorism policing: Evidence from the United Kingdom. *Journal of Empirical Legal Studies*, *8*, 728–761.

Ilan, J. (2016). Scumbags! An ethnography of the interactions between street-based youth and police officers. *Policing and Society*, *28*(6), 684–696.

Jackson, J. (2018). Norms, normativity, and the legitimacy of justice institutions: International perspectives. *Annual Review of Law and Social Science*, *14*, 145–165.

Jackson, J., & Bradford, B. (2019). Blurring the distinction between empirical and normative legitimacy? A methodological commentary on 'Police legitimacy and citizen cooperation in China'. *Asian Journal of Criminology*, *14*, 265–289.

Johnson, D., Wilson, D. B., Maguire, E. R., & Lowrey-Kinberg, B. V. (2017). Race and perceptions of police: Experimental results on the impact of procedural (in) justice. *Justice Quarterly*, *34*(7), 1184–1212.

Jonathan-Zamir, T., Mastrofski, S. D., & Moyal, S. (2015). Measuring procedural justice in police-citizen encounters. *Justice Quarterly*, *32*, 845–871.

Jones, T., Newburn, T., & Smith, D. J. (1996). Policing and the Idea of Democracy. *The British journal of criminology*, *36*(2), 182–198.

Justice, B., & Meares, T. L. (2014). How the criminal justice system educates citizens. *Annals of the American Academy of Political and Social Science*, *651*(1), 159–177.

Kelman, H. C., & Hamilton, V. L. (1989). *Crimes of obedience: Toward a social psychology of authority and responsibility*. Yale University Press.

Kochel, T., Parks, R., & Mastrofski, S. (2013). Examining police effectiveness as a precursor to legitimacy and cooperation with police. *Justice Quarterly*, *30*, 895–925.

Kyprianides, A., Bradford, B., Jackson, J., & Stott, C. (2022a). *Police generation of compliance among the homeless street population: Testing a boundary condition of procedural justice theory* [Manuscript submitted for publication].

Kyprianides A., Bradford, B., Jackson, J., Yesberg, J. A., Stott, C., & Radburn, M. (2020b). *On the identity dynamics of police legitimacy and public cooperation among a general population and a London street population* [Manuscript submitted for publication].

Kyprianides, A., Stott, C., & Bradford, B. (in press). "Playing the game": Power, authority and procedural justice in interactions between police and homeless people in London. *British Journal of Criminology*.

Langley, B., Ariel, B., Tankebe, J., Sutherland, A., Beale, M., Factor, R., & Weinborn, C. (2020). A simple checklist, that is all it takes: A cluster randomized controlled field trial on improving the treatment of suspected terrorists by the police. *Journal of Experimental Criminology*, *17*(4), 629–655.

Lenzi, M., Vieno, A., Gini, G., Pozzoli, T., Pastore, M., Santinello, M., & Elgar, F. J. (2014). Perceived teacher unfairness, instrumental goals, and bullying behavior in early adolescence. *Journal of interpersonal violence*, *29*(10), 1834–1849.

Loader, I., & Mulcahy, A. (2003). *Policing and the condition of England: Memory, politics and culture*. Oxford University Press.

MacQueen, S., & Bradford, B. (2015). Enhancing public trust and police legitimacy during road traffic encounters: Results from a randomised controlled trial in Scotland. *Journal of Experimental Criminology*, *11*(3), 419–443.

MacQueen, S., & Bradford, B. (2017). Where did it all go wrong? Implementation failure—and more—In a field experiment of procedural justice policing. *Journal of Experimental Criminology*, *13*(3), 321–345.

Madon, N. S., Murphy, K., & Sargeant, E. (2017). Promoting police legitimacy among disengaged minority groups: Does procedural justice matter more? *Criminology & Criminal Justice*, *17*(5), 624–642.

Martin, R., & Bradford, B. (2020). The anatomy of police legitimacy: Dialogue, power and procedural justice. *Theoretical Criminology*, *25*(4), 559–577.

Mazerolle, L., Antrobus, E., Bennett, S., & Tyler, T. R. (2013). Shaping citizen perceptions of police legitimacy: A randomized field trial of procedural justice. *Criminology*, *51*(1), 33–63.

Mehozay, Y., & Factor, R. (2017). Deeply embedded core normative values and legitimacy of law enforcement authorities. *Journal of Research in Crime and Delinquency*, *54*(2), 151–180.

Miller, H. & Redhead, R. (2019). Beyond "rights-based approaches"? Employing a process and outcomes framework. *The International Journal of Human Rights*, *23*, 699–718.

Murphy, K., & Barkworth, J. (2014). Victim willingness to report crime to police: Does procedural justice or outcome matter most? *Victims & Offenders*, *9*(2), 178–204.

Murphy, K., Cherney, A., & Teston, M. (2019). Promoting Muslims' willingness to report terror threats to police: Testing competing theories of procedural justice. *Justice Quarterly*, *36*(4), 594–619.

Murphy, K., Madon, N. S., & Cherney, A. (2017). Promoting Muslims' cooperation with police in counterterrorism: The interaction between procedural justice, police legitimacy and law legitimacy. *Policing: An International Journal*, *40*(3), 554–559.

Murphy, K., Madon, N. S., & Cherney, A. (2020). Reporting threats of terrorism: stigmatisation, procedural justice and policing Muslims in Australia. *Policing and Society*, *30*(4), 361–377.

Murphy, K., Sargeant, E., & Cherney, A. (2015). The importance of procedural justice and police performance in shaping intentions to cooperate with the police: Does social identity matter? *European Journal of Criminology*, *12*(6), 719–738.

Nagin, D.S., & Telep, C.W. (2017). Procedural justice and legal compliance. *Annual Review of Law and Social Science*, *13*, 5–28.

Nagin, D. S., & Telep, C. W. (2020). Procedural justice and legal compliance: A revisionist perspective. *Criminology & Public Policy*, *19*(3), 761–786.

Oliveira, T. R., Jackson, J., Murphy, K., & Bradford, B. (2021). Are trustworthiness and legitimacy "hard to win, easy to lose"? A longitudinal test of the asymmetry thesis of police-citizen contact. *Journal of Quantitative Criminology*, *37*, 1003–1045.

Owens, E., Weisburd, D., Amendola, K. L., & Alpert, G. P. (2018). Can you build a better cop? Experimental evidence on supervision, training, and policing in the community. *Criminology & Public Policy*, *17*(1), 41–87.

Papachristos, A. V., Meares, T. L., & Fagan, J. (2012). Why do criminals obey the law? The influence of legitimacy and social networks on active gun offenders. *The Journal of Criminal Law and Criminology*, *102*(2), 397–440.

Peacock, R. (2021). Dominance analysis of police legitimacy's regressors: Disentangling the effects of procedural justice, effectiveness, and corruption. *Police Practice and Research*, *22*(1), 589–605.

Pina-Sánchez, J., & Brunton-Smith, I. (2020). Reassessing the relationship between procedural justice and police legitimacy. *Law and Human Behavior*, *44*(5), 377–393.

Posch, K., Jackson, J., Bradford, B., & Macqueen, S. (2021). "Truly free consent"? Clarifying the nature of police legitimacy using causal mediation analysis. *Journal of Experimental Criminology*, *7*(4), 563–595.

President's Task Force on 21st Century Policing. (2015). *Final report of the President's Task Force on 21st Century Policing*. Off. Community Oriented Police Serv., US Department of Justice.

PytlikZillig, L. M., & Kimbrough, C. D. (2015). Consensus on conceptualizations and definitions of trust: Are we there yet? In E. Shockley, T. M. S. Neal, L. PytlikZillig, & B. Bornstein (Eds.), *Interdisciplinary perspectives on trust: Towards theoretical and methodological integration* (pp. 17–47). Springer.

Radburn, M., Savigar-Shaw, L., Stott, C., Tallent, D., & Kyprianides, A. (2022). How do police officers talk about their encounters with "the public"? Group interaction, procedural justice, and officer constructions of policing identities. *Criminology & Criminal Justice*, *22*(1), 59–77.

Radburn, M., & Stott, C. (2018). The social psychological processes of 'procedural justice': Concepts, critiques and opportunities. *Criminology & Criminal Justice*, *19*, 421–438.

Radburn, M., Stott, C., Robinson, M., & Bradford, B. (2016). When is policing fair? Groups, identity and judgements of the procedural justice of coercive crowd policing. *Policing and Society*, *28*, 647–664.

Reiner, R. (2010). *The politics of policing* (4th ed.). Prentice Hall/Harvester Wheatsheaf.

Savigar-Shaw, L., Stott, C., Radburn, M., Kyprianides, A., & Muscat, M. (2021). Procedural justice as a gift to the compliant: An ethnography of police-citizen interaction in police custody. *Policing and Society: A Journal of Policy and Practice*. Advance online publication.

Schwartz, G. L., & Jahn, J. L. (2020). Mapping fatal police violence across US metropolitan areas: Overall rates and racial/ethnic inequities, 2013–2017. *PloS One*, *15*(6), e0229686.

Sergeant, E., Murphy, K., & Cherney, A. (2013). Ethnicity, trust and cooperation with police: Testing the dominance of the process-based model. *European Journal of Criminology*, *11*(4), 500–524.

Skarlicki, D. P., & Folger, R. (1997). Retaliation in the workplace: The roles of distributive, procedural, and interactional justice. *Journal of Applied Psychology*, *82*(3), 434.

Skogan, W. G. (2008). Why reforms fail. *Policing and Society*, *18*(1), 23–34.

Stoutland, S. (2001). The multiple dimensions of trust in resident/police relations in Boston. *Journal of Research in Crime and Delinquency*, *38*, 226–256.

Sun, I. Y., Li, L., Wu, Y., & Hu, R. (2018). Police legitimacy and citizen cooperation in China: Testing an alternative model. *Asian Journal of Criminology*, *13*, 275–291.

Sunshine, J., & Tyler, T. R. (2003). The role of procedural justice and legitimacy in shaping public support for policing. *Law & Society Review*, *37*(3), 513–548.

Tankebe, J. (2009). Public cooperation with the police in Ghana: Does procedural fairness matter? *Criminology*, *47*(4), 1265–1293.

Tankebe J. (2013). Viewing things differently: the dimensions of public perceptions of police legitimacy. *Criminology*, *51*, 103–36.

Thibaut, J., & Walker, L. (1975). *Procedural justice: A psychological analysis*. Erlbaum

Thomas, K. J., Rodrigues, H., de Oliveira, R. T., & Mangino, A. A. (2020). What predicts pre-adolescent compliance with family rules? A longitudinal analysis of parental discipline, procedural justice, and legitimacy evaluations. *Journal of Youth and Adolescence*, *49*(4), 936–950.

Trinkner, R. (2019). Clarifying the contours of the police legitimacy measurement debate: A response to Cao and Graham. *Asian Journal of Criminology*, *14*, 309–335.

Trinkner, R., Cohn, E. S., Rebellon, C. J., & Van Gundy, K. (2012). Don't trust anyone over 30: Parental legitimacy as a mediator between parenting style and changes in delinquent behavior over time. *Journal of Adolescence*, *35*(1), 119–132.

Turner, J. C., Hogg, M. A., Oakes, P. J., Reicher, S., & Wetherell, M. (1987). *Rediscovering the social group: A self-categorisation theory*. Blackwell.

Tyler, T. R. (2006). *Why people obey the law*. Princeton University Press.

Tyler, T. R. (2017). Procedural justice and policing: A rush to judgement? *Annual Review of Law and Social Science, 13*, 29–53.

Tyler, T. R., & Blader, S. L. (2003). The group engagement model: Procedural justice, social identity, and cooperative behavior. *Personality and Social Psychology Review, 7*(4), 349–361.

Tyler, T. R., Degoey, P., & Smith, H. (1996). Understanding why the justice of group procedures matters: A test of the psychological dynamics of the group-value model. *Journal of Personality and Social Psychology, 70*, 913–930.

Tyler, T. R., & Fagan, J. (2008). Legitimacy and cooperation: Why do people help the police fight crime in their communities? *Ohio State Journal of Criminal Law, 6*, 231–275.

Tyler, T. R., Goff, P. A., & MacCoun, J. (2015). The impact of psychological science in policing in the United States: Procedural justice, legitimacy, and effective law enforcement. *Psychological Science in the Public Interest, 16*(3), 75–109.

Tyler, T. R., & Jackson, J. (2014). Popular legitimacy and the exercise of legal authority: Motivating compliance, cooperation and engagement. *Psychology, Public Policy and Law, 20*(1), 78–95.

Tyler, T. R., & Huo, Y. (2002). *Trust in the law: Encouraging public cooperation with the police and courts*. Russell Sage Foundation.

Tyler, T. R., & Trinkner, R. (2017). *Why children follow rules: Legal socialization and the development of legitimacy*. Oxford University Press.

Tyler, T. R., & Wakslak, C. J. (2004). Profiling and police legitimacy: Procedural justice, attributions of motive, and acceptance of police authority. *Criminology, 42*(2), 253–282.

Waddington, P. A. J., Williams, K., Wright, M., & Newburn, T. (2015). Dissension in public evaluations of the police. *Policing and Society, 25*, 212–235.

Walters, G. D., & Bolger, P. C. (2019). Procedural justice perceptions, legitimacy beliefs, and compliance with the law: A meta-analysis. *Journal of Experimental Criminology, 15*, 341–372.

Weitzer R., & Tuch SA (2005). Determinants of public satisfaction with the police. *Police Quarterly, 8*, 279–297.

Wheelock, D., Stroshine, M. S., & O'Hear, M. (2019). Disentangling the relationship between race and attitudes toward the police: Police contact, perceptions of safety, and procedural justice. *Crime & Delinquency, 65*(7), 941–968.

White, M. D., Mulvey, P., & Dario, L. M. (2016). Arrestees' perceptions of the police: Exploring procedural justice, legitimacy, and willingness to cooperate with police across offender types. *Criminal Justice and Behavior, 43*, 343–364.

Wolfe, S. E., Nix, J., Kaminski, R., & Rojek, J. (2016). Is the effect of procedural justice on police legitimacy invariant? Testing the generality of procedural justice and competing antecedents of legitimacy. *Journal of Quantitative Criminology, 32*(2), 253–282.

Worden, R. E., & McLean, S. J. (2017). Research on police legitimacy: The state of the art. *Policing: An International Journal, 40*(3), 480–513.

The Present and Future of Verbal Lie Detection

Aldert Vrij, Pär Anders Granhag, Sharon Leal, Ronald P. Fisher, Steven M. Kleinman, and Tzachi Ashkenazi

Abstract

The last thirty years has seen a transformation in deception research from passively observing subjects' nonverbal behavior to actively interviewing subjects to elicit verbal cues to deceit. Although significant progress has been made, there is still much work to do in the rapidly developing field of verbal lie detection. In this contribution, we briefly discuss the current status of the field. We outline the four interview protocols most frequently discussed in the scientific literature to date—Assessment Criteria Indicative of Deception (ACID), Cognitive Credibility Assessment (CCA), Strategic Use of Evidence (SUE), and Verifiability Approach (VA)—followed by the empirical support for these protocols. We then present ideas on how to move the field of verbal lie detection forward.

Key Words: deception detection, verbal lie detection, forensic interviewing, assessment criteria indicative of deception, cognitive credibility assessment, strategic use of evidence, verifiability approach

Solving crimes, preventing terrorist attacks, screening passengers at borders, assessing asylum claims, and vetting individuals for jobs all have in common that they involve interviewing subjects. The aim of such interviews is twofold: to obtain as much accurate information as possible and to determine whether the subject is telling the truth or lying. This chapter focuses on the lie detection part. In interviews, deception typically can be detected by analyzing speech and observing behavior. This chapter is limited to verbal lie detection. Nonverbal lie detection is relevant in situations where subjects cannot be interviewed and speech is thus unavailable, such as mass screening at airports (Vrij & Fisher, 2020; Vrij et al., 2019). However, for at least two reasons, we do not recommend observing nonverbal behavior in interview settings when speech is available. First, verbal cues to deceit are more diagnostic than nonverbal cues (Bond & DePaulo, 2006; DePaulo et al., 2003). Second, interviewers already experience cognitive load due to focusing on what the suspect says and, at the same time, thinking about the next question. If the mentally taxing task of observing nonverbal behavior is added to this, the cognitive challenge may become too much for interviewers (Patterson, 2006), and poor listening and questioning practices could be the result (Vrij & Fisher, 2020).

Until the late 1980s, lie detection through observing behavior was dominant in research and probably also in practice (Vrij, 2019). The introduction in the late 1980s of criteria-based content analysis (CBCA) started to change the focus in research from observing nonverbal behavior to analyzing speech (Köhnken & Steller, 1988). CBCA is a list of nineteen verbal criteria thought to occur more frequently in truthful than in deceptive statements. The most recent meta-analysis of CBCA, summarizing thirty-nine studies, found support for seventeen of the nineteen verbal criteria (Amado et al., 2016).

To obtain statements suitable for CBCA analyses, a standard interview protocol is used to elicit a free recall ("Please tell me all you remember"). We labeled this "passive interviewing" (Vrij & Granhag, 2012). Research in the last fifteen years has shown that verbal cues to deceit could become more transparent when specific interview protocols are used exploiting differences between truth tellers and lie tellers in their cognitive processing and the strategies (e.g., interviewing to detect deception; Vrij & Granhag, 2012). To date, four such interview protocols have been developed. The first section briefly introduces them. The second section discusses how research can move the field forward.

The Present State of Verbal Lie Detection: Interviewing to Detect Deception

This section introduces the four "interviewing to detect deception" protocols discussed most frequently in the scientific literature. Many empirical and overview articles as well as meta-analyses have been published about these interview protocols. Therefore, this section presents outlines of the protocols, similar to Vrij and Fisher (2016) and Vrij (2018). It also presents a summary of the empirical support for these interview protocols and discusses the similarities and differences between them. For more information about the interview protocols, see Colwell et al. (2013; for assessment criteria indicative of deception); Vrij et al. (2017; for cognitive credibility assessment); Hartwig et al. (2014; for the strategic use of evidence); and Palena et al. (2021; for the verifiability approach).

Assessment Criteria Indicative of Deception

The ACID (Assessment Criteria Indicative of Deception) interview procedure starts with an initial free recall in which an interviewee is invited to describe, in as much detail as possible, everything that happened during a specific period of time. This was the dominant question in deception research before the introduction of the interview protocols, labeled "passive interview style" in the previous section. In ACID, the initial free recall is followed by mnemonics, which are interview techniques that facilitate enhanced memory recall (Colwell et al., 2013). These mnemonics are derived from the Cognitive Interview (Fisher & Geiselman, 1992), an interview protocol designed to elicit more information from cooperative witnesses. Examples are recalling the event from the perspective of another person present during the event (e.g., "What could that person see?"), and reverse order recall, that is, reporting the event from the end to the beginning (e.g., "Report what you did last night beginning by describing what you did last, followed by what you did just before that?"). Truth tellers benefit from these mnemonics more than lie tellers and will, for example, provide more additional detail (Colwell et al., 2013). In addition, and unlike in the Cognitive Interview, in ACID a series of multiple-choice questions are asked in between the different mnemonics. These should be questions that lie tellers have not anticipated and are therefore not part of their rehearsed answers ("Did you notice anything unusual about the room"?). Again, truth tellers provide more details when answering these questions than lie tellers (Colwell et al., 2013).

The verbal cues frequently examined in ACID are perceptual details (what the person saw, heard, smelled, etc.), coherence (the extent to which different parts of a statement fit together in a reasonable way), and type-token ratio (TTR; ratio of unique words to the number of words in a statement) (Colwell et al., 2013).

Cognitive Credibility Assessment

Cognitive credibility assessment (CCA) comprises three elements: (1) Imposing cognitive load; (2) Asking unexpected questions, and (3) Encouraging interviewees to say more.

IMPOSING COGNITIVE LOAD

In interview settings lying is typically more mentally taxing than truth telling (see fMRI research, Christ et al. 2009). Investigators can exploit these different mental states by making the interview setting cognitively more difficult, for example, by asking interviewees to engage in a concurrent, second, task when discussing the event (e.g., remembering a six-digit number). Lie tellers, whose mental resources are more depleted, are less able than truth tellers to cope with additional requests (Debey et al., 2012), which impairs their story telling (Vrij et al., 2008).

ASKING UNEXPECTED QUESTIONS

Liars typically prepare themselves for possible interviews by preparing answers to questions they expect to be asked (Hartwig et al., 2007). Investigators can exploit this strategy by asking a mixture of anticipated and unanticipated questions. The difference in answers between the unanticipated and the anticipated questions is greater for truth tellers than for lie tellers (Lancaster et al., 2012).

ENCOURAGING INTERVIEWEES TO SAY MORE

In interviews, subjects do not provide all the information they know spontaneously (Fisher, 2010). One reason for this is that they do not know how much information is expected from them. An effective way to raise such expectations (Ewens et al., 2016) is to expose them to a detailed Model Statement, which is an example of a detailed account/story unrelated to the topic of the interview (Leal et al., 2015). A Model Statement results in more information from both truth tellers and lie tellers, but differences emerge in the quality of the information. Compared to lie tellers, after a Model Statement, truth tellers included more complications in their stories and these stories sounded more plausible (Vrij et al., 2018).

The verbal cues that are most frequently examined in CCA are "details," "plausibility" (likelihood that the activities happened in the way described), "consistency" (overlap between different parts of a statement), and, more recently, "complications" (an occurrence that affects the storyteller and makes a situation more complex ["Initially we did not see our friend, as he was waiting at a different entrance"; Vrij, Leal, Fisher, et al., 2020]).

STRATEGIC USE OF EVIDENCE

During interviews, truth tellers are generally forthcoming, whereas lie tellers are inclined to be avoidant (e.g., in a free recall, avoiding mentioning where they were at a specific time), or use denials (e.g., denying having been at a certain place at a specific time when asked directly; Granhag & Hartwig, 2008). When investigators ask questions related to the evidence without making the subject aware that they possess this evidence, these different strategies used by truth tellers and lie tellers result in truth tellers' accounts being more consistent with the evidence than lie tellers' accounts (statement–evidence consistency, Hartwig et al., 2014). In addition, when in interviews lie tellers start to realize that the interviewer may hold incriminating evidence against them, they are inclined to change their statement and try to provide an innocent explanation for this evidence. As a result, truth tellers show more overlap between different parts of a statement than lie tellers (within-statements inconsistencies; Hartwig et al., 2014).

One tactic integral to the SUE (strategic use of evidence) technique is the Evidence Framing Matrix (EFM), which helps to disclose individual pieces of evidence as tactical as possible. The EFM combines two dimensions: the *source* (from weak to strong) and the *specificity* of the evidence (from low to high or vague to precise). If a subject claims to not have purchased any traveling equipment, but there is CCTV footage showing how they pay for a suitcase, the EFM prescribes the following: "We have information (weak source) about you visiting a travel equipment store (low specificity)." Noting the subject's response, the interviewer then continues: "We have CCTV footage (strong source) of you visiting a travel equipment store (low specificity)." Finally, "We have CCTV footage (strong source) of you paying for a suitcase at Luggage Pro (high specificity)." If a subject stays with his initial aversive answer, he will display evidence-statement inconsistency. If he adjusts their statement as the evidence is presented, they will display within-statement inconsistency (Granhag et al., 2013).

VERIFIABILITY APPROACH

The idea behind the verifiability approach (VA) is that lie tellers have a dilemma to solve. On the one hand, they are motivated to provide many details, because detailed accounts are more likely to be believed (Bell & Loftus, 1989). On the other hand, they prefer to avoid mentioning too many details out of fear that investigators will check such details, which could subsequently give the lie away (Nahari et al., 2012). A strategy that incorporates both goals is to avoid mentioning details that can be verified. Details that can be verified are activities (1) carried out with, or (2) witnessed by named persons, (3) recorded on CCTV or photos, and (4) leave digital traces (e.g., phone calls) or physical traces (receipts). Lie tellers typically report fewer details that can be checked than truth tellers (Palena et al., 2021). This effect becomes stronger when an Information Protocol is used: Interviewees are asked, where possible, to include details in their statement that the investigator can check. Truth tellers, more than lie tellers, add checkable details in their accounts following such a request (Palena et al., 2021). The verbal cues most frequently examined in VA are verifiable details, unverifiable details, and ratio of verifiable details (verifiable details: verifiable + unverifiable details).

Empirical Support for the Four Interview Protocols

Of the four interview protocols, ACID is the least examined, and, unlike for the other three protocols, a meta-analysis is not available. The results should thus be interpreted with some caution, but the available ACID studies to date showed that approximately 75 percent of truth tellers and lie tellers were correctly classified with the tool (Vrij, 2018). In addition, compared to lie tellers, in ACID interviews truth tellers reported more perceptual details, told more coherent stories, and obtained a lower TTR (Colwell et al., 2013). Regarding TTR, honest statements tend to be longer and not-so-carefully phrased, whereas deceptive statements tend to be shorter and more carefully phrased (Colwell et al., 2013).

The three meta-analyses for the other three protocols examined slightly different issues. Accuracy rates in correctly classifying truth tellers and lie tellers were only reported for CCA. A meta-analysis of fourteen studies examining accuracy rates (based on human observers and computer software combined) revealed a superior accuracy rate in the CCA approach (71 percent) compared to the standard approach (56 percent) (Vrij et al., 2017). The 15 percent increment represented a medium-sized improvement (d = 0.42). A qualitative review of thirty-eight studies examining "verbal cues" (e.g., lack of detail, plausibility, and consistency) revealed that the CCA approach was more effective in eliciting verbal veracity cues than a standard approach (Vrij et al., 2016).

For SUE, a meta-analysis of eight studies showed a very large difference between truth tellers and lie tellers in statement—evidence consistency (d = 1.06), the only cue examined in that meta-analysis (Hartwig et al., 2014).

For VA, a meta-analysis of twenty studies showed that truth tellers reported more verifiable details than lie tellers (g = 0.42). The effect was moderated by the presence of the Information Protocol. The veracity effect was large when the Information Protocol was present (g = 0.80) but small when the Information Protocol was absent (g = 0.29). Truth tellers also reported a higher ratio of verifiable details than truth tellers (g = 0.49). Unverifiable details did not discriminate truth tellers from lie tellers (Palena et al., 2021).

A Comparison Between the Four Protocols

A common characteristic of the four protocols is their underlying basic structure. All protocols commence with an initial free recall (FR) followed by either posing an additional—different instruction regarding how to produce a second FR or asking specific follow-up questions regarding that FR. Examples of the additional-different instruction are in ACID a different perspective instruction; in CCA, a Model Statement or reverse-order production; and in VA the Information Protocol. Examples for the specific follow-up questions are in ACID and CCA asking unexpected questions and in SUE a follow-up request to clarify facts presented in the initial FR against newly presented evidence.

Another similarity between the four protocols is their theoretical and practical reliance on the differences between the information management strategies used by truth tellers and lie tellers (Hartwig et al., 2010); and specifically for lie tellers regarding the amount and type of information they provide (a dilemma which is not shared by truth tellers). This dilemma serves as a theoretical basis of the expected differences between truth tellers and lie tellers in ACID (using memory-enhancing techniques) and in CCA (especially with the subprotocols in the "Encouraging interviewees to say more" element). It also plays a central part in SUE and VA. For SUE, the dilemma for lie tellers is that they do not know what information the interviewer holds, and in VA, lie tellers do not know whether the interviewer is likely to check the information they provide.

An aspect that ACID and CCA have in common but separates them from SUE and the VA is independence/dependence on external knowledge, facts, and evidence. While ACID and CCA operate without reliance or access to external information, the actual or potential evidence is core aspects of SUE and the VA. In determining the veracity of a statement with ACID and CCA, someone needs only to analyze the statement itself. In contrast, SUE and the VA treat external information ("evidence") as a central principle in distinguishing truth tellers from lie tellers: in SUE, by presenting evidence to the subject and in the VA by the possibility of checking it. Understanding the similarities and differences between the different methods and presenting them theoretically as general principles, may enhance the development of additional interviews protocols that use the same principles in new ways.

The Future of Verbal Deception Research

Considerable progress has been made in the last thirty years in verbal deception research, but there is still a lot of work to do. The ideas we present in this section are the product of collaboration between researchers and practitioners and aim to optimize the research so that it becomes as applicable to practitioners as possible. Verbal deception research is an applied topic and the empirical results should be meaningful for practitioners. It is therefore important to carry out research that mirrors the challenges and circumstances found in real life as much as possible. Highly realistic research tells us more about whether the examined techniques will work in practice than research with low realism. In addition, practitioners will be more willing to accept the findings and incorporate the techniques in their own interviews when they come from highly realistic research.

We distinguish between seven categories of ideas: (1) The choice of deception scenario; (2) cross-cultural and individual differences; (3) the use of countermeasures; (4) the verbal cues to examine; (5) within-subjects and between-subjects comparisons and indicators; (6) debriefing lie tellers; and (7) external validation in realistic settings and implementations.

The Choice of Deception Scenario

The activities discussed in different types of interviews differ widely from each other. That is, a number of specific subjects are relatively unique to different activities in police, intelligence, border control, asylum seeking, and job-vetting interviews. This should be reflected in the experimental deception scenario, so that truth tellers (and lie tellers) discuss activities that are relevant for a particular domain. For example, in police interviews, subjects typically discuss their activities and whereabouts during a specific time period, but in intelligence interviews, subjects often discuss conversations they have overheard or took part in. Do the same differences between truth tellers and lie tellers occur when they discuss conversations instead of past activities?

In addition, in police interviews, subjects typically discuss their past activities, but in intelligence and border control interviews, subjects discuss intentions of future activities. Researchers examining intentions found to be one of the most diagnostic veracity cues. Episodic future thought (EFT) refers to mental images someone has of the to-be-carried-out activity at the planning stage of that activity. More truth tellers than lie tellers responded to having experienced such mental images when planning the activity, and truth tellers were more detailed than lie tellers when describing them (Granhag & Knieps, 2011). EFTs are specifically related to intentions and cannot be examined when describing past activities.

Another difference between police and intelligence interviews is the aim the lie teller wants to achieve. A crime suspect being investigated by the police may report a false alibi, while a deceptive intelligence source may report a fabricated event (conversation or activity). The police officer's belief in the suspect's false alibi serves only as a means for a different epistemological end—that the police officer will believe that the suspect could not have committed the crime. The intelligence officer's belief in the source's false report is the source's main epistemological goal (e.g., so that the source can be rewarded for the information he gave). Different methods and different veracity indicators may be effective to varying degrees in these two scenarios.

In deception research, truth tellers and lie tellers typically discuss activities that happened a short time ago. However, for example, in vetting interviews, subjects often discuss activities from a more distant past. Research has shown differences in findings between interviews taking place immediately after an event compared to interviews taking place after a delay. Differences between truth tellers and lie tellers in the number of details they report are more pronounced in immediate interviews than in delayed interviews (Harvey et al., 2017). Truth tellers tend to forget details over time (forgetting), whereas lie tellers do not take enough into account that memory fades over time (stability bias). As a result, truth tellers tend to report less information over time whereas lie tellers tend to report the same amount of information over time. This makes the difference in the amount of information reported between the two groups smaller over time.

In vetting interviews, intelligence interviews and source handlers interviews, investigators are very interested in the "Have you ever . . .?" scenario (e.g., "Have you ever taken drugs in your life?" (vetting), "Have you ever been involved in terror activity?" (intelligence), and "Have you ever disclosed our secret relationship?" (source handling). The "Have you ever . . . ?" scenario is challenging scenario for verbal deception research and, in fact, for any type of deception research (Nahari et al., 2019). In this scenario there is no specific space- and time-anchored event to discuss. The investigator is interested in the occurrence of a certain type of event, at an unknown place and time and with unknown people and circumstances. Since the only reply the investigator receives is a denial ("No"), there is no "story" or a report that could serve as working material for the interview protocol to operate upon. The lack of a validated protocol for this scenario is noteworthy since the stakes for making an incorrect veracity assessment are high. It could lead to introducing spies in an organization, relying on a source who has been doubled, and so on.

Most verbal deception studies were designed to distinguish between truth tellers and lie tellers when they describe events that they claim they have experienced. Sometimes, however, it is important to distinguish between truthful and untruthful reports that people offer about their own opinions, affiliations, or reasons for their acts. For example, in intelligence interviews it could be important to decide whether an informant is indeed as much against religious or ethnic extremism as they claim. In this example, the topic subjects discuss is not perceptual but conceptual. The perceptually oriented lie detection tools developed to date and discussed above are thus inadequate; what is needed in such scenarios are conceptually oriented tools to discriminate between truthful and false beliefs. This type of research is almost nonexistent (but see Leal et al., 2010, for an exception).

Psychologists have identified four types of lie: Outright lies, exaggerations, embedded lies, and omissions (DePaulo et al., 1996; Leins et al., 2013). Outright lies are lies in which the information that is conveyed is totally false. Exaggerations are distortions of the truth, such as overstating or understating facts. Embedded lies are lies in which the false information is incorporated in an otherwise truthful story. Omissions are lies by deliberately excluding relevant information. In the majority of deception studies, participants tell outright or embedded lies (Leins et al., 2013; Vrij, 2008), which may reflect the occurrence of such lies in real life (DePaulo et al., 1996). In contrast, practitioners are often interested in lies that occur when a person omits information. If evidence is available, omissions could be detected by comparing the statement with that evidence (Granhag & Hartwig, 2015). However, practitioners do not always possess relevant evidence. In such situations, detecting omissions is a challenge in verbal lie detection, because all information a subject provides is truthful. The question is whether someone can decipher from the truthful information a subject provides that they are hiding something. We are aware of only one publication in this domain (Leal et al., 2020). A difference emerged even in this challenging setting: Truth tellers reported more complications than lie tellers, possibly due to lie tellers' inclination to keep their stories simple. This important topic deserves more research and highlights the importance of ongoing collaborations between researchers and practitioners to identify gaps in deception research.

The key message of this section is that findings from one type of scenario should not automatically be generalized to another, and that each scenario type merits attention from researchers. This is the case even if no differences in findings are expected, because it is the only way to reassure practitioners that the findings are relevant to them.

Cross-Cultural and Individual Differences

Participants in detection deception experiments have typically been from Western, educated, industrialized, rich and democratic (WEIRD) societies (Henrich, Heine, & Norenzayan, 2010). Most people in the world do not belong to this group, and neither do most subjects interviewed by practitioners. In research, recruiting non-WEIRD participants is a major challenge, because most researchers live in WEIRD nations. The scarce cross-cultural research published to date has shown cross-cultural differences in speech. For example, in one experiment where Arab, British, and Chinese subjects were compared, British subjects provided more details than the Arab and Chinese subjects who did not differ from each other in the amount of detail they provided. This could be the result of different communication styles between the British versus Arab and Chinese participants. Such differences are well documented in the literature (Vrij, Leal, Mann, et al., 2021). The amount of detail provided has an effect on verbal cues to veracity: They are more likely to occur when subjects say more because words are the carriers of such cues (Vrij et al., 2007). In alignment with this, truth tellers provided more details than lie tellers, but the difference was most pronounced in the British sample (Leal et al., 2018).

In Leal et al. (2018) all participants were interviewed in their native language by native interviewers. However, in operational practice, subjects and interviewers often do not share the same native language. Subjects are then interviewed in the interviewer's native language which is for the subjects their second (or third) language, or they are interviewed in their own language through an interpreter who, as a group, have shown widely varying linguistic ability. In second-language research, a comparison between verbal veracity cues in native and second-language (nonnative) speakers has rarely been made. In one such experiment, the written texts of truth telling and lie telling native and nonnative speakers were compared regarding level of detail and plausibility (on 7-point rating scales) (Volz et al., 2020). It was found that native truth tellers' statements included more details and sounded more plausible than the statements of the other three groups which did not differ from each other. This pattern suggests that research findings obtained with native speakers may not generalize to nonnative speakers. However, more research is required.

Most second-language research focuses on the accuracy and bias in detecting deceit in native and nonnative speakers. In this research, observers can typically both hear and see the subject, and observers are thus exposed to a mixture of nonverbal and verbal cues. In terms of accuracy in detecting truths and lies, the results are mixed and no conclusion can be drawn. In terms of bias, nonnative speakers are typically perceived as less believable than native speakers (Akehurst et al., 2018; Evans & Michael, 2014), which could be the result of nonnative speakers' speech making a suspicious impression, their nonverbal behavior, or a combination of the two.

Research on interpreters has shown that interpreter-present interviews resulted in less information being elicited than in interpreter-absent interviews (Vrij, Leal, Mann, et al., 2017), due to a combination of interpreters not translating each detail that an interviewee provides and interviewees being less elaborative when they speak through an interpreter. In addition, differences between truth tellers and lie tellers were less pronounced in interpreter-present than in interpreter-absent interviews (Vrij, Leal, Mann, et al., 2017), possibly because interpreter-present interviews are easier for lie tellers as it reduces the cognitive load (i.e., they have more time to think as the interpreter translates their answers).

In different cultures, different verbal cues to veracity emerge (Taylor et al., 2014), which complicates verbal lie detection for interviewers. To promote the widest application of evidence-based practices, we think it is important to place emphasize research that seeks diagnostic cues on a cross-cultural basis. Focusing on details is an example of this concept as across cultures, truth tellers typically report more details than lie tellers (Leal et al., 2018). Details would thus be viewed as a cross-cultural veracity indicator. The same applies to complications, since truth tellers report more complications than lie tellers across cultures (Vrij et al., 2018; Vrij & Vrij, 2020).

Individual differences in personality variables may also affect accuracy. In the polygraph literature, individual differences were examined as early as the 1980s for extraversion/introversion and neuroticism (Bradley & Janisse, 1981) and psychopathy (Patrick & Iacono, 1989). For verbal deception detection, the Agreeableness factor of the Big Five personality traits model may affect accuracy, as this factor is highly related to cooperativeness. It could be that people low in Agreeableness will be less detailed (reporting fewer total details and complications) than their counterparts, which in turn could increase the chance that they will be regarded as lie tellers, regardless of their true veracity status.

The Use of Countermeasures

While the importance of transparency in government-sponsored research relating to interrogation and interviewing cannot be overstated, some government officials have expressed concern that sharing this research—especially the strategies and tactics that emerge from the research—can provide a dangerous advantage to individuals and groups with aims that are inimical to national and community security. A question naturally arises: when scientists and/or practitioners claim that a certain lie detection method is effective, is there a chance that a subject will read up about the method in an attempt to appear credible in interviews? The successful application of countermeasures seems to depend on the technique examined. Lie tellers could successfully implement countermeasures and did sound like truth tellers when informed about CBCA (Vrij et al., 2000). Their success was limited when informed about CCA (Vrij, Leal, Fisher, et al., 2020) or SUE (Luke, Hartwig, et al., 2016), because the differences between truth tellers and lie tellers became smaller after participants were informed about CCA and SUE. Lie tellers could not successfully use countermeasures when being informed about VA (Nahar et al., 2014). In fact, the difference between truth tellers and lie tellers became *more* pronounced after being informed about VA because it made truth tellers more than lie tellers report verifiable details. However, since these were all single experiments, we should interpret the results with caution. More countermeasures research is needed.

The Verbal Cues to Examine

Most verbal deception research examines verbal cues to truthfulness; that is, verbal cues that truth tellers report more frequently than lie tellers. For example, all nineteen CBCA criteria are cues to truthfulness. Only examining cues to truthfulness poses a problem for practitioners. Although the presence of such cues could indicate that a subject is telling the truth, the absence does not necessarily indicate deception. For example, the presence of verifiable details could indicate that the subject is telling the truth, but the absence does not necessarily indicate lying. Perhaps the truthful subject cannot back up their activities with verifiable details because they simply are not available (e.g., they paid for a meal with cash rather than with a credit card and did not keep the receipt). A practitioner would be in a much stronger position to determine that a subject is lying if they record cues that lie tellers are more likely to report (cues to deceit). Unverifiable details, however, are not related to deception (Palena et al., 2021).

Verbal cues to deceit are rare in deception research. We started to examine two of those: Common knowledge details and self-handicapping strategies (Vrij & Vrij, 2020). Common knowledge details refer to strongly invoked stereotypical information about events. Subjects can, for example, provide such information without actually having experienced the event ("The event had an Oscars theme so everybody was dressed up"). Truth tellers have personal experiences of an event and are likely to report these (DePaulo et al., 1996). If liars do not have personal experiences of the event they report or experiences of events related to the to-be-discussed event, they will draw upon general knowledge to construe the event (Sporer, 2016). Self-handicapping strategies refer to justifications as to why someone chooses not to provide information ("There isn't much to say about the actual bungee jump as it took only a few moments"). For lie tellers, not having to provide information is an attractive strategy. However, they are also concerned about their credibility and believe that admitting lack of knowledge and/or memory appears suspicious (Ruby & Brigham, 1998). A potential solution is to provide a justification for the inability to provide information.

The problem with common knowledge details and self-handicapping strategies is that they do not always occur. They are typically examined in a "travel" scenario where subjects report a trip they allegedly have made in the last twelve months. Making a trip is arguably a somewhat scripted activity, which makes common knowledge details more likely to occur ("We visited the famous market, after which we went to the beach. We had dinner in a Mexican restaurant"). And when the trip occurred not recently, it gives lie tellers the opportunity to include self-handicapping strategies ("I cannot remember which restaurants we went to in the evenings, as we went there three months ago"). The situation is different when, for example, a source calls his handler saying that he just overheard a conversation about the planning of an attack. Common knowledge details and self-handicapping strategies are unlikely to occur in that scenario. The search for cues to deceit that are likely to occur in many scenarios is urgent.

Within-Subjects and Between-Subjects Comparisons and Indicators

Verbal deception researchers typically use between-subjects designs. That is, they compare a group of truth tellers with a group of lie tellers. That research typically shows, for example, that truth tellers report more details than lie tellers. However, this information is not useful for practitioners because they typically do not have the luxury of comparing groups of truth tellers to groups of lie tellers. A subject's response needs to be compared to an absolute standard which is clearly not possible: How many details should a subject provide to be considered a truth teller?

The alternative is to compare different responses made by the same subject in a single interview (within-subjects comparisons). The answers these within-subjects comparisons provide are still not straightforward, but they offer a step in the right direction. For example, the Model Statement literature recommends starting an interview with a free narrative ("Tell me all you remember . . .") followed by the Model Statement followed by inviting the subject again to tell all they remember (Vrij et al., 2018). The number of additional complications (complications mentioned in the second recall but not in the first recall) is then used to assess whether the subject is lying or truth telling. The first recall controls for individual and situational differences which makes this method better than a between-subjects comparison, but the problem remains that there is no definitive metric for how many additional complications a subject needs to report to be considered a truth teller (Vrij, 2016). Another way to control for individual and situational differences is to use within-subjects indicators, such as ratio indicators. One such example is the proportion of complications: complications—(complications + common knowledge details + self-handicapping strategies) (Vrij et al., 2018). Again, the same problem remains that there is no definitive metric for what ratio score someone should achieve to be considered a truth teller. Resolving this metric problem would be a large step forward in verbal deception research.

Debriefing Lie Tellers

A common research strategy for applied cognitive psychologists is to think logically about how people should behave in a real-world setting. For example, a researcher might ask themself: if I were lying about an earlier experience, what underlying psychological processes would I engage? This is an odd research strategy. If we want to know what psychological processes lie tellers are engaged in, it is better to ask them to describe their thought processes. In other words, rather than *perspective-taking*, we should focus on *perspective-getting*. We sometimes ask experimental subjects about their strategies and underlying cognitive processes (Strömwall et al., 2006), but these postexperimental debriefing sessions may have limited value: They are very brief and use only cursory debriefing procedures; the Internal Review Board-approved experimental tasks about which lie tellers are debriefed are sometimes weak substitutes for real-world lying tasks, and the experimental participants (often university students) are generally not professional lie tellers.

We suggest that researchers explore real-world lying by debriefing experienced lie tellers. Such people can be found in abundance, either in the criminal population or as detainees in national security investigations. Predatory marketing and aggressive sales routinely involved gradations of deception; as a result, individuals involved in these activities might also serve as a source of valuable insights into thought processes and strategies.

Moreover, effective methods of debriefing people about their thought processes are available (e.g., Cognitive Interview [Fisher & Geiselman, 1992]; Critical Decision Method [Crandall et al., 2006]). Using such sophisticated debriefing tools on "professional" lie tellers should yield new insights into how they think in real situations. Success using this approach has already been demonstrated, as in a study to debrief criminals on why they admitted or denied guilt of serious crimes (Holmberg & Christianson, 2002).

External Validation in Realistic Settings and Implementations

Most research examining the efficacy of verbal lie detection interview protocols is laboratory based. Practitioners often find it difficult to accept the tested methods because it is possible that the findings obtained in the laboratory may be different from those that would be obtained in the field. A second concern (although less mentioned by practitioners) is that in most experiments, subjects are instructed to lie, whereas in real life people have the choice to do so. There are at least two ways to address these two concerns. First, to examine the interview protocols discussed earlier in this chapter in higher-stakes settings. For example, one successful simulation is the "cheating paradigm," which was developed for research on true and false confessions (Russian et al., 2005). Second, the approach we favor is to conduct field studies within organizations and agencies that use these interview protocols. It is hereby crucial to obtain ground truth through independent and objective validation data. One group of practitioners we collaborate with keep a database for intelligence interviews in which CCA is used. They also measure its success in cases where ground truth could be established. Based on more than sixty cases, a 90 percent accuracy rate was obtained (Vrij & Fisher, 2021). High accuracy rates derived in applied settings may help to convince field agents regarding the validity and efficiency of the interview protocols.

Conclusion

Verbal deception research has made tremendous progress in the last few decades, but now is not the time to become complacent. Four interview protocols have been developed that seem to distinguish truth tellers from lie tellers. They show similarities in their structure (free recall followed by an intervention) and focus on differences in information management strategies used by truth tellers and lie tellers. The four protocols differ in whether or not they rely on independent evidence. Understanding why different protocols work may result in the development of new protocols or techniques within these protocols.

The act of lying takes places in numerous ways and settings. This creates challenges for practitioners and research opportunities for scientists. Strong collaboration between practitioners and scientists in determining what these challenges are and how to properly research them should result in advanced knowledge that could be used to further improve verbal lie detection.

Acknowledgments

The time the first author spent working on this article was funded by the Centre for Research and Evidence on Security Threats (ESRC Award: ES/N009614/1). The authors have no conflict of interest to declare.

References

Akehurst, L., Arnhold, A., Figueiredo, I., Turtle, S., & Leach, A. M. (2018). Investigating deception in second language speakers: Interviewee and assessor perspectives. *Legal and Criminological Psychology*, *23*, 230–251.

Amado, B. G., Arce, R., Fariña, F., & Vilarino, M. (2016). Criteria-Based Content Analysis (CBCA) reality criteria in adults: A meta-analytic review. *International Journal of Clinical and Health Psychology*, *16*, 201–210.

Bell, B. E., & Loftus, E. F. (1989). Trivial persuasion in the courtroom: The power of (a few) minor details. *Journal of Personality and Social Psychology*, *56*, 669–679.

Bond, C. F., & DePaulo, B. M. (2006). Accuracy of deception judgements. *Personality and Social Psychology Review*, *10*, 214–234.

Bradley, M. T., & Janisse, M. P. (1981). Extraversion and the detection of deception. *Personality and Individual Differences*, *2*, 99–103.

Christ, S., E., Van Essen, D. C. Watson, J. M., Brubaker, L. E., & McDermott, K. B. (2009). The contributions of prefrontal cortex and executive control to deception: Evidence from activation likelihood estimate meta-analyses. *Cerebral Cortex*, *19*, 1557–1566.

Colwell, K., Hiscock-Anisman, C. K., & Fede, J. (2013). Assessment criteria indicative of deception: An example of the new paradigm of differential recall enhancement. In B. S. Cooper, D. Griesel, & M. Ternes

(Eds.) *Applied issues in investigative interviewing, eyewitness memory, and credibility assessment* (pp. 259–292). Springer.

Crandall, B., Klein, G., & Hoffman, R. R. (2006). *Working minds: A practitioner's guide to cognitive task analysis*. MIT Press.

Debey, E., Verschuere, B., & Crombez, G. (2012). Lying and executive control: An experimental investigation using ego depletion and goal neglect. *Acta Psychologica, 140*, 133–141.

DePaulo, B. M., Kashy, D. A., Kirkendol, S. E., Wyer, M. M., & Epstein, J. A. (1996). Lying in everyday life. *Journal of Personality and Social Psychology, 70*, 979–995.

DePaulo, B. M., Lindsay, J. L., Malone, B. E., Muhlenbruck, L., Charlton, K., & Cooper, H. (2003). Cues to deception. *Psychological Bulletin, 129*, 74–118.

Evans, J. R., & Michael, S. W. (2014). Detecting deception in non-native English speakers. *Applied Cognitive Psychology, 28*, 226–237.

Ewens, S., Vrij, A., Leal, S., Mann, S., Jo, E., Shaboltas, A., Ivanova, M., Granskaya, J., & Houston, K. (2016). Using the model statement to elicit information and cues to deceit from native speakers, non-native speakers and those talking through an interpreter. *Applied Cognitive Psychology, 30*, 854–862.

Fisher, R. P. (2010). Interviewing cooperative witnesses. *Legal and Criminological Psychology, 15*, 25–38.

Fisher, R. P., & Geiselman, R. E. (1992). *Memory enhancing techniques for investigative interviewing: The cognitive interview*. C. C. Thomas.

Granhag, P.A. & Hartwig, M. (2008). A new theoretical perspective on deception detection: On the psychology of instrumental mind-reading. *Psychology, Crime & Law, 14*, 189–200.

Granhag, P. A., & Hartwig, M. (2015). The Strategic Use of Evidence (SUE) technique: A conceptual overview. In P. A. Granhag, A. Vrij, & B. Verschuere (Eds.), *Deception detection: Current challenges and new approaches* (pp. 231–251). John Wiley & Sons.

Granhag, P. A., & Knieps, M. (2011). Episodic future thought: Illuminating the trademarks of forming true and false intentions. *Applied Cognitive Psychology, 25*, 274–280.

Granhag, P.A., Strömwall, L.A., Willén, R., & Hartwig, M. (2013). Eliciting cues to deception by tactical disclosure of evidence: The first test of the Evidence Framing Matrix. *Legal and Criminological Psychology, 18*, 341–355.

Hartwig, M., Granhag, P. A., & Luke, T. (2014). Strategic use of evidence during investigative interviews: The state of the science. In D. C. Raskin, C. R. Honts, & J. C. Kircher (Eds.), *Credibility assessment: Scientific research and applications* (pp. 1–36). Academic Press.

Hartwig, M., Granhag, P. A., & Strömwall, L. (2007). Guilty and innocent suspects' strategies during police interrogations. *Psychology, Crime, & Law, 13*, 213–227.

Hartwig, M., Granhag, P. A., Strömwall, L., & Doering, N. (2010). Impression and information management: On the strategic self-regulation of innocent and guilty suspects. *The Open Criminology Journal, 3*, 10–16.

Harvey, A., Vrij, A., Hope, L., Leal, S., & Mann, S. (2017). A stability bias effect amongst deceivers. *Law and Human Behavior, 41*, 519–529.

Henrich, J., Heine, S. J., & Norenzayan, A. (2010). The weirdest people in the world? *Behavioral and Brain Sciences, 33*, 61–83.

Holmberg, U., & Christianson, S-A. (2002). Murderers' and sexual offenders' experiences of police interviews and their inclination to admit or deny crimes. *Behavioural Sciences & the Law, 20*, 31–45.

Köhnken, G., & Steller, M. (1988). The evaluation of the credibility of child witness statements in German procedural system. In G. Davies & J. Drinkwater (Eds.), *The child witness: Do the courts abuse children?* (Issues in Criminological and Legal Psychology, no. 13) (pp. 37–45). British Psychological Society.

Lancaster, G. L. J., Vrij, A., Hope, L., & Waller, B. (2012). Sorting the liars from the truth tellers: The benefits of asking unanticipated questions. *Applied Cognitive Psychology, 27*, 107–114.

Leal, S., Vrij, A., Deeb, H., Hudson, C., Capuozzo, P., Fisher, R. P. (2020). Verbal cues to deceit when lying through omitting information. *Legal and Criminological Psychology, 25*, 278–294.

Leal, S., Vrij, A., Mann, S., & Fisher, R. (2010). Detecting true and false opinions: The Devil's Advocate approach as a lie detection aid. *Acta Psychologica, 134*, 323–329.

Leal, S., Vrij, A., Vernham, Z., Dalton, G., Jupe, L., Harvey, A., & Nahari, G. (2018). Cross-cultural verbal deception. *Legal and Criminological Psychology, 23*, 192–213.

Leal, S., Vrij, A., Warmelink, L., Vernham, Z., & Fisher, R. (2015). You cannot hide your telephone lies: Providing a model statement as an aid to detect deception in insurance telephone calls. *Legal and Criminological Psychology, 20*, 129–146.

Leins, D., Fisher, R. P., & Ross, S. J. (2013). Exploring liars' strategies for creating deceptive reports. *Legal and Criminological Psychology, 18*, 141–151.

Luke, T. J., Hartwig, M., Shamash, B., & Granhag, P. A. (2016). Countermeasures against the Strategic Use of Evidence technique: Effects on suspects' strategies. *Journal of Investigative Psychology and Offender Profiling, 13*, 131–147.

Nahari, G., Ashkenazi, T., Fisher, R. P., Granhag, P. A., Hershkovitz, I., Masip, J., Meijer, E., Nisin, Z., Sarid, N., Taylor, P. J., Verschuere, B., & Vrij, A. (2019). Language of Lies: Urgent issues and prospects in verbal lie detection research. *Legal and Criminological Psychology, 24*, 1–23.

Nahari, G., Vrij, A., & Fisher, R. P. (2012). Does the truth come out in the writing? SCAN as a lie detection tool. *Law & Human Behavior, 36*, 68–76.

Nahari, G., Vrij, A., & Fisher, R. P. (2014). The Verifiability Approach: Countermeasures facilitate its ability to discriminate between truths and lies. *Applied Cognitive Psychology, 28*, 122–128.

Palena, N., Caso, L., Vrij, A., & Nahari, G. (2021). The Verifiability Approach: A meta-analysis. *Journal of Applied Research in Memory and Cognition, 10*(1), 155–166.

Patrick, C. J., & Iacono, W. G. (1989). Psychopathy, threat, and polygraph test accuracy. *Journal of Applied Psychology, 74*, 347–355.

Patterson, M. L. (2006). The evolution of theories of interactive behavior. In V. Manusov & M. L. Patterson (Eds.), *The SAGE handbook of nonverbal communication* (pp. 21–39). SAGE.

Ruby, C. L., & Brigham, J. C. (1998). Can Criteria-Based Content Analysis distinguish between true and false statements of African-American speakers? *Law and Human Behavior, 22*, 369–388.

Russano, M. B., Meissner, C. A., Narchet, F. M., & Kassin, S. M. (2005). Investigating true and false confessions with a novel experimental paradigm. *Psychological Science, 16*, 481–486. doi: 10.1111/j.0956-7976.205.01560x.

Sporer, S. L. (2016). Deception and cognitive load: Expanding our horizon with a working memory model. *Frontiers in Psychology: Hypothesis and Theory, 7*, Article 420.

Strömwall, L. A., Hartwig, M., & Granhag, P-A. (2006). To act truthfully: Nonverbal behavior and strategies during a police interrogation. *Psychology, Crime & Law, 12*, 207–219.

Taylor, P. J., Larner, S., Conchie, S. M., & van der Zee, S. (2014). Cross-cultural deception detection. In P. A. Granhag, A. Vrij, & B. Verschuere (Eds.), *Detecting deception: Current challenges and cognitive approaches* (pp. 175–201). John Wiley & Sons

Volz, S., Reinhard, M-A., & Müller, P. (2020). Why don't you believe me? Detecting deception in messages written by non-native and native speakers. *Applied Cognitive Psychology, 34*, 256–269.

Vrij, A. (2008). *Detecting lies and deceit: Pitfalls and opportunities* (2nd ed.). John Wiley and Sons.

Vrij, A. (2016). Baselining as a lie detection method. *Applied Cognitive Psychology, 30*, 1112–1119.

Vrij, A. (2018). Verbal lie detection tools from an applied perspective. In J. P. Rosenfeld (Ed.), *Detecting concealed information and deception: Recent developments* (pp. 297–321). Elsevier: Academic Press.

Vrij, A. (2019). Deception and truth detection when analysing nonverbal and verbal cues. *Applied Cognitive Psychology, 33*, 160–167.

Vrij, A., & Fisher, R. P. (2016). Which lie detection tools are ready for use in the criminal justice system? *Journal of Applied Research in Memory and Cognition, 5*, 302–307.

Vrij, A., & Fisher, R. P. (2020). Unraveling the misconception about deception and nervous behaviour. *Frontiers in Psychology, section Personality and Social Psychology, 11*, 1377.

Vrij, A., & Fisher, R. P. (2021). Detecting deception. In C. Stott, B. Bradford, M. Radburn, & L. Savigar-Shaw (Eds.), *Making an impact on policing and crime: Psychological research, policy and practice* (pp. 105–124). Routledge.

Vrij, A., Fisher, R., Blank, H. (2017). A cognitive approach to lie detection: A meta-analysis. *Legal and Criminological Psychology, 22*, 1–21.

Vrij, A., Fisher, R., Blank, H., Leal, S., & Mann, S. (2016). A cognitive approach to elicit nonverbal and verbal cues of deceit. In J. W. van Prooijen & P. A. M. van Lange (Eds.), *Cheating, corruption, and concealment: The roots of dishonest behavior* (pp. 284–310). Cambridge University Press.

Vrij, A., & Granhag, P. A. (2012). Eliciting cues to deception and truth: What matters are the questions asked. *Journal of Applied Research in Memory and Cognition, 1*, 110–117.

Vrij, A., Hartwig, M., & Granhag, P. A. (2019). Reading lies: Nonverbal communication and deception. *Annual Review of Psychology, 70*, 295–317.

Vrij, A., Kneller, W., & Mann, S. (2000). The effect of informing liars about criteria-based content analysis on their ability to deceive CBCA-raters. *Legal and Criminological Psychology, 5*, 57–70.

Vrij, A., Leal, S., & Fisher, R. P. (2018). Verbal deception and the Model Statement as a lie detection tool. *Frontiers in Psychiatry, section Forensic Psychiatry, 9,* 492.

Vrij, A., Leal, S., Fisher, R. P., Mann, S., Deeb, H., Jo, E., Castro Campos, C., & Hamzeh, S. (2020). The efficacy of using countermeasures in a Model Statement interview. *European Journal of Psychology Applied to Legal Context, 12,* 23–34.

Vrij, A., Leal, S., Jupe, L., & Harvey, A. (2018). Within-subjects verbal lie detection measures: A comparison between total detail and proportion of complications. *Legal and Criminological Psychology, 23,* 265–279.

Vrij, A., Leal, S., Mann, S., Dalton, G. Jo, E., Shaboltas, A., Khaleeva, M., Granskaya, J., & Houston, K. (2017). Using the Model Statement to elicit information and cues to deceit in interpreter-based interviews. *Acta Psychologica, 177,* 44–53.

Vrij, A., Leal, S., Mann, S., Vernham, Z., Dalton, G., Serok-Jeppa, O., Rozmann, N., Nahari, G., & Fisher, R. P. (2021). "Please tell me all you remember": A comparison between British' and Arab' interviewees' free narrative performance and its implications for lie detection. *Psychiatry, Psychology, & Law, 28*(4), 546–559.

Vrij, A., Mann, S., Fisher, R., Leal, S., Milne, B., & Bull, R. (2008). Increasing cognitive load to facilitate lie detection: The benefit of recalling an event in reverse order. *Law and Human Behavior, 32,* 253–265.

Vrij, A., Mann, S., Kristen, S., & Fisher, R. (2007). Cues to deception and ability to detect lies as a function of police interview styles. *Law and Human Behavior, 31,* 499–518.

Vrij, A., & Vrij, S. (2020). Complications travel: A cross-cultural comparison of the proportion of complication as a verbal cue to deceit. *Journal of Investigative Psychology and Offender Profiling, 17,* 3–16.

Investigative Interviewing: A Review of the Literature and a Model of Science-Based Practice

Christian A. Meissner, Steven M. Kleinman, Amelia Mindthoff, Erik P. Phillips, and Jesse N. Rothweiler

Abstract

Investigative interviews are an essential tool for any criminal investigation and are conducted across a variety of contexts and subject populations. In each context, key psychological processes function to regulate communication between an interviewer and a subject—from developing rapport and trust to facilitating memory retrieval to assessing credibility. Research on investigative interviewing has dramatically increased to include assessing cooperative interviews with witnesses/victims, interviews with more resistant suspects and sources, and interviewing to detect deception. We review the extant research and discuss three fundamental challenges to eliciting the truth: (1) investigative biases, (2) the frailty of human memory, and (3) resistance to providing information. We then introduce a model of science-based investigative interviewing that encompasses both relational and informational tactics shown to be effective in developing rapport and trust, eliciting accurate information, and facilitating judgments of credibility. Finally, we discuss the policy and practice implications of this research.

Key Words: investigative interviewing, criminal investigations, rapport, memory retrieval, credibility assessment

Investigative interviews are defined as the systematic questioning of individuals for the purpose of collecting detailed and accurate accounts of a situation or event in support of a broader investigative decision (Meissner, 2021; Powell et al., 2005; St-Yves, 2014). Such interviews can encompass law enforcement engagements with individuals across a variety of contexts, including victim, witness, suspect, and source (or confidential informant) interviews. Investigative interviews are also conducted by intelligence and military personnel, to include interrogations of captured prisoners of war and the strategic debriefing of sources, informants, or personnel (often referred to as "subjects" for brevity). Investigative interviews also play an important role in inquiries conducted by independent government agencies, corporations, nonprofits, and schools/universities seeking to resolve conflicts or abusive practices.

In each of these varied contexts, psychological processes function to regulate communication between an interviewer and a subject. For example, social perception governs the amount of rapport and trust that develops between interactants. Motivational strategies lead subjects to resist an interviewer's questions and to offer deceptive responses. Investigative biases can lead to questioning tactics that influence the amount and accuracy of information recalled by interviewees. The characteristics of certain subjects can render them more vulnerable to persuasion or suggestion, including such factors as age, mental ability, or mental health.

Our scientific understanding of these psychological factors has evolved considerably over the past fifty years, as has the practice of investigative interviewing itself. In this chapter, we review the extant research on investigative interviewing and highlight trends and topics that have been examined. We then discuss three fundamental challenges to eliciting the truth: (1) investigative biases that influence an interviewer's behavior, (2) the frailty of human memory and the ease with which it can become corrupted, and (3) resistance to providing information that can produce deception and outright defiance by the interview subject. Finally, we introduce a model of science-based investigative interviewing that encompasses both relational and informational tactics shown to be effective for developing rapport and trust, eliciting accurate information, and facilitating judgments of credibility. We conclude by discussing the policy and practice implications of this research, including recent efforts at reform around the world.

50 Years of Research on Investigative Interviewing

The notion that interviewing strategies can influence the quality of information elicited was proposed more than a hundred years ago when Münsterberg (1908) contemplated the malleability of witness and suspect statements. It would, however, be decades before systematic, empirical research on investigative interviewing gained traction. The past fifteen years have produced the most dramatic increase in the number of studies conducted, as our search[1] for investigative interviewing articles published over the past fifty years (1970–2020) demonstrates an exponential growth in published research on the topic (see fig. 34.1).

The range of topics examined by scholars has similarly increased over the years. To further assess the state of the field, we employed VOSviewer (van Eck & Waltman, 2010) to render a mapping of the co-occurrence of keywords associated with articles published between 1970 and 2020. This visualization represents (1) the frequency with which

---

[1] We used the following search string in PsychINFO: investigative interview* OR (interview* AND interrogat*) OR (interview* AND decepti*) OR (interview* AND witness) OR (interrog* AND (confess* OR suspect)). Our search resulted in 4,485 records, from which we excluded 2,155 records for a final sample of 2,330 records.

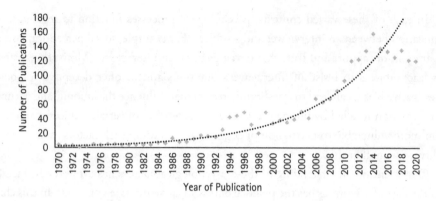

Figure 34.1 "Investigative interviewing" articles published each year from 1970 to 2020.

keywords occur in our search records (more frequent keywords are larger) and (2) the extent to which any two keywords were related (more closely related terms are proximate to one another). As displayed in figure 34.2, the investigative interviewing literature is multifaceted, with three primary clusters of overarching domains: (1) cooperative interviews with witnesses/victims, (2) interviews with more resistant suspects and sources, and (3) interviewing to detect deception.

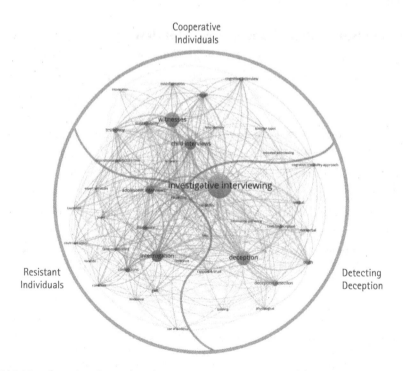

Figure 34.2 Map of prominent keywords in the investigative interviewing research literature.

Interviewing Cooperative Individuals

The literature on interviewing cooperative individuals is the largest subfield of the investigative interviewing literature. A strong emphasis is placed on witness recall together with a particularly robust literature on child interviewing (see Malloy et al., this volume). Additionally, development and assessment of the Cognitive Interview (CI) has garnered significant attention over the years and is closely associated with witness recall, child interviews, and, more recently, credibility assessment. Research on witness suggestibility and false memory are well represented within this cluster. Witness (courtroom) testimony is also a prevalent topic, suggesting that scholars are considering the implications of (in)appropriate investigative interviewing methods at the trial level. Finally, the influence of repeated interviewing and alcohol intoxication are receiving increased scrutiny.

Interviewing Resistant Individuals

The literature on interviewing more resistant individuals (e.g., criminal suspects, targets, and sources) has developed on a separate trajectory from that of the cooperative interviewee literature. One of the most prominent keywords within this cluster is "confessions," with a particular emphasis on "false confessions" and the influence of coercion and innocence as risk factors. Less emphasis has been placed upon recommended best-practices, such as developing rapport and trust, the strategic presentation of evidence, or subject resistance. Researchers have considered the trial-level implications of interrogation practices and confession evidence, as terms such as "courtroom," "judge," and "expert witness" are represented in this cluster. An emphasis on "adolescent (or juvenile) interrogations" has also been prominent; however, this term was strongly related to the "child interviews" term, suggesting that adolescent research spans both cooperative and resistant interview subject contexts.

Interviewing to Detect Deception

Within the deception domain, there has been a continued focus on the detection of deception and the utility of verbal and nonverbal cues to deception. An increasing number of studies have examined cognitive credibility approaches for interviewing to detect deception, while a comparable literature has amassed on physiological approaches. A smaller literature on investigative interview training appears within this cluster, suggesting that studies more frequently assess training to detect deception compared with the other interview contexts.

Investigative Interviewing across the Clusters

Although the term "investigative interviewing" is linked to all three research clusters, limited integration remains across these domains. This is arguably a function of the limited foci of research programs developed by scholars who often specialize in the study of certain topics and contexts. Nevertheless, certain fundamental processes likely transcend context. For example, rapport and trust appear crucial to the success of any investigative interview, whether it be with an adult or child, a witness or suspect. Similarly, the under-representation of training studies suggests that limited attention has been directed to field evaluations of evidence-based practices, particularly those involving interviews with cooperative and resistant subjects. Facilitating accurate and complete memory recall is also fundamental to interviewing witnesses, victims, suspects, or sources, and has increasingly been shown as linked to effective approaches for assessing credibility. As we note below, a comprehensive model of investigative interviewing that promotes the integration of topics across contexts is likely to further the advancement of research and to facilitate training and the dissemination of best practices.

Three Fundamental Challenges to Eliciting the Truth

Interviewers are likely to face several fundamental challenges in their attempts to elicit information, regardless of the context in which an interview is conducted. These challenges have the potential to prevent successful resolution of a case, as the manner in which interviewers respond to these challenges can alter the outcome of their investigation for better or for worse.

Investigative Biases—"We Know You Did It."

Research has shown that the mindset of an investigator, and in particular their investigative hypothesis, can dramatically influence the way they question a subject, the information and behaviors they elicit from the subject in response, and their assessments of the subject's credibility (Ask & Fahsing, 2019; Meissner & Kassin, 2004). Often referred to as tunnel vision or confirmation bias (Nickerson, 1998), such fundamental psychological processes in the investigative context have the potential to yield false information and false confessions. Initial investigative hypotheses have been shown to skew interpretation of evidence and serve only to reinforce an investigator's initial beliefs (Ask & Granhag, 2005; O'Brien, 2009). Biasing information can also lead interviewers to ask suggestive and leading questions rather than open-ended questions that allow the interview subject control of their response (Powell et al., 2012). In the context of an interview with a suspect, confirmation bias can lead to the use of more pressure-filled interrogation tactics—including maximization tactics that involve fabricating evidence and reinforcing a perception of guilt or minimization tactics that offer suggestive themes that assuage guilt and imply leniency in exchange for a confession (Kassin et al., 2010). This process of confirmation bias has been shown to increase the use of such tactics and therein increase the likelihood of a false confession (Narchet et al., 2011). Investigative biases can also influence perceptions of credibility, leading investigators to see deception in suspect denials and infer guilt from a coerced admission (Kassin et al., 2005; Meissner & Kassin, 2002).

Frailty of Human Memory—"I Can't Remember."

Regardless of the context, interview subjects will need to access their memory to effectively respond to investigative questions. Herein, the primary objective of any investigative interview is to elicit the most complete and reliable account of past events and/or the planning undertaken for future actions. In fact, many subjects report that they "can't remember" an event or detail in question. Rather than helping to prompt accurate recall, prodding with biased and suggestive questioning typically yields an account that aligns with an interviewer's mindset but is objectively false. Importantly, this approach can both corrupt a subject's memory and potentially interfere with future attempts to elicit the truth.

Decades of research have demonstrated that suggestive or leading questions by an interviewer can produce errors in memory reporting by witnesses—often referred to as the misinformation effect (Pickrell et al., 2016). Interrogative suggestibility, or the propensity for an interview subject to accept suggestive information provided by an interviewer (Gudjonsson, 1997) has also been shown to be associated with the likelihood of providing a false confession (Otgaar et al., 2021). Other psychological vulnerabilities can similarly increase the suggestibility of an interview subject, including age, mental illness, intellectual functioning, substance use, or certain personality characteristics (Gudjonsson, 2010).

Resistance to Providing Information—"I Don't Want to Talk to You"

While encountering resistance is a relatively routine experience for most interviewers, it nonetheless remains a topic that is poorly understood and absent from most training programs (Snook et al., 2021). It is not surprising, then, that there is no true consensus regarding how resistance appears in the interview room, the psychological sources of resistance, or even how to meaningfully define resistance. Here, we propose that resistance consists of both proactive and reactive behaviors displayed by the subject with the intent of moving away from cooperation and avoiding disclosure or disrupting the flow of an interaction.

Resistance is often discussed in the context of suspect interrogations (Vrij et al., 2017); however, witnesses and victims may also be reluctant to disclose information related to an investigation (Blasbalg et al., 2018). Scholars have identified a variety of resistance behaviors in investigative interviews including signs of physiological stress, physical disengagement, or reduced positive emotions (Guyll et al., 2019; Katz et al., 2012). Additionally, reluctant subjects might omit relevant information, offer outright resistance to requests for information or direct denials, or be generally less forthcoming in their responses (Hershkowitz et al., 2006). The extent to which these behaviors are indicative of cognitive, affective, or motivational processes has been of significant interest to scholars.

In the suspect interview context, Alison et al. (2014) identified five counterinterrogation behaviors from a set of 181 terrorism suspect interrogations, including *passive resistance* (e.g., maintaining silence), *passive verbal resistance* (e.g., claiming a lack of memory), *direct verbal resistance* (e.g., discussing unrelated topics), *retraction of prior statements*, and *direct refusal to engage* (e.g., "no comment" or engagement of rights). Kelly et al. (2019)

have similarly coded resistance (or engagement) in samples of police interrogations, with an additional focus on *affective responses* (e.g., the subject cried or became angry), *excuses or rationalizations* (e.g., blaming the victim or a co-conspirator), and *seeking information* from investigators (e.g., asking for details related to the incident or dispositional information). In general, scholars have found that certain interrogation tactics (such as accusatorial interrogation tactics; Meissner et al., 2015) can increase resistance while others (rapport-based, information-gathering approaches) are more likely to decrease resistance and increase cooperation (Alison et al., 2014). Similarly, supportive interviewing with child victims has been shown to reduce reluctance and facilitate disclosure (Saywitz et al., 2019).

Scholars have also examined the psychological processes associated with counterinterrogation behaviors. For example, resistance was described by Shepherd (1993) as involving two orthogonal dimensions related to both a subject's willingness to talk (relational) and their ability to recall the information (memory). Oleszkiewicz and Granhag (2019) add that resistance strategies can include both an affective and cognitive basis. Affective strategies are said to reflect a subject's negative emotional reaction to the available options or reactance to the perceived pressures of the interviewer (Knowles & Riner, 2007). Cognitive strategies, in contrast, involve the strategic regulation of information exchange based upon an instrumental evaluation of the potential consequences and a subjective evaluation of the evidence held by the interviewer.

A Model of Science-Based Investigative Interviewing

Decades of research have facilitated the development and assessment of effective approaches for conducting investigative interviews. As noted above, scholars have often focused on the evaluation of specific interviewing tactics or techniques (e.g., NICHD protocol, CI, and Strategic Use of Evidence). This focused development has proven important to furthering a science-based perspective; however, despite a few notable exceptions discussed below, there has been less of an emphasis on developing systematic frameworks or models that provide a comprehensive perspective across contexts.

Policing reforms in England and Wales led to the development of the PEACE model (see Bull & Rachlew, 2020). PEACE encompasses evidence-based practices such as good questioning, rapport-building, CI mnemonics, conversation management, presentation of evidence, and challenges regarding inconsistencies in the account (Snook et al., 2010). On a parallel track, a framework adopted by scholars in the United States has focused on a rapport-based, information-gathering approach (Brimbal et al., 2021; Meissner et al., 2015). This approach represents an evidence-based alternative to the biased and problematic questioning approaches that have been used with witnesses and victims (Fisher et al., 2014) and the accusatorial tactics that have long shaped customary practice in the interrogation of suspects (Kassin et al., 2010). Much like the PEACE model, information-gathering approaches place an emphasis on more productive questioning skills, the development of rapport, the use of cognitive mnemonics to improve recall, and

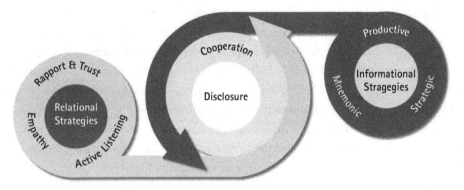

Figure 34.3 Model of science-based investigative interviewing that includes relational approaches that facilitate cooperation and informational approaches that increase disclosure and improve credibility assessment.

a strategic approach to challenging inconsistencies with evidence or investigative information (Brandon et al., 2019a).

Below we offer a novel framework of science-based investigative interviewing that brings together the extant literature, is reflective of key psychological processes and empirical models, and encompasses effective strategies for developing cooperation, eliciting information, and assessing credibility. As displayed in figure 34.3, the primary goals of the model reflect the twin objectives of *developing cooperation* and *eliciting disclosures*. In this context, the interviewer is dissuaded from seeking compliance or applying coercion that might otherwise compel a response (or provoke resistance). Rather, the initial goal is to develop rapport and trust and therein achieve a level of cooperation that allows the subject to maintain their autonomy in responding to questions. The interviewer is discouraged from simply seeking confirmation or an admission/confession that affirms a prevailing theory of the investigation. Instead, the interviewer should elicit the subject's most complete narrative by facilitating their memory recollection, asking questions in an unbiased manner, and using strategic questioning to address inconsistencies and facilitate assessments of credibility.

Relational Approaches That Facilitate Cooperation:
Relational approaches to investigative interviewing, discussed below, have been shown to effectively facilitate cooperation by interview subjects.

RAPPORT AND TRUST TACTICS
The term "rapport" has often been used to characterize the relationship between an interviewer and subject. Although investigators have long promoted the development of rapport in interviews, defining this concept and its related tactics has been surprisingly difficult (Russano et al., 2014). Only recently has research begun to systematically address the strategies and tactics that are most effective in the investigative interviewing context (Gabbert et al., 2021; Vallano & Compo Schreiber, 2015). In contrast to the coercive ethos that pervades accusatorial practices (Kassin et al., 2010), fostering a relationship with the subject appears key to inviting cooperation and ultimately achieving disclosure.

Rapport is an interactive concept that depends on both parties' attitudes and behaviors, which can vary over time. An interview is believed to begin absent rapport, with the interviewer attempting to develop rapport at the outset and working to maintain it throughout the interview (Walsh & Bull, 2012). One of the most prominent psychological models of rapport (Tickle-Degnen & Rosenthal, 1990) suggests that three elements are critical to a rapport-based interaction: *mutual attentiveness* (degree to which the interaction partners are focused on or interested in one another), *coordination* (the synchrony, balance, and harmony of the interaction between the interactants), and *positivity* (positive affect related to perception of another as friendly or caring). Duke et al. (2018) proposed a five-factor model of rapport in the investigative interview setting that expands this model to include aspects of *trust/respect* (interviewer appears trustworthy and acts respectfully toward the interview subject), *expertise* (the interviewer appears professional and competent), and *cultural similarity* (the interviewer and interview subject share an ethnicity, cultural background, or other characteristics). Research suggests that increased perceptions of rapport by the subject are more likely to yield cooperation and thereby increase information disclosure (Brimbal et al., 2019; Brimbal et al., 2021; Dianiska et al., 2021).

A recent review of the literature by Gabbert et al. (2021) evaluated more than thirty studies that examined various verbal, nonverbal, and paraverbal tactics to develop rapport. Among the most studied approaches for developing a relationship in the interview context, Gabbert and colleagues highlight the importance of showing interest in the interview subject. For example, Vallano et al. (2015) found that the most common rapport-building technique reported by investigators was to engage in "small talk" with the subject. Such an approach has been empirically supported in experimental studies (Kieckhaefer et al., 2014; Wachi et al., 2018).

Another effective rapport-building tactic involves the self-disclosure of personal information by the interviewer. Such disclosures have been shown to facilitate perceptions of liking (Collins & Miller, 1994) and to increase perceptions of rapport by the interview subject (Dianiska et al., 2021; Evans et al., 2014). Importantly, self-disclosures can also be used to build affiliation and common ground with an interview subject by highlighting similarities between the two. Attempts to build common ground have been shown to be effective in facilitating perceptions of rapport and ultimately increasing disclosure (Brimbal et al., 2019; Dianiska et al., 2021; Wachi et al., 2018), and investigators frequently report the use of such tactics (Goodman-Delahunty & Howes, 2016; Russano et al., 2014; Vallano et al., 2015).

Trust has generally been defined as a psychological state comprising the intention to accept vulnerability based upon positive expectations of actions taken by the individual being trusted (Rousseau et al., 1998). McAllister (1995) distinguished between two forms of trust: *cognitive trust* (i.e., perceptions of competence and reliability in predicting another's behavior) and *affective trust* (i.e., displays of benevolence and a positive emotional connection). One of the foundational principles of trust-building appears to be reciprocity—the social exchange of objects, items, or gestures that enable a general expectation of a future obligation and therein strengthens the relationship. In fact, reciprocity is a common tactic employed by investigative interviewers (Goodman-Delahunty & Howes, 2016), and research has substantiated its utility for increasing perceptions of trust and rapport (Matsumoto & Hwang, 2018).

ACTIVE LISTENING AND CONVERSATIONAL RAPPORT TACTICS

Active listening is key to successfully eliciting information in investigative interviews and has been proposed as central tactic for developing rapport (Abbe & Brandon, 2013). Rogers and Farson (1957) first coined the term "active listening," but it was later defined by Gordon (1975) as a set of verbal and nonverbal skills believed essential for effective communication. Such skills are considered foundational in interviewing frameworks such as the PEACE model (Clarke & Milne, 2016) and information-gathering approaches to investigative interviewing (Meissner et al., 2015; Meissner et al., 2017). There is also strong evidence for the efficacy of such skills. Active listening can both facilitate admissions in investigative interviews and enhance the effectiveness of certain interviewing strategies (e.g., rational arguments; Beune et al., 2009, 2011). Studies have also demonstrated that active listening improves relational engagement with the interviewer and facilitates confessions from guilty suspects (Cleary & Bull, 2018; Kebbel et al., 2006; Wachi et al., 2016).

Conversational rapport tactics, drawn from the motivational interviewing literature (Miller & Rolnick, 2012), have been shown to be effective in gaining a subject's cooperation and mitigating resistance (Alison et al., 2013; Alison et al., 2014). In particular, use of the OARS questioning approach—Open-ended questions, Affirmations (i.e., statements that highlight the subject's constructive statements, attributes, or experiences), Reflections (i.e., repeating a word or phrase offered by the subject, absent judgment or confrontation), and Summaries (i.e., a concise, yet detailed, review of what the subject has said)—can increase perceptions of rapport and indirectly facilitate the disclosure of information (Brimbal et al., 2021).

TACTICS FOR DEMONSTRATING EMPATHY

Active listening skills have also been associated with demonstrations of empathy (or empathic listening; Miller, 2018; Rogers, 1951). Studies suggest that people seek to be recognized, understood, and humanized by others. *Empathy* can be described as a process through which we let others know that we authentically see them and understand their situation. It broadly refers to considering a situation from another individual's perspective and involves understanding and attempting to humanize them (their thoughts, feelings, goals, beliefs, etc.). While sympathy imparts concern or even pity ("I feel bad for you"), empathy displays nonjudgmental acceptance of—although not necessarily agreement with—an individual's situation ("I see what you see, because I am here with you").

Scholars have systematically examined the use and function of empathy in investigative interviews. Dando and Oxburgh (2016) proposed a distinction between offering empathic comfort (e.g., providing a break, offering a tissue, and allowing a phone call) and empathic understanding (e.g., acknowledging the difficulty of the moment, paraphrasing a subject's words, and offering emotional labels). They found that female interviewers were more likely to engage in empathy and that empathic opportunities were often missed by investigators. Although the use of empathy may not directly relate to information elicitation in investigative interviews (Oxburgh et al., 2012), interviewers who demonstrate empathy are more likely to use appropriate and productive questioning tactics (open-ended and unbiased approaches) that yield greater information (Oxburgh et al., 2014). When incorporated within a framework for rapport-based interviewing, displays of empathy have been shown to facilitate perceptions of rapport and to increase the disclosure of information (Alison et al., 2013; Baker-Eck et al., 2021).

Research suggests that people prefer to interact with others who verify their beliefs about who they are and that people will actively seek feedback from others that confirms their self-concept (Swann Jr., 2011). To the extent that a person receives such confirmatory feedback (i.e., self-verification), they are more likely to reveal information and engage in further interactions with the listener. People also seek to maintain a positive self-concept or sense of self-integrity (Leary, 2007) and will respond positively to individuals who express positive things about their identity (i.e., self-affirmation). Such processes can be useful in an interview context to demonstrate empathy and are effective in facilitating information disclosure (Davis et al., 2016) and reducing interrogative suggestibility (Szpitalak & Polczyk, 2020).

Finally, a key element of empathy is the effort to adopt another person's perspective. While perspective-taking has become a popular theme, a far more effective approach involves *perspective-getting* (i.e., actively inquiring about another person's perspective; Eyal et al., 2018). Also known as *evocation* in the motivational interviewing literature (Miller & Rollnick, 2012), perspective-getting allows an interviewer both to demonstrate an empathic intent and to effectively draw out a subject's thoughts, emotions, and perceptions, therein facilitating rapport and mitigating resistance (Alison et al., 2013; Alison et al., 2014).

Informational Approaches That Increase Disclosure and Enhance Credibility Assessment: Informational approaches to investigative interviewing, discussed below, have been shown to significantly increase the disclosure of information by interview subjects and to improve the detection of deception.

PRODUCTIVE QUESTIONING TACTICS

Given prior research on the frailties of human memory and the extent to which biased and leading questions can induce both false memories and false confessions, scholars have turned to the evaluation of questioning tactics that can reduce bias and facilitate information disclosure (Baldwin, 1993). Questioning approaches have been studied in interviews of both children (Sternberg et al., 2002) and adults (Griffiths et al., 2011; Milne & Bull, 1999), leading to the development of best-practice protocols and the identification of productive questioning tactics.

With respect to children, research has demonstrated the importance of narrative-based, open-ended questions for increasing both the quantity and accuracy of information recalled (see Dickinson et al., this volume). A structured interview protocol for children, developed by researchers at the National Institute for Child Health and Human Development (NICHD), translates the available research into an evidence-based set of questioning tactics for use in everyday practice (Lamb et al., 2007). The NICHD protocol has been well studied and shown to be effective in both increasing the number of open-ended questions (and therein central details recalled by child interview subjects) and reducing the use of suggestive or leading questioning prompts (Benia et al., 2015).

Research on adult interview subjects has similarly suggested that interviewers frequently rely upon direct, closed-ended, and suggestive or leading questions (Fisher et al., 1987; Snook et al., 2012). As an alternative to such approaches, scholars have shown that interviewers can be trained to engage in more productive interviewing tactics that include open-ended questions and structured questioning strategies (i.e., a "funnel approach" that moves from broad open-ended questions to probes and appropriate closed-ended questions). Such productive interviewing tactics both increase the amount of information obtained and reduce the likelihood of bias (Griffiths et al., 2011; Soukara et al., 2009).

MNEMONIC QUESTIONING TACTICS

The use of productive questions can facilitate disclosure, but subjects may yet be limited in their ability to recall information even following multiple open-ended prompts. Mnemonic approaches can facilitate the cueing of memory (Tulving, 1983) over successive attempts at recall using a variety of approaches (Geiselman et al., 1986). For example, interviewers can alter the temporal nature of recall (e.g., asking subjects to recall in reverse order), change the perspective of the recall attempt (e.g., recall from another's perspective), offer a structured set of cues (e.g., recall events based upon a family tree, a calendar, or a timeline of key events; Hope et al., 2013), or ask subjects to retrieve using a more compatible sensory modality (e.g., drawing a sketch or creating a map; Vrij et al., 2018). The introduction of such mnemonic questioning approaches has been shown to substantially increase the information reported by interview subjects after having seemingly exhausted their initial free recall (Leins et al., 2014). Varying the presentation of such mnemonics across multiple retrieval opportunities can also significantly increase the amount of information recalled (Gilbert & Fisher, 2006).

Retrieval can also be enhanced by assisting the context-dependent nature of memory (Tulving & Thompson, 1973). Specifically, when the context encountered at encoding is matched at retrieval, contextual cues become available that facilitate recall. While reinstating the physical context has been shown to be increase recall, instructing interview subjects to mentally reinstate the context can produce comparable benefits (Smith & Vela, 2001).

Asking interview subjects to close their eyes has also been shown to improve memory recall for both children and adults (Natali et al., 2012; Vredeveldt & Penrod, 2013), likely because it facilitates concentration and reduces cross-modality distraction (Perfect et al., 2011).

These and other mnemonic questioning approaches have been combined into an evidence-based interview protocol by Fisher and Geiselman (1992) known as the Cognitive Interview. The CI is likely the most studied interview protocol, to include samples of child, adult, and elderly interview subjects across experimental, naturalistic, and field studies, and in contexts involving interviews with victims, witnesses, sources, and suspects (see Goldfarb & Fisher, this volume). The CI has been repeatedly shown to be effective in eliciting more information (without reducing the accuracy of such information; Memon et al., 2010). Further, the mnemonic components of the protocol have been shown to facilitate assessments of credibility (Mac Giolla & Luke, 2021).

STRATEGIC QUESTIONING TACTICS

Scholars have begun to design strategic questioning tactics to both effectively respond to the resistance strategies that interview subjects present and facilitate assessments of credibility (see Vrij et al., this volume). For example, evidence disclosure techniques have been developed to effectively challenge the information management strategies that suspects bring to an interview—namely, attempts to avoid providing certain information or to escape/deny their involvement. Withholding evidence until late in an interview and gradually presenting evidence to the interview subject has been shown to effectively reveal statement-evidence inconsistencies. These "strategic use of evidence" (Hartwig et al., 2005) and "tactical use of evidence" (Dando et al., 2013) approaches can substantially enhance an interviewer's ability to discriminate between deceptive and truth-telling subjects (Oleszkiewicz & Watson, 2021).

Another approach to countering the information management strategy of a subject has been drawn from the successes of a World War II German Luftwaffe (Air Force) interrogator named Hanns Scharff. He was widely known for his affable approach, but little was understood about his questioning methods until recently. Through systematic research and field validation (Granhag et al., 2016), the Scharff technique has proven to be an effective interrogation approach, particularly when questioning multiple subjects from the same organization. Beyond his storied friendly demeanor, Scharff appears to have employed four interrelated tactics: (1) *do not press for information* (lengthy narratives are offered in place of explicit questions); (2) *offer an illusion of knowing-it-all* (the narratives include previously known or suspected information); (3) *use of confirmations/disconfirmations* (rather than asking direct questions, the interviewer presents claims within the narrative the subject might confirm or disconfirm); and (4) *ignore new information* (important new information obtained from the subject via confirmations or disconfirmations is treated as already known or of little value). Studies confirm that the Scharff technique not only increases the amount of new information obtained but also leads the subject to underestimate the amount of information they revealed to the interviewer (Luke, 2021).

Finally, scholars have examined the value of asking unexpected questions regarding issues the subject would likely know if the account were truthful, including requesting spatial or temporal details or inviting greater specificity of information related to the experience. These inquiries are designed to counter a subject's strategy for preparing a simple and repeatable narrative that responds to anticipated questions. Research has demonstrated that asking unanticipated questions can lead to differences in the amount and type of information provided by deceptive versus truth-telling subjects (Vrij et al., 2009), and therein facilitate judgments of credibility (Mac Giolla & Luke, 2021). Similarly, the Verifiability Approach evaluates the frequency of (un)verifiable details offered by a subject and therein leverages the strategies used by deceptive versus truthful subjects (Nahari et al., 2014).

An Adaptive and Cyclical Interview Process

Investigative interviewing doctrine both in the United States and abroad remains mired in a false dilemma: should it be based on what is demonstrably effective in the real world (which is inherently complex) or on what can be effectively taught to a large number of entry-level practitioners (material that is essentially simple and linear)? There is perhaps a no more graphic illustration of a doctrine driven primarily by training requirements, and unchanged by its inability to meet the challenges posed by real-world requirements, than the frameworks set forth in the US Army Field Manual on interrogation (2006) and the accusatorial approach widely advocated for law enforcement (Inbau et al., 2013). Despite significant scholarship in the behavioral sciences that has unfolded in recent decades, the concepts and strategies described in these frameworks have remained fundamentally unchanged. They offer a linear, control-oriented, reactive model of interviewing that can be successfully taught to large numbers of trainees. Such linear-based models are founded on the erroneous premise that interviews have a defined beginning and end, that they consistently move forward through relatively disconnected phases, and that they are independent of their environment. Research suggests that the world, and importantly the interview context, is not so simple. Further, the majority of the recommended strategies in these approaches are unsupported by science and many have actually proven counterproductive (Brandon et al., 2019b; Vrij et al., 2017).

In contrast, the model presented here suggests that engagement between an interviewer and a subject represents a complex adaptive system involving a dynamic set of behaviors that emerge across a series of interactions (Steels, 2006). The model is adaptive to the variety of interviewing contexts and subject populations. It proposes a nonlinear interview process that incorporates the cycling of subsystems that respond to one another. Specifically, relational approaches to interviewing recognize the circularity of human interactions and place the principle of cooperation at the forefront of an interviewer's strategy, encouraging them to effectively understand and mitigate resistance as it occurs. When cooperation is demonstrated, informational approaches can be engaged to elicit reliable information from memory, leading to the disclosure of details that are of investigative or intelligence interest. This creates the opportunity for successfully assessing credibility via strategic questioning strategies that can be adaptively applied given an appropriate context and goal. Importantly, application of these interview strategies can be described as dynamic and cyclical, recognizing that investigators must often address and mitigate resistance in an interview context by utilizing relational strategies before reengaging informational strategies that facilitate disclosure. This cycle of resistance →cooperation →disclosure occurs numerous times throughout an interview and is likely a function of the specific topics addressed in an interview over time.

Moving Forward

It is clear that scholars have made significant progress in both understanding the challenges of conducting investigative interviews and developing effective, science-based approaches that encourage cooperation via rapport and trust, elicit accurate and reliable memories, and facilitate assessments of credibility. Our review of the literature suggests that three clusters of research topics have been engaged by scholars—interviewing cooperative individuals, interviewing resistant individuals, and interviewing to detect deception. Although there are some associations between these research clusters, such links could arguably be strengthened. For example, scholars in recent years have demonstrated the value of mnemonic questioning approaches for improving judgments of credibility. Research has also shown that the utility of rapport and trust-building tactics is in developing cooperation (and mitigating resistance), thereby indirectly supporting information disclosure objectives. Advancing practice will require greater integration across these domains to support the refinement of comprehensive models of investigative interviewing.

Further research is needed to better understand the variety of psychological factors that influence investigative interviewing. For example, we have limited knowledge regarding the important role of cross-cultural variation in tactics used for developing rapport and trust (Giebels & Taylor, 2012), in the ways that memory is shaped by culture (Wang, 2021), and in the extent to which cues to deception may vary across such contexts (Taylor et al., 2015). Recent years have seen a surge in scholarship on interpreted interviews (Goodman-Delahunty & Howes, 2019; Vrij et al., 2018) and assessments of credibility when a secondary or foreign language is presented (Elliott & Leach, 2016; Evans et al., 2013). Given increased migration and calls for international investigations, further research is needed to assess the effects of interpretation on rapport development, memory elicitation, and credibility assessment. More research is also needed on the effects of repeated interviews, including the influence of changing interviewers over time (La Rooy et al., 2010; Oleszkiewicz et al., 2017), as well as interviews for repeated events (e.g., victimization over time; Price & Connolly, 2021; Kontogianni et al., 2021). Finally, the COVID-19 pandemic has encouraged a move to video-based interviewing for many investigations (see Dickinson, et al., this volume)—while the psychological processes involved likely transcend the in-person context, further research is necessary to assess the impact of such a context change (Brown et al., 2021).

Influencing Policy and Practice

Over the past two decades, we have witnessed a considerable shift in investigative interviewing practices around the world. Child forensic interviewing practices have likely been most impacted by psycholegal scholarship, with specialized training required in many US jurisdictions and increased use of best practices around the world (La Rooy et al., 2015). In contrast, best practices for interviewing adult witnesses and victims, including the application of the Cognitive Interview, have not seen such wide adoption. The move to evidence-based investigative interviews of suspects and intelligence sources has proven even more challenging. Introduction of the PEACE framework in England and Wales was key to providing an initial alternative to accusatorial practices that have been shown to elicit false confessions (Meissner et al., 2014). Today, other countries, including the United States and Canada where accusatorial practices have been pervasive, have begun to shift practice toward a rapport-based, information-gathering approach (Meissner et al., 2017; Snook et al., 2010).

Still, significant barriers remain in the adoption of science-based investigative interviewing practices. Among the most vexing is what scholars refer to as the "toolbox approach" (Snook et al., 2020), a form of resistance to organizational change in which practitioners engage the piecemeal adoption of some evidence-based practices while retaining the use of problematic customary practices. In this context, supporting change requires that scholars offer a holistic model of investigative interviewing that negates any reliance upon accusatorial practices—one that can address resistance to cooperation absent the coercive strategies that can lead to false confessions and that incorporate strategies for reducing the influence of investigative biases and problematic questioning approaches.

The development and adoption of PEACE in England and Wales was the product of a collaboration between practitioners and scholars (Clarke & Milne, 2016). Similar collaborations have informed the science-based model of investigative interviewing presented in this chapter, including many of the techniques and efficacy studies conducted in support of the model (see Brandon et al., 2019a; Meissner et al., 2017). Such collaborations are critical for creating policy and implementing evidence-based practices (see Bornstein & Meissner, this volume), and have long been advocated within the investigative interviewing literature (Meissner et al., 2010). The successful translation of research to practice will require that scholars engage with practitioners to move research from the laboratory to the field.

Finally, whereas many countries have grappled with the transition to evidence-based interviewing practices, a recent collaboration between scholars, practitioners, and policymakers led to the development of a universal protocol for investigative interviewing

(Mendez et al., 2021). Designed as a set of six principles that offer a normative, evidence-based framework for investigative interviewing, the protocol was drafted primarily for policymakers and authorities responsible for developing policies and practices. The objective was to facilitate a global transition from the use of torture and other coercive interrogation tactics to the use of science-based investigative interviewing tactics. Realization of this goal will require continued advocacy, collaboration, and scholarship that effectively translates research to practice.

References

Abbe, A., & Brandon, S. E. (2013). The role of rapport in investigative interviewing: A review. *Journal of Investigative Psychology and Offender Profiling, 10*(3), 237–249.

Alison, L. J., Alison, E., Noone, G., Elntib, S., & Christiansen, P. (2013). Why tough tactics fail and rapport gets results: Observing Rapport-Based Interpersonal Techniques (ORBIT) to generate useful information from terrorists. *Psychology, Public Policy, and Law, 19*(4), 411–431.

Alison, L., Alison, E., Noone, G., Elntib, S., Waring, S., & Christiansen, P. (2014). The efficacy of rapport-based techniques for minimizing counter-interrogation tactics amongst a field sample of terrorists. *Psychology, Public Policy, and Law, 20*(4), 421–430.

Ask, K., & Fahsing, I. (2019). Investigative decision making. In R. Bull & I. Blandon-Gitlin (Eds.), *The Routledge international handbook of legal and investigative psychology* (pp. 84–101). Routledge.

Ask, K., & Grahnhag, P. A. (2005). Motivational sources of confirmation bias in criminal investigations: The need for cognitive closure. *Journal of Investigative Psychology and Offender Profiling, 2*(1), 43–63.

Baker-Eck, B., Bull, R., & Walsh, D. (2021). Investigative empathy: Five types of cognitive empathy in a field study of investigative interviews with suspects of sexual offences. *Investigative Interviewing: Research & Practice, 11*(1), 28–39.

Baldwin, J. (1993). Police interview techniques. *British Journal of Criminology, 33*(3), 325–352.

Benia, L. R., Hauck-Filho, N., Dillenburg, M., & Stein, L. M. (2015). The NICHD investigative interview protocol: A meta-analytic review. *Journal of Child Sexual Abuse, 24*(3), 259–279.

Beune, K., Giebels, E., Adair, W. L., Fennis, B. M., & Van Der Zee, K. I. (2011). Strategic sequences in police interviews and the importance of order and cultural fit. *Criminal Justice and behavior, 38*(9), 934–954.

Beune, K., Giebels, E., & Sanders, K. (2009). Are you talking to me? Influencing behaviour and culture in police interviews. *Psychology, Crime & Law, 15*(7), 597–617.

Blasbalg, U., Hershkowitz, I., & Karni-Visel, Y. (2018). Support, reluctance, and production in child abuse investigative interviews. *Psychology, Public Policy, and Law, 24*(4), 518–527.

Brandon, S. E., Arthur, J. C., Ray, D. G., Meissner, C. A., Kleinman, S. M., Russano, M. B., & Wells, S. (2019a). The high-value Detainee Interrogation Group (HIG): Inception, evolution, and outcomes. In M. A. Staal & S. C. Harvey (Eds.), *Operational psychology: A new field to support national security and public safety* (pp. 263–286). ABC-CLIO.

Brandon, S. E., Kleinman, S. M., & Arthur, J. C. (2019b). A scientific perspective on the 2006 US Army Field Manual 2–22.3. In M. A. Staal & S. C. Harvey (Eds.), *Operational psychology: A new field to support national security and public safety* (pp. 287–326). ABC-CLIO.

Brimbal, L., Dianiska, R. E., Swanner, J. K., & Meissner, C. A. (2019). Enhancing cooperation and disclosure by manipulating affiliation and developing rapport in investigative interviews. *Psychology, Public Policy, and Law, 25*(2), 107–115.

Brimbal, L., Meissner, C. A., Kleinman, S. M., Phillips, E. L., Atkinson, D. J., Dianiska, R. E., Rothweiler, J. N., Oleszkiewicz, S., & Jones, M. S. (2021). Evaluating the benefits of a rapport-based approach to investigative interviews: A training study with law enforcement investigators. *Law and Human Behavior, 45*(1), 55–67.

Brown, D., Walker, D., & Godden, E. (2021). Tele-forensic interviewing to elicit children's evidence—Benefits, risks, and practical considerations. *Psychology, Public Policy, and Law, 27*(1), 17–29.

Bull, R., & Rachlew, A. (2020). Investigative interviewing: From England to Norway and beyond. In S. J. Barela, M. Fallon, & G. Gaggioli (Eds.), *Interrogation and torture* (1st ed., pp. 171–196). Oxford University Press.

Clarke C., & Milne, R. (2016). Interviewing suspects in England and Wales. In D. W. Walsh, G. E. Oxburgh, A. D. Redlich, & T. Myklebust (Eds.), *International developments and practices in investigative interviewing and interrogation: Volume 2. Suspects* (pp. 101–118). Routledge.

Cleary, H. M. D., & Bull, R. (2018). Jail inmates' perspectives on police interrogation. *Psychology, Crime & Law, 25*, 157–170.

Collins, N. L., & Miller, L. C. (1994). Self-disclosure and liking: A meta-analytic review. *Psychological Bulletin, 116*(3), 457–475.

Dando, C. J., Bull, R., Ormerod, T. C., & Sandham, A. L. (2013). Helping to sort the liars from the truth-tellers: The gradual revelation of information during investigative interviews. *Legal & Criminological Psychology, 20*(1), 114–128.

Dando, C. J., & Oxburgh, G. E. (2016). Empathy in the field: Towards a taxonomy of empathic communication in information gathering interviews with suspected sex offenders. *European Journal of Psychology Applied of Legal Context, 8*(1), 27–33.

Davis, D., Soref, A., Villalobos, J. G., & Mikulincer, M. (2016). Priming states of mind can affect disclosure of threatening self-information: Effects of self-affirmation, mortality salience, and attachment orientations. *Law and Human Behavior, 40*(4), 351–361.

Dianiska, R. E., Swanner, J. K., Brimbal, L., & Meissner, C. A. (2021). Using disclosure, common ground, and verification to develop rapport and elicit information. *Psychology, Public Policy, & Law, 27*(3), 341–353.

Duke, M. C., Wood, J. M., Bollin, B., Scullin, M., & LaBianca, J. (2018). Development of the Rapport Scales for Investigative Interviews and Interrogations (RS3i), Interviewee Version. *Psychology, Public Policy, and Law, 24*(1), 64–79.

Elliott, E., & Leach, A.-M. (2016). You must be lying because I don't understand you: Language proficiency and lie detection. *Journal of Experimental Psychology: Applied, 22*, 488–499.

Evans, J. R., Houston, K. A., Meissner, C. A., Ross, A. B., LaBianca, J. R., Woestehoff, S. A., & Kleinman, S. M. (2014). An empirical evaluation of intelligence-gathering interrogation techniques from the United States Army field manual. *Applied Cognitive Psychology, 28*(6), 867–875.

Evans, J. R., Michael, S. W., Meissner, C. A., & Brandon, S. E. (2013). Validating a new assessment method for deception detection: Introducing a psychologically based credibility assessment tool. *Journal of Applied Research in Memory and Cognition, 2*, 33–41.

Eyal, T., Steffel, M., & Epley, N. (2018). Perspective mistaking: Accurately understanding the mind of another requires getting perspective, not taking perspective. *Journal of Personality and Social Psychology, 114*, 547–571.

Fisher, R. P., & Geiselman, R. E. (1992). *Memory-enhancing techniques for investigative interviewing.* C. C. Thomas.

Fisher, R. P., Geiselman, R. E., & Raymond, D. S. (1987). Critical analysis of police interview techniques. *Journal of Police Science and Administration, 15*(3), 177–185.

Fisher, R. P., Schreiber Compo, N., Rivard, J., & Hirn, D. (2014). Interviewing witnesses. In T. Perfect & S. Lindsay (Eds.), *The SAGE handbook of applied memory* (1st ed., pp. 559–578). SAGE.

Gabbert, F., Hope, L., Luther, K., Wright, G., Ng, M., & Oxburgh, G. (2021). Exploring the use of rapport in professional information-gathering contexts by systematically mapping the evidence base. *Applied Cognitive Psychology, 35*(2), 329–341.

Geiselman, R. E., Fisher, R. P., MacKinnon, D. P. and Holland, H. L. (1986). Enhancement of eyewitness memory with the cognitive interview. *American Journal of Psychology, 99*(3), 385–401.

Giebels, E., & Taylor, P. J. (2012). Tuning in to the right wavelength: The importance of culture for effective crisis negotiation. In M. St-Yves & P. I. Collins (Eds.), *The psychology of crisis intervention for law enforcement officers* (pp. 277–298). Editions Yvon Blais.

Gilbert, J. A., & Fisher, R. P. (2006). The effects of varied retrieval cues on reminiscence in eyewitness memory. *Applied Cognitive Psychology, 20*(6), 723–739.

Goodman-Delahunty, J., & Howes, L. M. (2016). Social persuasion to develop rapport in high-stakes interviews: Qualitative analyses of Asian-Pacific practices. *Policing and Society, 26*(3), 270–290.

Goodman-Delahunty, J., & Howes, L. M. (2019). High-stakes interviews and rapport development: practitioners' perceptions of interpreter impact. *Policing and Society, 29*, 100–117.

Gordon, T. (1975). *P.E.T.: Parent Effectiveness Training.* New American Library.

Granhag, P. A., Kleinman, S. M., & Oleszkiewicz, S. (2016). The Scharff technique: On how to effectively elicit intelligence from human sources. *International Journal of Intelligence and CounterIntelligence, 29*(1), 132–150.

Griffiths, A., Milne, B., & Cherryman, J. (2011). Question of control the formulation of suspect and witness interview question strategies by advanced interviewers. *International Journal of Police Science & Management, 13*(3), 255–267.

Gudjonsson, G. H. (1997). *The Gudjonsson Suggestibility Scales Manual.* Psychology Press.

Gudjonsson, G. H. (2010). Psychological vulnerabilities during police interviews. Why are they important? *Legal and Criminological Psychology, 15*(2), 161–175.

Guyll, M., Yang, Y., Madon, S., Smalarz, L., & Lannin, D. G. (2019). Mobilization and resistance in response to interrogation threat. *Law and Human Behavior, 43*(4), 307–318.

Hartwig, M., Granhag, P. A., Strömwall, L. A., & Vrij, A. (2005). Detecting deception via strategic disclosure of evidence. *Law and Human Behavior, 29*(4), 469–484.

Hershkowitz, I., Orbach, Y., Lamb, M. E., Sternberg, K. J., & Horowitz, D. (2006). Dynamics of forensic interviews with suspected abuse victims who do not disclose abuse. *Child Abuse and Neglect, 30*(7), 753–769.

Hope, L., Mullis, R., & Gabbert, F. (2013). Who? What? When? Using a timeline technique to facilitate recall of a complex event. *Journal of Applied Research in Memory and Cognition, 2*(1), 20–24.

Inbau, F. E., Reid, J. E., Buckley, J. P., & Jayne, B. C. (2013). *Criminal interrogation and confessions* (5th ed.). Jones & Bartlett Learning.

Kassin, S. M., Drizin, S. A., Grisso, T., Gudjonsson, G. H., Leo, R. A., & Redlich, A. D. (2010). Police-induced confessions: Risk factors and recommendations. *Law and Human Behavior, 34*(1), 3–38.

Kassin, S. M., Meissner, C. A., & Norwick, R. J. (2005). "I'd know a false confession if I saw one": A comparative study of college students and police investigators. *Law and Human Behavior, 29*(2), 211–227.

Katz, C., Hershkowitz, I., Malloy, L. C., Lamb, M. E., Atabaki, A., & Spindler, S. (2012). Non-verbal behavior of children who disclose or do not disclose child abuse in investigative interviews. *Child Abuse and Neglect, 36*(1), 12–20.

Kebbell, M. R., Hurren, E., & Mazerolle, P. (2006). *An investigation into the effective and ethical interviewing of suspected sex offenders.* Report to the Criminological Research Council and Crime and Misconduct Commission. Griffith University.

Kelly, C. E., Russano, M. B., Miller, J. C., & Redlich, A. D. (2019). On the road (to admission): Engaging suspects with minimization. *Psychology, Public Policy, and Law, 25*(3), 166–180.

Kieckhaefer, J. M., Vallano, J. P., & Schreiber Compo, N. (2014). Examining the positive effects of rapport building: When and why does rapport building benefit adult eyewitness memory? *Memory, 22*(8), 1010–1023.

Knowles, E. S. & Riner, D. D. (2007). Omega approaches to persuasion: Overcoming resistance. In A. R. Pratkanis (Ed.) *The Science of social influence: Advances and future progress* (1st ed., pp. 82–114). Psychology Press.

Kontogianni, F., Rubinova, E., Hope, L., Taylor, P. J., Vrij, A., & Gabbert, F. (2021). Facilitating recall and particularisation of repeated events in adults using a multi-method interviewing format. *Memory, 29*(4), 471–485.

Lamb, M. E., Orbach, Y., Hershkowitz, I., Esplin, P. W., & Horowitz, D. (2007). A structured forensic interview protocol improves the quality and informativeness of investigative interviews with children: A review of research using the NICHD Investigative Interview Protocol. *Child Abuse & Neglect, 31*(11–12), 1201–1231.

La Rooy, D., Brubacher, S. P., Aromäki-Stratos, A., Cyr, M., Hershkowitz, I., Korkman, J., Myklebust, T., Naka, M., Peixoto, C. E., Roberts, K. P., Stewart, H., & Lamb, M. E. (2015). The NICHD protocol: A review of an internationally-used evidence-based tool for training child forensic interviewers. *Journal of Criminological Research, Policy and Practice, 1,* 76–89.

La Rooy, D., Katz, C., Malloy, L. C., & Lamb, M. E. (2010). Do we need to rethink guidance on repeated interviews? *Psychology, Public Policy, and Law, 16,* 373–392.

Leary, M. R. (2007). Motivational and emotional aspects of the self. *Annual Review of Psychology, 58*(1), 317–344.

Leins, D. A., Fisher, R. P., Pludwinski, L., Rivard, J., & Robertson, B. (2014). Interview protocols to facilitate human intelligence sources' recollections of meetings. *Applied Cognitive Psychology, 28*(6), 926–935.

Luke, T. J. (2021). A meta-analytic review of experimental tests of the interrogation technique of Hanns Joachim Scharff. *Applied Cognitive Psychology*, *35*(2), 360–373.

Mac Giolla, E., & Luke, T. J. (2021). Does the cognitive approach to lie detection improve the accuracy of human observers? *Applied Cognitive Psychology*, *35*(2), 385–392.

Matsumoto, D., & Hwang, H. C. (2018). Social influence in investigative interviews: The effects of reciprocity. *Applied Cognitive Psychology*, *32*(2), 163–170.

McAllister, D. J. (1995). Affect- and cognition-based trust as foundations for interpersonal cooperation in organizations. *Academy of Management Journal*, *38*, 24–59.

Meissner, C. A. (2021). "What works?" Systematic reviews and meta-analyses of the investigative interviewing research literature. *Applied Cognitive Psychology*, *35*(2), 322–328.

Meissner, C. A., Hartwig, M., & Russano, M. B. (2010). The need for a positive psychological approach and collaborative effort for improving practice in the interrogation room. *Law & Human Behavior*, *34*, 43–45.

Meissner, C. A., & Kassin, S. M. (2002). "He's guilty!": Investigator bias in judgments of truth and deception. *Law and Human Behavior*, *26*(5), 469–480.

Meissner, C. A., & Kassin, S. M. (2004). "You're guilty, so just confess!" In G. D. Lassiter (Ed.) *Interrogations, confessions, and entrapment: Perspectives in law & psychology* (1st ed., pp. 85–106). Springer.

Meissner, C. A., Kelly, C. E., & Woestehoff, S. A. (2015). Improving the effectiveness of suspect interrogations. *Annual Review of Law and Social Science*, *11*(1), 211–233.

Meissner, C. A., Redlich, A. D., Michael, S. W., Evans, J. R., Camilletti, C. R., Bhatt, S., & Brandon, S. (2014). Accusatorial and information-gathering interrogation methods and their effects on true and false confessions: A meta-analytic review. *Journal of Experimental Criminology*, *10*(4), 459–486.

Meissner, C. A., Surmon-Böhr, F., Oleszkiewicz, S., & Alison, L. J. (2017). Developing an evidence-based perspective on interrogation: A review of the U.S. government's high-value detainee interrogation group research program. *Psychology, Public Policy, and Law*, *23*(4), 438–457.

Memon, A., Meissner, C. A., & Fraser, J. (2010). The Cognitive Interview: A meta-analytic review and study space analysis of the past 25 years. *Psychology, Public Policy, and Law*, *16*(4), 340–372.

Mendez, J. E., Thomson, M., Bull, R., Hinestroza, V., Namoradze, A. Z., Oxburgh, G., Perez Sales, P., Rachlew, A., Rytter, T., Schollum, M., Shaeffer, R., Ssekindi, R., Stein, L. M., Tait, S. (Contribs.). (2021). *Principles on effective interviewing for investigations and information gathering* [Online publication]. Norwegian Centre for Human Rights. https://www.apt.ch/en/resources/publications/new-principles-effective-interviewing-investigations-and-information

Miller, W. R. (2018). *Listening well: The art of empathic understanding*. Wipf and Stock.

Miller, W. R., & Rollnick, S. (2012). *Motivational interviewing: Preparing people for change* (3rd ed.). Guilford Press.

Milne, R., & Bull, R. (1999). *Investigative interviewing: Psychology and practice*. John Wiley & Sons.

Münsterberg, H. (1908). *On the witness stand*. Doubleday.

Nahari, G., Vrij, A., & Fisher, R. P. (2014). Exploiting liars' verbal strategies by examining the verifiability of details. *Legal and Criminological Psychology*, *19*(2), 227–239.

Narchet, F. M., Meissner, C. A., & Russano, M. B. (2011). Modeling the influence of investigator bias on the elicitation of true and false confessions. *Law and Human Behavior*, *35*(6), 452–465.

Natali, V., Marucci, F. S., & Mastroberardino, S. (2012). Long-term memory effects of eye closure on children eyewitness testimonies. *Applied cognitive psychology*, *26*(5), 730–736.

Nickerson, R. S. (1998). Confirmation bias: A ubiquitous phenomenon in main guises. *Review of General Psychology*, *2*(2), 175–220.

O'Brien, B. (2009). Prime suspect: An examination of factors that aggravate and counteract confirmation bias in criminal investigations. *Psychology, Public Policy, and Law*, *15*(4), 315–334.

Oleszkiewicz, S., & Granhag, P. A. (2019). Establishing cooperation and eliciting information: Semi-cooperative sources' affective resistance and cognitive strategies. In R. Bull & I. Blandón-Gitlin (Eds.) *The Routledge international handbook of legal and investigative psychology* (1st ed., pp. 255–267). Routledge Taylor & Francis Group.

Oleszkiewicz, S., Granhag, P. A., & Kleinman, S. M. (2017). Gathering human intelligence via repeated interviewing: Further empirical tests of the Scharff technique. *Psychology, Crime & Law*, *23*, 666–681.

Oleszkiewicz, S., & Watson, S. J. (2021). A meta-analytic review of the timing for disclosing evidence when interviewing suspects. *Applied Cognitive Psychology*, *35*(2), 342–359.

Otgaar, H., Schell-Leugers, J. M., Howe, M. L., Vilar, A. D. L. F., Houben, S. T., & Merckelbach, H. (2021). The link between suggestibility, compliance, and false confessions: A review using experimental and field studies. *Applied Cognitive Psychology, 35*(2), 445–455.

Oxburgh, G., Ost, J., & Cherryman, J. (2012). Police interviews with suspected child sex offenders: Does use of empathy and question type influence the amount of investigation relevant information obtained? *Psychology, Crime & Law, 18*(3), 259–273.

Oxburgh, G., Ost, J., Morris, P., & Cherryman, J. (2014). The impact of question type and empathy on police interviews with suspects of homicide, filicide and child sexual abuse. *Psychiatry, Psychology and Law, 21*(6), 903–917.

Perfect, T. J., Andrade, J., & Eagan, I. (2011). Eye closure reduces the cross-modal memory impairment caused by auditory distraction. *Journal of Experimental Psychology: Learning, Memory, and Cognition, 37*(4), 1008–1013

Pickrell, J. E., McDonald, D., Bernstein, D. M., & Loftus, E. F. (2016). Misinformation effect. In R. F. Pohl (Ed.), *Cognitive illusions: Intriguing phenomena in judgement, thinking and memory* (1st ed., pp. 406–423). Routledge.

Powell, M. B., Fisher, R. P., & Wright, R. (2005). Investigative interviewing. In N. Brewer & K. D. Williams (Eds.), *Psychology and law: An empirical perspective* (1st ed., pp. 11–42). Guildford Press.

Powell, M. B., Hughes-Scholes, C. H., & Sharman, S. J. (2012). Skill in interviewing reduces confirmation bias. *Journal of Investigative Psychology and Offender Profiling, 9*(1), 126–134.

Price, H., & Connolly, D. (2021). Children's memory for instances of repeated events: Applications to the experience of child victims and witnesses. In L. Baker-Ward, D. Bjorklund, & J. Coffman (Eds.), *The development of children's memory: The scientific contributions of Peter A. Ornstein* (pp. 115–131). Cambridge University Press.

Rogers, C. R. (1951). *Client-centered therapy*. Houghton-Mifflin.

Rogers, C. R., & Farson, R. E. (1957). *Active listening*. University of Chicago Industrial Relations Center.

Russano, M. B., Narchet, F. M., Kleinman, S. M., & Meissner, C. A. (2014). Structured interviews of experienced HUMINT interrogators. *Applied Cognitive Psychology, 28*(6), 847–859.

Rousseau, D. M., Sitkin, S. B., Burt, R. S., & Camerer, C. (1998). Not so different after all: A cross-discipline view of trust. *Academy of Management Review, 23*, 393.

Saywitz, K. J., Wells, C. R., Larson, R. P., & Hobbs, S. D. (2019). Effects of interviewer support on children's memory and suggestibility: Systematic review and meta-analyses of experimental research. *Trauma, Violence & Abuse, 20*(1), 22–39.

Shepherd, E. W. (1993). Resistance in interviews: The contribution of police perceptions and behaviour. *Issues in Criminological & Legal Psychology, 18*, 5–12.

Smith, S. M., & Vela, E. (2001). Environmental context-dependent memory: A review and meta-analysis. *Psychonomic Bulletin & Review, 8*(1), 203–220.

Snook, B., Barron, T., Fallon, L., Kassin, S. M., Kleinman, S., Leo, R. A., Meissner, C. A., Morello, L., Nirider, L. H., Redlich, A. D., & Trainum, J. L. (2021). Urgent issues and prospects in reforming interrogation practices in the United States and Canada. *Legal and Criminological Psychology, 26*(1), 1–24.

Snook, B., Eastwood, J., Stinson, M., Tedeschini, J., & House, J. C. (2010). Reforming investigative interviewing in Canada. *Canadian Journal of Criminology and Criminal Justice, 52*(2), 215–229.

Snook, B., Fahmy, W., Fallon, L., Lively, C. J., Luther, K., Meissner, C. A., Barron, T., & House, J. C. (2020). Challenges of a "toolbox" approach to investigative interview: A critical analysis of the RCMP's Phased Interview Model. *Psychology, Public Policy, & Law, 26*, 261–273.

Snook, B., Luther, K., Quinlan, H., & Milne, R. (2012). Let 'em talk! A field study of police questioning practices of suspects and accused persons. *Criminal Justice and Behavior, 39*(10), 1328–1339.

Soukara, S., Bull, R., Vrij, A., Turner, M., & Cherryman, J. (2009). What really happens in police interviews of suspects? Tactics and confessions. *Psychology, Crime & Law, 15*(6), 493–506.

Steels, L. (2006). Experiments on the emergence of human communication. *Trends in Cognitive Sciences, 10*, 347–349.

Sternberg, K. J., Lamb, M. E., Esplin, P. W., Orbach, Y., & Hershkowitz, I. (2002). Using a structure interview protocol to improve the quality of investigative interviews. In M. Eisen, J. A. Quas, & G. S. Goodman (Eds.) *Memory and suggestibility in the forensic interview* (1st ed., pp. 409–436). Erlbaum.

St-Yves, M. (2014). *Investigative interviewing: The essentials*. Carswell.

Swann Jr, W. B. (2011). Self-verification theory. In P. A. M. Van Lange, A. W. Kruglanski, & E. T. Higgins (Eds.), *Handbook of theories of social psychology* (2nd ed., pp. 23–42). SAGE.

Szpitalak, M., & Polczyk, R. (2020). Reducing interrogative suggestibility: The role of self-affirmation and positive feedback. *PLoS ONE, 15*(7), e0236088.

Taylor, P. J., Larner, S., Conchie, S. M., & Van der Zee, S. (2015). Cross-cultural deception detection. In P. A. Granhag, A. Vrij, & Verschuere, B. (Eds.), *Detecting deception: Current challenges and cognitive approaches* (pp. 175–201). John Wiley & Sons.

Tickle-Degnen, L., & Rosenthal, R. (1990). The nature of rapport and its nonverbal correlates. *Psychological Inquiry, 1*(4), 285–293.

Tulving, E. (1983). *Elements of episodic memory*. Oxford University Press.

Tulving, E., & Thomson, D. M. (1973). Encoding specificity and retrieval processes in episodic memory. *Psychological Review, 80*(5), 352–373.

US Department of the Army. (2006). *Human intelligence collector operations* (Field Manual 2-22.3). US Department of the Army.

Vallano, J. P., Evans, J. R., Schreiber Compo, N., & Kieckhaefer, J. M. (2015). Rapport-building during witness and suspect interviews: A survey of law enforcement. *Applied Cognitive Psychology, 29*(3), 369–380.

Vallano, J. P., & Schreiber Compo, N. (2015). Rapport-building with cooperative witnesses and criminal suspects: A theoretical and empirical review. *Psychology, Public Policy, and Law, 21*(1), 85.

van Eck, N.J., & Waltman, L. (2010). Software survey: VOSviewer, a computer program for bibliometric mapping. *Scientometrics, 84*, 523–538.

Vredeveldt, A., & Penrod, S. D. (2013). Eye-closure improves memory for a witnessed event under naturalistic conditions. *Psychology, Crime & Law, 19*(10), 893–905.

Vrij, A., Leal, S., Fisher, R. P., Mann, S., Dalton, G., Jo, E., Shabolta, A., Khaleeva, M., Granskaya, J., & Houston, K. (2018). Sketching as a technique to eliciting information and cues to deceit in interpreter-based interviews. *Journal of Applied Research in Memory and Cognition, 7*(2), 303–313.

Vrij, A., Leal, S., Granhag, P. A., Mann, S., Fisher, R. P., Hillman, J., & Sperry, K. (2009). Outsmarting the liars: The benefit of asking unanticipated questions. *Law and Human Behavior, 33*(1), 159–166.

Vrij, A., Meissner, C. A., Fisher, R. P., Kassin, S. M., Morgan III, C. A., & Kleinman, S. M. (2017). Psychological perspectives on interrogation. *Perspectives on Psychological Science, 12*(6), 927–955.

Wachi, T., Kuraishi, H., Watanabe, K., Otsuka, Y., Yokota, K., & Lamb, M. E. (2018). Effects of rapport building on confessions in an experimental paradigm. *Psychology, Public Policy, and Law, 24*(1), 36–47.

Wachi, T., Watanabe, K., Yokota, K., Otsuka, Y., & Lamb, M. E. (2016). Japanese suspect interviews, confessions, and related factors. *Journal of Police and Criminal Psychology, 31*(3), 217–227.

Wang, Q. (2021). The cultural foundation of human memory. *Annual Review of Psychology, 72*, 151–79.

Walsh, D., & Bull, R. (2012). Examining rapport in investigative interviews with suspects: Does its building and maintenance work? *Journal of Police and Criminal Psychology, 27*(1), 73–84.

Police Custody: A Legal Construct in Search of a Definition

Fabiana Alceste *and* Saul M. Kassin

Abstract

Police are only required to provide *Miranda* rights to criminal suspects during custodial interrogations. Other important legal safeguards, like the video recording of interrogations, are triggered by the same event. Over many decades, the US Supreme Court has refined the definition of police custody: when the totality of the objective circumstances of an interrogation are tantamount to arrest, as determined by a hypothetical reasonable person in the suspect's position. Until recently, however, this legal standard had not been subjected to the scrutiny of psychological and empirical testing. This chapter summarizes the case law surrounding the legal concept of custody, as well as the psychology of perceptions of custody and attributions of freedom. We discuss disparities in perceptions of custody between actors and observers, as well as between legal and lay participant groups. Finally, we make policy recommendations and identify avenues for future research.

Key Words: police custody, Miranda rights, criminal interrogations, custody, criminal interviews

Over the years, in light of the risk of wrongful convictions based on police-induced false confessions, two protective measures have been taken: the constitutionally framed requirement that police apprise suspects of their *Miranda* rights and the requirement passed in approximately half of all states that police video record the interrogation process in its entirety. Both protective measures are triggered by a state of "custodial interrogation."

In *Miranda v. Arizona,*[1] the US Supreme Court held that suspects who are in police custody have a constitutional right to silence and to counsel. In this landmark case, the Court ruled that any self-incriminating statements a defendant makes during a custodial interrogation may not be admitted as evidence unless certain safeguards were implemented—namely, that the suspect was apprised of these rights and then waived these rights voluntarily, knowingly, and intelligently. If these criteria are met, a confession taken from the suspect is admissible in court; if not, the confession is excluded.

---

[1] Miranda v. Arizona, 384 U.S. 436 (1966).

Over the years, a good deal of empirical research has examined the language of *Miranda* warnings, the extent to which juveniles and adults understand these rights and how to implement them, and whether these safeguards protect innocents who are accused and inclined to waive their rights from the risk of a coerced false confession (e.g., see Kassin et al., 2020; Smalarz et al., 2016; Weisselberg, 2017).

Initially, the Court's *Miranda* ruling was met by intense criticism from law enforcement officials, prosecutors, and "law-and-order" politicians who argued that criminals would routinely invoke their rights and escape prosecution (e.g., Cassell, 1996). It is now clear, however, that these dreaded effects never materialized. In fact, as a result of consistently high waiver rates as well as several post-*Miranda* rulings that have eroded the warning and waiver requirements, research has cast serious doubt as whether *Miranda* has had any protective effects. Hence, White (2001) complained of *Miranda*'s waning protection; Weisselberg (2008) "mourned" the death of *Miranda*, noting that it now functions as a safe harbor for police; and Kamisar (1962) concluded that *Miranda* has been "downsized and weakened in various ways" (p. 1021).

Miranda's failure can be seen most directly in the discovery of shocking numbers of police-induced false confessions taken in the United States after 1966. Although a prevalence rate cannot be calculated, two national databases provide informative data. As of mid-2021, the Innocence Project (IP) reported that false confessions contributed to 28 percent of the first 375 postconviction DNA exonerations in the United States (www.innocenceproject.org/). Within the National Registry of Exonerations (NRE), which tracks all wrongful convictions since 1989—by all means, not just DNA, thus yielding a larger and more diverse sample—false confessions contributed to 13 percent of more than 2,800 cases—and that number is nearly doubled in NRE's subsample of homicide cases (www.law.umich.edu/special/exoneration/Pages/about.aspx).

In the wake of these post-*Miranda* discoveries, the most significant recommendation for reform has been the proposed requirement that all interrogations be video recorded—the entire process, not just the confession. As stated in a American Psychology-Law Society Scientific Review Paper: "Without equivocation, our most essential recommendation is to lift the veil of secrecy from the interrogation process in favor of the principle of transparency" (Kassin et al., 2010, p. 25).

Historically, a policy of mandatory recording has proved a contentious source of debate. Various professional organizations have favored mandatory recording (e.g., American Bar Association, 2004; American Psychological Association, 2014) and surveys of individual law enforcement investigators in jurisdictions that have adopted the practice have yielded supportive results (e.g., Kassin et al., 2007; Sullivan 2008). Yet others, most aligned with law enforcement, have opposed recording on pragmatic or financial grounds or out of concern for how recording might inhibit or otherwise adversely affect police, suspects, judges, and juries (for an historical overview, see Drizin & Reich, 2003;

for a recent examination of states that mandate recording, see Bang et al., 2018; Sullivan, 2019).

Video recording as a means of protection has an inherent advantage over *Miranda* because it does not require the suspect to invoke it; waiver is not an option. It may also deter police from using coercive tactics (Kassin et al., 2014) and provide fact-finders with a more objective and accurate account of what transpired during the interrogation (Kassin et al., 2017)—all without inhibiting suspects (Kassin et al., 2020; for an overview of empirical arguments in favor of recording, see Kassin & Thompson, 2019). However, an important caveat accompanies this practice in the United States. In states that require video recording, the trigger point, as with *Miranda*, is custody. Only custodial interrogations must be recorded. Noncustodial interviews can be conducted off-camera.

What Does It Mean to Be in Custody?

In light of the consequential policies and practices that are at stake, the question we pose in this chapter is, What does it mean to be in custody? Over the years, courts in the United States have sought to define this elusive legal yet psychological concept.

"Interrogation" is defined as any type of police questioning that employs strategic tactics that might reasonably lead to self-incrimination on the part of a subject.[2] In *Miranda*, the Court defined custodial interrogation as "questioning initiated by law enforcement officers after a person has been taken into custody or otherwise deprived of his freedom of action in any significant way."[3] This definition specified two conditions under which legal safeguards may apply: custody or an alternative deprivation of freedom that is tantamount to custody. The Court later clarified that a person is in custody once they have been arrested—regardless of other circumstances.[4]

In the absence of arrest, the courts must apply a somewhat different test to determine whether the person experienced a restriction of freedom on par with custody.[5] Years of case law and Court decisions have yielded a two-pronged inquiry[6]—specifically, a consideration of (1) the totality of the *objective circumstances* of the suspect's situation, and (2) a determination of whether a *reasonable person* in that situation would have perceived a significant restriction on their freedom of action.

Objective Circumstances

Using a "totality of the circumstances" approach, judges seek to evaluate the presence or absence of certain factors that may influence a person's freedom in an interrogation.[7]

---

[2] Rhode Island v. Innis, 446 U.S. 291 (1980).

[3] *Id.* at 298.

[4] Orozco v. Texas, 394 U.S. 324 (1969).

[5] California v. Beheler, 463 U.S. 1121 (1983).

[6] Thompson v. Keohane, 516 U.S. 99 (1995).

[7] Berkemer v. McCarty, 468 U.S. 420 (U.S. 1984); Howes v. Fields, 132 S. Ct. 1181 (U.S. 2012); JDB v. North Carolina, 131 S. Ct. 2394 (2011).

Individuals who are under arrest clearly are in custody and not free to leave. Interrogations involving those who have not been arrested, however, may be more ambiguous, as the presence of traditionally "custodial" and "noncustodial" factors contribute to the ultimate inquiry. Given that each situation is unique,[8] courts generally regard the totality of the circumstances test as an "objective" way to weigh those factors in non-arrest scenarios.

Relevant Factors

Although there is no "official" list of factors that constitute custody versus freedom to leave, and although no one variable is dispositive, other than arrest, case law has pointed to several relevant circumstances. In *United States v. Griffin*,[9] the Eighth Circuit specifically cited the following factors: (1) whether police informed a suspect that they were free to leave; (2) whether the suspect's freedom of movement was not restrained by the police; (3) whether the suspect initiated contact with the police or was otherwise questioned voluntarily; (4) whether police used deceptive or coercive interrogation tactics, such as accusing or threatening the suspect or conducting the interrogation incommunicado; (5) whether the questioning took place in a police-dominated atmosphere; and (6) whether the interrogation concluded with the suspect's arrest. Three years later, the same circuit court clarified that the first three factors are generally indicative of noncustody, indicating that a suspect is free to leave, while the latter three suggest that the person was in custody and thus not free to leave.[10]

Many situations contain a unique combination of factors; hence, each must be weighed both individually *and* in the context of the totality of the circumstances. Illustrating that a single factor can be weighed differently depending on the situation, we next describe three cases that each contain the same indicator of police domination: the confiscation of a suspect's personal item. In two cases, *United States v. Longbehn* and *United States v. Adames*, the police confiscated the suspect's gun and car keys, respectively.[11] They also supervised the suspect's movements and, in the case of *Adames*, physically blocked the path on which he was walking. Such control over the suspects' movements, coupled with the confiscation of their personal items, led the courts to conclude that the defendants were in custody at the point of the questioning and were therefore not free to leave.

More recently, the First Circuit case of *United States v. Swan* yielded a different conclusion.[12] After driving herself to the police station, Defendant Swan had her cell phone confiscated in the parking lot by one of the detectives investigating her. When they entered the interview room, he said that she was not under arrest and that she did not

---

[8] People v. Antonio Torres, 25 Cal. App. 5th 162 (2018).
[9] United States v. Griffin, 922 F. 2d 1343 (8th Cir. 1990).
[10] United States v. Brown, 990 F.2d 397 (8th Cir. 1993).
[11] United States v. Longbehn, 850 F.2d 450 (8th Cir. 1988); United States v. Adames, 885 F. Supp. 610 (S.D.N.Y 1995).
[12] United States v. Swan, 842 F.3d 28 (1st Cir. 2016).

have to speak with them. She asked police when they would return her cell phone, but they retained possession even after it started ringing and Swan knew that her husband was calling. At the end of questioning, during which Swan made incriminating statements, the police returned her phone.

Once indicted by a grand jury, Swan moved to suppress these statements, claiming that she should have been advised of her *Miranda* rights because she was subjected to custodial interrogation. In contrast to *Longbehn* and *Adames*, the judge in this case ruled that Swan was not in custody. Considering all the aforementioned circumstances, the court concluded that a reasonable person would have felt free to leave. Even though the investigator confiscated her phone, which generally indicates custody, he eventually returned it and informed her that she was free to leave and did not have to talk if she did not wish to do so. This "free to leave" advisement has been cited in numerous cases as an especially potent counterforce that almost always outweighs other custodial factors.[13]

In *Howes v. Fields*, the Court affirmed the power of such an advisement of freedom to leave.[14] Randall Lee Fields, incarcerated for a previous crime, was brought in for questioning to a conference room in his Michigan jail. He was questioned at night for up to seven hours by armed investigators who used harsh tones and expletives and confronted him with an accusation of sexual abuse; he was literally in detention and not free to roam unsupervised. The Court agreed that these factors on their own would indicate that Fields was in custody and hence should be advised of his *Miranda* rights. But the Court also stated that the presence of certain noncustodial factors must also be taken into account. For example, the door to the conference room was sometimes open, Fields was not handcuffed or otherwise physically restrained, and importantly, the investigators told him that he was free to return to his cell if he did not want to cooperate. Writing for the majority, Justice Alito highlighted this free-to-leave advisement in ruling that Fields was not in custody and did not require *Miranda* warnings during this questioning.

Irrelevant Factors

As the totality-of-the-circumstances approach purports to provide an objective test, anything that would require investigators to make a subjective individualized assessment should not be considered when determining whether a suspect was in custody. The personal characteristics of the subject in question (e.g., intelligence, experience with law enforcement) are not weighed into the custody inquiry.[15] Furthermore, the subjective beliefs of either the interrogating officer or the suspect regarding the suspect's freedom to leave are not relevant.[16] The weight of the objective circumstances is therefore not to be

---

[13] California v. Beheler, 463 U.S. 1121; Howes v. Fields, 2012; Oregon v. Mathiason, 429 U.S. 492 (1977); cf. *Antonio Torres*, 25 Cal. App. 5th 162.

[14] *Fields*, 132 S. Ct. 1181.

[15] Yarborough v. Alvarado, 541 U.S. 652 (2004).

[16] Stansbury v. California, 511 U.S. 318 (1994).

considered from the perspective of the individual who was actually subjected to those circumstances. Instead, the custody inquiry is viewed from the perspective of a "reasonable person" in that suspect's position.[17] Put another way, "Would a reasonable person . . . have felt free simply to get up and walk out of the . . . room . . . at will?".[18]

The Reasonable Person Standard

The practice of framing beliefs and behaviors around "the reasonable person" rather than the actual individual in a given situation dates back to the 1800s. Writing on the common law of negligence torts, Justice Oliver Wendell Holmes (1881, p. 108) stated that the standard of care should be set by the "ideal average prudent man." Other early references to the so-called reasonable person standard also described it as a way to measure negligence (Gardner, 2015). If someone omitted an act of care and caution that a reasonable person could be expected to take, then that individual was deemed legally negligent and could be tried accordingly.[19]

Today, courts use the reasonableness construct not only to determine negligence but also to assess whether a suspect was in custody for interrogation purposes. Whether the totality of the circumstances culminates in a custodial or noncustodial situation is determined not in reference to the specific individual being questioned but rather through the hypothetical eyes of a reasonable person. The question is, "If encountered by a 'reasonable person,' would the identified circumstances add up to custody as defined in *Miranda*?"[20]

Who is the reasonable person, and why has the Court deemed this perspective preferable to the perspective of the individual being questioned? In the nineteenth century, Adolphe Quetelet, a Belgian sociologist, wrote about *l'homme moyen*: the reasonable man (Beirne, 1987; Quetelet, 1835). Quetelet's reasonable person was a hypothetical individual composed of the average characteristics of society. Though this is a potentially suitable way to think about this hypothetical person and their position, the courts have not adopted this as a relevant definition of the reasonable person. Rather, the reasonable person serves as a normative proxy rather than having to account for each individual's personal history, experiences, and characteristics that might influence their perceptions of freedom.[21] This standard aims to avoid placing on police and jurists the heavy burden of anticipating the "frailties or idiosyncrasies" of every person who walks into an interrogation room.[22] Instead they should examine the totality of the circumstances from the perspective of a single hypothetical reasonable person.

---

[17] *Berkemer*, 468 U.S. 420; *Stansbury*, 511 U.S. 318.

[18] *Yarborough*, 541 U.S. at 670.

[19] E.g., Blyth v. Birmingham Waterworks, 11 Ex. Ch. 781 (1856).

[20] *Thompson*, 516 U.S. at 113–114.

[21] *JDB*, 131 S. Ct. 261.

[22] People v. Rodney P. (Anonymous), 21 N.Y.2d 1, 10, 286 N.Y.S.2d 225, 233 N.E.2d 255 (1967).

The reasonable person standard has a long history. In a recent experiment aimed at its definition, Tobia (2018) asked one group of lay participants to estimate the "reasonable" number of different things (e.g., calories to consume each day, books read in a year, romantic involvements in a lifetime). For those same things, a second group was asked to estimate the "average" number; a third group estimated the "ideal" number. A consistent pattern was found across items: "Reasonable" amounts were greater than average but less than ideal. Tobia argued that perhaps "reasonableness" represents something of a hybrid construct, informed by what is normative and what is good.

In the context of determining custody, Who is this person? The effects of adopting a reasonable person standard to define custody in specific cases may be varied. Just as the objective circumstances can prove ambiguous to determine custody, so too is there disagreement when using the reasonable person standard: "Even if reasonable people could agree on the relevant factors to consider, they inevitably would disagree on how the relevant factors should be weighted" (Grano, 1979, p. 884). In *Yarborough v. Alvarado*,[23] even the Court recognized that the reasonable person standard does not yield uniform perceptions of custody the way a true objective test would ("fair minded jurists could disagree over whether Alvarado was in custody").[24]

The Psychology of Freedom and Custody

Labeling the custody inquiry an "objective" test does not capture the complexity of making attributions to another person's sense of restriction and freedom—an empirical social-psychological question. Research on the attributions people make for the behavior of self and others suggests that deciding how a "reasonable person" would feel in a particular situation is not straightforward. Beginning with Fritz Heider's (1958) pioneering work, attribution theorists have sought to understand how people explain the behavior of others by making attributions to factors that are both internal (e.g., personal traits) and external (e.g., situational pressures) to the actor.

One of the first signals to emerge from this literature is that actors and observers often diverge in their social perceptions, with observers focusing on the person as the person focuses the situation they are in. This divergence in perceptions is called the actor-observer effect (Jones & Nisbett, 1972; Watson, 1982). Specifically, research shows that when attempting to determine the causes of certain events or behaviors, actors focus externally on the factors of the situation that guided their behavioral decisions. In other words, they make situational attributions for their own behaviors—especially when the behavior or its outcome is deemed socially undesirable (e.g., Green et al., 1985). Observers, on the other hand, tend to attribute the causes of the actor's behaviors to dispositions of the actors themselves. As the focus of the observer's attention, the actor is visually salient, and

---

[23] *Yarborough,* 541 U.S. at 670.
[24] *Id.* at 664.

thus deemed more responsible for their behavior and the outcome of the situation (e.g., Harre et al., 2004).

Harvey et al. (1975) examined this actor-observer effect with specific regard to perceptions of freedom, the antithesis of custody. Using a variation of Milgram's (1963) obedience paradigm, Harvey et al. tested people's attributions for the teacher's administration of painful shocks to the learner. Two participants and a confederate were assigned to the following roles: the teacher, the observer, or the learner. Unbeknownst to the participants, the learner role was always assigned to the confederate, as in Milgram's original design. In the process of completing a word-association task, the teacher administered shocks to the learner while the observer and the experimenter watched the procedure. Also by random assignment, the learner exhibited moderate or severe distress in response to the shocks. If the teacher expressed discomfort with the situation or the wish to stop administering shocks, the experimenter gently, but firmly urged them to continue. (In reality, as in Milgram's study, the learner never received any electric shocks, though the teacher and observer were not aware of this deception.)

At the end of the study, Harvey et al. asked participants questions regarding the learner's freedom of choice and responsibility to continue administering painful shocks to the learner. Results showed an actor-observer difference. When the learner exhibited great distress, the observer assigned more freedom and responsibility to the teacher than the teacher attributed to themselves. The teacher, in turn, placed blame externally on the pressure of the situation and the dealer of that pressure: the experimenter. Harvey et al.'s (1975) demonstration of an actor-observer effect for perceptions of freedom was an important precursor to the psychological study of another applied topic: perceptions of custody.

Actor-Observer Differences in Perceptions of Custody

Although the psychology of custody is a nascent topic, some new empirical research has applied attribution theory and the actor-observer effect to the custody inquiry. Alceste et al. (2018) conducted a pair of two-phased experiments that examined both prongs of the custody inquiry described in *Thompson v. Keohane*[25]: the objective circumstances test and the reasonable person standard.

In the first experiment, participants sitting in the waiting area of the research lab witnessed a female confederate emerge from the inside room only to discover that the wallet she knew she entered the study with was missing from her bag. After the experimenter and confederate searched the room, the confederate said she would report the missing wallet to the university's Public Safety office. In the meantime, the experimenter and the actual participant began working on an unrelated cover story study. A few minutes later, a second confederate, a young male dressed as a plainclothes Public Safety officer,

---

[25] *Thompson*, 516 U.S. 99.

entered the lab and announced that he was investigating the missing wallet and had some questions about it. As far as participants were concerned, the stakes were real. A fellow student's wallet was missing and they were to be questioned as part of an investigation into possible theft.

At this point, the participant was randomly assigned to undergo one of two types of questioning sessions with this confederate posing as a security guard. In the "interview" session, participants encountered traditionally noncustodial circumstances: the experimenter remained in the room during the questioning; the room to the door remained open; the officer never accused the participant of stealing the wallet; and the questioning was brief. In contrast, participants in the "interrogation" encountered more restrictive custodial circumstances: the officer asked the experimenter to step out of the room so that he could question the participant alone; he then closed the door after the experimenter stepped out; he directly accused the participant of stealing the wallet; and the questioning session was significantly longer than the interviews. At the end of each session, the participant indicated their perceptions of how free they were to leave the situation. Importantly, all of the sessions were video recorded.

This first phase of the study examined the assumption that the objective circumstances influence perceptions of custody. For this assumption to be substantiated, participants in the noncustodial interview would have to report feeling significantly freer to leave than those in the more custodial interrogation. However, the results told a different story. Across the board, the majority of participants reported that they did not feel free to leave. Despite the objectively noncustodial factors present in the interview condition and the fact that the suspects in that condition reported feeling more like "witnesses" than "suspects," not a single participant asked the officer to stop, asked if they could leave, or attempted to walk out. The assumption that the objective circumstances of a noncustodial interview would yield the perception that one is free to leave was not substantiated.

In Phase 2, online participants served as observers and were randomly assigned to watch a recording of either an interview or an interrogation from Phase 1 after which they indicated their own perceptions of the actor and situation. This part of the study tested the second part of the custody inquiry. If online lay observers, a proxy for the reasonable person, agreed with Phase 1 participants in their perceptions of freedom, that result would support the proposition that the reasonable person standard provides an objective way to define the custody inquiry. Once again, however, the results did not support the assumptions of case law. In contrast to the uniform perceptions of custody versus freedom reported by the Phase 1 suspects in both conditions, the observers sharply differentiated between the two types of sessions. As the courts would predict, those who watched an interview indicated that the participant was significantly freer to leave than those who watched an interrogation. The fact that these perceptions diverge from those of the individuals who were personally subjected to Phase 1 questioning calls into question the utility of the reasonable person standard.

In a second study, Alceste et al. (2018) tested the presumed-controlling free-to-leave advisement present in numerous Supreme Court and lower court cases.[26] This experiment used the same cover story and missing wallet ploy. In this study, all student participants were assigned to the noncustodial interview condition from Study 1 and randomly assigned to receive or not receive an advisement from the Public Safety officer telling them that they were free to leave at any time. Specifically, they were told: "*Just so you know, you're free to leave. I'm not holding you here. If you don't want to talk to me or need to leave for any reason, you're free to do that*" (p. 393).

The results once again defied the courts' expectations. Compared to those in the no-advisement control condition, those who received the advisement were more likely to report that they were *objectively* free to leave the questioning. Indeed, they reported back exactly what they were told. However, there were no significant differences between the two groups on the more pressing *subjective* question concerning the extent to which they *felt* free to pick up and leave. As in the first study, participants in neither group felt free to terminate the session and leave. This finding may surprise those who set store by the presence of a reminder of freedom, as it runs counter to courts' repeated notion that the presence of such an advisement would make a reasonable person feel as though they were free to leave.

In both experiments by Alceste et al. (2018), Phase 2 observers reported not only their perception of how the actor felt, but also indicated whether they would feel free to leave if they were in the actor's position. In response to this question, observers' perceptions of freedom more closely resembled the perceptions of the Phase 1 actors. This result was consistent with previous research suggesting that perspective-taking exercises can attenuate the actor-observer effect by decreasing the perceived social distance between self and others (e.g., Galinsky et al., 2006; Galinsky & Moskowitz, 2000). At this point, it remains to be seen if the gap between some types of observers and the ordinary suspect is too wide for even the perspective-taking instruction to bridge. Specifically, in the aforementioned studies, the actors and the observers were both lay adults who were not professionals in the criminal justice system. However, in the real world, the perspectives of legal observers—namely, those of police and judges—are the ones that matter.

Relevant Observers' Perceptions of Custody

The divergence in custody perceptions between actors and observers may be particularly acute when one considers the differences that exist even among different observers themselves. Over the years, social perception research has shown that people's background experiences, beliefs, expectations, and motives may influence the way they interpret a particular behavioral event. In matters of custody, the perceptions of three categories of individuals are of particular relevance: police officers aiming to conduct an interview or

---

[26] E.g., *Beheler*, 463 U.S. 1121; *Fields*, 132 S. Ct. 1181; *Antonio Torres*, 25 Cal. App. 5th 162.

interrogation, trial judges who may later be called upon to determine whether a suspect was in custody for purposes of *Miranda* and video recording, and laypeople who may find themselves as a suspect in the crosshairs of an investigation.

Police officers enter a crime investigation motivated to gather information and acquire evidence—most notably a confession from a person of interest brought in for questioning. Their goal is to close the case. In real time, they seek to interrogate suspects. In so doing, they must determine at various points in time, for *Miranda* advisement and sometimes video recording purposes, if their suspect is in custody by evaluating the totality of objective circumstances and applying the reasonable person standard. As the Court put it, "Police must make in-the-moment judgments as to when to administer *Miranda* warnings."[27]

With numerous objective factors to consider, the judgment as to whether someone is in custody for the purposes of *Miranda* and video recording is often ambiguous.[28] This ambiguity provides fertile ground for motivated reasoning—often inspired, for example, by an officer's desire to elicit a confession (Ask et al., 2008; Kunda, 1990). On numerous occasions the Court has expressed skepticism in the law enforcement officer's ability to maintain objectivity regarding custody. In *Oregon v. Elstad*,[29] for example, the Court opined that "Police officers are ill-equipped to pinch-hit for counsel, construing the murky and difficult questions of when 'custody' begins or whether a given unwarned statement will ultimately be held admissible."[30]

Although recent research confirms that a vast majority of suspects waive their *Miranda* rights and that video recording does not in any way inhibit or otherwise adversely affect suspects (e.g., Kassin et al., 2019), many proponents of law-and-order politics have expressed the opinion that these safeguards may restrict law enforcement (e.g., Boetig et al., 2006; Cassell, 1996). In one post-*Miranda* case, dissenting Supreme Court justices went so far as to call the right against self-incrimination a " 'constitutional straitjacket' on law enforcement."[31]

After *Miranda* raised the stakes as to what constitutes a custodial interrogation, a good deal of debate has centered on how to define custody. Post-*Miranda*, the Court has progressively narrowed its definition and thereby reduced the number of factual situations in which a defendant would be entitled to protection. As noted earlier, for example, and in contrast to the findings reported by Alceste et al. (2018), questioning is consistently deemed noncustodial when police tell suspects they are free to leave. In the particularly controversial case of *Illinois v. Perkins*, the Court broke open a gaping loophole.[32] Lloyd

---

[27] *JDB*, 131 S. Ct. at 2402.
[28] E.g., *Yarborough*, 541 U.S. at 670.
[29] Oregon v. Elstad, 470 U.S. 298 (1985).
[30] *Id.* at 316.
[31] Orozco v. Texas, 394 U.S. 324, 328 (1969).
[32] Illinois v. Perkins, 496 U.S. 292 (1990).

Perkins, in jail for aggravated battery, received a visit to his cell by an undercover police officer posing as another prisoner. Without *Miranda*izing Perkins, this officer questioned him about a murder; Perkins confessed. It is hard to imagine a more "custodial" situation than being locked in jail, so the trial judge suppressed the confession and an appellate court affirmed. But then the Court reversed these prior rulings. The Court held that *Miranda* warnings are required to offset the inherent coerciveness of a police-dominated interrogation. Although the undercover agent sought to elicit a confession, although Perkins was incarcerated, and although no warnings were administered, the confession was voluntary and hence admissible because Perkins was not aware that he was speaking with a police officer.

Though some judges have expressed disdain for the protections afforded to suspects in custody, the trial judge's objective is decidedly different from that of police. Judges are the post hoc gatekeepers of confession evidence. Instead of real-time custody determinations, they assess the custody inquiry after the fact, often during suppression hearings. The goal of a trial judge is not to solve the case but rather to make a legally correct decision about whether someone was in custodial interrogation and required safeguards against self-incrimination. Here, a "correct" decision is one that follows from legal precedent, one that will not be overturned on appeal by a higher court (Guide to Judiciary Policy, 2014).

As shown by Alceste et al. (2018), lay adults differ in their judgments of custody, depending on their perspective. But how does age—specifically all the developmental vulnerabilities that come with being a minor—influence perceptions of freedom? Previous research shows that minors display an immaturity of judgment that may lead them to make poor legal decisions, such as falsely confess to escape the short-term pressure of an interrogation, not taking into account the long-term consequences of such behavior (Redlich & Goodman, 2003; Steinberg & Cauffman, 1996). For this reason, the Court has held that a young suspect perceives custody differently than an adult: "a reasonable child subjected to police questioning will sometimes feel pressured to submit when a reasonable adult would feel free to go."[33]

In a follow-up study after Alceste et al. (2018), new adolescents (mean age = 15.30 years) and adult participants (mean age = 35.22 years) were randomly assigned to watch either an interview or an interrogation from the original experiment, and then provided their perceptions of the subject's freedom to leave (Alceste, 2019). As in Alceste et al. (2018), overall, observers perceived less freedom in the interrogation versus interview conditions. Consistent with previous psychological literature and existing case law, juvenile observers perceived significantly less freedom for both interviews and interrogations than did adults. When asked how free they would feel to leave if they were in the subject's position, adolescents predicted that they would feel significantly less free than did adults.

---

[33] *JDB*, 131 S. Ct. at 2403.
United States v. Craighead, 539 F.3d 1073 (9th Cir. 2008).

Perceptions of Custody: A Comparison of Relevant Observers

To compare legal professionals and laypeople, and to assess the views of independent experts in the scientific study of how situations influence people's thoughts, feelings, and behaviors, Alceste and Kassin (2021) conducted a vignette study involving 875 police officers, judges, social psychologists, and lay adults. Each participant was randomly assigned to read about a police-suspect encounter that depicted a classic noncustodial interview, a classic high-custody interrogation, or a prototypical ambiguous situation containing a mix of custodial and noncustodial factors. After reading one of these vignettes, participants responded to questions pertaining to objective custody ("*How free was the suspect to leave?*"), subjective custody ("*How free to leave did the suspect feel?*"), and perspective-taking custody *("How free to leave would you have felt?")*.

Results revealed a great deal of disparity of custody perceptions among the four groups. In the low-custody scenario, social psychologists and laypeople alike reported that the suspect was less free to leave than did police and judges who read the same vignette. This result held true for all types of questions asked in the low-custody condition, including the perspective-taking question. Further challenging the courts' assumptions, the legal participants reported that they would feel significantly freer to leave than did nonlegal participants.

Alceste and Kassin also observed notable disparities within the samples of legal participants. Police reported believing that suspects in the low-custody vignette would feel significantly freer than judges did. In the prototypical ambiguous condition as well, police and judges varied greatly in their perceptions. This disparity is concerning, as the ambiguous vignette was the most realistic scenario of the three presented in the study. Interestingly, results showed that lay participants had an ally in social psychologists, who similarly appraised the low-custody situation as more restrictive than did police and judges. This group of experts in social influence and perception serve as an interesting arbiter of disagreements between legal professionals and laypeople.

Differences between and within legal participants were not limited to perceptions of freedom. As there is no universally accepted definition of a reasonable person, police and judges were asked to define this hypothetical entity for the purposes of the custody inquiry. Judges were significantly more likely to describe the reasonable person as someone possessing average characteristics and were particularly focused on intelligence. In contrast, police were more likely to define the reasonable person as someone who is mentally stable or of sound mind. Overall, this study showed that legal and lay observers differed in their custody perceptions in many ways. The potential downstream implications of these disparities are striking and potentially consequential.

Policy Implications

The stated purpose of the totality-of-the-circumstances and reasonable person standards is to make the custody inquiry as objective as possible—presumably for the purpose of maximizing what research psychologists would call interrater reliability. This is a worthy mission—the safeguards meant to protect those in custodial interrogation from undue harm and influence should not be allocated subjectively or unequally. Yet the current approach to determining custody and the required safeguards that follow is hardly objective. According to the research described in this chapter, perceptions of custody differ substantially between those who are being questioned by an authority figure and those who merely observe the session and stand in judgment (Alceste et al., 2018). Importantly, too, there are meaningful differences even among observers depending on their professional stature. For instance, police and judges, using themselves and case law as a baseline, tend to overrate how free a hypothetical suspect was and felt in a low-custody scenario, compared to social psychologists and laypeople (Alceste & Kassin, 2021).

Practically speaking, the fact that a potentially custodial situation can appear innocuous to legal professionals yet compulsory to the layperson means that suspects may feel legally compelled to endure the intensifying pressures of interrogation. In the eyes of the law, this suspect would not be afforded legal protections against self-incrimination. One potential avenue for reform would be to require the video recording of all police-suspect interactions, custodial and noncustodial alike. In a digital era in which police officers routinely wear body cameras, and in which interview rooms are routinely equipped for recording, there are no financial or other pragmatic barriers to a policy that requires full transparency, thereby eliminating the need for subjective human judgment.

With regard to legal professionals in particular, two troubling implications follow from the research. First, when police and the judges assert that a suspect was free to leave, that suspect will have been denied the two key legal safeguards against the risk of a coerced and possibly false confession—*Miranda* advisement and video recording. As confessions are powerfully incriminating to judges and juries, even when coerced (e.g., Kassin & Sukel, 1997; Wallace & Kassin, 2012), the decision to admit a confession into evidence all but ensures conviction at trial and increases the likelihood of a guilty plea (Redlich et al., 2018). Second, the finding that individual legal professionals can perceive the same potentially custodial situations so differently raises concerns about the equal administration of justice. In light of racial disparities throughout the criminal justice system, in domains ranging from routine traffic stops to long-term incarceration, the individual variability we had found provides a cause for concern about the risk that these judgments are biased by a defendant's race and other stereotyped characteristics.

What Next: Future Research

It is remarkable that no empirical attention has focused on "custody" until recently even though this psychologically rich construct has played a central role in criminal justice decision-making for well over fifty years. Still, our recent efforts have only scratched the surface. There are numerous interesting directions for future research. For example, rather than ask police and judges to define the reasonable person themselves, researchers might systematically vary a priori the definition of "reasonable person" and examine its effects on custody judgments. One possibility is to present normative and/or positive definitions to participants and ask them to judge custody based on these differing standards (Miller & Perry, 2012).

Normative definitions ask whether the risk multiplied by the magnitude of that harm is greater than the burden of removing the risk. This formula appeared as an early standard for the kinds of actions that are expected from reasonable people in society. In contrast, positive definitions, empirically derived, represent the kinds of actions the "average" person would take to avoid harm. In Alceste and Kassin (2021), the legal professionals used positive definitions of the reasonable, often average, person. Although the original definitions Miller and Perry described were derived from tort law, these definitions may be revised for the custody inquiry and presented to police officers and judges to determine if their perceptions of custody converge when using a single and specific definition.

Other empirical questions are raised by the effects of the COVID-19 pandemic on the practices of interrogation. The pandemic has forced numerous changes in norms, both socially and in the workplace, to keep institutions functioning while protecting from the virus. As such, various social distancing regulations have been implemented—such as conducting investigations virtually. One Marshall Project article titled "Your Zoom Interrogation is About to Start," describes how professional interviewing firms have responded to the pandemic by offering special training for private- and public-sector investigators on how to conduct remote interviews (Hager, 2020). At present, no data exist on how this remote questioning environment impacts the psychology of custody. As the Court's assumptions about the totality of circumstances and reasonable person standard have not held up in the research lab, one wonders about the effects in a virtual interrogation. Absent all sense of physical restraint, it is reasonable to assume that a virtual interrogation paradigm increases a suspect's sense of freedom, where leaving involves hanging up a phone or clicking a "Leave Meeting" button on a laptop. Research is needed to compare perceptions of custody and freedom in these alternative situations.

Conclusion

Custody is legal construct of immense significance but sorely in need of research. Serving as the trigger point for *Miranda* warnings and, more importantly, the video recording of interrogations in half of all states, the contrasting perceptions of police, their suspects, and later judges can markedly influence the course of an investigation. The legal safeguards, particularly video recording, can help to prevent and later identify wrongful convictions based on coerced false confessions. The Court has repeatedly sought to define "custodial interrogation" in objective terms in order to reduce subjectivity. The research described in this chapter, however, suggests that these attempts to concretize the custody inquiry have not held up as truly objective measures in the laboratory. At this point, more research is needed to inform the courts, policy, and practice with regard to this critical and largely psychological construct.

References

Alceste, F. (2019). *Different strokes for different but reasonable folks: Comparison of legally relevant observers' perceptions of custody* [Unpublished doctoral dissertation]. City University of New York.

Alceste, F., & Kassin, S. M. (2021). Perceptions of custody: Similarities and disparities among police, judges, social psychologists, and laypeople. *Law and Human Behavior, 45*(3), 197–214.

Alceste, F., Luke, T. J., & Kassin, S. M. (2018). Holding yourself captive: Perceptions of custody during interviews and interrogations. *Journal of Applied Research in Memory and Cognition, 7*(3), 387–397.

Ask, K., Rebelius, A., & Granhag, P. A. (2008). The 'elasticity' of criminal evidence: A moderator of investigator bias. *Applied Cognitive Psychology: The Official Journal of the Society for Applied Research in Memory and Cognition, 22*(9), 1245–1259.

Bang, B. L., Stanton, D., Hemmens, C., & Stohr, M. K. (2018). Police recording of custodial interrogations: A state-by-state legal inquiry. *International Journal of Police Science &Management, 20*(1), 3–18.

Beirne, P. (1987). Adolphe Quetelet and the origins of positivist criminology. *American Journal of Sociology, 92*(5), 1140–1169.

Boetig, B. P., Vinson, D. M., & Weidel, B. R. (2006). Revealing Incommunicado: ElectronicRecording of Police Interrogations. *FBI L. Enforcement Bull., 75*, 1.

Cassell, P. G. (1996). *Miranda*'s social costs: An empirical reassessment. *Northwestern University Law Review, 90*, 387–499.

Drizin, S. A., & Reich, M. J. (2003). Heeding the lessons of history: The need for mandatory recording of police interrogations to accurately assess the reliability and voluntariness of confessions. *Drake Law Review, 52*, 619–646.

Galinsky, A. D., Magee, J. C., Inesi, M. E., & Gruenfeld, D. H. (2006). Power and perspectivesnot taken. *Psychological Science, 17*(12), 1068–1074.

Galinsky, A. D., & Moskowitz, G. B. (2000). Perspective-taking: decreasing stereotypeexpression, stereotype accessibility, and in-group favoritism. *Journal of Personality and Social Psychology, 78*(4), 708–724.

Gardner, J. (2015). The many faces of the reasonable person. *Law Quarterly Review, 131*(Oct).

Grano, J. D. (1979). Voluntariness, free will, and the law of confessions. *Virginia Law Review, 65*(5), 859–945.

Green, S. K., Lightfoot, M. A., Bandy, C., & Buchanan, D. R. (1985). A general model of the attribution process. *Basic and Applied Social Psychology, 6*(2), 159–179.

Guide to Judiciary Policy. (2014). https://www.uscourts.gov/judges-judgeships/code-conduct-united-states-judges

Hager, E. (2020, June 20). Your Zoom interrogation is about to start. https://www.themarshallproject.org/2020/07/20/your-zoom-interrogation-is-about-to-start

Harre, N., Brandt, T., & Houkamau, C. (2004). An examination of the actor-observer effect in young drivers' attributions for their own and their friends' risky driving. *Journal of Applied Social Psychology, 34*(4), 806–824.

Harvey, J. H., Harris, B., & Barnes, R. D. (1975). Actor-observer differences in the perceptions of responsibility and freedom. *Journal of Personality and Social Psychology, 32*, 22–28.

Heider, F. (1958). *The psychology of interpersonal relations*. John Wiley & Sons.

Holmes, O. W., Jr. (1881). *The COMMON LAW*. Little, Brown.

Jones, E. E., & Nisbett, R. E. (1972). The actor and the observer: Divergent perspectives of the causes of behavior. In E. E. Jones, D. E. Kanouse, H. H. Kelley, R. E. Nisbett, S. Valins, & B. Weiner (Eds.), *Attribution: Perceiving the causes of behavior*. General Learning Press.

Kamisar, Y. (1962). What is an involuntary confession? Some comments on Inbau and Reid's criminal interrogation and confessions. *Rutgers Law Review, 17*, 728–759.

Kassin, S. M., Drizin, S. A., Grisso, T., Gudjonsson, G. H., Leo, R. A., & Redlich, A. D. (2010). Police-induced confessions: Risk factors and recommendations. *Law and Human Behavior, 34*, 3–38.

Kassin, S. M., Kukucka, J., Lawson, V. Z., & DeCarlo, J. (2014). Does video recording alter the behavior of police during interrogation? Mock crime-and-investigation study. *Law and Human Behavior, 38*, 73–83.

Kassin, S. M., Kukucka, J., Lawson, V. Z., & DeCarlo, J. (2017). Police reports of mock suspect interrogations: A test of accuracy and perception. *Law and Human Behavior, 41,* 230–243.

Kassin, S. M., Russano, M., Amrom, A., Hellgren, J., Kukucka, J., & Lawson, V. (2019). Does video recording inhibit crime suspects? Evidence from a fully randomized field experiment. *Law and Human Behavior, 43,* 44–55.

Kassin, S. M., Scherr, K. C., & Alceste, F. (2020). The right to remain silent: Realities and illusions. In R. Bull & I. Blandon-Gitlin (Eds.), *Routledge international handbook of legal and investigative psychology* (pp. 2–19). Taylor & Francis.

Kassin, S. M., & Sukel, H. (1997). Coerced confessions and the jury: An experimental test of the "harmless error" rule. *Law and Human Behavior, 21,* 27–46.

Kassin, S. M., & Thompson, D. (2019, August 1). Videotape all police interrogations—Justice demands it. *The New York Times* (Op-Ed). www.nytimes.com

Kunda, Z. (1990). The case for motivated reasoning. *Psychological Bulletin, 108*(3), 480.

Leo, R. A., & Thomas, G. C. (Eds.). (1998). *The Miranda debate: Law, justice, and policing.* Northeastern University Press.

Milgram, S. (1963). Behavioral study of obedience. *Journal of Abnormal and Social Psychology, 67*(4), 371–378.

Miller, A. D., & Perry, R. (2012). The reasonable person. *New York University Law Review, 87,* 323–392.

Quetelet, L. A. J. (1835). *Sur l'homme et le développement de ses facultés, ou Essai de physique sociale.* Bachelier, Imprimeur-libraire.

Redlich, A. D., & Goodman, G. S. (2003). Taking responsibility for an act not committed: The influence of age and suggestibility. *Law and Human Behavior, 27*(2), 141–156.

Redlich, A. D., Yan, S., Norris, R., & Bushway, S. (2018). The influence of confessions on guilty pleas and plea discounts. *Psychology, Public Policy, and Law, 24,* 147–157.

Rogers, R., Rogstad, J. E., Gillard, N. D., Drogin, E. Y., Blackwood, H. L., & Shuman, D. W. (2010). "Everyone knows their *Miranda* rights": Implicit assumptions and countervailing evidence. *Psychology, Public Policy, and Law, 16*(3), 300–318.

Smalarz, L., Scherr, K. C., & Kassin, S. M. (2016). *Miranda* at 50. *Current Directions in Psychological Science, 25,* 455–460. https://journals.sagepub.com/doi/10.1177/0963721416665097

Steinberg, L., & Cauffman, E. (1996). Maturity of judgment in adolescence: Psychosocial factors in adolescent decision making. *Law and Human Behavior, 20*(3), 249–272.

Sullivan, T. P. (2008). Recording federal custodial interviews. *American Criminal Law Review, 45,* 1297–1345.

Sullivan, T. P. (2019). Current report on recording custodial interrogations in the United States. *The Champion,* April, pp. 54–55.

Tobia, K. P. (2018). How people judge what is reasonable. *Alabama Law Review, 70,* 293–359.

Wallace, D. B., & Kassin S. M. (2012). Harmless error analysis: How do judges respond to confession errors? *Law and Human Behavior, 36,* 151–157.

Watson, D. (1982). The actor and the observer: How are their perceptions of causality divergent? *Psychological Bulletin, 92,* 682–700.

Weisselberg, C. D. (2008). *Mourning Miranda. California Law Review, 96,* 1521–1602.

Weisselberg, C. D. (2017). Exporting and importing *Miranda. Boston University Law Review, 97,* 1235–1291.

White, W. S. (2001). *Miranda*'s failure to restrain pernicious interrogation practices. *Michigan Law Review, 99*(5), 1211–1247.

Human Factors in Forensic Science: Psychological Causes of Bias and Error

Jeff Kukucka *and* Itiel E. Dror

Abstract

Forensic science evidence has long been accepted in court and is widely considered infallible. However, the forensic sciences have recently come under intense scrutiny, as forensic science errors have been implicated in an alarming number of wrongful convictions. In working to better understand and prevent such errors, researchers have discovered that they are often an unfortunate by-product of innate psychological processes. This chapter first reviews evidence that forensic science examiners, like all humans, are vulnerable to unconscious biases that can lead to erroneous judgments. Second, the chapter identifies barriers to mitigating the pernicious effects of bias in forensic laboratories and courtrooms, including widespread misconceptions about its causes and effects. Third, proposed reforms are offered to strengthen forensic science, with descriptions of some progress that has already been made in that regard.

Key Words: forensic science, bias, error, examiners, judgments, evidence

The forensic sciences encompass a wide range of disciplines with the common goal of analyzing physical evidence (DNA, fingerprints, bloodstain patterns, handwriting, shoeprints, etc.) to inform legal matters. Forensic science evidence can be a powerful tool in solving crimes, and it has long been accepted in court without opposition from the scientific community. However, the past decade has seen a dramatic shift, as the forensic sciences have come under scrutiny—including by the National Academy of Sciences (NAS; 2009) and the President's Council of Advisors on Science and Technology (PCAST; 2016), which noted a dearth of research establishing their validity and an alarming number of forensic science errors in known miscarriages of justice. Indeed, the National Registry of Exonerations (2020) has catalogued more than 650 cases in which a forensic science error contributed to the wrongful conviction of an innocent person. These errors—which are costly to the individual, to taxpayers, and to public safety—have prompted a wave of research to understand why they occurred and how to minimize them.

This chapter has three aims. First, we review evidence that forensic science examiners, like all humans, are vulnerable to unconscious biases that can lead to erroneous judgments. Second, we identify barriers to mitigating the pernicious effects of bias in forensic

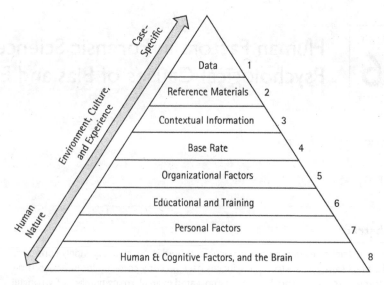

Figure 36.1 Eight Sources of Bias and Error in the Forensic Sciences.
Source: Dror (2020a).

laboratories and courtrooms, including widespread misconceptions about its causes and effects. Third, we discuss proposed reforms to strengthen forensic science, and we describe some progress that has already been made in that regard.

Causes of Bias and Error

Psychologists have long understood that humans do not process information in a purely objective way; rather, their judgments are colored by their idiosyncratic beliefs, motivations, expectations, and other contextual factors, which can lead people to interpret the same information in markedly different ways (i.e., *top-down processing*; Bruner & Goodman, 1947; Gregory, 1970). More recently, it has become clear that judgments of forensic evidence are likewise subject to outside influences, such that two experts—or even the same expert at two different points in time—can draw different conclusions from the same physical evidence depending on the context in which it is presented. Dror (2020a) identified eight sources of bias and error in the forensic sciences (see fig. 36.1). To date, empirical research has focused primarily on Levels 2–5 of this taxonomy. The next section first reviews the extant literature on these key sources of bias and error.

Reference Materials

In many forensic disciplines, examiners visually compare two stimuli (e.g., fingerprints, hairs, and bullets)—including one from the crime scene and one from a known individual (i.e., suspect)—and opine as to whether they share a common source (i.e., "match"). In other disciplines, such as blood pattern analysis, examiners compare the pattern from the crime scene against a pattern prototypical of a particular cause (e.g., gunshot) and opine as to whether they match. In either case, examiners must identify and compare features of the two stimuli that are likely to be indicative of a match or nonmatch.

Research suggests that the mere presence of reference material can alter examiners' judgment. Dror et al. (2011) found that fingerprint examiners identified different minutiae (i.e., features) in the same latent print when it was shown alongside a comparison print rather than in isolation, implying that the comparison print led examiners to miss or ignore minutiae that they would have otherwise deemed important. Fraser-Mackenzie et al. (2013) found that fingerprint examiners' decisions about the suitability of a latent print (i.e., whether it contained sufficient information for analysis) depended on whether and what type of comparison print was shown next to it. Taken together, these findings suggest that the mere presence of a comparison sample can influence whether and how an examiner performs a comparison. Reference materials can likewise affect interpretations of DNA evidence (i.e., knowledge of a suspect's DNA profile can guide decisions about a crime-relevant DNA mixture; Jeanguenat et al., 2017) and voice recordings (i.e., receiving a transcript can influence what people "hear" in a low-quality recording; Lange et al., 2011). To counteract such biases, Dror et al. (2015) recommended that examiners first analyze each stimulus in isolation before comparing them against each other (i.e., Linear Sequential Unmasking).

Contextual Information

It is well-established that people naturally seek out, select, and interpret information in ways that corroborate their preexisting beliefs (i.e., *confirmation bias*; Nickerson, 1998). The justice system is no exception; Kassin et al. (2013) coined the term "forensic confirmation bias" to describe situations where "an individual's pre-existing beliefs, expectations, motives, and situational context influence the collection, perception, and interpretation of evidence during the course of a criminal case" (p. 45). Simply put, forensic examiners should base their opinions solely on information that is relevant to the task at hand. This is hardly a novel idea; Hagan (1894) warned that examiners "must depend wholly upon what is seen, leaving out of consideration all suggestions or hints from interested parties [or] knowledge of the moral evidence or aspects of the case" (p. 82). Nevertheless, this issue was largely ignored until NAS (2009) called for "research programs on human observer bias and sources of human error in forensic examinations" (p. 24).

As shown in table 36.1, many studies have since found that irrelevant contextual information can impact judgments of forensic evidence. In some studies, examiners were swayed by information that implied guilt or innocence; for example, Dror and Charlton (2006) found that fingerprint examiners changed 17 percent of their own judgments of the same prints after learning of a suspect's confession or alibi. Even irrelevant demographic information can prompt bias. For example, Dror et al. (2021) found evidence of racial bias in an archival analysis of death certificates; then, in a follow-up experiment, they found that medical professionals more often ruled a child's death a homicide

Table 36.1 Index of Empirical Studies on Cognitive Bias in the Forensic Sciences

Discipline	Citation	Manipulation Type	Participants
Fingerprints	Dror et al. (2005)	Emotional context	Novices
	Dror et al. (2006)	Peer opinion	*Experts
	Dror & Charlton (2006)	Case information	*Experts
	Hall & Player (2008)†	Emotional context	Experts
	Langenburg et al. (2009)†	Peer opinion	Experts; novices
	Dror et al. (2011)	Reference materials	*Experts
	Fraser-Mackenzie et al. (2013)	Reference materials	Experts
	Langenburg et al. (2014)†	Case information	None (archival)
	Earwaker et al. (2015)	Emotional context	Experts
	Smalarz et al. (2016)	Case information	Novices
	Osborne & Zajac (2016)	Emotional context	Novices
	Stevenage & Bennett (2017)	Case information	Novices
	Quigley-McBride & Wells (2018)	Case information; evidence lineup	Novices
	Growns & Kukucka (2021)	Base rate	Novices
	Growns et al. (2022)	Base rate	Trainees
	Quigley-McBride (2020)	Case information; evidence lineup	Novices
	Kukucka, Dror et al. (2020)	Evidence lineup	Experts
Handwriting	Miller (1984)	Case information	Trainees
	Kukucka & Kassin (2014)	Case information	Novices
	Merlino (2015)	Peer opinion	Experts; novices
	Kouwenhoven (2018)	Case information; peer opinion	Novices
	Dror et al. (2020)	Adversarial allegiance	*Experts
Bloodstains	Taylor et al. (2016a)	Case information	Experts
	Taylor et al. (2016b)	Case information	Experts
	Osborne, Taylor, Healey, & Zajac (2016)	Case information	Experts; trainees
	Hugh & Satchell (2018)†	Case information	Trainees
Anthropology	Hartley et al. (2022)	Case information	Experts
	Nakhaeizadeh, Dror, & Morgan, (2014)	Case information	Experts; trainees
	Nakhaeizadeh, Hansen, & Dozzi (2014)	Case information	Experts; trainees
	Nakhaeizadeh et al. (2018)	Case information	Trainees
Firearms	Kersholt et al. (2010)†	Case information	Experts
	Mattijssen et al. (2020)	Peer opinion	Experts

Table 36.1 Continued

Discipline	Citation	Manipulation Type	Participants
Shoeprints	Kerstholt et al. (2007)†	Case information	Experts
	Sneyd et al. (2020)	Peer opinion	Novices
	Yu et al. (2021)	Case information	Experts
Pathology	Oliver (2017)	Case information	Experts
	Dror et al. (2021)	Case information	Experts
	Dror et al. (2022)	Case information	Experts
CSI	van den Eeden (2016; 2019)	Case information	Experts; trainees
	de Gruijter et al. (2017)	Case information	Experts
Hair	Miller (1987)	Evidence lineup	Trainees
DNA	Dror & Hampikian (2011)	Case information	Experts
Dog handling	Lit et al. (2011)	Case information	Experts
Arson	Bieber (2012)	Case information	Experts
Toxicology	Hamnett & Dror (2020)	Case information	Trainees
Bitemarks	Osborne et al. (2014)	Emotional context	Trainees; novices
	Chiam et al. (2021)	Case information	Experts
	Chiam et al. (2022)	Case information	Experts
Digital forensics	Sunde & Dror (2021)	Case information	Experts

Note. Citations denoted with † did not find any statistically significant cognitive bias effects. Experts denoted with * were unaware that they were participating in a study.

(rather than an accident) when the child was Black and found unresponsive by her mother's boyfriend, compared to when the child was White and found by her grandmother, even though the child's injuries were identical. Emotional context may also affect examiners' judgment; in two studies, participants more often judged the same fingerprints a "match" if they were shown alongside a gruesome photo rather than a neutral photo (Dror et al., 2005; Osborne & Zajac, 2016). In still other studies, examiners were influenced by knowledge of a peer's opinion; for example, Merlino (2015) found that 50 percent of forensic handwriting experts changed their initial opinion of two signatures after being told that another examiner had reached a different conclusion. As such, many have urged that examiners be shielded from *any* information that is potentially biasing and irrelevant to the task at hand (e.g., Kassin et al., 2013; National Commission on Forensic Science, 2015; PCAST, 2016).

Importantly, contextual information can shape not only an examiner's conclusion but also the process by which they reach that conclusion (Dror, 2009; Kukucka, 2014). For example, Hamnett and Dror (2020) recently found that forensic toxicology trainees who read an irrelevant case history prior to testing for the presence of opiates opted to perform different tests than those who did not. Future work should continue to examine the mechanism(s) by which context affects forensic judgments. Of particular note, a few studies have now utilized eye-tracking technology to better understand the processing strategies of forensic examiners (e.g., handwriting examiners, Merlino, 2015; anthropologists, Nakhaeizadeh et al., 2020). Though none of these studies has yet tested the impact of biasing context, eye-tracking studies from other expert domains (e.g., radiology; Fawver et al., 2020) and from basic cognitive psychology (e.g., Rajsic et al., 2015) have shown that contextual information can indeed alter processing strategies.

Some studies in table 36.1 have been criticized for using untrained novices or trainees (i.e., students training to become professional examiners) on the grounds that their findings may not generalize to experts (i.e., experienced professionals; e.g., Curley et al., 2020; Hackman et al., 2018; Lewis, 2016). Given the difficulty of collecting valid data from forensic experts (Dror, 2009; Kukucka, 2020), it is unsurprising that many researchers have instead recruited novices or trainees. However, as shown in table 36.1, studies of experts are hardly scarce. Moreover, van den Eeden et al. (2019) found that novices and experts were equally biased by case formation received prior to examining a mock crime scene. In fact, some have argued that experts may be *more* subject to bias than novices insofar as they are more reliant on cognitive shortcuts acquired from experience (e.g., selective attention; Chi, 2006; Dror, 2011; Walther et al., 2003). In any case, it appears that expertise does not grant immunity to bias, though this question merits further investigation.

A few studies in table 36.1 found no effect of contextual information. For example, Langenburg et al. (2009) found that knowledge of a peer's conclusion did not affect fingerprint judgments—but many participants in their study expressed suspicion as to its purpose and thus likely behaved unrealistically. Indeed, in most cases, experts who participated in these studies were aware that they were being tested (see table 36.1), which limits ecological validity. Kerstholt et al. (2007; Kerstholt et al., 2010) found no effect of contextual information on judgments made by shoeprint and firearms experts. These null effects could be due to highly standardized procedures that protected against bias, stimuli whose interpretation was less subjective, contextual information that was only weakly suggestive (e.g., the suspect owned a van and thus could have stolen large appliances), and/or the fact that participants knew they were being tested. Future research should aim to elucidate the "bias danger zone"—that is., the conditions under which the risk and impact of bias is greatest, such as the difficulty of the judgment or the nature of the contextual information.

Base Rate

The *low prevalence effect* is the phenomenon whereby rare stimuli are less likely to be detected during a visual search or comparison (see Horowitz, 2017). For example, studies have found that airport security were poorer at detecting weapons in luggage (Wolfe et al., 2013), radiologists were poorer at detecting cancerous lesions in CT scans (Nakashima et al., 2015), and laypeople were poorer at detecting facial mismatches (i.e., fake IDs; Papesh & Goldinger, 2014) when they occurred less than 10 percent of the time.

In most performance studies, forensic examiners analyzed similar numbers of matching and non-matching stimulus pairs (e.g., Tangen et al., 2011; White et al., 2015)—but in actual casework, matches may be normative or rare (see, e.g., Gardner et al., 2020). Regardless, if an examiner comes to expect a lopsided distribution of matches and nonmatches, they may be less adept at detecting whichever is rarer. Indeed, Growns and Kukucka (2021) recently found exactly that in a study of novices, each of whom evaluated one hundred fingerprint pairs that included either ten, fifty, or ninety matches. Compared to the equal prevalence condition, novices committed more false positive errors (i.e., misidentifying nonmatches as matches) when nonmatches were rare and more false negative errors (i.e., misidentifying matches as nonmatches) when matches were rare. Similarly, in the aforementioned study of bias in manner of death decisions, Dror et al. (2021) posited that the bias toward judging a Black child's death a homicide may stem from inaccurate or outdated base rate information. Base rate information could also undermine efforts to peer review (i.e., verify) forensic decisions, as explained below. In sum, base rate expectations can be problematic insofar as an examiner's experience in prior unrelated cases colors their judgment in the case at hand.

Organizational Factors

Finally, factors inherent to examiners' work environment—such as stress and pressure—may affect their accuracy or impartiality. Jeanguenat and Dror (2018) identified myriad potential stressors for forensic examiners, such as heavy workload, pressure to give results quickly, limited room for advancement, limited funding, and exposure to traumatic case details. Corroborating these points, Charlton et al. (2010) found that many fingerprint examiners held a strong fear of making mistakes and/or a strong desire to reach definitive conclusions (i.e., *need for closure*). Most recently, Almazrouei et al. (2020; Almazrouei et al., 2021) found that many examiners reported high levels of workplace-related stress—and 39 percent felt that stress influenced their performance (see also Levin et al., 2021). To mitigate any negative effects of stress on performance, Jeanguenat and Dror (2018) proposed that forensic labs take concrete steps to promote healthy work-life balance, such as offering flexible schedules, healthy nutrition, exercise initiatives, and mindfulness training—all of which have proven beneficial to employees in other domains. However, no research has yet examined the desirability, feasibility, or effectiveness of such interventions in the forensic sciences specifically.

Almazrouei et al. (2020) also found that examiners feel pressure to provide inculpatory evidence, with 14 percent strongly believing that their work is more appreciated if they find a "match" than if they do not. Relatedly, interdependence between forensic labs and police departments and/or prosecutors' offices could engender a pro-prosecution bias among examiners (e.g., Giannelli, 2010; Risinger et al., 2002; Robertson, 2010). In forensic psychology, for example, Murrie et al. (2013) found evidence of an *adversarial allegiance effect*, such that clinicians using the same measure assigned higher risk scores to the same offender if they believed they were working for the prosecution rather than the defense and vice versa. In the forensic sciences, Scherr and Dror (2020) found that examiners attributed wrongful convictions more to inadequate legal defense than to prosecutorial misconduct (when in fact the opposite is true), which they interpreted as evidence of ingroup favoritism that could cloud examiners' judgment. However, Dror et al. (2020) later found no evidence of an allegiance effect among forensic document examiners who were led to believe that they were working for either the prosecution or the defense. Future work should continue to explore whether and how allegiance effects color the opinions of forensic examiners across disciplines.

Barriers to Progress

It is clear that forensic examiners—like all people—are vulnerable to psychological biases that can unwittingly influence their judgments and increase the risk of error. However, the problem of bias and error does not start and end in forensic laboratories. Rather, wrongful convictions due to forensic science errors are the outcome of a chain of events that begins at a crime scene and ends in a courtroom or plea bargain process. In this section, we will describe how misunderstandings and/or overconfidence among examiners, police, lawyers, and jurors fail to safeguard against such miscarriages of justice.

Examiners' Understanding

Examiners' beliefs about bias presumably guide their efforts—or lack thereof—to design and implement bias countermeasures in their laboratories. Unfortunately, many examiners hold misconceptions about bias that are likely to preempt or undermine any such efforts (see Dror, 2020a). Some examiners have outright rejected the idea that bias affects their judgment—such as Leadbetter (2007), former chairman of the International Fingerprint Society, who wrote that any examiner who is "influence[d by] stories and gory images is either totally incapable . . . or is so immature that he/she should seek employment at Disneyland" (p. 231; see also Butt, 2013). Given the now-ample literature summarized in table 36.1, this position is no longer tenable—but nevertheless, many examiners continue to believe that they are immune to bias.

Instead, examiners often argue that irrelevant contextual information benefits their accuracy (e.g., Curley et al., 2020; Elaad, 2013; Oliver, 2018) and hence they actively seek it out (Gardner, Kelley, Murrie, & Blaisdell, 2019; Hamnett & Jack, 2019; Osborne, Taylor, & Zajac, 2016). This argument is dangerously misguided. To illustrate, Stevenage and Bennett (2019) found that students who had a priori knowledge of DNA evidence that implicated or exculpated a suspect made more accurate judgments of fingerprint pairs by simply agreeing with the DNA evidence. However, such an increase in accuracy is purely incidental; bias-tainted judgments—even if accurate—carry no independent probative value because they do not stem from examiners' unique expertise (see Dror, 2009; Kukucka, 2020; Thompson, 2011). In other words, bias may sometimes lead examiners to the right conclusion, but for the wrong reasons.

To better understand examiners' beliefs about bias, Kukucka et al. (2017) surveyed 403 examiners from twenty-one countries and found that most (71 percent) were concerned about cognitive bias in the forensic sciences as a whole—but fewer (52 percent) saw it as a problem in their own discipline, and still fewer (26 percent) felt that bias affects them personally. This pattern suggests a *bias blind spot* (Pronin et al., 2002), such that examiners see themselves as less biased than their peers. Moreover, only 49 percent of examiners felt they should be shielded from potentially biasing information, while 71 percent felt they could prevent bias by simply setting aside their expectations. The latter reflects a common misconception that bias is an ethical or motivational issue that can be avoided via training and/or willpower, which is simply not the case (Dror et al., 2013; Thompson, 2008). Although some errors are certainly due to incompetence and/or fraud (see Giannelli, 2007), cognitive bias can affect even skilled and honest examiners who are aware of the bias and motivated to correct it (see generally Wilson & Brekke, 1994). Thus, even if examiners recognize bias as a problem, their misperception of its controllability may beget ineffective efforts to address it.

Finally, some examiners may feel that reliance on technology mitigates bias. Technologies can surely facilitate efficient and accurate analyses, but they are unlikely to eradicate bias insofar as they supplement—not replace—human judgment (Dror & Mnookin, 2010). Moreover, some technologies may codify the biases of the humans who create them, as illustrated by recent concern over racial bias in facial recognition software (Lohr, 2018). In some cases, technology may even prompt bias; for example, Dror et al. (2012) found that fingerprint experts who used a computerized system to generate a rank-ordered list of potential matches to a latent print were more likely to select whichever prints appeared toward the top of the list as a match, regardless of accuracy. Thus, new technologies may alleviate some problems while creating others.

Legal Professionals' Understanding

After reaching a conclusion, examiners must communicate their conclusion to nonexperts (e.g., investigators, attorneys, and judges). van Straalen et al. (2020) recently found that these groups rated their own understanding of forensic reports as strong, yet their interpretations were noticeably flawed, as they tended to give examiners' conclusions more weight than was intended. For example, after reading a report, 26 percent of participants believed that the forensic evidence definitively implicated the suspect and 36 percent believed that it placed the suspect at the crime scene, when in fact neither was true. It is unclear whether these discrepancies are due to unclear reporting by examiners and/or misunderstanding by legal professionals, but in either case, such a communication breakdown is clearly problematic (see also Howes, 2017).

Similarly, Despodova et al. (2020) asked defense attorneys to evaluate a case file of evidence against a hypothetical client, including an autopsy report that was either patently biased (i.e., the medical examiner based his medical opinion on the defendant's confession) or unbiased. Regardless, they rated the autopsy as equally reliable, were equally confident in their client's guilt, and were equally likely to recommend a guilty plea. Moreover, only 47 percent of attorneys who read the biased autopsy said that they would ask about bias on cross-examination. Thus, even if attorneys are more skeptical of forensic science than the general public (Garrett & Mitchell, 2016), they may be unequipped to detect and attack unreliable forensic evidence. This problem is exacerbated by the fact that so many cases are settled by plea bargain (Redlich et al., 2017), which precludes any opportunity to scrutinize the forensic evidence and attack it when appropriate.

Jurors' Understanding

Do jurors give appropriate weight to forensic science evidence? Most studies have found jurors to be highly trusting of forensic evidence—even if the examiner used an unvalidated method (Koehler et al., 2016), even if they were forewarned of its limitations (McQuiston-Surrett & Saks, 2009), and especially if it was presented by a confident and credential expert (McCarthy-Wilcox & NicDaeid, 2018) or with a related but nonprobative photo (Sanson et al., 2020). For example, Koehler (2017) found that laypeople estimated an unrealistically low error rate of 0.0001 percent for both bite-mark comparison and microscopic hair comparison. Conversely, some data suggest that laypeople are skeptical of some forensic disciplines, with estimated accuracy rates at low as 57 percent (footwear comparison; Kaplan et al., 2020) or 65 percent (document examination; Ribeiro et al., 2019). Ribeiro et al. (2019) also found that jurors underestimated fingerprint examiners' accuracy (88 percent) relative to their actual accuracy rates in proficiency studies (97 percent; Tangen et al., 2011; Ulery et al., 2011). Thus, jurors may sometimes overvalue and sometimes undervalue forensic evidence—but importantly, for any forensic discipline whose error rate is unknown (National Academy of Science, 2009; see also Dror, 2020b), it is impossible to know if jurors are giving the evidence too much or too little weight.

Other studies have examined whether jurors discount dubious forensic science testimony. In two such studies (Crozier et al., 2020; Mitchell & Garrett, 2019), jurors rightly devalued the testimony of a forensic examiner who had exhibited a high error rate on laboratory-based proficiency tests—but they still gave considerable weight to this examiner's testimony. Moreover, if an examiner's proficiency was unknown, they assumed he was highly proficient. These findings raise the troubling possibility that jurors strongly trust forensic experts even when their documented accuracy is poor or unknown.

Three studies have specifically examined jurors' ability to recognize biasing influences on forensic science testimony. Scurich (2015) found that jurors were less persuaded by DNA evidence if the DNA expert testified that a detective had pressured him to give an inculpatory judgment. In contrast, Thompson and Scurich (2019) found that jurors rated a bite-mark expert as no less credible if he admitted that the suspect's criminal history could have influenced his opinion. Most recently, Kukucka, Hiley, and Kassin (2020) found that jurors devalued the testimony of a forensic examiner only if he explicitly admitted that the defendant's confession could have influenced his opinion—but not if he denied it (which is presumably the norm; Kukucka et al., 2017). Taken together, these findings suggest that jurors are largely unable to recognize and devalue biased forensic science testimony on their own—which is consistent with the broader literature on scientific expert testimony (e.g., Chorn & Kovera, 2019; McAuliff & Duckworth, 2010). Alternatively, jurors may be able to recognize overt sources of bias (i.e., pressure from investigators) but not subtler ones (i.e., biasing contextual information); future work should explore this possibility.

Cross-examination presents a potential safeguard against unreliable forensic testimony (see Edmond et al., 2014), but research has yielded mixed findings as to its efficacy. Some have found that cross-examination had little or no effect on a forensic expert's credibility (Garrett et al., 2020; Koehler, 2011), whereas others found that some strategies were more (e.g., emphasizing the subjectivity of the expert's opinion; Thompson & Scurich, 2019) or less (e.g., attacking the expert's credentials; Lieberman et al., 2008) effective than others. Future work should continue to examine which cross-examination strategies enable jurors to rightly discount dubious forensic testimony without creating a blanket skepticism that undercuts even valid forensic evidence. Relatedly, recent data from Martire et al. (2020) suggested that jurors may be unable—not unwilling—to critically evaluate forensic evidence, such that testimony from an opposing expert and/or judicial instructions may help sensitize them to invalid forensic testimony. Two studies (i.e., Eastwood & Caldwell, 2015; Mitchell & Garrett, 2021) have now found that opposing expert testimony was somewhat effective in this regard, though this question warrants further investigation.

Finally, jurors' trust in forensic experts' conclusions may depend on how those conclusions are framed. In a large content analysis, Bali et al. (2020) found that an overwhelming majority of examiners still express conclusions in categorical terms (i.e., as a "match" or "nonmatch"), even though this is widely considered inappropriate because it conveys an unwarranted degree of certainty (see also Cole & Barno, 2020). However, there is currently little consensus as to how examiners *should* express their conclusions (e.g., verbal scales, likelihood ratios, and random match probabilities) or how different conclusion types differentially influence jurors. Some have found that variations in reporting language (e.g., probabilistic vs. categorical statements) had little or no effect on the perceived strength of forensic conclusions (e.g., Garrett et al., 2018; Garrett et al., 2020; Thompson et al., 2018), whereas others have found that reporting language did have an effect and could create a problematic disconnect between what experts say and what jurors hear (Martire et al., 2014; Martire & Watkins, 2015; McQuiston-Surrett & Saks, 2008). As a middle ground, Thompson and Newman (2015) suggested that the effect of reporting language may vary between disciplines and/or depend on jurors' expectations, and future work should explore these possibilities.

Potential Solutions

The preceding section detailed a chain of events whereby (1) forensic examiners' misconceptions about cognitive bias limit measures to combat bias, thus spawning unreliable conclusions, (2) police and attorneys misinterpret the strength and/or reliability of forensic conclusions, and (3) jurors sometimes trust forensic evidence even when they should not. This final section describes procedural changes to reduce the risk of bias and error in the forensic sciences, including the potential benefits and challenges of each.

Blind Proficiency Testing

In the United States, the National Commission on Forensic Science (2016) has formally recommended regular proficiency testing as a quality control tool to estimate error rates and identify unreliable methodologies within and across forensic laboratories, as well as a precondition for accreditation. As it stands, many laboratories either create and distribute their own proficiency tests or contract an external organization to do so. However, scholars have noted that proficiency test results are only informative to the extent that the tests approximate actual casework (e.g., Dror, 2020b; Koehler, 2013; Mejia et al., 2020; Risinger et al., 2002)—and unfortunately, proficiency tests often fall short in two important respects.

First, proficiency tests tend to be less difficult than casework. Koertner and Swofford (2018) found that latent prints used in fingerprint proficiency tests were of higher quality and less complex than those seen in casework. Likewise, Kelley et al. (2020) found that fingerprint examiners were near-unanimous in their belief that proficiency tests were unrealistically easy. Accordingly, proficiency test data may suggest misleadingly low error rates; indeed, more than 96 percent of Kelley et al.'s examiners achieved perfect scores on their test (see also Gardner, Kelley, & Pan, 2020). Second, proficiency tests are not customarily blind; rather, examiners are typically aware that they are being tested. Consistent with the phenomenon of participant *reactivity*, examiners may behave in unrealistic ways—such as being more meticulous or less decisive—when aware that their performance is being monitored, which casts further doubt on the validity of these data.

Despite the logistical challenges of designing ecologically valid proficiency tests—such as knowing the ground truth of test samples, identifying samples of appropriate difficulty, and deciding when, if ever, to count inconclusive decisions as correct (see, e.g., Dror, 2020b; Dror & Scurich, 2020; Martire & Kemp, 2018; Mejia et al., 2020)—numerous laboratories have published accounts of their own implementation of blind proficiency testing programs (e.g., Hundl et al., 2020; Moral et al., 2019; Pierce & Cook, 2020; see also Gardner et al., 2021), detailing its costs and benefits and encouraging other labs to follow suit.

Relatedly, many forensic labs engage in *verification*—a form of peer review in which examiners' judgments are verified by a second examiner (see Ballantyne et al., 2017). Verification can be an effective means of detecting errors (e.g., Ulery et al., 2011; Wertheim et al., 2006). In practice, however, the verifying examiner is sometimes aware of the initial examiner's conclusion (Osborne & Taylor, 2018), which invites bias, as discussed above. Moreover, in some laboratories, it is customary to verify only "match" judgments, which may be self-defeating insofar as it creates a low prevalence effect (see above) that hinders verifiers' ability to detect errors. Despite its widespread use, there has been surprisingly little research on verification procedures and how to maximize their effectiveness; future research should address this gap.

Linear Sequential Unmasking

As explained above, exposure to reference materials and/or irrelevant contextual information can taint forensic examiners' judgments. To address these issues, Dror et al. (2015) proposed a procedure Linear Sequential Unmasking (LSU), which regulates the flow of information to examiners. Under LSU, examiners first analyze trace evidence from the crime scene in isolation, and they document their initial judgment and confidence before receiving any reference material or relevant context, thereby preventing the latter from guiding analysis of the former. Examiners may then revise their initial judgment in light of this new information—though not limitlessly, and only if they clearly document any such changes. LSU therefore does not preclude the possibility of bias, but it makes its potential effects more transparent.

More recently, Dror and Kukucka (2021) introduced Linear Sequential Unmasking—Expanded (LSU-E), which is a more versatile approach that can be implemented in any forensic discipline and enhances the quality of decision-making more broadly beyond mitigating bias. In short, LSU-E requires examiners to first form an opinion based solely on the actual data/evidence before receiving any other relevant information. Then, rather than exposing examiners to additional information in a random or incidental order, LSU-E provides three criteria—namely, objectivity, relevance, and biasing power—for optimizing the sequence of information in a way that maximizes the utility of the resultant decisions. Along the way, examiners must also document the justifications for, and any changes to, their decisions.

Several labs have now implemented variants of LSU, describing it as "not complex, overly time-consuming or expensive" (Found & Ganas, 2013, p. 158) and noting that it "increase[d] the value of the opinion to the court" (Archer & Wallman, 2016, p. 1276; see also Mattijssen et al., 2016; Stoel et al., 2014). Others have resisted, citing concerns over financial cost, existing backlogs of cases, and the difficulty of making sweeping decisions about what information is task-relevant (Charlton, 2013; Gardner, Kelley, Murrie, & Dror, 2019; Langenburg, 2017). As a middle ground, Dror et al. (2013) proposed a triage approach, where resource-intensive context management procedures are reserved for cases where the risk of bias is greatest (i.e., the "bias danger zone"; e.g., cases with complex evidence and/or strong contextual influences).

Other procedures may be used to avoid *bias cascade*—a phenomenon whereby biasing information from the crime scene later biases analytical work in the laboratory (Dror, 2018). Agencies can disrupt bias cascade by compartmentalizing the forensic workflow—for example, by ensuring that the person who collects evidence at the crime scene is not the same person who later examines that same evidence in the laboratory. Similarly, Thompson (2011) discussed a *case manager* model, wherein a second qualified examiner acts as an intermediary between investigators and the primary analyst, and in so doing, filters out any suggestive communications from investigators and helps them to properly understand the analyst's conclusion.

Evidence Lineups

In many forensic disciplines, examiners compare a sample from the crime scene against one sample from a known suspect. Whitman and Koppl (2010) argued that this procedure may inherently suggest guilt: Because police do not select suspects at random, examiners may infer the existence of other incriminating evidence (even without any specific knowledge) and thus be inclined to judge the samples as a "match."

This practice is analogous to an eyewitness "showup," where a witness views a single suspect photo and indicates whether or not that person was the culprit (see Wells et al., 2020). Eyewitness showups have likewise been criticized as inherently suggestive of guilt, and indeed, showups consistently yield poorer identification accuracy than lineups (e.g., Neuschatz et al., 2016; Wetmore et al., 2015), such that the use of showups is now strongly discouraged (National Academy of Science, 2014; Wells et al., 2020). Instead, eyewitnesses customarily view a photo lineup, which embeds the suspect's photo among known-innocent filler photos, such that the witness is unaware of the suspect's identity and it is possible for the witness to make a known error (i.e., misidentifying one of the filler photos as the culprit; Wells & Turtle, 1986).

In light of this, some scholars have proposed that forensic examiners likewise view an *evidence lineup* that embeds the suspect's sample among known-innocent fillers (e.g., Kassin et al., 2013; Risinger et al., 2002). In addition to mitigating bias, Wells et al. (2013) noted that evidence lineups would facilitate the estimation of error rates and expose incompetent examiners and/or flawed methodologies that produce high rates of filler identifications. In the first-ever study of evidence lineups, Miller (1987) found that trainees less often misjudged a nonmatching hair as a match if they compared it against a lineup of five hairs as opposed to a single suspect hair. Quigley-McBride and Wells (2018) provided a more comprehensive test of evidence lineups, finding that novices who viewed a fingerprint lineup made fewer correct identifications—but even fewer false identifications—than those who used the standard procedure, and that evidence lineups siphoned errors away from the suspect and onto filler samples (see also Quigley-McBride, 2020). Most recently, Kukucka, Dror, et al. (2020) found that fingerprint experts who viewed an evidence lineup produced more inconclusive judgments, but they were also somewhat less likely to miss a matching sample when one was present. In sum, there is mounting evidence that evidence lineups and eyewitness lineups produce similar effects on judgment, such that they may reap similar benefits in the forensic sciences.

The use of evidence lineups would surely present some challenges as well, such as how to generate appropriate filler samples, how to administer the lineup, and whether lineups should be used in all or only select cases (see Kukucka, Dror, et al., 2020; Quigley-McBride & Wells, 2018)—and the answers to these questions may well vary across disciplines. Despite this, at least some examiners appear quite open to the idea: For example, the American Board of Forensic Odontologists' (2018) current guidelines recommend that bite-mark examiners make identifications from "a dental lineup of dentition evidence . . . includ[ing] evidence from the person or persons of interest and from other individuals as foils," and some examiners report using evidence lineups in private practice (e.g., Langenburg, 2017, p. 2). Future research should continue to investigate the effectiveness, feasibility, and optimization of evidence lineups across forensic disciplines.

Beyond the Forensic Examiners

Each of the aforementioned "solutions" focuses on forensic examiners per se. However, examiners do not work in isolation; rather, they interact with myriad stakeholders who can both influence *them* and be influenced *by* them—including peers, supervisors, investigators, attorneys, judges, juries, accrediting bodies, and policymakers, among others (see Dror & Pierce, 2020). The complex causes of forensic science error will require an equally complex solution that engages as many stakeholders as possible—for example, by better educating jurors about the quality of forensic evidence, and by requiring investigators and attorneys to document their communications with examiners to increase transparency and accountability.

In so doing, collaboration between forensic and psychological scientists will be critical. Indeed, both forensic examiners (e.g., Found, 2015) and psychologists (e.g., Curley et al., 2020; Kukucka, 2020) have explicitly called for interdisciplinary efforts to develop guidelines that balance idealism and practicality, thereby strengthening forensic science without hamstringing it. Fortunately, some such efforts are already underway—including the Organization of Scientific Committees for Forensic Science (OSAC), a US federal organization that brings together forensic practitioners, psychologists, legal scholars, and statisticians to develop and disseminate best practice guidelines for all forensic science disciplines. Research collaborations will also prove critical in ensuring that such guidelines are grounded in empirical data, and as shown in table 36.1, studies of forensic expert performance have increased dramatically in recent years.

Though there is much more work left to be done, we are encouraged by the tremendous strides that have been made in the past decade, and we hope that the content of this chapter will inspire others to join us in the effort to strengthen forensic decision-making.

References

Almazrouei, M. A., Dror, I. E., & Morgan, R. M. (2020). Organizational and human factors affecting forensic decision-making: Workplace stress and feedback. *Journal of Forensic Sciences, 65,* 1968–1977.

Almazrouei, M. A., Morgan, R. M., & Dror, I. E. (2021). Stress and support in the workplace: The perspective of forensic examiners. *Forensic Science International: Mind and Law, 2*(1), Article 100059.

American Board of Forensic Odontology. (2018). *Standards and guidelines for evaluating bitemarks.* http://abfo.org/wp-content/uploads/2012/08/ABFO-Standards-Guidelines-for-Evaluating-Bitemarks-Feb-2018.pdf

Archer, M. S., & Wallman, J. F. (2016). Context effects in forensic entomology and use of sequential unmasking in casework. *Journal of Forensic Sciences, 61*, 1270–1277.

Bali, A. S., Edmond, G., Ballantyne, K. N., Kemp, R. I., & Martire, K. A. (2020). Communicating forensic science opinion: An examination of expert reporting practices. *Science & Justice, 60*, 216–224.

Ballantyne, K. N., Edmond, G., & Found, B. (2017). Peer review in forensic science. *Forensic Science International, 277*, 66–76.

Bieber, P. (2012). *Measuring the impact of cognitive bias in fire investigation.* International Symposium on Fire Investigation, Science and Technology. http://truthinjustice.org/Cognative_Bias_ARP.pdf

Bruner, J. S., & Goodman, C. C. (1947). Value and need as organizing factors in perception. *The Journal of Abnormal and Social Psychology, 42*, 33–44.

Butt, L. (2013). The forensic confirmation bias: Problems, perspectives, and proposed solutions: Commentary by a forensic examiner. *Journal of Applied Research in Memory and Cognition, 2*, 59–60.

Charlton, D. (2013). Standards to avoid bias in fingerprint examination: Are such standards doomed to be based on fiscal expediency? *Journal of Applied Research in Memory and Cognition, 2*, 71–72.

Charlton, D., Fraser-Mackenzie, P. A. F., & Dror, I. E. (2010). Emotional experiences and motivating factors associated with fingerprint analysis. *Journal of Forensic Sciences, 55*, 385–393.

Chi, M. T. H. (2006). Two approaches to the study of experts' characteristics. In K. A. Ericsson, N. Charness, P. J. Feltovich, & R. R. Hoffman (Eds.), *The Cambridge handbook of expertise and expert performance* (pp. 21–30). Cambridge University Press.

Chiam, S. L., Dror, I. E., Huber, C. D., & Higgins, D. (2021). The biasing impact of irrelevant contextual information on forensic odontology radiograph matching decisions. *Forensic Science International, 327*, 110997.

Chiam, S. L., Louise, S., & Higgins, D. (2022). "Identified", "probable", "possible" or "exclude": The influence of task-irrelevant information on forensic odontology identification opinion. *Science & Justice, 62*, 461–470.

Chorn, J. A., & Kovera, M. B. (2019). Variations in reliability and validity do not influence judge, attorney, and mock juror decisions about psychological expert evidence. *Law and Human Behavior, 43*, 542–557.

Cole, S. A., & Barno, M. (2020). Probabilistic reporting in criminal cases in the United States: A baseline study. *Science & Justice, 60*, 406–414.

Crozier, W. E., Kukucka, J., & Garrett, B. L. (2020). Juror appraisals of forensic evidence: Effects of blind proficiency and cross-examination. *Forensic Science International, 315*, 110433.

Curley, L. J., Munro, J., & Lages, M. (2020). An inconvenient truth: More rigorous and ecologically valid research is needed to properly understand cognitive bias in forensic decisions. *Forensic Science International: Synergy, 2*, 107–109.

De Gruijter, M., Nee, C., & De Poot, C. J. (2017). Rapid identification information and its influence on the perceived clues at a crime scene: An experimental study. *Science & Justice, 57*, 421–430.

Despodova, N. M., Kukucka, J., & Hiley, A. (2020). Can defense attorneys detect forensic confirmation bias? Effects on evidentiary judgments and trial strategies. *Zeitschrift für Psychologie, 228*, 216–220.

Dror, I. E. (2009). On proper research and understanding of the interplay between bias and decision outcomes. *Forensic Science International, 191*, e17–e18.

Dror, I. E. (2011). The paradox of human expertise: Why experts get it wrong. In N. Kapur (Ed.), *The paradoxical brain* (pp. 177–188). Cambridge University Press.

Dror, I. E. (2018). Biases in forensic experts. *Science, 360*, 243.

Dror, I. E. (2020a). Cognitive and human factors in expert decision making: Six fallacies and the eight sources of bias. *Analytical Chemistry, 92*, 7998–8004.

Dror, I. (2020b). The error in "error rate": Why error rates are so needed, yet so elusive. *Journal of Forensic Sciences, 65*, 1034–1039.

Dror, I. E., Champod, C., Langenburg, G., Charlton, D., Hunt, H., & Rosenthal, R. (2011). Cognitive issues in fingerprint analysis: Inter-and intra-expert consistency and the effect of a 'target' comparison. *Forensic Science International, 208*, 10–17.

Dror, I. E., & Charlton, D. (2006). Why experts make errors. *Journal of Forensic Identification, 56*, 600–616.

Dror, I. E., Charlton, D., & Peron, A. (2006). Contextual information renders experts vulnerable to making erroneous identifications. *Forensic Science International, 156*, 174–178.

Dror, I. E., & Hampikian, G. (2011). Subjectivity and bias in forensic DNA mixture interpretation. *Science & Justice, 51,* 204–208.

Dror, I. E., Kassin, S. M., & Kukucka, J. (2013). New application of psychology to law: Improving forensic evidence and expert witness contributions. *Journal of Applied Research in Memory and Cognition, 2,* 78–81.

Dror, I. E., & Kukucka, J. (2021). Linear sequential unmasking–expanded (LSU-E): A general approach for improving decision making as well as minimizing bias. *Forensic Science International: Synergy, 3,* 100161.

Dror, I. E., Melinek, J., Arden, J. L., Kukucka, J., Hawkins, S., Carter, J., & Atherton, D. (2021). Cognitive bias in forensic pathology decisions. *Journal of Forensic Sciences, 66,* 1751–1757. https://doi.org/10.1111/1556-4029.14697

Dror, I. E., & Mnookin, J. (2010). The use of technology in human expert domains: Challenges and risks arising from the use of automated fingerprint identification systems in forensics. *Law, Probability & Risk, 9,* 47–67.

Dror, I. E., Peron, A. E., Hind, S.-L., & Charlton, D. (2005). When emotions get the better of us: The effect of contextual top-down processing on matching fingerprints. *Applied Cognitive Psychology, 19,* 799–809.

Dror, I. E., & Pierce, M. L. (2020). ISO standards addressing issues of bias and impartiality in forensic work. *Journal of Forensic Sciences, 65,* 800–808.

Dror, I. E., Scherr, K. C., Mohammed, L. A., MacLean, C. L., & Cunningham, L. (2020). Biasability and reliability of expert forensic document examiners. *Forensic Science International, 318,* 110610.

Dror, I. E., & Scurich, N. (2020). (Mis)use of scientific measurements in forensic science. *Forensic Science International: Synergy, 2,* 333–338.

Dror, I. E., Thompson, W. C., Meissner, C. A., Kornfield, I., Krane, D., Saks, M., & Risinger, M. (2015). Context management toolbox: A linear sequential unmasking (LSU) approach for minimizing cognitive bias in forensic decision making. *Journal of Forensic Sciences, 60,* 1111–1112.

Dror, I. E., Wertheim, K., Fraser-Mackenzie, P., & Walajtys, J. (2012). The impact of human-technology cooperation and distributed cognition in forensic science: Biasing effects of AFIS contextual information on human experts. *Journal of Forensic Sciences, 57,* 343–352.

Dror, I. E., Wolf, D. A., Phillips, G., Gao, S., Yang, Y., & Drake, S. A. (2022). Contextual information in medicolegal death investigation decision-making: Manner of death determination for cases of a single gunshot wound. *Forensic Science International: Synergy.* doi:10.1016/j.fsisyn.2022.100285

Earwaker, H., Morgan, R. M., Harris, A. J., & Hall, L. J. (2015). Fingermark submission decision-making within a UK fingerprint laboratory: Do experts get the marks that they need? *Science & Justice, 55,* 239–247.

Eastwood, J., & Caldwell, J. (2015). Educating jurors about forensic evidence: Using an expert witness and judicial instructions to mitigate the impact of invalid forensic science testimony. *Journal of Forensic Sciences, 60,* 1523–1528.

Edmond, G., Martire, K., Kemp, R., Hamer, D., Hibbert, B., Ligertwood, A., Porter, G., San Roque, M., Searston, R., Tangen, J., Thompson, M., & White, D. (2014). How to cross-examine forensic scientists: A guide for lawyers. *Australian Bar Review, 39,* 174–197.

Elaad, E. (2013). Psychological contamination in forensic decisions. *Journal of Applied Research in Memory and Cognition, 2,* 76–77.

Fawver, B., Thomas, J. L., Drew, T., Mills, M. K., Auffermann, W. F., Lohse, K. R., & Williams, A. M. (2020). Seeing isn't necessarily believing: Misleading contextual information influences perceptual-cognitive bias in radiologists. *Journal of Experimental Psychology: Applied, 26,* 579–592.

Found, B. (2015). Deciphering the human condition: the rise of cognitive forensics. *Australian Journal of Forensic Sciences, 47,* 386–401.

Found, B., & Ganas, J. (2013). The management of domain irrelevant context information in forensic handwriting examination casework. *Science & Justice, 53,* 154–158.

Fraser-Mackenzie, P. A., Dror, I. E., & Wertheim, K. (2013). Cognitive and contextual influences in determination of latent fingerprint suitability for identification judgments. *Science & Justice, 53,* 144–153.

Gardner, B. O., Kelley, S., Murrie, D. C., & Blaisdell, K. N. (2019). Do evidence submission forms expose latent print examiners to task-irrelevant information? *Forensic Science International, 297,* 236–242.

Gardner, B. O., Kelley, S., Murrie, D. C., & Dror, I. E. (2019). What do forensic analysts consider relevant to their decision making? *Science & Justice, 59,* 516–523.

Gardner, B. O., Kelley, S., & Neuman, M. (2021). Latent print comparison and examiner conclusions: A field analysis of case processing in one crime laboratory. *Forensic Science International, 319,* Article 110642.

Gardner, B. O., Kelley, S., & Pan, K. D. (2020). Latent print proficiency testing: An examination of test respondents, test-taking procedures, and test characteristics. *Journal of Forensic Sciences, 65,* 450–457.

Gardner, B. O., Neuman, M., & Kelley, S. (2021). Latent print quality in blind proficiency testing: Using quality metrics to examine laboratory performance. *Forensic Science International, 324*, 110823.

Garrett, B. L., & Mitchell, G. (2016). Forensics and fallibility: Comparing the views of lawyers and jurors. *West Virginia Law Review, 119*, 621–638.

Garrett, B., Mitchell, G., & Scurich, N. (2018). Comparing categorical and probabilistic fingerprint evidence. *Journal of Forensic Sciences, 63*, 1712–1717.

Garrett, B. L., Scurich, N., & Crozier, W. E. (2020). Mock jurors' evaluation of firearm examiner testimony. *Law and Human Behavior, 44*, 412–423.

Giannelli, P. C. (2007). Wrongful convictions and forensic science: The need to regulate crime labs. *North Carolina Law Review, 86*, 163–236.

Giannelli, P. C. (2010). Independent crime laboratories: The problem of motivational and cognitive bias. *Utah Law Review, 2010*, 247–266.

Gregory, R. (1970). *The intelligent eye*. Weidenfeld & Nicolson.

Growns, B., Dunn, J. D., Helm, R. K., Towler, A., & Kukucka, J. (2022). The low prevalence effect in fingerprint comparison amongst forensic science trainees and novices. *PLoS ONE, 17*, e0272338.

Growns, B., & Kukucka, J. (2021). The prevalence effect in fingerprint identification: Match and non-match base rates impact misses and false alarms. *Applied Cognitive Psychology, 35*, 751–760.

Hackman, L., Davies, C., Langstaff, H., Swales, D., & NicDaeid, N. (2018). [Untitled commentary.] *Journal of Forensic Sciences, 63*, 1597.

Hagan, W. E. (1894). *A treatise on disputed handwriting and the determination of genuine from forged signatures*. Banks & Brothers.

Hall, L. J., & Player, E. (2008). Will the introduction of an emotional context affect fingerprint analysis and decision-making? *Forensic Science International, 181*, 36–39.

Hamnett, H. J., & Dror, I. E. (2020). The effect of contextual information on decision-making in forensic toxicology. *Forensic Science International: Synergy, 2*, 339–348.

Hamnett, H. J., & Jack, R. E. (2019). The use of contextual information in forensic toxicology: An international survey of toxicologists' experiences. *Science & Justice, 59*, 380–389.

Hartley, S., Winburn, A. P., & Dror, I. E. (2022). Metric forensic anthropology decisions: Reliability and bias-ability of sectioning-point-based sex estimates. *Journal of Forensic Sciences, 67*, 68–79.

Horowitz, T. S. (2017). Prevalence in visual search: From the clinic to the lab and back again. *Japanese Psychological Research, 59*, 65–108.

Howes, L. M. (2017). 'Sometimes I give up on the report and ring the scientist': Bridging the gap between what forensic scientists write and what police investigators read. *Policing and Society, 27*, 541–559.

Hugh, L., & Satchell, L. (2018). *Beginning with blood patterns: Surface material and case information effects on trainee analysts' judgments*. OSF. https://doi.org/10.31219/osf.io/xe8hq

Hundl, C., Neuman, M., Rairden, A., Rearden, P., & Stout, P. (2020). Implementation of a blind quality control program in a forensic laboratory. *Journal of Forensic Sciences, 65*, 815–822.

Jeanguenat, A. M., Budowle, B., & Dror, I. E. (2017). Strengthening forensic DNA decision making through a better understanding of the influence of cognitive bias. *Science & Justice, 57*, 415–420.

Jeanguenat, A. M., & Dror, I. E. (2018). Human factors effecting forensic decision making: Workplace stress and well-being. *Journal of Forensic Sciences, 63*, 258–261.

Kaplan, J., Ling, S., & Cuellar, M. (2020). Public beliefs about the accuracy and importance of forensic evidence in the United States. *Science & Justice, 60*, 263–272.

Kassin, S. M., Dror, I. E., & Kukucka, J. (2013). The forensic confirmation bias: Problems, perspectives, and proposed solutions. *Journal of Applied Research in Memory and Cognition, 2*, 42–52.

Kelley, S., Gardner, B. O., Murrie, D. C., Pan, K. D., & Kafadar, K. (2020). How do latent print examiners perceive proficiency testing? An analysis of examiner perceptions, performance, and print quality. *Science & Justice, 60*, 120–127.

Kerstholt, J., Eikelboom, A., Dijkman, T., Stoel, R., Hermsen, R., & van Leuven, B. (2010). Does suggestive information cause a confirmation bias in bullet comparisons? *Forensic Science International, 198*, 138–142.

Kerstholt, J., Paashuis, R., & Sjerps, M. (2007). Shoe print examinations: Effects of expectation, complexity and experience. *Forensic Science International, 165*, 30–34.

Koehler, J. J. (2011). If the shoe fits they might acquit: The value of forensic science testimony. *Journal of Empirical Legal Studies, 8*, 21–48.

Koehler, J. J. (2013). Proficiency tests to estimate error rates in the forensic sciences. *Law, Probability & Risk, 12*, 89–98.

Koehler, J. J. (2017). Intuitive error rate estimates for the forensic sciences. *Jurimetrics, 57*, 153–168.

Koehler, J. J., Schweitzer, N. J., Saks, M. J., & McQuiston, D. E. (2016). Science, technology, or the expert witness: What influences jurors' judgments about forensic science testimony? *Psychology, Public Policy, and Law, 22*, 401–413.

Koertner, A. J., & Swofford, H. J. (2018). Comparison of latent print proficiency tests with latent prints obtained in routine casework using automated and objective quality metrics. *Journal of Forensic Identification, 68*, 379–388.

Kouwenhoven, M. K. J. (2018). *Focus on the task at hand: Contextual bias in the forensic examination of handwriting* [Unpublished doctoral dissertation]. University of Otago.

Kukucka, J. (2014). The journey or the destination? Disentangling process and outcome in forensic identification. *Forensic Science Policy & Management, 5*, 112–114.

Kukucka, J. (2020). People who live in ivory towers shouldn't throw stones: A refutation of Curley et al. *Forensic Science International: Synergy, 2*, 110–113.

Kukucka, J., Dror, I. E., Yu, M., Hall, L., & Morgan, R. M. (2020). The impact of evidence lineups on fingerprint expert decisions. *Applied Cognitive Psychology, 34*, 1143–1153.

Kukucka, J., Hiley, A., & Kassin, S. M. (2020). Forensic confirmation bias: Do jurors discount examiners who were exposed to task-irrelevant information? *Journal of Forensic Sciences, 65*, 1978–1990.

Kukucka, J., & Kassin, S. M. (2014). Do confessions taint perceptions of handwriting evidence? An empirical test of the forensic confirmation bias. *Law and Human Behavior, 38*, 256–270.

Kukucka, J., Kassin, S. M., Zapf, P. A., & Dror, I. E. (2017). Cognitive bias and blindness: A global survey of forensic science examiners. *Journal of Applied Research in Memory and Cognition, 6*, 452–459.

Lange, N. D., Thomas, R. P., Dana, J., & Dawes, R. M. (2011). Contextual biases in the interpretation of auditory evidence. *Law and Human Behavior, 35*, 178–187.

Langenburg, G. (2017). Addressing potential observer effects in forensic science: A perspective from a forensic scientist who uses linear sequential unmasking techniques. *Australian Journal of Forensic Sciences, 49*, 548–563.

Langenburg, G., Bochet, F., & Ford, S. (2014). A report of statistics from latent print casework. *Forensic Science Policy & Management, 5*, 15–37.

Langenburg, G., Champod, C., & Wertheim, P. (2009). Testing for potential contextual bias effects during the verification stage of the ACE-V methodology when conducting fingerprint comparisons. *Journal of Forensic Sciences, 54*, 571–582.

Leadbetter, M. (2007). Letter to the editor. *Fingerprint World, 33*, 231.

Levin, A. P., Putney, H., Crimmins, D., & McGrath, J. G. (2021). Secondary traumatic stress, burnout, compassion satisfaction, and perceived organizational trauma readiness in forensic science professionals. *Journal of Forensic Sciences, 66*(5), 1758–1769. https://doi.org/10.1111/1556-4029.14747

Lewis, J. A. (2016). Minimizing cognitive bias in forensic document examination. *Journal of the American Society of Questioned Document Examiners, 19*, 33–36.

Lieberman, J. D., Carrell, C. A., Miethe, T. D., & Krauss, D. A. (2008). Gold versus platinum: Do jurors recognize the superiority and limitations of DNA evidence compared to other types of forensic evidence? *Psychology, Public Policy, & Law, 14*, 27–62.

Lit, L., Schweitzer, J. B., & Oberbauer, A. M. (2011). Handler beliefs affect scent detection dog outcomes. *Animal Cognition, 14*, 387–394.

Lohr, S. (2018, February 9). Facial recognition is accurate, if you're a white guy. *The New York Times*. https://www.nytimes.com/2018/02/09/technology/facial-recognition-race-artificial-intelligence.html

Martire, K. A., Growns, B., Bali, A. S., Montgomery-Farrer, B., Summersby, S., & Younan, M. (2020). Limited not lazy: A quasi-experimental secondary analysis of evidence quality evaluations by those who hold implausible beliefs. *Cognitive Research: Principles and Implications, 5*, 1–15.

Martire, K. A., & Kemp, R. I. (2018). Considerations when designing human performance tests in the forensic sciences. *Australian Journal of Forensic Sciences, 50*, 166–182.

Martire, K. A., Kemp, R. I., Sayle, M., & Newell, B. R. (2014). On the interpretation of likelihood ratios in forensic science evidence: Presentation formats and the weak evidence effect. *Forensic Science International, 240*, 61–68.

Martire, K. A., & Watkins, I. (2015). Perception problems of the verbal scale: A reanalysis and application of a membership function approach. *Science & Justice, 55*, 264–273.

Mattijssen, E. J. A. T., Kerkhoff, W., Berger, C. E. H., Dror, I. E., & Stoel, R. D. (2016). Implementing context information management in forensic casework: Minimizing contextual bias in firearms examination. *Science & Justice, 56*, 113–122.

Mattijssen, E. J., Witteman, C. L., Berger, C. E., & Stoel, R. D. (2020). Cognitive biases in the peer review of bullet and cartridge case comparison casework: A field study. *Science & Justice, 60*, 337–346.

McAuliff, B. D., & Duckworth, T. D. (2010). I spy with my little eye: Jurors' detection of internal validity threats in expert evidence. *Law and Human Behavior, 34*, 489–500.

McCarthy-Wilcox, A., & NicDaeid, N. (2018). Jurors' perceptions of forensic science expert witnesses: Experience, qualifications, testimony style and credibility. *Forensic Science International, 291*, 100–108.

McQuiston-Surrett, D., & Saks, M. J. (2009). The testimony of forensic identification science: What expert witnesses say and what factfinders hear. *Law and Human Behavior, 33*, 436–453.

Mejia, R., Cuellar, M., & Salyards, J. (2020). Implementing blind proficiency testing in forensic laboratories: Motivation, obstacles, and recommendations. *Forensic Science International: Synergy, 2*, 293–298.

Merlino, M. L. (2015). *Validity, reliability, accuracy, and bias in forensic signature identification.* National Institute of Justice. https://www.ncjrs.gov/pdffiles1/nij/grants/248565.pdf

Miller, L. S. (1984). Bias among forensic document examiners: A need for procedural changes. *Journal of Police Science and Administration, 12*, 407–411.

Miller, L. S. (1987). Procedural bias in forensic science examinations of human hair. *Law and Human Behavior, 11*, 157–163.

Mitchell, G., & Garrett, B. L. (2019). The impact of proficiency testing information and error aversions on the weight given to fingerprint evidence. *Behavioral Sciences & the Law, 37*, 195–210.

Mitchell, G., & Garrett, B. L. (2021). Battling to a draw: Defense expert rebuttal can neutralize prosecution fingerprint evidence. *Applied Cognitive Psychology, 35*, 976–987.

Moral, J., Hundl, C., Lee, D., Neuman, M., Grimaldi, A., Cuellar, M., & Stout, P. (2019). Implementation of a blind quality control program in blood alcohol analysis. *Journal of Analytical Toxicology, 43*, 630–636.

Murrie, D. C., Boccaccini, M. T., Guarnera, L. A., & Rufino, K. A. (2013). Are forensic experts biased by the side that retained them? *Psychological Science, 24*, 1889–1897.

Nakashima, R., Watanabe, C., Maeda, E., Yoshikawa, T., Matsuda, I., Miki, S., & Yokosawa, K. (2015). The effect of expert knowledge on medical search: medical experts have specialized abilities for detecting serious lesions. *Psychological Research, 79*, 729–738.

Nakhaeizadeh, S., Dror, I. E., & Morgan, R. (2014). Cognitive bias in forensic anthropology: Visual assessment of skeletal remains is susceptible to confirmation bias. *Science & Justice, 54*, 208–214.

Nakhaeizadeh, S., Hanson, I., & Dozzi, N. (2014). The power of contextual effects in forensic anthropology: A study of biasability in the visual interpretations of trauma analysis on skeletal remains. *Journal of Forensic Sciences, 59*, 1177–1183.

Nakhaeizadeh, S., Morgan, R. M., Olsson, V., Arvidsson, M., & Thompson, T. (2020). The value of eye-tracking technology in the analysis and interpretations of skeletal remains: A pilot study. *Science & Justice, 60*, 36–42.

National Academy of Sciences. (2009). *Strengthening forensic science in the United States: A path forward.* National Academies Press.

National Academy of Sciences. (2014). *Identifying the culprit: Assessing eyewitness identification.* National Academies Press.

National Commission on Forensic Science. (2015). *Ensuring that forensic analysis is based upon task-relevant information.* US Department of Justice. https://www.justice.gov/ncfs/file/818196/download

National Registry of Exonerations. (2020). *The national registry of exonerations.* http://www.law.umich.edu/special/exoneration/Pages/about.aspx

Neuschatz, J. S., Wetmore, S. A., Key, K. N., Cash, D. K., Gronlund, S. D., & Goodsell, C. A. (2016). A comprehensive evaluation of showups. In M. K. Miller & B. H. Bornstein (Eds.), *Advances in psychology and law* (pp. 43–69). Springer.

Nickerson, R. S. (1998). Confirmation bias: A ubiquitous phenomenon in many guises. *Review of General Psychology, 2*, 175–220.

Oliver, W. R. (2017). Effect of history and context on forensic pathologist interpretation of photographs of patterned injury of the skin. *Journal of Forensic Sciences, 62*, 1500–1505.

Oliver, W. R. (2018). Comment on Dror, Kukucka, Kassin, and Zapf (2018), "When expert decision making goes wrong." *Journal of Applied Research in Memory and Cognition, 7*, 314–315.

Osborne, N. K., & Taylor, M. C. (2018). Contextual information management: An example of independent-checking in the review of laboratory-based bloodstain pattern analysis. *Science & Justice, 58*, 226–231.

Osborne, N. K., Taylor, M. C., Healey, M., & Zajac, R. (2016). Bloodstain pattern classification: Accuracy, effect of contextual information and the role of analyst characteristics. *Science & Justice, 56*, 123–128.

Osborne, N. K., Taylor, M. C., & Zajac, R. (2016). Exploring the role of contextual information in bloodstain pattern analysis: A qualitative approach. *Forensic Science International, 260*, 1–8.

Osborne, N. K. P., Woods, S., Kieser, J., & Zajac, R. (2014). Does contextual information bias bitemark comparisons? *Science & Justice, 54*, 267–273.

Osborne, N. K. P., & Zajac, R. (2016). An imperfect match? Crime-related context influences fingerprint decisions. *Applied Cognitive Psychology, 30*, 126–134.

Papesh, M. H., & Goldinger, S. D. (2014). Infrequent identity mismatches are frequently undetected. *Attention, Perception, & Psychophysics, 76*, 1335–1349.

Pierce, M. L., & Cook, L. J. (2020). Development and implementation of an effective blind proficiency testing program. *Journal of Forensic Sciences, 65*, 809–814.

President's Council of Advisors on Science and Technology. (2016). *Forensic science in criminal courts: Ensuring scientific validity of feature-comparison methods.*

Pronin, E., Lin, D. Y., & Ross, L. (2002). The bias blind spot: Perceptions of bias in self versus others. *Personality and Social Psychology Bulletin, 28*, 369–381.

Quigley-McBride, A. (2020). Practical solutions to forensic contextual bias. *Zeitschrift für Psychologie, 228*, 162–174.

Quigley-McBride, A., & Wells, G. L. (2018). Fillers can help control for contextual bias in forensic comparison tasks. *Law and Human Behavior, 42*, 295–305.

Rajsic, J., Wilson, D. E., & Pratt, J. (2015). Confirmation bias in visual search. *Journal of Experimental Psychology: Human Perception and Performance, 41*, 1353–1364.

Redlich, A. D., Bibas, S., Edkins, V. A., & Madon, S. (2017). The psychology of defendant plea decision making. *American Psychologist, 72*, 339–352.

Ribeiro, G., Tangen, J. M., & McKimmie, B. M. (2019). Beliefs about error rates and human judgment in forensic science. *Forensic Science International, 297*, 138–147.

Risinger, D. M., Saks, M. J., Thompson, W. C., & Rosenthal, R. (2002). The *Daubert/Kumho* implications of observer effects in forensic science: Hidden problems of expectation and suggestion. *California Law Review, 90*, 1–56.

Robertson, C. T. (2010). Blind expertise. *New York University Law Review, 85*, 174–257.

Sanson, M., Crozier, W. E., & Strange, D. (2020). Court case context and fluency-promoting photos inflate the credibility of forensic science. *Zeitschrift für Psychologie, 228*, 221–225.

Scherr, K. C., & Dror, I. E. (2020). Ingroup biases of forensic experts: perceptions of wrongful convictions versus exonerations. *Psychology, Crime & Law, 27*, 89–104.

Scurich, N. (2015). The differential effect of numeracy and anecdotes on the perceived fallibility of forensic science. *Psychiatry, Psychology and Law, 22*, 616–623.

Smalarz, L., Madon, S., Yang, Y., Guyll, M., & Buck, S. (2016). The perfect match: Do criminal stereotypes bias forensic evidence analysis? *Law and Human Behavior, 40*, 420–429.

Sneyd, D., Schreiber Compo, N., Rivard, J., Pena, M., Stoiloff, S., & Hernandez, G. (2020). Quality of laypersons' assessment of forensically relevant stimuli. *Journal of Forensic Sciences, 65*, 1507–1516.

Stevenage, S. V., & Bennett, A. (2017). A biased opinion: Demonstration of cognitive bias on a fingerprint matching task through knowledge of DNA test results. *Forensic Science International, 276*, 93–106.

Stoel, R. D., Dror, I. E., & Miller, L. S. (2014). Bias among forensic document examiners: Still a need for procedural changes. *Australian Journal of Forensic Sciences, 46*, 91–97.

Sunde, N., & Dror, I. E. (2021). A hierarchy of expert performance (HEP) applied to digital forensics: Reliability and biasability in digital forensics decision making. *Forensic Science International: Digital Investigation, 37*, 301175.

Tangen, J. M., Thompson, M. B., & McCarthy, D. J. (2011). Identifying fingerprint expertise. *Psychological Science, 22*, 995–997.

Taylor, M. C., Laber, T. L., Kish, P. E., Owens, G., & Osborne, N. K. P. (2016a). The reliability of pattern classification in bloodstain pattern analysis, Part 1: Bloodstain patterns on rigid non-absorbent surfaces. *Journal of Forensic Sciences, 61*, 922–927.

Taylor, M. C., Laber, T. L., Kish, P. E., Owens, G., & Osborne, N. K. (2016b). The reliability of pattern classification in bloodstain pattern analysis, Part 2: Bloodstain patterns on fabric surfaces. *Journal of Forensic Sciences, 61*, 1461–1466.

Thompson, W. C. (2008). Beyond bad apples: Analyzing the role of forensic science in wrongful convictions. *Southwestern University Law Review, 37*, 1027–1050.

Thompson, W. C. (2011). What role should investigative facts play in the evaluation of scientific evidence? *Australian Journal of Forensic Sciences, 43*, 123–134.

Thompson, W. C., Grady, R. H., Lai, E., & Stern, H. S. (2018). Perceived strength of forensic scientists' reporting statements about source conclusions. *Law, Probability & Risk, 17*, 133–155.

Thompson, W. C., & Newman, E. J. (2015). Lay understanding of forensic statistics: Evaluation of random match probabilities, likelihood ratios, and verbal equivalents. *Law and Human Behavior, 39*, 332–349.

Thompson, W. C., & Scurich, N. (2019). How cross-examination on subjectivity and bias affects jurors' evaluations of forensic science evidence. *Journal of Forensic Sciences, 64*, 1379–1388.

Ulery, B. T., Hicklin, R. A., Buscaglia, J., & Roberts, M. A. (2011). Accuracy and reliability of forensic latent fingerprint decisions. *Proceedings of the National Academy of Sciences, 108*, 7733–7738.

van den Eeden, C. A. J., de Poot, C. J., & van Koppen, P. J. (2016). Forensic expectations: Investigating a crime scene with prior information. *Science & Justice, 56*, 475–481.

van den Eeden, C. A. J., de Poot, C. J., & van Koppen, P. J. (2019). The forensic confirmation bias: A comparison between experts and novices. *Journal of Forensic Sciences, 64*, 120–126.

van Straalen, E. K., de Poot, C. J., Malsch, M., & Elffers, H. (2020). The interpretation of forensic conclusions by criminal justice professionals: The same evidence interpreted differently. *Forensic Science International, 313*, 110331.

Walther, E., Fiedler, K., & Nickel, S. (2003). The influence of prior knowledge on constructive biases. *Swiss Journal of Psychology, 62*, 219–231.

Wells, G. L., Kovera, M. B., Douglass, A. B., Brewer, N., Meissner, C. A., & Wixted, J. T. (2020). Policy and procedure recommendations for the collection and preservation of eyewitness identification evidence. *Law and Human Behavior, 44*, 3–36.

Wells, G. L., & Turtle, J. W. (1986). Eyewitness identification: The importance of lineup models. *Psychological Bulletin, 99*, 320–329.

Wells, G. L., Wilford, M. M., & Smalarz, L. (2013). Forensic science testing: The forensic filler-control method for controlling contextual bias, estimating error rates, and calibrating analysts' reports. *Journal of Applied Research in Memory and Cognition, 2*, 53–55.

Wertheim, K., Langenburg, G., & Moenssens, A. (2006). A report of latent print examiner accuracy during comparison training exercises. *Journal of Forensic Identification, 56*, 55–93.

Wetmore, S. A., Neuschatz, J. S., Gronlund, S. D., Wooten, A., Goodsell, C. A., & Carlson, C. A. (2015). Effect of retention interval on showup and lineup performance. *Journal of Applied Research in Memory and Cognition, 4*, 8–14.

White, D., Jonathon Phillips, P., Hahn, C. A., Hill, M., & O'Toole, A. J. (2015). Perceptual expertise in forensic facial image comparison. *Proceedings of the Royal Society B: Biological Sciences, 282*, 1–8.

Whitman, G., & Koppl, R. (2010). Rational bias in forensic science. *Law, Probability & Risk, 9*, 69–90.

Wilson, T. D., & Brekke, N. (1994). Mental contamination and mental correction: Unwanted influences on judgments and evaluations. *Psychological Bulletin, 116*, 117–142.

Wolfe, J. M., Brunelli, D. N., Rubinstein, J., & Horowitz, T. S. (2013). Prevalence effects in newly trained airport checkpoint screeners: Trained observers miss rare targets, too. *Journal of Vision, 13*, 33–33.

Yu, Y., Luo, Y., Huang, L., & Quan, Y. (2021). The impact of contextual information on decision-making in footwear examination: An eye-tracking study. *Journal of Forensic Sciences, 66*, 2218–2231.

Psychological Barriers to the Detection of Child Sexual Abuse

Nicholas Scurich *and* Park Dietz

Abstract

Adults sexually abusing children where they work or volunteer has become painfully familiar not only to survivors of sexual abuse but also to their families, law enforcement, and the schools, churches, youth-serving organizations, and other institutions within which so many cases occur. In the aftermath of discovering that sexual abuse occurred, questions invariably arise as to why the abuse was not detected earlier. This chapter describes two different psychological phenomena that help to explain why child sexual abuse is difficult to recognize ex ante, and, paradoxically, why it is so easy to recognize ex post. These phenomena are "halo effects" and the "hindsight bias," respectively. This chapter reviews basic and applied research bearing on each as well as research on potential debiasing strategies. Halo effects and hindsight bias have significant implications for civil lawsuits that are occasioned by sexual abuse that occurs within organizations.

Key Words: sexual abuse, halo effects, hindsight bias, debiasing, grooming, foreseeability

A mother sits in an examination room with her pre-teenage daughter who is receiving treatment for a sports-related injury. The mother—herself a physician—notices something unusual about the attending physician:

> I remember, out of the corner of my eye, seeing what looked to be, potentially, an erection. And I just remember thinking, that's weird. That's really weird, poor guy—thinking, like, that would be very strange for a physician to get an erection in a patient's room while, you know, giving her an exam. (Smith & Wells, 2018)

The physician, it turned out, was Larry Nassar who pled guilty to ten counts of sexual abuse and was sentenced to up to 175 years in prison (Eggert & Householder, 2018). It was not until years later, when a newspaper published an article that accused Nassar of sexually abusing his female patients, that the mother thought to question her daughter about Nassar's examination. The daughter confirmed that Nassar had penetrated her during the examination. Nassar was convicted of sexually assaulting this victim. It is important to note that other victims and parents noticed Nassar's erection while he was examining patients (see Smith & Wells, 2018).

Although this situation raises a number of questions, perhaps the most fundamental question is this: How could the mother overlook such an obvious warning of danger to her child? Indeed, how could someone with medical training overlook the context—examination and treatment of a prepubescent child—in which his arousal became visible? And if viewing a sexually aroused physician touch a child under the guise of providing medical treatment does not raise the specter of sexual impropriety, then what behavior can be reasonably expected to do so, short of witnessing penetration?

This chapter attempts to shed light on these questions. Two different psychological phenomena help to elucidate why sexual abuse is difficult to recognize *ex ante* and, paradoxically, why it is so easy to recognize *ex post*. These phenomena are "halo effects" and the "hindsight bias." Each of these effects has been the subject of voluminous study in a variety of different domains, including the context of sexual abuse.

A key point is that these are psychological barriers rather than physical barriers to spotting sexual abuse. Failing to detect sexual abuse because it is never observed, a child victim never discloses, a preparator denies the behavior, and so on is unfortunate and not uncommon (Dietz, 2020; Scurich, 2020). Yet, it is a very different situation to view and/or have knowledge of behavior indicative of sexual abuse and fail to recognize it as such. Understanding these psychological effects will help to make clear why the mother described above—who had no incentive either to overlook the harm done to her daughter or to help the perpetrator avoid detection—failed to recognize a signal, and why that signal is so obvious, at least in hindsight.

These psychological phenomena also have significant implications for civil lawsuits that are occasioned by sexual abuse that occurs within organizations. Billions of dollars have been paid by organizations such as the Catholic Church, the Boy Scouts of America, USA gymnastics, and other organizations to victims of sexual abuse (e.g., Gjelten, 2018). Often the key legal issue in civil lawsuits related to sexual abuse is whether the organization should have been able to "foresee" and take "notice" that sexual abuse or impropriety was occurring and whether the organization took reasonable action to abate the behavior (for a discussion of litigation strategies, see Janci, 2020). These are issues that a jury would determine. Importantly, jurors have the luxury of hindsight: in many of these cases, there is no doubt about what occurred or when, but jurors are instructed to set aside this knowledge and make a judgment about foreseeability as if they did not know the outcome. As described below, a robust body of research finds that humans may not live up to this ideal and that reality may place defendants at a serious disadvantage when it comes to litigating what was "foreseeable" prior to the detection of sexual abuse.

Halo Effects

Thorndike (1920) coined the term "halo effect" a century ago. The halo effect is a cognitive bias in impression formation whereby the positive evaluation of one characteristic has a radiating effect on how other, nonrelated characteristics of the individual are evaluated. For example, one classic study found that physical attractiveness influenced evaluations of the target's personality, life satisfaction, and expected future personal and occupational success—despite the fact that no information about any of these attributes was provided (Dion et al., 1972). Physical attractiveness has also been found to influence culpability judgments, with attractive individuals being held less-responsible than unattractive individuals (Dion, 1973; Efran, 1974). Halo effects have been found to be cued by factors other than attractiveness, such as the described status of the target (Wilson, 1968), the name of the target (Harari & McDavid, 1973), and even one's mood when evaluating the target (Forgas, 2011). Studies have documented halo effects when making diagnoses of psychopathology, such that symptoms of one mental disorder influence the interpretation of other symptoms indicative of other mental disorders and vice versa (see, e.g., DeVries et al., 2017).

Halo effects are a means to achieving *cognitive consistency*, which roughly refers to a state in which attitudes, perceptions, beliefs, predictions, and thoughts are aligned. Cognitive consistency serves many important goals. As noted by Read and Simon (2012), cognitive consistency is "essential for reasons of parsimony and economy of effort, as well as to allow for the predictability of, and hence adaptability to, subsequent encounters" (p. 67). Indeed, the noted psychologist Leon Festinger "was convinced that the psychological need for cognitive consistency is as basic as hunger and thirst" (Gawronski, 2012, p. 652). But because the world is often not so neat, orderly, or unequivocal, humans engage in complicated reasoning processes to impose consistency. These processes involve *bidirectional reasoning* in which "decisions follow from evidence, and evaluations of the evidence shift toward coherence with the emerging decision" (Simon, Snow, & Read, 2004, p. 814; Greenspan & Scurich, 2016). As a result, perceptions and decisions become highly skewed toward one interpretation while alternatives are neglected or dismissed; hence consistency is achieved. This reasoning process occurs unconsciously—by which we merely mean outside conscious awareness—and is not intentional self-deception.

Halo effects can have serious practical consequences. As noted by Forgas and Laham (2016):

> Once unjustified initial expectations are formed about a person, they can easily become self-perpetuating with serious implications for how a target is treated. If we expect a person to have positive characteristics, we may selectively look for and find such features from the rich array of information available (a self-fulfilling prophecy), and positive impressions may in turn lead to preferential treatment in a range of domains: interpersonal relations, the work place, the health and legal systems, and even for decision making and consumer choices. (p. 286)

Returning to the context of child sexual abuse, could the halo effect explain the otherwise puzzling phenomenon of the "nice-guy" offender whom nobody suspects, as described by Lanning (2010)? "Nice guy" offenders often go unrecognized, hiding in plain sight:

> Many individuals do not prevent or recognize the sexual victimization of a child by a respected member of society because they cannot believe a man who is otherwise good, spiritual, generous, or seems to truly care for children could be a child molester; even a plea or jury verdict of guilt may be rejected by such supporters. Some accept the general proposition that such individuals can be child molesters, but just not the particular nice guy that they personally know and like. They might even rally to the support of the offender or blame the victim. (Lanning & Dietz, 2014, p. 9)

It is important to acknowledge that about 15 percent of detected sexual abuse is committed by strangers (Snyder, 2000). This means that in the vast majority of cases, child sexual abuse victims and their parents will have some prior knowledge of the perpetrator and thus have some initial impressions of the perpetrator. It is reasonable to assume that the majority of these impressions are either positive or indifferent but likely not negative (otherwise why would they leave their child with him?). Because these non-negative impressions shape the perception of the perpetrator and their interactions with the child, and because of the fundamental desire to achieve cognitive consistency, individuals will likely view problematic behaviors as innocuous and conjure up an explanation that does not lead to inconsistency ("dissonance") between the observed behavior and the perception of the individual. Hence, the mother described above viewed Nassar's erection not as a warning sign that something sexual was occurring since Nassar was by most accounts a well-liked and respected team doctor; those perceptions are incongruent and thus to be (unconsciously) explained away, overlooked, or interpreted as innocuous.

Empirical evidence supports this account (see, e.g., Winters & Jeglic, 2017). In one study (Scurich et al., 2022), we presented a large sample of adults with vignettes describing various interactions between a chief minister and several children who attend his church school and day camps. The minister had been a local resident his whole life, had a wife and three children, was well liked within the community, and was generally perceived as a pillar of the community. The interactions between the children and this minister included hugging ("hug"), taking certain children to lunch or dinner ("dinner"), sometimes wrestling with the children ("activities"), giving some children candy and gifts ("gifts"), and one time, at an overnight church retreat, sleeping in a bed with several young children (with other parents in the room) ("sleep"). The sample of participants was asked to rate different explanations of these interactions, including that he is a friendly guy, he is lonely, he loves kids, and he is a child molester, among other possible explanations. With regard to each of these interactions, the mean rating of the likelihood

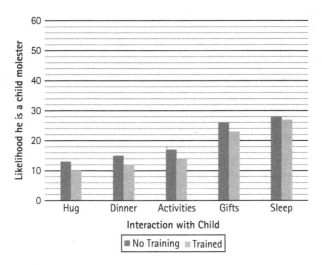

Figure 37.1 Participants' ratings of the likelihood that the minister is a child molester based on the described interaction between the minister and a child. Ratings were made on a 0–100% scale.

that the minister was a child molester was less than 30percent (see fig. 37.1) and all medians were less than 14 percent. Participants plainly did not interpret these interactions as motived by sexual desire.

In addition to the numerical ratings, participants were asked "has anything you read about [the minister] concerned you?"; 59 percent responded affirmatively to this question and were then asked to explain the cause of their concern. The open-ended responses varied widely, ranging from "playing favorites" and "being too friendly" to sleeping in the "same beds with boys." Only six (of 371) participants explicitly stated that they were concerned that John might be molesting children (i.e., used the term "molester" or "pedophile") and three participants stated that they believed John was engaged in grooming behavior (i.e., used the term "grooming"). In other words, 2 percent (9/371) of participants articulated a concern that John might be sexually abusing children after reading all five scenarios.

It could be argued that perhaps the participants in the study were simply unaware of what constitutes problematic, sexually motivated behaviors and this is what accounts for the low ratings. Winters and Jeglic (2017) noted:

> It may be that people were not able to identify the child molester who groomed because they are not aware of sexual grooming or what classifies as a grooming behavior. Thus, better educating children, parents, and community members about possible predatory behaviors could be greatly beneficial. Education could be provided to adults in the community through a variety of domains, such as pamphlets at locations frequented by caregivers, providing information to teachers and school staff, public service announcements, or websites geared toward families or education providers. . . . Providing people with a better understanding of the sexual grooming process and who the offenders are could aide in identifying these types of perpetrators prior to the commission of the abuse. (p. 731)

In the study described, approximately one-quarter of the sample had received specialized training on how to spot and report sexual abuse. All the interactions between the minister and the children described in the vignettes are widely recognized as "grooming" tactics used by child molesters (Samantha et al., 2006; Lanning & Dietz, 2014; Dietz, 2018). Yet, the mean ratings by these trained individuals never exceed 30 percent (gray bars in fig. 37.1). Despite their training and knowledge about what constitutes problematic, sexually motivated behaviors, they too were unable to detect problematic sexual behaviors when presented with such interactions. It is notable that their responses were in a hypothetical study, and thus their threshold for reporting should have been quite low since no consequences follow from a false allegation. Again, however, very few actually identified the behaviors as problematic. These findings speak to the powerful nature of halo effects. Sadly, there are also countless anecdotal accounts—supported by evidence presented in recent child sexual abuse litigation—of individuals verified to have undergone training programs to recognize sexual abuse who nonetheless failed to recognize or report all manner of pre-disclosure indicators, warning signs, and "red flags" (e.g., Lanning & Dietz, 2014).

This is an area ripe for more empirical research. Among other things, a more direct test of the halo effect account could be conducted in which the valence (positive or negative) of the perpetrator is experimentally manipulated to see whether that affects perceptions of behavior between him and children. One could hypothesize that individuals are more likely to recognize problematic sexual behaviors for negatively valanced men than positively valanced men. Future research might also manipulate the context in which the interactions occur and the relationship between the adult and the children (e.g., related vs. unrelated; school vs. church, etc.; see generally Smalarz et al., 2016). Additionally, future research might show participants videos of the interactions between adults and children to see if that affects the likelihood that halo effects can be broken.

Aside from the basic psychological questions, certainly more research ought to be conducted on the efficacy of training programs designed to spot sexual abuse. The findings reported above suggest that it is not enough to simply describe and explain what constitutes problematic sexual behaviors or "grooming" behaviors; individuals will need to spot those behaviors within the context of other knowledge and impressions about the target individual, and this is likely to compound the difficulty of the task considerably.

Hindsight Bias

The study described above had an additional component. After participants rated all the behaviors, they were told that the minister in question had pled guilty to sexually abusing numerous children and was currently in prison. Participants were then asked to reevaluate each of the five behaviors, and they were explicitly admonished to ignore the information about his criminal conviction. Given this instruction, one would expect the ratings to be identical to the previous ratings. However, the ratings significantly increased the second time around—for both participants with (see dark gray bars in fig. 37.2) and without training (see light gray bars in fig. 37.2) on how to spot problematic, sexually motivated behaviors. Simply put, participants could not ignore their knowledge of his conviction when assessing how they believe they would have felt without such knowledge. This is clear evidence of *hindsight bias*.

Hindsight bias refers to the tendency to overestimate how predictable an event is after learning the outcome of the event (Fischhoff, 1975). For example, after a political election, people believe their preelection estimates of the outcome were closer to the outcome than they actually were (Blank et al., 2003). Hindsight bias has been discussed in more than 800 scholarly articles across a variety of different domains including medicine, financial decision-making, consumer satisfaction, and within the legal domain (see Arkes, 2013; Roese & Vohs, 2012; Strohmaier et al., 2021) and using a variety of different experimental designs (Pohl & Erdfelder, 2016) and a variety of different stimuli such as written vignettes, visual stimuli (e.g., Bernstein & Harley, 2007), and auditory stimuli (e.g., Bernstein et al., 2012). Even individuals with specialized training and expertise engage in hindsight bias (Musch & Wagner, 2007). One notable study detected hindsight bias among actual judges making civil liability decisions, in which judges with outcome knowledge perceived the harm to be significantly more foreseeable than judges who did not receive outcome information and were thus more likely to render a finding of negligence (Oeberst & Goeckenjan, 2016). Another notable study detected hindsight bias in a sample of mental health professionals who gauged the dangerousness of a psychiatric

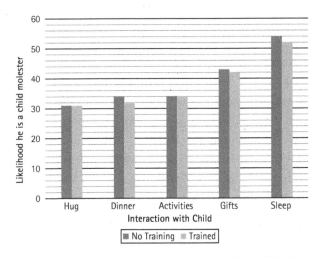

Figure 37.2 Participants' ratings made in hindsight of the likelihood that the minister is a child molester based on the described interaction between the minister and a child. Ratings were made on a 0–100% scale.

patient; again, outcome knowledge affected the perceived dangerousness and predictably of harm posed by the patient (Beltrani et al., 2018).

The underlying mechanisms for hindsight bias are the subject of debate and ongoing investigation. Two biases are proposed to play a dominant role: *recollection bias*, in which outcome information contaminates the encoding of the original judgment, and *reconstruction bias*, in which the inability to recall the original judgment leads to a rejudgment process that is contaminated by outcome information (see Erdfelder & Buchner, 1998; Hawkins & Hastie, 1990). As noted by Pohl and Erdfelder (2016), "Previous research has shown that reconstruction bias is the major determinant of hindsight bias, although recollection bias may also play a role under some conditions or for special populations such as older adults" (p. 437, internal citations omitted). Moreover, Roese and Vohs (2012) noted that "motivational factors fuel hindsight bias (particularly foreseeability) in two ways: first, by way of a need to see the world as orderly and predictable and, second, by way of a need to protect and enhance one's self-esteem" (p. 416).

Numerous debiasing strategies have been proposed to ward off hindsight bias. The "consider the opposite" outcome(s) is the most common approach (Roese & Vohs, 2012). Although there are some variants to the exact task, generally this approach asks participants to articulate *reasons* for their judgments about various explanations, and doing so tends to attenuate hindsight bias. For example, Arkes et al. (1988) had a group of 194 neuropsychologists rate the likelihood of three different medical diagnoses based on a description of a patient; half of the participants were told which diagnosis was correct and the other half were not given such information (thus one can compare the two estimates to assess hindsight bias). Moreover, half of the participants were instructed to give reasons for their numeric rating of each diagnosis while the other half were not instructed to do so. The result: "The frequency of subjects succumbing to the hindsight bias was lower in the hindsight-reasons groups than in the hindsight group not asked to list reasons" (Arkes et al., 1988, p. 305).

Researchers have investigated whether this and other debiasing techniques are effective within the legal context. These studies typically have mock jurors participate in a trial simulation in which some jurors are given an admonition either by the judge or the defense attorney to "consider the opposite," to "be aware of bias," or "try to reduce bias" or some variant (e.g., Kamin & Rachlinski, 1995; Smith & Greene, 2005); these admonitions are generally not effective at eliminating or even reducing the hindsight bias (Harley, 2007; but see Stallard & Worthington, 1998), and can actually increase the degree of hindsight bias when too many alternatives are to be considered (Sanna et al., 2002). The inability to eliminate hindsight bias through admonitions has led some to call for bifurcated trials in which jurors make relevant judgments about liability or negligence prior to learning information about the outcome, thus preventing information about the outcome from influencing judgments about the defendant's state of knowledge prior to the outcome (e.g., Horowitz & Bordens, 1990).

Whether hindsight bias can be reduced or eliminated in the context of child sexual abuse is an open empirical question. This context presents a heightened challenge given the personal and emotional nature of sexual abuse (see Azzopardi et al., 2019) and the desire to punish someone or something for the harm that has occurred (Foley & Pigott, 2000; Keller et al., 2010; Rogers & Ferguson, 2011). It seems likely that simple instructions to "consider the opposite" will be ineffective at reducing hindsight bias, though efficacy might depend on the specific instructions used and who delivers them (e.g., judge vs. defense attorney). It is also possible that having an expert in psychology explain via testimony the hindsight bias in detail could have some ameliorating effect. Again, these are empirical questions that ought to be tested. The potential usefulness of bifurcated trials should also be explored within this context.

Concluding Remarks

Much has been written about the legal implications of hindsight bias and what if anything ought to be done by lawyers and judges to mitigate it (e.g., Arkes & Schipani, 1994). As noted by Rachlinski (1998), "[g]eneric de-biasing strategies are unlikely to be available and the courts do not attempt to use them. Instead they have developed mechanisms for taking advantage of specific circumstances that allow them to reduce the influence of the hindsight bias" (p. 624). In our view, it is wise to move past general observations about hindsight bias and potential remedies, and focus on data specifically within the context of sexual abuse within organizations, such as schools, sports teams, churches, and youth-serving organizations and perhaps even more specifically with regard to particular cases. Lawyers litigating organizational sexual abuse cases might commission psychological researchers to conduct case-specific studies to understand how these phenomena might influence fact finders in their particular case and devise strategies to minimize their impact.

References

Arkes, H. R., Faust, D., Guilmette, T. J., & Hart, K. (1988). Eliminating the hindsight bias. *Journal of Applied Psychology*, *73*(2), 305–307.

Arkes, H. R., & Schipani, C. A. (1994). Medical malpractice vs. the business judgement rule: Differences in hindsight bias. *Oregon Law Review*, *73*, 587–605.

Arkes, H. R. (2013). The consequences of the hindsight bias in medical decision making. *Current Directions in Psychological Science*, *22*(5), 356–360.

Azzopardi, C., Eirich, R., Rash, C.L., MacDonald, S., & Madigan, S. (2019). A meta-analysis of the prevalence of child sexual abuse disclosure in forensic settings. *Child Abuse & Neglect*, *93*, 291–304.

Beltrani, A., Reed, A. L., Zapf, P. A., & Otto, R. K. (2018). Is hindsight really 20/20? The impact of outcome information on the decision-making process. *International Journal of Forensic Mental Health*, *17*(3), 285–296.

Blank, H., Fischer, V., & Erdfelder, E. (2003). Hindsight bias in political elections. *Memory*, *11*(4–5), 491–504.

Bernstein, D. M., & Harley, E. M. (2007). Fluency misattribution and visual hindsight bias. *Memory*, *15*(5), 548–560.

Bernstein, D. M., Wilson, A. M., Pernat, N. L. M., & Meilleur, L. R. (2012). Auditory hindsight bias. *Psychonomic Bulletin & Review*, *19*(4), 588–593.

DeVries, L. N., Hartung, C. M., & Golden, T. L. (2017). Negative halo effects in parent ratings of ADHD and ODD. *Journal of Psychopathology and Behavioral Assessment*, *39*(2), 179–188.

Dietz, P. (2018). Grooming and seduction. *Journal of Interpersonal Violence, 33*(1), 28–36.

Dietz, P. (2020). Denial and minimization among sex offenders. *Behavioral Sciences & Law, 38*(4), 571–585.

Dion, K. K. (1973). Young children's stereotyping of facial attractiveness. *Developmental Psychology, 9*, 183–188.

Dion, K. K., Berscheid, E., & Walster, E. (1972). What is beautiful is good. *Journal of Personality and Social Psychology, 24*, 285–290.

Efran, M. G. (1974). The effects of physical attractiveness on judgments in a simulated jury task. *Journal of Research in Personality, 8*, 45–54.

Eggert, D., & Householder, M. (2018). Larry Nassar sentenced to 40 to 175 years in prison; judge says "I just signed your death warrant". https://www.chicagotribune.com/sports/olympics/ct-larry-nassar-gymnastics-sentencing-20180124-story.html

Erdfelder, E., & Buchner, A. (1998). Decomposing the hindsight bias: A multinomial processing tree model for separating recollection and reconstruction in hindsight. *Journal of Experimental Psychology: Learning, Memory, and Cognition, 24*(2), 387–414.

Fischhoff, B. (1975). Hindsight≠ foresight: the effect of outcome knowledge on judgment under uncertainty. *Journal of Experimental Psychology: Human Perception and Performance, 1*, 288–299.

Foley, L. A., & Pigott, M. A. (2000). Belief in a just world and jury decisions in a civil rape trial. *Journal of Applied Social Psychology, 30*, 935–951.

Forgas, J.P. (2011). She just doesn't look like a philosopher . . .? Affective influences on the halo effect in impression formation. *European Journal of Social Psychology, 41*(7), 812–817.

Forgas, J. P., & Laham, S. M. (2016). Halo effects. *In Cognitive illusions: Intriguing Phenomena in Judgment, Thinking and Memory*. Routledge.

Gawronski, B. (2012). Back to the future of dissonance theory: Cognitive consistency as a core motive. *Social Cognition, 30*(6), 652–668.

Gjelten, T. (2018). The clergy abuse crisis has cost the Catholic Church $3 billion. https://www.npr.org/2018/08/18/639698062/the-clergy-abuse-crisis-has-cost-the-catholic-church-3-billion

Greenspan, R., & Scurich, N. (2016). The interdependence of perceived confession voluntariness and case evidence. *Law and Human Behavior, 40*(6), 650–659.

Harari, H., & McDavid, J. W. (1973). Name stereotypes and teachers' expectations. *Journal of Educational Psychology, 65*, 222–225.

Harley, E. M. (2007). Hindsight bias in legal decision making. *Social Cognition, 25*(1), 48–63.

Hawkins, S. A., & Hastie, R. (1990). Hindsight: Biased judgments of past events after the outcomes are known. *Psychological Bulletin, 107*(3), 311–327.

Horowitz, I., & Bordens, K. (1990). An experimental investigation of procedural issues in complex tort trials. *Law and Human Behavior, 14*, 269–285.

Janci, P.B. (2020). Helping# ChurchToo abuse victims hold religious entities accountable in civil cases. *Liberty University Law Review, 14*(2), 317–350.

Kamin, K., & Rachlinski, J. (1995). Ex post does not equal ex ante: Determining liability in hindsight. *Law and Human Behavior, 19*, 89–104.

Keller, L. B., Oswald, M. E., Stucki, I., & Gollwitzer, M. (2010). A closer look at an eye for an eye: Laypersons' punishment decisions are primarily driven by retributive motives. *Social Justice Research, 23*(2–3), 99–116.

Lanning, K. V. (2010). *Child molesters: A behavioral analysis* (5th ed.). National Center for Missing & Exploited Children.

Lanning, K. V., & Dietz, P. (2014): Acquaintance molestation and youth-serving organizations. *Journal of Interpersonal Violence, 29*(15), 2815–2838.

Musch, J., & Wagner, T. (2007). Did everybody know it all along? A review of individual differences in hindsight bias. *Social Cognition, 25*(1), 64–82.

Oeberst, A., & Goeckenjan, I. (2016). When being wise after the event results in injustice: Evidence for hindsight bias in judges' negligence assessments. *Psychology, Public Policy, and Law, 22*(3), 271–279.

Pohl, R. F., & Erdfelder, E. (2016). The phenomenon of hindsight bias. In R. F. Pohl (Ed.), *Cognitive illusions: Intriguing phenomena in judgement, thinking and memory* (pp. 424–445). Routledge/Taylor & Francis Group.

Rachlinski, J. J. (1998). A positive psychological theory of judging in hindsight. *University of Chicago Law Review, 65*(2), 571–625.

Read, S. J., & Simon, D. (2012). *Parallel constraint satisfaction as a mechanism for cognitive consistency.* In B. Gawronski & F. Strack (Eds.), Cognitive consistency: A fundamental principle in social cognition (pp. 66–86). Guilford Press.

Roese, N. J., & Vohs, K. D. (2012). Hindsight bias. *Perspectives on Psychological Science, 7*(5), 411–426.

Rogers, D. L., & Ferguson, C. J. (2011). Punishment and rehabilitation attitudes toward sex offenders versus nonsexual offenders. *Journal of Aggression, Maltreatment & Trauma, 20*(4), 395–414.

Samantha, C., Brown, S. & Gilchrist, E. (2006). Sexual grooming of children: Review of literature and theoretical considerations. *Journal of Sexual Aggression, 12*(3), 287–299.

Sanna, L. J., Schwarz, N., & Small, E. M. (2002). Accessibility experiences and the hindsight bias: I knew it all along versus it could never have happened. *Memory & Cognition, 30*, 1288–1296.

Scurich, N. (2020). Introduction to this special issue on underreporting of sexual abuse. *Behavioral Sciences & Law, 38*(4), 537–542.

Scurich, N., Güney, Ş., & Dietz, P. (2022). Hindsight bias in assessing child sexual abuse. *Journal of Sexual Aggression*, 1–15.

Simon, D., Snow, C.J., & Read, S.J. (2004). The redux of cognitive consistency theories: Evidence judgments by constraint satisfaction. *Journal of Personality and Social Psychology, 86*(6), 814–837.

Smith, A. C., & Greene, E. (2005). Conduct and its consequences: Attempts at debiasing jury judgments. *Law and Human Behavior, 29*(5), 505–526.

Smith, L., & Wells, K. (2018). Believed < the parents. https://www.npr.org/transcripts/669669746

Smalarz, L., Madon, S., Yang, Y., Guyll, M., & Buck, S. (2016). The perfect match: Do criminal stereotypes bias forensic evidence analysis? *Law and Human Behavior, 40*, 420–429.

Snyder, H. N. (2000). *Sexual assault of young children as reported to law enforcement: Victim, incident, and offender characteristics.* Bureau of Justice Statistics. http://www.bjs.gov/content/pub/pdf/saycrle.pdf

Stallard, M., & Worthington, D. (1998). Reducing the hindsight bias utilizing attorney closing arguments. *Law and Human Behavior, 22*, 671–682.

Strohmaier, N., Pluut, H., Van den Bos, K., Adriaanse, J., & Vriesendorp, R. (2021). Hindsight bias and outcome bias in judging directors' liability and the role of free will beliefs. *Journal of Applied Social Psychology, 51*(3), 141–158.

Thorndike, E. L. (1920). A constant error in psychological ratings. *Journal of Applied Psychology, 4*(1), 25–29.

Wilson, P. R. (1968). Perceptual distortion of height as a function of ascribed academic status. *Journal of Social Psychology, 74*, 97–102.

Winters, G. M., & Jeglic, E. L. (2017). Stages of sexual grooming: Recognizing potentially predatory behaviors of child molesters. *Deviant Behavior, 38*(6), 724–733.

First Steps on the Path to Wrongful Conviction: Phenomenology of Innocence, Police Stops, and Expectancies

Max Guyll, Kyle C. Scherr, Stephanie Madon, *and* Jessica Munoz

Abstract

Wrongful convictions represent a grave injustice. The innocent are punished, the guilty go free, and the postmortems that attend their occasional discovery typically reveal some shocking combination of incompetence, indifference, and malfeasance. Escaping notice, however, are myriad mundane influences that usually have negligible effects but which, like a feather falling on a balance, can sometimes tip the scale. In this chapter we highlight effects that could nudge the innocent onto paths that might ultimately lead to wrongful conviction. We begin by considering how the innocent are disadvantaged by an unwarranted sense of invulnerability. Next, we explore how police encounters and investigative stops can initially entangle the innocent in a criminal investigation. We then discuss how police may come to target an innocent suspect through the effects of expectancies, both justified and unjustified, and which may or may not operate outside awareness. We conclude by discussing future research directions.

Key Words: wrongful conviction, phenomenology of innocence, consensual encounters, stop and frisk, stereotypes, expectancies

Punishing innocent persons for crimes they did not commit goes against all values of a just society and cannot help but erode the people's trust in and commitment to the institutions of justice and law enforcement. Given the importance of preventing wrongful convictions, it is critical to recognize and understand the full range of processes that can contribute to their occurrence. It is relatively straightforward to understand how a wrongful conviction can result from incorrect evidence, such as a mistaken eyewitness identification, an incorrect forensic conclusion, or a lying, incentivized jailhouse informant. After all, incorrect information will increase the likelihood of an incorrect judgment. However, there are also a variety of less apparent forces that can potentially contribute to wrongful convictions. Counterintuitively, one set of forces can emerge from the innocent suspects themselves via psychological processes that result from their self-certain knowledge of being factually innocent. Other forces can emerge from the operation of routine law enforcement activities that increase the likelihood that innocent persons will be drawn under investigative scrutiny. Expectancies can compound the problem by influencing the strength of an investigator's belief that a suspect is guilty, which could then bias the interpretation of case facts or investigative strategies.

In this chapter, we begin by focusing on influences originating in the suspect, reviewing research and theory pertaining to how factual innocence can lead suspects to unwittingly increase their own risk of conviction. We subsequently shift focus to examine how effects stemming from law enforcement can increase the chances that innocent persons are targeted for investigation and how expectancies might influence the interpretation of available evidence to put innocents at risk of self-incrimination. We end by offering some directions for future research to further develop the empirical foundation pertaining to the processes we hypothesize.

Wrongful Conviction as a Person Perception Outcome

Wrongful convictions occur when actors in the criminal justice system come to suspect, investigate, prosecute, and convict an innocent person. Ultimately, wrongful convictions entail making incorrect judgments about people and, thus, can be seen as resulting from errors in person perception. Although general sources of person perception errors are so numerous that entire books are devoted to their consideration (e.g., Fiske & Taylor, 2021; Jussim, 2012; Kunda, 1999), we highlight several specific possibilities that could serve to increase the risk of conviction for innocent suspects during criminal investigations. We begin with innocent suspects themselves, and how they may come to provide law enforcement with information that causes them to be perceived as guilty.

Innocence and Increased Risk

Relative to the guilty, the innocent more frequently make choices and engage in behaviors that increase their risk of false confession and wrongful conviction. First, the innocent—believing that they have no reason to avoid talking with the police (e.g., Kassin & Norwick, 2004)—may willingly call attention to themselves by notifying police of a crime, coming forward to offer information about a crime, or offering themselves as a witness to a crime. In this manner, an innocent person is more likely to include themselves among the finite group of individuals who are both known to police and associated with a case. If police do not readily identify a suspect, they may consider these known individuals as possible perpetrators.

Second, in the event that the innocent do come under suspicion, they are likely to engage in a number of behaviors that increase their risk of conviction (Kassin, 2005, 2012; Scherr et al., 2020). In comparison to the guilty, the innocent are more likely to waive their constitutional protections, specifically their rights to silence and counsel, and more willing to cooperate with law enforcement by speaking freely and at length (Kassin & Norwick, 2004; Stromwall et al., 2006). In addition, because the innocent may not be particularly concerned about being perfectly consistent and precise, they may speak inexactly and unintentionally make inconsistent or factually incorrect statements. The police, however, may interpret such errors as intentional deceptions indicative of guilt (Masip et al., 2016).

Third, experimental evidence supports the idea that innocent persons behave in such a way as to elicit more coercive behavior from interrogators (Kassin et al., 2003). Specifically, interrogators questioned mock suspects who were either innocent or guilty of a mock crime, and all of whom denied guilt throughout questioning. Both interrogators and independent observers, all of whom were masked to the suspect's guilt status, rated interrogators as applying more pressure to the innocent suspects. Although suspect behaviors were not analyzed, one possible explanation for this effect is that the innocent might have been more assertive in their denials, which interrogators interpreted as a challenge to their authority, causing them to become more coercive in response (S. M. Kassin, personal communication, February 23, 2021).

Understanding the Phenomenology of Innocence

Theorizing regarding how the phenomenology of innocence operates to increase the risk of wrongful conviction has primarily been limited to how innocence may lead people to first place themselves in situations of greater risk and then how they might be led to falsely confess. Several general human characteristics have been highlighted for their potential to cause the innocent to voluntarily enter situations of greater risk. Just world theory, for instance, proposes that people generally believe that the world is just, which causes them to behave in accord with the idea that bad things only happen to bad people (Hafer & Begue, 2005; Lerner, 1980). Thus, innocent individuals may expose themselves to greater risk because they believe that as an innocent individual in a just world, they will not be unjustly punished. Consistent with this hypothesis, empirical research has found that the guilty report experiencing more stress than do the innocent, but that this difference becomes greater as participants more strongly endorse just world beliefs (Scherr & Franks, 2015).

Another general human characteristic is the illusion of transparency (Gilovich et al., 1998), which is the belief that one's internal state is obvious to others. The illusion of transparency discourages self-protective behaviors among the innocent because they believe that their innocence will be obvious to law enforcement who presumably only seek to punish the guilty. Self-presentational concerns may also encourage risky behavior among the innocent. Believing that an innocent person should have nothing to hide and be eager to fully cooperate, the innocent may behave in just such a manner in the hopes of causing others to correctly perceive them as innocent (Kassin, 2005, 2012)—a motivational process known as self-verification (Swann, 1987).

In the context of an interrogation, a belief in a just world and the illusion of transparency may encourage the innocent to confess. Specifically, being confident that the truth of their innocence will subsequently become known and that justice will ultimately prevail, they may hope that the effects of their confession will be undone, and that they will be shielded from punishment. By contrast, although self-verification motivations may promote cooperation (Swann et al., 2000), they should discourage false confession because confessing would naturally be seen as a behavior indicative of guilt, which is inconsistent with the self-view of an innocent person. Of course, the innocent are highly motivated to maintain their innocence in order to avoid the punishment and stigma associated with guilt. The observation that interrogations that produced documented false confessions averaged sixteen hours in length (Drizin & Leo, 2004) suggests that it often takes interrogators quite some time to overcome these obvious forces that encourage the innocent to deny guilt.

Cognitive-Emotional Models of Decision-Making

Theorists have also sought to understand how the phenomenology of innocence might influence decision-making and behavioral choices on a more general level. Subjective expected utility theory conceptualizes decision-making as a rational process wherein individuals seek to maximize their utility, which is the amount of satisfaction they experience (Mongin, 1998; Savage, 1954). Thus, when faced with a decision, people consider the utility and probability of the consequences that could flow from each choice, ultimately making the choice they expect to yield the greatest utility.

The interrogation decision-making model (Yang et al., 2017) applies a subjective expected utility framework to explore suspect decision-making during interrogation. Limited by the fact that the expected utility values are largely unknown, the model's chief contributions are that it promotes taking the perspective of a suspect undergoing an interrogation, encourages comprehensive consideration of factors affecting the decision to deny or confess guilt, and prompts separate evaluations for the innocent and the guilty. Subjective expected utility theory could also be applied to understand decision-making of the innocent when they tend to put themselves at greater risk prior to an interrogation, although this has not yet been done.

The behavior of innocent persons has also been studied from a stress and coping framework. Stress corresponds to a psychological experience in which a person perceives a situational threat that may tax or exceed their ability to effectively cope (Lazarus & Folkman, 1984). Although stress is often considered negative, it is actually an adaptive response that mobilizes an individual to engage in coping behaviors to address a threat. Applying these ideas to criminal suspects suggests that stress and the consequent mobilization to respond with self-protective behaviors should be greatest among those who perceive the most threat from being accused and those who expect the greatest difficulty in addressing the threat that an accusation of wrongdoing poses. In this regard, the innocent should be at a disadvantage relative to the guilty. Believing that their innocence is suffi-cient to protect them from harm, the innocent should feel less stress from an accusation, become less mobilized, and be less likely to cope in ways that maximize self-protection than do the guilty.

Empirical findings have generally supported these patterns with respect to the out-comes of behavioral choices and physiological responses. As detailed above, the innocent engage in less self-protective behaviors, a response that is consistent with the idea that they believe they face less threat and will be able to successfully cope with the accusation against them. Being innocent also causes one to exhibit less physiological mobilization. When accused, the innocent show less reactivity across a range of physiological measures (Guyll et al., 2013; Madon et al., 2017; Normile et al., 2018) indicating that the innocent perceive less threat in being accused than do the guilty.

However, the status of being innocent has not predicted decreased mobilization in terms of cognitive outcomes. Innocent and guilty individuals do not significantly differ with respect to how much attention they pay to accusation-relevant information or to how well they remember that information (Guyll et al., 2019; Madon et al., 2017). Thus, the innocent do not seem to be less cognitively mobilized than the guilty. Rather, the available research suggests that the primary means whereby innocence leads to increased risk is through the conscious behavioral choices that the innocent make. Although these choices might actually increase their risk of conviction, presumably the innocent make them because they believe they are the best way to cope with the situation of being falsely accused.

Making Contact with the Innocent

The foregoing discussion described how the phenomenology of innocence can lead the innocent to place themselves at greater risk, a topic that has received a fair degree of atten-tion in the empirical literature. However, the innocent are only able to behave contrary to their own self-interest because other forces had somehow previously brought them under suspicion, drawing them into the unfortunate spotlight associated with being a criminal suspect. Although thousands of documented wrongful convictions stand as prima facie evidence that innocent people can and do become entangled in criminal investigations (National Registry of Exonerations, 2021), the empirical literature has yet to focus on the ways in which the innocent come to be targets of investigation (see also Garrett & Crozier, this volume). This begs the question: *How do the innocent get into this mess in the first place?*

As noted at the beginning of this chapter, being "in this mess" corresponds to law enforcement having formed an incorrect impression about an innocent person, thereby highlighting the critical importance of person perception processes. However, the poten-tial for these processes to play any role at all presupposes that law enforcement has an innocent suspect as the object of their perception (Leo & Drizin, 2010). Therefore, we first explore how the routine law enforcement activities of consensual encounters and investigative detentions can cause innocent persons to become the objects of perception and subjected to unwarranted scrutiny. We then address how expectancies from a variety of sources have the potential to skew law enforcement toward a presumption of guilt. Where appropriate, we also note how these processes could be particularly problematic for minority individuals (see also Hunt, this volume; Prowse & Goff, this volume).

Consensual Encounters

A consensual encounter is a police interaction that is, by definition, noncustodial. Police may conduct a consensual encounter with anyone they wish, and they may use the encounter as an opportunity to question a person about possible criminal activity and request a search. Because people engaged in a consensual encounter are not detained, they have the option to terminate the encounter at any time and to refuse to be searched. Specifically, they have the legal right to refuse to answer questions, to refuse a search, and even to walk away. Simply put, they are always "free to go." Therefore, people engaged in a consensual encounter retain protective rights that obviate the relevance of the Fourth Amendment, which is only triggered by seizures and searches. However, being legally entitled to such rights is not the same as exercising them. As a result, law enforcement strategies and perceptual biases can combine with social influence forces operating on the individual to become entry points for the innocent to become entangled in a criminal investigation (see also Alceste & Kassin, this volume).

In the absence of Fourth Amendment protections, police may engage a person in a consensual encounter on nothing more than a hunch—a gut reaction, a vibe, an intuitive feeling (Carbado, 2017; Lerner, 2016). In other words, when it comes to consensual encounters, police may stop a person for questioning without cause, an ability that increases the likelihood of engaging with an innocent person. Although as we previously noted, people engaged in a consensual encounter retain all the rights of free individuals, they might not exercise these rights because of demand characteristics. Decades of psychological research have shown that people tend to comply with requests that are made by individuals who stand in positions of authority (Milgram, 1963). Police obviously have considerable authority over citizens, and that authority can make a request feel like a command—"what on their face are merely words of request take on color from the officer's uniform, badge, gun and demeanor" (Foote, 1960, p. 403). For example, of 16,228 motorists across a six-month period, all but *three* waived their right to refuse an unwarranted search of their vehicle (Bar-Gill & Friedman, 2012), an exceedingly strong compliance bias that laboratory research has replicated (Sommers & Bohn, 2019).

In addition, a consensual encounter can quickly escalate. If in the context of a consensual encounter a police officer develops the perception that a person may be involved in criminal activity or believes that the person poses a danger, then the consensual encounter can rapidly morph into an investigative detention or an arrest. Although transformation of the consensual encounter into an investigative detention does trigger Fourth Amendment protections, those protections have turned out to be more powerful in theory than in practice.

Investigative Detentions and the Reasonable Suspicion Standard

Unlike consensual encounters, an investigative detention is a custodial police interaction that triggers Fourth Amendment protections. In *Terry v. Ohio*,[1] the US Supreme Court ruled that police can stop and frisk someone if they have "specific and articulable facts" that suggest that the person is involved in criminal activity and poses a present danger; an "inchoate and unparticularized suspicion or 'hunch'" is insufficient. The significance of the Court's ruling is twofold. First, it created the reasonable suspicion standard as a midway point between a hunch and probable cause, thus lowering the degree of justification police needed to briefly detain someone for questioning and to conduct a frisk. Second, it calibrated Fourth Amendment protections by requiring police to have increasingly greater justification to conduct increasingly intrusive searches and seizures (Carbado, 2017). For instance, whereas the Court stated that stop-and-frisk requires reasonable suspicion of both criminal activity and a present danger, stop-and-question requires only reasonable suspicion of criminal activity. All in all, therefore, *Terry* weakened Fourth Amendment protections and increased police power (Lerner, 2006).

For the innocent, this ruling increased the likelihood that they could become the object of police attention and the target of suspicion. By way of analogy, if stop-and-question and stop-and-frisk are thought of as fishing nets that police use to catch criminals, the *Terry* ruling decreased the mesh size, making it more likely that innocent people will be scooped up. In essence, it comes down to a matter of probability. The more often that innocent people are stopped and come under police scrutiny, the more innocent persons who will become "known" to police. This provides an avenue whereby they could become entangled in an ongoing criminal investigation or become known for consideration as a potential suspect of a future crime. Thus, the reasonable suspicion standard increases the risk to innocent persons.

An additional factor making the reasonable suspicion standard problematic is the high degree of subjectivity involved in its application, with law enforcement permitted to rely upon the "totality of the circumstances" in making inferences about human behavior (Pelic, 2003). For example, the reasonable suspicion standard can be met by the perception of unusual sounds or smells, of activity occurring in a high-crime area, of normal activity taking place at an unusual time, of furtive movements, even by the presence of a car air freshener (Argiriou, as cited in Brown, 2012; Lerner, 2006). Thus, the definition of reasonable suspicion is open to individual construal and, therefore, vulnerable to biases, which could promote unnecessary contact with the innocent.

To illustrate, consider the fact that New York City police performed 4.4 million investigative detentions between 2004 and 2012, of which only 6 percent led to an arrest and 6 percent to a summons, suggesting that 88 percent were innocent and unnecessarily detained (Garrison, 2014). And, although 52 percent of these detentions involved a

---

[1] Terry v. Ohio, 392 U.S. 1 (1968).

frisk, only 1.5 percent of these searches yielded a weapon, indicating that the "specific and articulable facts" that are supposedly indicative of a present danger are very nonspecific. Thus, the reasonable suspicion standard is so overbroadly applied that it is actually highly predictive of innocence and not guilt.

Additionally worrisome is the potential for the reasonable suspicion standard to be applied in a discriminatory fashion. Whereas Whites comprised 33 percent of New York City's population, they accounted for only 10 percent of the investigative detentions. By contrast, Blacks comprised 23 percent of the city population but accounted for 52 percent of the detentions (Garrison, 2014). These differences in likelihood of being detained suggest that racial and ethnic biases may have led police to perceive or apply the reasonable suspicion threshold in ways that had a discriminatory effect. Although discriminatory actions can be intentional, they can also result from the effect of expectancies that operate outside awareness. We therefore turn to psychological theory related to expectancies and highlight how expectancies can lead to biased interpretation of the information to ultimately put innocents at risk of being targeted for criminal wrongdoing.

Expectancies

A fundamental principle of human behavior is that people infer meaning from context. They use their prior knowledge and beliefs to make sense of the world (Kunda, 1999; Ross & Nisbet, 2011). In short, people often engage in *top-down processing*, a quick and efficient information processing strategy whereby people interpret phenomena through the lens of their stored knowledge. Expectancies are a kind of stored knowledge that can influence people's judgments and behaviors (Trusz & Bąbel, 2016).

In general, expectancies can be beneficial because they allow people to efficiently formulate appropriate courses of action. For example, people's expectancies about the typical events that occur in a given situation (e.g., at a restaurant) or within a particular social interaction (e.g., doctor–patient interaction) provide a framework that enables them to interpret information and respond appropriately. However, expectancies can also lead people to make errors by biasing the way in which they process information. According to the confirmation bias, for example, people preferentially seek, interpret, and recall information in ways that confirm their preexisting beliefs (Findley & Scott, 2006; Snyder & Swann, 1978). Ultimately, this bias can cause people to believe that their expectancies have been confirmed to a greater extent than is justified (e.g., Nickerson, 1998; Willard et al., 2012). Decades of scientific research indicate that the confirmation bias contributes to a wide range of social problems including, for instance, academic underachievement, exaggerated perceptions of mental illness, miscalculations of audit risk assessment, misinterpretation of scientific evidence, stock market fluctuations, group disparities, and forensic errors (for reviews, see Jussim, 1986; Madon et al., 2011; Nickerson, 1998). The confirmation bias may also increase the chances that innocent people, especially racial and ethnic minorities, will come under police suspicion.

In the next section we consider several expectancies that have the potential to increase suspicion of an innocent person. We separate the expectancies according to whether or not they are appropriate for applying heightened scrutiny to the individuals whom the expectancy would bring under suspicion. General expectancies do not advance an investigation because they inappropriately bring large numbers of individuals under suspicion based on their group memberships. For example, if one expects without evidence that the perpetrator of a drive-by shooting is a Black male, it would be inappropriate to use the characteristics of "Black" and "male" as the sole criteria for investigating any given person because the likelihood is vanishingly small that any particular Black male is the perpetrator. Thus, the expectancy is of no meaningful value to an investigation. By contrast, investigatory expectancies have value for solving an investigation, either by focusing on a circumscribed set of individuals for justifiable reasons or by excluding whole groups of persons as possible suspects. For example, when investigating a sex crime, it would be appropriate to investigate known sex offenders residing in the area because there is a tenable prospect that the perpetrator is an individual within this group. Thus, the expectancy has value to the investigation.

General Expectancies:

General expectancies are those that do not advance an investigation because they are not based on evidence and they bring whole groups of people under suspicion, though any one individual from within that group has only an infinitesimal chance of being the perpetrator. General expectancies can be based on beliefs about all suspects, social groups, or the type of crime committed.

PRESUMPTION OF GUILT

A number of theoretical accounts propose that a presumption of guilt can lead people to interpret and respond to information in ways that ultimately cause them to confirm their preexisting guilt expectations (e.g., Bornstein & Greene, 2011; Findley & Scott, 2006; Kassin et al., 2003). A presumption of guilt would seem to be encouraged by some of the qualities associated with good police work, such as maintaining elevated levels of vigilance, skepticism, and suspicion (Phillips, 2020). Because the presumption of guilt corresponds to a belief, it has the potential to operate via the confirmation bias to increase suspicion and perceptions of threat and effectively lower the threshold for believing that the reasonable suspicion threshold has been surpassed in any given situation. Thus, a presumption of guilt could increase the number of individuals deemed suspicious enough to stop in the context of consensual encounters and investigative detentions and, consequently, increase the likelihood of entangling innocent persons in criminal investigations. Similarly, a presumption of guilt would encourage investigators to place individuals in lineups in the absence of other incriminating evidence, a tendency that dramatically increases the risk of mistaken eyewitness identifications (Wells et al., 2015), the factor that most commonly contributes to the wrongful conviction of DNA exonerees (Innocence Project, 2021).

A presumption of guilt could also lead to coercive interrogation practices that encourage false confession. Police training manuals, such as the *Reid Technique of Interviewing and Interrogation*, teach police that they can infer a suspect's innocence or guilt by virtue of observing the suspect's behavior (Inbau et al., 2013). However, the behaviors that are purported to be indicators of guilt are highly subjective and have no clear diagnostic value (Bond & DePaulo, 2006). Further compounding the problem is the fact that an interrogation situation can be dynamic, with the suspect displaying an array of diverse behaviors. Guided by their training, however, interrogators are made vulnerable to the confirmation bias in that the presumption of guilt may cause them to preferentially notice and remember the behaviors that supposedly indicate guilt over those that supposedly indicate innocence (Masip et al., 2016). As a consequence of misperceiving an innocent suspect to be guilty, an interrogator may proceed with a coercive interrogation, increasing the chance of a false confession and wrongful conviction.

RACIAL AND ETHNIC STEREOTYPES

The potential for bias is especially high for racial and ethnic minorities who may be judged on the basis of negative stereotypes. More than one hundred years of research in psychology has shown that people use stereotypes to form impressions of others, a process referred to as stereotyping. The process of stereotyping is borne from social categorization, is a fundamental feature of human cognition, and may be hardwired (Stolier & Freeman, 2016). Not surprisingly, therefore, people hold stereotypes about many social groups and their operation can influence person perception across a wide range of situations, including those encountered by law enforcement (Minhas & Walsh, 2018).

For several reasons, racial and ethnic stereotypes can put innocent minorities at risk of coming under police suspicion. First, some racial and ethnic stereotypes are associated with criminality. Blacks and Latinos, in particular, are stereotyped as being threatening, aggressive, hostile, and criminal (Aubé & Ric, 2019; Cottrell & Neuberg, 2005; Madon et al., 2001). Second, it can be difficult to control the effect of racial and ethnic stereotypes because their activation can be automatic, and they can levy their effects outside awareness (Fiske et al., 1991; Jones & Fazio, 2010; Stangor et al., 1992). In addition, the biasing effects of stereotypes are stronger when the behavior of an individual is open to multiple construals (Bodenhausen et al., 1994; Darley & Gross, 1983; Kunda & Sherman-Williams, 1993). Judgments of suspicious activity are often based on assessments of ambiguous behavior, such as waiting on sidewalk or walking through a neighborhood late at night. Thus, a stereotype could unconsciously bias a police officer to believe that the reasonable suspicion standard has been met, leading to an investigative detention, frisking, and generally greater scrutiny, but only for a racial or ethnic minority.

In addition to the vast experimental record demonstrating that stereotyping can lead to discriminatory treatment (e.g., Dovidio et al., 2010), a growing and consistent body of work indicates that the same effects occur in the criminal justice system. Indeed, across literatures using different samples and examining unique crimes, a robust theme emerges: Minority individuals, especially young, Black males, are subjected to discriminatory treatment throughout the investigatory process, including being more readily suspected of wrongdoing and more frequently stopped, detained, and arrested (D'Alessio & Stolzenberg, 2003; Kutateladze et al., 2014; Tonry, 2010). Thus, law enforcement more frequently engages with racial and ethnic minorities, thereby increasing the likelihood that the innocent from these groups will wrongly come under suspicion for having committed a crime. The heightened risk to the innocent from minority groups is perhaps best illustrated by the fact that they are disproportionately represented among those who have been exonerated of a wrongful conviction (Innocence Project, 2021; National Registry of Exonerations, 2021).

CRIME-SUSPECT STEREOTYPICAL CONSISTENCY

A crime stereotype is a set of beliefs people generally connect with a given crime. When one becomes aware that a particular crime has been committed, the beliefs that constitute that crime's stereotype are automatically activated. One set of beliefs within a crime stereotype are the characteristics of the typical perpetrator. For example, the criminal stereotype of date rape includes a White male perpetrator, that of prostitution includes a low-socioeconomic-status female perpetrator, and that of terrorism includes a Middle Eastern male perpetrator (Smalarz et al., 2016). When investigating a particular crime, the crime stereotype can serve as an informal criminal profile of the perpetrator, leading law enforcement to expect the perpetrator to have certain attributes, such as those related to race, ethnicity, social class, biological sex, and age. Thus, consistency between an innocent suspect's characteristics and those suggested by a crime stereotype could increase perceptions of guilt and risk of conviction. In other words, the degree of match between a suspects' or defendants' characteristics and those of the stereotypical perpetrator of a given crime has the potential to influence a host of legal judgments, including forensic analysis (Dror et al., 2021), evidence evaluation (Smalarz et al., 2018; Smalarz et al., 2016), ascribed motivation, criminal intent (Jones & Kaplan, 2003), and guilt judgments (McKimmie et al., 2013). Thus, innocent persons exhibiting such a match are at increased risk for wrongful conviction.

This effect is aptly illustrated by the high-profile investigation of the Madrid train bombing in 2004, which resulted in the arrest of Brandon Mayfield. FBI forensic examiners performed fingerprint comparisons with the knowledge that Mayfield was a follower of Islam and that he had provided legal counsel to a Muslim defendant charged with terrorism. The forensic examination falsely concluded that Mayfield's fingerprint matched those found on a bag of detonators recovered from the crime scene. Highlighting the potential effect of fitting the crime stereotype, a forensic examiner later acknowledged that the conclusion of a match might have received greater scrutiny if Mayfield had been like "the Maytag Repairman"—and advertising icon of the twentieth century that evokes a profoundly anodyne, White, native-born, American male (Department of Justice, Office of the Inspector General, 2006, p. 12; Smalarz et al., 2016).

Catalogued exonerations in the National Registry further suggest the idea that innocents who match criminal stereotypes may be at risk for wrongful conviction. White males represent only 31 percent of all exonerees, but make up 53 percent of exonerations for child sex abuse, a crime for which the stereotypical perpetrator is a White male. Racial and ethnic minorities represent 64 percent of all exonerees, but make up 82 percent of exonerations for drug-related crimes, for which the stereotypical perpetrators are minority individuals. Finally, although a total of only four exonerations for terrorism-related crimes exists, in all four cases the exonerees were Middle Eastern, Muslim men (National Registry of Exonerations, 2021). Taken together, the foregoing strongly suggests that innocents whose characteristics match a crime stereotype are at risk of being targeted for specific crimes.

Investigatory Expectancies

Investigatory expectancies are those that may advance an investigation because they identify individuals for whom group membership is predictive of guilt, rule out whole groups of individuals as suspects, or result from incriminating evidence.

RELATIONSHIP TO VICTIM

When someone is victimized, quite often the perpetrator is someone who is connected to or known by the victim. For example, in a considerable proportion of violent crimes against women, the perpetrator is a man who is romantically connected to the victim. One archival study found that more than half of American women from eighteen states who were killed between 2003 and 2014 were killed by men who were current or former intimate partners (Petrosky et al., 2017). A similar connection between victims and perpetrators characterizes other crimes as well, such as sexual assault and stalking (Bureau of Justice Statistics, 2021; Logan, 2022). Such associations are not new. Indeed, in the nineteenth century, the editor of the *New York Herald,* James Gordon Bennett, noted that husbands killing their wives was a common and easily forgotten crime (Schechter, 2021). Therefore, in cases such as murder wherein victims cannot provide information about the perpetrator, it is reasonable, even prudent, for the investigation to scrutinize as potential suspects individuals who were close to or knew the victim.

Unfortunately, the scrutiny applied to an innocent person by virtue of having a connection with the victim can sometimes shift from reasonable and prudent suspicion into an unfounded certitude of guilt, creating a tunnel vision that ignores other possible suspects. Such a process may have been responsible for the wrongful conviction of Darrell Parker. Parker, a forester who lived in Lincoln, Nebraska, returned home from work to find his wife murdered. After attending her funeral and burial in her home state of Iowa, the Nebraska police asked Parker to return to Nebraska to answer some questions, a request to which he agreed. However, rather than answering routine questions, Parker was subjected to a coercive interrogation by none other than John Reid, the developer of the Reid Technique, an interrogation method that presumes guilt and the chief goal of which is to obtain a confession.

After twelve hours of interrogation, Parker falsely confessed. He quickly recanted his confession but was nonetheless convicted and sentenced to life in prison. The true killer, Wesley Peery, had also been questioned about the murder but was discounted as a suspect as the investigation focused on Darrell Parker, likely because Parker was the victim's husband. Parker was not officially exonerated until 1991 based on information that Peery's attorneys had in their possession, but could not release until after his death, which occurred in 1988 (Starr, 2013).

The Parker anecdote is consistent with the well-documented effect of expectancies to affect perceptions. Parker's connection to the victim may have caused Reid to develop a false expectation that Parker was guilty of the murder. In turn, this expectation may have led Reid to interview Parker and to perceive him as being deceptive, setting the stage for a coercive interrogation, false confession, and wrongful conviction.

PRIOR CRIMINAL RECORD

Innocents can also be targeted in a criminal investigation on the basis of having a prior conviction. This idea—that prior convictions put innocents at risk—has been speculated as a factor associated with wrongful convictions for nearly a century (Borchard, 1932). Insomuch as a past conviction predicts subsequently committing a comparable offense, there is investigatory value in considering as potential suspects those who have previously committed similar crimes. As a consequence, an innocent person with a prior conviction might be presented to eyewitnesses, raising the possibility of a false identification and thereby becoming caught up in a criminal investigation (Gould et al., 2013).

In addition, for cases proving difficult to solve, a prior conviction could serve to keep an innocent person under suspicion through confirmation bias processes whereby police discount or ignore exculpatory evidence and interpret ambiguous or circumstantial evidence as inculpatory. In this manner it is possible that a deceptively convincing case could be built against an innocent suspect (Findley, 2012). Moreover, prior convictions can also disadvantage innocents during a jury trial by making them more resistant to offer first-hand testimony of their innocence because of fears that their credibility will be impeached and jurors will draw adverse inferences based on their prior record. Whereas 57 percent of DNA exonerees who had no prior record chose to testify on their own behalf at trial, among those who had a prior record this rate dropped to only 9 percent (Blume, 2008).

EVIDENCE

Another category of expectations that have investigatory value includes those that result from evidence that is gathered in the course of an investigation. For example, if an eyewitness accurately reports that the perpetrator is a young Black male, then the expectation that the perpetrator is a young Black male will also be accurate. Critically, however, the investigatory value of this expectation is only with regard to whom it excludes from suspicion. Specifically, investigators can rule out as suspects all persons who are not young

Black men. However, in and of itself, the knowledge that the perpetrator is a young Black man does no good in identifying the true perpetrator from among the general population of young Black men because all of them are actually innocent of the crime, with the single exception of the perpetrator. Thus, to the degree that an accurate, evidence-based expectation about the perpetrator's social group increases the perception of guilt for any one individual within the group, it does no better than an expectation based on a racial or ethnic stereotype, and correspondingly increases the risk to the innocent.

It also bears noting that the appropriateness of using an evidence-based expectation depends upon both the evidence and the action taken. The above example highlights evidence pointing only to a large group, and so it is only useful for excluding as suspects those who are not in that group and not for identifying suspects within that group. Other evidence, by contrast, might include a relatively small group of individuals, such as the perpetrator having tattoos signifying membership in a fringe group, in which case intense scrutiny of all individuals in the group may be reasonable. At the extreme, evidence and the resulting expectation can identify with nearly perfect accuracy the one true perpetrator, such as if recovered DNA matches a known person. Accordingly, as evidence points to fewer suspects, whether through highly identifying evidence such as DNA or through multiple, independent pieces of accurate evidence, relying on the resultant expectations will correspondingly pose less risk to the innocent.

The Self-Fulfilling Prophecy: Converting False Expectations into Convictions

As a private experience within the mind of an individual, a false expectation is—in and of itself—thoroughly impotent and devoid of the ability to do harm. The power of the false expectation derives from its effect on the behavior of the one who holds the expectation, for it is through behavior that the expectation might affect the treatment of the person to whom the expectation pertains. In contrast to expectancies themselves, expectancy-based behaviors provide the means to affect innocent suspects' outcomes in very real ways. This process describes the operation of a self-fulfilling prophecy, a well-documented interpersonal phenomenon wherein a false expectation about a person leads to its own fulfillment through the actions of the perceiver on the person (Merton, 1948; Rosenthal & Rubin, 1978). The anecdotal case of Darrel Parker reviewed above represents a prime example of a self-fulfilling prophecy in action. John Reid's false belief that Parker was guilty caused Reid to coerce a false confession from Parker which led to Parker's conviction, ostensibly proving the false belief to be true. Though we have considered a variety of different sources of false expectations of guilt, all of them have the potential to increase the risk to the innocent suspect, provided the perceiver has the opportunity to affect suspect treatment. Accordingly, wrongful convictions resulting from expectancies might be reduced in two ways. Training might increase awareness about how and when they are likely to occur, enabling law enforcement to reduce the development of such expectations in the first place. However, error and bias in person perception are unavoidable characteristics of human social cognition, perhaps suggesting that a better point to intervene may be in preventing the behavioral choices that could convey the harmful effects of a false belief. Enactment of critical decisions by law enforcement and prosecutors should only occur after deliberative and thorough consideration of the counterfactual condition that the true culprit has somehow escaped detection and that the suspect in custody is innocent.

Research Directions

In this chapter, we have proposed a number of processes that might contribute to the innocent being wrongfully convicted. The possibilities we have put forth have been based on direct evidence when available, but also on compelling anecdotes, reasoned analysis, and the inference that the same psychological processes documented by basic experimental research also operate among real suspects and law enforcement. Thus, substantial work remains to be done to maximize the quality of the scientific evidence that speaks to how and why the processes leading to wrongful conviction are triggered. For example, researchers should evaluate the extant research and (1) confirm by experimental tests any potentially causal relationships suggested by correlational research; (2) verify laboratory findings in the field; and (3) replicate findings based on samples of convenience with research in which participants are community members, suspects, or police, as appropriate.

Of the particular topics we discussed, researchers have most closely examined the phenomenology of innocence, perhaps because paradigms exist that enable experimental tests of hypotheses in laboratory settings with undergraduate samples (Kassin & Kiechel, 1996; Russano et al., 2005). A fruitful extension of this area of research relates to the possibility of transactional effects, wherein the innocent behave in a way that elicits more coercive treatment from investigators (Kassin et al., 2003). Researchers could code and compare the social interaction behaviors of innocent and guilty persons both from experimental manipulations and from actual interrogation tapes, assuming ground truth can be determined for the latter. Though lacking experimental controls, evaluating actual interrogation tapes would further allow examination of dynamic and reciprocal effects between suspects and interrogators, similar to other field interrogation research (e.g., Kelly et al., 2016). Experimental research could have actual police interrogators interrogate confederates trained to exhibit different suspect response behaviors to determine which behaviors elicit coercive treatment (see Kassin et al., 2003). Alternatively, the interrogators might watch stimulus videos of bogus interrogations in which suspect behaviors are manipulated, and then the interrogators could report their reactions to the suspect and how they would proceed with the interrogation.

It is also necessary to test the hypothesis that using a lower threshold for stopping individuals serves to increase the risk to innocent persons. Answering this question will likely require field research, police cooperation, and addressing a number of challenges, particularly standardization and operationalization of metrics across jurisdictions. For example, how might one measure the stopping threshold applied so that it might be compared across police departments? Another measurement issue involves how to assess how much risk there is to the innocent of being wrongfully convicted within a particular jurisdiction. Despite the challenges, such field research could yield major contributions. If police and scientists could form mutually supportive collaborations, it might be feasible to conduct quasi-experimental research. Perhaps existing variations in departmental policy could be used as a proxy manipulation for stopping thresholds, thereby enabling one to test whether such changes affected the risk to the innocent.

Meaningful research regarding the role of expectations on wrongful convictions likewise presents challenges. Because an expectation exists entirely within the mind of the individual, one can never be certain that it has been accurately measured. For this reason, experimental manipulations offer the surest way to investigate expectation effects. However, such experimental research would likely be of limited interest unless it were conducted with actual police who are naïve to a study's purpose, highly engaged in the procedures, and motivated to be accurate. Further, it is necessary to show that expectations not only bias perceptions but also investigatory behaviors in ways that would increase conviction risk for innocent persons. An additional issue that merits attention is the potential for inappropriate use of investigatory expectations. For example, is the knowledge that the suspect is of a particular ethnicity used only to exclude suspects who are of other ethnicities? Or does that knowledge serve to increase the suspicion for each potential suspect whose ethnicity happens to match that of the perpetrator? And might this effect be greater for some demographics, such as those related to suspect ethnicity?

Finally, the science of wrongful conviction will also benefit from the development of new experimental paradigms, particularly those that might be used with actual police and which activate psychological processes that are analogous to those operating in the field. Such paradigms could construct situations that tap the core elements of police-citizen interactions to identify what factors lead law enforcement to initiate interactions with some individuals over others. There are challenges to acquiring law enforcement samples to participate in research, especially the type of highly controlled, laboratory experiments that are prized among scientists for their ability to prove causal effects. However, to the degree that mutually respectful relationships can be forged between researchers and law enforcement, it is conceivable that access to that population might be expanded. Indeed, in the United States there are indications of a growing willingness among law enforcement to form such partnerships at the local, state, and federal level (e.g., Brimbal et al., 2021; Goldstein et al., 2019; Kassin et al., 2019). Experimentalists might even dare to imagine that police leadership might be willing to conduct experiments among their officers who participate under the belief that they are taking part in an actual police training exercise.

Conclusion

In this chapter, we considered an array of behavioral and psychological processes that could steer innocent individuals toward being viewed as suspects and possibly wrongfully convicted. We reviewed research and theory linking the psychological state associated with factual innocence to failures to engage in maximally self-protective behaviors. We outlined factors that guide police contact and interaction with the public, detailing how these factors can operate to increase the chances of entangling the innocent in a criminal investigation. We considered how a variety of expectancies, some justified and some unjustified, can lead law enforcement to falsely expect that a person is guilty. None of the behavioral and psychological processes we discussed is sure to cause police to target an innocent person or to produce a wrongful conviction. Indeed, they may do so only infrequently. However, even infrequent occurrences will yield appreciable numbers across many investigations, and even a single wrongful conviction constitutes a great tragedy for that innocent person. Accordingly, it is important to consider all possible processes whereby the innocent might be placed at greater risk of conviction, even if only by a small degree. Empirical investigation of these processes through both internally valid experimental research and externally valid field studies will provide a more comprehensive understanding of how wrongful convictions come to occur. Ultimately, such an understanding should be used to inform the development of safeguards to prevent or interrupt the sequence of events leading to wrongful conviction.

References

Aubé, B., & Ric, F. (2019). The socio-functional model of prejudice: Questioning the role of Emotions in the threat-behavior link. *International Review of Social Psychology, 32*(1), 1.

Bar-Gill, O., & Friedman, B. (2012). Taking warrants seriously. *Northwestern University Law Review, 106*(4), 1609–1674.

Blume, J. H. (2008). The dilemma of the criminal defendant with a prior record—Lessons from the wrongfully convicted. *Journal of Empirical Legal Studies, 5*(3), 477–505.

Bodenhausen, G. V., Sheppard, L. A., & Kramer, G. P. (1994). Negative affect and social judgment: The differential impact of anger and sadness. *European Journal of Social Psychology, 24*(1), 45–62.

Bond C. F., Jr., & DePaulo, B. M. (2006). Accuracy of deception judgments. *Personality and Social Psychology Review, 10*(3), 214–234.

Borchard, E. M. (1932). *Convicting the innocent: Errors in criminal justice.* Yale University Press.

Bornstein, B. H., & Greene, E. (2011). Jury decision making: Implications for and from psychology. *Current Directions in Psychological Science, 20*(1), 63–67.

Brimbal, L., Meissner, C. A., Kleinman, S. M., Phillips, E. L., Atkinson, D. J., Dianiska, R. E., Rothweiler, J. N., Oleszkiewicz, S., & Jones, M. S. (2021). Evaluating the benefits of a rapport-based approach to investigative interviews: A training study with law enforcement investigators. *Law and Human Behavior, 45*(1), 55–67.

Brown, Q. R. (2012). *Arizona v. Johnson*: Latest developments in the war on *Terry. University of Washington Bothell Policy Journal, 16*, 39–50.

Bureau of Justice Statistics. (2021). Generated using the NCVS Victimization Analysis Tool at www.bjs.gov (Number of rape/sexual assaults by victim-offender relationship, 1993-2019). https://www.bjs.gov/index.cfm?ty=nvat

Carbado, D. W. From stop and frisk to shoot and kill: *Terry v. Ohio*'s pathway to police violence. *UCLA Law Review, 64*(6), 1508–1553.

Cottrell, C. A., & Neuberg, S. L. (2005). Different emotional reactions to different groups: A Socio-functional threat-based approach to "prejudice." *Journal of Personality and Social Psychology, 88*(5), 770–789.

D'Alessio, S. J., & Stolzenberg, L. (2003). Race and the probability of arrest. *Social Forces, 81*(4), 1381–1397.

Darley, J. M., & Gross, P. H. (1983). A hypothesis-confirming bias in labeling effects. *Journal of Personality and Social Psychology, 44*(1), 20–33.

Dovidio, J. F., Hewstone, M., Glick, P., & Esses, V. M. (Eds.). (2010). *The SAGE handbook of prejudice, stereotyping and discrimination.* SAGE.

Drizin, S. A., & Leo, R. A. (2004). The problem of false confessions in the post-DNA world. *North Carolina Law Review, 82*(3), 891–1007.

Dror, I., Melinek, J., Arden, J. L., Kukucka, J., Hawkins, S., Carter, J., & Atherton, D. S. (2021), Cognitive bias in forensic pathology decisions. *Journal of Forensic Science, 66*(6), 2541–2544.

Findley, K. A. (2012). Tunnel vision. In B. L. Cutler (Ed.), *Conviction of the innocent: Lessons from psychological research* (pp. 303–323). American Psychological Association.

Findley, K. A., & Scott, M. S. (2006). The multiple dimensions of tunnel vision in criminal cases. *Wisconsin Law Review, 2006*(2), 291–398.

Fiske, A. P., Haslam, N., & Fiske, S. T. (1991). Confusing one person with another: what errors reveal about the elementary forms of social relations. *Journal of Personality and Social Psychology, 60*(5), 656–674.

Fiske, S. T., & Taylor, S. E. (2021). *Social cognition: From brains to culture.* SAGE.

Foote, C. (1960). The Fourth Amendment: Obstacle or necessity in the law of arrest? *The Journal of Criminal Law, Criminology, and Police Science, 51*(4), 402–408.

Goldstein, N. E. S., Cole, L. M., Houck, M., Haney-Caron, E., Holliday, S. B., Kreimer, R., & Bethel, K. (2019). Dismantling the school-to-prison pipeline: The Philadelphia Police School Diversion Program. *Children and Youth Services Review, 101*, 61–69.

Garrison, A. H. (2014). NYPD stop and frisk, perceptions of criminals, race and the meaning of *Terry v Ohio*: A content analysis of *Floyr, et al. v City of New York. Rutgers Race and the Law Review, 15*, 65–156.

Gilovich, T., Savitsky, K., & Medvec, V. H. (1998). The illusion of transparency: biased assessments of others' ability to read one's emotional states. *Journal of Personality and Social Psychology, 75*(2), 332–346.

Gould, J. B., Carrano, J., Leo, R., & Young, R. (2013). Predicting erroneous convictions: A social science approach to miscarriages of justice. Research report submitted to the US Department of Justice. https://www.ojp.gov/pdffiles1/nij/grants/241389.pdf

Guyll, M., Madon, S., Yang, Y., Scherr, K. C., Lannin, D., & Greathouse, S. (2013). Innocence and resisting confession during interrogation: Effects on physiologic activity. *Law and Human Behavior, 37*(5), 366–375.

Guyll, M., Yang, Y., Madon, S., Smalarz, L., & Lannin, D. G. (2019). Mobilization and resistance in response to interrogation threat. *Law and Human Behavior, 43*(4), 307–318.

Hafer, C. L., & Begue, L. (2005). Experimental research on just-world theory: Problems, developments, and future challenges. *Psychological Bulletin, 131*(1), 128–167.

Inbau, F., Reid, J., Buckley, J., & Jayne, B. (2013). *Criminal Interrogation and Confessions* (5th ed.). Jones & Bartlett.

Innocence Project. (2021). *DNA exonerations in the United States.* https://innocenceproject.org/dna-exonerations-in-the-united-states/

Jones, C. R., & Fazio, R. H. (2010). Person categorization and automatic racial stereotyping effects on weapon identification. *Personality and Social Psychology Bulletin, 36*(8), 1073–1085.

Jones, C. S., & Kaplan, M. F. (2003). The effects of racially stereotypical crimes on juror decision-making and information-processing strategies. *Basic and Applied Social Psychology, 25*(1), 1–13.

Jussim, L. (2012). *Social perception and social reality: Why accuracy dominates bias and self-fulfilling prophecy.* Oxford University Press.

Jussim, L. (1986). Self-fulfilling prophecies: A theoretical and integrative review. *Psychological Review, 93*(4), 429–445.

Kassin, S. M. (2005). On the psychology of confessions: Does innocence put innocents at risk? *American Psychology, 60*(3), 215–228.

Kassin, S. M. (2012). Why confessions trump innocence. *American Psychologist, 67*(6), 431–445.

Kassin, S. M., Goldstein, C. J., & Savitsky, K. (2003). Behavioral confirmation in the interrogation room: On the dangers of presuming guilt. *Law and Human Behavior, 27*(2), 187–203.

Kassin, S. M., & Kiechel, K. L. (1996). The social psychology of false confessions: Compliance, internalization, and confabulation. *Psychological Science, 7*(3), 125–128.

Kassin, S. M., & Norwick, R. J. (2004). Why people waive their *Miranda* rights: The power of innocence. *Law and Human Behavior, 28*(2), 211–221.

Kassin, S. M., Russano, M. B., Amrom, A. D., Hellgren, J., Kukucka, J., & Lawson, V. Z. (2019). Does video recording inhibit crime suspects? Evidence from a fully randomized field experiment. *Law and Human Behavior, 43*(1), 44–55.

Kelly, C. E., Miller, J., & Redlich, A. D. (2016). The dynamic nature of interrogation. *Law and Human Behavior, 40*(3), 295–309.

Kunda, Z. (1999). *Social cognition: Making sense of people.* Massachusetts Institute of Technology.

Kunda, Z., & Sherman-Williams, B. (1993). Stereotypes and the construal of individuating information. *Personality and Social Psychology Bulletin, 19*(1), 90–99.

Kutateladze, B., Andiloro, N., Johnson, B., & Spohn, C. (2014). Cumulative disadvantage: Examining racial and ethnic disparity in prosecution and sentencing. *Criminology, 52*(3), 514–551.

Lazarus, R. S., & Folkman, S. (1984). *Stress, appraisal, and coping.* Springer.

Leo, R. A., & Drizin, S. A. (2010). The three errors: Pathways to false confession and wrongful conviction. In G. D. Lassiter & C. A. Meissner (Eds.), *Police interrogations and false confessions: Current research, practice, and policy recommendations* (pp. 9–30). American Psychological Association.

Lerner, C. S. (2006). Reasonable suspicion and mere hunches. *Vanderbilt Law Review, 59*(1), 405–474.

Lerner, M. J. (1980). *The belief in a just world: A fundamental delusion.* Plenum.

Logan, T. (2022). Examining stalking assault by victim gender, stalker gender, and victim-stalker relationship. *Journal of Family Violence, 37*, 87–97.

Madon, S., Guyll, M., Aboufadel, K., Montiel, E., Smith, A., Palumbo, P., & Jussim, L. (2001). Ethnic and national stereotypes: The Princeton trilogy revisited and revised. *Personality and Social Psychology Bulletin, 27*(8), 996–1010.

Madon, S., Guyll, M., Yang, Y., Smalarz, L., Marschall, J., & Lannin, D. G. (2017). A biphasic process of resistance among suspects: The mobilization and decline of self-regulatory resources. *Law and Human Behavior, 41*(2), 159–172.

Madon, S., Willard, J., Guyll, M., & Scherr, K. C. (2011). Self-fulfilling prophecies: Mechanisms, power, and links to social problems. *Social and Personality Psychology Compass, 5*(8), 578–590.

Masip, J., Alonso, H., Herrero, C., & Garrido, E. (2016). Experienced and novice officers' generalized communication suspicion and veracity judgments. *Law and Human Behavior, 40*(2), 169–181.

McKimmie, B. M., Masters, J. M., Masser, B. M., Schuller, R. A., & Terry, D. J. (2013). Stereotypical and counter-stereotypical defendants: Who is he and what was the case against her? *Psychology, Public Policy, and Law, 19*(3), 343–354.

Merton, R. K. (1948). The self-fulfilling prophecy. *The Antioch Review, 8*(2), 193–210.

Milgram, S. (1963). Behavioral study of obedience. *The Journal of Abnormal and Social Psychology, 67*(4), 371–378.

Minhas, R., & Walsh, D. (2018). Influence of racial stereotypes on investigative decision-making in criminal investigations: A qualitative comparative analysis, *Cogent Social Sciences, 4*(1), Article 1538588.

Mongin, P. (1998). Expected utility theory. In J. B. Davis, D. W. Hands, & U. Mäki (Eds.), *Handbook of economic methodology* (pp. 342–350). Edward Elgar.

National Registry of Exonerations. (2021). *Exoneration detail list.* https://www.law.umich.edu/special/exoneration/Pages/detaillist.aspx

Nickerson, R. S. (1998). Confirmation bias: A ubiquitous phenomenon in many guises. *Review of General Psychology, 2*(2), 175–220. https://doi.org/10.1037/1089-2680.2.2.175

Normile, C.J., & Scherr, K.C. (2018). Police tactics and guilt status uniquely influence suspects' physiologic reactivity and resistance to confess. *Law and Human Behavior, 42*(6), 497–506.

Pelic, J. (2003). *United States v. Arvizu:* Investigatory stops and the Fourth Amendment. *Journal of Criminal Law and Criminology, 93*(4), 1033–1056.

Petrosky, E., Blair, J. M., Betz, C. J., Fowler, K. A., Jack, S. P. D., & Lyons, B. H. (2017). Morbidity and mortality weekly report. *Centers for Disease Control and Prevention, 66*(28), 741–746.

Phillips, S. W. (2020). The formation of suspicion: A vignette study. *International Journal of Police Science and Management, 22*(3), 274–284.

Rosenthal, R., & Rubin, D. B. (1978). Interpersonal expectancy effects: The first 345 studies. *Behavioral and Brain Sciences, 1*(3), 377–386.

Ross, L., & Nisbett, R. E. (2011). *The person and the situation: Perspectives of social psychology.* Pinter & Martin.

Russano, M. B., Meissner, C. A., Narchet, F. M., & Kassin, S. M. (2005). Investigating true and false confessions within a novel experimental paradigm. *Psychological Science, 16*(6), 481–486.

Savage, L. J. (1954). *The foundations of statistics.* John Wiley & Sons.

Schechter, H. (2021). *Maniac: The Bath School disaster and the birth of the modern mass killer.* Little A.

Scherr, K. C., & Franks, A. S. (2015). The world is not fair: An examination of innocent and guilty suspects' waiver decisions. *Law and Human Behavior, 39*(2), 142–151.

Scherr, K. C., Redlich, A. D., & Kassin, S. M. (2020). Cumulative disadvantage: A psychological framework for understanding how innocence can lead to confession, wrongful conviction, and beyond. *Perspectives on Psychological Science, 15*(2), 353–383.

Sommers, R., & Bohn, V.K. (2019). The voluntariness of voluntary consent: Consent searches and the psychology of compliance. *The Yale Law Journal, 128*, 1962–2033

Smalarz, L., Madon, S., & Turosak, A. (2018). Defendant stereotypicality moderates the effect of confession evidence on judgments of guilt. *Law and Human Behavior, 42*(4), 355–368.

Smalarz, L., Madon, S., Yang, Y., Guyll, M., & Buck, S. (2016). The perfect match: Do criminal stereotypes bias forensic evidence analysis? *Law and Human Behavior, 40*(4), 420–429.

Snyder, M., & Swann, Jr., W. B. (1978). Hypothesis-testing processes in social interaction. *Journal of Personality and Social Psychology, 36*(11), 1202–1212.

Stangor, C., Lynch, L., Duan, C., & Glas, B. (1992). Categorization of individuals on the basis of multiple social features. *Journal of Personality and Social Psychology, 62*(2), 207.

Starr, D. (2013, December 9). The interview: Do police interrogation techniques produce false confessions? *The New Yorker.* https://www.newyorker.com/magazine/2013/12/09/the-interview-7

Stolier, R. M., & Freeman, J. B. (2016). Neural pattern similarity reveals the inherent intersection of social categories. *Nature Neuroscience, 19*(6), 795–797.

Stromwall, L. A., Hartwig, M., & Granhag, P. A. (2006). To act truthfully: Nonverbal behavior and strategies during a police interrogation. *Psychology, Crime and Law, 12*(2), 207–219.

Swann, W. B. (1987). Identity negotiation: Where two roads meet. *Journal of Personality and Social Psychology, 53*(6), 1038–1051.

Swann, W. B., Jr., Milton, L. P., & Polzer, J. T. (2000). Should we create a niche or fall in line? Identity negotiation and small group effectiveness. *Journal of Personality and Social Psychology, 79*(2), 238–250.

Tonry, M. (2010). The social, psychological, and political causes of racial disparities in the American criminal justice system. *Crime and Justice, 39*(1), 273–312.

Trusz, S., & Bąbel, P. (Eds.). (2016). *Interpersonal and intrapersonal expectancies.* Routledge.

Wells, G. L., Yang, Y., & Smalarz, L. (2015). Eyewitness identification: Bayesian information gain, base-rate effect-equivalency curves, and reasonable suspicion. *Law and Human Behavior, 39*(2), 199–122.

Willard, J., Madon, S., Guyll, M., Scherr, K. C., & Buller, A. A. (2012). The accumulating effects of shared expectations. *European Journal of Social Psychology, 42*(4), 497–508.

Yang, Y., Guyll, M., & Madon, S. (2017). The interrogation decision-making model: A general theoretical framework for confessions. *Law and Human Behavior, 41*(1), 80–92.

PART III

Criminal Outcomes

Emerging Issues in the Psycholegal Study of Guilty Pleas

Allison D. Redlich, Tina M. Zottoli, Amy Dezember, Ryan Schneider, Mary Catlin, *and* Suraiya Shammi

Abstract

In the 2010 *Lafler v. Cooper* decision, the Supreme Court equated the US criminal justice system to one of guilty pleas. As addressed in this chapter, this is because guilty pleas make up the majority of criminal case outcomes (around 64 percent) and the majority of convictions (around 97 percent). In this chapter, common themes in guilty plea research are reviewed, including the psychology of guilty plea decision-making, the validity of guilty pleas, and false guilty pleas. Further, new data are presented, aimed at reconceptualizing guilty plea rates and measuring plea discounts. Researchers' choices about which dichotomous plea rate (prospective vs. retrospective) to examine and how to define plea discounts have implications for theories of plea decision-making and for advancing psycholegal scholarship on guilty pleas.

Key Words: guilty pleas, decision-making, false guilty pleas

Scholarly research on plea bargaining, particularly in the field of psychology and law, has increased tremendously over the past fifteen years. In part, this boom resulted from critiques of the field for a seemingly narrow focus on jury trials, a rare event compared to pleas (e.g., Ogloff, 2000). Almost all convictions in the United States are a result of guilty pleas, and plea bargaining is becoming more prevalent across the globe (Turner, 2017). In this chapter, we first provide an overview of topics and findings that plea researchers have concentrated on in the recent past. We then present new data on ways to conceptualize plea rates and discounts with the aim of moving this body of scholarship forward.

Common Themes in Guilty Plea Research

In *Brady v. United States*,[1] the Supreme Court of the United States upheld, for the first time, a guilty plea that was the product of a plea negotiation (i.e., a plea bargain). Prior to this decision, a guilty plea in open court was treated no differently than a confession

---

[1] Brady v. United States, 397 U.S. 742 (1970).

in police custody, and, as such, offers of leniency were considered coercive.[2] The Court's departure from its prior jurisprudence was practically unavoidable—by 1970, nearly 70 percent of criminal convictions in the United States were decided by guilty plea (Dervan, 2012). Today, the conviction-by-plea rate is about 95 percent or more (Devers, 2011).

Despite having supplanted the trial as the primary mechanism of criminal conviction, few of the rights that attach to defendants who go to trial have been formally extended to those who plead guilty (e.g., right to exculpatory evidence; Miller, 2019). Also, unlike trials, plea negotiations occur outside the view of the public (and sometimes the judiciary). In part due to the ambiguous attention to due process and secretive nature surrounding pleas, law journals teem with critiques of plea bargaining and arguments for reform (Covey, 2007; McCoy, 2005; White, 1971).

Against this backdrop, a burgeoning psycholegal research agenda has developed, with aims that include illuminating the oft-obscured plea process, understanding the plea decisions of defendants and attorneys, and testing the assumptions inherent to the validity of the plea process. Here we provide a thumbnail sketch of this research as it pertains to defendant decision-making, generally, and to questions surrounding the validity of guilty pleas, more specifically.

Psychology of Guilty Plea Decision-Making

When defendants decide whether they will plead guilty, they are choosing between a relatively certain outcome (i.e., the plea sentence) and the uncertainty of trial, which, if convicted, often results in a more severe sentence. It is perhaps not surprising that the likelihood to accept or reject a plea offer in this context depends largely on the sentencing differential between pleas and trial convictions (Schneider & Zottoli, 2019; Zimmerman & Hunter, 2018) and the perceived probability of conviction (Bordens, 1984; Bushway et al., 2014; Tor et al., 2010). Indeed, the most commonly referenced plea decision model, Shadow of the Trial (SOT; Bushway & Redlich, 2012), assumes that defendants and attorneys assess the value of a plea offer relative to the *expected value of trial* (i.e., the potential trial sentence multiplied by the probability of conviction). However, plea decisions can be complex and emotionally charged; myriad psychological factors—individual, normative, and structural—can influence how defendants evaluate their options and arrive at decisions (Bibas, 2004; Helm, 2018; Redlich et al., 2017). For instance, factual guilt, by itself, exerts a stronger influence on plea decisions than either conviction probability or plea discount (Tor et al., 2010; Wilford et al., 2020). Normative cognitive biases can also affect how defendants evaluate and respond to their options. Recent research suggest that defendants might overweigh low odds of conviction, such that they will settle for plea

---

[2] Bram v. United States, 168 U.S. 532 (1897).

deals that are worse than the expected value of trial when risk of conviction is perceived to be very low (Bartlett & Zottoli, 2021; Petersen et al., 2021).

System-factors that can influence defendant decisions include both jurisdiction-wide policies as well the individual decisions or actions of other legal actors (e.g., prosecutors and judges). For instance, defendants detained pretrial tend to plead guilty at higher rates and more quickly than those not detained (Dobbie et al., 2018; Sacks & Ackerman, 2012). If the plea leads to release, detained defendants may discount other important concerns, like negative collateral consequences (Edkins & Dervan, 2018). Pretrial detention may also be a factor in racial disparities in plea outcomes, as non-White defendants are more likely than White defendants to be held pretrial (Demuth, 2003).

Defendants are also typically at an informational deficit compared to the state. The constitutional right to material and exculpatory evidence[3] has not been formally extended to plea negotiations, and states vary considerably in terms of what the defense can access before pleading (Zottoli et al., 2019). Perhaps unsurprisingly, defendants and their attorneys feel their decisions are better-informed when they have access to evidence (Turner & Redlich, 2016; see also Luna & Redlich, 2020a), and in laboratory experiments, attorneys and mock-defendants adjust expectations for trial according to evidence strength (Bushway et al., 2014; Redlich et al., 2016). In one study, mock-defendants less certain about the evidence against them made more conservative estimates of their risk and were more likely to plead guilty than those who knew the evidence in their cases was weak (Faust, 2021).

In sum, although the guilty plea can be conceived of as a rational choice, there are a host of factors that affect defendants' assessments and tolerance of risk, and ultimate plea decisions. Insofar as they may affect a defendant's knowledge, understanding, and autonomy, many of these factors may also have implications for the validity of a guilty plea.

Validity of Guilty Pleas

Before accepting a guilty plea, in theory, a judge must be satisfied that the plea is voluntary and that defendants understand the procedural and constitutional rights they are waiving, and the legal consequences associated with their decision[4] (see Redlich, 2016). Most jurisdictions also require a sufficient factual basis for the charges (Zottoli et al., 2019). Finally, following *Padilla v. Kentucky*,[5] defendants must also be apprised of life-altering consequences (i.e., deportation).[6]

---

[3] Brady v. Maryland, 373 U.S. 83 (1963).

[4] *Brady*, 397 U.S. 742.

[5] Padilla v. Kentucky, 559 U.S. 356 (2010).

[6] Apart from the consequences mandated by Padilla, few states require communication of the many extralegal collateral consequences that may follow conviction, such as housing and employment restrictions (Zottoli et al., 2019). Although scholars argue that defendants should be made aware of these potential impacts (Bibas, 2011), only one study, to our knowledge, has examined how such information affects plea decisions. Edkins and Dervan (2018) found that knowledge of negative long-term consequences reduced the likelihood of mock-defendants pleading guilty, but only when plea offers did not entail immediate freedom.

The validity of a guilty plea is typically determined by oral plea colloquy or written tender of plea forms, and simple verbal or written affirmations are usually sufficient to satisfy the court (Redlich, 2016). There is good reason to believe, however, that these safeguards are inadequate. For instance, interviews with defendants who have pled guilty reveal substantial discrepancies between defendants' claims of knowledge and their actual legal and plea-specific knowledge (Redlich & Summers, 2012; Zottoli & Daftary-Kapur, 2019). Juvenile defendants, who show more pronounced deficits in legal knowledge and see their attorneys less frequently than adults, may be at even greater risk (Fountain & Woolard, 2018; Redlich & Shteynberg, 2016; Zottoli & Daftary-Kapur, 2019). In addition, although most individuals who were asked about their plea experiences said it was their own choice to plead guilty, not all were aware that guilty pleas *must* be voluntary (Redlich & Summers, 2012). Moreover, many who knew that, legally speaking, they had a choice, made it clear that, as a practical matter, they did not; most of these individuals referenced the substantially more severe punishments they would receive if they were convicted at trial (Zottoli & Daftary-Kapur, 2019).

Indeed, a common criticism leveled at plea bargaining is that sentence discrepancies are frequently so large as to be coercive (Caldwell, 2012; MacKenzie, 2007). Although estimating the plea discount is complicated (a point to which we return to below), the general consensus across studies is that plea discounts are steep. Estimates based on archival sentencing records range from 30 percent (federal; Kim, 2015) to 67 percent (New York; Yan & Bushway, 2018), and those based on interview data are even higher (e.g., 77 percent for adults convicted of felonies in New York City; Zottoli et al., 2016). Of course, plea bargains by definition involve offers of leniency,[7] and threatening a harsher sentence to encourage a plea is permissible as long as there is a statutory basis for the charge.[8] At the same time, the *Brady* Court stipulated that the plea process would be on shaky ground if offers of leniency were so large as to compel an innocent defendant, aided by competent counsel, to plead guilty. As we will discuss next, there is a growing empirical basis for questioning whether they have become so (Dervan, 2012).

FALSE GUILTY PLEAS

The language used by the *Brady* Court suggests that the legitimacy of plea bargaining rests on clear evidence of the defendant's guilt (Dervan, 2012). Even in permitting guilty pleas of defendants who wish to maintain their innocence (i.e., the so-called *Alford* plea[9]), the Supreme Court made explicit the condition that the record strongly evidenced guilt. However, the bar for establishing an evidentiary basis can be quite low (Redlich, 2016)— if required at all (Zottoli et al., 2019).

---

[7] *Brady*, 397 U.S. 742.
[8] Bordenkircher v. Hayes, 434 U.S. 357 (1978).
[9] North Carolina v. Alford, 400 U.S. 25 (1970).

Of course, there is much daylight between a factually deficient guilty plea and a false guilty plea—that is, a guilty plea by a factually innocent defendant. Nonetheless, it is beyond dispute that false guilty pleas do occur; as of this writing, 20 percent of exonerations documented in the United States since 1989 involved innocent defendants who pled guilty (National Registry of Exonerations, n.d.). Other indicators of plea-bargaining's "innocence problem" (Dervan, 2012) include high rates of self-reported false guilty pleas (Malloy et al., 2014; Redlich et al., 2010; Zottoli et al., 2016) and the frequency of *Alford* pleas (an estimated 76,050, or 6.6 percent, of state inmates in 2004 had entered *Alford* pleas; Redlich & Özdoğru, 2009). Finally, in a recent survey of US criminal defense attorneys, 90 percent ($n = 148$) reported having clients who pled guilty despite maintaining their innocence and 45 percent ($n = 74$) reported having advised a client they believed to be innocent to plead guilty (Helm et al., 2018).

Like guilty defendants, innocent defendants are more likely to plead guilty when there is a large differential between the plea and the trial sentence (Schneider & Zottoli, 2019), when the plea entails immediate freedom (Edkins & Dervan, 2018; Redlich & Shteynberg, 2016), and when the likelihood of conviction is perceived to be very high (Tor et al., 2010). At the same time, innocent defendants are more resistant to pleading guilty, and different cognitive processes appear to underlie the plea decisions of factually innocent and factually guilty defendants (Garnier-Dykstra & Wilson, 2021; Helm, 2018). Mounting data suggest that developmental factors are also important (Helm et al., 2017; Redlich & Shteynberg, 2016; Zottoli & Daftary-Kapur, 2019). As with research on false confessions (Kassin et al., 2010; see Redlich et al., 2017), as we better understand the phenomenon of false guilty pleas, the knowledge base can be used to inform policies and procedures aimed at maximizing true guilty pleas while minimizing false guilty pleas and preserving the autonomy of all defendants.

In sum, psychologists and other social scientists have been instrumental in making a typically closed-door legal process accessible to empirical study and in identifying a host of system- and defendant-level variables that influence guilty plea decisions. To date, most of this research has focused on defendants and has largely relied on single-point-in-time decisions (i.e., the decision to accept a plea offer). However, in recent years, increased attention has been given to other legal actors (e.g., prosecutors; see Kutateladze et al., 2016; Luna & Redlich, 2020b) and scholars have begun to highlight the complex and dynamic nature of the plea process (Helm & Zottoli, 2020). New methodologies are being developed to allow for the capture of multiple decision points and their cascading influences (e.g., Frazier & Gonzales, 2021) and interdisciplinary collaborations (e.g., with computational scientists, Zottoli et al., 2022) hold promise for the rapid expansion of complex modeling. Below, we highlight two emerging issues—conceptualizing plea rates and calculating plea discounts—to further drive plea scholarship forward.

Rethinking Plea Rates

As stated above, 95 percent or more of convictions are a result of guilty pleas, with the remainder the result of trial convictions (National Center for State Courts, Court Statistics Project, n.d.). This frequently cited ~95% rate comes from using the total number of guilty pleas as the numerator, and the total number of convictions as the dominator. For example, in the last iteration of the Bureau of Justice Statistics, State Court Processing Statistics (SCPS) of felony defendants, there were 32,300 convictions, of which 31,321 were plea convictions, or 97 percent (see Table 21, Reaves, 2013). With the exception of murder, which had a plea rate of 72 percent (51/70 instances), this high prevalence of pleas generally holds across various crime types.

But there is another way to calculate plea rates, one that is prospective, starting from the point of arrest/filing of charges. That is, to maintain the same numerator (total number of pleas) but use the number of defendants initially arrested or charged as the denominator. Again, using the SCPS data set to illustrate, we can see that pleas account for 64 percent of outcomes, or 31,321/48,939 (the total number of felony defendants) (Table 21, Reaves, 2013). The remainder from this 64 percent is made up of dismissed cases (25 percent); trial convictions (2 percent); trial acquittals (1 percent), and other nonconviction outcomes, such as diversion and deferred adjudication (9 percent; total equals 101 percent due to rounding error).

Thus, within the SCPS data set we get felony plea rates of 64 percent (going forward from number of defendants) to 97 percent (going backward from number of convictions). Thinking about plea rates from this 33-percentage-point gap, a number of new avenues of investigation are opened for plea scholars. For example, the decision point shifts from the defendant opting whether to accept or reject the plea offer to the prosecutor deciding whether to dismiss the case or go forward (offer a plea, offer a diversion option, etc.). By moving the study of decision-making to an earlier point in the criminal justice pipeline, it then becomes possible to examine a series of decisions over time and how each previous decision influences those that follow (e.g., in a cumulative manner; Kutateladze et al. 2014; Scherr et al., 2020).

Using data posted by Measures for Justice (MFJ; https://measuresforjustice.org/), we were able to calculate both plea rates (file and conviction) for three states that reported the data necessary for these calculations (for 2011–2015): Wisconsin (seventy-two counties; 0 missing); Arkansas (seventy-four counties; one missing); and North Dakota (forty-nine counties; four missing). To calculate the file-to-plea rates, the numerator was total number of guilty pleas for nonviolent and violent felonies and the denominator the total number of felonies filed. For conviction-plea rates, the numerator was total number of felony guilty pleas and the denominator was total number of convictions for nonviolent and violent felonies. (These variables were not available for misdemeanor offenses, though we would expect that both plea rates would be higher for these lower-level offenses than felonies [see Smith & Maddan, 2019].) Table 39.1 describes the mean and standard deviation, median, and range for both plea rates in these states.

Table 39.1 Mean and Standard Deviation, Median, and Range for Both Plea Rates in Wisconsin, Arkansas, and North Dakota

State	Plea/Felonies Filed	Plea/Felony Convictions
Wisconsin (72 counties)	Mean (SD): 74.80% (9.02) Median: 75.30% Range: 52.20% to 95.45%	Mean (SD): 98.35% (1.09) Median: 98.44% Range: 94.55% to 100%
Arkansas (74 counties)	Mean (SD): 67.01% (16.84) Median: 71.08% Range: 19.86% to 92.25%	Mean (SD): 83.98% (14.22) Median: 88.23% Range: 23.21% to 99.07%
North Dakota (49 counties)	Mean (SD): 71.75% (12.74) Median: 73.62% Range: 34.78% to 95.28%	Mean (SD): 94.82% (8.28) Median: 97.53% Range: 61.54% to 100%

The median shows that the file-to-plea rates range from about 71 percent to 75 percent, indicating that in half of the counties in these three states, roughly three-quarters of felony defendants with filed charges end up pleading guilty. Examining the ranges of file-to-plea rates, we see wide variation with a low of about one in five defendants eventually pleading out (20 percent), to other counties that approach five in five defendants (i.e., 92-95 percent).

The conviction-to-plea rate, especially for Wisconsin and North Dakota, is very much in line with the traditional 97 percent plea rate. For Wisconsin, all seventy-two counties have conviction-plea rates that are 95 percent or higher; there is very little variation. For North Dakota, although the range of rates is larger, half of the counties have conviction-plea rates that are 97.5 percent or higher. And indeed, ten of the forty-nine North Dakota counties have a 100 percent conviction-plea rate (not shown). Arkansas tells somewhat of a different story. The median conviction-plea rate is 88 percent which, although still a majority of cases, is lower than the standard 95–97 percent rate. There is also significant variability across the seventy-four Arkansas counties, ranging from a low of 23 percent to a high of 99 percent.

These data on plea rates raise a number of policy-relevant questions for researchers. For example, what factors account for such variation for either of the plea-rate types? Although space does not permit a more thorough analysis, one possibility is jurisdictional differences, such as county size. Notably, the 64 percent file-to-felony plea rate and the 97 percent conviction-plea rate calculated from the SCPS data pertain to the seventy-five largest counties in the United States. These rates might differ for smaller-sized counties (which make up most of the United States[10]). For example, Redlich et al. (2018) reported felony file-to-plea rates of 87.6 percent and 92.2 percent in two small–medium-sized upstate New York counties.

To explore this possibility, we computed correlations between county size and the two plea rates for each of the three states separately. In Wisconsin, there was a significant

---

[10] According to the US Census, 81 percent of US counties have fewer than 100,000 people.

correlation between county size and conviction-plea rate, $r = -0.39$, $p < 0.001$, but not file-to-plea rate, $r = 0.06$. Thus, the smaller the county in Wisconsin, the larger the conviction-plea rate (though as noted, the conviction-plea rate in Wisconsin had little variability). In Arkansas, neither correlation was significant (p's ≥ 0.30). In North Dakota, while conviction-plea rate and county size were not significantly correlated, $r = 0.19$, $p = 0.21$, file-to-plea rate and size were, $r = 0.33$, $p = 0.02$; indicating that larger size North Dakota counties had higher file-plea rates. Given that the SCPS data, which represent the largest counties in the United States, have an average file-plea rate of 64 percent, and given the somewhat larger file-plea rates found here of 67 percent to 75 percent (with much smaller-size counties), we might have expected to see significant, negative correlations between county size and file-plea rates. In contrast, the correlations were either nonsignificant, or positive. This may be because of the vast differences in county size. That is, 88 percent of the counties in our sample had populations less than 100,000, and 78 percent had less than 50,000. In contrast, the one county that appeared in our sample and the SCPS sample (i.e., Milwaukee[11]) has a population of nearly 1 million. Although county size is a gross measure, one that likely obscures a number of relevant nuances, these preliminary analyses underscore the importance of accounting for between-jurisdiction variations.

Our goal in presenting these two plea rate types is to continue to move plea scholarship forward. Whereas the conviction-plea rate will continue to be a useful variable for researchers to study as summarized in the first section of this chapter, the file-to-plea rate allows for an examination of decision-making prior to adjudication by a wider range of legal actors, in addition to the defendant. The data presented here also further emphasize the reliance on guilty pleas in our system. In all three states, there were individual counties in which the file-to-plea felony rate was 92 percent or more, indicating that only a combined 8 percent of initially filed felony cases were dismissed, found guilty at trial, were acquitted, or had some other nonconviction outcome. And, as noted, using this prospective plea rate allows for a more longitudinal approach; one that can help researchers identify how previous decisions affect subsequent decisions, both in isolation and cumulatively (Scherr et al., 2020).

We also note here that determining file-plea rates was quite difficult and cumbersome. Despite extensive searches, we could only find data for three states and only for felony offenses (although MFJ now has data from a total of sixteen states, most did not have the variables needed to compute this rate). Moreover, even for these three states, many steps were required to arrive at the data points needed to calculate the plea rates reported (more detail on these steps is available from the first author). Thus, we encourage criminal justice agencies to share, and researchers to report, rates of total number of defendants, number of cases dismissed, number of guilty pleas, and number of trials (and their

---

[11] Milwaukee, Wisconsin, has a file-plea rate of 71.67 percent and a conviction-plea rate of 94.55 percent.

outcomes). To wit, New Jersey just passed a bill requiring the Attorney General to "collect, record, analyze, and report certain prosecutorial and criminal justice data" including the filing and disposition of cases, and plea negotiations.[12] We also stress the need to do this for misdemeanor cases which make up the majority of criminal cases (see generally, Smith & Maddan, 2019).

Finally, another issue that limits the utility of both file- and conviction-plea rates is that they are dichotomous dependent variables, and thus power to detect differences and possible patterns of non-linearity is limited. Thus, in the next section, we discuss the continuous variable of plea discount, and the nuances to consider in measuring it as a second emerging topic.

Measuring Plea Discount

Although there is wide consensus that defendants who plead guilty generally receive less harsh sentences than defendants convicted at trial, there is less consensus on how to characterize or measure the direct benefit of a plea on defendants' sentences. Even though researchers use the term "plea discount" (or alternatively, "trial tax") to explain the benefit that defendants' receive in exchange for pleading guilty (or, alternatively, the increased severity in sentence they receive for exercising their right to trial), there is ambiguity on what exactly this term means, how to measure it, and what factors to consider (Kim, 2015; Yan & Bushway, 2018). For example, Yan (2022) estimated plea discounts using carceral sentences only or using both carceral and probation sentences. He found that when only carceral sentences were included, plea discount was 62.6 percent. However, when plea discount was estimated using the carceral and probation sentences (coded by their severity), plea discount dropped to 36.6 percent.

There are two main (but not mutually exclusive) theoretical frameworks commonly used when discussing and estimating plea discounts. First, the courtroom workgroup model argues that court actors' shared values and goals that create rules, or "going rates," determine the size of the plea discount (Alschuler, 1981; Bibas, 2004; Eisenstein & Jacob, 1977; Ulmer, 1997). Second is the SOT model, which, as noted, is rooted in rational choice and assumes that both the prosecutor and defendant seek to maximize their own outcomes, and thus the relative magnitude of the plea discount is directly guided by the rational behavior of defendants entering pleas (Bibas, 2004; Bushway & Redlich, 2012; Dezember & Redlich, 2019). These theoretical frameworks provide guidance on the variables that impact plea discounts but also highlight the different approaches to conceptualizing and measuring discounts.

Estimating the size of plea discounts is inherently challenging because defendants either plead guilty or go to trial, but not both. To partially address this challenge, one

---

[12] See https://legiscan.com/NJ/text/A1076/id/2203259

approach is to examine the differences between plea and trial sentences using regression modeling (e.g., Ulmer & Bradley, 2006; Ulmer et al., 2010). As Yan (2020) notes, however, this approach assumes that there is one unified sentencing process that exists for trials and pleas. Another approach has been to estimate the counterfactual trial sentence for defendants who pled guilty (Bushway & Redlich, 2012; Piehl & Bushway, 2007), which allows for different sentencing processes for plea convictions versus trial convictions (Yan, 2020). Both of these approaches to measuring plea discounts have methodological limitations—neither accounts for the possibility that defendants who go to trial may have different unobserved characteristics from defendants who pled guilty, such as risk preferences. Overall, Yan (2022) cautions researchers to carefully consider "the operationalization of plea discount or the trial penalty, since the way researchers quantify the discounts can directly affect the policy and theoretical implications" (p. 18). In the remainder of this section, we attempt to further this discussion by delineating which variables to use in pleas discount measurements and their possible implications.

If we think about sales discounts on retail items, there are two components—the starting or original price and the price that is actually paid; the difference between these two amounts is the discount. But, when considering a plea offer, identifying the start and endpoints is rarely that straightforward. For the starting point, or potential sentence, we could use the *maximum potential sentence for indicted charges* if convicted at trial or the *maximum potential sentence for plea charges* if convicted at trial. The former represents the total sentence the defendant faces if found guilty at trial of indicted charges and given the maximum sentence. The latter represents what the defendant perceives as the maximum potential sentence they could face at trial if they do not accept the plea offer. This distinction is important because there may be some cases in which the defendant knows or believes they are more likely to be convicted at trial of some charges (e.g., the plea charges) than others, which would make one of these operationalizations of plea discount more accurate than the other. Further, this difference in perspective on which charges/sentences are more likely to result in conviction could alter calculations under SOT—assuming defendants do indeed make decisions according to this model.

A second issue to consider when measuring plea discount concerns the charges used to calculate the potential maximum sentence for the starting value. The consideration is whether to use *all* (for either indicted or pleaded-to) charges, or *only the most severe charge*. On the one hand, using all charges represents the absolute maximum that a convicted defendant could possibly serve, particularly if they are made to serve the sentence for each of their charges consecutively. On the other hand, the top charge often has the most impact on sentencing decisions and, as a result, may drive the defendant's plea decision-making. The top charge also likely represents sentences in which each charge is served concurrently (i.e., in which the penalty for the top charges subsumes the penalties for the lesser charges).

A third issue is the endpoint. For the endpoint—or the sentence following conviction—one could use the maximum sentence the judge could give for the plea charges, prior to suspending any of the sentence, which we refer to here as the *maximum plea sentence*. This is the full length of the jail/prison sentence given by the judge as a result of the guilty plea prior to suspending any of the sentence (which is a common occurrence, see Sparks & Hill, 2014). For example, if the judge sentenced a defendant to twenty-four months with ten months suspended, the maximum plea sentence would be twenty-four months. This is important because even though the defendant may receive an immediate benefit of a shorter period of incarceration, the defendant could still serve the additional ten months if they violate the conditions of their plea (violates probation, fails drug test, etc.). Alternatively, another endpoint is the *minimum plea sentence*, which does not include the suspended sentence. Using the prior example, the defendant's actual incarceration sentence would be fourteen months, which represents the immediate sentence that the defendant has to serve as a result of their plea.

As an exercise, we identified eight ways to measure plea sentencing discounts in a sample of Virginia cases (*n* = 600) in which the defendant pled guilty. All measures consider the starting value (the starting potential sentence), the endpoint (the sentence upon conviction), and the charges included (all vs. the most serious), and were calculated by creating a percentage discount: [(starting value—endpoint value)/starting value]. Table 39.2 lists these eight measures with descriptive statistics for each and the proportions who received

Table 39.2 An Example of Eight Ways to Measure Plea Sentencing Discounts Across a Sample of Virginia Cases

Discount	Starting Value	Endpoint Value	Mean Discount (SD)	% Rc'd No Discount	% Rc'd Full Discount
1	Max. potential sentence for all indicted charges	Maximum plea sentence	72% (0.26)	6.0%	2.2%
2	Max. potential sentence for all plea charges	Maximum plea sentence	50% (0.33)	24.0%	1.8%
3	Max. potential sentence for most serious indicted charge	Maximum plea sentence	62% (0.30)	10.2%	2.2%
4	Max. potential sentence for most serious plea charge	Maximum plea sentence	49% (0.32)	22.4%	2.2%
5	Max. potential sentence for all indicted charges	Minimum plea sentence	95% (0.11)	0.4%	33.4%
6	Max. potential sentence for all plea charges	Minimum plea sentence	90% (0.17)	1.6%	27.9%
7	Max. potential sentence for most serious indicted charge	Minimum plea sentence	93% (0.13)	0.7%	31.2%
8	Max. potential sentence for most serious plea charge	Minimum plea sentence	88% (0.20)	2.4%	28.2%

no (0 percent) discount or received a full 100 percent discount. It is valuable to see the range in the average size of the plea discount across the different measurements, which runs from a low of 49 percent (Discount 4) to a high of 95 percent (Discount 5), highlighting the importance of the conceptualization of the variable and what factors the plea decision maker deems important.[13]

The discount measures that produced the largest average values (i.e., Discounts 5, 6, 7, and 8) highlight the greatest distances between the starting and endpoint values, with average discounts ranging from 88 percent to 95 percent. All these discounts use the *minimum plea sentence* as the endpoint measure. We also see that these discount measures have around one-quarter (Discount 8) to one-third (Discount 5) of individuals who received a full 100 percent discount. At the other end of the spectrum, for these four discount measures, few defendants (2.4 percent or fewer) did not receive any discount. In contrast, the discount measures that use the *maximum plea sentence* as the endpoint have smaller average discounts (range: 49 percent to 72 percent), much smaller percentages of defendants with a 100 percent discount (1.8 percent to 2.2 percent), and larger percentages of defendants receiving no discount (up to 24 percent). This is important because if researchers rely on *minimum plea sentence* rather than the *maximum plea sentence*, we will continue to see very large discounts (88 percent or higher; for example, see Dezember & Redlich, 2019), which may not reflect the true distance between the starting and endpoints, or accurately assess what legal actors consider when deciding whether to offer or accept plea deals. That is, whether the prosecutor, defense attorney, or defendant perceives the discount to be 49 percent or 95 percent from the original starting point has implications for models of plea decision-making, such as courtroom workgroup and SOT.

Further, for all measures of plea discount, regardless of how calculated, the range ran the gamut from 0 to 100 percent, allowing for a continuous variable with more explanatory power. Given that the majority of defendants plead guilty, whether we use the prospective 64 percent or retrospective 97 percent plea rate, the plea discount is useful in explaining the dichotomous plea decision. Thus, continuing to conceptualize and accurately measure plea discount is of emerging importance (see also Yan, 2020, 2022; Yan & Bushway, 2018).

Conclusions

Guilty pleas are ingrained in the justice systems of the United States and many other countries. It is often opined that the system would simply collapse if plea bargains were to be eliminated. Thus, it is noteworthy that psycholegal scholars have taken up the clarion call to research guilty plea decisions, processes, and consequences with such ardor. As

---

[13] We note here that another way to conceptualize plea discount is by determining the number of charges at indictment versus plea (e.g., defendants who are indicted on five charges but only plead to three charges). Calculating this charge discount resulted in an average 31 percent plea discount, which is quite different than the sentencing discounts shown in table 39.2.

we have reviewed in this chapter—and is evident in other chapters in this handbook of psychology and the law—psychological science has much to say about the legal system generally and pleading guilty, specifically. Our overview of research demonstrates how much has been learned in a short amount of time; our two exercises for ways forward in rethinking plea rates and conceptualizing plea discounts demonstrates how much more there remains to be learned.

References

Alschuler, A. W. (1981). The changing plea bargaining debate. *Columbia Law Review, 69*, 652–730.

Bartlett, J. M., & Zottoli, T. M. (2021). The paradox of conviction probability: Mock defendants want better deals as risk of conviction goes up. *Law and Human Behavior, 45*(1), 39–54.

Bibas, S. (2004). Plea bargaining outside the shadow of trial. *Harvard Law Review, 117*, 2463–2547.

Bibas, S. (2011). Regulating the plea-bargaining market: From caveat emptor to consumer protection. *California Law Review, 99*(4), 1117–1161. Retrieved from https://heinonline.org/HOL/Page?handle= hein.journals/calr99&id=1125&div=&collection=

Bordens, K. S. (1984). The effects of likelihood of conviction, threatened punishment, and assumed role on mock plea bargaining decisions. *Basic and Applied Social Psychology, 5*(1), 59–74.

Bushway, S. D., & Redlich, A. D. (2012). Is plea bargaining in the "shadow of trial" a mirage? *Journal of Quantitative Criminology, 28*, 437–454.

Bushway, S. D., Redlich, A. D., & Norris, R. J. (2014). An explicit test of plea bargaining in the "shadow of the trial". *Criminology, 52*(4), 723–754.

Caldwell, H. (2012). Coercive plea bargaining: The unrecognized scourge of the justice system. *Catholic University Law Review, 61*(1), 63–98.

Covey, R. D. (2007). Reconsidering the relationship between cognitive psychology and plea bargaining. *Marquette Law Review, 91*(1), 213–247.

Demuth, S. (2003). Racial and ethnic differences in pretrial release decisions and outcomes: A comparison of Hispanic, black, and white felony arrestees. *Criminology, 41*(3), 873–908.

Dervan, L. E. (2012). Bargained justice: Plea-bargaining's innocence problem and the brady safety-valve. *Utah Law Review, 51*, 51–97.

Devers, L. (2011). *Plea and charge bargaining*. Bureau of Justice Assistance, US Department of Justice.

Dezember, A., & Redlich, A. D. (2019). Plea bargaining in the shadow of the trial. In C. Spohn & P. Brennan (Eds.), *Sentencing policies and practices in the 21st century* (pp. 168–187). Routledge.

Dobbie, W., Goldin, J., & Yang, C. (2018). The effects of pre-trial detention on conviction, future crime, and employment: Evidence from randomly assigned judges. *American Economic Review, 108*(2), 201–240.

Edkins, V. A., & Dervan, L. E. (2018). Freedom now or a future later: Pitting the lasting implications of collateral consequences against pretrial detention in decisions to plead guilty. *Psychology, Public Policy, and Law, 24*(2), 204–215.

Eisenstein, J., & Jacob, H. (1977). *Felony justice: An organizational analysis of criminal courts*. Little, Brown.

Faust, T. (2022). *The impact of pre-plea access to evidence on estimates of conviction probability and plea decisions* [Unpublished master's thesis].

Fountain, E. N., & Woolard, J. L. (2018). How defense attorneys consult with juvenile clients about plea bargains. *Psychology, Public Policy, and Law, 24*(2), 192–203.

Frazier, A., & Gonzales, J. E. (2021). *Studying sequential processes of criminal defendant decision-making using a choose-your-own-adventure research paradigm* [Manuscript under review].

Garnier-Dykstra, L. M., & Wilson, T. (2021). Behavioral economics and framing effects in guilty pleas: A defendant decision making experiment. *Justice Quarterly, 38*(2), 224–248.

Helm, R. K. (2018). Cognitive theory and plea-bargaining. Policy Insights from the *Behavioral and Brain Sciences, 5*(2), 195–201.

Helm, R. K., Reyna, V. F., Franz, A. A., Novick, R. Z., Dincin, S., & Cort, A. E. (2018). Limitations on the ability to negotiate justice: Attorney perspectives on guilt, innocence, and legal advice in the current plea system. *Psychology, Crime and Law, 24*(9), 915–934.

Helm, R. K., Reyna, V. F., Franz, A. A., Novick, R. Z., Helm, R. K., Reyna, V. F., . . . Novick, R. Z. (2017). Too young to plead? Risk, rationality, and plea bargaining's innocence problem in adolescents. *Psychology, Public Policy, and Law, 24*(2), 180–191.

Helm, R. K., & Zottoli, T. M. (2020, March). *Models of plea decision-making* [Paper presentation]. Annual conference of the American Psychology and Law Society, New Orleans, LA.

Kim, A. C. (2015). Underestimating the trial penalty: An empirical analysis of the federal trial penalty and critique of the Abrams study. *Mississippi Law Journal, 84*(5), 1195–1256.

Kassin, S. M., Drizin, S., Grisso, T., Gudjonsson, G., Leo, R. A., & Redlich, A. D. (2010). Police-induced confessions: Risk factors and recommendations. *Law and Human Behavior, 34*, 3–38.

Kutateladze, B. L., Andiloro, N. R., & Johnson, B. D. (2016). Opening Pandora's box: How does defendant race influence plea bargaining? *Justice Quarterly, 33*(3), 328–496.

Kutateladze, B., Andiloro, N., Johnson, B., & Spohn, C. (2014). Cumulative disadvantage: Examining racial and ethnic disparity in prosecution and sentencing. *Criminology, 52*, 514–551.

Luna, S., & Redlich, A. D. (2020a). Unintelligent decision-making? The impact of discovery on defendant plea decisions. *Wrongful Conviction Law Review, 1*(3), 314–335.

Luna, S., & Redlich, A. D. (2020b). The decision to provide discovery: An examination of policies and guilty pleas. *Journal of Experimental Criminology, 17*, 305–320.

MacKenzie, G. (2007). The guilty plea discount: Does pragmatism win over proportionality and principle. *Southern Cross University Law Review, 11*, 205–223.

Malloy, L. C., Shulman, E. P., & Cauffman, E. (2014). Interrogations, confessions, and guilty pleas among serious adolescent offenders. *Law and Human Behavior, 38*(2), 181–193.

McCoy, C. (2005). Plea bargaining as coercion: The trial penalty and plea bargaining reform. *Criminal Law Quarterly, 50*, 67.

Miller, C. (2019). The right to evidence of innocence before pleading guilty. *U.C. Davis Law Review, 53*(1), 271–321.

National Center for State Courts. Court Statistics Project. http://www.courtstatistics.org/

National Registry of Exonerations. (n.d.). Exoneration registry. http://www.law.umich.edu/special/exoneration/Pages/about.aspx.

Ogloff, J. (2000). Two steps forward and one step backward: The law and psychology movement in the 20th century. *Law and Human Behavior, 24*, 457–483.

Piehl, A. M., & Bushway, S. D. (2007). Measuring and explaining charge bargaining. *Journal of Quantitative Criminology, 23*, 105–125.

Petersen, K., Redlich, A. D., & Norris, R. J. (2020). Diverging from the shadows: Explaining individual deviation from plea bargaining in the " Shadow of the Trial." *Journal of Experimental Criminology, 18*, 321–342.

Reaves, B. A. (2013). *Felony defendants in large urban counties, 2009-Statistical tables*. US Department of Justice, Office of Justice Programs, Bureau of Justice Statistics.

Redlich, A. D. (2016). *The validity of pleading guilty*. In M. K. Miller & B. Bornstein (Eds.), *Advances in psychology and law* (pp. 1–27). Springer International.

Redlich, A. D., Bibas, S., Edkins, V., & Madon, S. (2017). The psychology of defendant plea decision-making. *American Psychologist, 72*, 339–352.

Redlich, A. D., Bushway, S. D., & Norris, R. J. (2016). Plea decision-making by attorneys and judges. *Journal of Experimental Criminology, 12*(4), 537–561.

Redlich, A. D., & Özdoğru, A. A. (2009). *Alford* pleas in the age of innocence. *Behavioral Sciences and the Law, 27*(3), 467–488.

Redlich, A. D., & Shteynberg, R. V. (2016). To plead or not to plead: A comparison of juvenile and adult true and false plea decisions. *Law and Human Behavior, 40*(6), 611–625.

Redlich, A. D., & Summers, A. (2012). Voluntary, knowing, and intelligent pleas: Understanding the plea inquiry. *Psychology, Public Policy, and Law, 18*(4), 626–643.

Redlich, A. D., Summers, A., & Hoover, S. (2010). Self-reported false confessions and false guilty pleas among offenders with mental illness. *Law and Human Behavior, 34*(1), 79–90.

Redlich, A. D., Yan, S., Norris, R. J., & Bushway, S. D. (2018). The influence of confessions on guilty pleas and plea discounts. *Psychology, Public Policy, and Law, 24*, 147–157.

Sacks, M., & Ackerman, A. R. (2012). Pretrial detention and guilty pleas: If they cannot afford bail they must be guilty. *Criminal Justice Studies, 25*(3), 265–278.

Scherr, K., Redlich, A. D., & Kassin, S. M. (2020). Cumulative disadvantage: The compounding effect of innocents' decision-making from interrogations to the courtroom. *Perspectives on Psychological Science*. Advance online publication.

Schneider, R. A., & Zottoli, T. M. (2019). Disentangling the effects of plea discount and potential trial sentence on decisions to plead guilty. *Legal and Criminological Psychology*, 24(2), 288–304.

Smith, A., & Maddan, S. (Eds.). (2019). *The lower criminal courts*. Routledge.

Sparks, K. A., & Hill, B. A. (2014). Suspended sentence. In J. S. Albanese (Ed.), *The encyclopedia of criminology and criminal justice* (pp. 1–5). John Wiley & Sons.

Tor, A., Gazal-Ayal, O., & Garcia, S. M. (2010). Fairness and the willingness to accept plea bargain offers. *Journal of Empirical Legal Studies*, 7(1), 97–116.

Turner, J. I. (2017). Plea bargaining and international criminal justice. *University of the Pacific Law Review*, 48, 219–246.

Turner, J. I., & Redlich, A. D. (2016). Two models of pre-plea discovery in criminal cases: An empirical comparison. *Washington and Lee Law Review*, 73(1), 285–410.

Ulmer, J. T., (1997). *Social worlds of sentencing: Court communities under sentencing guidelines*. State University of New York Press.

Ulmer, J. T., & Bradley, M. S. (2006). Variation in trial penalties among serious violent offenses. *Criminology*, 44, 631–670.

Ulmer, J. T., Eisenstein, J, & Johnson, B. D. (2010). Trial penalties in federal sentencing: Extra- guidelines factors and district variation. *Justice Quarterly*, 27, 560–592.

White, W. S. (1971). A proposal for reform of the plea bargaining process. *University of Pennsylvania Law Review*, 119(3), 439–462.

Wilford, M. M., Wells, G. L., & Frazier, A. (2020). Plea-bargaining law: The impact of innocence, trial penalty, and conviction probability on plea outcomes. *American Journal of Criminal Justice*, 45, 554–575.

Yan, S. (2020). Estimating the size of plea discounts. In C. Spohn & P. Brennan (Eds.), *Sentencing Policies and Practices in the 21st Century* (pp. 188–207). Routledge.

Yan, S. (2022). What exactly is the plea discount? The sensitivity of plea discount estimates. *Justice Quarterly*, 39, 152–173.

Yan, S., & Bushway, S. D. (2018). Plea discounts or trial penalties? Making sense of the trial-plea sentence disparities. *Justice Quarterly*, 35(7), 1226–1249.

Zimmerman, D. M., & Hunter, S. (2018). Factors affecting false guilty pleas in a mock plea bargaining scenario. *Legal and Criminological Psychology*, 23(1), 53–67.

Zottoli, T. M., & Daftary-Kapur, T. (2019). Guilty pleas of youths and adults: Differences in legal knowledge and decision making. *Law and Human Behavior*, 43(2), 166–179.

Zottoli, T. M., Daftary-Kapur, T., Winters, G. M., & Hogan, C. (2016). Plea discounts, time pressures, and false-guilty pleas in youth and adults who pleaded guilty to felonies in New York City. *Psychology, Public Policy, and Law*, 22(3), 250–259.

Zottoli, T. M., Daftary-Kapur, T., Edkins, V. A., Redlich, A. D., King, C. M., Dervan, L. E., & Tahan, E. (2019). State of the States: A survey of statutory law, regulations and court rules pertaining to guilty pleas across the United States. *Behavioral Sciences & the Law*, 37(4), 388–434.

Zottoli, T. M., Helm, R. K., Edkins, V. A., & Bixter, M. T. (2022; manuscript under review). *Developing a plea decision model: Beyond the shadow of trial.*

Prosecutorial Misconduct

Margaret Bull Kovera *and* Melanie B. Fessinger

Abstract

Prosecutors have a complicated role in which they are tasked with convicting the guilty while also protecting the innocent. However, prosecutors sometimes abrogate their duties, which can result in miscarriages of justice. Prosecutorial misconduct includes activities like failure to disclose evidence favorable to the defense, improper argument (e.g., mentioning information not in evidence and denigrating the integrity of the defense attorney), and racial bias in jury selection. A variety of factors may contribute to the likelihood that prosecutors engage in misconduct, including a culture of competition, pressure to secure convictions, tunnel vision (a cognitive bias in which one gives more weight to evidence that supports the desired suspect), unguided prosecutorial discretion in deciding what evidence to disclose to the defense, and a lack of accountability. There is very limited empirical research that explores the antecedents of or remedies for prosecutorial misconduct, providing fertile ground for researchers to make substantial contributions toward understanding this particular cause of wrongful convictions.

Key Words: prosecutorial misconduct, decision-making, Brady violations, miscarriages of justice, tunnel vision, racial bias

Prosecutors serve a unique role in the criminal justice system. They have been referred to as the "ultimate gatekeeper" because in their role they shepherd a case through the criminal legal system from its inception to resolution (Armstrong & Possley, 1999). Prosecutors have many decision points throughout this process. They must decide whom to prosecute and for what crimes, whether sufficient evidence exists to carry a case forward, whether they should secure arrest and search warrants, whether to offer a plea to the defendant, whom to put on the witness stand, and what arguments they should make about the evidence in their case. While making each of these decisions, prosecutors are tasked not only with convicting the guilty but also with protecting the innocent by following fair procedures and ensuring that they do not abrogate defendants' constitutional rights.

Thus, prosecutors have a complicated role that requires them to wear different hats simultaneously. The Supreme Court described the complex position of prosecutors as focused on justice rather than securing convictions with the "twofold aim . . . that guilt shall not escape or innocence suffer."[1] Other descriptions of the prosecutor's role mirror this complexity. For example, the American Bar Association Model Rules of Professional Conduct explain that prosecutors have the responsibility as "a minister of justice and not simply that of an advocate. . . to see that the defendant is accorded procedural justice, that guilt is decided upon the basis of sufficient evidence, and that special precautions are taken to prevent and to rectify the conviction of innocent persons" (American Bar Association, 2020, p. 1323). The Ninth Circuit asserted that prosecutors "serve truth and justice first" and that their job "isn't just to win, but to win fairly, staying well within the rules."[2]

Yet the last few decades of data on wrongful convictions show us that sometimes prosecutors violate these rules, resulting in unfair wins. Consider, for example, the case of John Thompson, a young father in his early twenties who was convicted of murder and sentenced to death. While Thompson awaited execution, his appellate attorneys discovered that the prosecution had not disclosed to the defense that the blood stains found on the victim had a blood type that excluded Thompson as the perpetrator. In addition, an assistant district attorney had removed the blood samples from the evidence locker and destroyed them, never disclosing this exculpatory information to the defense. The attorneys also discovered additional undisclosed evidence that was favorable to the defense, including information about payments made to an informant who testified against Thompson. Thompson was eventually exonerated, and a civil jury awarded him $14 million as compensation for the fourteen years he was wrongly incarcerated on death row, yet the Supreme Court overturned this award, holding that an entire office could not be held responsible for improper actions by a single prosecutor.[3]

Although there are certainly examples of egregious misconduct on the part of prosecutors who abrogate their responsibility to seek justice, the exact prevalence of prosecutorial misconduct across all cases is difficult, if not impossible, to measure. Despite this difficulty, estimates of its occurrence in exoneration cases are relatively consistent. In a sample of the 2,400 exonerations that took place between 1989 and 2019, more than one-third involved prosecutorial misconduct of some form (Gross et al., 2020). In an analysis of eighty-six death row exonerations, nearly 20 percent involved prosecutorial misconduct (Warden, 2001). Among the first sixty-two individuals exonerated by DNA evidence, more than 40 percent of their cases involved prosecutorial misconduct (Dwyer et al., 2000). Prosecutorial misconduct also contributes to wrongful convictions indirectly because "[p]ractically speaking, the prosecutor is the first line of defense against many of the common factors that lead to wrongful convictions" (Joy, 2006, p. 407). Prosecutors oversee investigations, which makes it their duty to supervise the collection of eyewitness and confession evidence, the production of lab reports, and the use of informants and

---

[1] Berger v. United States, 295 U.S. 78 (1935).
[2] United States v. Kalfayan, 8 F.3d 1315 (9th Cir. 1993).
[3] Connick v. Thompson, 131 S. Ct. 1350 (2011).

cooperating witnesses (Joy, 2006). Thus, although there is variation in the prevalence estimates and description of ways in which prosecutorial misconduct affects exoneration cases, it is clear that it is a major contributing factor to wrongful convictions.

Prosecutorial misconduct is not just an issue limited to cases in which wrongful convictions occur and are discovered. It can still lead to miscarriages of justice when convictions are not wrongful but instead deny defendants their due process rights. Defendants have the right to fundamentally fair procedures which includes, among other things, that the prosecutors' behaviors comport with "fundamental ideas of fair play and justice."[4] Prosecutors who deny defendants those rights acts as ministers of injustice rather than justice (Joy, 2006). The abrogation of defendants' rights is still wrong even if done to secure a conviction of people who prosecutors believe to be guilty (Joy, 2006).

Therefore, it is important to consider prosecutorial misconduct at a broader level than merely wrongful conviction cases. Yet data on prosecutorial misconduct outside the context of wrongful convictions is even more difficult to obtain. In one study of 11,452 cases in which defendants alleged prosecutorial misconduct (Weinberg, 2003), appellate courts found that approximately 20 percent involved prosecutorial misconduct that warranted reversal, dismissal, or reduction in conviction and sentences. The courts found prosecutorial misconduct in thousands of other cases but ultimately ruled that it constituted harmless error (i.e., would not have affected the outcome of the case) and therefore upheld the convictions despite the misconduct. Other data show hundreds of defendants, some of whom were sentenced to death, who have had their convictions reversed or sentences reduced in part due to prosecutorial misconduct (Armstrong & Possley, 1999). Moreover, certain prosecutors are responsible for repeated instances of misconduct—several with more than a dozen cases of substantiated misconduct (Fair Punishment Project, 2016).

Available data on prosecutorial misconduct likely only reflect the tip of the iceberg. The numbers account only for official findings of misconduct which, according to the Innocence Project, likely represent "only a fraction of the misconduct that actually occurs" (Zack, 2020). In fact, the former Chief Judge of the Ninth Circuit remarked that some prosecutorial misconduct had "reached epidemic proportions in recent years."[5] In this chapter, we begin by defining prosecutorial misconduct and describing examples of it from real cases. We also discuss the limited psychological research on prosecutorial misconduct. We then discuss some potential psychological and institutional causes for prosecutors' misconduct and proposed interventions for discouraging prosecutorial behavior that does not serve justice. We conclude with a call for more research on this understudied topic.

---

[4] In re Oliver, 333 U.S. 257, 283 (1948).
[5] United States v. Olsen, 737 F.3d 625, 632 (9th Cir. 2013).

Forms of Prosecutorial Misconduct

Prosecutorial misconduct occurs when prosecutors deny defendants their due process rights to fundamentally fair procedures and can occur at virtually any point during a criminal prosecution, including grand jury proceedings, which are orchestrated solely by prosecutors[6] (Henning, 1999). According to the Supreme Court, it covers behaviors which "overstep the bounds of that propriety and fairness which should characterize the conduct of such an officer in the prosecution of a criminal offense."[7] It occurs when prosecutors seek an unfair advantage over defendants (Gershman, 2005) or when prosecutors "plac[e] a thumb on the scales of justice" which leads to unfair procedures, overrides the province of the fact-finder, and can result in convictions of innocent defendants (Joy, 2006, p. 406).

Prosecutorial misconduct appears in many forms. The Supreme Court has identified the failure to disclose exculpatory evidence to the defense,[8] the knowing use of perjured testimony,[9] making false statements about the evidence,[10] and misrepresenting the law to the jury[11] as improper prosecutorial conduct. Lower courts have added to this non-exhaustive list of the forms that prosecutorial misconduct can take, including failing to disclose incentives promised to informants in exchange for their testimony,[12] threatening to revoke immunity pledged to witnesses who provide testimony for the defense,[13] or making statements intended to provoke racial bias against the defendant.[14] Prosecutors also commit misconduct if they destroy or fail to preserve exculpatory evidence[15] or conduct themselves in "a thoroughly indecorous and improper manner."[16] Many of the cases that involve prosecutorial misconduct involve a combination of several forms of improper behavior (West, 2010). Due to length limitations, we will focus our review on three types of prosecutorial misconduct that have received the most scholarly attention: violations of rules governing discovery procedures, improper prosecutorial argument, and racial bias in the use of peremptory challenges.

Discovery (Brady) Violations

In *Brady v. Maryland*,[17] the Supreme Court held that prosecutors must disclose to the defense evidence that is favorable to the defendant (evidence that points to the defendant's

---

[6] *Oliver*, 333 U.S. 257.

[7] *Berger*, 295 U.S. at 84.

[8] Brady v. Maryland, 373 U.S. 83 (1963).

[9] Mooney v. Holohan, 294 U.S. 103 (1935).

[10] *Berger*, 295 U.S. 78

[11] Caldwell v. Mississippi, 472 U.S. 320 (1985).

[12] United States v. Doyle, 121 F.3d 1078 (7th Cir. 1997).

[13] United States v. Schlei, 122 F.3d 944 (11th Cir. 1997).

[14] United States v. Cannon, 88 F.3d 1495 (8th Cir. 1996).

[15] Arizona v. Youngblood, 488 U.S. 51 (1988).

[16] *Berger*, 295 U.S. at 84.

[17] *Brady*, 373 U.S. 83.

innocence) and material to the outcome of a case. Evidence is material "if there is a reasonable probability that, had the evidence been disclosed to the defense, the result of the proceeding would have been different.[18] The prosecutor's duty to disclose evidence favorable to the defense extends beyond evidence in the direct control of the prosecution to evidence uncovered by agents of the prosecution, including, but not limited to, the police.[19] Most known instances of prosecutorial misconduct occur in the form of suppressing exculpatory evidence (Dwyer et al., 2000).

The case of *Watkins v. Miller*[20] provides a clear example of a failure to disclose exculpatory information. Watkins was convicted for allegedly murdering an eleven-year-old child and was sentenced to sixty years in prison. The evidence presented against him at trial included an alleged secondary confession to a jailhouse informant and inconclusive blood type evidence. But several years after his conviction, Watkins discovered that the prosecutor had several pieces of evidence that pointed to his innocence that were not disclosed before trial. This evidence included a statement from an undisclosed eyewitness who saw the victim being abducted at a time for which the defendant had a solid alibi, a report that showed that another suspect had failed a polygraph examination about the case, and reports about other men who either confessed to killing the victim or were seen with blood on their clothes the night of her abduction. Several years later, a federal court found that the prosecutor committed misconduct in Watkins's case by failing to disclose this evidence. In holding so, the court noted, "[t]he United States Constitution requires a fair trial but not a perfect one. [The defendant] received neither, for the prosecutor in his murder case failed to disclose to [his] lawyers important information tending to show he was not guilty."[21] The court held that no reasonable jury would have convicted Watkins without the *Brady* violations and therefore overturned his conviction after he spent fourteen years incarcerated. Around 40 percent of the exoneration cases involving prosecutorial misconduct had instances like *Watkins* in which prosecutors failed to disclose exculpatory evidence before trial (Dwyer et al., 2000; West, 2010).

Brady violations that result from the failure to disclose exculpatory evidence to the defense seem to receive the most attention in discussions of prosecutorial misconduct, but the *Brady* rule is not limited to exculpatory information. Prosecutors also have an affirmative duty to disclose any evidence that could be favorable to the defense, including information that could be used to impeach the credibility of a prosecution witness[22] or to discredit the thoroughness of the police investigation.[23] Prosecutors typically rely on their own discretion to make determinations of whether evidence is favorable to the defense

---

[18] United States v. Bagley, 473 U.S. 667, 682 (1985).
[19] Kyles v. Whitley, 514 U.S. 419 (1995).
[20] Watkins v. Miller, 92 F. Supp. 2d 824 (S.D. Ind. 2000).
[21] *Id.* at 826.
[22] Giglio v. United States, 405 U.S. 150 (1972); Smith v. Cain, 565 U.S. 73 (2012).
[23] *Whitley*, 514 U.S. 419.

and thus needs to be disclosed.[24] These decisions rarely, if ever, are made after consultation with the court (Yaroshefsky & Green, 2012), and with relative impunity unless the defense discovers the previously undisclosed evidence and brings it to the attention of the court.[25]

Although most discussion of *Brady* violations focuses on the harm done to defendants by prosecutors' failure to disclose favorable evidence, the harm caused by these violations extends beyond defendants. By failing to turn over favorable evidence to defendants, the evidence is also withheld from juries. Withholding favorable evidence from jurors causes the jury to become a vehicle through which prosecutors' commit their bad acts, resulting in harm to individual jurors (e.g., when they discover they have wrongfully convicted an innocent defendant because of the prosecution's failure to disclose exculpatory evidence), as well as more generally to the institution of the jury (Kraeg, 2018). This damage to the citizenry's perceptions of the fairness of the criminal legal system may be compounded by the US Supreme Court's holding in *United States. v. Williams* that prosecutors need not present known exculpatory evidence to grand juries for their indictments to be valid (Bowman, 1993).[26]

Improper Argument

Another common form of prosecutorial misconduct is making improper arguments during trial (Balske, 1986; West, 2010). There are many forms of improper arguments, including expressing the prosecutors' personal opinions,[27] discussing facts not in evidence,[28] referencing the defendant's silence post-*Miranda*,[29] and appealing to jury's emotions or fears.[30] Although appellate courts often find that improper arguments constitute harmless error, two studies show that these types of statements may, in fact, affect jury decisions.

In the first study, researchers presented mock jurors with a prosecution closing argument that did or did not contain improper statements, including personal opinions and appeals to emotion (Platania & Moran, 1999). For example, the prosecutor either did or did not call the defendant "a cancer on the body of society" and mention that "[the defendant] himself believes in the death penalty." Mock jurors who were exposed to these improper statements were significantly more likely to recommend the defendant be sentenced to death than were those who were not exposed. In a second study, researchers replicated the finding that mock jurors were more likely to recommend a death sentence after being exposed to improper statements but found that the effect may be mitigated by

---

[24] *Bagley*, 473 U.S. 667.
[25] Pennsylvania v. Ritchie, 480 U.S. 39, 59 (1987).
[26] United States v. Williams, 112 S. Ct. 1735 (1992).
[27] United States v. Modica, 663 F.2d 1173 (2d Cir. 1981).
[28] United States v. Ainesworth, 716 F.2d 769 (10th Cir. 1983).
[29] Doyle v. Ohio, 426 U.S. 610 (1976). But cf. Salinas v. Texas, 369 S. W. 3d 176 (2013).
[30] Darden v. Wainwright, 477 U.S. 168 (1986).

specific jury instructions warning against the use of such statements (Platania & Small, 2010). Together, these studies show that improper arguments may not actually be harmless error as courts often find—especially in the absence of specific jury instructions. Moreover, improper argument from the prosecution may undermine citizens' faith in the jury system (Hagan, 1998).

Racial Bias in the Use of Peremptory Challenges

There are many other forms of prosecutorial misconduct that appear less often in appellate and exoneration cases. For example, prosecutors commit misconduct if they use their peremptory challenges, with which they typically can remove potential jurors from service without having to state a justification for doing so, to exclude prospective jurors on the basis of race alone. This racially driven use of peremptory challenges is a violation of the equal protection clause of the Fourteenth Amendment right[31] and warrants an automatic reversal of a defendant's conviction in some jurisdictions.[32] Similarly, attorneys may not use their peremptory challenges to remove jurors from service solely because of their gender.[33]

Despite the prohibitions in *Batson v. Kentucky*,[34] prosecutors show racial bias in their jury selection decisions. In experimental studies of mock voir dire, prosecutors were more likely to strike Black than White venire persons (Kerr et al., 1991; Sommers & Norton, 2007; see Hunt, this volume). Given that prosecutors face very limited accountability for their misuse of peremptory challenges to remove Black jurors from jury service, it is not surprising that the practice continues relatively unchecked, with archival analyses of prosecutors' use of peremptory challenges showing evidence of racial bias in real cases as well (Clark et al., 2007; Equal Justice Initiative, 2010; Rose, 1999). In North Carolina death penalty cases, even after controlling for variables like death penalty attitudes or previous experience with crime that should affect jury selection decisions, prosecutors were two and a half times more likely to use peremptory challenges to excuse Black venire persons than those who were not Black (Grosso & O'Brien, 2012). In an analysis of the use of peremptory challenges in a sample of Mississippi criminal cases, prosecutors were four and a half times more likely to remove Black than White potential jurors (DeCamp & DeCamp, 2020).

Why Do Prosecutors Commit Misconduct?

Research on prosecutorial misconduct is sparse, so explanations of the driving forces behind it are speculative at this point. Nevertheless, scholars have pointed to many

---

[31] Batson v. Kentucky, 476 U.S. 79 (1986).
[32] State v. Campbell, 772 N.W.2d 858 (Minn. Ct. App. 2009).
[33] J.E.B. v. Alabama ex rel. T.B., 511 U.S. 127 (1994).
[34] *Batson*, 476 U.S. 79.

different reasons why prosecutors may commit misconduct, hypotheses that can provide a fruitful avenue for future research on this topic. One scholar noted that prosecutors have both the motivation and opportunity to engage in misconduct because of a culture of competition, pressure to close cases, tunnel vision leading them to believe a defendant is guilty, unguided discretion, and a lack of punishment and accountability (Schoenfeld, 2005). In the next section, we discuss each of these explanations, in turn, and describe the limited experimental evidence that supports the notion that these variables contribute to prosecutorial misconduct.

Culture of Competition

One reason that prosecutors may commit misconduct is that they are operating within a culture of competition, in which there is a greater focus on winning cases than upholding defendants' rights and ensuring they are convicted only if guilty. The culture of competition that exists in prosecutors' offices has been well-documented by scholars and journalists. Prosecutors often keep score of their wins and losses, using them as measures of success (Armstrong & Possley, 1999; Bresler, 1996; Ferguson-Gilbert, 2001; Hagemann, 1996). Some have observed that prosecutors "recite conviction rates like boxers touting won-loss records" (Armstrong & Possley, 1999) and others keep track of their records like batting averages (Ferguson-Gilbert, 2001). Some prosecutors' offices keep physical tallies of wins and losses, with "each victory earning a prosecutor a green sticker next to his name, and each loss an embarrassing red one" (Armstrong & Possley, 1999).

Some prosecutors seem to be aware of how this culture of competition can lead to instances of misconduct. As one prosecutor noted, "[n]obody told us to cheat. Nobody told us to do wrong . . . It was to be smart, be tenacious, [be] the best prosecutor in the office" (Armstrong & Possley, 1999). Another acknowledged the importance of wins and losses, noting "[t]here are a lot of good prosecutors out there who want to win and can take a loss . . . And there are prosecutors who so don't want to lose that they would rather win dirty" (Armstrong & Possley, 1999). One prosecutor portrayed himself as a well-intentioned prosecutor who lost control in the heat of battle, driven to win by a complex blend of factors, including earning accolades of fellow prosecutors (Armstrong & Possley, 1999). Although these self-reports from prosecutors provide anecdotal evidence for the role that the competitive culture within prosecutors' offices plays in prosecutorial misconduct and the reports are compelling, they do not constitute evidence that a culture of competition *causes* misconduct. We are not aware of any empirical or experimental studies that provide that causal evidence.

Pressure

Prosecutors may engage in misconduct because they feel pressure to secure convictions. This pressure may come from themselves, their colleagues or superiors, or the public at large who often elect prosecutors into their positions. They may feel the need to convict a defendant to provide justice for victims or to please the public. This pressure may be especially felt in high-profile cases in which prosecutors feel the need to close a case quickly. In an experiment testing whether individuals are more likely to cut procedural corners when under increased pressure, researchers presented college students with case materials that were either less severe (assault) or more severe (murder) and had them decide whether to disclose relevant evidence to the defendant (Lucas et al., 2006). Participants who read the more severe case were more likely than participants who read the less severe case to believe the defendant was guilty, to say that attaining a conviction was personally important, and to withhold evidence from the defendant. Although this study was conducted with students playing the role of prosecutors rather than prosecutors themselves, it provides some preliminary evidence of how pressure may motivate misconduct that can serve as a foundation for future research in this area.

Tunnel Vision

Some scholars have proposed that prosecutorial misconduct arises from prosecutors' beliefs that most defendants are guilty. "From [the prosecutor's] perspective, bad guys are bad guys and whatever we need to do to put them away is OK" (Armstrong & Possley, 1999). Much like police officers' beliefs that the suspects whom they interrogate are guilty (Meissner & Kassin, 2002), which causes them to ask hypothesis- confirming questions that increase the rate at which suspects falsely confess (Kassin et al., 2003), prosecutors who believe a defendant is guilty may evaluate the evidence and the adjudication process through that lens (Yaroshefsky, 2013), a bias referred to as "tunnel vision" in legal scholarship (e.g., Findley & Scott, 2006; Hill, 2016). This biased evaluation of whether evidence favors a defendant's guilt or innocence is problematic because not every defendant is guilty.

Although the term "tunnel vision" has been described differently by different scholars, there is general agreement that it is comprised of a set of cognitive biases, including satisficing (a willingness to settle for a good enough outcome rather than work harder for the best outcome), the take-the-best heuristic (making a decision based on a small amount of information while ignoring the rest), the elimination-by-aspects heuristic (narrowing the set of suspects by considering the most important type of evidence first and eliminating the suspect for which that evidence is weakest), and confirmation bias (seeking information that confirms one's hypothesized suspect; Snook & Cullen, 2008). All these biases involve ignoring aspects of the evidence collected in the course of an investigation, which can lead to less-than-optimal decision-making. Although tunnel vision is generally thought to be one mechanism by which prosecutors may inadvertently commit misconduct (Findley & Scott, 2006; Reichart, 2016), other scholars view the tunnel vision process more positively, as decision-making shortcuts that people have developed to make decisions in complex situations in which cognitive resources are scarce, as is often the case in criminal investigations (Snook & Cullen, 2008).

Unguided Discretion

Prosecutors must disclose to the defense any material evidence that is favorable to the defendant. On first consideration, the mandate explicated in *Brady v. Maryland* (1963) and *United States v. Bagley* (1985) appears straightforward.[35] Yet for the prosecution to be compelled to disclose a piece of evidence, they must deem it both evidence of innocence and material evidence. Prosecutors have relatively unguided discretion to determine what evidence is exculpatory, and if exculpatory, whether it would materially affect the outcome of the case were it to be withheld from the defense (Joy, 2006). If evidence is determined to constitute *Brady* material, prosecutors also make decisions about *when* to disclose information to the defense. These decisions are typically made in private, with little guidance to prosecutors on how to make them or transparency among prosecutors in how they are made (Joy, 2006). For example, on the issue of when material evidence that is favorable to the defense should be disclosed, courts have held that "exculpatory and impeachment information no later than the point at which a reasonable probability will exist that the outcome would have been different if an earlier disclosure had been made."[36]

Prosecutors are essentially tasked with predicting whether a piece of evidence will affect the decisions of others and whether the timing of the disclosure will moderate this effect without benefit of policies or guidelines to inform these decisions (DeFrancis, 2002). Ethical rules for prosecutors send mixed messages about the role of prosecutors in litigation, requiring that prosecutors be both adversarial and a neutral seeker of justice, which results in unclear guidance for how prosecutors should make their disclosure decisions (Vorenberg, 1981; Zacharias, 1991). Moreover, scholars have concluded that current state-of-ethics rules provide an incomplete treatment of the ethical obligations governing prosecutors' professional conduct and fail to delineate a comprehensive list of what might be considered prosecutorial conduct (Green, 2003). We noted previously that there are several cognitive processes at work, especially under conditions of time pressure, that likely bias prosecutors' judgments about which evidence is exculpatory (Findlay & Scott, 2006). It is in the absence of clear guidance that these cognitive biases are most likely to operate, resulting in prosecutors failing to disclose material evidence that is favorable to the defense.

Lack of Punishment and Accountability

Perhaps one of the leading reasons why prosecutors commit misconduct is because they almost never experience negative consequences for doing so. Defendants who allege prosecutorial misconduct do not often find relief in appellate courts as appellate courts rarely

---

[35] Brady v. Maryland (1963) and United States v. Bagley (1985)
[36] United States v. Coppa, 267 F.3d 132, 142 (2d Cir. 2001).

substantiate such claims and, even if they do, often rule that such errors are harmless (Fisher, 1988). In one jurisdiction over an eight-year-span, more than 75 percent of the cases in which appellate courts found prosecutorial misconduct held that it constituted harmless error (Ridolfi & Possley, 2010). Even if appellate courts substantiate a defendant's claim of misconduct *and* find the error harmful, prosecutors are still unlikely to face personal consequences for such a ruling.

Hypothetically, there are several ways in which prosecutors could be held accountable or punished for committing misconduct. Practically, none of these are enforced with regularity. First and foremost, appellate courts that find prosecutorial misconduct are unlikely to identify the specific prosecutor by name (Ferguson-Gilbert, 2001). If they do identify the specific prosecutor, they are likely to do so in an unpublished opinion (Armstrong & Possley, 1999; Ferguson-Gilbert, 2001). Even those who are identified cannot be held civilly liable for their actions. In *Imbler v. Patchman*,[37] the Supreme Court ruled that prosecutors are immune from civil suits that arise from their conduct in their role as an advocate—even if their behavior is unlawful and malicious. In holding so, the court mentioned that other existing forms of punishments, including professional and criminal sanctions, would suffice as deterrents to misconduct.

Yet, professional and criminal sanctions for prosecutorial misconduct are exceedingly rare (Meares, 1995; Schoenfeld, 2005). State bar associations could, theoretically, discipline prosecutors who commit misconduct through the use of professional censures, temporary suspensions, or disbarment. In an investigation of nearly four hundred cases that were reversed due to prosecutorial misconduct, not a single prosecutor experienced a public sanction and only two were censured privately (Armstrong & Possley, 1999). Prosecutors are also virtually immune from criminal sanctions for misconduct. Cases of such a nature raise unique issues such as conflicts of interest, in that the prosecutor's office is generally the one that would have to pursue a criminal case of misconduct (Schoenfeld, 2005). As one prosecutor noted, "[p]rosecutors just don't prosecute prosecutors" and "we don't ask people to investigate their own family and prosecutors are like family" (Armstrong & Possley, 1999). As another prosecutor mentioned, "[i]t is one thing to prosecute bad guys for doing bad things . . . It is totally different to prosecute good guys for doing bad things" (Armstrong & Possley, 1999). In an unprecedented case in which three prosecutors were indicted for knowingly using false evidence which led to a wrongful conviction, all were eventually acquitted (National Registry of Exonerations, n.d.). In sum, prosecutors are unlikely to receive professional, civil, or criminal punishments for their misconduct. The lack of punishment for such behavior led one appellate court judge to conclude, "[t]he rules on the subject are pretend-rules."[38]

---

[37] Imbler v. Patchman, 424 U.S. 409 (1976).
[38] United States v. Antonelli Fireworks Co., 155 F.2d 631, 661 (2d Cir. 1946) (Frank, J., dissenting).

Interventions to Eliminate Prosecutorial Misconduct

Given that the prosecutorial context is rife with situational forces that promote misconduct, even the best-intentioned prosecutor may find it difficult to avoid committing some form of misconduct given the role of natural cognitive biases in their decision-making (Findley & Scott, 2006). Moreover, it is likely that the effectiveness of interventions intended to eliminate, or at least curtail, prosecutorial misconduct will depend on whether the misconduct is intentional or unintentional and whether the intervention targets the psychological causes of the misconduct that are relevant in a particular situation (e.g., competitive culture, pressure to close a case, tunnel vision, unguided discretion, and lack of accountability). Moreover, some potential remedies, like punishment, may only remedy misconduct that is intentional rather than inadvertent, requiring systemic change rather than individual rebuke to reduce misconduct significantly (Green & Yaroshefsky, 2017). Thus, although the specific interventions might change depending on the issue being addressed, implementing different policies and procedures for prosecutors to follow, coupled with supervision to ensure compliance with them, and consequences when they are not followed might begin to address the unchecked problem of prosecutorial misconduct.

For example, an effective remedy for the negative effects of a culture of competition and the problem of unguided discretion might be remedied by the adoption of new norms, policies, and procedures in prosecutors' offices. Heads of offices and professional organizations can communicate norms and change incentives for engaging in proper professional conduct. For example, to combat the need for guidance on how to make disclosure decisions, some scholars have recommended that prosecutors' offices adopt handbooks that provide their attorneys with guidelines that govern how prosecutors exercise their discretion (Joy, 2006). Unfortunately, there is little evidence suggesting that prosecutors' offices have followed these recommendations (Joy, 2006) or that prosecutors follow the professional codes of prosecutorial conduct adopted by the American Bar Association (ABA; 1993) and the National District Attorneys' Association (2009; Cohn, 2020). In response, some scholars have argued for greater sanctions for those prosecutors found to have engaged in misconduct (Rosen, 1987; Singleton, 2015; Sullivan & Possley, 2016), especially when the conduct cannot be characterized as a well-intentioned mistake (Murray et al., 2022).

Rather than providing better guidelines for exercising prosecutorial discretion or levying greater sanctions for violating standards of conduct in disclosing material that is favorable to the defense, perhaps the solution is to eliminate discretion altogether and enact open discovery that requires prosecutors to turn over their complete files to the defense. Although some jurisdictions practice open-file discovery, where prosecutors are obligated to disclose a wide array of materials early in the adjudication process, other jurisdictions operate under more of a closed-file system, permitting prosecutors to avoid disclosing information in their files until late in the process, if ever (Turner & Redlich,

2016). Survey data suggests that prosecutors who work in open-file jurisdictions (North Carolina) reported being more likely to disclose many types of evidence (with the exclusion of impeachment evidence), including exculpatory evidence, than were prosecutors who worked in closed-file jurisdictions (Virginia; Turner & Redlich, 2016). Although these data suggest that open-file discovery practices may reduce prosecutorial misconduct in comparison to closed-file discovery models, the data are self-reported so therefore may be representing what prosecutors know they *should* do under the laws of their state rather than what they actually do. Clearly, more data are needed to explore these issues.

Prosecutors can only turn over to the defense what is in their files, which may present an incomplete picture of evidence that could be collected if alternative suspects were considered and explored. Thus, additional reforms are likely needed in addition to open discovery. For example, a popular investigative technique in the Netherlands is the consideration of alternative scenarios of how the crime was committed that do not necessarily involve the primary suspect (Rassin, 2018). This direction to consider alternative scenarios is born out of the finding that people are biased assimilators of evidence, evaluating subsequently obtained evidence as more diagnostic of guilt after they have evaluated evidence of a suspect's guilt rather than of a suspect's innocence (Rassin, 2017; Rassin et al., 2010). A simple task in which investigators rated the evidence they obtained both for its support of the suspect's guilt and for an alternative scenario helped to reduce tunnel vision (Rassin, 2018). It remains to be tested whether such a strategy would reduce the likelihood of prosecutorial misconduct.

Correcting for the unconstitutional removal of venire persons on the basis of race may also require a systemic response to eradicate prosecutorial misconduct. Although the Supreme Court has outlined a process for attorneys to challenge race-based removal of venire persons from jury service,[39] in practice, these challenges are rarely successful (Gabbidon et al., 2008). It is relatively easy for attorneys to generate race-neutral explanations for challenging venire persons of a particular race (Sommers & Norton, 2007), which allows prosecutors to escape sanctions. Moreover, it is unclear whether race-biased peremptory challenges are the result of trial strategy (i.e., a conscious decision on the part of the prosecutor) or implicit bias about which the prosecutor is unaware (Kovera, 2019). If the latter is true, it will take some type of systemic change to prevent the operation of implicit racial bias as current efforts to train away implicit bias have proved unsuccessful (Lai et al., 2014; 2016). Instead of *Batson* challenges, which are intended to address misconduct after it has happened, perhaps a more fruitful approach may be to constrain the ability of prosecutors to defend their race-based challenges by forcing them to ask the same voir dire questions of all venire persons, regardless of race (Kovera, 2019).

---

[39] *Batson*, 476 U.S. 79; Miller-El v. Dretke, 545 U.S. 231 (2005); Snyder v. Louisiana, 552 U.S. 472 (2007).

Conclusion

Social scientific research has provided invaluable insight into many of the factors that contribute to wrongful convictions. Yet, despite its prevalence in exoneration cases, very limited research has focused on prosecutorial misconduct. To date, we know of only four studies that have examined this topic. Two of these studies showed that mock jurors' decisions are affected by improper arguments by prosecutors (Platania & Moran, 1999; Platania & Small, 2010). One study showed that participants playing the role of prosecutors were more likely to suppress exculpatory evidence in high- versus low-pressure cases (Lucas et al., 2006). Survey data suggest that prosecutorial misconduct may be less likely under open- versus closed-file discovery models (Turner & Redlich, 2016). Together, these four studies have begun an important line of research that we encourage researchers to continue, but we must highlight how little empirical research has been conducted to date on the causes and consequences of prosecutorial misconduct.

As previously discussed, prosecutorial misconduct, whatever form it takes, has the potential to abrogate all defendants' constitutional rights to due process (Joy, 2006) and increases the risk of the wrongful conviction of innocent defendants (Gross et al., 2020). In addition, prosecutorial misconduct is a contributing factor in a significant proportion of reversals in death penalty cases (Liebman et al., 2000). There are other dangers associated with prosecutorial misconduct. Not only is it associated with the wrongful conviction of the innocent; the presence of prosecutorial misconduct also is associated with the likelihood that the true perpetrators will not be identified or brought to justice (Weintraub, 2020) and could undermine the public's faith in the fairness of the legal system (Hagan, 1998; Joy, 2006). Given the host of negative outcomes associated with prosecutorial misconduct, it is crucial that psychological researchers begin to give the behavior the empirical attention that it deserves.

References

American Bar Association. (2020). *Model rules of professional conduct*. ABA. https://www.americanbar.org/groups/professional_responsibility/publications/model_rules_of_professional_conduct/rule_3_8_special_responsibilities_of_a_prosecutor/comment_on_rule_3_8/

American Bar Association. (1993). *ABA standards for criminal justice prosecution function and defense function* (3rd ed.). ABA. http://www.abanet.org/crimjust/standards/pfunc-toc.html

Armstrong, K., & Possley, M. (1999). The flip side of a fair trial, series: Trial and error, how prosecutors sacrifice justice to win, second in a five-part series. *Chicago Tribune*, January 12, 1.

Balske, D. N. (1986). Prosecutorial misconduct during closing argument: The arts of knowing when and how to object and of avoiding the "invited response" doctrine. *Mercer Law Review, 37*, 1033–1066.

Bresler, K. (1996). "I never lost a trial": When prosecutors keep score of criminal convictions. *Georgetown Journal of Legal Ethics, 9*(2), 537–546.

Bowman, G. W. (1993). Fifth Amendment—Substantial exculpatory evidence, prosecutorial misconduct and grand jury proceedings: A broadening of prosecutorial discretion. *The Journal of Criminal Law and Criminology, 88*(4), 718–743.

Clark, J., Boccaccini, M. T., Caillouet, B., & Chaplin, W. F. (2007). Five factor model personality traits, jury selection, and case outcomes in criminal and civil cases. *Criminal Justice and Behavior, 34*, 641–660.

Cohn, K. (2020). When the home team calls their own balls and strikes: The problem of *Brady* violations, accountability, and making the case for Washington state commission on prosecutorial conduct. *Seattle Journal for Social Justice, 19*(1), 161–200.

De Camp, W., & DeCamp, E. (2020). It's still about race: Peremptory challenge use on Black prospective jurors. *Journal of Research in Crime and Delinquency, 57*(1), 3–30.

DeFrances, C. J. (2002). *Prosecutors in state courts.* Bureau of Justice Statistics. https://bjs.ojp.gov/content/pub/pdf/psc01.pdf

Dwyer, J., Neufeld, P. J., & Scheck, B. (2000). *Actual innocence: Five days to execution and other dispatches from the wrongly convicted.* Doubleday Books.

Equal Justice Initiative. (2010). *Illegal racial discrimination in jury selection: A continuing legacy.* Equal Justice Initiative.

Fair Punishment Project. (2016). *America's top five deadliest prosecutors: How overzealous personalities drive the death penalty.* https://files.deathpenaltyinfo.org/documents/FairPunishmentProject-Top5Report_FINAL_2016_06.pdf

Ferguson-Gilbert, C. (2001). It is not whether you win or lose, it is how you play the game: Is the win-loss scorekeeping mentality doing justice for prosecutors? *California Western Law Review, 38*(1), 283–309.

Findley, K. A., & Scott, M. S. (2006). Multiple dimensions of tunnel vision in criminal cases. *Wisconsin Law Review, 2006*(2), 291–398.

Fisher, M. T. (1988). Harmless error, prosecutorial misconduct, and due process: There's more to due process than the bottom line notes. *Columbia Law Review, 88*(6), 1298–1324.

Gabbidon, S. L., Kowal, L. K., Jordan, K. L., Roberts, J. L., & Vincenzi, N. (2008). Race-based peremptory challenges: An empirical analysis of litigation from the U.S. Court of Appeals, 2002–2006. *American Journal of Criminal Justice, 33*, 59–68.

Gershman, B. L. (2005). *Prosecutorial misconduct* (2nd ed.). Thomas Reuters.

Green, B. (2003). Prosecutorial ethics as usual. *University of Illinois Law Review, 2003*, 1573–1604.

Green, B., & Yaroshefsk, E. (2017). Prosecutorial accountability 2.0. *Notre Dame Law Review, 92*, 51–116.

Gross, S. R., Possley, M. J., Roll, K. J., & Stephens, K. H. (2020). *Government misconduct and convicting the innocent: The role of prosecutors, police and other law enforcement.* National Registry of Exonerations. https://www.law.umich.edu/special/exoneration/Documents/Government_Misconduct_and_Convicting_the_Innocent.pdf

Grosso, C. M., & O'Brien, B. (2012). A stubborn legacy: The overwhelming importance of race in jury selection in 173 post-*Batson* North Carolina capital trials. *Iowa Law Review, 97*, 1531–1559.

Hagan, J. L. (1988). Prosecutorial misconduct during closing argument after *Darden v. Wainwright*: The guilty need not complain. *Houston Law Review, 25*(1), 217–244.

Hagemann, T. A. (1996). Confessions from a scorekeeper: A reply to Mr. Bresler. *Georgetown Journal of Legal Ethics, 10*(1), 151–158.

Henning, P. J. (1999). Prosecutorial misconduct in grand jury investigations. *South Carolina Law Review, 51*(1), 1–61.

Hill, A. (2016). Tunnel vision: How the system chooses its target. *Public Interest Law Reporter, 21*(2), 131–135.

Joy, P. A. (2006). Relationship between prosecutorial misconduct and wrongful convictions: shaping remedies for a broken system. *Wisconsin Law Review, 2006*(2), 399–430.

Kassin, S. M., Goldstein, C. C., & Savitsky, K. (2003). Behavioral confirmation in the interrogation room: On the dangers of presuming guilt. *Law and Human Behavior, 27*(2), 187–203.

Kerr, N. L., Kramer, G. P., Carroll, J. S., & Alfini, J. J. (1991). On the effectiveness of voir dire in criminal cases with prejudicial pretrial publicity: An empirical study. *The American University Law Review, 40*, 665–701.

Kovera, M. B. (2019). Racial disparities in the criminal justice system: Prevalence, causes, and a search for solutions. *Journal of Social Issues, 75*, 1139–1164.

Kreag, J. (2018). The jury's Brady right. *Boston University Law Review, 98*(2), 345–396

Lai, C. K., Maddalena, M., Lehr, S. A., Cerruti, C., Shin, J-Y. L., Joy-Gaba, J. A., Ho, A. K., Teachman, B. A., Wojcik, S. P., Koleva, S. P., Frazier, R. S., Heiphetz, L., Chen, E. E., R. N., Haidt, J., Kesebir, S., Hawkins, C. B., Schaefer, H. S., Rubichi, S., Sartori, G., . . . Nosek, B. A. (2014). Reducing implicit racial preferences: I. A comparative investigation of 17 interventions. *Journal of Experimental Psychology: General, 143*(4), 1765–1785.

Liebman, J. S., Fagan, J., & West, V. (2000). A broken system: Error rates in capital cases, 1973–1995. Columbia Law School, Public Law Research Paper No. 15.

Lucas, J. W., Graif, C., & Lovaglia, M. J. (2006). Misconduct in the prosecution of severe crimes: Theory and experimental test. *Social Psychology Quarterly, 69*(1), 97–107.

Meares, T. L. (1995). Rewards for good behavior: Influencing prosecutorial discretion and conduct with financial incentives. *Fordham Law Review, 64*(3), 851–920.

Meissner, C. A., & Kassin, S. M. (2002). "He's guilty!": Investigator bias in judgments of truth and deception. *Law and Human Behavior, 26*(5), 469–480.

Murray, B., Heaton, P. S., & Gould, J., (2022). Qualifying prosecutorial immunity through Brady claims. *Iowa Law Review, 107*(3), 1107–1158.

National District Attorneys Association. (2009). National District Attorneys Association prosecution standards, Standard 4.9 (3rd ed.). https://ndaa.org/wp-content/uploads/NDAA-NPS-3rd-Ed.-w-Revised-Commentary.pdf

Platania, J., & Moran, G. (1999). Due process and the death penalty: The role of prosecutorial misconduct in closing argument in capital trials. *Law and Human Behavior, 23*(4), 471–486.

Platania, J., & Small, R. (2010). Instructions as a safeguard against prosecutorial misconduct in capital sentencing. *Applied Psychology in Criminal Justice, 6*(2), 62–75.

Rassin, E. (2017). Initial evidence for the assimilation hypothesis. *Psychology, Crime & Law, 23*(10), 1010–1020.

Rassin, E. (2018). Reducing tunnel vision with a pen-and-paper tool for the weighting of criminal evidence. *Journal of Investigative Psychology and Offender Profiling, 15*(2), 227–233.

Rassin, E., Eerland, A., & Kuijpers, I. (2010). Let's find the evidence: An analogue study of confirmation bias in criminal investigation. *Journal of Investigative Psychology and Offender Profiling, 7*(3), 231–246.

Reichart, B. (2016). Tunnel vision: Causes, effects, and mitigation strategies. *Hofstra Law Review, 45*(2), 451–478.

Ridolfi, K. M., & Possley, M. (2010). *Preventable error: A report on prosecutorial misconduct in California 1997–2009.* Northern California Innocence Project.

Rose, M. R. (1999). The peremptory challenge accused of race and gender discrimination? Some data from one county. *Law and Human Behavior, 23,* 695–702.

Rosen, R. A. (1987). Disciplinary sanctions against prosecutors for *Brady* violations: A paper tiger. *North Carolina Law Review, 65,* 693–744.

Schoenfeld, H. (2005). Violated trust: Conceptualizing prosecutorial misconduct. *Journal of Contemporary Criminal Justice, 21*(3), 250–271.

Singleton, D. E. (2015). *Brady* violations: An in-depth look at higher standard sanctions for high-standard profession. *Wyoming Law Review, 15*(1), 139–164.

Snook, B., & Cullen, R. M. (2008). Bounded rationality and criminal investigations: Has tunnel vision been wrongfully convicted? In D. K. Rossmo (Ed.), *Criminal investigative failures* (pp. 71–98). Routledge.

Sommers, S. R., & Norton, M. I. (2007). Race-based judgments, race-neutral justifications: Experimental examination of peremptory use and the *Batson* challenge procedure. *Law and Human Behavior, 31,* 261–273.

Sullivan, T. P., & Possley, M. (2015). The chronic failure to discipline prosecutors for misconduct: Proposals for reform. *Journal of Criminal Law and Criminology, 105*(4), 881–946.

Turner, J. I., & Redlich, A. D. (2016). Two models of pre-plea discovery in criminal cases: An empirical comparison. *Washington and Lee Law Review, 73,* 285–408.

Vorenberg, J. (1981). Decent restraint of prosecutorial power. *Harvard Law Review, 94,* 1521–1573.

Warden, R. (2001). *How mistaken and perjured eyewitness identification testimony put 46 innocent Americans on death row: An analysis of wrongful convictions since restoration of the death penalty following* Furman v. Georgia. Center on Wrongful Convictions.

West, E. M. (2010). *Court findings of prosecutorial misconduct claims in post-conviction appeals and civil suits among the first 225 DNA exoneration cases.* Innocence Project. https://www.innocenceproject.org/wp-content/uploads/2016/04/pmc_appeals_255_final_oct_2011.pdf

Weinberg, S. (2003). *Breaking the rules: Who suffers when a prosecutor is cited for misconduct?* Center for Public Integrity. https://publicintegrity.org/politics/state-politics/harmful-error/breaking-the-rules/

Weintraub, J. N. (2020). Obstructing justice. The association between prosecutorial misconduct and the identification of true perpetrators. *Crime & Delinquency, 66*(9), 1195–1216.

Yaroshefsky, E. (2013). Why do *Brady* violations happen? Cognitive bias and beyond. *The Champion, 37*, 12–23.

Yaroshefsky, E., & Green, B. A. (2012). Prosecutors' ethics in context: Influences on prosecutorial disclosure. In L. C. Levin & L. Mather (Eds.), *Lawyers in practice: Ethical decision making in context* (pp. 269–292). University of Chicago Press.

Zacharias, F. C. (1991). Structuring the ethics of prosecutorial trial practice: Can prosecutors do justice? *Vanderbilt Law* Review, *44*(1), 45–114.

Zack, E. (2020). *Why holding prosecutors accountable is so difficult.* Innocence Project. https://innocenceproject.org/why-holding-prosecutors-accountable-is-so-difficult/

Jury Decision-Making

Lora M. Levett

Abstract

The US Constitution guarantees the right to a public trial by an impartial jury of one's peers in both criminal and civil contexts. This system is a cornerstone of our democracy but is not free from criticism. Researchers have spent decades investigating the jury, exploring what affects jurors' decisions, and how to increase the competence of this decision-making body. In this broad overview, the chapter first explores the theoretical underpinnings of juror and jury decision-making and discusses mathematical and explanation-based models at the juror and jury levels. Next, the chapter explores factors that influence the jury's decision, including the demographic and attitudinal characteristics of the legal participants, examples of evidentiary, extra-evidentiary, and trial factors, including the possibility of judges as alternative decision makers. Last, I summarize directions for future research and discuss some of the methodological difficulties jury researchers may encounter.

Key Words: jury decision-making, legal decision making, lay participation in the legal system, criminal and civil trials, evidence evaluation

Jury trials exist in a paradox in our American society (Bornstein & Greene, 2017). First, juries are considered central to the American democratic society (see Abramson, 1994). In the United States, the Sixth Amendment to the US Constitution guarantees the right to a "speedy and public trial, by an impartial jury of the State and district wherein the crime shall have been committed," and the Seventh Amendment guarantees the same right to a trial by jury for civil litigants. Thus, the jury places the execution of the law in the hands of the governed, with citizens assuming the responsibility of fact-finding, interpreting and applying the law, and rendering a decision that injects the community's sentiment and reinforces the notion that the community desires that the law be enforced. The jury serves as a protection against arbitrary rule (Abramson, 1994). It ensures that legal decisions reflect communities' sentiments of commonsense justice (Finkel, 1995), and increases civic engagement, satisfaction with the legal system, and perceptions of legitimacy of the criminal justice system (Gastil et al., 2002).

Simultaneously, critics have questioned the jury's ability to execute these weighty tasks (see Bornstein & Greene, 2017, for a review). These criticisms, some of which are exaggerations or "jury myths" and others that are well founded but have potential to be corrected through reforms to trial procedure, coexist with the idea that the jury is a cornerstone for a democratic system (Bornstein & Greene, 2017; Diamond, 2003). This paradox leads to several empirical questions about jury behavior. What influences the jury's decision? Do the factors that should legally influence the jury's decision do so? How might we improve the jury's decision?

Given the breadth of research in the area of jury decision-making, a full review of all possible areas is not feasible given the constraints of the chapter. However, the reader will find that other chapters in this volume address issues of juror and jury decision-making as they relate to the topic (see Hunt, on issues related to race; Peter-Hagene et al., on issues related to emotion; and Cutler & Krauss, on issues related to expert testimony, this volume). Here, I explore the broad literature in juror and jury decision-making with the first goal of understanding the overall theory behind how the jury makes decisions. Next, I explore the factors that influence decision-making. Last, I discuss implications of this work and directions for future research.

Theoretical Underpinnings

Jury scholars have engaged in substantial scholarship to provide a theoretical explanation of how jurors and juries make their decisions. This work generally integrates principles from social and cognitive psychology into the unique task given to juries at trial to create a model describing the decision-making process.

Models of Juror Decision-Making:

Current models typically vary on two dimensions—the method of modeling the decision (mathematical vs. explanation based) and the level of decision (individual vs. the group).

MATHEMATICAL MODELS

At the juror level, researchers using mathematical models of juror decision-making use formal equations to represent the juror's decision process. Generally, these models assume that jurors render decisions using a single "mental meter," or the cognitive representation of the jurors' belief that in all probability, the defendant committed the act in question (Hastie, 1993). At the beginning of trial, jurors start with a belief somewhere along the mental meter based on their values, preconceptions about the case, and the judge's instructions.

To update the mental meter throughout trial, jurors processing trial evidence identify probative pieces of information from that evidence. They then assign weight to that evidence and combine that weight with the previous value of the mental meter to update to a new belief in the defendant's guilt. At the end of the trial, jurors listen to jury instructions and use a combination of the jury instructions, severity of the crime, and personal attitudes and beliefs to create a threshold for conviction. They then compare the final value of the mental meter with their threshold for conviction to render a verdict. If the probability of the meter exceeds the threshold for conviction, the juror convicts; if not, the juror acquits (Hastie, 1993).

The most popular mathematical models are the algebraic, stochastic process, and Bayesian models (Hastie, 1993). Given the scope of this chapter, a full discussion of the nuances of these models is not possible (for a thorough review, see Devine, 2012). Generally, models differ in the mathematical formula used to weight evidence (e.g., an additive model vs. probability theory–based multiplicative model; Hastie, 1993), whether and how the mental meter freezes, and whether the outcome is a single value or a range of values to account for individual differences.

Research has shown mixed support for the mathematical models generally (Groscup & Tallon, 2009). In one study, researchers found the averaging model tested better fit the jurors' decisions than the additive model (Moore & Gump, 1995). A different study showed jurors tended to underutilize the probabilistic evidence compared to the Bayesian norms (Smith et al., 1996). The biggest critique of mathematical models is that they largely simplify the complicated and nuanced decision-making process (Hastie, 1993). Explanation-based models attempt to better account for this multifaceted process.

THE STORY MODEL

In explanation-based models, jurors use available information to create cause-and-effect explanations and then make subsequent decisions based on those explanations (Groscup & Tallon, 2009). These models account for the jurors' active role in the decision-making process, piecing together and making inferences about evidence. The most empirically supported model is the Story Model for Juror Decision-Making (Pennington & Hastie, 1988, 1993). According to the Story Model, jurors create a narrative to account for the trial evidence, incorporating their own perceptions and unique experiences into the narrative. This takes place in a sequence of three steps: story construction, learning verdict options, and story mapping.

In story construction, Jurors create multiple stories or narratives as they listen to trial evidence (Pennington & Hastie, 1993). In creating the narrative, jurors incorporate their own personal knowledge and experiences and their knowledge about what makes a complete story to fill in the blanks left by evidence. Typically, one story emerges as the best story resulting from three factors termed certainty principles: coverage, coherence, and uniqueness (Pennington & Hastie, 1993). A story's coverage depends on the amount of trial evidence it explains. A coherent story is plausible, complete, and consistent. If more than one study is high in both coverage and coherence, the lack of uniqueness would make either story less likely to be believed.

After determining which story is best, jurors learn the verdict options available to them through judicial instructions (Pennington & Hastie, 1993). This is a tough task given the difficulty jurors have in comprehending judicial instructions and often have preconceived notions about crime, law, or legal situations that interfere with their ability to learn the legal definitions in judicial instructions (Smith, 1991). After learning verdict options, jurors map their chosen story onto the possible options and determine the best match (Pennington & Hastie, 1993). If the best story favors a prosecution verdict, jurors determine whether their confidence in the story (determined by certainty factors) exceeds the threshold required for a guilty verdict (determined by judicial instructions and perceptions of the standard of proof). If no story matches an available verdict option or confidence is low, the juror renders a not guilty verdict.

Overall, research has shown support for the Story Model (e.g., Behl et al., 2013; Huntley & Costanzo, 2003; Pennington & Hastie, 1988). In two studies, stories jurors created mediated the relationship between evidence and verdict (Behl et al., 2013; Huntley & Costanzo, 2003). However, despite the comprehensiveness of the Story Model in accounting for the juror's decision-making process, it does not explain how jurors' stories may change or combine as a result of the deliberation process. Ultimately, jurors need to unanimously agree to render a verdict.[1] Similar to examining juror decision-making, jury researchers have used social and cognitive psychological methods to model the jury's decision.

Models of Jury Decision-Making:

Mirroring work modeling individual jurors' decisions, models of jury decision-making fall into the broad categories of mathematical and explanation-based theories.

MATHEMATICAL MODELS.

The verdict distribution of jurors' individual verdict preferences prior to deliberation is the best predictor of the jury's verdict (Devine et al., 2001). As such, most work examining jury deliberation uses mathematical modeling, predicting the final jury verdict based on this distribution. Like individual mathematical models, these models vary in the formula or methodology used to combine the verdict preferences into a final verdict (for a full review, see Devine, 2012). One of the most popular models is the Social Decision Scheme (SDS) model (Davis, 1973).

In the SDS model, the initial distribution of jurors' possible predeliberation preferences is modeled in a matrix representing guilty and not guilty verdicts, which are then combined into a final verdict. Several studies have shown that if two-thirds or more of a jury go into deliberation in agreement on a particular verdict, that verdict will likely be the final decision (Stasser et al., 1989). However, the majorities that are most likely to be successful are those that favor a not guilty verdict—especially in cases in which the jury is more divided at the onset of deliberation (Devine et al., 2001; MacCoun & Kerr, 1988).

Like individual models, criticisms of the group mathematical models include that they do not account for the complex process of deliberation. For example, one study showed that adding deliberation variables to the mathematical model almost doubled the amount of variance explained in the final verdict (Hastie et al., 1998). Mathematical

---

[1] Ramos v. Louisiana, 590 U.S. (2020).

models assume that all jurors have a predeliberation verdict preference; this may not be the case (Hanaford-Agor et al., 2002).

EXPLANATION-BASED MODELS

Given the shortcomings of group mathematical models, researchers have begun the process of integrating social psychological literature on group decision-making with the story model of juror decision-making and mathematical models to explain jury decision-making (see Levett & Devine, 2017, for a review). In showing how the story model may apply to the group decision-making process, one deliberation study may be reframed in light of research on the story (Holstein, 1985). In this study, data showed that fifteen "schematic interpretations," or a juror's attempt to explain what happened in the case, emerged in deliberations. These interpretations could be conceptualized as stories. Further, jurors reframed their schematic interpretations to account for other jurors' interpretations of the evidence in deliberation, essentially adapting their own stories to create a dominant, group story. The more schematic interpretations (or stories) presented in the deliberation, the likelihood of a hung jury increased (Holstein, 1985), indicating that if the stories lacked uniqueness, the likelihood of any story emerging as the dominant one decreased (Levett & Devine, 2017). Of course, this study is limited by the small sample size, but it provides a starting point for how the story model might operate in the deliberation context.

Based on a systematic review of the literature, Devine (2012) proposed a multilevel theory of jury decision-making that integrates decision-making across the juror and jury levels. The first stage of the model is termed the "Director's Cut" model, and it covers the individual juror's process prior to deliberation (Devine, 2012). This model posits that jurors put the case facts and beliefs about the case into a narrative, arranging sequences to form a "final cut" in a manner similar to how a film director creates movies (Devine, 2012). It builds on the story model of juror decision-making by going into greater depth on how individual differences, interpretations of evidence, and extra-evidentiary information (reviewed later in this chapter) may influence story creation, distinguishing between story construction processes for plaintiff/prosecution stories versus defense stories, and differently evaluating the best story.

The second stage uses the output of the Director's Cut model as input for the jury-level model, termed the "Story Sampling" model. The Story Sampling model describes the deliberation process as a collective search for the best story to describe the evidence (Devine, 2012). It accounts for the characteristics of jurors in explaining variation related to participating in deliberation and the types and frequency of information relayed by jurors in deliberation. It also incorporates information on deliberation style and other group dynamic variables in describing deliberation. For example, the model incorporates principles of informational influence (i.e., when people change their mind because of an actual change in attitude) and normative influence (i.e., when people change their mind publicly to agree with the group, but privately maintain their previous attitude) (Deutsch

& Gerard, 1955). In sum, the model integrates literature on juror decision-making and social psychological group processes to propose an integrative, explanation-based model that comprehensively explains the jury's decision. The model leads logically to several testable hypotheses to move our understanding of the jury's decision forward (see Devine, 2012, for a full discussion of those possibilities).

What Affects Jurors' Decisions?

In addition to modeling the juror and jury decision-making process, researchers have spent decades studying the factors that influence jurors' decisions and whether those factors are appropriate or inappropriate in their influence. Generally, these factors fall into three categories: characteristics of trial participants, evidentiary and extra-evidentiary factors, and trial factors.

Characteristics of Trial Participants:

Given the scope of this chapter, in this examination, I focus on a subset of each of the three categories, providing examples of how researchers have approached the study of how characteristics of trial participants, evidentiary and extra-evidentiary factors, and trial factors influence jurors' decisions.

DEMOGRAPHIC VARIABLES

In examining how the demographic characteristics of the jurors and trial participants affect juror and jury decision-making, researchers typically examine how the demographic characteristics directly affect decision-making or moderate the effects of other variables on jurors' decisions. These effects may vary based on the type of trial. For example, in most types of cases, juror gender does not have a strong effect on juror decision-making. However, in cases involving sexual assault or child sexual abuse, a meta-analysis showed that women were more likely than men to convict the defendant (Schutte & Hosch, 1997). Similarly, women were more likely than men to interpret more types of behaviors as sexual harassment (Rotundo et al., 2001).

Demographic characteristics of the defendant also may directly affect jurors' decisions. For example, one meta-analysis synthesized studies exploring the effect of attractiveness on jurors' judgments of guilt and sentence (Mazzella & Feingold, 1994). Results demonstrated that being physically attractive was beneficial to defendants, although other variables also affected this relationship (Mazzella & Feingold, 1994). Results from studies following the meta-analysis have been somewhat mixed (e.g., Gunnel & Ceci, 2010; see Devine, 2012, for a review).

Other defendant characteristics also affect jurors' perceptions and decision-making, including defendant remorse (e.g., Bornstein et al., 2002), criminal record (e.g., Wissler & Saks, 1985) and defendant socioeconomic status (SES; Mazzella & Feingold, 1994), and defendant race (Mitchell et al., 2005). These relationships may also depend on other trial, demographic, or attitudinal variables. For example, the effect of the defendant's prior criminal record may vary based on the content of the record compared to the current charge (see Devine, 2012, for a review). Similarly, effects of defendant SES may change based on the combination of SES and race (e.g., Espinoza & Willis-Esqueda, 2008). Effects of defendant race depends on the combination of defendant and juror race (see Hunt, this volume), and may be exacerbated by systematic suppression of minorities from participating in jury duty (see Kovera, 2019).

Attitudinal Variables

In addition to exploring the effects of demographic characteristics on legal outcomes, researchers have also explored how jurors' attitudes affect decision-making. First, jurors' attitudes may affect jurors' decision as direct effects. One meta-analysis combining twenty studies (thirty-two effects), showed a small relationship between authoritarianism and guilt, such that jurors who were higher in authoritarianism were also more conviction prone than jurors lower in authoritarianism (Narby et al., 1993). Similarly, Kassin and Wrightsman (1983) developed the first version of the Juror Bias Scale (JBS), which was later revised by Lecci and Myers (2002). The JBS measured jurors' tendencies to favor the prosecution or defense and related to verdict. Lecci and Myers (2002) revised the factor structure of the JBS and later went on to develop the Pretrial Juror Attitude Questionnaire (PJAQ; Lecci & Myers, 2008). The PJAQ contained six factors (conviction proneness, cynicism toward the defense, innate criminality, racial bias, social justice, and system confidence) and accounted for variance in jurors' judgments beyond those factors accounted for in legal authoritarianism measures or the JBS.

In addition to direct effects of attitudes on jurors' decisions, attitudes may also affect decisions through indirect effects. For example, in one study, jurors who viewed body-worn camera footage in one case were less likely than those who did not see such footage to believe the defendant was guilty of resisting arrest; this relationship was mediated by jurors' perceptions of moral outrage toward the officer (Saulnier et al., 2020). Similarly, examining jurors' sentences in a death penalty case showed that jurors with more fundamentalist attitudes (vs. less) were more likely to sentence the defendant to death because fundamentalism was associated with weighing aggravators more than mitigators (Yelderman et al., 2019).

Beyond direct and indirect attitudinal effects, the combination of juror characteristics and attitudes may also influence outcomes. In a meta-analysis examining jurors' decisions in child sexual abuse cases, researchers showed that mock jurors who had experienced abuse or knew someone who had been abused as a child were more empathetic toward child victims in a mock trial case than those jurors who did not have abuse experience or knowledge (Jones et al., 2020). Those jurors who were more empathetic toward child victims perceived those children as more credible and therefore were more likely to find the defendant guilty.

Similarly, other studies have shown that the chance to serve on a jury may be limited because of a jurors' attitudinal characteristics, and these attitudes may be related to demographics. For example, in examining decision-making in capital cases, jurors are required to be "death qualified" (Haney, 1984).[2] That is, jurors who would not impose the death penalty because of these attitudes and/or would not be able to impartially consider the evidence knowing that a death sentence is possible are excluded from the jury.

However, the changes resulting from excluding non-death qualified jurors are not just attitudinal. A meta-analysis showed evidence that the death qualification process also changes the demographic composition of the jury, with Black jurors and female jurors more likely than White jurors and male jurors to hold death penalty attitudes that would exclude them from serving on the jury (Filkins et al., 1998). Therefore, death qualified juries are generally more homogeneous in terms of attitudes and demographics, which is related to differences in the quality of decision-making. Death qualified jurors are more conviction prone than non-death qualified jurors (Cowan et al., 1984; Moran & Comfort, 1986) and juries containing both death qualified and non-death qualified jurors made higher-quality decisions than juries containing only death qualified jurors (Cowan et al., 1984).

In reviewing this research, one could note that the influence of demographic or attitudinal variables often depends on other characteristics of the case. That is, attitudes and demographics may influence outcomes, but how that information influences outcomes may vary depending on the type of evidence, extra-evidentiary information, or trial procedure.

Evidentiary Factors and Extra-Evidentiary Factors

Given that another piece of the puzzle in understanding jurors' decisions is understanding how they will interpret and use evidence, and how factors other than the evidence may influence their interpretations, we next turn to examining jurors interpret and use this information more broadly.

EVIDENTIARY FACTORS

The strongest predictor of a juror's decision is the strength of the evidence against the defendant. That is, across experimental and field studies, variations in strength of evidence reliably affect trial outcomes (Devine, 2012). However, looking beyond general measures of evidence begets more questions, especially when considering that cases with exceptionally strong or weak evidence are likely to resolve via plea agreement or withdrawing charges. Thus, cases that are heard by a jury are also the cases that may contain more equivocal evidence, necessitating the exploration of whether jurors can properly evaluate that evidence. Do jurors properly assign weight to reliable evidence and properly discount less reliable evidence? In this section, I review how jurors evaluate two types of evidence— eyewitness and confession evidence—as examples of the research conducted in this area.

---

[2] Wainwright v. Witt, 469 U.S. 412 (1985).

Eyewitness Evidence. In the majority of wrongful conviction cases documented by the Innocence Project, at least one eyewitness made an incorrect identification of the defendant (Innocence Project, 2021; see Smith & Wells, this volume). Importantly, once an identification is made, that identification must be properly evaluated for a just outcome to occur. That is, the fact-finder must recognize those conditions under which an eyewitness is more likely to be mistaken. However, to show that jurors can properly evaluate eyewitness evidence, we must test whether they can weigh identifications obtained under more ideal conditions more heavily than those obtained under less ideal conditions. Trial simulation methodologies allow for this type of test. These studies generally show that eyewitness evidence affects jurors' decisions (Loftus, 1980).

However, the evidence is mixed on whether variations in the factors that affect the quality of the identification appropriately affect jurors' decisions. In one study, researchers manipulated system and estimator variables (see Smith & Wells, this volume, for further discussion on this distinction) known to affect eyewitness accuracy and witness confidence (Cutler et al., 1990). They found that only eyewitness confidence affected jurors' decisions. Other research has replicated these findings, with some exceptions (e.g., Devenport & Cutler, 2004; Devenport et al., 2002). In these studies, variation in lineup composition (Devenport et al., 2002) and lineup composition and lineup instructions (Devenport & Cutler, 2004) affected jurors' ratings of the suggestiveness of the lineup but had limited or no effect on trial outcomes.

Thus, overall, variations in the quality of the eyewitness evidence do not reliably affect jurors' verdicts in appropriate ways. In addition, trial mechanisms designed to improve juror comprehension of evidence (expert testimony, cross examination, voir dire, closing arguments) seem limited in their ability to educate jurors about these factors (Bornstein & Greene, 2017), although training programs designed to teach jurors about factors affecting eyewitness accuracy may be more promising (Pawlenko et al, 2013).

Confession Evidence. False confessions also contribute to a significant number of wrongful convictions (Innocence Project, 2021). One a confession is admitted to evidence, if jurors determine that police coercion was a significant factor in obtaining the confession, the jury is responsible for weighing the confession appropriately given the conditions under which the confession was obtained. A false confession is more likely under coercive conditions (see Kassin et al., 2010, for a review). Therefore, theoretically, confessions obtained under those conditions should be weighed less than confessions obtained under less coercive conditions.

Survey research has shown that laypeople recognize that false confessions can occur (Chojnacki et al., 2008; Henkel et al., 2008). However, in other work, laypeople did not understand the factors leading to false confession (e.g., Blandón-Gitlin et al., 2011; Leo & Lui, 2009). Even though laypeople may believe that false confessions are possible, confession evidence is very persuasive in trial. Jurors in two studies did not weigh confession evidence differently in the presence of situational pressures to confess (Kassin & Sukel, 1997; Kassin & Wrightsman, 1980), and the effect of confession on verdict persisted even if jurors believed the confession was involuntary and that it did not affect their verdicts (Kassin & Sukel, 1997).

Recording the entirety of the interrogation and confession is a suggestion for improving jurors' evaluations of confession evidence because it affords jurors the opportunity to fully evaluate all the aspects of the confession. The recording should be equally focused on the interrogator and suspect (Lassiter et al., 2002). Videos focused solely on the suspect are more likely to result in judgments of confession voluntariness compared to videos focused equally on the suspect and interrogator. However, other factors that make the suspect salient (e.g., the suspect's race or sexual orientation) may undermine the efficacy of the equal focus perspective (Pickel et al., 2013; Ratclif et al., 2010).

Studies have demonstrated the promise of expert testimony for educating jurors about the quality of the confession evidence related to the content of the confession (Henderson & Levett, 2016) and the coerciveness of the interrogation tactics (Blandón-Gitlin et al., 2011). Conversely, educational jury instructions have not shown the same promise (e.g., Kassin & Wrightsman, 1981). However, this research question has not been as thoroughly tested—perhaps because judges may be more reluctant to include such instructions (Bornstein & Greene, 2017).

EXTRA EVIDENTIARY FACTORS

Some types of juror bias are inherent to the individual juror (e.g., use of stereotypes and/or attitudes that affect jurors' decisions that should not affect their decisions). Other forms of bias in jury decision-making are induced through the situation surrounding or occurring in the trial. Here, I explore two of these factors: pretrial publicity (PTP) and inadmissible evidence.

Pretrial Publicity. PTP, or information released to the public that may unfairly influence the jury, adversely affects jurors' decisions (American Bar Association, 2000). Such information could include information about the defendant's prior criminal record, character, inadmissible evidence, or admissible evidence that could lead the juror to infer that the defendant is guilty prior to trial. In short, PTP is any information (specific to the case or more generally related to topics in the case that could interfere with a juror's ability to fairly evaluate evidence and presume the defendant was innocent until proven guilty (Kovera & Levett, 2015).

Exposure to pro-prosecution PTP negatively affects jurors' decisions in both field studies and laboratory simulations. In a meta-analysis examining the relationship between PTP and jurors' decisions, researchers showed a small to medium effect of exposure to PTP on jurors' judgments, such that exposure to pro-prosecution PTP increased the probability that jurors would convict the defendant compared to jurors who were not exposed to PTP (Steblay et al., 1999). Further, this effect increased in magnitude as the ecological validity of the studies increased—those studies that closer mimicked real-world conditions had larger effects of PTP on jurors' decisions. Conversely, pro-defense PTP has not had the same consistent effect on jurors' decisions (see Bornstein et al., 2002; Ruva & McEvoy, 2008).

Given the strong effects of pro-prosecution PTP on jurors' decisions, researchers have turned to examining whether modifications to trial procedures or safeguards that could help jurors attenuate the bias introduced by PTP. This research has shown that some of the proposed safeguards are more or less effective. For example, instructing the jurors to ignore the PTP does not eliminate PTP effects (e.g., Bornstein et al., 2002). Similarly, another suggested safeguard is extending voir dire to allow judges and attorneys to identify jurors who have been biased by PTP; however, studies have also shown this safeguard is ineffective (Dexter et al., 1992). Further, in several studies, deliberation was also ineffective at attenuating bias due to PTP (Ruva & Guenther, 2015, 2017), and if the PTP is emotional in nature, deliberation may actually increase the effect of pro-prosecution PTP on jurors' decisions (Kerr et al., 1999; Kramer et al., 1990). However, one safeguard appears to be the most effective in attenuating the effect of PTP on jurors' decisions—a change of venue, or moving the trial to a community that has had no PTP exposure (or at least less PTP exposure). In this case, the most effective way to reduce bias is to ensure jurors have not been biased by the PTP in the first place.

Inadmissible Evidence. Similar to research on PTP, researchers have also investigated whether jurors can adequately disregard inadmissible evidence that is presented at trial. Overall, the results mirror the PTP literature. In one meta-analysis, researchers combined forty-eight studies and demonstrated that inadmissible evidence reliably effects jurors' decisions in the direction consistent with the bias introduced by the inadmissible evidence (Steblay et al., 2006). However, if judges provide a rationale for why the evidence is inadmissible, jurors may be more likely to comply with the request to disregard the evidence (Steblay et al., 2006). Simultaneously, though, admonitions may result in a backfire effect, or emphasis on the information that is supposed to be disregarded (Leiberman et al., 2009). Thus, similar to PTP, the best solution seems to be to prevent jurors from learning the extra-evidentiary information.

Trial Factors

EFFECTS OF TRIAL PROCEDURE ON JUROR DECISION-MAKING

We have explored intersections of trial factors with other factors affecting jurors' decisions previously in this chapter (e.g., the voir dire procedures in capital cases and effects of jurors' attitudes and demographics on decision-making). In addition to these intersections, characteristics of the trial itself can also affect the quality and content of the jury's decision. Research on several of these trial factors was inspired by US Supreme Court decisions ruling on the rules governing the jury processes.

For example, in *Williams v. Florida*,[3] the Court ruled that criminal juries could contain six jurors instead of twelve jurors, opining that juries of six and twelve members

---

[3] Williams v. Florida, 399 U.S. 78 (1970).

were functionally equivalent. Subsequently, psychologists investigated this assumption of functional equivalence. Combining these studies in a meta-analysis showed that smaller juries (vs. larger juries) had shorter, less thorough deliberations and were less accurate in evidence recall. However, juries rendered similar verdicts regardless of size, with the exception that larger juries were more likely to hang or not reach a decision than smaller juries (Saks & Marti, 1997).

EFFECTS OF JURY REFORMS ON DECISION-MAKING

Other trial factors intended to improve jury decision-making include improving jury instructions and allowing juror note taking or question asking. In some studies, note taking improved jurors' memories for complex evidence (e.g., Forsterlee et al., 2005), and in others, note taking had no effect (Heuer & Penrod, 1988, 1994). Similarly, revising jury instructions can improve verdict outcomes in reducing racial discrimination and increasing appropriate use of evidence, although the results here are also mixed and may depend other factors (Bornstein & Greene, 2017). Last, juror question appears to help jurors feel satisfied with the examination of witnesses (Heuer & Penrod, 1988, 1994). Thus, it appears that many of the reforms proposed to help jurors make better decisions have fewer or smaller effects on decision-making than anticipated by those championing them, but the effects also do not harm the decision-making process and may improve the jurors' subjective experiences (Kovera & Levett, 2015).

ARE JUDGES A BETTER ALTERNATIVE?

Given the shortcomings of the jury in decision-making, one must consider what viable alternative we have to the layperson as a legal decision maker. That is, one must consider the competence of the jury in the context of an alternative decision maker (Robbennolt & Eisenberg, 2017). In the United States, the most relevant comparison group is the judge. Most studies examining whether judges and juries agree on final verdict show high levels of agreement. In their seminal study, Kalven and Zeisel (1966) showed judges and juries agreed 78 percent of the time, with jurors tending to be more lenient compared to judges in cases of disagreement (Kalven & Zeisel, 1966), although other studies have not found evidence of jury leniency (Clermont & Eisenberg, 1992).

In considering evidence, judges and juries seem to have similar difficulty considering nuances of evidence in at least some areas. For example, in several studies judges and juries were similarly insensitive to variations in scientific evidence (e.g., Chorn & Kovera, 2019; Kovera & McAuliff, 2000). Also similar to jurors, judges also seem vulnerable to the effects of inadmissible evidence (Landsman & Rakos, 1994). Given the high levels of agreement on verdict and similar shortcomings in the evaluation of evidence, there is no strong evidence to believe that judges would be more competent decision makers than jurors.

Implications, Next Steps, and Future Directions for Research

To judge whether the jury is competent, the best question to ask is not whether the jury made the "right" or the "best possible" decision (Bornstein & Greene, 2017). Instead, one should consider whether the decision the jury made was reasonable in the context of the evidence provided (Bornstein & Greene, 2011). According to this metric, the jury is a generally competent decision-making body, albeit an imperfect one (Bornstein & Greene, 2017). Certainly, it is possible to improve the jury's decision, and doing so would increase just outcomes through reducing wrongful conviction and unjust civil judgments. However, to argue that the jury is incompetent is an overreach, especially when considered in context of the rate of judge–jury agreement and the strongest predictor of verdict (strength of evidence).

Given the limitations of the jury, it is important to continue the work to understand the theoretical mechanisms and factors that explain the jury's decision and to develop science-based mechanisms for improving the jury's decision. Given these goals, researchers integrate more of what we know about factors that affect jurors' decisions with the theoretical models for how jurors and juries make decisions. Further, knowing that the effects of trial participant characteristics and evidentiary and extra-evidentiary factors are often dependent on one another and/or the context in which the trial occurs, paying special attention to these interactions and the limitations of effects based on context is particularly important. In addition, much of the research in jury reform has been spurred by changes in procedure initiated by policymakers or the court (Kovera & Levett, 2014). Future research could attempt to reverse the process. That is, psychologists could work to identify the psychological mechanisms that could improve jurors' decisions, and then create the procedural reform based on the psychological mechanism, rather than responding to intuitive attempts at reform initiated by legal actors.

Methodologically, the area of jury decision-making presents some particularly difficult hurdles for researchers. The best designed study would likely include a large community member sample (preferably folks who reported for jury duty) viewing a live or videotaped trial and deliberating in groups. However, it is impossible for all jury studies to meet these criteria—especially when considering the number of juries and jurors required to obtain sufficient power to test the effects of manipulations on the jury's verdicts (see Giner-Sorolla et al., 2020, for a discussion of power and planning sample size). Instead, it will behoove us as jury researchers to carefully consider our research questions and how the results of those studies will be affected by our methodological choices. Then, we need to carefully justify our methodological choices and explain our limitations in light of those considerations. And above all, we need to replicate our work, using the same stimuli and then different stimuli to ensure generalizability.

As stated in the introduction, jury trials exist in a paradox in our modern society (Bornstein & Greene, 2017). They are simultaneously symbolic of the ideals of democracy and simultaneously flawed and imperfect. As researchers, we can work to improve the jury's decision by understanding the nuances of how juries decide and then working to create procedures and policies that will lead to a greater proportion of just outcomes.

Acknowledgments

This research was supported by grants from the National Science Foundation (NSF) to the author under Grant Number SBE -1123758. Any opinions, findings, and conclusions or recommendations expressed in this material are those of the authors and do not necessarily reflect the views of the NSF. The author has no known conflicts of interest to report.

References

Abramson, J. (1994). *We the jury: The jury system and the ideal of democracy*. Basic Books.

American Bar Association. (2000). *2003 edition: Model rules of professional conduct*. ABA.

Behl, J. D., Kienzle, M. R., & Levett, L. M. (2013). *A test of the story model of juror decision making* [Paper presentation]. Meeting of the American Criminology Society, Atlanta, Georgia.

Blandón-Gitlin, I., Sperry, K., & Leo, R. (2011). Jurors believe interrogation tactics are not likely to elicit false confessions: Will expert testimony inform them otherwise? *Psychology, Crime, & Law, 17*, 239–260.

Bornstein, B. H., & Greene, E. (2011). Jury decision making: Implications for and from psychology. *Current Directions in Psychological Science, 20*, 63–67.

Bornstein, B. L., & Greene, E. (2017). *The jury under fire: Myth, controversy, and reform*. Oxford University Press.

Bornstein, B. H., Rung, L. M., & Miller, M. (2002). Should physicians apologize for their mistakes? The role of remorse in a simulated malpractice trial. *Behavioral Sciences & Law, 20*, 393–409.

Bornstein, B. H., Whisenhunt, B. L., Nemeth, R. J., & Dunaway, D. L. (2002). Pretrial publicity and civil cases: A two-way street? *Law and Human Behavior, 26*, 3–17.

Chojnacki, D., Cicchini, M., & White, L. (2008). An empirical basis for the admission of expert testimony on false confessions. *Arizona State Law Journal, 40*, 1–45.

Chorn, J. A., & Kovera, M. B. (2019). Variations in reliability and validity do not influence judge, attorney, and mock juror decisions about psychological expert evidence. *Law and Human Behavior, 43*(6), 542–557.

Clermont, K. M., & Eisenberg, T. (1992). Trial by jury or judge: Transcending empiricism. *Cornell Law Review, 77*, 1124–1177.

Cowan, C. L., Thompson, W., & Ellsworth, P. C. (1984). The effects of death qualification on jurors' predisposition to convict and on the quality of deliberation. *Law and Human Behavior, 8*, 53–80.

Cutler, B. L., Penrod, S. D., & Dexter, H. R. (1990). Juror sensitivity to eyewitness identification evidence. *Law and Human Behavior, 14*, 185–191.

Davis, J. H. (1973). Group decision and social interaction: A theory of social decision schemes. *Psychological Review, 80*, 97–125.

Deutsch, M., & Gerard, H. B. (1955). A study of normative and informational social influences upon individual judgment. *Journal of Abnormal and Social Psychology, 51*, 629–633.

Devenport, J. L., & Cutler, B. L. (2004). The impact of defense-only and opposing eyewitness experts on juror judgments. *Law and Human Behavior, 5*, 569–576.

Devenport, J. L., Stinson, V., Cutler, B. L., & Kravitz, D. A. (2002). How effective are the cross-examination and expert testimony safeguards? Jurors' perceptions of the suggestiveness and fairness of biased lineup procedures. *Journal of Applied Psychology, 87*, 1042–1054.

Devine, D. J. (2012). *Jury decision making: The state of the science*. New York University Press.

Devine, D. J., Clayton, L. D., Dunford, B. B., Seying, R., & Pryce, J. (2001). Jury decision making: 45 years of empirical research on deliberating groups. *Psychology, Public Policy, and Law, 7*(3), 622–727.

Dexter, H. R., Cutler, B. L., & Moran, G. (1992). A test of voir-dire as a remedy for the prejudicial effects of pretrial publicity. *Journal of Applied Social Psychology, 22*, 819–832.

Diamond, S. S. (2003). Truth, justice, and the jury. *Harvard Journal of Law and Public Policy, 26*, 143–155.

Espinoza R. K. E., & Willis-Esqueda, C. (2008). Defendant and defense attorney characteristics and their effects on juror decision making and prejudice against Mexican Americans. *Cultural Diversity and Ethnic Minority Psychology, 14*, 364–371.

Filkins, J. W., Smith, C. M., & Tindale, R. S. (1998). An evaluation of the biasing effects of death qualification. In R. S. Tindale, L. Heath, J. Edwards, E. J. Posavac, F. B. Bryant, Y. Suarez-Balcazar, E. Henderson-King, & J. Myers (Eds.), *Theory and research on small groups* (pp. 153–175). Plenum Press.

Finkel, N. J. (1995). *Commonsense justice: Jurors' notions of the law.* Harvard University Press.

Forsterlee, L., Kent, L., & Horowitz, I. A. (2005). The cognitive effects of jury aids on decision making in complex civil litigation. *Applied Cognitive Psychology, 19*, 867–884.

Gastil, J., Deess, E. P., & Weiser, P. (2002). Civic awakening in the jury room: a test of the connection between jury deliberation and political participation. *The Journal of Politics, 64*, 585–595.

Giner-Sorolla, R., Carpenter, T., Lewis, N. A., Montoya, A. K., Aberson, C. L., Bostyn, D. H., Conrique, B. G. Ng, B. W., Reifman, A., Schoemann, A. M., & Soderberg, C. (2020). Power to detect what? Considerations for planning and evaluating sample size (Working paper). https://osf.io/d3v8t/

Groscup, J. L., & Tallon, J. (2009). Theoretical models of jury decision making. In J. D. Lieberman & D. A. Krauss (Eds.), *Jury psychology: Social aspects of trial processes: Vol. 1. Psychology in the courtroom* (pp. 41–65). Ashgate.

Gunnel, J. J., & Ceci, S. J. (2010). When emotionality trumps reason: A study of individual processing style and juror bias. *Behavioral Sciences & the Law, 28*, 850–977.

Hannaford-Agor, P. L., Hans, V. P., Mott, N. L., & Munsterman, G. T. (2002). Are hung juries a problem? (NCJ No. 201096). National Center for the State Courts.

Haney, C. (1984). On the selection of capital juries: The biasing effects of the death-qualification process. *Law and Human Behavior, 8*, 212–132.

Hastie, R. (1993). Algebraic models of juror decision processes. In R. Hastie (Ed.), *Inside the juror: The psychology of juror decision making* (pp. 84–115) Cambridge University Press.

Hastie, R., Schkade, D. A., & Payne, J. W. (1998). A study of juror and jury judgments in civil cases: Deciding liability for punitive damages. *Law and Human Behavior, 22*, 287–314.

Henderson, K. S., & Levett, L. M. (2016). Can expert testimony sensitize jurors to variations in confession evidence? *Law and Human Behavior, 40*(6), 638–649.

Henkel, L., Coffman, K, & Dailey, E. (2008). A survey of people's attitudes and beliefs about false confessions. *Behavioral Sciences and the Law, 26*, 555–584.

Heuer, L., & Penrod, S. (1988). Increasing jurors' participation in trials: A field experiment with jury note taking and question asking. *Law and Human Behavior, 12*, 231–261.

Heuer, L., & Penrod, S. (1994). Juror note taking and question asking during trials: A national field experiment. *Law and Human Behavior, 18*, 121–150.

Holstein, J. A. (1985). Jurors' interpretations and jury decision making. *Law and Human Behavior, 9*, 83–100.

Huntley, J. E., & Costanzo, M. (2003). Sexual harassment stories: Testing a story-mediated model of juror decision-making in civil litigation. *Law and Human Behavior, 27*, 29–51.

Innocence Project. (2021). Explore the numbers: Innocence project's impact. https://innocenceproject.org/exonerations-data/

Jones, T. M., Bottoms, B. L., & Stevenson, M. C. (2020). Child victim empathy mediates the influence of jurors' sexual abuse experiences on child sexual abuse case judgments: Meta-analyses. *Psychology, Public Policy, and Law, 26*(3), 312–332.

Kalven, H., & Zeisel, H. (1966). *The American jury.* University of Chicago Press.

Kassin, S. M., Drizin, S. A., Grisson, T., Gudjonsson, G. H., Leo, R. A., & Redlich, A. D. (2010). Police-induced confessions: Risk factors and recommendations. *Law and Human Behavior, 34*, 3–38.

Kassin, S. M., & Sukel, H. (1997). Coerced confessions and the jury: An experimental test of the "harmless error" rule. *Law and Human Behavior, 21*, 27–46.

Kassin, S. M., & Wrightsman, L. S. (1980). Prior confessions and mock juror verdicts. *Journal of Applied Social Psychology, 10*, 133–146.

Kassin, S. M., & Wrightsman, L. S. (1981). Coerced confessions, judicial instruction, and mock juror verdicts. *Journal of Applied Social Psychology, 11*, 489–506.

Kassin, S. M. and Wrightsman, L. (1983). The construction and validation of a juror bias scale. *Journal of Research on Personality, 17*, 423–442.

Kerr, N. L., Niedermeier, K. E., & Kaplan, M. F. (1999). Bias in jurors vs bias in juries: New evidence from the SDS perspective. *Organizational Behavior and Human Decision Processes, 80*, 70–86.

Kovera, M. B. (2019). Racial disparities in the criminal justice system: Prevalence, causes, and a search for solutions. *Journal of Social Issues, 75*(4) 1139–1164.

Kovera, M. B., & Levett, L. M. (2015). Jury decision making. In B.L. Cutler & P. A. Zapf (Eds.), *APA handbook of forensic psychology, Vol. 2. Criminal investigation, adjudication, and sentencing outcomes* (pp. 271–311). American Psychological Association.

Kovera, M. B., & McAuliff, B. D. (2000). The effects of peer review and evidence quality on judge evaluations of psychological science: Are judges effective gatekeepers? *Journal of Applied Psychology, 85,* 574–586.

Kramer, G. P., Kerr, N. L., & Carroll, J. S. (1990). Pretrial publicity, judicial remedies, and jury bias. *Law and Human Behavior, 14,* 409–438.

Landsman, S., & Rakos, R. F. (1994). A preliminary inquiry into the effects of potentially biasing information on judges and jurors in civil litigation. *Behavioral Sciences & the Law, 12,* 112–126.

Lassiter, G. D., Geers, A. L., Handley, I. M., Weiland, P. E., & Munhall, P. J. (2002). Videotaped confessions and interrogations: A simple change in camera perspective alters verdicts in simulated trials. *Journal of Applied Psychology, 87,* 867–874.

Lecci, L., & Myers, B. (2002). Examining the construct validity of the original and revised JBS: A cross-validation of sample and method. *Law and Human Behavior, 26,* 455–463.

Lecci, L., & Myers, B. (2008). Individual differences in attitudes relevant to juror decision making: Development and validation of the Pretrial Juror Attitude Questionnaire (PJAQ). *Journal of Applied Social Psychology, 15,* 656–672.

Lieberman, J. D., Arndt, J., & Vess, M. (2009). Inadmissible evidence and pretrial publicity: The effects (and ineffectiveness) of admonitions to disregard. In J. D. Lieberman & D. A. Krauss (Eds.), *Jury psychology: Social aspects of trial processes: Vol. 1. Psychology in the courtroom* (pp. 67–95). Ashgate.

Leo, R., & Lui, B. (2009). What do potential jurors know about police interrogation techniques and false confessions? *Behavioral Sciences and the Law, 27,* 381–399.

Levett, L. M., & Devine, D. M. (2017). Developing an explanation-based theory of jury decision making: Integrating individual and group models. In M.B. Kovera (Ed.), *The psychology of juries* (pp. 11–36). American Psychological Association.

Loftus, E. F. (1980). Impact of expert psychological testimony on the unreliability of eyewitness identification. *Journal of Applied Psychology, 65,* 9–15.

MacCoun, R.J., & Kerr, N.L. (1988). Asymmetric influence in mock jury deliberation: Jurors' bias for leniency. *Journal of Personality and Social Psychology, 54,* 21–33.

Mazzella, R., & Feingold, A. (1994). The effects of physical attractiveness, race, socioeconomic status, and gender of defendants and victims on judgments of mock jurors: A meta-analysis. *Journal of Applied Social Psychology, 24,* 1315–1344.

Mitchell, T. L., Haw, R. M., Pfeifer, J., & Meissner, C. A. (2005). Racial bias in juror decision-making: A meta-analytic review. *Law and Human Behavior, 29,* 621–637.

Moore, P. J., & Gump, B. B. (1995). Information integration in juror decision making. *Journal of Applied Social Psychology, 25,* 2158–2179.

Moran, G., & Comfort, J. C. (1986). Neither "tentative" nor "fragmentary": Verdict preference of impaneled felony jurors as a function of attitude toward capital punishment. *Journal of Applied Psychology, 71,* 146–155.

Narby, D. J., Cutler, B. L., & Moran, G. (1993). A meta-analysis of the association between authoritarianism and jurors' perceptions of defendant culpability. *Journal of Applied Psychology, 78,* 34–42.

Pawlenko, N. B., Safer, M. A., Wise, R. A., & Holfeld, B. (2013). A teaching aid for improving jurors' assessments of eyewitness accuracy. *Applied Cognitive Psychology, 27,* 190–197.

Pennington, N., & Hastie, R. (1988). Explanation-based decision making: Effects of memory structure on judgment. *Journal of Experimental Psychology: Learning, Memory, and Cognition, 14,* 521–533.

Pennington, N., & Hastie, R. (1993). The story model for juror decision making. In R. Hastie (Ed.), *Inside the juror: The psychology of juror decision making* (pp. 192–221). Cambridge University Press.

Pickel, K. L., Warner, T. C., Miller, T. J., & Barnes, Z. T. (2013). Conceptualizing defendants as minorities leads mock jurors to make bias evaluations in retracted confession cases. *Psychology, Public Policy, and Law, 19*(1), 56–69.

Ratcliff, J. J., Lassiter, G. D., Jager, V. M., Lindberg, M. J., Elek, J. K., & Hasinski, A. E. (2010). The hidden consequences of racial salience in videotaped interrogations and confessions. *Psychology, Public Policy, and Law, 16*(2), 200–218.

Robbennolt, J. K., & Eisenberg, T. (2017). Juries compared with what? The need for a baseline and attention to real-world complexity. In M. B. Kovera (Ed.), *The psychology of juries* (pp. 109–129). American Psychological Association.

Rotundo, M., Nguyen, D., & Sackett, P. R. (2001). A meta-analytic review of gender differences in perceptions of sexual harassment. *Journal of Applied Psychology, 86,* 914–922.

Ruva, C. L., & Guenther, C. C. (2015). From the shadows into the light: How pretrial publicity and deliberation affect mock jurors' decisions, impressions, and memory. *Law and Human Behavior, 39,* 294–310.

Ruva, C. L., & Guenther, C. C. (2017). Keep your bias to yourself: How deliberating with differently biased others affects mock-jurors' guilt decisions, perceptions of the defendant, memories, and evidence interpretation. *Law and Human Behavior, 41,* 478–493.

Ruva, C. L., & McEvoy, C. (2008). Negative and positive pretrial publicity affect juror memory and decision making. *Journal of Experimental Psychology: Applied, 14,* 226–235.

Saks, M. J., & Marti, M. W. (1997). A meta-analysis of the effects of jury size. *Law and Human Behavior, 21,* 451–467.

Saulnier, A., Burke, K. C., & Bottoms, B. L. (2020). The effects of body-worn camera footage and eyewitness race on perceptions of police use of force. *Behavioral Sciences & the Law, 37*(6), 732–750.

Schutte, J. W., & Hosch, H. M. (1997). Gender differences in sexual assault verdicts: A meta-analysis. *Journal of Social Behavior and Personality, 12,* 759–772.

Smith, B. C., Penrod, S. D., Otto, A. L., & Park, R. C. (1996). Jurors' use of probabilistic evidence. *Law and Human Behavior, 20,* 49–82.

Smith, V. L. (1991). Prototypes in the courtroom: Lay representations of legal concepts. *Journal of Personality and Social Psychology, 61,* 857–872.

Stasser, G., Kerr, N. L., & Davis, J. H. (1989). Influence processes and consensus models in decisions-making groups. In P. Paulus (Ed.), *Psychology of group influence* (2nd ed.) (pp. 279–326). Erlbaum.

Steblay, N. M., & Besirevic, J., Fulero, S. M., & Jimenez-Lorente, B. (1999). The effects of pretrial publicity on juror verdicts: A meta-analytic review. *Law and Human Behavior, 23,* 219–235.

Steblay, N. M., Hosch, H. M., Culhane, S. E., & McWethy, A. (2006). The impact on juror verdicts of judicial instruction to disregard inadmissible evidence: A meta-analysis. *Law and Human Behavior, 30,* 469–492.

Wissler, R. L., & Saks, M. J. (1985). On the inefficacy of limiting instructions: When jurors use prior conviction evidence to decide on guilt. *Law and Human Behavior, 9,* 37–48.

Yelderman, L. A., West, M. P., & Miller, M. K. (2019). Death penalty decision-making: Fundamentalist beliefs and the evaluations of aggravating and mitigating circumstances. *Legal and Criminological Psychology, 24*(1), 103–122.

Emotion and Legal Judgment

Liana C. Peter-Hagene, Samantha Bean, *and* Jessica M. Salerno

Abstract

When trials include emotionally evocative evidence such as gruesome photographs and victim impact statements, maintaining the balance between probative value and prejudicial effects can be difficult. Such evidence can rouse jurors' anger, disgust, outrage, or empathy. In turn, experienced emotions can, directly or indirectly, within or outside awareness, motivate decision makers to blame, punish, or forgive. These psychological processes can bias guilt or liability verdicts, where visceral reactions influence how jurors interpret facts or even motivate them to bypass careful consideration of these facts. Further, emotional displays from defendants (e.g., remorse) and victims (e.g., distress) influence judgments of credibility and legal decisions via cognitive (expectancy violation) or emotional (empathy) processes. The chapter describes the most recent scientific research on these topics, integrating work from social, cognitive, and legal psychology. The chapter concludes with recommendations for future research on emotion and prejudice, group processes, and emotion regulation in legal settings.

Key Words: jury decision-making, emotion, criminal trials, anger, disgust, outrage, empathy

Studying Emotion in Legal Settings

Through laws, procedures, and jury instructions, the legal system takes a complicated stance on emotion. Emotion is often vilified as an enemy to rationality but sometimes also characterized as an important part of legal decisions (Bandes & Blumenthal, 2012; Maroney, 2016). Many legal decisions involve emotionally evocative situations because legal transgressions and civil disputes often involve issues of morality, harm, and blame: violent crimes, injury, custody cases, child victims, and life-and-death decisions. Even when jurors, judges, and other legal decision makers ground their decisions in careful consideration of facts, their emotions motivate them to care about the decision and to take action (Bandes & Blumenthal, 2012; see also Levett, this volume). Thus, understanding how, when, and to what extent emotions influence legal judgments is crucial to developing informed legal policy.

Just as emotion research and theories can inform legal scholars, legal settings have much to offer emotion researchers: complex yet realistic scenarios and judgments; issues of blame, punishment, and harm; and plausibly emotional actors. Thus, studying emotion in legal contexts has the potential to (1) advance theoretical knowledge about how emotions are elicited, interpreted, regulated, and incorporated into decision-making processes; and (2) test psychological theories in realistic, complex, and ecologically valid settings with consequential real-world outcomes.

Our review is focused on recent developments in the growing area of emotion and legal judgment. Although we discuss implications for several types of legal decision makers, the bulk of the current research is focused on juror decision-making, and therefore is the primary focus of our research review. We discuss relevant legal precedent and scholarship; recent empirical developments; and future directions for the field.

Legal Perspectives

In this section, we will discuss courtroom decisions and legal precedent related to emotional evidence, as well as legal scholarship on emotion.

Legal Precedent Regarding Emotional Evidence

Rule 403 of the Federal Rules of Evidence outlines a balancing test for admissible evidence: It should be presented only if its probative value is not outweighed by unfair prejudicial effects.[1] The balancing test is especially relevant to emotional evidence such as victim impact statements and graphic visual evidence of injuries. In *Booth v. Maryland*,[2] the US Supreme Court held that victim impact statements (VIS) violated a defendant's constitutional Eighth Amendment rights, failing the probative/prejudicial balancing test. Four years later, however, the Supreme Court reversed the decision in *Payne v. Tennessee*[3]: Victim impact statements were deemed appropriate evidence of the emotional impact on the victims' family and of victims' uniqueness, and as a balancing factor for mitigating evidence in favor of the defendant.

Indeed, there is precedent that also favors defendants. The Supreme Court in *Lockett v. Ohio*[4] had granted defense attorneys in death penalty cases great leeway to introduce emotional mitigating evidence in support of a life sentence, and in *Riggins v. Nevada*,[5] the Supreme Court held that a mentally ill defendant must be allowed to testify without taking psychotropic drugs that could impact his ability to show remorse (Bandes, 2016).

Overall, a wide variety of court rulings on the admissibility of VIS has troubling implications for the equal distribution of justice. In some jurisdictions, VIS are highly limited (e.g., written text approved through a special hearing before the trial, evidence delivered by one family member capable of controlling their emotions, and factual testimony devoid of inflammatory comments).[6] In others, VIS are introduced only after sentencing, allowing victims their day in court, but precluding direct prejudice toward the

---

[1] Fed. R. Evid. 403.
[2] Booth v. Maryland, 482 U.S. 496 (1987).
[3] Payne v. Tennessee, 501 U.S. 808, 825–826 (1991).
[4] Lockett v. Ohio, 438 U.S. 586 (1978).
[5] Riggins v. Nevada, 504 U.S. 127 (1992).
[6] State v. Muhammad, 359 N.J. Super. 361 (2003).

defendant from impacting the sentencing (Myers et al., 2018). And yet in other jurisdictions, courts allowed, during the sentencing phase, highly emotional montages of victims' lives set to music or narrated by the victim's parents.[7] Recent efforts from victim advocacy groups have promoted Live Victim Photo Acts allowing pictures of murder victims before they died in the guilt phase of criminal trials, despite providing no probative information about the crime (e.g., Rychlak, 2016).

The tension between probative and prejudicial value also applies to crime scene or autopsy photographs. These can have probative value (e.g., nature of the wounds, forensic details, and level of harm), yet they also evoke emotional reactions in jurors and even judges (Maroney, 2006, 2011). Some courts found that gruesome photographs lacked probative value and were likely to incite emotions such as hatred and disgust,[8] whereas other courts saw probative value in photographs on their own[9] or as corroborating evidence to expert testimony.[10]

Occasionally, in trials with heightened emotional content, jurors receive curative instructions about how to process emotional evidence. In *Cargle v. State*,[11] the Oklahoma Appeals Court ruled that instructing jurors to keep their consideration of emotional victim impact statements "limited to a moral inquiry into the culpability of the defendant, not an emotional response to the evidence" was sufficient to eliminate prejudiced verdicts. It is reasonable to suspect, however, that most jurors (even judges) would have a hard time drawing the exact line that separates moral inquiry from emotional response. In *United States v. Treas-Wilson*,[12] the appellate court ruled that instructing jurors to "dispassionately" rely on gruesome photographs introduced into evidence was sufficient. Such rulings on the presumed effectiveness of jury instructions are not grounded in empirical research about people's ability to regulate emotions or about the types of emotion regulation strategies that work best. Some judges are aware of these limitations, calling curative instructions a legal "placebo" (Brown, 2011, p. 66).

Legal Scholarship on Emotions

Legal scholars have long pointed out an apparent double standard of the court system when it comes to emotions (Brown, 2011; Maroney, 2016). Folk beliefs that emotions are irrational, prejudicial bursts of feeling that compromise rational consideration of evidence have pervaded the legal system's relationship to affective processes even as evidence with high emotional impact is routinely allowed in high-stakes criminal and civil trials (Bandes & Blumenthal, 2012; Maroney, 2006). Maroney (2016) notes that understanding how the emotions that legal decision makers feel while making judgments can impact their

---

[7] Kelly v. California, 555 U.S. 1020 (2008); People v. Zamudio, 181 P.3d 105, 135 (Cal. 2008).
[8] Archina v. People, 307 P.2d 1083, 1095 (Colo. 1957).
[9] United States v. McRae, 593 F.2d 700, 707 (5th Cir. 1979).
[10] State v. Garcia, 663 P.2d 60, 64 (Utah 1983).
[11] Cargle v. State, 909 P.2d 806 (Okla. CR 1995).
[12] United States v. Treas-Wilson 3 F.3d 1406, 1410 (10th Cir. 1993).

decision-making processes is necessary for the law to function well. Instead of pitting reason against emotion, newer models must consider the law as a mechanism for more nuanced emotion regulation where specific emotions are either curbed or encouraged in different contexts to achieve the relevant legal purpose.

Current legal scholarship illustrates the variability in how emotions are regulated by rules and practice, supporting this call for more specific and nuanced approaches to emotion and law. Bandes and Salerno (2014) note that "emotion" is often used as an umbrella term to identify evidence considered improper or prejudicial. This is problematic because not all emotions function alike. In reality, different emotions convey different information about harm, danger, or morality, are associated with different information processing styles, and elicit different action tendencies—some desirable and some undesirable, depending on the specific legal context. Further, emotions can vary in intensity from mild arousal that guides and motivates rational decisions to overwhelming reactions that can drown out rational thought. Yet the law does not differentiate between the type and intensity of emotion based on psychological theory and research.

Overall, courts (with some exceptions) tend to view emotions as undesirable for legal decisions when *experienced* by the decision maker because they might cloud his or her judgment, but permissible when they are *displayed* by defendants and victims and used by decision makers to make inferences about harm and culpability. Legal decision makers are allowed to consider defendants' apparent emotions like anger and jealousy when deciding between murder and manslaughter, parents' and children's love and attachment when deciding custody cases, and plaintiffs' emotional suffering in civil trials (Maroney, 2006). Jurors are expected, even encouraged to consider the emotional displays of defendants at trial, and perceived displays of remorse from the defendant emerge as a crucial factor in death penalty sentencing trials (Bandes, 2016). Other legal decisions (parole and probation, noncapital sentencing, remanding juveniles to adult court) also openly account for displays of remorse.

Empirical Investigations of Emotion in Legal Decision Making

In this section, we review classic and recent empirical research on the effects of emotional evidence, emotional experiences of jurors, and emotion displays from victims and defendants on legal judgments. We also review strategies to reduce the unwanted effects of emotional evidence and we highlight the emerging field of group emotion and legal judgment.

Effects of Emotional Evidence on Legal Judgments

Anecdotal and qualitative evidence from actual trials suggest that jurors (and perhaps judges, Maroney, 2011) can experience strong emotions in reaction to trial evidence, sometimes powerful and long-lasting enough to threaten jurors' well-being (Antonio, 2005). The affect infusion model (AIM; Forgas, 1995) describes how emotional responses to evidence or testimony can affect judgments about a defendant. First, affective responses to evidence can influence decisions directly through a misattribution process. Jurors might notice that they feel angry or disgusted after seeing graphic evidence, wrongly attribute the anger or disgust to the defendant, and infer that they must feel this way because they think the defendant is guilty.

Second, affect can also influence jurors' decisions *indirectly* by biasing their systematic processing of case evidence in ways congruent with the affective valence. Angry or disgusted jurors might favor incriminating evidence and discount exculpatory details— which would lead them to a guilty verdict via effortful, but biased information processing. This indirect, biasing effect of emotional reactions to evidence is consistent with other information-processing models that account for the motivating power of emotion. For example, cognitive consistency models predict that initial verdict preferences influence the weight jurors give subsequent evidence, and emotion is a strong catalyst for these early decision leanings (Simon et al., 2015). That is, emotional reactions might lead them to prefer a given verdict and then pull their evaluations of subsequent evidence in line with that verdict preference. The culpable control model also posits that negative emotions, such as anger, elicit an automatic motivation to blame, which can instigate biased attention, recall, and interpretation of evidence consistent with blaming a target (Alicke, 2000).

GRUESOME PHOTOGRAPHS

The increased availability of video footage ensures that gruesome scenes such as the immediate aftermath of the Boston Marathon bombings or real-time police shootings are displayed to jurors in vivid, disturbing detail. In support of the AIM, Salerno (2017) found that gruesome photographs elicited more disgust and resulted in higher conviction rates when they were presented in color, but not when they were presented in black and white. This effect was particularly strong for jurors with higher awareness of their bodily sensations, who arguably were more likely to attend to their own bodily "gut reactions" of disgust and to rely on these cues to inform their guilt judgments (i.e., direct affect infusion). Disgust elicited by color photographs influenced verdicts via the indirect path as well, by making jurors less sensitive to the strength of defense evidence. These findings are in line with several prior findings that gruesome photographs affect legal judgments because they increase emotional reactions such as anger and disgust (Bright & Goodman-Delahunty, 2006, 2011; Salerno & Peter-Hagene, 2013), but also attributions of defendant negligence (Bright & Goodman-Delahunty, 2011; see Bornstein & Greene, 2017; Nunez et al., 2016, for review).

VIS

The theatrical features of some VIS intentionally target jurors' emotions: home movies, photo collages of the victim with family and friends, and evocative background music make it difficult for jurors (and even judges) to remain stoic (Myers et al., 2018). Mock jurors who watched videotaped VIS were four times more likely to vote for death than those who did not, an effect mediated by empathy and sympathy for the victim and anger at the defendant (Paternoster & Deise, 2011). In sexual assault cases, VIS increased sentence harshness by making jurors more upset and nervous (Wevodau et al., 2014).

Content analysis of actual VIS from capital trials reveals that two-thirds of them (67 percent) referred to the survivors' emotions, while far fewer mentioned physical (9 percent) or financial (4 percent) impact. Overall, VIS conveyed more sadness than anger, but the degree of sadness and anger expressed across multiple VIS in each trial did not significantly predict death penalty verdicts (Myers et al., 2018). In experimental studies, however, anger appears more likely than sadness to explain VIS effects on verdicts: mock jurors who saw angry versus sad VIS were more likely to apply the death penalty (Nunez et al., 2017).

Emotional Experiences and Legal Judgments

In addition to the effects of emotional evidence such as gruesome pictures and VIS, psychology and law research has found that specific emotional experiences influence legal judgments (Feigenson, 2016; Salerno, 2021). Even merely anticipating emotional reactions can affect jurors' verdict preferences in criminal (Wiener et al., 2014) and civil (Greene et al., 2016) cases. Next, we discuss specific emotions common to legal decisions.

ANGER

According to appraisal theories of emotion, anger is associated with increased desire to punish, increased certainty, and lowered motivation to process information carefully (Lerner & Keltner, 2001). In capital mock trials, jurors' fluctuations in anger during the trial predicted their willingness to assign the death penalty and to discount mitigating evidence presented by the defense (Georges et al., 2013). Qualitative interviews with prosecutors revealed that anger was the most prominent emotion they experienced, and that they were conflicted about resisting or accepting their emotions (Leiterdorf-Shkedy & Gal, 2019). Interviews and anecdotal evidence also indicate that anger is experienced by judges while serving on the bench (Maroney, 2011).

The prejudicial effect of anger is illustrated in research where emotions are "incidental" or unrelated to the case. Ask and Pina (2011) induced participants to feel angry or sad before reading about an ambiguous crime and found that anger, but not sadness, increased participants' attributions of intentionality and the severity of their punishment recommendations. Negative pretrial publicity increased jurors' propensity for guilty verdicts because it made them angry (Ruva et al., 2011). Even when incidental, anger can affect verdicts directly, by increasing perceptions of a defendant's moral blameworthiness, and indirectly, by reducing jurors' interest in a balanced consideration of both confirming and disconfirming evidence.

The importance of the indirect pathway is illustrated by an experiment where incidental anger *reduced* guilty verdicts. When judging a morally ambiguous crime (i.e., doctor killing terminally ill patient at the patient's request), angry (vs. non-angry) jurors were more likely to rely on their pretrial attitudes toward euthanasia, resulting in more lenient verdicts for jurors who believed euthanasia was morally permissible (Peter-Hagene & Bottoms, 2017). Thus, incidental anger increased the effect of pretrial attitudes, arguably because it increased reliance on heuristic processing (Bodenhausen et al., 1994), instead of increasing punitive tendencies for all jurors.

Yet anger might also make people more careful information processors. Angering (vs. neutral) trial information resulted in increased anger and a marked increase in guilty verdicts—but also in more systematic information processing perhaps due to its motivating effect (Semmler & Hurst, 2017). Similarly, angry participants were better at distinguishing weak from strong arguments (Moons & Mackie, 2007). Thus, anger can increase certainty, but it can also increase vigilance and motivation. When the answer is not obvious (and perhaps no clear heuristic cues direct decision makers to an easy answer), anger can actually promote more systematic processing.

EMPATHY

A meta-analysis of nine studies determined that empathy for child victims was a strong predictor of child witness credibility and guilty verdicts for defendants in child abuse cases (Jones et al., 2020). In death penalty cases, jurors' ability to identify with the victim made them more likely to sentence defendants to death (Sundby, 2002). Yet empathy can work for the defendant as well: jurors who were asked to empathize with a juvenile defendant were less likely to convict her compared to a control group (Haegerich & Bottoms, 2000).

MORAL OUTRAGE

When jurors evaluate a criminal act, they also evaluate the underlying moral transgression—and it is difficult for them to clearly separate the two aspects of their decisions. Neuroscience evidence indicates that decision-making in criminal contexts involves activity in dorsolateral prefrontal cortex regions responsible for decision-making, as well as activity in areas associated with emotion and moral outrage (amygdala, posterior cingulate cortex; Buckholtz et al., 2008). Feelings of moral outrage in response to a perceived *moral* transgression can also increase perceptions of *legal* guilt or liability in criminal (Salerno & Peter-Hagene, 2013; Saulnier et al., 2019) and civil trials (McCracken & Stevenson, 2017).

In contrast, when jurors do not see a criminal act as a moral transgression, they can acquit morally "blameless" defendants despite their indubitable legal guilt, a phenomenon known as jury nullification (Peter-Hagene & Bottoms, 2017). The moral emotions behind jury nullification have not been thoroughly investigated—but some evidence suggests that jurors' moral outrage against the law and the prosecution motivated jurors to disregard the law and acquit (Peter-Hagene & Ratliff, 2021).

Reducing the Effects of Emotional Evidence

Trials involve emotional evidence, but also instructions asking jurors to ignore their emotions. The conflict between the direct instructions to disregard emotions and the unavoidable psychological reality of emotional experience can prompt emotion regulation efforts (broadly defined as people's attempts to control the type, intensity, and expression of the emotions they experience; Gross & Thompson, 2007). Of these, attempts to suppress emotions and their expression appear to be an inefficient, effortful strategy that results in depletion and backfiring effects. In contrast, reappraisal of emotional stimuli in a less emotional light has emerged as a more successful emotion regulation strategy (Gross & Thompson, 2007; Maroney & Gross, 2014).

There is some evidence from mock jury studies to suggest that suppression would decrease performance for jurors and result in backfiring effects. Mock jurors saw emotional or neutral incriminating evidence regarding a defendant's past criminal behavior (Edwards & Bryan, 1997). The judge instructed half the jurors to disregard the evidence, while allowing the other half to rely on it. The emotional (but not neutral) evidence resulted in significantly higher guilt judgments only when it was accompanied by instructions to disregard it. Although this study did not rely on emotion regulation theories, and the authors found the results paradoxical, their findings evince emotion suppression effects: emotional evidence backfired when jurors tried to suppress it. Further, instructing jurors that statements from the victim's family are not evidence and should not be incorporated into verdict decisions were effective for jurors high in need for cognition but backfired for jurors low in need for cognition who were more likely to refer to emotional evidence in their verdict justifications after receiving limiting instructions (Matsuo & Itoh, 2017).

Several mock jury studies comparing the effectiveness of suppression and reappraisal instructions in reducing the emotional effects of gruesome photographs and emotional testimony found effects that were partially encouraging, partially concerning. Suppression instructions reduced the effect of graphic photographs on disgust, and in turn on convictions compared to a control condition and to reappraisal instructions—but they also decreased jurors' performance on a memory test of trial evidence (Peter-Hagene, 2022). Suppression also reduced the effect of emotional evidence for jurors high, but not low, in emotion regulation self-efficacy (i.e., jurors who believed they can regulate their emotions)—in line with positive effects of self-efficacy on performance in other domains (Bandura, 1977). Surprisingly, emotion reappraisal instructions had little direct or moderating effect on verdicts in all studies.

Individual Differences in Susceptibility to Emotion

Individual characteristics such as high need for affect, experiential versus rational processing, high bodily awareness, and high emotion dysregulation predict harsher sentencing and/or verdict decisions in death penalty (Stroud et al., 2014), murder (Salerno, 2017), sexual assault (Wevodau et al., 2014), battery (Gunnell & Ceci, 2010), and hate crime cases (Cramer et al., 2017). Individual differences in trait empathy predicted less support for capital punishment (Unnever et al., 2005).

Effects of Emotional Displays on Legal Judgments

Whereas experiencing emotion can influence one's own judgments and decisions, expressing that emotion can be a powerful tool to influence the decisions of others. Tearful testimony from victims, contrite statements of remorse from defendants, or passionate pleas from attorneys can enhance the content of their persuasive messages and sway jurors' verdicts. Theories of emotion as social information (e.g., van Kleef et al., 2011) explain that expressed emotions influence others in two ways: by rousing similar or complementary emotions in them (emotion contagion) or via inferential processes about the expresser of emotion (including the appropriateness of the emotion, which further depends on the decision maker's expectations).

As we discuss next, mock jury research largely confirms that jurors' inferences about the credibility of emotional victims, defendants, attorneys, and other jurors depend on whether the emotional display confirms of violates their expectations.

EMOTIONAL VICTIM EFFECT

Emotional displays typically increase adult and child victim credibility (the emotional victim effect), although instructions about the lack of diagnostic value of emotional displays for credibility might reduce these effects (Bollingmo et al., 2009). Victims of physical violence are evaluated more negatively when they expressed agentic (anger) compared to passive (sadness) emotion (Bosma et al., 2018). Perceivers expect victims of sexual assault to experience more negative emotions compared to victims of other crimes (Wrede & Ask, 2015). A recent meta-analysis revealed a positive moderate effect of sexual assault victims' emotional displays (versus neutral demeanor) on victim credibility across twenty studies, and this effect was equally strong for professionals in the legal system (law enforcement, judges, law students) and laypeople (students, community members; Nitschke et al., 2019). In civil trials, jurors pay attention to plaintiffs' emotional displays on and off the witness stand and discuss these as relevant to their verdicts during deliberation (Rose et al., 2010).

Although emotionality is a poor predictor of child accuracy and truthfulness (Katz et al., 2016), children fit the profile of psychologically vulnerable victims (e.g., Bederian-Gardner & Goldfarb, 2014) and thus legal decision makers expect displays of emotional distress (McAuliff & Kovera, 2012). Even child protective services professionals thought sad children were more credible, but angry children were less credible despite evidence that anger is a common response for victimized children (Wesse et al., 2013). Prosecutors consider children's emotional displays in their decision to press charges (Castelli & Goodman, 2014), and law students perceive emotional (vs. neutral) child victims as more credible (Landstrom et al., 2015).

The emotional victim effect appears to be mediated by increased compassion and confirmation of expectations, rather than negative affect (Ask & Landstrom, 2010; Landstrom et al., 2015). In further support, the emotional victim effect is stronger when people hold expectations of high emotion expressiveness from rape victims (Hackett et al., 2008), such as in more severe crimes (Justice & Smith, 2018; Lens et al., 2014), and when emotional displays were portrayed as consistent (Klippenstine & Schuller, 2012). Another study ruled out emotion contagion and empathy as mediators (Ask, 2018).

EMOTION DISPLAYS FROM DEFENDANTS

Defendant emotion can influence legal decisions when it is relevant to the moment when the crime was committed (e.g., provocation/heat-of-passion defenses). For example, politically conservative jurors were more lenient toward a male defendant who claimed he felt panic in response to the male victims' unwanted sexual advances (gay panic defense; Salerno et al., 2015). In cases involving police officers accused of lethal force, participants were more likely to vote guilty when a male officer was perceived as fearful (and, in turn, as less competent); for female officers, fearfulness did not predict verdict preferences, arguably because fear is more expected from women than men (Galeza et al., 2020).

Defendants' emotional displays during trial also influence verdicts. Defendants displaying sadness received fewer guilty verdict and were rated as more honest, particularly when the evidence against them was weak (Heath et al., 2004). Defendants perceived as remorseless or lacking in empathy received harsher sentencing recommendations for white-collar crimes (Cox et al., 2016) and were more likely to receive the death penalty (Cox et al., 2013). As with victim emotionality, perceived defendant remorse might not be a reliable source of information (Bandes, 2016), although some research indicates that people can distinguish genuine from fabricated remorse (ten Brinke et al., 2012).

EMOTION DISPLAYS FROM JURORS AND ATTORNEYS

These investigations support the general idea that expectations about appropriate or normative emotional displays are central to legal decisions—and these expectations might not be the same for everyone. Salerno and colleagues found that anger expression increased the persuasiveness of White and male jurors but decreased the persuasiveness of female and Black jurors during mock deliberations (Salerno & Peter-Hagene, 2015; Salerno et al., 2019). This happened because anger expression created a gender and racial gap in minority-opinion jurors' ability to exert social influence during deliberation. In neutral emotion conditions, holdout jurors' race and gender did not affect social influence, but in anger expression conditions, women and Black jurors were significantly less likely to sway other jurors' verdict preferences. The authors found support for justification-suppression models of prejudice, which predict that racial (and probably gender) prejudice is most likely expressed when people can attribute their judgmental biases to legitimate reasons not related to race (Crandall & Eshleman, 2003). More specifically, participants perceived the same level of emotion from White men as they did for women and African Americans, but perceptions of emotionality only decreased influence for women and Black holdouts. That is, displays of anger might provide a justification to dismiss a female or Black holdout and to deny them social influence. This extends to attorneys' closing arguments. People drew positive inferences from male attorneys' anger to justify hiring them, while they drew negative inferences from female attorneys' anger to justify not hiring them (Salerno et al., 2018).

Group Emotion and Legal Judgments

Empirical investigations of how jury deliberation might change the effects of experienced or witnessed emotions are rare and paint conflicting pictures. Emotional displays from a rape victim during videotaped testimony influenced individual jurors, but this effect was attenuated by deliberation because deliberation increased the credibility of victims displaying neutral or incongruent (i.e., happy) emotion and convictions (Dahl et al., 2007). In contrast, defendants' facial expressions of remorse and anger influenced verdicts before *and* after mock jurors deliberated (MacLin et al., 2009). Real capital jury deliberations were fraught with emotion. People often argued, grew frustrated with each other (Renaud, 2010), and made inferences about jurors' emotionality (Sundby, 2010). For example, when the majority favored death, life-leaning holdouts were characterized as emotionally weak and unstable.

Mock capital jurors often rely on emotion as a persuasive tactic to argue their point and to rebut opposing positions during deliberation (Lynch & Haney, 2015). Expressions of anger toward the defendant and empathy for the victim were expressed more freely and were qualified less than expressions of sympathy for the defendant. White male jurors were more likely to assert their emotional stance and more likely to police the emotions expressed by other jurors often in favor of White (vs. Black) defendants. Furthermore, White men are more likely to gain influence when they express anger (Salerno & Peter-Hagene, 2015, Salerno et al., 2019). Interracial interactions can be emotionally taxing and cognitively depleting (Richeson & Trawalter, 2005), and racially diverse juries are no exception (Peter-Hagene, 2019).

Future Research Directions

The field of emotion and law has now established effects of emotional evidence, emotion expression, and specific emotions on legal decisions of jurors, on which we can now build in incremental but important ways. For example, we know that anger, disgust, and sympathy mediate the effect of emotional evidence on verdicts, but there is no research that directly manipulates these specific emotions so that their effects can be disentangled. Classic appraisal theories of emotion can be used to formulate specific predictions for separate emotions beyond the classic distinction between anger and sadness. For example, it might be more useful, although arguably much more difficult, for psychology and law researchers to differentiate between anger and disgust, or compassion and empathy. Novel theories of emotion, in contrast, posit that distinct emotions do not exist as universal psychological entities triggered by specific events (e.g., moral transgressions) and associated with specific action tendencies (e.g., to punish), but rather are *constructed* ad hoc from components such as physiological arousal, cultural scripts, and environmental cues and then given a familiar label (e.g., anger; Barrett, 2017). This view of emotions could recast existing psychology and law findings in a new light and inspire novel research questions about emotional experiences and the interpretation of emotion expressions (Salerno, 2021).

It is important to integrate group decision-making with emotion research. How many of the effects observed in typical individual mock jury studies would withstand the deliberation process? Group dynamics, individual differences, memory facilitation or inhibition, error correction, leniency bias, and social influence are just a few of the factors that can reduce or exacerbate individual judgment effects during deliberation (Peter-Hagene et al., 2019). Would deliberation reduce the emotional victim effect or the effect of gruesome photographs when jurors have to go over the evidence, point by point, in the presence of others? Or would emotion contagion exacerbate the effects of emotional evidence throughout deliberation? Would deliberation make emotion regulation easier or more difficult for individual jurors to achieve? It is also important to learn more about the interpersonal dynamics on the jury, how jurors interpret each other's emotional displays, how they resolve conflict, whether the emotional tone of the group differs significantly as a function of group demographics, and whether that has a bearing on the quality of the legal decision.

In addition, emotion research could be better integrated with racial and anti-LGBTQ bias in legal decisions. An increasing body of evidence suggests emotional reactions are group-based. For example, African Americans elicit anger (Tapias et al., 2007), gay men and transgender individuals elicit disgust (DasGupta et al., 2009), and members of one's own racial group elicit empathy (Dovidio et al., 2010). What are the implications of this for how jurors (1) experience emotions, (2) perceive victims' and defendants' emotional expressions, and (3) allow emotions to influence their judgments?

Despite characterizations of jurors as passive receivers of emotional stimuli or instructions about emotions, social psychological research has shown that people are motivated and active, not passive, receivers and processors of information (Nickerson, 1998; Tamir, 2016). People avoid stimuli that would put them in a negative mood (English et al., 2017) and control their anger at someone more (but not less) powerful than themselves (Petkanopoulou et al., 2019). Future studies could develop novel questions about goals and motives in legal decision makers' willingness to regulate their emotions. For example, might jurors control their anger when the defendant belongs to their ingroup, but allow it to "take over" when the defendant belongs to a stigmatized outgroup?

Researchers should focus on other legal decision makers whose decisions are so important to trial outcomes, such as prosecutors and judges (Maroney, 2011; Maroney & Gross, 2014). Are judges better able than jurors to regulate their emotions? Are they more willing to do so because they recognize the importance of dispassionate decisions? How do they make decisions about allowing emotional evidence, and do they rely on research and expertise about the effects of emotional evidence on jurors?

Finally, future research should continue to test safeguards to the prejudicial or biasing effects of emotional evidence such as jury instructions, expert testimony about emotional evidence and about the diagnostic value of emotional displays from victims, and procedures for reducing the vividness of emotional evidence while maintaining its probative value.

References

Alicke, M. D. (2000). Culpable control and the psychology of blame. *Psychological Bulletin, 126*(4), 556–574.

Antonio, M. E. (2005). I Didn't Know It'd Be So Hard-Jurors' Emotional Reactions to Serving on a Capital Trial. *Judicature, 89,* 282–288.

Ask, K. (2018). Complainant emotional expressions and perceived credibility: Exploring the role of perceivers' facial mimicry and empathy. *Legal and Criminological Psychology, 23,* 252–264.

Ask, K., & Landström, S. (2010). Why emotions matter: Expectancy violation and affective response mediate the emotional victim effect. *Law and Human Behavior, 34*(5), 392–401.

Ask, K., & Pina, A. (2011). On being angry and punitive: How anger alters perception of criminal intent. *Social Psychological and Personality Science, 2*(5), 494–499.

Bandes, S. A. (2016). Remorse and criminal justice. *Emotion Review, 8*(1), 14–19.

Bandes, S. A., & Blumenthal, J. A. (2012). Emotion and the law. *Annual Review of Law and Social Science, 8,* 1–23.

Bandes, S., & Salerno, J. M. (2014). Emotion, proof and prejudice: The cognitive science of gruesome photos and victim impact statements, *Arizona State Law Journal, 46*(4), 1003–1056.

Bandura, A. (1977). Self-efficacy: Toward a unifying theory of behavioral change. *Psychological Review, 84*(2), 191–215.

Barrett, L. F. (2017). The theory of constructed emotion: An active inference account of interoception and categorization. *Social Cognitive and Affective Neuroscience, 12*(1), 1–23.

Bederian-Gardner, D., & Goldfarb, D. (2014). Expectations of emotions during testimony: The role of communicator and perceiver characteristics. *Behavioral Sciences & Law, 32*(6), 829–845.

Bodenhausen, G. V., Sheppard, L. A., & Kramer, G. P. (1994). Negative affect and social judgment: The differential impact of anger and sadness. *European Journal of Social Psychology, 24*(1), 45–62.

Bollingmo, G., Wessel, E., Sandvold, Y., Eilertsen, D. E., & Magnussen, S. (2009). The effect of biased and non-biased information on judgments of witness credibility. *Psychology, Crime & Law, 15*(1), 61–71.

Bornstein, B. H., & Greene, E. (2017). *The jury under fire: Myth, controversy, and reform.* Oxford University Press.

Bosma, A. K., Mulder, E., Pemberton, A., & Vingerhoets, A. J. (2018). Observer reactions to emotional victims of serious crimes: Stereotypes and expectancy violations. *Psychology, Crime & Law, 24*(9), 957–977.

Bright, D. A., & Goodman-Delahunty, J. (2006). Gruesome evidence and emotion: Anger, blame, and jury decision-making. *Law and Human Behavior, 30*(2), 183–202.

Bright, D. A., & Goodman-Delahunty, J. (2011). Mock juror decision making in a civil negligence trial: The impact of gruesome evidence, injury severity, and information processing route. *Psychiatry, Psychology and Law, 18*(3), 439–459.

Brown, T. R. (2011). The affective blindness of evidence law. *Denver University Law Review, 89,* 47–131.

Buckholtz, J. W., Asplund, C. L., Dux, P. E., Zald, D. H., Gore, J. C., Jones, O. D., & Marois, R. (2008). The neural correlates of third-party punishment. *Neuron, 60,* 930–940.

Castelli, P., & Goodman, G. S. (2014). Children's perceived emotional behavior at disclosure and prosecutors' evaluations. *Child Abuse & Neglect, 38*(9), 1521–1532.

Cox, J., Edens, J. F., Rulseh, A., & Clark, J. W. (2016). Juror perceptions of the interpersonal-affective traits of psychopathy predict sentence severity in a white-collar criminal case. *Psychology, Crime & Law, 22*(8), 721–740.

Cox, J., Clark, J. C., Edens, J. F., Smith, S. T., & Magyar, M. S. (2013). Jury panel member perceptions of interpersonal-affective traits of psychopathy predict support for execution in a capital murder trial simulation. *Behavioral Sciences & the Law, 31*(4), 411–428.

Cramer, R. J., Wevodau, A. L., Gardner, B. O., & Bryson, C. N. (2017). A validation study of the Need for Affect Questionnaire–Short Form in legal contexts. *Journal of Personality Assessment, 99*(1), 67–77.

Crandall, C. S., & Eshleman, A. (2003). A justification-suppression model of the expression and experience of prejudice. *Psychological Bulletin, 129*(3), 414–446.

Dahl, J., Enemo, I., Drevland, G. C., Wessel, E., Eilertsen, D. E., & Magnussen, S. (2007). Displayed emotions and witness credibility: A comparison of judgements by individuals and mock juries. *Applied Cognitive Psychology, 21*(9), 1145–1155.

Dasgupta, N., DeSteno, D., Williams, L. A., & Hunsinger, M. (2009). Fanning the flames of prejudice: The influence of specific incidental emotions on implicit prejudice. *Emotion, 9*(4), 585–591.

Dovidio, J. F., Johnson, J. D., Gaertner, S. L., Pearson, A. R., Saguy, T., & Ashburn-Nardo, L. (2010). Empathy and intergroup relations. In M. Mikulincer & P. R. Shaver (Eds.), *Prosocial motives, emotions, and behavior: The better angels of our nature* (pp. 393–408). American Psychological Association.

Edwards, K., & Bryan, T. S. (1997). Judgmental biases produced by instructions to disregard: The (paradoxical) case of emotional information. *Personality and Social Psychology Bulletin, 23*(8), 849–864.

English, T., Lee, I. A., John, O. P., & Gross, J. J. (2017). Emotion regulation strategy selection in daily life: The role of social context and goals. *Motivation and Emotion, 41*(2), 230–242.

Feigenson, N. (2016). Jurors' emotions and judgments of legal responsibility and blame: What does the experimental research tell us? *Emotion Review, 8*(1), 26–31.

Forgas, J. P. (1995). Mood and judgment: the affect infusion model (AIM). *Psychological Bulletin, 117*(1), 39–66.

Galeza, E., Bader, C., & Peter-Hagene, L.C. (2020, March). *Male, but not female officers are penalized by trial jurors when use of fatal force is attributed to fear* [Paper presentation]. Annual meeting of the American Psychology-Law Society, New Orleans, LA.

Georges, L. C., Wiener, R. L., & Keller, S. R. (2013). The angry juror: Sentencing decisions in first-degree murder. *Applied Cognitive Psychology, 27*(2), 156–166.

Greene, E., Sturm, K. A., & Evelo, A. J. (2016). Affective forecasting about hedonic loss and adaptation: Implications for damage awards. *Law and human behavior, 40*(3), 244–256.

Gross, J. J., & Thompson, R. A. (2007). Emotion regulation: Conceptual foundations. In J. J. Gross (Ed.), *Handbook of emotion regulation* (pp. 2–26). Guilford Press.

Gunnell, J. J., & Ceci, S. J. (2010). When emotionality trumps reason: A study of individual processing style and juror bias. *Behavioral Sciences & the Law, 28*(6), 850–877.

Hackett, L., Day, A., & Mohr, P. (2008). Expectancy violation and perceptions of rape victim credibility. *Legal and Criminological Psychology, 13*(2), 323–334.

Haegerich, T. M., & Bottoms, B. L. (2000). Empathy and jurors' decisions in patricide trials involving child sexual assault allegations. *Law and Human Behavior, 24*(4), 421–448.

Heath, W. P., Grannemann, B. D., & Peacock, M. A. (2004). How the defendant's emotion level affects mock jurors' decisions when presentation mode and evidence strength are varied. *Journal of Applied Social Psychology, 34*(3), 624–664.

Jones, T. M., Bottoms, B. L., & Stevenson, M. C. (2020). Child victim empathy mediates the influence of jurors' sexual abuse experiences on child sexual abuse case judgments: Meta-analyses. *Psychology, Public Policy, and Law, 26*(3), 312–332.

Justice, L. V., & Smith, H. M. (2018). Memory judgements: the contribution of detail and emotion to assessments of believability and reliability. *Memory, 26*(10), 1402–1415.

Katz, C., Paddon, M. J., & Barnetz, Z. (2016). Emotional language used by victims of alleged sexual abuse during forensic investigation. *Journal of Child Sexual Abuse, 25*(3), 243–261.

Klippenstine, M. A., & Schuller, R. (2012). Perceptions of sexual assault: Expectancies regarding the emotional response of a rape victim over time. *Psychology, Crime & Law, 18*(1), 79–94.

Landström, S., Ask, K., Sommar, C., & Willén, R. (2015). Children's testimony and the emotional victim effect. *Legal and Criminological Psychology, 20*(2), 365–383.

Leiterdorf-Shkedy, S., & Gal, T. (2019). The sensitive prosecutor: Emotional experiences of prosecutors in managing criminal proceedings. *International Journal of Law and Psychiatry, 63*, 8–17.

Lens, K. M., van Doorn, J., Pemberton, A., & Bogaerts, S. (2014). You shouldn't feel that way! Extending the emotional victim effect through the mediating role of expectancy violation. *Psychology, Crime & Law, 20*(4), 326–338.

Lerner, J. S., & Keltner, D. (2001). Fear, anger, and risk. *Journal of Personality and Social Psychology, 81*, 146–159.

Lynch, M., & Haney, C. (2015). Emotion, authority, and death: (Raced) negotiations in mock capital jury deliberations. *Law & Social Inquiry, 40*(2), 377–405.

MacLin, M. K., Downs, C., MacLin, O. H., & Caspers, H. M. (2009). The effect of defendant facial expression on mock juror decision-making: The power of remorse. *North American Journal of Psychology, 11*(2), 323–332.

Maroney, T. A. (2006). Law and emotion: A proposed taxonomy of an emerging field. *Law and Human Behavior, 30*(2), 119–142.

Maroney, T. A. (2011). The persistent cultural script of judicial dispassion. *California Law Review, 99*, 629–681.

Maroney, T. A. (2016). A field evolves: Introduction to the special section on law and emotion. *Emotion Review, 8*(1), 3–7.

Maroney, T. A., & Gross, J. J. (2014). The ideal of the dispassionate judge: An emotion regulation perspective. *Emotion Review, 6*(2), 142–151.

Matsuo, K., & Itoh, Y. (2017). The effects of limiting instructions about emotional evidence depend on need for cognition. *Psychiatry, Psychology and Law, 24*(4), 516–529.

McAuliff, B. D., & Bull Kovera, M. (2012). Do jurors get what they expect? Traditional versus alternative forms of children's testimony. *Psychology, Crime & Law, 18*(1), 27–47.

McCracken, E. W., & Stevenson, M. C. (2017). Rape perpetrator gender shapes liability judgments: Implications for disgust and moral outrage. *Translational Issues in Psychological Science, 3*(2), 153–166.

Moons, W. G., & Mackie, D. M. (2007). Thinking straight while seeing red: The influence of anger on information processing. *Personality and Social Psychology Bulletin, 33*(5), 706–720.

Myers, B., Nuñez, N., Wilkowski, B., Kehn, A., & Dunn, K. (2018). The heterogeneity of victim impact statements: A content analysis of capital trial sentencing penalty phase transcripts. *Psychology, Public Policy, and Law, 24*(4), 474–488.

Nickerson, R. S. (1998). Confirmation bias: A ubiquitous phenomenon in many guises. *Review of General Psychology, 2*(2), 175–220.

Nitschke, F. T., McKimmie, B. M., & Vanman, E. J. (2019). A meta-analysis of the emotional victim effect for female adult rape complainants: Does complainant distress influence credibility? *Psychological Bulletin, 145*(10), 953–979.

Nunez N., Estrada-Reynolds V., Schweitzer K., & Myers B. (2016). The impact of emotions on juror judgments and decision-making. In B. Bornstein & M. Miller (Eds.), *Advances in psychology and law* (pp. 55–93). Springer.

Nuñez, N., Myers, B., Wilkowski, B. M., & Schweitzer, K. (2017). The impact of angry versus sad victim impact statements on mock jurors' sentencing decisions in a capital trial. *Criminal Justice and Behavior, 44*(6), 862–886.

Paternoster, R., & Deise, J. (2011). A heavy thumb on the scale: The effect of victim impact evidence on capital decision making. *Criminology, 49*(1), 129–161.

Peter-Hagene, L. C. (2019). Jurors' cognitive depletion and performance during jury deliberation as a function of jury diversity and defendant race. *Law and Human Behavior, 43*, 232–249.

Peter-Hagene, L. C. (2022). *Emotion regulation strategies to reduce the effect of graphic evidence on disgust and verdicts* [Manuscript in preparation]. North Central College, Psychology and Neuroscience Department.

Peter-Hagene, L. C., & Bottoms, B. L. (2017). Attitudes, anger, and nullification instructions influence jurors' verdicts in euthanasia cases. *Psychology, Crime, and Law, 23*, 983–1009.

Peter-Hagene, L. C., & Ratliff, C. (2021). When jurors' moral judgments result in jury nullification: Moral outrage at the law as a mediator of euthanasia attitudes effects on verdicts. *Psychiatry, Psychology, & Law, 28*, 27–49.

Peter-Hagene, L. C., Salerno, J. M., & Phalen, H. (2019). Jury decision making. In N. Brewer & A. Douglas (Eds.), *Psychological science and the law* (pp. 338–366). Guilford Press.

Petkanopoulou, K., Rodríguez-Bailón, R., Willis, G. B., & van Kleef, G. A. (2019). Powerless people don't yell but tell: The effects of social power on direct and indirect expression of anger. *European Journal of Social Psychology, 49*(3), 533–547.

Renaud, T. (2010). The biggest bully in the room. *The Jury Expert, 22*, 23–26. Rose, M. R., Diamond, S. S., & Baker, K. M. (2010). Goffman on the jury: Real jurors' attention to the "offstage" of trials. *Law and Human Behavior, 34*(4), 310–323.

Richeson, J. A., & Trawalter, S. (2005). Why do interracial interactions impair executive function? A resource depletion account. *Journal of Personality and Social Psychology, 88*(6), 934–947.

Ruva, C. L., Guenther, C. C., & Yarbrough, A. (2011). Positive and negative pretrial publicity: The roles of impression formation, emotion, and predecisional distortion. *Criminal Justice and Behavior, 38*(5), 511–534.

Rychlak, S. (2016). I see dead people: Examining the admissibility of living-victim photographs in murder trials. *Vanderbilt Law Review, 69*, 1423–1455.

Salerno, J. M. (2017). Seeing red: Disgust reactions to gruesome photographs in color (but not in black and white) increase convictions. *Psychology, Public Policy, and Law, 23*, 336–350.

Salerno, J. M. (2021). The impact of experienced and expressed emotion on legal factfinding. *Annual Review of Law and Social Science*. Advance online publication. https://doi.org/10.1146/annurev-lawsocsci-021721-072326

Salerno, J. M., Najdowski, C. J., Bottoms, B. L., Harrington, E., Kemner, G., & Dave, R. (2015). Excusing murder? Conservative jurors' acceptance of the gay-panic defense. *Psychology, Public Policy, and Law, 21*(1), 24–34.

Salerno, J. M., & Peter-Hagene, L. C. (2013). The interactive effects of anger and disgust on moral outrage and jurors' verdicts. *Psychological Science, 24,* 2069–2078.

Salerno, J. M., & Peter-Hagene, L. C. (2015). One angry woman: Anger expression increases influence for men, but decreases influence for women, during group deliberation. *Law and Human Behavior, 39,* 581–592.

Salerno, J. M., Peter-Hagene, L. C., & Jay, A. C. (2019). Women and African Americans are less influential when they express anger during group decision making. *Group Processes & Intergroup Relations, 22,* 57–79.

Salerno, J. M., Phalen, H. J., Reyes, R. N., & Schweitzer, N. J. (2018). Closing with emotion: The differential impact of male versus female attorneys expressing anger in court. *Law and Human Behavior, 42*(4), 385–401.

Saulnier, A., Burke, K. C., & Bottoms, B. L. (2019). The effects of body-worn camera footage and eyewitness race on jurors' perceptions of police use of force. *Behavioral Sciences & Law, 37*(6), 732–750.

Semmler, C., & Hurst, J. (2017). The impact of state and trait anger on processing of evidential inconsistencies. *Psychiatry, Psychology and Law, 24*(4), 594–604.

Simon, D., Stenstrom, D. M., & Read, S. J. (2015). The coherence effect: Blending cold and hot cognitions. *Journal of Personality and Social Psychology, 109,* 369–394.

Stroud, C. H., Cramer, R. J., & Miller, R. S. (2014). A trait–affect model of understanding perceptions of expert witness testimony. *Psychiatry, Psychology and Law, 21*(3), 333–350.

Sundby, S. E. (2002). The capital jury and empathy: The problem of worthy and unworthy victims. *Cornell Law Review, 88,* 343–381.

Sundby, S. E. (2010). War and peace in the jury room: How capital juries reach unanimity. *Hastings Law Journal, 62,* 103–154.

Tamir, M. (2016). Why do people regulate their emotions? A taxonomy of motives in emotion regulation. *Personality and Social Psychology Review, 20*(3), 199–222.

Tapias, M. P., Glaser, J., Keltner, D., Vasquez, K., & Wickens, T. (2007). Emotion and prejudice: Specific emotions toward outgroups. *Group Processes & Intergroup Relations, 10*(1), 27–39.

ten Brinke, L., MacDonald, S., Porter, S., & O'Connor, B. (2012). Crocodile tears: Facial, verbal and body language behaviours associated with genuine and fabricated remorse. *Law and Human Behavior, 36*(1), 51–59.

Unnever, J. D., Cullen, F. T., & Fisher, B. S. (2005). Empathy and public support for capital punishment. *Journal of Crime and Justice, 28*(1), 1–34.

van Kleef, G. A., van Doorn, E. A., Heerdink, M. W., & Koning, L. F. (2011). Emotion is for influence. *European Review of Social Psychology, 22*(1), 114–163.

Wessel, E., Magnussen, S., & Melinder, A. M. D. (2013). Expressed emotions and perceived credibility of child mock victims disclosing physical abuse. *Applied Cognitive Psychology, 27*(5), 611–616.

Wevodau, A. L., Cramer, R. J., Clark, J. W., & Kehn, A. (2014). The role of emotion and cognition in juror perceptions of victim impact statements. *Social Justice Research, 27*(1), 45–66.

Wiener, R. L., Georges, L. C., & Cangas, J. (2014). Anticipated affect and sentencing decisions in capital murder. *Psychology, Public Policy, and Law, 20*(3), 263–280.

Wrede, O., & Ask, K. (2015). More than a feeling: Public expectations about emotional responses to criminal victimization. *Violence and Victims, 30*(5), 902–915.

Injustice in the Courtroom: How Race and Ethnicity Affect Legal Outcomes

Jennifer S. Hunt

Abstract

Race and ethnicity affect judgments and outcomes at many stages of the criminal justice and legal process, accumulating into significant disparities in incarceration rates for Black and Latinx defendants. This chapter provides an overview of recent research about the influence of race and ethnicity on trial outcomes and processes. Prosecutors often strike potential jurors of color, lowering diversity in juries. Juries with larger numbers of White jurors, in turn, may be more likely to convict defendants of color. Judges are more likely to give sentences involving incarceration to defendants of color, and both prosecutorial and jury biases contribute to racial disparities in the death penalty. Understanding biases in legal outcomes requires intersectional analyses that examine race in conjunction with other identities and consideration of multiple forms of bias (explicit, implicit, and structural). The chapter also discusses recent legal developments related to racial and ethnic disparities and directions for future research.

Key Words: legal decision-making, race, ethnicity, minority defendants, criminal trials

To witness the relation between race, ethnicity, and legal outcomes, one need only look at statistics about people incarcerated in the United States. As of 2019, Black men are 5.72 times more likely and Latino men are 2.54 times more likely, per capita, to be incarcerated than are White men (Carson, 2020). Similar patterns, although smaller in magnitude, are found for women (Carson, 2020) as well as juveniles in secure placements (Rovner, 2021). In addition to removing people from their families and communities, felony conviction and incarceration can have a range of negative—and often lifelong—effects, including loss of voting and parental rights, ineligibility for state benefits (e.g., food assistance) and educational loans, and restrictions on housing (Ewald, 2012). Given this, it is not surprising that scholars like Michelle Alexander (2010) view mass incarceration as "The New Jim Crow," that is, as the latest in an evolving series of forcible means by which the state is able to control and subjugate Black people, as well as other people of color.

Disparities in incarceration reflect the endpoint of a long series of criminal justice and legal processes, each of which may be influenced by racial bias, resulting in cumulative disadvantage (Kurlychek & Johnson, 2019; Kutateladze et al., 2014). For example, police overpatrol neighborhoods of color (e.g., Rios, 2011) and engage in racial profiling during traffic stops (e.g., Baumgartner et al., 2018). They are disproportionately likely to stop and conduct searches of people of color, arrest them, and use force against them (see Olson & Goff, this volume). If charged, Black and Latinx defendants are required to post higher bail and are more likely to be detained before trial (e.g., Martinez et al., 2020), which can increase willingness to accept plea offers and conviction at trial (see Redlich et al., this volume). Prosecutors have considerable discretion in charging crimes, and often file more serious charges for defendants of color than White defendants (e.g., Rehavi & Starr, 2014). If cases go to trial, White jurors and/or judges may be more likely to convict Black and Latinx defendants (e.g., Bradbury & Williams, 2013; see Levett, this volume). Black and Latinx defendants are more likely than White defendants to receive sentences that involve prison or jail time (e.g., King & Light, 2019). Importantly, racial biases at each stage are exacerbated by social inequalities that covary with race; for example, given the relationship between race and family wealth, defendants of color are less likely to be able to afford bail or legal representation (e.g., Clair, 2020).

This chapter examines the influence of race and ethnicity on trial judgments at the later stages of cumulative disadvantage: verdicts, which are decided by either juries or judges, and sentencing, which usually is determined by judges. These topics have been studied extensively by psychology and law researchers, primarily through experimental studies that manipulate defendant race/ethnicity and other trial features to examine differences in judgments and processes that may lead to discrimination. This research may be used to inform applied practice; for example, trial consultants may try to develop arguments that reduce the potential for stereotyping in a given case. In addition, some argue that applied law–psychology may contribute to racial and ethnic disparities through the use of risk assessment protocols that include factors that can be influenced by racial bias, such as previous arrests, which may reflect the overpolicing of neighborhoods of color (Desmarias & Zottola, 2019). This important debate falls outside the scope of this chapter.

Notably, the study of racial and ethnic disparities in trial outcomes and sentencing extends well beyond psychology into fields such as sociology, criminology, anticarceral feminism, and law. Research conducted by scholars in these fields often uses archival methods, such as large-scale analyses of actual case outcomes. In order to develop a full understanding of racial and ethnic disparities in legal outcomes, including when and why they are likely to occur, it is critical to take an interdisciplinary approach that aggregates findings and insights from all these fields.

This chapter provides an overview of recent research about the influence of race and ethnicity on trial outcomes and processes. After discussing important background concepts, the chapter examines the role of race in jury selection and deliberation and then reviews experimental and archival research on the effects of race and ethnicity on trial judgments, particularly verdicts, made by jurors and judges. Next, the chapter discusses research on racial disparities in sentencing, including capital (death penalty) sentences. Following the review of research, there is a brief discussion of recent legal developments related to racial and ethnic disparities. The chapter concludes with important directions for future research.

Key Concepts

A few overarching concepts are essential for analyzing and addressing racial/ethnic disparities in legal outcomes. Intersectionality refers to the ways in which power, privilege, and oppression are determined by the interplay of different social identities, including race, ethnicity, gender, sexual orientation, social class, nationality and citizenship status, (dis)ability status, and religion (Cooper, 2016). Intersectional effects occur at the group and individual level, with people's experiences, opportunities, and outcomes reflecting their intersectional position (Cole, 2009). Intersectionality entered legal discourse when critical race scholar Kimberlé Crenshaw (1989) examined how the existing sexual harassment law is ill-equipped to handle Black women's experiences, which reflect both gender and racial bias. Likewise, it is critical to use an intersectional approach when analyzing disparities in legal outcomes, because those outcomes reflect social identities in addition to race and ethnicity. For example, the incarceration statistics at the beginning of the chapter clearly show the interplay of race, ethnicity, and gender but tend to mask the ways in which social class contributes to "racial" differences.

Other important concepts relate to the nature of racial bias. Traditionally, racial bias has been conceptualized as explicit, that is, overt and intentional, with people deliberately making negative judgments or acting in a discriminatory manner due to racial animus. However, in the 1990s, social psychologists proposed that stereotypes and prejudice could also affect judgments and behavior through implicit processes, which are subtle, unintentional, difficult to control, and/or may not involve conscious awareness (Lane et al., 2007). Since then, there has been an explosion of research on implicit bias and the concept has been applied to legal contexts, including trial and sentencing judgments (e.g., (Kang et al., 2012; Levinson et al., 2014). Debates about whether explicit or implicit processes are more likely to affect legal outcomes are likely to be counterproductive. Instead, it is more appropriate to analyze ways in which both may contribute to biased outcomes.

In addition to individual biases, critical race theory emphasizes the importance of analyzing structural biases, that is, institutional policies or practices that perpetuate unequal outcomes across social groups (Delgado & Stefancic, 2017). For example, when municipalities like Ferguson, Missouri generate operational funds through tickets and fines, the burden tends to fall disproportionately on poor and lower-class individuals who are charged with minor legal infractions, such as expired registration, broken taillights, or loitering in public areas (Department of Justice, 2015; Mayson & Stevenson, 2020). When these individuals are unable to pay their fines or make court appearances during the workday, they may end up being arrested or jailed, making their situation even worse. Such practices are insidious because they do not require biased actors to create disparate outcomes across groups; they only require legal professionals to "follow the rules." Thus, structural biases are an important, and unrecognized, contributor to discriminatory legal outcomes (see also Olson & Goff, this volume).

Finally, as discussed earlier, cumulative disadvantage is a critical concept for understanding disparities in legal outcomes. Many biases in legal outcomes are small in magnitude. For example, in an analysis of arrests in Miami-Dade County, Florida, Martinez et al. (2020) found that Black defendants were required to pay 15 percent higher bonds than White defendants, and that each 1 percent increase in bond amount was associated with an 11 percent increase in pretrial detention time. Longer detention, in turn, increased the likelihood of conviction and incarceration, especially for Black defendants. Thus, even though the amount of bias at each stage was not large, over time, those small biases accumulated into substantial disparities. Findings like this illustrate the need to address even small disparities in legal outcomes.

Research on Race, Ethnicity, and Legal Outcomes

This section examines the influence of race and ethnicity on outcomes at several stages of the legal process, including jury selection and deliberation, trial verdicts, judicial decision-making, and sentencing.

Jury Selection

In *Peters v. Kiff*,[1] the Supreme Court held, "When any large and identifiable segment of the community is excluded from jury service, the effect is to remove from the jury room qualities of human nature and varieties of human experience."[2] Consistent with this assertion, jurors of color often have more negative attitudes toward the police and courts than do White jurors (e.g., Farrell et al., 2013), making them more receptive to defense arguments in criminal cases. Not surprisingly, people of color also have lower levels of explicit and implicit racial bias (Levinson et al., 2014). Thus, systematically excluding jurors of color may create more conviction-prone juries, especially for Black defendants.

During *voir dire* (jury selection), attorneys are allowed to use peremptory challenges to excuse potential jurors who they expect to be unsympathetic to their case. However, in *Batson v. Kentucky*[3] and subsequent cases (see section "Recent Legal Developments"), the Supreme Court held that excusing potential jurors on the basis of race violates the equal protection clause. Despite this ruling, prosecutors regularly use peremptory challenges to eliminate people of color, especially Black people, from juries. For example, a study of eight southern states by the Equal Justice Initiative (Stevenson, 2010) found that Black jurors are regularly challenged on pretextual grounds, frequently leading to all-White juries, even in capital cases. In some counties, there was virtually no representation of Black jurors. More

---

[1] Peters v. Kiff, 407 U.S. 493 (1972).
[2] *Id.* at 503.
[3] Batson v. Kentucky, 476 U.S. 79 (1986).

recently, a study by the Berkeley Law Death Penalty Clinic (Semel et al., 2020) found that prosecutors in California regularly used peremptory challenges against Black and Latinx potential jurors, often citing experience with or negative attitudes about the police and courts (see also Flanagan, 2018). It is important to note that defense attorneys are often more likely to use peremptory challenges against White jurors (e.g., DeCamp & DeCamp, 2020); however, due to the underrepresentation of people of color in jury pools, many juries still end up predominantly or entirely White (Hannaford-Agor & Waters, 2011).

Structural biases may exacerbate individual biases in jury selection. Attorneys are skilled at inferring implicit bias and tend to select jurors whose biases benefit their side. For example, prosecutors select more biased jurors and defense attorneys select less biased jurors for cases with Black defendants and White victims (Morrison et al., 2016). However, prosecutors often receive training about generating race-neutral explanations for peremptory challenges (Semel et al., 2020; Stevenson, 2010). Further, judges often are reluctant to overturn prosecutors' peremptory challenges, and challenges on *Batson* grounds are rarely effective (Gabbidon et al., 2008; Semel et al., 2020).

Effects of Jury Diversity on Verdicts and Deliberation

These findings raise the important question of how racial/ethnic diversity affects the functioning of juries. Both archival and experimental research reveal that jury diversity is associated with positive outcomes. Archival analyses show that when juries have few or no Black members, Black defendants are more likely to be convicted (Bradbury & Williams, 2013; Flanagan, 2018) and given the death penalty (Bowers et al., 2001). Flanagan (2018) found that each prosecutorial strike of a Black potential juror corresponded to a 2–3 percent increase in likelihood of conviction for Black male defendants. Conversely, juries with more Black members are less prone to conviction, overall and particularly for Black defendants (Bowers et al., 2001; Bradbury & Williams, 2013). In a similar vein, juries whose members represent greater numbers of race-gender intersections are less prone to conviction (Devine et al., 2016).

Experimental jury simulations suggest that diverse juries may be less conviction-prone because they promote better quality deliberation and sensitize jurors to the possibility of racial bias. Sommers (2006) manipulated diversity by constructing six-person mock juries with either six White people or four White people and two Black people. The diverse juries deliberated longer and discussed more pieces of evidence. They also were more likely to consider the potential influence of race on the case, which involved a Black defendant. A similar study by Peter-Hagene (2019) examined six-person juries that included either two White or two Black research confederates, who were trained to make identical, noncommittal contributions to the deliberations. Comparisons of the actual participants showed that deliberating in a diverse jury was more cognitively taxing than deliberating in an all-White jury, likely because participants were worried about appearing biased. However, this cost was offset by reductions in bias. The diverse juries discussed equivalent numbers of case facts for White and Black defendants; in contrast, the all-White juries discussed more facts when the defendant was White.

Sometimes, the benefits of diverse juries may be reduced by racialized processes within the jury. For example, consistent with the stereotype of "angry Black people," when Black jurors express anger during deliberations, they are coded as "emotional" and, as a result, their arguments have less influence on other jurors (Salerno et al., 2019). Overall, diverse juries may be challenging in terms of the effort required and the need to guard against intra-jury bias, but they can improve the quality of deliberation, especially in cases with defendants of color.

Juror and Jury Verdicts and Guilt Judgments

A key question is whether similarly situated defendants differ in their likelihood of being convicted at trial based on their race or ethnicity. As discussed below, racial or ethnic differences in jury verdicts can reflect explicit or implicit bias in a range of judgments, including the strength of the evidence, defendant credibility, or the standard of proof. However, biases in verdict judgments are likely to be smaller than biases at other stages of the criminal justice and legal process. Research consistently shows that the strongest predictor of verdicts is the strength of the evidence (Devine, 2012). Thus, race and ethnicity may skew guilt and verdict judgments, especially in cases with ambiguous evidence, but the potential for bias is relatively constrained.

ARCHIVAL STUDIES

There is relatively little archival research on the effects of race and ethnicity on convictions from jury trials, as the vast majority of convictions come from pleas (see Redlich et al., this volume). However, archival and observational studies on trial convictions provide some evidence of racial bias. An analysis of trials from state courts in major metropolitan areas in four states revealed an interaction between defendant race and jury racial/ethnic composition. Black defendants were more likely to be convicted by juries with higher proportions of White and Latinx jurors and less likely to be convicted by juries with higher proportions of Black jurors (Bradbury & Williams, 2013). Kutateladze and Lawson (2018) analyzed nearly 160,000 misdemeanor cases in New York City. Only a tiny fraction (0.2 percent) went to trial, but in those cases, Asian American defendants were more likely than White defendants to be convicted. Conviction rates were nonsignificantly higher for Black and Latinx compared to White defendants.

Smaller-scale studies have examined the effects of race for verdicts on specific charges. In an analysis of Michigan cases involving charges for having sex without disclosing HIV-positive status, Hoppe (2015) found that conviction rates were higher for Black men and, surprisingly, White women. Taking victim gender into account, conviction rates were highest for Black men who had sex with women, but lowest for Black men who had sex with men. This pattern suggests both racial bias and the devaluation of men presumed to be gay. Likewise, differences in conviction rates based on victim race were found in Florida cases involving "Stand Your Ground" laws, in which perceived threat of death or bodily harm can be used as a defense for killing another person (Ackermann et al., 2015). Defendants were more than twice as likely to be convicted if they had killed White victims rather than victims of color.

Finally, analyses of the National Registry of Exonerations (Gross et al., 2017) suggest that race plays an important role in wrongful conviction. As of 2016, Africans Americans were 47 percent of known exonerees, despite being 13 percent of the U.S. population. Based on catalogued exonerations, innocent Black people are several times more likely than Whites to be falsely convicted of several crimes, including murder, sexual assault, and drug crimes. Although several problematic practices, including racial profiling, eyewitness errors, and police misconduct, contributed to these wrongful convictions, there was evidence of jury bias in some of the cases (e.g., using all-White juries to convict Black defendants).

EXPERIMENTAL STUDIES

In experimental research on juror decision-making, racial and ethnic bias usually is operationalized in terms of the similarity-leniency effect, in which jurors make more lenient judgments about same-race versus other-race defendants. In this pattern, White jurors—who, as discussed earlier, are disproportionately likely to be seated on juries—tend to "go easier" on White defendants but make harsher judgments for defendants of color. Conversely, Black jurors and other jurors of color are likely to make more lenient judgments for Black or same race/ethnicity defendants, in part, due to the recognition that racial bias may have affected those defendants at earlier stages of the criminal justice and legal process (Sommers & Adekanmbi, 2008).

Evidence of the similarity-leniency effect was consistently found in experimental research conducted prior to 2005 (T. Mitchell et al., 2005). Subsequent research continues to show the similarity-leniency pattern for some combinations of mock juror and defendant races/ethnicities; for example, White jurors make harsher judgments for Latinx versus White defendants and Black jurors make harsher judgments for White versus Black defendants (Devine & Caughlin, 2014). In addition, Canadian research shows more negative judgments of Indigenous defendants (e.g., Clow et al., 2013; Maeder et al., 2015). In contrast, recent studies often find no differences between verdicts for Black and White defendants or the reverse of the similarity-leniency effect—that is, White jurors making more lenient judgments about Black rather than White defendants. For example, Shaw et al. (in press) examined both predeliberation individual verdicts and postdeliberation jury verdicts for White and Black defendants in a drug case. Across conditions, conviction rates were higher for the White defendant. Similar patterns were found for predeliberation and postdeliberation verdicts in a murder trial (Peter-Hagene, 2019).

There are several reasons why experimental studies on White mock jurors' judgments about Black defendants might show different patterns than archival studies, especially during the period in question (i.e., the 2010s and early 2020s). The most likely explanation involves people's awareness of discrimination against Black people in the criminal justice and legal systems, particularly since 2015 when Michael Brown was killed in by police in Ferguson, Missouri and the Black Lives Matter movement began. According to aversive racism theory (Gaertner & Dovidio, 1986), most people strive, although often fail, to avoid prejudice. When race is salient, people are aware of the potential of bias, and they try to correct for it. Applied to the jury context, mock jurors show bias against Black defendants when race is not salient in a trial, but not when it is salient (Sommers & Ellsworth, 2000; 2001). In periods of heightened sensitivity to anti-Black discrimination, race may be chronically salient to research participants, making them strive to make unbiased judgments and even overcorrect for perceived biases, thus favoring Black defendants (Wegener et al., 2000). The desire to avoid prejudice may be enhanced by social desirability concerns in which participants want to look good in front of researchers.

Other explanations involve the ways in which trial simulations differ from actual trials. In mock juror studies, race is often manipulated by using names associated with different racial/ethnic groups or photographs that differ across conditions. These manipulations provide far less information than actual jurors get during trials. Actual jurors are able to observe defendants' demeanor and mannerisms, hear their voices, and view their entire bodies; as a result, they have a much richer set of triggers for racial bias (as well as other biases, such as social class). For example, jurors may make more negative judgments of defendants who use African American Vernacular English (AAVE) rather than General American ("White") English (Kurinec & Weaver, 2019). In addition, mock jurors do not have significant stakes in their judgments; in contrast, actual jurors may worry about allowing potentially dangerous persons to reenter their communities, concerns that may be triggered by stereotypes linking Black people, especially men, with crime and violence (Welch, 2007). Finally, the use of the scientific method to hold everything in a case constant except race or ethnicity may obscure differences in defendants' positions that are likely to occur in actual cases. For example, Black and Afro-Latinx defendants are more likely than White defendants to be detained prior to trial (e.g., Martinez et al., 2020) and, due to prosecutorial discretion, may face more serious charges (e.g., Rehavi & Starr, 2014). Thus, in some cases, experimental research may be too "clean and sterile" to show real-world biases against Black defendants.

WHY AND WHEN BIAS OCCURS

Despite unexpected recent findings for White jurors judging Black defendants, experimental research on juror decision-making has provided considerable insight into the psychological processes that underlie racial/ethnic bias and trial contexts that facilitate biased judgments. Factors related to verdicts are discussed in this section; additional considerations related to jurors' decisions about whether to impose the death penalty are discussed later.

First, defendant race may influence jurors' interpretation or use of evidence. In cases with defendants of color, jurors may rely more on prosecution evidence (Abshire & Bornstein, 2003), interpret ambiguous evidence as indicative of guilt (e.g., Levinson & Young, 2010), or consider damaging evidence that has been ruled inadmissible (Hodson et al., 2005). Although jurors generally interpret evidence in stereotype-consistent ways, in some cases, jurors may be especially influenced by evidence that challenges stereotypes because it is novel and appears informative (Maeder & Hunt, 2011).

Another process that can contribute to juror bias involves attributions or explanations about why people engage in certain behaviors. When judging defendants from other racial/ethnic groups, jurors often make internal attributions for criminal behavior, explaining it in terms of lasting dispositional tendencies (e.g., "bad seed" or "inherently violent"). In contrast, jurors may give same-race defendants "the benefit of the doubt" by making external attributions that explain criminal behavior in terms of situational or unstable causes (e.g., "giving into peer pressure"; Rattan et al., 2012; Sommers & Ellsworth, 2000). Not surprisingly, internal attributions make defendants seem more blameworthy and likely to reoffend (Yamamoto & Maeder, 2017).

Importantly, racial and ethnic biases in juror decision-making can be explicit or implicit. In some cases, jurors may deliberately consider race when deciding a case; for example, in *Peña-Rodriguez v. Colorado*, a juror made the argument that "I think he did it because he's Mexican, and Mexican men take whatever they want."[4] However, in many cases, jurors may engage in implicit bias, unintentionally making judgments that are influenced by race or ethnicity (Kang et al., 2012). For example, jurors may be influenced by implicit racial stereotypes that link Blackness with guilt (Levinson & Young, 2010) or give more value to lives of White victims than victims of color (Levinson et al., 2014).

Finally, it is important to note that contextual factors (e.g., characteristics of particular trials) can increase or decrease the likelihood that racial bias will influence judgments. One moderating factor is race salience, which was discussed earlier. Another factor involves the specific charges in a trial, as different crimes are stereotypically associated with particular racial groups. Black and Latinx people tend to be associated with violent crimes, burglary, and drug crimes, whereas White defendants tend to be associated with fraud and embezzlement (Skorinko & Spellman, 2013). Jurors are more likely to convict, as well as recommend harsher punishment, when defendants are charged with crimes that are stereotypically associated with their racial/ethnic group.

---

[4] Peña-Rodriguez v. Colorado, 580 U.S. ___, 137 S. Ct. 855 (2017).

Judicial Decision-Making

Judges are a critical part of the trial process, and they have considerable potential to influence legal outcomes. However, most criminal cases are resolved through pleas rather than trials (see Redlich et al., this volume). Even when cases go to trial, the trier of fact usually is a jury rather than the judge. Thus, other than in bench trials, judges are most likely to influence criminal verdicts in indirect ways, such as decisions about pretrial release, the admissibility of evidence, and attorney motions.

Ethnographic studies of criminal court proceedings provide valuable insights on ways in which judges can perpetuate race and class inequalities. Judges often prioritize efficiency and decorum in proceedings (Clair, 2020; Gonzalez Van Cleve, 2016). As a result, they may resist procedural motions, make rulings after minimal discussion of case facts, and defer to recommendations from attorneys and other judicial officers. Further, judges often treat defendants who are poor and/or people of color with contempt, and silence defendants who attempt to ask questions or assert their rights. Judges therefore can exacerbate race and class biases in other parts of the legal process, including prosecutorial discretion, overstretched public defenders, and recommendations about bail and pretrial release.

Similar patterns have been found in other court settings. For example, an observational study of dependency court found that judges often shamed and silenced poor mothers of color who were trying to be reunited with their children (Lens, 2019). Likewise, in a study of probation hearings for domestic violence, judges made statements that reflected racial stereotypes (e.g., about Black fathers) and expressed skepticism about the progress of Black defendants and men (Romain Dagenhardt, 2020).

A recent study provided valuable insight into judges' understanding of the role of race in the legal process. Through interviews with fifty-nine judges in a northeastern state, Clair and Winter (2016) found the majority of judges were aware of racial disparities in legal outcomes, although they differed in whether they attributed them to differential treatment by the criminal justice and legal system or to factors outside the system, such as poverty. When asked how they tried to reduce the influence of race, most judges described noninterventionist strategies in which they monitored their own judgments for racial bias but did not address potential biases in the actions of other parties (e.g., question whether plea agreements were influenced by race, take a proactive role in jury selection). A minority of judges engaged in interventionist strategies in which they used their power to challenge others' actions and tried to create widespread equality. Notably, judges' choice of strategy varied across contexts, with more intervention in arraignments (e.g., detention decisions) and jury selection than in plea agreements or sentencing. Only a few judges consistently used interventionist strategies across stages. Thus, although it is laudable that judges are monitoring their judgments for potential bias, the pervasiveness and limited scope of noninterventionist strategies enables discriminatory outcomes to persist.

Sentencing

The vast majority of criminal sentences are determined by judges, with the notable exception of capital (death penalty) sentences, which are discussed in the next section. A prominent theoretical model, focal concerns theory perspective (Steffensmeier et al., 1998), asserts that judges consider three key issues when determining sentences: defendant blameworthiness, community protection, and the practical implications of particular decisions. Defendant race and ethnicity may be used as heuristics for evaluating blame and future recidivism, which is relevant to community protection; thus, negative stereotypes associating men of color, especially Black men, with criminal and violent behavior (Welch, 2007) may contribute to harsher sentencing.

Archival analyses of actual cases have repeatedly shown that, controlling for relevant factors—including factors that may themselves be affected by racial bias (e.g., criminal history)—Black and Latinx defendants are sentenced more harshly than White defendants. The effects of race and ethnicity are stronger for the categorical outcome of whether or not defendants are sentenced to prison or jail ("in-out" judgments) than for sentence length (Hauser & Peck, 2017; King & Light, 2019; O. Mitchell, 2005). Importantly, there is a growing tendency to examine intersectional patterns. Research examining the interactive effects of race, ethnicity, gender, and/or age generally finds that Black men, and to a lesser extent, Latino men, are sentenced most harshly (e.g., Elis, 2017; Freiburger & Sheeran, 2020; Lehmann & Gomez, 2021). Further, being younger reduces the severity of sentencing for White men and women, but increases severity for Black men (Freiburger & Hilinski, 2013; Steffensmeier et al., 2017), possibly due to stereotypes about young Black men being "superpredators." Findings about the interaction of race and gender for women have been mixed, with some studies showing more lenient outcomes for White women (e.g., Elis, 2017), some showing an absence of race effects for women (Steffensmeier & Demuth, 2006), and others showing more lenient outcomes for Black women (Doerner, 2015; Freiburger & Sheeran, 2020). Certain intersectional patterns are particularly relevant to specific groups; for example, Latinx defendants are especially likely to receive harsh sentences when they are not US citizens and when crimes are committed in areas with small Latinx populations (Ulmer & Konefal, 2019).

In many cases, sentencing disparities are result of beneficial treatment of White defendants relative to defendants of color; for example, White defendants are more likely to receive probation instead of jail (Freiburger & Hilinski, 2013; Freiburger & Sheeran, 2020), mitigating departures that reduce their sentences (Elis, 2017), and split sentences, which are partially served under community supervision (Lehmann & Gomez, 2021). In an analysis of more than 186,000 Florida cases, Lehmann (2020) found that sentencing disparities vary across types of crime, with Black defendants receiving especially severe sentences relative to White defendants for manslaughter, robbery, arson, and resisting arrest.

There has been much less research examining sentencing biases for other racial and ethnic groups, such as Asian Americans and Native Americans. Likely due to the "model minority" stereotype, Asian American defendants are less likely to receive sentences involving incarceration than are White, Black, or Latinx defendants (Franklin & Fearn, 2015; Johnson & Betsinger, 2009). However, leniency toward Asian American defendants varies across charges, and does not benefit noncitizens charged with immigration offenses (Wu & Kim, 2014). Findings for Native Americans are more mixed, in part due to the complexities of federal–tribal justice system integration (Ulmer & Bradley, 2018).

Finally, sentencing biases can reflect victim race, showing that greater value is placed on the lives and/or suffering of people from certain racial groups. For example, Pierce et al. (2014) found that prosecutors worked harder (e.g., gathered more evidence) on murder cases involving White woman victims compared to other race–gender combinations. Corresponding patterns were found for the sentences in those cases, with defendants receiving the harshest sentences for murdering White women and the most lenient sentences for murdering Black men (see also section "Capital Sentencing").

Effects of Sentencing Guidelines

In the late 1970s, widespread variability in sentencing across judges and jurisdictions led to the creation of sentencing guidelines in twenty-two states and the federal courts (Frase, 2019). These guidelines dictated ranges of sentences for different offenses, which varied based on factors such as crime severity and criminal history. For certain crimes, mandatory minimum sentences were specified. The imposition of sentencing guidelines reduced sentencing variability (Frase, 2019) but created new concerns related to disparities. Mandatory minimum sentences limited judicial discretion (e.g., for first-time offenders), and often indicated harsher sentences for offenses (e.g., possession of crack cocaine) or circumstances (e.g., crimes committed near public housing) that disproportionately applied to defendants of color (Frase, 2019; Schlesinger, 2011). In Florida, sentencing enhancements are given to defendants labeled "habitual offenders," a designation disproportionately given to Latinx and Black defendants (Caravelis et al., 2011). Finally, a major criticism is that sentencing guidelines simply move discretion from judges to prosecutors, who may select charges based upon their sentences (e.g., Frase, 2019; Yang, 2015).

In the 2000s, the Supreme Court held that sentencing guidelines are advisory, rather than required, for federal judges[5] and decreased appellate oversight.[6] However, significant racial and ethnic disparities have persisted over time and guideline changes (King & Light, 2019; Nowacki, 2015; Yang, 2015). Findings about the magnitude of those disparities are mixed, likely due to variability across studies in the years and jurisdictions of the cases, as well as the control variables used in analyses (e.g., whether citizenship is included).

---

[5] United States v. Booker, 543 U.S. 220 (2005).
[6] E.g., Kimbrough v. United States, 552 U.S. 85, 128 S. Ct. 558 (2007).

Some research finds decreases in disparities over time in federal and state courts (King & Light, 2019) and in states with presumptive (required) sentencing guidelines rather than voluntary or no sentencing guidelines (Wang et al., 2013). In contrast, two studies have found small but significant increases in federal sentences for Black and Latinx (relative to White) defendants (Nowacki, 2015; Yang, 2015). In Yang's (2015) study, the increase in sentencing disparities reflects, in part, an increase in prosecutorial charges involving binding mandatory minimums for Black defendants. In sum, although the exact effects of sentencing guidelines are not yet known, it seems clear that, regardless of whether they are required or advisory, they are not sufficient to eliminate the disproportionately harsh sentencing of defendants of color.

Capital Sentencing

Capital cases are distinct from other cases because if a defendant is convicted, the jury hears additional evidence and then decides whether to impose the death penalty or life in prison. Although only twenty-seven states still allow the death penalty (and three of those states have governor-imposed moratoria), death sentencing is critically important, given the high stakes and irreversible nature of state execution.

Because prosecutors do not seek the death penalty in all eligible cases, racial and ethnic disparities in the death penalty can reflect biases in prosecutorial charging decisions as well as in juries' trial judgments (e.g., O'Brien et al., 2016; Shatz et al., 2020). An extensive body of archival research generally shows one or both of two patterns of racial bias. First, the death penalty is more likely to be imposed when victims are White rather than Black or other people of color (e.g., O'Brien et al., 2016; Ulmer et al., 2020; cf. Jennings et al., 2014), reflecting a tendency for both prosecutors and juries to place greater value on the lives of White people, especially White women (e.g., Girgenti-Malone, 2019; Pierce et al., 2017). Second, research often shows Black defendants who are convicted of killing White victims are especially likely to be sentenced to death (Bjerregaard et al., 2017; Johnson et al., 2012; Shatz et al., 2020). Conversely, a recent analysis of death-eligible cases in North Carolina found that prosecutors are unlikely to seek the death penalty in cases involving Black defendants and Black victims (O'Brien et al., 2016). Although not all studies disentangle prosecutorial and jury influences, there is evidence that juries show racial bias in capital sentencing; for example, O'Brien et al. (2016) found that juries in North Carolina were significantly less likely to impose the death penalty when White defendants were convicted of killing Black victims. A landmark study known as the Capital Jury Project found that Black defendants are more likely to be sentenced to death when juries contain more White men; conversely, the presence of Black men in the jury reduces death sentences (Bowers et al., 2001).

There has been less research examining bias against Latinx defendants and victims; however, existing studies show relatively similar patterns. There is some evidence that Latinx defendants are more likely to receive the death penalty, especially when victims are

White (e.g., Shatz et al., 2020), and defendants are less likely to be sentenced to death when they kill Latinx versus White victims (Johnson, 2020). An analysis of California's "special circumstances" that make cases death-eligible shows that some factors, such as gang membership, drive-by shootings, and lying in wait, disproportionately apply to Latinx and Black defendants, facilitating capital charges (Grosso et al., 2019).

Consistent with archival research and providing stronger evidence for jury bias, experimental studies show mock jurors are more likely to give death sentences to Black than to White defendants, especially when victims are White (e.g., Lynch & Haney, 2009). Likewise, White mock jurors are more likely to recommend death for Latinx defendants from low socioeconomic backgrounds, especially when mitigating evidence is weak (Espinoza & Willis-Esqueda, 2015).

In addition to the processes discussed earlier, there are several reasons why racial and ethnic bias may occur in capital juries. Experimental research comparing noncapital and capital murder cases suggests that the mere option of the death penalty may increase racial bias in trial judgments (Glaser et al., 2015). Exacerbating this, because capital jurors must be death-qualified (i.e., willing to impose the death penalty if the case merits it), they are disproportionately likely to be White and men, and they tend to be higher than non–death-qualified jurors in both explicit and implicit racial bias (e.g., Levinson et al., 2014). In addition, White jurors are less likely to identify and/or be influenced by mitigating circumstances (which suggest the death penalty is inappropriate) for Black and Latinx defendants (Johnson et al., 2019; Lynch & Haney, 2009). Compared to Black jurors, White jurors also are more likely to see defendants as dangerous, cruel, and unremorseful, and to feel anger rather than empathy toward them (Bowers et al., 2004). They often have negative views of Black male victims as well, seeing them as non-innocent and blaming them to some extent for their victimization (Girgenti-Malone, 2019). Finally, failing to comprehend notoriously complex judicial instructions for determining capital sentences increases racial biases in those judgments (Lynch & Haney, 2009). Thus, many distinct issues must be addressed in order to reduce or eliminate persistent racial biases in death sentencing.

Recent Legal Developments

In this section, I review recent case law and legislation related to racial disparities in legal outcomes (for a more extensive review, see O'Brien & Grosso, 2020). Although there are some promising developments, unfortunately, most attempts at reform have been short-lived or had limited success. This pattern is consistent with research showing that racial biases accumulate across several stages of the criminal justice and legal process (Kurlychek & Johnson, 2019; Kutateladze et al., 2014; Martinez et al., 2020), suggesting a need to simultaneously enact change on multiple parts of the system in order to meaningfully reduce racial disparities and biases (O'Brien & Grosso, 2020).

Jury Selection

In *Batson v. Kentucky*,[7] the Supreme Court held that eliminating potential jurors on the basis of race violated defendants' rights under the equal protection clause. The *Batson* decision was extended to other social groups, such as Latinx people[8] and women,[9] in subsequent cases. However, as discussed earlier, the use of peremptory challenges to eliminate jurors based on race is a persistent issue (e.g., Semel et al., 2020), and *Batson* challenges are rarely successful (Gabbidon et al., 2008; Semel et al., 2020).

The Supreme Court has continued to affirm and strengthen the *Batson* framework. In *Foster v. Chatman*,[10] the Court reversed a decision by the Georgia Supreme Court, which held that the prosecutor's elimination of all potential Black jurors was not racially motivated, despite written evidence to the contrary (e.g., prosecution documents highlighting Black venire members). In *Flowers v. Mississippi*,[11] defendant Curtis Flowers had been tried six times for murder due to mistrials and prosecutorial misconduct. Across the five trials for which data on race were recorded, prosecutors used peremptory challenges to strike forty-one of forty-two Black venire members. The Supreme Court held that this pattern, along with inconsistencies in the number of questions and stated reasons for striking Black and White jurors, showed discriminatory intent. The fact that cases with such clear patterns of racial disparities made it to the US Supreme Court illustrates the ongoing challenges in enforcing *Batson*, leading some scholars to call for the elimination of peremptory challenges (e.g., Marder, 2012).

In an encouraging development, in recent years, high courts in Washington, Connecticut, and California have called for reforms in the use of peremptory challenges that address the role of implicit bias (Schwartzapfel, 2020). In 2020, the State of California enacted A.B. No. 3070, which enabled judges to consider implicit as well as deliberate biases in jury selection. The bill includes a list of reasons for striking potential jurors (e.g., distrusting law enforcement, receiving state benefits, and the ability to speak another language) that are presumed to be pretextual rationales for race-based challenges unless proven otherwise. Such structural changes to jury procedures have the potential to significantly reduce discrimination in jury selection and, by extension, legal outcomes. The Washington Supreme Court enacted similar changes in 2018 with General Rule 37, which applies to both criminal and civil trials.

Jury Deliberation

A recent case, *Peña-Rodriguez v. Colorado*,[12] addressing racial bias in jury deliberation has been characterized as "the new *Batson*" (Gonzalez, 2018). The defendant, Miguel

---

[7] *Batson*, 476 U.S. 79.
[8] Hernandez v. New York, 500 U.S. 352 (1991).
[9] J.E.B. v. Alabama ex rel. T.B., 511 U.S. 127 (1994).
[10] Foster v. Chatman, 578 U.S. ___, 136 S. Ct. 1737 (2016).
[11] Flowers v. Mississippi, 588 U.S. ___, 139 S. Ct. 2228 (2019).
[12] *Peña-Rodriguez*, 580 U.S. ___, 37 S. Ct. 855.

Peña-Rodriguez, was charged with unlawful sexual contact and harassment. He was convicted by a Colorado jury, but shortly after the verdict, two members of the jury informed the defendant attorney that an influential juror had made racist comments about the defendant and an alibi witness during deliberation (e.g., "nine times out of ten Mexicans were guilty of being aggressive towards women," calling the witness "an illegal"). Peña Rodriguez's request for a new trial was denied because a common rule of evidence, known as the impeachment rule, states that jurors' testimony may not be used to overturn a verdict. The majority opinion of the Supreme Court, written by Justice Kennedy, held that testimony by jurors about overt racial bias that cast "serious doubt on the fairness and impartiality of the jury's deliberations and resulting verdict" required an exception to the impeachment rule.[13]

Although *Peña-Rodriguez* establishes a substantive means of addressing racial biases in jury deliberation, legal commentators have argued that the ruling is incomplete. Because the ruling focuses on overtly racist statements, it does not address the influence of implicit or subtle biases on jury decision-making (Jolly, 2019; Sundquist, 2018) or the limited options for identifying and removing potential jurors with racist beliefs (Crump, 2019). In addition, jurors may not know about their ability to testify about racist statements that occur during deliberation (Spiess, 2018). Thus, there is reason to suspect that, on its own, *Peña Rodriguez* may not have a large effect on racial biases in legal outcomes.

Sentencing

Recent legislation and court cases related to racial disparities in sentencing have, in large part, focused on sentences for drug crimes. During the War on Drugs, the Anti-Drug Abuse Act of 1986,[14] equated 1 gram of crack cocaine to 100 grams of powder cocaine for sentencing purposes. Because the crack form of cocaine was much less expensive than the powdered form, people prosecuted for possession of it were disproportionately Black or other people of color, leading to a massive expansion of people of color in prison. As such, the Act created a lasting form of structural racism that has devastated communities of color (Kirk & Wakefield, 2018).

In 2010, under the so-called Fair Sentencing Act, Congress reduced the disparity between crack and powder cocaine to a 1:18 ratio. Both court cases[15] and the First Step Act of 2018 made that reduction apply retroactively for all but the lowest (Tier 3) charges. A recent case challenged that exception. Tarahrick Terry was sentenced to fifteen years in prison for possessing under 4 grams of crack, worth approximately $50, but, because of two minor drug charges in his teens, he was sentenced as a "career offender." The Supreme Court upheld his sentence, stating that the First Step legislation clearly did not include

---

[13] *Id.* at 869.

[14] Anti-Drug Abuse Act of 1986. https://www.congress.gov/bill/99th-congress/house-bill/5484

[15] Dorsey v. United States, 567 U.S. 260 (2012).

Tier 3 offenses, and only additional legislation could change that.[16] This decision illustrates how legislatively mandated disparities across drugs in sentencing guidelines can create powerful forms of structural racism.

Introduction of Research on Racial Disparities as Evidence

In an earlier section, I reviewed some of the considerable evidence that the outcomes of death penalty cases can be influenced by defendant and victim race. A lingering issue involves how such research may be used as evidence in legal cases, particularly in appeals of capital sentences. In a landmark case, *McCleskey v. Kemp*,[17] a divided Supreme Court held that defendants could not use statistical evidence of aggregate racial disparities in death penalty outcomes as evidence that their individual cases were affected by racial bias. Although this decision has been widely criticized (e.g., Maratea, 2019), the Supreme Court declined opportunities to revisit it in 2017 (Neklason, 2021).

Since *McCleskey*, several states have eliminated or imposed moratoria on the death penalty, at least in part due to concerns about racial disparities (Neklason, 2021). Two states, Kentucky and North Carolina, enacted legislation that allows defendants sentenced to death to use statistical data in their appeals. However, neither has been successful in providing meaningful relief (Donnelly, 2018). The Kentucky Racial Justice Act of 1998 allows defendants to use statistical evidence to show that capital charges were racially motivated, but it does not address biases in the trial itself. Given the limited data on charging and attempts by prosecutors to mask racial patterns, over ten years, it was used successfully by only one defendant (Donnelly, 2018). The North Carolina Racial Justice Act, enacted in 2009, allowed defendants to challenge capital sentences due to racial bias throughout the trial process. However, the Act was repealed retroactively in 2013. Recently, the North Carolina Supreme Court held the repeal could not be retroactive[18]; thus, the Act still may provide relief for defendants who petitioned for new hearings while it was law. Its quick repeal shows how legislative efforts to reduce racial bias in legal outcomes are vulnerable to the political climate.

Future Research on Race, Ethnicity, and Legal Outcomes

There are several important directions for scholars to continue to advance our understanding of the effects of race and ethnicity on legal outcomes (for a more extensive discussion, see Hunt, 2015). First, researchers who study disparities should expand the scope of legal outcomes that are examined. There has been extensive research on racial and ethnic bias in criminal outcomes. In comparison, there has been relatively little work on disparities in civil cases, which also have considerable potential for bias (Girvan & Marek, 2016).

---

[16] Terry v. United States, Docket 20-5904 (decided U.S., June 14, 2021).

[17] McCleskey v. Kemp, 481 U.S. 279 (1987).

[18] State v. Burke, No. 181-A93-4 (N.C. 2020); State v. Ramseur, No. 388A10 (N.C. 2020).

For example, an analysis of employment discrimination cases (Berrey et al., 2017) found evidence of several racial disparities; plaintiffs of color struggled to find attorneys willing to represent them, and Black defendants had a higher likelihood of having their cases end with a summary judgment in favor of their employer. In addition, there should be more research examining the role of race in specialty courts, such as family courts (Lens, 2019) and drug courts. Finally, the failure of a Kentucky grand jury to indict police officers for the death of Breonna Taylor is a reminder of the critical, yet understudied, role that grand juries can have in criminal cases related to race.

Psychologists should continue to improve the quality of experimental research on juror and jury decision-making, both to more accurately reflect actual trials and to resolve the disparities between experimental and archival findings discussed in this chapter. More experimental research needs to go beyond Black–White comparisons to examine biases against other racial and ethnic groups. Likewise, manipulations of the race/ethnicity of defendants and other trial participants need to be richer, going beyond simply a name or photo. Further, jury research needs to more critically engage with intersectionality, examining the ways in which race and ethnicity intersect with gender, social class, sexual orientation, immigration status, disability, and other important identities. Likewise, it needs to address the effects of cumulative disadvantage, for example, by including conditions that enable comparisons between defendants who not only differ in race/ethnicity but also in terms of pretrial release, quality of representation, and other aspects of cases that covary with race in actual trials.

Other important strategies for improving research involve increasing interdisciplinary collaborations and engaging in more multimethod and multistage studies. Scholars from several fields, including psychology, criminology, sociology, anticarceral feminism, and law, study racial/ethnic disparities in legal outcomes. However, in many cases, work in one discipline goes unseen by scholars in other disciplines. For example, psychological research often fails to cite ethnographic research that provides valuable insights into the mechanisms of racial/ethnic disparities (e.g., Clair, 2020; Gonzalez Van Cleve, 2016) or nonempirical legal scholarship by critical race theorists (e.g., Capers, 2014). Greater integration and collaboration across disciplines has the potential to expand our theoretical analyses, as well as quality, breadth, and depth of our work. In addition, studies that take multimethod approaches, combining qualitative methods, such as interviews, content analysis, or ethnography, with quantitative methods, has great potential to advance the field (e.g., Berrey et al., 2017). Likewise, research that includes multiple stages in the criminal justice and/or legal process helps to elucidate the many factors that contribute to racial/ethnic disparities in legal outcomes (Kurlychek & Johnson, 2019).

Finally, it is critical for scholars to continue developing and testing interventions to reduce racial/ethnic disparities (as well as disparities based on other social categories and intersectional positions) at different points in the criminal justice and legal process. For example, Schuller et al. (2009) found that asking mock jurors to reflect on the ways that race might affect their judgments reduced racial bias in their trial judgments, likely because it sensitized them to the potential for bias and motivated them to guard against it. Interventions and other insights from social scientists can be developed into policies, reforms, and structural changes, such as California A.B. No. 3070[19] and Washington GR 37,[20] which are aimed at reducing biases in legal outcomes (O'Brien & Grosso, 2020).

Conclusion

In the majority decision for *Peña-Rodriguez v. Colorado*, Justice Kennedy characterized racial bias as "a familiar and recurring evil that, if left unaddressed, would risk systematic injury to the administration of justice."[21] The research in this chapter supports this view, showing pervasive effects of race and ethnicity in jury selection, jury decision-making, and sentencing, including the death penalty. Throughout the criminal justice and legal process, these biases accumulate into substantial disparities, ending in a system of mass incarceration that disproportionately affects Black and Latinx defendants, as well as their families and communities. As social scientists, it is incumbent on us to study this "recurring evil" so that our knowledge can contribute to reforms that facilitate the administration of equal justice.

References

Abshire, J., & Bornstein, B. H. (2003). Juror sensitivity to the cross-race effect. *Law and Human Behavior, 27*(5), 471–480.

Ackermann, N., Goodman, M. S., Gilbert, K., Arroyo-Johnson, C., & Pagano, M. (2015). Race, law, and health: Examination of 'Stand Your Ground' and defendant convictions in Florida. *Social Science & Medicine, 142*, 194–201.

Alexander, M. (2010). *The new Jim Crow: Mass incarceration in the age of colorblindness.* New Press.

Baumgartner, F. R., Epp, D. A., & Shoub, K. (2018). *Suspect citizens: What 20 million traffic stops tell us about policing and race.* Cambridge University Press.

Berrey, E., Nelson, R. L., & Nielson, L. B. (2017). *Rights on trial: How workplace discrimination law perpetuates inequality.* University of Chicago Press.

Bjerregaard, B. E., Smith, M. D., Cochran, J. K., & Fogel, S. J. (2017). A further examination of the liberation hypothesis in capital murder trials. *Crime and Delinquency, 63*(8), 1017–1038.

Bowers, W. J., Brewer, T. W., & Sandys, M. (2004, Summer). Crossing racial boundaries: a closer look at the roots of racial bias in capital sentencing when the defendant is black and the victim is white. *DePaul Law Review, 53*(4), 1497–1538.

Bowers, W. J., Steiner, B. D., & Sandys, M. (2001). Death sentencing in black and white: An empirical analysis of the role of jurors' race and jury racial composition. *University of Pennsylvania Journal of Constitutional Law, 3*, 171–274.

Bradbury, M. D., & Williams, M. R. (2013). Diversity and citizen participation: The effect of race on juror decision making. *Administration & Society, 45*(5), 563–582.

Capers, I. B. (Ed.). (2014). Symposium: Twenty-plus years of critical race theory and criminal justice: looking backward, looking forward [Special issue]. *Ohio State Journal of Criminal Law, 12*(1), 1–114

---

[19] Juries: Peremptory Challenges, A.B. No. 3070 (Cal. 2020). https://leginfo.legislature.ca.gov/faces/billTextClient.xhtml?bill_id=201920200AB3070

[20] Jury Selection. GR 37 (Wash. Gen. Ct. 2018). https://www.courts.wa.gov/court_rules/?fa=court_rules.display&group=ga&ruleid=gagr37

[21] *Peña-Rodriguez*, 580 U.S. ___, 37 S. Ct. at 855.

Caravelis, C., Chiricos, T., & Bales, W. (2011). Static and dynamic indicators of minority threat in sentencing outcomes: A multi-level analysis. *Journal of Quantitative Criminology*, *27*(4), 405–425.

Carson, E. A. (2020). *Prisoners in 2019* (NCJ 255115). Bureau of Justice Statistics. https://bjs.ojp.gov/cont ent/pub/pdf/p19.pdf

Clair, M. (2020). *Privilege and punishment: How race and class matter in criminal court*. Princeton University Press.

Clair, M., & Winter, A. S. (2016). How judges think about racial disparities: Situational decision-making in the criminal justice system. *Criminology: An Interdisciplinary Journal*, *54*(2), 332–359.

Clow, K. A., Lant, J. M., & Cutler, B. L. (2013). Perceptions of defendant culpability in pretrial publicity: The effects of defendant ethnicity and participant gender. *Race and Social Problems*, *5*(4), 250–261.

Cole, E. R. (2009). Intersectionality and research in psychology. *American Psychologist*, *64*(3), 170–180.

Cooper, B. (2016). Intersectionality. In L. Disch & M. Hawkesworth (Eds.), *Oxford handbook of feminist theory* (pp. 385–406). Oxford University Press.

Crenshaw, K. W. (1989). Demarginalizing the intersection of race and sex: A Black feminist critique of anti-discrimination doctrine, feminist theory, and antiracist politics. *University of Chicago Legal Forum*, *1989*, 139–167.

Crump, L. (2019). Removing race from the jury deliberation room: The shortcomings of *Pena-Rodriguez v. Colorado* and how to address them. *University of Richmond Law Review*, *52*, 475–493.

DeCamp, W., & DeCamp, E. (2020). It's still about race: Peremptory challenge use on black prospective jurors. *The Journal of Research in Crime and Delinquency*, *57*(1), 3–30.

Delgado, R., & Stefancic, J. (2017). *Critical race theory: An introduction* (3rd ed.). New York University Press.

Department of Justice. (2015). *Investigation of the Ferguson Police Department*. https://www.justice.gov/sites/ default/files/opa/press-releases/attachments/2015/03/04/ferguson_police_department_report.pdf

Desmarais, S. L., & Zottola, S. A. (2019). Violence risk assessment: Current status and contemporary issues. *Marquette Law Review*, *103*, 793–817.

Devine, D. J. (2012). *Jury decision making: The state of the science*. New York University Press.

Devine, D. J., & Caughlin, D. E. (2014). Do they matter? A meta-analytic investigation of individual charac-teristics and guilt judgments. *Psychology, Public Policy, and Law*, *20*(2), 109–134.

Devine, D. J., Krouse, P. C., Cavanaugh, C. M., & Basora, J. C. (2016). Evidentiary, extra-evidentiary, and deliberation process predictors of real jury verdicts. *Law and Human Behavior*, *40*(6), 670–682.

Doerner, J. K. (2015). The joint effects of gender and race/ethnicity on sentencing outcomes in federal courts. *Women & Criminal Justice*, *25*(5), 313–338.

Donnelly, E. A. (2018). Can legislatures redress racial discrimination in capital punishment? Evaluating racial justice acts in response to *McCleskey*. *The Journal of Criminal Law*, *82*(5), 388–401.

Elis, L. (2017). Examining sentencing disparity in Virginia: The impact of race and sex on mitigating depar-tures for drug offenders. *Sociology of Crime, Law and Deviance*, *22*, 115–133.

Espinoza, R. K. E., & Willis-Esqueda, C. (2015). The influence of mitigation evidence, ethnicity, and SES on death penalty decisions by European American and Latino venire persons. *Cultural Diversity and Ethnic Minority Psychology*, *21*(2), 288–299.

Ewald, A. C. (2012). Collateral consequences in the American states. *Social Science Quarterly*, *93*(1), 211–247.

Farrell, A. P., Pennington, L. J. D. P., & Cronin, S. P. (2013). Juror perceptions of the legitimacy of legal authorities and decision making in criminal cases. *Law & Social Inquiry*, *38*(4), 773.

Flanagan, F. X. (2018). Race, gender, and juries: Evidence from North Carolina. *Journal of Law and Economics*, *61*(2), 189.

Franklin, T. W., & Fearn, N. E. (2015). Sentencing Asian offenders in state courts: The influence of a prevalent stereotype. *Crime & Delinquency*, *61*(1), 96–120.

Frase, R. S. (2019). Forty years of American sentencing guidelines: What have we learned? *Crime and Justice*, *48*, 79–129.

Freiburger, T. L., & Hilinski, C. M. (2013). An examination of the interactions of race and gender on sentenc-ing decisions using a trichotomous dependent variable. *Crime & Delinquency*, *59*, 59–86.

Freiburger, T. L., & Sheeran, A. M. (2020). The joint effects of race, ethnicity, gender, and age on the incarcera-tion and sentence length decisions. *Race and Justice*, *10*(2), 203–222.

Gabbidon, S. L., Kowal, L. K., Jordan, K. L., Roberts, J. L., & Vincenzi, N. (2008). Race-based peremp-tory challenges: An empirical analysis of litigation from the U.S. Court of Appeals, 2002-2006. *American Journal of Criminal Justice*, *33*(1), 59–68.

Gaertner, S. L., & Dovidio, J. F. (1986). The aversive form of racism. In J. F. Dovidio & S. L. Gaertner (Eds.), *Prejudice, discrimination, and racism* (pp. 61–89). Academic Press.

Girgenti-Malone, A. A. (2019). Empathy, distance, and blame: juror perceptions of black male homicide victims in capital cases. *Journal of Ethnicity in Criminal Justice, 17*(1), 57–79.

Girvan, E., & Marek, H. J. (2016). Psychological and structural bias in civil jury awards. *Journal of Aggression, Conflict and Peace Research, 8*(4), 247–257.

Glaser, J., Martin, K. D., & Kahn, K. B. (2015). Possibility of death sentence has divergent effect on verdicts for Black and White defendants. *Law and Human Behavior, 39*(6), 539–546.

Gonzalez, J. S. (2018). The new *Batson*: Opening the door of the jury deliberation room after *Peña-Rodriguez v. Colorado. St. Louis University Law Journal, 62*, 397–418.

Gonzalez Van Cleve, N. (2016). *Crook county: Racism and injustice in America's largest criminal court.* Stanford University Press.

Gross, S., Possley, M., & Stephens, K. (2017). *Race and wrongful convictions in the United States.* National Registry of Exonerations. http://www.law.umich.edu/special/exoneration/Documents/ Race_and_ Wrongful_Convictions.pdf

Grosso, C. M., Fagan, J. A., Laurence, M., Baldus, D. C., Woodworth, G. W., & Newell, R. (2019). Death by stereotype: Race, ethnicity, and California's failure to implement *Furman's* narrowing requirement. *UCLA Law Review, 66*, 1394.

Hannaford-Agor, P., & Waters, N. L. (2011). Safe harbors from fair-cross-section challenges? The practical limitations of measuring representation in the jury pool. *Journal of Empirical Legal Studies, 8*(4), 762–791.

Hauser, W., & Peck, J. H. (2017). The intersection of crime seriousness, discretion, and race: A test of the liberation hypothesis. *Justice Quarterly, 34*(1), 166–192.

Hodson, G., Hooper, H., Dovidio, J. F., & Gaertner, S. L. (2005). Aversive racism in Britain: The use of inadmissible evidence in legal decisions. *European Journal of Social Psychology, 35*(4), 437–448.

Hoppe, T. A. (2015). Disparate risks of conviction under Michigan's felony HIV disclosure law: An observational analysis of convictions and HIV diagnoses, 1992-2010. *Punishment & Society, 17*(1), 73–93.

Hunt, J. S. (2015). Race, ethnicity, and culture in jury decision making. *Annual Review of Law and Social Science, 11*, 269.

Jennings, W. G., Richards, T. N., Smith, M. D., Bjerregaard, B., & Fogel, S. J. (2014). A critical examination of the 'White victim effect' and death penalty decision-making from a propensity score matching approach: The North Carolina experience. *Journal of Criminal Justice, 42*(5), 384–398.

Johnson, B. D., & Betsinger, S. (2009). Punishing the "model minority": Asian-American criminal sentencing outcomes in federal district courts. *Criminology: An Interdisciplinary Journal, 47*(4), 1045–1090.

Johnson, S. L. (2020). The influence of Latino ethnicity on the imposition of the death penalty. *Annual Review of Law and Social Science, 16*, 421–431.

Johnson, S. L., Blume, J. H., Eisenberg, T., Hans, V. P., & Wells, M. T. (2012). The Delaware death penalty: an empirical study. *Iowa Law Review, 97*, 1925–1964.

Johnson, S. L., Blume, J. H., Hritz, A. C., & Royer, C. E. (2019). Race, intellectual disability, and death: An empirical inquiry into invidious influences on *Atkins* determinations. *UCLA Law Review, 66*, 1506–1531.

Jolly, R. L. (2019). The new impartial jury mandate. *Michigan Law Review, 117*, 713–760.

Kang, J., Bennett, M., Carbado, D., Casey, P., Dasgupta, N., Faigman, D., Godsil, R., Greenwald, A. G., Levinson, J. D., & Mnookin, J. (2012). Implicit bias in the courtroom. *UCLA Law Review, 59*, 1124–1186.

King, R. D., & Light, M. T. (2019). Have racial and ethnic disparities in sentencing declined? *Crime & Justice, 48*, 365–437.

Kirk, D. S., & Wakefield, S. (2018). Collateral consequences of punishment: A critical review and path forward. *Annual Review of Criminology, 1*, 171–194.

Kurinec, C. A., & Weaver, C. A., III. (2019). Dialect on trial: Use of African American Vernacular English influences juror appraisals. *Psychology, Crime & Law, 25*(8), 803–828.

Kurlychek, M. C., & Johnson, B. D. (2019). Cumulative disadvantage in the American criminal justice system. Annual Review of Criminology, 2, 291–319.

Kutateladze, B. L., Andiloro, N. R., Johnson, B. D., & Spohn, C. C. (2014). Cumulative disadvantage: Racial and ethnic disparity in prosecution and sentencing. *Criminology, 52*(3), 514–551.

Kutateladze, B. L., & Lawson, V. Z. (2018). Is a plea really a bargain? An analysis of plea and trial dispositions in New York City. *Crime and Delinquency, 64*(7), 856–887.

Lane, K. A., Kang, J., & Banaji, M. R. (2007). Implicit social cognition and law. Annual Review of Law and Social Science, *3*, 427–451.

Lehmann, P. S. (2020). Race, ethnicity, crime type, and the sentencing of violent felony offenders. *Crime and Delinquency, 66*(6–7), 770–805.

Lehmann, P. S., & Gomez, A. I. (2021). Split sentencing in Florida: Race/ethnicity, gender, age, and the mitigation of prison sentence length. *American Journal of Criminal Justice, 46*(2), 345–376.

Lens, V. (2019). Judging the other: The intersection of race, gender, and class in family court. *Family Court Review, 57*(1), 72–87.

Levinson, J. D., Smith, R. J., & Young, D. M. (2014). Devaluing death: An empirical study of implicit racial bias on jury-eligible citizens in six death penalty states. *New York University Law Review, 89*, 513–581.

Levinson, J. D., & Young, D. M. (2010). Different shades of bias: Skin tone, implicit racial bias, and judgments of ambiguous evidence. *West Virginia Law Review, 112*, 307–350.

Lynch, M., & Haney, C. (2009). Capital jury deliberation: Effects on death sentencing, comprehension, and discrimination. *Law and Human Behavior, 33*(6), 481–496.

Maeder, E. M., & Hunt, J. S. (2011). Talking about a black man: The influence of defendant and character witness race on jurors' use of character evidence. *Behavioral Sciences & Law, 29*(4), 608–620.

Maeder, E. M., Yamamoto, S., & McManus, L. A. (2015). Race salience in Canada: Testing multiple manipulations and target races. *Psychology, Public Policy, and Law, 21*(4), 442–451.

Maratea, R. J. (2019). *Killing with prejudice: Institutionalized racism in American capital punishment.* New York University Press.

Marder, N. S. (2012). *Batson* revisited. *Iowa Law Review, 97*, 1585–1612.

Martinez, B. P., Petersen, N., & Omori, M. (2020). Time, money, and punishment: Institutional racial-ethnic inequalities in pretrial detention and case outcomes. *Crime and Delinquency, 66*(6–7), 837–863.

Mayson, S. G., & Stevenson, M. T. (2020). Misdemeanors by the numbers. *Boston College Law Review, 61*, 971–1044.

Mitchell, O. (2005). A meta-analysis of race and sentencing research: Explaining the inconsistencies. *Journal of Quantitative Criminology, 21*, 439–466. https://doi.org/10.1007/s10940-005-7362-7

Mitchell, T. L., Haw, R. M., Pfeifer, J. E., & Meissner, C. A. (2005). Racial bias in mock juror decision-making: A meta-analytic review of defendant treatment. *Law and Human Behavior, 29*(6), 621–637.

Morrison, M., DeVaul-Fetters, A., & Gawronski, B. (2016). Stacking the jury: Legal professionals' peremptory challenges reflect jurors' levels of implicit race bias. *Personality and Social Psychology Bulletin, 42*(8), 1129–1141.

Neklason, A. (2021). The "death penalty's *Dred Scott*" lives on. *The Atlantic.* https://www.theatlantic.com/politics/archive/2019/06/legacy-mccleskey-v-kemp/591424/

Nowacki, J. S. (2015). Race, ethnicity, and judicial discretion: The influence of the *United States v. Booker* decision. *Crime and Delinquency, 61*(10), 1360.

O'Brien, B., & Grosso, C. M. (2020). Criminal trials and reforms intended to reduce the impact of race: A review. *Annual Review of Law and Social Science, 16*, 117–130.

O'Brien, B., Grosso, C. M., Woodworth, G., & Taylor, A. (2016). Untangling the role of race in capital charging and sentencing in North Carolina. *North Carolina Law Review, 94*, 1997–2045.

Peter-Hagene, L. (2019). Jurors' cognitive depletion and performance during jury deliberation as a function of jury diversity and defendant race. *Law and Human Behavior, 43*(3), 232–249.

Pierce, G. L., Radelet, M. L., Posick, C., & Lyman, T. (2014). Race and the construction of evidence in homicide cases. *American Journal of Criminal Justice, 39*(4), 771–786.

Pierce, G. L., Radelet, M. L., & Sharp, S. (2017). Race and death sentencing for Oklahoma homicides committed between 1990 and 2012. *Journal of Criminal Law & Criminology, 107*(4), 733–756.

Rattan, A., Levine, C. S., Dweck, C. S., & Eberhardt, J. L. (2012). Race and the fragility of the legal distinction between juveniles and adults. *PLoS One, 7*(5), Article e36680.

Rehavi, M. M., & Starr, S. B. (2014). Racial disparity in federal criminal sentences. *Journal of Political Economy, 122*(6), 1320.

Rios, V. M. (2011). *Punished: Policing the lives of Black and Latino boys.* New York University Press.

Romain Dagenhardt, D. M. (2020). Observing gender and race discourses in probation review hearings. *Feminist Criminology, 15*(4), 492–515.

Rovner, J. (2021). *Racial disparities in youth incarceration persists.* The Sentencing Project. https://www.sentencingproject.org/ publications/racial-disparities-in-youth-incarceration- persist/

Salerno, J. M., Peter-Hagene, L. C., & Jay, A. C. V. (2019). Women and African Americans are less influential when they express anger during group decision making. *Group Processes & Intergroup Relations*, *22*(1), 57–79.

Schlesinger, T. (2011). The failure of race neutral policies: How mandatory terms and sentencing enhancements contribute to mass racialized incarceration. *Crime & Delinquency*, *57*(1), 56–81.

Schuller, R. A., Kazoleas, V., & Kawakami, K. (2009). The impact of prejudice screening procedures on racial bias in the courtroom. *Law and Human Behavior*, *33*(4), 320–328.

Schwartzapfel, B. (2020, May 11). A growing number of state courts are confronting unconscious racism in jury selection. *The Marshall Project*. https://www.themarshallproject.org/2020/05/11/a-growing-number-of-state-courts-are-confronting-unconscious-racism-in-jury-selection

Semel, E., Downard, D., Tolman, E., Weis, A., Craig, D., & Hanlock, C. (2020). *Whitewashing the jury box: How California perpetuates the discriminatory exclusion of Black and Latinx jurors*. Berkeley Law Death Penalty Clinic. https://www.law.berkeley.edu/wp-content/uploads/2020/06/Whitewashing-the-Jury-Box.pdf

Shatz, S. F., Pierce, G. L., & Radelet, M. L. (2020). Race, ethnicity, and the death penalty in San Diego County: The predictable consequences of excessive discretion. *Columbia Human Rights Law Review*, *51*, 1070–1098.

Skorinko, J. L., & Spellman, B. A. (2013). Stereotypic crimes: How group-crime associations affect memory and (sometimes) verdicts and sentencing. *Victims & Offenders*, *8*(3), 278–307.

Sommers, S. R. (2006). On racial diversity and group decision making: Identifying multiple effects of racial composition on jury deliberations. *Journal of Personality and Social Psychology*, *90*(4), 597–612.

Sommers, S. R., & Adekanmbi, O. O. (2008). Race and juries: An experimental psychology perspective. In G. S. Parks, S. Jones, & W. J. Cardi (Eds.), *Critical race realism: Intersections of psychology, race, and law* (pp. 78–93). New Press.

Sommers, S. R., & Ellsworth, P. C. (2000). Race in the courtroom: Perceptions of guilt and dispositional attributions. *Personality and Social Psychology Bulletin*, *26*(11), 1367–1379.

Sommers, S. R., & Ellsworth, P. C. (2001). White juror bias: An investigation of prejudice against Black defendants in the American courtroom. *Psychology, Public Policy, and Law*, *7*(1), 201–229.

Spiess, N. A. (2018). *Peña-Rodriguez v. Colorado*: A critical, but incomplete, step in the never-ending war on racial bias. *Denver Law Review*, *95*, 809–841.

Steffensmeier, D., & Demuth, S. (2006). Does gender modify the effects of race-ethnicity on criminal sanctioning? Sentences for male and female White, Black, and Hispanic defendants. *Journal of Quantitative Criminology*, *22*(3), 241–261.

Steffensmeier, D., Painter-Davis, N., & Ulmer, J. (2017). Intersectionality of race, ethnicity, gender, and age on criminal punishment. *Sociological Perspectives*, *60*(4), 810–833.

Steffensmeier, D., Ulmer, J., & Kramer, J. (1998). The Interaction of Race, Gender, and Age in Criminal Sentencing: The Punishment Cost of Being Young, Black and Male. *Criminology*, *36*(4), 763–797.

Stevenson, B. (2010). *Illegal racial discrimination in jury selection: A continuing legacy*. Equal Justice Initiative.

Sundquist, C. B. (2018). Uncovering juror racial bias. *Denver Law Review*, *96*, 309–351.

Ulmer, J., & Bradley, M. S. (2018). Punishment in Indian Country: Ironies of federal punishment of Native Americans. *Justice Quarterly*, *35*, 751–781.

Ulmer, J. T., & Konefal, K. (2019). Sentencing the other: Punishment of Latinx defendants. *UCLA Law Review*, *66*, 1716–1761.

Ulmer, J. T., Kramer, J. H., & Zajac, G. (2020). The race of defendants and victims in Pennsylvania death penalty decisions: 2000–2010. *Justice Quarterly*, *37*(5), 955–983.

Wang, X., Mears, D. P., Spohn, C., & Dario, L. (2013). Assessing the differential effects of race and ethnicity on sentence outcomes under different sentencing systems. *Crime & Delinquency*, *59*, 87–114.

Wegener, D. T., Kerr, N. L., Fleming, M. A., & Petty, R. E. (2000). Flexible corrections of juror judgments: Implications for jury instructions. *Psychology, Public Policy, and Law*, *6*(3), 629–654.

Welch, K. (2007). Black criminal stereotypes and racial profiling. *Journal of Contemporary Criminal Justice*, *23*(3), 276–288.

Wu, J., & Kim, D.-Y. (2014). The model minority myth for noncitizen immigration offenses and sentencing outcomes. *Race and Justice*, *4*(4), 303–332.

Yamamoto, S., & Maeder, E. M. (2017). Defendant and juror race in a necessity case: An ultimate attribution error. *Journal of Ethnicity in Criminal Justice, 15*(3), 270–284.

Yang, C. S. (2015). Free at last? Judicial discretion and racial disparities in federal sentencing. *The Journal of Legal Studies, 44*, 75–111.

Law, Psychology, and Wrongful Convictions

Brandon L. Garrett *and* William Crozier

Abstract

The study of psychology in law is integrally linked to wrongful convictions. Archival research and case studies of cases in which the wrong person was convicted of a crime provide real-life examples of errors that psychologists seek to understand. In turn, psychological research, particularly laboratory studies, provide explanations for how these errors can occur, making it easier to detect and address wrongful convictions in the future. This chapter discusses how eyewitness evidence, forensic evidence, false confessions, informant testimony, alibi evidence, police technology, plea bargaining, and features of the adversarial legal system can result in wrongful convictions—and how research has led to recommendations to avoid them. However, the work is not complete, and we make recommendations for how new research can address gaps in our current understanding, especially in areas where legal protections in the United States are currently inadequate.

Key Words: wrongful convictions, legal errors, biases, judgments, decision-making

Wrongful convictions uncovered around the world, including with the benefit of new technology such as DNA testing, have sparked renewed awareness of the sources of error in criminal cases, and a new generation of legal and scientific research, as well as law and policy reform (Garrett et al., 2021). Exonerations, including in death penalty cases, but also in low-level criminal cases, are now common globally, exposing and sparking new debates about "the fallibility of human justice" (Amnesty International, 2015). These exonerations have attracted substantial and mainstream media attention, in newspapers, films, podcasts, books, and other print and digital media (Scheck et al., 2000). Researchers in law, criminology, psychology, and in a range of other disciplines, have documented the scale and nature of those wrongful convictions and they have conducted research into the causes of wrongful convictions. In turn, contributions from wrongful conviction research, which, in addition to law and psychology, has involved interdisciplinary contributions from criminology, genetics, neuroscience, and statistics, among the relevant fields, have impacted the law. These impacts have been seen through expert reports in individual cases, policy recommendations that have impacted judicial and police practices, and judicial rulings and legislation designed to improve criminal procedure.

This chapter begins by describing archival research studying wrongful convictions and then turning to experimental research regarding underlying causes of evidentiary error and wrongful convictions. The chapter discusses key areas in which such research has been conducted in the past and turns to emerging and underdeveloped areas of interest in law and psychology, including as notions of wrongful convictions expand and causes are examined across different stages in the criminal legal process. New work in psychology has moved beyond errors in evidence collection to examine interactions in areas that legal researchers and practitioners have long identified as important, including screening, plea bargaining, and postconviction law.

The interchange between law and psychology will ideally grow still more productive in the future. We conclude by discussing common themes, including improved documentation, debiasing, and blinding, across areas of law and psychology research regarding the identification and prevention of wrongful convictions. The intersection of law and psychology has been particularly productive in the area of wrongful convictions research, with decades of research resulting in concrete changes to law enforcement practices, statutes, and judicial doctrine. However, in the years ahead, far more can be done to both enrich psychological research, better connect it to legal research and practices, reorient legal rules, and understand the causes and cures for wrongful convictions.

Wrongful Convictions Research

In a first generation of work studying wrongful convictions, a body of archival and descriptive research analyzed characteristics of known wrongful conviction cases. Early work was case study–oriented (Borchard, 1932) and documented the existence of wrongful convictions, which many legal professionals and members of the public doubted could occur. That work later became systematized and involved studies of defined sets of cases, focusing on exonerations, in which there was a legal decision to overturn a conviction based in part on newly discovered evidence of innocence. One particular area of focus has been DNA exonerations. DNA exoneration cases have been of special interest due to their prominence but also the clarity of the evidence of innocence in those cases, in which new DNA technology arrived and shed new light on closed cases (Garrett, 2011). Beginning with the first postconviction DNA exonerations in the United States in 1989, modern DNA testing has led to more than 370 exonerations. There is no comparable body of postconviction DNA exonerations elsewhere in the world, although there have now been DNA exonerations in many countries (Garrett, 2017).

A body of empirical research has now explored the facts underlying DNA exonerations in the United States (Garrett, 2011; see also http://www.convictingtheinnoc ent.com/). Additional research has studied still broader groups of exonerations. The best-known collection of data concerning all exonerations (both DNA and non-DNA) in the United States is reported by the National Registry of Exonerations, which documents more than 2,700 individuals who have been exonerated since 1989. The current count of all exonerations is frequently updated and may be found on the National Registry's website (https://www.law.umich.edu/special/exoneration/Pages/about.aspx). The Death Penalty Information Center (DPIC) maintains an archive of death row exonerations in the United States. Still, additional work has examined sets of exonerations in a number of countries around the world, as increasingly documented by scholars in, for example, Australia, China, Germany, and Switzerland (Garrett et al., 2021). These sets of exonerations, and the research conducted to examine them, have underscored how eyewitnesses can misidentify innocent suspects, forensic evidence can be unreliable and flawed, confessions can be false, and informants can lie on the stand. Organizations have created easy-to-navigate websites for members of the public to learn about the causes behind and people impacted by wrongful convictions. A more recent set of studies has examined the psychological effects of wrongful conviction, including behavioral health consequences (Brooks & Greenberg, 2020; Grounds, 2004).

A second body of research has turned from this archival work to focus on the causes of wrongful convictions, including work at the intersection of law and psychology, and using a range of methods. Archival research has examined characteristics of exoneration cases but also detailed how evidence became altered or erroneous during those criminal investigations (Garrett, 2011). Qualitative research has studied the attitudes and culture of actors that can produce wrongful convictions. Experimental research, including memory experiments and mock jury experiments, have tested mechanisms that can produce errors in criminal investigations and adjudications. Theoretical research has examined sources for cognitive errors and statistical errors that underlie wrongful convictions. Applied research has examined what changes in police practice and law might better safeguard against wrongful convictions.

Accuracy and Evidence

The growing numbers of wrongful conviction cases and the lessons learned from those cases have impacted police practices and created a new focus on accuracy in criminal investigations. This is reflected in police policies and guidelines that state an abiding interest in accurate and impartial evidence collection. The International Association of Chiefs of Police (IACP) has taken an active role in promoting the consideration of ways to improve the "accuracy and thoroughness" of police investigations, including through training, supervision and policy (IACP, 2013). In the past, traditional police manuals lacked attention to rules designed to promote reliability in investigations. A 1990s study of such manuals found that "none of the training materials addresses the importance of investigating, recording, or reporting exculpatory facts to avoid punishment of a possibly innocent arrestee" (Fisher, 1993, p. 30). However, a general interest in accuracy is not enough: specific practices must be addressed. Research in law and psychology has driven such change in law and in practice. Perhaps the most prominent such areas is in the area of eyewitness evidence, in which thousands of studies have been conducted.

Eyewitness Evidence

In 2014, the National Academy of Sciences summarized the scientific research as follows: "it is well known that eyewitnesses make mistakes, and their memories can be affected by various factors including the very law enforcement procedures designed to test their memories" (National Research Council, 2015, p. 1). A lineup is designed to be a memory test, but when law enforcement conduct such procedures improperly, they can alter an eyewitness's memory when trying to merely test it (Greenspan & Loftus, 2020).

Eyewitness misidentifications documented in early work examining reported wrongful convictions (Borchard, 1932) occurred in more than 70 percent of postconviction DNA exonerations in the United States (Garrett, 2011), including the first death-row DNA exoneration, in which five eyewitnesses misidentified Kirk Bloodsworth. A large number of DNA exoneration cases involve testimony from victim-witnesses, which is one reason eyewitness errors are so prominent in those cases. Most of those cases involved eyewitnesses who testified with a high degree of confidence at trial but following highly suggestive police lineup procedures and earlier red flags concerning unreliability (Garrett, 2011). Unfortunately, even if it is the product of false confidence, inflated by police suggestion and reinforcement, testimony by an eyewitness who is very confident in the courtroom is an extremely convincing piece of evidence to jurors (Garrett et al., 2020). However, it is important to carefully consider the lessons that can be drawn from DNA exoneration cases. For example, some researchers have misstated what can be gleaned from the patterns in DNA exonerations, including references to the initial confidence expressed by eyewitnesses in those cases (Berkowitz et al., 2022). The records of initial confidence in those DNA exoneration cases were rarely contemporaneously documented or preserved. Instead, witness testimony at criminal trials forms the basis for our understanding of the evidence in such cases (Berkowitz et al., 2022). Thus, real care should be taken when generalizing from archival research to the phenomenon studied in experimental settings.

Decades of psychology research have demonstrated through laboratory and field-based studies that eyewitnesses can come to misidentify innocent people as the perpetrator of the crime (National Research Council, 2015). The National Research Council (NRC) Report made five key recommendations: (1) training all law enforcement officers on variables that can affect eyewitness identifications; (2) adopting "blind" lineup and photo array procedures; (3) providing officers who do administer the procedures with standardized witness instructions; (4) documenting witness's stated level of confidence at the time of an identification; and (5) videotaping the witness identification process.

In 2020, the American Psychology and Law Society (AP-LS) updated the influential scientific review paper that digests eyewitness research to make recommendations for improving eyewitness identification procedures (Wells et al., 2020). New recommendations included (1) the need for reasonable suspicion before conducting an identification procedure; (2) the need to conduct a pre-lineup interview of the witness; (3) video recording the entire procedure; (4) avoiding repeated identification attempts with the same witness and same suspect; and (5) avoiding the use of showups when possible and improving how showups are conducted when they are necessary.

Less familiar to a psychology audience, but highly influential to legal audiences, the American Law Institute (2019), as part of its Principles of Policing Project, adopted principles for law enforcement concerning eyewitness identifications, adding that agencies should not conduct identification procedures without a suspect (trawling) or conduct an identification without a "substantial basis" to place a witness in a lineup procedure. Particularly important are recommendations that can improve the accuracy of eyewitness identification procedures, such as conducting procedures blind or blinded. In contrast, once cases go forward in the criminal system, it is challenging to educate jurors regarding the factors that can contaminate eyewitness memory (Garrett et al., 2019).

Responding to this large body of eyewitness memory research, a number of jurisdictions have reconsidered traditional rulings regarding eyewitness evidence, states have enacted statutes requiring changes made in lineup procedures, and still additional states have adopted model policies, or otherwise promoted new practices by law enforcement (Albright & Garrett, 2022). Perhaps most prominent and ambitious judicial action was the ruling of the New Jersey Supreme Court in *Henderson v. New Jersey*,[1] which revised the entire legal framework for reviewing eyewitness evidence. Many states have also passed responsive legislation, adopted new jury instructions, and embraced expert testimony on eyewitness evidence. Thus, this is an area in which psychological research has had a deep and growing impact on law and on police practices.

Forensic Evidence

A growing body of research at the intersection of psychology and law is examining the forensic evidence commonly used to link evidence to suspects in criminal cases. A wide range of forensic disciplines, as detailed in a landmark 2009 National Academy of Sciences report, have lacked grounding in foundational scientific research (National Research Council, 2009). That report highlighted the role that forensic evidence played in wrongful conviction cases, including in DNA exoneration cases. An analysis of forensic trial testimony, cited by the 2009 report, further detailed how DNA testing set exonerees free, but many were originally convicted based on flawed forensics (Garrett & Neufeld, 2009).

One important and growing area of research, noted in the 2009 NRC Report, examines how cognitive biases can impact the subjective decision-making by forensic experts that are comparing evidence and deciding whether to link it to evidence in a criminal

---

[1] State v. Henderson, 208 N.J. 208 (2011).

case—and, in turn, whether those decisions influence other investigators. For example, one study found that if fingerprint examiners were given irrelevant contextual information about a set of fingerprints (that they were the prints from a known incorrect identification), then those examiners were more likely to say that the two prints did not match—even though the examiners had concluded the two prints did match previously in their career (Dror et al., 2006).

This process is broadly known as "forensic confirmation bias"—the tendency for experts' and investigators' decision-making to be influenced by task-irrelevant information (Kassin et al., 2013). A series of studies have shown how task-irrelevant information can bias forensic experts, in disciplines ranging from fingerprint evidence (Dror et al., 2006) to medical death investigations (Dror et al., 2021) to blood pattern analysis (Taylor et al., 2016) even to DNA testing (Dror & Hampikian, 2011). The type of biasing information can vary as well, including other evidence such as a confession (Kukucka & Kassin, 2014). Another such source of bias can come from favoring the side that retains them, termed "adversarial allegiance" (Murrie et al., 2013). Another source of bias can be the forms that police use to submit evidence to them, which commonly call for task-irrelevant information (Gardner et al., 2019).

A second body of research has examined how jurors perceive forensic evidence. At a basic level, forensic evidence is very convincing to jurors. Despite the perception that forensic evidence is scientific, highly accurate, and objective, most forms used to link evidence to individuals (apart from nuclear DNA testing) are subjective and prone to human error. However, laypeople intuitively believe that error rates are extremely low for a range of forensic methods; jurors estimated in one study that the error rate for fingerprint comparisons was 1 in 5.5 million and for bite-mark comparisons it was one in a million (Koehler, 2017). Jurors give far less weight to evidence when they hear about error rates as actually measured in properly conducted studies (Koehler, 2017), but there appear to be some limitations in lay understanding of those rates and statistics (Garrett et al., 2020). Further, for fields like DNA testing, which involve probabilistic presentations, and as other forensic disciplines move toward probabilistic conclusions, it will be important to continue to study how laypeople perceive statistics. People may fall prey to fallacies, including the "prosecutor's fallacy," that a probability that a person is included in a population instead refers to a probability of guilt (Thompson & Schumann, 1987).

Information about the expert's ability is also potentially useful to inform jurors' perceptions of forensic evidence quality. When mock jurors heard information about the proficiency of an expert witness, based on realistic and challenging tests, they could calibrate how they weight the evidence (Crozier et al., 2020; Mitchell & Garrett, 2019). It is important to note, though, that information about error rates and proficiency are not a panacea, and other measures are important as well. Examiners should present testimony that is as scientifically accurate as possible, and not use language that overstates their findings. Work on experts shows that defense experts can also be helpful in countering misunderstood and misperceived forensic evidence as (Mitchell & Garrett, 2021).

Although we know forensic errors can lead to wrongful convictions, archival research examining criminal cases has found that forensic evidence often has little influence on the case outcomes given the range of other factors in play, particularly during plea negotiations (Baskins & Sommers, 2010). To be sure, errors in forensics may not come to light until years later, resulting in costly audits and reviews (Garrett, 2021). To improve the integrity of the forensic process, procedures can be instituted through policy to improve the flow of information to officers, including procedures that selectively blind them to irrelevant and potentially biasing information (Dror, 2016). Blind verification and proficiency testing can create a quality-oriented culture of error detection and correction. There is still a need for clearer and research-informed standards for forensic reports and testimony to improve juror understanding of forensic evidence and forensic experts—particularly their weaknesses and limitations. Moreover, research and policy needs to address the manner in which criminal cases are typically resolved through plea negotiations, without substantial discovery or adversarial process.

False Confessions

Many long doubted that an innocent person could falsely confess, but in recent years a large body of such false confessions has come to light (Garrett, 2011). Psychologists have long been able to demonstrate research participants falsely confessing in laboratory paradigms (e.g., Kassin & Kiechel, 1996; Russano et al., 2005). However, psychologists have simultaneously struggled to provide guidance on how to tell a true from a false confession (Kassin et al., 2005). As such, real-life false confessions are fairly difficult to identify, and detection often relies on strong exonerating evidence. In the DNA exoneration cases, almost all those false confessions were extremely detailed and were alleged to contain details that only the culprit could have known; they were contaminated statements, and the jury had the misimpression that these people had confessed in detail (Garrett, 2011). Constitutional rules require only very deferential review of police interrogations, however, focusing on the well-known *Miranda v. Arizona* warnings[2] and the requirement that the confession be voluntary under the entirety of the surrounding circumstances.

A large and growing body of research has studied how such false confessions occur. Some risk factors, such as use of coercive interrogation tactics, fall under the control of the investigators. Other factors, such as the demographics of the suspect, do not. A related body of research examines vulnerable populations, including juveniles and persons with behavioral health limitations, who may be particularly susceptible to coercion and to falsely confess. An AP-LS scientific review paper has set out detailed recommendations regarding how to prevent coerced and false confessions (Kassin et al., 2010). A number

---

[2] Miranda v. Arizona, 384 U.S. 436 (1966).

of jurisdictions have responded to this research and these recommendations by adopting legal reforms, including by videotaping interrogations and by reforming the training and procedures that officers use to conduct interrogations of suspects.

Videotaping in particular has been broadly endorsed as a useful reform (Kassin et al., 2010). Videotaping—or merely audiotaping if videotaping is not available—allows experts and legal actors to evaluate the coerciveness of the interrogation after the fact, rather than rely on contested reports between the investigators and the suspect. Additionally, recorded interrogations allow for other missteps in the interrogation beyond a coerced confession, such as investigators inadvertently disclosing nonprivileged information about a case to the suspect, and then having heightened suspicion of the suspect when they repeat that information. This process, known as contamination, can lead to more credible false confessions (Alceste et al., 2020; Leo, 2013), which in turn can lead to a greater chance of wrongful conviction (Alceste et al., 2019). However, merely recording interrogations does not prevent investigators from engaging in abusive, coercive, and misleading practices that may secure false confessions. Nor does videotaping necessarily improve how lawyers, judges, and jurors view interrogation evidence, even if it does document abuses in a way that may be more salient to those audiences. Front-end legal reforms to interrogation practices are needed, as well as reforms to legal standards for judicial gatekeeping and use of interrogation evidence at trial. More research on how to conduct interviews and interrogations in a way that produces high-quality information is needed.

Informant Evidence

The risk of wrongful conviction is one of the best-known costs of informant use: "Our judicial history is speckled with cases where informants falsely pointed the finger of guilt at suspects and defendants, creating the risk of sending innocent persons to prison."[3] However, constitutional criminal procedure has long permitted a wide variety of uses of information testimony, despite long-standing concerns with the reliability of such evidence. The reliability issues posed by informant use are not addressed well by constitutional criminal-procedure rules. In general, the US Supreme Court has emphasized that cross-examination may bring out any unreliability in informant statements (Slobogin, 2007). Informants have a wide range of motivations to lie or provide unreliable evidence. As one scholar (Roth, 2016) explains:

> Informant lies come in several forms. A jailhouse informant may fabricate a fellow prisoner's admission. Accomplices may admit to participating in a crime but minimize their own involvement while inflating the roles played by others. Some may admit guilt but fabricate the involvement of others. Others may lie about the identity of participants out of loyalty or fear or to conform their stories to the narratives law enforcement already constructed (pp. 765–766).

---

[3] United States v. Bernal-Obeso, 989 F.2d 331, 333 (9th Cir. 1993).

In general, courts have assumed that jurors can understand well that such witnesses may be inherently unreliable.

Researchers have examined DNA exonerations in which false informant testimony played a role, including several witnesses who received incentives, such as jailhouse informants. Those informants often testified that they had overheard the defendant confess to specific nonpublic details concerning the crime, which we now know to have been false postexoneration (Garrett, 2011). Just in recent years, there is a small body of evidence studying how jurors perceive such informant evidence, suggesting that neither cross-examination nor jury instructions are effective at responding to informant testimony (Neuschatz et al., 2008). The American Law Institute (ALI) has recommended reforms in response to these dangers of undocumented, unregulated, and unreliable uses of informants, and several jurisdictions have enacted reforms, including requirements that databases be maintained to track use of informants and that judges conduct reliability review (American Law Institute, 2022).

Alibi Evidence

One would hope that an innocent person would be able to clear themselves by presenting law enforcement with a solid alibi. Doing so is easier said than done. Many of the wrongful convictions that have been identified and overturned have included alibi evidence that was quite powerfully supported and nevertheless, did not sway the jury (Garrett, 2011). Take, for instance, the case of Wilton Dedge, who was at work during the entire day of a crime, with multiple coworkers verifying this; he was convicted of a crime that occurred far away, based on implausible testimony by a jailhouse informant who claimed he had undertaken a high-speed adventure using his motorcycle to commit the offense during the workday (Garrett, 2011).

The failure to properly investigate the alibi may contribute to wrongful conviction, but police agencies have long lacked requirements regarding whether or how to investigate evidence that may be chiefly of assistance to the defense. Recently, policing recommendations have emphasized the law enforcement obligation to investigate all evidence, including alibi evidence. However, police may be cognitively biased to focus on evidence that supports their case.

Further, even if an alibi is presented at trial, jurors may still not give it the weight it deserves. Laypeople tend to be suspicious of alibis, and if they think a defendant is guilty—say, from other evidence—tend to rate the alibi as less believable (Olson, 2013). Indeed, the type of cues that people tend to believe are diagnostic of an accurate alibi, such as consistency across time, can occur for reasons beyond deception—such as simple memory errors and forgetting (Crozier et al., 2017), which can be very common in alibi generation (Cardenas et al., 2021; Charman et al., 2019). Despite recognition that memory problems can cause an alibi provider to inadvertently include inaccurate details, Portnoy et al. (2020) found that people tend not to believe that it occurs. Research has found that

90 percent of a sample comprised of college students expressed belief the suspect was lying if they changed their alibi after a police interview (Culhane et al., 2008). Other work has found that a sample of law enforcement officers and college students preferred an alibi that did not change to one that did change, even one that changed to become stronger than the original (Culhane & Hosch, 2012).

Far more work needs to be done to address the challenges posed by investigating alibis, and how they are received by lawyers and jurors, and a range of legal rules should be reexamined concerning how alibi evidence is introduced, or not, in investigations and trials.

Police Technology

Unfortunately, in the past, many policing technologies have been a "black box" to which little access is provided to legal actors; indeed, law enforcement itself may lack sufficient access to evaluate the technology (e.g., see Karp, 2019, regarding facial recognition technology). Sometimes this has been because policing agencies purchase technology from third-party vendors who retain rights and deem their product to be proprietary. Further, law-enforcement–created databases have often been limited, for example, so that they bar judicial or defense access (Murphy, 2010). Doing so can make the reliability of the evidence entirely unknown to legal actors. Aside from transparency concerns, police technology may inadvertently create difficulties in investigations that raise cognitive questions of relevance to the intersection of law and psychology. Take, for instance, technology designed to aid in eyewitness lineup generation. Recent programs are able to search through thousands of photographs to identify lineup fillers that match a suspect's photographs. While this would save time for investigators and potentially lead to more formulaic, even lineups, it may also lead to lineups that are more difficult for eyewitnesses.

Recent work by Bergold and Heaton (2018) found that algorithmic searches through larger databases for fillers led to worse eyewitness performance. Specifically, lineups created from larger databases resulted in fewer correct identifications of the suspect, and more selections of innocent fillers than lineups created from smaller databases. Performance dropped for suspect-absent lineups as well—participants who viewed databases from larger databases resulted in fewer correct rejections and more selections of innocent fillers. In actual cases, these drops in performance would likely lead to wrongful convictions. Similarly, research has suggested that forensic databases that produce large numbers of candidates may fatigue lab examiners, causing them to be less likely to select a correct choice the farther down that list it appears (Dror & Hampikian, 2011).

Thus, large databases and algorithmic technology may in fact create new challenges to accuracy in criminal investigations. For black box algorithms, little is known about the degree to which they result in false hits that risk wrongful convictions. Far more work should be done to study the impacts of databases and search on expert decision-making.

The Adversary Process: Prosecution and Defense Lawyering

Much of the research discussed concerning wrongful convictions focuses on evidence considered at criminal trials, and although important lessons have been learned about the psychology of jury decision-making (Bornstein & Greene, 2011), our system largely consists of cases resolved through negotiated dispositions in plea bargains. As the US Supreme Court has put it, "criminal justice today is for the most part a system of pleas, not a system of trials."[4] Whereas legal scholars have long studied the criminal system as a system of plea bargaining, psychologists have been slower to engage with the practical realities of criminal adjudication in the United States (Edkins, 2011). In recent years, more work has examined the factors that impact plea bargaining, including guilty pleas by innocent persons (Redlich, 2016; Redlich et al., 2017). Further work has examined the role of defense lawyers and prosecutors. Research has documented the role of inadequate defense lawyering in wrongful conviction cases (Garrett, 2011). Studies have looked at the role of confirmation bias in prosecutorial decision-making (Linden et al., 2019). A body of work has begun to engage with the degree to which strength of evidence, versus other case processing concerns, impacts plea and sentencing outcomes (Kramer et al., 2007; Kutateladze et al, 2015).

Fortunately, recent work has begun to focus on the broader footprint of the criminal system, including arrest decision-making, the impact of low-level criminal enforcement (Crozier et al., 2020), and pretrial decision-making and detention (Desmarais et al., 2020; Scurich & Krauss, 2020). Each of the stages of the system can play a role in wrongful conviction cases, because arrests, pretrial detention, and other collateral consequences can place enormous pressure on individuals to plead guilty, despite their innocence (Bowers, 2007). Important work has examined implicit bias in police encounters (Voigt et al., 2017). Further work has examined legal decisions of juvenile defendants (Viljoen et al., 2005).

Still additional work examines psychological and legal factors that affect judicial behavior, which is relevant to judicial decisions at trial but also on appeal and postconviction. Research has studied, for example, the ways in which judges find error to be harmless, including by dwelling on seemingly "overwhelming" evidence of a defendant's guilt (Mitchell, 1994). Judges have done so even in cases in which we later learned, with the benefit of postconviction DNA testing, that the convicted person was innocent (Garrett, 2008). The US Supreme Court has not clearly recognized a freestanding right of a convict to claim innocence, which might allow a convict to challenge wholly unreliable evidence gathering or analysis by law enforcement. Nevertheless, innocence claims are litigated in state and federal court. In response to wrongful conviction cases, as well as research regarding wrongful convictions, states also have relaxed rules of finality to make it easier

---

[4] Lafler v. Cooper, 566 U.S. 156, 170 (2012).

to obtain access to evidence like DNA testing postconviction, and to reopen convictions based on new evidence of innocence (Garrett, 2011). There is far more law and psychology work that could be done to examine postconviction rules and outcomes.

Conclusion

One common theme in this chapter has been the growing intersection of law and psychology research in the area of wrongful convictions. This intersection has produced a rich body of scholarship and noteworthy impact on policy and law in a short period of just a few decades. Nevertheless, there is much unexplored and much work to be done. Some of the new directions involve evidentiary topics, like alibi and informant evidence, which is more challenging to study and has been far less examined than eyewitness evidence, which so readily lends itself to memory experiments. However, other new directions involve stages of the real-world criminal process that are complex, require knowledge of criminal procedure and institutional practice, and would benefit from closer collaboration between legal and criminal legal practitioners and researchers. For example, several of the areas discussed all implicate the role of cognitive bias in criminal investigations. In its Canons of Police Ethics, the IACP makes clear: "The law enforcement officer shall be concerned equally in the prosecution of the wrong-doer and the defense of the innocent. He shall ascertain what constitutes evidence and shall present such evidence impartially and without malice." This canon is reflected in state law and in the policies or codes of ethics of an increasing number of policing agencies. The general problem of cognitive bias in police investigations has received growing attention due to scientific research as well as evidence that officers make errors leading to wrongful convictions. Of course, cognitive biases affect all human behavior, and the mental shortcuts we rely on are extremely useful and time-saving mechanisms. Officers may face large caseloads that place great demands on their time and that make efficiency a high priority, which makes them prime candidates to rely on such mental shortcuts that result in the cognitive biases we see implicated in many wrongful conviction cases (see Guyll et al., this volume, for a related discussion).

A growing body of evidence has shown how cognitive biases can affect officers in negative ways, but it also points toward concrete changes that can reduce the negative influence of such biases. For example, officers analyzing evidence from crime scenes can be "vulnerable to cognitive and contextual bias" (National Research Council, 2009, p. 8). Officers' prior views about a suspect's guilt may affect how they evaluate evidence (Charman et al., 2017). Officers also can share information that can bias other officers; for example, sharing the results of forensic testing can cause officers to place undue weight on other evidence in a case, such as an eyewitness identification (Kassin et al., 2013). Improved documentation and disclosure can also address these sources of bias. In rulings such as *Brady v. Maryland* and *United States v. Bagley*,[5] the US Supreme Court held that

---

[5] Brady v Maryland, 373 U.S. 83 (1963); United States v. Bagley, 473 U.S. 667 (1985).

officers must disclose to prosecutors and the defense any evidence that is material and exculpatory, including evidence that would impeach the credibility of witnesses. Despite such constitutional rulings, the concealment of exculpatory evidence continues to occur, including in a series of high-profile exonerations, those brought to light by postconviction DNA testing (Garrett, 2011). The full extent of the problem of inadequate discovery in criminal cases cannot be readily known. Simply put, concealed evidence may never come to light, even during postconviction litigation. Although constitutional rulings create a mandatory minimum legal standard, it is not highly informative to officers, who before any trial cannot be sure what evidence may or may not later be material. Law and psychology research can, it is hoped, inform improved practices that are not constitutionally required but can prevent errors and injustices in criminal cases.

Many of the recommendations flowing from law and psychology research have in common the need to better document, including through electronic recording, a wide range of evidence used in criminal cases. Human memory is fallible, and persons ranging from witnesses to trained and professional observers like police officers will recall conversations and events imperfectly. Second, witnesses, jurors, judges, officers, and lawyers are all human and subject to cognitive biases. One person's biases about a case may also affect others, such as when an officer unconsciously conveys to an eyewitness which person in a lineup is the suspect. There are techniques available to avoid such biases, which agencies should explore and implement in policy and through training. Blinded lineups make use of an officer who does not know which person is the suspect, making it impossible to provide any suggestion, intentionally or not, to an eyewitness. Blind proficiency testing or verification in forensic analysis can provide an additional level of independent review of conclusions. Independent review by outside lawyers or experts can provide a safeguard against error.

Over the past two decades, new evidence concerning wrongful convictions, and a growing body of research concerning their cases, has already resulted in an innocence revolution in research and in criminal procedure. Those insights will only grow as researchers in law, psychology, and other disciplines collaborate, engage with criminal legal actors and policymakers, and further explore how criminal investigations can and do go wrong.

References

Albright, T., & Garrett, B. L. (2022). The law and science of eyewitness evidence. *Boston University Law Review, 102*, 511–630.

Alceste, F., Crozier, W. E., & Strange, D. (2019). Contaminated confessions: How source and consistency of confession details influence memory and attributions. *Journal of Applied Research in Memory and Cognition, 8*(1), 78–91.

Alceste, F., Jones, K. A., & Kassin, S. M. (2020). Facts only the perpetrator could have known? A study of contamination in mock crime interrogations. *Law and Human Behavior, 44*(2), 128–142.

American Law Institute. (2019). Eyewitness identification. Principles of Policing. ALI.

American Law Institute (2022). *Informant testimony* [Manuscript in preparation]. Principles of Policing. ALI.

Amnesty International. (2015). Amnesty international report 2015/2016: The state of the world's human rights. https://www.amnesty.org/download/Documents/POL1025522016ENGLISH.PDF

Baskin, D., & Sommers, I. (2010). The influence of forensic evidence on the case outcomes of homicide incidents. *Journal of Criminal Justice, 38*(6), 1141–1149.

Bergold, A. N., & Heaton, P. (2018). Does filler database size influence identification accuracy? *Law and Human Behavior, 42*(3), 227–243.

Berkowitz, S. R., Garrett, B. L., Fenn, K. M., & Loftus, E. F. (2022). Convicting with confidence? Why we should not over-rely on eyewitness confidence. *Memory, 30*(1), 10–15.

Borchard, E. M. (1932). Judicial relief for peril and insecurity. *Harvard Law Review, 45*(5), 793–854.

Bornstein, B. H., & Greene, E. (2011). Jury decision making: Implications for and from psychology. *Current Directions in Psychological Science, 20*(1), 63–67.

Bowers, J. (2007). Punishing the innocent. *University of Pennsylvania Law Review, 156*(5), 1117.

Brooks, S. K., & Greenberg, N. (2020). Psychological impact of being wrongfully accused of criminal offences: A systematic literature review. *Medicine, Science and the Law, 61*(1), 44–54.

Cardenas, S. A., Crozier, W., & Strange, D. (2021). Right place, wrong time: the limitations of mental reinstatement of context on alibi-elicitation. *Psychology, Crime & Law, 27*(3), 201–230.

Charman, S. D., Kavetski, M., & Mueller, D. H. (2017). Cognitive bias in the legal system: Police officers evaluate ambiguous evidence in a belief-consistent manner. *Journal of Applied Research in Memory and Cognition, 6*(2), 193–202.

Charman, S., Matuku, K., & Mosser A. (2019). The psychology of alibis. In B. Bornstein & M. Miller (Eds.), *Advances in psychology and law* (pp 41–72), Springer.

Crozier, W., Garrett, B. L., & Krishnamurthy, A. (2020). The transparency of jail data. *Wake Forest Law Review, 55*, 821–855.

Crozier, W. E., Strange, D., & Loftus, E. F. (2017). Memory errors in alibi generation: How an alibi can turn against us. *Behavioral Sciences & the Law, 35*(1), 6–17.

Culhane, S. E., & Hosch, H. M. (2012). Changed alibis: Current law enforcement, future law enforcement, and layperson reactions. *Criminal Justice and Behavior, 39*(7), 958–977.

Culhane, S. E., Hosch, H. M., & Kehn, A. (2008). Alibi generation: Data from US Hispanics and US non-Hispanic whites. *Journal of Ethnicity in Criminal Justice, 6*(3), 177–199.Desmarais, S. L., Zottola, S. A., Duhart Clarke, S. E., & Lowder, E. M. (2020). Predictive validity of pretrial risk assessments: A systematic review of the literature. *Criminal Justice and Behavior, 48*, 398–420.

Dror, I. E. (2016). A hierarchy of expert performance. *Journal of Applied Research in Memory and Cognition, 5*(2), 121–127.

Dror, I. E., Charlton, D., & Péron, A. E. (2006). Contextual information renders experts vulnerable to making erroneous identifications. *Forensic Science International, 156*(1), 74–78.

Dror, I. E., & Hampikian, G. (2011). Subjectivity and bias in forensic DNA mixture interpretation. *Science & Justice, 51*(4), 204–208.

Dror, I., Melinek, J., Arden, J. L., Kukucka, J., Hawkins, S., Carter, J., & Atherton, D. S. (2021). Cognitive bias in forensic pathology decisions. *Journal of Forensic Sciences, 66*, 1751–1757.

Edkins, V. A. (2011). Defense attorney plea recommendations and client race: Does zealous representation apply equally to all? *Law and Human Behavior, 35*(5), 413–425.

Fisher, S. Z. (1993). Just the facts, ma'am: Lying and the omission of exculpatory evidence in police reports. *New England Law Review, 28*, 1–61.

Gardner, B. O., Kelley, S., Murrie, D. C., & Dror, I. E. (2019). What do forensic analysts consider relevant to their decision making? *Science & Justice, 59*(5), 516–523.

Garrett, B. L. (2008). Judging innocence. *Columbia Law Review, 108*(1), 55–142.

Garrett, B. L. (2011). *Convicting the innocent.* Harvard University Press.

Garrett, B. L. (2017). Towards an international right to claim innocence. *California Law Review, 105*(4), 1173–1221.

Garrett, B. L. (2021). *Autopsy of a crime lab.* University of California Press.

Garrett, B. L., Crozier, W. E., & Grady, R. (2020). Error rates, likelihood ratios, and jury evaluation of forensic evidence. *Journal of Forensic Sciences, 65*(4), 1199–1209.

Garrett, B. L., Helfer, L. R. & Huckerby, J. (2021). Closing international law's innocence gap. *Southern California Law Review, 95*, 311–364.

Garrett, B. L., Liu, A., Kafadar, K., Yaffe, J., & Dodson, C. S. (2020). Factoring the role of eyewitness evidence in the courtroom. *Journal of Empirical Legal Studies, 17*(3), 556–579. https://doi.org/10.1111/jels.12259.

Garrett, B. L., & Neufeld, P. J. (2009). Invalid forensic science testimony and wrongful convictions. *Virginia Law Review, 95*, 1–97.

Greenspan, R. L., & Loftus, E. F. (2020). Eyewitness confidence malleability: Misinformation as post-identification feedback. *Law and Human Behavior, 44*(3), 194–208.

Grounds, A. (2004). Psychological consequences of wrongful conviction and imprisonment. *Canadian Journal of Criminology and Criminal Justice, 46*, 165–182.

International Association of Chiefs of Police. (n.d.). Law enforcement code of ethics. https://www.theiacp.org/resources/law-enforcement-code-of-ethics

Karp, J. (2019, November 3). *Facial recognition technology sparks transparency battle.* Law360. https://www.law360.com/articles/1215786/facial-recognition-software-sparks-transparency-battle

Kassin, S. M., Drizin, S. A., Grisso, T., Gudjonsson, G. H., Leo, R. A., & Redlich, A. D. (2010). Police-induced confessions: Risk factors and recommendations. *Law and Human Behavior, 34*(1), 3–38.

Kassin, S. M., Dror, I. E., & Kukucka, J. (2013). The forensic confirmation bias: Problems, perspectives, and proposed solutions. *Journal of Applied Research in Memory and Cognition, 2*(1), 42–52.

Kassin, S. M., & Kiechel, K. L. (1996). The social psychology of false confessions: Compliance, internalization, and confabulation. *Psychological Science, 7*(3), 125–128.

Kassin, S. M., Meissner, C. A., & Norwick, R. J. (2005). "I'd know a false confession if I saw one": A comparative study of college students and police investigators. *Law and Human Behavior, 29*(2), 211–217.

Koehler, J. J. (2017). Intuitive error rate estimates for the forensic sciences. *Jurimetrics, 57*(2), 153–168.

Kramer, G. M., Wolbransky, M., & Heilbrun, K. (2007). Plea bargaining recommendations by criminal defense attorneys: Evidence strength, potential sentence, and defendant preference. *Behavioral Sciences & the Law, 25*(4), 573–585.

Kukucka, J., & Kassin, S. M. (2014). Do confessions taint perceptions of handwriting evidence? An empirical test of the forensic confirmation bias. *Law and Human Behavior, 38*(3), 256–270.

Kutateladze, B. L., Lawson, V. Z., & Andiloro, N. R. (2015). Does evidence really matter? An exploratory analysis of the role of evidence in plea bargaining in felony drug cases. *Law and Human Behavior, 39*(5), 431–442.

Leo, R. A. (2013). Why interrogation contamination occurs. *Ohio State Journal of Criminal Law, 11*, 193–217.

Lidén, M., Gräns, M., & Juslin, P. (2019). From devil's advocate to crime fighter: Confirmation bias and debiasing techniques in prosecutorial decision-making. *Psychology, Crime & Law, 25*(5), 494–526.

Mitchell, G. (1994). Against overwhelming appellate activism: Constraining harmless error review. *California Law Review, 82*, 1335–1370.

Mitchell, G., & Garrett, B. L. (2019). The impact of proficiency testing information and error aversions on the weight given to fingerprint evidence. *Behavioral Sciences & Law, 37*(2), 195–210.

Mitchell, G., & Garrett, B. L. (2021). Battling to a draw: Defense expert rebuttal can neutralize prosecution fingerprint evidence. *Applied Cognitive Psychology, 35*, 976–987.

Murphy, E. (2010). Databases, doctrine, and constitutional criminal procedure. *Fordham Urban Law Journal, 37*(3), 803–836.

Murrie, D. C., Boccaccini, M. T., Guarnera, L. A., & Rufino, K. A. (2013). Are forensic experts biased by the side that retained them? *Psychological Science, 24*(10), 1889–1897.

National Research Council (US). (2009). *Strengthening forensic science in the United States: A path forward* (NCJ No. 228091). National Academy Press.

National Research Council. (2015). *Identifying the culprit: Assessing eyewitness identification.* National Academies Press.

Neuschatz, J. S., Lawson, D. S., Swanner, J. K., Meissner, C. A., & Neuschatz, J. S. (2008). The effects of accomplice witnesses and jailhouse informants on jury decision making. *Law and Human Behavior, 32*(2), 137–149.

Olson, E. A. (2013). "You don't expect me to believe that, do you?" Expectations influence recall and belief of alibi information. *Journal of Applied Social Psychology, 43*(6), 1238–1247.

Portnoy, S., Hope, L., Vrij, A., Ask, K., & Landström, S. (2020). Beliefs about suspect alibis: A survey of lay people in the United Kingdom, Israel, and Sweden. *The International Journal of Evidence & Proof, 24*(1), 59–74.

Redlich, A. D. (2016). The validity of pleading guilty. In B. Bornstein & M. Miller (Eds.), *Advances in psychology and law* (pp. 1–26). Springer.

Redlich, A. D., Bibas, S., Edkins, V. A., & Madon, S. (2017). The psychology of defendant plea decision making. *American Psychologist, 72*(4), 339–352.

Roth, J. A. (2016). Informant witnesses and the risk of wrongful convictions. *American Criminal Law Review, 53*, 737.

Russano, M. B., Meissner, C. A., Narchet, F. M., & Kassin, S. M. (2005). Investigating true and false confessions within a novel experimental paradigm. *Psychological Science, 16*(6), 481–486.

Scheck, B., Neufeld, P. J., & Dwyer, J. (2000). Actual innocence: Five days to execution and other dispatches from the wrongly convicted. Doubleday Books.

Scurich, N., & Krauss, D. A. (2020). Public's views of risk assessment algorithms and pretrial decision making. *Psychology, Public Policy, and Law, 26*(1), 1–9.

Slobogin, C. (2007). Lying and confessing. *Texas Tech Law Review, 39*, 1275–1293.

Taylor, M. C., Laber, T. L., Kish, P. E., Owens, G., & Osborne, N. K. (2016). The reliability of pattern classification in bloodstain pattern analysis—Part 2: bloodstain patterns on fabric surfaces. *Journal of Forensic Sciences, 61*(6), 1461–1466.

Thompson, W. C., & Schumann, E. L. (1987). Interpretation of statistical evidence in criminal trials: The prosecutor's fallacy and the defense attorney's fallacy, *Law and Human Behavior, 167*, 169–71.

Voigt, R., Camp, N. P., Prabhakaran, V., Hamilton, W. L., Hetey, R. C., Griffiths, C. M., Jurgens, D., Jurafsky, D., & Eberhardt, J. L. (2017). Language from police body camera footage shows racial disparities in officer respect. *Proceedings of the National Academy of Sciences, 114*, 6521–6526.

Viljoen, J. L., Klaver, J., & Roesch, R. (2005). Legal decisions of preadolescent and adolescent defendants: Predictors of confessions, pleas, communication with attorneys, and appeals. *Law and Human Behavior, 29*(3), 253–277.

Wells, G. L., Kovera, M. B., Douglass, A. B., Brewer, N., Meissner, C. A., & Wixted, J. T. (2020). Policy and procedure recommendations for the collection and preservation of eyewitness identification evidence. *Law and Human Behavior, 44*(1), 3–36.

INDEX

For the benefit of digital users, indexed terms that span two pages (e.g., 52–53) may, on occasion, appear on only one of those pages.

Note: Tables and figures are indicated by *t* and *f* following the page number

American Psychology-Law
Society (AP-LS), 4, 10–11,
71–72, 117, 769–70
American Society of Addiction
Medicine (ASAM), 420–21
Americans with Disabilities Act
(ADA), 226–27
amicus curiae, 4, 174–75
amplified strategies, 334, 335t,
337–38
anatomically correct (AC) dolls,
250
anchoring effect, 240
anger emotion in legal settings,
211, 731–32
Annual Security Report (ASR),
497–98
antidepressant medication, 230
Anti-Drug Abuse Act (1986), 757
anxiety disorder, 191–92, 229–30
applied psychology, 4, 19, 102,
365
appropriate practice, 119
AsPredicted, 81–82, 88
Association for Psychological
Science (APS), 26
Association of Family and
Conciliation Courts
(AFCC), 237–38, 246–47
Association of the State and
Provincial Psychology
Boards (ASPPB), 368, 371
Atkins evaluations, 192–98, 201
Atkins v. Virginia, 192–93
ATR (Atypical Response) scale,
264–65
attachment theory, 191, 252–53
attention deficit hyperactivity
disorder (ADHD), 207, 338
attenuated reliability, 349–50
attitudes in FMHA, 104
attorney emotion in legal
settings, 735
attorney-selected psychological
expert witnesses, 67
AUCs (areas under the curve),
311–12
Australian and New Zealand
Association of Psychiatry,
Psychology, and Law, 4
autism spectrum disorder
(ASD), 454
autonomy, 102–3, 512–13, 516,
518, 523
avoidance behavior, 211

B
Barefoot v. Estelle, 51, 317–18
Batson v. Kentucky, 698, 745–46,
756
Baxstrom v. Harold, 316–17
Bazelon, David, 4
behavioral difficulties, 192
behavioral variant of FTD
(bvFTD), 295
Bell, Monica, 528–29
Bennett, James Gordon, 665
Berkeley Law Death Penalty
Clinic, 745–46
best interests of the child,
242–48
Best Practices for Forensic
Mental Health Assessment,
4
bias/biasability. *See also* forensic
science bias and errors
adversarial allegiance, 64,
104–5, 353–58, 627–28, 771
adversary bias, 239
allegiance bias, 105–7
blind spot, 105, 240, 628–29
child custody evaluation,
238–42
cognitive bias, 104–9, 161
in competence-to-stand-trial
evaluation, 159–63
conceptual bias, 332
confirmation bias, 239, 240,
586
debiasing strategies, 105
explicit bias, 239
hindsight bias, 104–5, 239,
240, 648–51, 649f
implicit bias, 110–11, 140, 239,
527, 534, 704, 744, 746,
747, 750, 756, 776
investigative interviewing, 586
judgment bias, 239
juror bias, 180
language in forensic report
writing, 140–43
racial bias in preemptory
charges, 698
recollection bias, 650
reconstruction bias, 650
structural bias, 746
tunnel vision, 586, 700–1
violence risk assessment and
management, 313–14, 318–19
wrongful conviction
expectancies, 661–67

bias blind spot, 105, 240, 628–29
bias cascade, 633–34
bias susceptibility, 107–8
bidirectional reasoning, 645
bipolar disorder, 191–92, 230
black box algorithms, 775
Black Lives Matter movement,
21
Black's Law Dictionary (Garner),
372
Bland, Sandra, 537–38
blind lineup, 769
blind proficiency testing, 632–33
Bloodsworth, Kirk, 769
board certification of testifying
expert labor, 369–70
Booth v. Maryland, 727
Boston Marathon bombings,
730
Boy Scouts of America, 644
Brady, James, 173–74
Brady v. Maryland, 695–96,
777–78
Brady v. United States, 677–78,
680
Brady violations, 695–97
brain functioning, 170
Breyer, Stephen, 172–73
Brief Psychiatric Rating Scale
(BPRS), 157
Brown, James L., 531–32
Brown, Michael, 537–38
Brown v. Board of Education, 4
Buck v. Davis, 45

C
California Rules of Evidence,
491
California Supreme Court, 317
Campus SaVE Act, 497–98,
502–3
Capital Jury Project, 754
capital mitigation, 6
capital punishment, 27–28, 30,
46, 190, 199–200, 733. *See
also* death penalty
capital sentencing
adaptive behavior and,
194–96, 195t
Atkins evaluations, 192–98, 201
death penalty cases, 65, 187–89,
189t, 192–98
forensic mental health
assessment, 190–92, 196,
201

complainant, defined, 496, 498–99
compliance behavior, 551–53
complicated mild TBI, 293
COMPSTAT for Justice, 539
conceptual bias, 332
conditional release, 6, 181
confession evidence and jury decision-making, 717–18
confirmation bias, 239, 240, 586
constitutional rights, 679
Convention Against Torture (CAT), 261–62
The Conversation, 26
cooperation development in investigative interviewing, 589–95
coordination in rapport, 590
correctional officers, 8
correctional rehabilitation, 404–6. *See also* justice-involved persons with serious mental illness
Correctional Service of Canada, 314
correctional treatment inefficiency, 40
counseling psychology, 13–14
counterfactual analysis, 533–35
Court Review journal, 25–27
COVID-19 pandemic
child protection community and, 450
digital impact of, 87, 451, 452, 458–59
FMHA and, 112–13
impact on courts, 485
impact on incarcerated persons, 380–81
practices of interrogation, 618
public health impact, 21
social distancing recommendations, 451
video-based interviewing, 596–97
Crane v. Kentucky, 282
Crenshaw, Kimberlé, 744
The Crime of Punishment (Menninger), 38
crime-reduction policy, 552–53
crime-suspect stereotypes, 664–65
criminal justice system, 30–31
criminal liability, 38, 376

criminalness-mental illness relationship, 404–6, 405f
criminal recidivism, 28
criminal responsibility evaluations
civil commitment and conditional release, 181
expert testimony and, 56–57
field reliability, 179–80
future research directions, 182–83
insanity defense, 171–73, 174–77
mock juror studies, 180–81
neuroscience and, 175
pleas and acquittals, 175–77
presentation of, 170–71
research design, 177–78
review of practices, 179
substance use and, 174–75
volitional prong in, 173–74
criminal sanctions for prosecutorial misconduct, 701–2
crisis intervention team (CIT), 423
crisis of confidence, 71
criteria-based content analysis (CBCA), 566, 574–75
critical interrogation tactics, 63
critical race theory, 744–45
cruel and unusual punishment, 531
cultural similarity in rapport, 590
curricula vitae (CV), 367
custodial interrogation, 604
cyclical investigative interviewing, 595–96

D
Dassey v. Dittman, 278
data gathering and interpretation in FMHA, 103, 104, 109–10
Daubert criteria, 57–60, 63–64, 90, 245, 344
Daubert v. Merrell Dow Pharmaceuticals, 57–59, 162–63, 371–72
day before analysis, 205
Dear Colleague Letter (DCL), 496–97, 498–500
death penalty
based on a risk assessment, 46

ethnic/racial legal considerations and, 752, 754–55
jurisprudence, 27–28
mock juror studies, 180
SCOTUS cases, 187–89, 189t, 192–98
sentencing, 65, 187–89, 189t, 192–98
Death Penalty Information Center (DPIC), 767–68
death qualification, 19, 27–28
debiasing strategies, 105
decarceration movement, 44
decision-making, 307, 549–50, 657, 737. *See also* adolescent decision making; jury decision-making
The Decline of the Rehabilitative Ideal (Allen), 55
decriminalizing mental illness, 155
Dedge, Wilton, 774
defendant emotion in legal settings, 734–35
defense lawyering, 776–77
defensiveness, 328–29
dementia, 294–95
Department of Homeland Security (DHS), 259–60
Department of Justice (DOJ), 259, 484–85
Department of Veterans Affairs, 368–69
depression and occupational functioning, 230. *See also* major depressive disorder
desert-based sentencing, 42–44, 46–48
DeShaney v. Winnebago County, 533
Detailed Assessment of Posttraumatic Stress (DAPS), 212, 213
determination in FMHA, 104
deterrence-driven regimes, 36–37
developmental immaturity, 275–76
developmental psychologists, 56–57
Diagnostic and Statistical Manual of Mental Disorders (DSM-5), 146, 265–66
diagnostic impression in civil litigation case study, 214–16